THE MARINE FAUNA OF THE BRITISH ISLES AND NORTH-WEST EUROPE

VOLUME 1

Introduction and
Protozoans to Arthropods

The Marine Fauna
of the
British Isles and
North-West Europe

VOLUME 1

Introduction and
Protozoans to Arthropods

Edited by

P. J. HAYWARD AND J. S. RYLAND

Marine, Environmental and Evolutionary Research Group,
School of Biological Sciences,
University College of Swansea

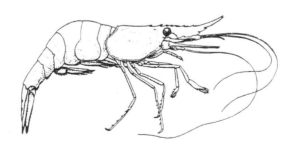

CLARENDON PRESS · OXFORD

1990

Oxford University Press, Walton Street, Oxford OX2 6DP

Oxford New York Toronto
Delhi Bombay Calcutta Madras Karachi
Petaling Jaya Singapore Hong Kong Tokyo
Nairobi Dar es Salaam Cape Town
Melbourne Auckland
and associated companies in
Berlin Ibadan

Oxford is a trade mark of Oxford University Press

Published in the United States
by Oxford University Press, New York

British Library Cataloguing in Publication Data
The marine fauna of the British Isles and North-West Europe.
1. Europe. Coastal waters. Marine organisms
I. Hayward, P. J.   II. Ryland, J. S.
574.94
ISBN 0–19–857356–1

Library of Congress Cataloging in Publication Data
The Marine fauna of the British Isles and North-West Europe / edited
by P. J. Hayward and J. S. Ryland.
p.   cm.
Includes bibliographical references and index.
Contents: v. 1. Introduction and protozoans to arthropods—v.
2. Molluscs to chordates.
1. Marine fauna—Great Britain.   2. Marine fauna—Europe.
I. Hayward, P. J. (Peter Joseph)   II. Ryland, J. S. (John Stanley)
QL255.M29   1990   591.92'13—dc20   90–7629
ISBN 0–19–857356–1 (v. 1)
ISBN 0–19–857515–7 (v. 2)

Printed in Great Britain by
Butler & Tanner Ltd, Frome, Somerset

PREFACE

THIS work was conceived in 1969 by members of the Zoology Department of the University College of Swansea, during the annual marine field course, then held at Galway, Ireland, over the period of the autumn equinoctial tides. It was an exciting time of expansion for marine biology, in which field studies seemed to have an increasingly important role to play. The traditional marine field class had long been an integral part of zoology teaching at most British universities, but by 1969 marine ecology was a fast-growing discipline attracting more students and researchers than ever before. This was matched by a renascent amateur interest, partly stimulated by the increasing popularity of SCUBA diving, and partly by a new awareness of the need for marine resources management and conservation programmes. Correct identification of species is a necessary prerequisite for any research in the field, or based on specimens collected in the field. Our Galway courses were served by the small but excellent *Guide to the sea shore*, by John Barrett and C. M. Yonge, while the more scholarly, but older and poorly illustrated, *Littoral fauna of the British Isles*, by N. B. Eales, provided dichotomous keys and an introduction to the specialist literature increasingly needed to identify the catch. As more ecologists and students visited an ever widening spectrum of shores, and investigated more habitats, the shortcomings of available identification keys became increasingly obvious. Yet, for many groups the specialist literature, dating from the mid- to late-nineteenth century, employed obsolete and unscientific terminology, and was frequently difficult to use. In the past two decades, stimulated partly by need and partly by the availability of new methods of study, there has been a great deal of systematic revision, and many new insights into the biology of marine animals. The fruits of this work can be seen, for example, in the new series of *Synopses of the British fauna*, published at first by the Linnean Society of London, alone, and later jointly with the Estuarine and Brackish Water Sciences Association. However, there remains an urgent need for an illustrated identification manual which bridges the considerable gap between the semi-popular field guides, a number of which are now available, and the specialist treatises or series of synopses. Moreover, whereas the works of Eales and of Barrett and Yonge dealt solely with intertidal faunas, their successor single volume needs also to cover the common species of the sublittoral. These volumes are designed to fill the gap, providing dichotomous keys, illustrations, brief descriptions, and notes on distributions for the most frequently occurring intertidal and subtidal marine organisms.

The Introduction deals essentially with the marine environment of the British Isles and adjacent areas of the North Sea and north-east Atlantic. Most of the animal species occurring here are found also on the coast of mainland Europe. North of Bergen the marine fauna becomes increasingly Arctic in character, while many north-west European species reach their southern limits on the coast of Brittany. These two points mark the limits of coverage of this book. In some groups a few species known only from either the extreme northern or southern parts of this region have been excluded, at least partly because of continuing uncertainty over their taxonomic identity. For most groups, however, the keys provided will suffice for the identification of all but the rarest coastal species occurring between Bergen and Brittany.

The years, over which preparation of this book have been spread, have seen many changes.

The Zoology Department of the University College of Swansea has now been amalgamated with others into its School of Biological Sciences. The Marine Biology honours BSc degree, instituted in 1975, flourishes, and the new Marine, Environmental and Evolutionary Research Group sustains most of the marine research interests of the School. In Britain as a whole, despite constraints imposed by financial cutback, field studies are regarded as an important component in secondary and tertiary level biology teaching, as well as of numerous higher education programmes, and amateur interest continues to grow. Conservation is perceived as an urgent priority around the coasts and in the shallow seas of western Europe, and it seems that marine environmental and management studies will continue to grow in importance.

With just three exceptions, all of the contributors to this work are, or have been, associated with the former Departments of Zoology and Oceanography, at Swansea. The roll expanded steadily as the book developed, while one or two of the original participants regrettably felt obliged to withdraw their commitment during its long gestation. One of the original few, David N. Huxtable, deserves special mention. A gifted and devoted student of marine biology, David early developed considerable expertise with the Anthozoa, and acquired an impressive knowledge of the species found in south Wales, north Devon, and on the Galway coast. As a graduate student he worked tirelessly on the behaviour of burrowing sea anemones, but made time also to produce a draft key to the British marine hydroids, which he intended to develop into the first modern account of this group. David Huxtable's promising career was tragically ended by a fatal accident in 1974. It is fitting that we remember him now, as our joint venture finally achieves publication.

Swansea   P. J. H.
1989   J. S. R.

ACKNOWLEDGEMENTS

The editors wish to express their appreciation of the many, patient undergraduate students who have participated in testing these identification keys through many drafts. We wish to thank the illustrators for their long hours of detailed and painstaking work, and also Mr. M. R. Tootill, course leader in Scientific Illustration at Blackpool and the Fylde College, for his much valued help in encouraging graduate illustrators to take on this task. We are grateful to the Natural Environment Research Council for the generous award of a grant towards illustration costs. Mrs. Margaret Thomas and Mrs. Nancy Taylor gave indispensable support with their swift and efficient typing, and we deeply appreciate their efforts.

In several instances the text has benefited from the critical attention of specialist colleagues from other institutions. The section on Stauromedusae owes much to the freely given expertise of Mr. P. G. Corbin (MBA, Plymouth), who also advised on sandeels. Professor A. A. Myers (University College, Cork) critically reviewed the text for Amphipoda, and Dr. D. M. Holdich (University of Nottingham) suggested improvements to parts of Chapter 9.

Finally, we should like to thank all of the contributors for their work over many years, and special thanks are reserved for the Oxford University Press for its remarkable patience during the long gestation of this book.

The editors are pleased to acknowledge the cited sources from which the following figures have been redrawn:

Fig. 2.1
Prorocentrum lima, Sinophysis ebriola, Thecadinium petasatum, Amphidinium scissum, A. britannicum, A. herdmanae, Gyrodinium lebourae, Oxyrrhis marina, Herdmania litoralis, Katodinium asymmetricum, Glenodinium monensis, Gonyaulax polyedra, Polykrikos lebourae, Adenoides eludens, Amphidiniopsis swedmarkii: after Dodge (1982). *Gymnodinium arenicolus, Pontosphaera roscoffensis, Trachelmonas abrupta:* after Dragesco (1965). *Cyathomonas truncata:* after Hollande (1952). *Tetraselmis convolutae:* after Parke and Manton (1967). *Urceolus cyclostomus, Petalomonas mediocanellata:* after Huber-Pestalozzi (1955). *Sphenomonas elongata, Pentamonas spinifera:* after Lackey (1962).

Fig. 2.6
Stephanopogon colpoda: after Dragesco (1963a). *Tracheloraphis phoenicopterus, Geleia fossata, Remanella rugosa, Prorodon marinus:* after Dragesco (1960). *Kentrophoros latum, Pseudoprorodon arenicola, Conchostoma longissima:* after Fenchel (1969). *Metacystis truncata, Coleps tesselatus, Lachrymaria coronata, Spathidium procerum, Mesodinium pulex, Loxophyllum verrucosum, Litonotus fasciola:* after Kahl (1930–35). *Coelosomides marina:* after Faure-Fremiet (1950).

Fig. 2.7
Scaphidiodon navicula, Discotricha papillifera: after Dragesco (1965). *Paranassula microstoma, Chlamydodon triquetrus, Dysteria aculeata:* after Kahl (1930–35).

Hypocoma acinetarum: after Deroux (1975). *Heliochona sessilis:* after Fenchel (1965b). *Ancistrocoma pelseneeri:* after Kozloff (1946). *Conidophrys pilisuctor, Foettingeria actiniarum, Gymnodiniodes inkystans, Chromidina elegans:* after Chatton and Lwoff (1935). *Ephelota gemmipara, Acineta tuberosa, Discophrya lyngbyei:* after Kahl (1933–34).

Fig. 2.8
Frontonia marina, Uronema marinum, Platynematum denticulatum, Cyclidium glaucoma, Vorticella nebulifera, Zoothamnium alternans, Scyphidia patellae, Pyxicola ligiae, Leiotrocha patellae, Trichodina ophiotrichis: after Kahl (1930–35). *Pleuronema coronatum:* after Dragesco (1960). *Peniculostoma mytili, Ancistrum mytili, Hemispeira antedonis:* after Fenchel (1965b). *Anoplophryopsis ovata:* after de Puytorac (1954). *Epistylis gammari:* after Fenchel (1965b).

Fig. 2.9
Blepharisma clarissimum, Metopus contortus, Condylostoma arenarium, Peritromus faurei, Caenomorpha levanderi, Licnophora auerbachi, Saprodinium halophilum, Urostrongylum caudatum, Holosticha arenicola, Trachelostyla pediculiformis, Aspidisca pulcherrima: after Kahl (1930–35). *Lagotia viridis:* after Das (1949). *Strombidium sauerbreyae:* after Faure-Fremiet (1960). *Tintinnopsis beroidea:* after Marshall (1969). *Diophrys scutum:* after Dragesco (1963b).

Fig. 4.3
Diagrams mainly after Millard (1975).

Fig. 4.5

Ectopleura dumortieri colony: after Lagardère and Tardy (1980, *Cah. Biol. mar.*, **21**). *Hybocodon prolifer*: after Agassiz (1862). *Sarsia loveni*, *Sarsia tubulosa*: after C. Edwards (1978, *JMBA*, **58**).

Fig. 4.6

Podocoryne borealis, *P. carnea*: after C. Edwards (1977, *JMBA*, **52**).

Fig. 4.7

Rhizorhagium roseum: after Russell (1907) and W. J. Rees (1938, *JMBA*, **23**). *Garveia nutans*, *Dicoryne conferta*: after Allman (1871). *Dicoryne conybeari*: after Ashworth and Ritchie (1917). *Leuckartiara octona*: after W. J. Rees (1938, *JMBA*, **23**).

Fig. 4.8

Bougainvillia ramosa: after Allman (1871). *B. pyramidata*, *B. britannica*: after C. Edwards (1964, *JMBA*, **44**). *B. muscoides*: after W. J. Rees (1938, *JMBA*, **23**).

Fig. 4.9

Proboscidactyla stellata: after Hincks (1872). *Eudendrium capillare*: after Allman (1871).

Fig. 4.22

Monotheca obliqua: ♀ gonotheca after Lister (1838); ♂ gonotheca after J.-M. Gili i Sarda (1982, *Tret. Inst. Catalana Hist. Nat.*, **10**).

Fig. 4.23

Polyplumaria flabellata: gonotheca after Billard (1906). *Schizotricha frutescens*: gonotheca after Vervoort (1946, *Fauna Ned.*).

Fig. 4.24

Aglaophenia acacia: colony after Allman (1883).

Fig. 4.26

Alcyonium glomeratum: after Manuel (1981).

Fig. 4.27

Swiftia pallida: polyp after Manuel (1981).

Fig. 6.30

Branchellion borealis, *Calliobdella lophii*, *Calliobdella nodulifera*, *Ganymedebdella cratere*, *Janusion scorpii*: after Leigh-Sharpe (1914, 1915, 1917, 1933). *Brumptiana lineata*: after Llewellyn and Knight-Jones (1984). *Branchellion torpedinis*: after Harding (1910). *Hemibdella soleae*: after Llewellyn (1965). *Heptacyclus myoxocephali*, *Malmiana bubali*: after Srivastra (1966).

Fig. 6.31

Malmiana yorki: after Srivastra (1966). *Pontobdella muricata*: after Llewellyn (1966). *Pontobdella vosmaeri*: after Llewellyn (1966) and Harding (1910). *Platybdella anarrhichae*: after Leigh-Sharpe (1916). *Pterobdellina jenseni*: after Bennicke and Bruun (1939). *Sanguinothus pinnarum*: after de Silva and Burdon-Jones (1961).

Fig. 7.1

Echiurus echiurus, *Bonellia viridis*, *Maxmuelleria lankesteri*: after Stephen and Edmonds (1972). *Halicryptus spinulosus*, *Priapulus caudatus*, *Thalassema thalassemum*: after Shipley (1910). *Amalosoma eddystonense*: after Saxena (1986). *Siboglinum* sp.: after A. J. Southward *et al.* (1986). *Siboglinum fjordicum*: after

Webb (1963). *Siboglinum holmei*: after E. C. Southward (1963). *Siboglinum norvegicum*: after Ivanov (1963).

Fig. 7.2

Aspidosiphon muelleri, *Golfingia elongata*, *Golfingia vulgaris*, *Nephasoma minuta*, *Nephasoma rimicola*, *Onchnesoma squamatum* *Phascolion strombi*, *Phascolosoma granulatum*, *Sipunculus nudus*. *Thysanocardia procera*: after Gibbs (1977).

Fig. 7.3

Loxosomella nitschei: after Ryland (1961, *Sarsia*, **1**). *L. antedonis*: after Ryland and A. P. Austin (1960, *Proc. Zool. Soc. Lond.*, **133**). *Barentsia mutabilis*: after Ryland (1961, *Ann. Mag. nat. Hist.*, **13** (3)). Other *Barentsia* spp. drawn from photographs in P. Emschermann (1972), unpublished, 'Key for the determination of the Barentsiidae of the World'. *Pedicellina cernua*: colony after Brien (1959, *Traite de Zoologie* **5**(1)). Other *Pedicellina species*: after Ryland (1965, *Trans. Roy. Soc. N.Z.*, **6**).

Fig. 8.4

All figures after Sars (1903, 1918).

Fig. 8.5

All figures after Sars (1911).

Fig. 8.6

All figures after Sars (1911).

Fig. 8.7

All figures after Sars (1911).

Fig. 8.8

All figures after Sars (1911).

Fig. 8.9

Botrillophilus brevipes, *Notodelphys allmani*, *Doropygus pulex*, *Enterocola bilamellata*, *Ascidicola rosea*, *Notopterophorus papilio*, *Modiolicola insignis*, *Lichomolgus agilis*, *Sabelliphilus elongatus*, *Eunicicola clausi*: after Sars (1921). *Thespesiopsyllus paradoxus*: after J. Bresciani and J. Lützen (1962, *Vidensk. Medd. dansk. naturh. Foren.*, **124**). *Splanchnotrophus brevipes*: after A. Hancock and A. M. Norman (1863, *Trans. Linn. Soc.*, **24**). *Leptinogaster histrio*: after C. Bocquet and J. H. Stock (1958, *Arch. zool. exp. gen.*, **96**). *Ergasilus gibbus*, *Holobomolochus confusus*, *Acanthochondria cornuta*: after Kabata (1979).

Fig. 8.10

Artotrogus orbicularis, *Cancerilla tubulata*: after Sars (1921). *Lernaeocera branchialis*: after T. Scott and A. Scott (1913, *British Parasitic Copepoda*, London). *Hatschekia cluthae*, *Caligus elongatus*, *Lepeophtheirus pectoralis*, *Clavella adunca*, *Haemobaphes cyclopterina*: after Kabata (1979). *Nicothoe astaci*, *Sarsilenium crassirostris*, *Eurysilenium truncatum*: after W. H. Leigh-Sharpe (1928, *Parasitology*, **17**). *Lamippe rubra*: after J. Bresciani and J. Lützen (1962, *Vidensk. Medd. dansk, naturh. Foren.*, **124**). *Aspidoecia normani*: after H. J. Hansen (1897), *Choniostomatidae*, Copenhagen). *Phyllocola petiti*: after D.-Deboutteville and Laubier (1960). *Thaumaleus rigidus*: after Malaquin (1901). *Thaumaleus malaquini*: after M. Caullery and F. Mesnil (1914), *Bull. Scient. Fr. Belg.*, **48**). *Monstrilla* *helgolandica*: after P. Pelseneer (1914, *Bull. Scient. Fr. Belg.*, 48).

Fig. 8.11
Lepas hilli, L. anserifera: after Broch (1960).

Fig. 8.12
Chthalamus montagui, C. stellata: partly after Southward (1976).

Fig. 8.14
All figures after Hoeg and Lutzen (1985).

Fig. 8.15
All figures after Hoeg and Lutzen (1985).

Fig. 8.16
All figures after Hoeg and Lutzen (1985).

Fig. 9.8
All figures after Tattersall and Tattersall (1951).

Fig. 9.9
All figures after Tattersall and Tattersall (1951).

Fig. 9.17
Acidostoma obesum, Hippomedon denticulatus, Lysianassa ceratina, Lysianassa plumosa, Nannonyx goesi, Lepidepecreum longicorne: after Lincoln (1979).

Fig. 9.18
Perriella audouiniana, Socarnes erythrophthalmus, Scopelocheirus hopei, Tryphosella sarsi, Orchomene nana, Orchomene humilis: after Lincoln (1979).

Fig. 9.19
Tmetonyx cicada, Tryphosites longipes, Ampelisca brevicornis, Ampelisca gibba, Ampelisca macrocephala: after Lincoln (1979).

Fig. 9.20
Ampelisca spinipes, Ampelisca typica, Ampelisca tenuicornis, Haploops tubicola: after Lincoln (1979). *Iphimedia obesa, Iphimedia minuta*: after Myers, McGrath and Costello (1987).

Fig. 9.21
Iphimedia perplexa, Iphimedia spatula: after Myers, McGrath and Costello (1987). *Pereionotus testudo, Amphilochus manudens, Amphilochus neapolitanus, Amphilochus spencebatei, Colomastix pusilla*: after Lincoln (1979).

Fig. 9.22
Gitana sarsi, Peltocoxa damnoniensis, Paramphilochoides odontonyx, Leucothoe spinicarpa: after Lincoln (1979). *Leucothoe incisa, Leucothoe lilljeborgi*: after Myers and Costello (1986).

Fig. 9.23
Metopa alderi, Metopa pusilla, Stenothoe monoculoides, Stenothoe marina, Stenothoe valida, Stenula rubrovittata, Parametopa kervillei: after Lincoln (1979).

Fig. 9.24
Orchestia gammarellus, Orchestia mediterranea, Talorchestia deshayesii, Talorchestia brito: after Lincoln (1979).

Fig. 9.25
Hyale nilssoni, Hyale perieri, Hyale pontica, Chaetogammarus marinus, Chaetogammarus pirloti, Chaetogammarus stoerensis: after Lincoln (1979).

Fig. 9.26
Eulimnogammarus obtusatus, Gammarus chevreuxi, Gammarus crinicornis, Gammarus duebeni, Gammarus finmarchicus, Gammarus insensibilis: after Lincoln (1979).

Fig. 9.27
Gammarus locusta, Gammarus oceanicus, Gammarus salinus, Gammarus tigrinus, Gammarus zaddachi, Pectenogammarus planicrurus: after Lincoln (1979).

Fig. 9.28
Abludomelita obtusata, Allomelita pellucida, Ceradocus semiserratus, Cheirocratus assimilis, Cheirocratus intermedius, Cheirocratus sundevallii: after Lincoln (1979).

Fig. 9.29
Elasmopus rapax, Gammarella fucicola, Maera grossimana, Maera othonis, Maerella tenuimana, Melita gladiosa: after Lincoln (1979).

Fig. 9.30
Melita palmata, Melita hergensis, Bathyporeia elegans, Bathyporeia guilliamsoniana, Bathyporeia nana, Bathyporeia pelagica: after Lincoln (1979).

Fig. 9.31
Bathyporeia pilosa, Bathyporeia sarsi, Bathyporeia tenuipes, Urothoe elegans, Urothoe marina, Urothoe poseidonis, Urothoe brevicornis: after Lincoln (1979).

Fig. 9.32
Argissa hamatipes, Monoculodes carinatus, Perioculodes longimanus, Pontocrates altamarinus, Pontocrates arenarius, Synchelidium haplocheles, Westwoodilla caecula: after Lincoln (1979).

Fig. 9.33
Harpinia antennaria, Harpinia pectinata, Harpinia crenulata, Metaphoxus fultoni, Metaphoxus pectinatus, Phoxocephalus holbolli: after Lincoln (1979).

Fig. 9.34
Megaluropus agilis, Melphidippella macra, Liljeborgia kinahani, Liljeborgia pallida, Eusirus longipes, Apherusa bispinosa, Apherusa cirrus: after Lincoln (1979).

Fig. 9.35
Apherusa clevei, Apherusa jurinei, Apherusa henneguyi, Gammarellus homari, Gammarellus angulosus, Calliopius laeviusculus: after Lincoln (1979).

Fig. 9.36
Parapleustes bicuspis, Stenopleustes nodifer, Atylus falcatus, Atylus swammerdami, Atylus guttatus, Atylus vedlomensis: after Lincoln (1979).

Fig. 9.37
Dexamine spinosa, Dexamine thea, Guernea coalita, Tritaeta gibbosa, Ampithoe rubricata, Ampithoe ramondi: after Lincoln (1979).

Fig. 9.38
Ampithoe gammaroides, Ampithoe helleri, Amphitholina cuniculus, Sunamphitoe pelagica, Lembos longipes, Lembos websteri: after Lincoln (1979). *Aora gracilis*: after Myers and Costello (1984).

Fig. 9.39
Leptocheirus pilosus, Leptocheirus hirsutimanus, Microdeutopus anomalus, Microdeutopus chelifer,

Microdeutopus gryllotalpa, Microdeutopus versiculatus: after Lincoln (1979).

Fig. 9.40
Gammaropsis maculata, Gammaropsis nitida, Gammaropsis palmata, Gammaropsis sophiae, Isaea elmhirsti, Isaea montagui: after Lincoln (1979).

Fig. 9.41
Photis longicaudata, Megamphopus cornutus, Microprotopus maculatus, Protomedeia fasciata: after Lincoln (1979). *Photis pollex, Photis reinhardi*: after Myers and McGrath (1981).

Fig. 9.42
Corophium acherusicum, Corophium acutum, Corophium affine, Corophium arenarium, Corophium bonelli, Corophium crassicorne: after Lincoln (1979).

Fig. 9.43
Corophium insidiosum, Corophium lacustre, Corophium sextonae, Corophium multisetosum, Corophium volutator: after Lincoln (1979). *Siphonoecetes kroyeranus, Siphonoecetes striatus*: after Myers and McGrath (1979).

Fig. 9.44
Unciola crenatipalma, Unciola planipes, Chelura terebrans: after Lincoln (1979). *Ericthonius fasciatus, Ericthonius rubricornis, Ericthonius punctatus, Ericthonius difformis*: after Myers and McGrath (1984).

Fig. 9.45
Ischyrocerus anguipes, Jassa falcata, Jassa ocia, Jassa marmorata, Jassa pusilla, Parajassa pelagica, Microjassa cumbrensis: after Lincoln (1979).

Fig. 9.46
Dyopedos monacanthus, Dyopedos porrectus, Dulichia fulcata, Podocerus variegatus: after Lincoln (1979). *Hyperia galba*: after Sars (1894).

Fig. 10.11
All figures after Selbie (1915).

Fig. 10.22
All figures after Ingle (1980).

Fig. 10.24
Cancer bellianus: after Christiansen (1969).

Fig. 10.27
Pilumnus spinifer: after Christiansen (1969).

Fig. 10.28
Geryon affinis: after Christiansen (1969).

Fig. 11.22
Polyxenus lagurus, Thalassisobates littoralis, Ommatoiulus sabulosus, Brachyiulus pusillus: after Blower (1985). *Necrophloeophagus longicornis, Hydroschendyla submarina, Geophilus fucorum seurati, Strigamia maritima*: after Eason (1964).

Fig. 12.3
Partly after Fretter and Graham (1962).

Fig. 12.20
Aplysia punctata, Berthella plumula, Alderia modesta, Elysia viridis, Limapontia capitata, Tritonia hombergi, Cuthona caerulea, Polycera quadrilineata: after Thompson and Brown (1976).

Fig. 12.21
Colpodaspis pusilla, Retusa obtusa, R. truncatula, R. umbilicata, Roxania utriculus, Cylichna cylindracea, Scaphander lignarius: whole animals after Thompson and Brown (1976).

Fig. 12.22
Philine aperta, P, scabra, P, catena, P, punctata, Berthella plumula: whole animals after Thompson and Brown (1976).

Fig. 12.24
Alderia modesta, Hermaea dendritica, H. bifida, Limapontia capitata, L, senestra, L, depressa: after Thompson and Brown (1976).

Fig. 12.26
Goniodoris castanea, G. nodosa: after Thompson and Brown (1976).

Fig. 12.27
Palio dubia: after Thompson and Brown (1976).

Fig. 12.28
Rostanga rubra, Jorunna tomentosa: after Thompson and Brown (1976).

Fig. 12.29
Embletonia pulchra: after Thompson and Brown (1976).

Fig. 12.32
Tergipes tergipes, Tenellia adspersa: after Thompson and Brown (1976).

Fig. 13.18
Sepiola aurantiaca, Sepietta oweniana, S. neglecta: after Jaeckel (1968).

Fig. 13.20
Todaropsis eblanae, Todarodes sagittatus: after B. J. Muus (1963, *Fisches d'identification du zooplancton*, **96**).

Fig. 14.1
Phoronis hippocrepia (top left) and *P. muelleri*: after Cori (1932, 1939). *P. hippocrepia*: whole animal and LS lophophore base (top right) after C. Dawydoff (1959, *Traite de Zool.*, **5**(1)). *P, psammophila*: after Selys-Longchamps (1907). *P. ovalis* (left): after Harmer (1917, *Q. J. micros. Sci.*, **62**). *P. ovalis* lophophore: after Cori (1932, 1939). *P. pallida*: after Silen (1952, *Ark. Zool.*, **4**(4)). All nephridia after C. C. Emig (1974, *Z. zool. Syst. Evolut.-forsch.*, **12**).

Fig. 14.5
All figures after Davidson (1886–88).

Fig. 15.1
Partly after Dales (1969 (ed) *Practical Invertebrate Zoology*. London)

Fig. 15.2
Partly after Dales (1969 (ed) *Practical Invertebrate Zoology*. London)

Fig. 15.10
Globiferous pedicellariae ossicles: after Mortensen (1927).

Fig. 16.1
Figure A: after Stebbing (1970A); Figures B–F, and L: after Horst (1927–39); Figure G: after Brambell and

Cole (1939); Figure M: after Burdon-Jones and McIntyre (1960).

Fig. 16.2
Open body diagrams after P. Mather (1984, 'A Coral reef handbook', Brisbane).

Fig. 16.3
Diagrams after P. Mather (1984, 'A Coral reef handbook', Brisbane).

Fig. 16.4
Diazona colony: after Thompson (1933, *Fish, Scotl. Sci. Invest.*). *Polycitor*: after Kott (1952). All others: after Berrill (1950).

Fig. 16.6
All after Berrill (1950), except *A. densum*, *A. 'nordmanni'*: after Medioni (1970b); *A. pallidum*: after Van Name (1945, *Bull. Am. Mus. nat. Hist.*, **84**).

Fig. 16.7
Perophora: after Lister (1834). *D. spongiforme*: zooid clusters after Kott (1952). *A. obliqua*: after Alder and Hancock (1905). *A. prunum*: after Van Name (1945, *Bull. Am. Mus. nat. Hist.*, **84**).

Fig. 16.8
Didemnid zooids all after Lafargue (1968, 1975a, 1976), except *D. maculosum*: after Medioni (1970a).

Fig. 16.9
Didemnid zooids all after Lafargue (1968, 1975b), except *Polysyncraton bilobatum* (right): after Medioni (1970a); *Leptoclinides faeroensis*: after Millar (1966).

Fig. 16.11
Whole ascidians *S. coriacea*, *C. mollis*, *P. fibrosa* and *P. gracilis*: after Alder and Hancock (1907); body walls: after Van Name (1945, *Bull. Am. Mus. nat. Hist.*, **84**), except *P. pomaria*, *P. rustica* and *P. gracilis*: after Berrill (1950).

Fig. 16.12
Body walls of *D. variolosus* and *S. socialis*: after Lacaze-Duthiers and Delage. Body wall of *D. grossularia*: after Van Name (1945, *Bull. Am. Mus. nat. Hist.*, **84**).

Fig. 16.13
Whole ascidians *M. claudicans*, *P. microcosmos* (upper), *P. tessellata*, *P. squamulosa* and *B. echinata* after Alder and Hancock (1907). *P. microcosmos* (lower) and *E. arenosa* after Thomson (1932, *Fish. Scotl. Sci. Invest.*). Body walls of *M. claudicans* and *P. microcosmos* after Berrill (1950). *P. squamulosa* body wall: after Lacaze-Duthiers and Delage. Remainder after Lacaze-Duthiers.

Fig. 17.15
Callionymus reticulatus: after H. W. Chang (1951, *JMBA.*, **30**).

ILLUSTRATORS

GRAHAM AUSTIN
Blackpool and the Fylde College
Figs. 8.4–8.8, 9.26–9.46.

F. T. BANNER
Dept. of Geological Sciences, University College, London
Figs. 2.2–2.5.

SIMON CHEW
Blackpool and the Fylde College
Figs. 6.2–6.18, 16.6, 16.7, 16.10–16.12.

DANIEL COLE
Blackpool and the Fylde College
Figs. 6.2–6.18, 16.5.

NIGEL GERKE
Carmarthen School of Art
Figs. 12.4–12.19.

R. GIBSON
Dept. of Biology, Liverpool Polytechnic
Figs. 5.1–5.4.

TONI HARGREAVES
Blackpool and the Fylde College
Figs. 15.1–15.5, 15.10, 15.11.

P. J. HAYWARD
School of Biological Sciences, University College of Swansea
Figs. 1.1–1.5, 3.1–3.11, 4.2, 6.1, 6.28, 6.29, 8.1, 8.9, 9.10–9.15, 11.1, 11.22, 11.29, 12.1–12.3, 12.20–12.32, 13.1, 13.18–13.20, 14.2–14.4, 14.13, 14.14, 16.2–16.4 16.8, 16.9.

PHYLLIS KNIGHT-JONES
School of Biological Sciences, University College of Swansea
Figs. 6.19–6.27.

PAUL J. LLEWELLYN
School of Biological Sciences, University College of Swansea
Figs. 4.1, 4.3–4.31, 6.2, 6.3, 6.9, 6.11, 6.30, 6.31, 7.1, 7.2, 8.2, 8.3, 8.10–8.16, 9.1–9.7, 9.16–9.25, 9.27–9.48, 10.1–10.28, 11.2–11.20, 11.23–11.25, 11.27, 11.28, 11.30–11.32, 13.2–13.17, 15.1, 15.2, 15.6–15.9, 15.12–15.14, 16.1, 16.5, 16.10, 16.11, 16.13, 17.1–17.18.

JULIET POWELL
Carmarthen School of Art
Figs. 2.1, 2.6–2.9.

P. J. A. PUGH
School of Biological Sciences, University College of Swansea
Figs. 11.2–11.16.

J. S. RYLAND
School of Biological Sciences, University College of Swansea
Figs. 7.3, 14.1, 14.5–14.12, 14.15.

NATHALIE YONOW
School of Biological Sciences, University College of Swansea
Figs. 9.8, 9.9, 11.17–11.21.

CONTENTS

CONTRIBUTORS

F. T. BANNER
Dept. of Geological Sciences, University College London
Chapter 2, Sarcodina.

P. F. S. CORNELIUS
Dept. of Zoology, British Museum (Natural History), London
Chapter 4, Hydrozoa (with J. S. Ryland).

P. E. J. DYRYNDA AND ELIZABETH A. DYRYNDA
School of Biological Sciences, University College of Swansea
Chapter 3.

P. ELLIOTT
School of Biological Sciences, University College of Swansea
Chapter 11, Coleoptera (with P. E. King).

R. GIBSON
Dept. of Biology, Liverpool Polytechnic
Chapter 5, Nemertea (with E. W. Knight-Jones).

P. J. HAYWARD
School of Biological Sciences, University College of Swansea
Chapter 1; Chapter 12, Polyplacophora and Scaphopoda; Chapter 13, Bivalvia.

M. J. ISAAC
Dept. of Extra Mural Studies, University College of Swansea
Chapter 8, Ostracoda and Copepoda; Chapter 9, Leptostraca, Cumacea, and Tanaidacea.

P. E. KING
School of Biological Sciences, University College of Swansea
Chapter 11, Pycnogonida, Insecta (with P. Elliott, Alison Smith and Sarah L. A. Wheeler),
Tardigrada (with C. I. Morgan).

E. W. KNIGHT-JONES
School of Biological Sciences, University College of Swansea
Chapter 2, Mastigophora, Ciliophora (with J. M. Wright);
Chapter 5, Nemertea (with R. Gibson); Chapter 6, Hirudinea;
Chapter 7, Priapulida, Sipuncula, Echiura, and Pogonophora;
Chapter 16, Hemichordata.

PHYLLIS KNIGHT-JONES
School of Biological Sciences, University College of Swansea
Chapter 6, Sabellariidae, Sabellidae, Serpulidae, and Spirorbidae.

P. MAKINGS
School of Biological Sciences, University College of Swansea
Chapter 9, Mysidacea.

R. L. MANUEL
Dept. of Zoology, University of Oxford
Chapter 4, Anthozoa.

C. I. MORGAN
Field Studies Council Research Centre, Popton Fort
Chapter 11, Tardigrada (with P. E. King).

J. MOYSE
School of Biological Sciences, University College of Swansea
Chapter 8, Cirripedia;
Chapter 10, Reptantia; Chapter 15, Echinoidea, Asteroidea.

E. NAYLOR
School of Ocean Sciences, University College of North Wales
Chapter 9, Isopoda.

A. NELSON-SMITH
School of Biological Sciences, University College of Swansea
Chapter 6, Polychaeta (except for Sabellariidae, Sabellidae, Serpulidae, and
Spirorbidae), Oligochaeta.

P. J. A. PUGH
School of Biological Sciences, University College of Swansea
Chapter 11, Arachnida.

J. S. RYLAND
School of Biological Sciences, University College of Swansea
Chapter 4, Scyphozoa, Hydrozoa (with P. F. S. Cornelius);
Chapter 7, Entoprocta; Chapter 14; Chapter 16, Urochordata;
Chapter 17.

G. SMALDON
formerly University College of Swansea
Chapter 9, Caprellidea; Chapter 10, Natantia.

ALISON SMITH
School of Biological Sciences, University College of Swansea
Chapter 11, Diptera (with P. E. King).

P. A. TYLER
Dept. of Oceanography, University College of Swansea
[*present address: Dept. of Oceanography, University of Southampton*]
Chapter 15, Ophiuroidea, Holothurioidea.

SARAH L. A. WHEELER
School of Biological Sciences, University College of Swansea
Chapter 11, Collembola (with P. E. King).

G. D. WIGHAM
Department of Biological Sciences, Polytechnic South-West
Chapter 12, Prosobranchia.

R. G. WITHERS
formerly University College of Swansea
Chapter 9, Gammaridea.

J. M. WRIGHT
formerly University College of Swansea
Chapter 2, Ciliophora (with E. W. Knight Jones).

NATHALIE YONOW
School of Biological Sciences, University College of Swansea
Chapter 12, Opisthobranchia, Pulmonata.

1 INTRODUCTION

FROM Shetland to Scilly, the British Isles extend through 11 degrees of latitude, a distance of about 1250 km. Between eastern England and western Ireland they range through 13 degrees of longitude, about 900 km. The northern and western boundaries of this region face the open Atlantic; oceanic influences, locally modified by geographical and topographical factors, largely modulate the character of the marine environment. The eastern side of the British Isles bounds a shallow epicontinental sea; oceanic influences in the North Sea decrease towards the south, where the proximity of the European landmass has a different modifying effect. In the south, the complex hydrography of the Channel results in rapidly changing physical characteristics along its length, again with discernible environmental consequences. The Irish Sea, and major embayments such as the Bristol Channel, Liverpool Bay, the Scottish firths, and the Wash, are also characterized by particular physical conditions and, if geography is stretched to include the Channel Isles, the Gulf of St. Malo exemplifies further modifications of the marine environment. The effects of major physical factors are everywhere mediated by local geographical and topographical influences. Thus, throughout the region there exist marked gradients in the marine environment which are reflected in profuse variation in the characteristics of different marine habitats, with consequent effects on the nature of the marine fauna. Good illustrations of this have been provided by Holme (1961, 1966) and Cabioch (1968) in their studies of the environmental characteristics, bottom deposits, and benthic fauna of the Channel.

The marine fauna of the British Isles is rich and varied. The coastline encompasses almost all types of temperate intertidal habitat, from hypersaline and brackish lagoons, estuaries, and coastal marsh and mudflats, to sandy and rocky shores with every degree of exposure and widely varying profile. Subtidal habitats are equally diverse. Each local habitat reflects prevailing environmental factors and is further characterized by its biota. Thus the marine fauna itself demonstrates gradients of change throughout the British Isles.

The sea has been of economic importance throughout the histories of the nations inhabiting the British Isles, and marine science has an increasing significance today. Long-established fishing traditions have developed into major industries which now demand careful international management, based on continuous research and monitoring. Industrialization and urban development, particularly of coastal wetlands and estuaries, have had a profound impact on both inshore and offshore habitats. Improved ecological understanding is necessary if the effects of current levels of development are to be assessed accurately. This is needed with increasing urgency; coastal barrage schemes, for example, almost certainly leading to further industrialization, will have profound effects on marine habitats over very wide areas. Environmental quality is accorded increasing importance for both economic and aesthetic reasons, and marine biological research is important in this context, not only in view of the need to measure and control the effects of urban, industrial, and radioactive effluents, but also because some marine ecosystems are useful as early indicators of environmental contamination.

One field of marine research with a long history is that concerned with fouling organisms. Rapid, dense, and persistent growth of sessile invertebrates, leading to extensive fouling of harbours, docks, the hulls of ships, and power station water intake systems, continues to be a problem. Toxic substances, such as organo-tins, used to control fouling may also adversely affect the naturally occurring fauna, especially in enclosed waters. The development of offshore structures for oil drilling, mineral extraction, and power generation is likely to increase during the rest of the present century, and marine fouling research will continue to be important. The impact of such future developments on marine habitats and their animal communities will require continuous monitoring. A final consideration, perhaps likely to loom larger in the future, is marine biology as a leisure pursuit. Academic research is long established, and will certainly continue, but there is a rapidly expanding amateur interest at least partly fuelled by the growing popularity of scuba diving.

Study or use of marine habitats needs to be informed and considerate. Increased access to our marine heritage must be accompanied by habitat awareness and responsibility. The adverse effect of visitors on the marine biota is not a new phenomenon, and the deterioration of shores in Torbay in the Victorian era was recorded by Edmund Gosse (1907, *Father and son*), but the number of people able to visit the coast is hugely greater now.

Whatever short-term exigencies may dictate, it is certain that marine biology will continue to expand steadily as both an academic and applied discipline, and will contribute increasingly to other, more specialized fields of biological science. Specialization must be founded upon a basic background in marine biology, which undoubtedly needs to be more widely taught. This book is designed to provide a broad introduction to the marine fauna of the British Isles, and is intended to enable students and specialists to identify accurately most, at least, of the organisms they are likely to encounter during the course of marine biological field-work, survey or monitoring programmes, or detailed ecological research. It provides a series of keys, taxonomic descriptions, and illustrations, together with short notes on habitat, occurrence, and distribution, for almost all of the major groups of benthic marine animals. The breadth of coverage varies from group to group. For some, such as the Cnidaria and Mollusca, treatment is broad and excludes only the rarest species; for certain others, such as the Platyhelminthes, extensive coverage is not possible within a work of this kind. In these latter cases, an introduction is given to demonstrate sufficiently the variety and number of species likely to be encountered, and to guide the user to specialist literature. For some groups of animals, such as the fish and Bryozoa, there are good modern texts available and the selection included here encompasses only the most widespread and ecologically most significant inshore species. However, for certain other groups, such as Mollusca and Decapoda, both of which have a good modern literature, coverage is still extensive as these generally conspicuous animals tend to be preferentially collected by students and amateurs. As a general rule the text includes, for most groups, a preponderance of the species occurring from the shore to about 50 m depth. Coverage of subtidal species varies from group to group, but it is hoped that intertidal faunas have been more than adequately dealt with. The plankton is not included; it has deservedly received extensive treatment in the *Fiches d'identification du zooplancton* (Conseil International pour l'Exploration de la Mer, Copenhagen). Similarly, sea birds and mammals have a wide literature of their own, which could not be improved upon here.

The remaining sections of this introductory chapter deal briefly with those features of the marine environment most important to an understanding of the nature of local marine habitats, together with a discussion of distribution patterns. Good introductions to marine biology and ecology are provided by, for example, Yonge (1949), Lewis (1964), Barnes and Hughes (1982), King (1975) and Price *et al.* (1980), while more specialist reviews are provided in the volume edited by Moore and Seed (1985). The five volume treatise edited by Kinne (1970–84) is the most comprehensive review of marine ecology presently available.

A detailed series of maps of the British sea area has been provided by Lee and Ramster (1981).

HYDROGRAPHY

The primary distinction between the sea areas to the west and to the east of the British Isles (Fig. 1.1) is related to the proximity in the west of the edge of the European continental shelf, generally accepted to coincide with the 200 m isobath. From the Celtic Sea the edge of the shelf trends north-eastwards close to the western coasts of Ireland and Scotland, turning abruptly south-east north of the Shetlands as the edge of a deep trough, the Rinne, which flanks the western and southern coast of Norway. The 100 m isobath follows a similar route, but lies closer inshore in the south-west, extends into the southern Minch between the Hebrides and mainland Scotland, and subsequently continues south-east from Shetland to Aberdeen before turning east, marking the edge of a broad arc of deep shelf situated between north-east Scotland and the Rinne. Beyond 200 m depth, topographic features of the sea floor influ-

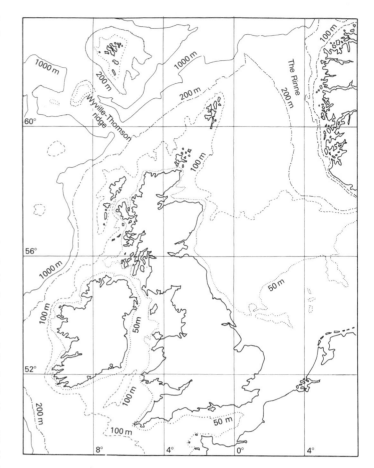

Fig. 1.1 Bathymetric map of the British sea area

ence the deep water circulation of the north-east Atlantic. The deep channel between the Shetland-Hebrides shelf and the Faeroes is interrupted by a north-west trending ridge, the Wyville Thomson ridge, which forms a barrier affecting the free interchange between cold water of the deep Norwegian Sea and the warmer water of the north-east Atlantic. However, shallow water circulation patterns are more regularly related to the 200 m or 100 m isobaths. Much of the sea floor of the central and southern Irish Sea lies below the 50 m isobath, as do the central and western areas of the English Channel. To the east, the Southern Bight of the North Sea is mostly shallower than 50 m while the central region lies between 50 m and 100 m depth. Thus, the west of the British Isles is characterized by a great and relatively rapid shallowing towards the coast, while the North Sea shoals gradually and gently towards the south.

There are no marked areas of strong upwelling around the British Isles. The region is characterized by fluctuating gradients of changing physical factors related to the residual flow of the North Atlantic drift. The rate of flow, volume, and course of the North Atlantic drift vary from year to year, and surface current patterns may similarly be modified by seasonal effects such as wind and temperature. However, the gross features of the circulation are relatively constant. The North Atlantic drift passes north-eastwards along the western coasts of Ireland and Scotland. A portion is deflected into the Celtic Sea, and from there both northwards into the Irish Sea and eastwards along the

Channel. These two elements of the circulation are particularly variable. North of Scotland the flow divides; the larger part continues north-eastwards but a portion turns southwards into the North Sea. It is thought that from the Hebrides to Shetland and into the North Sea much of the water of the North Atlantic drift flows along the 200 m isobath, and as it flows southwards in the North Sea is partly influenced by the 100 m isobath. Circulation within the North Sea is variable, but important features are a northern, clockwise flow, which incorporates northward-flowing water originating from the Kattegat, and a smaller anticlockwise gyre in the south, which varies considerably according to the volume of water flowing eastwards through the Dover Strait and the southward-flowing coastal current which passes down the eastern side of Britain. This eastern coastal current represents a portion of the North Atlantic drift which passes between Orkney and Shetland, and between Orkney and mainland Scotland. The volume of this flow, and its degree of deflection towards the eastern coast, vary greatly from year to year. It should be noted that the circulation patterns described above all relate to surface currents, and all may be influenced and modified by water movements at greater depth.

Surface waters are characterized by their plankton species, and the distribution and abundance of indicator species in a particular year give a rough guide to the origins of the different water masses. Most simply, through late spring to autumn, this allows distinction to be made between resident plankton communities in the North Sea, English Channel, and certain large embayments such as the Bristol Channel and Morecambe Bay, and oceanic species marking influxes of fresh oceanic water. In regions of mixing a plankton community characterized by the chaetognath *Sagitta elegans* is found, and the distribution and extent of '*elegans* water' each year gives an approximate indication of the direction and volume of residual currents of the North Atlantic drift.

TEMPERATURE AND SALINITY

Temperature is probably the most important of the major physical environmental factors which mediate the life histories of marine organisms. Its effects are expressed in different distribution patterns, rates of growth, and in the timing of reproductive cycles. Sea surface temperatures around the British Isles vary considerably through the year (Fig. 1.2), and both the range and the pattern of isotherms differ between the western shores and the shallow North Sea.

During the winter months the surface temperature gradient for the whole region trends roughly east–west. In the eastern North Sea, along the German and Danish coasts, mean winter surface temperature is typically less than 3°C. North–south isotherms extend almost to the middle of the North Sea, but near the east coasts of England and Scotland they are sharply deflected to run east–west, influenced by warmer Atlantic water in the northern North Sea and warmer flows through the Dover Strait. However, from the Thames estuary to Caithness, inshore waters have a mean winter temperature of only 5° or 6°C. Winter minima increase steadily westwards along the Channel, and in

the Western Approaches the winter mean reaches 10°C. Off the west coast, winter isotherms again tend to align north–south and most of the west coast of England has a mean winter low of 7° to 8°C. In the Bristol Channel and Morecambe Bay it is often lower than this; in Morecambe Bay, in particular, the winter low may match that for east coasts and, under certain meteorological conditions, approaches the very low values obtained for the Danish coast. The western coast of Ireland is the warmest in the region and from Donegal southwards the mean winter low ranges from 9° to 10°C.

During the summer the temperature gradient runs approximately north–south on both sides of the British Isles, with highest values, of 18°C and upwards, obtained along the south-east coast of the North Sea, and a summer mean declining from 17° to 13°C northwards along eastern Britain. On the west coast the highest mean summer temperatures, up to 16°C, are found in relatively enclosed areas, such as Morecambe Bay, while for western Ireland 14° to 15°C is normal for the whole coast. Thus, annual range in sea surface temperature may be as much as 12°C off south-eastern England, or as little as 5° along the west coast of Ireland.

For intertidal species air temperature may be as significant a factor in their distribution as sea temperature. The seasonal pattern of air temperature over the British Isles is very similar to, though less complex than, that for sea surface temperature (Fig. 1.2). In winter there is a gradient from a mean of 3.9° in the east to 7.2°C in south-west Cornwall. In summer it extends north–south, from 13° in Orkney to 17°C off the south-east coast of England.

Mean bottom seawater temperatures for the whole of the North Sea and the western shelf are only a little lower, in winter, than those of the surface. The distribution of isotherms is not dissimilar to that for surface temperature, and a vertical range of 1° to 2°C occurs over the whole region. During summer, vertical ranges in temperature are naturally greater, and differ between west and east coasts. On the west coast the pattern of isotherms is similar to that for surface temperature, with a vertical range of 2°C in the central Irish Sea and up to 6° in the south-west Celtic Sea. In the North Sea a body of very cold water lies on the bottom over much of the central and northern part of the region, giving a steep gradient in mean bottom temperature from 17°C off the Netherlands coast to less than 7° off southern Norway where a vertical range of as much as 13° has been recorded.

Salinity is regarded as the second most important physical characteristic of the marine environment. Throughout the British sea area total concentration of dissolved salts has a low range of about 31 to 35‰ (g/kg) (Fig. 1.3). The 35‰ isohaline marks the boundary of Atlantic oceanic water; values lower than this reflect the mixing of oceanic water with varying proportions of water from other sources. Surface and bottom salinity differ little; for both, values of 34–35‰ pertain throughout most of the Irish Sea and the North Sea. In major embayments, in the German Bight, and along the southern shores of the North Sea a mean summer surface salinity as low as 30‰ may be further reduced to 29‰ by winter river outflows, while bottom salinities

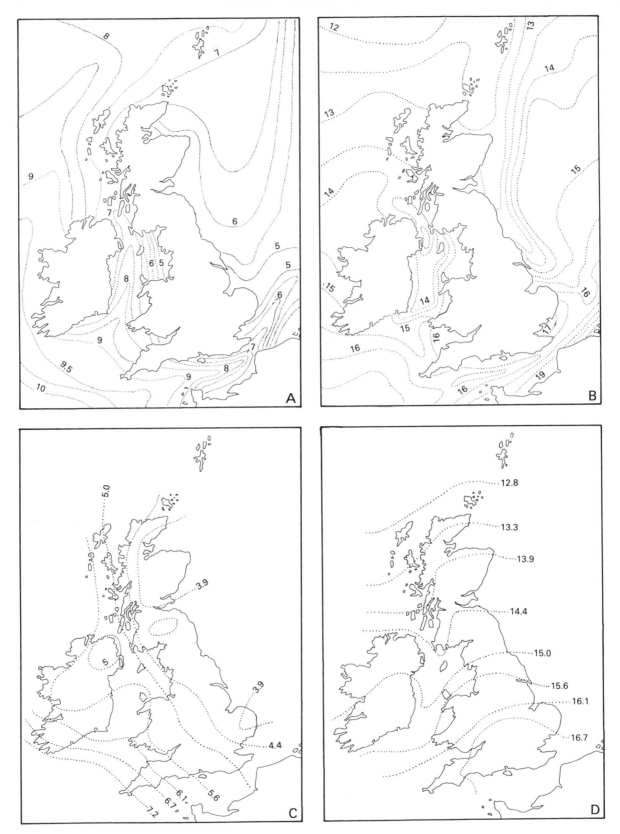

Fig. 1.2 Temperature, degrees centigrade. A Mean winter sea surface temperature. B Mean summer sea surface temperature. C Mean winter air temperature. D Mean summer air temperature.

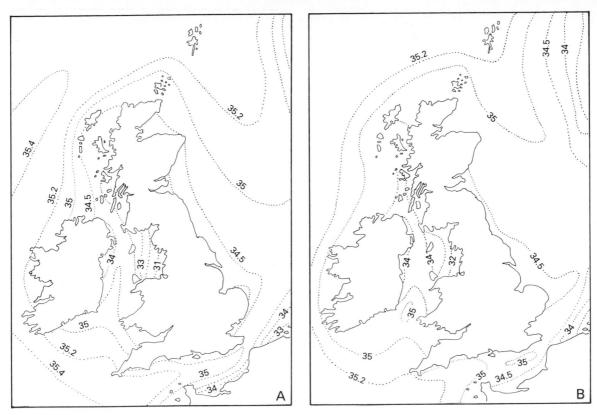

Fig. 1.3 Mean surface salinity (‰). A Winter. B Summer.

of as little as 27‰ may similarly be depressed to 23‰. However, over much of the British sea area, seasonal variation in both surface and bottom salinity is related to the penetration of oceanic water, having a salt concentration in excess of 35‰, into the English Channel and northern North Sea during the winter months.

Temperature/salinity profiles are used together to define the limits of particular water bodies, which may be further characterized by other properties, such as nutrient content and plankton communities. Temperature/salinity profiles of the water column during the summer months sometimes indicate a sharp boundary, or thermocline, between warm surface waters, often of slightly lower salinity, and cold deeper waters. The thermocline has biological significance in both preventing the interchange of nutrients between upper and lower water layers, and in limiting the vertical migration of organisms. Regular vertical mixing of water resists the establishment of a thermocline, and it has been shown that the likelihood of mixing can be predicted by the equation $\log_{10}(H/U^3)$, where H is water depth at a particular point, and U the maximum tidal stream velocity at that point. Values of less than 2 indicate a regime of continual mixing and no thermocline, whereas sea areas with values of 2 or more tend to be layered during the summer months. The transition boundary between layered and non-layered waters tends to be sharp, and such boundaries constitute what are referred to as oceanic fronts. In the British sea area this boundary $[\log_{10}(H/U^3) \geqslant 2]$ coincides with the limits of unmixed Atlantic oceanic water, except in the southern North

Sea. Here, the boundary extends well south of the unmixed Atlantic waters, perhaps influenced by a deep-lying body of cold water at the bottom of the north and central North Sea. Thus, the southern part of the North Sea, the coastal waters of eastern England, the Channel, Bristol Channel, and much of the Irish Sea are unlayered, mixed, and often turbid throughout the year. Where these warm, shallow waters are high in dissolved organic nutrients, as off south-east England and the Netherlands, high marine productivity results, and such areas tend to be important nursery grounds for benthic fish.

MARINE PRODUCTIVITY

Plankton productivity, measured in terms of the average daily production of organic carbon over the sea surface, is the most important biological factor determining the distribution and biomass of marine organisms. Generally, productivity is highest in shallow seas, off large estuaries or in regions of upwelling, and lowest in polar waters and over the great ocean basins. The primary source of organic carbon is through photosynthetic fixation by phytoplankton, and the rate of production is dependent on light, temperature, and the availability of nutrient salts, principally of nitrate and phosphate, for phytoplankton growth. Light available for photosynthesis penetrates to a far greater depth in clear oceanic water than in the often turbid waters of shallow seas. However, high productivity demands a high level of nutrients, and in oceanic waters there is a continual loss of nutrients as organisms die and sink to depths beyond which photosynthesis is impossible.

Each sea area is characterized by a particular type of production cycle (Cushing 1975), dependent upon prevailing physical environmental factors and biological factors, especially the period of delay between the initiation of phytoplankton growth and the appearance of planktonic herbivores. In the temperate north-east Atlantic plankton productivity displays characteristic seasonal peaks. As daylength and sea temperature rise in early spring phytoplankton growth increases rapidly, developing a 'bloom', which around Britain peaks between late April and May. This growth is fuelled by nutrient levels enhanced by winter stirring—the overturn of coastal waters by wind and storm, bringing dissolved organic materials to the sea surface. The phytoplankton bloom is followed by a bloom of grazing zooplankton, the peak of which coincides with the decline of the phytoplankton. The effects of intensive grazing are enhanced by a decrease in nutrients, and the phytoplankton bloom declines swiftly through June. An important factor in reducing nutrient levels is the summer thermocline, which effectively prevents mixing of surface and deeper waters, and there is a consequent net loss of nutrients from the upper layers. In late autumn the thermocline breaks down, vertical mixing begins again, and there is a second, smaller productivity peak which eventually declines as both daylength and temperature drop with the onset of winter.

In the British sea area winter nutrient levels are highest in the southern North Sea, off the Thames Estuary and the Wash, and in the northern Irish Sea. Values for both phosphate and nitrate are lowest in the central and northern North Sea, in the Celtic Sea, and off western Britain beyond the 100 m isobath. In these latter areas, also, a summer thermocline is characteristic. The shallow coastal waters of the British Isles show little summer layering of the water column and here productivity is highest, achieving an average daily rate of at least $500\,mg\,C\,m^{-2}$, and often very much more. In these areas light penetration is perhaps an important limiting factor, with photosynthesis occurring only in the top few metres of water.

TIDES

Tides are a significant factor in the ecology of marine organisms, as well as an important consideration for marine biologists. All coastlines are subjected to regular vertical changes in sea level, although in some parts of the world these are so small at times as to be scarcely discernible. Around the British Isles tidal ranges are variable, sometimes complexly so, and some coastlines experience often spectacular tidal amplitudes. The pattern of variation in tidal range around Britain and Ireland, and its effect on the ecology of intertidal marine organisms have been discussed at length by Lewis (1964), while King (1975) presents a detailed account of tidal theory and the principles of tidal prediction.

Tidal movements of the oceans result from the mutual gravitational attraction of the earth, moon, and sun. Tidal predictions are based on the known, regular movements of the three bodies, but tidal forces are subject to modification by meteorological influences, among others, and actual tidal effects may vary considerably from prediction. The tide-producing, or tractive, force is the resultant of two opposing agencies: the gravitational forces exerted by the sun and the moon, and a centrifugal force generated by the rotation of the earth. The tractive force varies in tune with the earth's yearly orbit of the sun, the 28 day orbit of the moon, and the 24 hour rotation of the earth itself. Analysis of tidal rhythms shows that the components attributable to the sun and to the moon are distinct and separable; when both are aligned with the earth their separate gravitational forces combine to give maximum tidal effect, resulting in the fortnightly spring tides. At the first and last quarter of the moon, the two forces are to some extent opposed; tidal effects are then dampened, resulting in the low-amplitude neap tides. Overall, however, the moon is the dominating influence on tidal rhythms, and is responsible for the mean tidal period of around 12 hours, giving two high and two low tide periods in each day, a tidal pattern referred to as semi-diurnal. The two high tides of a single day may not be of equivalent height and, similarly, the two low tides may be unequal; this phenomenon of diurnal inequality is related to the declination of the moon relative to different points on the earth's surface. Generally, around the British Isles the degree of diurnal inequality is slight compared with that in certain other parts of the world.

The tide-producing tractive force gives rise to tidal streams in the oceans, characterized by wave forms whose velocity is dependent upon water depth and gravitional force (King 1975). Where these tidal streams impinge on continental land masses and are subject to the modifying effects of shelf and coastal topography, reflection of the wave sets up the oscillating system which gives rise to the tides. In enclosed basins, such as the Bristol Channel, these oscillations are particularly marked, and their period can be shown (King 1975) to be dependent entirely on water depth and the length of the basin. When the period of oscillation is close to the mean tidal period very large tidal amplitudes may result; at points in the Bristol Channel, for example, spring tide ranges of 10 m or more are usual.

The tidal cycles at different points around the British Isles can be correlated by reference to a further modifying effect of the centrifugal force generated by the earth's rotation, the Coriolis force. In the northern hemisphere the Coriolis force results in moving bodies, such as tidal streams, being deflected by a measurable amount to the right of their path. Thus, as the Atlantic flood tide flows into the northern part of the North Sea, the tidal stream is deflected towards the coasts of Scotland and England; the deflection is reversed as the ebb flows northwards again. The resulting complex movement of water in the North Sea, through a tidal cycle of 12 hours, can best be described by reference to three nodal, or amphidromic, points around which tidal streams and successive changes in tidal elevation appear to move in an anticlockwise direction. These amphidromic points may be fixed by plotting co-tidal times, viz., lines joining points on the surface of the North Sea where high tide occurs at precisely the same time. The co-tidal lines are seen to radiate from three points (Fig. 1.4): one situated midway between East Anglia and the coast of the Netherlands, a second in the central North Sea, and a third close to the south-west coast of Norway.

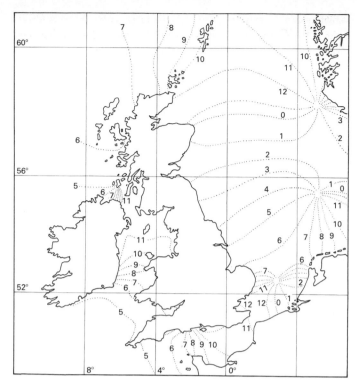

Fig. 1.4 Co-tidal lines and amphidromic points

At each amphidromic point there is no tidal fluctuation in sea level, and tidal range increases progressively away from the point. The anticlockwise flow of the three North Sea amphidromic systems is synchronized to the extent that from Caithness to Sheppey, high water occurs successively later down the whole of the east coast. Off the western British Isles co-tidal lines tend to be correlated with amphidromic systems of the north Atlantic; there is no simple progression of high tide times, tidal range is highly variable and often rather low. In the Channel, combined effects of the Coriolis force, and the frictional drag on the tidal stream as it passes eastwards along a shallowing and narrowing trough, result in inequalities in tidal range on each side of the Channel. On both ebb and flow, vertical movement of the tide tends to be higher on the south than on the north shore of the Channel. The amphidromic system is poorly developed, but can be plotted with reference to an inland point in southern England.

Tidal phenomena have been extensively studied around the British Isles, particularly with regard to their significance for intertidal marine ecology. Lewis (1964) presented a detailed account of tidal cycles and their variation around the coasts of Britain and Ireland, and only a general introduction to the topic is intended here. The tidal range for a given locality refers to the vertical variation in sea level throughout a tidal period. The 28 day cycle of neap and spring tides oscillates about a mean tidal level (MTL), and four important standard levels may be recognized: mean high water of spring (MHWS) and neap (MHWN) tides, and mean low water of spring (MLWS) and neap (MLWN) tides. These levels refer to the mean heights in any year, while 'extreme' levels (e.g. ELWS) refer to the lowest tides of the year. Two important features of tidal cycles are related to the astronomical and gravitational factors discussed above. Firstly, tidal range changes progressively, with each tidal period, throughout the spring/neap cycle, with the highest spring tides of each cycle occurring about $1\frac{1}{2}$ days after the full and new moon. Secondly, spring and neap tidal amplitudes, also, change progressively through the year, with the greatest spring amplitude occurring at the time of the equinoctial tides, in late March and late September, when the sun passes the earth's equator. The fact that the tidal period, between two high tides, is on average greater than 12 hours results in tides becoming progressively later each day. This cycle coincides with the neap/spring cycle of $14\frac{1}{2}$ days, and thus at any locality spring tides occur at approximately the same time of day on each cycle, this time advancing by 1 or 2 hours in the course of a complete year.

The tidal range, MHWS–MLWS, varies most commonly between 3–7 m; in the Bristol Channel and the Gulf of St. Malo it may be greater than 10 m, while along the Channel coast it may be only 1.5–3 m. Smallest tidal ranges, from 0.5 to 1.5 m, are found along the south-west shores of Scotland. The effect of the tidal cycle on a particular shore is expressed as successive periods of emersion and immersion, of varying duration, the consequences of which for the intertidal fauna and flora are mediated by topographic and climatic factors. The latter—rain, freshwater runoff, wind, sunshine, and air temperature—will vary in intensity according to latitude and the time of day at which low tides, especially low springs, occur. Barometric pressure and wind strength may have profound effects on tides. A combination of low pressure and onshore winds can result in low tides not reaching predicted levels, while unusually high pressure may depress the tide below its expected minimum. The tide has an influence on the broad distribution of marine organisms, both vertically and horizontally, and also a profound effect on the zoned distribution of the intertidal fauna and flora. This aspect of marine ecology continues to be of particular interest to marine biologists (Lewis 1964; Stephenson and Stephenson 1972).

GEOLOGY

Sedimentary and igneous rocks of all geological ages contribute to the structure of the British Isles, are represented in coastal topographies, and provide sources of material for marine deposits. Generally, youngest and least resistant rocks outcrop along the south-eastern coasts; here, excluding man-made structures such as groynes and port installations, intertidal hard substrata tend to be relatively impermanent, and typically with low and rounded profiles. The geological age of rocks increases steadily northwards and westwards; coastal outcrops are correspondingly harder, more resistant to erosion and, depending on the geomorphology of each region, more or less precipitous. The igneous intrusions of south-western England, and the Precambrian metamorphic series of north-west Scotland and the Western Isles, are exceptionally hard. These rocks weather less readily than sedimentary rocks and the effect of coastal erosion is to produce smooth, rounded profiles which provide few opportunities for habitat diversity. Generally, the limestone shores of north-east and south-west England, South Wales, and southern and western Ireland support the richest intertidal faunas. The physical and chemical erosion of limestone, particularly when well-bedded, leads to the development of maximum diversity of intertidal rocky habitats. However, shores of slate, interbedded sandstones and marls, or fissile shales, when protected from high levels of marine erosion, often support faunas almost as rich as those of limestone shores.

The nature of the marine fauna developed along a certain coastline, including both intertidal and subtidal elements, is also dependent on coastal topography, which is itself related both to regional geomorphology and hydrography. Thus, shallowing, retrenched coastlines tend to be areas of marine deposition characterized by sandy beaches and offshore bars. When sheltered from the prevailing swell such areas may accumulate the finest deposits, giving rich faunas of soft-bottom invertebrates and high populations of demersal fish. Rocky promontories may develop a hard substratum fauna, but this is often impoverished through the scouring effect of a high sand-table. High-energy depositing coastlines are characterized by coarse gravel deposits, frequently with a high proportion of shell which may support a diverse and dense community of encrusting organisms. Salient coastlines of promontories, frequently associated with offshore islets, stacks or reefs, are erosional coastlines typically fully exposed to the Atlantic swell; the magnitude, and hence erosional effect, of a swell is related to its 'fetch', the distance of uninterrupted sea surface over which it develops. Deposition on such coasts is localized, and limited to short, coarse-grained, high-energy beaches between promontories. Offshore, the bottom is typically of bedrock, boulders and cobbles, and patches of coarse gravel. Both intertidal and subtidal habitats are richly populated; seaweed cover is typically dense and animal diversity high. Estuarine and lagoonal habitats, finally, develop where coastal topography and regional drainage patterns interact to give conditions of extreme shelter and permit continual deposition of land-derived erosional products. Three exceptions to this may be noted, however. Drowned ria coastlines, such as those found in south-west England, typically have extensive, sheltered, fully marine inlets in which both rate of freshwater runoff and sedimentation is too low to encourage the development of estuarine conditions. Fjords are drowned glacial valleys, often very deep and typically with a shallow barrier, or 'threshold', close to the seaward mouth, which may to some extent result in different physical conditions between the benthic environment of the fjord and that of the adjacent sea. The deep sea lochs of western Scotland may be regarded as fjords. Finally, sheltered lagoons may develop, as on the south coast of Devon, where storm beaches on a high-energy coast isolate narrow stretches of coastline, along which lenses of seawater are trapped, to freshen to brackish conditions through slow, persistent freshwater seepage.

The varying rock types of Britain and Ireland thus give rise to differing coastal forms and provide different opportunities for the development of marine habitats. Similarly, the rock and soil type of a particular region, together with its coastal topography and drainage pattern will influence the nature of the offshore, subtidal environment, with consequent effects for the marine

fauna. These influences are modified by other factors of the physical marine environment, and strong tidal streams, exposure to heavy swell, and various climatic features may result in erosional products being deposited at sites remote from their origin. However, in very few areas is the nature of the offshore environment predominantly determined by proximate, presently acting influences. Instead, the most important factor determining the nature of the marine benthic environment around the British Isles is the Pleistocene glaciation of north-western Europe. Much of the North Sea, the Channel, and the Irish Sea is floored with thick deposits of mixed clay, sand, and gravel which has been continuously reworked and redistributed by hydrographical factors since the retreat of the ice sheets. Much of the eastern half of the North Sea is covered with sand and gravel deposits predominantly of Pleistocene age, sorted by tidal streams and currents, with its present-day distribution related to prevailing current patterns, and augmented to a varying degree by post-Pleistocene erosion. Central areas of the North Sea have extensive muddy bottoms, probably consisting predominantly of fine particles transported from other areas of the sea, although again this will be augmented to some extent by post-Pleistocene sediments. However, muddy areas along the southern coast of the North Sea are in all likelihood entirely derived from post-glaciation river borne sediments.

Westwards along the Channel sediments steadily coarsen, as tidal streams increase in velocity. The western half of the Channel has extensive areas of coarse gravel and large deposits of dead shell, their distribution again related to prevailing current regimes (Cabioch 1968). The exposed western coasts of Ireland and Scotland have offshore bottoms of boulders, gravel and coarse sand, with patches of bare bedrock, and are not influenced to any degree by glacial deposits. Sands and gravels, on the western coasts of the British Isles, have a high content of shell debris and other organic carbonates, while eastern benthic sand deposits are predominantly of silica.

ANIMAL DISTRIBUTIONS

The marine faunas of the British Isles are not everywhere the same. A survey of a moderately sheltered rocky shore on the coast of Northumberland will reveal a slightly different suite of species from a similar survey on the coast of south Devon. Similarly, dredge hauls from the Firth of Clyde and the western English Channel may be equally rich in species, but different groups of species will occur in each haul. Certain familiar species occur commonly on all British coasts; certain others may have very limited distributions, being restricted, for example, to north-east or south-west coasts. Many species may simply be more common at one geographical extreme than the other, occurring with diminishing frequency along a north–south or east–west gradient. No marine species is truly ubiquitous, and even the commonest and most widely distributed species do not occur at constant frequency or density over the whole of their geographical range. Similarly, widely distributed species rarely display the same population structure, or the same reproductive cycle, over the whole of their range. Distribution pattern is part of the array of biological features characterizing each individual species, and patchiness is characteristic of all species distribution patterns.

The distribution of a particular marine organism can be defined at different levels, and discontinuities—patchiness—may occur on more than one scale. At the broadest level, each species occupies a particular geographical range, which may be very extensive or very limited. Some large pelagic fish, planktonic cnidarians, or benthic molluscs with very protracted larval stages may be truly pan-oceanic in distribution; abyssal molluscs and echinoderms may be widely distributed over entire ocean basins; many intertidal or shallow sublittoral organisms are distributed along the whole length of one or more continental margins. Conversely, for example, perhaps a majority of bryozoans, with only short swimming larval stages, have relatively restricted geographical distributions; viviparous intertidal prosobranchs may occur as groups of polymorphic or allopatric species, distributed successively along a continental margin or through a chain of islands; shallow-water or intertidal animals of oceanic islands are sometimes specifically distinct from those of the next island or the nearest continental land mass. Within the limits of its geographical range, each species is further restricted by a series of physical, biological, and ecological factors, which generally result in a concentration of populations in habitats particular to each species. These factors are frequently complexly interrelated, but it is often possible to isolate them and thus to define successive scales of patchiness. For example, within the north-east Atlantic region a particular species may be limited by lowest winter sea surface temperatures to parts of western Norway, the Western Isles of Britain, and the west coast of Ireland. It may then be further restricted to moderately exposed rocky shorelines free of estuarine or other freshwater influence; resource competition may confine the same species to a particular vertical zone, from parts of which it may be excluded by predation, parasitism, habitat disturbance, or other ecological factors.

The study of animal and plant distributions is formally defined as biogeography. At its broadest, biogeography plots the geographical distribution of species, describes and analyses types of pattern, and attempts to explain determined patterns in terms of the biology, ecology, and evolutionary history of the organisms. At this level biogeography is largely an academic and intellectual pursuit. However, by shifting its emphasis towards the study of local distributions, within the defined geographical boundaries of particular species, and of the ecological requirements of each species, biogeography becomes a necessary discipline for the marine biologist. Marine biogeography has a long history in British marine biology, the first attempt to describe patterns of marine distributions being Forbes and Godwin-Austen (1859, *The natural history of the European seas*). Early interest was doubtless stimulated by certain features of Britain's marine faunas. The latitudinal extent of the British Isles, and the major hydrographic differences between eastern and western coasts result in rather different faunal assemblages in the west and in the east, and observable faunal changes from south to north. Discontinuities in the distribution of particular species,

or assemblages of species, may be further emphasized by changes in substratum or habitat. It has long been known that, while certain elements of the British marine fauna comprise species which range far to the north, others are widespread in the western Mediterranean and along the coasts of north-west Africa instead; each of these elements displays different distributions around the British coasts (Fig. 1.5).

Biogeographers divide the marine realm into 'provinces', each characterized by a certain minimum proportion of autochthonous, or endemic, species, whose evolutionary origins, or the largest part of whose evolutionary history, are inferred to lie within that province. Such provinces may also be defined by physical barriers, such as land masses, deep sea trenches, or divergent current systems, and may display clear boundaries in the form of abrupt changes in fauna. In the north-east Atlantic region, influenced for much of its extent by the Gulf Stream drift, there appear to be no major biogeographic boundaries, although a few abrupt hydrographic boundaries, such as the Wyville Thomson Ridge, do correlate with equally abrupt changes in bottom fauna. However, the fauna of the western Mediterranean and north-western Africa is clearly different from that of northern and western Norway, and the particular interest of the faunas of the British Isles derives from the fact that they are largely a mixture of northern cold water (or boreal) species, and southern warm water (or lusitanian) species. There are very few marine animals endemic to the British Isles, although for some, such as the Dog whelk *Nucella lapillus*, the British Isles is the centre of their distributional range. However, many southern species reach their northernmost limits in British waters, and perhaps as many northern species are close to their southern limits here. Probably for few species can an actual furthest limit be demonstrated; the geographical ranges of most species probably contract and expand in concert with long-term climatic cycles, and distant population outliers may persist or disappear according to purely local environmental factors. Instead, most species will show a gradual range attenuation, to north and south, which is modified by local factors and influenced by the physiological and ecological characteristics of each species. The resulting overlay of distribution patterns provides a rich testing ground for all aspects of biogeographical research. Particularly interesting examples are provided by intertidal organisms. Many lusitanian species reach their northern limits around south-western and western Britain. The extent of their distribution and the persistence or relative abundance of their populations vary widely between species, suggesting different tolerances to different environmental factors. The top shell *Gibbula umbilicalis*, for example, has an almost continuous distribution from the Isle of Wight westwards and northwards to Orkney, including all coasts of Ireland, while *Monodonta lineata* occurs on the west coasts of Ireland and Wales and around the Cornubian peninsula, but occurs only sporadically on the east coast of Ireland. *Balanus perforatus*, a lowshore barnacle, is found on the Pembrokeshire coast, around the south-west peninsula of England, and eastward to the Isle of Wight, but is entirely absent from Ireland. Conversely, the echinoid *Paracentrotus lividus* is abundant along the western coasts of Ireland, but, apart from sporadic

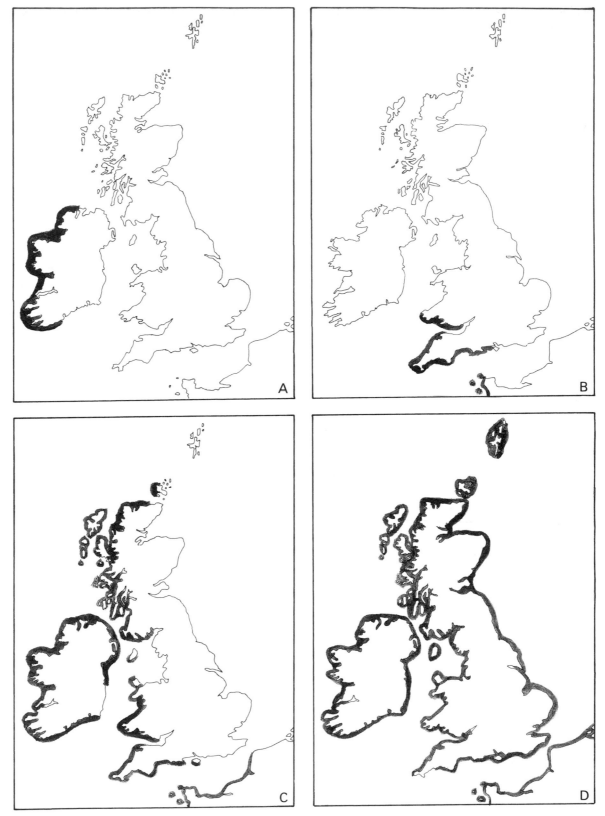

Fig. 1.5 Contrasting distributions in four intertidal animals: A *Paracentrotus lividus*. B *Balanus perforatus*. C *Gibbula umbilicalis*. D *Semibalanus balanoides* [after Lewis 1964].

records from Devon and the Channel Isles, occurs nowhere on the coasts of England and Wales.

Biogeography is a multifaceted discipline with an extensive specialist literature. The most complete descriptive account of marine biogeographic provinces is that of Briggs (1974). Lewis's *Ecology of rocky shores* (1964) discusses the factors influencing the geographical and ecological distributions of intertidal organisms. More recently, Earll and Farnham (in Earll and Erwin 1983) have presented a detailed account of the distribution patterns of primarily sublittoral organisms; Earll and Erwin (1983) also include a comprehensive bibliography of distributional studies of the British marine faunas. Such a diverse subject as marine biogeography cannot be given a comprehensive treatment here, but the remaining pages of this introductory chapter are devoted to a brief consideration of different levels of distribution, and of the factors most important in determining them. This treatment is intended merely to demonstrate the importance of observed distributional patterns to both the identification and descriptive ecology of marine organisms.

The geographical distribution of a particular species reflects both its evolutionary history and its present-day ecological tolerances. The ultimate barrier to the expansion of any species is its own physiology, and on the broadest scale the distribution of each species tends to be limited by physical environmental factors, the most important of which is probably temperature (Gunter 1957). Most marine animals are able to live within a fairly broad temperature range. So-called stenothermal organisms may tolerate an annual temperature range of only 4° or 5°C; such narrow ranges of temperature are not found close inshore anywhere around the British Isles. Most shallow-water temperate organisms are, rather, eurythermal, and are able to tolerate annual temperature ranges of 10°C or even 15°C. Temperature affects all physical and biological processes, which tend to proceed more quickly as temperature rises; metabolic rates in marine animals may be doubled by a 10°C temperature rise. Thus, growth, reproduction, and metabolic rate of a particular species may vary across its geographical range, affecting both its adaptive and competitive potential in different ways, with consequent effects on its relative abundance, reproductive output, and overall biomass at different places. All biological processes function most efficiently within an often narrow optimum temperature range, and all reproductive stages of marine organisms are mediated by temperature, with critical or optimal temperatures for all stages, from oogenesis, to maturation, spawning, fertilization, and embryogeny. Thus, certain apparently widely distributed species may achieve maximum population level over only a small part of their geographical range and may breed successfully only in certain optimum habitats. Elsewhere, populations may be sustained by larval drift or adult dispersal, with the population structure related to the reproductive output of populations in neighbouring, or remote, habitats, and to the survival of dispersive stages. Some widely distributed species exist as a series of physiological races, with each race adapted to annual temperature regimes, or other climatic conditions, existing in its immediate vicinity. Local physiological adaptation is particularly likely to occur when

suitable habitat for the species is not present over the whole of its geographical range, but is distributed as discrete areas, each separated by areas of unsuitable habitat.

The continental shelf edge is a significant barrier to expansion for many benthic species; but, for certain offshore species, adapted to a narrow range of fairly low temperatures, the outer continental shelf is a migration pathway. Consequently, certain decapods, molluscs, and echinoderms, for example, occurring offshore around the British Isles, may be distributed in similar habitats as far south as the coasts of West Africa. Major river outflows, or deltas, may be important barriers to similar migration of coastal species. Current systems may act as barriers to geographical expansion, particularly when they are associated with upwellings, when abrupt temperature changes may enhance the effect. Earll and Farnham (1983) suggested that the anticlockwise, southern North Sea gyre may be responsible for limiting the northwards expansion of the immigrant prosobranch *Crepidula fornicata* along the eastern coasts of England, simply by preventing the northward movement of planktonic larvae. Other good examples may be found in the Isles of Scilly. Both the southern, warm water barnacle *Balanus perforatus*, and the northern cold water *Semibalanus balanoides* are rare around the Lizard peninsula, and the latter is absent from the Scilly Isles. The southern limpet *Patella depressa* does not occur in the Scilly Isles, and the northern winkle *Littorina littorea* occurs only rarely. These curious distributions are explained by a clockwise current eddy off the Lizard which ensures that dispersing larvae, whatever their origin, are swept away from the Scilly Isles (Crisp and Southward 1958). For the most part, however, current systems are most important as pathways for migration and, although some intertidal organisms show clear range attenuation, or even marked geographical limits, in British waters, the hydrographic conditions experienced by the British Isles generally favour broad distributions of marine benthic organisms in the British sea area.

The evolutionary history of each species is often reflected in its geographical distribution, as is the history of its environment. Climate and environment change through time. Species adapt to change, or migrate, or become extinct; environmental change may lead to the fragmentation of continuous distributions, leaving isolated populations surviving in reduced areas of optimum habitat. Evidence of formerly wide distributions for particular species may be preserved in sediments and fossil deposits, indicating long-term changes in the species' geographical ranges. However, such change may also be observed on far shorter time scales. In recent time, the severe winter of 1962–3 caused local extinctions of many intertidal or shallow sublittoral species (Crisp 1964). In some instances, the affected areas were soon recolonized by immigrant populations, and through larval dispersal from adjacent areas. In others, the immediate result was a marked contraction in geographical range, which has been regained subsequently by some organisms, while others seem to have suffered a permanent range contraction. Periodic change in climatic and hydrographic factors is reflected in periodic change and fluctuation in marine benthic faunas. For example, in the early 1920's the western

English Channel experienced substantial influxes of oceanic water and was characterized by high levels of dissolved phosphorus in winter, a rich spring macroplankton, the chaetognath *Sagitta elegans*, and large herring populations. A marked change in the 1930's, perhaps related to rising sea temperature, gave rise to a regime of low winter phosphorus and poor spring macroplankton, characterized by *Sagitta setosa* and pilchards, with total disappearance of the herring. A number of benthic bivalve species, perhaps only established during the 1920's, disappeared from the western Channel during the 1930's (Holme 1966), and a number of northern species, such as *Antalis entalis*, became locally extinct along the south-west coasts of England.

Continuous adaptation to environmental change may lead ultimately to the reproductive isolation of populations of a particular species over its geographical range, and eventually to allopatric speciation, the appearance of distinctly different, locally adapted species derived from a common ancestor. What may be allopatric species groups can be seen in certain intertidal littorinids, and among the intertidal species of the bryozoan genus *Alcyonidium*. Subsequent contraction in the geographical range of one or more of an allopatric species group may result in relict populations. Good examples are difficult to demonstrate among marine organisms, but evidence can be found through reference to fossil deposits. A newly recognized case is the bryozoan *Hippoporidra edax* which develops distinctive nodulated colonies on small gastropod shells, occupied by hermit crabs (Taylor and Cook 1981). *H. edax* is common in Pliocene deposits of western Europe and the eastern United States, but living populations are restricted today to the south-eastern USA and the Gulf of Mexico. In the eastern Atlantic, four closely similar, allopatric species are distributed from the coasts of West Africa to the south-west British Isles, where *H. lusitania* has a limited distribution from the Gulf of St. Malo and the western end of the Channel, to the Isle of Man.

Within the broad limits of its geographical range each species occurs in a particular habitat, defined by the particular, optimum conditions for its growth and reproduction. Bordering each area of optimum habitat may be a zone of suboptimal habitat in which the species is able to exist, but in which it does not achieve maximum growth or longevity, or is unable to achieve maximum reproductive output, or is at a competitive disadvantage to other species. The optimum habitat may be limited by physical and/or biological factors. The most simple demonstration of this is with reference to substratum. Level-bottom communities around the British Isles change in composition as the substratum changes. As fine muds intergrade with silty sand, which then trends to progressively coarser sand, both the species composition of the benthic fauna and the relative abundance of species change. Certain species of infaunal polychaetes, bivalve molluscs, and echinoderms decline in relative abundance, perhaps at different rates, eventually to be replaced by others. Such patterns are ultimately related to current and tidal effects and change in response to these around the whole of the British Isles.

Substratum has an important influence on the distribution of sessile organisms. For example, as the limestones and shales of southern England give way eastwards to soft chalk and clay, patterns of faunal change occur, perhaps reinforced by gradients of change in other factors, such as temperature. Hard-substratum sessile species, crevice-dwelling species, and rock borers may be discontinuously distributed along a coastline, with breaks occurring where rock type changes or gives way to unconsolidated substrata. Limestones are the most richly colonized rocks, being sufficiently resistant to erosion to enable populations to persist, yet eroding sufficiently along bedding or jointing planes to provide crevices, gullies, and pools, thus increasing the diversity of local habitat. Softer limestones, shales, and marls will have a different fauna of boring organisms from crystalline limestones, but fewer encrusting species. The hard igneous and metamorphic rocks of western Scotland provide the least diversity of habitat, and sessile faunas will flourish only where the smoothly eroded rock surfaces are provided with local shelter.

The vertical zonation of intertidal rocky shore organisms is a further expression of local distribution patterns varying in response to environmental factors, a theme which was studied exhaustively by Lewis (1964). The barnacle belts and seaweed zones of rocky shores, with their attendant fauna, are sensitive indicators of local environmental conditions. Gently sloping shores with maximum shelter from wave and swell are characterized by a narrow supralittoral barnacle belt, and a broad midshore region dominated by the brown algae *Fucus serratus* and *Ascophyllum nodosum*. Such shores have perhaps the richest intertidal faunas. As exposure increases and the shore profile steepens, the fucoid algae give way to shrubby red algae and a different, less diverse fauna. The extreme is seen in storm-beaten western promontories where the barnacle belt extends some tens of metres above high water mark, and the algal zones are reduced to a narrow fringe of exposure resistant species, such as *Alaria esculenta*. While the geographical distribution of intertidal species may be defined by gross environmental factors, particularly sea temperature, local distribution patterns are determined by the availability of habitat, mediated by the effects of exposure, shore aspect, tidal factors, and climate. Air temperature, rainfall, and sunshine, in relation to the magnitude, duration, and time of daily low tide periods, have important effects on the distribution of intertidal species, which differ between northern and southern, and eastern and western coasts of Britain.

A final aspect of local distribution patterns may be termed 'ecological distribution'. The occurrence of parasitic and symbiotic species is naturally dependent on the distribution of their hosts. Similarly, epiphytic and epizootic species occur only where their preferred plant or animal substratum occurs. The persistence of such species may depend on the biological characteristics of their substratum. For example, the brown seaweed *Fucus serratus* supports a rich and characteristic fauna of bryozoans, hydroids, tubeworms, sponges, and sea squirts, with their associated predators. However, this community develops only where sheltered conditions allow the *Fucus* plant to achieve maximum size and bushiness, and where the cover of seaweed is also at a maximum. In turbulent conditions, plants tend to be small, spindly, and sparsely distributed; the epiphytic fauna may be only minimally developed, or quite absent, not simply as a result of harsher environmental characteristics, but also through the narrower range of microhabitats provided by the *Fucus* population.

REFERENCES

Barnes, R. S. K. and Hughes, R. N. (1982). *An introduction to marine ecology*. Blackwell Scientific Publications, Oxford.

Briggs, J. C. (1974). *Marine zoogeography*, McGraw Hill, New York.

Cabioch, L. (1968). Contribution à la connaissance des peuplements benthiques de la Manche Occidentale. *Cahiers de Biologie Marine*, **5**, Supplement.

Crisp, D. J. (ed.) (1964). The effects of the severe winter of 1962–63 on marine life in Britain. *Journal of Animal Ecology*, **33**, 165–210.

Crisp, D. J. and Southward, A. J. (1958). The distribution of intertidal organisms along the coasts of the English Channel. *Journal of the Marine Biological Association of the U.K.*, **37**, 157–208.

Cushing, D. H. (1975). *Marine ecology and fisheries*. Cambridge University Press.

Earll, R. and Erwin, D. G. (1983). *Sublittoral ecology*. Clarendon Press, Oxford.

Earll, R. and Farnham, W. F. (1983). Biogeography. In: *Sublittoral ecology* (ed. R. Earll and D. G. Erwin). Clarendon Press, Oxford.

Forbes, E. and Godwin-Austen, R. (1859). *The natural history of the European Seas*. Van Voorst, London.

Gosse, E. W. (1907). *Father and son; A study of two temperaments*. William Heinemann, London.

Gunter, G. (1957). Temperature. In J. W. Hedgpeth (ed.) Treatise on marine ecology and paleoecology. *Geological Society of America, Memoir* **67**.

Holme, N. A. (1961). The bottom fauna of the English Channel. *Journal of the Marine Biological Association of the U.K.*, **41**, 361–397.

Holme, N. A. (1966). The bottom fauna of the English Channel. Part II. *Journal of the Marine Biological Association of the U.K.*, **46**, 401–93.

King, C. A. M. (1975). *Introduction to physical and biological oceanography*. Edward Arnold, London.

Kinne, O. (1970). *Marine ecology. Vol. 1, Environmental factors, Part 1*. John Wiley, London.

Kinne, O. (1971). *Marine ecology. Vol. 1, Environmental factors, Part 2*. John Wiley, Chichester.

Kinne, O. (1975). *Marine ecology. Vol. 2, Physiological mechanisms, Part 1*. John Wiley, Chichester.

Kinne, O. (1975). *Marine ecology. Vol. 2, Physiological mechanisms, Part 2*. John Wiley, Chichester.

Kinne, O. (1976). *Marine ecology. Vol. 3, Cultivation, Part 1*. John Wiley, Chichester.

Kinne, O. (1977). *Marine ecology. Vol. 3, Cultivation, Part 2*. John Wiley, Chichester.

Kinne, O. (1977). *Marine ecology. Vol. 3, Cultivation, Part 3*. John Wiley, Chichester.

Kinne, O. (1978). *Marine ecology. Vol. 4, Dynamics*. John Wiley, Chichester.

Kinne, O. (1982). *Marine ecology. Vol. 5, Ocean management, Part 1*. John Wiley, Chichester.

Kinne, O. (1983). *Marine ecology. Vol. 5, Ocean management, Part 2*. John Wiley, Chichester.

Kinne, O. (1984). *Marine ecology. Vol. 5, Ocean management, Part 3*. John Wiley, Chichester.

Kinne, O. (1984). *Marine ecology. Vol. 5, Ocean management, Part 4*. John Wiley, Chichester.

Lee, A. J. and Ramster, J. W. (ed.) (1981). *Atlas of the seas around the British Isles*. Ministry of Agriculture, Fisheries and Food, London.

Lewis, J. R. (1964). *The ecology of rocky shores*. English Universities Press, London.

Moore, P. G. and Seed, R. (1985). *The ecology of rocky coasts: Essays presented to J. R. Lewis*. Hodder and Stoughton, London.

Price, J. H., Irvine, D. E. G., and Farnham, W. F. (1980). *The shore environment*, 2 Vols. Academic Press, New York and London.

Stephenson, T. A. and Stephenson, A. (1972). *Life between tidemarks on rocky shores*. W. H. Freeman, San Francisco.

Taylor, P. D. and Cook, P. L. (1981). *Hippoporidra edax* (Busk 1859) and a revision of some fossil and living *Hippoporidra* (Bryozoa). *Bulletin of the British Museum* (*Natural History*), *Geology* **35**(3), 243–51.

Yonge, C. M. (1949). *The Sea Shore*. Collins, London.

NOTES FOR THE USER

The following chapters provide dichotomous keys for the identification of the inshore components of the British and northwest European marine fauna: namely, selected groups of free-living protozoans, through littoral and benthic macro-invertebrates, to coastal fishes. The chapters follow usual systematic order, and only a minimum basic knowledge of animal types is required to select the chapter appropriate for a particular specimen. Within each chapter, major animal groups are introduced at the level of phylum, class, or order, depending mostly on the size of the group and its relative significance in the marine fauna. For each such group, a brief introductory account is given, designed to familiarize the user with the basic morphology of the organisms, the terminology required to use the keys, and an outline classification of the group. These introductory passages are supplemented by labelled diagrammatic figures at the beginning of each chapter. Within each animal group primary keys, set across the full page width, enable the user to identify the family (in most cases) to which each specimen should be referred. Family accounts then follow in numbered sequence, each usually beginning with a short confirmatory diagnosis. A secondary key, set to column width, carries identification to the level of species. In some cases, these keys may lead only to selected exemplar genera. The descriptions usually follow the key in alphabetical order of species, except in a few instances in which the author has followed a systematic sequence of clearly contrasted species. The species descriptions are mostly brief, highlighting those characteristics which, together with short notes on their biology, ecology, and geographical distribution, confirm the identification arrived at through the key.

It must be stressed that this is essentially an identification manual. Care has been taken to ensure that each species is accorded its correct, current taxonomic designation, with the author who introduced its name correctly cited. Note that parentheses around an author's name indicate that the species is now referred to a genus different from that to which it was originally assigned. References to original descriptions, or to subsequent synonymies, have rarely been included and only when there has been a recent change from a very well-known name. In the case of the most familiar and best studied groups, such as the Mollusca, no literature citations are given at all, but in many cases a reference is given to a description in a monograph. The selection of literature provided after the introduction to each group includes, apart from specific works cited in text, the most recent, or useful, further sources. In the case of especially rare species, not included here, these reference lists will enable the user to continue the process of identification. For certain groups in which there is no convenient monograph at all, the accounts in this book have sometimes been expanded to include greater detail and/or some of the rarer species.

2 PROTOZOA

PROTOZOA form a subdivision of the Kingdom Protista, which comprises organisms not divided into different kinds of cells. Their general characters are treated in most introductory textbooks of biology, so knowledge of these can be assumed. Their diversity in the sea is vast, but here we omit the five exclusively parasitic phyla recognized by Levine *et al.* (1980). We deal only with benthic representatives of the two remaining phyla, Sarcomastigophora (flagellates and rhizopods) and Ciliophora (ciliates).

Most flagellates live in the plankton, and only orders which have non-parasitic representatives in the benthos are shown in the following classification.

PHYLUM SARCOMASTIGOPHORA

With a single type of nucleus (except in many Foraminiferida). Locomotion by flagella or pseudopodia.

A. Subphylum Mastigophora

Typically with one or more flagella throughout most of life cycle.

Class I Phytomastigophorea

With chloroplasts, or obviously related to forms which have chloroplasts.

Order 1 Dinoflagellida

Usually with two flagella, one transverse and often in an equatorial groove (*annulus*) and the other directed backwards (rarely forwards) and often in a longitudinal groove (*sulcus*). Body with or without armour of cellulose plates. Chloroplasts brown, green, or absent.

Order 2 Cryptomonadida

Two flagella arising subapically in ventral groove at mouth of a gullet. Shape more or less oval with one flattened side. Chloroplasts brown, red, yellow, blue, or absent.

Order 3 Chrysomonadida

With one anterior flagellum bearing a row of fine hairs (*mastigonemes*) on each side and one trailing flagellum without hairs. Chloroplasts absent or yellow-brown, with chlorophyll a and c, and fucoxanthin.

Order 4 Heterochlorida

Very like chrysomonads, but chloroplasts are yellow-green with little or no chlorophyll c, and no fucoxanthin. Pseudopodia may be developed, as well as flagella.

Order 5 Prymnesiida

With two similar flagella lacking hairs and sometimes with a third filament for attachment (*haptonema*). Chloroplasts yellow-brown, lacking chlorophyll b in this and all preceding orders. Body covered with fine scales, which are calcified in Coccolithophoridae and can then be seen by light microscopy.

Order 6 Euglenida

Typically with one or two flagella projecting from an anterior invagination. Colourless or with green chloroplasts, which contain both chlorophylls a and b in this and the two orders following. Leedale (1967) recognizes several suborders, which are treated here as families.

Order 7 Volvocida

With two or four smooth apical flagella, green chloroplasts and a cellulose cell wall.

Order 8 Prasinomonadida

With one, two, four, or eight similar flagella, which like body are typically covered with rows of fine scales. Some have a theca, but not of cellulose.

Class II Zoomastigophorea

Lacking chloroplasts and not obviously related to algae. Most orders are parasitic and not listed here.

Order 1 Choanoflagellida

With one terminal flagellum surrounded by a ring (*collar*) of fine tentacles.

Order 2 Kinetoplastida

With one or two flagella, and a DNA-rich body (*kinetoplast*) which lies near the kinetosome(s) and connects with the (single) mitochondrion.

Flagellates are abundant and ecologically important in the sea, but most are so small that individuals are difficult to identify without culture methods. Electron microscopy is necessary to determine many of their characters, so their taxonomy is relatively new, incomplete, and needing more specialist study. An easy introduction to wild populations, however, may be obtained from a study of sandy beaches, for some common flagellates are 'psammophilic' (living characteristically between sand grains) and sufficiently large to identify without much difficulty. The following account is mostly confined to psammophilic species. They can be extracted by the ice-water technique, as follows. Sand samples from the lower wet levels of beaches are placed on to medium-mesh plankton netting or muslin fine enough to retain most of the sand grains. The netting is supported in sieves or funnels above small basins containing a little seawater. Frozen seawater is then placed on top of the sand and, within half an hour, abundant Protozoa and other representatives of the interstitial fauna will have been carried down into the basins by the melt water, helped by their own movements. They can be observed under a dissecting microscope and pipetted out for more detailed study by transmitted (preferably cool) light, either in a solid watchglass (low power objectives only) or under a supported coverslip. Vaselined margins will support coverslips and also prevent evaporation.

LITERATURE

Sleigh (1973) gives a good introduction to Protozoa, wisely using for phytoflagellates the botanical terminations for names of higher taxa (-ales for orders and -aceae for families). Dodge (1982) is best for identifying dinoflagellates, as the nomenclature in Lebour (1925) needs updating. Some other flagellates from sandy beaches are described or listed by Lackey (1962), Lackey and Lackey (1963), Dragesco (1965), and Parke and Manton (1967). For recent papers on most phytoflagellate groups see Parke and Dixon (1976).

The illustrations reproduced in Fig. 2.1 have been redrawn from the following sources: Dodge (1982), Dragesco (1965), Hollande (1952), Huber-Pestalozzi (1955), Lackey (1962), and Parke and Manton (1967).

REFERENCES

Butcher, R. W. (1967). An introductory account of the smaller algae of British coastal waters. Part IV. Cryptophycea. *Fishery Investigations. Ministry of Agriculture, Fisheries and Food.* Series IV, **4**, 1–54.

Dodge, J. D. (1982). *Marine dinoflagellates*, 303 pp. H.M.S.O., London.

Douglas, A. E. (1985). Growth and reproduction of *Convoluta roscoffensis* containing different naturally occurring algal symbionts. *Journal of the Marine Biological Association of the U.K.,* **65**, 871–9.

Dragesco, J. (1965). Étude cytologique de quelques flagelles mesopsammiques. *Cahiers de Biologie marine,* **6**, 83–115.

Ettl, H. and Green, J. C. (1973). *Chlamydomonas reginae* sp. nov. (Chlorophyceae), a new marine flagellate with unusual chloroplast differentiation. *Journal of the Marine Biological Association of the U.K.,* **53**, 975–85.

Hollande, A. (1952). Classe des Cryptomonadines. *Traité de Zoologie,* Vol. I, fasc. 1, (ed. P. P. Grassé), pp. 285–308. Masson et Cie, Paris.

Huber-Pestalozzi, G. (1955). Das Phytoplankton des Süsswassers. 4 Teil. Euglenophyceen. *Die Binnengewässer,* Vol. 16, (ed. A. Thienemann). 606 pp. E. Schweizerbart, Stuttgart.

Lackey, J. B. (1962). Three new colourless Euglenophyceae from marine situations. *Archiv für Mikrobiologie,* **42**, 190–5.

Lackey, J. B. and Lackey, E. W. (1963). Microscopic Algae and Protozoa in the waters near Plymouth in August 1962. *Journal of the Marine Biological Association of the U.K.,* **43**, 797–805.

Lebour, M. V. (1925). *The dinoflagellates of northern seas.* Plymouth Marine Biological Association.

Leedale, G. F. (1967). *Euglenoid flagellates.* Prentice-Hall, New Jersey.

Parke, M. and Dixon, P. S. (1976). Check-list of British marine Algae, 3rd revision. *Journal of the Marine Biological Association of the U.K.,* **56**, 527–94.

Parke, M. and Manton, I. (1967). The specific identity of the algal symbiont in *Convoluta roscoffensis. Journal of the Marine Biological Association of the U.K.,* **47**, 445–64.

Reid, P. C. (1972). Dinoflagellate cyst distribution around the British Isles. *Journal of the Marine Biological Association of the U.K.,* **52**, 939–44.

Sleigh, M. A. (1973). *The biology of Protozoa.* Edward Arnold, London.

KEY TO FAMILIES OF FLAGELLATES FOUND IN BEACH SAND

1. With one or more transverse grooves encircling body, and generally with a longitudinal groove (**sulcus**) along ventral side (typical dinoflagellate)   **8**

   Transverse groove absent or on apical margin   **2**

2. Forming spherical or oval cysts, which lack flagella but may bear radiating spines.   Perhaps 8. **Gonyaulacidae**

   With one or more flagella   **3**

3. Crawling by worm-like extensions and contractions and/or with one large apical flagellum sometimes accompanied by another which may be much shorter (typical euglenoid)   **16**

   Not showing propagated waves of contraction. With two or more flagella of similar size   **4**

4. Oval, < 15 μm long, with a comparatively large green chloroplast   **15**

   Chloroplasts yellowish, brownish, red or absent   **5**

5. Cells > 25 μm long, protected by a few (often two) thin thecal plates   **6**

   Cells appear naked or may bear many light-reflecting plates (coccoliths)   **12**

6. Most of body protected by two saucer-like plates, which meet sagittally   **7**

   With more than two major plates and lacking a sagittal suture

   Adenoides amongst 9. **Oxytoxidae**

7. With no trace of groove round body   1. **Prorocentridae**

   Terminal groove encircles anterior end   2. **Dinophysidae**

8. With a single transverse groove (**annulus**)   **9**

   With four or eight such grooves   5. **Polykrikidae**

9. With distinct thecal plates protecting dorsoventrally flattened body.

   Annulus surrounds anterior end   *Amphidiniopsis* amongst 9. **Oxytoxidae**

   Thecal plates absent or difficult to distinguish   **10**

10. Either with annulus near posterior end, or with an apical notch which is distinct from
    sulcus   6. **Lophodiniidae**

    With annulus equatorial or situated anteriorly, apical notch absent or formed by anterior
    prolongation of sulcus   **11**

11. Thecal plates difficult to demonstrate and may be indistinguishable in *Glenodinium
    monensis*, but in this species sulcus extends equally short distances fore and aft of
    annulus, which is equatorial   7. **Peridiniidae**

    Thecal plates absent. Sulcus extends posteriorly much further than anteriorly, from
    annulus which is anterior or equatorial or spiralling   3. **Gymnodiniidae**

12. Cells rounded or oval, and covered with oval calcareous plates

    Perhaps 12. **Pontosphaeridae**

    Cells naked, and oval or elongated, sometimes with ends somewhat pointed   **13**

13. With two flagella arising together from mouth of an anterior subterminal gullet (typical
    cryptomonad)   **14**

    With two flagella, separated by a small tentacle, arising on either side of a posterior
    depression   *Oxyrrhis* in 4. **Pronoctilucidae**

14. Gullet simple   10. **Cryptomonadidae**

    Gullet differentiated into two regions   11. **Cyathomonadidae**

15. With two flagella arising from an apical papilla   13. **Chlamydomonadidae**

     With four flagella arising from an apical notch   14. **Prasinocladidae**

---

16. With no anterior cytopharynx or other invagination, except a narrow-necked reservoir from which flagella emerge   **17**

     With a cytopharynx, or tapering siphon alongside the anterior reservoir 16. **Heteronematidae**

---

17. With cuticle marked by spiral striations. Often 'metabolic' (performing euglenoid movements). Some colourless but others have green chloroplasts and (near base of flagellum) a red stigma, but may be enclosed in a brown test (*Trachelomonas*)   15. **Euglenidae**

     Cuticle may form ridges and grooves but never fine striae. Non-metabolic. Chloroplasts absent.   17. **Sphenomonadidae**

Class **Phytomastigophorea**

Order **Dinoflagellida**

1 PROROCENTRIDAE

Body without grooves, completely enclosed by two lateral plates, which meet sagittally and are usually perforated by small trichocyst pores.

Prorocentrum lima (Ehrenberg) Dodge   FIG. 2.1
[DODGE 1982: 30]

Oval, 32–50 μm long, indented anteriorly, with pores distributed fairly uniformly. Two plate-like chloroplasts. The only prorocentrid recorded abundantly from sand, sometimes as *Exuviella marina*. Figures (2.1) show side and edge views.

Europe; America; Australasia.

2 DINOPHYSIDAE

Annulus anterior, usually bounded by thin collar formed by thecal plates. Most of body covered by two lateral plates.

Sinophysis ebriola (Herdman) Balech   FIG. 2.1
[DODGE 1982: 56]

Flattened laterally, ellipsoidal, 32–43 μm long. Annulus almost terminal, surrounding a collar which is high but only about 0.3 × diameter of cell. Without chloroplasts.

Port Erin; Brittany; Boulogne; Wood's Hole.

Thecadinium petasatum (Herdman) Kofoid and Skogsberg   FIG. 2.1
[DODGE 1982: 57]

Flattened laterally, ellipsoidal, 25–33 μm long, figured (2.1) from right side and ventrally. Annulus forms Y-shaped junction with sulcus, and lacks any thin collar. Ovoid nucleus lies posteriorly. Many chloroplasts radiate from central pyrenoid.

Port Erin; south-west Scotland; Brittany.

Thecadinium semilunatum (Herdman)
[DODGE 1982: 58]

As above, but larger (50–64 μm long) and lacks chloroplasts.

Port Erin; Folkestone.

3 GYMNODINIIDAE

Naked forms, without any trace of thecal plates. The psammophilic species are mostly flattened dorso-ventrally, never laterally, for laterally flattened '*Amphidinium*' included in Lebour (1925) are now placed in other genera and other families.

---

1. Annulus anterior, so that forepart of cell (*epicone*) is <0.5 × size of remainder (*hypocone*)   **5**

     Annulus more equatorial   **2**

2. Annulus spirals for >0.2 of body length   *Gyrodinium lebourae*

     Annulus with little or no spiral displacement   **3**

3. Sulcus extends length of cell   *Gymnodinium arenicolus*

     Sulcus does not extend on to epicone   **4**

4. With chloroplasts   *Gymnodinium incertum*

     Without chloroplasts   *Gymnodinium variabile*

5. With chloroplasts   **6**

     Without chloroplasts (but may contain pigmented food vacuoles)   **14**

6. Chloroplast arrangement radiating   **7**

     Chloroplasts not radiating   **11**

7. Annulus spiralling, so that on right side it becomes almost equatorial before joining sulcus   **8**

     Annulus bilaterally symmetrical   **9**

8. Length >36 μm, nucleus spherical and central   *Amphidinium britannicum*

     Length <37 μm, nucleus ovoid and posterior   *Amphidinium ovum*

9. Epicone about 0.5 × width of hypocone. Nucleus crescent-shaped   *Amphidinium herdmanae*

     Epicone about 0.3 × width of hypocone. Nucleus ovoid   **10**

10. Only one chloroplast, peripherally arranged but
connecting with a central pyrenoid   *Amphidinium carterae*

Numerous chloroplasts radiating from central
pyrenoid   *Amphidinium operculatum*

11. Sulcus as long as cell, notching
both ends   *Amphidinium corpulentum*

Sulcus not extending on to epicone   **12**

12. Epicone <0.3 × width of hypocone. Sulcus reaches
end of hypocone   *Amphidinium lacustre*

Epicone about 0.5 × width of hypocone. Sulcus
extends <0.7 × length of hypocone   **13**

13. Almost globular   *Amphidinium globosum*

Oval, flattened   *Amphidinium ovoideum*

14. Body spindle-shaped. Both ends pointed
                                       Amphidinium sphenoides

Ends not sharply pointed   **15**

15. Widely bifurcate posteriorly   *Amphidinium bipes*

Posterior end not widely bifurcate   **16**

16. Posterior end notched by sulcus   **17**

Posterior end not notched by sulcus   **18**

17. Cytoplasm colourless but may contain coloured
granules   *Amphidinium flexum*

As above, but more transparent   *Amphidinium pellucidum*

18. Flattened dorso-ventrally   **19**

Nearly circular in cross-section   **20**

19. Length 1.1 × breadth   *Amphidinium latum*

Length 3 × breadth   *Amphidinium scissum*

20. Length 2 × breadth   *Amphidinium crassum*

Length 1.2 × breadth   *Amphidinium manannini*

Amphidinium bipes Herdman
[DODGE 1982: 63]

About 30 × 22 μm, squarish anteriorly and widely bifurcate posteriorly, somewhat flattened. Bilaterally symmetrical. Annulus forms shallow V-shape ventrally.

   Port Erin; south-west Scotland; Yorkshire; south-east England.

Amphidinium britannicum (Herdman) Lebour   FIG. 2.1
[DODGE 1982: 68]

Asymmetrically oval, about 40–60 μm long. Epicone nearly 0.5 × size of hypocone. Flattened. Nucleus central. Chloroplasts radiating, but no pyrenoid.

   Port Erin; south-west and east Scotland; Yorkshire; southern England.

Amphidinium carterae Hulburt
[DODGE 1982: 69]

Oval, 11–24 × 6–17 μm, flattened. Annulus forms V ventrally. Epicone small and asymmetric, extending to left, without any anterior extension of sulcus. Nucleus posterior. Chloroplast with peripheral lobes connected to a central pyrenoid.

   Widespread round Britain and world, in pools and salt marshes as well as sand.

Amphidinium corpulentum Kofoid and Swezy
[DODGE 1982: 69]

Oval, about 35 × 18 μm, flattened. Epicone broad and 0.2 × length of cell. Annulus forms shallow V. Sulcus extends length of cell. Chloroplasts many and discoid.

   South-east Britain; California.

Amphidinium crassum Lohmann
[DODGE 1982: 64]

Oval, 23–43 × 11–24 μm, not flattened. Bilaterally symmetrical. Epicone conical, with sulcus reaching apex. Annulus straight ventrally, not forming V.

   Western Europe; eastern USA; Adriatic.

Amphidinium flexum Herdman
[DODGE 1982: 64]

Rounded-rectangular, 42–60 × 28–40 μm, flattened. Epicone broad and low, slightly grooved by sulcus, which extends to bilobed hind end.

   Round most of Britain; Belgium.

Amphidinium globosum Schroder
[DODGE 1982: 70]

Globular 8–16 × 7–14 μm. Bilaterally symmetrical. Annulus forms shallow V ventrally. Several discoid chloroplasts.

   Adriatic; southern England.

Amphidinium herdmanae Kofoid and Swezy   FIG. 2.1
[DODGE 1982: 70]

Oval, 25–50 × 17–25 μm, flattened. Annulus forms V ventrally. Sulcus runs to hind end, but not on to epicone. Nucleus posterior, crescent-shaped. Many chloroplasts radiate from central pyrenoid.

   Forms brown patches on wet sand at many places round Britain.

Amphidinium lacustre Stein
[DODGE 1982: 72]

Ovoid, 15–23 × 10–18 μm, not flattened. Epicone a tiny button surrounded by a wide annulus. Sulcus runs length of hypocone. Nucleus posterior. Chloroplasts few.

   Adriatic; Belgium; Prawle Point, Devon. In brackish and freshwater sites.

Amphidinium latum Lebour
[DODGE 1982: 66]

Almost round in ventral view, 13–19 × 11–17 μm, flattened.

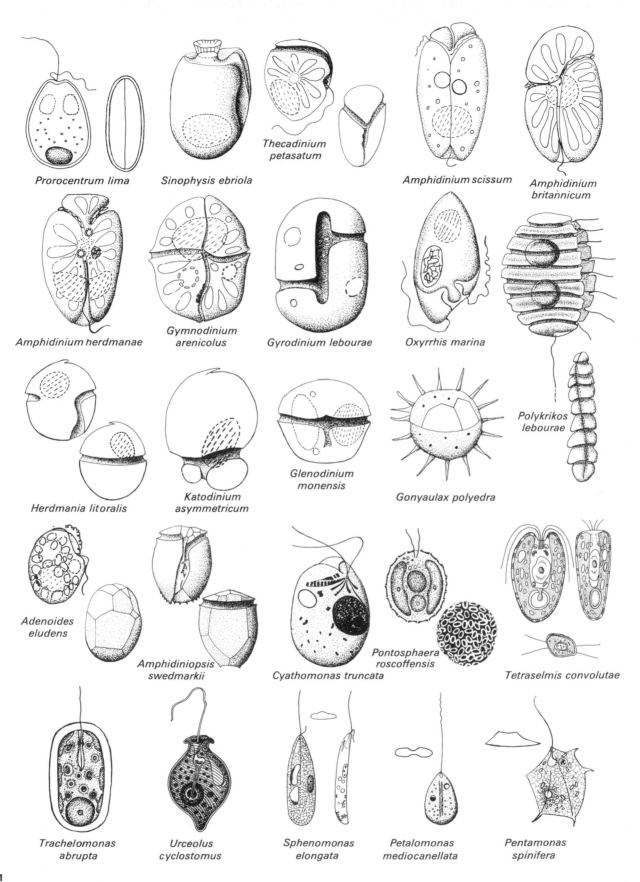

Prorocentrum lima

Sinophysis ebriola

Thecadinium petasatum

Amphidinium scissum

Amphidinium britannicum

Amphidinium herdmanae

Gymnodinium arenicolus

Gyrodinium lebourae

Oxyrrhis marina

Polykrikos lebourae

Herdmania litoralis

Katodinium asymmetricum

Glenodinium monensis

Gonyaulax polyedra

Adenoides eludens

Amphidiniopsis swedmarkii

Cyathomonas truncata

Pontosphaera roscoffensis

Tetraselmis convolutae

Trachelomonas abrupta

Urceolus cyclostomus

Sphenomonas elongata

Petalomonas mediocanellata

Pentamonas spinifera

Fig. 2.1

Epicone short and flat, notched by sulcus. Annulus wide, not forming a V. Nucleus anterior. No chloroplasts.

Port Erin; Cullercoats; south-east England; Belgium.

Amphidinium manannini Herdman
[DODGE 1982: 66]

Broadly ovoid, about 20 μm long, somewhat pointed posteriorly, not flattened. Epicone short and broad. Annulus not forming V. Nucleus posterior. No chloroplasts.

Port Erin; south-west Scotland; Belgium.

Amphidinium operculatum Claparède and Lachmann
[DODGE 1982: 73]

Ovoid, 15–50 × 10–30 μm, flattened. Epicone small, bent to left, 0.3 × breadth of cell. Annulus forms V. Sulcus runs length of hypocone. Nucleus posterior. Many chloroplasts radiate from central pyrenoid.

Wet beaches from Norway to Naples; Baltic; New England.

Amphidinium ovoideum Lemmermann
[DODGE 1982: 73]

Ovoid, 17–23 × 14–19 μm, flattened. Epicone small, bent to left. Sulcus only 0.7 × length of hypocone. Nucleus posterior. Many chloroplasts scattered throughout cell.

Baltic; Belgium; salt marsh in Solway Firth.

Amphidinium ovum Herdman
[DODGE 1982: 74]

Ovoid, 24–36 × 16–26 μm, flattened. Epicone broad and asymmetrical, the annulus being lower on right side. Sulcus as long as hypocone, notching posterior end. Nucleus posterior. Many chloroplasts radiate from centre.

Port Erin; south Wales; south-west Scotland; south-east England.

Amphidinium pellucidum Herdman
[DODGE 1982: 67]

Ovoid, 50–60 × 35 μm, flattened, may be pointed posteriorly. Annulus forms V ventrally. Sulcus as long as body. Cytoplasm transparent, colourless or with pigmented vacuoles.

Port Erin; west Scotland; Belgium; Brittany.

Amphidinium scissum Kofoid and Swezy   FIG. 2.1
[DODGE 1982: 67]

Elongated ovoid, 50–60 × 30 μm, flattened. Like *A. pellucidum* but less bulky and less transparent. Cell surface may be striated.

Port Erin; south-west Scotland; south-east England; California.

Amphidinium sphenoides Wolff
[DODGE 1982: 68]

Spindle-shaped, 35–60 × 12–15 μm. Annulus almost straight, forming very shallow V. Sulcus extends halfway along both epicone and hypocone. No chloroplasts.

Sand at Port Erin, but also planktonic and may parasitize diatoms; Plymouth; Helgoland; Barents Sea; Wood's Hole.

Gymnodinium arenicolus Dragesco   FIG. 2.1
[DRAGESCO 1965: 109; DODGE 1982: 90, as *G. variable*]

Rounded in ventral view, 20–40 μm long, flattened. Annulus equatorial, with no displacement by spiralling. Sulcus as long as body, notching both poles. With chloroplasts and pyrenoids.

Brittany.

Gymnodinium incertum Herdman
[LEBOUR 1925: 41; DODGE 1982: 85]

Oval, 15 μm long, flattened. Hypocone smaller than epicone, because annulus is slightly displaced posteriorly on right side. Sulcus not indenting epicone or reaching hind end. Several large pale green chloroplasts.

Port Erin.

Gymnodinium variabile Herdman
[LEBOUR 1925: 41]

Rounded, about 40 μm long, flattened. Sulcus usually short, scarcely indenting epicone, but sometimes reaching hind end. Protoplasm colourless or pale yellow, with or without pigmented granules. May be a complex of species.

Port Erin.

Gyrodinium lebourae Herdman   FIG. 2.1
[LEBOUR 1925: 53; DODGE 1982: 102]

Oval, about 15 μm long, flattened. Annulus displaced at least 0.3 of body length.

Port Erin, and perhaps South Africa.

4 PRONOCTILUCIDAE

Few genera, of uncertain relationships and affinities. One psammophilic species.

Oxyrrhis marina Dujardin   FIG. 2.1
[DODGE 1982: 111]

Oval, 10–35 × 8–30 μm. Flagella arise either side of tentacular lobe, which stems from middle of depression near hind end. Colourless. Without thecal plates.

In sand and pools round Britain and much of world.

5 POLYKRIKIDAE

With multiple annuli and sulci, as if each individual comprised a chain of four or eight gymnodinioid zooids. One genus.

Polykrikos lebourae Herdman   FIG. 2.1
[DODGE 1982: 118]

Flattened laterally, up to 60 μm long, with eight annuli, two nuclei and many chloroplasts. The only flattened *Polykrikos*, and the only one found interstitially. Figures (2.1) show right side and ventral edge.

Wet sand off Britanny and most of Britain.

6 LOPHODINIIDAE

Covered with delicate theca of polygonal plates, which are best studied by scanning electron microscopy. Includes two sand-living genera.

1. Epicone slightly smaller than hypocone **Herdmania litoralis**

   Epicone much larger than hypocone **2**

2. Not much flattened. Without an apical notch. Hypocone bilaterally symmetrical **Katodinium fungiforme**

   Flattened dorso-ventrally. Cell apex notched. Hypocone bilaterally asymmetrical **Katodinium asymmetricum**

Herdmania litoralis Dodge   FIG. 2.1
[DODGE 1982: 125]
Rounded in ventral view, 25–35 μm long, flattened dorso-ventrally, notched apically. Annulus incomplete ventrally on right side. Without chloroplasts. Figures (2.1) show ventral and dorsal views.

Round most of Britain.

Katodinium asymmetricum (Massart) Loeblich   FIG. 2.1
[DODGE 1982: 127]
Length 10–22 μm. Epicone rounded with apical notch. Hypocone asymmetrical, larger on left side of sulcus. Without chloroplasts.

Katodinium glandula (Herdman) Loeblich, length 17–35 μm, may be separated from this only by its larger size range (Dodge 1982), which seems an insufficient distinction.

In wet sand and salt marshes round south and south-west Britain; Belgium; France; eastern USA.

Katodinium fungiforme (Anissimowa) Loeblich
[DODGE 1982: 128]
As above, but 11–15 μm, lacking apical notch and asymmetry of hypocone.

In wet sand and salt marsh pools from Russia; Britain; France.

7 PERIDINIIDAE
Species in this and related families of 'peridinians' (suborder Peridiniina) are mostly distinguished by their patterns of thecal plates, but these are difficult to see in *Glenodinium*, the only genus represented in sand (by one species).

Glenodinium monensis Herdman   FIG. 2.1
[DODGE 1982: 49]
Discoid, 23–5 μm long. Annulus equatorial, sometimes forming almost flat spiral. Sulcus short, but indenting both epicone and hypocone. Plasma yellowish-green. No chloroplasts or thecal plates described.

Port Erin; southern England.

8 GONYAULACIDAE
Three genera, all planktonic. Many phytoflagellates encyst, but *Gonyaulax* and some other peridinians have cysts that are particularly distinctive, with radiating processes. The cyst of *Gonyaulax polyedra* (Fig. 2.1) is common in intertidal sediments off Wales and western Ireland (Reid 1972).

9 OXYTOXIDAE
Heterogeneous assemblage, with thecal plates and reduced epicone.

1. Flattened dorsoventrally **2**

   Flattened laterally **4**

2. Length 30–40 μm **Amphidiniopsis kofoidii**

   Length 43–60 μm **3**

3. Thecal plates covered with rows of small projections **Amphidiniopsis hirsutum**

   Only a few small processes projecting posteriorly **Amphidiniopsis swedmarkii**

4. Lateral compression slight; thecal plates distinct; epicone small but prominent **Roscoffia capitata**

   Strongly flattened; thecal plates difficult to see; epicone minute or flattened **5**

5. Annulus oblique, with dorsal loop almost apical and junction with sulcus displaced posteriorly **Adenoides eludens**

   Annulus transverse **Adenoides kofoidii**

Adenoides eludens (Herdman) Balech   FIG. 2.1
[DODGE 1982: 241]
Ovoid, 27–30 × 20–5 μm. Hypocone covered with 11 thin plates. Many brown chloroplasts. Figured (2.1) from right side, showing optical section and surface.

Port Erin; North Wales; southern England; Brittany.

Adenoides kofoidii (Herdman)
[DODGE 1982: 241]
Subquadrangular, with rounded corners, 25–40 × 25 μm. Annulus adjoins anterior margin. No details available of thecal plates.

Port Erin.

Amphidiniopsis hirsutum Balech
[DODGE 1982: 248]
Ovoid, 48–51 × 36–44 μm, epicone bluntly pointed, almost flat, nearly as wide as hypocone. Thecal plates with rows of small projections. Cytoplasm colourless.

Brittany; southern England.

Amphidiniopsis kofoidii Woloszynska
[DODGE 1982: 247]
As above, but 30–40 × 23–6 μm. Thecal plates with small pores, lacking projections. Cell contains chloroplasts and pigment granules.

Baltic; southern England.

Amphidiniopsis swedmarkii Balech   FIG. 2.1
[DODGE 1982: 248]

As above, 43–60 × 30–8 μm; with two or more short posterior processes. Figures (2.1) show ventral and dorsal view.

Brittany; southern England; Port Erin; south-west Scotland.

Roscoffia capitata Balech
[DODGE 1982: 249]

Cell 32–4 × 24–6 μm, like *Amphidiniopsis* but with epicone only 0.6 × width of hypocone.

Brittany.

Order **Cryptomonadida**

10 CRYPTOMONADIDAE

Several genera (Butcher 1967). *Cryptomonas* has been observed in sand at Plymouth and Roscoff, but perhaps not identified to species.

11 CYATHOMONADIDAE

One species, often placed in this order, although it stores oil, not starch.

Cyathomonas truncata (Fresenius) Fisch   FIG. 2.1
[HOLLANDE 1952: 303]

About 20 × 12 μm, laterally compressed. Anterior depression leads into deep gullet, surrounded by horseshoe-shaped band of trichocysts.

Freshwater and (at Plymouth) marine sand or mud (Lackey and Lackey 1963).

Order **Prymnesiida**

12 PONTOSPHAERIDAE

Parke and Dixon (1976) list 16 families in this order (= Haptophyceae). Several of these could be regarded as 'coccolithophorids', having body scales calcified and visible by light microscopy. One such species is recorded from sand.

Pontosphaera roscoffensis Chadefaud and
   Feldman   FIG. 2.1
[DRAGESCO 1865: 87]

Ovoid, about 16 × 14 μm, covered with discoid coccoliths up to 2.5 μm across. Two anterior flagella. Central leucosin body, posterior nucleus and, on each side, a large yellow-brown chloroplast. Figures (2.1) show optical section above, and surface view below.

Brittany, occasionally forming brown coatings over fine sand. Cells also attach to the alga *Cladophora*.

Order **Volvocida**

13 CHLAMYDOMONADIDAE

Several marine genera and many species.

Chlamydomonas reginae Ettl and Green
[ETTL AND GREEN 1973: 975]

Ovoid 12–22 × 9–18 μm. Chloroplast cup-shaped, with its sides characteristically fissured in this species by 10–16 longitudinal slits. These are long but do not extend to the anterior margin, which is not lobed.

Brittany.

Order **Prasinomonadida**

14 PRASINOCLADIDAE

Motile cells superficially like chlamydomonads.

Tetraselmis convolutae Parke and Manton   FIG. 2.1
[PARKE AND MANTON 1967: 445]

Freeliving cells ovoid, 8–13 × 6–10 μm, flattened and somewhat quadrangular in transverse section, with an anterior lobe of the chloroplast adjoining the cell wall in each rounded corner.

Brittany, Channel Islands and perhaps South Wales. Symbiotic with flatworm *Convoluta roscoffensis*, which forms green patches on sand surface. The Welsh material presents taxonomic problems (Douglas 1985).

Order **Euglenida**

15 EUGLENIDAE

Rarely recorded from sand. Leedale (1967) restricts this group to forms which have one flagellum so short that it does not emerge from an anterior invagination. It is associated there with the base of another flagellum which is usually emergent and is motile throughout its length during swimming.

Euglena obtusa Schmitz
[LEEDALE 1967: 23]

Length 80–150 μm. Both flagella non-emergent. Many flat irregularly arranged chloroplasts, each with its own pyrenoid.

In mud on shores of estuaries, e.g. Avon near Bristol, creeping by worm-like movements to surface when tide is out.

Euglena viridis Ehrenberg
[DRAGESCO 1965: 89; LEEDALE 1967, 25]

Length 50–80 μm. Cylindrical with posterior end generally pointed but often initiating waves of contraction that travel forward. Nucleus posterior to a central pyrenoid, from which many chloroplasts radiate.

Brittany, in saprobic and brackish conditions high on beach.

Trachelomonas abrupta Swivenko sensu
   Dragesco   FIG. 2.1
[DRAGESCO 1965: 91]

Oval, about 30 μm long. Theca brown with terminal aperture from which flagellum emerges. About 12 discoid yellow-green chloroplasts lie in contact with cell membrane. Each is attached by a short stalk to a separate pyrenoid situated deeper in the cell, as optical section shows (Fig. 2.1).

Brittany; brackish water in sand.

16 HETERONEMATIDAE

Lacking chloroplasts. With cytostome separate from invagination which contains the flagellar base(s). In this family and many species of the next, much of the anterior flagellum points stiffly forward during swimming, with only the distal part moving actively.

---

1. Body wall rigid, with longitudinal grooves but no striations. Cytostome forms mouth of tapering siphon **Entosiphon cuneatiformis**

   Body capable of changing shape, wall with spiral striations. Cytostome associated with cytopharynx flanked by ingestion rods **2**

2. With one emergent flagellum. Body coated with silt particles and/or with anterior end enlarged and funnel-shaped **7**

   With two emergent flagella. Without a silt coating, and tapering or rounded anteriorly **3**

3. Anteriorly directed flagellum shorter than the other **4**

   Anteriorly directed flagellum longer than the other **5**

4. Body subcylindrical, rounded posteriorly, with rows of granules between pellicular striations. **Dinema griseolum**

   Body spindle-shaped. Striations without rows of granules **Dinema litorale**

5. Posterior flagellum lies free from cell **Heteronema acus**

   Posterior flagellum pressed close to cell, usually lying in a groove **6**

6. Posteriorly rounded or sometimes tapering, but without an excentric posterior process. Cytoplasm granular **Peranema trichophorum**

   Usually rounded posteriorly, with an excentric process. Cytoplasm homogeneous and transparent **Peranema cuneatum**

7. Without coating of silt particles **Urceolus cyclostomus**

   With coating of silt particles **8**

8. Almost spindle-shaped, tapering posteriorly but truncated and fairly broad anteriorly **Urceolus sabulosus**

   Ovoid, rounded posteriorly, tapering anteriorly **Urceolus pascheri**

Dinema griseolum Perty

[HUBER-PESTALOZZI 1955: 535]

Elongated 76–80 × 30–40 μm, ends rounded. Anterior flagellum about 1 × body length, trailing one 1.5 × body length.

Freshwater, Plymouth sediment. See Lackey and Lackey (1963) for marine occurrences of colourless euglenoids from this and the next family (which are known mostly from freshwater).

Dinema litorale Skuja

[HUBER-PESTALOZZI 1955: 536]

Spindle-shaped, flattened, metabolic, 80–95 × 27–38 μm. With broad groove along one side. Flagella as above.

Baltic. Plymouth sediment.

Entosiphon cuneatiformis Lackey

[LACKEY 1962: 193]

Discoid, diameter about 40 μm, thickness 15–20 μm. Ventral surface flat, dorsal with four longitudinal grooves separating five lobes. Siphon short, like a wedge driven into the cytoplasm. Anterior flagellum 30 μm long, trailing one 60 μm.

Coasts of USA.

Heteronema acus (Ehrenberg) Stein

[HUBER-PESTALOZZI 1955: 510; Leedale 1967: 60]

Spindle-shaped 45–50 × 8–20 μm, ends rounded. Anterior flagellum exceeds body length, trailing one half as long.

Plymouth sediment. Also freshwater.

Peranema cuneatum Playfair

[HUBER-PESTALOZZI 1955: 475]

Wedge-shaped 25–70 × 5–15 μm, sometimes with excentric process projecting from broad hind end.

Plymouth sediment. Freshwater in Australia.

Peranema trichophorum (Ehrenberg) Stein

[HUBER-PESTALOZZI 1955: 473]

Spindle-shaped or subcylindrical 22–70 × 12–20 μm. Very metabolic. Anterior flagellum thick, at least as long as body. Posterior flagellum much thinner, lying in groove or stuck to cell surface, difficult to see. Cytopharynx flanked by two ingestion rods.

Plymouth sediment. Widely distributed in freshwater.

Urceolus cyclostomus (Stein) Mereschowski FIG. 2.1

[HUBER-PESTALOZZI 1955: 480]

Spindle- or flask-shaped 26–50 × 17–30 μm. Plymouth sand or mud. Also freshwater.

Urceolus pascheri Skvortzow

[HUBER-PESTALOZZI 1955: 483]

Ovoid 11–18 × 5–15 μm, coated with silt particles, narrowing anteriorly.

Plymouth sand or mud. Freshwater in northern Manchuria.

Urceolus sabulosus Stokes

[HUBER-PESTALOZZI 1955: 482]

Spindle-shaped, but truncated or even widening anteriorly, about 58 μm long, coated with silt particles.

Plymouth sand, mud, and sediment. Widely distributed in freshwater.

17 SPHENOMONADIDAE

Colourless, but with no special cytostome. Cell more or less rigid, usually with keels, grooves, or protrusions.

1. With one emergent flagellum   **2**

    With two emergent flagella   **5**

2. With laterally projecting pointed processes   ***Pentamonas spinifera***

    Without such processes   **3**

3. Length less than 13 μm, not much flattened, without longitudinal furrows   ***Petalomonas pusilla***

    Length more than 29 μm, flattened, with longitudinal furrow(s)   **4**

4. With a furrow on both sides   ***Petalomonas mediocanellata***

    With a furrow on one side   ***Petalomonas excavata***

5. Anterior flagellum usually shorter than the other, never longer   **6**

    Anterior flagellum always longer than the other   **8**

6. Cell spindle-shaped. Pellicle longitudinally striated   ***Anisonema pusillum***

    Cell oval. Pellicle smooth   **7**

7. Anterior flagellum equals body length   ***Anisonema ovale***

    Anterior flagellum is double body length   ***Anisonema emarginatum***

8. Markedly flattened. Outline ovoid, wider posteriorly   ***Notosolenus apocamptus***

    Not flattened, or with body elongated or tapering posteriorly   **9**

9. With eight fairly sharp longitudinal keels   ***Tropidoscyphus octocostatus***

    With longitudinal keels that are inconspicuous and rounded in cross-section   **10**

10. With four keels, so quadrangular in cross-section. Length about twice breadth   ***Sphenomonas quadrangularis***

    With three inconspicuous keels on one side and the other side flattened. Length about 3 × breadth   ***Sphenomonas elongata***

Anisonema emarginatum Stokes
[HUBER-PESTALOZZI 1955: 526]

About 14 × 10 μm. Flagellum which trails posteriorly is not much longer than the other.

    Plymouth sand or mud. Freshwater in USA.

Anisonema ovale Klebs
[HUBER-PESTALOZZI 1955: 526]

About 11 × 7 μm, rounded at each end. Posterior flagellum 1.5 × the other.

    Plymouth sand or mud. Also in freshwater.

Anisonema pusillum Stokes
[HUBER-PESTALOZZI 1955: 527]

About 11 × 5 μm, pointed at each end, flattened. Posterior flagellum 3 × length of the other.

    Plymouth sediment. Freshwater in USA.

Notosolenus apocamptus Stokes
[HUBER-PESTALOZZI 1955: 529; LEEDALE 1967: 57]

Outline ovoid but bluntly triangular, 6.5–10.5 μm long, pointed anteriorly, very flattened. Shallow longitudinal furrow occupies middle of dorsal surface. Anterior flagellum 1.5 × body length.

    Plymouth sand or mud. Freshwater in USA.

Pentamonas spinifera Lackey   FIG. 2.1
[LACKEY 1962: 194]

Flattened, about 10 μm thick. Outline irregularly pentagonal, about 80 × 40 μm, with three or four backwardly curved spines projecting from right and posterior edges. Left side forms either a spine or an angular point or a convex curve. Flagellum about 0.8 × cell length.

    Plymouth sand or mud. Both coasts of USA.

Petalomonas excavata Skuja
[HUBER-PESTALOZZI 1955: 488]

Slightly flattened, almost oval 30–5 × 22 μm wide, 16–18 μm thick, with mid-longitudinal furrow on one side.

    Plymouth sediment. Latvia.

Petalomonas mediocanellata Stein   FIG. 2.1
[HUBER-PESTALOZZI 1955: 489]

Broadly ovoid, flattened, 34–9 × 22–6 μm, 8–10 μm thick, with a mid-longitudinal furrow on each side.

    Plymouth sand, mud, and sediment. Widely distributed in freshwater.

Petalomonas pusilla Skuja
[HUBER-PESTALOZZI 1955: 488]

Ellipsoidal 5–12 × 2–4 μm, slightly flattened, without a furrow.

    Plymouth sand, mud, and sediment. Sweden.

Sphenomonas elongata Lackey   FIG. 2.1
[LACKEY 1962: 191]

Length 40–70 μm, about 3 × greatest width. Flattened. Slightly concave ventrally in longitudinal section. Dorsal side bears three rounded longitudinal keels (see cross-section). Flagella tenuous, anterior 0.5 and posterior 0.15 × body length.

    Plymouth sand or mud. Both coasts of USA.

Sphenomonas quadrangularis Stein
[HUBER-PESTALOZZI 1955: 458]

Broadly spindle-shaped, about 30 μm long, with four rounded longitudinal keels, so cross-section is cruciform. Anterior flagellum twice body length.

    Plymouth sediment. Also freshwater.

Tropidoscyphus octocostatus Stein
[HUBER-PESTALOZZI 1955: 516]
Broadly spindle-shaped, 36–65 μm long, with eight longitudinal ridges spiralling slightly. Anterior flagellum 1.5–2 × body length. Posterior flagellum much smaller.

Plymouth sand or mud. Also freshwater.

B Subphylum **Sarcodina**

Comprises Sarcomastigophora which produce *pseudopodia* (or related forms of protoplasmic flow) for locomotion and various other functions; flagella, if present at all, occur only in short-lived, early developmental stages.

Superclass **Rhizopoda**

Contains dominantly benthic sarcodines (only some of the Granulorecticulosea, order Foraminiferida, are planktonic), which may be naked, or possess an external flexible *pellicle*, or an extracytoplasmic *sheath*, or even a rigid exoskeleton (a *test*). In the naked Gymnamoebia and Acarpomyxea, locomotion is achieved by changes in cell shape, as none possess a rigid sheath or test. Some (e.g. in suborder Thecina of the order Amoebida) merely ripple an external pellicle, but others produce more extended locomotor structures, ranging from short, blunt, sub-conical projections (*subpseudopodia*, in Amoebida of the suborders Acanthopodina and Conopodina) to lobose extensions, which may be flexible and finger-like (*dactylopodia*, as in floating forms of the Conopodina and Tubulina) or broadly lobe-shaped or even knob-like (*lobopodia*, also in the Amoebida). In some, lobopodia may furcate distally, to produce long, slender filaments; a fringe of short fine filaments may trail from the posterior edge of the cell (some Flabellina) or resemble bristles (*villi*, as in some Peliobiontida). Adhesive, *uroid*, villous, knob-like protrusions characterize the trailing, posterior edges of some motile forms of Acarpomyxea (order Leptomyxida). In the Testacealobosia, an external organic sheath is formed around the cell; in the Trichosida, impermanent, ephemeral apertures form in the fibrous, flexible sheath and short dactylopodia extrude from them, but locomotion is still achieved by rippling of the surface and development of broad lobopodia beneath the pellicular sheath; the Arcellinida have a rigid test with a permanent aperture, and only from this opening do lobopodia emerge. The pseudopodia of the Filosea are characteristically long, slender, filiform and branching (*filopodia*) and those of the Granulorecticulosea are not only slender and branching, but also anastomose, forming ephemeral, reticulate networks (*reticulopodia* or *myxopodia*) and are characteristically granular. All these forms of pseudopodia are believed to differ quite fundamentally from the slender, radiating, relatively stiff *axopodia* of the superclass Actinopoda (which possess distinctive axial filaments, around which the cytoplasm of the pseudopodium flows). The Actinopoda are nearly all planktonic, and are not treated here.

NOTES ON COLLECTING BENTHIC MARINE RHIZOPODA

The techniques of collection of the naked rhizopods (gymnamoebid Lobosea, Acarpomyxea) and those with temporary, uncemented sheaths (trichosid Testacealobosia) necessarily differ from those for rhizopods with permanent, rigid tests (arcellinid Testacealobosia, gromiid Filosea, foraminiferid Granuloreticulosea), and each is described separately below.

1. NAKED AMOEBIDS

Naked marine or estuarine amoebids live on or near the surface of muds, in the water-saturated interstices of silts and sands, and sometimes on algal fronds. It is not practical to study the amoebids directly in the field, and it is usual to collect small samples of the water-saturated sediment in sterile jars and then to inoculate a suitable nutrient agar, in petri dishes. Suitable agar media (Page 1970, 1973) include:

A. *Cerophyl-seawater agar* (CS)

10 g Bacto-agar per litre; fluid base is 1 g Cerophyl boiled for 5 min in filtered natural sea-water (to normal salinity, 35‰, or in 75%, 50%, etc. dilutions), with Cerophyl particles then removed by filtration. Medium autoclaved before introduction to sterile petri dishes. Inoculation, with sterile seawater and sample, transfers both amoebae and accompanying bacterial flora, for amoebid nutrition, and cultures can be maintained.

B. *Malt extract—yeast extract seawater agar* (MYS)

0.1 g malt extract, 0.1 g yeast extract, 15 g Difco Bacto-agar per litre. Same technique. Living amoebae are studied in ordinary wet mounts on glass slides using a reversing microscope, or in hanging drops on the underside of cover glasses by an ordinary biological microscope. Permanent preparations can be made by standard cytological fixation and staining techniques: Nissenbaum's or Bouin's fixatives, and Feulgen-fast green, Kernechtrot, Periodic acid-Schiff and alcian blue stains are useful.

2. TESTATE AMOEBIDS, FILOSIDS, AND FORAMINIFERIDS

Testate amoebids and other small genera can be collected and studied by methods used for the naked forms, but the living, larger testate genera may be collected directly in sediments of salt-marsh pools, creeks, estuaries, beaches, and rock-pools and on firm substrates (dead shell, seaweeds, pebbles, etc.) inshore and offshore. Dead, empty tests are found commonly in finer sediment accumulations such as muddy areas or the troughs of sand ripples.

Collection in the littoral can be done by hand. For offshore collecting a simple dredge can be made by removing the bottom of a galvanized iron bucket, replacing it with a fine metal screen of 5 mm mesh size and covered with a strong linen or hessian bag. This improvised dredge will sieve out large material and collect finer fragments in the bag, which should be easily removable. The weight of coarse material in the body of the bucket is usually enough to keep the dredge on the sea-bed, but additional lead weights are advantageous.

A. *Collection of living specimens*

Techniques have been described in detail by Arnold (1974) and by Boltovskoy and Wright (1976). At its simplest, sediment (or appropriate firm substrate fragments) may be collected in clean, translucent, screw-top, wide-mouth jars; the jars should never have been washed using detergents or other surfactants, as these are rapidly toxic even in trace quantities. About 100 g, collected from the top 1–2 cm of sediment, in a 250 ml jar with about 100 ml of *in situ* water, is appropriate. The jars can then be stored in natural light but in a cool place until required. Euryhaline and eurythermal species can survive for weeks in this environment, but stenohaline, stenothermal open marine species need early attention. The natural bacterial flora collected with the sediment or other substrata will provide nutrients.

If specimens are to be preserved, 70% alcohol is best introduced immediately upon collection; 5% or 10% sea-water formalin may be used, but it must be buffered to pH 7.5–8.5 (with, e.g. hexamine) to prevent dissolution of calcareous tests.

To determine which of the testate rhizopods (in preserved material) were living at the time of collection, a standard technique is to wash away the preserving solution by wet-sieving or decanting with tap water and distilled water, and then to immerse the material in a 5% w/v aqueous solution of Rose Bengal for about half an hour; this stains proteins pink. The material is then washed free of surplus stain, and can be wet-mounted; specimens which appear to be pink internally, through their translucent tests, are considered to have been alive (or recently so) at the time of collection.

Subsamples of living specimens may be examined in a petri dish in sea-water at × 20 to × 50 magnification using a binocular stereo microscope and incident light. Smaller, individual specimens may be transferred using a fine-grade paintbrush to a normal or recessed glass slide, in a drop of the *in situ* seawater, and observed under a compound microscope using incident or transmitted light; a combination of phase condenser and Köhler's illumination can reveal pseudopodia well (see Banner and Williams 1973, plates 8 and 9). It may be some hours before pseudopodial extrusion occurs.

Permanent mounts may be made after fixation and staining, but recessed slides must be used; most recessed slides are deep enough for only the smallest Foraminiferida, and a deeper recess may be made from thin rings of perspex tubing cemented to plain glass slides.

B. *Collection of tests*

The simplest way to obtain large quantities and variety of foraminiferal tests is to collect fine sediment from the littoral or offshore: the finer the sediment, the more dead tests will have accumulated (on beaches of medium-sized or coarse sand, the best collecting sites are in the troughs of ripples or at the strandlines of the tide). The sediment should be sieved, and the 0.2–0.5 mm size-fraction examined; muddy sediment can be stirred with an excess of water and the suspended mud decanted off. The mud-free sediment should be dried and the tests picked out with a grade 0 artist's paintbrush, using a blackened petri dish as a sorting tray, and a microscope with incident light and

× 20 or × 40 magnification. Tests may be dry-mounted (using a weak solution of gum tragacanth or gum arabic as an adhesive) into plastic or cardboard slides. Such slides may be hand made by punching holes (approx. 1 cm diameter) in a 25 mm × 75 mm strip of thin, strong cardboard, sticking this on to a cardboard base of the same size upon which exposed, developed and fixed photographic bromide paper has been glued, and covering with a standard thin glass microscope slide. The bromide paper emulsion, when dampened, will provide adequate adhesion for small, fragile tests, without extra adhesive.

REFERENCES

Alexander, S. P. and Banner, F. T. (1984). The functional relationship between skeleton and cytoplasm in *Haynesina germanica* (Ehrenberg). *Journal of Foraminiferal Research*, **14**, 159–70.

Arnold, Z. M. (1974). Field and laboratory techniques for the study of living foraminifera. *Foraminifera*, **1**, 153–206.

Banner, F. T. and Culver, S. J. (1978). Quarternary *Haynesina* n.gen. and Paleogene *Protelphidium* Haynes. *Journal of Foraminiferal Research*, **8**, 177–207.

Banner, F. T. and Williams, E. (1973). Test structure, organic skeleton and extrathalamous cytoplasm of *Ammonia* Brünnich. *Journal of Foraminiferal Research*, **3**, 49–69.

Bé, A. W. H. (1967). *Fiches d'identification du Zooplankton*, No. **108**. Foraminifera: families Globigerinidae and Globorotaliidae. Counseil permanent International pour l'Exploration de la Mer, Copenhagen.

Boltovskoy, E. and Wright, R. (1976). *Recent foraminifera*. Dr. W. Junk B. V., The Hague.

Brönnimann, P. and Whittaker, J. (1986). On the morphology of *Paratrochammina* (*Lepidoparatrochammina*) *haynesi* (Atkinson) from south Cardigan Bay, Wales. *Révue de Paléobiologie*, **5**, 117–25.

Brönnimann, P. and Whittaker, J. (1987). A revision of the foraminiferal genus *Adercotryma* Loeblich & Tappan with a description of *A. wrighti* sp. nov. from British Waters. *Bulletin of the British Museum* (*Natural History*): *Zoology*, **52**, 19–28.

Brönnimann, P., Zaninetti, L., and Whittaker, J. (1983). On the classification of the Trochamminacea. *Journal of Foraminiferal Research*, **13**, 202–18.

Chardez, D. (1977). Thécamoebiens du mesopsammon des plages de la Mer du Nord. *Révue Verviétoise d'histoire naturelle*, **34**(4/6), 18–34.

Cushman, J. A. (1931). The foraminifera of the Atlantic Ocean, part VIII. *Bulletin of the U.S. National Museum*, **104**, 1–179.

de Saedeleer, H. (1934). Beitrag zur Kenntnis der Rhizopoden: morphologische und systematische Untersuchungen und ein Klassifikationsversuch. *Mémoires du Musée royale d'histoire naturelle de Belgique*, **60**.

Farmer, J. N. (1980). *The Protozoa*. C. V. Mosby Co, St. Louis.

Feyling-Hanssen, R. W., Jørgensen, J. A., Knudsen, K. L., and Andersen, A.-L. L. (1971). Late Quaternary foraminifera from Vendsyssel, Denmark and Sandness, Norway. *Bulletin of the Geological Society of Denmark*, **21**, 67–317.

Golemansky, V. (1974). Psammonobiotidae fam. nov. Une nouvelle famille de Thecamoebiens du psammal supralittoral des mers. *Acta Protozoologica*, **13**, 137–42.

Haynes, J. R. (1973). Cardigan Bay recent Foraminifera. *Bulletin of the British Museum* (*Natural History*): *Zoology*, Supplement, **4**, 1–245.

Haynes, J. R. (1981). *Foraminifera*. MacMillan, London and Basingstoke.

Hedley, R. H. (1958). A contribution to the biology and cytology of *Haliphysema* (Foraminifera). *Proceedings of the Zoological Society of London*, **130**, 569–76.

Hedley, R. H. (1962). *Gromia oviformis* (Rhizopodea) from New Zealand, with comments on the fossil Chitinozoa. *New Zealand Journal of Science*, **5**, 121–36.

Höglund, H. (1947). Foraminifera in the Gullmar Fjord and the Skagerak. *Zoologiska bidrag fran Uppsala*, **26**, 1–328.

Jepps, M. (1942). Studies on *Polystomella* Lamarck. *Journal of the Marine Biological Association of the U.K.*, **25**, 607–66.

Jepps, M. (1956). *The Protozoa, Sarcodina*. Oliver and Boyd, 183 pp.

Jones, R. W. (1984). A revised classification of the unilocular Nodosariida and Buliminida (Foraminifera). *Revista Española de Micropaleontologia*, **16**, 91–160.

Knight, R. (1986). A novel method of dark field illumination for a stereomicroscope and its application to a study of the pseudopodia of *Reophax moniliformis* Siddall (Foraminiferida). *Journal of Micropalaeontology*, **5**, 83–90.

Knight, R. and Mantoura, R. F. C. (1985). Chlorophyll and carotenoid pigments in Foraminifera and their symbiotic algae. *Marine Ecology, Progress Series*, **23**, 241–9.

Knudsen, K. L. (1973). Foraminifera from postglacial deposits of the Lundergård area, in Vendsyssel, Denmark. *Bulletin of the Geological Society of Denmark*, **22**, 255–82.

Le Calvez, J. (1935). Les gamètes de quelques foraminifères. *Compte rendu de l'Academie des Sciences Paris*, **201**, 1505–7.

Le Calvez, J. (1947). *Entosolenia marginata*; foraminifère apogamique ectoparasite d'un autre foraminifère *Discorbis vilardeboanus*. *Compte rendu de l'Academie des Sciences, Paris*, **224**, 1448–50.

Levine, N. D. *et al.* (1980). A newly revised classification of the Protozoa. *Journal of Protozoology*, **27**, 37–58.

Levy, A., Mathieu, R., Poignant, A., Rosset-Moulinier, M., and Rouvillois, A. (1975). Sur quelques foraminifères actuels des plages de Dunkerque et des environs: neotypes et espèce nouvelle. *Révue de Micropaleontologie*, **17**, 171–81.

Lewis, K. B. (1970). A key to the recent genera of the Foraminiferida. *Bulletin of the New Zealand Department of Scientific and Industrial Research*, **196** (*N.Z. Oceanographic Institute memoir*, **45**).

Loeblich, A. R. and Tappan, H. (1964). *Treatise on invertebrate paleontology, Part C, Protista 2, Sarcodina*. University of Kansas Press.

Leoblich, A. R. and Tappan, H. (1984). Suprageneric classification of the Foraminiferida (Protozoa). *Micropaleontology*, **30**, 1–70.

Mathieu, R., Momeni, I., Poignant, A., Rosset-Moulinier, M., Rouvillois, A., and Ubaldo, M. (1971). Les representants des Miliolacea dans les sables des plages des environs de Dunkerque. Rémarques sur les espèces signalées par O. Terquem. *Révue de Micropaleontologie*, **14**, 157–66.

Murray, J. W. (1971). *An Atlas of British recent foraminiferids*. Heinemann, London.

Murray, J. W. (1973). *Distribution and ecology of living benthic Foraminiferids*. Heinemann, London.

Murray, J. W. (1979). *British near-shore foraminiferids*. Academic Press, London.

Myers, E. H. (1937). The life-cycle of *Spirillina vivipara* Ehr., with notes on the morphogenesis, systematics and distribution of the foraminifera. *Journal of the Royal Microscopical Society of London*, **56**, 120–46.

Page, F. C. (1967). Taxonomic criteria for limax amoebae, with descriptions of 3 new species of *Hartmannella* and 3 of *Vahlkampfia*. *Journal of Protozoology*, **14**, 499–521.

Page, F. C. (1969). *Platyamoeba stenopodia* n.gen., n.sp., a freshwater Amoeba. *Journal of Protozoology*, **16**, 437–41.

Page, F. C. (1970). Two new species of *Paramoeba* from Maine. *Journal of Protozoology*, **17**, 421–7.

Page, F. C. (1971a). A comparative study of five freshwater and marine species of the Thecamoebidae. *Transactions of the American Microscopical Society*, **90**, 157–73.

Page, F. C. (1971b). Two marine species of *Flabellula* (Amoebida, Mayorellidae). *Journal of Protozoology*, **18**, 37–44.

Page, F. C. (1972). *Rhizamoeba polyura* n.gen., n.sp., and uroidal structures as a taxonomic criterion for amoebae. *Transactions of the American Microscopical Society*, **91**, 502–13.

Page, F. C. (1973). *Paramoeba*: a common marine genus. *Hydrobiologia*, **41**, 183–8.

Page, F. C. (1974a). Some marine *Platyamoeba* of East Anglia. *Journal of the Marine Biological Association of the U.K.*, **54**, 651–64.

Page, F. C. (1974b). A further study of taxonomic criteria for limax amoebae, with descriptions of new species and a key to genera. *Archiv für Protistenkunde*, **116**, 149–84.

Page, F. C. (1976a). A revised classification of the Gymnamoebia (Protozoa, Sarcodina). *Zoological Journal of the Linnean Society*, **58**, 61–77.

Page, F. C. (1976b). Some comparative notes of the occurrence of Gymnamoebia (Protozoa, Sarcodina) in British and American habitats. *Transactions of the American Microscopical Society*, **95**, 385–94.

Page, F. C. (1977). The genus *Thecamoeba* (Protozoa, Gymnamoebia): species distinctions, locomotive morphology, and protozoan prey. *Journal of Natural History*, **11**, 25–63.

Page, F. C. (1979). *Vexillifera armata* n.sp. (Gymnamoebia, Paramoebidae), an estuarine amoeba with distinctive surface structures and trichocyst-like bodies. *Protistologica*, **15**, 111–22.

Page, F. C. (1980a). A key to marine species of *Vannella* (Sarcodina, Gymnamoebia), with descriptions of new species. *Journal of the Marine Biological Association of the U.K.*, **60**, 929–46.

Page, F. C. (1980b). A light- and electron-microscopical comparison of limax and flabellate marine amoebae belonging to four genera. *Protistologica*, **16**, 57–78.

Page, F. C. (1983). *Marine Gymnamoebae*. Institute of Terrestrial Ecology, Cambridge.

Rosset-Moulinier, M. (1971). Étude systématique et écologique des Elphidiidae et des Nonionidae du littoral Breton. 1. Les *Elphidium* du groupe *crispum* (Linnée). *Révue de Micropaleontologie*, **14**, 76–81.

Rosset-Moulinier, M. (1985). Importance écologique des foraminifères agglutinées appartenant aux genres *Remaneica*, et *Deuterammina*. *Révue de Micropaleontologie*, **28**, 205–12.

Schultze, M. S. (1854). *Uber den organismus der Polythalamien (Foraminiferen), nebst Bemerkungen über die Rhizopoden im Allgemein*. Engelmann, Leipzig.

Sheehan, R. and Banner, F. T. (1973a). *Trichosphaerium* an extraordinary testate Rhizopod from coastal waters. *Estuarine and Coastal Marine Science*, **1**, 245–60.

Sheehan, R. and Banner, F. T. (1973b). The pseudopodia of *Elphidium incertum*. *Revista Española de Micropaleontologia*, **4**, 31–63.

KEY TO CLASSES WITH MARINE SPECIES

1. Pseudopodia hyaline, lobose or more or less filiform, produced from a broad, hyaline zone or lobe of cell body   **2**

    Pseudopodia very slender, streaming from main mass of cell (not from a conspicuous hyaline lobe)   **3**

2. Usually uninucleate (if multinucleate, not a flattened or branching plasmodium)   **1. Lobosea**

    Small plasmodia or much expanded, similar uninucleate forms, usually branching (sometimes forming a reticulum of coarse branches)   **2. Acarpomyxea**

3. With hyaline, non-granulate filopodia, usually branching, rarely (if ever) anastomosing   **3. Filosea**

    With granulohyaline branching and anastomosing reticulopodia   **4. Granuloreticulosea**

Class 1 Lobosea

This class contains protozoa which are enteric (parasitic), freshwater, estuarine, and marine in habitat. Brackish water and marine genera occur in both subclasses—the naked, non-testate GYMNAMOEBIA and the sheathed, often testate TESTACEALOBOSIA. The suprageneric classification used here is adapted from those given by Page (1976a) and by Levine *et al.* (1980).

Subclass Gymnamoebia

Only two orders contain marine or estuarine species:

1. Locomotion by steady flow within the cytoplasm; no flagellate stage of development   **Amoebida**

    Locomotion by more or less eruptive, hyaline, hemispherical bulges; usually with a temporary flagellate developmental stage   **Schizopyrenida**

Order Amoebida

This order contains many of the so-called **limax amoebae** (which, just as in the class Acarpomyxea, are monopodial, cylindrical or subcylindrical in locomotor form, with a more or less hemispherical, unflattened anterior end), as well as ovate or flabellate forms, and many which are broadly lobed or branched (like the popular image of *Amoeba – recte Chaos –* itself). All suborders contain estuarine or marine species, but records of the latter are few, reflecting the low level of research activity which this order has attracted. Page (1979) believes that "coastal and estuarine species constitute one [ecological] group, over against freshwater/soil species on the other hand": the former are essentially marine, and can all be cultured in diluted sea water media.

KEY TO SUBORDERS

1. With broadly or narrowly extruded lobopodia only   **2**

    With subpseudopodia, usually from broad hyaline lobe   **4**

2. With pellicle, which may wrinkle with rolling movements; normally unbranched   **Thecina**

    Without pellicle or pellicle-like layer   **3**

3. Body a branched or unbranched cylinder   **Tubulina**

    Body flattened, broad, sometimes discoid   **Flabellina**

4. Subpseudopodia blunt, digitiform or mamilliform, normally unbranched   **Conopodina**

    Subpseudopodia finely tipped, filiform, often furcate   **Acanthopodina**

Suborder **Thecina**

KEY TO MARINE GENERA
IN LOCOMOTOR (BENTHIC) FORMS

---

1. Form ovoid; thick pellicle forms parallel ridges or thick folds (anterior hyaloplasmic zone continues in lateral strips to posterior) **Thecamoeba**

   Form flattened ovoid to flabellate, with anterior hyaloplasm depressed and flatter than the posterior granuloplasm ('thinner dorsoventrally'); thinner pellicle forms no strong ridges 2

---

2. Pellicle forms transitory parallel wrinkles or thin folds; posterior granuloplasmic zone sometimes spatulate; no surface glycostyle **Platyamoeba**

   No pellicular wrinkles; posterior granular zone never drawn out or spatulate; surface has glycostyles of pentagonal pattern (electron microscopy) **Vannella**

I THECAMOEBIDAE

With characters as for the suborder. The locomotor forms vary from ovoid to flabellate: grossly similar flabellate forms, lacking pellicles, belong to the Suborder Flabellina (q.v.).

Thecamoeba orbis Schaeffer   FIG. 2.2
[PAGE 1974*a*: Figs. 13, 14, 19, 40–46; 1977: 49, Fig. 54]
The locomotor form characters are as for genus; floating form with radiating, clavate, thick, hyaline lobopodia. Known from intertidal sediments of the Wash (Hunstanton) and North Sea (Brancaster), and from estuaries (R. Stour, 20‰ salinity). Ingests diatoms, will feed on bacteria.

   T. hilla Schaeffer, known from the intertidal, North Sea (Mersea, Essex), differs in its less strong pellicular folds and partial enclosure of the posterior *granuloplasm* by stronger lateral "horns" of *hyaloplasm* from the anterior end.

Platyamoeba flabellata Page   FIG. 2.2
[PAGE 1974a: 653, I, A–G]
Shape of the locomotor form is as for the genus, variable from flattened ovoid to broadly flabellate, sometimes with posterior granular area elongate into bluntly spatulate form. Floating form with slender, curved lobopodia, equal in length to the diameter of the central mass from which they radiate, and of almost equal thickness throughout their length.

   Known from southern North Sea intertidal (low beach at Harwich, tidal pools at West Mersea, Essex). *P. flabellata*, alone among the known British species, has a contractile vacuole and is the most tolerant of low salinities in laboratory studies, tolerating even freshwater; however, other species, lacking a contractile vacuole (*P. bursella*, *P. plurinucleolus*), found naturally in seawater, can also survive in salinities as low as 3‰).

   Platyamoeba is one of the commonest of marine amoebids (rivalled only by *Paramoeba* of the Conopodina), but it is often very difficult to distinguish from the rarer *Vannella*, especially in marine isolates, without electron microscopy of the cell surface; the *glycostyles* on the surface of the latter are only about 120 nm (0.12 μm) long.

Vannella aberdonica Page   FIG. 2.2
[PAGE 1980*a*: 936–8, Figs. 4C–F, 5, 7B–C]
The locomotor form has a shape very similar to that of *P. flabellata*; in outline, it varies from semicircular to flabellate, with straight or concave, rarely convex, posterior edge to the granuloplasmic zone, and a broadly convex edge to the thinner, anterior hyaloplasmic zone. The glycostyles of the cell surface may be associated with phagocytosis. The amoebid moves sluggishly, travelling only $1\frac{1}{2}$ to 4 times its body length (about 9 μm) per minute (at 23°C). The floating form is unusual, being thickly flattened, rather twisted, always lacking pseudopodia (the floating forms of other species, e.g. *V. anglica*, *V. septentrionalis*, have radiating, slender, curved pseudopodia like those of floating *Platyamoeba*).

   V. aberdonica is known from the shore of the North Sea (at Aberdeen); other species (*V. anglica*, *V. septentrionalis*) are estuarine; Page (1980*a*) gives a key to these species.

Suborder **Tubulina**

This suborder contains terrestrial or freshwater Amoebidae (including *Amoeba*, *Chaos*), the parasitic Entamoebidae, and the family Hartmannellidae, which has terrestrial, freshwater, and marine representatives. While the Amoebidae are polypodial, the Hartmannellidae are monopodial (*limax*) in form.

I HARTMANNELLIDAE

This family comprises monopodial (*limax*) gymnamoebae which move by steady protoplasmic flow, sometimes with a gentle hemispherical bulging to either side at the anterior (hyaloplasmic) end.

Hartmannella hibernica Page   FIG. 2.2
[PAGE 1980*b*: 62–4, 75, Figs. 3–4, 16–17, 27–31]

The small, slender locomotor form (length: breadth ratio 1.7–5.0, mean 2.8–3.1) moves sluggishly, with frequent stops and changes of direction. It has been found in sandy beaches of the Atlantic coast of Ireland (salinity around 35‰) and has been cultured at about 26‰. The floating form has 5–12 hyaline, blunt, slender pseudopodia, of length not quite as great as the diameter of the central mass of the cell from which they radiate.

H. abertawensis, from the sandy beaches of Swansea Bay (salinity about 32‰), and which has also been cultured at about 26‰, has a locomotor form rather more slender than, but otherwise very similar to, *H. hibernica*; however, its floating form is irregularly rounded.

Suborder **Flabellina**

The locomotor form of these amoebids is flattened and broad, grossly resembling the shapes adopted by locomotor *Platyamoeba* and *Vannella* (Thecina, Thecamoebidae) but, like the Hartmanellidae (Tubulina), it possesses no pellicle. One family (Flabellulidae) contains marine species.

I FLABELLULIDAE

No subpseudopodia are produced during normal locomotion, but the amoebid rapidly changes its monopodial form (from spatulate to flabellate), often with eruptive cytoplasmic flow.

Flabellula citata Schaeffer   FIG. 2.2
[PAGE 1971*b*: 37–44, Figs. 1–9, 25–30; 1980*b*: 68–70; Figs. 5–6]

The locomotor form is usually fan-shaped (flabellate), but its shape changes with movement more variously than in the Thecinid *Platyamoeba* or *Vannella*, sometimes stretching anterio-posteriorly to become longer than broad. The anterior hyaloplasmic zone is flattened ('dorso-ventrally depressed') and extrudes short, stubby lobopodia (subpseudopodia) from its leading edge; the zone may be temporarily divided by clefts or 'rifts', and its outline can become deeply scalloped. The posterior granuloplasmic zone is thicker and often depressed ovoid in form; it contains food vacuoles, while the nucleus is usually in the anterior hyaline zone. Hyaloplasm passes back along the sides of the advancing amoeba and gathers at the posterior end, where fine, uroidal filaments (*pseudovilli*) are often extruded (to lengths up to that of the entire cell diameter) and adhere to the substratum. Feeding (ingestion of bacteria) occurs both anteriorly and posteriorly. The floating form is apparently short-lived; it is irregularly spherical, often with a few, short subpseudopodia.

F. citata, the type species of *Flabellula*, probably is universally distributed in the sea, and has been recorded from the intertidal beach at Brancaster, Norfolk (North Sea). *F. trinovantica* Page, from the Blackwater estuary, Essex, has been described in locomotion by Page (1980*a*) 'it puts out a broad, hyaline lobe, draws its posterior end rapidly forwards into the main cell mass, balls up, and then puts out another hyaline lobe, often in a different direction … (achieving) the locomotive rate per minute 0.8 to 4.5 times the length of the amoeba'.

Suborder **Conopodina**

These gymnamoebids have locomotor forms which are longer than broad, with their greatest breadth often (but not always) at the hyaline (anterior) end; blunt, finger-like lobopodia emerge and point anteriorly from this hyaloplasmic zone. The floating forms usually possess slender, radiating hyaline pseudopodia. It contains the single family Paramoebidae, of which some genera (e.g. *Mayorella*) are freshwater, others (e.g. *Vexillifera*) are both freshwater and estuarine, and one (*Paramoeba*) is marine.

I PARAMOEBIDAE

Paramoeba pemaquidensis Page   FIG. 2.2
[PAGE 1970: 421–7, Figs. 1–10, 16, 19–25; 1973: 183–7, Figs. 1, 2]

The locomotive form is normally thickest at the anterior, hyaloplasmic end, from which blunt, short, finger-like pseudopodia and short, stubby 'subpseudopodia' extrude. The floating form has long, slender pseudopodia radiating to twice the central-body diameter in length. The species is known from sandy beaches of the Wash (Hunstanton) and the North Sea (Brancaster, north Norfolk Coast, and Mersea, Essex).

Vexillifera armata Page   FIG. 2.2
[PAGE 1979: 111–22, Figs. 1–11, 13–20, 22, 24–9]

The locomotor form is similar to that of *Paramoeba*, but the anterior, hyaline pseudopodia are elongate, slender, and dactylopod-like, while bluntly conical subpseudopodia, also produced from the anterior hyaline lobe, are often carried back to the posterior end, to give the whole amoeba a spiny outline. Page (1979) reported that 'the pseudopodia start as blunt projections of the hyaline zone, elongate rapidly and become thinner and more or less linear, with a more or less constant diameter along much of their length.... When it has reached its full length, often greater than the length of the main cell mass, the pseudopodium may bend, rarely may become helical, and usually is carried back along the sides to be resorbed posteriorly; this accounts for the spiny appearance of the amoeba. The cell moves by advance of the broad hyaline lobe from which the subpseudopodia are produced. The lobe may narrow as it is pushed forward, so that the cell as a whole sometimes is urn-shaped, but generally the hyaline area is more flattened than the posterior mass.' Even more sluggish than *Vannella*, *Vexillifera armata* is recorded to travel only its own body length, or less, each minute (at 19°C). The floating form is 'usually irregularly rounded, with hyaline pseudopodia, if any, usually unevenly distributed' (Page 1979).

The locomotor cell surface of *Vexillifera* possesses ultramicroscopic, hexagonal glycostyles, slightly shorter than those of *Vannella* (where the glycostyles are pentagonal); *Vexillifera armata* is the only species of its genus to possess trichocyst-like bodies.

V. armata occurs in beaches of the Bristol Channel and the

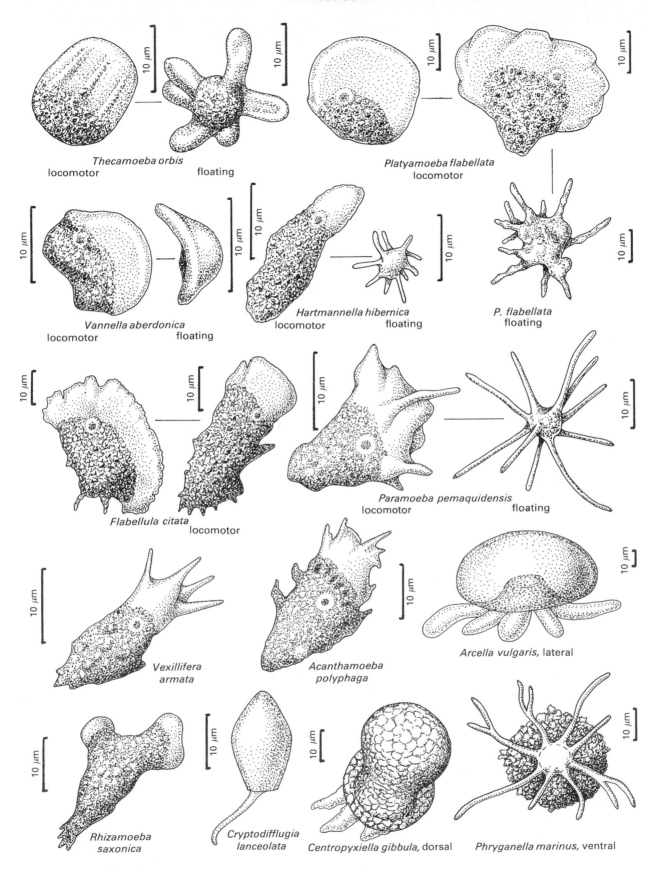

Thecamoeba orbis
locomotor   floating

Platyamoeba flabellata
locomotor

Vannella aberdonica
locomotor   floating

Hartmannella hibernica
locomotor   floating

P. flabellata
floating

Flabellula citata
locomotor

Paramoeba pemaquidensis
locomotor   floating

Vexillifera armata

Acanthamoeba polyphaga

Arcella vulgaris, lateral

Rhizamoeba saxonica

Cryptodifflugia lanceolata

Centropyxiella gibbula, dorsal

Phryganella marinus, ventral

Fig. 2.2

Kingsbury estuary, probably with a salinity of about 28‰ or less; it has been cultured at about 26‰.

Suborder **Acanthopodina**

The short, usually pointed subpseudopodia, spread from hyaline origins over the surface of the locomotor cell, give it a characteristic spiny or thorny appearance, especially over the anterior hyaline cap. Two families are contained here. The Echinamoebidae, with finally pointed, filiform or spiny subpseudopodia (and where the hyaline border does not extend around the entire cell periphery but is often confined, with the subpseudopodia, to the anterior end), is terrestrial only. The Acanthamoebidae contains only one genus (*Acanthamoeba*) and one species of this is known from a variety of terrestrial (pond, ditch, soil, enteric, etc.) and estuarine habitats.

I ACANTHAMOEBIDAE

Acanthamoeba polyphaga (Puschkarew)   FIG. 2.2

This is the only species known to occur in a marine habitat. Page (1976*b*) records it from estuaries where salinity ranged from 26 to 29.5‰. Other records of this extraordinarily euryhaline species are from leaf litter, soil, moss, surfaces of crop plants, and from a human corneal lesion. Other species of *Acanthamoeba* (e.g. *A. castellani*) are known to be pathogenic. Farmer (1980) refers to *A. polyphaga* as 'a smaller version of *A. castellani*'.

Order **Schizopyrenida**

Containing only one family, the Tetramitidae. There is one genus, *Vahlkampfia*, which has species recorded from tidal pools and estuaries (*V. damariscottae* Page) but even this does not yet seem to be firmly recorded from British waters. *Vahlkampfia* spp. known from Britain (e.g. *V. aberdonica* Page) are terrestrial or enteric.

Subclass **Testacealobosia**

This subclass contains Rhizopoda with hyaline, broad, typically unbranched pseudopodia (*lobopodia*, *dactylopodia*, etc.), which also possess an exoskeletal sheath of non-living materials, either continuous, with a permanent aperture through which pseudopodia are extruded (order ARCELLINIDA) or discontinuous, with ephemeral apertures for the transitory extrusion of dactylopodia (order TRICHOSIDA).

Order **Arcellinida**

This order contains many (the remainder are members of the Filosea) of the species loosely and incorrectly grouped together by micropalaeontologists and some biologists as 'Thecamoebians' because they are 'amoebids', in the loose sense, with 'thecae' or 'tests'—the rigid or flexible outer skeleton which may be preserved in sediments after the death and decay of the protozoan cell. They are only remotely related to *Thecamoeba*, Amoebida (see above). The sheaths of all Testacealobosia are quite external to, and separately contain, the cell and its outer pellicular membrane. The foundation of the sheath appears to be a *glycocalyx* of mucoproteins or 'tectin', which may become many layered and fibrous but flexible, or strengthened and thickened by agglutination of extraneous, inorganic particles such as silt.

The Arcellinida are almost entirely freshwater, but some species occur in beach sediments or in estuaries; many of these occurrences may be due to transportation from freshwater environments, but representatives of two suborders have been recorded from Belgian beaches at interstitial salinities of between 30‰ and 32‰ (Chardez 1977), and may well occur in the British intertidal.

KEY TO SUBORDERS WITH PROBABLE MARINE SPECIES

1. Lobopodia broad or slender, but not anastomosing into sheet-like forms   **Arcellina**

   Lobopodia (or dactylopodia) slender, sometimes bifurcating or proximally anastomosed into narrow or broad sheets of hyaloplasm   **Cryptodifflugina**

Suborder **Arcellina**

Both families which probably contain marine species possess tests with a single, ventral aperture.

KEY TO FAMILIES WITH PROBABLE MARINE SPECIES

1. Test hemispherical, dorsally domed, ventrally flattened, with central aperture possessing invaginated margin; little or no agglutinated material in rigid organic test wall   **1. Arcellidae**

   Test oviform, flattened ventrally with laterally placed aperture with everted margin; some or much agglutinated material in test wall   **2. Centropyxidae**

1 ARCELLIDAE

Arcella vulgaris Ehrenberg FIG. 2.2
[LOEBLICH AND TAPPAN 1964: C22–3; JEPPS 1956: 56, 59, 64]
The brown, translucent test occurs quite frequently in estuarine sediments, but its possible marine ecology is unknown. The lobopodia are few and sometimes become spatulate during locomotion. The cell body is centrally situated in the test, above the aperture, and appears to be attached to the inner surface of the test by thin strands of hyaloplasm. Other, freshwater *Arcella* spp. may have inflated, bulbous tests, even with dentate margins.

2 CENTROPYXIDAE

Flask-shaped tests with broadly flaring margins to the ventrally and laterally situated aperture; they are similar to the supra-littoral Psammonobiotidae, but the latter are 'chitinoid', not agglutinating, and extrude cryptodifflugiid-like, filiform pseudopodia.

Centropyxiella gibbula Valkanov FIG. 2.2
[CHARDEZ 1977: 25, Fig. 19, 1, 6]
The body of the test is finely sandy, but the aperture (*pseudostome*) has an everted, reflexed margin with a broad, flaring, very sandy collar, equal in diameter to that of the main test body. It is known from the beach at Ostende.

C. golemanskyi appears to be more widely distributed (common in beaches at Ostende, Mariakerke, and Middelkerke); the test is more depressed and flatter, the test body being yellowish, transparent, and non-agglutinating, while the narrow collar is sandy.

Suborder **Cryptodifflugina**

The slender pseudopodia (like elongate dactylopodia) fuse proximally for part of their length. The tests are agglutinating and small (c. 0.1 mm) or non-agglutinating and very small (15–18 μm).

KEY TO FAMILIES

1. Test very small (c. 15–20 μm), transparent, not agglutinating		**1. Cryptodifflugiidae**
Test small (c. 0.1 mm), agglutinating silt grains		**2. Phryganellidae**

1 CRYPTODIFFLUGIIDAE

Cryptodifflugia lanceolata Golemansky FIG. 2.2
[CHARDEZ 1977: 27, Figs. 14, 1, 25]
The translucent, thin, organic test is compressed and lanceolate (unlike the ovoid, freshwater type species of the genus, *C. oviformis* Penard) and extrudes slender pseudopodia to a length greater than that of the test. It occurs rarely in beaches at Ostende, Mariakerke, Raversijde, Nieuport, and Sint-Idesbald.

2 PHRYGANELLIDAE

Phryganella marinus Chardez FIG. 2.2
[CHARDEZ 1977: 27, Fig. 20, I, 1]
The slender, hyaline pseudopodia extend radially from the central, simple, ventral aperture, and sometimes bifurcate distally. The organic 'theca' agglutinates poorly sorted silt grains. Occurs commonly in beaches at Blankenberge, Ostende, Mariakerke, Raversijde, and Middelkerke.

Order **Trichosida**

The extracellular sheath (*glycocalyx*) is flexible and, in the locomotor form, contains a mesh of secreted spicules. There is only one family.

1 TRICHOSPHAERIIDAE

Trichosphaerium sieboldi Schneider FIG. 2.3
[JEPPS 1956: 88–90; SHEEHAN AND BANNER 1973a: 245, I–IV]
Varies greatly in shape (globular, ovoid, lobulate, discoid, hemi-spherical, completely irregular) and in size (0.01 mm to 0.2 mm or more). A sheath of radially or subradially arranged calcite spicules, embedded in a coat of mucin, is immediately exterior to the body of the cell. The sheath is flexible and conforms to each movement of the cell body; short, finger-shaped pseudopodia (dactylopodia) penetrate the sheath, and, on retraction, leave temporary, circular apertures filled with mucin. Locomotion is by rolling of the cell body or by rippling of the sheath; the dactylopodia appear to be chemo-sensory or mechano-receptive, not locomotory.

The floating form is believed to be a short-lived, 'duck-foot shaped' sporont generation (superficially resembling a small locomotor *Paramoeba*), which develops into a sub-globular sporont with a few, short dactylopodia emerging radially through a flexible, non-spicular glycocalyx. After plasmotomy, this benthic sporont releases biflagellate gametes which are believed to produce the typical, spicular, schizont locomotor form figured here.

Typical, spicular form occurs on *Zostera*, in algal mats, in surface layers of algal-rich fine sediments, on dead shells, sublittoral; cosmopolitan. Becomes very abundant in marine aquaria (where specimens appear to naked eye as shining, white specks at salinities ranging from 27‰ to 40‰, in temperatures from freezing point to 40°C.

Class 2 Acarpomyxea

The naked, non-testate amoebids in this class comprise a wide diversity of uninucleate (like typical Lobosea) and multinucleate (*plasmodial* or *syncytial*) species, which usually (but not always) branch, and have lobose advancing tips in locomotor forms which show no reversals of cytoplasmic streaming. *Rhizamoeba*, although placed here following Levine *et al.* (1980) and Page (1980*a*), has little but its occasional plurality of nuclei to distinguish it from the Hartmannellidae (Tubulina), where it once was placed.

KEY TO ORDERS

1. Subcylindrical, 'limax' or thin polyaxial sheet-like forms   **Leptomyxida**

   Amoeboid forms with branching pseudopodia, used for very slow locomotion or for flotation   **Stereomyxida**

Order Leptomyxida

1 LEPTOMYXIDAE

Rhizamoeba saxonica Page   FIG. 2.2
[PAGE 1974*b*: 167, Figs. 29–35; 1980*a*: 74, Figs. 12, 48–56]
The slender locomotor form is monopodial (*limax*) or sometimes broadly branching (often by simple bifurcation), with a narrow, anterior hyaline zone (not unlike *Hartmannella*), and a lengthy granuloplasmic zone which extrudes adhesive filaments (*pseudovilli*) not only at its posterior end (as does *Flabellula*) but also at any point around the cell periphery.

   This is the only known marine species of *Rhizamoeba* (from the mouth of the Blackwater Estuary, Essex) and the only amoebid (of any Class) yet known (electron microscopically) to possess a continuous coating of lenticular collosomes just inside the plasma membrane (maybe associated with the ability to extrude pseudovilli from anywhere over the cell surface; both pseudovilli and collosomes concentrate at the posterior end).

Order Stereomyxida

Contains the single family Stereomyxidae and two genera (*Stereomyxa* Grell, *Corallomyxa* Grell) which are multilobed, each lobe extruding multibranched, aborescent pseudopodia. So far, known only in shallow, tropical seas (coral reefs).

Class 3 Filosea

The pseudopodia of the Filosea are long (extending beyond the cell body from one to three or more cell diameters) and multibranched, and are made of clear, non-granulate cytoplasm. The cell body is usually enclosed in a simple, flask-shaped test made of organic material (sometimes, but only in freshwater species, with siliceous scales).

Order Gromiida

The test always has a distinct aperture.

1 GROMIIDAE

The tests of the Gromiidae are always dominantly organic, and lack siliceous scales or plates, but commonly incorporate agglutinated inorganic grains. A few marine species (*Lecythium minutum*, *Ditrema marina*) were figured from the Belgian coast by de Saedeleer (1934) but are not yet recorded firmly from British waters.

Gromia oviformis (Dujardin)   FIG. 2.3
[HEDLEY 1962: 121, Figs. 1–7; SHEEHAN AND BANNER 1973*b*: 31, VI, 13–14]
Brown, flask-shaped tests of acid mucopolysaccharide; test shape varies from ovoid to flattened, spheroidal to broadly lobed.

   Attached by pseudopodia extruded from the aperture (i.e. test is naturally orientated apertural-side down) on kelp hold-fasts, *Corallina*, stones and rock-faces, and in muddy or sandy sediments, in rock pools and shallow coastal waters. Cosmopolitan.

Class 4 Granuloreticulosea

Possess very long pseudopodia (commonly more than three times the cell diameter) which branch and anastomose to form reticulate networks (Fig. 2.3): *granules* (which are probably phagocytotic or pinocytotic vesicles) stream along the pseudopodia towards and away from the cell body. Taxa which possess organic or mineralized tests with definite apertures (through which extrathalamous cytoplasm may be extruded and from which pseudopodia may emerge) are grouped in the order Foraminiferida; these occur in all marine and estuarine habitats, and about 200 valid species have been recorded from British waters. Many contain photosymbionts (Knight and Mantoura 1985), which enable these heterotrophs to contribute significantly to benthic primary bioproduction.

   No planktonic species (of the superfamily Globigerinacea, suborder Rotaliina) are endemic to British waters; therefore, only benthic species are described here. The 40 species which have been chosen for description exemplify something of the diversity of morphology which exists in British foraminifera, as well as the range of habitats they occupy.

   The known families and genera of the Foraminiferida were quite recently monographed by Murray (1971, 1979) and by Haynes (1973), so they are treated less exhaustively than the Lobosea, for which no monograph yet exists. The classification adopted below is much simplified from those employed by Loeblich and Tappan (1964, 1984) and Haynes (1981).

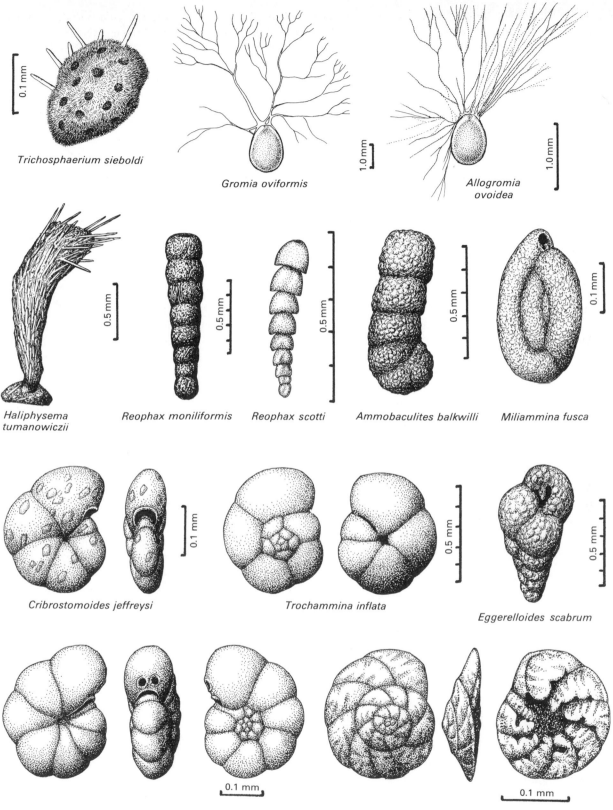

Trichosphaerium sieboldi

Gromia oviformis

Allogromia ovoidea

Haliphysema tumanowiczii

Reophax moniliformis

Reophax scotti

Ammobaculites balkwilli

Miliammina fusca

Cribrostomoides jeffreysi

Trochammina inflata

Eggerelloides scabrum

Jadammina macrescens

Remaneica helgolandica

Fig. 2.3

Order **Foraminiferida**

KEY TO LIVING BENTHIC SUBORDERS

1. Test material organic (mucopolysaccharides and mucoproteins), sometimes with adventitious organic material **Allogromiina**

Test built of inorganic particles (silt or mud or sand-grains, or sponge spicules, mica flakes, etc.) cemented by secreted organic, siliceous, ferric or calcareous material upon the organic endoskeleton **Textulariina**

Test of secreted calcium carbonate (calcite) built as an imperforate, 'porcellaneous' wall upon an organic base **Miliolina**

Test of secreted calcium carbonate (calcite or aragonite), built as a perforate, transparent or translucent ('hyaline') wall upon a very thin, often very inconspicuous, organic base **Rotaliina**

Suborder **Allogromiina**

I ALLOGROMIIDAE

Allogromia ovoidea Rhumbler   FIG. 2.3
The appearance is much as *Gromia oviformis* (Gromiidae), but it is smaller and with characteristic granular, reticulate pseudopodia.

Lives attached by pseudopodia to algae, *Zostera*, and hard or sedimentary substrates in shallow coastal waters.

Pleurophrys blanckenbergi, recorded from the Belgian coast, has a very small (less than 0.1 mm), well-agglutinated, ovate test.

Suborder **Textulariina**

The tests may consist of a single flask-shaped or tubular chamber (i.e. they are *monothalamous*), which may be enlarged or lengthened during growth, or may be many-chambered (*poly-*

thalamous), new chambers being added in a regular manner (particular to each taxon) as the cell grows. Because many taxa build tests lacking calcium carbonate, representatives of this suborder occur in all benthic habitats, even where the pH is so low and the partial pressure of carbon dioxide is so high that the calcareous tests of Rotaliina or Miliolina would be dissolved. Textularine tests cemented by thick layers of organic material are particularly common in marsh environments; where there is little adventitious matter, the tests are often flexible, and are commonly distorted. Tests with ferric or calcareous cements are rigid and relatively undistortable (so that the regular growth mode of polythalamous tests is more readily recognizable) and the latter, particularly, often characterize sublittoral and open marine shelf environments. As with the other suborders of the Foraminiferida, the examples described here are merely a selection from hundreds of extant species: more complete lists may be found in Haynes (1973, 1981) and Murray (1973, 1979).

KEY TO REPRESENTATIVE FAMILIES

1. Test monothalamous, tubular or branching, not enrolled **1. Astrorhizidae**

   Test polythalamous **2**

2. Chambers arranged in a straight or curved single series **2. Hormosinidae**

   Chambers coiled, in part at least **3**

3. Chambers coiled in high spire, test elongate **3. Textulariidae**

   Chambers coiled in a low spire, test more or less biconvex **4**

4. Test coiled in many planes (similar to Miliolidae, q.v.) **4. Rzehakinidae**

   Test coiled in a single plane (planospiral) or in a simple, low spire (trochospiral) **5. Lituolidae**

1 ASTRORHIZIDAE

Tubular or branching tests are built of detrital material cemented into rigid and/or flexible sheaths over an organic extracellular wall; pseudopodia are extruded from a simple aperture at the growing end of the test.

Haliphysema tumanowiczii Bowerbank — FIG. 2.3
[HEDLEY 1958: 569, I–III; HAYNES 1981: 84, 9:6]

Test built of sponge spicules and quartz grains, cemented by acid mucopolysaccharide to an organic ('mucoprotein') extracellular wall; attached to substratum by a proximal 'basal disc' of shell material, then growing upwards, freely from attachment area. The test thickens with growth, so that it is thin and flexible proximally, thick and rigid distally; pseudopodia extrude from simple aperture at distal end and, apparently, collect diatoms for ingestion.

Reproduction by budding off multinucleate or uninucleate individuals from distal end; these subspherical daughter cells have their own tests and a short free existence before attachment and development as sedentary individuals.

Occurs below LWST, especially in kelp zone, attached to *Laminaria, Phyllophora, Delesseria* and other algae, hydroids, stones, and dead shells.

2 HORMOSINIDAE

Tests of agglutinated quartz or other debris, built as a series of enlarging *chambers* from the first-formed chamber (*proloculus*) to the final stage of growth (when reproduction occurs); each chamber separated from the succeeding by a *septum*, penetrated by a *septal aperture*, these structures once having been the *terminal face* and *final aperture* of the growth stage that chamber represents; chambers added in a single series (*uniserial*) to produce a rectilinear, straight or curved, free-living, unattached test.

---

1. Test large, built of quartz grains and scattered sponge spicules; intercameral sutures weakly depressed — ***Reophax moniliformis***

   Test small and delicate, organic wall thinly coated with mud and mica flakes, sutures strongly depressed — ***Reophax scotti***

Reophax moniliformis Siddal — FIG. 2.3
[MURRAY 1971: 19, II; HAYNES 1973: 24, III, 17; KNIGHT 1986: 83–90, I, II]

Brown, ferruginous, brittle tests often with obscure sutures, built of silt and sponge debris; aperture large and round.

LWST to deep water of inner shelf, but common in intertidal marshes.

Reophax scotti Chaster — FIG. 2.3
[MURRAY 1971: 17, I]

Delicate test, mostly of organic material, thin; flexible, easily crushed and distorted.

In muddy inshore sediments.

3 TEXTULARIIDAE

Tests coiled in a high, elongate spiral, from two to many chambers in each whorl. Aperture in terminal face of last chamber but situated at suture between that chamber and the penultimate one. In life, usually mobile over the substratum by means of pseudopodia extruded through aperture (which is then facedownwards on substratum).

Eggerelloides scabrum (Williamson) — FIG. 2.3
[FEYLING-HANSSEN *et al.* 1971: 192, XV, 5; HAYNES 1973: 44, II, 7–8]

Three chambers in each whorl (except in first whorl, which has more); wall of angular quartz silt cemented by organic material (usually giving a brownish colour to test); aperture modified into loop-shape due to development of a *tooth* projecting inwards from anterior side of aperture.

Intertidal to deeper inner shelf waters, usually in muddy sediments; can tolerate waters of low oxygen content and salinities as low as 20‰.

4 RZEHAKINIDAE

Proloculus followed by, and enclosed by, tubular chambers, each about one half-whorl in length, added in varying planes (c.f. Miliolidae, q.v.).

Miliammina fusca (Brady) — FIG. 2.3
[MURRAY 1971: 21, III; HAYNES 1973: 54, II, 9–10]

Brown-grey test built of silt, quartz and mud, cemented rigidly on to a thick organic wall; terminal aperture a rounded hole at end of last chamber, partly constricted by a short, stubby tooth projecting from its basal sutural side.

Strongly euryhaline: common in tidal marshes, hyposaline lagoons and brackish estuaries, in silty and sandy sediment. Cosmopolitan.

5 LITUOLIDAE

Test is coiled in a low, compressed spiral (at least in the early growth stages—the later states may uncoil). Aperture is in the basal suture of the last chamber, or in the area of the terminal face, or both; sometimes with additional apertures in the sutures of one side or other of the test.

KEY TO REPRESENTATIVE GENERA

---

1. Test initially coiled, later uncoiling and uniserial — ***Ammobaculites***

   Test coiled throughout — **2**

---

2. Test coiled in a single plane (*planospiral*) bilaterally symmetrical   ***Cribrostomoides***

Test coiled in a low spire (*trochospiral*), bilaterally asymmetrical: one side displaying all chambers of all whorls, i.e. *evolute*; the other side wholly or partly with the early whorls concealed by the later whorls, i.e. more or less *involute*   **3**

3. Chambers empty, simple, uncomplicated   **4**

Chambers with internal 'buttresses' caused by fluting and invagination of the septa and chamber margins   ***Remaneica***

4. Aperture a sutural slit at base of last chamber, on the involute side   ***Trochammina***

Aperture a basal, sutural slit with additional apertural holes in the area of terminal face   ***Jadammina***

Ammobaculites balkwilli Haynes   FIG. 2.3
[HAYNES 1973: 25, II, 2, 3]
Fragile wall coarsely agglutinated, of angular quartz and other mineral grains in matrix of fine silt; sutures obscure in early, coiled part, but more clearly depressed in uncoiled, rectilinear part; aperture large and round, in terminal face.

Intertidal marshes; rare in open sea.

Cribrostomoides jeffreysi (Williamson)   FIG. 2.3
[MURRAY 1971: 23, IV; HAYNES 1973: 29, II, 5–6]
Compressed, bilaterally symmetrical test, involute equally on both sides; wall brownish, of very fine detrital material set in organic matrix, often with larger quartz grains scattered in wall surface; aperture a slit, symmetrical to periphery of early part of last whorl, set very near base of terminal face but with a thin projecting *lip* surrounding it, both above and below (the latter lip often concealed by overhang of the terminal face).

Stenohaline, LWST to deeper waters of inner shelf.

Jadammina macrescens (Brady)   FIG. 2.3
[MURRAY 1971: 41, XIII, 1–5; HAYNES 1973: 41, II, 14–16]
Compressed, bilaterally asymmetrical test, involute on one side, partly evolute on the other; wall brown, of very fine detrital material in organic matrix, flexible; after death, often deformed, crushed, flattened or otherwise distorted; aperture a basal, sutural slit in last chamber, extending from involute side of periphery, plus one or more additional openings in the area of the terminal face.

Hyposaline, intertidal marshes, muddy or sandy sediments. Cosmopolitan. Strongly euryhaline and eurythermal.

Remaneica helgolandica Rhumbler   FIG. 2.3
[HÖGLUND 1947: 212; HAYNES 1973: 43, V, 19; LEVY *et al.* 1975: 171–81; ROSSET-MOULINIER 1985: 205–12, 1]
Compressed, very thin test, attached by its flattened or concave involute side, evolute side being weakly domed; wall brownish, of very fine silt and mud particles in relatively thick, organic matrix; aperture a slit along inner suture of final chamber on involute, attached side, with additional sutural slits in intercameral sutures of that side (apertures are often very obscure); margins of chambers invaginated, forming series of peripheral, internal buttresses (which can be seen externally as plications of the sutures and the periphery).

Attached to hydroids and dead shells below LWST.

Trochammina inflata (Montagu)   FIG. 2.3
[HAYNES 1973: 37, IV, 15–17; 1981: 111, Figs. 6:10, 8:10, pl. 11 B, 5]
Wall brownish, rigid, of fine detrital material embedded in organic (iron-rich?) matrix; evolute side flat (or very slightly convex or concave), involute side strongly vaulted and convex with a deep central hollow (*umbilicus*) where inner ends of chambers meet; aperture a narrow slit in basal suture of involute side of last chamber, from near umbilicus almost to periphery. *Trochammina* has recently been revised, and several new, related genera have been described (Brönnimann *et al.* 1983), some (such as *Paratrochammina*, *Lepidoparatrochammina*) from British waters (Brönnimann and Whittaker 1986, 1987).

Euryhaline and eurythermal; occurs frequently in muddy or silty sediments of intertidal marshes, and in similar sediments of the littoral and just below MLWST (the last occurrences may be due to offshore transport from the littoral zone or from estuaries).

Suborder **Miliolina**

Relatively stenohaline and stenothermal, usually characterized by milky-white, porcellaneous, imperforate tests of calcium carbonate (as micro-crystalline calcite). Rarely, the tests of some structurally simple forms may possess superficial coatings of adventitious, inorganic material (mud, silt, etc.) but they are usually white and polished in appearance. In life, some thin-walled species may be pale pink in colour due to pigmentation of the cytoplasm, and others may be pale honey-coloured or very pale golden-brown (due to the colour of the inner, 'chitinoid' organic lining of the test showing through the translucent calcareous outer wall). The cytoplasm of the cell is wholly internal, except for the granuloreticulopodia which extrude, through the aperture, for attachment, feeding, and locomotion; consequently, in life, specimens are attached apertural-end downwards, usually to hard substrates. Few species are known commonly to inhabit areas of salinity less than 28‰, and the suborder as a whole characterizes the open sea; however, dead tests are frequently transported shorewards by wave-drift and occur as part of the biogenic component of most shore sands and silts. The milifrom test is particularly resistant to solution and mechanical abrasion, and even resists digestion by bottom-detritus feeders (tests occur in decapod faecal pellets and have been found in the gut of *Gobius*, for example).

Miliolines develop large and structurally very complex skeletons (1 cm or more in diameter) in shallow tropical seas, but only the structurally simpler forms occur in British waters; even among these, the application of generic names to the many described species is much disputed, so only the commonest are described here.

KEY TO BRITISH FAMILIES

1. Proloculus followed by a single, long, tubular or spreading, undivided chamber   **1. Fischerinidae**

   Proloculus followed by a series of tubular or reniform chambers, separated by septa   **2**

2. Chambers added in a planospiral coil (usually evolute) or randomly, in any plane   **2. Nubeculariidae**

   Chambers added in regularly varying planes, relative to each other, about the axis of greatest length of the whole test; usually two chambers per whorl, but they are added regularly and successively in planes (at 120° or 144°, for example) from one another, at least in the early growth-stages; usually involute   **3. Miliolidae**

1 FISCHERINIDAE

Cornuspira selseyensis Heron–Allen and Earland   FIG. 2.4
[HAYNES 1973: 48, IX, 15; 1981: IIB, 11]
White, planospiral test; post-prolocular coil with series of ribs or corrugations, marking successive intervals of addition to the tubular chamber during growth; aperture a simple, terminal hole. Test more or less evolute, displaying proloculus and early whorls. Prolocular size varies: specimens with large proloculus have fewer whorls than specimens of comparable total size and a small proloculus; the former (*megalospheric*) probably represents the *gamont* (haploid) and the latter (*microspheric*) the *schizont* (diploid) generation.

Habitat is unusual for this suborder: it is common in tide pools and some marshes, and it is an exceptionally euryhaline and eurythermal species. Also known below L W S T as an inner shelf species.

Tests of similar shape but which are glassy and perforate belong to the quite different suborder Rotaliina (Spirillinidae, q.v.).

2 NUBECULARIIDAE

Spirophthalmidium acutimargo emaciatum Haynes FIG. 2.4
[HAYNES 1973: 50–2, V, 11; IX, 11; 1981: IIB, 12; IX, 1]

Thin, delicate, compressed test with acute, carinate periphery; composed of evolute planospire of chambers, two to each whorl; terminal end of last chamber produced as slender tube-like neck, ending in circular, rimmed aperture. Test wall thin, translucent; white after death but pink cytoplasm may be seen through it in life.

Occurs below L W S T on hard substrates (dead bivalve shells, hydroid stems, *Flustra foliacea* bases, etc.).

3 MILIOLIDAE

At least thirty species of Miliolidae occur in British coastal and shelf waters, but the great majority must be considered to be beyond the scope of this work as their habitats are unknown in any detail and their taxonomy is much disputed. The whole family is ripe for synoptic study and revision (see Mathieu *et al.* 1971). The genera included in the following key are those which may be diagnosed and named unequivocally, and in which the commoner species may be included without serious morphological disagreement with the type species. If specimens do not conform fully to the descriptions given here, Haynes (1973) and Murray (1973, 1979) may be consulted for other available names in the species group, and Loeblich and Tappan (1964) and Lewis (1970) for applicable generic names.

KEY TO COMMON GENERA

1. Adult test flattened, compressed, early stages involute, last pair of chambers in one plane   **Massilina**

   Adult test globose   **2**

2. Two chambers only, visible externally	**Pyrgo**
More than two chambers visible externally	**3**

3. Three chambers visible externally	**Triloculina**
More than three chambers visible externally	**4**

4. Adult test with five chambers visible externally, test regularly formed: aperture with narrow tooth	**Quinqueloculina**
Test variable in shape between individuals; aperture with a broad plate	**Miliolinella**

Massilina secans (d'Orbigny)   FIG. 2.4
[HAYNES 1973: 53, V, 3–4; 1981: Fig. 8:2, 5–9, 8:3, 6–13]
Thick-walled, white, compressed test; early chambers coiled like *Quinqueloculina*, followed by a mature stage of planospiral, compressed chambers with acutely-angled peripheral margins and smooth surfaces (except for weak striations parallel to growth direction). Aperture elongate, parallel-sided and extends through full height of terminal face of last chamber; furnished with narrow, thickened rim and prominent, high, narrow tooth-plate (which bifurcates distally to form a 'Y' in apertural view).

A stenohaline and stenothermal inner shelf species, occurring on algae and *Zostera* below LWST in shallow waters.

Pyrgo williamsoni (Silvestri)   FIG. 2.4
[FEYLING-HANSSEN *et al.* 1971: 196, 11, 8–9; MURRAY 1973: 71, XXVII, 5–7]
Globose, ovoid, thick-walled, white test, almost completely involute (only last two chambers visible), with rounded margins and weakly depressed but distinct sutures, otherwise smooth and shiny. Aperture rounded, with toothplate which may be spatulate or bifurcate, but always slender proximally, at its junction with innermost margin of aperture.

Lives on firm substrates (hydroids, *Flustra*, shell, etc.) below LWST in inner shelf waters.

Triloculina trihedra Loeblich and Tappan   FIG. 2.4
[FEYLING-HASSEN *et al.* 1971: 196, 11, 7; HAYNES 1973: 80, IX, 3–4]
White, smooth-surfaced test with three chambers visible externally, approximately triangular in cross-section, with bluntly (rounded) acute angles and sides slightly convex or concave. Sutures clearly depressed. Aperture a high arch, furnished with a tooth.

Habitat in off-shore and inner shelf coastal waters.

Quinqueloculina seminulum (Linnaeus)   FIG. 2.4
[MURRAY 1973: 65, XXIV, 1–6; HAYNES 1973: VII, 14–19; 1981: Fig. 5.1]
White, thick-walled, smooth-surfaced test with five chambers visible externally (four seen in one side view, three if specimen turned over), sub-triangular in section with flattened sides and subangular to broadly rounded edges. Sutures only weakly depressed and may be indistinct, so that innermost chamber of outer whorl may be difficult to see: however, even if only three chambers may be recognized in each case when the test is viewed from two sides, it may be determined as *Quinqueloculina* (in *Triloculina*, three chambers are visible on one side, but only two on the other). The aperture is a high arch with a thin toothplate, which is usually not bifurcate except at its extreme distal tip.

This species has been very extensively recorded, as it is the type species of the genus, but not all records are correct because of confusion with other, smooth-walled species of *Quinqueloculina*. To avoid any error here, the illustration is copied from that of the neotype (Loeblich and Tappan 1964).

Specimens referable with confidence to this stenohaline species occur on firm substrates below LWST on the inner shelf and in coastal waters around southern Britain. May burrow in silt and mud to a depth of 10–15 cm.

Quinqueloculina dimidiata Terquem   FIG. 2.4
[MURRAY 1973: 61, XXII, 5–8]
This binomen was originally used for tests found on Dunkirk beach: the type specimens are lost, but Murray (1973) applies the name in the sense used here to a small species with very oblique sutures, a thin, translucent test and a rounded periphery in cross-section, which is atypical in that its high, rounded aperture entirely lacks a toothplate.

Its habitat is also atypical for the genus in that it occurs in the intertidal zone as well as below LWST (mud flats, salinity 30–5‰, *teste* Murray 1973).

Quinqueloculina bicornis (Walker and Jacob)   FIG. 2.4
[MURRAY 1973: 57, XX, 1–5; HAYNES 1973: 67, VII, 18; 1981: Fig. 8:12, 3–4]
Globose test with rounded chambers, surface characterized by longitudinal *costae* (ribs). Aperture is a high, parallel-sided arch with a prominent, non-bifurcating toothplate. *Q. bicornis angu-*

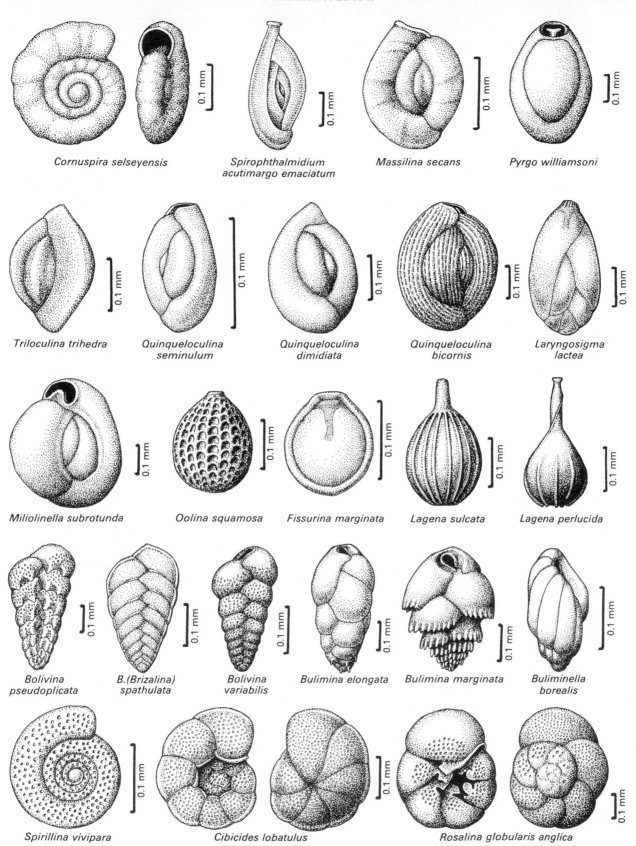

Cornuspira selseyensis

Spirophthalmidium
acutimargo emaciatum

Massilina secans

Pyrgo williamsoni

Triloculina trihedra

Quinqueloculina
seminulum

Quinqueloculina
dimidiata

Quinqueloculina
bicornis

Laryngosigma
lactea

Miliolinella subrotunda

Oolina squamosa

Fissurina marginata

Lagena sulcata

Lagena perlucida

Bolivina
pseudoplicata

B.(Brizalina)
spathulata

Bolivina
variabilis

Bulimina elongata

Bulimina marginata

Buliminella
borealis

Spirillina vivipara

Cibicides lobatulus

Rosalina globularis anglica

Fig. 2.4

lata (Williamson) differs in being more slender and in possessing fewer, stronger costae.

Occurs on the inner shelf in the sea of the Hebrides, Irish Sea, Celtic Sea, and English Channel.

Miliolinella subrotunda (Montagu)   FIG. 2.4
[MURRAY 1973: 73, XXVIII, 5–6; HAYNES 1973: 56, V, 5–6, 12–13; 1981: Fig. 8:12, 17–18]

Globose, ovoid test, with white and polished surface (in juvenile specimens pale pink protoplasm may be seen through translucent walls). Three, four, or five reniform chambers may be visible externally, as there is considerable morphological variation between individuals (due largely to variable growth rates, variations in rate of chamber enlargement, and differences in degree to which successive chambers cover earlier ones), but coiling mode essentially quinqueloculine. Aperture a high arch, partly closed by a broad, lunate, basal, flap-like plate.

Lives both below LWST on the innermost shelf and intertidally in rock-pools, on dead shell, hydroids, *Flustra foliacea*, and other firm surfaces.

Suborder Rotaliina

Although stenothermal, stenohaline species greatly outnumber eurythermal, euryhaline ones, representatives of this suborder occur in almost all brackish and fully marine environments. As with all benthic foraminifera, dead tests are subjected to transport by waves and tidal currents, and an association of tests does not necessarily represent the living population. For example, species of *Elphidium*, *Haynesina*, and *Ammonia*, which are often represented by very large numbers of living individuals in salt-marsh pools, in estuaries and on tidal flats, are often accompanied by dead tests of open-marine species which have been drifted inshore by wave and current transport. Most species of the Rotaliina possess tests which, in life, have a glassy (hyaline) appearance: after death, the test surface becomes progressively etched by solution and erosion, and the test wall becomes opaque and white. This, as well as species diversity, the presence or absence of protoplasm in the tests, and the recognition of non-adherent tests in (or not in) life position, provides an indication of the autochthoneity or allochthoneity of the material.

Some rotalines (superfamily Globigerinacea) are holoplanktonic, yet their dead tests are still found, occasionally, in littoral and sublittoral fine sediments. However, as they occur only sparsely in the plankton of shelf seas, they are omitted from this work [reference may be made to Bé (1967) for those which may be found].

The gross shape and coiling mode of the test of benthic rotalines broadly reflect the microhabitat and degree of mobility of the living organism. As in the Textulariina and Miliolina, genera with apertures terminal to the unithalamous or high-spired polythalamous tests (e.g. *Fissurina*, *Bolivina*, *Bulimina*, *Buliminella*) attach themselves by pseudopodia to a firm substratum, apertural end down, and have limited mobility in an area from which nutrients are gathered by pinocytosis and phagocytosis within the adherent pseudopodial webs. The test is free-standing, growing by the addition of new chambers at the apertural end, adjacent to the substratum (note that the species are figured here according to long-established but misleading convention, inverted from their life attitudes). Monothalamous planospiral tests (*Spirillina*) have a similar posture and life habit. Polythalamous tests reflect greatest mobility in planospiral coiling modes (e.g. *Haynesina*, *Elphidium*); these genera crawl actively over firm substrata and can burrow in fine silts and muds, often to several centimetres depth; their pseudopodia are vigorously locomotory, as well as being chemosensory and trophic. Trochospiral forms are more usually on firm substrates, apertural side downwards, and those with rounded peripheries (e.g. *Ammonia*) are the more mobile; those with markedly flattened apertural sides (the more evolute side, misleadingly called 'dorsal', in *Cibicides*, and the more involute, 'ventral' side in *Rosalina*) becoming virtually immobile in the mature stage of life, particularly in the spreading genus *Planorbulina*. The adherent sides of *Cibicides*, *Rosalina*, and *Planorbulina* may all grow closely to fit the shape of the underlying substratum; if this is curved or ridged (e.g. a bivalve shell), then the surface of the foraminiferal test is deformed accordingly.

The classification of the Rotaliina is, on the whole, satisfactory at generic level, but, at suprageneric level it is much disputed: the comprehensive classifications in current specialist use (e.g. Loeblich and Tappan 1964) are extremely difficult (in some cases, impossible in practice) to apply. Far too much emphasis has been placed upon supposed differences in the ultra-microscopic structure of the walls and septa: the significance of these differences has never been established, and they are usually impossible to see unless the specimens are elaborately prepared and examined under very high magnification, or polarized light, or electron microscopy. Consequently, the classification used here is not that sometimes favoured by the specialist, but is based upon the external morphocharacters which may be seen, without especial preparation, at magnifications of × 100 or less in common British species; it may still prove to be as valid as any other, in many cases at least.

The following key aids determination of the families to which the commoner British species and genera may be assigned. Specialists would group these families differently, into superfamilies based on criteria not always mentioned here: this key is designed for application by the student with a good hand-lens or a low-powered microscope only. For further information and more complete lists, Haynes (1973, 1981) and Murray (1973, 1979) are among the authors who may be consulted. The rarer and deeper-water genera have been omitted: if specimens do not exactly agree with the key and illustrations, they should not be identified from the information given here alone. Many of the more obvious skeletal shapes have evolved independently in different lineages: for example, terminal apertures have been acquired not only by the Glandulinidae, Polymorphinidae, and Nodosariidae, but by the very distantly related Uvigerinidae—a family closely related, in fact, to the Buliminidae—and by genera of the Bolivinitidae not listed here. Therefore, mention of any particular morphocharacter in relation to a particular family, genus, or species does not imply that no other Rotaline

KEY TO REPRESENTATIVE FAMILIES

1. Test with terminal aperture   **2**

   Test with sutural primary aperture   **4**

2. Terminal aperture with internal tube (which may often be seen through the translucent or transparent wall)   **1. Glandulinidae**

   Aperture without an internal tube   **3**

3. Aperture radiate (i.e. a small hole surrounded by a cluster of very small radiating slits), coiling milioline or biserial   **Polymorphinidae** (p. 44)

   Coiling not milioline or biserial. Test unilocular, or in a single series, or (initially at least) in a flat spire (planospire)   **2. Nodosariidae**

4. Aperture an elongate, curved, often comma-shaped slit; typically situated at basal suture of last chamber, but extended up into apertural face and broadening there (rarely, the basal apertural construction leads to fusion of apertural lips basally, isolating apertural opening in area of face); almost all genera high-spired   **5**

   Primary aperture basal, not elongate into apertural face; almost all genera are low-spired   **7**

5. Test biserial (two chambers per whorl, set as alternating pairs), at least in early growth stage   **3. Bolivinitidae**

   Test with more than two chambers per whorl   **6**

6. Test with three chambers per whorl (triserial)   **4. Bullminidae**

   Test with three or more chambers per whorl   **5. Turrilinidae**

7. Test unilocular, non-septate   **6. Spirillinidae**

   Test multilocular, septate   **8**

8. Test planospiral   **10. Elphidiidae**

   Test trochospiral (more evolute one side than on the other)   **9**

9. Test a complex coil with annular 'chamberlets'   **9. Planorbulinidae**

   Test a simple, single coil   **10**

10. Primary aperture extends from peripheral part of basal suture into the spiral suture of the more evolute side   **7. Cibicididae**

    Primary aperture in the basal suture of the last chamber, on the more involute side of the test   **8. Discorbidae**

foraminifera possess it; however, the combinations of morphocharacters described here can be taken to be effectively definitive for the family and generic names to which they are applied.

1 GLANDULINIDAE

Multiloculate genera of the Glandulinidae are rare in British waters: the only genera frequently encountered (and then usually as dead tests) are the unilocular ovoid *Oolina* and compressed *Fissurina*. The POLYMORPHINIDAE may be very similar, superficially, to the multiloculate Glandulinidae but are very rare in British waters; however, a family diagnosis is included in the above key for comparison.

Oolina squamosa (Montagu)   FIG. 2.4
[HAYNES 1973: 110, XIV, 14; XV, 4, 5; 1981: 11B, 29]
Meridional costae separated by discontinuous, curved secondary costae, producing a characteristic fish-scale pattern. Aperture a simple, round hole at one pole of ovoid test.

Stenohaline, found over the whole continental shelf, although possibly most commonly on the inner shelf, in shallower, coastal waters. In the similar species, *O. hexagona* (Williamson) the meridional costae are zig-zag and joined by straight secondary costae, to produce a hexagonal pattern over the ovoid test.

Fissurina marginata (Walker and Boys)   FIG. 2.4
[MURRAY 1973: 97, XXXIX, 4–6; HAYNES 1973: 96–7]
The acute margin of the compressed, subcircular, translucent test is furnished with a double carina. Aperture a narrow slit within this double carina at the oval end.

This species is stenohaline and inhabits the inner shelf. It is one of the very few foraminifera known to live, sometimes at least, as an ectoparasite; Le Calvez (1947) has described how it feeds on the extrathalamous cytoplasm of certain Discorbidae. At reproduction (which can be every ten days) *F. marginata* leaves its host, constructs a hemispherical 'chitinoid' cyst, and dissolves its internal tube; the cytoplasm then leaves the test to enter the main volume of the cyst. The single nucleus divides; each daughter cell secretes a new test, free from the parent, and returns to the host discorbid to reinfest it.

Laryngosigma lactea (Walker and Jacob)   FIG. 2.4
[HAYNES 1973: 100, Figs. 6–12; 1981: Fig. 9:7, 28–9]
Initial chambers formed in a quinqueloculine spire, about 144° apart, but each successive chamber further from base of test even though all strongly embrace earlier chambers; later chambers added biserially, about 150° apart, so that the biserial spire becomes twisted, appearing sigmoidal in cross-section. Aperture radiate, with an internal (*entosolenian*) tube. Wall smooth, thin, very finely perforate, translucent or transparent.

According to Haynes (1973), many specimens lose their septa by resorption (during reproduction?) and even the side of the test which is attached to the substratum may be resorbed, leaving a spreading 'peripheral flange'.

Recorded attached to sand grains in Carmarthen Bay; originally described (and subsequently recorded) from the English Channel coasts and the Scilly Isles.

2 NODOSARIIDAE

Large, multiloculate Nodosariidae are commonest on the outer continental shelf and on the continental slope and rise; small multiloculate genera (e.g. *Dentalina*) and uniloculate forms (e.g. *Lagena*) are not common even on the inner shelf, except as dead tests. Nothing is known of their biology. The suggestion that species of *Lagena* could represent the first chambers of multiloculate Nodosariidae is frequently made, but often the *Lagena* species possess patterns of costae and spines which are not known in species of other Nodosariidae. The possibility cannot be disproved that this surface sculpture differs between sexual (diploid) and asexual (haploid) generations, and that one of these generations alone could be *Lagena*. Nominal species of *Lagena* are very numerous and have been diagnosed merely on test shape and differences in surface sculpture: the unilocular genera have been extensively revised by Jones (1984), who illustrates many British taxa.

Lagena perlucida (Montagu)   FIG. 2.4
[HAYNES 1973: 86, XII, 5; MURRAY 1973: 85, XXXIII, 1–3; JONES 1984: 132, VII, 10]
Aperture a round hole with crenulate border (seen to be radiate if viewed from above at high magnification) at the end of a long neck bearing spiral or oblique costae; aboral part of test with short, thick costae arranged meridionally.

Known from the Celtic Sea and the English Channel; a similar distribution is recorded for *L. semistriata* (Williamson), which has twice as many, but weaker, aboral costae; and *L. tenuis* (Bornemann), which has been found off Plymouth, is similar to *L. perlucida* but more slender and elongate.

Lagena sulcata (Walker and Jacob)   FIG. 2.4
[MURRAY 1971: 87, XXXIV, 5–8; HAYNES 1973: 90, XXII, 9; 1981: Fig. 9: 6, 13; JONES 1984: 131, VI, 20–4]
Aperture a round hole at the end of a long neck, but, quite atypically for the Nodosariidae, is apparently not radiate. Costae meridional and strong, fusing near base of neck, forming the margins of sculptured channels which may function to direct streaming of extrathalamous cytoplasm to and from the aperture.

L. substriata Williamson is more slender, less ovoid, and has more numerous, weaker costae; it has a crenulate aperture at the end of a spirally costate neck (like *L. perlucida*). *L. gracilis* Williamson also has fine meridional costae over the whole test, but there are fewer of them than in *L. substriata*, and they are not twisted on the neck. All these species appear to be stenohaline, inhabitants of the open shelf, but nothing precise is known of their habitats.

3 BOLIVINITIDAE

The common British species of this family belong to one or two genera only. *Bolivina* possesses crenulate sutures, the proximal portion of each chamber wall being lobulate; the generic name *Brizalina* has been used for those species which do not possess such crenulations and lobulations, but which, in morphologically extreme forms, have smooth sutures heavily thickened by glassy shell material. This taxonomic separation is one of convenience only, as the biological significance of this difference in shell structure is quite unknown. Because of this, and because some species exist where the distinction is difficult to make, *Brizalina* is used here as a subgenus of *Bolivina*. Each species of the Bolivinitidae possesses a funnel-shaped toothplate inside its aperture, and the shape of the toothplate seems to be remarkably constant in each species; as the toothplate must be in intimate contact with the cytoplasm, it may prove to be more significant for taxonomy than the shape of the sutures, but much more study is required.

In all known cases, *Bolivina sensu lato* is marine; individuals live aperture downwards on firm substrata, the pseudopodial net extruded from the aperture acting as an anchoring and locomotor mechanism as well as a food-gathering and excretory organ. All living species observed by the writer are pigmented in life— usually pale pink.

Bolivina pseudoplicata Heron-Allen and Earland FIG. 2.4
[FEYLING-HANSSEN *et al.* 1971: 243, XVII, 11; MURRAY 1973: 107, XLIII, 1–7]

Coarsely perforate, otherwise glassy test, characterized by deeply and broadly depressed sutures irregularly bounded by narrow, raised ridges; longitudinal suture (which runs between each chamber-pair of the biserial test) particularly marked by offset, lateral ridges, discontinuously developed between successive chambers, with smaller, weaker ridges developed parallel to main ones but closer to test periphery (further from longitudinal suture); gross appearance is of 'scooped out' sutures bordered (on sides nearest apertural end of test) by narrow, scalloped crenulations. In cross-section, the test is about twice as broad as thick, with convex sides and bluntly acute peripheral margins.

The Plymouth inshore area is the type locality for this species, which has also been recorded from the Bristol Channel, Irish Sea (Carmarthen Bay) and the North Sea, from depths ranging from 10 m to nearly 100 m.

Bolivina (Brizalina) spathulata Williamson FIG. 2.4
[MURRAY 1973: 111, XLV, 1–4]

Compressed, leaf-shaped hyaline test, more than three times as broad as thick, with gently convex sides and sharply acute peripheral margins. Surface smooth, except for weakly depressed intercameral sutures (which may be thickened and glassy in their most anterior parts).

B. (*B.*) *subaenariensis* (Cushman) is similar but has longitudinal costae on initial half of test; *B. striatula* Cushman has similar costae, but is thick, with a cross-section closer to that of *B. pseudoplicata*. Some specimens of *B.* (*B.*) *spathulata* have intercameral sutures narrowly depressed at the peripheral margin of the test, which then develops a serrated outline like that of *B.* (*B.*) *superba* Emiliani, a rare species which has been recorded by Haynes (1973).

Occurs on the inner shelf below about 10 m depth, from the English Channel north to Shetland.

Bolivina variabilis (Williamson) FIG. 2.4
[MURRAY 1973: 113, XLVI, 1–3; HAYNES 1973: 141, X, 8; 1981: 11B, 13]

Test slender, very coarsely perforate; sutures broadly and deeply depressed; periphery lobulate, rounded, not acute.

B. pseudopunctata Höglund is similar but its chambers are less high and much less coarsely perforate; *B. britannica* Macfadyen is even more finely perforate and also has a more compressed test and in cross-section an acutely angled periphery.

This species perhaps occurs all round the British Isles, and southerly records from the inner shelf are confirmed by Haynes (1973) and Murray (1973).

4 BULIMINIDAE

Like the Bolivinitidae, the Buliminidae are characterized by high-spired tests with elongate, loop- or comma-shaped apertures furnished with toothplates which are often elaborate in structure. The test walls are so finely perforate that the perforations can rarely be seen under magnifications of less than × 500; the walls are thin, transparent or translucent, and may be very smooth or with longitudinal rib-like costae of varying strengths.

All common species are strongly stenothermal and stenohaline and are very difficult indeed to culture. All live below LWST in shelf waters, where they may be very abundant (Murray, 1973, records that *Bulimina elongata* comprises up to 69% of the living foraminifera in some samples from the Bristol Channel).

Bulimina elongata d'Orbigny FIG. 2.4
[HAYNES 1973: 116, X, 9–11; MURRAY 1973: 117, XLVIII, 1–8]

Test elongate, up to six whorls coiled in a high spire, translucent and smooth, except for scattered short spines on early chambers. It appears to be identical to the species originally recorded from Middle Miocene strata of the Vienna Basin, and is reputed to be extremely widespread in the north-west European shelf seas (as well as in the Mediterranean and the Bay of Biscay).

Several 'varieties' have been named: they differ in the rate of chamber enlargement (producing short, ovoid, or long slender tests) and could be true subspecies or phenotypic variants resulting from different growth rates. Very short, stout forms, with rapidly tapering initial ends, are sometimes referred to a distinct species, *B. gibba* Fornasini.

Bulimina marginata d'Orbigny FIG. 2.4
[FEYLING-HANSSEN *et al.* 1971: 235, VI, 17–18; MURRAY 1973: 119, XLIX, 1–7]

This is the type species of *Bulimina*, originally described from the Adriatic, and specimens identical to those remaining in the d'Orbigny collections in Paris are very widespread on the continental shelves and slopes of the world ocean. The deeply incised sutures, fringed with a border of short spines, and the excavated apertural face with its asymmetrically situated, comma-shaped, lipped, and toothed aperture, are characteristic. It occurs widely on the inner continental shelf, and specimens are often transported inshore, on to beaches or into estuary mouths.

5 TURRILINIDAE

Buliminella borealis Haynes   FIG. 2.4

[FEYLING-HANSSEN *et al.* 1971: 234, VI, 15; HAYNES 1973: 114]

Test smooth, very finely perforate, translucent, very tightly coiled (10 to 12 chambers in last whorl) in a high spire. Aperture similar to that of *Bulimina*, situated at anterior end of a long, broad, concave depression which occupies almost all of terminal face of last chamber. The initial end of the test may be almost wholly embraced by the last whorl in megalospheric (haploid?) generations, but is usually less covered and more slowly tapering in microspheric (diploid?) generations.

Recorded below LWST all around British coasts (the type area is Carmarthen Bay) but its transported, dead tests are also sedimented in estuarine muds.

6 SPIRILLINIDAE

Spirillina vivipara Ehrenberg   FIG. 2.4

[LOEBLICH AND TAPPAN 1964: 600, Figs. 475, 1–2; MURRAY 1973: 145, LX, 1–2]

Test planospiral, non-septate, glassy, thick relative to its size, and coarsely perforate. Evolute on both sides (more so on one side than on the other) and slightly biconcave; periphery rounded. Aperture a simple, basal opening at end of coiled chamber. *S. vivipara runiana* Heron-Allen and Earland differs from *S. vivipara sensu stricto* in having even coarser perforations, confined to the spiral suture.

Life cycle described by Myers (1937); megalospheric tests are those of the schizont (this is the opposite situation to that of the milioline analogue *Cornuspira* (q.v.): an additional contrast is that the gametes of *Spirillina vivipara* are amoeboid, while those of the Miliolina—as known from some genera, at least—are flagellate).

This species occurs attached to firm substrata in coastal and inner shelf waters. The original types (and the neotype, designated by Leoblich and Tappan 1964) are from the Caribbean; it may be that the species described and figured here should be distinguished as *S. perforata* (Schultze), as suggested by Haynes (1973), but that species, which was originally described from off Mozambique, needs typification and redescription.

Planispirillina (e.g. *P. terquemi* Silvestri) is granulate over one side, and *Sejunctella* (e.g. *S. lateseptata* (Terquem)) has its whorls separated by a sheet of crystalline calcite (see Levy *et al.* 1975).

7 CIBICIDIDAE

The extension of the basal, sutural aperture into and along the spiral suture of the more evolute ('dorsal') side of the test permits extrusion of cytoplasm and the formation of reticulopodial nets in that area. Consequently, the species normally live with the evolute side next to the substratum, where pseudopodia attach the test and can be used for food gathering. Different species of the genus *Cibicides* appear to have very different degrees of mobility. A few have biconvex tests, with the more evolute side growing regularly and independently of the form of the substratum, suggesting that the organism is continuously mobile. More commonly, others, like *C. lobatulus* (described below), have tests with evolute sides which vary greatly in shape, depending largely on the substratum on which the animal lived: this implies that 'adult' *C. lobatulus* moves little, if at all, from the site it occupies.

Cibicides lobatulus (Walker and Jacob)   FIG. 2.4

[FEYLING-HANSSEN *et al.* 1971: 260, IX, 9–14; MURRAY 1973: 175, LXXIII, 1–7]

Test white, finely perforate, convex and domed on involute side, flat or concave or irregularly concave-convex on evolute side, with an acutely angled margin. Aperture in basal suture of last chamber, around periphery of previous whorl, extending backwards in the spiral suture for two or more chambers; partly covered by a thin lip.

Very widely distributed on the inner shelf, attached to a great variety of firm substrata. It seems to prefer environments of high energy and tolerates salinities at least as low as 32‰. Its dead tests are common in beach sands. Northerly areas of lower temperatures have populations of larger, thicker-walled individuals than those areas of high temperature (and probably more rapid growth).

Heterolepa (e.g. *H. ubaldoae*; Levy *et al.* 1975) differs from *Cibicides* in extending its aperture along the spiral suture of the last chamber only and in not being permanently attached to a single substratal site: consequently, it is normally biconvex, and it never deforms according to the topography of its substratum.

8 DISCORBIDAE

In contrast to the Cibicididae, the primary aperture in the Discorbidae extends along the basal suture from the periphery of the penultimate whorl on to the more 'ventral' (more involute) side of the test, which is attached to the substratum. The aperture is furnished with a flange-like lip, which usually broadens towards the depression (the *umbilicus*) where the innermost ends of the chambers almost meet, to form a broad flap partly covering this umbilicus. All the primary apertures of the last whorl can extrude cytoplasm through the umbilicus to the exterior, and additional apertures for cytoplasmic extrusion are often developed in the innermost (umbilical) parts of the intercameral sutures on the ventral side (as *supplementary, sutural apertures*). Because the involute side of the tests is in continuous contact with the substratum and the evolute side with the surrounding seawater, there are different numbers of perforations, of different sizes, in the test walls of the two sides; the involute side may lack perforations entirely, or they may occupy a very reduced area, while the dorsal side usually possesses perforations uniformly spread over the surfaces of the chambers of the last whorl, at least. As the test grows by the addition of new chambers, additional shell material is added to the surfaces of the earlier chambers (this happens in all multiloculate Rotaliina), and the perforations in the walls of the early whorls usually become sealed by the added calcium carbonate. Many Discorbidae also possess thick, internal, organic linings to the calcareous test: these linings are also added to during growth, so that the cytoplasm of the early whorls of an 'adult' individual becomes effectively sealed off from the outer environment (the only communication between early and late chambers being via the septal apertures). In contrast, the cytoplasm of the last-formed chambers, where both the calcareous and the organic walls are thin and where the perforations remain open, is in intimate contact with the surrounding seawater, both by pseudo-podial extrusion through the apertures and by the extrusion of a very thin layer of extramural cytoplasm (over the later chambers) which can exchange solutes through the perforations to the internal cytoplasm. It is from this extramural cytoplasmic layer that pseudopodia, themselves, may often arise (Banner and Williams 1973). 'Feeding cysts' develop as the animal gathers detritus around itself by pseudopodial action.

KEY TO EXEMPLIFYING GENERA

1. Test plano-convex; attached firmly to substratum	**Rosalina**
Test biconvex, not firmly attached to substratum	**2**
2. Umbilicus open, with multiple or composite umbilical plugs and pillars	**Ammonia**
Umbilicus closed by a smooth, broad plug	**Gavelinopsis**
(for other genera, see Loeblich and Tappan 1964, and Haynes 1973, 1981).	

Rosalina globularis anglica (Cushman)   FIG. 2.4

Test flattened on its involute side, with a deep umbilicus partly closed by flap-like extensions of apertural lips; evolute side convex, with narrowly incised sutures, periphery bluntly rounded or bluntly acute. Perforations cover later chambers of evolute side, except at periphery and at intercameral sutures; coarser perforations may be present on the involute side (in which case they are confined to limited areas of the chamber walls near the umbilicus) but that side may be imperforate.

R. globularis sensu stricto (the type species of *Rosalina*) is believed to be uniformly and equally perforate on both sides of the test (Loeblich and Tappan 1964, Haynes 1973.) and to lack the imperforate peripheral margin and intercameral sutures of *R. globularis anglica*, a taxon first described by Cushman (1931) on deformed specimens obtained from off Nose Head, Moray Firth. Very irregularly growing specimens, in which the later chambers occupy about half of one whorl, have also been called *R. irregularis* (Rhumbler) (e.g. Haynes 1973). Specimens with completely imperforate involute sides have been referred to as *R. anomala* Terquem (Haynes 1973), but this species has not been redescribed since the type specimens (now lost) were described a century ago: it cannot be identified with certainty (see Levy *et al.* 1975; cf. Haynes, 1981, Fig. 12.7).

Specimens of *R. globularis anglica* adapt themselves, during growth, to the shape of the substratum to which they are attached: consequently, tests may vary considerably in shape from the regularly growing specimen illustrated here. Some wrap themselves around the slender 'stems' of hydroids, and become hemicylindrical in form. The taxon characterizes both inshore and offshore areas of the shelf, where currents have a high enough velocity to prevent burial of the chosen substratum and provide a constant supply of suspended detritus. It is steno-haline.

The inner whorls of the evolute side are characteristically brick-red or deep rose-red in colour; this pigmentation is in the calcareous wall and in the underlying organic wall, and it persists long after the death of the cell. In living specimens, the last chambers are also pale pink, and the periphery of the test characteristically possesses a loose 'fringe' of the detritus which the pseudopodia have collected.

Ammonia batava Hofker   FIG. 2.5

[BANNER AND WILLIAMS 1973: 49–69, I, 1–2; HAYNES 1981: VIII, 2]

Test biconvex, thick and glassy, especially over early whorls of evolute side, and around the umbilicus of the domed involute side. Walls very finely perforate, except in the sutures and around the umbilical margins, where the perforations are sealed by thick, glassy deposits of shell material. Aperture at the basal suture, extending into the umbilicus; bordered by a narrow lip, which enlarges into a flange at the umbilical margin, where it becomes thickened (during chamber addition) to develop into a nodular mass. These nodules, on the apertural flanges of the very early chambers, emerge through the umbilicus as a composite 'plug'.

Cytoplasm is extruded from the apertures and umbilicus, to form a thin extramural sheath over the involute side (especially over the later chambers) and from this the pseudopodia arise as free-standing nets.

A. batava inhabits firm and mobile substrata in coastal waters of salinities of about 30‰ to 34‰. *A. tepida* (Cushman) is a smaller, thinner walled, yellow- or greenish-brown species which has markedly less thickened sutures and lips, and much weaker umbilical plugs: it is euryhaline and eurythermal, and inhabits salt-marshes and estuaries, tolerating a salinity range from 4‰ to at least 30‰. *A. beccarii* (Linnaeus) is a large, very ornate, many-chambered Mediterranean species which, though frequently recorded from British seas, is not yet proven to occur there (see Haynes 1981).

Gavelinopsis praeggeri (Heron-Allen and Earland) FIG. 2.5
[LOEBLICH AND TAPPAN 1964: 568–579, Figs 456.4; HAYNES 1981: 2B, 33]

Test delicate, translucent or transparent; evolute side subconical and domed, involute side weakly convex or flattened; periphery sharply acute, with a delicate keel. Sutural aperture runs along the base of the last chamber from near periphery of penultimate whorl to the umbilicus. The umbilicus is almost entirely filled with a smooth, glassy plug, only a narrow slit between it and the innermost ends of the last two or three chambers remaining open for cytoplasmic extrusion from those chambers.

The test is pale pink when the cell is alive. This species occurs, involute side down, on pebbles, dead shell, and similar substrata. It is stenohaline, an open marine, inner shelf species.

9 PLANORBULINIDAE
Planorbulina mediterranensis d'Orbigny FIG. 2.5
[LOEBLICH AND TAPPEN 1964: 693–694, Figs. 560, 561; MURRAY 1973; 179, LXXV, 1–6]

The initial whorl is very similar to *Cibicides*, and is attached, evolute-side downwards; later chambers are added in annuli (alternating in position from annulus to annulus, like bricks in a wall) and are evolute on both sides. Each of the later chambers has two apertures; new chambers are added over the opposed apertures of each of two earlier chambers. The wall is equally coarsely perforate on both sides of the test, but the perforations of the earlier chambers become sealed by secondarily deposited shell material. The outline of the test varies from subcircular to subquadrate; the attached side adopts its general shape from the substratum of attachment, and the individual chamber sides are flattened (those of the unattached, initially involute, side are convex with more depressed sutures). In life, the cytoplasm is pink or pale green; anastomosing pseudopodia are extruded to a distance nearly equal to the test diameter.

The reproductive cycle has been studied by Le Calvez (1935); a temporary cyst is produced to enclose the test during schizogony, up to 100 embryonts are then produced by vegetative division of the parent nucleus and cytoplasm and by dissolution of much of the parental shell-material. During gamogony, when biflagellate gametes are released, the parent loses its pigmentation.

A stenohaline species, widespread on firm substrates in areas of high current velocities or wave energies, especially on the inner shelf.

10 ELPHIDIIDAE
The planospiral, 'hyaline' species of this family often have umbilical plugs and pillars, sometimes of quite complex structures. In the morphologically simplest taxa (*Haynesina*), a basal, sutural aperture extends across the periphery of the penultimate whorl into each umbilicus, where relict, sutural apertures of earlier chambers also open (analogous situation to *Ammonia*). In more complex forms (e.g. *Elphidium*) the sutural apertures are partly or wholly sealed externally and complex canal systems develop in the septa. In each case, extrathalamous cytoplasm is extruded from both the aperture and from the umbilical area, producing pseudopodia from the external cytoplasmic covering. In general terms, the more complex the skeleton, the more stenohaline is the species: *H. germanica* and *E. williamsoni* are euryhaline species of estuaries and salt-marsh pools, while *H. depressula* and *E. crispum* occupy the mouths of estuaries or offshore habitats.

Haynesina depressula (Walker and Jacob) FIG. 2.5
[BANNER AND CULVER 1978: 200–201, X; HAYNES 1973: 209, XXII, 8–11; 1981: 11B, 22; Figs. 12.1(5) and 12.9 (18–19)]

The very thin, translucent wall is milky white even in fresh, living or only recently dead material, and the perforations are ultramicroscopic in size. Test shape may be very similar to that of *Haynesina germanica* (below), but is typically more compressed, more evolute, with a broader area of umbonal thickening and micro-tubercles, and higher chambers. The primary aperture is a very thin sutural slit, very difficult to see.

It occurs below LWST on the inner shelf and is believed to be stenohaline.

Haynesina germanica (Ehrenberg) FIG. 2.5
[BANNER AND CULVER 1978: 184–200, IV–IX; ALEXANDER AND BANNER 1984: 159–170, I–VI]

Test glassy, finely perforate, planospiral, equally involute on each side, with fine, short, conical micro-tubercles massed along basal chamber sutures, umbilical parts of intercameral sutures, and the umbilici themselves, where the tubercles may coalesce into composite plugs. Primary aperture in basal suture of last chamber, extending over periphery of previous whorl and into each umbilicus equally. As in *H. depressula*, relict apertures open in the umbilical ends of the intercameral sutures of the last few chambers. All apertures are very small and usually very difficult to see, but the micro-tubercles which surround them are more easily visible. The tubercles probably act as a sieve and disaggregation tool for particles drawn into the umbilicus and apertures by the extrathalamous protoplasm.

In life, yellowish or greenish brown cytoplasm is visible through the translucent chamber walls. Cytoplasm is extruded from primary and relict apertures to form an extramural layer over the last few chambers, at least, and from this layer recticulopodia may extend radially for a distance of two or more test diameters. *H. germanica* is euryhaline and flourishes in salt-marsh and intertidal mudflat pools and creeks, in the upper centimetre of mud, and on filamentous algae; it also occurs offshore in bays and coastal waters near estuaries, tolerating a range of salinities at least from 5‰ to 33‰, but is rare on the open shelf. Cultured populations have withstood anoxic (even reducing) conditions for several weeks.

H. germanica and *H. depressula* (like *Ammonia batava* and *A. tepida*) exemplify closely related species which inhabit quite different environments. The same is true for comparative species of *Elphidium*, described below.

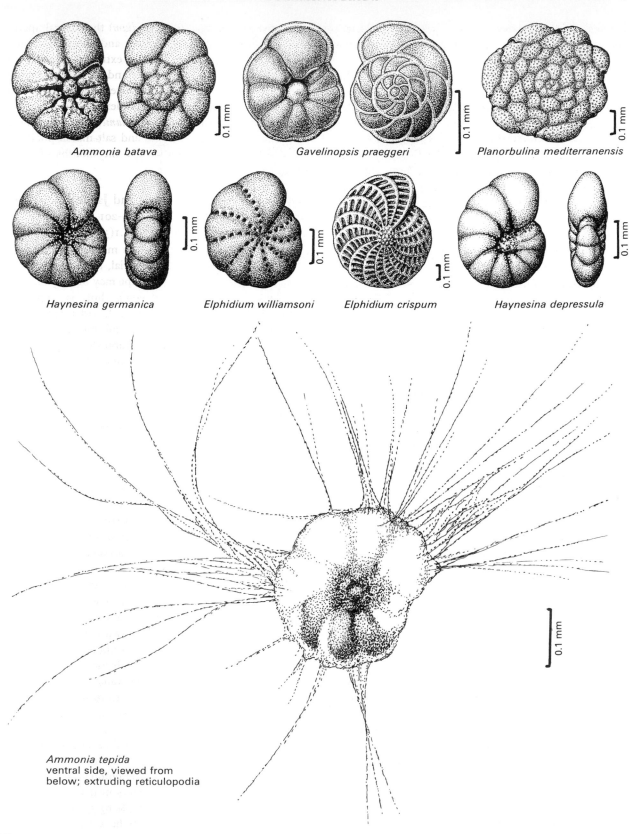

Ammonia batava

Gavelinopsis praeggeri

Planorbulina mediterranensis

Haynesina germanica

Elphidium williamsoni

Elphidium crispum

Haynesina depressula

Ammonia tepida
ventral side, viewed from
below; extruding reticulopodia

Fig. 2.5

Elphidium williamsoni Haynes.   FIG. 2.5
[HAYNES 1973: 199, XXII, 6, XXIV, 14–16; 1981: 11B, 16; VIII, 11]

The glassy, finely perforate test closely resembles *Haynesina germanica* in shape, but has secondary apertures developed in the intercameral sutures; these multiple, sutural apertures separated from each other by tiny, ridge-like extensions of the posterior margin of the chamber which is anterior (i.e. succeeds in growth direction) to that suture. The sutural ridges house backward-pointing extensions of the intracameral cytoplasm (called *retral processes*) which characterize *Elphidium* and closely related genera. Primary aperture at the suture (base) of last chamber, extending from umbilicus to umbilicus, as a series of discrete, separate, small holes (*cribrate* aperture).

Cytoplasm is extruded from the primary aperture and the umbilical areas to form an extramural cytoplasmic layer from which radial or reticulate nets of granulopodia extend for up to four test diameters in distance.

This species is strongly euryhaline, and inhabits muddy pools in intertidal marshes; it can withstand a salinity range of at least 30‰ (i.e. from at least 3‰ to 33‰), and has even been found living in moist mud a few centimetres below the sediment surface of pools which have otherwise dried out. It also occurs on filamentous algae in marsh pools and in estuaries. In life, the cytoplasm is typically pigmented brownish-green.

E. incertum (Williamson) has a similar rounded test periphery but has shorter, few retral processes; it also occurs in low salinity (hyposaline) environments. *E. exoticum* (Haynes), of marshes and offshore coastal waters, has retral processes like those of *E. williamsoni* but the test is compressed and thinner, and the umbilici are flat and not granular. *E. margaritaceum* (Cushman) also has short retral processes and a compressed test, but is covered in tiny granule-like tubercules; it occurs below LWST. *E. gerthi* Voorthuysen is an offshore species similar to *E. incertum* but with distinct, fused umbilical plugs and a more angular periphery.

Elphidium crispum (Linnaeus)   FIG. 2.5
[LOEBLICH AND TAPPAN 1964: 632–633; ROSSET-MOULINER 1971: 76–81; MURRAY 1973: 155, LXIV, 1–6]

Glassy, very finely perforate test, with acute, keeled margin, strongly marked sutures and long, strong retral processes. Cribrate, basal aperture at base of a curved, narrowly triangular, apertural face. The biconvexity of the test causes part of it to be raised from a firm substratum (to which remainder of test is attached by locomotory pseudopodial nets); food-gathering pseudopodial nets then extend, from free-standing keeled margin, into surrounding seawater, where they entrap diatoms, small flagellates and ciliates, and even small swimming arthropods, like flies in a spider's web.

Smaller specimens, with smooth umbilical plugs, are sometimes referred to as *E. macellum* (Fichtel and Moll); the typical *E. crispum* has a large, distinctly pitted pair of glassy umbilical plugs. The periphery occasionally bears short, radial spines of glassy calcite.

The species is stenohaline and lives in the more southerly parts of the inner shelf, both in areas of calm water and in those of high current and wave energy. The reproductive cycle is an alternation between outwardly similar multinucleate, diploid schizonts (internally microspheric) and uninucleate, haploid gamonts (internally megalospheric), the latter capable of producing free, biflagellate gametes similar to those of *Planorbulina*. In British waters, the life span of each individual is believed to be about one year.

PHYLUM CILIOPHORA

All ciliates except *Stephanopogon* have two types of nuclei, *macronuclei* and *micronuclei*, and all without exception have, during at least part of their lives, an *infraciliature*. This is a subsurface arrangement of *microtubules* and *fibrils*, which are associated with ciliary basal bodies called *kinetosomes*. Cilia grow out from the kinetosomes, and function in locomotion and food-gathering. Most cilia are arranged in rows (*kineties*) which can be blackened by silver. Each kinety then appears as a succession of dots (the kinetosomes) linked by threads. Compound ciliary organelles are seen best in *Euplotes* and other Hypotrichida (Fig. 2.9, bottom). These have ventral cilia forming dense tufts or *cirri*, which function like legs. Anteriorly and round the left side of the buccal cavity they have an *adoral zone* of *membranelles* (AZM), each membranelle made up of close-set rows of cilia acting together to form a paddle. Within the buccal cavity and along its right side is a row of cilia which beat metachronally to produce an undulating movement, forming what is now termed the *paroral membrane* (pm). The dorsal cilia of *Euplotes* are sparse, but nevertheless arranged in kineties (k). Silver staining reveals these as a fine web, but shows the crowded kinetosomes of large membranelles and cirri as broad black bars and spots.

Other useful categories of ciliature are *oral* and *somatic*, i.e. associated with mouth and rest of body. The *cytostome* (here termed mouth for brevity) is a hole in the *pellicle* through which food passes into the endoplasm. It may lead into a non-ciliated tube (*cytopharynx*) which may be surrounded by a basket (*cyrtos*) of fine fibres (in *Scaphidiodon* and *Paranassula*—Fig. 2.7, top). The pellicle around the mouth (and elsewhere) may contain *toxicysts*, which can discharge enzymes to paralyse and cytolyse prey. The mouth may be superficial, or in a ciliated depression which may be shallow (*atrium*) or deeper (*buccal cavity, vestibulum*) or tubular (*infundibulum*). In 'higher' ciliates, e.g. *Euplotes* and *Peritrichia*, the buccal ciliature tends to emerge onto an expanded oral area (*peristome*) which may partially encircle the anterior end.

Marine ciliates may be classified as follows (Corliss 1979).

Class I Kinetofragminophorea

Oral cilia form mere fragments of kineties, not much modified from somatic ciliation.

Subclass I Gymnostomatia

Mouth anterior or anterolateral, flush with body surface (most of Fig. 2.6).

Order I Primociliatida

Nuclei only one type.

Order 2 Karyorelictida

Macronuclei diploid (or oligoploid), each usually with one large nucleolus. Ploidy refers to multiplication of N chromosome number. Most ciliates have very large polyploid macronuclei, containing many N sets and many small nucleoli, whereas diploid macronuclei have diameters only $2-5 \times$ those of micronuclei. Karyorelictids possess them in considerable numbers (usually about twice number of micronuclei), either scattered throughout body or clumped to form a nuclear complex. This may have a bounding membrane and then looks like a single larger nucleus, but staining shows its make-up (see *Tracheloraphis*).

Order 3 Prostomatida

Microphagous, with mouth apical or subapical.

Order 4 Haptorida

With toxicysts for larger prey, apical or subapical mouth, and often a cytopharyngeal apparatus for swallowing.

Order 5 Pleurostomatida

Mouth slit-like, along 'ventral' edge of flattened body.

Subclass II Vestibuliferia

Mouth at bottom of deep ciliated depression (Fig. 2.6, bottom, right).

Order I Trichostomatida

Like prostomatid gymnostomes, except for having the ciliated vestibulum. The only vestibuliferan order found in the sea, also including several families endocommensal in land vertebrates. Related Colpodida are known only from freshwater or land soils, whilst Entodiniomorphida include rumen ciliates.

Subclass III Hypostomatia

Mouth ventral, often leading to cytopharyngeal cyrtos. Diverse group of microphagous or algivorous or ecto- or endocommensal forms (a few of latter lack mouth) (most of Fig. 2.7).

Order I Synhymeniida

With perioral or postoral transverse band ('*frange*') of longer cilia arising in pairs ('*pseudomembranelles*').

Order 2 Nassulida

Frange less extensive.

Suborder I Nassulina

With cyrtos for ingesting filamentous algae. Body cylindrical and uniformly well ciliated.

Suborder 2 Microthoracina

Ciliation reduced. Body flattened.

Order 3 Cyrtophorida

With cyrtos. Body often flattened, ciliated only ventrally.

Suborder I Chlamydodontina

Ventral cilia 'thigmotactic' (specialized for adhesion) with no other prominent adhesive organelle.

Suborder 2 Dysteriina

With ventral adhesive 'podite' often protruding conspicuously.

Suborder 3 Hypocomatina

Commensal on various hosts. Ventral surface flat with thigmotactic organ. Can mostly protrude sucking tube.

Order 4 Chonotrichida

Vase-shaped, with collars within which rows of cilia run towards mouth, but otherwise unciliated and attached, mostly to Crustacea.

Suborder I Exogemmina

External budding.

Suborder 2 Cryptogemmina

Internal budding.

Order 5 Rhynchodida

Without mouth. Parasites attached to host by anterior sucking knob.

Order 6 Apostomatida

Parasites, especially of Crustacea, with spiralling widely spaced kineties.

Suborder I Apostomatina

Small mouth surrounded by '*rosette*' (area of pellicle, perhaps secretory).

Suborder 2 Astomatophorina

Without mouth. Body may be vermiform.

Suborder 3 Pilisuctorina

Mature forms impaled on crustacean setae.

Subclass IV Suctoria

Mostly attached, catching and absorbing prey through suctorial tentacles. Larvae ciliated, but lose cilia after attachment (Fig. 2.7, bottom).

Order 1 **Suctorida**

The only order in this subclass.

Suborder 1 **Exogenina**

Buds arise and develop externally.

Suborder 2 **Endogenina**

One or more larvae complete development within an invaginated pouch, and emerge swimming.

Suborder 3 **Evaginogenina**

Single pouch invaginates but is then everted to become an external bud.

Class II **Oligohymenophorea**

Typically with few small membranelles on left side of buccal cavity and paroral membrane on right (Fig. 2.8 top).

Subclass 1 **Hymenostomatia**

Somatic ciliation fairly uniform. Buccal cavity small, and may be absent.

Order 1 **Hymenostomatida**

Typical of class and subclass. Two out of fourteen families have marine representatives. Lack of scutica (see below) separates from next order.

Order 2 **Scuticociliatida**

The *scutica*, of kinetosomes arranged in shape of a hook or whip, is seen only during cell division, in newly developing oral field.

Suborder 1 **Philasterina**

Mostly with one or more particularly long caudal cilia.

Suborder 2 **Pleuronematina**

Very large paroral membrane projects like a sail.

Suborder 3 **Thigmotrichina**

All commensals, mostly of molluscs and echinoderms, with mouth posterior or reduced.

Order 3 **Astomatida**

Without mouth. All parasites or endocommensals.

Subclass 2 **Peritrichia**

Body like inverted bell or cone or short cylinder, with reduced somatic ciliation (Fig. 2.8, lower half). Peristomial ciliature encircles apical area, before plunging into an infundibulum.

Order 1 **Peritrichida**

The only order in this subclass.

Suborder 1 **Sessilina**

Mostly attached semi-permanently, some by stalks. A few secondarily free-swimming.

Suborder 2 **Mobilina**

Capable of crawling about on an aboral attachment disc, which incorporates rings of denticles and cilia.

Class III **Polyhymenophorea**

AZM prominent, often extending out of buccal cavity around anterior end of body (Fig. 2.9).

Subclass 1 **Spirotrichia**

The only subclass, with characters of class.

Order 1 **Heterotrichida**

Mostly large, some highly contractile.

Suborder 1 **Heterotrichina**

Generally well-ciliated, mobile forms.

Suborder 2 **Clevelandellina**

Parasitic in gut of land animals, but *Nyctotherus* is also recorded from a tropical marine mollusc.

Suborder 3 **Armophorina**

Top-shaped, anteriorly rounded, with reduced ciliation and rigid pellicle. Mostly with caudal spine.

Suborder 4 **Folliculinina**

Attached loricate 'bottle-animalcules'.

Suborder 5 **Licnophorina**

Short cylinders, with ciliation reduced to basal ring for attachment and distal ring formed by AZM. Ectocommensal.

Order 2 **Odontostomatida**

Small, compressed, with reduced ciliation and thick pellicle, often bearing spines.

Order 3 **Oligotrichida**

Top-like, with AZM round anterior end like blades of helicopter. Somatic ciliation reduced. Mostly planktonic.

Suborder 1 **Oligotrichina**

Mostly not loricate.

Suborder 2 **Tintinnina**

All loricate.

Order 4 **Hypotrichida**

Flattened, with cirri on ventral surface.

Suborder 1 **Stichotrichina**

Cirri small, arranged in two or more longitudinal rows.

Suborder 2 **Sporadotrichina**

Cirri large, arranged in localized groups.

There are over 7000 named 'species' of ciliates and most major groups are represented in the sea. This account includes at least one species from each of these groups, including the commoner families. Most of these species can be obtained from sand collected near low water, using the ice-water technique and examination methods described for flagellates. Most of the remainder are epibiont (ectocommensal) or parasitic forms, obtained by searching the hosts on which they are common. Older hosts from crowded populations are most likely to be infested. Ecology and distribution were treated by Fenchel (e.g. 1965a, b, 1969) in the Øresund, Fauré-Fremiet (1950) and Dragesco (1960, 1963 a and b) at Roscoff. The northern and southern parts of our area are thus well-covered and, to save space later, it may be noted that all species described in the following pages are probably common on suitable shores from Brittany to Sweden, unless otherwise stated. Final identification of species will usually need staining with fuchsin and silver, to reveal nuclei and kineties (Wright 1983). Above all it will need long searches in the literature, including recent papers.

The figures reproduced in Figs. 2.6–2.9 have been redrawn from various sources, but principally from Dragesco (1960, 1963a, b, 1965), Fenchel (1965a, b, 1969), and Kahl (1930–35, 1933–34).

REFERENCES

Kahl (1933–4) gave a short introduction to marine ciliates, which is well-illustrated (with keys) but lacks an index. Later (Kahl 1930–5) he completed a wider treatment, which has an index to nearly 3000 species, but there the marine forms must be sought out from among numerous freshwater species. Corliss (1979) explains the changed and advancing taxonomy, with details of all families, about 1000 figures of genera, and nearly 3000 references to the all-important original papers and monographs. Some of these are cited here, but Corliss (1979) should be consulted for a complete bibliographic treatment.

Chatton, E and Lwoff, A. (1935). Les Ciliés apostomes. Morphologie, cytologie, éthologie, évolution, systématique. Première partie. Aperçu historique et général. Etude monographique des genre et des espèces. *Archives de Zoologie experimental et generale, Paris*, **77**, 1–453.

Corliss, J. O. (1979). *The ciliated protozoa, characterization, classification and guide to the literature*, (2nd edn). Pergamon, London and New York.

Das, S. M. (1949). British Folliculinidae. *Journal of the Marine Biological Association of the U.K.*, **28**, 382–93.

Deroux, G. (1975). Les dispositifs adhésifs ciliaires chez les Cyrtophorida et la famille des Hypocomidae. *Protistologica*, **10**, 379–96.

De Puytorac, P. (1954). Contribution à l'étude cytologique et taxonomique des infusoires astomes. *Annales des sciences naturelles, zoologie* (11), **16**, 85–270.

Dragesco, J. (1960). Ciliés mésopsammiques littoraux. Systématique, morphologie, écologie. . *Travaux de la Station biologique de Roscoff (n.s.)*, **12**, 1–356.

Dragesco, J. (1963a). Compléments à la connaissance des ciliés mésopsammiques de Roscoff. I. Holotriches. *Cahiers de Biologie marine*, **4**, 91–119.

Dragesco, J. (1963b). Compléments à la connaissance des ciliés mésopsammiques de Roscoff. II. Hétérotriches. III. Hypotriches. *Cahiers de Biologie marine*, **4**, 251–75.

Dragesco, J. (1965). Ciliés mésopsammiques d'Afrique Noire. *Cahiers de Biologie marine*, **6**, 357–99.

Fauré-Fremiet, E. (1950). Ecologie de ciliés psammophiles littoraux. *Bulletin biologique de la France et de la Belgique*, **84**, 35–75.

Fenchel, T. (1965a). Ciliates of Scandinavian molluscs. *Ophelia*, **1**, 71–173.

Fenchel, T. (1965b). On the ciliate fauna associated with the marine species of the amphipod genus *Gammarus* J. G. Fabricius. *Ophelia*, **2**, 281–303.

Fenchel, T. (1969). The ecology of marine microbenthos. IV. Structure and function of the benthic ecosystem, its chemical and physical factors and the microfauna communities, with special reference to the ciliated protozoa. *Ophelia*, **6**, 1–182.

Hadzi, J. (1951). Studien über Folliculiniden. *Dela Slov. Akad. Znan. Umet. Hist. Nat. Med.*, **4**, 1–390.

Kahl, A. (1930–35). Urtiere oder Protozoa. I. Wimpertiere oder Ciliata (Infusoria). In *Die Tierwelt Deutschlands*, parts **18** (1930), **21** (1931), **25** (1932), **30** (1935), (ed F. Dahl), pp. 1–886. Fischer, Jena.

Kahl, A. (1933–34). Ciliata libera et ectocommensalia. Ciliata entocommensalia et parasitica Suctoria. In *Die Tierwelt der Nord-und Ostsee* Lief. **23** (1933), 29–46; **26** (1934), 147–226, (ed G. Grimpe and E. Wagler).

Kent, W. S. (1880–82). *A Manual of the Infusoria*. D. Bogue, London. 3 vols.

Khan, M. A. (1969). Fine structure of *Ancistrocoma pelseneeri* (Chatton et Lwoff), a rhynchodine thigmotrichid ciliate. *Acta Protozoologica*, **7**, 29–47.

Kozloff, E. N. (1946). Studies on ciliates of the family Ancistrocomidae Chatton and Lwoff. IV. *Biological Bulletin*, **91**, 200–9.

Lackey, J. B. and Lackey E. W. (1963). Microscopic algae and Protozoa in the waters near Plymouth in August 1962. *Journal of the Marine Biological Association of the U.K.*, **43**, 797–805.

Marshall, S. M. 1969. *Fiches d'identification du zooplankton*. Nos. 117–27. Protozoa. Order Tintinnida. Conseil permanent International pour l'Exploration de la Mer, Copenhagen.

Wright, J. M. (1983). Sand dwelling ciliates of South Wales. *Cahiers de Biologie marine*, **24**, 187–214.

Class **Kinetofragminophorea**

Subclass **Gymnostomatia**

Order **Primociliatida**

1 STEPHANOPOGONIDAE

Lacking nuclear dimorphism. Occurring interstitially in sand (this applies to occurrence of all subsequent families too, unless otherwise stated). One genus, few species.

KEY TO REPRESENTATIVE MARINE FAMILIES

NB. Families are in numbered sequence, and in Figs. 2.6–2.9 the number of the family precedes the name of each exemplifying species.

1. With conspicuous adoral zone of membranelles (Spirotrichia—Fig. 2.9) — **48**
   Without conspicuous AZM — **2**

2. Mostly with tentacles and lacking cilia during trophic life — **28**
   Mostly without tentacles, always with cilia — **3**

3. Body mostly unciliated except for oral ciliature — **4**
   Body well-ciliated — **5**

4. Body sometimes contractile, often bell-shaped, with peristomial groove running round oral disc (Peritrichia—Fig. 2.8, bottom) — **41**
   Body stiff, vase-shaped, usually attached to Crustacea (Chonotrichia) — **26**

5. With mouth — **6**
   Without mouth — **9**

6. Mouth on surface, or in depression that lacks compound ciliary structures — **7**
   Mouth in ventral buccal cavity, which contains a paroral membrane and/or several small membranelles (Hymenostomatia—Fig. 2.8, top half) — **33**

7. Mouth apical or subapical (Fig. 2.6) — **8**
   Mouth ventral (Hypostomatia—Fig. 2.7, upper parts) — **20**

8. Mouth flush with surface (Gymnostomatia) — **10**
   Mouth in a vestibulum (Vestibuliferia) — **12. Coelosomididae**

9. If freeliving in sand, perhaps *Kentrophoros* (Loxodidae) — **13**
   If parasitic, perhaps — **27 or 33**

10. Two or more nuclei of only one type. Body compressed, flask-shaped, asymmetrical, length 2–3 × breadth. Mouth an apical slit (Primociliatida) — **1. Stephanopogonidae**
    With two types of nuclei, macro- and micronuclei — **11**

11. Macronuclei only 2–5 × diameters of micronuclei, each with one large nucleolus. Several of each type. Body usually slender and elongated (Karyorelictida) — **12**
    Macronucleus much larger than micronuclei, and with several or many nucleoli — **14**

12. With narrow neck that does not taper anteriorly. Apex bilaterally symmetrical. Mouth apical — **2. Trachelocercidae**
    Apex tapering and curved asymmetrically. Mouth subapical — **13**

13. Ciliation uniform, but cilia longer near mouth, which is small and near (not on) concave side **3. Geleiidae**

Body laterally compressed, ciliated on one side. Mouth absent or slit-like on concave edge **4. Loxodidae**

14. Mouth slit-like, along convex anterior edge of laterally compressed body (Pleurostomatida) **11. Amphileptidae**

Mouth apical **15**

15. With toxicysts around mouth (Haptorida) **18**

Toxicysts absent or somatic **16**

16. Pellicle covered with opaque rectangular plates **7. Colepidae**

Mostly without pellicular plates **17**

17. Cilia round mouth much longer than most somatic cilia. Lorica may be secreted **5. Metacystidae**

Ciliation fairly uniform **6. Prorodontidae**

18. Body rotund. Cilia form mere girdles **10. Didiniidae**

Body more elongated and uniformly ciliated **19**

19. Tapering anteriorly to small oval mouth **8. Enchelyidae**

Truncated anteriorly, with wide, slit-like, transverse or oblique mouth **9. Spathidiidae**

20. Freeliving, usually with a cytopharyngeal basket **21**

Ecto- or endocommensals lacking such a basket **25**

21. With adhesive podite protruding posteroventrally **17. Dysteriidae**

Without such a podite **22**

22. Ovoid, ciliated densely and uniformly **14. Paranassulidae**

Flattened **23**

23. Outline rounded. Few kineties **15. Microthoracidae**

Shaped like right shoe. Many kineties **24**

24. With narrow striated canal round lateral and frontal margins **16. Chlamydodontidae**

Without such a canal **13. Scaphidiodontidae**

25. Living on suctorians, peritrichs, ophiuroids, or tunicates **18. Hypocomidae**

On other hosts **27**

26. Body bottle-shaped, attached directly (without stalk) to amphipods   **19. Heliochonidae**

    Body leaf-like, attached by thin stalk to amphipods or *Nebalia*   **20. Stylochonidae**

27. With an anterior knob attached to and sucking from gills of bivalve molluscs

                                                                               21. Ancistrocomidae

    Without such a knob   **28**

28. Mature stage lacks cilia   **29**

    Mature stage retains cilia, with kineties spiralling round body (Apostomatida)   **30**

29. Without tentacles, but impaled upon crustacean seta   **22. Conidophryidae**

    With tentacles, mostly epizoic on various hosts (Suctoria—Fig. 2.7, bottom)   **31**

30. Mouth present and surrounded by rosette pattern. Hosts Crustacea and actinians

                                                                               23. Foettingeriidae

    Mouth absent, body vermiform, hosts amphipods, isopods, squid, and octopus

                                                                               24. Opalinopsidae

31. Pointed peripheral tentacles around clump of short ones which end in suckers. Buds
    develop externally (Exogenina)   **25. Ephelotidae**

    Tentacles all similar. Buds develop from an invaginated pouch   **32**

32. Buds complete development in pouches, from which the ciliated larvae swim (Endo-
    genina). Adults stalked, with tentacles in a few bunches   **26. Acinetidae**

    Bud arises as a pouch, but this is everted and becomes an external bud (Evaginogenina)

                                                                               27. Discophryidae

33. With mouth and buccal cavity   **34**

    Without mouth (Astomatida)   **36. Buetschliellidae**

34. Commensal with molluscs or echinoderms   **39**

    Freeliving   **35**

35. With one or a few long tail cilia, and some with large paroral membrane projecting
    like a sail   **36**

    Lacking such characters, mostly large with mouth in anterior third of body   **28. Frontoniidae**

36. Paroral membrane like sail (Pleuronematina)   **38**

    Membrane not projecting much (Philasterina)   **37**

37. Body flattened, sparse ciliature limited to ventral surface   **30. Cinetochilidae**

    Ciliated sparsely but more uniformly, though with bare anterior pole   **29. Uronematidae**

38. Length 45–180 μm, densely ciliated   **31. Pleuronematidae**

     Length 15–60 μm, sparsely ciliated   **32. Cyclidiidae**

39. Body laterally compressed, kidney-shaped. Marginal depression surrounds equatorial mouth. In mantle cavity of *Mytilus*   **33. Peniculostomatidae**

     More cylindrical, usually tapering anteriorly, with posterior mouth   **40**

40. In respiratory chambers of molluscs or holothurians   **34. Ancistridae**

     Attached to asteroids and *Antedon* by kineties of aboral cilia. These do not form a ring, which should prevent confusion with similar but unrelated ectocommensals (see below)   **35. Hemispeiridae**

41. Mostly ectocommensal, like short cylinders, distal end surrounded by peristomial groove, basal end with ring of cilia for crawling and attachment   **46**

     Like inverted bell, cone, or cylinder; incapable of crawling, attached semi-permanently to rocks or other organisms (Sessilina)   **42**

42. Secreting a protective case (lorica)   **43**

     Not loricate   **44**

43. Blue or green ciliate visible within transparent bottle-shaped lorica, which sticks to substratum by one side and lacks a stalk   **53**

     Usually unpigmented, lorica of various shapes, with or without stalk   **40. Vaginicolidae**

44. With stalk   **45**

     Without stalk, attached directly to substratum   **39. Scyphidiidae**

45. Stalk very contractile, some colonial   **37. Vorticellidae**

     Stalk not contractile   **38. Epistylidae**

46. Within basal attachment ring of cilia there is an inner ring of denticles (Mobilina)   **47**

     Without denticles. Oral ring is an AZM   **50**

47. Denticles smooth   **41. Leiotrochidae**

     Denticles linked to their neighbours by hooks   **42. Trichodinidae**

48. Body mostly covered with cilia, at least on ventral side, not top-shaped, without ventral cirri (most Heterotrichidae)   **53**

     Body mostly bare or with ventral cirri   **49**

49. Body like spinning top or hourglass   **50**

     Body flattened   **52**

50. Body a short cylinder, mostly unciliated but with AZM forming a distal ring, whilst basal ring of cilia surrounds an attachment disc. Ectocommensal on echinoderms, polychaetes, and molluscan gills   **49. Licnophoridae**

Body top-shaped, mostly with AZM surrounding wide anterior end, tapering or rounded posteriorly   **51**

51. Body twisted anteriorly like Metopidae (see below). Buccal ciliature spiralling to posterior mouth. Mostly with long caudal spine   **47. Caenomorphidae**

Body not twisted. AZM forms circle or shallow spiral anteriorly (Oligotrichida)   **57**

52. Ventral side bears cirri, which are used for walking (Hypotrichida)   **58**

Small forms lacking cirri, with thick pellicular armour generally bearing posterior spines (Odontostomatida)   **50. Epalxellidae**

53. Blue or green, in lorica attached to stones or other organisms   **48. Folliculinidae**

Non-loricate, usually unpigmented   **54**

54. Flattened, ciliated only ventrally   **46. Peritromidae**

Ciliation not confined to one side   **55**

55. Anterior end twisted to left. Posterior end pointed or with long caudal cilia. Length about 2 × breadth   **44. Metopidae**

Not markedly twisted, mostly cylindrical, many vermiform   **56**

56. Generally slender, with narrow inconspicuous peristome running down anterior half of body and facing laterally   **43. Spirostomidae**

Mostly less slender, with peristome situated and facing more anteriorly

45. Condylostomatidae

57. With lorica shaped like vase, bell, or amphora   **52. Codonellidae**

Mostly non-loricate   **51. Strombidiidae**

58. Often elongated, with cirri inconspicuous and arranged in longitudinal or spiralled rows   **59**

Oval forms, with cirri few, conspicuous, and not arranged in longitudinal rows   **60**

59. With a few spiralled rows of small cirri   **53. Strongylidiidae**

With a row of cirri along right margin, another along left and (in some species) intermediate rows   **54. Holostichidae**

60. Membranelles of AZM reduced in number and size, enclosed centrally on ventral surface. Dorsal surface distinctly ribbed and lacking cilia   **55. Aspidiscidae**

AZM usually conspicuous along anterior margin and round left side for about half length of body. Dorsal ribs less conspicuous, but each bears a sparse row of cilia ('bristles')   **56. Euplotidae**

Stephanopogon colpoda Entz   FIG. 2.6
[DRAGESCO 1963a: 101]
Ciliated only on flattened ventral side, 12–14 kineties. Anterior end bent towards right. Mouth apical, slit-like, with three pointed anteroventral lobes. Length about 60 μm.

Stephanopogon mesnili Lwoff has four inconspicuous anteroventral lobes.

Order **Karyorelictida**

2 TRACHELOCERCIDAE
Mouth apical. Body bilaterally symmetrical and often elongated, with long neck. At least 3 genera and many species. Comparatively small macronuclei of these and other karyorelictids may perhaps be a relict character, consistent with possibly primitive sand environment to which order is confined.

Tracheloraphis phoenicopterus (Cohn)   FIG. 2.6
[KAHL 1930: 118]
Length 600–1300 μm, oval in cross-section, with 22–26 kineties and a non-ciliated dorsal area occupying about one-quarter of circumference. Nuclear complex (nc) includes about six micronuclei and more macronuclei.

Wright (1983) gives a key to over 40 species, differing in colour and numbers of nuclei and kineties. Some have nuclei distributed along length of body.

3 GELEIIDAE
Apex tapering and bent to left. Subapical mouth near concave side. At least two genera.

Geleia fossata Kahl   FIG. 2.6
[DRAGESCO 1960: 230]
Length 300–500 μm. Cytoplasm pale yellow. Enlarged drawings show anterior end with ventral mouth, and stained complex of two macronuclei and a micronucleus.

Many other species (Dragesco 1960). Small oval *Ciliofaurea mirabilis* Dragesco and related forms are sometimes placed in this family.

4 LOXODIDAE
Body laterally compressed, ciliated only on right side. With two marine genera plus *Loxodes* (which is known only from freshwater). This and *Remanella* have apex bent ventrally, with slit-like mouth on concave edge.

Remanella rugosa Kahl   FIG. 2.6
[KAHL 1935: 824]
Length 180–400 μm, with 14–15 kineties on right side. Two macro- and one micronucleus. Muller's corpuscles (like statocysts) are located near dorsal edge.

Kentrophoros latum Raikov   FIG. 2.6
[FENCHEL 1969: 88]
Length 500—600 μm, without mouth, each end tapering symmetrically. Upper surface covered with symbiotic bacteria (rods

0.5 × 5 μm) which genus crops by phagocytosis. Longitudinal ridge along centre. Nuclear complex of two micronuclei surrounded by nucleoli and chromatin bodies.

Order **Prostomatida**

5 METACYSTIDAE
Mostly less than 100 μm long, often loricate, often free-swimming but capable of attachment by caudal cilia or (in *Metacystis*) a caudal vesicle. Mostly freshwater but a few *Metacystis* are marine.

Metacystis truncata Cohn   FIG. 2.6
[KAHL 1930: 146]
Length 30 μm, recorded from North Sea and from sediment at Plymouth.

6 PRORODONTIDAE
Oval or cylindrical, with mouth at or near apex and an anterodorsal 'brush' of cilia. At least 10 genera (e.g. *Plagiocampa*, *Urotricha*) and many species, mostly freshwater but also in marine sands.

Prorodon marinus Claparède and Lachmann   FIG. 2.6
[DRAGESCO 1960: 68]
Oval 100–200 μm long, with round macronucleus and posterior contractile vacuole. Planktonic and in Tamar sediment.

Pseudoprorodon arenicola Kahl   FIG. 2.6
[KAHL 1935: 809, FENCHEL 1969: 87]
Vermiform 310–1200 μm long, with macronucleus like string of beads extending throughout most of body. Posterior contractile vacuole. *Helicoprorodon gigas* Fauré-Fremiet (1950) is just as large.

7 COLEPIDAE
Small scavengers, mostly barrel-shaped, with pellicle marked by rows of rectangular plates. Many freshwater and several marine species. *Tiarina* (few species) is more slender, more pointed posteriorly and more planktonic.

Coleps tesselatus Kahl   FIG. 2.6
[KAHL 1930: 136]
Length 50–70 μm, marked by about 11 transverse grooves. One terminal spike projects forward and three backwards.

Coleps pulcher Spiegel and *Coleps similis* Kahl, 100 and 60 μm long respectively, also in sand, have only three transverse grooves, so plates between are elongated longitudinally.

Order **Haptorida**

8 ENCHELYIDAE
Body tapering anteriorly to small oval mouth, sometimes on flexible neck. At least 24 mostly marine genera. *Lacrymaria* often found interstitially (Dragesco 1963a).

Lacrymaria coronata Claparède and Lachmann   FIG. 2.6
[KAHL 1930: 95]
Length 90–150 μm, with 18–23 slightly spiralling kineties, one oval, central macronucleus, and a posterior contractile vacuole.

9 SPATHIDIIDAE
Often flattened, with truncated anterior end bearing slit-like mouth on transverse or oblique marginal ridge, which is not ciliated. At least 15 genera, mostly freshwater. *Spathidium* has numerous freshwater and a few marine species (Kahl 1933: 59). *Homalozoon caudatum* Kahl (1935: 819) was figured too by Fenchel (1969: 86).

Spathidium procerum Kahl   FIG. 2.6
[KAHL 1930: 164]
Vermiform, 250–410 μm long, anteriorly cylindrical, posteriorly flattened. Macronucleus long but spirally coiled. Posterior contractile vacuole. Mouth ridge bears toxicysts.

10 DIDINIIDAE
Mostly small (100 μm), rounded, planktonic and/or freshwater. Four out of eleven genera occur in sea (Kahl 1933: 56, gives nine species) and one in sand.

Mesodinium pulex Claparède and Lachmann   FIG. 2.6
[KAHL 1930: 127]
Length 20–30 μm. Anterior cone with apical mouth often bearing four to eight short tentacles, separated from rounded posterior by equatorial groove from which two rings of cilia arise, one projecting anteriorly, the other posteriorly. Often planktonic (named from jerky swimming).
   Mesodinium cinctum Calkins, seems to have a third equatorial girdle of shorter cilia.
   Mesodinium pupula Kahl is more slender (like Russian doll), and has fore and hind body of similar size. In other species these are very unequal (Dragesco 1963*a*).

Order **Pleurostomatida**

11 AMPHILEPTIDAE
Mouth slit along ventral (convex) edge of flattened body. Six genera represented in sea (Kahl 1933, 61), particularly *Loxophyllum*, which has thin margins, loaded with trichocysts (toxicysts?). These may be clumped, particularly dorsally. *Litonotus* has edges without thin margins, except posteriorly in some species. *Heminotus* is 1 or 2 mm long, attenuated at both ends. *Amphileptus* is ciliated on both sides (others only on right).

Loxophyllum verrucosum (Stokes)   FIG. 2.6
[KAHL 1931: 201]
Length 110–250 μm, contractile, distinguished by large marginal spines. Macronuclei, four to seven, in an irregular line. One to six contractile vacuoles arranged dorsally.
   Swansea Bay. Kahl (1933: 62) described 20 spp., six of which are recorded from Britain (Wright 1983).

Litonotus fasciola Wrzesniowski   FIG. 2.6
[KAHL 1931: 194]
Length 100 μm, with each end flattened and tapering. Posterior contractile vacuole.
   Helgoland, Plymouth, also in freshwater.

Subclass **Vestibuliferia**
Order **Trichostomatida**

12 COELOSOMIDIDAE
Cylindrical marine forms with apical vestibulum. The only other vestibuliferan family well-represented in the sea is the Plagiopylidae, which are kidney-shaped, with mouth anterior but not apical. Kahl (1933: 74) gives five marine species of *Plagiopyla* and ten of *Sonderia*, but these seem uncommon in sand.
   There are two genera of Coelosomidae and few species.

Coelosomides marina Anigstein   FIG. 2.6
[FAURÉ-FREMIET 1950: 47]
Ovoid, about 200 μm long, transparent in life. Macronucleus oval.

Conchostoma longissimum Fauré-Fremiet   FIG. 2.6
[FENCHEL 1969: 88]
Vermiform, length 400–800 μm, with macronucleus almost as long and band-like. Posterior contractile vacuole.

Subclass **Hypostomatia**
Order **Synhymeniida**

13 SCAPHIDIODONTIDAE
Frange of membranelles which gave order its name is inconspicuous in this mostly marine family. Two genera.

Scaphidiodon navicula (Müller)   FIG. 2.7
[DRAGESCO 1965: 385]
Length 70–100 μm. Cytopharyngeal apparatus obvious. About 36 kineties confined to ventral side, seen by transparency in main figure, which is a dorsal view. Ovoid macronucleus, micronucleus. Five or six contractile vacuoles. Posterior projection characteristic of genus is seen best in lateral view.

Chilodontopsis vorax (Stokes)
[WRIGHT 1983: 200]
Length 140–220 μm, like *Scaphidiodon* but ciliated on both sides, without posterior projection and with fewer or no contractile vacuoles.

Order **Nassulida**

14 PARANASSULIDAE
A small entirely marine family, not easy to separate from the mainly freshwater nassulids.

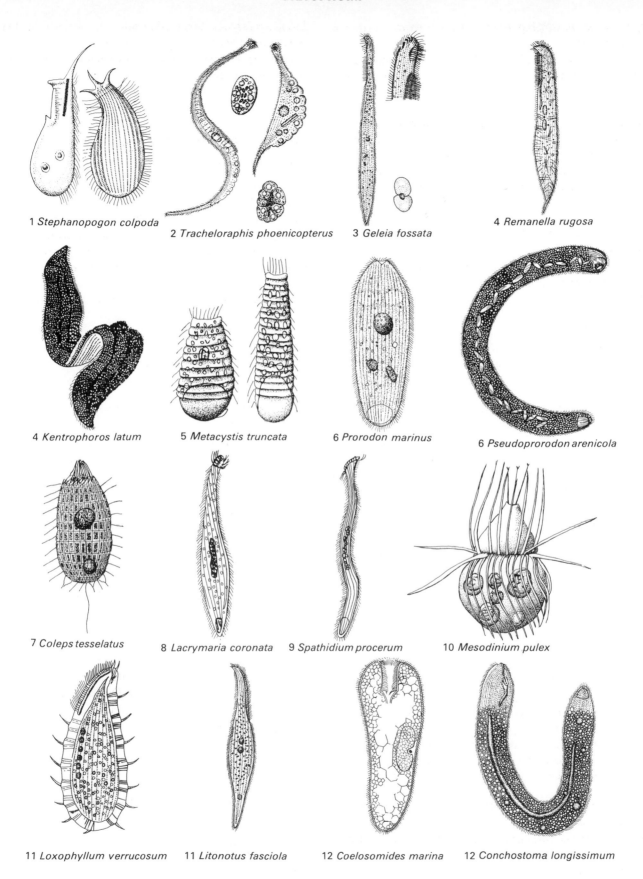

1 *Stephanopogon colpoda*

2 *Tracheloraphis phoenicopterus*

3 *Geleia fossata*

4 *Remanella rugosa*

4 *Kentrophoros latum*

5 *Metacystis truncata*

6 *Prorodon marinus*

6 *Pseudoprorodon arenicola*

7 *Coleps tesselatus*

8 *Lacrymaria coronata*

9 *Spathidium procerum*

10 *Mesodinium pulex*

11 *Loxophyllum verrucosum*

11 *Litonotus fasciola*

12 *Coelosomides marina*

12 *Conchostoma longissimum*

Fig. 2.6

Paranassula microstoma Kahl   FIG. 2.7
[KAHL 1931: 221]
Length 70–110 μm, about 75 kineties, oval macronucleus, one dorsal contractile vacuole. Pellicle criss-crossed with longitudinal and circular striations. Found regularly though sparsely at four places off Helgoland. Colourless, which must help to distinguish from species of *Nassula* (Kahl 1933: 66).

15 MICROTHORACIDAE
Small, flattened, with thick pellicle and reduced ciliation. In freshwater or moss etc., with only one marine species.

Discotricha papillifera Tuffrau   FIG. 2.7
[DRAGESCO 1965: 389]
Length 40–60 μm. Cilia form ventral cirri in a pattern of longer and shorter rows. Mouth near left side. Macronucleus rounded, with one micronucleus. In fine sand.

Order Cyrtophorida

16 CHLAMYDODONTIDAE
Ciliated ventral side only. Two genera. Most species of *Chlamydodon* have a cross-striated marginal canal about 4 μm wide (Kahl 1933: 67).

Chlamydodon triquetrus Müller   FIG. 2.7
[KAHL 1931: 231]
Length 75–120 μm. Macronucleus oval and central. Several contractile vacuoles. Larger forms (250 μm) with more filaments in cyrtos were separated by Kahl as var. *major*. At Swansea (Wright 1983) both large and small forms were green.

17 DYSTERIIDAE
Ciliated ventral side only. This and related families (*s.o. Dysteriina*) characterized by adhesive podite. Six genera, mainly marine, with many more related Hartmannulidae and Plesiotrichopidae. Kahl (1933: 69) included 37 marine species, mostly of *Dysteria*.

Dysteria aculeata Claparède and Lachmann   FIG. 2.7
[KAHL 1931: 258]
About 40 μm long. Mouth with cytopharyngeal basket is ventral, but anterior and towards right side. Along left side is a keel pointed at each end.
   Planktonic and in mud, Norway, Marseille, and estuary of Plym.
   Dysteria monostyla Ehrenberg-Stein, similar but lacking keel, is recorded just as widely.

18 HYPOCOMIDAE
Cytopharyngeal suctorial tube protrudes from body. On suctorians, vorticellids, ophiuroids, tunicates. Three genera. Few species.

Hypocoma acinetarum Collin   FIG. 2.7
[DEROUX 1975: 391]
Length 35–50 μm, with 20 kineties, forming ventral area for crawling, including attachment organelle posteriorly. Latter is associated with a ventral invagination. Sucking tube extends antero-ventrally. Macronucleus very long, U-shaped. Figure shows an individual swollen after feeding, with kineties silver-stained.
   Parasitic on the suctorian *Ephelota* in current-swept places.
   Hypocoma parasitica Grüber, living on vorticellids in sheltered harbours, lacks the postero-ventral invagination.

Order Chonotrichida
Suborder Exogemmina

19 HELIOCHONIDAE
Epibiont. Direct attachment without stalk is seen in most of six families of Exogemmina, but heliochonids are alone amongst them in bearing many spines round distal margins.

Heliochona sessilis Plate   FIG. 2.7
[FENCHEL 1965b: 286]
Length about 60 μm; bottle-shaped, attached to gills of *Gammarus locusta* and *G. oceanicus*. Distal funnel, with many spines, may take form of lophophore or horse's hoof.
   Heliochona scheuteni (Stein), which is very similar, is attached to outer rami of pleopods of the same gammarids (Fenchel 1965b).

Suborder Cryptogemmina

20 STYLOCHONIDAE
Epibiont. In this suborder most families have stalks and marginal spines.

Stylochona coronata Kent   FIG. 2.7
[KENT 1880–1882: Plate 33]
Length about 60 μm, with second inner funnel. On legs of *Gammarus* off Jersey.
   Corliss (1979) lists 45 genera of Chonotrichida, half with more than one species. Kahl (1935) illustrates 19 species.

Order Rhynchodida

21 ANCISTROCOMIDAE
Mostly on gills or mantle epithelium of molluscs, attached by anterior sucking tube. Pyriform or more elongated. Well-ciliated, except mid-dorsally and posteriorly.

Ancistrocoma pelseneeri Chatton and Lwoff   FIG. 2.7
[KOZLOFF 1946: 189; KHAN 1969: 29]
Length 40–100 μm, 14 kineties. Like fat cucumber, on gills of *Mya*, *Macoma*, etc.
   Fenchel (1965a) gives details of 15 species from 11 of 25 rhynchodid genera listed by Corliss (1979), including two Sphenophryidae. The latter lose cilia as adults, but may fall so abundantly from *Cardium* gills that some of the banana-shaped cells are likely to be bearing ciliated buds, which drag them about.

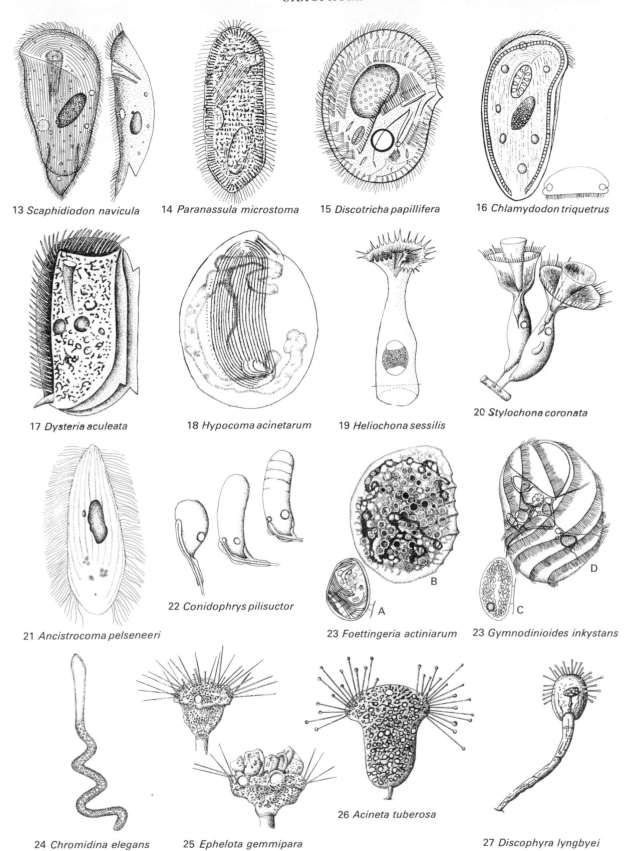

13 *Scaphidiodon navicula*

14 *Paranassula microstoma*

15 *Discotricha papillifera*

16 *Chlamydodon triquetrus*

17 *Dysteria aculeata*

18 *Hypocoma acinetarum*

19 *Heliochona sessilis*

20 *Stylochona coronata*

21 *Ancistrocoma pelseneeri*

22 *Conidophrys pilisuctor*

23 *Foettingeria actiniarum*

23 *Gymnodinioides inkystans*

24 *Chromidina elegans*

25 *Ephelota gemmipara*

26 *Acineta tuberosa*

27 *Discophyra lyngbyei*

Fig. 2.7

Order **Apostomatida**

Suborder **Pilisuctorina**

22 CONIDOPHRYIDAE

Ectoparasites on Crustacea. *Conidophrys* impales itself on host seta, from which it sucks nourishment.

Conidophrys pilisuctor Chatton and Lwoff   FIG. 2.7
[CHATTON AND LWOFF 1935: 697, FENCHEL 1965*b*: 298]
Cylindrical unciliated mature stage, length 20–30 μm, divides into smaller parts (tomites) each of which develops cilia, swims off, finds another crustacean seta, loses cilia, and starts growing. Found on amphipods and isopods, e.g. *Gammarus*, *Idotea*.

Suborder **Apostomatina**

23 FOETTINGERIIDAE

Mouth small, absent in some stages. Kineties in widely spaced spirals. Many genera, mostly with single species.

Foettingeria actiniarum Claparède   FIG. 2.7
[CHATTON AND LWOFF 1935: 309]
Up to 400 μm across, with nine kineties and mouth on flattened ventral surface, common in coelenteron of actinians. Adult moves to outside of host, encysts and divides into tomites, each of which emerges and swims away, to form another cyst (Fig. A) attached to *Gammarus* or *Caprella*. This hatches when host is eaten by actinian and starts to grow. Figure B is of this stage, fixed and stained to show branching macronucleus, and also showing most of the kineties in profile along one side. In larger specimens the kineties elongate and form spirals, so there appear to be more than nine.

Gymnodinioides inkystans Minkiewicz   FIG. 2.7
[CHATTON AND LWOFF 1935: 34; FENCHEL 1965b: 298]
Encysts (Fig. C) on gills of *Pagurus* or pleopods of *Gammarus*. Hatches when host moults and feeds on exuvial fluids within cast skin, growing rapidly. Figure D shows size and organization 29 h after hatching. When full-grown forms a mucus cyst within which it divides repeatedly to form folded chain of up to 64 tomites. Each of these swims off to find new crustacean host, without intervention by actinian.

Suborder **Astomatophorina**

24 OPALINOPSIDAE

Mouth absent. Kineties spiralled. Vermiform, attached to host tissue by anterior end, strobilating tomites posteriorly.

Chromidina elegans (Foettinger)   FIG. 2.7
[CHATTON AND LWOFF 1935: 405]
Length 30–1200 μm. In kidney of *Sepia elegans*. Mediterranean.

Subclass **Suctoria**

Order **Suctorida**

Suborder **Exogenina**

25 EPHELOTIDAE

Large epibionts, with dimorphic tentacles, producing multiple larvae synchronously. Most of 11 families with exogenous budding produce them singly.

Ephelota gemmipara Hertwig   FIG. 2.7
[KAHL 1934: 203]
Body 220–250 μm across, on stalk 1500 μm long, with long pointed tentacles arranged around a mid-distal group of short suctorial tentacles. Tentacles are mostly lost during budding (see second figure). Often abundant, especially on *Obelia* in tide pools.

Suborder **Endogenina**

26 ACINETIDAE

Many loricate, mostly stalked epibionts. The three other families of Endogenina lack stalks.

Acineta tuberosa Ehrenberg   FIG. 2.7
[KAHL 1934: 209]
Lorica thin and inconspicuous, because filled by body. Length 50–100 μm, including short stalk. Capitate tentacles in two or three bundles. On algae, hydrozoans, bryozoans, etc.
    Many other genera and species.

Suborder **Evaginogenina**

27 DISCOPHRYIDAE

Largest and most marine of four families with evaginative budding. Simple, sometimes stalked, rarely loricate.

Discophrya lyngbyei Ehrenberg   FIG. 2.7
[KAHL 1934: 206 (as *Corynophrya*)]
About 50 μm across, non-loricate, stalked, with tentacles not in bundles. On algae and hydroids. Several species.

Class **Oligohymenophorea**

Subclass **Hymenostomatia**

Order **Hymenostomatida**

28 FRONTONIIDAE

Mouth in anterior third of body. Of 14 families in this order only this and the Ichthyophthiridae (fish parasites) have marine species.

Frontonia marina Fabre-Domergue   FIG. 2.8
[KAHL 1931: 319; DRAGESCO 1960: 263]
Length 185–500 μm, with long postoral and preoral sutures (lines where kineties converge), ovoid macronucleus, one to four micronuclei, one contractile vacuole.
    Several species in sand (Dragesco 1960), one commensal in pharynx of Mediterranean *Amphioxus* (Kahl 1931: 320).

Order **Scuticociliatida**

Suborder **Philasterina**

29 URONEMATIDAE

Bald apex distinguishes these from 11 other families in this suborder, several of which have a long caudal cilium. Most Philasterina are marine. Like the first *Philaster*, several Philasteridae (family not included here) are histophagous and associated with echinoderms, molluscs, sponges, etc.

Uronema marinum Dujardin   FIG. 2.8
[KAHL 1931: 356]
Length 30–50 μm, with about 15 kineties. Mouth near equator, with paroral membrane distinct but not projecting far. Macronucleus rounded, one micronucleus. Posterior contractile vacuole and long caudal cilium are often seen in scuticociliates.

30 CINETOCHILIDAE

Small, flattened, ciliated only ventrally and sparsely, with one or more caudal cilia. Mostly freshwater.

Platynematum denticulatum Kahl   FIG. 2.8
[KAHL 1935: 833]
Length 50–60 μm, with caudal cilium and a few (variable) teeth near mouth and posteriorly.
   In sand at Kiel and probably Helgoland.

Suborder **Pleuronematina**

31 PLEURONEMATIDAE

With paroral membrane projecting and curling around subequatorial mouth. Mostly with several long stiff caudal cilia. Three genera.

Pleuronema coronatum Kent   FIG. 2.8
[DRAGESCO 1960: 272]
Length 70–90 μm with 40 kineties. Macronucleus ovoid, one micronucleus. One posterior contractile vacuole.

32 CYCLIDIIDAE

Small, ovoid, sparsely ciliated, often with bald apex. Paroral membrane not quite as prominent as above, and mouth often more anterior. Mostly with one long caudal cilium. Four genera.

Cyclidium glaucoma Müller   FIG. 2.8
[KAHL 1931: 376]
Length 25–30 μm. Mouth equatorial. From sand on Drake's Island, Plymouth, and also in plankton. A few other marine and many freshwater species (Kahl 1931).

33 PENICULISTOMATIDAE

Laterally flattened, reniform, mouth in ventral margin with typical hymenostome ciliature (species below is therefore separated from freshwater Conchophthiridae which have reduced oral ciliature). Commensal in bivalves and echinoids.

Peniculistoma mytili (DeMorgan)   FIG. 2.8
[FENCHEL 1965a: 81]
Length 110–176 μm. Large macronucleus, two or three micronuclei. Posterior contractile vacuole.
   Abundant in mantle cavity of large *Mytilus*.

Suborder **Thigmotrichina**

34 ANCISTRIDAE

Thigmotactic ciliature not distinct from other somatic kineties. Mouth near or at posterior end, but paroral membrane runs ventrally nearly length of body. Eleven genera, with molluscs and a holothurian.

Ancistrum mytili (Quennerstedt)   FIG. 2.8
[FENCHEL 1965a): 99]
Flattened, ovoid. Length 60–90 μm. Right side convex and left concave with 13–16 and 25–28 kineties, respectively. Left side is viewed in figure (Fig. 2.8). Macronucleus sausage-shaped, one micronucleus.
   Abundant in mantle cavity of *Mytilus*. Fenchel (1965a) describes many other ancistrids, most of which are more tapering anteriorly, but *Protophrya ovicola* Kofoid, abundant with *Littorina*, is more oval.

35 HEMISPEIRIDAE

Mouth posterior. *Ancistrospira* and *Plagiospira* are with bivalves and like Ancistridae, but with distinct thigmotactic kineties confined to anterior half of body on dorsal side. In *Hemispeira* this trend goes further.

Hemispeira antedonis (Cuenot)   FIG. 2.8
[FENCHEL 1965a: 110]
Length about 30 μm, laterally flattened, figured here from left side. Cilia of paroral membrane form a long distal fringe. Thigmotactic kineties form a close-set apical field (here basal).
   On *Antedon*, especially in corners between arms and pinnules.

Order **Astomatida**

36 BUETSCHLIELLIDAE

Found in polychaetes, so probably the most marine of 11 astome families, the others occurring mainly in freshwater and land hosts (e.g. Clitellata and molluscs).

Anoplophryopsis ovata de Puytorac   FIG. 2.8
[DE PUYTORAC 1954: Fig. 59]
Length 105–160 μm, with rod-like macronucleus almost as long, one micronucleus, about three contractile vacuoles in a row and 67 kineties.
   In *Lysidice ninnetta* dredged near Ile d'Oleron.

Subclass **Peritrichia**

Order **Peritrichida**

Suborder **Sessilina**

37 VORTICELLIDAE

With contractile stalks. Often epibiont. Eleven genera, mostly with one or few species. Only *Vorticella* and *Haplocaulus* are non-colonial.

Vorticella nebulifera Müller   FIG. 2.8
[KAHL 1935: 736]
Body 50–60 μm long, stalk much longer, spiralling on contraction. Macronucleus strap-shaped. Transverse striations on body separate this from *Vorticella patellina* Müller, and the three-cornered profile from *Vorticella marina* Greef, which has body more rounded, with a constriction behind peristome. Kahl's (1935) keys include over 30 marine *Vorticella* species, and many other peritrichs.

Attached to algae etc. Helgoland, Plymouth.

Zoothamnium alternans Claparède and Lachmann
[KAHL 1935: 748]   FIG. 2.8
Length of zooids about 50 μm, of whole colony several mm. Instant contraction of whole colony characterizes genus, small zooids and branching pattern this species.

Epizoic on *Cancer pagurus* etc.

38 EPISTYLIDAE

With non-contractile stalks. Mostly epibiont. Five genera. Mostly freshwater species.

Epistylis gammari Precht   FIG. 2.8
[FENCHEL 1965b: 285]
Length of zooids about 60 μm, of colony up to 600 μm. On *Gammarus oceanicus* from Oresund, always on antennae. Several other peritrichs occur on *Gammarus*.

39 SCYPHIDIIDAE

Without stalk, mostly epibiont, attached to substratum by disc. Five genera.

Scyphidia patellae Cuenot   FIG. 2.8
[KAHL 1935: 670]
Length 30–45 μm, beaker-shaped. On mantle-edge of *Patella vulgata*, northern France.

40 VAGINICOLIDAE

Loricate, solitary, mostly epibiont, with or without stalk. Nine genera.

Pyxicola ligiae Cuenot   FIG. 2.8
[KAHL 1935: 790]
Lorica about 50 μm long, stalk 25 μm. Lorica outline rounded. On gill lamellae of isopod *Ligia oceanica*.

Suborder **Mobilina**

41 LEIOTROCHIDAE

Denticles of basal ring without spikes. Not obviously distinct from Urceolariidae except that *Urceolaria* (common on molluscs and polychaetes) has macronucleus simple and rounded. On molluscs and echinoderms. One genus, few species.

Leiotrocha patellae (Cuenot)   FIG. 2.8
[KAHL 1935: 657; FENCHEL 1965: 129]
Body rounded, 50 μm across. Denticles smooth, spindle-shaped, 12–16 in ring, small figure (Fig. 2.8) shows three of them. Other figures (latero-basal views) show H-shaped macronucleus stained with Feulgen and kinetosomes stained with silver. On 'gill' filaments of *Patella*.

42 TRICHODINIDAE

Denticles with hooked spikes. On echinoderms, polychaetes, molluscs, and fish gills.

Trichodina ophiotricis Fabre-Domergue   FIG. 2.8
[KAHL 1935: 661, as *Cyclochaeta*]
Disc-shaped, 50 μm across. Sausage-shaped macronucleus. Smaller figure shows two of denticles which form basal ring. On *Ophiothrix* from west coast of France.

Class **Polyhymenophorea**

Subclass **Spirotrichia**

Order **Heterotrichida**

Suborder **Heterotrichina**

43 SPIROSTOMIDAE

Elongated. Six genera, mostly freshwater but *Gruberia* is marine. Latter contracts without twisting, unlike *Spirostomum*. *Blepharisma* is not markedly contractile.

Blepharisma clarissimum Anigstein   FIG. 2.9
[KAHL 1932: 447 FENCHEL 1969; 89]
Length 180–400 μm, 7–10 × breadth. Apex pointed and curved, posterior rounded with contractile vacuole. Ciliated uniformly, except that line of membranelles (AZM) extends along left edge of peristome for half body length, i.e. from apex to mouth. Macronucleus a string of 15–50 oval elements throughout most of body. Kahl (1932) describes eight other marine *Blepharisma*.

44 METOPIDAE

With apex twisted. Some with caudal cilia or pointed tail. Six or seven genera, with many species of *Metopus*, but mostly from freshwater.

Metopus contortus Quennerstedt   FIG. 2.9
[KAHL 1932: 417; FENCHEL 1969: 91]
Oval, 100–160 μm long, with oval macronucleus, posterior contractile vacuole and caudal tuft 0.3–0.5 × long as body.

45 CONDYLOSTOMATIDAE

Mostly large, somewhat contractile. Wide buccal cavity faces anteriorly, like scoop. Three genera.

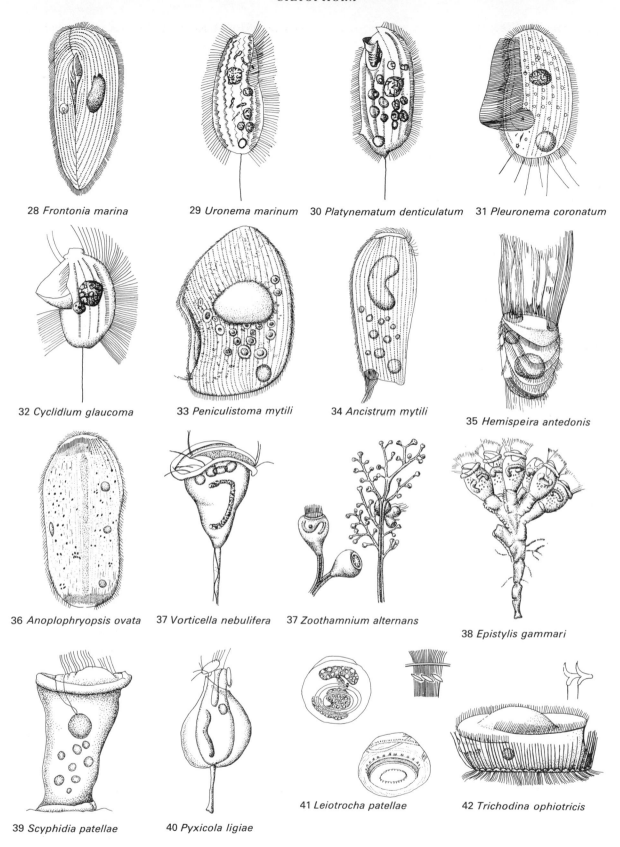

28 *Frontonia marina*

29 *Uronema marinum*

30 *Platynematum denticulatum*

31 *Pleuronema coronatum*

32 *Cyclidium glaucoma*

33 *Peniculistoma mytili*

34 *Ancistrum mytili*

35 *Hemispeira antedonis*

36 *Anoplophryopsis ovata*

37 *Vorticella nebulifera*

37 *Zoothamnium alternans*

38 *Epistylis gammari*

39 *Scyphidia patellae*

40 *Pyxicola ligiae*

41 *Leiotrocha patellae*

42 *Trichodina ophiotricis*

Fig. 2.8

Condylostoma arenarium Spiegel FIG. 2.9
[KAHL 1932: 455]
Length 300–600 µm. About 26 kineties. Macronucleus a string of about 12 beads. Posterior rounded, with contractile vacuole. *Condylostoma tenuis* Faure-Fremiet is full of green symbionts (Dragesco 1963*b*).

46 PERITROMIDAE
Flattened, ciliated only ventrally. Edges and a few dorsal prominences bear small spines. One genus.

Peritromus faurei Kahl FIG. 2.9
[KAHL 1932: 482; FENCHEL 1969: 91]
Oval, length 70–150 µm, with 19–23 kineties. Remarkably contractile. Two oval macronuclei. In Swansea sand with two other species (Wright 1983).

Suborder **Armophorina**

47 CAENOMORPHIDAE
Top-shaped, with spiral AZM encircling body, caudal tuft (or spine) and some apical cilia, but other ciliation reduced. Three genera, mostly freshwater.

Caenomorpha levanderi Kahl FIG. 2.9
[KAHL 1932: 431; FENCHEL 1969: 91]
Length 80–120 µm. Mouth at base of posterior spine. Two rows of cirri anteriorly. Elongated ovoid macronucleus. Marseille harbour; and in sulphide layers of fine sand at Helsingor.

Suborder **Folliculinina**

48 FOLLICULINIDAE
Lorica transparent, attached, bottle-shaped, often epibiont. Body usually blue or green, protruding peristomial wings to feed, withdrawing rapidly on disturbance. Mostly marine, 38 genera each with one or a few species, some with specific substrata, e.g. *Pebrilla paguri* Giard.

Lagotia viridis Wright FIG. 2.9
[DAS 1949: 390, as *Folliculina*]
Body extends to length 400 µm, yellowish green. Peristomial lobes with rounded ends but discrete tips. Lorica about 250 µm long, with mouth tube at right angles to ampulla. On green algae in rock pools.
Kahl (1932), and Das (1949) described other common species. Hadzi (1951) revised nomenclature.

49 LICNOPHORIDAE
Oral and basal ciliary rings at each end of short unciliated body. One genus, several species, mostly marine and epizoic.

Licnophora auerbachi (Cohn) FIG. 2.9
[KAHL 1932: 486]
Length 80–120 µm. Widespread on various hosts (asteroids, ophiuroids, molluscs).

Order **Odontostomatida**

50 EPALXELLIDAE
Small, somewhat compressed laterally. Mouth on left but near edge. Pellicle rigid, often ridged like armour. Ciliation patchy. Three genera, mostly freshwater.

Saprodinium halophilum Kahl FIG. 2.9
[KAHL 1932: 527; FENCHEL 1969: 91]
Size 40–50 µm. Genus mostly has terminal thorns on posterior teeth, but this species has left teeth often lacking thorns, and on right (Fig. 2.9, upper figure) only one posterior tooth which bears a short thorn. In sulphide sands only.

Order **Oligotrichida**
Suborder **Oligotrichina**

51 STROMBIDIIDAE
Top-like, with AZM forming incomplete apical circle. Most of body unciliated. Rarely loricate. Mostly planktonic and marine. Four genera. Many species of *Strombidium*.

Strombidium sauerbreyae Kahl FIG. 2.9
[KAHL 1932: 497; FAURÉ-FREMIET 1950]
Length 80–100 µm, flattened dorsoventrally. AZM curves back to equator and two thigmotactic cirri arise on left of mouth. One of several sand species.

Suborder **Tintinnina**

52 CODONELLIDAE
With a tubular or cup-shaped lorica which may include agglutinated particles. Body top-like, with AZM forming apical circle. Nearly all planktonic, predominantly marine. Perhaps most neritic of 13 families in suborder.

Tintinnopsis beroidea Stein FIG. 2.9
[MARSHALL 1969: 6]
Lorica cylindrical, 34–100 × 18–36 µm, bluntly pointed or rounded aborally. Planktonic, but also in sand at Drake's Island, Plymouth (Lackey and Lackey 1963) with a few other 'tintinnids'.

Order **Hypotrichida**
Suborder **Stichotrichina**

53 STRONGYLIDIIDAE
Mostly elongated, with few spiralled rows of ventral cirri. Three genera. Few marine species.

Urostrongylum caudatum Kahl FIG. 2.9
[KAHL 1932: 556; FENCHEL 1969: 91]
Length 100–250 µm. 'Tail' a narrow extension of left side of body. Great length of anterior membranelles should distinguish from *Epiclintes ambiguus* (Müller) (Kahl 1932: 569).

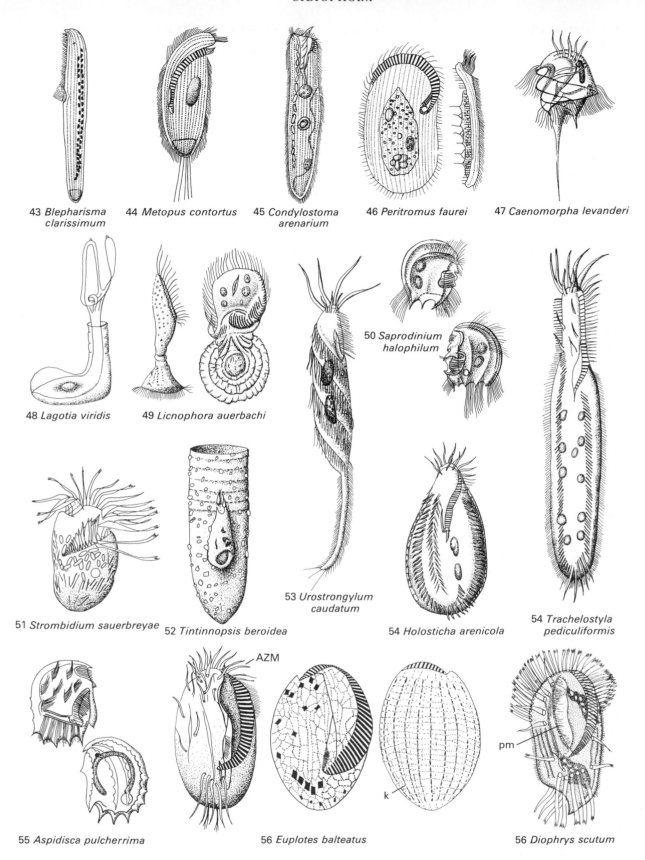

43 *Blepharisma clarissimum*

44 *Metopus contortus*

45 *Condylostoma arenarium*

46 *Peritromus faurei*

47 *Caenomorpha levanderi*

48 *Lagotia viridis*

49 *Licnophora auerbachi*

50 *Saprodinium halophilum*

51 *Strombidium sauerbreyae*

52 *Tintinnopsis beroidea*

53 *Urostrongylum caudatum*

54 *Holosticha arenicola*

54 *Trachelostyla pediculiformis*

55 *Aspidisca pulcherrima*

56 *Euplotes balteatus*

56 *Diophrys scutum*

Fig. 2.9

54 HOLOSTICHIDAE

Ventral cirri in right and left marginal rows, usually with various numbers of rows in between, two in *Holosticha*, one or two in *Keronopsis*, none in *Trachelostyla*, one in *Amphisiella* (Dragesco 1963*b*). Both *Holosticha* and *Trachelostyla* have several marine species (Kahl 1932).

Holosticha arenicola Kahl   FIG. 2.9
[KAHL 1932: 583; FENCHEL 1969: 89]

Length 70–100 *μ*m, ovoid, or slimmer and more rectangular. Two macro- and two micronuclei. Transverse row of 7–10 enlarged cirri at posterior end. Frontal cirri (three) enlarged and distinct from anterior cirri of central rows (not so in *Keronopsis*).

Trachelostyla pediculiformis (Cohn)   FIG. 2.9
[KAHL 1932: 596; FENCHEL 1969: 89]

Length 100–250 *μ*m, peristomial region particularly elongated and thin. Numerous macro- and two micronuclei. Transverse cirri five. Several frontal cirri. In *Trachelostyla caudata* Kahl (1932: 597) the posterior region too is elongated.

Suborder **Sporadotrichina**

55 ASPIDISCIDAE

Small, flattened. Dorsal side without cilia, often ribbed like armour. AZM not projecting beyond body margins, mostly covered by transparent fold from right of peristome. Few genera. Several marine species.

Aspidisca pulcherrima Kahl   FIG. 2.9
[KAHL 1932: 648]

Length 60–70 *μ*m. Transverse cirri six, frontals seven, as in most related species. Dorsal side (right figure) with four toothed ribs. Hind margin bears five teeth, lacking in other *Aspidisca*.

56 EUPLOTIDAE

Anterior membranelles of AZM enlarged to form conspicuous projecting fringe. Dorsal side with low ribs and sparse ciliation. Seven genera, predominantly marine.

Euplotes balteatus (Dujardin)   FIG. 2.9
[KAHL 1932: 635; WRIGHT 1983: 207]

About 80 *μ*m long, oval. Left figure views cirri and membranelles ventrally. Others show ventral and dorsal patterns of silver staining (see introduction). Ten fronto-ventral and five transverse cirri are typical of genus.

Diophrys scutum Dujardin   FIG. 2.9
[KAHL 1932: 624; DRAGESCO 1963*b*: 266]

Length 150–200 *μ*m. Genus has three 'rudder-cirri' arising marginally, behind and to right of transverse five.

3 PORIFERA

THE **Porifera** or Sponges are sedentary, aquatic, fundamentally radially symmetrical invertebrates. They possess a minimal diversity of cells and the simplest grade of metazoan organization (Hyman 1940; Brien 1973; Bergquist 1978). They are filter feeders characterized by an internal monolayer of flagellated *choanocytes* collectively circulating one or more unidirectional water streams through the *aquiferous system*, a network of pores, canals, and chambers perforating the body.

The group is also notable among the larger macroscopic phyla for being particularly difficult to identify at the species level. The 5000 or so Recent species are categorized into four classes, principally according to the composition and structure of the skeletal elements:

The exclusively marine **Calcarea** possess a skeleton of calcium carbonate spicules. The group presents considerable taxonomic difficulties at all levels (Burton 1963), and only a few of the better understood species are included in this guide.

The **Hexactinellida** possess a skeleton of six-rayed spicules. They typically occur in very deep marine waters; there are no records for coastal shelf waters around the British Isles.

The **Demospongiae** represent some 95% of the global sponge fauna and include the only freshwater species. Almost all possess a skeleton of siliceous spicules, which are either *monaxons* (single-rayed) or *tetraxons* (four-rayed) (Fig. 3.1). This is sometimes supplemented or entirely replaced by an organic, *collagenous* skeleton of flexible *spongin* fibres. A few species are without a skeleton.

The **Sclerospongiae** is a small marine group characterized by a massive calcareous skeleton. There are no known British representatives.

Sponge organization is graded in complexity (Fig. 3.1). The simplest, most primitive scheme is the *asconoid* arrangement. The body consists of one or more simple, thin walled, tubular units, each with a central cavity opening apically as a single, exhalant *osculum*. Inhalant canals lined by specialized *pinacocytes* bridge the *mesohyl* between the *pinacoderm* and the *choanoderm* (Fig. 3.1). The choanoderm lines the cavity as a simple layer. The asconoid arrangement occurs in the *olynthus*, the post-settlement phase of calcareous sponges, and also in the adults of the Leucosoleniidae.

The *syconoid* organization entails a folding of the sponge wall, with the choanoderm localized to lining side chambers arising from a central cavity. These interdigitate with cavities lined by pinacoderm, extending from the outside of the sponge. The result is that the mesohyl is significantly thicker than in asconoid sponges. In addition to examples from the Calcarea such as *Sycon*, this condition is also portrayed by *Plakina*

monolopha, which is a member of the Demospongiae (Brien 1973).

The most advanced and complex organization, the *leuconoid* arrangement, entails a further annexation of the choanoderm into discrete *chambers*. Each is fed from *incurrent canals*, passing from incurrent pores, the *ostia*, and entering the chamber through pores, the *prosopyles*. Water exits via a single *apopyle* leading to an *excurrent canal*. Tributary excurrent canals coalesce with others, ultimately converging on one or more excurrent apertures or *oscula*. The aquiferous system of a leuconoid sponge can be very complex, and is often accompanied by a considerable thickening of the mesohyl, and in many cases, a loss of the radial symmetry shown by asconoid and syconoid sponges. The leuconoid condition is encountered in many Calcarea, e.g. *Leuconia*, as well as in virtually all other sponges.

In British waters, sponges frequently occur alongside hydroids, colonial anthozoans, bryozoans, and ascidians. By evolutionary convergence, these groups have acquired common growth patterns and gross forms. It can be easy at first sight to confuse sponges with some members of these other groups. Growth occurs along growing fronts in encrusting sponges, at terminal points in arborescent forms, and more generally across the surface of massive, mound forms. Growth is often indeterminate in that there is no definitive maximum size, the ultimate size being governed by external agents such as the hydraulic stresses of water motion, by predation, or disease. Growth often involves the repetitive addition of units or individuals of a standard template, but these are not so rigidly defined as the polyps and zooids of the other colonial phyla. An advantage of such a *modular* growth scheme is a high capacity for survival in terms of the regeneration of partly damaged sponges. It is believed that for many sponges, in the short-term, colonization by growth is more important than that by sexual reproduction and that some clones may persist for hundreds of years.

With regards to sexual reproduction, individual sponges are usually hermaphroditic, but not necessarily simultaneously. Amoeboid cells of the mesohyl develop into gametes. Spermatozoa are released from, and enter the sponge via the aquiferous system. Fertilization and embryogenesis are internal within the mesohyl. Short-lived, lecithotrophic, ciliated larvae are released, again via the aquiferous system, and metamorphosis follows settlement. Growth and reproduction are seasonally programmed. In common with freshwater sponges, some marine examples produce gemmules which facilitate overwintering, although most species are evident as a year round feature.

In total 70 species, representing 32 families of the Calcarea and Demospongiae are included in this guide. This constitutes

Sponge organization

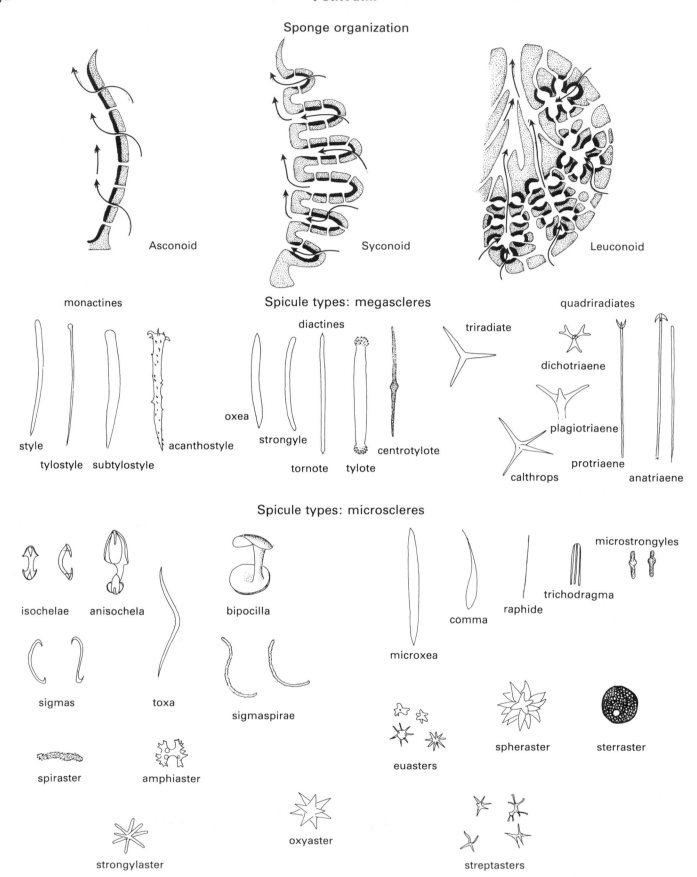

Asconoid   Syconoid   Leuconoid

Spicule types: megascleres

monactines

diactines

triradiate

quadriradiates

dichotriaene

oxea

plagiotriaene

style

strongyle

tylostyle   subtylostyle

acanthostyle

tornote   tylote

centrotylote

protriaene

calthrops

anatriaene

Spicule types: microscleres

microstrongyles

isochelae   anisochela

bipocilla

comma

raphide

trichodragma

microxea

sigmas   toxa

sigmaspirae

spheraster   sterraster

euasters

spiraster   amphiaster

strongylaster

oxyaster

streptasters

Fig. 3.1

approximately one-third of the British continental shelf sponge fauna. The species included are those considered to be the most common species, together with some particularly distinctive rarer ones.

CRITERIA USED IN IDENTIFICATION

Sponge taxonomy is founded on the form and occurrence of different spicule types. However, whereas many species can be identified according to spicules alone, others cannot and require an integrated approach involving a range of criteria. Problems are frequently exacerbated by an often considerable intraspecific variability in characteristics.

Gross form can be a useful character in the case of species having specific forms, e.g. spheres, funnels, or arborescent patterns. Other species are highly variable, or share very common forms, e.g. encrusting patches or sheets, or irregularly massive mounds or plates. Yet others have combined forms, e.g. encrusting sheets bearing erect papillae or fronds.

In view of the capacity for indeterminate growth shown by many species, maximum size values are of only limited use and those specified in this guide should not be regarded as being definitive.

Surface morphology can be very helpful since it is often more consistent than gross form. Whereas some species are smooth, most are rough in some way, e.g. because of cratering, papillae, or spines, which are the points of spicules projecting through the sponge surface.

The occurrence of visible pores can be useful. Whereas inhalant pores are usually invisible to the naked eye, the oscula are often visible. They may be small or large in number, scattered or grouped; armoured with spines or simple; flush with the surface or raised upon papillae or chimneys.

The consistency of the sponge can also be useful. Some species are characteristically either delicate or firm, although most fall between the two extremes. The skeletal composition has the major bearing on consistency, species with dense-packed spicules being particularly firm, and those with a high content of spongin fibres often being delicate.

Some sponges produce significant quantities of mucus, the exudation of which from collected specimens can be very noticeable, particularly if there is damage. Many sponges undergo some degree of gross contraction when removed from water. This may result in a considerable reduction in size, a much firmer consistency, and surface changes such as the closure of oscula.

Sponges are among the most colourful of invertebrates, in life being dominated by browns, oranges, reds, and yellows; and occasionally vivid white, blues, and even black. In a few cases, the colour is sufficiently unusual and consistent to serve as a good diagnostic character. However, a wide range of colour variants usually occurs. The presence of endosymbiotic algae can also tint or even transform the gross colour, e.g. by imparting green, blue, yellow, or red hues.

Many sponges produce and accumulate secondary metabolites such as alkaloids or terpenoids. Many of these substances are toxic, in some cases acutely so, serving defensive roles against infection, overgrowth, or predation. The more volatile of these substances can combine to generate characteristically strong and distinctive aromatic odours, but which can be difficult to describe in the absence of more familiar equivalents. Biochemical analysis has revealed that secondary metabolites can, individually or in combination, be species specific. The clear potential of this as a form of biochemical fingerprinting for taxonomic purposes has been examined by Bergquist and Wells (1983).

Also with potential is the use of gel electrophoresis in the determination of genetic differences between species. This technique has been applied to British species of *Suberites* by Solé-Cava and Thorpe (1986).

However, still the most important character for the determination of species is the structure of the skeleton. In many species, different spicule types are localized and ordered, e.g. radially, whereas in others, the arrangement is more random. In some species, the sponge body is distinctly divided into an *ectosome*, or skin, and a *choanosome*. Species containing spongin fibres but no spicules also often exhibit distinctive structuring of the fibres.

In most Demospongiae, as opposed to the Calcarea, the spicules are categorized by size into megasleres and microscleres (Fig. 3.1). There is very considerable variation in form, and some variants, restricted to particular families, have specific names. However, most spicules fall into one of the general categories shown in Fig. 3.1. Those of the Calcarea, and the megascleres of Demospongiae, are mostly classified according to the number of axes and points they possess, e.g. monaxons can be either *monoactines* or *diactines*, according to the number of points. Thereafter, the classification is according to the form of the ends, whether any swellings occur, or whether the surface is thorny or otherwise. Within each category of spicule there can be considerable inter- and intraspecific variation in form, e.g. the shape and curvature of the shaft, the point, any swellings, and the distribution of thorns. Still greater diversity is encountered in the microscleres. The range of spicules known for each species is described in this guide, but size ranges, which can vary considerably, are only included in the absence of reliable alternatives for identification.

With reference to ecological characteristics, marine sponges are most widespread in shallow sublittoral waters, but some species are characteristic of shaded areas on the lower shore. Essentially sublittoral species can occur intertidally, but are confined to exceptionally well-shaded crevices and caves. In the absence of comprehensive data, vertical distribution is very difficult to specify for most species. Whereas the littoral and shallow sublittoral distribution of species is quite well known, beyond the regular diving depths, i.e. 30–40 m, data are far more limited. Since few species are definitively depth zoned within the 0–40 m depth range, and the distinction between truly sublittoral and littoral species is not clear, depth range is not considered a particularly useful character for identification purposes.

Most sponges are typically epilithic, although many are equally able to colonize artificial materials such as concrete or fibreglass. Some species are characteristic of biogenic materials, e.g. macro-algae, the tubes of polychaetes, or mollusc shells. In many localities, heavy silting precludes sponges from colonizing upwardly orientated facets. However, certain species are morphologically adapted to tolerate silting, and can commonly occur on such surfaces.

Sponges flourish most prolifically under conditions of strong tide combined with weak wave exposure, e.g. in tidal rapids systems. In such cases, the intrinsic *active* filtration system is sometimes supplemented by extrinsically induced *passive* filtration. Massive forms characteristic of strong currents often degenerate if transferred to weak current conditions. Many species thrive in wave-induced water motion, e.g. in the surge gullies of the shallow sublittoral zone. Although most species are exclusively marine, many extend into estuaries and other brackish waters.

Geographical distributions and frequencies of occurrence or abundance are very difficult to specify in the absence of comprehensive information for the British coasts. Therefore geographical localization cannot be reliably used as an aid to identification.

IDENTIFICATION

Ideally, the true form and colour of the species when alive, *in situ*, and submerged should be recorded by divers using an underwater camera with electronic flash and colour transparency film. The photographs should show the gross form, the dimensions, the surface detail and the colour. Many species substantially alter their appearance once they are collected because of contraction, and may not fully recover their natural state even if resubmerged. Few thrive in aquaria, most rapidly deteriorate, although they may persist in a diminished, atypical form for many months. The existence of a noticeable odour or of mucus in the freshly collected sponge should be recorded.

It is important to take a sufficiently large sample to portray surface characteristics, skeletal structure, and to provide adequate quantities of spicules and spongin for analysis, i.e. the whole sponge in the case of small forms, or a substantial scraping in the case of encrusting forms, removal with the substrate being advised for very thin encrusters. In view of the regenerative capacity of sponges, the removal of part of a sponge will not usually kill the remainder, and this is the only practical solution for the sampling of very large forms. Collected sponges should be placed in rigid containers to avoid crushing.

Whereas gross form and the skeletal elements can be retained by drying the sponge, surface form and colour are lost. Surface characteristics may even change, e.g. smooth surfaces in life can become spiny when dried as internal spicules rupture through. Preservation should be undertaken very soon after collection. Formalin is a good short-term preservative for all sponges, and a good long-term preservative for Demospongiae. It preserves form and certainly colour better than ethanol. However, because of its tendency to decalcify, it is not suitable for Calcarea beyond a very few days. Seventy per cent ethanol is the safe long-term preservative for all sponges, but this usually quickly leaches out

or changes the natural colour. It also leaches out toxins which some sponges produce, and although hazards are undocumented, skin contact with ethanol extracts should be avoided. For the same reason, the tongue testing of sponges for taste or surface texture should not be undertaken.

Although not generally required by this key, should the examination of the skeletal structure be desired, thick sections of the sponge should be made along the appropriate axis using a razor blade, the disposition of spicules or spongin fibres being examined by means of a low-power compound microscope ($\times$ 100). To analyse the form of spicules or spongin fibres, the sponge tissue must be digested out. Small cubes of sponge representing all sections from the surface to the interior should be submerged in a digesting agent. If it is not clear whether the specimen is a calcareous sponge or not, this can be established by immersing a sub-sample in dilute hydrochloric acid, in which calcareous spicules would dissolve. The best all-round agent for spicule extraction is sodium hypochlorite or any household bleach containing this substance. Whereas some species digest very quickly, others may take 12 h, and some will not digest, but will break down when boiled in nitric acid (not for calcareous sponges). The third option is to use an enzyme such as pepsin or trypsin (Fry and Gray, 1987). It is important to note that if a framework of spongin fibres exists, it may partially or completely disintegrate when exposed to digesting agents. Once digested, the dissolved materials should be washed out with several changes of water, always allowing sufficient time for the tiny microscleres, as well as the larger megascleres, to settle down before decanting. Temporary aqueous mounts can be examined microscopically; for permanent mounts the spicules should be dehydrated through alcohols and mounted in an appropriate agent, although because of closer refractive indices, detail may be less clear in permanent as opposed to temporary mounts. For examination, magnifications of $\times$ 100 to $\times$ 1000 are required, the latter for some microscleres. Scanning electron microscopy is a very effective way of examining fine detail on spicules, but not for routine identification. Usually the combination of spicules present, and the detailed structure of some of these, should be sufficient for determination; however, sizes are important in some cases, and appropriate ranges of these are provided in the key where necessary. Usually the dominant spicule types are immediately apparent, but rarer types may be much more difficult to see. It is important to note that some sponges do incorporate spicules released from their neighbours into their own bodies.

LITERATURE

Substantial reviews of the biology and ecology of the Porifera have been provided by Hyman (1940), Brien (1973) and Bergquist (1978). The most detailed of these, which also provides most coverage of the European fauna is that of Brien (1973), who with Bergquist (1978) and Hartman (1982), provide comprehensive systematic classifications covering all sponges. The classification scheme down to the family level and much of the terminology used in this key is largely in accordance with the scheme presented in Bergquist (1978).

Much of what is known of the British sponge fauna today is the result of studies undertaken during the last century; early monographs applying to the British fauna were prepared by Johnston (1842), Bowerbank (1864, 1866, 1874, 1882), and Topsent (1894, 1896, 1900). The monographs of Bowerbank are still the most comprehensive works specifically referring to the British Isles. However, Arndt (1935) produced an important work, in German, covering north-west coasts of Europe, with detailed descriptions and illustrations of spicules for virtually all known British species, citing previous references, and covering known geographical distributions. British sponge taxonomy has changed little since that time, and much of the information provided for individual species in this guide is derived from this work, which should be referred to if further information is required. Synonyms are only provided in this guide if the name differs from that used by Arndt. For the Calcarea, the systematics of which are still under review, Burton (1963) prepared a major monograph covering all species known globally, including those found in Britain. An important current development is the Sponge Guide of the Marine Conservation Society in Britain (Ackers *et al.* 1985). Now in its fourth version, this working guide is the product of the collation of field data on the form, habitat, and geographical distribution of species, presented alongside detailed descriptions and underwater colour photographs of the live sponges.

The majority of sponge illustrations featured in this guide have been prepared from original underwater photographs. Others are based on the illustrations of Bowerbank (1874, 1882) and in some cases, the illustrations of Vosmaer (1931–35) and photographs featured in Ackers *et al.* (1985). Most spicule illustrations are after Arndt (1935).

Further useful literature is included in the following bibliography.

Ackers, R. G., Moss, D., Picton, B. E., and Stone, S. M. K. (1985). *Sponges of the British Isles* (4th edn). Marine Conservation Society, Ross-on-Wye.

Arndt, W. (1935). Porifera. *Tierwelt der Nord-und Ostsee*. Teil 3a, pp. 1–140, Leipzig.

Bergquist, P. R. (1978). *Sponges*. Hutchinson, London.

Bergquist, P. R. and Wells, R. J. (1983). *Marine natural products* 4, (ed. P. J. Scheuer). Academic Press, New York, pp. 1–50.

Bowerbank, J. S. (1864). *A monograph of the British Spongiadae*, I. Ray Society, London.

Bowerbank, J. S. (1866). *A monograph of the British Spongiadae*, II. Ray Society, London.

Bowerbank, J. S. (1874). *A monograph of the British Spongiadae*, III. Ray Society, London.

Bowerbank, J. S. (1882). *A monograph of the British Spongiadae*, IV. Ray Society, London.

Brien, P., Lévi, C., Sarà, M., Tuzet, O., and Vacelet, J. (1973). Spongiaires. *Traité de Zoologie*, **III**, 1–716.

Burton, M. (1963). *A revision of the classification of the calcareous sponges*. British Museum (Natural History), London.

Fry, W. G. (ed) (1970). *The biology of the Porifera*. Academic Press, London.

Fry, P. D. and Gray, D. (1987). An enzymatic technique for the separation of spicules from alcohol-preserved sponge tissue. pp 93–99. In *Taxonomy of Porifera*, (ed. J. Vacelet and N. Boury-Esnault). Springer-Verlag, Berlin.

Harrison, F. W. and Cowden, R. R. (eds.) (1976). *Aspects of sponge biology*. Academic Press, New York.

Hartman, W. D. (1982). *Porifera*. In: *Synopsis and classification of living organisms* 1, pp. 641–666 (ed. S. P. Parker). McGraw-Hill, New York, pp. 641–66.

Hiscock, K., Stone, S. M. K., and George, J. D. (1984). The Marine Fauna of Lundy. Porifera (Sponges): a preliminary study. *Annual Report of the Lundy Field Society*, 34, 16–35.

Hyman, L. H. (1940). *The invertebrates: Protozoa through Ctenophora*. McGraw-Hill, New York.

Johnston, G. (1842). *A history of British sponges and lithophytes*. Edinburgh.

Levi, C. and Bourry-Esnault, N. (eds.) (1979). Sponge biology. *Colloques Internationaux du Centre National de la Récherche Scientifique*, No. 291.

Solé-Cava, A. M. and Thorpe, J. P. (1986). Genetic differentiation between morphotypes of the marine sponge *Suberites ficus* (Demospongiae: Hadromerida). *Marine Biology*, 93, 247–53.

Topsent, E. (1894). Étude monographique des Spongiaires de France. 1. Tetractinellida. *Archives de Zoologie Expérimentale et Générale*. Séries 3, **2**, 259–400.

Topsent, E. (1896). Étude monographique des Spongiaires de France. 2. Carnosa. *Archives de Zoologie Expérimental et Générale*. Séries 3, **3**, 493–590.

Topsent, E. (1900). Étude monographique des Spongiaires de France. 3. Monaxonida. *Archives de Zoologie Expérimental et Générale*. Séries 3, 8, 1–331.

Vacelet, J. and Boury-Esnault, N. (eds.) (1987). *Taxonomy of Porifera*. Springer-Verlag, Berlin.

Vosmaer, G. (1931–35). The Sponges of the Bay of Naples. *Capita Zoologica*, 3–5 and 5–1.

KEY TO FAMILIES[1]

1. Spicules wholly calcareous (Class Calcarea)—for further identification of the Calcarea, use the key to species[2] (p. 78)

   Spicules siliceous or absent   **2**

---

2. Spicules absent   **3**

   Spicules numerous   **6**

---

3. No skeleton. Encrusting and pigmented   **4**

   Spongin fibre network, tough and elastic (spongy)   **5**

---

4. Surface lobed and velvety   **5. Oscarellidae**

   Surface very smooth   **32. Halisarcidae**

---

5. Spongin without inclusions   **31. Aplysillidae**

   Spongin full of sand grains   **30. Dysideidae**

---

6. Spicules are all small (<100 μm) and include triaenes   **6. Plakinidae**

   Many spicules are large (>100 μm)   **7**

---

7. Megascleres include tetraxons, microscleres are asters of some kind   **8**

   Spicules not as above   **10**

---

8. Microscleres include sterrasters   **8. Geodiidae**

   No sterrasters present   **9**

---

9. Calthrops absent   **7. Stellettidae**

   Calthrops present   **9. Pachastrellidae**

---

10. Megascleres are triaenes and oxeas, microscleres are sigmaspirae   **10. Tetillidae**

    Spicules not as above   **11**

---

11. Megascleres are calthrops, microscleres include toxas   **9. Pachastrellidae**

    Spicules not as above   **12**

---

12. Megascleres are tylostyles or subtylostyles, usually with at least superficial radial organization   **13**

    Spicule form and arrangement not as above   **16**

---

13. Sponge spherical, showing strong radially symmetrical arrangement of spicules throughout, megascleres very long subtylostyles, microscleres are asters   **14. Tethyidae**

    Not as above   **14**

---

14. Sponge forms a cushion from which arise numerous long papillae, microscleres absent
    12. Polymastiidae

    Not as above
    15

15. Sponge massive or encrusting; microscleres usually absent, but microstrongyles can occur
    11. Suberitidae

    Sponge massive or boring, microscleres include spirasters
    13. Clionidae

16. Without cheloid microscleres
    17

    With cheloid microscleres or, if not, with at least three other microsclere types
    24

17. Skeleton contains axial tracts of substantial spongin fibres, and megascleres which may be monaxons, oxeas, styles, or strongyles; these may be twisted in form. Sponge erect with flexible consistency, surface rough to touch with projecting spicules (Axinellida)
    18

    Not as above
    20

18. Acanthostyles occur, sponge branching
    17. Raspailiidae

    Acanthostyles absent, sponge branching or cup-shaped
    19

19. Very long styles present (some > 1.5 mm), sponge branching
    16. Hemiasterellidae

    Styles not exceptionally long (usually < 1.5 mm), sponge branching or cup-shaped
    15. Axinellidae

20. Acanthostyles occur, or styles with toxas, sponge usually thin encrusting
    25. Crellidae (*Spanioplon*)

    27. Hymedesmiidae (*Hymedesmia brondstedi*)

    29. Clathriidae (several species)[3,4]

    Acanthostyles absent
    21

21. Oxeas, if present, not stout, spongin does not occur as substantial fibres. Spicules without regular arrangement, except at the surface in some species
    22

    Skeleton dominated by stout oxeas with or without substantial quantities of spongin fibre
    23

22. Skeleton principally of slender oxeas, sometimes with styles
    18. Halichondriidae

    Skeleton principally of styles, although oxeas may occur
    19. Hymeniacidonidae

    23. Biemnidae (*Hemimycale columella*)

23. Tangential dermal spicule skeleton occurs, spongin occurs in very small quantities at the spicule joints imparting very delicate consistency to the sponge
    21. Adociidae
    (easily confused with the Haliclonidae)

    Spongin typically evident as heavy fibres imparting a fairly tough but flexible consistency
    20. Haliclonidae
    (easily confused with the Adociidae)

24. Cheloid microscleres absent, sigmas, commas, and other forms do occur   **23. Biemnidae**

    Cheloid microscleres present   **25**

25. Without acanthostyles   **26**

    With acanthostyles   **27**

26. With anisochelae and often a number of other microsclere types   **22. Mycalidae**

    Without anisochelae   **24. Desmacidonidae**

27. With toxas   **29. Clathriidae**

    Without toxas   **28**

28. Sponge mound, massive, or branched in form, often exceeding 20 mm in thickness, with a variety of microscleres   **26. Myxillidae**

    Sponge forming thin (<20 mm) or very thin patches or sheets   **29**

29. Endosomal skeleton includes an array of acanthostyles orientated vertically away from the attachment surface and embedded basally in a layer of spongin fibre

    27. Hymedesmiidae[4].

    Endosomal skeleton of acanthostyles not arranged as above, spongin not present in substantial quantities   **28. Anchinoidae[4].**

NOTES

[1] This key has been developed as a practical aid for the identification of the 70 species included in the guide. It is by no means systematically complete, several families are omitted, and the key may not work for species not included in this guide.

[2] The classification of families within the Calcarea involves criteria other than gross structure or the skeletal elements, for example the larval pattern, which are inappropriate for an identification key. A single key is provided in the species section, covering the eight species from four families that are included in this guide.

[3] This includes members of the Order Poecilosclerida which do not possess chelate microscleres.

[4] These three families are particularly difficult to separate for practical identification purposes.

Class **Calcarea**

Skeleton composed solely of calcareous spicules that are not differentiated by size into megascleres and microscleres. Exclusively marine.

KEY TO SPECIES

1. Sponge composed of delicate, thin-walled tubes (<1 mm diameter)   **2**

    Sponge more substantial and solid   **4**

2. Sponge composed of a mass of tubes forming a tight anastomosing meshwork, tri-actines with rays equal in length   **Clathrina coriacea**

    Sponge composed of a more loose array of mainly erect tubes, triactines with rays unequal in length   **3**

3.	Erect tubes little branched	**Leucosolenia botryoides**
	Erect tubes frequently branched	**Leucosolenia complicata**

4.	Gross shape a flattened sac	**Scypha compressa**
	Not as above	**5**

5.	Gross shape cylindrical or vase-shaped with a single terminal osculum	**6**
	Gross shape encrusting or massive, usually several oscula	**7**

6.	Cylindrical or vase-shaped, fairly sharply tapered terminally, terminal osculum often armoured by a circlet of spines	**Sycon ciliatum**
	Cylindrical or slightly tapering, with a terminal osculum	**Ute ensata**

7.	Surface smooth to touch	**Leuconia nivea**
	Surface distinctly rough to touch	**Leuconia gossei**

Sub-class **Calcinea**

Triactines, if present, have rays that are approximately set at equal angles and are equal in length.

Order **Clathrinida**

The asconoid grade of organization is retained at the adult stage. Therefore, the sponge consists of delicate, thin-walled tubes.

I CLATHRINIDAE

Clathrina coriacea (Montagu)   FIG. 3.2

Sponge consists of a characteristically clathrate or mesh-like, anastomosing mass of simple, delicate tubes. Diameter to 25 mm, thickness to 10 mm. Surface detail sub-microscopic. Oscula not distinct. Colour white. Skeleton typically a mixture of triradiates, quadriradiates and oxeas, but the last may be absent.

Epilithic, cryptic low-littoral, and shallow sublittoral. Common, all coasts.

Sub-class **Calcaronea**

Triactines with rays of unequal length, set at unequal angles.

Order **Leucosolenida**

Asconoid structure occurs throughout life. Sponge composed of very thin tubes.

2 LEUCOSOLENIIDAE

Leucosolenia botryoides (Ellis and Solander)   FIG. 3.2

Sponge composed of an encrusting holdfast of thin tubes, from which arise erect (oscular) and little-branched tubes, each bearing a single, terminal osculum. Sponge clearly visible to the naked eye, often 10 mm in diameter and height. Surface minutely hispid. Consistency very delicate. Colour translucent white. Skeleton includes triradiates and quadriradiates.

Epilithic and epibiotic on algae. Common, all coasts.

Leucosolenia complicata (Montagu)   FIG. 3.2

Sponge composed of a more or less extensive encrusting holdfast of reticulating ascon tubes from which arise erect tubes bearing lateral branches. Erect elements bear terminal oscula. Sponge often diminutive to the naked eye. Surface of tubes minutely hispid. Consistency very delicate. Colour translucent white. Skeleton of triradiates, quadriradiates, and oxeas.

Epilithic and epibiotic on algae and sessile invertebrates. Cryptic low-littoral, sublittoral. Common.

Order **Sycettida**

Syconoid or leuconoid structure, with choanocytes localized to choanocytic chambers.

3 SYCETTIDAE

Sycon ciliatum (Fabricius)   FIG. 3.2

Sponge characteristically cylindrical in form, more or less tapering as a vase. Attached to the substratum at one end, and with a single, terminal osculum at the other, this often being fringed by a circlet of spines. Up to 50 mm in length and 7.5 mm wide. Delicate to firm, but flexible. Colour pure or off-white. Skeleton of triradiates, quadriradiates, and oxeas.

Sponge occurs singly or in clusters on rock or seaweeds, in the cryptic low-littoral, and in the sublittoral. Very common, all coasts.

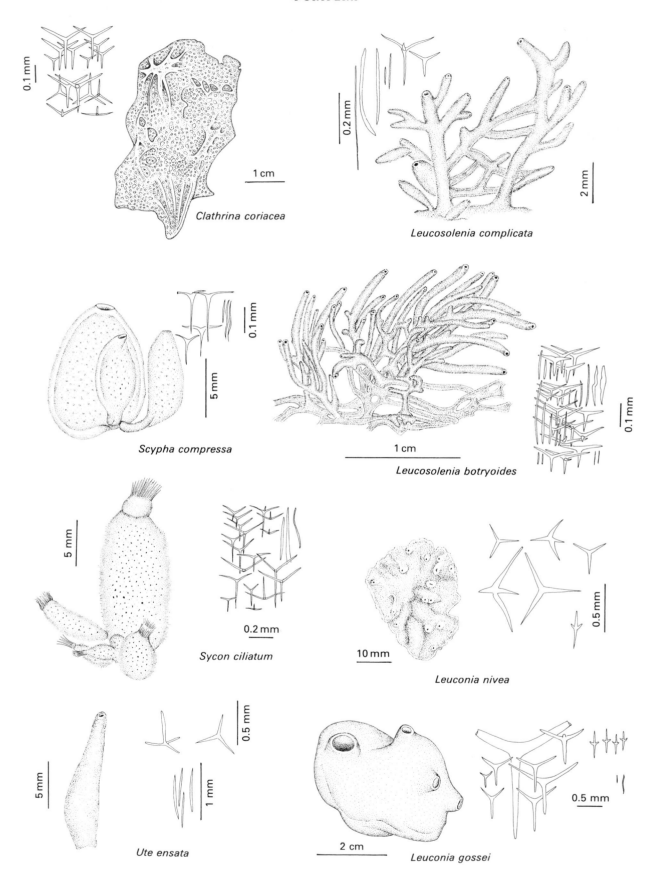

Clathrina coriacea

Leucosolenia complicata

Scypha compressa

Leucosolenia botryoides

Sycon ciliatum

Leuconia nivea

Ute ensata

Leuconia gossei

Fig. 3.2

4 GRANTIIDAE

Scypha (*Grantia*) *compressa* (Fabricius)   FIG. 3.2

Sponge a laterally compressed sac, tapering at both ends, attached basally, and with a single, usually terminal osculum. Typically 10–20 mm high, 5–10 mm wide, and 2.5 mm thick. Surface lightly hispid. Consistency firm but flexible. Colour white or off-white. Skeleton of triradiates, quadriradiates, and oxeas.

Occurs individually or collectively upon rock or seaweeds, in the sublittoral or the lower littoral where it may feature on open surfaces as well as in crevices. Very common, all coasts.

Ute ensata (Bowerbank)   FIG. 3.2

Sponge tubular and elongate, sessile or substipitate with an apical osculum. Even and non-hispid surface. Firm but friable consistency. Colour whitish. Skeleton of triradiates, quadriradiates, and oxeas.

Epilithic, also on stones and shells in the littoral and sublittoral.

Leuconia gossei (Bowerbank)   FIG. 3.2

Encrusting or irregularly massive form, with undulating ridges that can impart a near cerebriform appearance. Surface slightly rough to touch. Oscula naked. Consistency firm. Colour white or off-white. Skeleton of triradiates, quadriradiates, and oxeas.

Epilithic, lower littoral, and sublittoral.

Leuconia gossei (Bowerbank)   FIG. 3.2

Encrusting or irregularly massive form, with undulating ridges that can impart a near cerebriform appearance. Surface slightly rough to touch. Oscula naked. Consistency firm. Colour white or off-white. Skeleton of triradiates, quadriradiates, and oxeas.

Epilithic, lower littoral, and sublittoral.

Class **Demospongiae**

Sponges with siliceous spicules, in many species divisible into megascleres and microscleres. Megascleres are usually monaxons or tetraxons, but are triaxons in one subclass. Hexaxons do not occur. In some cases the skeleton is supplemented, dominated, or may even consist entirely of spongin. In a very few species, the skeleton is absent.

Subclass **Homoscleromorpha**

Spicules often triactines, frequently supplemented by diactines and tetractines. No differentiation into megascleres and microscleres, all spicules being small (<100 μm), and without regional differentiation. One genus has neither spicules nor spongin.

Order **Homosclerophorida**

Definition as for the subclass.

5 OSCARELLIDAE

Spicules and spongin absent, but pattern for larval development consistent with the subclass.

Oscarella lobularis (Schmidt)   FIG. 3.3

Encrusting sheet with rounded lobes, sponge to 100 mm across. Surface smooth, oscula sometimes visible. Gelatinous consistency, but lobes can be fairly firm. Colour usually strongest in the lobes: often yellowish or brownish, sometimes with other tints; occasionally entirely red, violet, blue, or green. No spicules or spongin skeleton.

Epilithic, or epibiotic on algae, cryptic low-littoral, or sublittoral.

6 PLAKINIDAE

Spicules present.

Plakina monolopha Schulze   FIG. 3.3

Irregularly rounded or lobed mounds, sometimes penetrated by rounded cavities. Sponge to 150 mm across. Surface finely tuberculate, oscula in clusters. Spicules include highly characteristic tetractinal variants resembling candelabras. Also somewhat irregular and twisted oxeas.

Epilithic. Sublittoral.

Subclass **Tetractinomorpha**

Where present, megascleres are tetraxons or monaxons. Microscleres usually asters, but sigmas, raphides, microxeas, and other types can occur.

Order **Choristida**

Microscleres are asters and sometimes microxeas. Megascleres are tetractines and oxeas. In some genera, tetractines or microscleres, or both, are absent, only oxeas remaining.

7 STELLETTIDAE

Megascleres are tetractines and oxeas, microscleres are asters but not sterrasters.

1. Contains orthotriaenes and strongylasters   ***Stelletta grubii***
   Contains dichotriaenes and plagiotriaenes
   Stryphnus ponderosus

Stelletta grubii Schmidt   FIG. 3.3

Massive and rounded. Diameter and height to 150 mm. Surface smooth or slightly rough, occasionally embedded with extraneous bodies including parts of adjacent sessile biota, or even small stones. Oscula sometimes in groups, sometimes separated. Consistency firm. Colour brown or violet, sometimes whitish, greenish, or reddish. Megascleres are oxeas and orthotriaenes, also some styles, tylostyles, and strongyles. Microscleres are strongylasters and oxyasters.

Epilithic, sublittoral.

Stryphnus ponderosus (Bowerbank)   FIG. 3.3

Massive, lobed or plate form. Width and height to 200 mm, thickness to 75 mm. Surface smooth with scattered oscula. Colour violet, black, brown, or whitish. Core whitish but aquiferous channels can be pigmented. Megascleres are dichotriaenes, plagiotriaenes, and oxeas. Microscleres are amphiasters and oxyasters.

Epilithic, sublittoral.

8 GEODIIDAE

Megascleres are triaenes and oxeas, microscleres include sterrasters.

Pachymatisma johnstonia (Bowerbank in Johnston) FIG. 3.3

Massive, rounded in form, ranging from small patches, through mounds to thick plates. Smooth surface, oscula distinct and often in lines. Diameter to 150 mm, height to 100 mm. Colour of surface bluish to violet-grey, sometimes whitish in part, translucent in small sponges; always whitish within. Distinct skin, 1 mm thick. Megascleres are strongyles, and also orthotriaenes, usually with straight rays. Microscleres are microstrongyles, oxyasters with a few elongate rays, and characteristic sterrasters which are near spherical, 90–200 μm long and 70–160 μm broad. Microrhabds and centrotylotes often occur.

Epilithic, sublittoral.

9 PACHASTRELLIDAE

Microscleres include calthrops and also streptasters. Euasters are absent.

---

1. Black or dark grey encrusting sheets, no asters
                                             Dercitus bucklandi

   Whitish to light grey sheet or mound, asters present
                                             Poecillastra compressa

---

Dercitus bucklandi (Bowerbank)   FIG. 3.3

Encrusting to massive, to 500 mm in diameter and 50 mm in thickness. Surface smooth and even with scattered oscula of variable size. Consistency fairly firm. Colour dark grey to black, characteristic when combined with the gross form. Megascleres are calthrops. Microscleres are microxeas and toxas.

Epilithic, sublittoral.

Poecillastra compressa (Bowerbank)   FIG. 3.3

Encrusting or massive. Diameter to 75 mm. Surface even, or pitted. Oscula small and scattered. Consistency fragile. Colour white, yellowish, or light grey. Megascleres are oxeas and calthrops. Microscleres are centrotylotes, amphiasters and spirasters.

Epilithic, sublittoral.

Order **Spirophorida**

Radial skeleton results in a spheroid form. Megascleres triaenes and oxeas. Sigmaspirae are microscleres that are characteristic of the order.

10 TETILLIDAE

Definition as for the order.

Tetilla cranium (Müller)   FIG. 3.3

Spherical or ovoid, sometimes egg-shaped. Diameter to 50 mm. Surface finely hispid and with conuli. Oscula single or in a small group, or not visible. Colour off-white or yellowish. Radially symmetrical skeleton. Megascleres are anatriaenes, protriaenes and oxeas. Microscleres are sigmaspirae.

Epilithic, cryptic lower littoral and sublittoral; sometimes on *Axinella infundibuliformis*.

Order **Hadromerida**

Megascleres are tylostyles or subtylostyles, with at least superficial radial organization. If present, microscleres are asters or microxeas. Spongin often occurs but not as fibres.

11 SUBERITIDAE

Megascleres are tylostyles, subtylostyles, or sometimes styles. Microscleres usually absent, but can occur.

---

1. Thin encrusting   **2**

   Massive   **4**

2. Surface hispid, shaft of tylostyle narrower than the
   terminal basal swelling   **Prosuberites epiphytum**

   Surface smooth   **3**

3. Very soft consistency, gelatinous internally, endophytes often cause bright blue-green or orange-yellow colour, shaft of tylostyle narrower than basal swelling, which is terminal   **Terpios fugax**

   Fairly firm consistency, shaft of tylostyle in part broader than the basal swelling, which is sub-terminal   **Pseudosuberites sulphureus**

4. Sponge mound composed of anastomosing plates imparting a brain-like appearance   **Suberites massa**

   Sponge with a rounded, fairly even surface   **5**

5. Spicules consist of tylostyles alone   **Suberites carnosus**

   Other spicule types occur also   **6**

6. Spicules include centrotylote strongyles   **Suberites ficus**

   Centrotylote strongyles do not occur   **Suberites domuncula**

Prosuberites epiphytum (Lamarck)   FIG. 3.4

Thin encrusting patches, diameter to 150 mm. Surface finely hispid and uneven, oscula not visible. Firm consistency. Megascleres are only tylostyles with discrete spheroid heads, and narrower, gradually tapering and curved shafts. Microscleres absent.

Epilithic, cryptic low-littoral, and sublittoral.

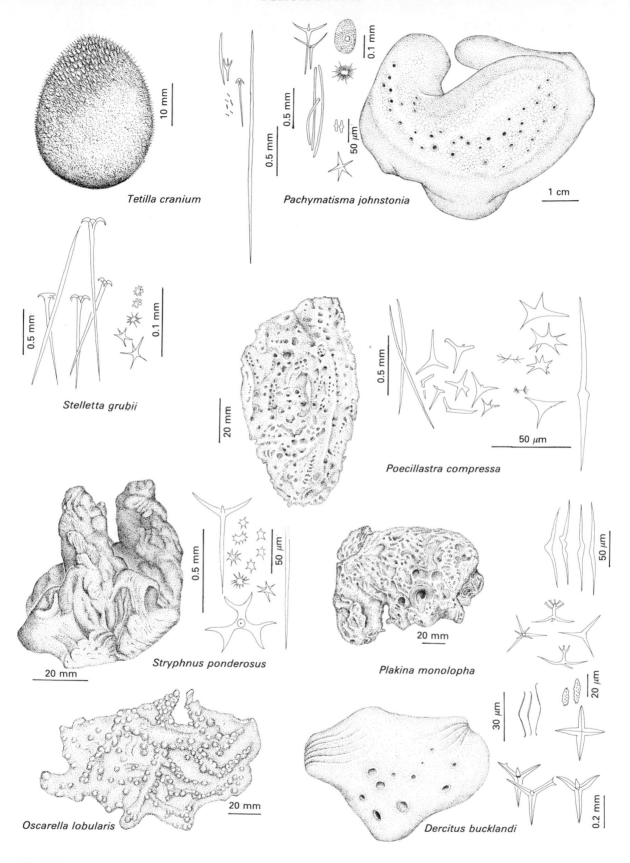

Tetilla cranium

Pachymatisma johnstonia

Stelletta grubii

Poecillastra compressa

Stryphnus ponderosus

Plakina monolopha

Oscarella lobularis

Dercitus bucklandi

Fig. 3.3

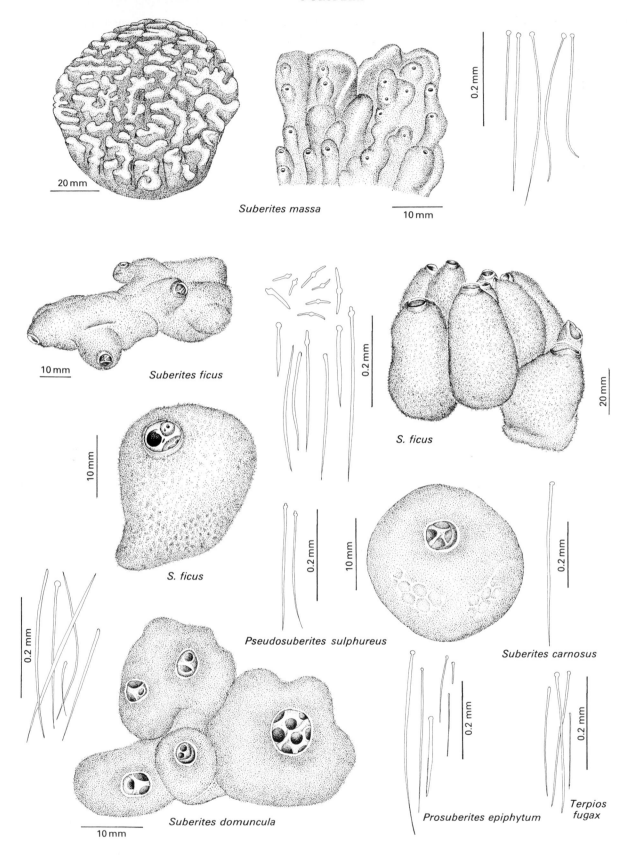

Suberites massa

Suberites ficus

S. ficus

S. ficus

Pseudosuberites sulphureus

Suberites carnosus

Suberites domuncula

Prosuberites epiphytum

Terpios fugax

Fig. 3.4

Pseudosuberites sulphureus (Bowerbank) FIG. 3.4

Thin encrusting patches, diameter to 130 mm. Colour light to dark yellow. Megascleres are tylostyles, thickest half-way along the shaft although the basal swelling approaches this maximum diameter. Microscleres absent.

Epilithic, cryptic low littoral, and sublittoral.

Suberites carnosus (Johnston) FIG. 3.4

Typically spheroid and anchored by a short stalk, sometimes encrusting or irregularly massive, to 150 mm in height. In the spheroid form usually a single, apical osculum. Surface even, almost smooth. Contraction substantial. Consistency soft when dilated, firm when contracted. Colour yellow to brown. Megascleres are exclusively tylostyles with egg-shaped basal swellings and spindle-shaped shafts.

On stones and rock. Common.

Suberites domuncula (Olivi) FIG. 3.4

Massive, rounded spheroid or lobed form, to 200 mm wide and 100 mm high. Surface even but slightly rough. One or more distinct oscula. Consistency firm yet elastic. Colour typically orange, but can be whitish, blue or red, or a mixture. Megascleres include curved tylostyles, the terminal basal swelling appearing three-lobed in optical section. A second swelling may occur below this on the shaft. Styles and oxeas also occur.

Epilithic, sometimes in cryptic low-littoral, but more usually sublittoral. Common, all coasts.

Suberites ficus (Esper) FIG. 3.4

Massive, highly variable form. Often spheroid or lobed, sometimes clubbed, fig-shaped, or elongate (hanging down), or encrusting. Size can exceed 300 mm. Surface even but slightly rough. One or more large oscula. Consistency firm, yet elastic. Out of water, contraction substantial and the sponge becomes firm. Colour grey or orange-red, and yellow within the core. Endophytic chlorophytes may cause dark-green patches. Megascleres include tylostyles and styles, both usually curved. In the tylostyles, the single basal swelling can occur terminally, or a little way down the shaft. Oxeas also occur. Microscleres, sometimes absent, can be centrotylote microstrongyles.

Epilithic, also on stones and shell, often exceeding the size of the initial substrate so becoming free-standing. Occasionally in the cryptic low-littoral, more commonly in the sublittoral. Common, all coasts.

Suberites massa Nardo FIG. 3.4

Massive, hemispheroid, or irregular, composed of anastomosing ridges bearing small oscula. Surface slightly rough. Diameter to 250 mm, height to 150 mm. Consistency fairly firm. Contraction significant out of water; the ridged gross structure becomes more apparent and the oscula close. Colour bright orange to whitish yellow; in illuminated situations the top can be purple or brown. Megascleres are tylostyles, each with a spheroid basal swelling, characteristically much wider and distinct from the slender, tapering shaft which may be straight or curved.

Epilithic, also on stones and shell, occasionally in the lower littoral, more widely in the sublittoral. Locally abundant in turbid, brackish water zones of some southern estuaries, otherwise uncommon.

Terpios fugax Duchassaing and Michelotti FIG. 3.4

Thin encrusting patches, to 50 mm across. Smooth surface, oscula not visible. Very soft in consistency. Colour fundamentally ochre-yellow or bright brown. However symbiotic algae can frequently impart a deep blue-green or bright orange-yellow cast. Megascleres are all tylostyles, each with a slender shaft, usually smoothly curved, gradually tapering to a point. Basal swelling spheroidal but variable.

Epilithic, typically in cryptic low-littoral situations, also sublittoral. Common.

I2 POLYMASTIIDAE

Megascleres tylostyles or subtylostyles, always in two or three size categories; styles can also occur. Microscleres usually absent. Characteristic cushion-formed massive body covered with large erect papillae, some bearing an osculum, others ostia.

---

1. Erect papillae solid, broad-based, and fairly steeply tapering, usually opaque seen underwater; surface of base and papillae smooth **Polymastia boletiformis**

   Erect papillae delicate with a gradual taper, often translucent seen underwater, surface of base rough, and of papillae smooth **Polymastia mammillaris**

Polymastia boletiformis (Lamarck) FIG. 3.5
(ARNDT, 1935 as *P. robusta*)

Cushion-formed or massive, upper surface bearing numerous robust and steeply tapering, cylindrical papillae. Diameter of sponge to 100 mm, papillae typically 20 mm long but can reach 120 mm. Surface of base and papillae smooth. Ostia and oscula confined to papillae, the latter often visible in live specimens. Firm consistency, papillae flexible. Colour orange, ochre-yellow, dark grey, or green. Papillae not translucent, nor significantly paler when seen underwater. Megascleres tylostyles, mostly with distinct but irregular basal swellings, and spindle formed shafts. No microscleres.

Epilithic, often upward facets of rock, sublittoral. Common.

Polymastia mammillaris (Müller) FIG. 3.5

Cushion formed with numerous subcylindrical, fairly slender, gradually tapering papillae. Diameter of base to 120 mm, thickness 10 to 20 mm; height of papillae to 120 mm. Surface of base rough, whereas papillae are smooth, Papillae bear ostia or oscula, the latter often visible in live specimens. Base firm in consistency, papillae are flexible. Colour orange, yellow, pink, or grey, the papillae being paler and sometimes translucent. Interior of base orange. Megascleres include stout and spindle-formed tylostyles, most with sub-terminal basal swellings. Styles also occur. Microscleres are absent.

Sufficiently tolerant of silting to occur on upper facets of rock, base may at times be covered with sediment, sublittoral. Common.

13 CLIONIDAE

Sponges that can excavate extensive burrows within calcareous substrates, or can form massive colonies on these and on non-calcareous materials. Megascleres are tylostyles and sometimes oxeas, and microscleres are spirasters, amphiasters, and thorny microxeas. Inhalant and exhalant papillae always feature at the surface, in the case of burrowing sponges, protruding through circular holes at the surface of the substrate.

1.	Sponge partly or wholly massive	*Cliona celata*
	Sponge entirely penetrant	2
2.	Megascleres only tylostyles	*Cliona lobata*
	Megascleres tylostyles and often oxeas	3
3.	Oxeas smooth, fine, mainly in bundles	*Cliona celata*
	Oxeas spindle-shaped and finely thorned	*Cliona vastifica*

Cliona celata Grant   FIG. 3.5

In the penetrant form, the sponge burrows into limestone or mollusc shells such as those of oysters and scallops, excavating and filling a network of galleries. Vital communication is maintained via papillae protruding through circular pores, to 3 mm across, each papilla bearing ostia or an osculum. This form can outgrow its substrate and so progress to the massive form. Similar mound forms can occur upon non-calacareous rocks, filling crevices or, in extreme cases, growing as thick, rounded plates, up to 1 m across, 250 mm thick and 500 mm high. The surface of mound sponges is uniformly covered by flat-topped papillae bearing ostia, and by large rimmed oscula, often arranged in lines across the sponge, along the crest in the case of plate forms. Consistency very firm and inflexible. Sponge contracts significantly when out of water, papillae being withdrawn. Colour often bright to deep yellow. Megascleres include tylostyles with distinct, sub-terminal basal swellings, the shafts being somewhat spindle-formed and in the lower half, curved. Oxeas are fine, mostly in bundles, and often absent. Microscleres are spirasters, and occur solely in young sponges.

Sublittoral. Burrowing and massive forms occur in both wave-exposed, open coast sites and in silty estuaries. Very common.

Cliona lobata Hancock   FIG. 3.5

Only known in the penetrant form, size of sponge dependent on that of its substrate, a mollusc shell or other calcareous material. Papillae numerous and very small, for example 0.4 mm in diameter, these being linked by a network of internal galleries. Colour gold-yellow, papillae paler. Megascleres are smooth tylostyles, these being overall slightly spindle-formed, and straight or curved. Basal swelling three-lobed or egg-shaped, often a sec-ondary sub-terminal swelling of the same thickness, and occasionally a third in the central section of the shaft. Spirasters straight, or have one to nine spirals, partly or wholly covered with thorns.

Only where calcareous substrates occur, lowest shore, and sublittoral.

Cliona vastifica Hancock   FIG. 3.5

Only known in the penetrant form, bores into mollusc shells and other calcareous substrates. Papillae may be arranged in lines, numerous. Diameter of these 0.5 to 0.8 mm. Colour red, orange, yellowish. Tylostyles mostly with rounded basal swellings, shafts mostly straight, very finely thorny; acanthoxeas spindle-formed, slightly curved, symmetrical, often with a cover of fine thorns. Microscleres are thorny spirasters, some fairly straight; either wholly covered with spines, or with these in a line.

Sublittoral.

14 TETHYIDAE

Massive, spherical sponges with a distinctly radially symmetrical skeleton, and a distinct cortical region. Megascleres include very long subtylostyles, also styles. Microscleres are asters.

Tethya aurantium (Pallas)   FIG. 3.5

Massive, spherical, with a holdfast of rootlike projections. Diameter to 60 mm. Surface with tubercles, polygonal in shape. Osculum often single and apical, ostia submicroscopic. Consistency very firm. Colour yellow or orange. Megascleres are styles and subtylostyles, the latter being straight, spindle-formed, and sometimes very long (1.5–2.7 mm). Microscleres include spirasters and strongylasters, the latter having 9–12 rays.

Epilithic, occasionally cryptic low-littoral, usually sublittoral. Common.

Order **Axinellida**

Skeleton of spicules and a substantial proportion of spongin fibres, subdivisible into two components: a more concentrated and central, axial skeleton of spicules and fibres, and a more superficial extra-axial skeleton in which the spicules are held by spongin in plumose or plumoreticulate arrays. The two are often discernible physically in that the latter is noticeably more flexible than the former. Megascleres are some combination of oxeas, styles, tylostyles, and strongyles. Spicules often sinuous. Microscleres can be trichodragmas or asters. Sponge surface usually rough with projecting spicules.

15 AXINELLIDAE

Main skeletal tracts are of spongin fibres enclosing megascleres. These are in part condensed into an axial skeleton, and in part consist of extra-axial plumose or plumoreticulate elements leading to the surface. Megascleres monactines, diactines, or both.

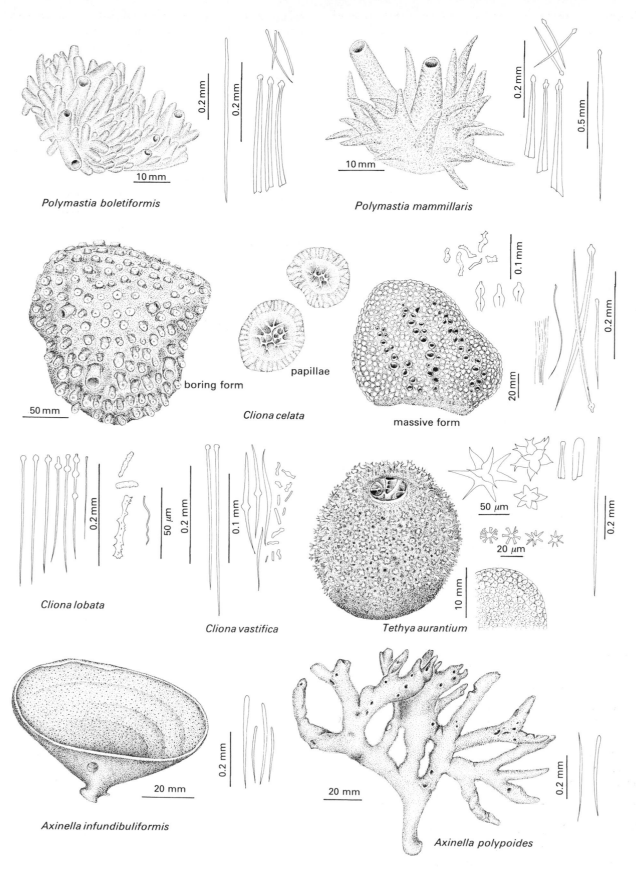

Polymastia boletiformis

Polymastia mammillaris

boring form

papillae

Cliona celata

massive form

Cliona lobata

Cliona vastifica

Tethya aurantium

Axinella infundibuliformis

Axinella polypoides

Fig. 3.5

1. Erect, funnel or fan-shaped **2**

   Erect, ramifying and branched **Axinella polypoides**

2. Edge of funnel or fan, thick or rounded
   Axinella infundibuliformis

   Edge of funnel or fan, tapered and sharp
   Phakellia ventilabrum

Axinella infundibuliformis (Linnaeus)   FIG. 3.5

Funnel- or sometimes fan-shaped, rim thick and rounded. Short stalk. Diameter of funnel to 250 mm. Surface even, and finely hispid, oscula numerous and scattered over entire surface. Colour ochre-yellow with a brownish tint. Megascleres include styles, most with an abrupt curvature near the base, and a point that is finely drawn out but somewhat short. Oxeas are slightly curved. Microscleres are trichodragmas.

Epilithic, sublittoral.

Axinella polypoides Schmidt   FIG. 3.5
(ARNDT, 1935 as *Axinella distorta*)

Erect and ramifying, branches flattened, partly anastomosing, ends rounded. Height to 150 mm. Firm but flexible. Colour pale brown. Surface smooth, oscula small, scattered. Megascleres include curved styles, and oxeas, also curved but more slender.

Epilithic, sublittoral.

Phakellia ventilabrum (Johnston)   FIG. 3.6

Funnel- or fan-shaped, edge is tapered and is much sharper than in *Axinella infundibuliformis*, to which it is otherwise similar. Height to 450 mm, thickness to 5 mm. Surface usually smooth, sometimes rough and finely hispid with small scattered oscula. Colour pale yellow (in alcohol). Megascleres are strongyles and styles, both twisted and irregular in form.

Epilithic, sublittoral.

16 HEMIASTERELLIDAE

Megascleres are monactines, diactines, or both, these being enclosed in spongin fibres that radiate upwards in a plumose fashion. Microscleres can include asters and microxeas.

---

1. Sponge erect, with a cluster of short, club-ended branches; oxeas solid and with drawn-out points
   Stelligera rigida

   Sponge erect, with slender dichotomous branches; oxeas slender, of uniform thickness and with steeply tapering points   **Stelligera stuposa**

Stelligera rigida (Montagu)   FIG. 3.6

Erect form, short-stalked and with numerous short, broad branches, sometimes part flattened, and with thickened ends. Height to 50 mm. Surface spiny, oscula small. Sponge often covered with a layer of silt. Consistency moderately firm and flexible.

Colour ochre to orange-yellow. Megascleres include some very large styles (to 3 mm in length), oxeas with long, drawn-out points, and some strongyles. Microscleres are asters.

Epilithic, sublittoral.

Stelligera stuposa (Montagu)   FIG. 3.6

Erect, tree form, branches bifurcating, rounded in section. Height to 180 mm. Surface spiny with small oscula. Consistency fairly firm but flexible. Sponge charged with mucus. Colour pale brown or yellow. Megascleres include very long and solid styles, to 1.87 mm in length, thickness at the base to 0.25 mm. Strongyles are unequal ended, one end being less rounded and more drawn out than the other; oxeas are uniformly slender along their length, and with steeply tapering points. Microscleres are spherasters.

Epilithic, sublittoral.

17 RASPAILIIDAE

Axial skeleton of spongin fibres enclosing monactines, diactines, or both. Extra-axial skeleton of radial or plumose fibres extending from the axis to the surface where long terminal styles project as spines. Very small acanthostyles occur. True microscleres are absent.

---

1. Low profile, irregular branching shrub form, colour carmine red   **Raspailia aculeata**

   Not as above   **2**

2. Tree form, fairly slender branches, colour pale yellow-brown   **Raspailia hispida**

   Tree form, stout branches, colour dark reddish-brown   **Raspailia ramosa**

Raspailia aculeata (Johnston)   FIG. 3.6

Low, irregular shrub form, the branches arising from a small crustose holdfast and an irregular column. Height to 250 mm. Surface uneven, oscula small. Consistency fragile. Colour carmine-red. Megascleres are styles, tylostyles, and oxeas. Sometimes a proportion of styles take the form of anisostrongyles. Acanthostyles are straight, occasionally curved, and spinose all over, the spines being small.

Epilithic, sublittoral.

Raspailia hispida (Montagu)   FIG. 3.6

Tree-formed, branches long and slender, mostly forked, sometimes a little flattened. Whole sponge to 350 mm high, branches to 130 mm. Surface even, but somewhat hispid and with small oscula. Consistency fairly soft, and elastic. Colour yellow-brown. Megascleres include curved styles, acanthostyles that are straight and wholly thorned, and oxeas.

Epilithic, sublittoral, often with *R. ramosa*. Common.

Raspailia ramosa (Montagu)   FIG. 3.6

Tree-formed, branches digitate, fan-shaped, or irregular but with well-rounded ends. Height of sponge to 150 mm, length of

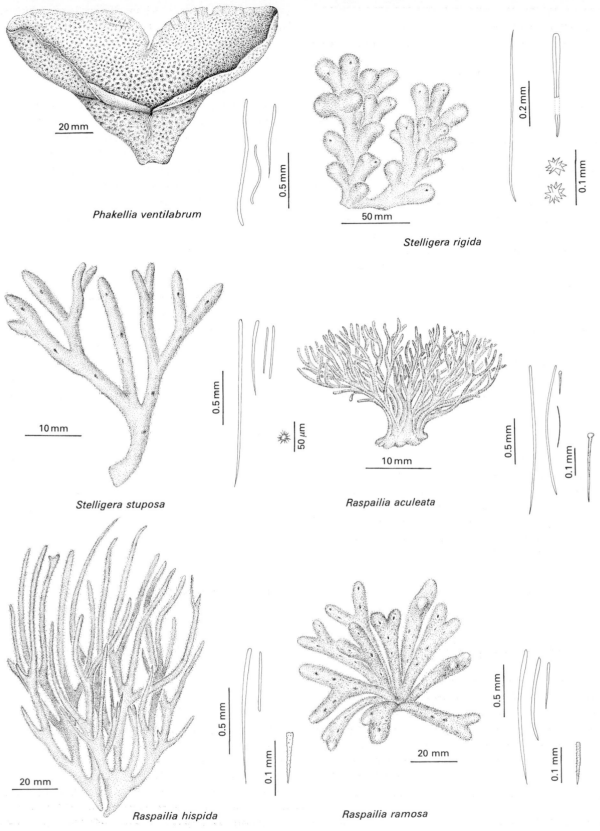

Phakellia ventilabrum

Stelligera rigida

Stelligera stuposa

Raspailia aculeata

Raspailia hispida

Raspailia ramosa

Fig. 3.6

branches to 25 mm. Surface even but hispid, oscula small but distinct in life. Consistency flexible. Colour dark reddish-brown. Megascleres styles, somewhat curved, and occasionally with a basal swelling. Strongyles are lightly curved. Oxeas occur. Acanthostyles are entirely thorny, and straight.

Epilithic, sublittoral. Often with *R. hispida*. Common.

Order **Halichondrida**

Megascleres oxeas, styles, or strongyles. No microscleres. Spicule skeleton structured at the surface—a layer of tangential dermal spicules can be evident. The endosomal skeleton with spicules in disarray is termed 'halichondroid'.

18 HALICHONDRIIDAE

Principal megascleres oxeas, although styles may occur. Subdermal spaces separate the often reticulated dermal skeleton from the randomly arranged endosome.

---

1. A cluster of tall conical projections arising from a cushion-like base often hidden by sediment
   Ciocalypta penicillus

   Sheet encrusting, massive or erect and branching   **2**

2. Sponge often produces slender digits (diameter 5 mm or less), or flat, thin fronds; soft and pliable, not readily fractured by twisting. Out of water, surface can have a translucent, whitish, delicate appearance; odour often weak or absent   **Halichondria bowerbanki**

   Not as above, although sponge sometimes forms thick anastomosing digits (10 mm or more); firm and rubbery, quite readily fractured by twisting. Out of water, surface not translucent or delicate in appearance; odour strong   **Halichondria panicea**

Ciocalypta penicillus (Bowerbank)   FIG. 3.7

Encrusting cushions giving rise to hollow, slender and tapering projections that are characteristic in form. Diameter of the cushion to 100 mm, the projections typically being 50 mm high, and basally 5 mm thick. The upper surface of the cushion is rough. There is a dermal membrane, as in *Halichondria panicea*, this being particularly evident in the digits. Consistency of the projections is fairly firm but flexible. Colour brownish or whitish-yellow, digits may be translucent. Megascleres are styles or oxeas, either may predominate and in some cases one may occur without the other. They are usually curved. A little spongin occurs.

Sponges typically grow on upward-facing rock surfaces, sometimes with only the digits showing, the base being covered by sand or silt. Common.

Halichondria bowerbanki Burton   FIG. 3.7

Gross form highly variable, can be sheet-encrusting, if so, usually fairly thin patches (often less than 5 mm thick, diameter to 100 mm); otherwise massive, usually of mound form (to

250 mm in thickness, 1 m across). Sheet and mound forms often give rise to elongate processes, slender and digitate, or flattened as expanded fronds. Surface smooth to slightly rough, oscula large and distinct in massive forms, not so in sheet forms. Consistency soft and pliable. Odour as for *H. panicea* but much weaker, or absent. Colour pale yellow or yellow-white. Megascleres are fairly slender, curved oxeas. Microscleres absent.

Mainly on rock, but often epibiotic on seaweeds and sessile animals, e.g. on the tubes of *Sabella pavonina* (Polychaeta). Usually sublittoral, but sometimes found in well-shaded cryptic situations in the lowest littoral zone. Open coast, and outer and mid zones of silty estuaries, alongside *Halichondria panicea* with which it can be readily confused.

Halichondria panicea (Pallas)   FIG. 3.7

Gross form highly variable, can be encrusting to various thicknesses, or irregularly massive, sometimes spherical, or mound-formed, or occurring as upright masses, anastomosing lobes, or digits. Thickness of encrusting sheets is from approximately 2.5 mm, and the horizontal extent from a few centimetres to a metre or more; erect plates can be to 350 mm in height; anastomosing digits from 10 mm in diameter. Surface smooth to slightly rough, oscula are large and prominent, often as raised craters, arranged as lines along the crests of some erect forms. Consistency firm, a little flexible or rubbery, but can be fractured if twisted significantly. Characteristic strong pungent odour. Megascleres are only oxeas, elongated, slender, spindle-formed, a little curved, or bent in the middle, very gradually pointed.

Occurs on rocks and on some of the larger seaweeds, e.g. kelp stipes. The encrusting sheet forms are typical of the lower littoral zone, where the species can be abundant in cryptic and semi-cryptic situations. More massive forms are confined to the sublittoral. Open coasts and outer zones of estuaries. Very common, all coasts (can easily be confused with *H. bowerbanki*, with which it often occurs, particularly in the outer zones of estuaries).

19 HYMENIACIDONIDAE

Megascleres are styles, sometimes with oxeas, microscleres being absent. The ectosomal skeleton is often structured, with spicule brushes protruding beyond the sponge surface. Significant subdermal cavities may separate the ectosome from the endosome, the skeleton of which is not organized. Spongin may occur. The surface of the sponge characteristically bears short erect processes.

Hymeniacidon perleve (Montagu)   FIG. 3.7
[ARNDT, 1935 as *H. sanguinea*]

Encrusting or cushion-formed, occasionally rounded. To 150 mm across, and 20–50 mm thick. Surface uneven, usually covered with small erect processes, but sometimes smooth. Oscula sparse and to 2 mm diameter. Consistency fairly firm but springy. Colour yellow, orange-yellow, orange-red, blood red, or superficially green. Megascleres are all lightly curved styles with long drawn-out points. Sometimes two size categories occur.

Epilithic. Tolerant to desiccation, can occur on open surfaces

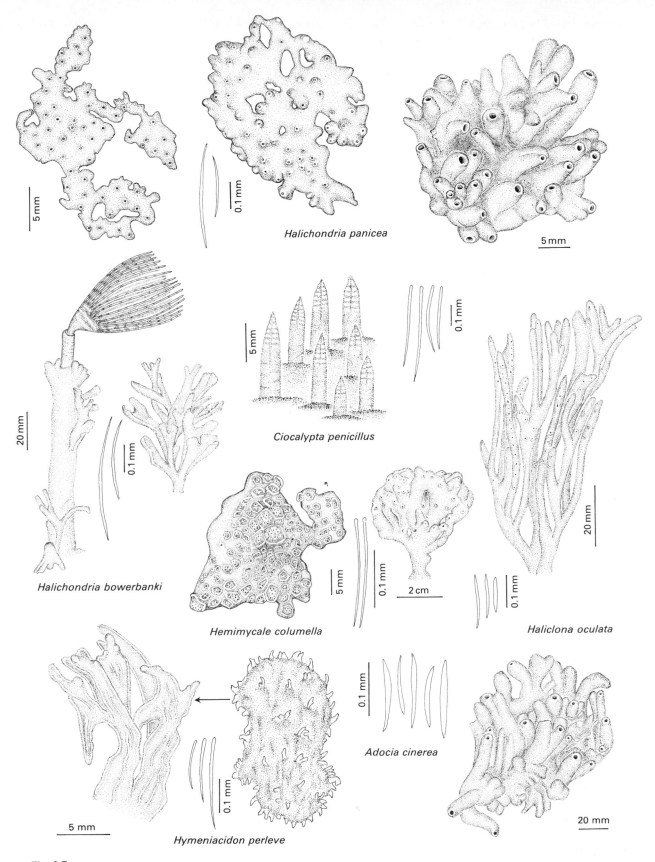

Halichondria panicea

Ciocalypta penicillus

Halichondria bowerbanki

Hemimycale columella

Haliclona oculata

Adocia cinerea

Hymeniacidon perleve

Fig. 3.7

in the mid-littoral zone. Most common in cryptic low-littoral; also sublittoral. Can occur on upward-facing rocks in silty estuaries such that the main body of the sponge is smothered, the bright orange papillae alone protruding through the silt layer. Most common on the open coast.

Order **Haplosclerida**

Skeleton reticulated, the pattern being isodictyal with rectangular or triangular meshes, sided by single spicules, spicule bundles, or constructed entirely of spongin fibre without spicules. Principal spicules usually fairly stout oxeas or strongyles, in both cases relatively uniform in length within a species. Microscleres occur in some cases.

20 HALICLONIDAE

Megascleres typically oxeas, stout in appearance and of uniformly small size. These are arranged within an isodictyal skeleton consolidated by spongin, either in small quantities at the joints of spicule meshes or as more substantial fibres. In some species, spongin is the predominant skeletal component. Microscleres usually absent.

N.B. A number of species occur in British waters, but the identity of most is not clearly defined, a prominent exception being the species given below.

Haliclona oculata (Pallas)   FIG. 3.7

Limited encrusting holdfast gives rise to a stalked tree form with digitate branches, mostly round in section and with rounded ends; branches typically numerous, but occasionally, under sheltered conditions, flattened, antler-shaped, and few in number. Height of sponge to 300 mm, diameter of branches about 7 mm. Oscula small but distinct, often slightly raised, frequently ordered into lines along the branches. Consistency fairly tough, but easily compressible and very flexible. Colour in life pale brown, sometimes yellowish, greenish, rose, or purple. Megascleres are spindle-formed, mostly curved, sturdy oxeas.

Epilithic, often on upwardly orientated facets, even under silty conditions. Sublittoral, occasionally cryptic low-littoral. On the open coast and in outer sections of estuaries. Very common.

21 ADOCIIDAE

Megascleres often in multispicular tracts with an isodictyal arrangement. Oxeas and strongyles can occur. Microscleres can be sigmas and toxas. All species have a tangential dermal spicule skeleton. Spongin occurs, but to a much lesser degree than in the Haliclonidae. See note for the Haliclonidae.

Adocia cinerea (Grant)   FIG. 3.7

Encrusting, cushion form with chimney-formed conical elevations, or short branches. Height to 35 mm, horizontal extent to 200 mm. Surface even but overall slightly rough. Oscula scattered, located upon the chimneys, diameter 1 to 2 mm. Consistency very soft, delicate, and compressible, but form readily springs back after light squeezing. Colour whitish violet, blood red, dark purple, reddish brown, orange, brown, ash-grey, or

bright yellow. Skeleton a three- or four-sided meshwork of individual oxeas joined at their ends by small quantities of spongin, hence the soft consistency. Oxeas slender (for a Haplosclerid), curved, seldom straight, cylindrical with short points, and smooth. No microscleres.

On rock and stable stones. Sublittoral and cryptic low-littoral. On open coasts and in outer sections of estuaries.

Order **Poecilosclerida**

Skeleton always composed of both spicules and spongin fibre. Considerable diversity in the form of spicule assemblages. Megascleres a variety of monactines or diactines, often spinose. The many microsclere types include chelas, sigmas, and toxas.

22 MYCALIDAE

Diffuse, radially arranged, plumoreticulate spicule and fibre skeleton in which megascleres are monactines, i.e. styles or subtylostyles. Microscleres always include anisochelae, as well as often some combination of sigmas, toxas, raphides, isochelae, and other cheloid variants, in fact up to seven microsclere types in a single species.

---

1. Encrusting patch form, surface porous in appearance, but smooth. Colour yellow or deep red
   Mycale macilenta

   Mound form, surface warty and solid in appearance. Colour scarlet red, or pink   ***Mycale rotalis***

Mycale macilenta (Bowerbank)   FIG. 3.8

Encrusting, greatest diameter to around 50 mm. Surface even but generally of porous appearance. Soft consistency. Colour yellowish or deep red. Megascleres include subtylostyles, mostly straight and a little spindle-formed, with slightly formed elliptical basal swellings. Microscleres include anisochelae of three size categories. Also sigmas of two sorts, and toxas with a gentle curve and broad crook in their middle. Trichodragmas are absent.

On rock and shells, sublittoral. Common, all coasts.

Mycale rotalis (Bowerbank)   FIG. 3.8

Sheet to massive, mound form. Diameter to 50 mm. Surface rounded and warty. Oscula sometimes evident. Consistency soft. Colour scarlet red to rose. Megascleres are subtylostyles with elliptical basal swellings. Shaft spindle-formed, point somewhat short. Microscleres include anisochelae of three size categories; sigmas of two sizes, these being slender. Toxas and trichodragmas are absent.

Epilithic, sublittoral.

23 BIEMNIDAE

Plumoreticulate skeleton of smooth styles with some spongin. Microscleres abundant and diverse, including sigmas, microxeas, toxas, commas, and other varieties.

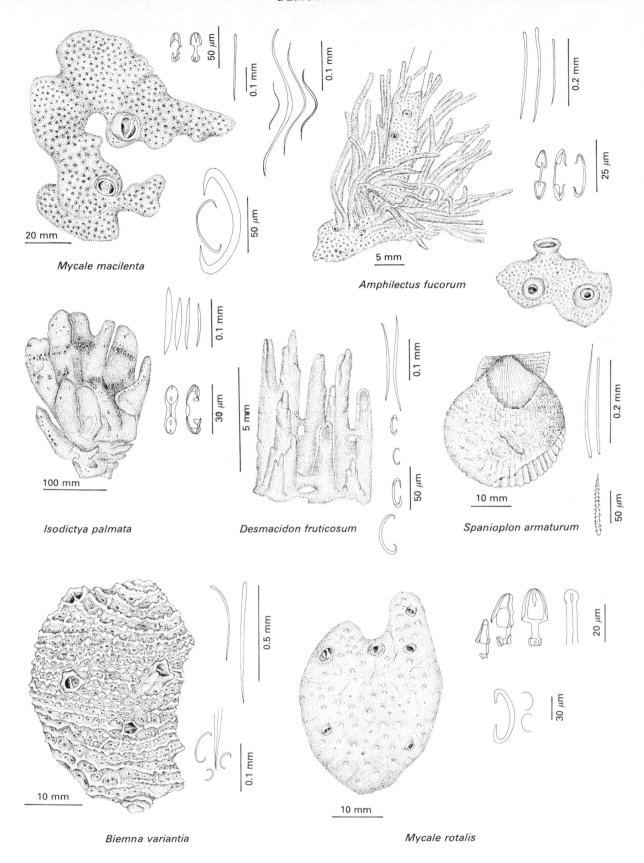

Mycale macilenta

Amphilectus fucorum

Isodictya palmata

Desmacidon fruticosum

Spanioplon armaturum

Biemna variantia

Mycale rotalis

Fig. 3.8

1. Sponge a uniform light greyish colour; surface rough with conical elevations. A diversity of microscleres
   Biemna variantia

   Sponge surface pink or yellowish with whitish rimmed craters. No microscleres   **Hemimycale columella**

Biemna variantia (Bowerbank)   FIG. 3.8
Young sponges encrusting or massive, mature ones being fan- or cup-shaped. Diameter to 80 mm. Surface rough with conical elevations, oscula sparse and scattered. Consistency soft and flexible. Colour light grey, sometimes yellowish. Skeleton is of anastomosing spongin fibres and numerous spicules. Megascleres are styles. Microscleres are sigmas, raphides, trichodragmas, and commas.

On rock and stones, sublittoral.

Hemimycale columella (Bowerbank)   FIG. 3.7
[ARNDT, 1935 as *Stylotella columella*]
Thick encrusting or irregularly massive. Thickness from 10 mm, diameter to 300 mm. Surface characteristically cratered, each enclosing one or more pores. The ridges sometimes give a honeycombed effect, less pronounced as the sponge contracts out of water. Oscula small (1 mm in diameter) and often indistinct. Colour pink or yellowish foundation, the ridges of the craters are conspicuously whitish. Megascleres are styles, slightly curved, with slightly expanded bases; mixed with a few strongyles.

Epilithic, sublittoral.

24 DESMACIDONIDAE

Reticulate or plumoreticulate skeleton, and diactinal megascleres of a uniform type throughout the sponge. Microscleres can be sigmas and chelae.

---

1. Colour orange-pink, sponge with grooved, broad extensions orientated towards the water surface. Megascleres tornotes, microscleres anchorate isochelae   **Desmacidon fruticosum**

   Not as above, microscleres palmate isochelae   **2**

2. Colour usually bright orange, megascleres are styles
   Amphilectus fucorum

   Colour yellow-grey (in alcohol), megascleres are oxeas   **Isodictya palmata**

Amphilectus fucorum (Esper)   FIG. 3.8
Form variable: encrusting patches, 5 mm thick; when growing on substrates of limited area, e.g. tubes of *Sabella* (Polychaeta), can give rise to numerous slender erect digits, 3 mm in diameter and up to 100 mm long. Otherwise can be massive. Surface generally even and finely rough. Oscula usually scattered in encrusting and massive forms, sometimes raised on flat-topped chimneys in encrusting forms, and in approximate lines along branches of erect forms. Consistency delicate and very flexible. Colour usually bright orange, sometimes reddish, yellow-brown, or grey-brown. Megascleres are slightly curved styles, 135–480 μm long, 3–19 μm thick. Microscleres are palmate isochelae, 14–18 μm long.

On rock, or frequently as an epibiont on red scrub algae or kelp, or on *Sabella* tubes. Occasionally cryptic low littoral, but typically shallow sublittoral. Common.

Desmacidon fruticosum (Montagu)   FIG. 3.8
Encrusting to massive, mound form, characterized by vertical extensions, often grooved, usually orientated towards the water surface, irrespective of the axis of the substrate. Surface finely hispid. Oscula small and scattered. Colour a characteristic yellowish pink. Substantial mucus content. Megascleres are tornotes. Microscleres are anchorate isochelae and sigmas.

Epilithic, sublittoral. Common.

Isodictya palmata (Johnston)   FIG. 3.8
Erect, with digitate, compressed, often fused branches. Height to 340 mm. Surface somewhat rough. Oscula numerous, often localized to the branch edges, 1–6 mm in diameter. Consistency very elastic. Colour mostly bright yellow-grey (in alcohol). Megascleres oxeas. Microscleres palmate isochelae with curved, waisted shafts.

Epilithic, sublittoral.

25 CRELLIDAE

Principal choanosomal skeleton of smooth diactinal megascleres structured in plumose or plumoreticulate fibrous tracts, often echinated by acanthostyles. Dermal skeleton often a dense layer of acanthostyles. Encrusting forms have a layer of acanathostyles attached to the basal layer of spongin close to the attachment surface. Microscleres are isochelae, sigmas, and rarely anisochelae.

Spanioplon armaturum (Bowerbank)   FIG. 3.8
Thin encrusting patches, diameter can be 30 mm, surface smooth, oscula minute. Colour ochre-yellow. Megascleres include strongyles, styles, and acanthostyles that are entirely thorny.

Epilithic, cryptic low littoral, and sublittoral.

26 MYXILLIDAE

Endosomal skeleton a regular reticulum of monactinal megascleres, styles, or acanthostyles, perhaps with echinating acanthostyles. Ectosomal spicules are diactinal. Diversity of microscleres which may occur include arcuate isochelae, sigmas, anisochelae, bipocilli, forceps, and others. Toxas and palmate isochelae do not occur.

1.　Microscleres are anisochelae and bipocilli　　**2**

　　Microscleres are not as above　　**3**

2.　Sponge thin encrusting, megascleres include tor-
　　notes　　***Iophon hyndmani***

　　Sponge massive, megascleres include tylotes
　　　　Iophon pattersoni

3.　Tornotes end in a simple, steeply tapering point, no
　　thorns　　***Myxilla fimbriata***

　　Tornote ends are covered with thorns　***Myxilla incrustans***

　　Tornote ends each have three thorns　***Myxilla rosacea***

Iophon hyndmani (Bowerbank)　　FIG. 3.9

Thin crust, partly with raised anastomosing branches. Diameter of crust to 50 mm, height of branches to 200 mm. Surface uneven, bristly, oscula and ostia microscopic. Colour light yellow or purple. Megascleres are acanthostyles and slender tornotes. Microscleres are anisochelae and bipocillae.

Epilithic, sublittoral.

Iophon pattersoni (Bowerbank)　　FIG. 3.9

Massive and irregular. Greatest diameter to 30 mm. Surface uneven but smooth. Colour dark brown. Megascleres include acanthostyles, sparsely thorny throughout their length; also tylotes. Microscleres are anisochelae and small bipocilli.

Epilithic, sublittoral, all coasts.

Myxilla fimbriata (Bowerbank)　　FIG. 3.9

Cushion-formed. Size to 80 mm. Surface even, and a little rough. Oscula scattered. Consistency variable in firmness, somewhat elastic. Colour orange in life, brown to black in alcohol. Megascleres joined by small amounts of spongin; include acanthostyles and tornotes with simple ends. Microscleres are spatulate isochelae.

Epilithic, sublittoral, all coasts.

Myxilla incrustans (Johnston)　　FIG. 3.9

Encrusting, irregularly massive or lobed. Height to 90 mm, diameter to 115 mm. Scattered oscula, often on the peaks of conical humps. Moderately firm consistency. Produces a lot of mucus. Colour yellow to orange, or brownish. Megascleres are joined by small quantities of spongin; they include acanthostyles with sparse scattered thorns, and tornotes, most with sparsely thorny ends. Microscleres are spatulate isochelae and sigmas, typically with a quarter spiral.

Epilithic, often in cryptic low-littoral situations, but mainly sublittoral. Common.

Myxilla rosacea (Lieberkühn)　　FIG. 3.9

Encrusting, sometimes branched. Size to 60 mm. Surface overall pitted and somewhat rough. Oscula sometimes visible. Consistency firm but somewhat flexible. Colour typically a dull rose-red, otherwise orange or brownish yellow. Megascleres linked by small quantities of spongin at the joints, include acanthostyles with scattered thorns; tornotes, mostly with triple-thorned ends. Microscleres include spatulate isochelae and sigmas.

Epilithic, sublittoral. All coasts.

27 HYMEDESMIIDAE

All have a thin, sheet-encrusting growth form. Endosomal megascleres are acanthostyles, orientated vertically and attached by the base to the substratum with spongin, i.e. the characteristic 'hymedesmoid' arrangement. Smaller accessory acanthostyles stand among principal ones. Ectosomal spicules smooth, often diactines or monactines, occurring individually or grouped, and orientated vertically or strewn without organization throughout the thin body. Usually more slender than the principal spicules. Substantial diversity of microscleres can include a variety of isochelae, sigmas, forceps, as well as many peculiar forms which characterize the genera.

1.　Sponge light brown and very thin, slimy to touch out
　　of water. No microscleres　***Hymedesmia brondstedi***

　　Sponge not this colour. Isochelae present　　**2**

2.　Sponge vivid turquoise-blue in life. Isochelae with
　　strongly curved shafts and rounded teeth
　　　　Hymedesmia paupertas

　　Sponge reddish. Isochelae with rounded shaft and
　　elongate teeth　　***Hymedesmia pansa***

　　* A number of other related species occur in British waters.

Hymedesmia brondstedi Burton　　FIG. 3.10
[ARNDT, 1935 as *Stylopus dujardini*]

Very thin encrusting patches, diameter to 25 mm, thickness to 0.5 mm. Colour yellowish or brownish. Surface very smooth, feels slimy to touch out of water. Oscula sometimes not visible, or small and scattered. Skeleton of acanthostyles with spherical heads, overall thorny, 83–220 μm in length. Tornotes and strongyles also occur, one end of these often being larger than the other. Microscleres absent.

On rock, stones, also shells; sublittoral. All coasts, common.

Hymedesmia paupertas (Bowerbank)　　FIG. 3.10

Thin encrusting patches. Diameter to 150 mm, thickness 3 mm. Surface hispid, sometimes smooth; cratered effect evident in live specimens *in situ*. Colour deep turquoise-blue. Megascleres include two kinds of acanthostyles. The larger ones are 300–550 μm long, with a distinctly pronounced basal swelling, 12 μm in diameter, a slightly curved shaft, bearing sparsely distributed, small, robust thorns. The second, smaller category are 120–160 μm long, with a weakly pronounced basal swelling, 5 μm in diameter, and covered with densely packed, long thorns. Strongyles are straight, slender, 220–320 μm long and 3–5 μm thick. One end is thicker than the other. Microscleres are isochelae with strong curved shafts.

Epilithic, sublittoral.

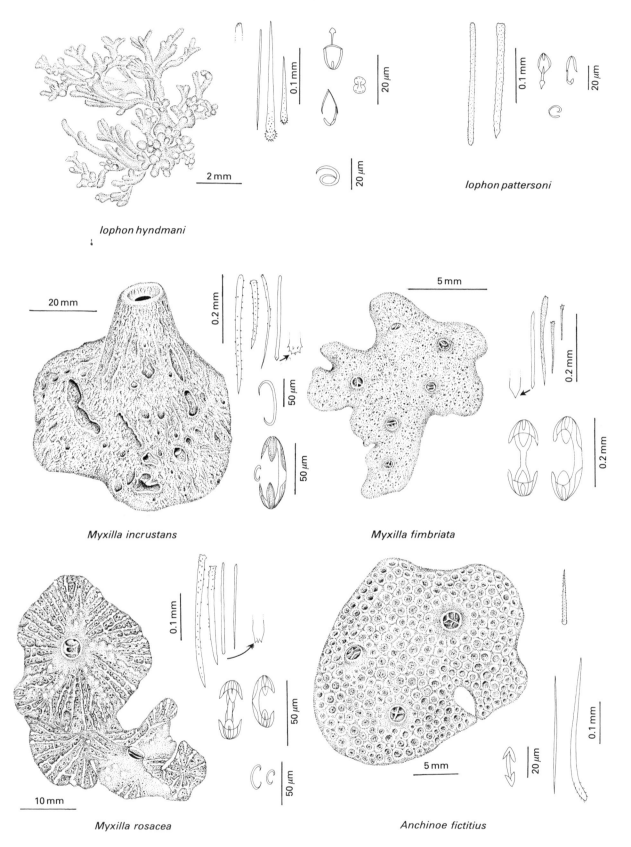

Iophon hyndmani

Iophon pattersoni

Myxilla incrustans

Myxilla fimbriata

Myxilla rosacea

Anchinoe fictitius

Fig. 3.9

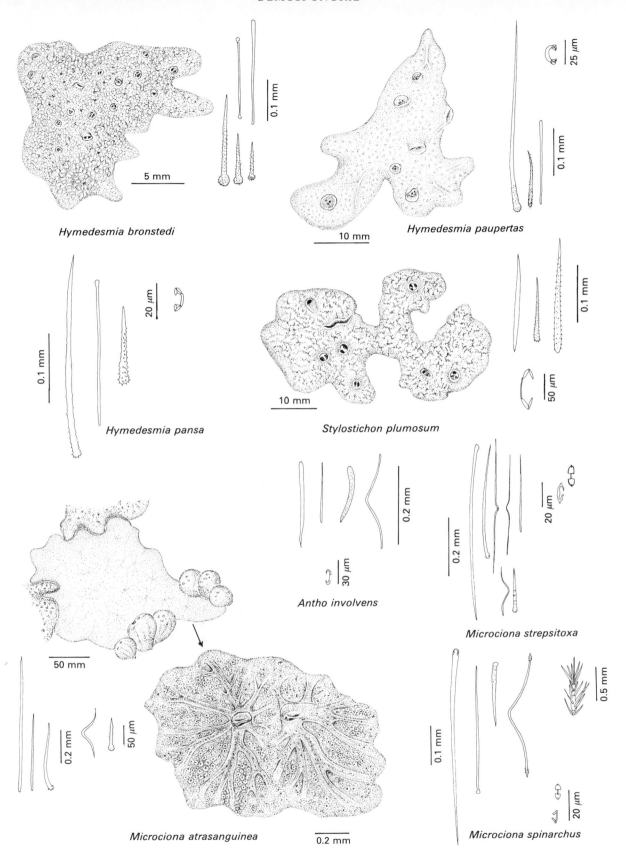

Hymedesmia bronstedi

Hymedesmia paupertas

Hymedesmia pansa

Stylostichon plumosum

Antho involvens

Microciona strepsitoxa

Microciona atrasanguinea

Microciona spinarchus

Fig. 3.10

Hymedesmia pansa Bowerbank   FIG. 3.10

Thin fleshy encrusting patches, to 35 mm across and 5 mm thick. Surface smooth. Oscula not known. Colour light pink (in alcohol). Megascleres include acanthostyles of two sorts. The larger is 155–300 μm long and 6–9 μm wide, with lightly curved shaft; the basal swelling and approximately half the length are thorny. The second kind is 90–120 μm long, 4–7 μm thick, straight or slightly curved, and thorny over its entire length, the thorns of the shaft being recurved basally. Other megascleres are intermediates between strongyles and subtylo-tornotes. They are very thin, straight. Whereas one end is rounded, or sometimes even significantly swollen, the other is abruptly pointed. Microscleres are arcuate isochelae, with a curved shaft.

Epilithic, sublittoral.

28 ANCHINOIDAE

Principal endosomal skeleton of plumose to plumoreticulate columns of diactines echinated by styles or acanthostyles. Ectosomal spicules diactinal, often as in the endosome. Microscleres are isochelae and sigmas. There is no dense ectosomal layer of spicules, and spongin fibre is not a major component of the skeleton. These negative characters distinguish the group from the Crellidae, with which it can be confused.

---

1. Bright pink or red, sheet encruster, surface having a cratered appearance in life   **Anchinoe fictitius**

   Dull yellow or orange, patch encruster. Surface smooth with scattered oscula.   **Stylostichon plumosum**

Anchinoe (Phorbas) fictitius (Bowerbank)   FIG. 3.9

Encrusting sheet form, can be extensive, to 500 mm in diameter, to 15 mm in thickness. Surface with a cratered effect in life (similar to *Hemimycale columella*). Oscula small and scattered. Colour vivid light red or pink. Megascleres include two size categories of acanthostyles. In the larger, the thorns are confined to the basal region, and the smaller category are wholly thorny. Tornotes also occur. Microscleres are arcuate isochelae.

Epilithic, sublittoral.

Stylostichon plumosum (Montagu)   FIG. 3.10

Thick encrusting sheet to irregularly massive form. Diameter to 100 mm. Surface often smooth, but can be papillate. Oscula distinctive and scattered. Consistency firm. Colour dull yellow to dark, reddish orange. Living sponges have a very characteristic strong odour. Megascleres include acanthostyles of two size categories. Oxeas are present. Microscleres are two toothed isochelae.

Epilithic, sublittoral.

29 CLATHRIIDAE

Megascleres dominated by styles or acanthostyles. These are organized into unispicular or multispicular tracts, also containing spongin which can occur in substantial quantities in some species. The tracts also support echinating acanthostyles.

Styles also occur as accessory ectosomal spicules, these usually being finer than the endosomal ones. There are no diactinal megascleres. Microscleres occur as palmate isochelae and toxas. All species covered here form encrusting sheets.

---

1. Fairly thick (can exceed 10 mm), deep red encrusting sheets with rounded edges, containing stout styles and also toxas   **Ophlitaspongia seriata**

   Thin encrusting sheets, orange or red   2

2. Colour orange or orange-red   3

   Colour deep red   4

3. Colour orange-red, often conspicuously wrinkled, sheet form. Stout acanthostyles, toxas devoid of thorns   **Antho involvens**

   Colour orange, usually smooth. More slender acanthostyles. Toxas with thorny ends occur   **Microciona spinarcus**

4. Many toxas exceptionally slender with curvature confined to the central section   **Microciona strepsitoxa**

   All toxas exhibit a typically gradual curvature   **Microciona atrasanguinea**

Antho involvens (Schmidt)   FIG. 3.10

Thin encrusting patches or sheets. Smooth, sometimes wrinkled, slightly hispid. Scattered small oscula, not easily seen. Colour orange-red. Megascleres are acanthostyles, sparsely covered with thorns. Also styles and subtylostyles. Microscleres are toxas and palmate isochelae.

Epilithic, sublittoral.

Microciona atrasanguinea Bowerbank   FIG. 3.10

Thin encrusting patches or sheets, diameter can be 200 mm, thickness < 2.5 mm. Surface finely hispid. Oscula tiny, scattered. Detailed examination of submerged sponges often reveals a web-like pattern of raised exhalant channels, converging on each osculum. Colour dark red. Megascleres include curved styles; acanthostyles usually curved and with thorns confined to the basal swelling, occasionally the thorns are absent. Smaller acanthostyles are straight and thorny over their entire length. Microscleres are toxas and two-toothed isochelae.

Epilithic, cryptic littoral, sublittoral. Common.

Microciona spinarcus Carter and Hope   FIG. 3.10

Thin encrusting patches, diameter to 25 mm. Surface even, only hispid in places. Colour orange. Megascleres include long styles that are slightly curved, sometimes with slight basal swellings, which can be slightly thorny. Acanthostyles are slightly to strongly curved, and almost entirely, but sparsely thorny. Microscleres include very slender toxas which are characteristically terminally thorny and also isochelae.

Sublittoral.

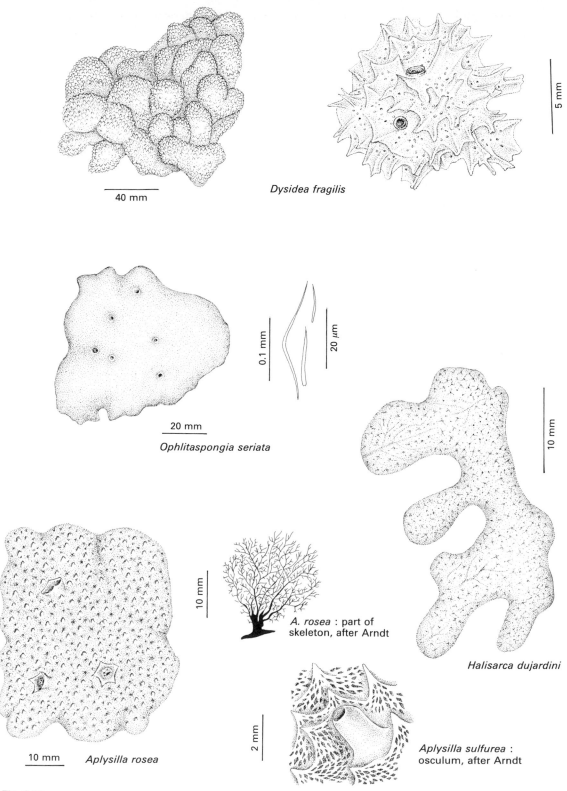

40 mm

Dysidea fragilis

5 mm

20 mm

Ophlitaspongia seriata

0.1 mm

20 µm

10 mm

10 mm

A. rosea : part of skeleton, after Arndt

Halisarca dujardini

10 mm

Aplysilla rosea

2 mm

Aplysilla sulfurea : osculum, after Arndt

Fig. 3.11

Microciona strepsitoxa Hope   FIG. 3.10

Thin encrusting patches. Thickness to 1 mm. Surface smooth when live, spiny when dry. Oscula numerous. Colour scarlet red. Megascleres include subtylostyles with slight basal swellings, sometimes somewhat thorny and lightly curved. Tylostyles have more distinct basal swellings which are also slightly thorny, and a slender shaft. Acanthostyles or acanthotylostyles are overall thorny. Many toxas are very slender, with the curvature confined to the central section. Isochelae occur.

Epilithic, sublittoral.

Ophlitaspongia seriata (Grant)   FIG. 3.11

Encrusting patches with rounded edges. Diameter to 75 mm, thickness to 12.5 mm. Surface even, partly hispid. Oscula small but distinct, numerous and scattered. Colour dark, dull red. Megascleres are rather broad styles. Microscleres are toxas.

Epilithic, sublittoral.

Order **Dictyoceratida**

No spicules present, but there is a well-developed organic skeleton of spongin fibres. This always forms an anastomosing network of differentiable primary and secondary fibres. The order includes the commercially exploited *Spongia* (Fam. Spongiidae, not found in the British Isles).

30 DYSIDEIDAE

Choanocyte chambers very large (40 μm), and often oval with a wide exhalant opening, a form of chamber termed 'eurypylous'. Fibres of spongin skeleton reticulate and laminated. Foreign materials often incorporated in quantity into the fibres.

Dysidea fragilis (Montagu)   FIG. 3.11

May be irregularly encrusting with rounded edges, 50 mm across, and from 7.5 mm in thickness; otherwise a lobed mass, up to 300 mm across and in height under favourable conditions. Surface characteristically covered with conuli, 1.5 mm in height, 2–2.5 mm across the base. Oscula are distinct and scattered, and sometimes raised, they may be 2–5 mm wide. Colour brownish or greyish white, sometimes reddish brown or other colours. Characteristic subtle odour. There are no spicules. The skeleton is a meshwork of spongin fibres, of the order of 100–200 μm in diameter, and characteristically incorporates foreign hard material, sand grains, spicules of other sponges, foraminifera, etc.

Epilithic, cryptic low littoral, and sublittoral.

Order **Dendroceratida**

No mineral spicules, skeleton usually entirely of spongin fibres characteristically arranged in a dendritic pattern, rarely anastomosing. Skeleton absent in one family.

31 APLYSILLIDAE

Spongin skeleton present.

---

1. Colour red, surface conuli well-separated (towards 5 mm), oscula not raised   **Aplysilla rosea**

Colour yellow, surface conuli dense packed (1 mm), oscula on raised chimneys   **Aplysilla sulfurea**

Aplysilla rosea Schulze   FIG. 3.11

Small, flat encrusting patches. Diameter to 40 mm, thickness to 5 mm. Surface with thin conuli, 2–3 mm high and 5 mm apart. Colour rose or cherry red. Skeleton without spicules, composed of tree-like systems of branched spongin fibres.

Epilithic, littoral, or sublittoral.

Aplysilla sulfurea Schulze   FIG. 3.11

Small, flat encrusting patches. Thickness 3–6 mm. Surface covered with conuli, 0.5–1 mm in diameter and about 1 mm apart. Oscula distinct, 1–2 mm wide, each located upon a raised chimney. Colour in life pale to dark sulphur-yellow. In alcohol, gradually changes to a patchy blue. No spicules. Skeleton consists of smooth, tree-formed system of branching fibres.

Epilithic, cryptic low-littoral, sublittoral.

32 HALISARCIDAE

No spongin skeleton.

Halisarca dujardini Johnston   FIG. 3.11

Encrusting, diameter to 400 mm, thickness to 5 mm. Surface smooth and slimy. Oscula sparse, sometimes raised. Colour dull yellowish brown or whitish. No spicules or distinct spongin fibres, although very fine fibrils do occur.

Epilithic, epibiotic on algae. Cryptic low-littoral, sublittoral.

4 CNIDARIA

THE Cnidaria (formerly known as Coelenterata) are most obviously characterized by their *radial*, or sometimes more strictly *biradial*, *symmetry* (p. 101). The basic structure is saclike with a single terminal opening, the mouth, which also functions as an anus. The internal space is the *coelenteron* or *gastrovascular cavity*, which may be subdivided by radially arranged partitions, the *mesenteries* or *septa*. The mouth is surrounded by a circle or circles of *tentacles*. The body wall consists of only two layers of cells, ectoderm and endoderm, between which is the *mesogloea*. The mesogloea ranges from a non-cellular membrane in hydroids, to a thick fibrous layer in anemones, and a jelly-like filling in medusae. The musculature, formed from epithelio-muscular cells, may be well-developed. All cnidarians are characterized by the presence, especially on the tentacles, of stinging capsules, *cnidae* or *nematocysts*, of various types. These capsules are unique to the phylum. Nematocysts consist basically of a capsule with an armed or naked thread coiled inside it. When stimulated the thread is fired by eversion.

Two basic structural types of cnidarian are recognized: a *polyp* is sessile, more or less cylindrical, has the mouth at the free, distal end, and thin mesogloea; a *medusa* is free-swimming, bell shaped to discoid, with the convex surface upward and the mouth and tentacles on the under surface. Larger forms are referred to as jellyfish. Cnidarian species may be exclusively medusoid, exclusively polypoid, or pass through both polypoid and medusoid phases. The medusae are often reproductive, producing gametes; on fertilization the zygote develops into a *planula* larva. Polyps (though not of Cubozoa, the box jellyfish) may propagate asexually by fission (longitudinal or transverse) or by budding new polyps from themselves. Such buds in the freshwater *Hydra*, for example, may separate from the parent polyp; but in marine cnidarians the buds usually do not separate, leading to the formation of a *colony*. Medusae rarely bud. Many colonies of polyps build a common skeleton which may be chitinous or calcareous, internal or external.

Although the main types of cnidarian are readily recognized, the manner in which they are grouped for classification varies. In this book the most familiar classification, recognizing four classes, is retained.

Class I Scyphozoa

Marine. The pelagic medusoid stage predominates in most orders and the sessile polyp (*scyphistoma*) is usually very small. Coelenteron divided into four by *septa*. Marginal tentacles in a single (or variously modified) whorl surround the mouth, which is generally situated at the end of a tubular *manubrium*. Few scyphistoma stages have been described (Fig. 4.1). They are generally naked but the type known as *Stephanoscyphus* has a funnel-shaped chitinous periderm. Scyphistomae may produce more scyphistomae from stolons by budding, and produce young medusae (*ephyrae*) by transverse fission (*strobilation*), either singly or in simultaneous groups.

In medusae, four endodermal interradial *septa* partly divide the coelenteron into a central stomach and four perradial *pouches*; these pouches give rise to *radial canals* which join the marginal *ring canal*. Endodermal gonads are borne on the septa or pouches. The margin usually bears some reduced tentacles (*rhopalia*) enclosing statoliths. The upper surface of the medusa is *exumbrellar* or *aboral*; the under surface is *subumbrellar* or *oral*. The subumbrellar surface usually contains four invaginated interradial *funnels*. The mouth hangs at the end of a quadrangular, tubular *manubrium*, and the corners of the mouth may be prolonged as oral arms. There is no velum (cf. Hydrozoa).

There are four orders. Three of these (Coronatae, Semaeostomeae, and Rhizostomeae) are jellyfish and should be identified using Russell (1970). The fourth order, Stauromedusae, are sessile and are included here (p. 101).

Class II Cubozoa

Box jellyfish (single order, Cubomedusae). Medusae often roughly square in section. One or more interradial tentacles hang from *pedalia* at each corner, and perradial sense organs are situated on each side of the bell.

Class III Hydrozoa

Characterized by the alternation of attached, asexually replicating, typically colonial *polyps* and pelagic, sexually reproducing *medusae*, the latter perhaps best being regarded as the adult. However, in contrast to Scyphozoa, the medusa is generally small and may be suppressed, while the polyp tends to propagate into conspicuous colonies. In neither polyp nor medusa is the coelenteron septate. Free medusae are most commonly budded from polyps, are radially (or tetramerally) symmetrical, and have the subumbrellar space partially enclosed by a thin shelf or *velum*. The mouth is at the end of a tubular *manubrium*. Four perradial *canals* (and sometimes others) connect the gastric cavity with a *ring canal* in the bell margin. No rhopalia. The polyps are radially symmetrical and are generally colonial, the coelenterons being continuous from polyp to polyp. There is generally a *chitinous* (or sometimes calcareous) *exoskeleton*. New polyps are budded from adnate stolons or from other polyps. Many are polymorphic.

The principal order is the Hydroida (p. 107); others are not included being either exclusively tropical or pelagic. However, a pleustonic (floating on the sea's surface) representative of another order (Siphonophora, p. 159) and an aberrant athecate hydroid (p. 116) may be stranded on Atlantic beaches. These are the Portuguese man-o'-war *Physalia*, and by-the-wind-sailor *Velella* respectively. One representative of the small order Limnomedusae (*Proboscidactyla*), the polyp stage of which lives on the tube rim of sabellid polychaetes, is keyed with the hydroids and described on p. 159.

Class IV Anthozoa

Marine. Exclusively polypoid; solitary or colonial. Gastrovascular cavity divided by 6, 8, or numerous longitudinal, radially arranged septa termed *mesenteries*; terminated distally by the *oral disk* from which, between the mesenteries, arise the hollow tentacles. Symmetry secondarily *biradial*; the mouth and *actinopharynx* descending from it, elongate in section, one or both ends modified as ciliated grooves or *siphonoglyphs*. Mesenteries are thickened and convoluted at their free edge as *mesenteric filaments* and may include well-formed retractor muscles; gonadal cells, derived from endoderm, develop within them. Fertilization is usually external. Dispersal is by pelagic larvae, usually *planulae*, but asexual propagation by external budding, fission, fragmentation, and (apparently) some form of internal budding or parthenogenesis is widespread. Many contain internal skeletal material of various kinds or secrete a calcareous exoskeleton.

Divided into 2 subclasses:

1. Octocorallia or Alcyonaria. Mesenteries 8; tentacles pinnate. Classification into orders is dubious but includes Alcyonacea (soft corals), Gorgonacea (sea fans), and Pennatulacea (sea pens).

2. Hexacorallia or Zoantharia. Mesenteries 6 or multiples of 6; tentacles simple. Orders include Actiniaria (anemones), Corallimorpharia (jewel anemone), Scleractinia (corals), Zoanthidea (zoanthids), and Ceriantharia (tube anemones).

Class Scyphozoa

Order Stauromedusae

Attached Scyphozoa which develop directly from the scyphistoma. Each consists of a *bell* (umbrella or *calyx*) and a more or less distinct aboral stalk which terminates in an *adhesive disk*. As in other scyphozoans, symmetry is tetramerous and defined in terms of the disposition of the four stomach pouches in the *perradii* and their separating septa in the *interradii*. Between these main axes lie eight *adradii*. The mouth is tetramerous with the angles lying in the perradii. The septa of the bell are rounded in section and effectively hollow, the oral surface being indented as four tapering, interradial *funnels* (pits or infundibula). The bell typically has eight adradial marginal *arms* (lobes), each supporting a cluster of knobbed hollow *tentacles* (secondary tentacles). In some genera eight per- and interradial marginal *primary tentacles* (anchors) are present, used for temporary attachment when the animal moves in a looper caterpillar fashion, transferring the stalk disk to a new position. No rhopalia. Gonads are borne on the septal walls as eight separate half gonads or pairs may be partially or completely fused in the perradii. Gametes are shed into the water; zygotes develop into unciliated vermiform planula larvae from which the scyphistoma develops after a period of attached encystment.

Most species occur on the lower shore attached to algae, *Zostera*, and stones. The sexes are separate and all evidence points to their being annuals.

LITERATURE

Brief descriptions, with synonymies but not illustrations, of all the British Stauromedusae except one were given by Kramp (1961). The remaining species, *Lucernariopsis cruxmelitensis*, was described by Corbin (1978). Berrill (1962) has given a good account of *Haliclystus salpinx*, and Eales (1938) erroneously redescribed *Lucernariopsis campanulata*. The ecology of four species in the Plymouth area was discussed by Corbin (1979).

Berrill, N. J. (1962). The biology of three New England Stauromedusae, with a description of a new species. *Canadian Journal of Zoology*, **40**, 1249–62.

Corbin, P. G. (1978). A new species of the stauromedusan genus *Lucernariopsis* (Coelenterata: Scyphomedusae). *Journal of the Marine Biological Association of the U.K.*, **58**, 285–90.

Corbin, P. G. (1979). The seasonal abundance of four species of Stauromedusae (Coelenterata: Scyphomedusae) at Plymouth. *Journal of the Marine Biological Association of the U.K.*, **59**, 385–91.

Eales, N. B. (1938). *Lucernaria discoidea*, a new species from the Channel Islands. *Journal of the Marine Biological Association of the U.K.*, **23**, 167–70.

Johnston, G. (1847). *A history of the British zoophytes*, edn 2. 2 vols, Van Voorst, London.

Kramp, P. L. (1961). Synopsis of the medusae of the world. *Journal of the Marine Biological Association of the U.K.*, **40**, 292–303.

Naumov, D. V. (1961). Scyphomedusae of the seas of the USSR (in Russian). *Opred Faune SSSR*, **75**: 1–98.

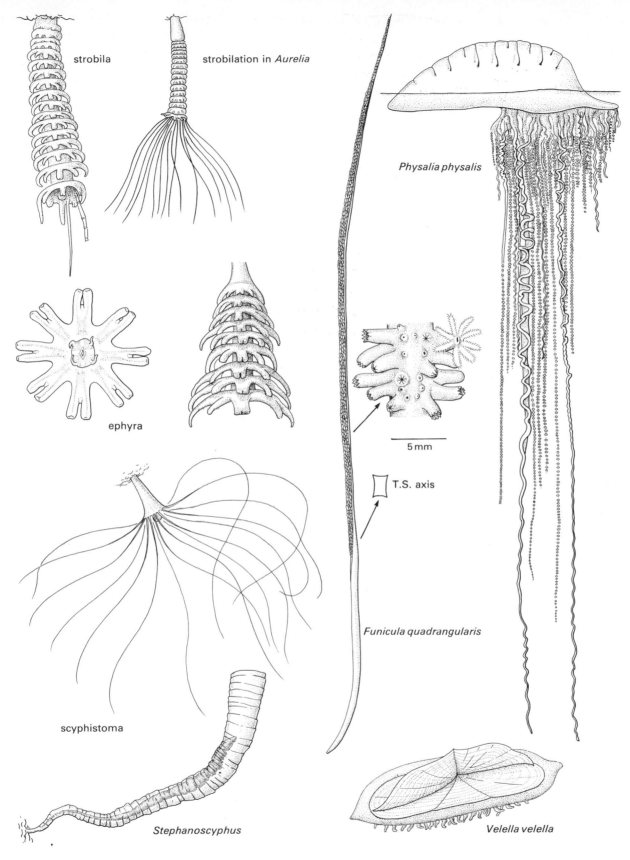

strobila

strobilation in *Aurelia*

ephyra

scyphistoma

Stephanoscyphus

Physalia physalis

5 mm

T.S. axis

Funicula quadrangularis

Velella velella

Fig. 4.1

KEY TO SPECIES

---

1. Arms absent; >20 tentacles in each octant of bell margin, in one to three rows; gonads horseshoe-shaped; bell <10 mm in diameter   ***Depastrum cyathiforme***

   Arms present; arm tentacles numerous, in eight bunches; gonads various; mature bell >10 mm in diameter   **2**

---

2. Arms cruciformly arranged in four pairs; deep and shallow sinuses alternating
   Lucernaria quadricornis

   Eight equal, radially-arranged arms; inter-arm sinuses equal   **3**

---

3. Well developed marginal primary tentacles (anchors) present in each sinus (*Haliclystus*)   **4**

   Primary tentacles typically absent in adult   **5**

---

4. Marginal primary tentacles large, trumpet-shaped, with thickened rim and a central rudimentary tentacle   ***Haliclystus salpinx***

   Marginal primary tentacles kidney-shaped, shortly stalked, aboral to the margin
   Haliclystus auricula

---

5. Peduncle short; arms short and wide, with up to 80 tentacles; gonad halves united (presenting in oral view a perradial, cruciform arrangement)   ***Craterolophus convolvulus***

   Peduncle about as long as height of the bell (though it may be involuted within the base of the bell), arms distinct, with up to 35 tentacles; gonad halves separate or partially separate, extending adradially to arm tips (*Lucernariopsis*)   **6**

---

6. Bell to 35 mm diameter; colour variable but uniform, with 1–4 bright turquoise spots seen in interradii midway down bell; aboral surface papillate; a globular swelling at the base of each tentacle of outermost tentacle row; gonad halves linear, separate
   Lucernariopsis campanulata

   Bell to 18 mm diameter; colour maroon with conspicuous white spots on disk in pattern of maltese cross; white flecks in V-formation seen in aboral interradii; a swollen band at base of outermost tentacle row encircling outer half of arm; gonad halves united perradially at base, Y-shaped in oral view; characteristically displays 'stalkless' posture with stalk involuted within the bell   ***Lucernariopsis cruxmelitensis***

---

1 CLEISTOCARPIDAE

Gonads united by a transverse, circumferential membrane which divides each of the stomach pouches into outer and inner chambers.

Craterolophus convolvulus (Johnston)   FIG. 4.2
[KRAMP 1961: 303; JOHNSTON 1847, 248, as *Lucernaria campanulata*]
Bell vase- or urn-shaped, 25(–30) mm high and 25(–30) mm diameter with short stalk, 5(–8) mm, and wide basal disk; adradial arms short, wide, equidistant, with 60–80 tentacles in clusters having radial diameter greater than transverse diameter; per- and interradial primary tentacles absent in adults, inconspicuous in bells <9 mm diameter. Gonad halves united, evenly lobed along each side, extending perradially to the bell margin, seen as four 'feathers' in oral view. Non-translucent; grey, green, brown, or red coloured, sometimes with whitish spots (nematocyst storage vesicles) along mid-line of gonad.

Low intertidal and shallow sublittoral, on algae and *Zostera*; all coasts; rarely numerous. Two generations a year; peak abundance April, secondary peak September at Wembury (Corbin 1979). North Atlantic: New England, Iceland, Denmark, Brittany.

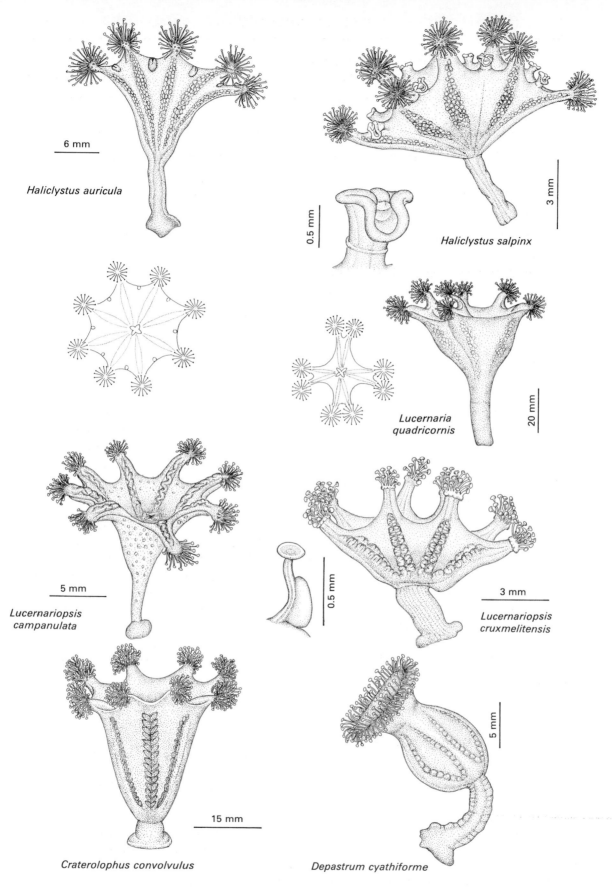

Haliclystus auricula

Haliclystus salpinx

Lucernaria quadricornis

Lucernariopsis campanulata

Lucernariopsis cruxmelitensis

Craterolophus convolvulus

Depastrum cyathiforme

Fig. 4.2

Depastrum cyathiforme (M. Sars)   FIG. 4.2
[KRAMP 1961: 301]
Bell goblet-shaped, 10(–12) mm high and 8(–10) mm diameter; stalk about as long as bell, 12(–14) mm, flexible, contractile. Arms absent; 8–15 tentacles in 1–3 rows in each adradial octant of the bell margin; bell constricted below the tentaculate rim. Gonads lyrate, with transverse folds when ripe. Grey-brown, ripe gonads whitish to pinkish.

Low intertidal and shallow sublittoral, usually under or among stones and boulders (never on algae); local, fairly common in parts of Isle of Man; gonads April to September. North Atlantic: Norway, British Isles south to Scilly, and Brittany.

2 ELEUTHEROCARPIDAE

Perradial stomach pouches simple.

Haliclystus auricula (Rathke)   FIG. 4.2
[KRAMP 1961, 292; JOHNSTON 1847, 246, as *Lucernaria*]
Bell funnel-shaped, 15(–20) mm high and 25(–30) mm diameter; stalk as long as the bell, 15(–20) mm. Arms adradial, with 30–60(–100) tentacles in each adradial tuft; per- and interradial primary tentacles ovoid, reverted, conspicuous (dorsally grooved with central projecting tentacular knob in young specimens). Half gonads separate, extending adradially to arm tips; seen as eight linear-lanceolate 'leaves' in oral view; follicles individually visible, in about four linear series. Body translucent, pale to deep grey, green, yellow, brown, red, or purple; a few whitish spots (nematocyst storage vesicles) near perradial margins.

Low intertidal and shallow sublittoral; on algae and *Zostera*; all coasts; widespread, the most numerous British species. One generation a year; peak abundance June–July at Wembury (Corbin 1979). North Atlantic and North Pacific.

Haliclystus salpinx Clark   FIG. 4.2
[KRAMP 1961, 294; BERRILL 1962, 1250]
Bell broadly funnel-shaped, generally 20–25(–30) mm high and 20–25(–30) mm in diameter, the stalk as long as the height of the bell; adradial arms moderately prominent, with 60–70(–100) slender tentacles in each cluster; primary tentacles very large, prominent, and columnar, distally trumpet-shaped with a thickened rim except at its most proximal point, with a short capitate tentacle in the centre and having a narrow ridge encircling the column near the base. Gonad halves separate, meeting at the vertex of the funnel, almost reaching the margin adradially; follicles individually visible, in about four linear series. Pink-red in colour. Specimens described by Berrill (1962) from Maine were small (8–9 mm high, 15–20 tentacles).

Low intertidal and sublittoral; to about 5 m, on *Laminaria*, other algae, and *Zostera*. North Atlantic and North Pacific (see Naumov 1961, as *Octomanus monstrosus*). Not yet recorded in British waters though known from the vicinity of Bergen, Norway.

Lucernaria quadricornis Müller   FIG. 4.2
[KRAMP 1961, 295; JOHNSTON 1847, 244, Pl. 45, as *L. fascicularis*]

Bell funnel-shaped, 60(–70) mm high and 70(–80) mm diameter; stalk a little longer than height of bell but very contractile. Arms arranged in four pairs; deep perradial sinuses alternating with narrow, shallow interradial sinuses; up to 140 tentacles in each cluster, thin stalks, small heads. Primary tentacles typically absent in adults; present in young and irregularly persisting in some adults in some populations (e.g. Isles of Scilly). Gonad halves linear-lanceolate, extending adradially almost to arm tips, with transverse folds when ripe, luminescent in dark when stimulated. Specimens are very flaccid; symmetrical oral view seldom presented. Non-translucent, green-black to brown-black, gonads cream-orange in aboral view.

Low intertidal and sublittoral to 550 m; under stones and boulders at British localities, also on algae further north; local but may be numerous in subarctic waters; mainly northern in British Isles but south to Isles of Scilly.

L. bathyphila Haeckel is a less obviously cruciform, deepwater species (see Naumov 1961). Stalk short; bell large, goblet-shaped, to 80 mm high and 60 mm wide, with very short arms; perradial sinuses scarcely wider and deeper than interradial; gonads club-shaped, not reaching the end of the arms. Arctic, but a single specimen taken from the Faroe-Shetland Channel in 1880.

Lucernariopsis campanulata (Lamouroux)   FIG. 4.2
[KRAMP 1961, 298; EALES 1938, as *Lucernaria discoidea*]
Bell funnel-shaped, 20(–25) mm high and 30(–35) mm diameter; stalk 20(–25) mm, ending in a disk; entire aboral surface papillated (nematocyst storage vesicles). Adradial arms long, the per- and interradial sinuses of equal size; up to 45 tentacles, all except the short inner ones with discoid ends, and each of the outermost with a basal, glandular swelling. Small primary tentacles present in young specimens (<9 mm diameter), typically absent in adults. Gonad halves separate, linear, extending to the arm tips; in oral view appearing coiled, as adradial 'ropes'. Generally translucent, uniformly green, brown, or red; 1–4 bright turquoise spots (nematocyst storage vesicles) situated deeply at the base of each of the four interradial funnels of oral surface, most clearly seen in oral or lateral view.

Low intertidal and shallow sublittoral; on algae and *Zostera*; all coasts but scarce bordering North Sea; north-west France. Single generation per year; peak abundance September–October at Wembury (Corbin 1979).

Lucernariopsis cruxmelitensis Corbin   FIG. 4.2
Bell widely funnel-shaped, 8 mm high and 12(–14) mm diameter; stalk 8 mm, but the base of the bell characteristically involuted around the stalk, presenting in life a 'stalkless' appearance; basal disk broad. Arms well-developed and equidistant; up to 35 tentacles per cluster, each with a rounded (not discoid) head; a swollen, glandular band encircles the outer half of the arm at the level of the tentacle bases. Primary tentacles absent in adults, present in young (<7 mm diameter) specimens. Gonad halves thick, linear, united perradially at the base, extending adradially to the arms; with swellings along their length, in oral view appearing as thick 'ropes'. Translucent, maroon in colour, orally

with a conspicuous maltese cross of bright white spots (nematocyst storage organs) in the perradii and delimited by the gonads.

Low intertidal and shallow sublittoral; usually on *Chondrus* and *Gigartina*, rarely *Zostera*; south-west England from Swanage to north Devon, Atlantic coasts of Ireland; one generation per year with peak abundance in late winter (Wembury, South Devon: Corbin 1979).

Class **Hydrozoa**

Order **Hydroida**

Hydrozoans typified by sessile *polyp* and free-swimming *medusa* generations in the life cycle. Almost all are marine. The hydroid stage is either solitary or *colonial*, and either buds free medusae or has sessile structures representing vestigial medusae. Gametes liberated from the medusae or from their sessile counterparts fuse to form zygotes which develop into *planula* larvae. The planula settles and develops into a *primary polyp* from which a new colony grows, completing the life cycle.

The skeleton is nearly always external to the tissues, but in the Hydractiniidae it secondarily forms an underlying mat. Over most of the colony the skeleton comprises a branching tube of chitinous material termed the *perisarc*. The tube of tissue inside is the *coenosarc* and consists of the usual three cnidarian layers. The colonies formed by most hydroids comprise (1) a basal portion, the *hydrorhiza*, which might be *stolonal*, mat-like, or a fibrous mass of aggregated tubes, and usually (2) an erect stem which in many species is branched (Fig. 4.3). Usually a colony comprises several to many erect shoots of well-defined growth habit joined basally by a stolon lacking polyps. In a few hydroids, however, colonies start growing stolonally, subsequently sending up erect shoots, and having feeding and sometimes also reproductive polyps on both components of the colony. The stolon functions to anchor the erect shoots and, early in colony development, to space them apart.

The main stem or *hydrocaulus* may fork, the side branches being called *hydrocladia*. The branching pattern may be regular or irregular, bushy, *pinnate* (feather-like), or have branches arising all round the stem, recalling a bottle brush; or it may be a combination of these patterns. The first level of branching is termed *first order*, those arising from them *second order*, and so on. Many hydrocauli and hydrocladia are *flexuose* (zigzag). Stems and branches comprising a single tube are termed *monosiphonic* or simple, and those of two or more fused together are called *polysiphonic* or compound (fascicled in older literature).

Most hydrocauli and hydrocladia have *annuli* or rings at regular or irregular intervals, which may be *transverse*, if at right angles to the axis of the skeletal tube, or *oblique*. Annuli are roughly circular grooves in the exoskeleton which permit limited bending of the mostly stiff outer tube. The positions of the annuli on the stems and branches are termed *nodes* and the intervening portions *internodes*. Annuli occur also in the *pedicels* or stalks of many polyps.

The polyps originate from the coenosarc and their *enterons* are continuous with it. Thus a meal obtained by one can be shared around the colony. There are several kinds of polyps, the feeding polyps or *hydranths* being usually the largest and most conspicuous. In very polymorphic forms the feeding polyps, which may lack tentacles, are termed *gastrozooids*. Hydranths are borne on the hydrocladia, and often on hydrocauli, stolons, and other hydrorhizae depending on the species. In the suborder Thecata the hydranths can in most families contract within a robust protective perisarcal cup, the *hydrotheca*, though in some thecates this has degenerated to a mere collar. In the suborder Athecata there are no true hydrothecae, there being at most a frail often deciduous extension of the stem perisarc termed a *pseudohydrotheca*. These occur in just a few species and are clearly secondary in origin. In the thecates the margin or *rim* of the hydrotheca may be *smooth* or *even*, *undulating*, *crenulate*, *indented*, *cusped*, *denticulate*, or *castellate* (Fig. 4.3). Some cusps are themselves deeply indented at the apex so that the rim has alternating deep and shallow *embayments* between the points, the *bimucronate* condition. In some families the hydrothecal *aperture* is closed by a lid or *operculum* of one to several flaps. In many genera new hydrothecae grow inside old ones so that a chain or nest of *renovated hydrothecae* or *renovated hydrothecal rims* becomes built up.

Some groups of thecates have the hydrotheca free and on a short *pedicel*, which is often *annulated*. The hydrothecae in others can be considered as a series showing progressive incorporation of the theca into the perisarc tube. Hydrothecae lacking a stalk are termed *sessile*, those in which part or all of the adjacent or *adcauline* wall is fused with the perisarc of the stem or branch are termed *adnate* or *fused*, and those in which the outer or *abcauline* wall also becomes incorporated to a varied extent are described as *sunken*. Hydrothecal pedicels in some genera of Campanulariidae have two unusually deep annuli at the top, delimiting a *subhydrothecal spherule* and permitting great lateral movement. In some genera the hydrotheca has internally near the base a *diaphragm* which may be *transverse* if at right angles to the hydrothecal axis or *oblique*. A small *hydropore* in the centre allows continuity with the coenosarc below. *True diaphragms* are continuous with the hydrothecal wall, *false diaphragms* arise later as outgrowths from it. Hydrothecae of some thecates have *internal septa* of irregular structure which partition them into chambers of varied shape. They are most prevalent in the Sertulariidae and Aglaopheniidae.

The hydranth comprises a short but often very extensile body or *column*. The mouth, often on a raised *hypostome*, is terminal and functions also as an anus. There are almost always numerous tentacles. They surround the mouth in one or two rings, circlets or *whorls*, or in an *oral* (upper) whorl around the mouth and an *aboral* (lower) one more basally on the column. In some genera they are scattered over much of the column, or may be disposed in several more or less loosely defined whorls, or partly in whorls and partly scattered. Hydranths of thecates usually have a single whorl in which alternate tentacles are directed upwards and downwards, an arrangement termed *amphicoronate*, but in some species all point the same way. Short ectodermal *webs* join the tentacles basally in some thecates: in some groups their presence

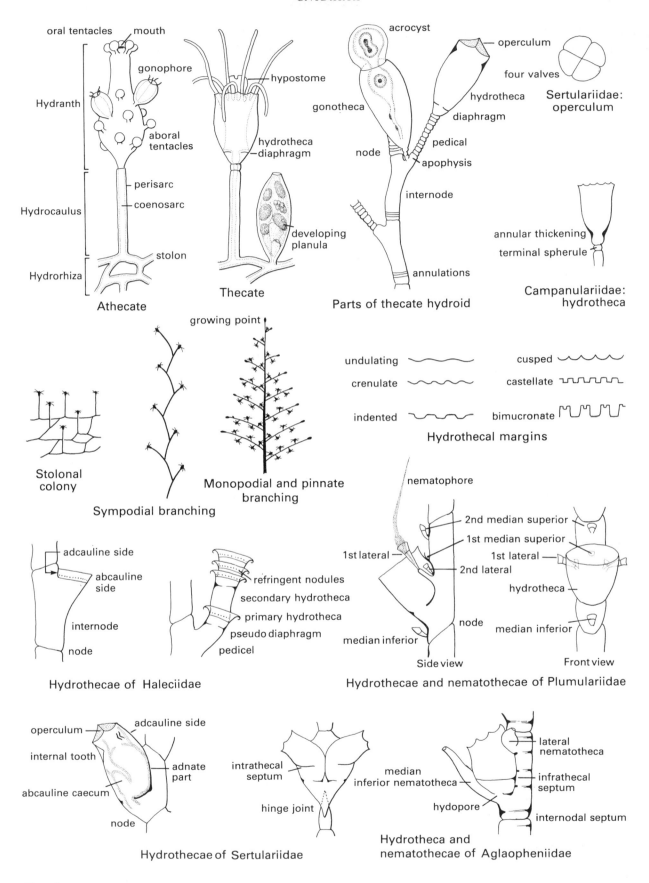

oral tentacles   mouth

gonophore

Hydranth

aboral
tentacles

perisarc

Hydrocaulus   coenosarc

stolon

Hydrorhiza

Athecate

hypostome

hydrotheca
diaphragm

developing
planula

Thecate

acrocyst

operculum

gonotheca   four valves

node   hydrotheca

diaphragm   **Sertulariidae:
                    operculum**

pedical

apophysis

internode

annular thickening

terminal spherule

annulations

Parts of thecate hydroid   **Campanulariidae:
                                    hydrotheca**

growing point

undulating   cusped

crenulate   castellate

indented   bimucronate

Hydrothecal margins

**Stolonal
colony**

**Monopodial and pinnate
branching**

Sympodial branching

nematophore

adcauline side   2nd median superior

abcauline   refringent nodules   1st median superior

side   secondary hydrotheca   1st lateral   1st lateral

internode   primary hydrotheca   2nd lateral

pseudo diaphragm   hydrotheca

node   pedicel   node   median inferior

                                    median inferior

                                    Side view   Front view

Hydrothecae of Haleciidae   **Hydrothecae and nematothecae of Plumulariidae**

operculum   adcauline side

internal tooth   lateral
                                    intrathecal   nematotheca
abcauline caecum   adnate   septum   median
                        part   inferior nematotheca   infrathecal
                                                                        septum
                        node   hinge joint   hydopore
                                                                        internodal septum

Hydrothecae of Sertulariidae   **Hydrotheca and
                                                    nematothecae of Aglaopheniidae**

Fig. 4.3

has been regarded as a family characteristic, in others it varies within a genus. *Capitate* tentacles have knobbed tips and occur in some athecate families but most, termed *linear*, are either parallel-sided almost throughout their length or taper barely perceptibly to the pointed tip. *Moniliform* tentacles have the nematocysts in groups, giving a banded appearance; *cateniform* tentacles have them in a spiral, and in *filiform* tentacles they are scattered irregularly. Other arrangements occur. In some species of thecates all three are to be found and they have little use in identification.

Nematophores occur on the stems and branches of some athecates and in many species of the thecate families Plumulariidae, Aglaopheniidae, Campanulinidae, Haleciidae, and Zygophylacidae. These are minute extensile polyps which usually lack mouths and tentacles but are armed with numerous nematocysts. They are thought to defend the colony against predation and settlement by larvae. Those of most thecate genera have a surrounding perisarc cup, the *nematotheca*, which may be sessile and immovable, termed *fixed*, or on a short movable pedicel and *mobile*, but in some genera the nematophores are *naked*.

In the Hydractiniidae occur long, atentaculate polyps called *dactylozooids* comprising *spiral zooids*, which coil up, and *tentaculozooids*, which remain roughly straight.

Increase in size by hydroid colonies is by growth ('vegetative reproduction'), in which new branches and polyps, the 'individuals' or modules, are added to the colony. The life cycle of most hydroids involves a succession or 'alternation' of generations in which one or other of the generations includes a sexual phase. Species retaining the basic life cycle produce medusae by asexual budding. In the Hydrozoa the medusae are called *hydromedusae* (see Russell 1953, for descriptions). Most are less than 20 mm across in contrast to true jellyfish or *scyphomedusae* almost all of which attain 100 mm or more at maturity. Most species of hydromedusae were first described separately from, and in ignorance of, their hydroid stages and the two were only later linked, usually by rearing. Even in some British species the hydroid and medusa have still to be connected. The medusae, when present, are the sexual phase of the life cycle. Each medusa is either male or female, bearing gonads from which spermatozoa or ova are typically discharged into the sea. The zygotes resulting from fertilization develop in the plankton into minute planulae which settle to grow into new hydroid colonies and so complete the life cycle. However, in many species the medusa is reduced and remains attached to the hydroid in a variety of vestigial states such as *eumedusoids* and *sporosacs*. The latter are secondarily released in some species. *Gonomedusoids*, a kind of eumedusoid found in *Gonothyraea*, have vestigial radial canals and tentacles, but in the more widespread sporosacs these are absent and the medusa is reduced to a mere sac of gonadal tissue. A sporosac held external to the gonothecal aperture and lacking medusoid features is termed an *acrocyst*.

In many athecates medusae are budded from unmodified feeding hydranths which may, in some species, regress as the medusae develop. In other athecates, however, and in all thecates, medusae and their vestigial derivatives are borne on specialized polyps, lacking mouth or tentacles, termed *blastostyles*. In the thecates these are enclosed in corresponding *gonothecae* but in athecates they are naked. A blastostyle or other kind of polyp bearing gonophores and sporosacs or medusae was termed a *gonozooid* in older literature. In thecates the blastostyle and gonotheca together are sometimes referred to as a *gonangium*.

The gonothecae usually differ between species and, in species not releasing medusae, often between male and female. Such differences can be useful in identification. The differences between 'male' and 'female' gonothecae can usually be related to their different roles. (It is of course the enclosed sporosacs which actually are male or female.) Female gonothecae tend to have wider apertures to allow the egress of mature planulae, whereas male gonothecae, from which spermatozoa are released, usually have narrower apertures. A typical planula might be 1 mm long and 0.2 mm wide. In species which liberate medusae there is no such distinction between male and female gonothecae, the medusae of the two sexes being identical when liberated. Only later do the medusae develop sexual differences. In some genera of thecate hydroids the gonangia are protected in modified branches such as the *coppiniae* (muff-like tangles of elongate reduced hydrothecae) and *scapi* (sing., *scapus*) of some Lafoeidae, and the *corbulae* and *phylactocarps* of some Aglaopheniidae. These features are often helpful in identification.

Species not releasing medusae may be *gonochoric* or *dioecious*, having the gonophores all of one sex, or *monoecious*, having those of both sexes on any colony, as in *Plumularia setacea*. The former is the more common though in some species both conditions are known. The spermatozoa of species having sessile gonophores are released into the sea and presumably find their way to the ova which are fertilized and subsequently develop *in situ*, typically into planulae. In some species of Tubulariidae development continues further, resulting in a considerably modified swimming polyp, the *actinula*. Most gonothecae (restricted to thecates) terminate in a simple circular opening through which the planulae eventually escape. However in, for example, many species of *Diphasia*, the embryos develop in a protective *brood chamber* formed from a chitinous extension from the end of the gonotheca. In other thecates, for example *Orthopyxis* and several of the Sertulariidae, planulae mature in a gelatinous sac or *acrocyst* (see above).

The two suborders which are both well-represented around British coasts can be distinguished thus:

Suborder ATHECATA (ANTHOMEDUSAE; formerly Gymnoblastea), releasing so-called *anthomedusae*. Hydroida in which the hydranths are not protected by true hydrothecae, or the gonangia by gonothecae; and in which the gonads of the medusae are usually borne on the manubrium.

Suborder THECATA (LEPTOMEDUSAE; formerly Calyptoblastea), releasing so-called *leptomedusae*. Hydroida in which hydrotheca and gonotheca are fundamentally present, although the hydrotheca is reduced in some families; and in which the gonads of the medusae are usually borne on the radial canals.

There are exceptions in both these groupings. Thus in the thecate families Haleciidae and Plumulariidae the hydrotheca is usually too small to accommodate the hydranth, while several species of athecates have an extension of the perisarc enveloping much of the hydranth and termed a *pseudohydrotheca*. But these exceptions are clearly secondary and the classification is largely valid.

Most hydroids occur sublittorally. A few only are characteristic of the shore; most of the species found there being stragglers from sublittoral strongholds. In the first 0–15 m hydroids grow abundantly on *Laminaria* and other algae. They continue below this, often in a thick turf in association with Bryozoa, to a depth of 30–40 m around British coasts. Many occur much deeper, almost to the greatest depths of the ocean, but only in shallower waters do hydroids normally form dense communities.

Intertidally hydroids occur most commonly in rock pools, particularly just below the surface, and in moist situations such as in wide crevices and beneath overhangs and algae. Others grow on the blades of brown and red algae, and on eel grass. Most thrive best in places of moderate water movement where feeding opportunities are greatest, and the richest dredge hauls are often made in turbulent waters off headlands or in narrow straits.

Hydroids seem particularly sensitive to human pollution, and along the south-east coast of England and around some other heavily populated and industrialized areas they may be less common than formerly. Many species are tolerant of reduced salinity, silty conditions, and temperature fluctuation but most have rather narrow limits of tolerance. A few, not included here, occur exclusively in fresh water, and some are parasitic.

Hydroids are best collected by removing them from their substrata with forceps and placing them in collecting vessels. Many will survive well in aquaria but cleanliness and temperature control are crucial. Anaesthetization can be achieved with menthol crystals, 15% $MgSo_4.7H_2O$ or 7.5% $MgCl_2.6H_2O$, or with very dilute formalin or ethanol. Colonies for preservation should be fixed first in 8% formaldehyde solution (i.e. a 20% solution of commercial formalin) for 24 h and transferred to 70% methylated ethanol for permanent storage. Formaldehyde is harmful and should be handled with care. The perisarc of most hydroids can be stained effectively with borax carmine and the tissues with haematoxylin. Gurr's hydramount or equivalent is an adequate mountant and has the great advantage that specimens can be transferred into it from water, ethanol, or formalin. Canada balsam or synthetic resin are permanent over tens of years but preparation takes longer. Care should be taken not to squash the hydrothecae and hence distort their shape: it is advisable to support the coverslip, and short lengths of thicker monofilament nylon fishing line are ideal for this purpose. Many details of hydroids can be seen in unstained material using phase contrast or interference microscopy.

LITERATURE

The most complete monograph in English is Hincks' *A history of the British hydroid zoophytes* (1868), now out of date in nomenclature and terminology but with excellent plates. Allman's (1871–2) monograph on the athecates is accurately illustrated in colour. Useful and more recent books covering the hydroid fauna of the North Sea and eastern English Channel are those by Broch (1928, in German), Kramp (1935, in Danish), Vervoort (1946, in Dutch) and Leloup (1952, in French). Brinckmann-Voss (1970, in English) has described the Mediterranean capitate Athecata in a volume notable for its coloured plates, but only a few British hydroids come within its scope. Russell's monographs on medusae (1953, 1970) include descriptions and illustrations of the hydroids of all species having a medusa stage in the life cycle. A volume by Cornelius on the Thecata and their medusae in the Linnean Society's *Synopses of the British Fauna* is in preparation. The best general introductions to the group are those by Naumov (1969) and Millard (1975), both in English, by Werner (1984) in German, and by Bouillon (in press) in French. Bouillon *et al.* (1987) have provided accounts of several biological aspects.

Allman, G. J. (1871, 1872). *A monograph of the gymnoblastic or tubularian hydroids*. London, Ray Society, Vol. I, part (1871) 1–154; Vol. I, remainder (1872) 155–231; Vol. II (1872) 232–450.

Allman, G. J. (1883). Report on the Hydroida dredged by HMS Challenger during the years 1873–1876. Pt. 1. Plumularidae. *Report on the Scientific Results of the Voyage of HMS Challenger*. Zoology, Vol. 7.

Boero, F. and Cornelius, P. F. S. (1987). First records of *Eudendrium glomeratum* (Cnidaria: Hydroida) in British and Irish Waters, and taxonomic comments. *Irish Naturalists Journal*, **22**, 244–6.

Bouillon, J. (ed.), (1989). *Traité de Zoologie: 3 (2), Cnidaires, Cténaires*. Paris, Masson.

Bouillon, J., Boero, F., Cicogna, F., and Cornelius, P. F. S. (1987). *Modern trends in the systematics, ecology, and evolution of hydroids and hydromedusae*. Clarendon Press, Oxford.

Broch, H. (1928). Hydrozoa, I. *Tierwelt der Nord- und Ostsee*, **36**, 1–100.

Brinckmann-Voss, A. (1970). Anthomedusae/Athecatae (Hydrozoa, Cnidaria) of the Mediterranean. Part I. Capitata. *Fauna Flora Golfo Napoli*, **39**, 1–96.

Cornelius, P. F. S. (1975a). The hydroid species of *Obelia* (Coelenterata, Hydrozoa: Campanulariidae), with notes on the medusa stage. *Bulletin of the British Museum (Natural History)* Zoology, **28**, 249–93.

Cornelius, P. F. S. (1975b). A revision of the species of Lafoeidae and Haleciidae (Coelenterata: Hydroida) recorded from Britain and nearby seas. *Bulletin of the British Museum (Natural History)* Zoology, **28**, 373–426.

Cornelius, P. F. S. (1979). A revision of the species of Sertulariidae (Coelenterata: Hydroida) recorded from Britain and nearby seas. *Bulletin of the British Museum (Natural History)* Zoology, **34**, 243–321.

Cornelius, P. F. S. (1982). Hydroids and medusae of the family Campanulariidae recorded from the eastern North Atlantic, with a world synopsis of genera. *Bulletin of the British Museum (Natural History)* Zoology, **42**, 37–148.

Edwards, C. (1964a). The hydroid of the anthomedusa *Bougainvillia britannica*. *Journal of the Marine Biological Association of the U.K.*, **44**, 1–10.

Edwards, C. (1964b). On the hydroids and medusae *Bougainvillia pyramidata* and *B. muscoides*. *Journal of the Marine Biological Association of the U.K.*, **44**, 725–52.

Edwards, C. (1966). The hydroid and the medusa *Bougainvillia principis*, and a review of the British species of *Bougainvillia*. *Journal of the Marine Biological Association of the U.K.*, **46**, 129–52.

Edwards, C. (1972). The hydroids and the medusae *Podocoryne areolata, P. borealis* and *P. carnea. Journal of the Marine Biological Association of the U.K.*, **52**, 97–144.

Edwards, C. and Harvey, S. M. (1975). The hydroids *Clava multicornis* and *C. squamata. Journal of the Marine Biological Association of the U.K.*, **55**, 879–86.

Evans, F. O. (1978). The marine fauna of the Cullercoats district. 6. Coelenterata and Ctenophora. *Reports of the Dove Marine Laboratory*, (3) **19**, 1–165.

Hamond, R. (1957). Notes on the Hydrozoa of the Norfolk coast. *Journal of the Linnean Society* (Zoology), **43**, 294–324.

Hincks, T. (1868). *A history of the British hydroid zoophytes*, 2 vols. Van Voorst, London.

Kramp, P. L. (1935). Polypdyr (Coelenterata) I. Ferskvandspolypper og Goplepolypper. *Danmarks Fauna*, **41**, 1–207.

Leloup, E. (1952). Coelentérés. *Faune Belge*, 1–283.

Millard, N. A. H. (1975). Monograph of the Hydroida of southern Africa. *Annals of the South African Museum*, **68**, 1–513.

Naumov, D. V. (1969). Hydroids and hydromedusae of the U.S.S.R. *Fauna U.S.S.R.*, **70**, 1–660. (Israel Program for Scientific Translation, cat. no. 5108).

Russell, F. S. (1953). *The medusae of the British Isles. Anthomedusae, Leptomedusae, Limnomedusae, Trachymedusae and Narcomedusae.* Cambridge University Press, Cambridge.

Russell, F. S. (1970). *The medusae of the British Isles, II. Pelagic Scyphozoa, with a supplement to the first volume on hydromedusae.* Cambridge University Press, Cambridge.

Sars, G. O. (1874). Bidrag til Kundskaben om Norges Hydroider. *Forhandlinger i Videnskabsselskabet i Kristiania*, (1873), 91–150.

Svoboda, A., Cornelius, P. F. S., and Picton, B. E. (in press) The European and Mediterranean species of *Aglaophenia* (Cnidaria, Hydrozoa). *Zoologische Mededelingen.*

Teissier, G. (1965). *Inventaire de la faune marine de Roscoff. Cnidaires-Cténaires.* Roscoff, France.

Vervoort, W. (1946). Hydrozoa (CI). A. Hydropolypen. *Fauna Nederland*, **14**, 1–336.

Werner, B. (1984). Stamm Cnidaria, Nesseltiere. *Lehrbuch der Speziellen Zoologie. Band I: Wirbellose Tiere. 2 Teil: Cnidaria, Ctenophora ... Priapulida*, (ed. A. Kaestner). Gustav Fischer, Stuttgart, pp. 11–305.

IDENTIFICATION

Hydroids as a group exhibit much convergence in morphology and, in addition, many species vary in response to environmental conditions. Problems like these bedevil identification keys. Further, many of the characters employed by specialists are minute and inconvenient for general use in identification; or perhaps only appear at one stage in the life cycle. Such characters are avoided here whenever possible, but these problems should be borne in mind when using the keys.

The rarely reported *Proboscidactyla* is for convenience included in the key to athecates but in the text is in its more usual position in a separate order, the Limnomedusae (p. 159), of which it is the only representative included.

Most species of hydroids vary greatly in colony size, in most other dimensions, and in morphological detail. The descriptions given attempt to cover this variation, but the appearance of many species can differ markedly from one habitat to another. This should be remembered. The colony sizes given are normal maxima. Larger colonies might occasionally be found but a majority will be smaller, particularly if young, broken, or growing in suboptimal conditions. Populations in the north are often composed of individuals which are bigger both in detail and in overall colony size than those of the same species in the south, even within British waters.

KEY TO SUBORDERS
(medusa characters omitted)

1. Hydranth with no well-defined hydrotheca; sometimes a weak pseudohydrotheca (delicate extension of the stem perisarc); gonotheca usually lacking, gonophores borne on unspecialized hydranths, on reduced hydranths (blastostyles) or directly on stolon, stem, or pedicel   **Athecata**

   Hydranth with usually large, robust hydrotheca of definite shape, though in some groups too small to accommodate hydranth; gonophores borne on blastostyles and protected by a gonotheca   **Thecata** (p. 126)

Suborder **Athecata**

Hydroida fundamentally lacking well-defined hydrotheca and gonotheca. Tentacles capitate or linear, scattered over hydranth, in oral and aboral whorls, or inserted in one whorl, typically continuing to increase in number after hydranth becomes functional.

KEY TO FAMILIES

The pelagic species *Velella velella* (Fig. 4.1) is not included in the key: see 3. VELELLIDAE (p. 116).

---

1. Some or all of tentacles capitate (club-tipped), very short in the worm-shaped *Candelabrum*   **2**

   Tentacles all linear (tips not clubbed)   **4**

---

2. Hydranth large, solitary, worm-shaped   **5. Candelabridae**

   Colony a normal hydroid, erect or stolonal   **3**

---

3. Hydranth with capitate tentacles scattered over much of column or in up to about six loose whorls; linear tentacles present or absent; colony erect or stolonal   **6. Corynidae**

   Hydranth with single oral whorl of four to five capitate tentacles and aboral whorl of four to five shorter, linear ones; colony stolonal   **4. Cladonematidae**

---

4. Tentacles scattered over much of hydranth; or only two tentacles, sometimes forked   **5**

   Tentacles numerous, clearly in one or two whorls   **6**

---

5. Colony minute, stolonal; hydranths less than 1 mm high; tentacles two, sometimes forked; probably on worm tube [not athecates, but included here for convenience]

   Proboscidactylidae (p. 159)

   Colony large, erect, stolonal, or hydrorhizal; hydranths more than 1 mm; tentacles about 10 or more   **7. Clavidae**

---

6. Tentacles in one whorl, or in two closely adjacent whorls seeming to be one   **7**

   Tentacles in two clearly separate whorls   **10**

---

7. Hypostome narrowing below and widening above, obconical to spherical; never a medusa stage   **8. Eudendriidae**

   Hypostome conical to domed; with or without medusa   **8**

---

8. Hydranths borne on definite, perisarc-covered stem, erect, branched in some species; rarely stolonal   **9. Bougainvilliidae**

   Hydranths on stolonal network or sheet-like hydrorhiza; rarely on short erect stems   **9**

---

9. Hydrorhiza an open network of stolons; sometimes with short erect stems of up to about four hydranths; only hydranths and gonophores represented   **11. Pandeidae**

   Hydrorhiza from a closely anastomosing mat to completely sheet-like; erect stems never present; usually with polyp-types additional to hydranths and gonophores

   10. Hydractiniidae

---

10. Hydranths solitary, massive, up to about 100 mm thick, anemone-like, floppy, lacking normal hydroid perisarc sheath   **1. Corymorphidae**

    Usually colonial or aggregated, hydranths atop rigid perisarc-covered stems; more typically hydroid-like in appearance   **2. Tubulariidae**

---

1 CORYMORPHIDAE

Large, solitary, anemone-like hydroids with massive, cylindrical hydrocaulus ensheathed in delicate, non-supportive perisarc; usually with basal anchoring filaments; hypostome conical; tentacles in oral and aboral whorls; gonophores attached above aboral tentacles, usually on branched blastostyles; fixed sporosacs or released medusae.

Corymorpha nutans M. Sars   FIG. 4.4
[HINCKS 1868, 127, Pl. 22; ALLMAN 1872, 208, 388, Pl. 19; RUSSELL 1953, 84, as *Steenstrupia*]

Hydranth very large, solitary, translucent, white to pale red, faintly lined, anemone-like, floppy, to about 10 cm; elongate, cylindrical to tapering upwards, in life often with upper end recurved and nodding; often with bent, basalmost part in substratum; closely sheathed basally in thin, transparent, deciduous perisarc tube; terminal region red with lower whorl of about 32 long, thick, white, non-contractile tentacles; upper group of about 80 finer, shorter ones. Developing medusae attached just above lower group, on 15–20 branched stalks; mature medusa with just one long tentacle and pointed apex.

Anchored in silt to gravel; coastal, to at least 100 m; throughout British Isles; Mediterranean to northern Norway.

2 TUBULARIIDAE

Solitary or colonial, with erect stems, perisarc extending to base of hydranth. Hydranth large, hypostome conical, tentacles in oral and aboral whorls, the former sometimes capitate when young; gonophores often in branched clusters attached between tentacle whorls; or fixed sporosacs and free medusae known; often an actinula stage.

---

1. Many more oral tentacles than aboral; stems not fused   **Tubularia larynx**

   Oral and aboral tentacles roughly similar in number; stems sometimes fused   **2**

2. Oral tentacles in one whorl   **3**

   Oral tentacles in two whorls   **4**

3. Hydranths as high as wide, or taller; stems erect, often fused basally; up to about 45 mm **Tubularia indivisa**

   Hydranth wider than high; lower parts of stems often procumbent, not fused basally; up to about 25 mm
                                                     Tubularia bellis

4. Hydranths solitary, up to about 20 mm
                                         Ectopleura dumortieri

   Hydranths grouped in colonies, up to about 50 mm
                                          Hybocodon prolifer

Ectopleura dumortieri (Van Beneden)   FIG. 4.5
[HINCKS 1868, 124, Pl. 21; RUSSELL 1953, 76; BRINCKMAN-VOSS 1970, 22]

Hydranths solitary, not clumped; stems narrow, to about 25 mm, exceptionally 100 mm; seldom branched, horn-coloured, nar-rowing basally; some annuli, especially near base; joined by stolons. Hydranth large, reddish; tentacles of oral whorl short, up to about 24, said to be in two circlets of about 12; aboral whorl up to about 30, longer. Gonophores in branched clusters inserted above aboral whorl of tentacles; medusae released.

Recorded on other hydroids, *Flustra*, wood; shallow coastal; all temperate to tropical oceans; reported from southern Scotland southwards.

Hybocodon prolifer Agassiz   FIG. 4.5
[RUSSELL 1953, 79; NAUMOV 1969, 233]

Colony a group of a few often sinuous, unbranched hydrocauli, up to about 50 mm but often shorter; stems tapering basally, widening up to about 1.5 mm distally; perisarc horn-coloured, sometimes longitudinally lined; ringed at top. Hydranth large, deep orange-red; tentacles in two whorls, oral in two circlets of 16, upper half length of lower; aboral whorl up to about 30, much longer. Gonophores in branched clusters inserted just above aboral whorl; developing medusae with asymmetrical apical point and single cluster of about three tentacles.

Substrata little known, recorded once on sponge *Desmacidon*; lower shore pools to sublittoral; medusae throughout British Isles, northern boreal circumpolar.

Tubularia bellis Allman   FIG. 4.4
[HINCKS 1868, 122, Pl. 21; ALLMAN 1872, 409, Pl. 22]

Colony short, up to about 25 mm. Erect stems sparsely branched, often partly procumbent, coenosarc orange to red-orange, grading darker basally; widely ringed for much of basal part; with creeping stolon; tips of stems slightly dilated, pale, lightly corrugated. Hydranth wider than high, column scarlet; tentacles about 15–20 in oral whorl, 20 in aboral; spread of aboral whorl in life about 10 mm. Gonophores in short clusters of four to five above aboral tentacles; ♂ and ♀ with four protruding and conspicuous distal conical processes; central column scarlet. Dispersive stage an actinula.

In rock pools and on rocks, mid to lower shore; recorded Shetlands, south-west Ireland, North Sea oil rigs; probably overlooked.

From *T. larynx* by shorter gonophore clusters, proportionate width of hydranth, procumbent tendency of stem bases, and their widely spaced annuli.

Tubularia indivisa Linnaeus   FIG. 4.4
[HINCKS 1868, 115, Pl. 20; ALLMAN 1872, 400, Pl. 20]

Stems clustered, stiff, pale horn, sinuous; annuli sparse; often fused together basally in intertwined groups, usually 30–150 (exceptionally to 400) mm. Hydranth pale pink to scarlet, large, drooping, about 40 white oral tentacles, 20–30 aboral. Gonophores in three to four pendulous branches with up to about 20 retained, reduced medusae each releasing a single actinula larva, which walks on its ten arms and settles – sometimes on an adult's stem – to grow into a new colony; no planula.

On various solid substrata; lower shore pools to at least 280 m; common throughout British Isles.

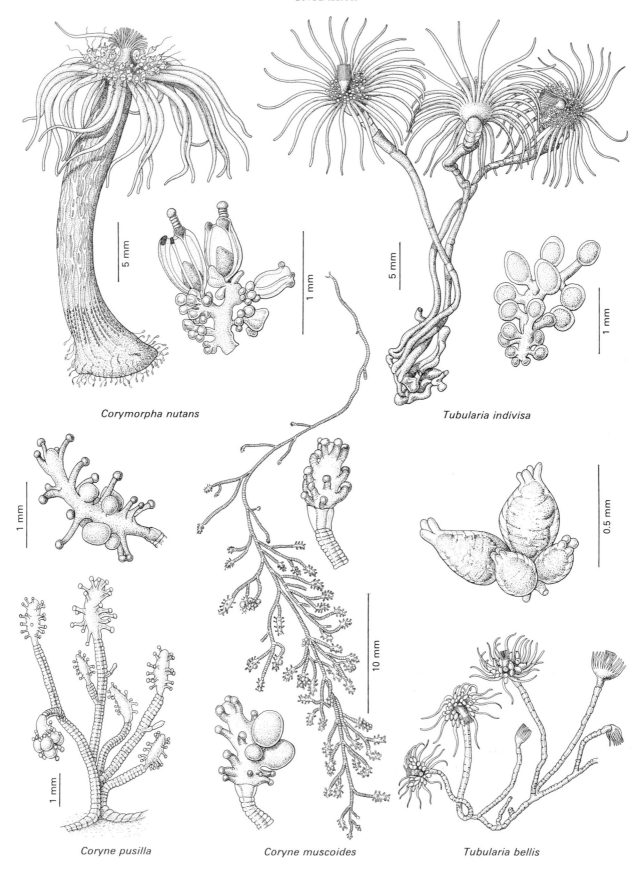

Corymorpha nutans

Tubularia indivisa

Coryne pusilla

Coryne muscoides

Tubularia bellis

Fig. 4.4

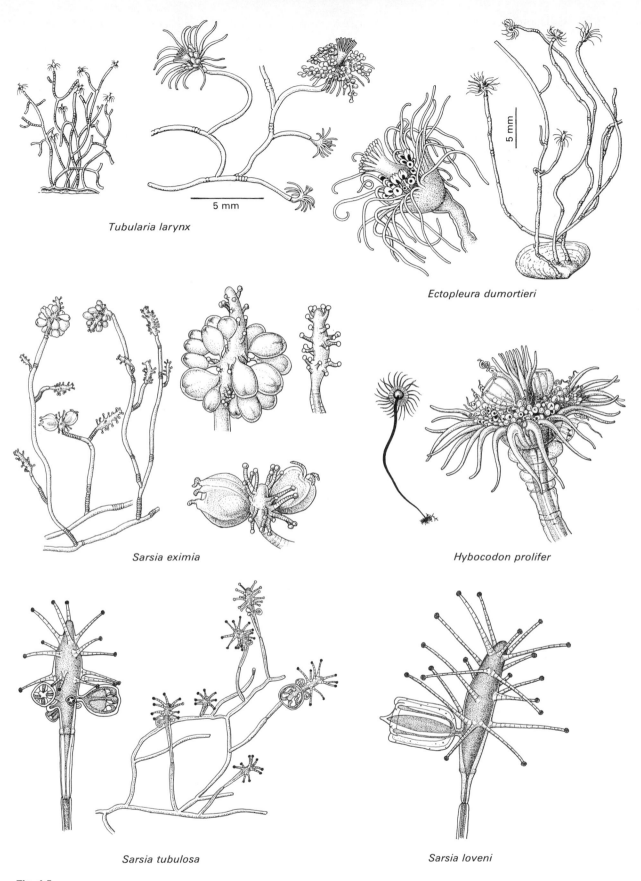

Tubularia larynx

Ectopleura dumortieri

Sarsia eximia

Hybocodon prolifer

Sarsia tubulosa

Sarsia loveni

Fig. 4.5

Tubularia larynx Ellis and Solander   FIG. 4.5
[HINCKS 1868, 118, Pl. 21; ALLMAN 1872, 406, Pl. 21]
Colony a loose collection of separate, occasionally forked stems up to about 45 mm, topped by large hydranths. Each hydranth rose-red, 14–20 white oral and about 20 aboral tentacles. Stems straw coloured, with numerous spaced annuli. Gonophores in long clusters, supporting about 20 retained reduced medusae, each with four low tubercles distally, and releasing a single, floating, actinula which lacks tentacles on liberation. No planula.

On other hydroids and solid substrata; lower shore to at least 100 m; common throughout British Isles; tolerant of slightly reduced salinity.

T. larynx is in general smaller, more forked, and more annulated than *T. indivisa*, has the stems not fused, and hydranths typically with fewer tentacles.

3 VELELLIDAE

Hydranth pleustonic, floating at the sea surface. Float flattish, chambered, chitinous, bearing a triangular fin; the blastostyles and tentacles below it, concentric around the mouth.

Velella velella (Linnaeus). By-the-wind-sailor   FIG. 4.1
[KIRKPATRICK, P.A. and PUGH, P.R., 1984, *Syn. Br. Fauna*, 29, 142].
Float flat, oval, membranous, raised diagonally as a flange-like fin or 'sail'; up to 100 mm in length; deep blue. The central mouth hangs below, surrounded by reproductive blastostyles and marginal tentacles.

May occur stranded in large numbers on south-westerly coasts, in all seasons, and occasionally as far north as the Hebrides during summer, following persistent southerly or south-westerly winds. Occasionally in Faroe Islands.

4 CLADONEMATIDAE

Colonies stolonal, hydranths arising directly from stolon, with or without perisarc; oral whorl of capitate tentacles, with or without aboral whorl of short linear ones; gonophores inserted on hydranth. Medusa released.

Cladonema radiatum Dujardin   FIG. 4.6
[HINCKS 1868, 62, Pl. 11; ALLMAN 1872, 357, Pl. 18; RUSSELL 1953, 105; BRINCKMANN-VOSS 1970, 77]
Colony a stolon giving off single hydranths or supporting loosely branched, slender stems up to about 30 mm high, each branch long and terminating in a hydranth; perisarc light horn to transparent, smooth. Hydranth naked, 1 mm high, whitish to pale red, rounded above, tapered below, often changing shape; with four to five stout, short, straight, capitate, oral tentacles, held symmetrically and usually at right angles to body, and four to five shorter, narrower, linear ones about half-way down hydranth, alternating in position with distal ones. Gonophores up to 3 per hydranth, inserted singly above aboral tentacles; releasing distinctive swimming medusa which also attaches by its tentacles.

Habits little known. On stones and weed, especially perhaps *Laminaria* and eel grasses; recorded intertidally, in caves, and in aquaria; probably not deep; all British and Irish records from the south; Mediterranean to Kattegat.

5 CANDELABRIDAE

Large, solitary, worm-shaped hydranths with thin, flexible perisarc closely ensheathing basalmost region; tentacles capitate, numerous, scattered over hydranth; attachment by stumpy basal organs; gonophores on special blastostyles borne directly on hydranth. No medusa stage.

Candelabrum cocksi (Cocks)   FIG. 4.6
[HINCKS 1868, 77, Pl. 12; ALLMAN 1875, *Phil. Trans. Roy. Soc.* (B), 165, 549; both as *Myriothela*; also formerly called *Arum*]
Solitary, worm-shaped, up to 50 mm when contracted but extending up to 100 mm; upper part cylindrical, pointed above, upper half covered in 200 or more minute club-tipped tentacles of a variety of reds, pinks, purples, browns, and white giving in life a mottled and banded appearance; lower down with many pinkish-horn branched processes each supporting several pink gonophores; liberating an actinula larva which walks on its 15–20 long, capitate tentacles. Monoecious; basal region bulbous, four-fifths covered in thin perisarc, dark horn to grey, with ten or more short extensions for attachment.

Habits little known. Recorded under stones and algae from ELWS to about 3000 m; in Britain most records south-west England, but sparingly reported north to Arctic Ocean.

C. phrygium (Fabricius) from deeper water is often regarded as a distinct species.

6 CORYNIDAE

Colonial, with erect stems and firm perisarc reaching at least to hydranth base; hypostome conical; tentacles capitate, some species with small linear aboral tentacles; gonophores borne on hydranth amongst or below tentacles; reproduction by sporosacs or free medusae.

---

1. Perisarc closely ringed throughout; gonophores producing sporosacs (*Coryne*)   **2**

   Perisarc mostly smooth; gonophores producing medusae (*Sarsia*)   **3**

2. Colony elongate, up to about 150 mm, hydranth usually with thin deciduous perisarc sheath basally, diagnostic if present   ***Coryne muscoides***

   Colony short, 25 mm or less, hydranth always naked
                                                          Coryne pusilla

3. Perisarc nearly smooth throughout; slightly rugose in places but not usually ringed   ***Sarsia tubulosa***

   Perisarc ringed in places   **4**

4. Colony stolonal   ***Sarsia loveni***

   Colony with erect, branched shoots   **5**

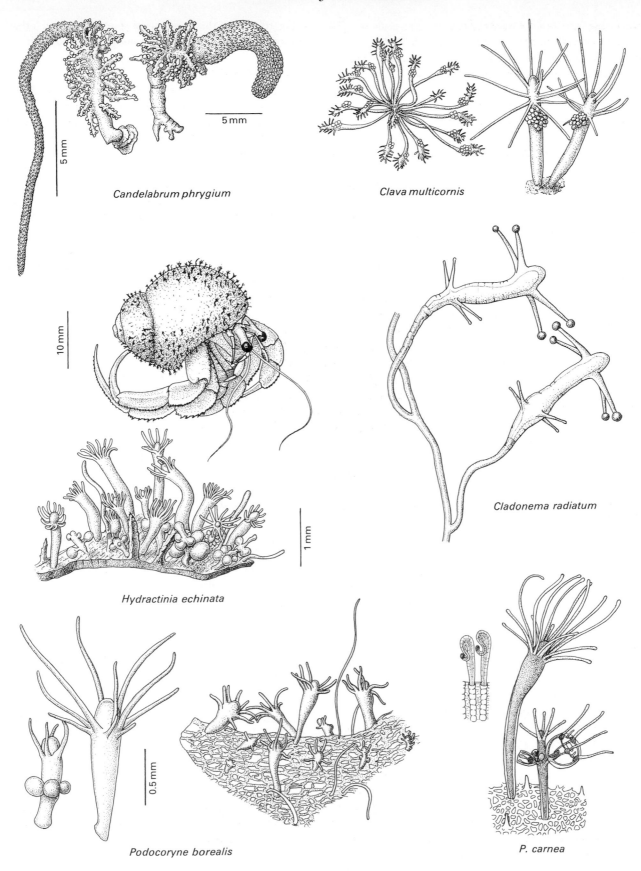

Candelabrum phrygium

Clava multicornis

Cladonema radiatum

Hydractinia echinata

Podocoryne borealis

P. carnea

Fig. 4.6

5. Colony tall, with erect, frequently branched stem up
to about 100 mm; stems pale brown to dark brown;
medusae borne amongst tentacles, released **Sarsia eximia**

Colony short, with erect shoots up to about 40 mm,
usually branched only two–three times; stems light
coloured to pale brown; medusae in whorl below
capitate tentacles, not released **Sarsia loveni**

(Several other *Sarsia* species are omitted)

Coryne muscoides (Linnaeus)   FIG. 4.4
[HINCKS 1868, 41, Pl. 8; ALLMAN 1872, 268, Pl. 4, both as *C. vaginata*; BRINCKMANN-VOSS 1970, 49]
Colony long, branched, up to about 150 mm. Stem pale to dark brown, closely ringed throughout; forked occasionally, especially near base; with numerous short side branches sometimes themselves branched. Hydranths terminal, long, pink to rose coloured, tapered basally; up to about 30 tentacles sometimes (? always) in three to four distinct whorls, white, stout, capitate tips sometimes red; tip of supporting branch with diagnostic (but deciduous) membranous perisarc sheath (pseudohydrotheca) into which hydranth can partly to wholly withdraw. Gonophores spherical, attached direct to hydranth amongst tentacles. Dispersive stage a planula.

On brown algae, lithophytes, and other substrata; lower shore to about 2 m below LWST; numerous records north to Isle of Man, Northern Ireland, Norfolk, Orkneys, but status around mainland Scotland and north-east England unclear.

Coryne pusilla Pallas   FIG. 4.4
[HINCKS 1868, 39, Pl. 7; ALLMAN 1872, 266, Pl. 4; NAUMOV 1969, 257; BRINCKMANN-VOSS 1970, 51]
Colony a loose tangle but not bushy, up to about 25 mm. Hydrocaulus sinuous, forked three to four times; perisarc pale horn to mid-brown, ringed throughout, lacking a pseudohydrotheca. Hydranth long, hardly tapering, flesh to red, sometimes with white dots; with up to about 30 long, thick, capitate tentacles scattered over length sometimes in loose to distinct whorls. Gonophores globular, scattered among tentacles in lower half of hydranth. Dispersive stage an almost spherical planula.

Typically on brown algae; mid to lower shore; all around British Isles; at least from northern Norway to Cape Verde Islands.

Sarsia eximia (Allman)   FIG. 4.5
[HINCKS 1868, 50, Pl. 9; ALLMAN 1871, Pl. 5; 1872, 282, both as *Syncoryne*; RUSSELL 1953, 50]
Colony a collection of erect, narrow, straw-coloured to brown, branched stems up to about 100 mm; sometimes creeping and stolonal. Main stem sometimes forked, ringed at base, otherwise smooth; branches tending to arise on one side of stem, with numerous rings basally, smooth above, sometimes themselves branching. Hydranths long, bright pink to red; up to about 30 straight, capitate tentacles, four just below mouth and rest scattered. Gonophores on short stalks in axils of tentacles over most of hydranth, each producing a single medusa.

On rocks, floating structures, *Laminaria*, and other algae; lower shore, probably to shallow coastal; all around British Isles.

Sarsia loveni (M. Sars)   FIG. 4.5
[NAUMOV 1969, 257, as *Coryne*; EDWARDS 1978, *J. mar. biol. Ass., U.K.*, **58**, 307]
Colonies erect, irregularly branched, up to about 40 mm, or limited to an anastomosing stolon; stems colourless to pale yellow, corrugated irregularly, annulated above and below origins of branches and near stem bases, smooth elsewhere. Hydranths pink to pale pink with 16–30 slender, capitate tentacles, scattered or in up to about four whorls. Gonophores in form of retained, reduced medusae, reddish, two to three on short stalks below lowermost tentacles. Dispersive stage a planula.

On rocks, stones, and weed; around LWST and offshore to 200 m; recorded Plymouth, north-east England, west Scotland, Norway, and Kattegat; tolerant of reduced salinity; other records problematic.

Sarsia tubulosa (M. Sars)   FIG. 4.5
[HINCKS 1868, 52, Pl. 7, as *Syncoryne sarsii*; 1868, 57; ALLMAN 1871, Pl. 6; 1872, 279, all as *S. pulchella*; NAUMOV 1969, 252, as *Coryne*; EDWARDS 1978, *J. mar. biol. Ass., U.K.*, **58**, 302]
Colony of hydranths on pedicels arising singly from an anastomosing, mesh-like stolon, to about 10 mm; or erect, slightly branched, up to about 30 mm; stems mainly smooth. Pedicels unringed, slightly rugose; perisarc thin, translucent horn-coloured. Hydranths bright orange through brownish pink to pink; narrowing below; with up to about 20 long, white, capitate tentacles in distal half, in loose whorls. Sometimes a loose, delicate perisarc sheath over basal third of hydranth. Gonophores attached singly on short stalks in one irregular whorl below lowermost tentacles. Medusa released. Hydranths occasionally bud in laboratory.

On rocks, stones, and weeds; rock pools on lower shore, occasionally sublittoral; tolerant of reduced salinity; around British Isles; circum-polar boreo-arctic.

7 CLAVIDAE
Solitary or colonial; hydranths with conical hypostome, tentacles filiform, scattered; firm perisarc on hydrorhiza only or on erect stems also; fixed sporosacs or free medusae.

---

1. Colony stolonal or encrusting; hydranths attached directly to basal structure **Clava multicornis**

Colony tall, erect, with long branches ensheathed in perisarc; hydranths terminal **Cordylophora caspia**

Clava multicornis (Forsskål)   FIG. 4.6
[HINCKS 1868, 2, Pl. 1; ALLMAN 1872, 246, Pl. 2; now held to include *C. squamata* and other nominal species (Edwards and Harvey 1975)]
Colony of active, naked, fleshy hydranths in small groups; varied

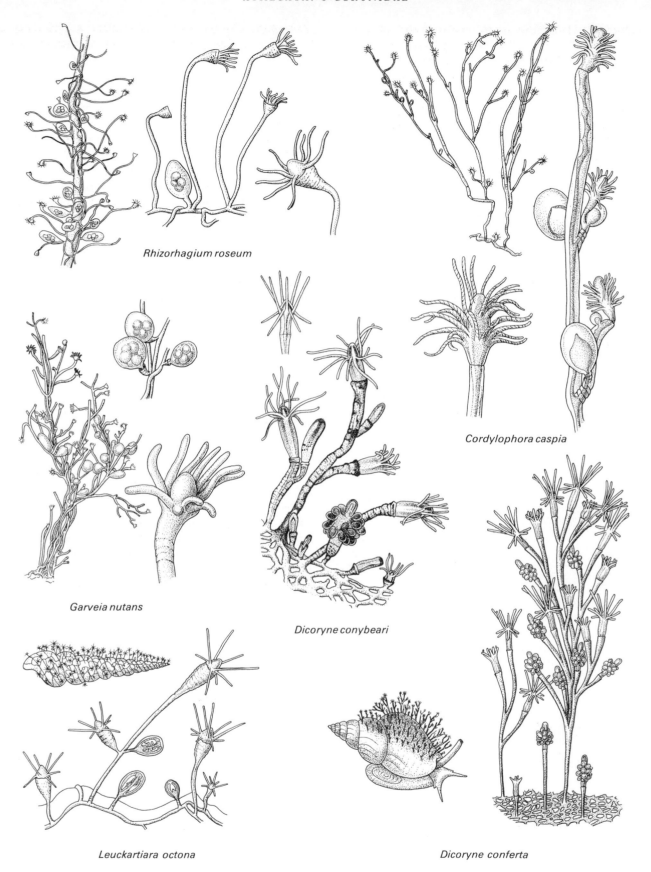

Rhizorhagium roseum

Cordylophora caspia

Garveia nutans

Dicoryne conybeari

Leuckartiara octona

Dicoryne conferta

Fig. 4.7

in morphology. Hydranths up to about 30 mm when fully extended, white through pink to red and brown, even bright blue, often bulging below; up to about 30 thick, white tentacles scattered over upper part, tips slightly dilated. Basal hydrorhiza varied from a stolon through an anastomosing network to an encrusting mass. Gonophores clustered on short branches below tentacles, forming prominent collar. Dispersive stage a large planula, one to two from each gonophore.

Often on *Ascophyllum* and other algae; intertidal, MTL to ELWS; also on and under stones and in rock pools; tolerant of emersion and of brackish water; all around British Isles.

Cordylophora caspia (Pallas)   FIG. 4.7
[HINCKS 1868, 16, Pl. 3; ALLMAN 1871, Pl. 3; 1872, 252, all as *C. lacustris*]
Stems to about 100 mm, loosely and occasionally branched from alternate sides, light horn to light brown; each branch ringed basally. Hydranths terminal, white to pale pink, long, tapered below; hypostome conical but truncate above; 12–16 long, colourless, rather straight, linear, extensile tentacles inserted irregularly over upper half of hydranth. Gonophores pear-shaped, on short stalks, up to about three on each final branch. Dispersive stage a planula.

On various substrata, often in shade; brackish to nearly fresh water; shallow depths; widespread, likely to occur all around British Isles.

8 EUDENDRIIDAE
Colonial, stems erect, usually branched; perisarc extending to hydranth base. Hydranth with flared to globose hypostome atop short constriction; one or more whorls of tentacles beneath it; fixed sporosacs, often on a blastostyle; ♂ gonophore often a

---

1. Colony tall, arborescent; polysiphonic at least basally   **2**

   Colony at most a loose shrubby tangle of haphazardly branched stems; monosiphonic throughout   **3**

2. Most branches monosiphonic; colony polysiphonic only basally; even main stems slender, branches often long and tending upwards; ♂ gonophores in short chains, ♀ in circlet of three to four at hydranth base   ***Eudendrium ramosum***

   All but distal branches polysiphonic; stems thick, trunk-like, branches short, pointing in all directions; ♂ gonophores single spheres in clusters on and below hydranth, ♀ inserted singly along each pedicel   ***Eudendrium rameum***

3. Colony up to about 10 mm, in life forming a whitish mat; hydranth whitish; tentacles of fertile hydranths persisting   ***Eudendrium album***

   Colony up to about 30 mm; not whitish; hydranth brownish-yellow to olive; tentacles of fertile hyd-ranths often regressing   ***Eudendrium capillare***

---

short chain of sporosacs, ♀ usually single; no medusa stage. An additional species, *Eudendrium arbusculum* Wright, has been redescribed by Hincks (1868) and Hamond (1957).

Eudendrium album Nutting   FIG. 4.9
[NUTTING 1898, *Ann. Mag. nat. Hist.* (7) 1, 362; LELOUP 1952, 124]
Colony short, delicate, main shoots dark brown basally, to about 10 mm; can form dense white downy patches. Stems mono-siphonic, loosely forked. Branches frequent, pale horn, fading distally, irregular, final branches long; ringed above axils in lower parts, elsewhere tending to smooth throughout. Hydranths minute, tapered below, white to whitish, reported sometimes lightly tinged with pink to brown, perhaps from food contents; hypostome bulbous; tentacles 20–32, linear, one whorl. Male gonophores ovoid, pale yellow-orange, on hydranths with tentacles retained, in whorled clusters of chains of two to three, or singly, attached below hydranth; female similar but inserted singly, not in chains. Dispersive stage a planula.

On stones and on *Sertularia*; about 10–40 m; reported only Plymouth, Roscoff, off Belgium, and north-east North America.

From *E. capillare* by smaller size of colony and hydranth, colour of hydranth, relative retention of tentacles on fertile hydranths and, at least in British Isles, possibly a difference in reproductive season (January–May recorded in *E. album*, March–September in *E. capillare*).

Eudendrium capillare Alder   FIG. 4.9
[HINCKS 1868, 84, Pl. 14; ALLMAN 1872, 335, Pl. 14; LELOUP 1952, 124; NAUMOV 1969, 263; MILLARD 1975, 82]
Colony short, delicate, stolon loosely branched to anastomosing, shoots to about 30 mm, monosiphonic; branching loose, irregular. Stems and branches thread-like, of uniform width, sinuous, pale horn to transparent; ringed basally and above axils; final branches rather long. Hydranth tapered below, recorded as yellowish-brown, horn-coloured, and pale grey-olive; hypostome bulbous, white; tentacles 14–30, long, linear, in one circlet. Male gonophores ovoid, grey-olive, in chains of two to four, clustered on hydranths lacking tentacles through rapid atrophy; female pear-shaped, red-orange, inserted singly but clustered on hydranths with tentacles reduced or lacking. Dispersive stage a planula.

On other hydroids and invertebrates, shells, algae, rock, and other substrata; LWST to about 100 m, sometimes deeper; around British Isles; north and south Atlantic.

Eudendrium rameum (Pallas)   FIG. 4.8
[HINCKS 1868, 80, frontispiece; ALLMAN 1872, 334; LELOUP 1952, 126; NAUMOV 1969, 264]
Colony large, bushy, with a fibrous basal mass; trunk and major forks thick, to 100 mm, occasionally 250 mm, rigid out of water. Main stems dark brown, repeatedly branched, thinning to mono-siphonic only distally; minor branches much ringed basally, sinuous to straight. Hydranths roughly alternate on finer branchlets, on long, sinuous, tightly ringed pedicels; red, tapering below; hypostome bulbous; tentacles 20–24, in one

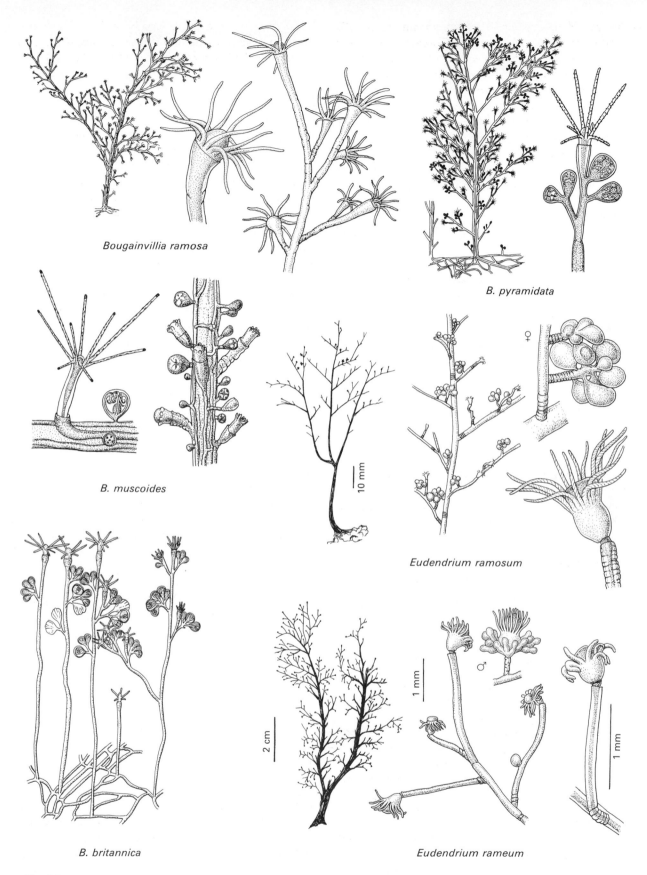

Bougainvillia ramosa

B. pyramidata

B. muscoides

10 mm

♀

Eudendrium ramosum

B. britannica

2 cm

1 mm

♂

1 mm

Eudendrium rameum

Fig. 4.8

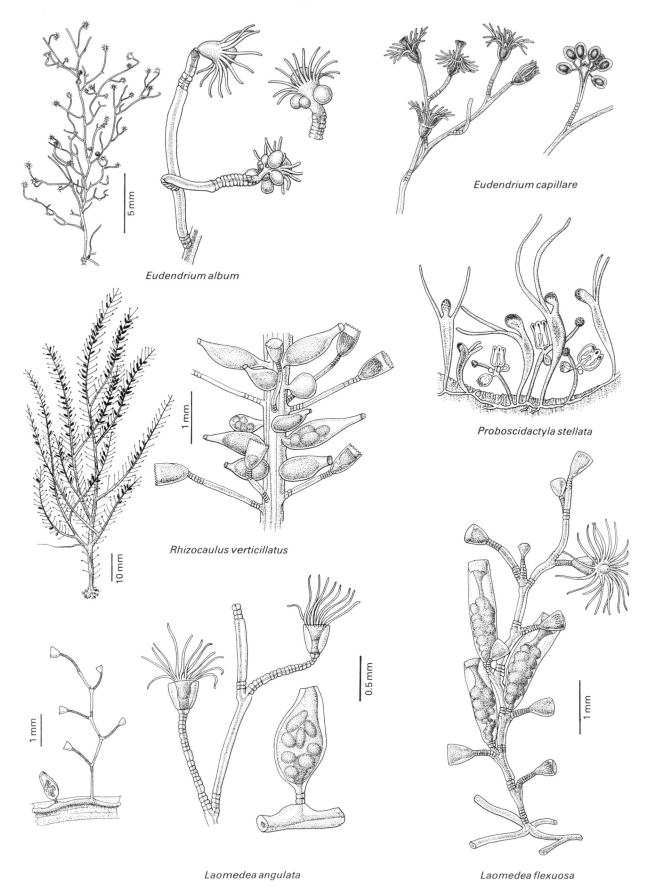

Eudendrium capillare

Eudendrium album

Proboscidactyla stellata

Rhizocaulus verticillatus

Laomedea angulata

Laomedea flexuosa

Fig. 4.9

whorl, stout but tapering, filiform, held roughly horizontally, perhaps slightly amphicoronate. Gonophores ovoid, yellow, short-stalked, on and below hydranths in clusters of up to about 15 (male) or several inserted singly along each pedicel (female). Male gonophores two-chambered. Dispersive stage a planula.

On various solid substrata; about 5–100 m, sometimes deeper; common around British Isles; near-cosmopolitan.

Eudendrium ramosum (Linnaeus)　　　　　FIG. 4.8

[HINCKS 1868, 82, Pl. 13; ALLMAN 1872, Pl. 13; LELOUP 1952, 127; NAMOUV 1969, 266; MILLARD 1975, 85]

Colony tall, much branched, typically alternately, often with numerous long monosiphonic main shoots arising from lower region; polysiphonic only near base; limp out of water. Erect stems up to about 100 mm, occasionally 200 mm, dark to red-brown, narrow, branches arising acutely and often turning upwards to lie roughly parallel with primary branch; branches and pedicels ringed basally, pedicels long, roughly alternate. Hydranth large, vermilion to pink, tapered below; hypostome spherical, white; tentacles up to about 24, occasionally to 30, straight, filiform, white, in one whorl, held roughly horizontally but slightly amphicoronate. Male gonophores on hydranths, in chains of two to three spherical sporosacs, smallest proximally; female in circlet of about three to four at base of hydranth, sometimes another circlet below, pear-shaped on short stalk; supporting hydranths atrophy. Dispersive stage a planula.

On variety of substrata; about 5–200 m, sometimes deeper; common around British Isles; widespread in Atlantic.

From *E. rameum* by branching mostly monosiphonic, more slender habit, and limpness out of water; gonophores diagnostic when present. *E. glomeratum* Picard, recorded from Plymouth, south Devon, and Ireland is described by Boero and Cornelius (1987).

9 BOUGAINVILLIIDAE

Colonies erect and branched, sometimes stolonal; perisarc often extending part-way up hydranth as pseudohydrotheca; hydranth with conical hypostome and one whorl of linear tentacles; fixed sporosacs or medusae.

---

1. Parts of stem polysiphonic　　　　　　　　　　**2**

   Stem monosiphonic throughout　　　　　　　　**5**

2. Stem of tightly packed tubes; branches few, polysiphonic; gonophores borne directly on stem
   　　　　　　　　　　　　　　Bougainvillia muscoides

   Stem of less orderly tubes; branches many, most monosiphonic　　　　　　　　　　　　　　　**3**

3. Main stem of loosely packed, twisted tubes; colony up to about 25 mm, bushy　　　***Garveia nutans***

   Main stem of tightly packed, straight tubes; colony 40 mm plus, arborescent　　　　　　　　　**4**

4. Colony with thick stem, straight and erect-looking growth habit, regularly arranged branches; several erect growths in a typical colony; hydranth tentacles six to 14　　　　　***Bougainvillia pyramidata***

   Colony with more slender stem, less straight and erect-looking; usually just one erect stem per colony; hydranth tentacles up to about 20　　***Bougainvillia ramosa***

5. Colony arising from a closely anastomosing stolonal mat　　　　　　　　　　　　　　　　　**6**

   Branches of stolon widely spaced　　　　　　　**7**

6. Erect shoots up to about 10 mm, slightly corrugated, little branched, tentacles about 12; released sporosacs having single ciliated process　***Dicoryne conybeari***

   Erect shoots up to about 20 mm, smooth, much branched, tentacles up to 16, sometimes 20; released sporosacs having two ciliated processes　***Dicoryne conferta***

7. Tentacles up to about 16; with medusa
   　　　　　　　　　　　　　　Bougainvillia britannica

   Tentacles up to about 24; no medusa　***Rhizorhagium roseum***

Bougainvillia britannica Forbes　　　　　FIG. 4.8

[HINCKS 1868, 96, Pl. 17, as *Perigonimus linearis*; EDWARDS 1964a, 1966, 145; RUSSELL 1970, 237; formerly called *Atractylis linearis*]

Colony an anastomosing stolon with rather distant, erect shoots to about 15 mm, usually arising from stolon junctions; some branches at acute angle, each ending in a hydranth. Perisarc of shoots horn-coloured, smooth above, wrinkled below, slightly sinuous. Hydranth club-shaped with short conical hypostome, white; tentacles six to about 16, long, straight, linear, amphicoronate; lower parts of older hydranths sheathed in wrinkled pseudohydrotheca. Gonophores spherical to pear-shaped, two to three together near top of shoot or in branched clusters of up to about six; each in persistent perisarc sheath. Dispersive stage a medusa.

On gastropod and bivalve shells; coastal; medusa recorded all around British Isles and southern Norway.

Bougainvillia muscoides (M. Sars)　　　　　FIG. 4.8

[REES, W.J. 1938, *J. mar. biol. Ass., U.K.*, 23, 2; EDWARDS 1964b, 725; 1966, 146]

Mature colony erect, to about 20 mm, polysiphonic, up to about seven tubes, thinning above, arising from network of stolons. Erect shoots brown; branches short, sinuous, rather few. Hydranths pink to red, borne directly on stems and branches and also terminally, not on pedicels, each extending out from upturned end of perisarc tube or from its side, elongate, up to 1.0 mm, cylindrical with conical hypostome; tentacles eight to 12, straight, linear, in one amphicoronate circlet, upper ones the longer. Gonophores small, spherical to pear-shaped, on short stalks, often in lines, borne directly on perisarc tubes of stem and branches, red to white; far outnumbering hydranths. Dispersive stage a medusa.

On other hydroids, *Ascidia* and *Sabella*; probably about 20–60 m; reported Firth of Clyde and north of British Isles, widespread Norway.

Bougainvillia pyramidata (Forbes and Goodsir)   FIG. 4.8
[EDWARDS 1964*b*, 725; 1966, 145; RUSSELL 1970, 242]

Colonies erect, main stems straight or nearly so, to about 40 mm, polysiphonic, distally thinning to straight, poly- to monosiphonic branches. Perisarc pale horn, translucent, corrugated at branch bases. Hydrorhiza of anastomosing stolons, varied and irregular, often with some parallel-running tubes. Branches markedly regularly arranged, arising acutely and spirally, in several vertical planes; varied in length, upper often longer than some lower; some secondary to tertiary branching, monosiphonic, in same arrangement. Hydranths on tips and sides of branches, in older colonies missing from main trunk; with thin, transparent pseudohydrotheca; cylindrical, short, hardly projecting beyond theca; pink; hypostome rounded, white; club-shaped when contracted; tentacles straight, linear, six to 14, in one amphicoronate circlet, upper ones the longer. Gonophores below hydranths and on stems and branches; stalked, singly or in branching clusters of one to about five; each pear-shaped, pink, within persistent perisarc sheath; occasionally borne directly on stolon. Dispersive stage a medusa.

Recorded on *Ascidiella*, *Virgularia*, and *Tubularia*, 30–80 m; medusa mainly near deeper water, west Scotland, Irish Sea, south-west Ireland. In somewhat deeper water than *B. ramosa*, but some overlap.

Bougainvillia ramosa (Van Beneden)   FIG. 4.8
[HINCKS 1868, 109, Pl. 19; ALLMAN 1871, Pl. 9; 1872, 311; RUSSELL 1953, 153; EDWARDS 1966, 115]

Colony tall, erect, stolon anastomosing; from short, wholly monosiphonic, little-branched stems to much-branched, polysiphonic, arborescent colonies with thick trunks; to about 100 mm. Branches numerous, somewhat regularly arranged, often alternate and in loose spiral; some secondary and even tertiary branching. Perisarc straw coloured to light brown, corrugated at branch bases; thin pseudohydrotheca over hydranth to tentacle bases. Hydranths terminal on branches, tapered, pale pink, hypostome tall-conical; tentacles up to about 20, straight, linear, in one amphicoronate circlet, lower ones the shorter. Gonophores pear-shaped to ovoid, on stalks one-third to one-half their length, attached below hydranths singly or up to about three in small branched cluster. Dispersive stage a medusa.

On variety of substrata; lower shore probably to about 50 m; common all around British Isles.

Dicoryne conferta (Alder)   FIG. 4.7
[HINCKS 1868, 105, Pl. 18; ALLMAN 1871, Pl. 8; 1872, 293; NAUMOV 1969, 218; MILLARD 1975, 101]

Colony moss-like, stolon anastomosing; with single stalked hydranths or erect, monosiphonic, branched stems arising frequently, to about 20 mm. Branching acute; perisarc smooth, brown, tubular, distending slightly distally. Hydranths pale brown, cylindrical with conical hypostome; tentacles up to 16, rarely 20, straight, linear, in one amphicoronate circlet, lower ones the shorter; contracting partly within perisarc tube which then bulges out. Gonophores stalked, ovoid, in clusters of up to about 15, on blastostyles which lack tentacles but have large extensile hypostome; arising from stolons or stems, releasing distinctive sporosacs with two ciliated processes.

On shells of living gastropods and empty ones with or without hermit crabs; 5–300 m; scattered records around British Isles, mostly northerly; Barents Sea to southern Africa.

Dicoryne conybeari (Allman)   FIG. 4.7
[HINCKS 1868, 107, Pl. 18; ALLMAN 1871, Pl. 10; 1872, 307; all as *Heterocordyle*]

Colony encrusting, moss-like; stolon anastomosing, with single stalked hydranths or erect, monosiphonic, branched stems arising frequently, to about 10 mm. Branching irregularly acute, some second order; perisarc transversely corrugated, pale brown, distending slightly distally. Hydranths pale brown, slightly dilated above, with about 12 straight, linear tentacles in one amphicoronate circlet, upper ones the longer; contracting partly within perisarc tube. Gonophores ovoid to pear-shaped, inserted singly along most of length of blastostyles which arise from the stolon and bear nematocysts terminally; releasing distinctive sporosacs with one ciliated process.

On shells of gastropods, including those adopted by hermit crabs; coastal; sparsely recorded around British Isles, perhaps mostly in south.

Garveia nutans (Wright)   FIG. 4.7
[HINCKS 1868, 102, Pl. 14; ALLMAN 1871, Pl. 12; 1872, 297; LELOUP 1952, 119, as *Bimeria*]

Colonies erect, bushy, to about 25 mm, often in dense patches. Stems polysiphonic thinning above to monosiphonic, branching mainly from alternate sides of stem; perisarc pale brown, slightly corrugated on branches, sometimes bent sharply just below hydranth, continuing over it as thin, short, funnel-shaped cup. Hydranth fat pear-shaped, bright orange-red, tentacles about ten, short, in one whorl held all at same elevation, yellow to orange. When disturbed all hydranths hang down. Gonophores deep orange, ovoid with apical truncated point, grouped on mid-region of stem and main branches, each on short stalk. Dispersive stage a planula.

On various subtrata, lower shore to about 30 m; reported Plymouth to Shetlands, probably common.

Rhizorhagium roseum M. Sars   FIG. 4.7
[RUSSELL, E.S. 1907, *Ann. Mag. nat. Hist.* (7) **20**, 52, as *Wrightia coccinea*; NAUMOV 1969, 205, as *Perigonimus*]

Colony reptant, with anastomosing stolon. Erect stems, sometimes branching, to about 25 mm but often shorter; straight to kinked, sparsely ringed; perisarc thin, horn coloured to brown, sometimes widening below hydranth to form false hydrotheca. Hydranth often held at sharp angle to pedicel, cylindrical, rounded below, up to about 1.0 mm, bright pink, sometimes grading to whitish on hypostome, with up to about 24 short whitish tentacles in single whorl held nearly horizontally; hypostome broad. Gonophores ovoid, borne on short stalks on stolon. Dispersive stage a planula.

On wide variety of substrata; typically 50–200 m; common along coast of Norway, in Britain recorded only south-east and south-west Scotland. (A second species, *R. album* Rees, recorded only north Cornwall, in a rock pool: Rees, W. J., 1938, *J. mar. biol. Ass., U.K.*, **23**, 9.)

10 HYDRACTINIIDAE

Colonial, stolonal to hydrorhizal; polyps polymorphic; hydranths (gastrozooids) naked, tentacles linear, in one or more whorls; hydrorhiza often including chitinous spines; reproduction by fixed sporosacs or free medusae.

---

1. Tentacles in two whorls of about eight; tentacles in lower whorl shorter than those in upper; reproduction by sporosacs.   ***Hydractinia echinata***

   Tentacles in one whorl of about 16, often alternately short and long; reproduction by medusae   **2**

2. Hydranth 10–15 mm   ***Podocoryne borealis***

   Hydranth up to about 5.5 mm   ***Podocoryne carnea***

Hydractinia echinata (Fleming)   FIG. 4.6
[HINCKS 1868, Pl. 4; ALLMAN 1872, 345, Pls. 15, 16; LELOUP 1952, 112; NAUMOV 1969, 223]

Colony a white to pale pink encrusting mat supporting short polyps of four kinds. Hydranths up to about 13 mm, slender, widening upwards, with upper circlet of about eight long, blunt tentacles and immediately below it a circlet of about eight shorter ones; hypostome a steep cone. Gonozooids shorter than hydranths, with few, stubby, terminal tentacles and ring of yellow to white (♂) or pink (♀) gonophores. Also long, slender, white dactylozooids; active, coiling and beating, sometimes in unison. Basal crust about 3 mm thick; with numerous blunt conical chitinous spines, about 2 mm high with jagged edges, mingled amongst polyps. Dispersive stage a planula.

On gastropod shells inhabited by hermit crabs, sometimes also on other solid substrata; MTL probably to about 30 m; common throughout British Isles; recorded Arctic to Morocco.

Podocoryne borealis (Mayer)   FIG. 4.6
[ALLMAN 1872, 349, Pl. 16, as *P. carnea*; EDWARDS 1972, 111]

Colony encrusting, stolon closely anastomosing, perisarc translucent. Hydranths single, 10–15 mm, numerous, cylindrical to club-shaped, perisarc collar at very base only; hypostome conical to rounded; one whorl of up to 16 long, colourless, filiform tentacles often slightly dilated at tip, often alternating short and long. Perisarc spines smooth, amongst hydranths. Gonophores pear-shaped, on some hydranths, which are often smaller than infertile ones; to about 20 in a close cluster, about one-third

from top of hydranth which is narrower from there up; in varied developmental stages; hydranth regressing as gonophores mature. Most colonies include tentaculozooids, resembling small isolated tentacles arising direct from stolon with or without minute basal perisarc collar. No spiral zooids recorded. Medusa released.

On shells of gastropods, barnacles, and larger crustaceans; also shells occupied by hermit crabs and even on hydroids, *Aphrodita*, and on aquarium glassware; coastal, to at least 100 m; all British coasts; southern Norway and Iceland to Belgium.

Podocoryne carnea (M. Sars)   FIG. 4.6
[HINCKS 1868, 29, Pl. 5; RUSSELL 1953, 121; EDWARDS 1972, 123]

Colony encrusting, stolon closely anastomosing to coalescent, perisarc translucent. Hydranths white to pink, up to 5.5 mm, cylindrical to club-shaped in life, no basal perisarc collar; hypostome conical to rounded; tentacles up to 16, sometimes 20, in one whorl, often alternating longer and shorter, filiform with slightly swollen tip. Perisarc spines smooth, arising from hydrorhiza amongst hydranths; said to be occasionally absent from colonies living on gastropods. Gonophores variable in size, on shorter hydranths having fewer tentacles, in clusters of up to about ten, about one-third from top of hydranth which is narrower from there up; hydranth regresses as gonophores mature. Spiral zooids in some colonies, especially around apertures of gastropod shells occupied by hermit crabs; short, hydranth-like, curling actively, lacking tentacles and defined hypostome. Tentaculozooids may be present. Medusae released.

On shells of several living gastropods, especially *Nassarius reticulatus*, and on those with hermit crabs; also on bivalves, barnacles, larger crustaceans, and possibly stones; intertidal pools to about 50 m; around British Isles, north to mid-Norway.

11 PANDEIDAE

Colonies stolonal to shortly erect; hydranths with one whorl of filiform tentacles; perisarc varied in development, sometimes absent; medusae released.

Leuckartiara octona (Fleming)   FIG. 4.7
[HINCKS 1868, 90, Pl. 16 as *Perigonimus repens*; REES, W. J., 1938, *J. mar. biol. Ass. U.K.*, **23**, 12; RUSSELL 1953, 195]

Greatly varied, growth probably influenced by habits of host substratum. Colony creeping, stolon branched or in open anastomosis; erect stems short to long, to about 3 mm; up to four hydranths on each, often one; hydranths terminal or at each branching; perisarc thin, pale horn, corrugated, often ringed at base, extending over hydrant to base of tentacles as a wrinkled pseudohydrotheca, loose- to close-fitting depending on recent feeding. Hydranths small, cylindrical to tapered, white, hypostome conical; tentacles four to ten, in one circlet, long, straight, linear, stiff, amphicoronate, lowermost much the shorter; retracting largely within theca. Gonophores subsessile to stalked, on stolon and/or up to five per erect stalk, ovoid to pear-shaped. Medusa released.

On various substrata, often *Turritella* and *Corystes*, also other hydroids, *Aphrodita*, *Agonus*, spider crabs, *Dentalium*, *Scaphander* and other gastropods; 0–200 m; common around British Isles and to north-west Europe; near-cosmopolitan.

Suborder **Thecata**

Hydroida with well defined hydrotheca (reduced in some genera) and gonotheca; tentacles always linear, inserted in one whorl and not increasing in number after rupture of deciduous hydrothecal cap. Medusa typically with gonads overlying radial canals; usually having statocysts, sometimes ocelli.

KEY TO FAMILIES

1. Hydrotheca bilaterally symmetrical, sometimes only slightly so   **2**
   Hydrotheca fundamentally radially symmetrical   **5**

2. Hydrothecae on one side of stem; colony not stolonal   **3**
   Hydrotheca on both sides of stem, or colony stolonal   **4**

3. Hydrotheca always large enough to accommodate hydranth; hydrotheca usually with conspicuous adherent nematotheca in mid-line; rim with about eight deep clefts and cusps; gonotheca in protective basket or unprotected   **10. Aglaopheniidae**
   Hydrotheca usually too small to accommodate hydranth; no nematothecae adherent to hydrotheca in mid-line; rim usually smooth; gonotheca always unprotected
       9. Plumulariidae

4. Colony largely erect, hydrothecae sessile to adnate, on both sides of erect stems; no medusa   **8. Sertulariidae**
   Colony stolonal, hydrothecae on pedicels arising from stolon; medusa released
       1. Laodiceidae

5. Hydrotheca closed by conical operculum of several roughly triangular flaps (may be deciduous)   **6**
   Hydrotheca lacking operculum   **9**

6. Hydranths tubular, lacking pedicel   **2. Campanulinidae**
   Hydranths tapered below, with pedicel   **7**

7. Operculum delimited basally by creased hinge-line   **8**
   Operculum not delimited basally by creased hinge-line
       5. Phialellidae, also *Opercularella* (p. 127)

8. Colony stolonal   **2. Campanulinidae**
   Colony short, but erect   **4. Lovenellidae**

9. Hydrotheca pedicellate   **3. Campanulariidae**
   Hydrotheca sessile (except in the tiny and stolonal *Hydranthea*, p. 140)   **10**

10. Hydrotheca short, far too small to accommodate the large hydranth, often renovated in chains   **7. Haleciidae**

Hydrotheca deep, tubular, easily accommodating the slender hydranth, sometimes renovated   **6. Lafoeidae**

I LAODICEIDAE

Colonial, stolonal; hydrotheca with conical or gabled operculum, sessile to pedicellate; hydranth with single whorl of linear tentacles and conical hypostome, withdrawing wholly within hydrotheca; gonotheca as hydrotheca but larger. Medusa released.

Modeeria rotunda (Quoy and Gaimard)   FIG. 4.12
[HINCKS 1868, 208, Pl. 39, as *Calycella fastigiata*; EDWARDS 1973, *J. mar. biol. Ass., U.K.*, **53**, 582; formerly called *Stegopoma fastigiatum*]

Colony creeping; single hydrothecae on short to long pedicels arising at frequent but irregular intervals from a branching or anastomosing stolon. Hydrotheca large, up to 1.75 mm, tubular, tapering below into a smooth pedicel of varied length; distinctively gabled above, two halves of operculum meeting in a straight ridge; no diaphragm. Gonothecae rather scarce, similar to hydrothecae in structure, shape, and origin from stolon, but larger and lacking pedicel. Dispersive stage a medusa.

Usually on other hydroids; about 30–300 m, perhaps deeper; all around British Isles; widespread in western Europe.

2 CAMPANULINIDAE

Small colonies, stolonal or with short erect stems; hydrotheca deep, cylindrical; with conical operculum of several triangular flaps, with or without hydrothecal diaphragm; hydranth slender, fully contracting within hydrotheca; hypostome conical; some species with nematophores; reproduction by sporosacs or medusae.

The scope of this family has been much debated and is still uncertain (synopsis in Millard 1975). For example, hydroids having hydrothecae of the *Cuspidella* form are known to be produced by medusae which are referred to distinct families. Their affinities are poorly understood and they are referred to the genus *Cuspidella* for convenience.

1.	Colony mostly erect	***Opercularella lacerata***
	Colony stolonal	**2**
2.	Hydrotheca with pedicel	***Calycella syringa***
	Hydrotheca sessile	***Cuspidella* spp.**

Calycella syringa (Linnaeus)   FIG. 4.13
[HINCKS 1868, 206, Pl. 39]

Hydrocaulus a creeping stolon, smooth. Hydrothecae arising individually, up to about 1 mm including pedicel; long, cyl-

indrical, rounded below; rim scalloped into a low operculum of eight to nine slender projections, each delimited by a fold; operculum deciduous, often folded inwards; pedicels varied in length, twisted into three or more whorls. Gonotheca smooth, ovoid, on short, one- or two-ringed pedicel attached to stolon; developing gonophores contained in acrocysts projecting singly from the gonothecal apertures.

On other hydroids and algae; coastal; near-cosmopolitan; common throughout British Isles; often on stranded material.

Two closely similar nominal species of uncertain validity, *Calycella gracilis* Hartlaub and *C. hispida* (Nutting), are discussed by Cornelius (in prep.) along with some little-known forms referred to *Campanulina* which might also be confused with the present species.

Opercularella lacerata (Johnston)   FIG. 4.13
[HINCKS 1868, 194, Pl. 30]

Main stem erect, to about 20 mm, slender, slightly flexuose, repeatedly branched; perisarc annulated to sinuous throughout; giving rise at nodes to short, two- to five-ringed pedicels. Hydrotheca widest in middle, tapering basalwards, with conical operculum of nine to 12 long, pointed flaps not demarcated from hydrotheca; sometimes a hydrotheca growing inside an older one. Gonothecae axillary or on stolon; male 'subcylindrical' (Hincks); female large, obconical, with wide aperture; smooth-walled. Dispersive stage a planula.

On various substrata; 0–50 m; widespread in British Isles; Mediterranean to Arctic.

Cuspidella spp.   FIG. 4.12
[e.g. HINCKS 1868, 209, Pls 39, 40]

Colony stolonal; hydrothecae sessile, 0.25–2.2 mm high, cylindrical, walls often with one to several widely spaced rings; operculum conical, with eight to 12 flaps demarcated from hydrotheca by thin crease; basal half of hydrotheca sometimes procumbent. Hydranth very extensile.

On various substrata; seldom intertidal, but to considerable depths.

Several distinctive species of hydromedusae are known to have similar hydroid stages and these have been assigned to various species of *Cuspidella*. Differences between them are still debated so that only a generalized description can be given. For further comment and references see Calder (1970, *J. Fish. Res. Bd. Canada*, **27**, 1501) and Millard (1975).

3 CAMPANULARIIDAE

Colonies stolonal or erect; hydrotheca pedicellate, bell-shaped, fundamentally radially symmetrical, with 'true' or 'false' dia-

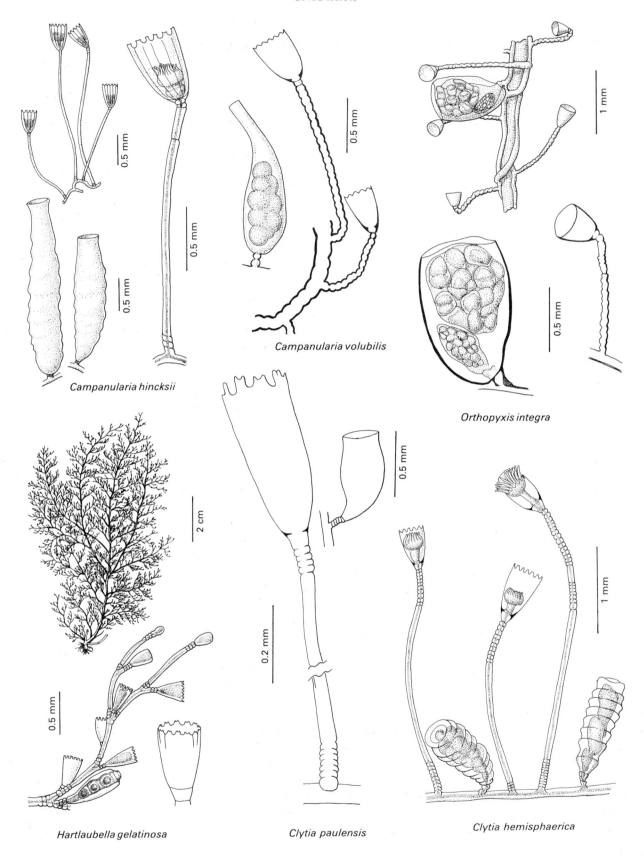

Campanularia hincksii

Campanularia volubilis

Orthopyxis integra

Hartlaubella gelatinosa

Clytia paulensis

Clytia hemisphaerica

Fig. 4.10

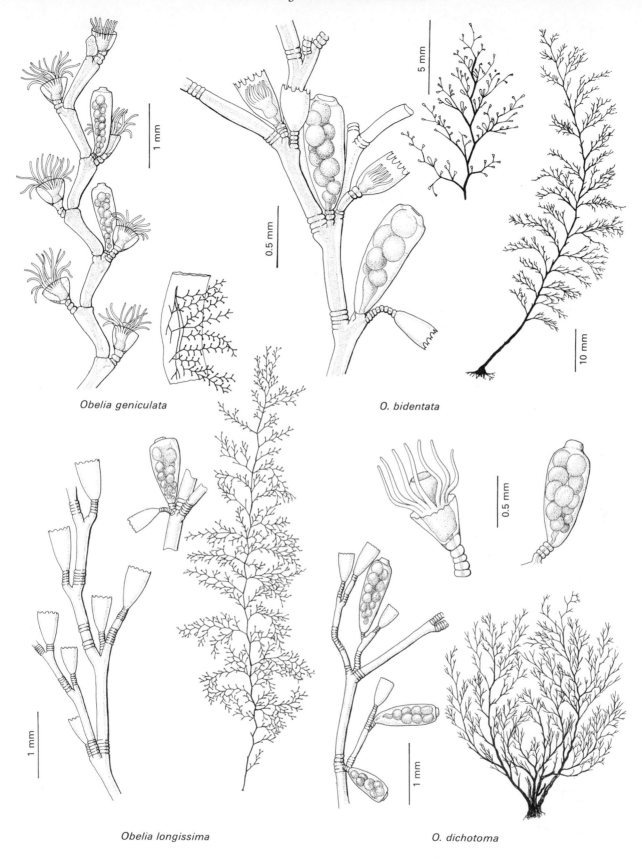

Obelia geniculata

O. bidentata

Obelia longissima

O. dichotoma

Fig. 4.11

phragm, without operculum; hydranths with pear-shaped to spherical hypostome atop narrow constriction; tentacles linear, inserted in one whorl, amphicoronate; reproduction by sporosacs, gonomedusoids or free medusae.

Some species are morphologically among the most varied of all hydroids, and a few will key out in more than one place. Care should be taken when identifying young colonies which might lack adult characters.

1. Colony with erect stems each supporting several to many hydrothecae   **2**

    Colony mainly stolonal, each stem or pedicel supporting one or few hydrothecae   **15**

2. Hydrothecal rim even, sinuous, or crenulate   **3**

    Hydrothecal rim definitely cusped (but often abrading even in *Gonothyraea* spp., *Hartlaubella gelatinosa*, and *Obelia longissima*)   **8**

3. Internodes curving   **4**

    Internodes quite straight, or only slightly curving   **6**

4. Hydrotheca thickened; internode usually asymmetrically thickened   ***Obelia geniculata***

    Hydrotheca and internode unthickened   **5**

5. Hydrotheca usually at least one and a half times long as broad, rim sinuous to crenulate; aperture of mature gonotheca raised; releasing medusae
    Obelia dichotoma (but see also ***O. longissima***)

    Hydrotheca not much longer than broad; rim even; end of mature gonotheca flatly truncate; releasing planulae   ***Laomedea flexuosa***

6. Internodes usually rigidly straight, rather long; terminal tendrils present in autumn; gonotheca on stolon; releasing planulae (found only on eel grasses)   ***Laomedea angulata***

    Internodes at least slightly curving; terminal tendrils unusual in nature; gonothecae usually axillary; releasing medusa   **7**

7. Colony very long, stem brown to black, monosiphonic except sometimes towards base, in older colonies side branches ceasing growth at roughly uniform length but this gradually decreasing distalwards
    Obelia longissima

    Colony loosely fan-shaped, stem polysiphonic basally, pale to mid-brown, never black; side branches not uniform in length, growth of many continuing indefinitely   ***Obelia dichotoma***

8. Hydrothecal cusps sharp (Fig. 4.3., p. 108)   **9**

    Hydrothecal cusps blunt; square, notched or rounded   **11**

9. Hydrothecal rim with embayments between cusps all roughly same depth   ***Clytia hemisphaerica***

    Hydrothecal rim usually bimucronate (Fig. 4.3)   **10**

10. Mature colony tall and bushy, with scores or hundreds of hydranths; main stem polysiphonic; with second- and often third-order branching; gonothecal aperture usually raised, slightly narrower than gonotheca   ***Obelia bidentata***

    Mature colony small, only up to about 20 hydranths; stem monosiphonic; unbranched, of first-order branching only; gonothecal aperture not raised, as broad as gonotheca   ***Clytia paulensis***

11. Hydrothecal rim with rounded cusps   **12**

    Hydrothecal rim with square cusps, often notched (abrade easily)   **13**

12. Mature colony large, main stem polysiphonic; most hydrothecae with sub-hydrothecal spherule; no medusa stage   ***Rhizocaulus verticillatus***

    Mature colony not usually large, always monosiphonic; no spherule; medusae released
    Clytia hemisphaerica

13. Central stem dark brown to black   ***Obelia longissima***

    Central stem pale   **14**

14. Small slender colony, stem monosiphonic; main stem forked, but no true secondary branching; medusae retained as sessile gonomedusae, when mature held external to gonotheca   ***Gonothyraea loveni***

    Large bushy colony, stem polysiphonic; with some second- and third-order branching; large ova, developing into planulae within gonotheca; no medusa
    Hartlaubella gelatinosa

15. Sub-hydrothecal spherule present (Fig. 4.3)   **16**

    Sub-hydrothecal spherule absent   **18**

16. Hydrothecal rim even   ***Orthopyxis integra***

    Hydrothecal rim cusped or undulating   **17**

17. Hydrotheca > 0.5 mm long, typically with lines running down from rim   ***Campanularia hincksii***

    Hydrotheca < 0.5 mm long, without lines
    Campanularia volubilis

(Very young and still stolonal colonies of *Rhizocaulus verticillatus* are similar but with much larger hydrotheca and hydranth)

18. Hydrothecal rim bimucronate (Fig. 4.3); south Essex southwards   *Clytia paulensis*

Hydrothecal rim with uniform embayments; widespread   *Clytia hemisphaerica*

Campanularia hincksii Alder   FIG. 4.10
[HINCKS 1868, 162, Pl. 20; CORNELIUS 1982, 53]
Unbranched, often long pedicels topped by hydrothecae rising at irregular intervals from a tortuous stolon; to about 15 mm. Hydrothecae large, bell-shaped with parallel sides; length $1\frac{1}{3}$–$2\frac{1}{4}$ × breadth; rim castellate, with eight to 15 blunt, notched to deeply cleft cusps; gaps deep, curved, with line from centre of each nearly to base of hydrotheca (not from cusp as occasionally in *C. volubilis*); basal diaphragm conspicuous, stout. Pedicel long; a spherule below hydrotheca; shaft smooth to sinuous, usually ringed basally and sometimes in middle. Male and female gonothecae uniform but female usually longer, borne on stolon; loosely tubular, sides crimped in a succession of shallow rings; tapering gradually upwards, end truncate, sometimes flared; aperture wide, terminal. Dispersive stage a planula.

On hydroids and hard substrata; about 10–200 m, perhaps deeper; in British Isles fairly common off all coasts; widespread, but considered scarce Belgium and Netherlands; north to about Lofoten Islands and Iceland.

Campanularia volubilis (Linnaeus)   FIG. 4.10
[HINCKS 1868, 160, Pl. 24; CORNELIUS 1982, 55]
A small species. Colony stolonal with unbranched pedicels up to about 5 mm at irregular intervals, each topped by a single hydrotheca. Pedicels spirally grooved to smooth, a globular subhydrothecal spherule distally. Hydrotheca bell-shaped, parallel-sided, rounded below; rim with 10–12 shallow, blunt, triangular cusps; reportedly sometimes with fine longitudinal striae associated with cusps (not with gaps as in *C. hincksii*). Male and female gonothecae alike, scarce, borne on stolon or on hydrothecal pedicels, flask-shaped, smooth; aperture narrows when mature, at end of short to long neck. Dispersive stage a planula.

On other hydroids; sub-littoral, 5–100 m or more. Common from southern England north to arctic; not reliably reported north-west France, Belgium, or Netherlands; once Channel Isles.

Clytia hemisphaerica (Linnaeus)   FIG. 4.10
[HINCKS 1868, 143, Pl. 24, as *C. johnstoni*; CORNELIUS 1982, 73; medusa formerly known as *Phialidium hemisphaericum*]
Stems unbranched or slightly branched, up to about 10 mm, arising from creeping stolon. Pedicels long, variously annulated. Hydrothecae large, deep, bell-shaped; rim with 10–14 rounded, symmetrical, triangular cusps. Gonothecae borne on hydrorhiza or less often on hydrocaulus, long-ovoid to cylindrical, smooth

through corrugated to strongly annulated transversely; truncate at top; on short pedicels; medusa released.

On plant and animal substrata, intertidal to deep sublittoral; on all British and Irish coasts, one of our commonest hydroids and medusae; nearly cosmopolitan.

The hydroid of *Clytia gracilis* Sars (not illustrated) has been reported sparingly from southern England but extensively from Scandinavia and also from the Mediterranean. It is slightly smaller, with the cusps on the hydrothecal rim sharp and inclined to one side. In *C. hemisphaerica* they are bluntly pointed and symmetric. See also the scarce *C. paulensis*.

Clytia paulensis (Vanhöffen)   FIG. 4.10
[MILLARD 1975, 221; CORNELIUS 1982, 88]
Colony largely stolonal; single or occasionally branched. Pedicels up to 1.5 mm, arising at irregular intervals, the few branches upward-curved basally and roughly parallel with primary pedicel; ringed basally, below hydrotheca and sometimes centrally, rest smooth. Hydrotheca usually more elongate than in *C. hemisphaerica*, slightly smaller, length/breadth ratio usually 3–4 but exceptionally 1.5; rim with seven to 11 rounded bimucronate cusps, the embayments between them slightly bulging; diaphragm oblique; longitudinal folds in hydrothecal wall can look like striations. Gonotheca reportedly cylindrical, tapered gradually below and slightly above, smooth; rim flared, truncate, aperture wide; on stolon on short ringed stalk; one to three medusa buds. Medusa presumed released.

On other hydroids and animals; lower shore to 200 m; around British Isles reported only Suffolk, Essex, and south Devon, also from warmer parts of northern French coast; apparently absent Roscoff, reappearing Glénan archipelago southwards; widespread in warm oceans.

Gonothyraea loveni (Allman)   FIG. 4.12
[HINCKS 1868, 181, Pl. 25; CORNELIUS 1982, 92]
Stems erect, arising from creeping stolon; irregularly branched; to about 30 mm. Colourless to pale horn, annulated at base and above origins of branches. Hydrothecae alternate, bell-shaped, margin with about 14 blunt cusps, often with minute median notch; pedicels usually ringed throughout. Male and female gonothecae similar, male slightly narrower; axillary, on short pedicels; long, obconical, truncate distally; containing several male or female vestigial medusae which project from the gonotheca in twos or threes as the planulae develop.

On stones and algae, particularly browns; often in pools; tolerant of brackish water; MTL to 200 m; common around British Isles; all coasts of Europe. A second nominal species, *G. hyalina* Hincks, has been separated as having longer hydrothecae and internodes and is said to form the deeper populations.

Hartlaubella gelatinosa (Pallas)   FIG. 4.10
[HINCKS 1868, 151, Pl. 26, as *Obelia*; CORNELIUS 1982, 95]
Colony erect, bushy, to about 350 mm; one to several main shoots, sometimes forked, arising from a dense network of stolon threads occasionally aggregated into a basal fibrous mass. Main stems rather thick, darker than branches; polysiphonic, with up

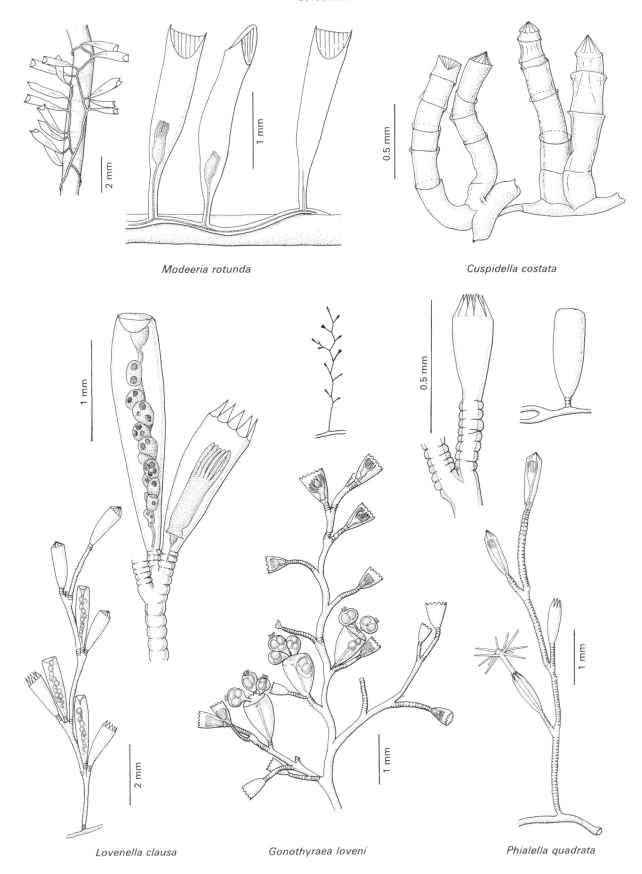

Modeeria rotunda

Cuspidella costata

Lovenella clausa

Gonothyraea loveni

Phialella quadrata

Fig. 4.12

to 20 perisarc tubes basally, thinning out above. Side branches numerous, tending to be in right-angled pairs, successively on opposite sides of stem (as also in *Obelia bidentata*); branches straight, polysiphonic basally, monosiphonic and flexuose distally; with short branchlets at each flexure, each with about six hydrothecae; occasionally further branchlets. Hydrothecae bell-shaped, thin-walled, small, rim castellate with about 12–14 blunt cusps each slightly indented in unworn specimens, but rim often abraded smooth; pedicels varied in length, ringed throughout or with smooth central portions. Male and female gonothecae similar, axillary, long-ovoid, flat-topped with raised terminal aperture. Dispersive stage a planula.

Intertidal to 15 m or deeper, often in gentle current; tolerant of silt and of brackish water; southern Scotland, Oslo Fjord, and Denmark south to Mediterranean and Black Seas. See also *Obelia bidentata* and *O. longissima*.

Laomedea angulata Hincks FIG. 4.9
[HINCKS 1868, 170, Pl. 24; CORNELIUS 1982, 98]
Colony a series of short shoots arising regularly from a long, rather straight stolon. Erect shoots monosiphonic, narrow, rigidly zigzag, to about 15 mm; not forked; internodes straight to very slightly curving, rather long, annulated basally; often long terminal tendril in autumn. Hydrotheca on long, ringed pedicel; length about 1.5 times maximum breadth, thin-walled; rim even. Gonotheca always on stolon; long-ovoid, wide in middle, tapering above, wall thickened distally; aperture terminal, narrow, reportedly narrower in male than in female. Dispersive stage a planula.

Recorded only on eel grasses; ELWS to about 8 m; known today from south coast of England southwards but reliable 19th century records north to Isle of Man; status in Ireland unclear.

Laomedea flexuosa Alder FIG. 4.9
[HINCKS 1868, 168, Pl. 33; CORNELIUS 1982, 105]
Stems flexuose, monosiphonic, usually unbranched, arising from creeping stolon; to about 35 mm; internodes curving, annulated at base and above origin of each pedicel; perisarc horn-coloured. Hydrothecae alternate, large, cup-shaped, rims even; on annulated pedicels. Female gonotheca subcylindrical, narrowing proximally, truncate distally, sides smooth to slightly sinuous; male slightly to much shorter, slightly tapered distally towards narrow truncate aperture; on ringed axillary pedicels. Dispersive stage a planula.

On stones and weeds; mid-shore to about 40 m, occasionally to 90 m; one of the commonest British hydroids; all European coasts, recorded south to Ghana. Young colonies of several other campanulariids can be similar.

Obelia bidentata Clarke FIG. 4.11
[Syn. *O bicuspidata* Clarke]
[LELOUP 1952, 157, as *Laomedea*; CORNELIUS, 1975a, 260]
Mature colony comprising several erect main stems, sometimes slightly zigzag, polysiphonic but slender, to about 150 mm, sometimes forked; minor lateral branches tending to be in right-angled pairs, successively on opposite sides of stem (as also in *Hartlaubella gelatinosa*) but this arrangement often obscured. Minor branches delicate, shallowly zigzag, with graceful sigmoid downward curvature in life; pinnate, branchlets alternate, monosiphonic, flexuose, bearing hydrothecal pedicels at nodes; sometimes themselves branched (3rd order) and even branched again (4th order). Hydrotheca two to three times as long as broad, cylindrical to bell-shaped; sometimes slightly asymmetric; diaphragm oblique from some angles; rim with 10–20 cusps, usually bimucronate. Gonotheca long-obconical with slightly raised aperture. Dispersive stage a medusa.

On inert substrata such as wood, shells, wrecks and on sandy bottoms, sometimes algae; tolerant of brackish water; sublittoral to at least 200 m, rarely intertidal in pools; also stranded. Around British Isles known from Wash, north Norfolk, parts of southern North Sea, Sheppey, and once near Portsmouth; also warmer parts of northern French coast, Belgium, and Netherlands; temperate- to warm-water global.

Obelia dichotoma (Linnaeus) FIG. 4.11
[HINCKS 1868, 156, Pl. 28; 159, Pl. 30, as *O. plicata*; CORNELIUS 1990, *J. nat. Hist.*, 24]
Colonies varying from solitary unbranched, through much branched, monosiphonic stems of up to 50 m high, to older loosely fan-shaped to elongate colonies with stem polysiphonic basally; these reaching about 350 mm in height and sometimes in breadth, perhaps occurring especially in calm habitats. Branches shallowly zigzag, lower ones nearly as long as main stem; older branches and stems dark, younger parts colourless to pale horn. Internodes nearly straight, tubular, with many short branches arising at nodes; solitary, monosiphonic stems similar, lacking branches; hydrothecal pedicels arising at nodes, ringed, slightly tapered. Hydrotheca wide-conical to long bell-shaped, often slightly polyhedral in section; wall thin; rim crenulate to smooth; often with about 15 fine striae running basally from indentations on rim, best seen with side-lighting. Gonotheca obconical, tapering basally; truncate distally, with short terminal collar. Medusae released in summer.

On animal, plant, and inert substrata; intertidal to about 100 m; throughout British Isles; near-cosmopolitan.

Obelia geniculata (Linnaeus) FIG. 4.11
[HINCKS 1868, 149, Pl. 25; CORNELIUS 1975a, 272]
Erect stems to about 50 mm arising from long, rather straight stolon; usually zigzag, sometimes branched; annulated at each flexure. Perisarc thickened asymmetrically, with internal projections at upper end of each internode. Hydrothecae alternate, cup-shaped, often thickened, sometimes asymmetrically, little longer than wide; rim even; on short, slightly tapering, annulated pedicels. Gonothecae long, obconical, with wide aperture atop short terminal collar; axillary, on short pedicels. Medusa released in summer.

Usually on algae, especially *Laminaria* and *Fucus*; MTL to sublittoral; common; all British coasts; nearly cosmopolitan.

Obelia longissima (Pallas)   FIG. 4.11
[HINCKS 1868, 154, Pl. 27; 157, Pl. 29, as *O. flabellata*; CORNE-
LIUS 1990, *J. nat. Hist.*, 24]
Colony typically single-stemmed, exceptionally to about
350 mm, occasionally with main stem forked; monosiphonic
except in older colonies when basal parts of main stem polysiphonic; main stem and branches gracefully curving, flexible.
Stem and older branches brown to black, younger branches pale
horn to darker; internodes of both stem and branches long,
tubular; branches decreasing gradually in length along colony;
arising singly or in twos or threes, usually one of the branchlets
smaller than the other(s) but not always; branches themselves
branched. Hydrotheca elongate, obconical to long bell-shaped,
sometimes slightly asymmetric; thin-walled; rim shallow-cas-
tellate to blunt-cusped, 11–17 cusps but often abraded even;
sometimes slightly flared; not polygonal in section; hydrothecal
pedicels slightly tapered, ringed, arising at nodes. Gonotheca
obconical, tapering below; end truncate, usually with short
collar. Medusae released in spring in British waters.

On plant and inert substrata, including rock and sand; intertidal pools to about 30 m or more; all British coasts; probably
near-cosmopolitan. Fully grown colonies are among the most
graceful of all British hydroids.

Orthopyxis integra (Macgillivray)   FIG. 4.10
[HINCKS 1868, 164, Pl. 31, as *Campanularia*; CORNELIUS 1982,
60]
Tortuous stolon with many erect pedicels, up to 10 mm. Pedicel
corrugated, with a spherule below hydrotheca. Hydrotheca bell-
shaped, rim even; wall often greatly, and frequently asymmetrically, thickened; a shelf projecting inwards at base forming
spherical cavity. Gonotheca borne on stolon; shortly stalked,
cylindrical, irregularly ovoid with a wavy profile; top truncate,
aperture wide. Planulae develop within gonotheca at first but
later protrude in an acrocyst.

On algae, especially reds, and on a wide variety of inert
substrata; LWST to offshore; rarely in deep intertidal pools;
widespread in British Isles, but seldom recorded Ireland, Irish
Sea, or western Scotland; nearly cosmopolitan.

Rhizocaulus verticillatus (Linnaeus)   FIG. 4.9
[HINCKS 1868, 167, Pl. 32, as *Campanularia*; CORNELIUS 1982,
67]
Stem erect, polysiphonic, infrequently and irregularly forked;
to about 10 cm. Very young colonies stolonal. Hydrotheca bell-
shaped, rim with 10–16 blunt cusps; on long pedicels, typically
spirally grooved, arranged in whorls of four to six, reminiscent
of horse-tails (*Equisetum*). Male and female gonothecae alike,
flask-shaped with distal neck of varied length, narrowing
abruptly to short two-ringed stalk below; on stem. Dispersive
stage a planula.

On shells and stones; 20–600 m; all British coasts; to Arctic.

4 LOVENELLIDAE
Colonies stolonal or forming short, branched, erect shoots;
hydrotheca basically radially symmetrical, with thin diaphragm,

pedicellate, walls thin, sometimes collapsing; operculum conical,
of many triangular flaps, or frail and collapsing; hydranth extensile, contracting within hydrotheca, with single whorl of linear
tentacles with or without basal web, hypostome conical. Gonotheca cylindrical, thin-walled, radially symmetrical. Reproduction by medusae where known.

Lovenella clausa (Lovén)   FIG. 4.12
[HINCKS 1868, 177, Pl. 32]
Colony comprising either single pedicels or short erect hydrocauli arising from a stolon; up to about 25 mm; branches of
pedicel arising slightly down from top of internode. Pedicels
with two to five rings below hydrotheca, rest of perisarc sinuous
throughout. Hydrothecae long and narrow, thin-walled; often
with two to three renovated hydrothecae inside oldest, based on
the transverse hydrothecal diaphragm in characteristic way,
inner hydrothecae narrower and longer than outermost; roughly
cylindrical, sometimes slightly asymmetric, tapering slightly
towards base, widest at aperture; rim scalloped into eight to ten
cusps; operculum of eight to ten triangular flaps, each with
well-demarcated, rounded base. Gonotheca elongate, axillary,
tapering from truncate end towards base; sides often slightly
sinuous; aperture broad, extending whole width of end. Dispersive stage a medusa.

Often on *Turritella communis* and other molluscs, once *Dentalium*; once on *Fucus*; LWST to 50 m. Scattered records throughout British and Irish waters; Denmark to southern Spain.

5 PHIALELLIDAE
Colonies erect, short, branched; hydrothecae radially symmetrical, with conical operculum of many triangular flaps not
delimited basally; hydranth retracting within hydrotheca, with
single whorl of linear tentacles and conical hypostome; gonotheca cylindrical, borne on stem. Medusa released.

Phiallela quadrata (Forbes)   FIG. 4.12
[HINCKS 1868, 189, Pl. 38, as *Campanulina repens*; RUSSELL
1953, 315]
Stems erect, rising from a creeping stolon, to about 5 mm; simple
or alternately forked. Perisarc distinctly annulated throughout.
Hydrotheca obconical, with operculum of long, triangular segments which are not obviously delimited basally from hydrotheca. Gonotheca large, shaped like inverted bottle, usually
borne on stolon, on short annulated pedicel; medusae released.

Coastal; on various substrata; common. Medusa recorded
off all coasts except eastern and south-eastern England, but
distribution of the hydroid stage less well-known.

6 LAFOEIDAE
Colony stolonal or erect; hydrotheca bell-shaped to tubular,
deep, radially symmetrical, with or without diaphragm, pedicellate or sessile to adnate, rim even, lacking operculum;
hydranth contracting wholly within hydrotheca, with conical
hypostome and single whorl of filiform tentacles; gonothecae
usually aggregated beneath modified protective hydranths in a
scapus or *coppinia* (orderly tangle of elongate, modified hydro-

1. Colony mainly stolonal **2**

   Colony mainly erect **3**

2. Hydrotheca with occasional rings, tubular, adherent, never with defined pedicel, upward-curving from stolon, diameter up to about 175 μm; stolon tortuous; minute, typically on another hydroid, often *Abietinaria abietina*   ***Filellum serpens***

   Hydrotheca not ringed; pedicel kinked, straight, or absent, arising at right angles from stolon, diameter about 350 μm upwards; stolon straighter; larger, on wide variety of substrata   ***Lafoea dumosa***

3. Hydrothecae tubular, in four to eight regular and parallel rows, partly adnate and outward-turning distally; never a pedicel   ***Grammaria abietina***

   Hydrothecae typically tapered below, in two or more rows, entirely free, usually pedicellate   ***Lafoea dumosa***

---

thecae); reproduction usually by fixed sporosacs, sometimes by released medusae.

Filellum serpens (Hassall)   FIG. 4.13
[HINCKS 1868, 214, Pl. 41; CORNELIUS 1975*b*, 378; formerly called *Coppinia* spp.]
One of the simplest thecates. Colony a tortuous stolon, irregularly branched, from which long tubular upward-curving hydrothecae arise at close, irregular intervals to a height of about 1.5 mm. Hydrotheca slightly wider than stolon, basal quarter to one-third adnate; rim even, usually slightly flared; often with one to several renovations; no operculum or diaphragm. Gonothecae protected in hermaphrodite coppinia. Dispersive stage a planula.

Epizoic, especially on *Abietinaria* spp. but also on other sertulariid hydroids, shells, and other inert substrata; sublittoral to edge of continental shelf; common throughout British Isles; cosmopolitan.

Grammaria abietina (M. Sars)   FIG. 4.13
[HINCKS 1868, 212, Pl. 41; CORNELIUS 1975*b*, 382]
Colony erect, branching irregular to nearly pinnate; stem and nearly all branches polysiphonic; up to about 100 mm. Hydrotheca long, tubular, merging with stem; variably outward-curving; rim even, circular, often renovated, frequently slightly flared. Hydrothecae in four to eight longitudinal rows, alternate in adjacent rows; if four rows, often in decussate pairs. Gonothecae protected in hermaphrodite coppiniae resembling muffs. Dispersive stage a planula.

On both silty and rocky substrata; 10–250 m; a cold water species, Shetland south to Northumberland but apparently not west coast of Scotland southwards; also Denmark north to Arctic Ocean.

Lafoea dumosa (Fleming)   FIG. 4.13
[HINCKS 1868, 200, Pl. 41; CORNELIUS 1975*b*, 385]
Colony either stolonal and simple or erect with stems irregularly forked and polysiphonic, sometimes both; to about 100 m.

Hydrotheca long, up to about 1 mm, smooth; narrowing slightly to form a pedicel, sometimes kinked towards the base; more or less sessile on hydrocaulus, no diaphragm, in erect colonies arising irregularly to semi-regularly from all or just two sides; rim plain, without operculum, occasionally renovated. Gonothecae borne in somewhat rare coppinae. Dispersive stage a planula.

On various substrata; intertidal to offshore; all coasts but scarce east English Channel and southern North Sea; not recorded Belgium.

7 HALECIIDAE

Colony erect, procumbent or stolonal; hydrotheca usually shorter than wide, too small to accommodate hydranth, cylindrical; rims even, often renovated; lacking operculum; hydrothecal desmocytes (formerly termed punctae) large, persistent after death, often birefringent; usually no pedicel; hydranths larger than hydrothecae, hypostome conical, with single whorl of filiform tentacles; nematophores in some species (none included here); male and female gonothecae usually dissimilar, often with associated hydranths; reproduction usually by fixed sporosacs, sometimes by eumedusoids and free-swimming medusae.

---

1. Hydrothecal rim recurved **2**

   Hydrothecal rim straight **4**

2. Colony minute, up to 20 mm, comprising one or a few erect shoots; monosiphonic throughout   ***Halecium tenellum***

   Colony large, usually over 20 mm, arborescent; polysiphonic in older parts **3**

3. Internodes uniform in length, perisarc smooth, seldom ringed; nodes oblique   ***Halecium muricatum***

   Internodes varied in length, perisarc sinuous, often ringed; nodes roughly transverse   ***Halecium labrosum***

4. Colony regularly pinnate, in one plane, branches neatly parallel; never stolonal   ***Halecium halecinum***

   Colony irregular, branches not precisely parallel; or not in one plane; or stolonal **5**

5. Colony polysiphonic basally, erect **6**

   Colony monosiphonic throughout, erect or stolonal **7**

6. Colony much taller than wide; main stem usually unforked; side branches straight, uniform in length, regularly arranged, to one side of stem; limp out of water   ***Halecium sessile***

   Colony bushy, spreading sideways as well as upward; main stem often forked; side branches irregular in shape, length, and arrangement; stiff out of water   ***Halecium beanii***

7. Colony stolonal, minute; often on *Flustra*   ***Hydranthea margarica***

   Colony erect **8**

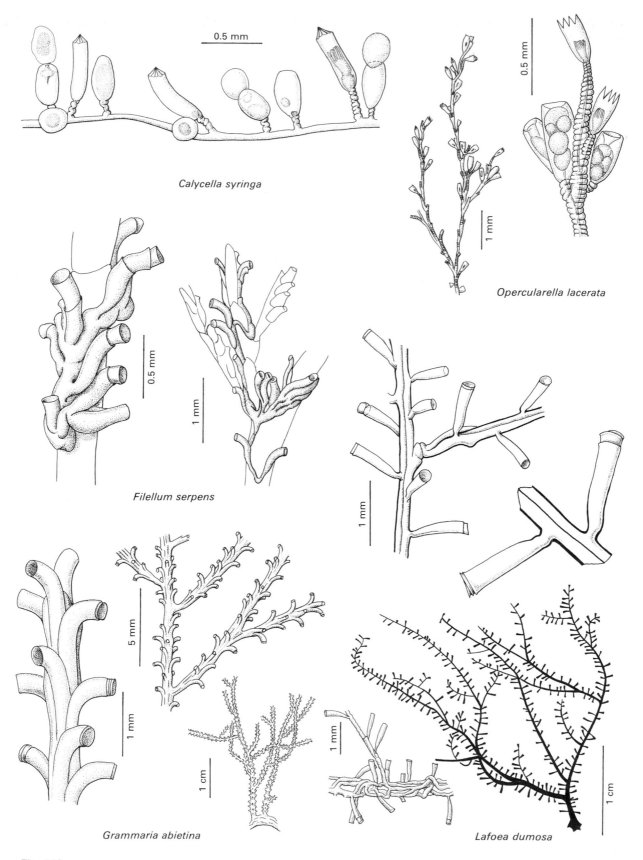

0.5 mm

Calycella syringa

0.5 mm

1 mm

Opercularella lacerata

0.5 mm

1 mm

Filellum serpens

1 mm

5 mm

1 mm

1 cm

Grammaria abietina

1 mm

1 cm

Lafoea dumosa

Fig. 4.13

8. Internodes dissimilar in shape and length, sometimes lightly corrugated; axils of branchlets >45°
          Halecium lankesteri

Internodes roughly uniform in shape and length,
smooth; axils <45°   **Halecium sessile**

Halecium beanii (Johnston)   FIG. 4.14
[HINCKS 1868, 224, Pl. 43; CORNELIUS 1975*b*, 391]
Colony erect, irregularly branched, finer branches more delicate in habit than in *H. halecinum*; to about 200 mm. Stems and larger branches compound, tapering; branches alternate, often themselves branched, variously zigzag, jointed at short intervals. Hydrothecae alternate, one borne below each joint, shortly tubular, widening a little towards aperture, rim plain; often renovated; too small to accommodate hydranths. Gonothecae borne on hydrocladia, male elongate-ovoid, on short pedicels; female kidney-shaped, with short tube on concave side, two hydranths projecting from its aperture, containing four to six ova. Dispersive stage a planula.

On other hydroids and shells; 5–100 m depth; common throughout British Isles; nearly cosmopolitan.

Halecium halecinum (Linnaeus). Herring-bone hydroid
              FIG. 4.14
[HINCKS 1868, 221, Pl. 42; CORNELIUS 1975*b*, 393]
Colony arising from small spongy mass of fibres, stiffly erect, regularly pinnate, irregularly forked; to 250 mm. Stems and branches polysiphonic basally, tapering and monosiphonic distally. Branches alternate, parallel, equally spaced, sometimes branched pinnately, axes variously zigzag, nodes transverse; internodes short, stout. Hydrothecae alternate, collar-like, rim plain; two to eight in nested series marking successive hydrothecal renovations; too small to accommodate hydranths. Gonothecae borne on upper sides of branches; male ovoid, slender, tapering below to short pedicel of one to two rings; female oblong, tapering below, broad and truncate above, with short tubular upward-pointing aperture at one upper corner; with two to three hydranths issuing from the aperture. Dispersive stage a planula.

On stones and shells; coastal; common off all coasts; widely distributed in Atlantic.

Halecium labrosum Alder   FIG. 4.14
[HINCKS 1868, 225, Pl. 44; CORNELIUS 1975*b*, 396]
Colony erect, to about 50 mm, imperfectly pinnate; all but final branches polysiphonic. Main branches slightly flexuose, the finer side-branches alternate, with characteristic curve near base. Internodes unequal; much of perisarc often wrinkled or smooth. Hydrothecae sessile, on prominent processes; short, rim strongly recurved, up to about 12 renovations common. Gonotheca on stem, on short pedicel; apparently without the gonothecal hydranths present in some *Halecium* spp.; male ovoid to elongate, tapering below and sometimes also above, aperture small, terminal; female ovoid, large, rather thick-walled, up to

1.5 mm long, narrowing basally, aperture terminal on short often ill-defined collar. Dispersive stage a planula.

Epizoic on various invertebrates, perhaps also on inanimate substrata; 5–200 m; a northern species, recorded south to southern England; also Roscoff but not Scillies, Channel Isles, Belgium, or Netherlands; from British Isles and Denmark northwards.

Halecium lankesteri (Bourne)   FIG. 4.14
[CORNELIUS 1975*b*, 399]
Colony a collection of erect, monosiphonic shoots, limp out of water, joined by a branching stolon; up to about 80 mm; usually unbranched but sometimes imperfectly pinnate. Internodes unequal in length, usually a hydrotheca on each but sometimes up to ten athecate internodes between hydrothecae; bases of branches on characteristic processes. Hydrothecae alternate, short, cylindrical, walls straight and divergent; rims even, not flared; up to about five renovations. Gonothecae on short pedicels below hydrothecae; male cylindrical, aperture terminal, narrow, female kidney-shaped with aperture at end of tube in centre of concave side, with one to two protruding hydranths. Dispersive stage a planula.

On stones, other hydroids, crabs, bryozoans, and algae; LWST to about 50 m; a southern species reaching south-west Wales and Norfolk; not reported from Ireland; probably overlooked, may occur more widely.

Halecium muricatum (Ellis and Solander)   FIG. 4.15
[HINCKS 1868, 223, Pl. 43; CORNELIUS 1975*b*, 402]
Colony large, erect, up to 200 mm, imperfectly pinnate; main stem and larger branches rather straight but haphazard; all but final branches polysiphonic; branches alternate. Internodes equal; nodal annuli inclined successively left and right, or all transverse. Hydrothecae alternate, on final, monosiphonic, branches; each on short process, usually delimited by deep, irregular annulus; short, rims even, usually flared; up to about six renovations. Male and female gonothecae similar, flattened-ovoid with nine to 15 somewhat irregular rows of 100–200 μm spines; on short pedicels on major branches. Dispersive stage a planula.

Mostly on rocks and shells but reported once on red algae; 10–1350 m; arctic to boreal, reaching south-west Scotland, Isle of Man, Norfolk, central North Sea, Denmark, and west Sweden; possibly Ulster but no Irish records this century, and no English Channel records since Hincks (1868).

Halecium sessile (Norman)   FIG. 4.15
[HINCKS 1868, 227, 229, Pl. 44, including *H. plumosum*; CORNELIUS 1975*b*, 406]
Colonies monosiphonic, up to about 50 mm, or polysiphonic in older parts, up to about 300 mm; loosely pinnate; branches alternate, arching, sparsely branched and branched again; larger colonies limp when out of water. Stem shallowly zigzag; nodal annuli transverse or sloping alternately left and right. Internodes approximately equal but shorter distally, often differing in length between colonies. Hydrotheca on short process distal on internode, directed upwards; short; walls straight, divergent; rim

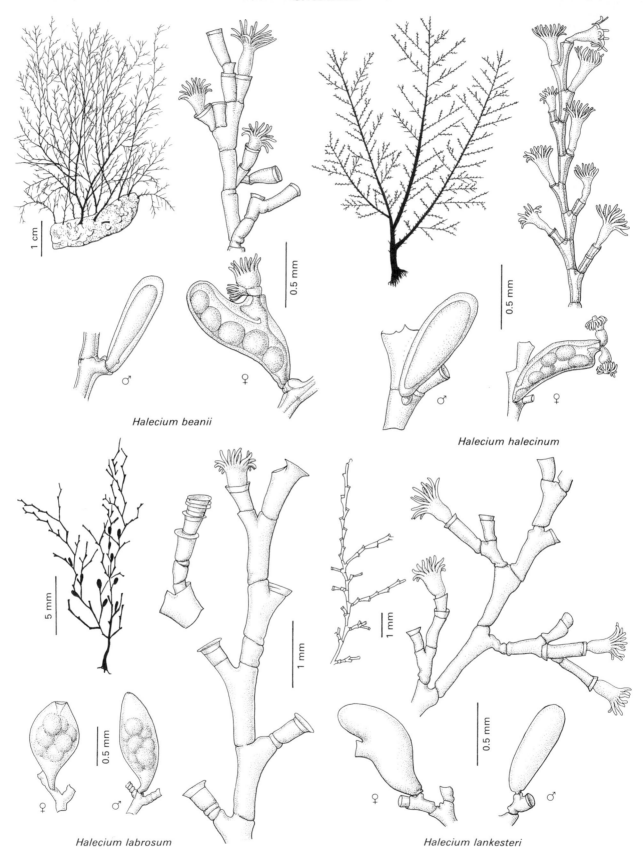

Halecium beanii

Halecium halecinum

Halecium labrosum

Halecium lankesteri

Fig. 4.14

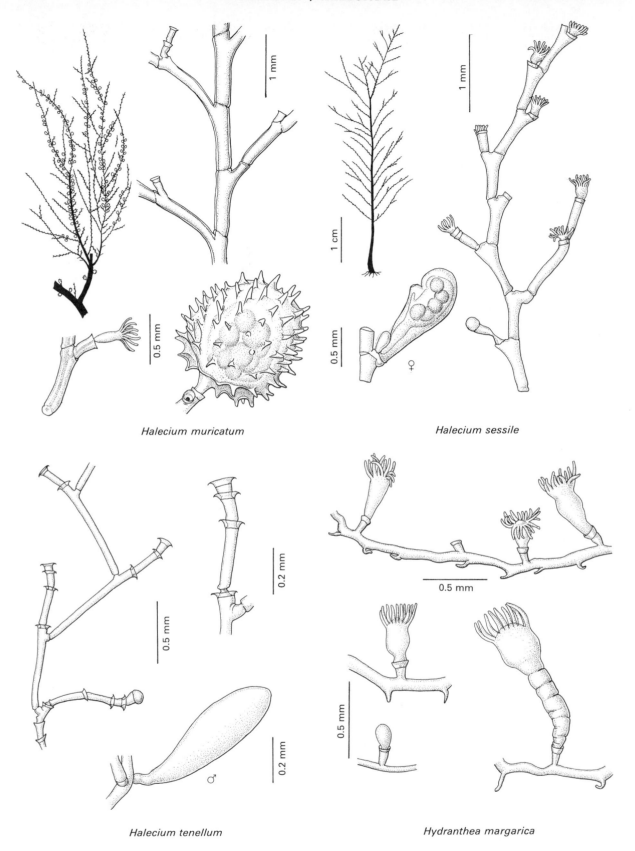

Halecium muricatum

Halecium sessile

Halecium tenellum

Hydranthea margarica

Fig. 4.15

even, not flared; with characteristic annular thickening of perisarc below hydrotheca, wedge-shaped in optical section; renovations common, very short, giving diagnostic appearance. Male gonotheca tubular, often slightly curved, aperture terminal; female kidney-shaped, aperture at end of short tube on concave side. Dispersive stage a planula.

Recorded on *Sabellaria* tubes and algae but probably on other substrata; LWST to edge of continental shelf; occurring throughout European seas including whole of British Isles; not Baltic; reportedly cosmopolitan. *H. plumosum* may prove to be distinct [Cornelius, P. F. S., *Syn. Br. Fauna* (in prep.)]

Halecium tenellum (Hincks)   FIG. 4.15
[HINCKS 1868, 226, Pl. 45; CORNELIUS 1975*b*, 409]
A small species. Erect shoots up to 20 mm, delicate, monosiphonic, irregularly branched, some branches apparently arising through hydrothecae. Stem zigzag; internodes usually straight, long, and narrow, one to three wrinkles top and bottom grading to wrinkled throughout. Hydrothecae one per internode, each on prominent, often long process; tubular, short, rim flared. Male gonotheca ovoid, flattened in one plane, aperture narrow, terminal; female similar, slightly larger and proportionately broader; no protruding hydranths. Dispersive stage a planula.

On other hydroids and on bryozoans; LWST to 500 m; nearly cosmopolitan; probably throughout British Isles, but sparsely recorded.

Hydranthea margarica (Hincks)   FIG. 4.15
[HINCKS 1868, 100, Pl. 19; CORNELIUS 1975*b*, 412]
Colony a stolon bearing single, plump, yellowish white polyps at irregular intervals. Hydrotheca very short, up to about 0.5 mm excluding pedicel, walls straight, slightly divergent; rim even; diaphragm concave; on short unringed pedicel inserted on stolon; hydranth 0.5 mm or more long, widest just below conical hypostome; 20–30 tentacles, amphicoronate, joined by small basal web. Large nematocysts, 30–40 μm long, on web and throughout hydranth and stolon tissues. Gonotheca poorly known, resembling hydrotheca, on short basally-tapered pedicel; male and female gonophores similar; vestigial medusa retained, spherical, 0.5 mm, with four conspicuous, branched, orange gastrovascular ('radial') canals.

Most frequently on *Flustra* and other bryozoans, but also on mollusc shells, other hydroids, *Laminaria* holdfasts, and bare rock; offshore; from Roscoff to Shetlands but apparently no east coast records north of Norfolk; no Irish records; elsewhere recorded only from Mediterranean and Seychelles, so evidently overlooked.

8 SERTULARIIDAE
Colonies erect; hydrothecae in two or more rows (secondarily one in adult *Hydrallmania*), often closely spaced, usually sessile to adnate or wholly sunk within perisarc, occasionally pedicellate (though not in European species), bilaterally symmetrical, rim often cusped, usually with operculum of one to four flat flaps (never conical); hydrothecae usually with flat floor perforated by pore, but 'true' diaphragm in a few species having pedicellate hydrothecae; hydranth tubular, with conical hypostome and single circlet of linear tentacles, completely retracting within hydrotheca, in some genera folding on retraction to form on one side a pocket or *abcauline caecum* (Fig. 4.3); nematothecae absent; gonophores usually fixed sporosacs, rarely releasing a medusoid.

Young colonies of some species differ in character from adults and such species key out in more than one place.

1.	Hydrothecal rim even or notched, never cusped	**2**
	Hydrothecal rim cusped, not notched	**13**
2.	Hydrotheca totally contained within perisarc or nearly so	**3**
	Terminal quarter or more of hydrotheca projecting from perisarc	**6**
3.	Branches all round stem	***Thuiaria thuja***
	Branches in one plane	**4**
4.	Branches mostly opposite	***Thuiaria articulata***
	Branches mostly alternate	**5**
5.	Hydrothecal apertures directed outward (young, pinnate colony prior to acquiring adult growth habit)	***Thuiara thuja***
	Hydrothecal apertures directed upward	***Selaginopsis fusca***
6.	Hydrothecae apparently uniseriate (in one row)	***Hydrallmania falcata***
	Hydrothecae biseriate or tetraseriate (triseriate in occasional specimens of *Diphasia fallax*)	**7**
7.	Hydrothecal surface with fine transverse ridges (rarely also in *Tamarisca tamarisca*)	***Diphasia delagei***
	Hydrothecal surface not finely ridged	**8**
8.	With axillary hydrothecae (see text for distinctions)	***Abietinaria abietina*** and **A. filicula**
	Without axillary hydrothecae	**9**
9.	Side-branches narrower than main stem; colony regularly pinnate	**10**
	Side-branches same width as main stem; colony irregularly pinnate, or not pinnate at all	**12**
10.	Inner wall of hydrotheca almost or completely adnate	***Diphasia nigra***
	Inner wall of hydrotheca at most three-quarters adnate	**11**
11.	Hydrothecal flexure about 45°; sides of main stem approximately parallel	***Diphasia alata***
	Hydrothecal flexure about 90°; sides of main stem constricted below each hydrotheca	***Diphasia pinaster***
12.	Hydrotheca half adnate; flexure abrupt, about 45° (see text for distinctions)	***Diphasia attenuata*** and **D. rosacea**

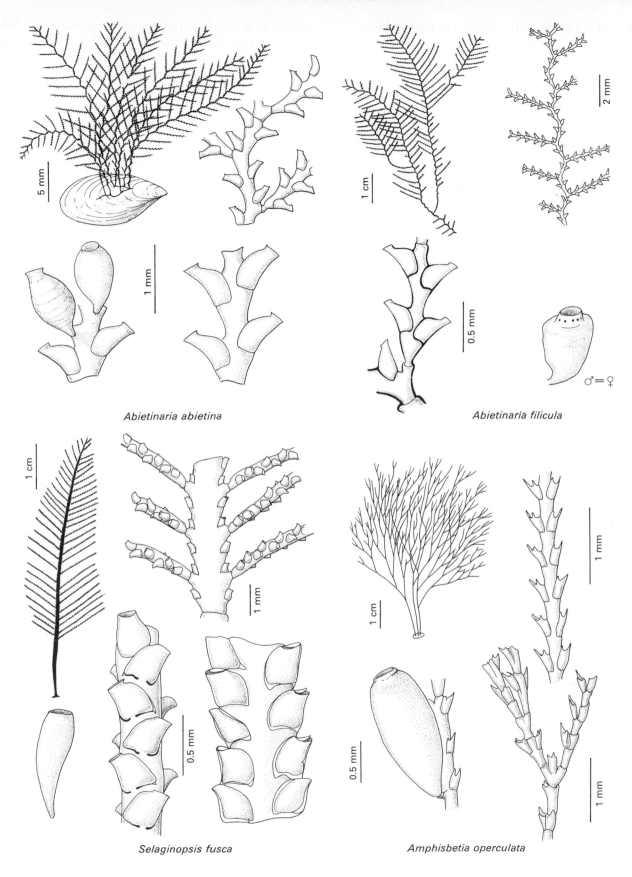

Abietinaria abietina

Abietinaria filicula

Selaginopsis fusca

Amphisbetia operculata

Fig. 4.16

Hydrotheca two-thirds or more adnate; flexure
gradual, <45°   ***Diphasia fallax***

13. Cusps on hydrothecal rim two to three, one some-
times minute   **14**

    Cusps on hydrothecal rim four   **20**

14. Two hydrothecal cusps   **15**

    Three hydrothecal cusps   **19**

15. Hydrothecae in (sub) opposite pairs (also sometimes
Sertularia cupressina)   **16**

    Hydrothecae alternate   **18**

16. Hydrothecal cusps markedly unequal
                                                  Amphisbetia operculata

    Hydrothecal cusps approximately equal   **17**

17. Nodal annuli all transverse, except sometimes basal-
most   ***Dynamena pumila***

    Transverse and oblique nodal annuli approximately
alternating   ***Sertularia distans***

18. One (rarely both) cusps on hydrothecal rim long (see
also young *Amphisbetia operculata*)   ***Sertularia cupressina***

    Both cusps on hydrothecal rim short (young colonies,
or rather common aberrant branches on mature col-
onies)   ***Hydrallmania falcata***

19. Hydrothecae approximately straight, length:breadth
ratio about 2:1   ***Symplectoscyphus tricuspidatus***

    Hydrothecae curving outwards, length:breadth ratio
about 4:1   ***Tamarisca tamarisca***

20. Hydrothecae rugose (for distinctions see text)
                              Sertularella rugosa and ***S. tenella***

    Hydrothecae smooth   **21**

21. Three (rarely, one, two, or four) low rounded projections sub-distally on inside of hydrothecal wall;
internodal perisarc and hydrothecal wall usually
smooth   ***Sertularella gaudichaudi***

    No projections on inside of hydrothecal wall; inter-
nodal perisarc and hydrothecal wall usually undu-
lating to rugose   ***Sertularella gayi*** and ***S. polyzonias***

Abietinaria abietina (Linnaeus)   FIG. 4.16
[HINCKS 1868, 266, Pl. 55, as *Sertularia*; CORNELIUS 1979,
251]
Stems thick, arising from a basal stolon; main stem to 300 mm;
slightly flexuose, sometimes forked; side branches alternate,
straight, close, regularly pinnately arranged, equidistant. Hydrothecae large, crowded, alternate, bulbous below, narrowing
above into a short tubular neck which is free and out-turned;
aperture oblique, rim even, shallow notch just below, on inner

side (cf. *A. filicula*). Male and female gonothecae similar, shortly
stalked, borne at base of hydrothecae; ovoid, smooth, or slightly
wrinkled, with a plain, short, tubular aperture. Embryos yellow,
developing into planulae within an external acrocyst.

On shells and stones; 10 m to offshore, often found on strandline; all coasts, common; arctic to Mediterranean.

See also young *Hydrallmania falcata*.

Abietinaria filicula (Ellis and Solander)   FIG. 4.16
[HINCKS 1868, 264, Pl. 53, as *Sertularia*; CORNELIUS 1979,
253]
Colony erect, pinnate, much branched, smaller in detail and less
robust than *A. abietina*; up to about 100 mm. Stem flexuose to
straight; branches same width as stem, alternate; some secondary
branching. Hydrothecae biseriate, subalternate to alternate, on
stems and branches and in axils; flask-shaped, bulbous below,
neck said to be more distinct than in *A. abietina*; one- to two-
thirds adnate; aperture circular, even-rimmed, usually inclined
towards stem; notch below aperture on inner side reportedly
deeper than in *A. abietina*. Male and female gonothecae similar,
elongate-ovoid, aperture terminal, wide, circular, on short collar.
Dispersive stage assumed to be a planula larva.

Substrata not recorded; 5–550 m but mostly shallower than
50 m; formerly recorded all around British Isles but all recent
records are from Isle of Man and Norfolk northwards.

Remarkably similar to the much commoner *A. abietina* but
considerably smaller in all dimensions; see also young
Hydrallmania falcata.

Amphisbetia operculata (Linnaeus)   FIG. 4.16
[HINCKS 1868, 263, Pl. 44, as *Sertularia*; CORNELIUS 1979,
271]
Colony recalling tuft of fine, wavy hair; to 100 mm; hydrocaulus
filamentous, slightly flexuose; branching alternate to sub-dichot-
omous. Hydrothecae arranged in subopposite pairs, small; aperture sloping inwards towards stem, its outer angle pointed and
the sides minutely one- to three-cusped. Gonotheca ovoid,
smooth, with terminal, plain, circular, aperture; operculum a
simple flap. Reduced medusoids develop within gonotheca,
briefly planktonic.

On brown algae, often *Laminaria digitata* stipes; LWST,
often in pools in south-west, and sublittoral; widely distributed,
north to Shetlands.

Diphasia alata (Hincks)   FIG. 4.17
[HINCKS 1868, 258, Pl. 48; CORNELIUS 1979, 267, as *D.
pinastrum*]
Colony robust, erect, up to about 150 mm, regularly pinnate
with long, straight, closely set, parallel branches; often some
secondary branching; main stem thicker than branches, straight,
usually monosiphonic throughout. Hydrothecae opposite or
nearly so, in two rows; long, S-shaped, two-thirds adnate, distal
third sharply out-turned at about 90° with immediate upward
flexure of about 45°; internal thickening at point of outward
flexure apparent in optical section; aperture broad, rim even to
sinuous; operculum a single flap, attached on inner side. Male

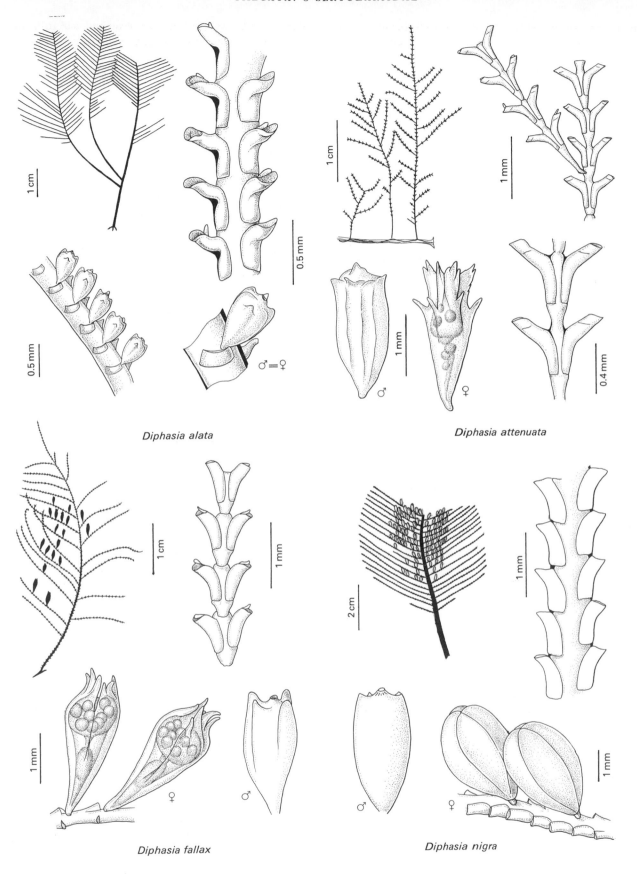

Diphasia alata

Diphasia attenuata

Diphasia fallax

Diphasia nigra

Fig. 4.17

and female gonothecae alike, cylindrical with quadrangular section, tapering below; aperture terminal, slightly raised, surrounded by four perisarc ridges ending in rounded points. Dispersive stage a planula.

Substrata unknown (once 'worm tubes'); recorded 7–140 m; scattered British Isles records: Shetlands, Hebrides, Argyll, south-west England, south-west Ireland, also north-west France; mid-Norway to Azores.

Diphasia attenuata (Hincks)   FIG. 4.17
[HINCKS 1868, 247, Pl. 49; CORNELIUS 1979, 256]
Colony erect, to about 50 mm, bending, pinnate with branches spaced apart; monosiphonic throughout; stem and branches similar in width, both sometimes ending in tendrils; some secondary branching; axils about 65°. Hydrothecae in two rows, in opposite pairs, tubular, half to two-thirds adnate, gradually (not sharply) out-turned; aperture roughly circular, but rim with deep notch on inner side; single-flapped operculum attached on inner side. Male gonotheca cylindrical, with six longitudinal ridges ending in points; females hexagonal, with one to three whorls of six tubular to conical spines distally; aperture on small terminal cone. Dispersive stage a planula.

Usually on other hydroids; sublittoral at least to edge of continental shelf; all around British Isles but reportedly commonest in south and west.

Possibly conspecific with *D. rosacea*. Spines of *attenuata*-type female gonothecae may be joined by longitudinal ridges and in some specimens tend to point upward as in *rosacea*.

Diphasia fallax (Johnston)   FIG. 4.17
[HINCKS 1868, 249, Pl. 49; CORNELIUS 1979, 260]
Colony erect, pinnate, monosiphonic, to about 100 mm; stem and branches straight to gently curved; some secondary branching; main stem slightly thicker than branches; terminal tendrils frequent. Hydrothecae recorded in two rows in Europe but often triseriate in arctic; opposite to subopposite, on stem and branches; short, tubular, at least three-quarters adnate, slightly out-turned above; aperture circular, rim even, single-flapped operculum attached on inner side. Nodal annulus below each pair of hydrothecae. Gonothecae on branches; male elongate, widest above, with four erect spines (one to all of which may be bifid) surrounding raised tubular aperture; female similar but longer, with slender neck above and teminal aperture, four long conical processes joining above aperture to form brood-chamber protecting an acrocyst. Sometimes monoecious. Dispersive stage a planula larva.

Recorded on other sertulariid hydroids but substrata generally little known; probably 20–250 m; in British waters today recorded only north of a line passing from the Clyde to Heligoland. Some more southerly early 19th century records. Currently arctic to southern North Sea.

Diphasia nigra (Pallas)   FIG. 4.17
[HINCKS 1868, 255, Pl. 52, as *D. pinnata*; CORNELIUS 1979, 265]
Colony large, stiffly erect, to about 200 mm, robust and rigidly

pinnate, main stem thicker than branches; said to be deep red in life, preserved colonies brown to black. Hydrothecae tubular, wholly adnate but gently out-curved; rim even; operculum circular, attached on inner side; hydrothecae alternate, each nearly contiguous with next above. Gonothecae of both sexes borne on the branches; male gonotheca ovoid, tapering below to short pedicel, aperture on short terminal cone surrounded by about four blunt spines; female similar but larger, lacking spines, inverted pear-shaped, with four longitudinal grooves meeting above, contents rose-red. Dispersive stage a planula.

Recorded on mussels but probably also on other substrata; about 80 m and deeper; a warm-water Atlantic species known from south-west England, north-west France and western English Channel; once reported Northumberland.

Diphasia pinaster sensu Hincks   FIG. 4.18
[HINCKS 1868, 252, Pl. 50; CORNELIUS 1979, as *D. margareta*]
Colony erect, untidily pinnate, up to about 150 mm; branches long, as wide as main stem in young colonies but less so in older ones; some secondary branching. Hydrothecae biseriate, opposite grading to sub-opposite towards base of colony; each sharply out-turned in middle, half to three-quarters adnate; one or two inward projections of perisarc at angle of bend; aperture oblique, circular, even-rimmed, usually with inner notch; operculum circular, attached on inner side. Male gonotheca ovoid, tetrangular, with spine on each upper corner, aperture small, on distal cone; female very large, long-ovoid, tetrangular, with row of one to three spines on each corner, aperture small, terminal. Dispersive stage a planula.

75–900 m; recorded Bergen southwards; all around British Isles, reportedly commonest in south.

Diphasia rosacea (Linnaeus)   FIG. 4.18
[HINCKS 1868, 245, Pl. 48; CORNELIUS 1979, 269]
Stems gently curving, delicate, irregularly and unequally branched; to about 25 mm. Perisarc transparent or pale yellow. Hydrothecae in pairs, long, tubular, upper portion free and out-turned; aperture oblique, rim even with slight notch on inner side; operculum circular, attached on inner side. Male gonotheca club-shaped, curved towards the base, with eight longitudinal ridges which end in spinous points of equal size around the slender tubular aperture. Female gonotheca pear-shaped, shortly stalked, long, with eight longitudinal ridges terminating in spines, the outer on each side being much the longest, incurved, narrow, the rest shorter, crowded, and convergent. When mature the processes forming a distal brood chamber in which planulae develop in a protected acrocyst.

On hydroids and shells; lower intertidal to about 80 m; common around British Isles; arctic to South Atlantic.

Dynamena pumila (Linnaeus)   FIG. 4.20
[HINCKS 1868, 260, Pl. 53, as *Sertularia*; CORNELIUS 1979, 271]
Stems short, erect, up to about 30 mm; usually unbranched, arising from creeping stolon; straight to gently curving. Stem and branches identical, internodes short, each bearing an

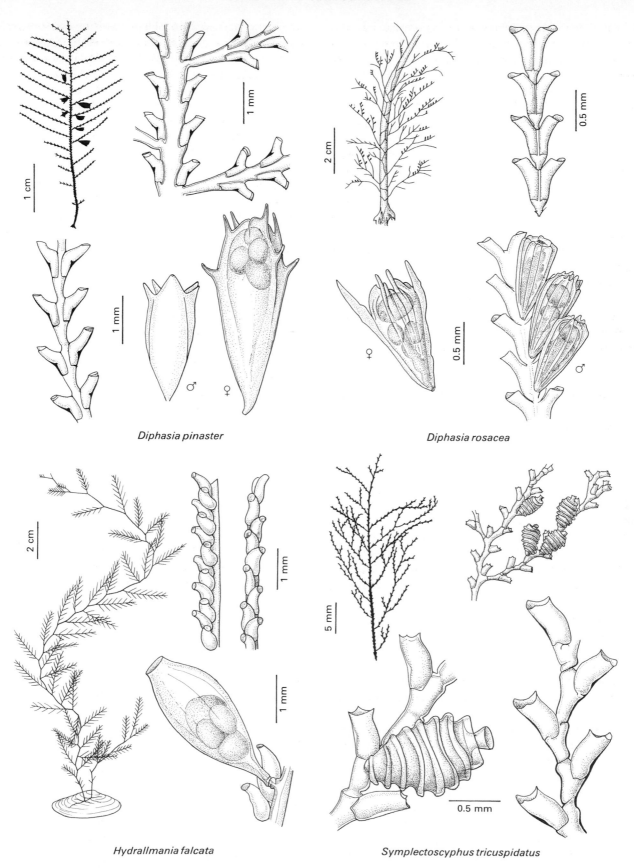

Diphasia pinaster

Diphasia rosacea

Hydrallmania falcata

Symplectoscyphus tricuspidatus

Fig. 4.18

opposed pair of hydrothecae which in profile forms an inverted triangle. Hydrotheca short, tubular, half adnate, free and out-turned in distal half, tapering slightly towards aperture which is cleft and two-cusped. Perisarc horn-coloured. Gonotheca arising just below a hydrotheca, subsessile, irregularly ovoid, aperture wide, on short collar. Male gonotheca sometimes said to be more slender than female. Dispersive stage a planula brooded in an acrocyst.

On brown algae and rocks, sheltered to moderately exposed shores; MTL to shallow sublittoral. Common on all rocky coasts around British Isles; Arctic to western France. Tolerant of brackish conditions.

Hydrallmania falcata (Linnaeus) FIG. 4.18
[HINCKS 1868, 273, Pl. 58; CORNELIUS 1979, 273]
Main stems very tall, in open spiral, to at least 0.5 m; arising from a basal stolon; monosiphonic, occasionally forked; lateral branches spirally arranged, regularly pinnate, hydrocladia alternate, nodal annuli oblique. Hydrothecae tubular, contiguous in groups of four to ten; in one row (actually, two closely set rows) along the hydrocladia, with a short gap at each annulus; rim even to minutely cusped, oblique. Male and female gonothecae alike, ovoid, tapering below to a short stalk, with slightly tubular neck. Dispersive stage a planula.

On shells and stones, particularly in sandy areas; 20–100 m; common off all British coasts; Arctic to south-west Europe.

Selaginopsis fusca (Johnston) FIG. 4.16
[HINCKS 1868, 272, Pl. 50, as *Sertularia*; NAUMOV 1969, 431, as *Abietinaria*]
Colony a small group of stiffly pinnate, erect stems up to about 80 mm. Main stem slightly thicker than branches. Dark brown to black, shiny when dry; branches alternate, straight, of slightly differing lengths. Hydrothecae on both stem and branches, biseriate, small, short and wide, vertically touching next, apertures successively directed left and right giving four-rowed appearance; nine-tenths to wholly sunk; aperture oblong, transverse, directed upwards; operculum a single flap, attached on inner side. Gonotheca described as elongate pear-shaped, smooth; with aperture terminal, rather broad; on short pedicel; borne on branches in one row. Dispersive stage unknown.

On other hydroids and stones; 40–200 m; north-east England and north-east Scotland, south to Scarborough in 19th century but present limit unknown; north to Iceland and Barents Sea.

Sertularella gaudichaudi (Lamouroux) FIG. 4.19
[HINCKS 1868, 234, Pl. 47, as *S. fusiformis*; CORNELIUS 1979, 282]
Stem rather short, erect, usually unbranched, monosiphonic throughout, slightly zigzag, to about 35 mm. Perisarc smooth to rugose. Hydrotheca one per internode, tubular, tapering or flask-shaped; with subterminal constriction, one-third to half adnate, walls smooth to rugose; aperture four-cusped with four-flapped operculum, transverse to oblique; two to four low, rounded projections on inside of hydrothecal wall near aperture. Gonothecae ovoid, length twice breadth, annulated throughout or smooth basally; aperture terminal, three to four cusped; female said to be slightly larger than male. Planula released.

On inert substrata, intertidal and coastal; probably all around British Isles but no Irish records.

Sertularella gayi (Lamouroux) FIG. 4.19
[HINCKS 1868, 237, Pl. 46; CORNELIUS 1979, 284]
Stems erect, loosely pinnate; to 250 mm; branching irregular, small branches roughly alternate; stems, main forks and larger branches polysiphonic; smaller branches monosiphonic, annuli oblique, internodes short. Hydrothecae distant, alternate, one to each internode; out-turned, walls frequently sinuous proximally, narrowing above to a four-cusped aperture; operculum four-flapped. Tissues often sulphur-yellow. Gonotheca elongate-ovoid, widest in middle, tapering to top and base, aperture small with two or more cusps. Dispersive stage a planula.

Sublittoral, possibly sometimes intertidal; widespread in north Atlantic and common off all coasts of British Isles to edge of continental shelf. Possibly conspecific with *S. polyzonias*. Similarity to that species makes identification of occasional short intertidal specimens difficult.

Sertularella polyzonias (Linnaeus) FIG. 4.19
[HINCKS 1868, 235, Pl. 46; CORNELIUS 1979, 287]
Stems erect, irregularly branched; to 50 mm; colony more shrubby than in *S. gayi*; main stem and branches monosiphonic. Smaller branches with oblique annuli, internodes short. Hydrothecae alternate, one to each internode, out-turned, bulging below, narrowing slightly to four-cusped aperture; operculum four-flapped. Tissues often sulphur-yellow. Male and female gonothecae alike, ovoid, shortly stalked, strongly wrinkled above grading to smooth below, tapering to base and top; aperture small with four cusps. Dispersive stage planulae developing in external acrocyst.

On shells and algae; intertidal to 50 m, sparsely to 300 m; all British coasts; widely distributed in North Atlantic. Possibly conspecific with *S. gayi*.

Sertularella rugosa (Linnaeus) FIG. 4.19
[HINCKS 1868, 241, Pl. 47; CORNELIUS 1979, 290]
Stems arising from basal stolon, to 20 mm, unbranched or sparingly and irregularly branched; or, in many colonies, hydrothecae attached directly to stolon; some colonies mixed. Stems monosiphonic, annulated above base and between hydrothecae; perisarc horn-coloured. Hydrothecae alternate, barrel-shaped, crowded on stem, deeply ridged, narrowing above, with notch near top on outer side; aperture outward-facing, with four minute cusps and a four-flapped operculum. Male and female gonothecae alike, large, ovoid, strongly annulated; aperture four-cusped. Dispersive stage a planula larva.

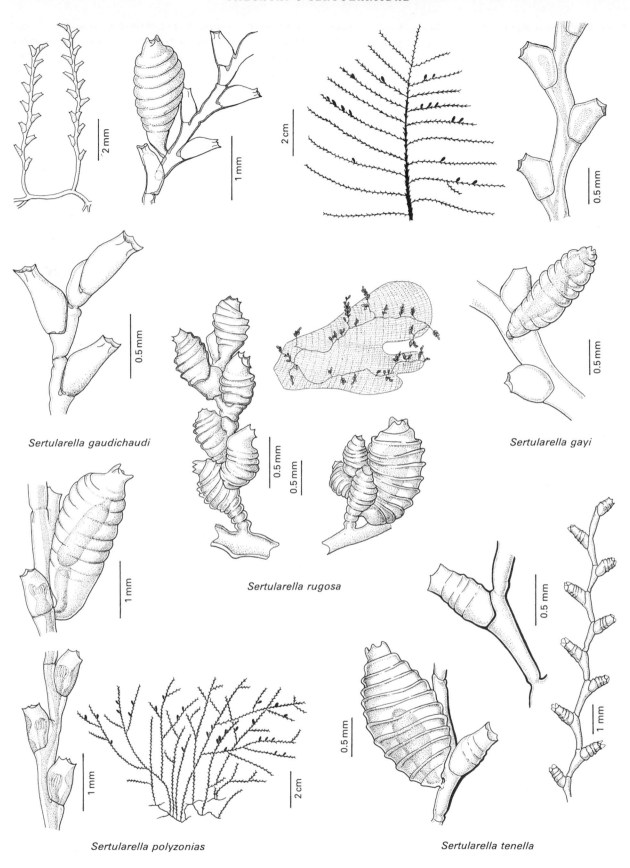

Sertularella gaudichaudi

Sertularella gayi

Sertularella rugosa

Sertularella polyzonias

Sertularella tenella

Fig. 4.19

On bryozoans, particularly *Flustra foliacea*, also algae and other substrata; LWST to about 50 m; found all around British Isles, widespread in Europe. See also *S. tenella*, which might prove conspecific.

Sertularella tenella (Alder)   FIG. 4.19
[HINCKS 1868, 242, Pl. 47; CORNELIUS 1979, 292]
Colonies usually comprising upright stems connected by tortuous basal stolons, but hydrothecae sometimes borne directly on stolon. Erect stems monosiphonic, usually unbranched, to 20 mm, zigzag with varied angle. Hydrothecae alternate, quarter adnate; walls with three to six shallow ridges usually complete and conspicuous but sometimes slight and on outer part of hydrotheca only, or entirely absent; aperture transverse, four-cusped, no notch on outer side as in *S. rugosa*; operculum four-flapped. Male and female gonothecae probably similar, large, ovoid, rugose, aperture terminal, three to four spined; similar to those of *S. rugosa*. Dispersive stage a planula.

On other hydroids; 10–150 m, perhaps deeper; reported all around British Isles, widespread in north Atlantic.

S. tenella is said to lack a notch below the hydrothecal rim on the outer (abcauline) side and *S. rugosa* to have one, but intermediate material occurs and the two may prove conspecific.

Sertularia cupressina Linnaeus   FIG. 4.20
[HINCKS 1868, 270, Pl. 57; CORNELIUS 1979, 294]
Stems arising from short basal stolon; growth form varied; long and bushy, to 0.5 m, gradually tapering. Young colonies pinnate. main stems straight, sometimes forked, stout but monosiphonic, side-branches alternate but giving impression of spiral arrangement; hydrocladia on each branchlet sub-branched dichotomously, fan-shaped. Hydrothecae alternate, tubular, only slightly out-turned; rim typically with one or two long, sharp cusps; operculum frail, two-flapped. Male and female gonothecae alike, on hydrocladia, short-stalked, elongate, rectangular, tapering below; when mature usually prolonged into one to two sharp spines above, typically one on each side; aperture central, slightly raised. Planulae developing in an acrocyst.

A common and often abundant sublittoral species, characteristically on sand, sometimes at ELWS and in low-shore pools on flat shores; to at least 100 m; found all round British Isles, widespread in Europe. Harvested commercially as 'whiteweed'.

S. argentea Linnaeus is often regarded as conspecific: reputed differences discussed by Cornelius (*Syn. Br. Fauna*, in prep.).

Sertularia distans Lamouroux   FIG. 4.20
[HINCKS 1868, 262, Pl. 53, as *S. gracilis*; CORNELIUS 1979, 296]
Colony comprising numerous short, dark, hair-like, erect, sometimes branched stems, to about 15 mm, joined by a stolon; resembles the commoner *Dynamena pumila* but delicate with longer cusps on the hydrothecal rim. Hydrothecae in opposite pairs, in two rows, tubular, sharply to gradually out-curved, length:breadth ratio from 2 to 4; half adnate, less in the longer hydrothecae; aperture two-cusped, occasionally with minute

third cusp on outer margin; rim sometimes renovated; operculum two-flapped; hydrothecae of a pair often contiguous, but this can vary along a stem; nodes of two kinds, oblique (or 'hinge') and transverse in side view (see Fig. 4.3: *D. pumila* has only transverse nodes); oblique nodes situated at the base of the stem and then between every two to three pairs of hydrothecae, transverse nodes separating most other pairs. Another difference from *D. pumila* is that in the present species the hydranth is provided with an abcauline caecum. Male and female gonothecae alike, ovoid, tapered below; walls smooth, thin; aperture broad, terminal, usually on short collar; borne below hydrotheca on stem or, reportedly, on stolon; presence or absence of acrocyst debated. Dispersive stage presumably a planula.

On various plant, animal, and inert substrata; intertidal to 60 m; warmer-water species, regular south coast England, to north-west Wales, Norfolk, and probably as far as Yorkshire; records from further north need scrutiny owing to similarity of *D. pumila*; not yet reported Ireland, Belgium, Netherlands.

Symplectoscyphus tricuspidatus (Alder)   FIG. 4.18
[HINCKS 1868, 239, Pl. 47, as *Sertularella*; CORNELIUS 1979, 301]
Stem erect, up to 150 mm, monosiphonic, loosely pinnate, with some secondary branching; main stem and branches similar, both slightly zigzag; typically three to five hydrothecae on stem between base of one branch and next; perisarc slightly rugose. Stem annuli usually between every one to two hydrothecae, transverse to slightly oblique. Hydrothecae tubular to barrel-shaped, one-third to half adnate, length two to three times breadth, wall smooth to coarsely rugose; outer side usually forming continuous curve with stem below; rim tricuspid, roundly cleft to varied extent; operculum three-flapped; hydrothecal renovations common. Male and female gonothecae alike, elongate-ovoid with seven to nine washer-shaped annular ridges; aperture narrow, terminal, atop short tube, rim even, slightly flared; on short pedicel below hydrotheca. Dispersive stage unknown.

On other hydroids; coastal to 200 m and deeper; cold water form, since 1900 only confirmed Moray Firth northwards; south to Northumberland in mid-19th century.

Tamarisca tamarisca (Linnaeus)   FIG. 4.20
[HINCKS 1868, 254, Pl. 51, as *Diphasia*; KRAMP 1935, 174, as *Sertomma*; CORNELIUS 1979, 304]
Colony 150 mm or more, erect, robust but straggly; monosiphonic throughout; growth habit recalling finer branches of tamarisk tree; branches alternate or occasionally opposite, widely spaced, in one plane, same width as stem. Hydrothecae on both stem and branches, (sub)opposite, in two rows; very large, up to 1.6 mm long; tubular, half adnate, variously outward-curving; rim three-cusped, sometimes renovated; operculum three-flapped. Male gonotheca kite-shaped, flattened, tapering to short pedicel below, two upper corners about 90°; aperture terminal, circular, on short tube. Female gonotheca conical, distal end hidden by two large, ragged flaps cut into several fingers meeting above the true aperture and a third, smaller, flap tucked in

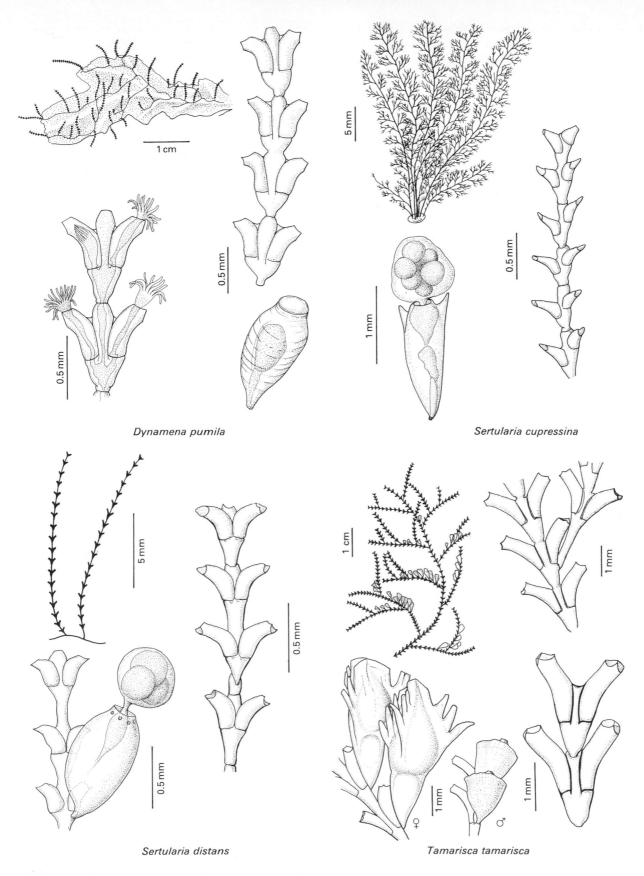

Dynamena pumila

Sertularia cupressina

Sertularia distans

Tamarisca tamarisca

Fig. 4.20

between the other two. Usually dioecious, sometimes monoecious. Dispersive stage a planula.

Substratum apparently unrecorded; 10–250 m; local throughout British Isles; north to Arctic Ocean.

Thuiaria articulata (Pallas)   FIG. 4.21
[HINCKS 1868, 277, Pl. 60; CORNELIUS 1979, 276, as *Salacia*]
Colony tall, rigid, regularly pinnate, up to 250 mm; older parts dark brown to black. Stem flat and wide; branches narrower, usually opposite, on short processes. Hydrothecae on stems and branches, in two rows, apertures of those in each closely set row pointing successively left and right; nearly or wholly sunk within perisarc; tubular, tapered above, aperture directed outwards; base of hydrotheca flat, bottom inner corner angular in side view; aperture circular, smooth; operculum one-flapped, attached on lower edge. Male and female gonothecae alike, in one to two rows on branches; cylindrical, often bulging on one side, tapered sharply below; aperture circular, wide; pedicel short; planulae brooded in an acrocyst.

On stones and shells; 18–300 m; frequent north of a line roughly passing through Dublin and London, scarcer and in deeper water in south; arctic to northern boreal, circumpolar, south to Brittany. See also *Selaginopsis fusca* and young colonies of *T. thuja*.

Thuiaria thuja (Linnaeus).
'Bottle brush hydroid'   FIG. 4.21
[HINCKS 1868, 275, Pl. 59; CORNELIUS 1979, 280, as *Salacia*]
Adult colony 50–250 mm, in form of bottle brush; branches all round stem, usually dichotomous, pale horn; stem dark brown to black, slightly zigzag; branches on basal third to three-quarters, usually dropping off. Young colony pinnate, abrupt change to bottle brush arrangement of branches when about 20 mm high. Adult branches inserted close together, branched three to four times, tips blunt. Hydrothecae on branches only, alternate, biseriate (rarely, triseriate); entirely sunk within branch, cylindrical but tapering above; operculum circular, attached on lower side. Male and female gonothecae alike, ovoid to obconical, smooth to slightly rugose, tapering below and more sharply above; aperture circular, often on short collar; no pedicel; acrocyst in female. Dispersive stage a planula.

Young, still pinnate, colonies have zigzag stems and alternate branches whereas similar sized colonies of *T. articulata* have straight stems and opposite branches. See also *Selaginopsis fusca*.

On shells and similar substrata; 2–800 m; northern, reported growing south to Clyde and Farne Islands; often cast up on strand line from Yorkshire northwards, occasionally drifting south as far as Norfolk; in 19th century recorded from Ireland and western English Channel.

9 PLUMULARIIDAE
Colonies erect, often regularly pinnate; hydrothecae in one row, usually too small to accommodate hydranth; hypostome of hydranth conical, tentacles linear, inserted in single whorl; nematothecae usually movable; gonophores nearly always fixed

1. Main stem monosiphonic throughout **2**
   Main stem polysiphonic, at least at base **8**

2. Each branch with a single hydrotheca, the branch functioning as a pedicel **Monotheca obliqua**
   Several hydrothecae per branch **3**

3. Colony comprising plumes with alternately arranged branchlets **4**
   Colony comprising plumes with opposite branchlets, or with erect stems threadlike, or with branching distant, not plumose **7**

4. Usually more than one hydrocladium arising per stem internode; one annulus between successive hydrothecae **Kirchenpaueria pinnata**
   One hydrocladium arising from each stem internode; two or three annuli between successive hydrothecae **5**

5. Nematothecae absent; one naked nematophore below each hydrotheca, none above a hydrotheca or in the hydrocladial axil **Kirchenpaueria similis**
   Nematophores in nematothecae, occurring above and below a hydrotheca and in the hydrocladial axil **6**

6. A pair of nematothecae above the hydrotheca, one below it, and one on the short internode; female gonotheca flask-shaped, with a slender neck **Plumularia setacea**
   A single nematotheca above the hydrotheca, one below it, none on the short internode; female gonotheca barrel-shaped. (Young colony, yet to acquire polysiphonic stem) **Ventromma halecioides**

7. Branching pinnate **Halopteris catharina**
   Colony not pinnate, usually a collection of unbranched threads **Antennella secundaria**

8. Mature colony not exceeding 50 mm **Ventromma halecioides**
   Mature colony more than 50 mm **9**

9. Hydrocladia arising all round main stem **10**
   Hydrocladia arranged in two rows, occasionally three **11**

10. Main stem forked **Nemertesia ramosa**
    Main stem not forked **Nemertesia antennina**

11. Colony rigid; main stems almost perfectly straight; forking and sub-branching uniform at about 45° **Polyplumaria flabellata**
    At least final branches limp; main stems not perfectly straight, forking and sub-branching dissimilar in angle **Schizotricha frutescens**

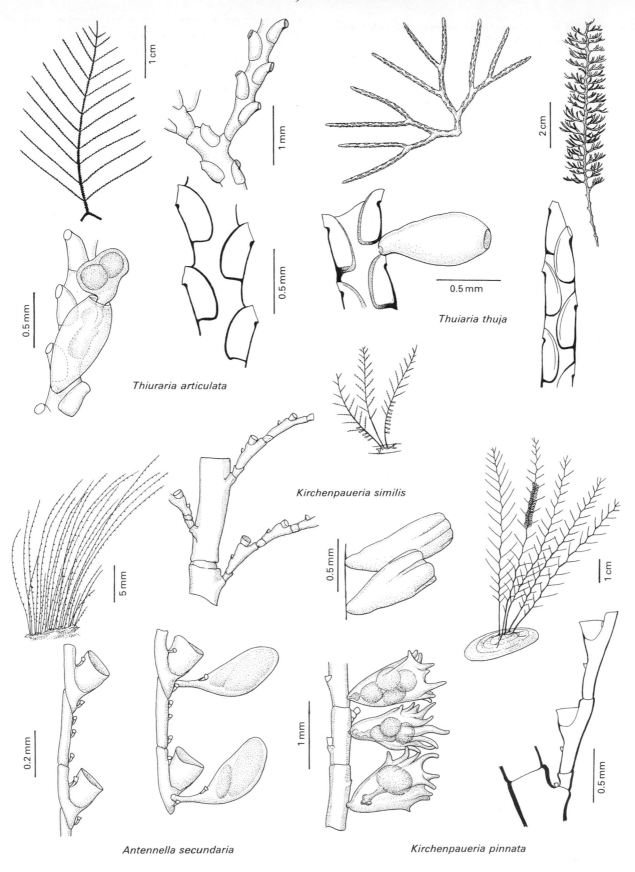

Thiuraria articulata

Thuiaria thuja

Kirchenpaueria similis

Antennella secundaria

Kirchenpaueria pinnata

Fig. 4.21

sporosacs; gonothecae not protected by basket-shaped structures; dispersive stage a planula.

Antennella secundaria (Gmelin)   FIG. 4.21
[MILLARD 1975, 332]

Colonies a bunch of hair-thin threads, usually unbranched, to about 30 mm; tissues often greenish-yellow. Hydrothecae in one row, one transverse and one oblique annulus between them; thin walled, cup shaped, parallel sided, one-third to half (sometimes two-thirds) adnate; slightly flared distally; rim even, transverse. Associated nematothecae: one median below hydrotheca, another below that, and one each side and just above hydrotheca. Gonothecae below a hydrotheca, singly or in pairs, male curved, pear-shaped, on short pedicel; female similar, larger; often monoecious.

On variety of substrata; LWST (rarely) to 100 m; in British Isles north to Mull and Norfolk, probably overlooked; widespread in warm water.

Halopteris catharina (Johnston)   FIG. 4.23
[HINCKS 1868, 299, Pl. 66, as *Plumularia*; also known as *Schizotricha catharina*]

Colony of delicate, erect, pinnate fronds, with hydrocladia more widely spaced than in most plumulariids; branching usually opposite, straight, parallel; to 40 (–100) mm; tissues colourless. Hydrothecae on hydrocladia in one row, separated by one transverse and one oblique constriction; cup-shaped, walls parallel to slightly divergent, one-third to half adnate; hydrothecae on stem also; usually, perhaps always, with two nematothecae each side of hydrotheca, upper pair smaller than lower; one median nematotheca below hydrotheca and one to two more below that. Male gonotheca ninepin-shaped, female much broader; aperture of both terminal, wider in female; inserted below hydrotheca.

On variety of substrata; in large intertidal pools and sublittoral to at least 150 m; widespread, all British coasts. See also *Ventromma halecioides*.

Kirchenpaueria pinnata (Linnaeus)   FIG. 4.21
[HINCKS 1868, 295, Pl. 65, as *Plumularia*]

Pinnate stems clustered on branched basal stolon; commonly 30 (–100) mm; white to pale yellow; hydrocaulus straight to slightly zigzag, annulated at intervals; hydrocladia alternate, several to each stem internode, bearing hydrothecae on the stem side; hydrothecae wide and short with plain rim, separated by a single oblique to transverse annulus. Nematophores sessile, minute, one below and sometimes one above each hydrotheca; usually one in axil of hydrocladium; no nematothecae. Gonotheca pear-shaped to roughly ovoid, contiguous, in double row, attached to main stem, stalked; usually with several spinous projections of varied length at the top.

On stones and algae; in pools, MLW to sublittoral; common off all British coasts; Iceland to Mediterranean.

'*Plumularia echinulata* Lamarck' was held by Hincks (1868) to differ in having a combination of one branch per stem internode, just one annulus between hydrothecae, and a nematophore above the hydrotheca; but intermediates occur and the status of *echinulata* needs clarifying. See also *K. similis*.

Kirchenpaueria similis (Hincks)   FIG. 4.21
[HINCKS 1868, 303, Pl. 55, as *Plumularia*]

Pinnate stems clustered on branched basal stolon; 30–60 mm; stem slightly zigzag to straight; hydrocladia alternate, one per stem internode; hydrothecae wide and short, rim even; two annuli between succesive hydrothecae. Nematophores sessile, naked, minute, one below each hydrotheca; none above hydrotheca or in axils of branches; no nematothecae. Gonothecae inverted pear-shaped to ovoid, separated, in double row attached to main stem; said sometimes to have spinous projections as in *K. pinnata*.

Little known; recorded widely, but similarity to *K. pinnata* makes separation dubious and the two might prove conspecific.

Monotheca obliqua (Saunders in Johnston)   FIG. 4.22
[HINCKS 1868, 304, Pl. 58, Millard 1975, 396, both as *Plumularia*]

Colony comprising minute, erect, unbranched stems joined by a stolon, to 10 mm. Each stem zigzag, internodes gently curving, each bearing short hydrothecal pedicel on a distal process; each branch reduced to a single pedicel supporting a hydrotheca. Hydrothecae large, bell-shaped, in older parts of colony having two chambers delimited by vertical septum in outer quarter; rim even, sinuous, often dipping on abcauline side. Nematothecae minute, two immediately above and behind hydrotheca, one below it, one to two in each pedicel axil and one on each stem internode. Gonotheca imperfectly known: male reportedly tapering both ends, smooth-walled, aperture terminal, small; female reportedly cylindrical, truncate above with wide aperture, tapering below; on stem below hydrothecal pedicel.

Habitat and distribution little known. Recorded on weed, sponges; intertidal pools on lower shore to about 15 m; widespread in warmer parts of North Atlantic but in British Isles apparently recorded only English and Bristol Channels. Probably overlooked.

Nemertesia antennina (Linnaeus), 'Sea beard'   FIG. 4.22
[HINCKS 1868, 280, Pl. 61, as *Antennularia*]

Forms clumps of up to about 50 stems, orange-buff, stiffly erect, up to 250 mm; almost never branched; each stem a colony, growing with others from a sponge-like, fibrous communal mass of living and dead hydrorhizae. Hydrocladia short, in whorls of six to ten, inserted on distinct apophyses, straight to slightly incurved; with alternating short, athecate and longer, thecate internodes. Hydrothecae short and wide, rims even. Nematophores elongate, two immediately above each hydrotheca, one below, one on the short internode; and two at the base of each hydrocladium. Gonothecae borne singly, on apophyses in axils of hydrocladia, male and female alike but distinguishable by colour of contents (male whitish, female orange), curved ovoid, subpedicellate; aperture subterminal, circular, facing stem. Usually one planula per female gonotheca.

On shells and sandy bottoms; inshore to deeper water;

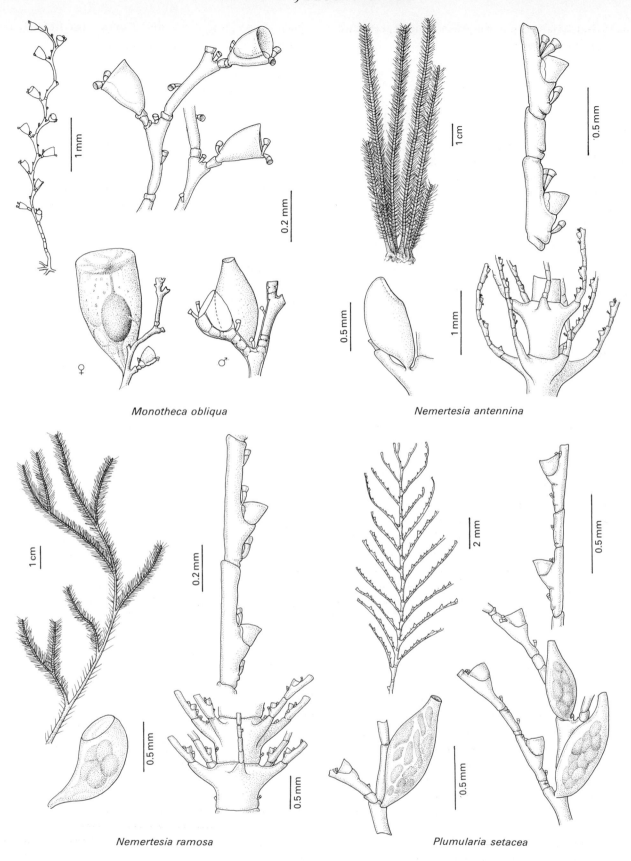

Monotheca obliqua

Nemertesia antennina

Nemertesia ramosa

Plumularia setacea

Fig. 4.22

common in British waters; in North Atlantic found at least from Iceland to northwest Africa.

Nemertesia ramosa (Lamouroux) FIG. 4.22
[HINCKS 1868, 282, Pl. 62, as *Antennularia*]

Stems yellow-buff, erect, up to 150 mm; thick, occasionally and irregularly branched and sub-branched, arising singly from a dense fibrous hydrorhizal mass. Hydrocladia on apophyses, in whorls of six to ten, long; jointed, with straight internodes of uniform length, a hydrotheca on each. Hydrothecae small, distant, separated by a single joint; no athecate internodes. Nematophores elongate; arrangement as in *N. antennina* except that at base of hydrocladia there may be as many as six, with another on the stem a little above origin of each hydrocladium. Gonothecae on apophyses in axils of hydrocladia, curved-ovoid, smooth; aperture facing main stem.

Similar in habitat to *N. antennina*; inshore to deeper water; common throughout British Isles; in north Atlantic from Iceland at least to north-west Africa.

Plumularia setacea (Linnaeus) FIG. 4.22
[HINCKS 1868, 296, Pl. 66]

Colony pinnate, stem pale horn; hydrocladia alternate, one from each stem internode, immediately below each joint; branchlets with thecate internodes separated by one, occasionally two, athecate internodes. Hydrotheca short, wide, rim plain. Nematothecae elongate, two abreast above and behind each hydrotheca, one below it, and one on short internode; another axillary, at origin of hydrocladium, and one on each stem internode. Monoecious (at least in British waters). Gonothecae axillary; female ampullate, smooth, when mature usually with long tubular neck; male narrower and smaller, less attenuate above and tapering to fine point with minute orifice, lower on stem than female gonothecae.

On algae, pool sides, and rock faces on the shore, and on variety of substrata sublittorally; common off all British coasts; nearly cosmopolitan, north to Iceland.

Polyplumaria flabellata G. O. Sars FIG. 4.23
[SARS 1874, 101; ALLMAN 1874, *Trans. Zool. Soc., Lond.*, 8, 479, as *Diplopteron insigne*]

Colony strikingly regularly pinnate; main stem and branches forking always at about 45°; up to about 350 mm. Main stems polysiphonic, pale to dark horn; primary and secondary forkings opposite, hydrocladia stiff. Hydrothecae monoseriate, short-tubular, thin-walled, tapering slightly basally; length about 1.5 times breadth; rim even, sometimes slightly flared; one-third to half adnate; inclined at about 45°. Two small nematothecae on short lateral processes beside hydrotheca where it joins branch, and two to three (–four) median nematothecae, typically one to two above hydrotheca and one below. One or two annular constrictions between hydrothecae. Male and female gonothecae similar, inverted pear-shaped, obliquely truncate above; aperture large; four small nematothecae near base; pedicellate, attached near branch base.

30–800 m; in British Isles recorded Shetland, western Scot-

land, North Sea, Plymouth, Scillies; also Roscoff; north to Iceland.

Schizotricha frutescens (Ellis and Solander) FIG. 4.23
[HINCKS 1868, 307, Pl. 67, as *Plumularia*; also known as *Polyplumaria frutescens*]

Colony dark, stiffly erect, pinnately branched, up to about 150 mm. Main stem polysiphonic, forked in some specimens; hydrocladia limp, arising in two to three rows; insertion both alternate and opposite; some secondary and even tertiary branching of hydrocladia. Hydrothecae uniseriate, annulus between every one to three; tubular to goblet-shaped, tapering basally; thin-walled; entirely adnate; aperture broad, rim even or dipping down slightly near stem. One lateral nematotheca each side of hydrothecal rim and one to two median nematothecae below hydrotheca (medians sometimes lost, minute pores showing sites). Male and female gonothecae similar; inverted pear-shaped, truncate above; aperture terminal, wide, transverse to slightly oblique; two small basal nematothecae.

Usually on rocks and stones, but reported once on a sponge; 30–1000 m; known throughout British Isles but few records from eastern English Channel and southern North Sea; Iceland to Biscay.

Ventromma halecioides (Alder) FIG. 4.23
[HINCKS 1868, 306, Pl. 67, as *Plumularia*]

Colony a group of small, pinnate shoots and connecting stolon; main stem often branched, polysiphonic basally; up to about 50 mm, sometimes longer in still waters. Hydrocladia spaced more widely than in most Plumulariidae (but cf. *Halopteris catharina*), alternate, rather short, bearing only three to seven hydrothecae, terminal one directed outwards. Hydrothecae uniseriate on stem and branches, two to three annuli between them; short, length equal to or less than width; walls divergent, straight to slightly flared; rim even; entirely adnate. One median nematotheca above and one below each hydrotheca, and one nematotheca in each hydrocladial axil; small, deciduous. Male gonotheca cylindrical, elongate to broad, end more or less truncate, aperture terminal, wide, developing late. Female gonotheca barrel-shaped, walls with nine to 12 grooves; sharply tapered and in-curved basally; attached near hydrocladial base, sometimes on stolon.

Often on other hydroids, also algae, eel grasses, and stones; intertidal pools and lagoons, and LWST to shallow sublittoral, probably 20 m maximum; scattered around British Isles; nearly cosmopolitan in boreal to tropical waters.

10 AGLAOPHENIIDAE

Colonies erect, main stems forked in some species; feather-shaped, at least in side shoots; hydrothecae usually completely adnate, with deeply cleft and cusped margin, often having an adnate nematotheca in midline; all nematothecae immovable; hydranth where known uniform, small, with conical hypostome and ten tentacles, withdrawing totally into hydrotheca; gonothecae unprotected, or protected in loose to closed baskets

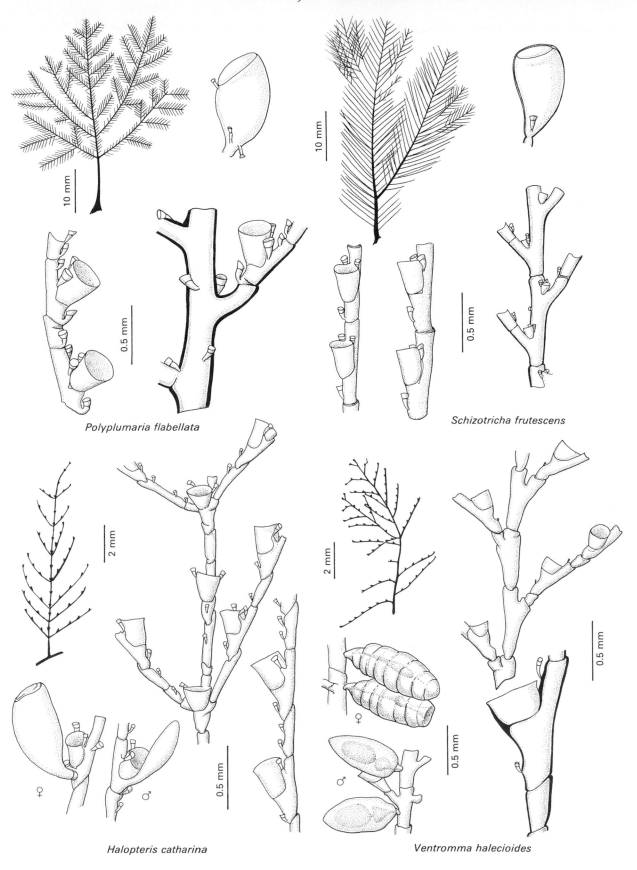

Polyplumaria flabellata

Schizotricha frutescens

Halopteris catharina

Ventromma halecioides

Fig. 4.23

formed from modified branchlets, called *phylactocarps* and *corbulae*; no medusa stage in European species.

---

1. Main stem polysiphonic   **Lytocarpia myriophyllum**

   Main stem monosiphonic   **2**

2. Median nematotheca on outer wall of hydrotheca long, pointed, free for most of length, projecting well above hydrothecal rim   **Gymnangium montagui**

   Median nematotheca adnate for much of length, not pointed; projecting at most only slightly above hydrothecal rim   **3**

3. Colony a collection of plumes on a basal stolon   **4**

   Several plumes on a common stem   **6**

4. Median nematotheca free for about half of length and reaching nearly to hydrothecal rim, tubular   **Aglaophenia tubulifera**

   Median nematotheca much shorter, adnate most of length, never reaching hydrothecal rim, usually gutter-shaped   **5**

5. With prominent recurved intra-hydrothecal septum (Fig. 4.24)   **Aglaophenia kirchenpaueri**

   Lacking prominent recurved intra-hydrothecal septum   **Aglaophenia pluma**

6. Colony with an erect, branching main stem; plumes arising in opposite pairs [or with one of pair forming a reproductive corbula (Fig. 4.23)]   **Aglaophenia acacia**

   Colony with basal stolon straggling across substratum; plumes arising singly from stem; sometimes dichotomous   **Aglaophenia pluma**

Aglaophenia acacia (Allman)   FIG. 4.24
[ALLMAN 1883, 38; SVOBODA *et al.* in press]

Fully grown colony tall, recorded up to about 150 mm; adjacent erect stems close together on short stolon; monosiphonic throughout. Major branches pinnate, widely spaced on stem, typically paired; or, with one of a pair modified into a basket-like corbula and bent back over partner; sometimes both are corbulae; at point of branching stem bends vertically, resulting in a repeated trifid arrangement. Secondary branches with single row of hydrothecae and associated nematothecae – one median, adnate to hydrotheca (excepting basalmost on hydrocladium) and not reaching rim, two beside aperture. Hydrotheca deep, length > 1.7 times breadth; rim nine-cusped, outermost longest, grading to innermost which is shortest; intrathecal septum indistinct. Gonophores in basket-like corbula, formed from seven to 12 pairs of ribs, the first and last of which may be free.

On hard substrata; probably 25–820 m; once south-east Ireland, once west Scotland; otherwise eastern Atlantic from northern France to Azores and Canaries.

Aglaophenia kirchenpaueri (Heller)   FIG. 4.24
[SVODOBA *et al.* in press]

Colony a collection of broad, unbranched, erect plumes, up to 200 mm in Spain but perhaps usually 20–50 mm off British coasts; stolon much branched. Main stem monosiphonic, unbranched. Hydrocladia nearly to base, alternate, rather long and straight. Hydrothecae not deep, with one median adnate nematotheca and one each side of aperture. Hydrotheca length:breadth ratio 1.1–1.25; nine marginal cusps, outer longest grading to inner shortest; with prominent recurved intrathecal septum below which hydranth can completely retract; median nematotheca not reaching rim. Up to ten corbulae per erect shoot; ribs of mature corbula not always completely fused, occasionally some free; with oval openings between ribs in male, more usually closed in female; eight to ten pairs of ribs per corbula.

In Mediterranean recorded on rock, coralline algae, gorgonians, and *Cystoseira*; 1–90 m but little information in British Isles; recorded only Lundy, Plymouth, and south-east Ireland, otherwise known west European and Mediterranean coasts south to Morocco and Cape Verde islands.

Aglaophenia pluma (Linnaeus)   FIGS. 4.24, 25
[HINCKS 1868, 286, Pl. 63; SVOBODA *et al.* in press]

Colony comprising one to several erect plumes, to about 80 mm, joined by branched stolon; main stem monosiphonic; some colonies branching dichotomously and reaching at least 150 mm. Hydrocladia slightly curving, alternate. Hydrothecae not deep, of varied proportions; rim with nine cusps of varied length; intrathecal septum indistinct; median nematotheca not reaching hydrothecal rim, gutter-shaped (not tubular), basal connection to hydrotheca clearly visible; one lateral nematotheca each side of rim. Dioecious. Male corbula with gaps between the five to eight ribs, female with ribs fused.

Often on *Halidrys siliquosa* but also reported on rock, gravel, *Sargassum*, and *Laminaria*; LWS and deep intertidal pools to about 20 m, locally abundant; from western Scotland southwards, unproven Shetlands; east to Isle of Wight, no reports from east coast of Britain in past 100 years; south at least to South Africa, possibly cosmopolitan.

It seems that two, probably more, species have been confused under the name *pluma* in British waters. One of these has recently been identified as *A. parvula* Bale. In the hydrotheca of *A. pluma*, all the marginal teeth have single points (Fig. 4.25), but in *A. parvula* the teeth of the second pair from the adcauline end have equal or subequal double points (Fig. 4.25). In the British Isles *A. parvula* has been recorded from south-west England, south-west Wales and southern Ireland; south to South Africa, and Australia.

Aglaophenia tubulifera (Hincks)   FIGS. 4.24, 4.25
[HINCKS 1868, 288, Pl. 63, 64; SVOBODA *et al.* in press]

Colony comprising one to several erect, almost always unbranched, monosiphonic plumes joined by an infrequently branched stolon; to about 60 mm; long forked colonies not recorded (cf. *A. pluma*), branching of main stem exceptional. Hydrocladia

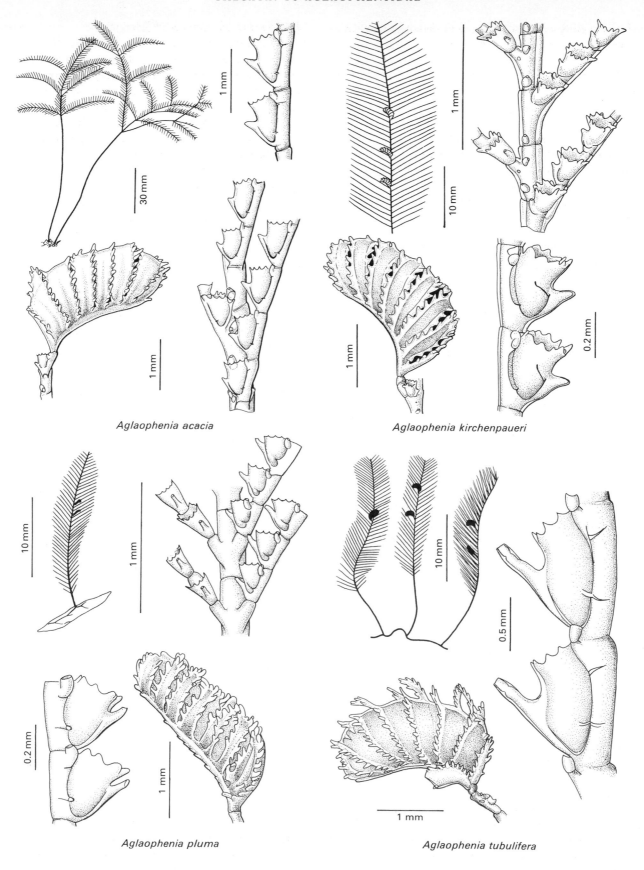

Aglaophenia acacia

Aglaophenia kirchenpaueri

Aglaophenia pluma

Aglaophenia tubulifera

Fig. 4.24

straight to slightly curving, alternate, absent basally. Hydrothecal length:breadth ratio about 1.7 (excepting basalmost on each hydrocladium); rim nine-cusped, median (outer) cusp longest; intrathecal septum indistinct. Median nematotheca long, tubular distally; with diagnostic distal egg-shaped region of lumen delimited by internal subdistal annulus; usually extending to level of hydrothecal rim. Dioecious; up to 12 corbulae per erect plume; corbula with 8–13 ribs.

On rocks, boulders, and pebbles; from 10 (usually 20) to at least 80 m; Irish Sea north to western Scotland; south to Cape Verde Is.

Gymnangium montagui (Billard)   FIG. 4.25
[HINCKS 1868, 292, Pl. 63, as *Aglaophenia pennatula*; formerly called *Halicornaria pennatula*]

Colony of one to several large erect plumes, to about 150 mm, tapering above; stem monosiphonic, thick, dark, gently bending. Branches in two rows but both directed to some extent forwards; alternate, closely set, slightly curved, parallel. Hydrothecae in one row, small, cup-shaped, margin with one cusp on each side; a long hollow spine (nematotheca) on outer side, curving upward, rising well above level of aperture; prominent intrathecal septum. Nematothecae small, one each side of hydrothecal aperture at junction between hydrotheca and stem. Gonotheca poorly known, (?) male and female alike, pear-shaped, smooth, borne on stem; not enclosed in corbula.

On algae, shells, and rock; coastal; in north-east Atlantic recorded from Morocco to Galway and Isle of Arran.

Lytocarpia myriophyllum (Linnaeus)   FIG. 4.25
[HINCKS 1868, 290, Pl. 64, as *Aglaophenia*; also formerly known as *Thecocarpus*]

Stems arising from a fibrous mass, erect, solitary; colony plumose, dull horn, up to 300 mm (to 1 m in Mediterranean). Stem polysiphonic, swelling out into oblong knobs at intervals, forked in some colonies; hydrocladia alternate, close together, in two rows on same face of stem. Hydrothecae large, cylindrical; rim wavy, often with large outer cusp. Two lateral, suberect nematothecae projecting a little above hydrothecal rim; another anterior in position, curved and spinous, with terminal orifice, inserted near hydrothecal base. Gonothecae in pairs on modified hydrocladia, protected by numerous long, toothed, unfused ribs which form a loose, open basket (phylactocarp).

Sublittoral on sandy bottoms; widely distributed in British Isles; northern Norway to Mediterranean.

Order **Limnomedusae**

Hydranths small, sessile, often solitary (*Proboscidactyla* is an exception); tentacles few or absent; lacking hydrotheca or gonotheca. Releasing medusae.

1 PROBOSCIDACTYLIDAE

Colonies minute, athecate, stolonal; perisarc absent. Polyps of two kinds: gastrozooids, with two linear (rarely, forked) tentacles and large bulbous hypostome atop long 'neck'; gonozooids lacking mouth or tentacles, bearing gonophores.

Proboscidactyla stellata (Forbes)   FIG. 4.9
[HINCKS 1868, 36; 1872, *Ann. Mag. nat. Hist.*, (4) 10, 313, both as *Lar sabellarum*; RUSSELL 1953, 386]

Colony minute, a series of single, naked gastrozooids of quasi-humanoid form, arising from an anastomosing stolon. Gastrozooids less than 1 mm high, cylindrical in middle, tapering finely below; with two long tentacles (rarely, forked); hypostome on short neck, bulbous, with prominent apical patch of nematocysts and two-lipped mouth; spontaneously active. Gonophores on sides of capitate dactylozooids arising from stolon, pear-shaped, on short stalks, single, lacking perisarc covering; young medusa with six (not usual four) radial canals and four tentacles.

Hydroid stage seldom recorded (probably overlooked), only around rim of sabellid tubes; presumably shallow water; medusa recorded all round coast of British mainland and south-west Ireland, north-west France, and Norway.

Order **Siphonophora**

Floating or swimming hydrozoan colonies in which medusae are not released. The polyps (*zooids*) exhibit a high degree of polymorphism. Zooids are budded from a stem (*siphosome*) derived from the primary polyp. The only genus included, *Physalia*, belongs to the suborder **Cystonectae** in which the zooids are crowded below a large float (*pneumatophore*).

1 PHYSALIIDAE

Physalia physalis (Linnaeus).
Portuguese man o'war   FIG. 4.1
[KIRKPATRICK, P.A. and PUGH, P.R., 1984, *Syn. Br. Fauna*, 29, 26]

Pneumatophore elongate-ovoid, thin-walled, crested, up to about 300 mm in length; blue, suffused pink when living. Various types of polyps including dactylozooids with long tentacles hang from one end, below the float. In the sea the tentacles trail behind and below the float, often for tens of metres. Viewed against the light the tentacles appear beaded, the 'beads' being batteries of nematocysts extremely virulent to humans.

May appear on south-westerly beaches during summer following prolonged southerly or south-westerly winds; intermittent.

Class **Anthozoa**

Polypoid coelenterates with no medusoid stage (Fig. 4.26). Anthozoan polyps consist of a cylindrical body or *column*, closed at the distal end by the transverse *oral disk*. The hollow tentacles arise from the disk, usually being arranged in concentric rings or *cycles*. At the centre of the disk is the mouth which leads to the throat or *actinopharynx*, a laterally compressed tube, with one or both angles modified as ciliated gutters (*siphonoglyphs*) projecting into the body cavity (*coelenteron*). This cavity is divided into alcoves by radially arranged *mesenteries*, which are attached to the internal surfaces of the disk, body wall, and base. Some mesenteries reach the actinopharynx and are termed *perfect*; those that do not are *imperfect*. Mesenteries commonly

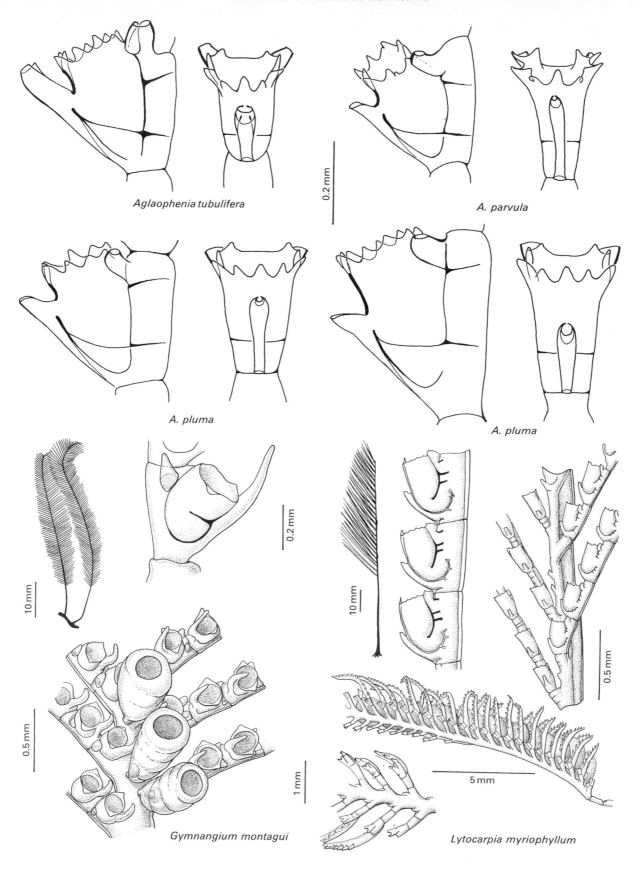

Aglaophenia tubulifera

A. parvula

A. pluma

A. pluma

Gymnangium montagui

Lytocarpia myriophyllum

Fig. 4.25

arise in pairs of equal size. The free, inner edge of a mesentery is formed into a convoluted *mesenteric filament*. The base of a polyp may take the form of an adherent disk, as in most anemones, or it may be confluent with a common basal mass of tissue, *coenenchyme*, as in many colonial forms.

Anthozoan polyps are very contractile and most of them can also retract their tentacles and oral disk into the body when disturbed. They are thus capable of changing their size and shape between extremes that would be impossible in most other animals. Except in the colonial octocorals, where the form of the colony is more important than that of the polyps, the keys and descriptions apply to 'open' polyps with expanded tentacles. Measurements also apply to specimens in this condition but in such contractile animals are only a rough guide to relative size: differences of 50% either way are quite possible. Tentacle length is a useful recognition feature and is expressed in relation to the disk diameter of a healthy, well-expanded specimen: *long* tentacles are longer than disk diameter; *moderate* tentacles are half to equalling disk diameter; and *short* tentacles are less than half diameter.

Colour is, unfortunately, rarely an accurate guide to identification. Many anemones are so variable in this respect that it is best, if one can do so, to ignore this attractive aspect of their appearance and concentrate on other features when trying to identify them.

LITERATURE

Until recently the only account of British octocorals was in Johnston's *British Zoophytes* (1847), but detailed descriptions accompanied by clear line drawings of all our Anthozoa have been provided by Manuel (1981, 1988). The anemones had been earlier monographed by Stephenson (1928, 1935), and these volumes must be consulted for their beautiful colour plates; underwater photographs are included in the Marine Conservation Society's guide (Manuel 1983). Gosse's (1860) account of the anemones is now mainly useful for its compendium of early records, although it too has interesting colour plates in a very different style. Nomenclature has changed considerably since then.

Gosse, P. H. (1860). *Actinologia Britannica. A history of the British sea anemones and corals.* Van Voorst, London.

Johnston, G. (1847). *A history of the British zoophytes*, edn. 2. Van Voorst, London, 2 vols.

Manuel, R. L. (1981, revised 1988). British Anthozoa. *Synopses of the British Fauna.* N.S., **18**, 1–241.

Manuel, R. L. (1983). The Anthozoa of the British Isles – a colour guide, 2nd edn. Produced for the Marine Conservation Society by R. Earll.

Shaw, P. W., Beardmore, J. A., and Ryland, J. S. (1987). *Sagartia troglodytes* (Anthozoa:Actiniaria) consists of two species. *Marine Ecology, Progress Series*, **41**, 21–8.

Stephenson, T. A. (1928–35). *The British sea anemones*. London: The Ray Society; Vol. 1 (1928), Vol. 2, 426 pp. (1935).

KEY TO SUBCLASSES

1. Always colonial; polyps with eight pinnate tentacles arranged in a single cycle (Fig. 4.26); most colonies contain calcareous particles (*sclerites* or spicules) and some have a rod-like axial skeleton **Octocorallia**

   Solitary or colonial; polyps with at least 12 tentacles which are arranged in at least two cycles and never pinnate; sclerites absent but stony corals have a limestone skeleton **Hexacorallia** (p. 164)

Subclass **Octocorallia (Alcyonaria)**

Colonial anthozoans; polyps (or *zooids*) with eight pinnate tentacles arranged in a single cycle. Polyps comprise retractile distal *anthocodium* and proximal, more skeletalized *anthostele* into which the anthocodium retracts. A short, wart-like anthostele is termed a *calyx*. One siphonoglyph. Most octocorals contain internal calcareous *sclerites* or *spicules*; some have a rod-like skeletal *axis*. Gastrovascular cavities linked by endoderm-lined channels (*solenia*).

KEY TO ORDERS AND FAMILIES

1. Colony free, living upright with its base in mud or sand; overall shape a spike or feather-like, consisting of a very long modified axial polyp forming the stem and supporting the secondary polyps (Sea pens: PENNATULACEA) **2**

   Colony attached to a substratum; polyps arising singly **4**

2. Colony a spike. Polyps not in fused lateral series (leaves) but clustered around the stem **5. Funiculinidae**

   Colony pinnate (even if long and thin); polyps in fused lateral series (leaves) **3**

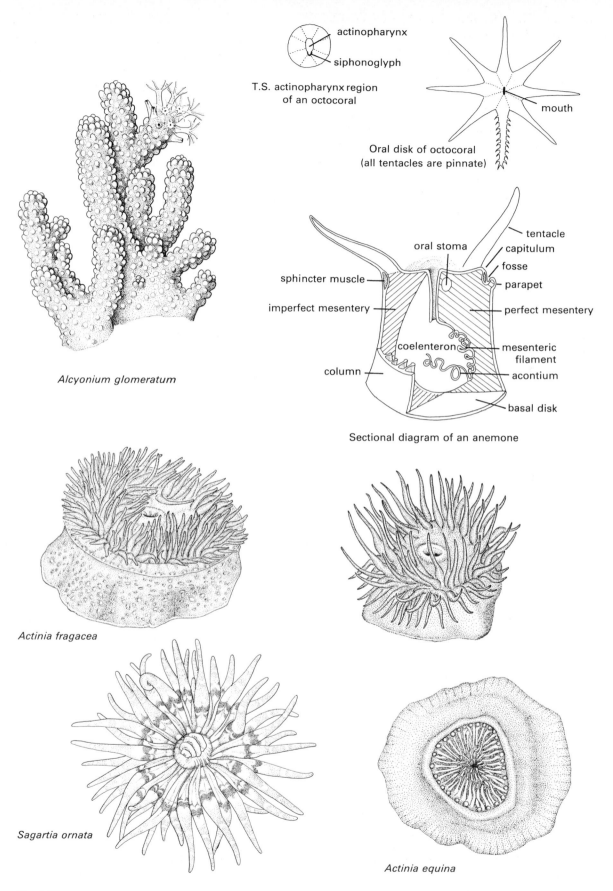

actinopharynx

siphonoglyph

T.S. actinopharynx region
of an octocoral

mouth

Oral disk of octocoral
(all tentacles are pinnate)

Alcyonium glomeratum

oral stoma

tentacle

capitulum

fosse

sphincter muscle

parapet

imperfect mesentery

perfect mesentery

coelenteron

mesenteric
filament

column

acontium

basal disk

Sectional diagram of an anemone

Actinia fragacea

Sagartia ornata

Actinia equina

Fig. 4.26

3. Colony red; leaves long **6. Pennatulidae**

   Colony whitish or yellowish; leaves short **7. Virgulariidae**

4. Colony tree-like, with branching axial skeleton (Sea fans: GORGONACEA) **5**

   Colony massive or encrusting, not tree-like, no axial skeleton **6**

5. Colony small, to 150 mm tall, with few branches; always white; spicules of polyp in eight arrow-heads **3. Paramuriceidae**

   Colony usually large, to 300 × 400 mm, with numerous branches; typically pink but occasionally white; no spicules in retractile portion of polyp **4. Plexauridae**

6. Polyps arising from a creeping stolon of coenenchyme (STOLONIFERA) **1. Clavulariidae**

   Polyps arising from a massive, fleshy, often lobed mass of coenenchyme (ALCYONACEA) **2. Alcyoniidae**

Order Stolonifera

Cylindrical polyps arising from a ribbon-like stolon or sheet spreading over solid surfaces. Polyps never budded from other polyps. Tentacular portion of polyp retractile within a stiffened, proximal portion (*anthostele*).

1 CLAVULARIIDAE

Skeleton of usually separate spicules; a cuticle on the stolon.

Sarcodictyon roseum (Philippi)   FIG. 4.27

[Syn. *S. catenata* Forbes in Johnston]

Stolon typically forming a narrow creeping band, often branched or with lateral expansions; often overgrown by other organisms; usually red, sometimes yellowish or colourless. Polyps up to 10 mm; white, arising singly at close intervals; when closed they leave a low mound on the stolon, which is then very inconspicuous.

   On rocks or shells; LWST to offshore; common on all coasts, but easily overlooked; south to Mediterranean.

Order Alcyonacea

Soft corals. Colonies encrusting, lobate, or arborescent. Coenenchyme filled with sclerites (spicules). Basal portion of colony often lacking polyps; anthocodia distally. Secondary polyps arise from solenia. Polyps non-retractile, retractile within anthosteles, or able to withdraw into coenenchyme.

2 ALCYONIIDAE

Colony fleshy, with spindle-shaped sclerites. Polyps generally dimorphic (feeding *autozooids*; inhalent, non-tentaculate *siphonozooids*), though not in the British species.

1. Thick, stubby lobes; polyps similar in colour to rest of colony **Alcyonium digitatum**

   Longer, slender lobes; white polyps contrast with pale orange-yellow to deep red colony mass **Alcyonium glomeratum**

Alcyonium digitatum Linnaeus.   FIG. 4.27
Dead men's fingers

Colonies form massive growths; shape irregular but usually in form of thick, fleshy, finger-like lobes up to about 200 mm; young colonies form thin encrustation. Translucent polyps evenly distributed over colony surface; expanding to height of 10–15 mm. Colonies typically white or dull orange, but yellowish or even brownish forms occur; polyps usually similar in colour to the rest of the colony. Gonads ripening autumn–winter, pink.

   Attached to rocks, shells, and stones; LWST to about 50 m; common on all coasts; Iceland to western Europe.

Alcyonium glomeratum (Hassall)   FIG. 4.26
[Formerly known as *A. couchii* (Johnston)]

General colony shape as in *A. digitatum* but the lobes slender, not more than 20 mm wide, often branched, and long (to 300 mm). Colour from deep red to pale orange-yellow, with contrasting white polyps; the latter feature distinguishes immediately from *A. digitatum*.

   In gullies or caves sheltered from strong wave action; below about 10–15 m; south and west coasts as far north as Scotland; south to Biscay.

Order Gorgonacea

Sea fans. Arborescent colony attached (usually) to a solid substratum by a basal plate. Fans commonly grow in directional

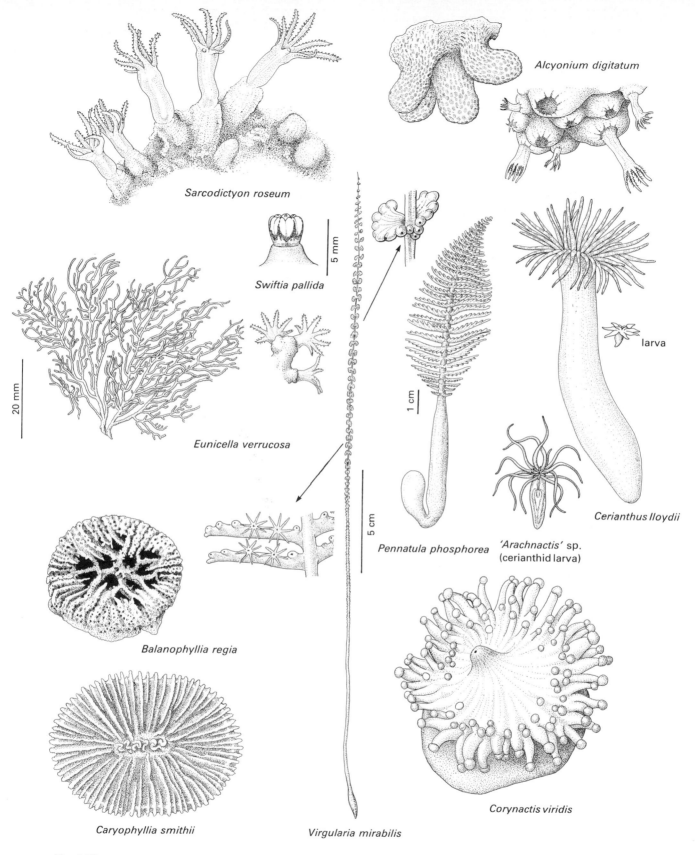

Sarcodictyon roseum

Alcyonium digitatum

Swiftia pallida

5 mm

larva

Eunicella verrucosa

20 mm

Cerianthus lloydii

Balanophyllia regia

1 cm

Pennatula phosphorea

'*Arachnactis*' sp.
(cerianthid larva)

5 cm

Caryophyllia smithii

Virgularia mirabilis

Corynactis viridis

Fig. 4.27

currents and branch in one plane, orientated perpendicular to the current. Peripheral axial epithelium secretes a skeletal *axis* of *gorgonin* (horny proteinaceous material) with or without nonspicular calcareous matter, or of fused sclerites surrounded by gorgonin. Thin coenenchyme (*rind*) contains spicules and, sometimes, strands of gorgonin. Polyps usually monomorphic. British representatives belong to suborder HOLAXONIA in which the axis comprises an inner *medulla* of spongy material surrounded by a *cortex* of gorgonin bundles; both regions may include nonspicular calcification.

3 PARAMURICEIDAE
Medulla chambered. Anthocodial sclerites arrayed in chevrons; neck between anthocodium and anthostele more or less devoid of spicules; polyp retracts into protruding anthostele.

Swiftia rosea Madsen   FIG. 4.27
A small, sparsely branched sea fan up to about 150 mm; always white or pale greyish in colour. Eight chevrons of spicules on the anthocodium.

On steep slopes or cliff faces below about 10 m; widespread but local, west Scotland and Ireland; also Biscay and Mediterranean.

4 PLEXAURIDAE
Axis with wide, chambered medulla and a horny, more or less calcified cortex. Rind thick, perforated by canals. Sclerites include warty spindles and short clubs. Polyps either completely retractile, or anthocodia withdraw into anthosteles.

Eunicella verrucosa (Pallas)   FIG. 4.27
Colony erect, fan-like, branching profusely, mostly in one plane. Polyps arising from thin layer of coenenchyme which covers horny axial skeleton. Usually pink but white or yellowish specimens occur occasionally. Up to 300 mm high. Anthocodia without chevrons of sclerites.

Attached to rocks at depths from about 10 m (less in Channel Isles); south and west coasts, locally common; to northern Ireland, (?) west of Scotland; south to north-west Africa and the Mediterranean.

Order Pennatulacea
Sea pens. Only octocoral order adapted for life in soft substrata. Secondary, dimorphic polyps (*zooids*) arise from the *rachis* of the elongate, primary axial polyp (*oozooid*), which proximally is dilated as a terminal bulb or *peduncle*. Gastrovascular cavity of primary polyp lacks mesenteries but contains four longitudinal canals that enclose the horny, calcified skeletal *axis*. *Autozooids*, often in lateral rows, are typical octocoral polyps, but lack a siphonoglyph; *siphonozooids*, which pump water into the colony and control its turgor, small and degenerate but with a well-developed siphonoglyph. There are two suborders; SESSILIFLORAE in which the polyps are borne on the rachis itself; and SUBSESSILIFLORAE in which polyps are fused in pinnately arranged leaves.

Suborder Sessiliflorae

5 FUNICULINIDAE
Elongate sea pens. Autozooids laterally and ventrally on the rachis. Siphonozooids few. Axis quadrangular.

Funiculina quadrangularis (Pallas)   FIG. 4.1
Large sea pen, can exceed 2 m. Autozooids irregularly arranged on rachis or in short oblique rows, retractile within toothed calyces; white to pink. Axis white, diagnostically quadrangular in section, with concave faces and acuminate angles.

In the muddy bottom of sea lochs and elsewhere; 20 m to deep water; west and north coasts of Ireland and Scotland; north Atlantic, perhaps world-wide.

Suborder Subsessiliflorae

6 PENNATULIDAE
Pinnate sea pens. Leaves bilaterally symmetrical along rachis; each leaf containing a single row of fused anthocodia, the outermost being the oldest. Siphonozooids confined to rachis.

Pennatula phosphorea Linnaeus   FIG. 4.27
Axial polyp rather stout and fleshy, divided into bulbous peduncle, anchoring the colony, and distal, polyp-bearing rachis. Normal polyps (autozooids) elongated and graduated in size, fused together in bunches to form triangular leaves in two opposing lateral rows on rachis. Colour deep red (owing to presence of red sclerites) and height of whole colony up to about 250 mm.

Living erect in mud or sand below about 15 m; local, on all coasts except south; widespread in north Atlantic.

7 VIRGULARIIDAE
Slender pinnate sea pens. Leaves small, bilaterally symmetrical along rachis. Axis rounded in section.

Virgularia mirabilis (Müller)   FIG. 4.27
Axial polyp very long and slender, up to 0.6 m. Polyps in small clusters of three to eight in two opposing lateral rows on rachis; spicules absent; colour off-white to creamy yellow.

Standing erect in soft mud into which the whole colony can withdraw when disturbed; in sheltered localities, i.e. harbours and sea lochs, below about 10 m, or in deeper open water; locally common on all coasts; north Atlantic and Mediterranean.

Class Hexacorallia (Zoantharia)
Solitary, aggregated, or colonial anthozoans. Some (Scleractinia) secrete calcareous exoskeleton. Cylindrical polyps usually with mesenteries in multiples of six, disposed in *pairs* (two complementary adjacent mesenteries) and *couples* (two mirror-image mesenteries, formed more or less simultaneously, on opposite sides of the axis of symmetry). The space between members of a pair is the *endocoel*, that between pairs the *exocoel*. The *directive mesenteries* are at opposing ends of the actinopharynx. Longi-

KEY TO ORDERS

1. Polyp solitary, living in soft tube buried in bottom sediment; tentacles of two types: long, marginal in three to four cycles; and short, labial from top of actinopharynx   **Ceriantharia**

   Polyps solitary or colonial, living attached to rocks or buried in soft sediments but never inhabiting a tube; tentacles all of one type, arising from the oral disk   **2**

2. Polyps with calcareous skeleton fixed to substratum   **Scleractinia** (p. 116)

   Polyps with no calcareous skeleton   **3**

3. Polyps colonial, arising from an encrusting basal mass of coenenchyme (not always easily observed); tentacles in two cycles (easily observed)   **Zoanthidea** (p. 166)

   Polyps not colonial (not permanently joined at bases) but sometimes living in dense aggregations   **4**

4. Tentacles not arranged in distinct cycles but in radial rows, each tentacle with a prominent spherical knob on the tip; polyps typically gregarious   **Corallimorpharia**

   Tentacles usually arranged in three or more distinct cycles, not knobbed (except in rare species not included here); polyps gregarious or solitary   **Actiniaria** (p. 168)

tudinal muscles typically endocoelic (i.e. facing one another). Often with an annular *sphincter muscle* at the top of the column which can close the polyp with the disk and tentacles withdrawn. Endodermal zooxanthellae sometimes present and abundant. Hexacorals found around the British Isles are classified into five orders: Actiniaria (anemones), Corallimorpharia (jewel anemone), Scleractinia (corals), Zoanthidea (zoanthids), and Ceriantharia (tube anemones).

Order **Ceriantharia**

Tube anemones. Solitary anthozoans, with an elongate (up to 1 m) column, that live in a felt-like tube of mucus, cnidae, and mud, buried to the level of the oral disk in soft sediment. Single siphonoglyph (conventionally designated dorsal). Aboral end contains a pore; rounded (no basal disk). Tentacles of two kinds: short *labial tentacles* encircling the mouth; long *marginal tentacles* around periphery of disk. Arrangement of mesenteries distinctive, coupled but not in pairs, added during life from the ventral intermesenteric space; lacking retractor muscles. Nematocysts include a distinctive type known as *ptychocysts*. Pelagic *arachnactis* larvae develop tentacles and mesenteries before settling.

8 CERIANTHIDAE
Characters as given for the order.

Cerianthus lloydii Gosse   FIG. 4.27
Column cylindrical, elongate, with rounded basal end; up to 150 mm. Disk markedly concave, with short labial tentacles. Marginal tentacles long and slender, to about 70; up to 50 mm

in length. Tentacles not retractile within column. Disk and tentacles shades of brown, or white, sometimes vivid green; marginal tentacles often finely barred; column brown or greyish.

In soft felt-like tubes of their own manufacture; tube buried, often deeply, in mud, sand, or gravel. The cerianthid is not attached to tube and can retract very rapidly when disturbed. Common on all British coasts where suitable substrata occur; LWST to offshore; Greenland and Spitzbergen to (?) Mediterranean.

Order **Corallimorpharia**

A small order of anemone-like anthozoans, most easily distinguished by the radial arrangement of tentacles which are often knobbed (*capitate*). Sphincter muscle weak. Basal disk present but lacking basilar muscles. Solitary or weakly colonial (incomplete fusion resulting in polystomeality). Cnidom as in Scleractinia.

9 CORALLIMORPHIDAE
Tentacles simple, each provided with an *acrosphere* (terminal knob). two to eight tentacles in radial lines arising from each endocoel, alternating with a single marginal tentacle arising from the exocoel.

Corynactis viridis Allman. Jewel anemone   FIG. 4.27
Column usually short and squat, but sometimes elongate, usually overlapped by oral disk. Tentacles short to moderate, increasing in size towards the margin—arranged in radial rows; each with prominent spherical knob (acrosphere) at its tip. Disk about 10 mm diameter; span of tentacles to 25 mm. Colours varied,

often brilliant: white, orange, red, brown, emerald green, etc., in various combinations, with disk, tentacles, and acrospheres often in contrasting colours.

Uncommon in shaded places near LWST; common and often abundant in depths below 5 m on south and west coasts, often occurring in dense aggregations beneath rocky overhangs, in caves, and similar places; northern Scotland to south-west Europe and the Mediterranean.

Order Scleractinia

Stony corals. Solitary or colonial. Polyp morphology similar to actinians but siphonoglyphs lacking. Most important characteristic is the secretion of a calcareous (aragonitic) exoskeleton. Skeleton of a solitary polyp (or colony) is the *corallum*: that of polyps comprising a colony the *corallite*; the calcification between corallites the *coenosteum*. Radial *sclerosepta* are deposited as ridges between the mesenteries of the polyp, and the living tissues of the polyp can be retracted between the sclerosepta.

Only solitary corals are found intertidally or (with one rare exception) in shallow waters around the British Isles; but there are deep water colonial species such as *Lophelia pertusa* along the continental edge and extending into deep sea lochs and Norwegian fjords (see Manuel 1981). Two solitary corals are included.

---

1. Tentacles yellow, without distinct terminal knobs;
    disk without a contrasting pattern   **Balanophyllia regia**

    Tentacles rarely yellow, with small but distinct terminal knobs; disk usually with a contrasting pattern
    Caryophyllia smithii

---

10 DENDROPHYLLIIDAE

Corallum with porous walls. Free margin of septa granular or dentate.

Balanophyllia regia Gosse   FIGS. 4.27, 4.28

Polyp with up to about 48 rather short tentacles. Overall colour rich translucent golden yellow, often shading to orange or scarlet around the mouth. Span of tentacles about 25 mm. Corallum broad and low, about 10 mm across and usually less in height; texture porous, spongy, and brittle, much less durable than other British corals. Septa of the 4th cycle meeting and extending to centre (an arrangement termed the Pourtalès plan); not raised, surface irregular.

Attached to rocks in caves or surge-gullies around LWST; to 25 m; south-west England and Pembroke; southward to Morocco, Canary Isles, and Mediterranean.

11 CARYOPHYLLIIDAE

Corallum with solid walls; septa raised (exsert), margins smooth; never arranged in Pourtalès plan (see *Balanophyllia*).

Carophyllia smithii Stokes and Broderip. Devonshire cup-coral   FIGS. 4.27, 4.28

Polyp with up to 80 moderate or long, tapering tentacles, each ending in a prominent spherical knob. Colour variable, usually translucent; white, orange, red, brown, pink, emerald green, in various combinations; a zigzag ring of denser colour usually encircling the mouth. Corallum up to 15 mm diameter and about the same in height; hard, dense, not perforated as in *Balanophyllia*.

An epizoic barnacle, *Megatrema anglicum* (p. 355), is commonly attached to the corallum.

On rocks and shells; LWST in south and west, down to about 100 m where often in great abundance; all coasts except eastern England; to south-west Europe and Mediterranean.

Order Zoanthidea

Solitary or (all British forms) colonial, arising from flat stolons or basal mat containing canals lined with endoderm; or immersed in *coenenchyme*. No skeleton but many incorporate sand particles into the body wall. Actinopharynx with a single siphonoglyph, regarded as ventral. Differ structurally from anemones in the arrangement of mesenteries; in most, apart from the *directives*, pairs comprise one perfect and one imperfect mesentery; dorsal directives imperfect, ventrals perfect. New mesenteries arise laterally to the ventral directives. Tentacles in two cycles, corresponding to endocoels and exocoels. Mainly tropical; most (including the British *Isozoanthus*) have zooxanthellae.

All British zoanthids belong to the type known as *macrocnemic* in which mesenteries of the 5th couple (the dorsal directives being 1st) are perfect.

---

1. Polyps minute, to 3 mm diameter and 10 mm in height; not more than 22 tentacles. (Squashes of tentacles viewed microscopically show endoderm cells with dense zooxanthellae)   **Isozoanthus sulcatus**

    Fully developed polyps larger than 2 mm diameter. (No zooxanthellae)   2

2. Colony in association with a hermit crab, or free
    Epizoanthus incrustatus

    Colony in association with sponges or gorgonians, or on shell, rocks, etc.   3

3. Tentacles colourless, minutely capitate **Epizoanthus couchii**

    Tentacles yellowish (rarely white), tapering to fine points   **Parazoanthus axinellae**

---

12 EPIZOANTHIDAE

Mesenteries macrocnemic; oral sphincter muscle in the mesogloea; polyps sand encrusted.

Epizoanthus couchii (Johnston)   FIG. 4.28

Polyps arising from a thin encrustation of coenenchyme, which forms an irregular network or sheet that is usually hidden by silt or overgrown by other organisms. Polyps up to 15 mm tall

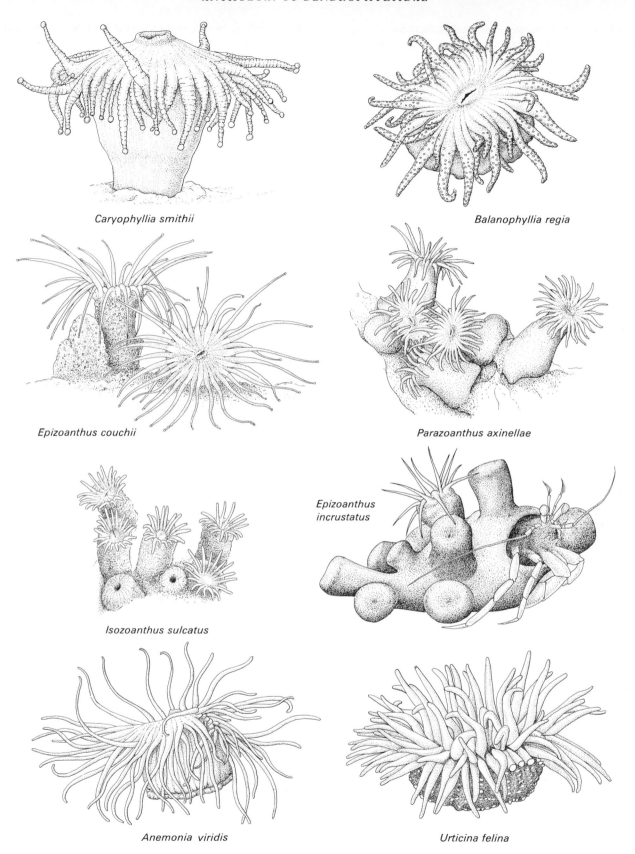

Caryophyllia smithii

Balanophyllia regia

Epizoanthus couchii

Parazoanthus axinellae

Isozoanthus sulcatus

Epizoanthus incrustatus

Anemonia viridis

Urticina felina

Fig. 4.28

and 5 mm diameter; column typically encrusted with fine sand grains; up to 32 long tentacles, arranged in two cycles, transparent and colourless except for a tiny white knob at the tip. Column and disk translucent buff, the latter usually flecked with white.

Found on rocks and shells, to at least 100 m, very occasionally on the shore; common and widespread off all coasts except North Sea; inconspicuous and easily overlooked; also recorded France.

Epizoanthus incrustatus (Düben and Koren)   FIG. 4.28

Colonies on shells occupied by hermit crabs, where they form carcinoecia of rather few polyps directed upwards and outwards; or form small polyp clusters lying free on the bottom. Polyps to about 15 × 6 mm (more in free form), with up to 48 tentacles.

Recorded on all coasts but few recent records; mostly in deep water; north Atlantic.

13 PARAZOANTHIDAE

Mesenteries macrocnemic; oral sphincter endodermal; polyps sand encrusted.

Isozoanthus sulcatus (Gosse)   FIG. 4.28

Basal coenenchyme thin and irregular, usually hidden from view by layer of silt or other encrusting organisms. Polyps small, rarely more than 10 × 3 mm, with a tentacle span of about 6 mm. Disk and tentacles purplish or reddish brown. The only European zoanthid to contain zooxanthellae.

Colonies of this tiny species are often extensive, typically occurring on horizontal, silt-covered rocks at depths down to about 24 m; occasionally in shore pools. Polyps inconspicuous when expanded; very sensitive, retracting and becoming virtually invisible at the slightest disturbance. Probably common on south and west coasts; Norway to France.

Parazoanthus axinellae (Schmidt)   FIG. 4.28

Colonies unmistakable; clusters of bright yellow polyps arise from a more or less conspicuous, encrusting mass of coenenchyme. Polyps to 20 × about 7 mm, with 26–34 moderately long tentacles arranged in two distinct cycles. Most specimens yellow, shading to orange around the mouth, occasionally white.

Attached to rocks, gorgonians, sponges, shells, etc.; 6–100 m; south and west coasts, locally abundant; south to Mediterranean.

P. anguicomus (Norman) is a similar species which has been confused with *P. axinellae* under the name *P. dixoni* Haddon and Shackleton. It is a whitish, slightly larger species with 34–44 tentacles and found in deeper water.

Order Actiniaria

The anemones form the largest order of anthozoans and the most important in British waters. Although they have a reputation for being difficult to identify this is largely a consequence of using unreliable and superficial features such as shape and colour. Before using the key it is important that the terms described below are understood.

The cylindrical *column* of an anemone is often divided into distinct regions. The major part is the (proximal) *scapus*, which varies greatly in texture but is always thicker-walled than other parts. In many genera the top edge of the scapus folds inwards to form a distinct, permanent rim, the *parapet*, which encloses a groove or *fosse*. Between the fosse and the oral disk is a delicate, thin-walled zone, the *capitulum*. This arrangement can easily be observed on the beadlet anemone *Actinia*. A less common arrangement is for the scapus to lead directly (without parapet and fosse) to a distal region of smooth texture, the *scapulus*. This usually occurs in genera which have the scapus covered with *periderm*, a cuticle-like material secreted by the anemone. The scapulus is always naked and retractile. Other anemones show no differentiation of the column at all.

Various features may be present on the scapus: hollow warts or *verrucae*; flattened adhesive *suckers*, differentiated by their pale colour; or solid *tubercles* of varying appearance. A few species possess a ring of specialized hollow warts, *acrorhagi*, on the parapet or in the fosse. *Cinclides* are tiny apertures in the column wall that are often visible as raised mounds or tiny dark dots. The periderm, when present, may be tough and closely adherent or thin, paper-like, and only loosely attached; it often incorporates foreign material. Other species may secrete a thin, non-adherent sheath of soft mucus, which should not be confused with true periderm.

The proximal end of the anemone may be a flattened, adherent *basal disk* forming, by muscular action, a distinct and permanent angle (*limbus*) at its junction with the column wall. Alternatively the base may be rounded, with no sign of a limbus. This usually occurs in burrowing forms which use the rounded base (*physa*) as a digging organ.

The tentacles are arranged on the disk in concentric cycles, the innermost being primary, the next secondary, and so on. The number of tentacles in each cycle increases progressively. Commonly there are six tentacles in cycle 1, six in cycle 2, 12 in cycle 3, 24 in cycle 4, and so on. This is a *hexamerous* arrangement; but other numerical arrangements can occur [see for instance, *Urticina* (p. 174) and *Stomphia* (p. 174)]. The distinction between the perfect and imperfect mesenteries is very marked in some anemones, there being none of intermediate size. Such clearly defined large and tiny mesenteries are respectively *macrocnemes* and *microcnemes*.

Some anemones possess thread-like organs, *acontia*, originating on the mesenteries, which can be discharged through the cinclides (or sometimes the mouth) when the animal is disturbed. Care must be taken to avoid confusing acontia with mesenteric filaments, which may protrude through wounds.

Asexual division is common in some species, occurring in one of three ways: *transverse fission* (across the column) is rare; *longitudinal fission*, which normally results in two anemones of roughly equal size; and *pedal laceration*, in which small portions of the column tear off at the limbus, eventually growing a disk, tentacles, and other parts. Recently it has been shown in several anemones that the brooded young found in the coelenteron are genetically identical to the parent. This implies that they are not sexual progeny, as previously supposed, but the product of either internal budding, automixis, or parthenogenesis. Specimens resulting from asexual division typically have an irregular

KEY TO SPECIES OF ACTINIARIA

1. Anemones with a distinct adherent basal disk which forms a limbus at its junction with the column. Tentacles numerous, 48 or more in adults. Typical anemones which attach to firm substrata. **2**

   Anemones with no basal disk but sometimes capable of firm basal adhesion; proximal end rounded when free, never with a limbus. Tentacles 36 or fewer. Mostly burrowing forms with more or less elongate columns, capable of fast retraction when disturbed **25**

2. Column divisible into scapus and capitulum between which are parapet and fosse (may disappear in extreme extension) **3**

   Column divisible into scapus and scapulus, or undivided. Never with parapet and fosse **14**

3. Acontia absent; verrucae present on column, or acrorhagi in parapet region, or both **4**

   Acontia present (fairly readily discharged through cinclides on scapus); no verrucae or acrorhagi **11**

4. Never with verrucae on column; acrorhagi present in parapet region **5**

   Verrucae present on column; acrorhagi present or absent **7**

5. Acrorhagi in fosse, usually of contrasting colour to column (nearly always blue); tentacles readily retractile (*Actinia*) **6**

   Acrorhagi on parapet, same colour as column; tentacles not readily retractile
   Anemonia viridis (p. 172)

6. To 50 mm diameter; column and tentacles variously coloured but not often spotted
   Actinia equina (p. 172)

   To 100 mm diameter, column red with regular greenish spots; tentacles red or purplish
   Actina fragacea (p. 172)

7. Tentacles rather stout, decamerously (i.e. 10 + 10 + 20 etc.) arranged (*Urticina*) **8**

   Tentacles not very stout, hexamerously or irregularly arranged **9**

8. Scapus with numerous verrucae usually covered with debris; tentacle span up to 200 mm; colour variable with many combinations **Urticina felina** (p. 174)

   Verrucae smaller and rarely with adherent debris; tentacle span up to 300 mm; colour usually pale **Urticina eques** (p. 174)

9. A distinct small red spot on each verruca **Anthopleura ballii** (p. 172)

   No red spots on verrucae **10**

10. Tentacles regularly hexamerous, in four or five cycles. Acrorhagi absent; often verrucae on the parapet **Bunodactis verrucosa** (p. 172)

    Tentacles irregular, apparently in only two or three cycles. Spherical acrorhagi present in the fosse **Anthopleura thallia** (p. 172)

11. Tentacles very numerous, presenting a fluffy appearance; mouth with prominent ribbed lips extending a little on to disk; may be large (up to 250 mm high)   **Metridium senile** (p.176)

    Tentacles never more than about 200. Small, column not exceeding about 20 mm diameter   **12**

12. Column brownish or greenish, usually with vertical stripes of orange, yellow, or white. Mouth inconspicuous, without prominent lips   **Haliplanella lineata** (p. 174)

    Column without vertical stripes (apart from tonal differences at insertion of mesenteries)   **13**

13. Column greatly elongated in extension; in this state the parapet and fosse disappear and the capitulum is very long, often equal to scapus   **Diadumene cincta** (p. 174)

    Column never greatly elongate; capitulum relatively short; parapet and fosse permanent. Mouth with prominent ribbed lips extending on to disk   **Metridium senile** (p. 176)

14. Acontia absent; column smooth, no suckers or tubercles. Offshore species   **15**

    Acontia present (not always readily discharged); column with or without suckers or tubercles. If offshore, then tubercles present or acontia fairly readily discharged   **16**

15. Tentacles hexamerously (i.e. $6+6+12+24$, etc.) arranged; can be shed by pinching off at base; span of tentacles up to 300 mm or more   **Bolocera tuediae** (p. 172)

    Tentacles distinctively arranged, the first two cycles differing in number (i.e. $6+10$ or $12+16$ or 18, etc.); cannot be shed; tentacle span not exceeding 60–70 mm

    Stomphia coccinea (p. 174)

16. Base broadly expanded into two lobes which embrace hermit crab. Acontia usually magenta, sometimes white; freely discharged   **Adamsia carciniopados** (p. 177)

    Base normal, often broad but never expanded into lobes. Acontia always white   **17**

17. Column divisible into scapus and scapulus; scapus with tubercles and typically covered with periderm   **Hormathia coronata** (p. 178) and **Cataphellia brodricii** (p. 177)

    Column not divisible into regions; tubercles absent but scapus often rough or wrinkled, sometimes with periderm   **18**

18. Body wall rather tough and thick; cinclides only on proximal part of column. Anemone usually associated with hermit crab   **Calliactis parasitica** (p. 177)

    Body wall soft, smooth, and not very thick; cinclides not restricted to lower column. Anemone not associated with hermit crab   **19**

19. Column with suckers that appear as distinct pale spots, often with debris stuck to them   **20**

    Suckers absent   **22**

20. Tentacles nearly always irregularly arranged. Suckers rarely have adherent debris

    Sagartia elegans (p. 176)

    Tentacles regularly hexamerous. Suckers usually with adherent debris   **21**

21. Column never trumpet-shaped (disk not much wider than column). Suckers usually rather inconspicuous **Sagartia ornata** (p. 176) and **S. troglodytes** (p. 177)

Column often trumpet-shaped in extension (disk much wider than column). Suckers usually large and prominent **Cereus pedunculatus** (p. 176)

22. Tentacles long and stout, not readily retracted into column. Anemone predominantly brown **Aiptasia mutabilis** (p. 174)

Tentacles of more 'normal' proportions, readily retracted into column. Anemones not brown. **23**

23. Acontia readily discharged; tentacles never very long, always plain white **Actinothoe sphyrodeta** (p. 176)

Acontia not very readily discharged; tentacles often long, always patterned (*Sagartiogeton*) **24**

24. Extended column pillar-like, to 120 mm high; up to 200 tentacles arranged hexamerously; column grey or buff with vertical stripes **Sagartiogeton undatus** (p. 177)

Rarely exceeding 30 mm when extended; irregular arrangement of tentacles owing to occurrence of pedal laceration; always with some orange coloration on column and disk **Sagartiogeton laceratus** p. 177)

25. Column stout, typically pear-shaped. Tentacles up to 36 with seven in inner cycle **Mesacmaea mitchellii** (p. 178)

Column slender, more or less cylindrical. Tentacles of first cycle four, six, or eight **26**

26. Tentacles very long, at least half column length. Anemone very small, rarely more than 15 × 2 mm. In isolated lagoons or tidal creeks **Nematostella vectensis** (p. 180)

Tentacles less than half column length; column (when full grown) substantially larger than above. Found in the open sea **27**

27. Tentacles 12 (6 + 6), with 'V' or 'W' markings on them. Burrowing anemones **28**

Tentacles 16 or more, never with 'V' or 'W' markings. Burrowing or crevice dwelling anemones **29**

28. Anemones up to 300 × 30 mm; tentacles much longer than disk diameter when expanded; a small multi-lobed organ (*conchula*) projecting from one corner of mouth **Peachia cylindrica** (p. 178)

Anemone small, up to 50 × 5–6 mm; tentacles always shorter than disk diameter: no conchula **Halcampa chrysanthellum** (p. 178)

29. Anemone inhabiting holes in rocks **Edwardsiella carnea** (p. 180)

Anemone burrowing in mud or sand (*Edwardsia*) **30**

30. Scapus with eight longitudinal rows of tubercles; tentacles 16 (8 + 8), colourless with spots and bands of buff and red-brown **Edwardsia claparedii** (p. 178)

Scapus lacking rows of tubercles; tentacles 32 (in three cycles), translucent buff or pink with white markings **Edwardsia timida** (p. 178)

arrangement of tentacles and other parts, and this can be a useful feature for identification. For example, *Sagartia elegans* habitually multiplies by pedal laceration and fission and hence most specimens are markedly irregular; *Sagartia troglodytes*, on the other hand, never reproduces by fission and is thus always hexamerous, this being the normal arrangement in sexually produced individuals of that species.

Identification of anemones improves greatly with practice! Once a few species can be recognized by their facies alone, identification of others becomes easier. Certain superficial characters are often present which can be misleading: e.g. a white line across the disk, sometimes running on to the tentacles can occur in almost any species, and has no importance whatsoever in identification. As stated earlier, the coloration is seldom diagnostic but, with practice, certain colour patterns or combinations which are characteristic of a species can be recognized.

Suborder **Nynantheae**

Mesenteric filaments with ciliated tracts; retractor muscles facing into endocoels.

14 ACTINIIDAE

Tentacles simple, one arising from each endocoel and each exocoel. Mesenteries not divided into macrocnemes and microcnemes. Sphincter muscle endodermal. Acontia absent.

Actinia equina (Linnaeus). Beadlet anemone   FIG. 4.26
Column smooth, its height and diameter about equal, up to about 50 mm. Prominent acrorhagi in the fosse, which may be hidden by overhanging tentacles. Tentacles of moderate length, hexamerously arranged, to about 200. Colour various shades of red, green, orange, or brown; acrorhagi, and a line on the limbus, typically blue but occasionally white or pink. Column occasionally spotted or streaked with pale colour; tentacles sometimes different colour from column. Reproduction by viviparity common.

A typical shore form extending from high on the shore (HWN) to shallow water offshore, on rocks, in pools, etc; common on all coasts; Arctic to West Africa and Mediterranean.

Actinia fragacea Tugwell   FIG. 4.26
Strawberry anemone
[Formerly known as *A. equina* var. *fragacea*]
Compared with *A. equina* this species is larger, up to 100 mm column diameter. Column red, with regular greenish flecks, like the pips on a strawberry; tentacles red or purplish.

Occurs on the lower shore; widespread but local.

Anemonia viridis (Forsskål)   FIG. 4.28
Opelet or snakelocks anemone
[Formerly known as *A. sulcata* (Pennant)]
Column smooth, usually wider than high, to about 50 mm diameter; parapet with inconspicuous acrorhagi. Disk wide, often wavy, with up to 200, irregularly arranged, long and sinuous tentacles arising in rather crowded fashion from its rim; although retractile, the tentacles are rarely retracted. Span of tentacles to

150 mm or more. Column brown or greyish, acrorhagi similar; tentacles brown, grey or bright grass green, usually with purple tips and sometimes streaked with white or crimson. Contains zooxanthellae.

On the shore in pools and other places open to the light, and down to about 20 m; south and west, north to Scotland, and reaching south-west Norway (Dons, C. 1945, *K. Norske Vidensk. Selsk. Forh.*, 12, 11–4); south-west Europe and Mediterranean.

Anthopleura ballii (Cocks)   FIG. 4.29
Column from tall and trumpet-shaped to short and squat; to about 70 mm high; small verrucae arranged in neat vertical rows, each terminating at the parapet in a rounded or conical acrorhagus. Disk wide; tentacles moderate to long, fairly stout, to about 96; arranged hexamerously; tentacle span up to 100 mm. Column yellow, purple, brown, or orange, palest proximally; acrorhagi and verrucae paler, each verruca tipped with a tiny but distinct red spot. Disk and tentacles brown or translucent yellow, pink, or greyish, sometimes suffused with vivid green; disk with a vague dark pattern, the whole minutely flecked with white. Contains zooxanthellae.

In holes or crevices, buried in gravel, etc; mid-shore pools and lower shore to about 25 m; south and west coasts as far north as Isle of Man, rather local; south-west Europe to Mediterranean.

Anthopleura thallia (Gosse)   FIG. 4.29
Column typically tall, up to 50 × 20 mm. Verrucae prominent, in irregular rows and increasing in size towards the parapet, usually with debris stuck to them; small spherical acrorhagi present in fosse. Tentacles moderate in length, irregularly arranged in two or three cycles, up to about 100. Column olive green, brown, grey, or reddish; verrucae darker, acrorhagi white or pink; disk and tentacles almost any colour: olive, grey, brown, pink, violet, etc., usually with a dark pattern on the disk and pale opaque spots on the tentacles. Reproduces by longitudinal fission.

In pools and crevices on shores exposed to strong wave action; MTL to LWST; extreme south-west, local; also Atlantic coast of France.

Bolocera tuediae (Johnston)   FIG. 4.29
Column smooth and featureless. Tentacles moderate to long, thick, in some states with longitudinal grooves; capable of detaching from the base, where a constriction marks the position of a sphincter muscle; to 200; hexamerously arranged. Whole anemone dull pink, orange, or brownish; very large, up to 300 mm or more across the tentacles.

Sublittoral, 20 to at least 2000 m; all coasts but rare in the south; north Atlantic and Arctic.

The reason for shedding tentacles is not known; they do not regenerate into new anemones.

Bunodactis verrucosa (Pennant)   FIG. 4.29
Column typically tall, to 80 × 30 mm, but usually about half this. Verrucae prominent and arranged in up to 48 neat vertical

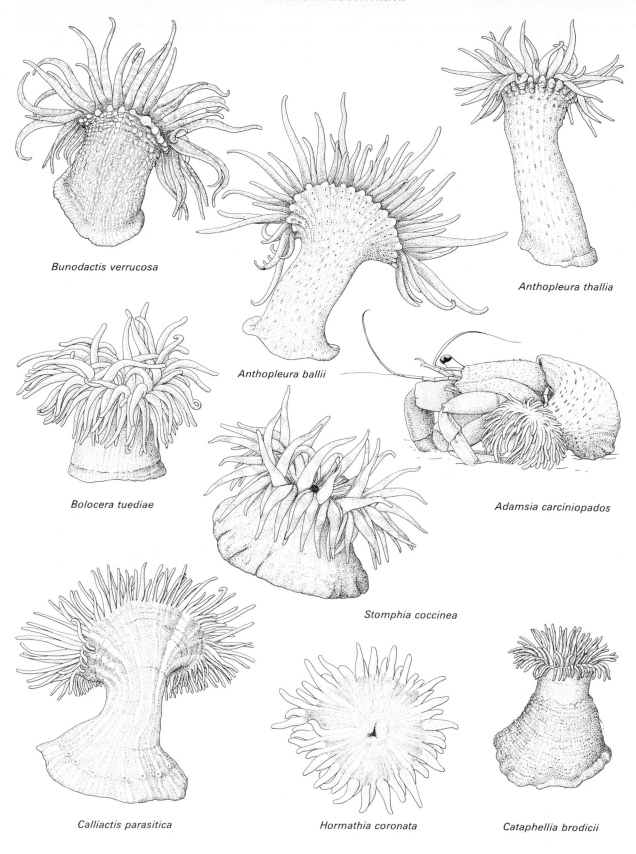

Bunodactis verrucosa

Anthopleura ballii

Anthopleura thallia

Bolocera tuediae

Adamsia carciniopados

Stomphia coccinea

Calliactis parasitica

Hormathia coronata

Cataphellia brodicii

Fig. 4.29

rows, from limbus to parapet. Tentacles moderate to long, rather stiffly held, hexamerously arranged, up to 48 (rarely more). Column grey or pink, verrucae darker with the six principal rows usually white; disk and tentacles grey, green, pink, brown, or purplish, with a dark pattern in the disk and opaque pink, white, or grey spots on the tentacles. Reproduction by viviparity common.

A typical shore form found in crevices, pools (especially *Corallina* pools) or attached to bedrock beneath a layer of sand or gravel; rarely found below the tidal zone; south and west coasts, locally common; to south-west Europe and Mediterranean.

Urticina felina (Linnaeus). Dahlia anemone FIG. 4.28
[Formerly known as *Tealia felina*]
Column typically rather short and squat, with a firmly adherent base, to about 100 mm diameter; verrucae numerous on scapus, not usually arranged regularly in rows; nearly always with adhering gravel, shell, or other debris. Tentacles stout, short or moderate in length, arranged in multiples of ten, up to about 160; their span up to about 200 mm. Colour variable: red, blue, green, white, brown, purple, yellow, etc., in various combinations; column plain or with irregular patches of different colours, verrucae usually grey; disk usually patterned with red lines; tentacles usually banded, sometimes plain (e.g. white).

In pools and crevices, usually around low water mark, occasionally midshore in deep, shaded pools, on rocky shores, common; offshore to at least 100 m; Arctic to Biscay.

Urticina eques (Gosse)
[Formerly known as *Tealia felina* var. *lofotensis*]
Similar to *U. felina* but tentacles relatively longer, verrucae reduced in size and rarely with adherent debris. Colour usually pale: red, yellowish, or cream. Often larger than *U. felina*, with a tentacle span of 300 mm or more.

Typically offshore, LWST to at least 400 m; all coasts (doubtful English Channel); to Arctic.

15 ACTINOSTOLIDAE
Mesenteries not divided into macrocnemes and microcnemes. Sphincter muscle mesogloeal. Acontia absent.

Stomphia coccinea (Müller) FIG. 4.29
Column smooth, to about 70–80 mm diameter. Tentacles moderate in length, and unusually arranged: 6 + 10 or 12 + 16 or 18, etc. Colour variable, white, red, orange, buff; column irregularly blotched, tentacles usually banded.

On stones and shells (especially *Modiolus*); 10–400 m; all coasts except south; Arctic-boreal.

16 AIPTASIIDAE
Sphincter muscle mesogloeal but weak, or absent. Acontia present. Mesenteries not divided into macrocnemes and microcnemes.

Aiptasia mutabilis (Gravenhorst) FIG. 4.31
[Formerly known as *A. couchii* (Cocks)]
Column typically tall and trumpet-shaped, flaring out to the wide oral disk which bears up to 100 long, rather stout tentacles. Height of column to about 100–120 mm, span of tentacles to 150 mm. Cinclides fairly prominent when column well-extended; acontia emitted rather reluctantly. Although capable of doing so, this anemone rarely retracts its tentacles; when disturbed it contracts in a series of short jerks. Overall colour brown, usually with opaque white (or appearing bluish) lines on the disk. Contains zooxanthellae.

Under stones, beneath overhangs, in lower shore pools, but more abundant in the shallow sublittoral amongst *Laminaria* and *Saccorhiza* holdfasts; to about 30 m. Restricted to extreme south-west coasts; also Channel Isles and south to Mediterranean.

17 DIADUMENIDAE
Sphincter muscle endodermal and weak, or absent. Acontia present. Mesenteries not divided into macrocnemes and microcnemes.

Diadumene cincta Stephenson FIG. 4.31
Column smooth, long and slender when fully extended and not divided into regions; in contraction the parapet, fosse, and capitulum become distinct. Oral disk about same diameter as column, with up to about 200 irregularly arranged long, slender tentacles. Column typically about 60–70 × 5–10 mm. Reproduction by pedal laceration is habitual. Whole anemone dull orange (rarely buff), translucent at the distal end so that the deep orange actinopharynx usually shows through; cinclides visible as dark dots on scapus; disk and tentacles often with a characteristic faint greenish caste, rarely splashed with opaque white.

On stones, mussels, growing through sponges, etc.; sometimes in water of variable salinity; on the shore and sublittoral down to about 40 m; reported from all coasts but usually very local, occurring in aggregations; also Netherlands and France.

Haliplanella lineata (Verrill) FIG. 4.31
[Formerly known as *Aiptasiomorpha* or *Diadumene luciae* (Verrill)]
Column smooth, never much taller than wide, divided into scapus and capitulum, with a prominent, permanent parapet and fosse; usually about 10–20 mm diameter but can be larger. Oral disk a little wider than column; tentacles long, arranged irregularly, up to about 100. Overall texture rather delicate. Reproduction by longitudinal fission is habitual. Column typically olive green, with prominent longitudinal stripes of orange or sometimes yellow or white. Capitulum, disk and tentacles translucent grey sparingly spotted with opaque white; disk sometimes with crimson blotches.

On stones, shells, pier piles, etc., usually intertidal; reported from all British coasts, very local; often in harbours and in water of variable salinity; widely distributed through Europe, including Mediterranean, and rest of world.

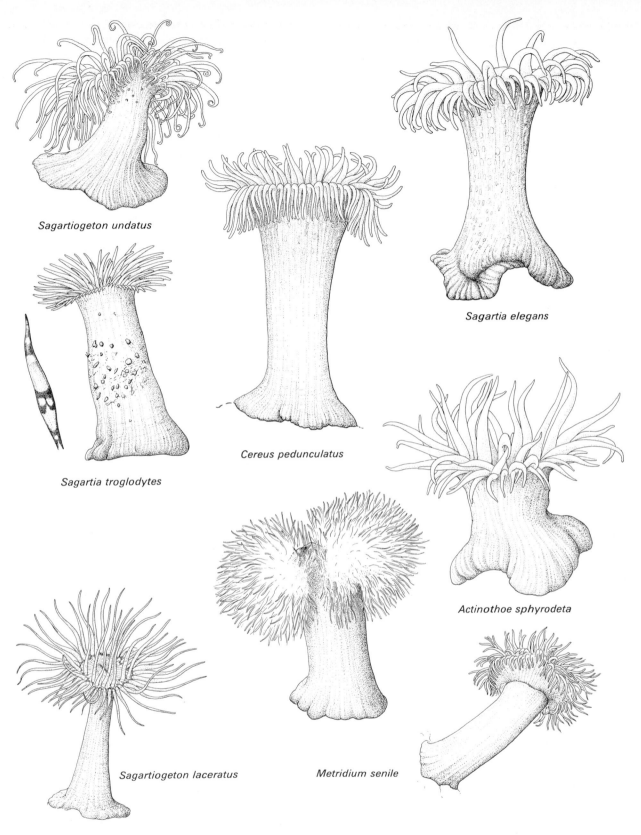

Sagartiogeton undatus

Sagartia troglodytes

Cereus pedunculatus

Sagartia elegans

Actinothoe sphyrodeta

Sagartiogeton laceratus

Metridium senile

Fig. 4.30

18 METRIDIIDAE

Sphincter muscle mesogloeal. Acontia present. Mesenteries not divided into macrocnemes and microcnemes. Column divided into scapus and capitulum, with parapet and fosse.

Metridium senile (Linnaeus). Plumose anemone FIG. 4.30
An anemone of very variable form. Base wider than column, often irregular (result of pedal laceration); column with smooth scapus and long capitulum; in full expansion the parapet may be visible as a prominent collar. Oral disk wide; tentacles variable in length and number. Colour plain but for one or two white bars often present near the base of each tentacle; commonest colours white and orange. Two forms or morphs can be recognized, although there is no genetic evidence for these being varieties justifying taxonomic recognition (Bucklin, A., 1985, *J. mar. biol. Ass. U.K.*, **65**, 14–157).

Var. *dianthus* (the plumose form): column taller than wide, up to 0.5 m. Oral disk wide, lobate; tentacles rather short, very numerous, creating a fluffy effect. Large specimens typically occur in sites where they can project into strong tidal currents.

Var. *pallidum*: a small shore form, often found in brackish water; column low, to 25 mm across base, usually no taller than wide. Oral disk not lobed; up to about 200, long tentacles.

In overhangs, caves, and beneath boulders on the lower shore, and on pier piles and rock faces to at least 100 m; common and widespread on all coasts; Scandinavia to Biscay.

19 SAGARTIIDAE

Sphincter muscle mesogloeal. Acontia present. Mesenteries not divisible into macrocnemes and microcnemes. Column not divided into scapus and capitulum; never with parapet and fosse.

Actinothoe sphyrodeta (Gosse) FIG. 4.30
Column typically short and squat but can become taller than wide, to 20 × 15 mm. Up to about 120 moderate to long tentacles, rather stout at base and sharply tapering; irregularly arranged. No suckers. Cinclides visible as dark dots on the upper column; acontia readily emitted. Column white to greyish; disk white, yellow, or orange; tentacles pure white; a vague dusky pattern sometimes present at the tentacle bases. Distinguished from white specimens of *Sagartia* spp. by the lack of suckers and its habit of attaching to the surface of the substratum, not inserting its base into a hole or crevice. Reproduces freely by longitudinal fission.

On open rock faces exposed to wave or tidal action; sometimes on *Laminaria* or *Himanthalia* buttons; occasional on the shore at LWST in caves, etc.; commoner in sublittoral down to at least 50 m; south and west coasts, north to Shetland; also south to Biscay.

Cereus pedunculatus (Pennant). Daisy anemone FIG. 4.30
Column taller than wide in extension, typically narrowest just above broad basal disk, flaring out to wide oral disk; tall or short, depending on situation. Oral disk very wide, up to 120 mm but more usually 40–50 mm. Tentacles short, rather small, very numerous, 500–700 in an average specimen, more than 1000 in

a large one; arranged hexamerously. Cinclides present high on the column; acontia freely emitted. Column grey, brown, purple, etc., darkest distally where the suckers form prominent pale spots, usually with adhering debris; very pale pink or yellow specimens are occasionally found. Disk and tentacles usually richly patterned in various colours: grey, purple, bluish, red, brown, and yellow typically present, adding to the effect of a speckled dark brown disk; often flecked with white. Various elements may be lacking and plain brown specimens are not uncommon. 'Rayed' specimens (cf. *Sagartia*) are also frequent. Contains zooxanthellae. Viviparous, often producing numerous young when collected.

In holes and crevices, typically in pools, rarely in places that dry out at low water; also commonly buried in sand or mud with the disk expanded at the substrate surface; from MTL down to at least 50 m; south and west coasts north to Scotland; locally abundant; south-west Europe and Mediterranean.

Sagartia elegans (Dalyell) FIG. 4.30
Base wider than column; column taller than wide in full extension, flaring to the broad oral disk. Suckers prominent, especially distally; only rarely with adherent debris. Cinclides just visible on upper part of column; acontia emitted from them freely. Up to about 200 tentacles, moderate in length, arranged irregularly owing to frequent occurrence of pedal laceration. Tentacle span to about 60 mm.

Colour of oral disk and tentacles variable, five varieties being recognized:

1. disk and tentacles all white; no pattern: var. *nivea*;
2. disk orange, tentacles white; no pattern: var. *venusta*;
3. disk variable, tentacles rose-pink or magenta: var. *rosea*;
4. disk variable, tentacles dull orange: var. *aurantiaca*;
5. disk and tentacles patterned; var. *miniata*.

The pattern on *miniata* consists of broken concentric dark rings, the tentacles barred and often with B-shaped marks at their base; all this on a variegated ground of white, orange, brown, etc. Occasionally alternate groups of radii may be light and dark, giving a rayed effect. Varieties 1–4 may have a trace of this pattern on the disk, particularly 3 and 4, and all sorts of intermediate forms occur. Varieties 1, 2, and 5 are common; 4 is rare.

A common species, in pools or under stones, beneath rocky overhangs, typically with its base inserted into a hole or crevice, so that only the disk is visible; on the shore, and extending to at least 50 m; all coasts, locally abundant; Scandinavia to Mediterranean.

Sagartia ornata (Holdsworth) FIG. 4.26
[MANUEL 1981, 146, as *S. troglodytes* var. *ornata*; see SHAW *et al.* 1987].
Column widest basally, rarely tall; diameter of base usually less than 15 mm. Tentacles long, up to four to five cycles. Suckers inconspicuous, often without adherent debris; cinclides few, but large and easily observed. Lower part of column may be covered by loose investment of mucus and detritus, forming

a sheath. Column and oral disk translucent shades of green or brown. Pattern at base of tentacles rather similar to that in *S. troglodytes* and some specimens may be difficult to place in their correct species. Viviparous young are produced asexually, building up aggregations of identical anemones.

In holes, crevices, and under stones, and in *Laminaria* hold-fasts; also found on stones, shells, and *Zostera* over muddy sand flats, including brackish localities; all British coasts.

Sagartia troglodytes (Price in Johnston)   FIG. 4.30
[MANUEL 1981, 146, as *S. troglodytes* var. *decorata*; see SHAW *et al.* 1987].

Anemones known by this name in the literature comprise two separate and distinct species, *S. troglodytes* and *S. ornata* (Holdsworth); the varietal name *decorata* applied to the former should lapse (Shaw *et al.* 1987).

Column typically broadest at base, only slightly overlapped by oral disk; usually a tall pillar up to 120 mm and 50 mm diameter. Tentacles moderate in length, to about 200, neatly arranged in the usual hexamerous pattern (cf. *S. elegans*). Suckers forming small and inconspicuous pale spots but often with adherent debris; cinclides on upper part of column, acontia not readily emitted. Column typically dull in colour, very variable: green, brown, grey, buff, etc. Colour of disk and tentacles exceedingly variable: white, black, grey, brown, green, lilac, purple, orange; usually with a speckled pattern, or trace of one; usually with conspicuous, or at least discernible, B-shaped markings at the base of tentacles. Sometimes the rayed effect described for *S. elegans* occurs. Unlike *S. elegans* this species never occurs in any reddish shades (except for dull orange on disk or tentacles). Reproduces sexually, and populations are therefore more variable than those of *S. ornata*; the two may occur together.

Typically buried in sand or silty mud, attached to a stone or shell up to 150 mm below, in full or reduced salinity; also in pools, crevices, kelp holdfasts on rocky shores; from MTL to 50 m; all coasts; Scandinavia to Mediterranean.

Sagartiogeton laceratus (Dalyell)   FIG. 4.30
General form similar to *S. undatus* but smaller, rarely more than 30 by 15 mm basal disk diameter; tentacles arranged irregularly, owing to habitual reproduction by pedal laceration. No suckers. Column patterned as *S. undatus*; cinclides usually visible as dark spots on upper column; acontia not readily emitted. A loose covering of mucus and particles may invest lower column. This species, unlike *S. undatus*, has some orange coloration in the column and disk, and pale chevrons on a dark ground near the tentacle bases. Tends to occur in small groups.

On hard substrata; sublittoral, to at least 100 m; all coasts; Scandinavia to Biscay.

Sagartiogeton undatus (Müller)   FIG. 4.30
Column in full extension a pillar up to 120 mm high and 20 mm diameter, becoming very low in contraction. Oral disk wider than column, with an unusually wide mouth; tentacles up to 200, long, slender, graceful, arranged hexamerously. No suckers.

Column grey or buff, with regular vertical stripes of brown flecks of variable intensity; cinclides forming conspicuous dark spots on upper column; acontia not readily emitted. Disk and tentacles translucent grey or buff, with a pattern of dark grey or brownish markings and cream spots; often with irregular dark radial wedges; tentacles with two dark longitudinal stripes. Easily distinguished from *Sagartia troglodytes*, with which it gets confused, by its lack of suckers and the long striped tentacles. Pedal laceration not recorded.

Typically buried in sand or gravel, attached to a stone or shell 100–150 mm down, or in crevices or holes in rocks, lower shore and sublittoral to at least 100 m; all coasts, frequent but rarely abundant; Scandinavia to Mediterranean.

20 HORMATHIIDAE
Sphincter strong, mesogloeal. Acontia present. Mesenteries not divisible into macrocnemes and microcnemes; only 6 or 12 pairs perfect. Column tough, tuberculate, cuticular. Often on detached substrata, crustaceans, or pagurid-inhabited shells.

Adamsia carciniopados (Otto)   FIG. 4.29
[Formerly *A. palliata* (Bohadsch)]
Base broadly expanded, forming two lobes which embrace and overlap a shell inhabited by the hermit crab *Pagurus prideauxi*; the two lobes meet dorsally and the oral disk lies beneath the crab. Remainder of column very short; oral disk elliptical, tentacles short and slender, up to 500. Colour mainly white, proximal part of column often rusty brown; mostly with numerous pink or magenta spots on column; cinclides present on lower column, through which pink, rarely white, acontia are freely emitted. Typical size of anemone *en masse* about 30–50 mm diameter. Can secrete chitinous extension to the shell, circumventing the need for the pagurid to change shells.

Occasional LWST, common sublittorally at all depths on sandy or gravelly substrata; all coasts; Norway to Mediterranean.

Calliactis parasitica (Couch)   FIG. 4.29
Column taller than wide, its texture firm and cartilaginous; tentacles moderate in length, rather slender and numerous, up to about 700. Typically 50–80 × 30–50 mm, but can become larger. Acontia readily emitted from cinclides just above limbus. Ground colour cream, yellow, or buff, more or less densely blotched and streaked with reddish or greyish brown, tending to form vertical stripes; often with additional spots of red or purple; usually with short vertical yellow lines rising from limbus. Disk and tentacles plain or with a simple pattern of cream streaks and broken brown lines.

Typically found on whelk (*Buccinum undatum*) shells inhabited by hermit crab *Pagurus bernhardus* but occasionally on stones or empty shells; rarely intertidal; locally common offshore at depths to about 60 m; southern coasts, north to Bristol Channel and west of Ireland; south-west Europe and Mediterranean.

Cataphellia brodricii (Gosse)   FIG. 4.29
Column taller than wide, usually with a broad base; up to

60 × 40 mm; scapus with numerous small dark tubercles, usually concealed by a dense, wrinkled layer of brown periderm; scapulus naked. Oral disk small, with about 100 short to moderate tentacles arranged in a neat and distinct hexamerous pattern. Column beneath periderm brownish or pink, scapus with six dark patches linked to the disk pattern of dark purplish brown primary endocoels, overlain with spots and streaks of gold and cream; lining of actinopharynx blackish; tentacles grey-brown with darker bands. Cinclides visible as tiny dark spots just above the limbus. Acontia emitted reluctantly. Viviparous.

A very cryptic anemone found in crevices or attached to bedrock beneath sediments, under stones; etc.; from LWST to 20 m; Devon, Cornwall, south-west Ireland, France.

Hormathia coronata (Gosse)   FIG. 4.29

General form and size very similar to *Cataphellia brodricii*, but lacks cinclides (acontia can protrude only through the mouth). Coloration generally paler or more reddish than in *C. brodricii*; disk pattern often absent or obscured by irregular white patches; actinopharynx lining red or buff. Viviparity has been recorded.

Usually found on shells, worm tubes, or other organic substrata; sublittoral only; south and west coasts, rather local; Ireland and western Scotland to south-west Europe and Mediterranean.

21 HALOCLAVIDAE

Basilar muscles lacking; column generally elongate, generally divided into scapus and physa. Sphincter weak or lacking. Single siphonoglyph. No acontia. Mesenteries not differentiated into macrocnemes and microcnemes.

Mesacmaea mitchellii (Gosse)   FIG. 4.31

Column turnip-shaped, divided into scapulus and scapus, the latter usually encrusted with sand or gravel; base rounded, used for digging, capable of becoming a disk without a limbus and able to adhere firmly to a solid surface; up to 70 × 35 mm. Tentacles long, up to 36, with seven in inner cycle, these usually held inwards over the mouth. Scapus orange, brown, flesh-coloured, etc.; scapulus, disk, and tentacles brownish or grey, patterned with white, cream, or dark grey, the tentacles with V- or W-shaped markings.

Buried in sand or gravel with just the disk and tentacles protruding; always sublittoral, 15–100 m south and west coasts; to mid-Scotland; south-west Europe and Mediterranean.

Peachia cylindrica (Reid)   FIG. 4.31
[Formerly known as *P. hastata* Gosse]

Column elongated when buried but contracting to short sausage-shape when dug up, about 50–60 × 15–20 mm; may attain 300 mm when fully extended; indistinctly differentiated into physa, scapus, and capitulum. Disk of similar diameter to column with a small lobed organ, the *conchula*, protruding from one corner of the mouth; tentacles 12 in two cycles, very long in an expanded, buried specimen (spanning up to 150 mm) but remaining short in an unburied one. Column pinkish buff or brown, with irregular dashes of darker brown; disk patterned with white, buff, and brown, forming V- and W-shaped markings; disk sometimes plain white.

Burrowing in sand or gravel, occasionally on the lower shore but mainly sublittoral; all coasts; western Europe and Mediterranean.

22 HALCAMPIDAE

Column lacking a base; typically an elongate cylinder divisible into physa, scapus, and capitulum. Scapus may be cuticular and bear adhesive papillae (*tenaculi*). Sphincter mesogloeal. Mesenteries divisible into macrocnemes and microcnemes. Tentacles few.

Halcampa chrysanthellum (Peach)   FIG. 4.31

Column elongated and worm-like, becoming less so when dug up; usually 30–40 × 4–5 mm but may be larger. Disk small, tentacles 12, always short or moderate; fewer than the mesenteries. Column white, pink, or buff, with translucent longitudinal stripes; disk and tentacles variable, usually with a pattern of V- and W-shaped markings in various shades of brown, buff, white, etc., sometimes bright yellow, sometimes all white.

Burrows in sand or gravel; occasional at LWST (e.g. in *Zostera*) but mainly sublittoral; all coasts; further distribution beyond France uncertain.

23 EDWARDSIIDAE

Column vermiform, differentiated into two or more regions. Basal end rounded, its structure variable. Sphincter, acontia, basilar muscles absent; cinclides may be present. Eight macrocnemes and at least four microcnemes present; tentacles few. Some genera characterized by *nemathybomes*, pockets in the column wall containing batteries of large nematocysts; they may or may not be visible without sectioning. The condition of the *ciliated tracts* (on the mesenteric filaments) provides a generic character.

Edwardsia claparedii (Panceri)   FIG. 4.31
[Formerly known as *E. callimorpha* (Gosse)]

Column elongated and wormlike, up to 60–70 × 5 mm; divisible into three regions; naked, rounded basal physa (usually with adherent sand grains when freshly dug up; without cinclides); long cylindrical scapus, covered with a thin brownish or reddish layer of periderm, bearing eight longitudinal rows of more or less prominent tubercles (underlying nemathybomes); and short, naked scapulus. Disk small, 16 long and slender tentacles, arranged 8 + 8. Ciliated tracts short. Column buff or translucent flesh-colour, disk speckled with buff or cream with various dark markings and orange dots, sometimes with white streaks or all white; tentacles colourless and transparent except for spots and bands of buff and red-brown.

Burrowing in mud or muddy sand; LWST to sublittoral, often in or around *Zostera* beds; south and west coasts, local.

Edwardsia timida Quatrefages is similar to *E. claparedii* but usually more slender, and the column lacks the rows of tubercles; physa with cinclides. Disk small; tentacles long and slender, up to 32 (usually 20–28) arranged in three cycles. Column with white markings.

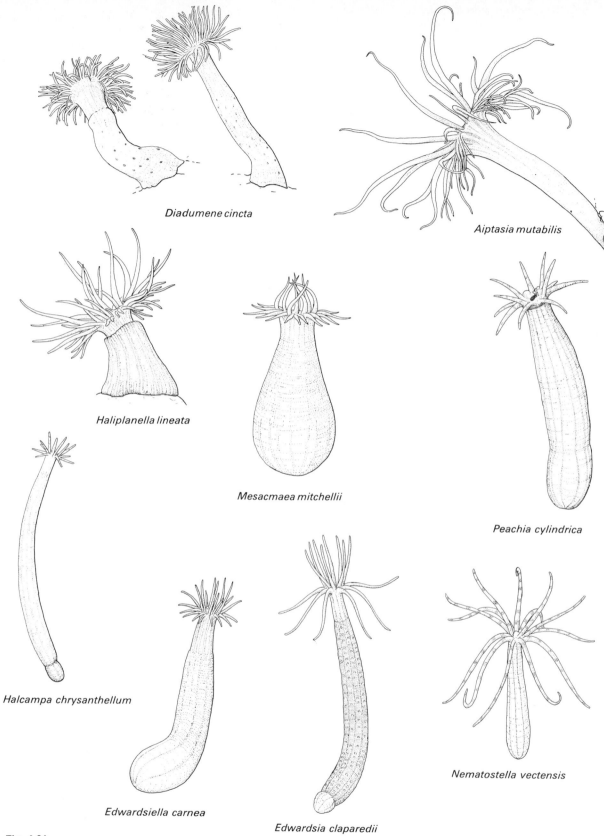

Fig. 4.31

Recorded only from lower shore in muddy coarse sand or gravel; south and west coasts only, very local.

Edwardsiella carnea (Gosse)   FIG. 4.31
[Formerly known as either *Fagesia* or *Milneedwardsia*]
Column cylindrical, up to 20 × 3–4 mm, divided into scapus, which lacks nemathybomes and bears a thick rough layer of brownish periderm, and naked scapulus; basal end of scapus rounded, usually naked, adherent to the substratum (no physa). Disk small, up to about 34 moderate to long, slender tentacles. Ciliated tracts short. Whole anemone translucent orange; white or yellow marks on scapulus and disk.

In holes and crevices in rocks, often in large local aggregations; always in shaded places, caves, beneath overhangs, etc., MTL to shallow water; all coasts, but mostly in south and west; Scandinavia to France, perhaps Mediterranean.

Nematostella vectensis Stephenson   FIG. 4.31
Column moderately elongated, up to 15 × 1.5 mm (rarely more), differentiated into physa, scapus, and capitulum, thickest proximally. Disk small, 10–18 tentacles arranged irregularly owing to habitual reproduction by transverse fission, rarely retracted, almost as long as column when fully extended. No nemathybomes. Ciliated tracts long but broken into discrete sections. Whole anemone transparent, colourless except for occasional white marks on distal parts.

Burrowing in fine mud or attached to plant life in brackish lagoons and tidal creeks (not in the open sea); several localities on south and east coasts; very local (and declining through loss of habitat) but abundant where found.

5 PLATYHELMINTHES, NEMATODA, NEMERTEA

A. PHYLUM PLATYHELMINTHES

THE platyhelminths, or flatworms, are bilaterally symmetrical, pseudocoelomate animals with soft, dorso-ventrally flattened bodies. The body shows marked cephalization, but is unsegmented, although in the Cestoda serial budding, or strobilization, of identical proglottids posterior to the scolex gives rise to an apparently segmented body. The outer body wall is a ciliated epithelium in freeliving flatworms, and a non-ciliated syncytial tegument in parasitic forms; no class includes species with an outer cuticle. The bulk of the flatworm body consists of a heterogeneous parenchyma in a liquid matrix. The digestive tract is characteristically incomplete; in most groups an anus is lacking, and the entire gut is absent in many symbiotic or parasitic species. Excretion, and perhaps osmoregulation, are carried out by single-celled protonephridia, or flame cells. Most species of flatworm are hermaphroditic. Reproductive structures, reproductive behaviour, and life cycles are often complex and display numerous adaptive features throughout the phylum.

Five classes may be recognized among the Platyhelminthes. The Aspidogastraea, Digenea, Monogenea, and Cestoda are entirely parasitic, and their range of hosts includes many marine species, particularly among the decapods, molluscs, and fish. The class Turbellaria comprises the freeliving flatworms, one small proportion of which is found in marine habitats.

Class **Turbellaria**

The turbellarian flatworms comprise 12 orders, all of which include marine species. Many are small, simple animals and some families are known only from a very few specimens, of very few species, from limited microhabitats. A number of groups within the Turbellaria consist of species entirely interstitial in habit. However, the class also includes many large and spectacular species, familiar in shallow marine environments throughout the world. The Acoela includes *Convoluta*, often sufficiently abundant on suitable intertidal sands to give a greenish coloration to the beach. The Tricladida is predominantly composed of freshwater or terrestrial species, but includes a minority of marine species. Finally, the Polycladida, which is exclusively marine, includes the most striking and largest of the freeliving flatworms. The black and white banded *Prostheceraeus vittatus* (Montagu) is the most familiar example found on British shores.

Turbellarians are delicate, often fragile animals which deteriorate rapidly following collection. Many species will fragment and disintegrate upon handling. Some may be recognized when alive by distinctive colours or patterns, but for the most part identification is based on internal morphological features and requires correct procedures for fixation and microscopical preparation. Suitable techniques are given in detail by Prudhoe (1982), and Ball and Reynoldson (1981), who also provide comprehensive keys and descriptions to British Tricladida and Polycladida.

Class **Aspidogastrea**

This small group of flukes was for long regarded as intermediate between the Monogenea and the Digenea, which were formerly regarded as subclasses of a single class, Trematoda. All three groups are now accorded class status, although the Aspidogastrea seem to be closely similar to the Digenea. Aspidogastreans have a cylindrical, often wormlike body, with a ventral haptor, or holdfast, which may consist of an extensive, alveolate organ extending for much of the body length, a linear series of small suckers, or a series of thick, transverse ridges. The mouth is surrounded by a buccal funnel, but the body as a whole lacks hooks and anchors. The gut comprises pharynx, oesophagus, and one or two caeca. Development is mostly direct, although an intermediate host is used by a few species. Adult worms are endoparasites of both freshwater and marine molluscs, and also occur in fishes and turtles.

Class **Digenea**

The Digenea comprises the majority of the parasitic flukes formerly united in the Class Trematoda. The adults of almost all species are endoparasites of vertebrates, and more than half parasitize fish. Development is indirect, and life cycles often complex, with a series of larval stages involving one or more intermediate hosts, which are frequently invertebrates. The adult body form is greatly varied, but typically has one or two attachment suckers, and may bear hooks or spines. The gut consists of a pharynx, oesophagus, and one or two intestinal caeca, which may be complexly branched. Most digeneans are hermaphroditic; the life cycle includes as many as five morphologically distinct larval stages, at least one of which, the cercaria, has a short freeliving existence. Many species of intertidal molluscs, particularly gastropods, are intermediate hosts for digenean parasites of fish or seabirds. Certain molluscs, such as *Littorina littorea* and *Hydrobia* species, may be host to populations of several digenean species. The class includes more than 1500 genera worldwide. An extensive specialist literature is required for identification; the most useful texts for the north-east Atlantic area are given below.

Class **Cestoda**

Adult cestodes are intestinal parasites of vertebrates, with many species occurring in the freshwater and marine fishes. Larval stages require an intermediate host, which may be vertebrate or invertebrate. The bilaterally symmetrical, flattened, tapeworm body consists of an anterior scolex, armed with hooks and suckers for attaching to the host, an unsegmented neck region, and a chain of identical units called proglottids, which are serially budded from the neck region. Ripe, egg-bearing proglottids are shed from the posterior end of the worm, and each proglottid undergoes growth, sexual maturation, and self-fertilization as it proceeds posteriorly. The morphology of the reproductive system is widely used in classifying tapeworms. Systematic study of marine cestodes requires an extensive specialist literature.

Class **Monogenea**

The monogenean flukes are predominantly ectoparasites of fishes, especially marine fishes, and occur particularly within the gill chamber and close to the operculum of the host. Body form is very varied, with many specialized adaptations. Typically, there is an anterior attachment organ (prohaptor) consisting of one or more suckers, and an often complex posterior opisthohaptor, which may consist of one to six muscular suckers, in combination with sclerotized hooks or anchors. The opisthohaptor is frequently important in identification. The gut consists of a buccal cavity, pharynx, oesophagus, and one or two variably modified caecae. The life cycle involves only a single host; a ciliated onchomiracidium larva hatches from the egg and attaches to its definitive host, where it gradually assumes adult form without intermediate larval stages, and without larval replication. More than 1000 species of Monogenea have been described, worldwide. There is a considerable specialist literature, examples of which are listed below.

Ball, I. R. and Reynoldson, T. B. (1981). British Planarians. *Synopses of the British Fauna* (n.s.) **19**. Cambridge University Press, for the Linnean Society of London and the Estuarine and Brackish Water Sciences Association.

Dawes, B. (1968). *The Trematodes, with special reference to British and other European Forms.* Cambridge University Press.

Erasmus, D. (1972). *The Biology of Trematodes.* Crone, Russak: New York.

Prudhoe, S. (1982). British Polyclad Turbellarians. *Synopses of the British Fauna* (n.s.) **26**. Cambridge University Press, for the Linnean Society of London and the Estuarine and Brackish Water Sciences Association.

Schmidt, G. D. (1982). Platyhelminthes. *In: Synopsis and classification of living organisms*, Vol. 1, (ed. S. P. Parker). New York: McGraw-Hill, New York, pp. 717–822.

Yamaguti, S. (1963). *Systema Helminthum*, Vol. 4: *Monogenea and Aspidocotylea.* Interscience, New York.

Yamaguti, S. (1975). *A synoptical review of life histories of digenetic Trematodes of vertebrates.* Keigaku, Tokyo.

B. PHYLUM NEMATODA

The Nematoda is one of the largest of the invertebrate phyla. Nematode worms occur in every possible environment, and there are both freeliving and parasitic forms in every marine habitat. Freeliving marine nematodes may be particularly abundant in intertidal muds and fine sands, and also in and among algal holdfasts. They are commonly no more than a few millimetres in length, with slender, vermiform bodies. The nematode body wall consists of an outer cuticle and an underlying layer of longitudinal muscle; circular muscles do not occur, and the worm has a rather stiff appearance which distinguishes it from other worms in mixed samples. The anterior mouth is terminal, but the anus is subterminal, and nematodes typically have a slender, often curled, postanal tail. Sensory setae or papillae are found at the anterior and posterior ends, and may be present also elsewhere along the length of the body.

The study of marine nematodes has long been hampered by difficulties in identification. Platt and Warwick (1983) provided a pictorial key to marine genera, which cannot be improved upon here. They also describe methods and techniques for collecting and handling marine species, together with descriptions and illustrations of the British species of one subclass, the Enopla.

Gerlach, S. A. and Riemann, F. (1973). The Bremerhaven checklist of aquatic nematodes. A catalogue of Nematoda Adenophorea excluding the Dorylaimida. 1. *Veröffentlichungen des Instituts fur Meeresforschung in Bremerhaven*, Supplement **4**, Part 1.

Gerlach, S. A. and Riemann, F. (1974). The Bremerhaven checklist of aquatic nematodes. A catalogue of Nematoda Adenophorea excluding the Dorylaimida. 2. *Veröffentlichungen des Instituts fur Meeresforschung in Bremerhaven*, Supplement **4**, Part 2.

Heip, C., Vincx, M., Smol, N., and Vranken, G. (1982). The systematics and ecology of free-living marine nematodes. *Helminthological Abstracts* (Series B), **51**, 1–31.

Platt, H. M. and Warwick, R. M. (1980). The significance of free living marine nematodes to the littoral ecosystem. In: *The shore environment*, Vol. 2. *Ecosystems* (eds. J. H. Price, D. E. G. Irvine, and W. F. Farnham). Academic Press, London, pp. 727–59.

Platt, H. M. and Warwick, R. M. (1983). Freeliving marine nematodes. Part 1, British Enoplids. *Synopses of the British Fauna* (n.s.) no. **28**. Cambridge University Press, for the Linnean Society of London and the Estuarine and Brackish Water Sciences Association.

C. PHYLUM NEMERTEA

Nemerteans occur under stones, in sand, mud, and rock crevices, amongst turf algae, kelp holdfasts, trawled hydroids, and other dense populations of sedentary animals. Ideally they should be studied alive, noting colours, pigment patterns, head shape, positions of *mouth* and *proboscis pore*, numbers and distributions of *eyes* and *cephalic grooves*, and the presence or absence of a *caudal cirrus*. Some internal organs (e.g. the *cerebral ganglia* or *proboscis stylets*) can often be distinguished by transmitted light, particularly in pale or translucent species which have been gently compressed under a supported glass slide. MgCl$_2$ (0.3 N) can be used as a narcotic during this process and washed away afterwards to allow recovery. Although the broad classification of the phylum also uses characters revealed only by histological sectioning, the study of living material is sufficient for the identification of many species. A considerable number of species have indeed been described from external features alone, with no details of internal anatomy; this has led to several such forms being taxonomically misplaced. Proper study needs microscopy and drawings from life, followed by histological examination. Species identification of preserved material is particularly difficult, and often scarcely practicable.

LITERATURE

Gibson (1982a) gives descriptions of all nemertean species recorded from Britain, with a full bibliography. Other small palaeonemerteans which may well occur here (e.g. in sea lochs) are described by Hylbom (1957) and Brunberg (1964); Brunberg also included some colour plates, as did such beautifully illustrated monographs of the last century as McIntosh (1873–74). Several of our figures are derived from the Naples monograph by Bürger. For relevant changes in nomenclature and taxonomy since those times see Gibson (1982a, b, 1985). For a worldwide synopsis of families and genera see Gibson (1982b). Small interstitial species occurring amongst sand grains (e.g. *Arenonemertes, Ototyphlonemertes*) are not treated here, for they have scarcely been studied in Britain and are poorly known worldwide. They are however not uncommon and anyone seeking to tackle them may find a lead in papers by Friedrich (1935, 1949) and Mock (1978).

Brunberg, L. (1964). On the nemertean fauna of Danish waters. *Ophelia*, **1**, 77–111.

Friedrich, H. (1935). Studien zur Morphologie, Systematik und Ökologie der Nemertinen der Kieler Bucht. *Archiv für Naturgeschichte*, **4**, 293–375.

Friedrich, H. (1949). Über zwei bemerkenswerte neue Nemertinen der Sandfauna. *Kieler Meeresforschungen*, **6**, 68–72.

Gibson, R. (1982a). British Nemerteans. *Synopses of the British Fauna*, **24**, 1–212. Cambridge University Press.

Gibson, R. (1982b). Nemertea. In: *Synopsis and classification of living organisms*, (ed. A. P. Parker). McGraw-Hill, New York, **1**, 823–46.

Gibson, R. (1985). The need for a standard approach to taxonomic descriptions of nemerteans. *American Zoologist*, **25**, 5–14.

Hylbom, R. (1957). Studies on palaeonemerteans of the Gullmar Fiord area (west coast of Sweden). *Arkiv for Zoologi, Uppsala*, **10**, 539–82.

McIntosh, W. C. (1873–74). *A monograph of the British annelids, Part I. The nemerteans*. Ray Society, London.

Mock, H. (1978). *Ototyphlonemertes pallida* (Keferstein, 1862) (Hoplonemertini, Monostilifera). *Mikrofauna des Meeresbodens*, **67**, 559–70.

PHYLUM NEMERTEA

Unsegmented, bilaterally symmetrical, ciliated acoelomate worms, with separate mouth and anus, a closed blood system, and an eversible muscular proboscis contained within a dorsal fluid-filled chamber, the rhynchocoel. Classification uses internal characters, as follows. Two classes.

Class I **Anopla**

Mouth below or posterior to cerebral ganglia. Longitudinal nerve cords embedded in body wall. Proboscis without stylets. Two orders.

Order 1 **Palaeonemertea**

Outermost muscles of body wall circular. Nerve cords either external to these muscle layers or embedded in the longitudinal musculature.

Order 2 **Heteronemertea**

Body wall muscles in three layers, outer and inner longitudinal, middle circular. Nerve cords lie just outside the middle layer.

Class II **Enopla**

Mouth anterior to cerebral ganglia and usually united with proboscis pore. Nerve cords internal to body wall musculature. Proboscis usually armed with stylets. Two orders.

Order 1 **Hoplonemertea**

Body worm-like. Gut straight. No posterior sucker. Two suborders.

Suborder Monostilifera: One functional stylet, flanked by pouches containing reserve stylets, as shown for *Nemertopsis flavida* in Fig. 5.3L.

Suborder Polystilifera: Many stylets on a rasping pad (also flanked by accessory pouches), as shown for *Paradrepanophorus crassus* in Fig. 5.4P.

Order 2 **Bdellonemertea**

Body leech-like, with a posterior sucker. Gut sinuous. Proboscis without stylets.

KEY TO FAMILIES

The higher classification of nemerteans, particularly at the family level, is in general not soundly established and requires extensive re-evaluation. Recent attempts to resolve such systematic problems with the Heteronemertea (Gibson 1985) demonstrated the need for much more detailed information on the anatomy of the greater proportion of recognized species; with few exceptions the grouping of nemertean genera into families can only be achieved on a very provisional basis and is principally done for convenience rather than on secure morphological grounds. The present key, designed to avoid the need for extensive histological studies, inevitably has its limitations and applies only to those taxa described in the succeeding text.

1. Pigmented body with conspicuous rectangular pattern of white lines   **22**
   Without such a pattern   **2**

2. With longitudinal grooves on opposite sides of head   **17**
   Without longitudinal grooves on head   **3**

3. With four eyes forming a rectangle   **9**
   Eyes two, none, or more than four   **4**

4. Elongated body densely pigmented dorsally but pale ventrally   **12**
   Without such a marked difference between darker and paler surfaces   **5**

5. Flattened, leech-like body with posterior ventral sucker (Fig. 5.4Q). In mantle cavity of bivalve
   molluscs   **16 Malacobdellidae**
   Body much longer than wide, without sucker. Not with bivalves   **6**

6. With two small eyes. Parasitic on gills or eggs of crabs. Proboscis very short and reduced
   (Fig. 5.3G)   **9 Carcinonemertidae**
   Eyes rarely two, usually four, many or none. Freeliving. Proboscis at least one third length
   of body   **7**

7. Mouth indistinct, in front of brain, usually opening with proboscis pore at or near anterior tip.
   Proboscis armed with one or more stylets. TS shows lateral nerves internal to body wall
   muscle layers (Enopla, Hoplonemertea)   **8**

   Mouth usually distinct, below or behind brain, well separated from proboscis pore. Proboscis
   not armed with stylets. Lateral nerves embedded in or external to body wall muscle layers
   (Anopla)   **16**

8. With four eyes arranged to form corners of a square or rectangle. Mostly small worms (less
   than 20–30 mm long), with or without distinctive colour patterns or markings on dorsal surface;
   markings, when present, often restricted to head and may partially mask the eyes   **9**

   Eyes usually 0 or more than 4, often numerous. Body often long and slender, frequently much
   coiled. Rarely with distinct colour pattern, but often with dorsal surface more deeply pigmented
   than ventral   **12**

9. Body soft, slender, colour pattern when present restricted to head or consisting of one or two dark but narrow longitudinal stripes (Fig. 5.4A–N)   **13 Tetrastemmatidae**

   Without colour pattern or with pattern extending full body length; if striped, stripes are pale on darker background   **10**

10. Body soft, delicate, without colour pattern   **11**

    Body firm, stout, with distinct colour pattern of transverse bands, marbled or pale longitudinal bands (Fig. 5.3M)   **12 Prosorhochmidae**

11. Head rounded or diamond-shaped, without distinct terminal notch, eyes small. Mid- to lower-shore, typically associated with algae (Fig. 5.4A–N)   **13 Tetrastemmatidae**

    Head somewhat bilobed, with terminal notch, front pair of eyes significantly larger than rear pair. Upper shore, rarely found other than in summer months when mature individuals give birth to live young (Fig. 5.3N)   **12 Prosorhochmidae**

12. Live body length more than 40 × width. Proboscis sheath not reaching beyond middle of body. Head distinct with many eyes, or very slender, indistinct, with four minute eyes (Fig. 5.3I–L)   **11 Emplectonematidae**

    Live body length usually less than 20 × width. Proboscis sheath reaches to or almost to posterior tip of body. Eyes two or numerous   **13**

13. Eyes numerous, arranged in four longitudinal rows on head. Proboscis armed with several stylets (Polystilifera)   **14**

    Eyes not as above, proboscis armed with single stylet   **15**

14. Dorsally marked with colour pattern of pale longitudinal stripes (Fig. 5.4O)   **14 Drepanophoridae**

    Dorsal body surface without pattern of longitudinal stripes (Fig. 5.4P)   **15 Paradrepanophoridae**

15. Body stout, thick, somewhat dorsoventrally flattened, very contractile. Head with median dorsal longitudinal ridge or swelling. Proboscis large relative to size of body (Fig. 5.3H)   **10 Cratenemertidae**

    Body soft, delicate, not strongly contractile. Head without median dorsal longitudinal ridge or swelling. Proboscis comparatively small relative to size of body (Fig. 5.3A–G)   **8 Amphiporidae**

16. With distinct longitudinal grooves on opposite sides of head   **17**

    Without longitudinal grooves on head, either entirely without grooves or with single transverse furrow encircling rear of head   **20**

17. With longitudinal median groove on upper and lower surfaces of head (Fig. 5.2S)   **7 Valenciniidae**

    With lateral longitudinal grooves on each side of head   **18**

18. With caudal cirrus   **19**

    Without caudal cirrus (Fig. 5.2F–M)   **6 Lineidae**

---

19. Head more or less pointed, body distinctly flattened dorso-ventrally, broad with sharp lateral margins (Fig. 5.2A–D)   **5 Cerebratulidae**

    Head rounded or pointed, body not distinctly flattened dorso-ventrally, more or less slender with rounded lateral margins (Fig. 5.2N–Q)   **6 Lineidae**

---

20. With numerous eyes along borders of rounded head. Body long, slender, marked by narrow interrupted dark longitudinal stripes (Fig. 5.2R)   **7 Valenciniidae**

    Without eyes. Either without obvious colour pattern or with well-marked pattern of longitudinal and/or transverse white bands   **21**

---

21. With transverse furrow encircling rear of head. Head broad, bluntly pointed (Fig. 2E)
                                                                             5 Cerebratulidae

    Without transverse furrow at rear of head. Head rounded or, if pointed, extremely slender
                                                                                          22

---

22. Head rounded, usually forming distinct anterior lobe. With strikingly marked colour pattern of white transverse and/or longitudinal bands (Fig. 5.1J–R)   **4 Tubulanidae**

    Head slender, pointed, or rounded. Without colour pattern of transverse and/or longitudinal bands   **23**

---

23. Mouth far behind brain, four or five body widths from anterior end (Fig. 5.1B–E)
                                                                             2 Cephalothricidae

    Mouth just behind brain, less than four and usually less than two body widths from anterior end   **24**

---

24. Head long, slender, tapering to point, body thickest in posterior half (Fig. 5.2T)
                                                                             7 Valenciniidae

    Head rounded, body either thickest in anterior half or of more or less uniform width throughout
                                                                                          25

---

25. Head not delimited from trunk. Body long, slender, tapering gradually from thicker anterior regions (Fig. 5.1A)   **1 Carinomidae**

    Head usually forming distinct lobe. Body of more or less uniform thickness for most of its length   **26**

---

26. Head with rhynchodaeum visible internally as a triangular shape at its obtusely blunt tip (Fig. 5.1F)   **3 Hubrechtidae**

    Rhynchodaeum not distinguishable or not forming triangular shape (Fig. 5.1J–R)
                                                                             4 Tubulanidae

Class **Anopla**

Order **Palaeonemertea**

1 CARINOMIDAE

Remarkable in possessing muscle fibres (circular and longitudinal) within the epidermis. Anteriorly the nerve cords lie just below the epidermal basement membrane, but posteriorly they move deeper into the inner longitudinal muscle layer. Only one genus.

Carinoma armandi (McIntosh) FIG. 5.1A

Up to 20 cm long, threadlike when extended. Head rounded in front, flattened and slightly enlarged behind the tip. No grooves or eyes. Body mostly cylindrical, anterior part whitish, middle pale buff, posterior end flattened, translucent and somewhat pointed. Superficially resembles *Tubulanus linearis*, but lacks cerebral organs.

In sand near LW, amongst tubes of *Lanice*. Known only from Southport and St. Andrews.

2 CEPHALOTHRICIDAE

Head somewhat pointed, with mouth four or five body-widths distant from the anterior tip. Also with no cerebral organs, and nerve cords situated in the inner longitudinal muscle layer throughout. Most cephalothricids lack an inner circular muscle layer. Species separation difficult. Key below follows Gibson (1982*a*).

---

1. On disturbance contracts into a tight spiral (*Callinera* of the Tubulanidae also does this) **2**

   On disturbance may contract into a tight knot, but does not coil spirally **3**

2. Up to 15 cm long and 1 mm or more wide, with an incomplete layer of inner circular muscle fibres in the foregut region ***Procephalothrix filiformis***

   Up to 1 cm long and 0.2 mm wide, without inner circular muscles ***Cephalothrix arenaria***

3. Up to 30 cm long, 0.5–1 mm wide, translucent white, yellowish, or greyish ***Cephalothrix linearis***

   Up to 6 cm long, 0.5 mm wide, whitish or translucent tinged with orange, red, or purple on tip of head ***Cephalothrix rufifrons***

Cephalothrix arenaria Hylbom FIG. 5.1B
[HYLBOM 1957: 555]

Length 6–10 mm. Translucent with yellowish tinge. Characterized mainly by its small size.

Common in fine clean sand, 4 m depth, near Kristineberg, Sweden.

Cephalothrix linearis (Rathke) FIG. 5.1C

Length 10–30 cm, width 0.5–1 mm. Head long, bluntly pointed.

Lower shore and sublittoral, burrowed in coarse sand or mud, or among *Laminaria* holdfasts, *Corallina*, on hydroids or beneath stones. Britain, Sweden, Mediterranean, Greenland, eastern North America, Japan.

Cephalothrix rufifrons (Johnston) FIG. 5.1D

Length 5–6 cm, width 0.5 mm or less. Head (a) rounded at tip, usually tinged with reddish hue to varying degrees. Sketch (b) shows cerebral ganglia, seen by transparency, mid-way between mouth and terminal proboscis pore.

Gregarious, common intertidally beneath boulders, usually in clean coarse sand, and amongst *Corallina* in pools, occasionally in brackish water. Dredged to depths of 30 m. Britain, Sweden, Mediterranean.

Procephalothrix filiformis (Johnston) FIG. 5.1E

Length up to 15 cm, width 1 mm or more. Head bluntly pointed, white or translucent, body yellowish white or orange, often darker posteriorly.

Under stones or in muddy gravel from midshore to 40 m or more depth. St. Andrews, western Ireland, Channel Islands, France.

3 HUBRECHTIDAE

With a sensory cerebral organ on each side of head. Otherwise typically palaeonemertean except in having a mid-dorsal blood vessel. *Hubrechtia* (from Naples) has an inner circular muscle layer, but *Hubrechtella* lacks this.

Hubrechtella dubia Bergendal FIG. 5.1F
[HYLBOM 1957: 557; BRUNBERG 1964: 83]

Body up to 1.5 cm long, 0.5 mm wide, white, translucent anteriorly but not in the tapering extensible posterior part. Head not wider than body, rounded at front but flattened when creeping. Slight constriction in mouth region. The short rhynchodaeum can usually be seen as a triangular shape at the tip of the head. The proboscis and rhynchocoel are half the length of the body.

In surface of sublittoral muds, at depths from 8–100 m or more. Sweden, Norway, Denmark.

4 TUBULANIDAE

Some are brown or red and may bear conspicuous white stripes. Others are small and translucent enough to show the cerebral organs by transmitted light. These organs are embedded one on each side in the constriction separating the rounded, somewhat flattened head from the more or less cylindrical body. Cerebral organs are lacking, however, from *Callinera* and *Carinesta*. The nerve cords usually lie just below the basement membrane of the epidermis, as in most palaeonemerteans, but *Carinina* (alone amongst nemerteans) has the nerve cords within the epidermis, outside the thin basement membrane.

1. Brown or reddish with transverse white rings and usually also longitudinal white stripes ... **2**

   Without such conspicuous white stripes ... **6**

2. Head colour and pattern like that of body ... **3**

   Head white ... **4**

3. With four longitudinal stripes (mid-dorsal, mid-ventral and two lateral) ... *Tubulanus superbus*

   With three such stripes (mid-dorsal and two lateral) ... *Tubulanus annulatus*

4. White head lacks markings and is followed by a dark unconstricted collar of brownish red. Rest of body yellowish ... *Tubulanus albocapitatus*

   White head bears two black pigment patches ... **5**

5. Up to 1.5 cm long, with up to 18 transverse rings. Indistinct mid-dorsal longitudinal stripe as a series of white flecks present or absent ... *Tubulanus banyulensis*

   Up to 10 cm long, with 40 or more rings and three or four longitudinal stripes ... *Tubulanus nothus*

6. Richly pigmented, brown, orange or red ... **7**

   Pale yellow, pink, grey, milky, or translucent ... **10**

7. Up to 30 cm or more long and 5 mm wide. Dark reddish brown ... **8**

   5 cm or less in length, 2 mm wide. Red-orange or red-brown ... **9**

8. Head wider than body ... *Tubulanus polymorphus*

   Head about the same width as body ... *Tubulanus theeli*

9. Vermillion or reddish brown, with minute specks of white ... *Tubulanus inexpectatus*

   Uniformly orange, or paler ventrally ... *Tubulanus miniatus*

10. Head rounded and flattened, broader than body or marked off by a slight constriction in which a cerebral organ opens on each side ... **11**

    Head pointed, narrow, and not marked off from body, without cerebral organs ... **13**

11. Length up to 15 cm ... *Tubulanus linearis*

    Length up to 3 cm, width 0.3–2 mm, translucent yellowish with a sudden change to a lighter tinge about halfway along body ... **12**

12. Thin, 0.3–0.5 mm wide, lives interstitially in sand ... *Carinina arenaria*

    Stout, usually about 1 cm long, 1 mm wide, lives in mud ... *Carinina coei*

13. Posterior part of proboscis sheath partly surrounded (ventrally and laterally) by a mass of transverse muscles (distinguishable through skin, close behind head) ... *Callinera buergeri*

    Not as above ... *Carinesta anglica*

Callinera buergeri Bergendal ... FIG. 5.1G
[HYLBOM 1957: 552; BRUNBERG 1964: 83]
Length 9–30 mm, width 0.3–1.5 mm. Head translucent, pointed, not broadened or marked off from body. Proboscis pore ventral, about one body-width from tip of head. Mouth two or three body-widths further back. Body whitish, rounded anteriorly, somewhat flattened posteriorly, hind end (partly missing in Figure) often coiled spirally.

Mud at depths of 6–50 m, especially in polluted situations. Sweden, Norway, Denmark.

Carinesta anglica Wijnhoff
Inadequately described. Head elongated and pointed, becoming wrinkled when contracted. Body translucent, whitish anteriorly, tinged rosy-brown posteriorly.

Sand or muddy sand at low water, near Plymouth.

Carinina arenaria Hylbom ... FIG. 5.1H
[HYLBOM 1957: 542]
Length 7–15 mm, width 0.3–0.5 mm. Body yellowish, translucent, posterior part with lighter tinge.

Clean coarse sand, 4 m depth, West Sweden.

Carinina coei Hylbom ... FIG. 5.1I
[HYLBOM 1957, 543; BRUNBERG 1964: 79]
Length about 10 mm, width 1–2 mm. Otherwise like *C. arenaria*.

Mud, depths 20–30 m. Sweden, Denmark.

Hylbom (1957) gives a key to six North Sea and Baltic species of *Carinina*, which need sectioning for their identification.

Tubulanus albocapitatus Wijnhoff ... FIG. 5.1J
Length about 1.5 cm, width 0.5 mm. Head small and white, followed by belt of dark brownish red. Body yellowish, but reddish brown dorsally, with white lines mid-dorsally and laterally, and forming 11 transverse rings. Not well-described.

Muddy sand or gravel at 50–60 m depth. Plymouth.

Tubulanus annulatus (Montagu) ... FIG. 5.1K
Length up to 75 cm or more, width 3–4 mm. Brown or reddish with about 50 white rings and three longitudinal lines (no mid-ventral line). Head broad and rounded, same colour as body.

Occasionally intertidal under rocks or in sand or mud at LW, more commonly sublittoral to depths of 40 m or more. With a wide geographic range in northern hemisphere, from Pacific coast of North America, North Sea, and Mediterranean coasts of Europe.

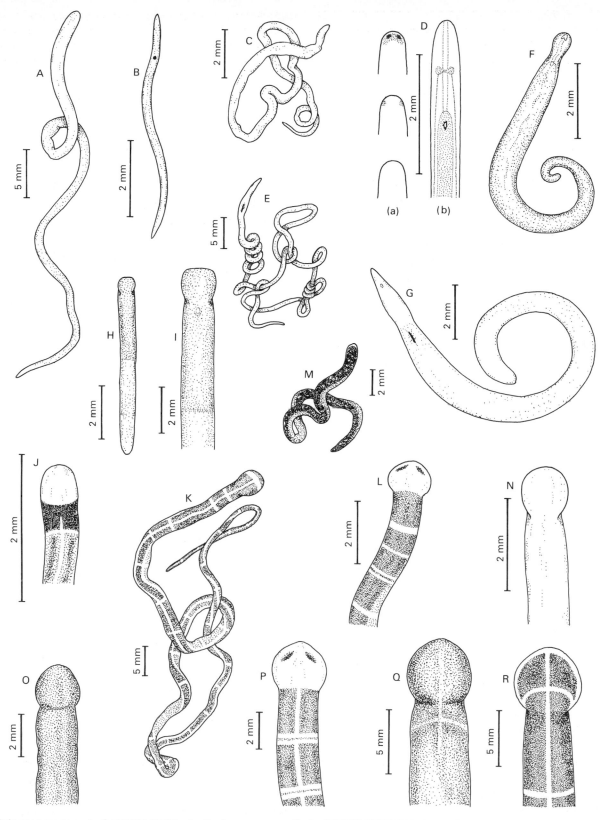

Fig. 5.1 Palaeonemertea. 1, CARINOMIDAE: A. *Carinoma armandi*. 2, CEPHALOTHRICIDAE: B. *Cephalothrix arenaria*, C. *C. linearis*, D. *C. rufifrons*, E. *Procephalothrix filiformis*. 3. HUBRECHTIDAE: F, *Hubrechtella dubia*. 4, TUBULANIDAE: G. *Callinera buergeri*, H. *Carinina arenaria*, I. *C. coei*, J. *Tubulanus albocapitatus*, K. *T. annulatus*, L. *T. banyulensis*, M. *T. inexpectatus*, N. *T. linearis*, O. *T. miniatus*, P. *T. nothus*, Q. *T. polymorphus*, R. *T. superbus*.

Tubulanus banyulensis (Joubin)   FIG. 5.1L

Length 1–1.5 cm, width 1–1.5 mm. Head rounded with two black markings anteriorly. Body tapering, reddish or greenish, with ventral surface sharply contrasting pink or yellow. Up to 18 white rings, sometimes with indistinct mid-dorsal longitudinal stripe formed as a series of flecks. Not well described.

    Dredged from 4–16 m depth. West Ireland, Mediterranean.

Tubulanus inexpectatus (Hubrecht)   FIG. 5.1M

Length up to 3.5 cm, width 1 mm. Tip of head colourless, body red or red-brown, paler ventrally, with minute specks of white. Not well described.

    Clean gravel at 90 m depth. West Ireland, Capri.

Tubulanus linearis (McIntosh)   FIG. 5.1N

Length up to 15 cm, width 0.5–1 mm. Body translucent white, often tinged orange or yellow-brown posteriorly.

    Sand at LW and sublittorally. Britain, Mediterranean.

Tubulanus miniatus (Bürger)   FIG. 5.1O

Length 3–4.5 cm, width 2 mm. Body orange-red. Inadequately described.

    Dredged from 40–70 m depth. Naples, Plymouth.

Tubulanus nothus (Bürger)   FIG. 5.1P

Length up to 10 cm, width 2.5 mm. Resembles *T. annulatus* but with the head white and bearing two curved black patches anteriorly, and sometimes with an inconspicuous mid-ventral line.

    Dredged. Naples, Plymouth.

Tubulanus polymorphus Renier   FIG. 5.1Q

Length up to 50 cm or more, width 5 mm. Head rounded, much wider than body. Body uniformly reddish or orange-brown. In alcohol or formalin loses colour except for a dark band in the region of the foregut and nephridia. There is a lateral sensory organ on each side, near the posterior margin of the band. In this region too there is a dorsal muscle-cross between the outer and inner circular muscle layers of the body wall, but no ventral muscle-cross.

    Sand and gravel down to 50 m depth or more. Britain, Scandinavia, Mediterranean, and westwards to Pacific coast of North America.

Tubulanus superbus (Kölliker)   FIG. 5.1R

Length up to 75 cm or more, width 5 mm. Similar to *T. annulatus* but with up to 200 white rings and a distinct mid-ventral white line in addition to the other three longitudinal stripes.

    Sand or gravel down to 80 m or more depth, occasionally intertidal. Sweden, Britain, Mediterranean.

Tubulanus theeli (Bergendal)

[HYLBOM 1957: 549; BRUNBERG 1964: 82]

Length 3 cm or more, width 1–1.5 mm. Reddish brown and like *T. polymorphus*, but with head usually not broader than body

and with both dorsal and ventral muscle-crosses in the foregut region.

    Sand or gravel, 20–35 m depth. West Sweden, Denmark.

Order **Heteronemertea**

The classification of heteronemertean families follows that proposed by Gibson (1985).

5 CEREBRATULIDAE

Proboscis when everted has in its wall an arrangement of muscle layers like that of the body wall (i.e. a middle layer of circular muscles between outer and inner layers of longitudinal fibres). Most have body somewhat flattened, with lateral edges often sharp and fin-like. Some swim readily, with undulations in the sagittal plane. *Cerebratulus* has a horizontal slit along each side of the head, ending posteriorly in the aperture of a cerebral organ (figured for *C. marginatus*).

---

1. With a longitudinal groove on each side of head and a caudal cirrus posteriorly   **2**

   Without longitudinal cephalic grooves or a caudal cirrus   ***Oxypolia beaumontiana***

2. Posterior end wider than anterior, not tapering at its rear   ***Cerebratulus fuscus***

   Posterior end narrower than anterior, body tapering gradually hindwards   **3**

3. Mottled with dark and pale markings, especially near anterio-dorsal margins   ***Cerebratulus pantherinus***

   Not mottled   **4**

4. Greyish brown, greyish green, slate-blue, or brown, with whitish lateral margins   ***Cerebratulus marginatus***

   Pink or yellowish   **5**

5. Head yellowish, narrower than trunk   ***Cerebratulus roseus***

   Head white-tipped, swollen   ***Cerebratulus alleni***

Cerebratulus alleni Wijnhoff

[GIBSON 1982a: 75]

Poorly described, without measurements recorded. Head swollen with white tip, body otherwise pink.

    Sand at LW, Plymouth.

Cerebratulus fuscus (McIntosh)   FIG. 5.2A

Length up to 15 cm, width 2–5 mm. Yellowish, pinkish, or greyish brown. Tapers anteriorly to a bluntly pointed head, with four to 13 eyes on each side. Caudal cirrus originates from a broad, almost square posterior end. Readily autotomizes posteriorly. Swims readily. Sketch of head shows reddish cerebral ganglia by transparency.

    Sand or shelly gravel at LW and to 50 m or more depth; as deep as 1590 m off Portugal. Fairly common, Alaska, Florida, Greenland, Britain, Mediterranean, South Africa.

Cerebratulus marginatus Renier   FIG. 5.2B
Length up to 100 cm, width to 25 mm or more, tapering towards
both ends. Often recorded in the literature as eyeless, for eyes
are small and inconspicuous. Otherwise similar to *C. fuscus*.
Swims actively. Head illustrated in side-view shows canal of
cerebral organ opening into cephalic slit.

Sand or mud sublittorally at depths of 20–150 m or more,
rarely at LW. Fairly common, widely distributed in northern
hemisphere from Japan eastwards to Europe.

Cerebratulus pantherinus Hubrecht   FIG. 5.2C
Length 4–7 cm or more. Not well described. Marked antero-
dorsally by a mottled pattern of brown, green, yellow, and white.

Sand at 50 m depth or deeper. Plymouth, Roscoff, Naples.

Cerebratulus roseus (Delle Chiaje)   FIG. 5.2D
Length up to 50 cm, width 5–6 mm. Caudal cirrus may be 2 cm
long. No eyes. Pink in foregut region, otherwise yellowish, with
colourless lateral margins. Not well described.

In limestone burrows and sand, LW to 30 m depth. Plymouth,
Mediterranean.

Oxypolia beaumontiana Punnett   FIG. 5.2E
Length about 12 cm, width 5 mm. Head flat and pointed,
bounded by a transverse furrow in front of mouth. Body white
anteriorly, tinged with brown or red posteriorly.

Intertidally and to 50 m depth, on soft rocks well-covered by
colonial invertebrates. Plymouth.

6 LINEIDAE

Proboscis with only two muscle layers; in everted position these
are outer circular and inner longitudinal muscles. All members
of this family have a horizontal slit along each side of head, as
in *Cerebratulus*.

1. With a caudal cirrus   2
   Without a caudal cirrus   7

2. Body up to 20 cm long, bright red, with head tinged
   yellow near tip. Lateral sensory organs present.
   Rhynchocoel has lateral pouches in foregut region
                                          Micrella rufa
   Mostly smaller, not red tipped with yellow anteriorly.
   Without lateral organs or lateral pouches to rhyn-
   chocoel (Genus *Micrura*)   3

3. Reddish or brownish with transverse white bands
                                       Micrura fasciolata
   Without transverse white bands   4

4. Body milky white   ***Micrura lactea***
   Body pigmented   5

5. Head with two lateral rows of eyes, five to eight in
   each   ***Micrura scotica***
   Head mostly white or white-tipped, without eyes   6

6. Bright red dorsally, white or pink ventrally. Head
   bears a reddish patch anteriorly   ***Micrura aurantiaca***
   Dark purplish-brown dorsally, somewhat paler ventrally. Otherwise white head bears a transverse band
   of yellow   ***Micrura purpurea***

7. Body thick, wrinkled, more or less cylindrical,
   speckled with brown or green   ***Euborlasia elizabethae***
   Body thin, smooth, threadlike or ribbonlike, not
   speckled   8

8. With two pale stripes dorsally, extending the length
   of the body   ***Lineus bilineatus***
   Without conspicuous longitudinal stripes   9

9. Body mostly white or pale coloured   10
   Body darkly pigmented   11

10. Head sharply pointed with deep cephalic slits.
    Without eyes   ***Lineus acutifrons***
    Head bluntly rounded with shallow cephalic slits.
    With eyes   ***Lineus lacteus***

11. Body dark brown, black, or green   12
    Body reddish or mid-brown   13

12. Black or dark brown, except for younger specimens
    usually over a metre long and may reach 20–25 m or
    more   ***Lineus longissimus***
    Green to greenish black, less than 10 cm long
                                          Lineus viridis

13. If disturbed contracts without coiling   ***Lineus ruber***
    If disturbed contracts into tight spiral coils
                                       Lineus sanguineus

Euborlasia elizabethae (McIntosh)   FIG. 5.2F
Length up to 30 cm, width 5–6 mm. Body rounded, but becomes
flattened posteriorly when contracted. Head tapering, bluntly
pointed, white or pale yellow, bearing on each side a short
horizontal cephalic slit, which continues internally as a canal.
Body brown, speckled with paler shades and regularly marked
with pale transverse belts.

Sand or mud, LW to 50 m depth. Herm (Channel Islands),
Mediterranean.

Lineus acutifrons Southern   FIG. 5.2G
Length (estimated) up to 15–17 cm, width 5–7 mm, depending
upon degree of contraction. White anteriorly, gradually becom-

ing pink, red, or brown posteriorly, or red in front and pink behind. Head acutely pointed, without eyes. Inadequately described.

Sand near LW, western Ireland

Lineus bilineatus (Renier)   FIG. 5.2H
Length up to about 70 cm, width 6 mm. Body reddish brown, purplish, or chocolate, paler in juveniles, marked with two white or yellowish longitudinal dorsal stripes adjoining the mid-dorsal line. On the head these diverge, outlining an elongate triangular shape. No eyes.

Lower middle shore to sublittoral. Fairly common on gravel, sand, mud, amongst coralline algae, under stones, or between mussels and oysters. Scandinavia, Britain, North America, South Africa.

Lineus lacteus (Rathke)   FIG. 5.2I
Length to 60 cm, width 1–2 mm. Head bears six to 15 eyes in a dorso-lateral row on each side. Body pink anteriorly, fading to white or pale yellow posteriorly. Mouth unusually far behind cerebral ganglia and not indicated in illustration, which shows cerebral organs behind ganglia, with canals opening into lateral slits, and rhynchodaeum running to end of snout.

Low water and sublittoral on gravel, sand, or stones. Britain, Mediterranean, Black Sea.

Lineus longissimus (Gunnerus)   FIG. 5.2J
Length commonly 5–15 m, occasionally up to 30 m or more, width about 5 mm. Head bears ten to 20 eyes in a row on each side, but these are usually obscured by the dark pigmentation of the body. Colour olive-brown to black, often with an iridescent sheen.

Fairly common under rocks or on mud, sand, or shell sediments; LW and sublittorally. Iceland and the Atlantic, North Sea, and Baltic coasts of Europe.

Lineus ruber (Müller)   FIG. 5.2K
Length up to about 8 cm, rarely more, width 2–3 mm. Head with two to eight eyes in an irregular row on each side. Body reddish brown, paler ventrally. When irritated contracts by becoming shorter and broader without coiling. Larvae 10–15 per egg string, weakly photopositive for only a short time after emergence.

Very common intertidally on muddy sand under stones, but also amongst barnacles and mussels, on rock pool algae, in laminarian holdfasts, etc. Extends sublittorally and into brackish water. Circumpolar in northern hemisphere.

Lineus sanguineus (Rathke)   FIG. 5.2L
Length up to 20 cm, width 2–3 mm. Very similar to *L. ruber* but with four to six eyes on each side, arranged further back and more regularly, and when irritated contracts into tight spiral coils.

Intertidal under rocks embedded in black mud. Scandinavia, western Europe, Britain.

Lineus viridis (Müller)   FIG. 5.2M
Like *L. ruber* but dark olive-green to greenish black, or occasionally pale green and sometimes lighter ventrally. Larvae small, 400–500 per egg string, strongly photopositive for two to three weeks after emergence.

Locally abundant on mud below midshore boulders. Britain, Mediterranean, and widespread in the northern hemisphere.

Micrella rufa Punnett
[GIBSON 1982*a*: 98]
Length up to 20 cm, width 2–3 mm. Head pointed, with shallow cephalic slits but no eyes. Body uniformly bright red, shading into a yellowish tinge near tip of head.

Mud at LW, near Plymouth.

Micrura aurantiaca (Grube)   FIG. 5.2N
Length up to 8 cm, width 1.5–2 mm. Head white, bluntly tapered, without eyes, usually with an antero-dorsal spot of red, violet, or brown. Body rounded and red dorsally, flattened and white or pink ventrally. Caudal cirrus small and translucent, often indistinct.

Beneath stones in rock pools and sublittorally from coralline grounds. Plymouth, Herm, Mediterranean.

Micrura fasciolata Ehrenberg   FIG. 5.2O
Length 10–15 cm, width 1–4 mm. Usually reddish brown, with white transverse bars, sometimes yellowish, greenish brown, or purple, with the white bars indistinct or lozenge-shaped. Head white, or coloured but white-tipped, with three to 12 eyes in a row on each side.

Sand, gravel, mud, rocks, with *Pomatoceros* tubes, or in laminarian holdfasts, LW to 80 m depth. Scandinavia, Britain, Mediterranean.

Micrura lactea (Hubrecht)   FIG. 5.2P
Length up to 9 cm, width 1–1.5 mm. Eyes absent. Milky-white overall, sometimes tinged pink, yellow, or brown.

Dredged from depths of about 30 m. Port Erin, Plymouth, Mediterranean.

Micrura purpurea (Dalyell)   FIG. 5.2Q
Length up to 20 cm, width 2–3 mm. Head with transverse band of yellow. Snout whitish or translucent. Eyes absent. Body dark purplish brown, often appearing iridescent, similar but sometimes paler ventrally.

Sand, gravel, mud, or rocks, LW to 40 m depth. Scandinavia, Britain, Mediterranean.

Micrura scotica Stephenson
[GIBSON 1982*a*: 107]
Length 6.5 cm, width 2.5 mm. Head tapering, red-tipped, with a row of five to eight eyes on each side. Anterior body light brown, tinged purple. Posteriorly only the gut and its caeca are similarly pigmented, the body otherwise appearing pale, especially at margins. Inadequately described.

Dredged from about 30 m depth, Firth of Clyde.

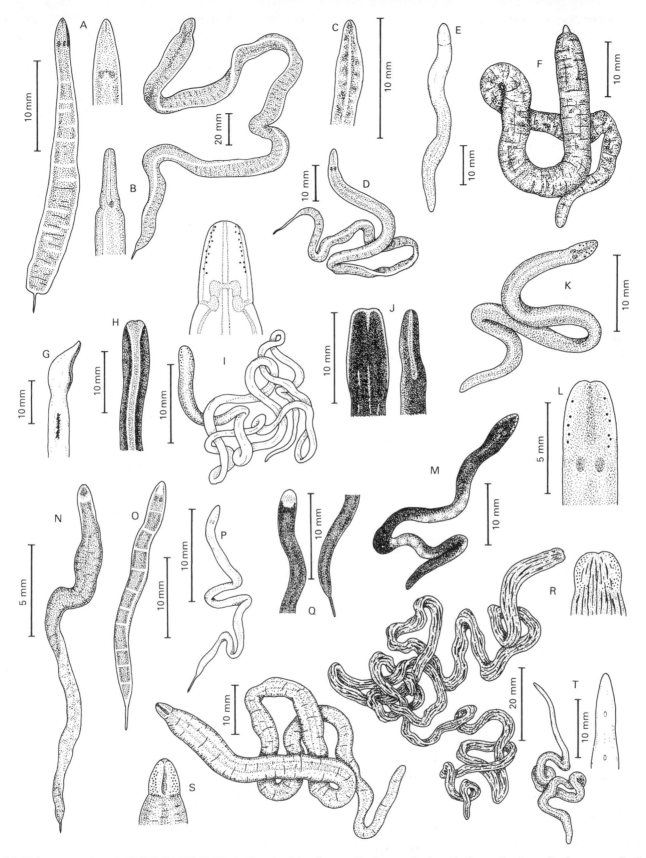

Fig. 5.2 Heteronemertea. 5, CEREBRATULIDAE: A. *Cerebratulus fuscus*, B. *C. marginatus*, C. *C. pantherinus*, D. *C. roseus*, E. *Oxypolia beaumontiana*. 6, LINEIDAE: F. *Euborlasia elizabethae*, G. *Lineus acutifrons*, H. *L. bilineatus*, I. *L. lacteus*, J. *L. longissimus*, K. *L. ruber*, L. *L. sanguineus*, M. *L. viridis*, N. *Micrura aurantiaca*, O. *M. fasciolata*, P. *M. lactea*, Q. *M. purpurea*. 7, VALENCINIIDAE: R. *Baseodiscus delineatus*, S. *Poliopsis lacazei*, T. *Valencinia longirostris*.

7 VALENCINIIDAE

Proboscis with only two muscle layers, the outer of longitudinal and the inner of circular fibres when everted. Horizontal lateral cephalic grooves absent. N.B. The minute palaeonemertean *Callinera* may key out here, for its tapering head resembles *Valencinia* (see 4. TUBULANIDAE).

1.	With longitudinal stripes	***Baseodiscus delineatus***
	Without longitudinal stripes	**2**
2.	With a mid-dorsal and a mid-ventral cephalic furrow	***Poliopsis lacazei***
	Without cephalic furrows	***Valencinia longirostris***

Baseodiscus delineatus (Delle Chiaje)   FIG. 5.2R

Length up to 100 cm or more, width 2–4 mm. Head slightly bilobed, with numerous eyespots. Body light brown marked with interrupted reddish-brown longitudinal stripes which are occasionally fused, five to 12 stripes dorsally, fewer and paler ventrally.

Sublittoral on shells or gravel with sand or mud, Plymouth; worldwide in tropical and subtropical latitudes.

Poliopsis lacazei Joubin   FIG. 5.2S

Length up to 50 cm, width 5–8 mm. Head with about 40 small eyes on each side of the mid-dorsal furrow. Body bulky, cylindrical, wrinkled when contracted, pink to greyish red anteriorly, yellowish posteriorly.

Uncommon but widespread. Mostly dredged from 40–50 m depth on sand or shelly substrata (Plymouth, Calais, Mediterranean, Mauritius), rarely intertidal (Chile).

Valencinia longirostris Quatrefages   FIG. 5.2T

Length up to 15 cm, width 2–3 mm. Proboscis pore (see Figure) about halfway between mouth and tip of head, which is slender, whitish, without eyes or grooves. Body thickest posteriorly, mostly pink, yellowish grey, or brown.

In sand or among roots of sea-grasses, 1–10 m depth. Jersey, Mediterranean.

Class Enopla

Order Hoplonemertea

Suborder Monostilifera

8 AMPHIPORIDAE

Mostly plump species with many eyes and two pairs of cephalic grooves. Colours usually drab, variable, and without distinctive patterns. Rhynchocoel extends almost whole length of body and has wall of circular and longitudinal muscles forming separate layers.

1.	Head bears mid-dorsal longitudinal ridge	
		Amphiporus hastatus
	Head without longitudinal ridge	**2**
2.	Eyes form four longitudinal rows	***Amphiporus allucens***
	Eyes not arranged in four longitudinal rows	**3**
3.	Less than six eyes	**4**
	More than six eyes, usually more than 20	**5**
4.	Only two large eyes near tip of head. Body length less than 20 × width	***Amphiporus bioculatus***
	With two anterior eyes, plus a few more further back. Body length more than 30 × width	***Amphiporus elongatus***
5.	Eyes form separate anterior and posterior groups on each side of head. Posterior cephalic furrows meet dorsally to form backwards pointing V, which is located behind the cerebral ganglia	***Amphiporus lactifloreus***
	Eyes form single continuous row on each side. Posterior cephalic furrows form V located above cerebral ganglia	***Amphiporus dissimulans***

Amphiporus allucens Bürger   FIG. 5.3A

Length 4–4.5 cm, width 2.5–3 mm. Pale yellow anteriorly with pink ganglia. Most of body red. Eyes form double row on each side. Only one pair of transverse cephalic grooves, which meet mid-ventrally. Inadequately described.

Dredged from 20–30 m depth. Plymouth, Naples.

Amphiporus bioculatus McIntosh   FIG. 5.3B

Length 8–10 cm, width 5–6 mm. One pair of large eyes near tip of head. Originally described as orange or brownish, paler ventrally, head reddish. Other reports of widely differing colour forms indicate that the species needs much more investigation.

Sand or *Laminaria* holdfasts, LW to 30 m depth. Britain, Roscoff, possibly eastern North America.

Amphiporus dissimulans (Riches)   FIG. 5.3C

Length 5–7.5 cm, width 1–2 mm. Head oval with many eyes around dorsolateral margins. Posterior furrows meet dorsally over cerebral ganglia, the latter visibly pink by transparency. Body pink, orange, yellowish, or brownish, often darker posteriorly.

Shells, mud, sand, or gravel, LW to 40 m depth. Britain, Scandinavia.

Amphiporus elongatus Stephenson   FIG. 5.3D

Length 7.5 cm, width less than 1 mm, tapering to bluntly pointed head. Two eyes anteriorly, three others between the cephalic furrows. Body yellow, with whitish lateral margins. Poorly described.

Sand, Firth of Clyde.

Amphiporus hastatus McIntosh   FIG. 5.3E

Length 9–10 cm, width 3–20 mm. Head with numerous eyes, a mid-dorsal pale longitudinal ridge and only one pair of cephalic grooves meeting dorsally and ventrally as forward pointing Vs, anterior to cerebral ganglia. Colour pinkish, yellowish, reddish, or brownish, the ventral surface and head being paler.

Sand, mid-tide to 35 m depth. Atlantic North America, Greenland, Britain, Mediterranean, Scandinavia.

Amphiporus lactifloreus (Johnston)   FIG. 5.3F

Length up to 10 cm, usually less, width about 2 mm. Head broad but bluntly pointed, with many eyes in two groups on each side. Posterior cephalic furrows meet mid-dorsally as backward pointing V behind cerebral ganglia. Colour variable depending upon reproductive state and gut contents; typically pinkish with paler head, tail, and lateral margins, posteriorly green, brown, grey, or black.

Locally abundant in sand or gravel, from just below *Pelvetia* zone to 250 m or more depth. Britain, North Atlantic, Mediterranean.

9 CARCINONEMERTIDAE

On gills or egg masses of crabs. With two eyes and no cephalic furrows. Rhynchocoel wall lacks muscles and is remarkably short, extending only a little way behind the cerebral ganglia. Proboscis reduced, weak, without reserve stylets.

Carcinonemertes carcinophila (Kölliker)   FIG. 5.3G

Juveniles on gills 1.5 cm long, maturing on eggs 2–7 cm long. Body yellowish, orange, or reddish.

On *Carcinus*, *Liocarcinus*, Xanthidae, and Galatheidae. Britain, north Atlantic.

10 CRATENEMERTIDAE

Generally like amphiporids, but with wall of rhynchocoel composed of single layer of interwoven longitudinal and circular muscle fibres. N.B. *Amphiporus hastatus* may also key out here because of its mid-dorsal longitudinal cephalic ridge (see 8. AMPHIPORIDAE).

Nipponnemertes pulcher (Johnston)   FIG. 5.3H

Length up to 9 cm, width 1–5 mm. Head distinct, with many eyes and a mid-dorsal longitudinal ridge. Two pairs of transverse furrows, the anterior fused ventrally and possessing many short, forwardly directed secondary ridges; the posterior furrows fuse dorsally to form a backward pointing V. Brown or reddish, especially dorsally.

Sublittorally on sand, gravel, or shells down to 569 m depth, occasionally beneath stones at extreme LW. Greenland, Britain, Roscoff, Chile, Antarctica.

11 EMPLECTONEMATIDAE

Elongate forms, with rhynchocoel restricted to anterior half of body.

1. Head narrow, with two pairs of eyes and two pairs of cephalic furrows. Length up to 4 cm   **Nemertopsis flavida**

   Head broader than body, with numerous small eyes and indistinct transverse cephalic furrows. Length often 20–40 cm (Genus *Emplectonema*)   **2**

2. Up to 20 cm long, with numerous sickle-shaped spicules scattered in the skin. Reddish, paler posteriorly   **Emplectonema echinoderma**

   Up to 50 cm long or more, without spicules. Densely pigmented dorsally, much paler ventrally   **3**

3. Speckled dorsally, with short longitudinal streaks of brown. Central stylet straight   **Emplectonema neesii**

   Greyish-green or blue-green dorsally. Central stylet curved   **Emplectonema gracile**

Emplectonema echinoderma (Marion)   FIG. 5.3I

Length up to 20 cm, width 1–2.5 mm. Head a rounded diamond-shape, with about 20 small eyes on each side. Body yellowish or orange-red, paler posteriorly, sometimes with dorsal longitudinal streaks of pigment on head. Skin contains many transparent refractive spicules (a in Figure). Sketch (b) on right, which has neck widened by compression, indicates how rhynchocoel and mouth open together, ventral to cerebral ganglia and just behind cerebral organs.

Lower shore and shallow water in sand, with stones or *Zostera*. Madeira, Mediterranean, uncommon in Britain.

Emplectonema gracile (Johnston)   FIG. 5.3J

Up to 50 cm long, 3–4 mm wide. Head rounded and rather flattened, with 20–30 eyes on each side. Usually greenish dorsally, pale ventrally. Produces much mucus when irritated. Central stylet curved, with a long slender basis.

On shore amongst boulders, on silt, gravel or sand, in crevices, laminarian holdfasts, or *Mytilus* beds. Also dredged to 100 m depth. Britain, North America, Chile, northern Europe, Mediterranean, Russia, Japan.

Emplectonema neesii (Örsted)   FIG. 5.3K

Length up to 50 cm, occasionally 1 m or more, width 5–6 mm. Head rounded with many eyes. Body flattened but fairly bulky, pale yellowish-brown finely streaked with darker bown dorsally, much paler ventrally. Sometimes more uniformly reddish. Central stylet straight, basis short.

On the shore in crevices, under boulders, amongst *Mytilus*, and on sand, silt, gravel or shingle, also dredged to 30 m or more depth. Iceland, Britain, Mediterranean.

Nemertopsis flavida (McIntosh)   FIG. 5.3L

About 4 cm long and 0.5 mm wide, tapering towards both ends. Head somewhat like *Amphiporus elongatus*, with four eyes and the posterior pair of cephalic furrows forming a V dorsally.

White, yellowish pink, or reddish brown, with pale margins and translucent snout.

Intertidal, under stones and in rock pools, in holdfasts, and dredged to 300 m depth. Denmark to Mediterranean, possibly also from South Africa.

12 PROSORHOCHMIDAE

Ill-defined assemblage of generally small species, including the terrestrial *Argonemertes dendyi* which has the circular and longitudinal muscles of its rhynchocoel wall interwoven, as in the Cratenemertidae. In *Oerstedia* and *Prosorhochmus* the rhynchocoel muscles form separate layers. Cephalic grooves usually shallow or indistinguishable in marine forms.

---

1. Body somewhat flattened, pale without patterns of pigment, tapering posteriorly, with head as wide as or wider than body. Ovoviviparous, juveniles emerging through anus. **Prosorhochmus claparedii**

   Body cylindrical, bearing patterns of pigment, tapering towards both ends. Not ovoviviparous.
   Oerstedia dorsalis

Oerstedia dorsalis (Abildgaard) FIG. 5.3M
Length usually 1–1.5 cm, occasionally 3 cm, width 1–2 mm. Head rounded but narrow, not demarcated from body. Eyes four, in a square. Body cylindrical, marbled, or transversely banded with shades of brown, often speckled with white or yellow, sometimes with a pale mid-dorsal stripe. Usually paler ventrally. Colour forms *O. immutabilis* and *O. nigra* may be distinct species.

Common, often abundant amongst rock-pool algae or dredged from mud, gravel, sand, stones, or shelly sediments, to 80 m or more depth. Widespread in northern hemisphere from Pacific North America eastwards to Europe.

Prosorhochmus claparedii (Keferstein) FIG. 5.3N
Length up to 3.5–4 cm. Head may appear bilobed, with a terminal notch. Eyes four, in a transversely elongated rectangle, anterior pair larger than the others. Body pale yellow or orange. Rhynchocoel and brooded young may be seen through body wall.

Under stones and in rock crevices, upper and lower shore and sublittorally. Britain, France, Spain, Mediterranean, Adriatic.

13 TETRASTEMMATIDAE

Small slender nemerteans, which include the freshwater species of *Prostoma*. Rhynchocoel extends throughout body, its walls having two separate muscle layers.

---

1. Dark red stripe extends mid-dorsally throughout body
   Tetrastemma herouardi

   No dark mid-dorsal longitudinal stripe 2

2. Head with mid-dorsal patch of pigment 3
   Head without mid-dorsal patch of pigment 6

3. Cephalic pigment patch subquadrangular, covering some eyes 4
   Cephalic pigment patch crescentic, between eyes 5

4. Patch reddish, covering only anterior half of area between eyes **Tetrastemma longissimum**
   Patch black or dark brown, covering most of area between eyes **Tetrastemma melanocephalum**

5. Patch a simple crescent, its ends pointing anteriorly. Body slender, 1.5 cm long and 1 mm wide, greenish
   Tetrastemma coronatum
   Crescent usually bears a third median point. Body bulky, 4 cm long and 2 mm wide, brownish
   Tetrastemma peltatum

6. With two longitudinal brown streaks joining anterior and posterior eyes on each side of head
   Tetrastemma vermiculus
   Without longitudinal streaks joining eyes 7

7. With a transverse band of pigment just behind head
   Tetrastemma robertianae
   Without such a transverse band of pigment 8

8. Head diamond-shaped and wider than most of body 9
   Head not diamond-shaped, not wider than body 10

9. Anterior eyes much bigger than others
   Tetrastemma ambiguum
   Eyes all of similar size
   Tetrastemma cephalophorum

10. Body stout, cylindrical, broadest near posterior end
    Tetrastemma beaumonti
    Body somewhat flattened, of uniform width or tapering posteriorly 11

11. Shining whitish gland cells present between anterior eyes **Tetrastemma helvolum**
    Without such a conspicuous mass of gland cells 12

12. Proboscis with four accessory stylet pouches visible when compressed in transmitted light
    Tetrastemma quatrefagesi
    Only two accessory stylet pouches 13

13. Eyes distinct, moderately large, body tapering posteriorly **Tetrastemma candidum**
    Eyes minute, body not tapering posteriorly
    Tetrastemma flavidum

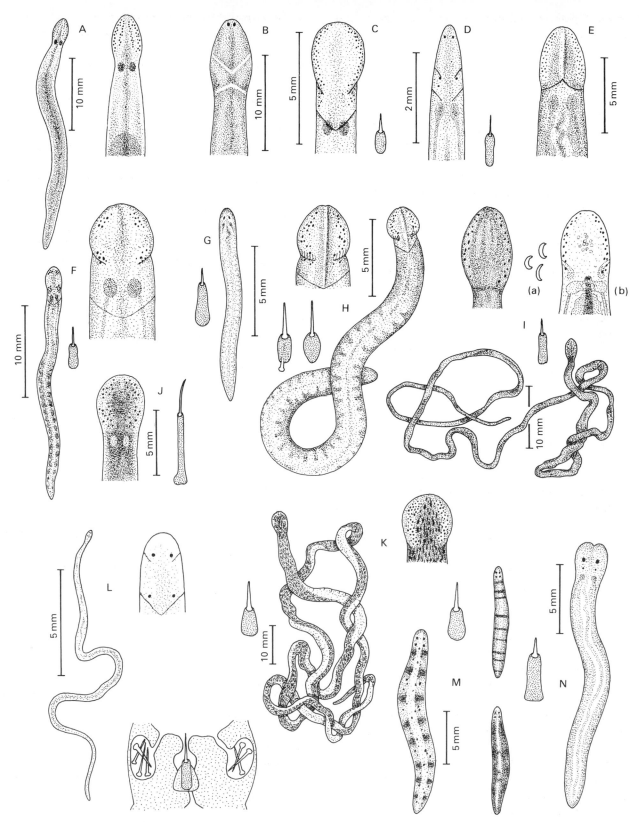

Fig. 5.3 Hoplonemertea. 8, AMPHIPORIDAE: A. *Amphiporus allucens*, B. *A. bioculatus*, C. *A. dissimulans*, D. *A. elongatus*, E. *A. hastatus*, F. *A. lactifloreus*. 9. CARCINONEMERTIDAE: G. *Carcinonemertes carcinophila*. 10. CRATENEMERTIDAE: H. *Nipponnemertes pulcher*. 11, EMPLECTONEMATIDAE: I. *Emplectonema echinoderma*, J. *E. gracile*, K. *E. neesii*, L. *Nermertopsis flavida*. 12, PROSORHOCHIMIDAE: M. *Oerstedia dorsalis*, N. *Prosorhochmus claparedii*.

Tetrastemma ambiguum Riches   FIG. 5.4A
Length 1–1.5 cm. Pale yellow, usually tinged reddish brown dorsally.

Sublittoral to 60 m depth, on sand, mud, limestone fragments, and stones. Plymouth.

Tetrastemma beaumonti (Southern)   FIG. 5.4B
Length 0.3–0.6 cm. Remarkably stout posteriorly, tapering towards head. Anterior eyes usually larger than others. Whitish, occasionally tinged pink.

Dredged from 3–20 m depth on gravel and sand. Atlantic coast of Ireland, possibly Isle of Man.

Tetrastemma candidum (Müller)   FIG. 5.4C
Length 1–3cm, width 1 mm. Four eyes equally distinct. Lacks clearly diagnostic characters. Colours seem extremely variable (yellowish, orange, reddish, greenish, whitish), perhaps including unrecognized species. Apart from being more restless and actively moving, easily confused with *T. flavidum*.

Mid-shore to depths of 55 m or more; from rock pool algae, in *Ascophyllum* bladders, under rocks on shells or gravel, with colonial invertebrates. Apparently circumpolar in northern hemisphere.

Tetrastemma cephalophorum Bürger   FIG. 5.4D
Length 1.5 cm, width 1.5–2 mm. Head diamond-shaped, with four large eyes. Reddish brown dorsally, pale yellowish laterally and ventrally.

Shell gravel or stones at 10–15 m depth. Britain, Mediterranean.

Tetrastemma coronatum (Quatrefages)   FIG. 5.4E
Length up to 1.5 cm, width 0.5–1 mm. Head blunt, with shallow cephalic furrows posteriorly and a dark crescent between eyes. Otherwise pale, usually greenish.

With intertidal algae, tubicolous polychaetes, stones and sandy detritus to 40 m depth. Scandinavia, Britain, Mediterranean, Black Sea.

Tetrastemma flavidum Ehrenberg   FIG. 5.4F
Length up to 1.5 cm, width 0.5–0.75 mm. Body rather flattened, head rounded or slightly tapered with four small eyes. Typically bright pink, sometimes tinged yellowish or reddish, or translucent. May be confused with *T. candidum*.

LW to depths of 100 m in mud, sand, gravel, or amongst laminarian holdfasts. Britain, Scandinavia, Mediterranean, Red Sea (N.B. British records of this species are confused).

Tetrastemma helvolum Bürger   FIG. 5.4G
Length up to 2 cm, width less than 1 mm. Like *T. candidum* but generally longer and more slender. Light honey-yellow, head paler.

Dredged 4–80 m depth from coralline, muddy, shelly, or sandy sediments, or amongst algae. Britain, Mediterranean.

Tetrastemma herouardi (Oxner)   FIG. 5.4H
Length up to 0.6 cm, width 0.75 mm. Pale transparent pink, with single mid-dorsal stripe of dark red.

With algae and sedentary invertebrates. Britain, Roscoff.

Tetrastemma longissimum Bürger   FIG. 5.4I
Length may exceed 2 cm, width 1 mm. Like *T. coronatum* but brownish yellow. Head generally distinct from body, almost colourless but with transverse band of red between the eyes.

With algae, shells, or sand; intertidal and sublittoral to 20 m depth. Britain, Mediterranean.

Tetrastemma melanocephalum (Johnston)   FIG. 5.4J
Length 3–6 cm, width 2–2.5 mm, with dark subquadrangular pigment patch on head. Body yellowish, sometimes reddish brown.

Common in various intertidal habitats, with rock pool algae, in crevices, on sand, and to 40 m depth. Scandinavia, Britain, Mediterranean, Madeira, Canary Islands, Black Sea.

Tetrastemma peltatum Bürger   FIG. 5.4K
Up to 4–5 cm long, 2 mm wide, with dark three-pronged crescent of pigment on head, and anterior eyes much larger than others. Body brownish, sometimes greenish posteriorly.

Plymouth, Adriatic, Mediterranean, Chile.

Tetrastemma quatrefagesi Bürger   FIG. 5.4L
Up to 0.6 cm long. Transparent yellowish, not clearly distinguishable from *T. flavidum*.

Tetrastemma robertianae McIntosh   FIG. 5.4M
Up to 3–3.5 cm long, 0.7–1 mm wide. Anterior eyes larger than others. Transverse brown band around body behind head, may be incomplete ventrally. From it, two dorsolateral brown stripes run backwards longitudinally.

Shallow sublittoral to 70 m depth on mud, shelly gravel, and stones. Britain, Scandinavia.

Tetrastemma vermiculus (Quatrefages)   FIG. 5.4N
Up to 2 cm long, 0.8 mm wide. Head oval, with two pairs of cephalic furrows. Body yellowish, pinkish, or pale orange. Brown longitudinal streak joins anterior and posterior eyes on each side of head.

Lower shore and to 40 m depth in rocky places. Scandinavia, Britain, Mediterranean, Madeira, Atlantic North America, Gulf of Mexico.

Suborder **Polystilifera**

14 DREPANOPHORIDAE

Cerebral sense organs each with two sensory canals and a glandular appendage. Mouth and proboscis pore adjacent but separate. Cephalic furrows subdivided into secondary slits (as in most benthic Polystilifera and some Amphiporidae and Cratenemertidae).

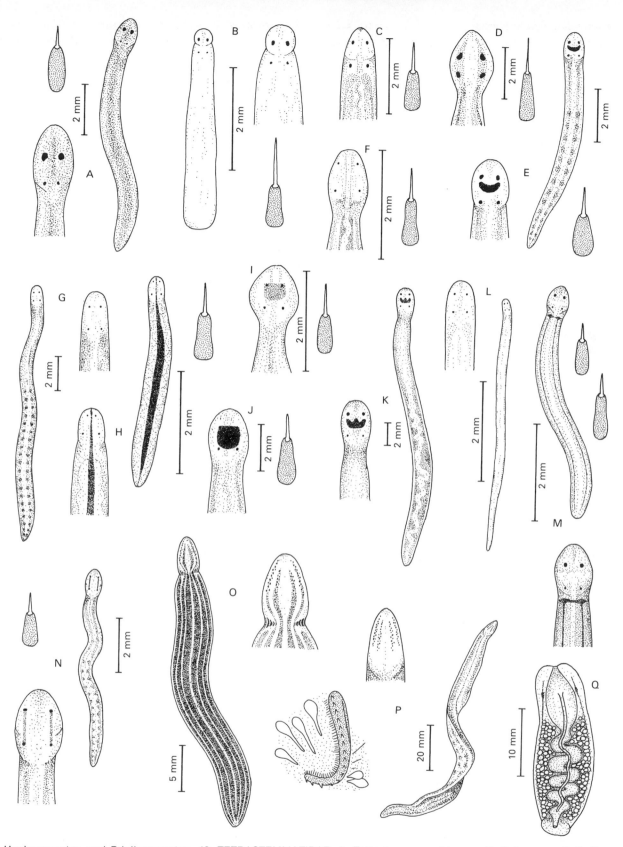

Fig. 5.4 Hoplonemertea and Bdellonemertea. 13, TETRASTEMMATIDAE: A. *Tetrastemma ambiguum*, B. *T. beaumonti*, C. *T. candidum*, D. *T. cephalophorum*, E. *T. coronatum*, F. *T. flavidum*, G. *T. helvolum*, H. *T. herouardi*, I. *T. longissimum*, J. *T. melanocephalum*, K. *T. peltatum*, L. *T. quatrefagesi*, M. *T. robertiana*, N. *T. vermiculus*. 14, DREPANOPHORIDAE: O. *Punnettia splendida*. 15, PARADREPANOPHORIDAE: P. *Paradrepanophorus crassus*. 16, MALACOBDELLIDAE: Q. *Malacobdella grossa*.

Punnettia splendida (Keferstein)   FIG. 5.4O

Up to 5 cm long and 5 mm wide. Body flattened, reddish brown, dorsally with five longitudinal whitish stripes and thin lateral margins which are also whitish. Head spatulate, demarcated by a transverse cephalic furrow on each side, each containing seven to eight secondary slits which are longitudinal (i.e. transverse to the furrow). Eyes about 70, in longitudinal rows. Swims actively when irritated.

Sublittorally to 40 m depth, with algae, gravel, or stones. Plymouth, Channel Islands.

15 PARADREPANOPHORIDAE

Cerebral sense organs each with one sensory canal and no glandular appendage. Otherwise similar to Drepanophoridae except that mouth and proboscis pore may share a common opening, whilst cephalic furrows may or may not include secondary slits. N.B. From arrangement of eyes *Amphiporus allucens* may also key out here (see 8. AMPHIPORIDAE).

Paradrepanophorus crassus (Quatrefages)   FIG. 5.4P

Up to 16 cm long and 9 mm wide. Body flattened but bulky, tapering to both ends. Brownish, paler ventrally. Head demarcated by white cephalic furrows with brown secondary slits. Mouth and proboscis adjoining but separate. Eyes in four longitudinal rows.

Under stones just below LW and to 5 m depth, between worm-tubes and rocks. Secretes a thin parchment tube, fixed to underside of boulders. Lough Ine (Ireland), Mediterranean.

Order **Bdellonemertea**

16 MALACOBDELLIDAE

Body broad, flattish and short, with a posterior ventral sucker. Rhynchocoel opens into foregut, which is barrel-shaped. Intestine sinuous. Proboscis lacks stylets. One genus, entocommensal in bivalves.

Malacobdella grossa (Müller)   FIG. 5.4Q

Up to 4 cm long and 15 mm wide. Rhynchocoel as long as body and straighter than gut. Immature specimens whitish, mature females with greenish grey ovaries, mature males with pinkish testes.

Particularly common in *Mya truncata* and *Zirfaea crispata*, but also occurs in many other host bivalve species. Usually only a single worm per host, typically on or between gill lamellae, exceptionally up to five individuals in a single host. Widely distributed on the coasts of Europe, Atlantic, and Pacific North America.

6 ANNELIDA

THE annelids or 'true' worms form a major animal group, typically of elongated cylindrical shape and mostly ranging in length from 10 mm to 150 mm (although some are microscopic and a few exceed 1 m); the body is characteristically made up of a series of ring-like segments, indicated externally by annular constrictions. The relatively simple gut normally passes down the body from an anterior subterminal mouth to a posterior terminal anus. The first segment (*prostomium*) (Fig. 6.1) is situated above and in front of the mouth, the second (buccal segment or *peristomium*) surrounds it and the last (*pygidium*) encircles the anus. The segments in between (which, in the growing worm, are added to the body just anterior to the pygidium) primitively more or less resemble each other, each containing a similar complement of organs. This may be expressed externally by a segmental series of similar pores or protruding structures, particularly those used in locomotion. Movement is normally achieved by the action of body-wall muscles on the fluid-filled coelomic (body) cavity, producing peristaltic waves of contraction or sigmoid rippling of the body. In the polychaetes, which are entirely aquatic and regarded as the basic annelid stock, a typical body segment carries on each side a *parapod* (Fig. 6.1) comprising various well-developed fleshy lobes and a large number of chitinous bristles (*chaetae*); in unhurried locomotion on a solid substratum, these may function like short legs and, in many, they also aid swimming as the body flexes more rapidly in a horizontal plane. In the oligochaetes, fleshy outgrowths are lacking and the chaetae are fewer; amongst aquatic species, they may still be numerous and quite long, although the more familiar earthworms have only few, short enough to be almost invisible. The leeches (Hirudinea) lack bristles; using their terminal suckers, they may move along a solid surface by 'looping'. When swimming, the dorso-ventrally flattened body reflects this action by flexing in a vertical plane.

Although the anterior end of oligochaetes and leeches carries sense-organs, its external appearance is smooth and uncomplicated. Most polychaetes have a head bearing a variety of appendages, often numerous and sometimes (in specialist sedentary species) forming a conspicuous fan- or brush-like structure which may be the only part of the body normally protruded from a tube or burrow constructed to shelter the rest of the animal. In these worms, the body tends to be divided into an anterior 'thoracic' region which is stouter and more complex than the posterior 'abdomen'. Apart from a region modified for reproductive purposes which may be permanent, present only during the breeding season or invisible from the exterior, the body segments of oligochaetes and leeches all appear essentially similar except in size.

The Myzostomaria are a problematical group of a few small, disklike parasites (or commensals) of echinoderms, atypical or degenerate in many features but generally thought to have derived from polychaetes. See Pettibone 1982, Dales 1963, Grassé 1959.

REFERENCES

Dales, R. P. (1963). *Annelids.* Hutchinson University Press, London

Grassé, P. P. (ed.) (1959) *Annélides. Traité de Zoologie,* 5(I). Masson et Cie, Paris.

Pettibone, M. H. (1982). Annelida. In *Synopsis and classification of living organisms,* Vol. 2 (ed. S. P. Parker), pp. 1–61. McGraw-Hill, New York.

A. Class **Polychaeta**

The largest group of annelid worms, all aquatic and almost entirely marine. They are mainly freeliving; some are commensal and very few are parasitic. The body form varies widely, reflecting a range of habit from pelagic, through crawling with occasional swimming, to active burrowing or tube-dwelling. There are a number of well-defined families but no widely recognized or consistent scheme of higher taxa. Traditionally, the polychaetes have been divided into the Errantia (free-moving, with a large number of similar segments and a head bearing relatively few well-differentiated short appendages, often with hard jaws) and the Sedentaria (burrow- or tube-dwelling, with a limited number of segments, the body often divided into two or more distinct regions, and a head sometimes lacking appendages but often with many similar elongated ones, not possessing jaws). However, many species do not correspond well with the definition of their group and some clearly fall between the two. More recently, several distinct schemes have been proposed uniting the families into various hierarchies of orders, suborders, and superfamilies. For ease of reference by a user unfamiliar with the niceties of polychaete taxonomy, families included here have been arranged individually in alphabetical order.

Of the segments forming the *head* (Fig. 6.1), the *prostomium* (which is normally seen as a flattened sphere projecting forwards above the mouth) has *antennae* (often one mid-dorsally and one or more pairs antero-laterally) which are essentially tactile and a pair of *palps* ventrally, preceding or flanking the mouth, which are chemosensory and used mainly in feeding. One or more pairs of *eyes*, often large and frequently having a lens, are mounted dorsally. Ciliated *nuchal organs* of various designs and functions may pass back dorsally from the rearward edge of the prostomium. The *peristomium* usually has incorporated with it a number of anterior body-segments, although this is not immediately obvious. Their appendages may have originated in several ways but they can be referred to, generally, as *tentacles*. These may be short or long, flexible (and perhaps contractile or retractable) or rigid although, quite often, they are similar to the antennae. Tentacles may be mobile and ciliated for food-gathering; amongst the more specialized tubeworms, they are stiff and feathery, forming a funnel-like *branchial crown* used to generate a current for respiration as well as suspension feeding. The anterior part of the gut very often can be everted through the mouth to form a *proboscis*. Its lining is frequently elaborated into fleshy or cuticular papillae, hard ridges, or chitinous teeth; in the more rapacious errant species there may be two or four dark, chitinous, opposable *jaws* opened and closed by strong muscles (and, in large nereids, capable of giving a nasty nip to the finger of an incautious collector!). The arrangement of teeth on the proboscis of nereids, or the pattern of the elaborate pharyngeal jaws of eunicids, is important in their identification. Some burrowers (e.g. glycerids) use a relatively enormous proboscis as a kedge-anchor to help draw them through the sand.

The *parapod* (Fig. 6.1) inserted on each side of a typical body-segment can be divided into dorsal and ventral parts (*rami*) known as the *notopod* (mnemonic: contains the word 'top') and *neuropod* (note that the nerve cord is ventral), respectively. The major part of each is usually a fleshy lobe containing a bundle of bristles (*chaetae*, often referred to as setae); hence, those in the dorsal bundle are called *notochaetae* and those in the ventral bundle, *neurochaetae*. The lobes are usually supported internally by strong chitinous rods, *acicula*, whose outer end sometimes protrudes like a short, stout bristle. Each lobe may be subdivided and more than one bundle of chaetae may be present; alternatively, one entire ramus (most often, the notopod) may be lacking. Each ramus, if present, typically has a *cirrus* associated with it. They are usually tactile, resembling a small antenna, although the dorsal one may be modified into a paddle-blade, a branching gill or a protective scale. In burrow- or tube-dwelling worms, the fleshy lobes and other appendages may be much reduced.

Chaetae occur in a variety of forms. They may be *simple* (all in one piece) or *jointed* (also called compound), usually with a short terminal part (often hooked) hinged to a longer shaft. The simplest in form are fine, hairlike *capillary* chaetae; other simple chaetae may be stout, distally serrated, or hooked. Often a straight shaft has a swelling, decorated with coarse teeth, from which the blade-like end region tapers away at an angle. In species which swim well, especially the sexual epitokes of various errant families, they may be flattened to resemble oars. Burrowing species often have stout hooked chaetae, or *crochets*, by which they can anchor themselves to the walls of the burrow. Tubeworms use, for this purpose, *uncini* which are small chitinous plates whose outer edge is serrated, mounted in a stacked row within the groove of a parapod modified in the form of parallel swollen lips: the arrangement is known as a *torus* and resembles a short, closed zip-fastener. The usual layout is for

notopods to have a bundle of normal bristles and the associated neuropods to have such a row of uncini or crochets. In the most specialized tubeworms, the arrangement in the 'abdomen' is the reverse of that in the 'thorax'. Pierre Fauvel (from whose encyclopaedic publications on the polychaetes of the French coast much of the information included in the species descriptions below has been taken) relied very heavily on features of the chaetae in devising his keys. However, as many details can be seen only under the higher magnifications of a compound microscope, they are mostly utilized here for the separation of otherwise similar species or to provide the final confirmation of an identification.

A *chaetiger* (chaetigerous segment) is one which bears chaetae and, usually, at least some other components of a parapod. The term is used here particularly when the precise location of a characteristic feature is needed (e.g. the special, stout tube-boring chaetae on the 5th chaetiger of *Polydora*). Because the number of segments incorporated with the peristomium is not readily apparent, it would only be confusing to refer to the *n*th segment. Similarly, where the number of readily visible segments is small and may be diagnostically important, the information is given in terms of chaetigers; where a worm may have several hundred segments, the number involved in the head makes little difference and reference is then made to the number of segments. Chaetae occur only infrequently on the peristomium and not on the pygidium which, however, often has a pair of *anal cirri*. In some groups, the anus is surrounded by papillae or lobes whose form and number may be important in identification. Almost invariably, it is necessary to have the head end of a broken specimen before a full identification can be made; in these, the posterior end is also necessary. When assessing the number of worms in a sample containing many broken specimens, it is usual to count only heads.

Details of the circumstances in which a polychaete was found—especially any apparent close association with another organism and the nature of a burrow or tube—may be helpful in confirming its identity. Whenever possible, an attempt should be made to identify the specimen whilst it is still alive, noting its coloration and characteristic movements. On some occasions, it may then be possible to release the animal unharmed. If it proves impossible to identify the worm alive (perhaps because dissection of some structure is necessary), or the intention is to preserve the collection for future reference, it is best where possible to relax the animals with a narcotizing agent first. This is particularly useful when it is desirable to have the proboscis everted. A good general-purpose reagent is 7.5% magnesium chloride in sea water; individual specimens can usually be relaxed by slowly adding 70% ethanol to their water. As soon as the worms fail to respond to touch, they should be fixed in 10% sea water formalin for at least 24 h. It is inadvisable to leave them in formalin indefinitely, because the vapour is unpleasant (perhaps even dangerous) for subsequent workers bent over the dishes. Its acidity also rapidly destroys calcareous structures. Wash the specimens with fresh water and transfer to 70% ethanol for storage. Note that this is not, by itself, an adequate initial fixative. Colours are rapidly lost in alcohol and, where

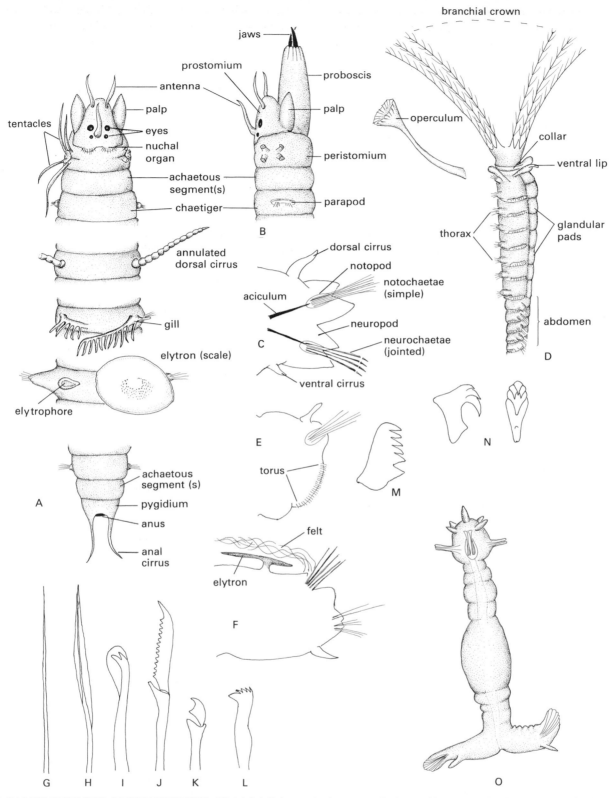

Fig. 6.1 (MAJOR FEATURES OF POLYCHAETES); *Histriobdella*) a. typical errant polychaete (dorsal view), with various modifications of the dorsal cirrus b. same, anterior end (lateral), showing everted proboscis c. parts of the basic parapod d. a sabellid fanworm (lateral); serpulid operculum e. half-section of tubeworm thorax, showing arrangement of simple chaetae (dorsal) and uncini in torus (ventral) f. half-section of *Aphrodita aculeata,* showing felt of notochaetae covering elytra g. simple capillary chaeta h. simple 'winged' (lance-like) chaeta i. hooded and hooked simple chaeta j. jointed chaeta with long, toothed blade k. jointed chaeta with short, hooked blade l. crochet m. uncinus with single row of teeth n. uncinus with complex arrangement of teeth—lateral and face-view o. *Histriobdella homari,* entire worm

they are particularly important, you might consider using 1–2%
aqueous propylene phenoxytol.

REFERENCES

Chambers, S. (1985). *Polychaetes from Scottish waters. 2. Aphroditidae, Sigalionidae and Polydontidae*. Royal Scottish Museum, Edinburgh.

Clark, R. B. (1960). *Fauna of the Clyde sea area: polychaetes*. Scottish Marine Biological Association, Millport.

Day, J. H. (1967). *A monograph of the Polychaeta of southern Africa*. British Museum (Natural History), London (2 vols.).

Fauchauld, K. (1977). *The polychaete worms*. (Science series, No. 28). Los Angeles County Natural History Museum.

Fauvel, P (1923). Polychètes errantes. *Faune de France*, 5. Féderation français des Sociétés de Sciences naturelles, Paris.

Fauvel, P. (1927). Polychètes sédentaires. *Faune de France*, 16. Fédération français des Sociétés de Sciences naturelles, Paris.

Garwood, P. R. (1981). Marine fauna of the Cullercoats district, 9. Polychaeta Errantia, *Reports of the Dove Marine Laboratory*, third series, No. 22. University of Newcastle upon Tyne.

Garwood, P. R. (1982). Marine fauna of the Cullercoats district, 10. Polychaeta Sedentaria. *Reports of the Dove Marine Laboratory*, 3rd series, No. 23. University of Newcastle upon Tyne.

George, J. D. and Hartmann-Schröder, G. (1985). Polychaetes: British Amphinomida, Spintherida and Eunicida. *Synopses of the British Fauna* (new series), No. 32. Leiden: E. J. Brill, for the Linnean Society of London and the Estuarine and Brackish Water Sciences Association.

Hartmann-Schröder, G. (1971). Annelida, Borstenwürmer, Polychaeta. *Die Tierwelt Deutschlands*, 58. Gustav Fischer, Jena.

Holthe, T. (1986). Polychaeta Terebellomorpha. Marine invertebrates of Scandinavia, No. 7. Norwegian University Press, Oslo.

Jones, M. L. (1977). A redescription of *Magelona papilliconis* F. Müller. *In*: Reish, D. J. and Fauchald, K. (editors). *Essays on polychaetous annelids*, 247–66. Los Angeles, University of Southern California.

Pettibone, M. H. (1963). Marine polychaete worms of the New England region. I. Aphroditidae through Trachochaetidae, *Bulletin of the U. S. National Museum*, No. 227, 1–356.

Smaldon, G. and Lee, E. W. (1979). *A synopsis of methods for the narcotization of marine invertebrates*. (Information series, Natural History, No. 6). Royal Scottish Museum, Edinburgh.

Tebble, N. and Chambers, S. (1982). *Polychaetes from Scottish waters, 1. Polynoidae*. Royal Scottish Museum, Edinburgh.

KEY TO FAMILIES

1. Dorsal surface covered with overlapping scales, a dense coat of felted or fur-like chaetae (which conceal such scales) or transverse ridges of bristles — **2**
   Dorsal surface not so covered (N.B. tufts of gills in various forms, or stiff chaetae, may project dorsally from the lateral parapodia) — **3**

2. Large, broad worms covered dorsally by a dense, greyish-brown felt; **or** medium-sized, with overlapping dorsal scales fringed and partly covered by a tangled chaetal fur; **or** various sizes but more elongated, most covered by overlapping scales and bearing typical chaetae in lateral bundles (N.B. such scales are readily shed by many species) — **3. Aphroditidae**
   Small, oval, flattened body in which each segment bears dorsally a range of bristles and branching gills extending from each side almost to mid-line; a crest extends along dorsal mid-line for a few segments behind head — **2. Amphinomidae**
   (*Euphrosyne foliosa* is the only species included here)

3. Small, with elongated lateral processes at one end giving an anchor- or pick-like body form, lacking chaetae — **4**
   Lacking such body form — **5**

4. Extremely small (2 mm or less) with indistinct segmentation, lacking parapods. Body bifurcates posteriorly into thick lateral processes each terminating in a sucker; head bears a number of short appendages. Found amongst the eggs or in the branchial cavity of lobsters — *Histriobdella homari* (see **8. Eunicidae**)

Small (up to 20 mm) with segmentation emphasized by elongated paddle-like parapods. Prostomium extended to each side, resembling a pick-head; second segment bears a whip-like appendage on each side, stiffened by a long aciculum and usually swept back along the body, whose length it nearly equals. Of delicate, transparent appearance, swimming in the plankton *Tomopteris helgolandica* (**26. Tomopteridae**)

5. Segmentation of body indistinct, indicated largely by rows of spherical capsules. Parapods simple, uniramous, and with few chaetae **22. Sphaerodoridae**

Segmentation of body usually indicated distinctly by transverse constrictions, prominent parapods, or both. Spherical capsules lacking **6**

6. Anteriorly, antennae short or absent; tentacles and palps short or absent (N.B. spionids that have lost their palps may key out here) **7**

Anteriorly, antennae, tentacles, or palps well-developed **17**

7. Stout but soft and fragile worm with a smooth, more or less cylindrical mid-region lacking typical parapods but bearing specialized appendages dorsally (anteriorly, a pair of curved wings or fins and posteriorly three large fans or paddles). In life, always occupies a leathery tube buried in clean sand, with each end opening at the surface *Chaetopterus variopedatus* (**6. Chaetopteridae**)

Lacking such specialized appendages **8**

8. Prostomium either conical, with four minute terminal antennae, or more or less rectangular with four small antennae, one at each anterior corner **9**

Prostomium not so **10**

9. Body cylindrical, at least anteriorly; parapods small. Prostomium conical, annulated, with four minute antennae forming a cross at its tip. Often reddish **10. Glyceridae**

Body flattened; parapods well-developed, biramous with well-separated lobes. Prostomium not annulated, more or less rectangular with four small antennae, one at each anterior corner. Usually grey or white **14. Nephtyidae**

10. Body not divided into distinct regions; segments not markedly longer than wide; prostomium conical, without appendages or with a short median antenna only **8. Eunicidae I**

Body usually divided into distinct regions or some body segments much longer than wide; prostomium variable **11**

11. Some body segments much longer than wide; anterior end obliquely flattened or hooded, lacking appendages or bearing a frilled membranous crown **12**

Segments may be multiannulate, mostly shorter than wide and often with wrinkled, reticulated epidermis in anterior region; posteriorly, they may be more elongated and narrower. Anterior end more or less conical, lacking appendages, reminiscent of an earthworm **13**

12. Posterior end in the form of a funnel, a more or less oblique plate, or spoon-like. The elongated segments are usually in posterior part of body **13. Maldanidae**

 Posterior end simple, rounded. Segments elongated in anterior mid-region but becoming progressively shorter posteriorly **18. Oweniidae**

13. Numerous (more than 11) pairs of tufted gills dorsally along middle or posterior parts of body. Neuropod consists of a simple torus containing a single row of stout crochets not hooded at tip. All but the first few segments 5-annulated **4. Arenicolidae**

 Gills, if present, usually numerous simple lobes, paddle-shaped or cirriform structures; if tufted, no more than four pairs anteriorly. Crochets may be lacking, inserted in notopodial bundles, or in multiple rows on a papillated torus; if in a simple torus, their tips are hooded. Segments simple or with fewer than five annuli **14**

14. Dorsal and/or ventral tori present, containing crochets in rows **15**

 Parapods biramous as small lobes or reduced to bundles of fine chaetae; no tori, crochets absent **16**

15. Anterior region broad and flattened, with lateral parapods; posteriorly, body narrower and more cylindrical with dorsal parapods. Anterior neuropod in the form of a torus bearing several rows of crochets and a fringe of post-chaetal papillae. A number of segments at junction of the two body regions may also bear a row of papillae ventrally. Gills, chaetae, and parapodial appendages may be sufficiently numerous to give a brush-like appearance to the dorsal surface posteriorly **17. Orbiniidae**

 Anterior region usually with markedly wrinkled epidermis, posterior region smooth with rather elongated segments, body cylindrical and of much the same diameter throughout. Simple tori present, crochets small. Parapods not prominent: superficial resemblance to an earthworm. Two or more pairs of prominent genital spines may occur mid-dorsally in anterior region **5. Capitellidae**

16. Long cirriform gills on many of body segments, inserted on ventral parapods but sweeping upwards and backwards. Segments may be multiannulate but rarely with reticulated epidermis. Conical prostomium may be prolonged anteriorly in a short fingerlike process. Anus surrounded by papillae, may be enclosed in a short tube or hood **16. Opheliidae**

 Gills either absent, or tufted and restricted to no more than four anterior segments. Parapods lateral, occasionally bearing short cirri. All segments multiannulate, with markedly reticulated epidermis. Prostomium blunt and T-shaped or bilobed. Pygidium usually with four to five elongated cirri **21. Scalibregmidae**

17. Elongated, typically worm-like. Segments more or less alike throughout, body not divided into distinct regions (except in epitokes). Prostomium usually well-developed, with sensory appendages but none markedly long or specialized. Parapods usually well-developed, adapted for active movement **28**

 Often short and relatively broad-bodied; frequently divided into regions which are distinctly different. Prostomium reduced, with appendages which are either numerous and specialized or very long (or both). Parapods often reduced; mainly burrowing or tubicolous forms **18**

18. Head with two long palps; a few filamentous gills may be present, but anterior end lacks numerous filamentous appendages **19**

Head with numerous bristles, tentacles, or feathery appendages **21**

19. Body not divided into distinct regions (although some appendages, e.g. gills, may occur on only one part of it) **23. Spionidae**

Body divided into distinct regions **20**

20. Body in two regions distinctly different from each other; anterior end like a duck's bill; occupies burrows but no permanent tube **12. Magelonidae**
    (*M. mirabilis* is the only species included here)

Body in three regions distinctly different from each other; anterior end blunt, often with a funnel-like terminal mouth; occupies a tough, membranous permanent tube **6. Chaetopteridae**

21. Anterior end with feathery appendages, normally stiff and arranged in two semicircles, forming a funnel **22**
    Anterior appendages not feathery **23**

22. Occupying a straight, sinuous, or coiled calcareous tube; one appendage often modified as a stalked plug (operculum) sealing tube when worm is retracted into it **32**

Usually occupying a more or less erect tube of cemented fine sediment (in one species, of thick mucus; some small species are free-living); no operculum **28. Sabellidae**

23. Anterior appendages tentacle-like **24**
    Anterior appendages stiff bristles **26**

24. Tentacles usually originate from behind head. Body not divided into distinct regions. Gills simple, elongate, may be present along much of body **7. Cirratulidae**

Tentacles inserted on head. Body clearly divided into a swollen anterior and more slender posterior region. Often one or more pairs of branched gills behind the tentacles **25**

25. Tentacles retractile **1. Ampharetidae**
    Tentacles not retractile **25. Terebellidae**

26. Body covered with papillae and more or less encased in mucus, often encrusted with sediment particles which do not form a definite tube. Prostomium and buccal segment cylindrical and retractile, not markedly truncated. Anterior chaetae usually directed forwards, making a cage around head **9. Flabelligeridae**

Body not papillated, in life always occupying a rigid tube of cemented sand-grains. Anterior end obliquely truncated with a crown of stout flattened chaetae, sealing tube when worm is retracted into it. **27**

27. Anterior chaetae arranged in a comb-like series on either side, crossing in the midline. Most posterior part of body short, spoon-shaped, segmented but mostly lacking chaetae. Tube free, solitary, a smooth elongated cone open at each end   **19. Pectinariidae**

    Anterior chaetae arranged in three concentric semicircles on each side. Most posterior part of body a long, unsegmented anal tube lacking chaetae and reflected forwards along ventral side of worm. Tubes attached to solid substrata, with a rough surface and open at only one end, either forming part of a massive reef or more or less solitary on stones and shells
    27. Sabellariidae

28. Parapods uniramous, with leaf-like or globular cirri; four antennae (at front of head) and sometimes a median one (which may be further back); no palps; two to four pairs of tentacles; proboscis jawless but bears papillae   **20. Phyllodocidae**

    Parapods uni- or biramous but cirri not leaf-like or globular when present; usually two antennae (may be none or three); two palps present, usually short and stout; tentacles absent or various; Proboscis often bears dark chitinous jaws, spines, or teeth   **29**

29. Parapods clearly biramous, with dorsal and ventral lobes more or less equal. Four pairs of tentacles, may be quite long but not divided into sections, distinct from dorsal cirri of adjacent segments. Proboscis with a pair of jaws and small scattered teeth
    15. Nereidae

    Parapods appear uniramous (some elements of missing lobe may still be present); tentacles absent or, if present, not as four pairs   **30**

30. First three or four body segments lack chaetae, compressed into a more or less distinct short region behind the head, bearing six to eight pairs of relatively long tentacles. Palps moderately long and divided into two sections. Proboscis without jaws or with simple horny lips   **11. Hesionidae**

    Tentacles absent or, if present, as one or two pairs only. Palps not divided into two sections and usually squat. Proboscis with at least one large tooth, usually with complex jaws   **31**

31. Head with three relatively long antennae. Two pairs of tentacles followed by dorsal cirri down the rest of the body, all usually long and divided into many sections   **24. Syllidae**

    Head with two short antennae or none, five long tentacles or none. Feathery gills may be present on part of the body but dorsal cirri not prominent   **8. Eunicidae II**

32. Tube straight or sinuous. Thorax with more than four chaetigers   **29. Serpulidae**

    Tube helical, usually coiled flat against substratum. Thorax with three or four chaetigers
    30. Spirorbidae

---

1 AMPHARETIDAE

The body is divided into two regions, a broader and shorter anterior one with biramous parapods (notopod as a conical boss with a bundle of long capillary chaetae, neuropod with a row of simple spear-like chaetae or, more usually, uncini) and a posterior region with neuropodial flaps bearing a row of uncini, the notopod being vestigial or lacking. These worms generally resemble terebellids but can retract their tentacles completely and have simple gills (a group of four on each side in the species included here). Many new species have recently been collected from deep dredging (Holthe 1986).

1. Posterior region (lacking bundles of long chaetae but well-developed neuropodial flaps) not much longer than broader anterior region, with about 12–15 segments. A prominent bundle of stiff golden 'collar chaetae' in front of gills on each side of head region.

Gills free more or less to the base. At least two anal cirri **2**

Posterior region long and narrow, with 50 or more segments. No 'collar chaetae'. A pair of stout nuchal hooks protruding from thoracic membrane dorsally, just behind gills (Fig. 6.2b). Gills united by a web-like membrane for more or less half their length. No anal cirri **3**

2. Twelve posterior chaetigers, mostly bearing only neuropodial flaps with uncini. Anus surrounded by numerous cirri (of which one on each side may be larger than the others). Tentacles bear small papillae, giving them a slightly feathery appearance. Prostomium pointed, without prominent ridges. Uncini with eight to ten teeth in two rows (Fig. 6.2d)
Ampharete acutifrons

Fifteen posterior chaetigers. Notopodial boss of anterior region bears a small club-like dorsal cirrus which remains as a vestige posteriorly. Two anal cirri, of variable length. Tentacles smooth or lightly ringed. Prostomium rectangular, with a prominent glandular ridge on each side. Uncini with five to seven teeth in a single row (*sim.* Fig. 6.2c)
Amphicteis gunneri

3. Four anterior segments have a row of fine spear-like chaetae as the neuropod. Posterior margin of thoracic membrane cut into 10–20 well-defined teeth (Fig. 6.2b). Web joining gills poorly developed. Body of medium length (30–60 mm) *Melinna cristata*

Three anterior segments with a row of spear-like chaetae; these are lacking from one segment before uncinigerous tori appear. Posterior margin of thoracic membrane either entire or cut into four to eight indistinct teeth. Web joining gills may extend as far as two-thirds their length. Small (15–20 mm)
Melinna palmata

Ampharete acutifrons Grube (includes *A. grubei*) FIG. 6.2
Fourteen anterior and twelve posterior chaetigers. 15–35 mm long generally, may reach 80 mm in arctic waters. Pointed prostomium with two small ridges outlining an irregular pentagonal area. Two eyes. Peristomium narrow and can be partially retracted into segments behind it. Buccal tentacles bear small papillae, giving them a pinnate appearance. Ten to fifteen long golden 'collar chaetae' on each side in front of gills, arranged in a fan pointing stiffly forwards. Four tapering cirriform gills, free to the base, are arranged in a group on each side. The first parapod is a tiny achaetous tubercle behind gills; uncini occur from third chaetiger. The notopod is a simple conical boss bearing a transverse row of uncini with nine to ten teeth arranged in two parallel rows. In the posterior region, the neuropod is a palette-shaped flap with a cirriform prolongation at the upper angle; uncini have eight to ten teeth arranged in two rows more irregularly (d). On the first four or five posterior segments, a blunt tubercle occurs above the flap but capillary chaetae are lacking. Pygidium with numerous anal cirri, of which one on each side is usually longer than the rest. Amongst adults, males are greenish white, females pale salmon-pink; blood greenish. Tube membranous, covered with sand-grains.

At low water, in muddy sand amongst sea-grasses, and sublittorally. Circum-Arctic, European coasts to the Mediterranean, including the Baltic Sea.

Amphicteis gunneri (Sars)

Seventeen anterior and fifteen posterior chaetigers, 20–40 mm long. Prostomium rectangular because of two prominent divergent glandular crests. Two groups of small, simple eyes. Peristomium long ventrally. Buccal tentacles smooth or lightly ringed. Eight to ten blunt or pointed golden 'collar chaetae' on each side in front of gills. A group of four tapering gills on each side, more or less fused at base, well-separated by a skin fold. Uncini occur from chaetiger four. The notopod is a long conical boss bearing capillary chaetae and with a little club-shaped dorsal cirrus; anteriorly, the neuropod is a flattened, stalked button bearing a transverse row of uncini, each with a single row of five to seven teeth and a hooked heel. Posteriorly, the neuropod is a more flattened flap with a very short, blunt dorsal extension. The notopod is represented only by the dorsal cirrus. Pygidium with two anal cirri of variable length. Yellowish white or pink, with white spots and brown blotches. Gills green with bands of brown, white, and yellow; blood green. Tube membranous.

At low water and in the sublittoral to considerable depths, on mud or muddy sand. Circum-Arctic, most European coasts to the Mediterranean; mid-Atlantic, Gulf of Mexico, southern Africa, Antarctic.

Melinna cristata (Sars) FIG. 6.2

Sixteen anterior chaetigers, including a first rudimentary one; about 50 posterior ones. 30–60 mm long, becoming very thin posteriorly. Prostomium slightly trilobed, without glandular crests. Several eyespots on each side. Peristomium mostly covered by a collar-like extension of the next segment ventrally. Few smooth buccal tentacles. Each group of four long filiform gills united by a palmar membrane for up to half their length. Chaetigers two to five have a deep dorsal depression covered by a thoracic membrane with a posterior border cut into 10–20 well-defined teeth (b). Behind the gills on each side of chaetiger four, a chitinous nuchal hook (b). Laterally on chaetigers 2, 3, 5, and 6 the neuropod is represented by a transverse row of fine spear-like chaetae. From chaetiger six, typical notopods (a conical boss bearing a bundle of capillary chaetae, lacking a cirrus); from the seventh, neuropodial tori bearing a row of triangular uncini, each with four teeth in a single row. Posteriorly, the neuropod is a rectangular flap without a cirriform extension; the notopod is represented by a vestigial tubercle. The pygidium lacks cirri; anus terminal, in a small funnel. Yellowish or pinkish-white, gills blotched with olive-green; blood red. Tube membranous, cylindrical, fairly thickly encrusted with mud.

On the shore and sublittorally on muddy bottoms, often amongst sea-grasses. Most north-west European coasts, Arctic; north Pacific, sub-Antarctic.

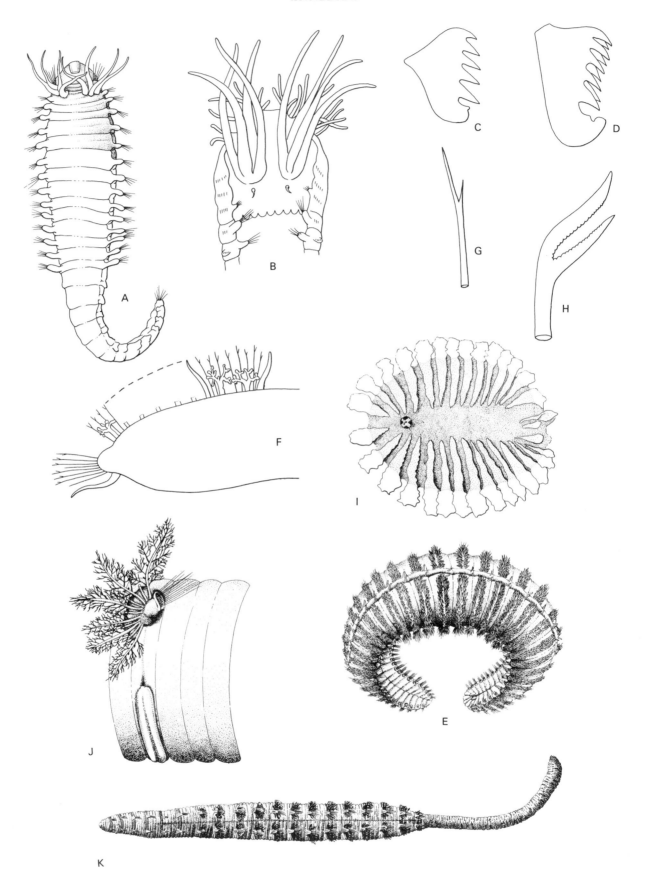

Fig. 6.2 (AMPHARETIDAE, AMPHINOMIDAE, ARENICOLIDAE) a. *Ampharete grubei*—entire worm, dorsal (after Uschakov) b. *Melinna cristata*—anterior end, dorsal c. *M. palmata*—uncinus d. *Ampharete acutifrons*—uncinus (after Fauvel) e. *Euphrosyne foliosa*—entire worm (after McIntosh) f. *E. foliosa*—half TS g. *E. foliosa*—notochaeta h. *E. foliosa*—toothed notochaeta (after Fauvel) i. *Spinther miniaceus*—entire worm (dorsal) j. *Arenicola marina*—lateral view of one segment in branchial region (after Ashworth) k. *A. marina*—entire worm, dorsal

Melinna palmata Grube   FIG. 6.2

Sixteen anterior chaetigers, including a first rudimentary one; about 60 posterior segments. 15–20 mm long, body very narrow posteriorly. Prostomium markedly trilobed, without glandular crests. Several eyespots on each side. Peristomium mostly covered by a ventral collar-like extension of the next segment. Few, smooth buccal tentacles. Each group of four long, tapering, annulated gills is bound together by a web for up to two-thirds their length. The thoracic membrane behind them has a posterior border which is either entire and a little concave or cut into four to eight indistinct, rounded teeth. A nuchal hook is present on each side behind the gills. Laterally on chaetigers 2, 3, and 5 there is a transverse row of fine spear-like chaetae, but they are lacking from chaetiger six. From the sixth, typical notopods commence and, from the seventh, neuropodial tori bearing a row of triangular uncini with four or five teeth in a single row (c). Posteriorly the neuropod is a rectangular flap without a cirriform extension; the notopod is represented by a vestigial tubercle. The pygidium lacks cirri; anus terminal, in a small funnel. Pale or brownish pink, blotched with red. Gills greenish with brown bands; blood red. Tube membranous, cylindrical, thickly coated with mud.

At low water in mud amongst sea-grasses, also sublittoral on muddy bottoms. Western European coasts, also Mediterranean; Black Sea, Arabian Gulf.

2. AMPHINOMIDAE

The body is often fairly short, flattened, and oval in plan view. The prostomium is reduced but, in the mid-dorsal line, the caruncle which is typical of this family (a nuchal organ in the form of a crest) extends backwards for several segments. The dorsal surface is covered to various extents by rows of simple chaetae, gills, and cirri. There is an eversible proboscis without jaws or papillae. Most members of the family are carnivorous, sucking the tissue fluids of sessile invertebrates, and may be brightly coloured to match them. Some (confined to northern waters or the tropics and thus not included here) have a more typically worm-like, elongated body; of these, the 'fire-worms' (*Hermodice*) have hollow poison-chaetae which break after penetrating the skin, causing intense irritation. The genus *Spinther* contains worms which are either specialized amphinomids or close relatives: they are small, flattened, almost circular and live on sponges (Fig. 6.2i; see George and Hartmann-Schröder 1985).

Euphrosyne foliosa Audouin and Milne Edwards FIG. 6.2
Body an elongated oval shape, convex dorsally (e). 30–36 chaetigers; 10–30 mm long, up to 10 mm wide. Prostomium continues back along the ventral surface, with two large dorsal and two smaller ventral eyes. A thick, cylindrical median antenna is inserted between the dorsal eyes; two lateral antennae, half its size, are inserted ventrally. The mouth is ventral, flanked anteriorly by a pair of palps reduced to flattened cushions. The caruncle extends back to chaetiger five and is divided into three longitudinal lobes, the middle one as a projecting crest with ciliated bands down each side. The notopods spread across the dorsal surface leaving only a small bare region down the mid-line (f). On each side there are seven to nine gills, each branching

dichotomously from a stout base, the branches terminating in variously enlarged tips. Two dorsal cirri, one at the inner end of the row of gills, the other between the 2nd and 3rd gill from that end. Notochaetae, much longer than gills, in an irregular row anterior to them; all bifurcated, of two kinds—some with very unequal smooth branches (g), others with the branches more equal and toothed internally (resembling the partly opened mouth of a shark) (h). Neurochaetae around edge of body, all bifurcated with smooth unequal branches becoming shorter the more ventrally they are inserted. One ventral cirrus below the bundle of neurochaetae. Anus small, dorsal to a pair of short, thick anal cirri. Colour orange, brick-red, or vermilion.

Under stones, amongst shells and algae or in crevices on bottoms of various types, from low water to moderate depths. Most north-west European coasts; Mediterranean, Red Sea.

3. APHRODITIDAE

A large family characterized by the elytra (scales) which cover much of the dorsal surface. Representatives of three main subgroups (often listed as separate families) are included here. The aphroditids proper (Hermioninae in Fauvel) have few segments and an oval body which may be quite large. They are slow-moving, burrowing, or creeping on soft bottoms where they feed on living animals, carrion, or detritus. Some notochaetae are fine and extremely long, intertwining to form a felt which completely covers the back in *Aphrodita* (called 'sea mouse' but more closely resembling a large hairy slug); in others this is less well-developed and may be torn away when collecting the worm from mud or cleaning it up, or may be lacking. The Polynoinae are the most numerous and typical scale-worms, whose shape may be oval and flattened or cylindrical and elongated; they are generally quite small. Elytra usually occur on every second or third segment, the others having a long dorsal cirrus. The effect is often of a Viking boat with oars extended beyond the shields protecting its crew. Elongated worms may lack scales posteriorly. As in the aphroditids, all the chaetae are simple. The polynoids are carnivorous, having four large chitinous teeth in pairs above and below the opening of the eversible proboscis. They are often commensal with animals living in tubes or burrows, when their elytra are usually smooth; those with strongly ornamented elytra are more likely to be freeliving. The Sigalioninae have an elongated body with very many segments, appearing tetragonal in cross-section. Elytra occur on alternate segments in the anterior part of the body but then on every segment, right to the tail end. There are no dorsal cirri, although all but the first parapods have a cirriform gill inserted dorsally, on the stalk of the elytra if these are present. Parapods also typically carry, along the upper edge, a row of three ctenidia (ciliated cup-shaped or leaf-like protuberances). Some or all of the neurochaetae are jointed. Like the polynoids, sigalionids have four chitinous hooks in the proboscis; they are carnivores, usually moving fast on sandy bottoms.

See Tebble and Chambers 1982; Chambers 1985.

N.B. In most species, the elytra are easily shed during collection; their position is shown by the mushroom-shaped 'stalk' (elytrophore) (Fig. 6.3b–f), which is the basal portion of the modified dorsal cirrus.

1. Large, broad and flattened oval-bodied worm whose dorsal surface is covered with a greyish-brown felt and fringed by stout iridescent bristles **Aphrodita aculeata**

   Dorsal scales more or less visible   **2**

2. Medium size, flattened, and oval-bodied. Dorsal scales are visible but partially covered by chaetal 'fur'; body fringed laterally by tangled chaetae **Laetmatonice filicornis**

   Size varies, but generally shorter and more slender; dorsal scales not at all covered by chaetae, body fringed laterally only by straight chaetae of normal length and, often, by elongated dorsal cirri   **3**

3. Elytra (scales) inserted on alternate segments, one segment in three, or lacking posteriorly; segments not bearing elytra have dorsal cirri, elongated and protruding dorso-laterally. Prostomium always bears three antennae, one median (anterior) and two lateral, usually smaller (Fig. 6.3a–c). Body mostly short, flattened, and oval, though not very broad; 12, 15, or 18 pairs of elytra (Polynoinae)   **4**

   Elytra inserted on alternate segments anteriorly and on every segment posteriorly; segments not bearing elytra lack dorsal cirri, but almost all segments bear dorsally a ciliated cirriform gill on each side, beneath the elytron if present (except *Pholoë*). Prostomium bears vestigial or one to three visible antennae (Fig. 6.3d–f). Body usually long and slender, with up to c. 150 pairs of elytra (Sigalioninae)   **15**

4. Elytra (15 pairs) leave an appreciable number of posterior body segments (c. 10–50) uncovered   **5**

   Elytra cover substantially whole length of body   **6**

5. Posterior quarter body length (8–20 segments) uncovered. Length 30–40 mm **Lagisca extenuata**

   Posterior half body length (c. 50 segments) uncovered. Length 30–120 mm. Typically shares tube of terebellid *Eupolymnia* **Polynoë scolopendrina**

6. Twelve pairs of elytra   **7**

   More than twelve pairs of elytra   **8**

7. Elytra scarcely overlap and leave dorsal surface uncovered in mid-line; mostly smooth and unfringed **Lepidonotus clava**

   Elytra overlap considerably, covering entire dorsal surface; with numerous prominent papillae, and fringed along external border **Lepidonotus squamatus**

8. Fifteen pairs of elytra   **9**

   More than fifteen pairs of elytra   **14**

9. Elytra transparent, not overlapping markedly and lacking prominent papillae or pigmentation, not strongly fringed. Fragile worms typically found on echinoids   **10**

   Elytra opaque, often with brownish markings, prominent papillae, or a fringed external border. Sturdy appearance   **11**

10. Antennae and cirri bear short spines   **Adyte assimilis**

    Antennae and cirri smooth   **Subadyte pellucida**

11. Lateral antennae inserted subterminally. Antennae, palps. and cirri smooth. Elytra smooth and unfringed, banded brown with darker spots. Normally found on spatangoids or asteroids   **Malmgrenia castanea**

    Lateral antennae inserted ventrally. Antennae, palps, and cirri hairy or spiny   **12**

12. No elytra on last four segments; their external border finely fringed, surface covered with small papillae, greyish white with a central black spot. Shares tube of terebellid or *Chaetopterus*   **Gattyana cirrosa**

    Body completely covered with elytra, variously decorated   **13**

13. *Harmothoë* spp. are not easy to separate; these are the commonest around the British Isles:

    a: Elytra not fringed; papillae absent or numerous but so small as to be inconspicuous:
    Elytra brown with black circular, semicircular, or chevron pattern; worm medium size (10–35 mm), often shares tube or burrow   **H. lunulata**

    Elytra pale yellowish with broad brown band around posterior edge; dorsal cirri and ventral setae very long, giving marked lateral fringe to body; fairly large (30–60 mm), often shares tube or burrow   **H. longisetis**

    b: Elytra fringed with only few hairs or weak spines; papillae generally small but may become large near free edge:
    First pair of elytra almost white, often with central black spot; most dark brown with greenish sheen, becoming paler and marbled with lighter spots towards posterior end; worm fairly small (c. 15 mm)   **H. spinifera**

    Elytra greyish to dark brown with purplish sheen, sometimes with white outer edge; worm fairly large (30–50 mm), may share tube or burrow **H. imbricata**

    Elytra greyish to violet brown, either lighter or darker in centre; worm large (60–80 mm) and broad   **H. (Eunoë) nodosa**

    c: Elytra well-fringed with strong spines, variously covered with papillae which may be large near free edge; generally brownish; worm fairly small (12–25 mm)   **H. impar**

14. Eighteen pairs of translucent off-white elytra; worm large (80–90 mm) but fairly broad **Alentia gelatinosa**

Approximately 20–70 pairs of small elytra; worm large (35–220 mm) and slender; shares terebellid tubes **Lepidasthenia argus**

15. No median antenna, lateral antennae vestigial. Elytra (150 pairs or more) fringed with 10–20 feathery papillae (Fig. 6.3i) **Sigalion mathildae**

Median antenna present, elytra lack feathery fringe **16**

16. Median antenna present but short (as are other anterior processes). Elytra (40–60 pairs) fringed with stout, simple, or moniliform papillae (Fig. 6.3j). Small (10–20 mm) **Pholoë minuta**

Median antenna long, short lateral antennae (or processes resembling lateral antennae) present. Large (50–200 mm), c. 150 pairs of elytra **17**

17. Body rectangular in section, elytra fail to meet in mid-line or only barely do so. Some jointed ventral chaetae have banded tips, but none are bifid **Leanira tetragona**

Body oval in section, elytra overlap well and completely cover the dorsal surface. Some jointed ventral chaetae have bifid tips, but none are banded **18**

18. Elytra have a fringe of simple spines and are opaque, covered with small conical tubercles (Fig. 6.3g) **Sthenelais boa**

Elytra are smooth, translucent, and mostly lack a fringe, but are notched in the external edge (Fig. 6.3h) **Sthenelais limicola**

APHRODITINAE

Aphrodita aculeata (Linnaeus)

Body oval, more pointed to the rear; dorsal surface convex and completely covered by a close 'felt' of fine chaetae, ventral surface forms a flattened sole. About 40 segments; 100–200 mm long, 30–70 mm wide. Prostomium spherical, with two sessile eyes and a single tiny antenna between them. Two long awl-shaped palps; two pairs of subequal tentacles, shorter than the palps. Fifteen pairs of smooth elytra, tightly overlapping (and hidden beneath the felt). In addition to the very long, fine chaetae forming this covering, the notopod bears short, thick, dark-coloured bristles which poke up through it and fine, silky, iridescent ones forming a fringe around its edge. Long dorsal cirri project through this fringe from the segments not bearing elytra. The neuropod carries a small number of short, stout bristles extending laterally, and a short ventral cirrus. Spiny or pinnate chaetae occur on first and last chaetigers. Dorsal felt dark-grey; flanks iridescent from blue through green and yellow to bronze; sole brownish yellow.

Sublittoral in sand or muddy sand; rarely, stranded at low tide. Most north-west European coasts, Mediterranean.

Laetmatonice filicornis Kinberg FIG. 6.3

Body a broad oval with 34–36 chaetigers; length 20–35 mm. Dorsal felt loose, variably developed. Prostomium rounded, divided into three lobes. Two eyes on short stalks. The antenna long; two palps, nearly as long, covered with fine papillae. Two pairs of filamentous tentacles, shorter than the palps. Fifteen pairs of smooth interlocking elytra, visible through the felt. Dorsal cirri (on segments not bearing elytra) long and thin; the notopod on those segments provides the felt-forming chaetae whilst, on elytron-bearing segments, it has stouter ones with a multibarbed tip like a harpoon (m), rarely enclosed between two long valves. The neuropod has a few strong chaetae with a spur near the tip, from which there runs a terminal fringe of fine, stiff filaments (n). In the first few chaetigers there are also fine pinnate chaetae. Dorsal surface often bluish or violet, seen through the grey felt.

On muddy bottoms to considerable depths. Most north-west European coasts; Pacific.

N.B. *L.* (= *Hermione*) *hystrix* (Savigny) is generally similar but larger (50–60 mm long) and without a dorsal felt. Its elytra are smooth, brownish with a slight iridescence. It occurs on shell and gravel bottoms along western coasts (also the Mediterranean and Indian Ocean).

POLYNOINAE

Adyte (= *Scalisetosus*) *assimilis* (McIntosh)

Body elongated, narrow and fragile, about 40 segments, 18–20 mm long. Prostomium in two rounded lobes; four eyes, the anterior pair larger and with a lens. Median antenna long, lateral ones shorter. Palps thick, brown; tentacles short. Antennae, palps, and tentacles smooth. Dorsal cirri relatively short. Antennae, tentacles, and dorsal cirri terminate in an elongated point; ventral cirri short and awl-shaped. Elytra (15 pairs) rounded or oval, transparent, finely dotted and with fine papillae around free edge. Notochaetae short, slightly curved, with a row of fine spines. Neurochaetae longer and finer; near the tip a moderate swelling with a webbed spur, beyond which a row of fine spines runs to slightly hooked tip. Nephridial papillae not visible. Pale coloured, with a longitudinal brownish or greenish band dorsally.

In shallow sublittoral, on *Echinus*. Western European coasts.

Alentia (= *Halosydna*) *gelatinosa* (Sars)

Body straight-sided, narrowing at each end and flattened, with 43 chaetigers; 80–90 mm long. Prostomium divided into two rounded lobes, each bearing two large eyes on outer side; a semicircular nuchal fold covers it posteriorly like a high collar. Median and lateral antennae subequal, shorter than palps which are smooth and tapering. Tentacles subequal, almost as long as palps; antennae and tentacles also smooth, with a subterminal swelling and pointed tip. Dorsal cirri similar, extending beyond chaetae; ventral cirri short and tapering. Elytra (18 pairs) large, soft, with a brown reticulated pattern; free surface covered with numerous small, truncated, brownish papillae. Notochaetae few and delicate, very finely toothed towards tip. Neurochaetae numerous and long, with a broader finely toothed region towards tip, which is lightly bifid in those more ventrally inserted. Nephridial papillae more or less prominent, ventral to parapod in mid-region. Ventral side orange, dorsal side marked with transverse brown and white bands; elytra a translucent dirty white or brownish.

Under stones, sometimes in *Nerine* burrows, on muddy bottoms in the shallow sublittoral. Around most British coasts; north-east Atlantic.

Gattyana cirrosa (Pallas)   FIG. 6.3

Body broad, not narrowing markedly at ends, with 34–36 chaetigers; 25–50 mm long, 5–10 mm wide. Prostomium with well-marked frontal horns; four little black eyes, first pair looking downwards. Median antenna as long as palps, lateral ones half as long. Tentacles a little shorter than palps, decorated with papillae like the antennae (c). Dorsal cirri extend about as far as chaetae; ventral cirri shorter. Fifteen pairs of elytra, none on last four chaetigers but covering whole body. Their free edge fringed with short hair-like processes; surface appears smooth but is covered with many little conical processes, some with two or four cusps. The notopod has many long, delicate, finely spined chaetae; neurochaetae are longer and thicker, with a spiny blade. Nephridial papillae prominent, cylindrical. Two long anal cirri. Colour milky or greyish white, sometimes broken by a black spot in the middle of each elytron.

In the tube of terebellid or chaetopterid worms. On most British coasts; Arctic, north Atlantic, north Pacific.

Harmothoë spp.   FIG. 6.3

General characters are as follows. Only noteworthy variations from these will be given for the individual species listed, although it should be appreciated that the relative lengths of contractile structures such as antennae may be deceptive.

Body short, straight-sided or narrowing at the rear end, with 35–40 chaetigers. Prostomium divided in front to produce two conical lobes (frontal horns). Four eyes. One median antenna and two shorter lateral antennae. Two stout palps, two pairs of long tentacles with small chaetae around their base. Dorsal cirri more or less long, ventral cirri short. Antenna, tentacles, and cirri usually have a pointed tip and subterminal swelling, and are covered with small elongated or knobbed processes; palps are smooth or bear finer papillae in longitudinal rows. Notochaetae are short and stout, bearing distally numerous rows of spines; neurochaetae longer, finer, also spiny and often slightly bifid at the tip (o). Fifteen pairs of overlapping elytra cover the whole body dorsally and are inserted from the 2nd to the 32nd chaetiger, more or less alternately. Nephridial papillae more or less prominent, ventral to the parapods. Two long anal cirri.

Harmothoë imbricata (Linnaeus)

Body 30–50 mm long. Dorsal cirri extend well beyond chaetae. Elytra appear smooth to the unaided eye but, on closer inspection, are covered with small conical tubercles; they are fringed along their free edge with short hairs, more abundantly in young specimens. Large worms also have, on the rearward margin, a

row of large, roughly globular nodules on a short stalk. Coloration varies from mottled grey-black through bluish grey to brown or brownish purple with metallic glints. The elytra may have a darker centre and lighter spots around the edge. Some specimens have a broad chestnut band down the middle of the back and white down each side.

At low water in kelp holdfasts or tubes of terebellid and chaetopterid worms; on stony or shelly bottoms to considerable depths. European coasts from the Arctic to the Mediterranean; Indian Ocean, North Pacific.

Harmothoë impar Johnston
Includes *H. reticulata* (Claparède.)

Body 12–25 mm long. Prostomium deeply cleft to make frontal horns prominent. Dorsal cirri extend beyond chaetae. Elytra easily shed, strongly fringed on their free edge, mostly covered with chitinous tubercles and spiny outgrowths of varied shape, although these are sometimes missing from a few elytra or in young specimens. Tubercles may be enmeshed in a reticular colour-pattern. Notochaetae bear strong spines, well-separated. Dorsal coloration greenish brown, darker at the head end, with a complex pattern of stripes and spots; elytra often have a yellowish spot in the middle; reticular pattern orange-brownish. Ventrally, pale and iridescent. Bioluminescent.

At low water under stones, amongst shells or in kelp holdfasts; offshore to some depth. North-western European coasts, Mediterranean.

Harmothoë longisetis (Grube)

Body 30–60 mm long. Prostomium bilobed but frontal horns blunt or absent. Antennae slender, relatively small. Dorsal cirri extend beyond chaetae. Elytra easily shed, delicate, appearing smooth but actually covered with very many small conical processes and bearing a few very short hairs along free edge. Ventral coloration silvery white; back pale, perhaps with transverse brown bands. Head appendages and cirri may be brown. Elytra pale yellow with a chestnut band around posterior edge, or may be colourless. Bioluminescent.

At low water and in shallow sublittoral, under stones and particularly in tubes of chaetopterids, terebellids, and even *Arenicola*. North-western European coasts, Mediterranean.
N.B. British records are probably of *H. glabra* (Malmgren), with characters as described above; more southerly records may be of *H. longisetis* proper, which differs in some characters.

Harmothoë lunulata (delle Chiaje)

Body 10–35 mm long. Prostomium bilobed but frontal horns not well-marked. Antennae and tentacles relatively short. Dorsal cirri extend only as far as chaetae. Elytra smooth and unfringed, decorated with very variable patterns. Notochaetae few and very short. Coloration very variable: ventral side with a median dark-red band and transverse brownish stripes posteriorly; elytra with brownish markings in circular, semicircular, or 'V' shapes, sometimes broken, with a central black spot. Head reddish, antennae and cirri with brown markings. Bioluminescent.

At low water, under stones or in crevices; most frequently

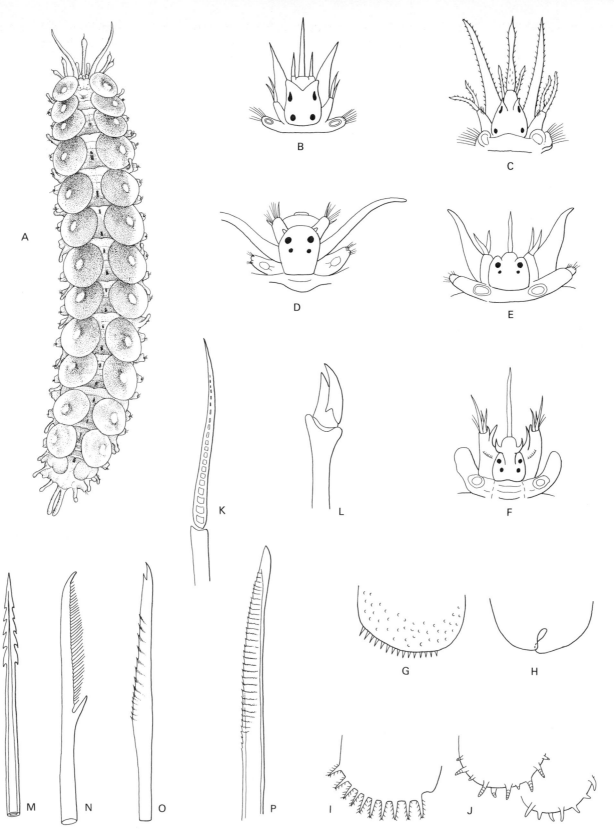

Fig. 6.3 (APHRODITIDAE) a. *Lepidonotus clava*—entire worm (dorsal) b. *Malmgrenia castanea*—anterior region c. *Gattyana cirrosa*—anterior region d. *Sigalion mathildae*—anterior region e. *Pholoë minuta*—anterior region f. *Sthenelais boa*—anterior region g. *S. boa*—posterior edge of elytron h. *S. limicola*—posterior edge of elytron i. *Sigalion mathildae*—posterior edge of elytron j. *P. minuta*—posterior edge of elytron k. *Leanira tetragona*—jointed neurochaeta l. *S. boa*—jointed neurochaeta m. *Laetmatonice filicornis*—'harpoon' chaeta n. *L. filicornis*—neurochaeta o. *Harmothoë imbricata*—neurochaeta p. *Eunoë nodosa*—notochaeta

commensal with various annelids or holothurians. Western coasts of Europe (northern records need checking) to Meditterranean.

Harmothoë (= Eunoë) nodosa (Sars)

May reach a length of 60–80 mm and width of 25–30 mm. Prostomium with slight frontal horns. Dorsal cirri extend well beyond chaetae. Free edge of elytra may or may not be fringed; their free surface covered with spiny chitinous papillae and often, also, with large conical or globular nodules. Elytra coloured grey or purple-brown, often with a lighter or darker spot in the middle; antennae and cirri reddish with a brown band and white tip.

On bottoms of gravel and muddy sand to considerable depths. Arctic and northern Europe.

Harmothoë spinifera (Ehlers)

Body about 15 mm long. Dorsal cirri extend only as far as chaetae. Surface of elytra ornamented with small rounded tubercles, their free edge with a few short hairs. Neurochaetae may have strongly bifid tips. Ventral side colourless anteriorly, greenish behind. Dorsal side with transverse dark stripes. First pair of elytra very pale with a black spot, contrasting strongly with the others which are dark brown or black with a metallic greenish glint; colouring becomes more pale and mottled posteriorly. Antennae, palps, and cirri brownish.

Under stones, in crevices and in kelp holdfasts at low water, also in shallow sublittoral. Western coasts of Europe to Mediterranean.

Lagisca extenuata (Grube)

Body quite narrow in last third of its length, about 40–50 segments; 30–40 mm long, 8–10 mm wide. Prostomium bilobed, with sharp frontal horns; four eyes. Median antenna long, lateral ones half that length. Tentacles similar to median antenna in length and form, as are dorsal cirri (which extend beyond chaetae). Ventral cirri short. Antennae, tentacles, and cirri ornamented with long papillae. Elytra do not cover the last 8–15 segments, which form a sort of tapering tail. They bear little conical chitinous tubercles over the entire surface, a posterior row of large globular warts and a fringe of long processes. Notochaetae numerous, stout, spiny, and directed dorsally; upper and lower neurochaetae with a single pointed tip, middle ones bifid. Two papillated anal cirri. Short nephridial papillae. Coloration very variable: usually the underside is pale and iridescent, the back covered with brownish bands forming a complex design. Elytra marbled in brown and grey or reddish, usually with a lighter spot in the middle. Head reddish with a pale transverse band. Antennae and cirri ringed with brown.

Under stones and amongst rocks throughout the tidal zone, also offshore to some depth. European coasts from the Arctic to the Mediterranean.

Lepidasthenia argus Hodgson

Body narrow and straight-sided, with more than 200 segments; 35–215 mm long. Prostomium bilobed, but not forming frontal horns. Four eyes. Median antenna long, fairly thick, with subterminal swelling and pointed tip; lateral ones almost as long, but more slender. Palps stout. Tentacles and dorsal cirri similar to antennae; appendages smooth. Dorsal cirri extend as far as chaetae, ventral cirri much smaller. Elytra (22–67 pairs) smooth, translucent, and unfringed, covering sides of body to the rear end but leaving uncovered a large part of the back. Notopod reduced to a small protuberance with four or five long, smooth chaetae which may often be altogether absent. Many neurochaetae, upper ones longer and with a long spiny region, middle ones stouter and shorter, lower ones more delicate; all have bifid tips. Two short anal cirri. Nephridial papillae very prominent below ventral cirri. Fawn coloured, with a brown band across each segment; a red mid-line down the underside. Antennae and cirri with a brown ring below tip. Elytra with a dark spot in middle and a white crescent around posterior edge.

South-western coasts of Britain, commensal in the tube of *Amphitrite*.

Lepidonotus clava (Montagu)   FIG. 6.3

Body of uniform width, last parapods relatively large, with 26 chaetigers; 25–30 mm long (a). Prostomium bilobed but without frontal horns. Four eyes. Median antenna shorter than palps, lateral ones half its length; tentacles and dorsal cirri about as long as median antenna. All smooth, with a marked subterminal swelling and pointed tip; palps stout, tapering, with longitudinal rows of small papillae. Ventral cirri short, thick, with a pointed tip; first one larger, with a swollen tip, directed fowards. Elytra (12 pairs) overlap only in young specimens; they extend to rear end but leave part of back uncovered. The first four pairs carry widely scattered chitinous tubercles, large and small; the rest are almost smooth; none are fringed. Notochaetae fine, with spines along most of their length; neurochaetae long and stout, with a small swelling below tip bearing a large spur and several rows of small spines. Two anal cirri similar to dorsal cirri. In adults, nephridial papillae well-developed in most segments. The back dark-coloured, with white blotches; elytra marbled in brown, chestnut, and yellowish white, with a large white spot in the middle. Appendages with a dark ring below the subterminal swelling and sometimes another near the base.

Under stones in the tidal zone. Western Europe to Mediterranean; Indian Ocean, north Pacific.

Lepidonotus squamatus (Linnaeus)

Similar to *L. clava* except for very minor differences in relative lengths of appendages and chaetae, but the elytra overlap considerably, covering entire dorsal surface; they all bear many chitinous tubercles of various types, large and small, and are strongly fringed around the free edge. Coloration variable but often pale yellowish with a dark spot in the middle of the elytra; larger tubercles are brownish, making a mosaic pattern.

Under stones on the shore; amongst old shells or serpulid tubes in the shallow sublittoral and to considerable depths. North-western European coasts; north Pacific.

Malmgrenia castanea McIntosh FIG. 6.3

Body broad, narrowing posteriorly, with 36–41 chaetigers; 18–20 mm long. Prostomium pear-shaped, without frontal horns. Four eyes, front pair almost invisible from above. Median antenna a little longer than palps, lateral ones half as long (b). Palps smooth, stout, short. Tentacles shorter than palps, dorsal cirri similar (extending about as far as chaetae); ventral cirri slender and short. Elytra (15 pairs) smooth except for a small group of rounded tubercles on anterior (hidden) part; not fringed. Notopod small, with a few short blunt chaetae bearing rows of ill-defined small spines; neurochaetae about as thick but longer, with a short spiny blade terminating in a weak hook. Two long anal cirri. Nephridial papillae not visible. Coloration very variable; underside pink, brownish, or purple, back light brown. Elytra with transverse chestnut bands and dark spots.

Found around the mouth and in the ambulacra of *Spatangus* or, less often, on sea-stars. European coasts from the Arctic to the Mediterranean.

Polynoë scolopendrina Savigny

Body narrow, with 80–100 segments; 30–120 mm long. Prostomium with ill-defined frontal horns. Four eyes, forward pair larger but scarcely visible from above. Median antenna fairly long, with only a slight subterminal bulge and covered with short knobbed processes. Tentacles and dorsal cirri similar, lateral antennae and ventral cirri shorter. Palps of variable length, bearing rows of fine papillae. Elytra (15 pairs) cover only front half of body and do not all overlap across mid-line; they have a broad band of little tubercles across the anterior (partly hidden) portion and a few short knobbed processes around the free edge. Segments not bearing elytra have a row of three tubercles across their dorsal surface. Notochaetae are small, spiny, and often blunt-ended; the neuropod contains one large, bluntly pointed bristle in more anterior segments and numerous smaller ones with a short, spiny blade and delicately bifid tip. Two short papillated anal cirri. Cylindrical nephridial papillae. Rather variably coloured: underside usually light brown, becoming darker towards rear, with a white or reddish mid-ventral line; back a mottled brown. Elytra also mottled brown with a central dark spot surrounded by a paler area.

At low water under stones, in crevices and, particularly, commensal with *Eupolymnia* or *Lysidice*. North-western Europe, Mediterranean.

Subadyte (= *Scalisetosus*) *pellucida* (Ehlers)

Body rather narrow, very fragile, with about 40 segments; about 30 mm long. Prostomium bilobed but the anterior protuberances rounded, not forming horns. Four eyes, anterior pair much larger. Median antenna long, drawn out into an elongated tip; lateral ones and tentacles a little shorter. These and similar dorsal cirri decorated with short knobbed processes. Palps tapering and smooth. First ventral cirrus very long, remaining ones short. The anterior of 15 pairs of elytra overlap in the middle; further back they leave mid-dorsal surface bare. Elytra transparent, free surface dotted with small processes and, occasionally, a few larger rounded tubercles. Their edge may be finely papillated but not conspicuously fringed. Elytra readily shed. Notochaetae short but thick, blunt-ended, with several webbed spurs; neurochaetae longer, with a more prominent webbed spur on a subterminal swelling, from which transverse rows of fine spines run to the bifid tip. Two long anal cirri. Nephridial papillae small. Body translucent, back yellowish with light brown transverse bands, occasionally with whitish blotches. Elytra finely dotted with yellow, white, pink, brown, or purple.

Shallow sublittoral, on echinoderms. Western coasts of Europe, Mediterranean.

SIGALIONINAE

Leanira (= *Sthenolepis*) *tetragona* (Oersted) FIG. 6.3

Body narrow, tetragonal in section, with up to 300 segments; up to 200 mm long and 7 mm wide. Prostomium wide, rounded and bilobed; no visible eyes. Median antenna long, with two small fingerlike ctenidia at its base. Slender, shorter lateral antennae; a long dorsal and short ventral tentacle on each side. Two very long tapering palps. No dorsal cirri. Elytra (about 150 pairs) covering entire body, but only barely meeting in the mid-line; transparent and fringed with long papillae along their free edge. One cirriform gill inserted on the elytrophore or above each parapod except the foremost; three cup-shaped ctenidia along dorsal edge of each parapod. Each ramus has several short fingerlike processes. Notochaetae long, fine and spiny; neurochaetae jointed, with a smooth or spiny shaft and a tapering terminal segment having a ladderlike internal structure (k). Short awl-like ventral cirri. Colourless. In deep water on muddy bottoms.

Off north-western British coasts; Arctic, North Sea, north Atlantic, Mediterranean.

Pholoë minuta Fabricius FIG. 6.3

Body oblong, with a convex dorsal surface and a flat ventral surface having a longitudinal gutter; 45–70 segments, 10–20 mm long. Prostomium small and rounded; four small eyes. Median antenna short, papillated; palps short and stout, smooth (e). Two pairs of tentacles, much shorter than palps, with scattered papillae. Elytra (40–60) showing concentric rings and fringed by long, more or less moniliform processes (j). Only more posterior ones meet at mid-line. Parapods covered with short papillae. Notochaetae fine, curved, lightly toothed; neurochaetae fewer, much longer and thicker, jointed; shaft swollen and toothed at its outer end and the terminal segment as a short hook. Two threadlike anal cirri. Back a pale pink, elytra speckled with rusty brown.

At low water under stones; in the shallow sublittoral amongst old shells. North-western Europe; Pacific.

Sigalion mathildae Audouin and Milne Edwards FIG. 6.3

Body cylindrical, rolling up into a spiral when disturbed. About 200 segments, 100–150 mm long and 4–5 mm wide. Prostomium longer than its width, rounded anteriorly. Four very small eyes, often not visible. No median antenna, lateral antennae very small; palps long and smooth. First chaetiger directed forwards beneath prostomium, with a small dorsal and a rudimentary ventral tentacle. Elytra rectangular, smooth and colourless, fringed with 10–20 pinnate papillae (i). A cirriform gill inserted on the elytrophore or above each parapod. Along dorsal edge of each parapod, three ciliated mushroom-like ctenidia. Notopod elongated, with only one fingerlike process dorsally above a bundle of numerous long, fine, curved chaetae. Neurochaetae of various types: most dorsally, a few stout, simple, and pinnate ones—the rest jointed, having a terminal region of several segments, often strongly recurved. Greyish white in colour; underside iridescent, with a prominent red mid-ventral blood-vessel.

At low water, 150–200 mm beneath the surface of fine sand. North-western Europe, Mediterranean.

Sthenelais boa (Johnston)   FIG. 6.3

Body narrow, with more than 150–200 segments; 100–200 mm or more long. Prostomium rounded, with four black eyes; two button-like nuchal organs at its rearward margin. One long, smooth median antenna mounted on a swollen base which also bears two fingerlike ctenidia resembling short lateral antennae (f). Two long, smooth palps. Chaetiger one directed forwards beneath prostomium; it bears on each side one short, true lateral antenna on its internal (anterior) edge, a ctenidium dorsally at base of antenna and one long dorsal, one short ventral tentacle. Elytra cover the whole body, overlapping in the mid-line as well as down each side, giving the worm a snakelike appearance; they are covered with small, flattened tubercles and have a fine fringe around the free edge (g). On all but the most anterior few segments, a long cirriform gill; dorsal edge of each parapod has a row of three mushroom-shaped ctenidia. All but the foremost chaetiger have a notopod with several fingerlike processes and a bundle of numerous long, fine chaetae; the uppermost neurochaetae are simple, short, and pectinate, the rest jointed with a stout shaft and a hooked tip (l) becoming larger and more slender ventrally. Two long anal cirri. Coloration ranges from pale grey to yellow or brownish, sometimes with transverse rusty or dark brown bands; occasionally bright orange.

At low water in muddy sand amongst sea-grasses or under stones. On western coasts of Europe to the Mediterranean.

Sthenelais limicola (Ehlers)   FIG. 6.3

Body narrowing posteriorly, with about 120–200 segments; 50–100 mm long. Prostomium round and broad, with four black eyes of which anterior pair are markedly larger. Median antenna smooth and very long, with a pair of stout fingerlike ctenidia on its base. Chaetiger one directed forwards under prostomium, bearing on each side three processes which represent a short lateral antenna, a long dorsal tentacle, and a short ventral tentacle; dorsally a ctenidium in the form of a long ciliated crest. Elytra cover whole body, overlapping in the mid-line; they are unfringed but have a deep notch in the outer edge (h). On all but the most anterior few segments, a long cirriform gill; dorsal edge of each parapod has a row of three mushroom-shaped ctenidia, also small globular ctenidia between the parapods.

All notopods except foremost carry fingerlike processes, more numerous and longer in anterior part of body. Notochaetae are long and flexible; the uppermost neurochaetae are simple, small, and pinnate, the rest jointed with a stout shaft and a hooked terminal segment becoming longer and more slender ventrally. Two long anal cirri. Colourless and transparent, with a large brown blotch on each elytron forming, towards the front, an inverted 'V'-shape across the back.

Sublittoral, on sandy or muddy bottoms. Off coasts around the southern half of Britain; Atlantic, Mediterranean.

4 ARENICOLIDAE

Lugworms are so familiar as to require little detailed description. They are relatively stout worms with a cylindrical body made up of short segments, each (except the first three or four) superficially divided into five annuli. The notopod is a conical swelling bearing a bundle of relatively large, more or less spiny simple chaetae; the neuropod, a simple torus (Fig. 6.2j) containing a single row of crotchets with one large and one to three subsidiary terminal teeth, not hooded. Body divided into an anterior region lacking gills, then a mid-region with branching, tufted gills each inserted dorsal to the notopod; in the best-known species, this is followed by a narrower 'tail' region lacking both gills and chaetae. Lugworms occupy a fairly deep burrow in sand or muddy sand whose head end is indicated at the surface by a shallow conical depression; the characteristic coiled worm-cast appears at the top of the tail-shaft. Since a healthy worm adds to this cast regularly at 30–45 min intervals, the worm density in a given area is indicated at low tide by the number of such casts on the surface unless obliterated by, for example, heavy rain.

Branchiomaldane vincenti Langerhans (the only species in a genus not considered here in detail) is smaller, with biannulate segments and gills having 1–4 unbranched filaments. It occupies a mucus tube amongst lower-shore algae on south-western British shores.

---

1. Nineteen chaetigerous segments anteriorly, of which
    the last 13 bear paired tufted gills, followed by a
    narrower posterior region lacking gills and chaetae
                                                 Arenicola marina

    30–60 chaetigerous segments, 20–40 bearing gills;
    no achaetous 'tail'   **2**

2. First 11–12 chaetigers lack gills; 20–30 pairs of gills
    posteriorly   **Arenicolides branchialis**

    First 15–16 chaetigers lack gills; 30–40 pairs of gills
    posteriorly   **Arenicolides ecaudata**

Arenicola marina (Linnaeus)   FIG. 6.2

Thick anterior region of 19 chaetigers, of which the last 13 bear gills (j); a 'tail' region present, narrower and more fragile, lacking chaetae and gills (k). Body 150–200 mm long. Prostomium small, three-lobed. Notochaetae markedly spiny. Flesh-pink when young, becoming greenish yellow; stains yellow when handled. Severed tail region, or gut extruded from damaged specimen, may cause confusion.

On lower shore in clean to muddy sand, exposed or sheltered. An important bait species, said to be the best for bass-fishing. North-west European coasts from the Arctic to the Mediterranean.

Arenicolides branchialis Audouin and Milne Edwards (= *Arenicola grubei* Claparède)

Body of moderate thickness, narrowing at each end, 30–45 chaetigers, 150–200 mm long. First 11–12 chaetigers without gills then 20–30 pairs; no 'tail'. Prostomium truncated, without lateral lobes. Notochaetae with few spines. Very dark green or black with a metallic glint, occasionally reddish brown or deep yellow-brown.

In sediments filling cavities between rocks or stones on the lower shore; casts much finer than *A. marina*. Western Europe and Mediterranean.

Arenicolides ecaudata Johnston

Body of moderate thickness, narrowing at each end, 40–60 chaetigers, 120–250 mm long. First 15–16 chaetigers without gills, then 30–40 pairs; no 'tail'. Prostomium truncated, without lateral lobes. Notochaetae without spines.

In rich mud between stones or in rock crevices at low water; casts much finer than *A. marina*. Western Europe.

5 CAPITELLIDAE

Very common, widespread worms with long, slender bodies. Head end conical, without appendages. Their cylindrical shape, reddish brown colour and rather insignificant parapods make them the most earthworm-like of polychaetes. A short, relatively broad anterior region has short segments, most of which bear capillary chaetae only; the long posterior region has more elongated segments with small hooded crochets in simple tori, which may be visible only when they catch the light.

---

1. A single genital pore dorsally between chaetigers 8 and 9, at the centre of four stout chaetae (or pairs of chaetae) arranged in a diagonal cross (Fig. 6.5a) (*except* in female *C. capitata*, which lacks these spines). Anterior region of nine or ten chaetigerous segments **2**

    Four or more paired genital pores dorsally on last segments of anterior region or early segments of posterior region, without associated spines (Fig. 6.5b). Anterior region of 12 chaetigerous segments **3**

2. Long, slender worm (up to 100 mm, 90 or more segments). Only capillary chaetae in first six chaetigers. Blood-red, in muddy sand or rich mud **Capitella capitata**

    Short (about 10 mm, 35–45 segments). Only capillary chaetae in first four or five chaetigers. Almost colourless, in relatively clean sediments amongst stones **Capitomastus giardi**

3. Long crochets in last six segments of anterior region. Genital pores on last four anterior segments. Segments of posterior region at first long and cylindrical, then shorter and bead-like, finally bell-shaped with parapodial swellings increasing their width posteriorly (Fig. 6.4b). Single long, stout anal process **Heteromastus filiformis**

    Chaetigers of anterior region bear bundles of capillary chaetae only; no parapodial lobes or swellings. Genital pores on seven to twenty anterior segments of posterior region. Posterior segments more or less uniform. No anal process **Notomastus latericeus**

Capitella capitata (Fabricius) FIGS. 6.4, 6.5

Ninety or more segments, 20–100 mm long. Body rather fragile, narrowing at each end (6.4a) and capable of considerable expansion or contraction. Anterior region usually of nine chaetigerous segments, of which first six carry capillary chaetae only; the last two carry only hooded crochets, while the 7th may bear capillary chaetae, crochets, or both. Posterior segments bear only crochets which, in the first few, are twice as long as in the rest. A single genital pore opens mid-dorsally between chaetigers 8 and 9, in the female on an oval swelling, in the male in the middle of four stout chaetae (or bundles of chaetae)—'genital spines'—arranged in a diagonal cross (6.5a). No gills or branchial lobes. Blood-red colour.

At low water and offshore, in muddy sand or rich mud and under stones; often indicates polluted conditions. European coasts from Arctic to the Mediterranean, widespread elsewhere around Atlantic and Pacific coasts.

Capitomastus (= *Capitellides*) *giardi* (Mesnil)

From 35 to 45 segments, 10 mm long. Two regions of body very distinct. Anterior region usually of nine chaetigerous segments, of which first six carry capillary chaetae only; from the 7th they carry long, slender hooded crochets like those of posterior region. In that region, segments are markedly longer than in anterior part; dorsal rami at first bear seven or eight crochets, ventral ones eight to ten, but these numbers diminish posteriorly. The single genital pore, opening mid-dorsally between segments 8 and 9, is surrounded by a pair of genital spines on each segment, in both sexes. No gills or branchial lobes. Almost colourless, tinged with pale pink.

At low water, amongst stones. Irish Sea, Western Approaches, English Channel.

Heteromastus filiformis (Claparède) FIG. 6.4

About 140 segments, 100 mm long. Body quite thin. Anterior region of 12 chaetigerous segments, of which 2nd–6th bear only short, stout capillary chaetae and 7th–12th, long hooded crochets. Posterior segments at first long, cylindrical and biannulate, then shorter and rounded, finally bell-shaped, with swollen parapodial ridges at posterior end (b). Abdominal crochets are shorter, stouter, and more strongly toothed. Branchial lobes occur on parapodia from about the 80th segment. Four

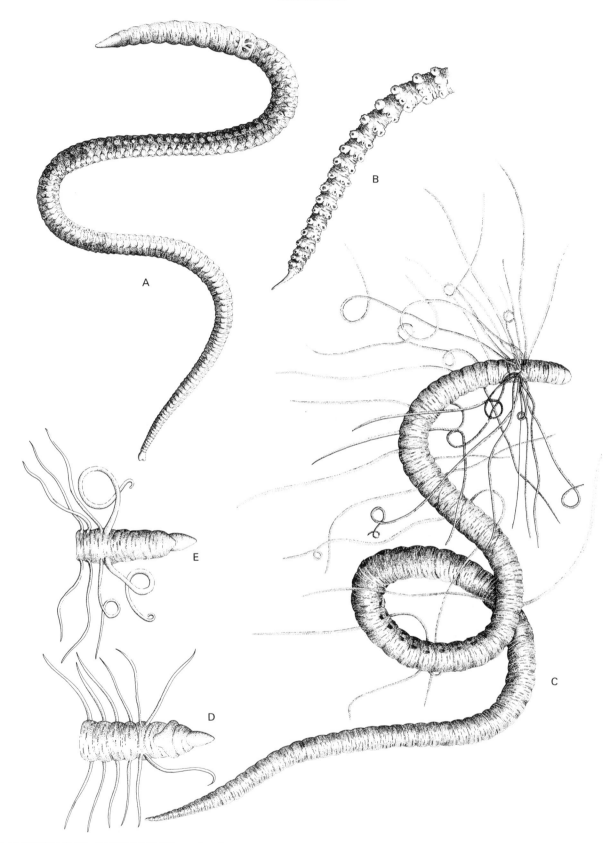

Fig. 6.4 (CAPITELLIDAE, CIRRATULIDAE) a. *Capitella capitata*—entire worm b. *Heteromastus filiformis*—posterior region c. *Cirratulus cirratus*—entire worm d. *C. filiformis*—anterior region e. *Tharvx marioni*—anterior region

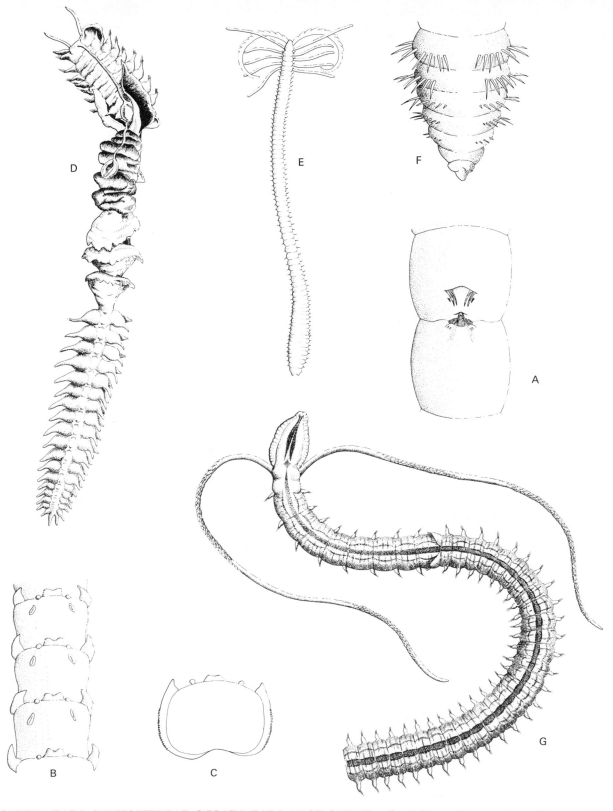

Fig. 6.5 (CAPITELLIDAE 2, CHAETOPTERIDAE, CIRRATULIDAE 2, MAGELONIDAE) a. *Capitella capitata*—male genital apparatus b. *Notomastus latericeus*—dorsal view of first abdominal segments to show genital pores c. *N. latericeus*—abdominal TS (after Day) d. *Chaetopterus variopedatus*—entire worm, dorsal e. *Dodecacerium concharum*—entire worm (after Fauvel) f. *Chaetozone setosa*—posterior end (after Hartmann-Schröder) g. *Magelona mirabilis*—anterior part of worm (after McIntosh)

pairs of genital pores, on chaetigers 9–12; no genital spines. Pygidium has a single long, stout terminal process. Anterior region dull red, posterior reddish green or yellow.

Lower shore to shallow sublittoral, in muddy sand. North Sea, English Channel, north-east Atlantic, Mediterranean.

Notomastus latericeus M. Sars FIG. 6.5

From 100 to 150 segments, 150–300 mm long. A very fragile worm, difficult to remove intact from its very contorted gallery in the sediment. Anterior region of 12 chaetigerous segments whose integument has a reticulated appearance; all bear capillary chaetae. Posterior region bears hooded crochets; between dorsal and ventral rami on each side there is a button-like lateral organ. Simple gills are formed by extensions of the rami along most of the posterior region (c). Paired genital pores dorsally on numerous (seven to twelve) anterior segments of posterior region (b): no genital spines. Pygidium terminates in a membranous flap. Anterior region purple or dark red, becoming brighter or yellowish posteriorly; posterior region colourless and transparent.

Lower shore to deep sublittoral, in clean or muddy sand, often amongst sea-grasses. European coasts from the Arctic to the Mediterranean.

6 CHAETOPTERIDAE

Soft and fragile worms with a body divided into three distinct regions. Prostomium small and often indistinct; mouth terminal, lacking a proboscis. Two conspicuous palps. Anterior region of a few segments bearing notopods only; middle and posterior regions have biramous parapods. Segments of mid-region few, elongated, and may bear much-modified structures; posterior region of many segments, all alike. Chaetiger 4 carries extra-large spines. Notochaetae mostly few, deeply embedded. Neuropods carry uncini. The worms occupy tough permanent tubes.

---

1. Large and thick (150–250 mm long, 10–25 mm wide) with relatively small palps but various large, highly specialized structures dorsally in the mid-region. Tube opaque, whitish, not annulated.
   Chaetopterus variopedatus

   Of medium length (20–60 mm) and slender (up to 2 mm wide). Palps relatively large, mid-region without large specialized appendages. Tube translucent, yellowish, often annulated **2**

2. Chaetigerous segments 60–70, less than 40 mm long. Anterior region has more than 10 chaetigers, mid-region usually has more than 10 chaetigers
   Phyllochaetopterus anglicus

   Chaetigerous segments 140–150, undamaged adult more than 40 mm long. Anterior region has 9–10 chaetigers, mid-region usually fewer than 10 chaetigers **Spiochaetopterus typicus**

Chaetopterus variopedatus (Renier) FIG. 6.5

Large, stout, although fragile worm (150–250 mm long, up to 25 mm wide) (d). Mouth in the form of a funnel whose lower edge protrudes forwards. Dorsally, two relatively short thread-like palps. Anterior region usually of 9 (8–12) chaetigers, flattened and bearing only notopods as triangular lappets with a small fan of spear-like chaetae (chaetiger 9 has rudimentary neuropods). Chaetiger 4 has several greatly enlarged chaetae. Mid-region of five segments; first of these very elongated and bears dorsally a pair of curved fins supported by an embedded bundle of fine chaetea; second has dorsally a feeding-cup formed from the notopods, fused in the mid-line. Dorsal elements of parapods of remaining segments have each fused to form three large rounded paddles. The ventral element of the parapods of all five segments have fused to form sucker-like structures fringed with uncini. Posterior region has 20–70 chaetigers in which the notopods form slender fingerlike structures pointing upwards and supported by fine embedded chaetae; the neuropods are made up of a latero-ventral fin with a small lateral cirrus, and a more ventral fin partly fused with that of the other side. Each bears three rows of pectinate uncini. Yellowish or greenish white; mature females pinkish. Certain parts of the worm, and the mucus which it secretes abundantly, give off a bluish luminescence. Tube circular in section, made up of many layers of flexible whitish membrane. The central part forms a flattened U-shape in clean or muddy sand; each end is narrower but open and protrudes slightly above the surface.

Around or below low water. Cosmopolitan.
(N.B. Because the worm breaks up easily when disturbed and can readily regenerate lost parts, some specimens may show marked anomalies).

Phyllochaetopterus anglicus Potts (= *P. socialis* Claparède)

Thin worm of medium length (20–40 mm long, 1–2 mm wide), 60–70 chaetigers. Mouth a semicircular or straight slit; two very short tentacles and a pair of large palps, often spiralled or rolled up. Anterior region usually of 13 (10–18) chaetigers, rather flattened, bearing dorsally chaetae of various spear-like forms. Chaetiger 4 has a single greatly enlarged chaeta on each side. Ventrally, a glandular cushion extends over last half of the region. Mid-region of 7–24 segments. The lobes of the notopods comprise bilobed leaf-like flaps dorsally, supported by embedded fine chaetae, and gill-like crescents laterally. Neuropods also have two lobes, a tiny lateral one and a large ventral one partly fusing with that of the other side, each bearing finely toothed triangular uncini. Posterior region of numerous short segments; notopods small, erect, and cylindrical, with only one or two lanceolate chaetae; neuropods simple flanges joined to the notopod by a transverse ridge and bearing pectinate uncini. Yellowish, with red markings anteriorly. The tube is of a tough translucent yellow plastic-like material, often annulated. As the worms often break and regenerate, several can sometimes be found in one tube, or side-branches are made.

At low water on rocks; dredged from the sublittoral. Sometimes tubes form an extensive 'turf'. Irish Sea, south-west Britain, north-east Atlantic, Mediterranean.

Spiochaetopterus typicus Sars

Long, thin worm (50–60 mm long, up to 2 mm wide), 140–150 chaetigers. Mouth funnel-like, with a fleshy lower lip. Two very long palps, often spiralled. Anterior region of 9–10 chaetigers, rather flattened, bearing dorsally long spear-like chaetae. Chaetiger 4 has a single greatly enlarged chaeta on each side. Ventrally, two glandular cushions occupy posterior half of this region. Mid-region of 2–10 very elongated segments with foliaceous notopods supported by capillary chaetae and simple neuropods containing fine-toothed uncini. Posterior region of many short segments with small cylindrical notopods each bearing a few lanceolate chaetae; neuropods contain fine-toothed triangular uncini. Yellowish, with brown and white glandular patches. Tube of a tough translucent yellow plastic-like material with regular annulations.

In both shallow and deep water on bottoms of sand, mud, and gravel. Northern waters.

7 CIRRATULIDAE

Worms generally living in mud or rock crevices, with a more or less cylindrical body usually tapering at each end. The first three segments lack parapods and chaetae. On one of the first to fourth chaetigers are inserted either a pair of long, coiled palps or a number of finer tentacular filaments (some species not included here have a single long median tentacle); laterally on a number of segments there are also long, contractile gill-filaments. These filaments, protruding from the mud or crevice like a number of small worms, are often all that can be seen of the animal. The palps and some of the gills may be shed in the disturbance of collection, but a few gills usually remain. The anus tends to be dorsal, leaving the pygidium as a terminal button or cone.

1. One of the first few segments bears a pair of palps markedly larger than the threadlike gills **2**

    One of the first few segments bears few to numerous tentacles of similar size to the gills (which occur throughout most of the body **4**

2. Stout chaetal spines present, particularly posteriorly. Fewer than 100 segments **3**

    Fine capillary chaetae only. More than 200 segments. ***Tharyx marioni***

3. Spines form almost a complete ring around posterior segments, each tapering to a simple point (Fig. 6.5f). Gills on numerous (at least 20) segments. Body relatively thin, narrowing posteriorly ***Chaetozone setosa***

    Spines inserted laterally, having either a spoon-shaped tip or a short toothed blade. Gills on only four to six anterior segments. Body relatively thick, broad, and flattened posteriorly ***Dodecaceria concharum***

4. Eight or fewer tentacles in a cluster on each side of first chaetigerous segment. Segments relatively long and distinct **5**

Many more than eight tentacles on each side of first chaetiger. Segments short and tightly packed together. Gills and tentacles roll up tightly when animal is disturbed ***Cirriformia tentaculata***

5. Prostomium blunt, with four to eight large black eyes on each side; following three segments (which lack chaetae) similar to each other, with normal straight margins (Fig. 6.4c). Large blunt chaetae present in middle and posterior segments in addition to capillary ones ***Cirratulus cirratus***

    Prostomium pointed, without eyes; second achaetous segment behind it is heart-shaped dorsally, with a lobe extending back in the mid-line over the third (Fig. 6.4d). Chaetigerous segments bear capillary chaetae only

    Cirratulus filiformis

Chaetozone setosa Malmgren FIG. 6.5

Body with 70–90 segments, 20–25 mm long. Prostomium conical, pointed, without eyes. Two large palps, grooved, very long and fragile, inserted on anterior edge of first chaetiger. Gills on a large number of segments throughout about first half of body. Chaetigers throughout body bear capillary chaetae; in posterior region, simple pointed stout chaetae are inserted in a transverse series which, towards rear end, almost encircles each segment (f). Grey, brownish- or bluish-black.

On muddy bottoms in the shallow sublittoral. European waters from the Arctic to the Mediterranean.

Cirratulus cirratus (Müller) FIG. 6.4

Body with 75–130 segments, 30–120 mm long. Prostomium a blunt cone with a row of four to eight large black eyes on each side, sometimes meeting in mid-line. Two to eight grooved tentacles inserted on anterior edge of first chaetigerous segment on each side, again sometimes meeting in the mid-line (c). Gills of much the same size as tentacles, from first chaetiger almost to tail end. Chaetigers throughout body bear capillary chaetae. Stout, bluntly pointed chaetae also occur ventrally from chaetiger 10–12 and dorsally from 20–23; posteriorly, ventral ones (two or three per ramus) are larger and darker than dorsal ones. Orange, pinkish- or brownish-red; tentacles and gills red or yellow.

Lower shore, in mud or muddy sand beneath or between rocks. Most north-west European coasts, also in south Atlantic.

Cirratulus filiformis Keferstein FIG. 6.4

Body with 150–200 segments, 30–42 mm long. Prostomium pointed, without eyes; the second of three achaetous segments behind it is roughly heart-shaped dorsally, with a lobe overlapping the third in the mid-line (d). One or two tentacles inserted on anterior edge of first chaetigerous segment on each side. Gills of much the same size as tentacles, from chaetiger one to tail end. Throughout the body, chaetae are capillaries only. Brownish or greenish yellow.

Lower shore, amongst lithothamnia or in rock crevices. Irish Sea, Channel, and North Sea.

Cirriformia (= *Audouinia*) *tentaculata* (Montagu)

Body with 300 or more very short, tightly packed segments; 150–200 mm long. Body tends to be flattened or concave ventrally. Prostomium a blunt cone without well-developed eyes but bearing several pigment-spots. On 6th–7th chaetigers (rarely 4th–5th), very numerous tentacular threads in two groups which may meet in mid-line. Gills from chaetiger one almost to tail end. Chaetigers throughout the body bear capillary chaetae. Stout, bluntly pointed chaetae also occur on all but the first few, ventrally sooner than dorsally; ventral ones are larger and darker. Orange, reddish brown, or greenish bronze; tentacles and gills red.

Lower shore, in rich mud under stones, in muddy sand, or amongst sea-grasses. Most north-west European coasts.

Dodecaceria concharum Oersted   FIG. 6.5

Body with 45–80 segments, 20–60 mm long. Body cylindrical but becoming flattened and broader posteriorly (e). Prostomium small, without eyes in adult; next (buccal) segment is long, achaetous, and triannulate ventrally; it bears on its posterior edge a pair of large, wrinkled, grooved and coiling palps, also a pair of much more slender gill filaments. The first three or four (rarely five) chaetigers also carry a pair of gills (e). In the first six or seven chaetigers there are only capillary craetae but subsequently there are also both stout and finer crochets with tips hollowed like small spoon-bowls; capillary chaetae become fewer posteriorly. In young specimens, the stouter chaetae have a short, broad-toothed blade rather than a spoon-end. Brownish or blackish green; eggs green.

At low water, in galleries excavated amongst lithothamnia, in soft rock or old shells. These sedentary forms are parthenogenetic females. Pelagic epitokes with two large eyes, palps reduced or absent, fewer stout chaetae but bundles of long capillaries, occur more rarely and can be of either sex, yellowish in colour. They seem always to be parasitized by a long gregarine. Most north-west European coasts from the Arctic to the Mediterranean.

Tharyx marioni (de St Joseph)   FIG. 6.4

Body with 200 segments or more, 35–100 mm long, very thin. Prostomium a blunt cone without eyes; three following, achaetous segments relatively long. Two large, grooved, and coiling palps inserted in anterior edge of first chaetiger (e). Gills on about the first half of body from chaetiger 1. Chaetigers throughout the body bear only capillary chaetae. Reddish brown, eggs greenish.

At low water, amongst lithothamnia and in rock crevices. Irish Sea, Channel, North Sea.

8 EUNICIDAE

All members of this family have a strong, muscular, eversible proboscis with black chitinous jaws, often numerous and elaborate but arranged in the same basic plan. The body is usually elongated and typically worm-like, with distinct although small parapods in which dorsal elements are reduced and ventral ones well-developed. However, the presence and arrangement of appendages, including gills, is so variable that the family has been divided into sub-groups which some workers regard as families in their own right. Here, purely for practical purposes, it has been divided into two groups which emerge from the general key separately. *Histriobdella homari*, a parasite of lobsters, also keys out separately on the basis of its bizarre external appearance; it is included in this family because of its jaw structure. See George and Hartmann-Schröder (1985).

'EUNICIDAE I'

This group comprises the subfamilies Arabellinae and Lumbrinereinae, plus *Nematonereis* from the Eunicinae. All have a conical prostomium with either no appendages or only a single median antenna. There are never gills; the notopod is either completely absent or represented only by a small button-like dorsal cirrus and, sometimes, an aciculum. The first body-segment (following the peristomium) has neither parapods nor chaetae. Pectinate chaetae (like a flattened brush) are found only in *Nematonereis*.

---

1. Short median antenna (Fig. 6.6b); short dorsal cirri and pectinate chaetae (Fig. 6.6d) present
    Nematonereis unicornis

    No prostomial appendages; dorsal cirri rudimentary or absent, no pectinate chaetae.   **2**

2. Chaetae all simple (mostly with a long, thin, curved blade); no crochets   **3**

    Simple or jointed hooded crochets (Fig. 6.6m, n) present   **4**

3. One very large, plain, blunt chaeta present in the lower bundle of each parapod (Fig. 6.6j)   ***Drilonereis filum***

    Chaetae all much the same size   ***Arabella iricolor***

4. Jointed crochets present in the first 20–30 chaetigerous segments, simple crochets in the remainder; usually well under 300 mm long   ***Lumbrineris latreilli***

    No jointed crochets   **5**

5. Simple crochets lacking from first 1–5 chaetigers, present in remainder, acicula yellow; may be large (up to 400 mm long)   ***Lumbrineris tetraura***

    Simple crochets lacking from first 22–35 chaetigers, present in remainder; acicula black; usually under 30 mm long   ***Lumbrineris fragilis***

Arabella iricolor (Montagu)   FIG. 6.6

Body cylindrical, narrowing to a point at each end, with about 400 segments; up to 500–600 mm long. Prostomium a blunt cone without appendages but with four eyes in a transverse row at

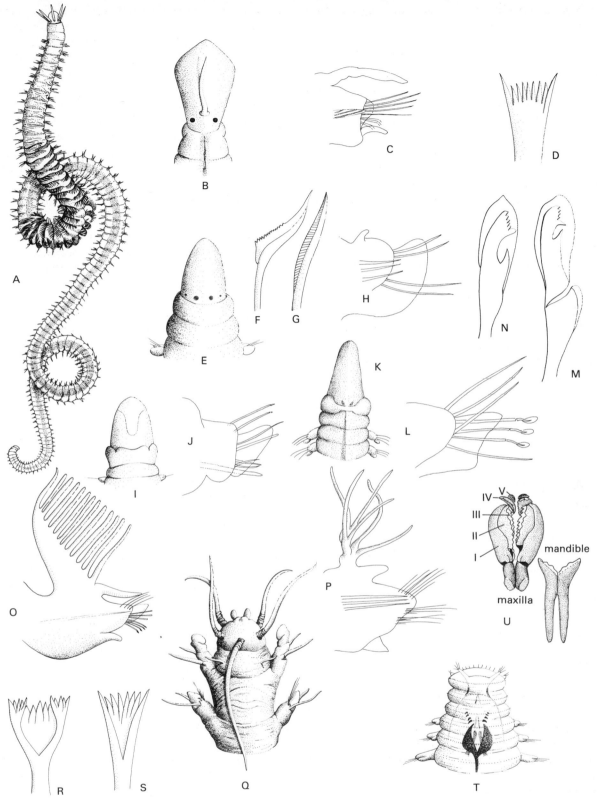

Fig. 6.6 (EUNICIDAE) a. *Marphysa belli*—enitre worm (partly after McIntosh) b. *Nematonereis unicornis*—head c. *N. unicornis*—anterior parapod d. *N. unicornis*—tip of brush-ended (pectinate) chaeta e. *Arabella iricolor*—head f. *A. iricolor*—toothed geniculate chaeta g. *A. iricolor*—winged chaeta h. *A. iricolor*—anterior parapod i. *Drilonereis filum*—head (after Fauvel) j. *D. filum*—parapod k. *Lumbrineris latreilli*—head l. *L. latreilli*—anterior parapod m. *L. latreilli*—jointed hooded crochet n. *L. latreilli*—simple hooded crochet o. *Marphysa belli*—parapod with gill (after Fauvel) p. *M. sanguinea*—parapod with gill (after McIntosh) q. *Onuphis conchylega*—anterior end r. *O. conchylega*—triple brush-ended (pectinate) chaeta s. *Marphysa sanguinea*—pectinate chaeta t. *Ophryotrocha puerilis*—anterior end u. Upper and lower jaw elements (*Onuphis conchylega*), conventionally numbered

rearward edge (e). Lower edge of peristomium thrown into several longitudinal folds. Jaws with a pair of large hooks; two long posterior supports, one elongated middle element. In front of hooks, four pairs of elements asymmetrically toothed. Parapods with two lobes, the postero-ventral one an elongated conical shape (h). Dorsal cirri small tubercles, no ventral cirri. Several yellow acicula to each parapod, ending in a fine protruding point. Chaetae all simple, short, and strong, ending in a curved blade sometimes toothed at its base (f,g). Pygidium with four short anal cirri. Pinkish grey, iridescent; sometimes four longitudinal rows of dark spots on the fore segments (lost in alcohol).

At low water and in the shallow sublittoral, in muddy sand. Coasts of south-west Britain, Europe to the Mediterranean; Red Sea, Arabian Gulf, Indo-Pacific.

Drilonereis filum (Claparède)   FIG. 6.6

Slender cylindrical body with very numerous segments, 80–160 mm long. Prostomium forming a flattened blunt point, without appendages and usually lacking eyes, often depressed along its dorsal mid-line; two dark nuchal organs at its rearward edge dorsally (i). Lower edge of peristomium thrown into numerous longitudinal folds. Jaws with a pair of large hooks; two long posterior supports, one short broad middle element overlapping their forward ends. In front of the hooks, two to three pairs of elements reduced to single teeth. Parapods simple low swellings in first few chaetigers, becoming two-lobed and longer further back (j). Dorsal cirri reduced to little buttons. Numerous yellow acicula to each parapod, ending in a fine protruding point. Chaetae all simple, mostly with a curved blade at tip, but one very large, straight, blunt-ended one occurs ventrally in each parapod. Four anal cirri. Yellowish, pink, or dirty green, strongly iridescent.

At low water and below in muddy sand, often associated with *Cirriformia tentaculata*. On southern and western coasts of Britain, Europe to the Mediterranean; Red Sea, Arabian Gulf.

Lumbrineris fragilis (O. F. Müller)

Cylindrical body with about 300 segments, much the same width throughout its length of 150–350 mm. Prostomium a pointed cone with neither appendages nor eyes (*sim.* Fig. 6.6k); two small nuchal organs (may be withdrawn from view). Lower edge of peristomium thrown into a few longitudinal folds. Jaws with a pair of large hooks; a pair of supports form a shield shape behind (with no middle element). In front of hooks, two pairs of triangular plates, points inwards. Parapods with two lobes, postero-ventral one an elongated conical shape (*sim.* Fig. 6.6h). Dorsal cirri indistinct or absent. A few black acicula with fine tips dorsally. Chaetae all simple: in first 60–100 chaetigers there are those with curved blades and, from chaetiger 22–35, also hooded crochets. The more posterior parapods bear only these crochets. Pygidium a four-lobed button. Orange, yellow, or brown (becoming grey in alcohol), iridescent.

Sublittoral, on bottoms of muddy sand or gravel. West coast of Europe from the Arctic to the Mediterranean; north Pacific.

Lumbrineris latreilli Audouin and   FIG. 6.6
Milne Edwards

As *L. fragilis* but smaller (50–300 mm long) (k). Acicula yellow. Curved, bladed simple chaetae occur in first 40–60 chaetigers and, in first 20–30, jointed chaetae with a short end-section in the form of a hooded hook (m); in remaining segments, simple hooded crochets (n). Pygidium with four short, unequal anal cirri. Pink, orange, or brown; iridescent.

At low water and below, amongst sea-grasses in muddy sand, in gravel, or in black mud under stones. On most European coasts from Iceland to the Mediterranean; north Atlantic, Red Sea, Indo-Pacific.

N.B. *L. gracilis* Ehlers also has jointed crochets (in the first 10–15 chaetigers); it is smaller (30–50 mm long) and very slender, occurring along western shores.

Lumbrineris tetraura (Schmarda) (= *Lumbriconereis impatiens* Claparède)

As *L. fragilis* but large (300–400 mm long and with more than 500 segments). Acicula yellow. Curved, bladed, simple chaetae occur in first 40–80 chaetigers; no jointed crochets, simple ones from chaetiger 1–5. Four short anal cirri. Pale pink or red, iridescent.

At low water, in clean or only slightly muddy sand, shell gravel, or algal holdfasts, to considerable depths. Cosmopolitan.

Nematonereis unicornis (Grube)   FIG. 6.6

Body threadlike, often thrown into many bends, with 300–400 segments, about 150–200 mm long. Prostomium blunt-ended, bearing dorsally a single short antenna flanked by a pair of large eyes (b) (juveniles may also have two small eyespots). Jaws consist of a pair of large hooks with a single median support behind and two pairs of toothed elements in front. Dorsal cirri fingerlike, extending laterally a little beyond parapods; ventral cirri short, pear-shaped. Acicula dark; those protruding like chaetae occur from about chaetiger 20 and are tipped with a small hooded hook. Chaetae in upper bundle of each parapod (c) simple bladed and brush-ended (d); in lower bundle, they are jointed, with a short end-section having a toothed edge and terminating in a small hooded hook. Anal cirri slender, two long and two short. Body pale pink in front, orange or greenish behind, iridescent.

At low water and in the shallow sublittoral, under stones on muddy sand or in rock-crevices. On south-western coasts in Britain; north-east Atlantic, Mediterranean; Indian Ocean.

'EUNICIDAE II'

Includes the subfamilies Dorvilleinae, Eunicinae except *Nematonereis*, and Onuphinae. The prostomium has numerous appendages, usually two antennae, two palps, and zero to five tentacles. The notopod is reduced but may contain a few chaetae; gills may also be present dorsally.

1. Gills (and usually tentacles) present   **2**

   Gills and tentacles absent (short, stout dorsal cirri may be present but are not readily confused with gills)   **5**

2. Gills a pair of single fingerlike filaments on most segments, more or less resembling dorsal cirri; worm may be occupying a tube which it carries around   **3**

   Most or all of gills have a number of filaments, arranged either in a tuft or as the teeth of a comb; worm does not occupy a free tube   **4**

3. First body-segment lacks parapods but carries a pair of short tentacles dorsally. Tube membranous, encrusted with shell-fragments or coarse sand-grains   ***Onuphis conchylega***

   First body-segment lacks both parapods and tentacles; tube transparent, horny   ***Hyalinoecia tubicola***

4. Gills comb-like (Fig. 6.6o), on about 20 segments of anterior half of body; dorsal cirri long. Large (up to 200 mm long), fairly sturdy   ***Marphysa belli***

   Gills as a tuft (Fig. 6.6p), on most segments of body; dorsal cirri short. Very large (may be well over 300 mm long) but readily breaks up   ***Marphysa sanguinea***

5. Palps, antennae, and dorsal cirri reduced to short unjointed papillae; translucent, whitish; black jaws visible within body, resembling a closed pair of tongs (Fig. 6.6t)   ***Ophryotrocha puerilis***

   Palps relatively prominent; antennae with three or four sections, dorsal cirri with two sections. Brightly coloured in life, details of jaws not visible within body   ***Dorvillea rubrovittata***

Dorvillea (= *Staurocephalus*) *rubrovittata* (Grube)

Body narrowing at each end, 15–30 mm long, with a flattened ventral surface, dorsally convex; 40–50 very distinct segments. Two short, broad palps, curling backwards; two short antennae, unjointed in juveniles but with three or four sections in adults. Buccal segment twice as long as next, both achaetous. Jaws not visible through body-wall. First chaetiger without dorsal cirrus; on the following ones, this cirrus cylindrical, in two parts—a long basal section strengthened by an aciculum and a shorter, conical end-section. Ventral cirri fingerlike. Parapods small but long, bluntly conical, with chaetae in two bundles: in the upper one, simple, stout, flattened, finely toothed, and blunt-ended; in the lower, finer, jointed, with a hooded bidentate blade. Yellow cross-banded with greenish yellow in juveniles, reddish orange in adults (colourless in alcohol).

On the lower shore, under stones and amongst small algae; in the shallow sublittoral amongst old shells. South and west coasts of Britain, northern seas, north-east and tropical Atlantic, Mediterranean.

Hyalinoecia tubicola (O. F. Müller)

Body rather square in section, 60–120 mm long, with about 80–120 segments. Two large globular palps; two ovoid frontal antennae. Five occipital antennae on a short annulated basal section; the two most anterior short, lateral ones about one-third longer (reaching back to the 9th–10th chaetiger) and middle one longer again. Buccal segment almost the same size as the following. Anterior edge of lower jaw element dull white. Gills all simple, fingerlike, starting on 22nd–26th segment and at first very small, then longer than dorsal cirri (which become much smaller around chaetiger 30). Ventral cirri awl-shaped, stout but short, on first three chaetigers. Ventral element of each parapod resembles a flattened cirrus until 13th–16th chaetiger, then much smaller as far as 20th. On first two chaetigers, the parapods contain fine bristles and simple or bidentate crochets (which may appear jointed); from the 3rd, they have short lance-like bristles and brush-ended chaetae, together with two stout chaetae each having two hooded terminal teeth. Acicula yellow. Body yellowish in alcohol, iridescent.

The worm occupies an unattached horny tube resembling the quill of a feather, open at each end but with internal mitre-valves. Offshore on sandy or muddy bottoms. Around most of the British coast; more or less cosmopolitan.

Marphysa belli (Audouin and Milne Edwards)   FIG. 6.6

Body slender, 100–200 mm long, 200–300 segments (a). Anterior edge of prostomium smoothly rounded. Five antennae, indistinctly annulated, subequal, and scarcely extending beyond head. Buccal segment twice as long as following one. Dorsal cirri long, fingerlike; ventral cirri similar but shorter. Gills prominent, like a coarse comb with 10–18 teeth (o), from 12th–15th to about 35th chaetiger. Conical parapods with two bundles: in the upper, fine lance-like chaetae and brush-ended ones; below, jointed chaetae with a hooded bidentate hook together (in anterior third of body) with some having a long, pointed outer element. Bidentate, hooded, dark, stout chaetae from about 35th chaetiger. Acicula black. Body pinkish or purplish grey, iridescent, with bright red gills.

On the lower shore in muddy sand, often amongst sea-grasses, frequently associated with the capitellid *Notomastus latericeus*. Western coasts of Britain, Europe to the Mediterranean.

Marphysa sanguinea (Montagu)   FIG. 6.6

Body broad, flattened, 300–600 mm long, breaks up very readily; 300 segments or more. Anterior edge of prostomium bilobed. Antennae smooth or faintly annulated, short; median one slightly longer. Buccal segment twice as long as following. Dorsal cirri smooth, short, conical; ventral cirri short, blunt tubercles. Gills first simple, then as a tuft of four to seven filaments (p). Parapods with two bundles: in the upper, fine flattened bristles and brush-ended chaetae (some with very fine, numerous teeth; others—especially in the posterior region—with much larger, fewer teeth: s); below, jointed chaetae with a long pointed outer element. Bidentate stout chaetae dark; acicula black. Body pinkish grey, iridescent; gills bright red.

Occupies a mucus-lined gallery in muddy sand under stones and in rock crevices on the lower shore, also amongst old shells sublittorally. Valued as angling bait in the Channel Isles ('verm') and can bite painfully when harassed. Western coasts of Britain; more or less cosmopolitan.

Onuphis conchylega Sars   FIG. 6.6

Body cylindrical, 100–150 mm long, with more than 150 segments. Two ovoid frontal antennae, five occipital ones on a short annulated basal section; posterior lateral of these reach back to the 5th–6th segment, median one a little longer. Buccal segment shorter than following one, with two slender tentacles. First two chaetigers large, with parapods extending forwards on each side of head (q). Anterior edge of lower jaw element white, porcelain-like. Dorsal cirri slender and fingerlike on anterior chaetigers, same length as gills back to 18th–20th then much shorter, disappearing at about chaetiger 30. Gills simple (or, very rarely, bifid) from 11th–13th chaetiger to end of body. Ventral cirri fingerlike on first two chaetigers and directed forwards; globular from chaetiger 3 back. Posterior lip of parapod cirriform until 14th chaetiger. On first two chaetigers, flattened simple bristles and large crochets; from the 3rd, chaetae apparently jointed, with a single-toothed (rarely bidentate) tip as 'blade'. From chaetiger 4, parapods contain toothed or curved lance-like chaetae, chaetae with a triple brush-end (r) and also, from 9th–12th, stout chaetae with a hooded bidentate tip. Colour very variable: anterior segments often cross-banded with violet/brown on a yellowish brown background. Rust-coloured blotches at base of parapods.

Worm occupies a flattened, membranous tube covered with shell-fragments embedded in silt, which it drags around with it. On sandy or muddy bottoms in the shallow sublittoral and offshore. Around most of the British coast; cosmopolitan.

Ophryotrocha puerilis Claparède and Mecznikow FIG. 6.6

Body 3–10 mm long, slightly attenuated at rear; 20–30 segments, each with a ciliated ring around it. Antennae and palps form a pair of small, elongated papillae at each side of rounded prostomium. Buccal segment much the same size as following, both achaetous. Parapods bluntly conical. Dorsal and ventral cirri reduced to small rounded lobes. One to three stout simple chaetae dorsally; two to four jointed chaetae with a short pointed blade inserted lower down, with a single simple pointed one ventrally. One straight aciculum. Colourless or whitish; jaw apparatus visible through body-wall as a black shape resembling a closed pair of tongs (t). The whole worm is reminiscent of a small maggot.

Amongst sedentary animals and algae in the intertidal of sheltered shores; sometimes in the body-cavity of holothurians. All around the British coast; cosmopolitan, often appears in marine aquaria.

Histriobdella homari van Beneden   FIG. 6.1

(Because of its unique shape, this worm emerges separately in the key to families, not in those to other eunicids)

Very small (0.25–0.5 mm long) with a slender body of five unequal segments. Head and 4th (genital) segment swollen, globular; posterior end broadly bifurcated, giving the worm the appearance of a pick-axe or anchor. Head bears five tentacular appendages, with median one inserted anteriorly. At rear of head, a pair of stouter appendages each bear a terminal sucker. The jaws consist of two long ventral elements, ending anteriorly in a toothed part with a large hook at each side, and a single long dorsal element with further toothed pieces in front of it. No parapods or chaetae. The paired posterior processes each bear a small cirriform tubercle midway along their rearward edge and a terminal sucker; the anus lies dorsally between them. The sexes are separate, with complicated genital organs visible within the body.

Parasitic amongst the eggs or in the branchial cavity of lobsters; surprisingly agile. South and west coasts of Britain, northwest Europe.

9 FLABELLIGERIDAE

Also known as Chlorhaemidae. The body is short and spindle-shaped, covered with small papillae and characteristically encrusted with sand or mud grains incorporated into mucus secreted by these papillae, or completely sheathed in clear mucus. Some chaetae of anterior segments are long and directed forwards, often forming a cage around the head. Two thick palps and a number of slimmer simple gills are borne on a buccal tube formed from the prostomium and peristomium and can be retracted with it. Flabelligerids typically feed on particles on the sand or mud surface, living under stones or in shallow burrows and creeping around only slowly; *Flabelligera* species are commensals of sea-urchins, feeding on faecal material.

1. Cephalic cage of numerous long chaetae more or less encloses anterior end. Stout, curved, and hooked chaetae may be prominent ventrally on posterior segments. Buccal tube short, not very extensible   **2**

   Cephalic cage represented by only one to three collar chaetae on each side. Chaetae throughout body are capillaries. Buccal tube long and mobile
   Diplocirrus glaucus

2. Body completely encased in a thick, clear mucus sheath. In posterior half of body, each segment has one or two prominent composite chaetae with a darker, curved blunt-ended tip. Anteriorly, two groups of 20–30 ciliated gill-filaments. May be found amongst spines of echinoids   *Flabelligera affinis*

   Body encrusted with grains of sand or mud. All but the most anterior segments have a row of stout curved spines on each side ventrally. Anteriorly, a row of four fingerlike gills on each side   *Pherusa plumosa*

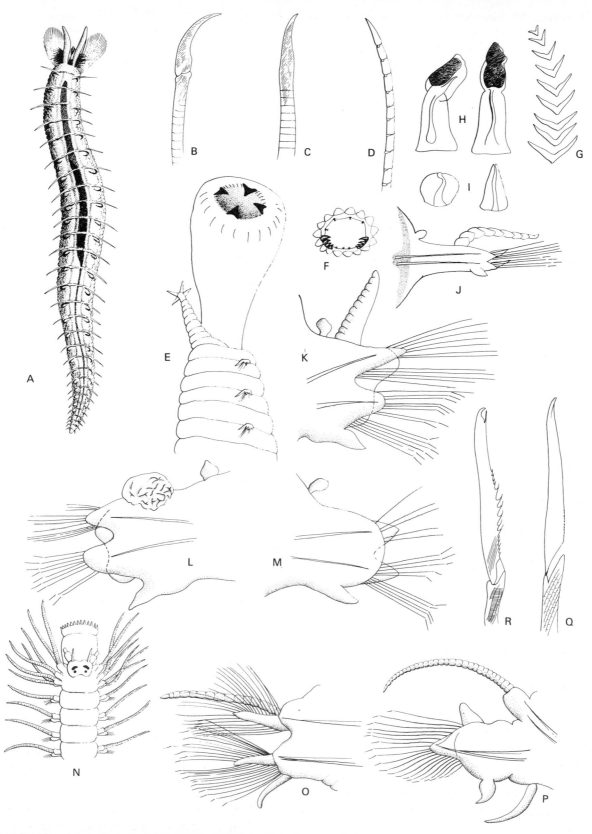

Fig. 6.7 (FLABELLIGERIDAE, GLYCERIDAE, HESIONIDAE) a. *Flabelligera affinis*—entire worm b. *F. affinis*—jointed hook c. *Pherusa plumosa*—simple hook (after Hartmann-Schröder) d. *Diplocirrus glaucus*—pseudoarticulated neurochaeta e. *Glycera tridactyla*—anterior end f. *Goniada maculata*—jaws (after Day) g. *G. maculata*—chevrons of proboscis h. *Glycera alba*—papillae of proboscis i. *G. rouxi*—papillae of proboscis j. *G. rouxi*—mid-region parapod (after Day) k. *G. alba*—mid-region parapod, from rear l. *G. gigantea*—mid-region parapod, from front m. *G. capitata*—mid-region parapod, from rear n. *Kefersteinia cirrata*—anterior region o. *Ophiodromus flexuosus*—parapod p. *Nereimya punctata*—parapod q. *N. punctata*—jointed chaeta (after Fauvel) r. *K. cirrata*—jointed chaeta (after Hartmann-Schröder)

Diplocirrus glaucus (Malmgren)   FIG. 6.7

Body with 20–30 (rarely 50) segments, 20–25 mm long. Body swollen and fairly smooth anteriorly, posterior region like a string of beads, with a marked constriction between each segment. Papillae small, fingerlike, more or less bent over at tip and well-spaced. Buccal tube long and retractile, four flattened gills inserted on anterior edge of tube and four much more slender cirriform ones behind them. There are four eyes and two long palps, broader than first type of gills. One to three long, forward-directed collar chaetae on first chaetiger, clearly divided into short sections like telescope-segments, iridescent. Chaetae of subsequent segments (d) become progressively shorter; all are of the capillary type and annulated. Notopods surrounded at their base by a circle of larger papillae. Pearly grey or silvery white.

Sublittoral, on muddy or sandy bottoms. Northern European coasts.

Flabelligera affinis Sars   FIG. 6.7

Body with 30–50 segments, 20–60 mm long (a). Papillae have an elongated or club-shaped tip on a long flexible stalk. Buccal tube short. Two pairs of eyes, almost fused. Two groups of 20–30 delicate, ciliated cirriform gills. Two broad palps with thick wrinkled edges. Four bundles of long chaetae, 60–120 altogether, project forwards from the first chaetiger to form a cephalic cage. Notopods bear fine capillary chaetae and are surrounded by longer papillae. From chaetiger 25, the neuropod contains one or two stout jointed (or apparently jointed) chaetae with an annulated stalk and a short, curved, blunt-ended tip of darker colour (b); each is surrounded by a bundle of five to six short, straight capillary chaetae of which only the point protrudes from the skin. Body greenish, gills green. Palps yellow or orange, gut bright red (visible by transparency). Body encased in mucus which is clear unless stained with mud.

At low water, under stones and amongst algae; young specimens often found amongst the spines of echinoids. Also sublittoral, on muddy bottoms. Northern European coasts including the western Baltic and Western Approaches.

Pherusa (= *Stylarioides*) *plumosa* (Müller)   FIG. 6.7

Body with 25–70 segments, 50–60 mm. The more posterior segments rather more clearly demarcated. Body well-covered with papillae which have either the same thickness throughout or a slightly swollen tip, better developed on the dorsal surface and around parapods. Buccal tube short. Four brown eyes, anterior pair larger than the posterior. Eight fingerlike gills in a semicircular row, more or less divided into two groups. Two broad palps with thick wrinkled edges. Cephalic cage formed from long chaetae of the first three chaetigers, directed forwards, annulated and weakly iridescent. Parapodial lobes scarcely developed. From chaetiger 4, capillary chaetae in a bundle dorsally and, ventrally, a transverse row of sigmoid spines (c) of variable shape, together with finer chaetae. Deep orange or rusty yellow when young; adults greenish, dark brown, or steel grey. Encrusted with sand or mud-grains, giving an appearance of sandpaper; cephalic chaetae may be festooned with mucus, as though with cobwebs.

At low water in muddy rock crevices, amongst mussels or under stones; also sublittoral on muddy bottoms. European coasts from the Arctic possibly to the Mediterranean.

10 GLYCERIDAE

Long, slender worms with numerous segments, appearing even more numerous because they are further subdivided by annular constrictions; often red, pink, or flushed with pink anteriorly. The anterior end bears a small, elongated, tapering, and multiannulate prostomium at the end of which are four minute antennae (Fig. 6.7e); other anterior appendages and the parapods are relatively insignificant. A living specimen will soon evert a long, thick proboscis from beneath the base of the prostomium. The genus *Goniada* (of which only one species is included here) is distinguished from *Glycera* by the chitinous chevrons ranged along each side of the proboscis near its base, resembling good-conduct stripes on the sleeves of a military jacket, and by the circlet of many-toothed jaw-pieces around its terminal mouth. In *Glycera*, the mouth is armed with four large fang-like jaws arranged in a cross; some species deliver a bite which is said to resemble a bee-sting. The nature of the papillae scattered over the proboscis may also be diagnostic.

In *Goniada*, the posterior part of the body is broader, flattened and bears biramous parapods; these are uniramous in the rounded anterior part. *Glycera* has a rounded body throughout; the first two chaetigers bear uniramous parapods but, otherwise, they are all biramous. In some species this is obvious, because each ramus bears a separate pre-chaetal and post-chaetal lappet. However, others have a single post-chaetal lappet extending across both rami. The dorsal surface of the parapods may or may not bear gills; in some species, these are retractile and thus may not be visible, especially in preserved specimens (the key takes account of this). There is a dorsal cirrus which is small and globular; the ventral cirrus is elongated but nevertheless small. Glycerids are carnivores burrowing actively in clean or muddy sand. When swimming, the body is thrown into spiral undulations; they may coil up tightly when disturbed (see Pettibone 1963).

---

1. Body divided into two distinct regions, posterior part being broader and more flattened. Parapods uniramous anteriorly, biramous posteriorly. Mouth (at end of a large eversible proboscis) armed with two large and numerous small jaw-pieces in a circle (Fig. 6.7f). Segments divided into two by an annular constriction   ***Goniada maculata***

Body uniform throughout, although tapering posteriorly. All parapods more or less obviously biramous. Proboscis armed with four large fang-like jaws arranged in a cross (Fig. 6.7e). Segments divided by two or three annular constrictions   **2**

2. Gills visible, inserted dorsally on parapods over most of body **3**

  Gills either absent or retracted (especially in preserved specimens) **4**

3. Gills fairly long, fingerlike (Fig. 6.7j,k); worm small to moderately large (under 200 mm long) **6**

  Gills short and globular (Fig. 6.7l); worm very large (over 200 mm long) ***Glycera gigantae***

4. Parapods have two post-chaetal lappets, one to each ramus (Fig. 6.7l). Body segments biannulate. Prostomium with ten or more annulations **5**

  Parapods have single large post-chaetal lappet, extending across both rami (Fig. 6.7 m). Body segments triannulate. Prostomium with eight (rarely up to eleven) annulations

  Glycera capitata

5. Prostomium with 12–14 annulations, each secondarily divided into two; worm large (over 200 mm) and greyish. Gills globular when protruded ***Glycera gigantea***

  Prostomium with 10–12 annulations; worm moderately large (up to 200 mm) and reddish. Gills fingerlike when protruded ***Glycera rouxi***

6. Papillae on proboscis resemble a fingertip, having a bent upper part bearing a chitinous 'nail' (Fig. 6.7h) **7**

  Papillae on proboscis elongated or globular, but do not bear a chitinous plate (Fig. 6.7i) ***Glycera rouxi***

7. Prostomium with eight to ten annulations. Worm small (30–75 mm), milky white ***Glycera alba***

  Prostomium with 14–18 annulations. Worm of medium size (60–100 mm), pinkish ***Glycera tridactyla***

Glycera alba (Müller) FIG. 6.7

Body with 100–150 biannulate segments, 30–75 mm long. Prostomium with eight to ten annulations. Papillae on proboscis may be simple, globular, or conical, but include many resembling a fingertip with an oblique chitinous 'nail' (h). Parapods with two post-chaetal lappets, upper fairly long and triangular, lower short and rounded (k). Gills non-retractile, fingerlike (k). Milky white.

At low water and in the shallow sublittoral. West of Britain, North Sea, Channel, north Atlantic.

Glycera capitata Oersted FIG. 6.7

Body with 140–170 triannulate segments, 30–75 mm long. Prostomium with eight to eleven annulations. Papillae on proboscis simple, mostly elongated but some globular. Parapods with single large post-chaetal lappet (m). No gills. Greyish, flushed with pink anteriorly.

Shallow sublittoral. Arctic, north-west Europe, Atlantic; Pacific, Antarctic. (*G. lapidum* Quatrefages is very similar).

Glycera gigantae Quatrefages FIG. 6.7

Large (300–400 biannulate segments, 200–350 mm long). Prostomium with 12–14 annulations, each with a secondary constriction. Papillae on proboscis simple, mostly elongated but some globular. Parapods with two post-chaetal lappets, both short and rounded (1). Gills retractile, globular (1). Greyish, flushed with pink anteriorly.

At low water and in the shallow sublittoral, often amongst rocks. South and west of Britain, north-east Atlantic.

Glycera rouxi Audouin and Milne Edwards FIG. 6.7

Body with 200–250 biannulate segments, 100–200 mm long. Prostomium with ten to twelve annulations. Papillae on proboscis simple, conical or globular (i). Parapods with two post-chaetal lappets, upper fairly long and triangular, lower short and rounded (j). Gills retractile, fingerlike (j). Reddish.

Most British coasts, north-west Europe to the Mediterranean.

Glycera tridactyla Schmarda (= *G. convoluta* Keferstein) FIG. 6.7

Body with 120–180 biannulate segments, 60–100 mm long. Prostomium with 14–18 annulations (e). Papillae on proboscis resemble a fingertip with an oblique chitinous 'nail'; a few are simple, short, and rounded. Parapods with two post-chaetal lappets, upper fairly long and triangular, lower short and rounded. Gills non-retractile, fingerlike. Pink, iridescent.

Intertidal and shallow sublittoral; rolls up at the slightest touch. South and west of Britain, Atlantic coast to the Mediterranean; Red Sea.

Goniada maculata Oersted FIG. 6.7

About 200 biannulate segments, 50–100 mm long. Prostomium with ten annulations. Proboscis with two large multitoothed jaws, three smaller ones ventrally and four yet smaller ones dorsally (f); a row of seven to eleven chitinous chevrons on each side at base (g); various small papillae anteriorly, none bearing a chitinous plate. Parapods in anterior half of body uniramous (but with two to three lappets); in flattened posterior half, biramous with rami well-separated. No gills (but dorsal cirrus is fairly large). Pale green or yellowish, becoming orange posteriorly, often flecked with brown.

Low water to deep sublittoral. Arctic, north-west Europe including most British coasts; north Pacific, Arabian Gulf.

11 HESIONIDAE

Worms resembling centipedes (N.B. some hesionids are short and cylindrical but are rarely, if at all, found in British waters and have thus not been included here). Prostomium simple or bilobed with four eyes, two or three antennae, and two palps each divided into two sections. Eversible proboscis with or without chitinous jaws or fringing papillae. First three or four body segments compressed into a short, more or less distinct region bearing six to eight pairs of tentacles, usually annulated. Dorsal lobe of parapods less well-developed than ventral, mostly very reduced. Dorsal cirri mostly long and annulated; ventral cirri shorter. Dorsal chaetae, if present, simple and slender;

ventrally, stouter jointed chaetae. Pygidium with two anal cirri. Active but fragile worms, some carnivorous but others commensal with burrowing worms, asteroids, or shrimps.

---

1. Dorsal lobe of parapod scarcely developed except for cirrus (Fig. 6.7p); tentacles and dorsal cirri both long and annulated　　　　　　　　　　　　　　**2**

   Dorsal lobe only slightly less well-developed than ventral (Fig. 6.7o); tentacles and dorsal cirri short and only feebly annulated, if at all　**Ophiodromus flexuosus**

2. Eight pairs of tentacles; jointed chaetae of neuropod with saw-toothed blade coarsely bifurcated at its tip (Fig. 6.7r)　　　　　　　　　　　**Kefersteinia cirrata**

   Six pairs of tentacles; jointed chaetae with straight-edged or finely toothed blade delicately bifurcated at its tip (Fig. 6.7q)　　　　　　**Nereimyra punctata**

Kefersteinia cirrata (Keferstein)　　　　FIG. 6.7

Body slender, fragile, 20–75 mm long; 36–65 chaetigers. Prostomium short and square; anterior pair of eyes large, with lens. Two short antennae, palps a little longer and thicker. Proboscis cylindrical with a large circular terminal opening bordered by a fringe of about 40 fine papillae (n). Eight pairs of long annulated tentacles; the base of each, and of each long annulated dorsal cirrus, reinforced by two to three acicula. No dorsal chaetae. Ventral lobe well-developed, bearing jointed chaetae with cross-striated shaft and a broad saw-like blade with a bifurcated tip (r). Coloration varies according to age and sex—yellow, brownish, purple, or scarlet; transparent anteriorly, with whitish cirri.

At low water and in the shallow sublittoral in rock-crevices, under stones, amongst shells and worm-tubes, or in kelp holdfasts. On most British coasts; north-west Europe to the Mediterranean.

Nereimyra (= *Castalia*) *punctata* (O. F. Müller)　FIG. 6.7

Body thick anteriorly, becoming slender towards the rear (10–25 mm long, 3–4 mm wide); 40–50 chaetigers. Prostomium broad and bilobed; anterior pair of eyes large, with lens. Palps a little larger than the two short antennae. Proboscis rather globular, with a ventral opening fringed by about a dozen well-spaced pointed papillae; horny folds dorsally and ventrally resemble jaws. Six pairs of long annulated tentacles. Dorsal lobe of parapod contains only two to four small capillary chaetae and a long, annulated cirrus whose base is reinforced by acicula (p). Ventral lobe well-developed, bearing jointed chaetae with cross-striated shaft, a long blade with a straight or only very fine-toothed edge and a slightly bifurcated tip (p,q). Dorsally, yellowish with darker transverse bands; ventrally, salmon-pink with a brown band down the mid-line.

At low tide and in deeper water in rock-crevices, kelp holdfasts, or amongst worm-tubes and shells. All around Britain; Atlantic coast of Europe.

Ophiodromus flexuosus delle Chiaje　　　FIG. 6.7

Body fairly stout (35–70 mm long, 3–4 mm wide) but fragile; 55–60 chaetigers. Prostomium broad, oval, with three antennae, median one very short; palps rather longer than lateral antennae. Proboscis globular, constricted around its opening, with neither papillae nor jaws. Six pairs of tentacles, short and not annulated. Parapods more nearly biramous (o); dorsal lobe with numerous long, fine capillary chaetae, dorsal cirri not much longer than these and feebly articulated. Ventral lobe a little larger and bearing a fan of stouter, long, jointed chaetae with cross-striated shaft and a long, thin, fine-pointed blade. Dorsal surface dark brown with transverse iridescent turquoise bands; ventral surface yellowish or brownish with a paler longitudinal line. Head white with red eyes, cirri banded in brown and white. The colours rapidly disappear in alcohol.

In burrows of other worms, the ambulacra of *Astropecten* or on the surface of muddy sand below low-water mark. All around Britain; north-west Europe to the Mediterranean.

12 MAGELONIDAE

Worms with a long, slender body divided into two distinct regions by an intervening segment different from the others. Prostomium flattened, like a duck's bill, often wider than the rest of the body; no antennae, no eyes. A pair of long, thick palps fringed with papillae down one side are inserted ventrally at the base of the prostomium (Fig. 6.5g). (N.B. These may be missing, damaged or regenerating atypically, as they form an important part of the diet of bottom-feeding fish.) Mouth ventral, with a very large proboscis. Parapods biramous with well-developed lappets. Probably only one species occurs in northern European waters.

Magelona mirabilis (Johnston)　　　FIG. 6.5

[*M. papillicornis* McIntosh *non* F. Müller (Jones 1977)]

Body threadlike, long (50–170 mm, up to 2.5 mm wide), rather square in section, ca. 150 chaetigers. Anterior region of eight chaetigers bears only capillary chaetae. Chaetiger 9 has greatly developed dorsal lappets (g) which almost meet in the mid-line; special chaetae, paddle-shaped and terminating in a fine pointed process, form a broad fan with longer spear-shaped ones in each half of parapods. The remaining chaetigers have smaller, incurved parapodial lappets and bear relatively few, short hooded chaetae with double hooks. There are two small anal cirri. Palps and anterior region pink, posterior region greenish grey with white blotches.

Burrowing in clean sand at low water and sublittorally, apparently without a tube. All around Britain, north-west Europe to the Mediterranean.

13 MALDANIDAE

Polychaetes which, with their long, cylindrical bodies usually truncated at one or both ends, and with very elongated segments swollen at one end by parapodial lobes, are well described by their popular name of bamboo-worms.

The prostomium lacks appendages and the head consists of a

median keel lying between a pair of nuchal slits. This keel may be strongly convex, giving a hood-like appearance (Fig. 6.8k), or flattened and incorporated into an oblique cephalic plate whose membranous rim is notched or cut into numerous teeth (Fig. 6.8f). The mouth is ventral; there is a small globular eversible proboscis. The biramous parapods bear a bundle of hair-like chaetae dorsally; ventrally there are single, simple stout chaetae (in the anterior few segments) or many-toothed crochets in a single or double row, set in a swollen transverse torus. Tori occur at the anterior end of the first eight or nine segments and towards the posterior end of the remaining ones. A few pre-anal segments lack chaetae but retain the parapodial swellings. Glandular bands or patches are scattered over the anterior and middle part of the body. The pygidium may be in the form of a funnel fringed with cirri (of which one in the ventral mid-line is usually the largest), when the anus opens terminally in the centre of the funnel, often on a conical protuberance (Fig. 6.8d,g); or an oblique plate similar to the cephalic plate, when the anus is dorsal and opens outside the plate (Fig. 6.8p); or spoon-like (as in *Petaloproctus*, not included here). Maldanids live in mucus tubes encrusted with particles of sediment, usually head-down in sandy or muddy bottoms.

Attempts at identification are difficult if the specimen is incomplete. The relative length and shape of segments, and the degree to which the parapodial lobes protrude, depends on the way in which non-living specimens died or were preserved. Segments may swell at one end to form a sheath partly enclosing adjacent ones; this should not be confused with the relatively thin, delicate collars characteristic of *Rhodine*.

1. Head a more or less oblique, flattened cephalic plate with a notched or toothed rim **2**

   Head rounded, with no encircling rim **4**

2. Anus terminal, within a pygidial funnel fringed with cirri **3**

   Anus dorsal, inserted outside a flattened pygidial plate not fringed with cirri ***Maldane sarsi***

3. Rim of cephalic plate cut into 7–14 teeth posteriorly (Fig. 6.8b). Pygidial funnel long, striated longitudinally, fringed by numerous cirri either more or less of equal size or alternating large and small fairly regularly (Fig. 6.8d). Parapods of three pre-anal segments lack chaetae ***Euclymene lumbricoides***

   Rim of cephalic plate continuous except for a notch on each side and one posteriorly (Fig. 6.8f). Pygidial funnel short, smooth, fringed by a few large cirri amongst more numerous small ones (Fig. 6.8g). Parapods of five pre-anal segments lack chaetae ***Euclymene robusta***

4. Posterior edge of last few segments extended as a collar (Fig. 6.8q). Crochets of mid-region parapods inserted in a double row ***Rhodine loveni***

   No collars. Crochets inserted in single rows **5**

5. First three chaetigerous segments bear ventrally a single simple stout chaeta (Fig. 6.8m) on each side. More than 20 segments, medium size (over 50 mm long) ***Nicomache lumbricalis***

   All chaetigerous segments bear ventrally two or more comparatively large crochets (Fig. 6.8j). Fewer than 20 segments, very small (5 mm long or less) ***Micromaldane ornithochaeta***

Euclymene lumbricoides (Quatrefages) FIG. 6.8

Nineteen chaetigerous segments plus three achaetigerous pre-anal segments (c), up to 150 mm long. Rim of cephalic plate cut into 7–14 teeth posteriorly (a,b). Nuchal slits straight, extending about half-way back across plate. First three chaetigers bear ventrally on each side only a single simple stout chaeta; following ones, crochets in a single row. Pygidium a long, longitudinally striated funnel fringed by 30–40 cirri either all much the same size or fairly regularly alternating between larger and smaller ones (c,d). Anus central within funnel. Tube thick, encrusted with small stones or shell fragments. Pinkish or pale brown with red and white glandular bands.

At low water, amongst sea-grasses and stones on sand. Western coasts of Britain and Europe to the Mediterranean.

Euclymene robusta Arwidsson FIG. 6.8

Nineteen chaetigers plus five achaetigerous pre-anal segments (e), up to 150 mm long. Rim of cephalic plate with one notch on each side and a less marked one posteriorly (f). Nuchal slits straight, extending back across most of plate. First three chaetigers bear ventrally on each side a single simple stout chaeta; following ones, crochets in a single row. Pygidial funnel short, smooth, fringed by a few long cirri amongst many short ones (g). Anus central within funnel. Tube thick, rigid, encrusted with sand and shell fragments. Yellow-brown with various red bands and patches.

At low water and in shallow sublittoral. West of Britain, north-west Europe (*E. oerstedi* (Claparède) is similar but variable, apparently because of the frequency with which atypical regenerating specimens are found.)

Maldane sarsi Malmgren FIG. 6.8

Nineteen chaetigers plus two achaetigerous pre-anal segments (p), 50–100 mm long. Cephalic plate with a markedly convex keel, its rim having a notch on each side (o). Nuchal slits short and divergent. The first chaetiger bears ventrally neither a single stout chaeta nor crochets; subsequent segments have crochets in a single row. Pygidium a plate with a rim notched on each side, sometimes wavy or weakly toothed ventrally. Anus opens on a wrinkled tubercle above dorsal edge of plate (p). Tube encrusted with mud-particles. Anterior region brown with darker patches, posterior paler.

At low water and in shallow sublittoral on shell-gravel, sandy or muddy bottoms. North-west Britain, North Sea, north-west Europe.

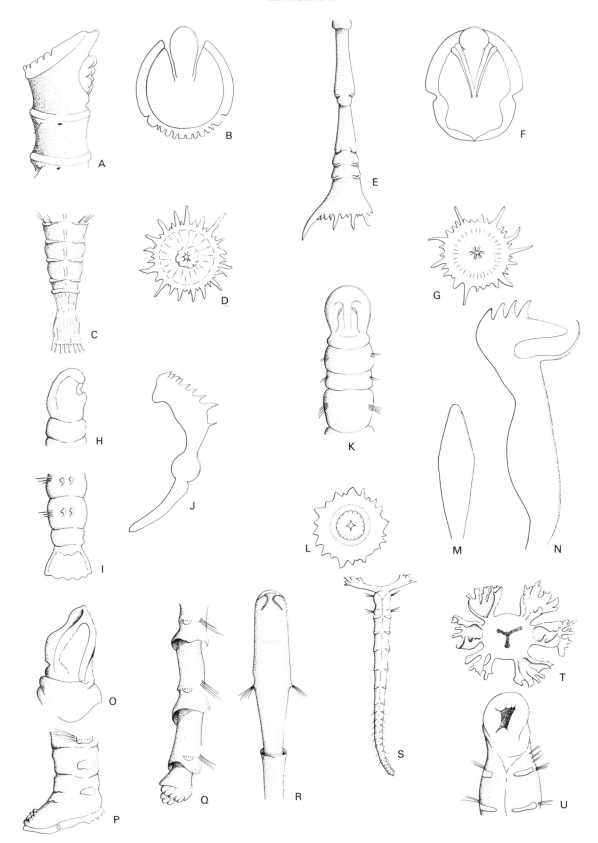

Fig. 6.8 (MALDANIDAE, OWENIIDAE) a. *Euclymene lumbricoides*—anterior region (lateral) b. *E. lumbricoides*—cephalic plate c. *E. lumbricoides*—posterior region d. *E. lumbricoides*—pygidial funnel e. *E. robusta*—posterior region f. *E. robusta*—cephalic plate g. *E. robusta*—pygidial funnel h. *Micromaldane ornithochaeta*—anterior region (lateral) i. *M. ornithochaeta*—posterior region j. *M. ornithochaeta*—crochet k. *Nichomache lumbricalis*—anterior region (dorsal) l. *N. lumbricalis*—pygidial funnel m. *N. lumbricalis*—anterior neurochaeta n. *N. lumbricalis*—crochet o. *Maldane sarsi*—anterior region (dorsolateral) p. *M. sarsi*—posterior region q. *Rhodine loveni*—posterior region r. *R. loveni*—anterior region (dorsal) s. *Owenia fusiformis*—entire worm t. *O. fusiformis*—crown u. *Myriochele heeri*—anterior region (ventral)

Micromaldane ornithochaeta Mesnil   FIG. 6.8

Thirteen to seventeen chaetigers plus one achaetigerous pre-anal segment (i). Very small (3–5 mm). Head rounded like a hood (h), without a membranous rim. Nuchal slits fairly long, curved. All chaetigerous segments bear ventrally a few relatively large crochets in a single row (j). Pygidium a short funnel with an irregularly fringed or wavy rim (i). Anus central within funnel. Tube encrusted with sand-grains. Colourless.

At low water amongst algal holdfasts and lobes of lithothamnia. South-west Britain, Irish Sea, Atlantic coast of Europe.

(Fauvel suggested that this species may merely be a young stage of *Nicomache*.)

Nicomache lumbricalis (Fabricius)   FIG. 6.8

Body with 22–23 chaetigers plus two achaetigerous pre-anal segments, 60–160 mm long. Head rounded like a hood (k). Nuchal slits short and curved. First three chaetigers bear ventrally on each side a single simple stout chaeta (m); following ones, crochets (n) in a single row. Pygidium a short funnel fringed by 15–25 short cirri, all about the same size (l). Anus central within the funnel. Tube thick, straight, or sinuous, encrusted with sand-grains. Reddish brown along back and sides of anterior end.

At low water and in shallow sublittoral. Around most of Britain, Irish Sea, Arctic, North Sea, north-west Europe.

Rhodine loveni Malmgren   FIG. 6.8

Forty chaetigers, up to 100 mm long. Head rounded like a hood (r). Nuchal slits short, horseshoe-shaped. Anterior segments (including buccal segment) bear hair-like chaetae dorsally; crochets ventrally in a single row, from fifth segment and in a double row in the mid-region. The anterior edge of the first few segments and, more conspicuously, the posterior edge of the last few is extended as a collar encircling the next segment (q). Pygidium small, not forming a funnel or plate, terminating in small papillae surrounding anus (q). Tube transparent or encrusted with silt particles and sand-grains. Yellowish- or greyish-brown with red patches.

Shallow sublittoral to medium depths, often in brackish water. North-west Britain, Arctic, North Sea, west Baltic, Atlantic coast of Europe to Mediterranean.

14 NEPHTYIDAE

Medium or large, active worms with smooth, pearly, whitish dorsal and ventral surfaces. Well-bristled yellowish parapods are set very laterally, increasing their flattened appearance. Their swimming is characteristic, with a rapid lateral wriggling starting from the rear and increasing in amplitude towards the head. The prostomium has four very small antennae inserted at its anterior corners; there is a large eversible proboscis, bearing papillae which are usually prominent, with which the worm can burrow rapidly in muddy sand. The parapods have fairly large, flattened, and sometimes subdivided lobes. On all but the first few segments, there is a reddish, sickle-shaped gill between the noto- and neuropodial lobes (Fig. 6.9c, d). The dorsal cirrus is usually vestigial, the ventral cirrus small. There is a single long tail-filament. Large specimens are used for bait and are called 'catworms' by anglers.

---

1. Dorsal and ventral cirri of first chaetigerous segment of equal length (about as long as posterior antennae)   **4**

   Dorsal cirrus of first chaetiger smaller than ventral cirrus (usually reduced to a mere tubercle)   **2**

2. In posterior parapods, the branchial cirrus is as long as the gill (Fig. 6.9c). Some posterior chaetae sharply bent (Fig. 6.9e). Body more or less oval in section

   Nephtys cirrosa

   Branchial cirrus markedly shorter than gill (Fig. 6.9d). Some chaetae curved but not sharply bent (Fig. 6.9f). Body markedly rectangular in section   **3**

3. In anterior parapods, a small globular process at the point where aciculum reaches surface of each lobe, most obvious in notopodium. Papillae of proboscis prominent, especially at anterior end. Worm large (up to 200 segments, 200 mm long)   ***Nephtys hombergi***

   No acicular cap. Papillae of proboscis are very small, except for a single very large one dorsally. Worm of medium size (up to 70 segments, 65 mm long)

   Nephtys incisa

4. A single very large papilla present mid-dorsally on everted proboscis. Ventral cirrus of parapod relatively large (approx. same size as gill)

   Nephtys longosetosa

   The everted proboscis has numerous papillae but not a single very large one mid-dorsally. Ventral cirrus of parapod shorter than gill   ***Nephtys caeca***

Nephtys caeca Fabricius   FIG. 6.9

Body with 90–150 segments, 150–250 mm long (a). Proboscis with numerous papillae but no large mid-dorsal one. Dorsal and ventral cirri of first chaetigerous segment are of more or less equal size, as long as posterior antennae. Chaetae in posterior parapods strongly toothed, some are curved (f), but none are sharply bent. Branchial cirri are shorter than gills (*sim*.d).

Intertidal and at low water. Common and widespread (all around Britain; Arctic and north Atlantic).

Nephtys cirrosa Ehlers   FIG. 6.9

Body with 90–95 segments, 60–100 mm long; body relatively thin. Proboscis with numerous papillae, including a large mid-dorsal one (b). Dorsal cirrus of first chaetigerous segment reduced to a small tubercle on each side; ventral cirrus close to posterior antenna and rather longer than it. Chaetae in posterior parapods very finely toothed, some geniculate (sharply bent) (e). In posterior segments, branchial cirrus is as long as the rather slender gill (c).

Intertidal and at low water. All around Britain, Atlantic coast of Europe.

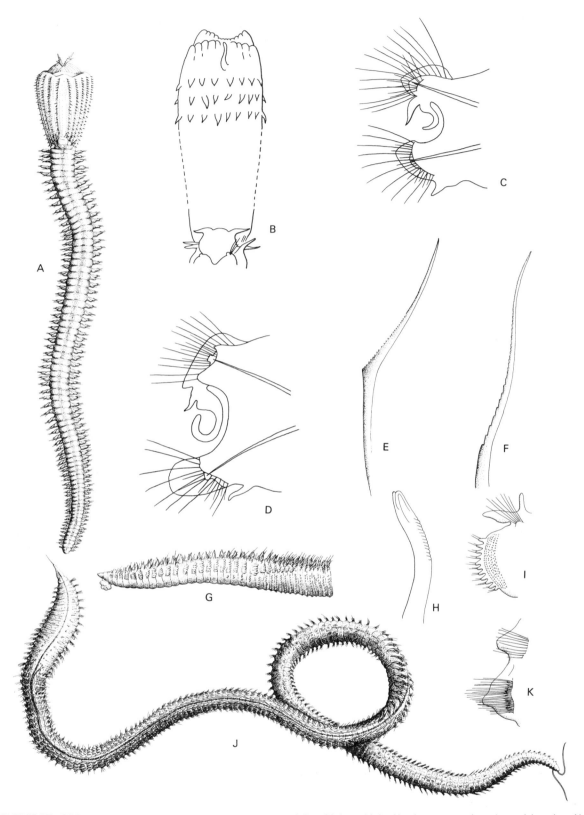

Fig. 6.9 (NEPHTYIDAE, ORBINIDAE) a. *Nephtys caeca*—entire worm (after McIntosh) b. *N. cirrosa*—proboscis and head c. *N. cirrosa*—posterior parapod d. *N. hombergi*—parapod from mid-region e. *N. cirrosa*—geniculate posterior chaeta f. *N. caeca*—curved posterior chaeta g. *Orbinia latreilli*—anterior end h. *O. latreilli*—crochet (after Fauvel) i. *O. latreilli*—parapod with postchaetal papillae (after Fauvel) j. *Scoloplos armiger*—entire worm k. *S. armiger*—typical parapod (after Hartmann-Schröder)

Nephtys hombergi Savigny
FIG. 6.9

Body with 90–200 segments, 100–200 mm long; body markedly rectangular in section. Proboscis with prominent papillae, including a large mid-dorsal one. Dorsal cirrus of first chaetigerous segment reduced to a small tubercle; ventral cirrus as long as posterior antennae. Amongst anterior parapods, point where the aciculum reaches surface is marked by a small globular fleshy cap, most obvious in notopod (d). Posterior chaetae finely toothed; some curved but none sharply bent. Branchial cirri shorter than gills (d).

Intertidal and at low water. Common and widespread (all around Britain, north-west Europe, Mediterranean).

Nephtys incisa Malmgren

Body with 60–70 segments, 25–65 mm long; rectangular in section. Proboscis with numerous but very small papillae, except for very large mid-dorsal one. Ventral cirrus of first chaetigerous segment as long as posterior antenna, dorsal cirrus smaller. Rami of parapods very well-separated (about two or three times height of a noto- or neuropod). Chaetae in posterior parapods finely toothed, none sharply bent. Branchial cirri short.

Sublittoral, in shallow to deep water. Around much of Britain (? rare in south-west), north-west Europe, Mediterranean.

Nephtys longosetosa Oersted

Body with 90–120 segments, 50–150 mm long. Anterior papillae of proboscis quite elongated, one in mid-dorsal region particularly long. Dorsal and ventral cirri of first chaetigerous segment are of more or less equal size, as long as posterior antennae. Posterior chaetae strongly toothed; some curved but none sharply bent. Branchial cirri short and slim. Ventral cirri are relatively large (about as long as gills).

Sublittoral, in shallow water. West coast of Britain, Atlantic coast of Europe.

15 NEREIDAE

Members of this family are perhaps more similar to each other than in any other. It is thus more likely that the key will mislead its users, who must consequently be prepared to retrace their steps if the first identification arrived at seems implausible.

Nereids are very 'typical' errant polychaetes, having a long slender body with very many similar segments. The prostomium bears two ovoid palps, each with a small terminal button, at the anterior corners of the small prostomium; between them are two small antennae and, on the dorsal surface, four eyes arranged in a rectangle. A large eversible proboscis has two curved chitinous jaws at its anterior end and, usually, scattered small horny teeth (paragnaths) over its surface which, although on the outside when it is everted is, of course, the lining when it has been withdrawn. They form various groups on the dorsal surface, of which the only ones of general use in identification lie laterally in the proximal part, just anterior to the palps. In the equivalent region ventrally, the paragnaths usually form a continuous transverse band. Their arrangement has been used in the key below only as a confirmatory character as it is not always easy to persuade the worm to evert its proboscis; the best technique is to apply pressure behind the head with a fingertip or by rolling a pencil or seeker-handle up its body but, if applied clumsily, this may seriously injure the worm. All that can be done with a dead specimen is to cut open the buccal region from the mouth mid-ventrally, pinning open the flaps thus created to reveal the groups of paragnaths in inverted order. Figs. 6.11c–e illustrate the way in which the regions of an everted proboscis are conventionally numbered and how they are arranged in a retracted proboscis opened up in this way. There are four pairs of tentacles lateral to and slightly behind the prostomium. The parapods are generally biramous, with dorsal and ventral cirri; chaetae occur in a single bundle dorsally and two, superior and inferior, ventrally. Simple bristles may be present but the jointed ones are more important and are divided on the basis of the socket at the end of the shaft, which may be symmetrical (*homogomph*) or asymmetrical, with the tooth on one side larger than the other (*heterogomph*); and on the blade, which may be short, like a bill-hook or pruning-saw, or long like a lance. Stout chaetae with a paddle-like blade which seems fused with its shaft, rather than articulating on it, occur on epitokes (see below) but also occur occasionally in the more familiar forms. The usual pattern is for the notopod to contain homogomph jointed chaetae with a lance-like blade; each bundle in the neuropod contains chaetae with both bill-hook blades and lance-like blades but whereas, in the superior bundle, the former are heterogomph and the latter homogomph, in the inferior one both are heterogomph. Exceptions are mentioned in the species descriptions. There are two anal cirri. Most nereids produce a tenuous mucous tube in which sand-grains become embedded. At maturity, they usually become transformed into a pelagic epitoke (*heteronereis*) which shows sexual dimorphism; individual details are not given and must be sought in more specialist texts but, generally, anterior sense-organs are enlarged, parapodia in the posterior region are modified for more efficient swimming and the anus becomes surrounded by papillae.

1. Dorsal lappets of parapod markedly longer than ventral lappets, especially in posterior part of body (Fig. 6.10g, h) — **2**

   Dorsal lappets more or less same size as ventral ones (Fig. 6.10f) — **4**

2. Dorsal lappets broad and leaf-like, at least in mid-region (Fig. 6.10g); tentacles short (all but rearmost pair no longer than body-width) (Fig. 6.10b) — **3**

   Dorsal lappets long but narrow, not leaf-like (Fig. 6.10h); tentacles long (all longer than body-width, rearmost may be one-quarter of body-length) (Fig. 6.10e); small worm (60 mm long or less) — ***Platynereis dumerili***

3. Dorsal cirri long, extending beyond lappets (which are broadest in mid-region); large worm (up to 200 mm long) — ***Nereis fucata***

   Dorsal cirri insignificant (Fig. 6.10g); lappets broad throughout, giving a frilly edge to body; very large (may be well over 200 mm long) — ***Nereis virens***

4. Dorsal cirri extend beyond lappets   **5**

    Dorsal cirri shorter than lappets   **7**

5. Antennae markedly shorter than palps; on proximal dorsal surface of everted proboscis, two patches of large paragnaths (Fig. 6.10d); a medium-sized cylindrical worm (up to 120 mm long)   ***Nereis pelagica***

    Antennae same length as, or only slightly shorter than palps   **6**

6. Tentacles all the same length (about equal to body-width); on proximal dorsal surface of everted proboscis, two patches of small paragnaths (Fig. 6.11b); a small, delicate, flattened worm (less than 80 mm long)   ***Nereis zonata***

    Posterior pair of tentacles longer than others, extending back to about chaetiger 6; on proximal dorsal surface of everted proboscis, two transverse chitinous ridges resembling eyebrows (Fig. 6.11a); a large, stout worm (over 100 mm long) with a markedly arched back   ***Perinereis cultrifera***

7. Most tentacles longer than body width (Fig. 6.10c); antennae more or less as long as palps; large worm (200–300 mm long) with a 'broad-shouldered' appearance   ***Nereis irrorata***

    Most tentacles only as long as body width or shorter (posterior pair may be an exception); antennae markedly shorter than palps   **8**

8. A medium-sized worm (60–100 mm long) of normal tapering shape; socket at tip of shaft in compound chaetae of notopod is markedly asymmetrical (heterogomph condition) (Fig. 6.10k)   ***Nereis diversicolor***

    A long worm (200–500 mm) of more or less constant width; socket of notopodial compound chaetae symmetrical (homogomph condition) (Fig. 6.10i)
    Nereis longissima

Nereis (= *Hediste*) *diversicolor* O. F. Müller   FIG. 6.10

Body rather flabby, flattened, and tapering rearwards, with a prominent dorsal blood-vessel; 60–120 m long, 90–120 chaetigers. Antennae much shorter than palps, which are medium length but not stout. Tentacles about as long as body width, rearward pair slightly more. Parapods with short, thick lappets about equal in length dorsally and ventrally (f); dorsal cirri shorter than lappets. Posteriorly, one large paddle-like chaeta in each neuropod (k). Colour variable—greenish, yellowish, or orange.

Intertidal, making burrows in black muddy sand, often under brackish conditions. Commonly used as bait by anglers (known by them as 'ragworm', together with *Perinereis cultrifera*). Around most British coasts; north-west Europe to the Mediterranean.

Nereis (= *Neanthes*) *fucata* (Savigny)   FIG. 6.10

Body tapering both anteriorly and posteriorly; long parapodial appendages give it a broad, flattened appearance; 100–200 mm long, 90–120 chaetigers. Antennae and palps of same length, rather short (b). Tentacles slightly shorter than body-width, rearward pair slightly longer. Dorsal lappets markedly larger than ventral, broad and leaf-like in mid-region. Dorsal cirri extend beyond lappets. Two long anal cirri. Bright pink or yellowish, with a white line passing longitudinally down each side of dorsal blood-vessel; parapods whitish.

Commensal with hermit-crabs in whelk shells, also freeliving. On most British coasts; north-west Europe to the Mediterranean.

Nereis (= *Neanthes*) *irrorata* (Malmgren)   FIG. 6.10

Body broad in first few segments, then becomes slender and rather flattened; 200–300 mm long, 130–140 chaetigers. Palps and antennae about same (medium) size. Length of tentacles slightly greater than body width, rearward pair longer, reaching back to about chaetiger 15 (c). Dorsal lappets as long as ventral ones anteriorly, becoming progressively longer posteriorly from chaetiger 25, with small brown and white glandular areas visible. Dorsal cirri short, about as long as lappets. A pair of long anal cirri. Brick-red with scattered grey and white spots.

Occupies a delicate mucus tube in rock crevices, under stones or amongst eel-grass. South-west coasts of Britain; Atlantic and Mediterranean, coasts of Europe.

Nereis (= *Eunereis*) *longissima* (Johnston)   FIG. 6.10

Body long, rather flattened, with very regular segmentation, tapering very little to front or rear; 200–500 mm long, more than 200 chaetigers. Antennae much shorter than the palps. Tentacles shorter than body-width, except rearward pair which are rather longer. Dorsal and ventral parapodial lappets of much the same length; dorsal cirri as long as lappets. Acicula black. The most posterior segments lack chaetae with bill-hook blades ventrally but, from chaetiger 65–70 rearwards, each notopod has one or two paddle-shaped chaetae with a stout shaft and short, narrow blade (i). The everted proboscis bears paragnaths only as two small patches on the proximal dorsal surface; they are pale and hard to see. Blue-grey or pinkish.

At low water and in the shallow sublittoral in muddy sand or rich mud amongst eel-grass. Around most British coasts; Atlantic coast of Europe.

Nereis pelagica Linnaeus   FIG. 6.10

Body smooth, cylindrical, tapering only a little rearwards; peristomium noticeably wider than the next segment; prominent dorsal blood-vessel; 60–210 mm long, 80–100 chaetigers. Palps unusually large, antennae markedly shorter (d). Tentacles about as long as body-width, all much the same. Dorsal lappets slightly longer than ventral; dorsal cirrus quite long, especially towards rear when it is three or four times as long as lappets. Golden or bronze, often with a greenish metallic sheen.

At low water amongst algae, in kelp holdfasts and mussel

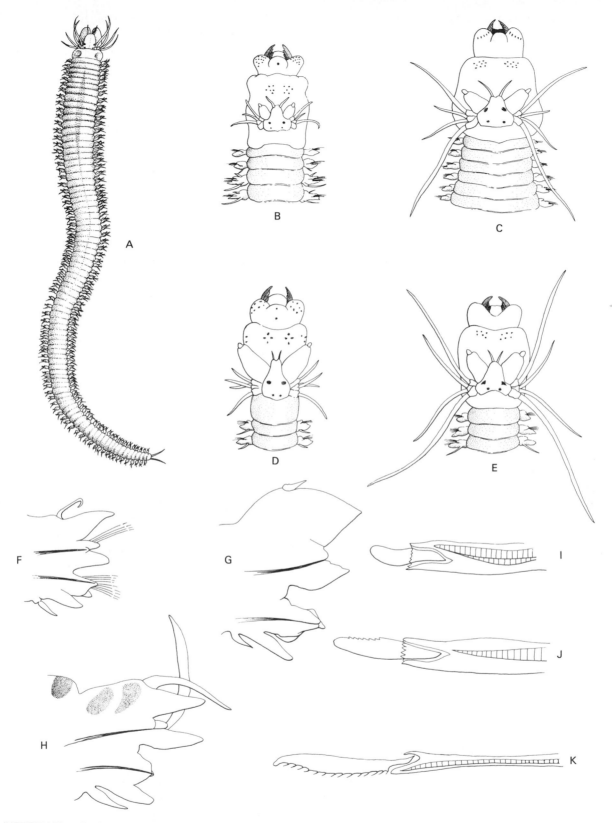

Fig. 6.10 (NEREIDAE) a. *Perinereis cultrifera*—entire worm, dorsal b. *Nereis fucata*—anterior end with proboscis c. *N. irrorata*—anterior end with proboscis d. *N. pelagica*—anterior end with proboscis e. *Platyneris dumerili*—anterior end with proboscis (after Fauvel) f. *Nereis diversicolor*—parapod g. *N. virens*—parapod (after Hartmann-Schröder) h. *Platynereis dumerili*—parapod (after Hartmann-Schröder) i. *Nereis longissima*—paddle-like chaeta of posterior notopod (after Fauvel) j. *N. zonata*—paddle-like chaeta of posterior notopod (after Fauvel) k. *N. diversicolor*—paddle-like chaeta of posterior neuropod (after Fauvel)

beds; very active. On most British coasts; Arctic, north-west Europe to the Mediterranean; south Pacific.

Nereis (= Neanthes) virens (Sars)   FIG. 6.10

Body long and wide, dorsal surface of segments with a flabby, wrinkled appearance; 200–300 mm or more long, 100–175 chaetigers or more. Antennae shorter than palps. Tentacles about as long as body-width except rearward pair, which reach back to about chaetiger 8. Dorsal lappet very large and leaf-like (g), giving a frilly edge to body, so that the worm superficially resembles an extremely large phyllodocid. Dorsal cirri insignificant. Jointed chaetae all long and thin (none with a blade like a paddle or bill-hook), also numerous fine simple chaetae. Dark green with a bluish iridescence; parapodial lappets fringed in yellow.

Occupies a mucus-lined burrow in black muddy sand; swims vigorously, with a graceful sinusoidal motion. Taken commercially and much valued by anglers as bait ('king rag'). On most British shores, particularly in the south and west; Atlantic coast of Europe.

Nereis zonata Malmgren   FIGS. 6.10, 6.11

Body slender, slightly flattened, tapering rearwards; 30–80 mm long, 80–100 chaetigers. Palps rather short, antennae the same size or slightly shorter (Fig. 6.11b). Tentacles about as long as body-width. Dorsal lappets slightly longer than ventral; dorsal cirri quite long, about twice as long as lappets. Around chaetiger 25–30, one or several large paddle-like chaetae in the notopod (Fig. 6.10j). Fawn, pink, or yellow, occasionally with whitish transverse bands.

In the shallow sublittoral amongst shells, stones, and worm-tubes. Around most British coasts; Arctic, north-west Europe to the Mediterranean; Adriatic, Indo-Pacific.

Perinereis cultrifera (Grube)   FIGS. 6.10, 6.11

Body flattened ventrally and well-arched dorsally, tapering gently but steadily rearwards (Fig. 6.10a); 100–250 mm long, 100–125 chaetigers. Antennae rather stout, shorter than palps. Tentacles about as long as body-width, rearward pair slightly longer. Dorsal lappets slightly longer than ventral, dorsal cirrus slightly longer again. Glandular patches can be seen on more posterior notopods. Acicula dark. Two long anal cirri. When everted, two transverse dark chitinous ridges like a pair of eyebrows can be seen on proximal dorsal surface of proboscis (Fig. 6.11a): these are diagnostic. Bronze-green with bright-red dorsal vessel and parapods.

Makes galleries in the mud filling rock-crevices, under stones and amongst eel-grass; swims clumsily by throwing its body into S-shapes. Commonly used as bait by anglers (known as 'ragworm' together with N. diversicolor). All around British coasts; north-west Europe to the Mediterranean; Indian Ocean.

Platynereis dumerili Audouin and Milne Edwards
FIG. 6.10

Body becoming very slender at the rear; 20–60 mm long, 70–90 chaetigers. Antennae short, not quite as long as palps. Tentacles

very long (e): rearmost pair may reach one-quarter of body length. Dorsal lappets markedly larger than ventral, with dark glandular patches, becoming longer and narrower towards rear. Dorsal cirri longer than lappets. Acicula black. Posteriorly, each notopod has one or two jointed chaetae with a blade resembling a bill-hook (as opposed to the usual arrangement, with a long lance-like blade). Two long anal cirri. Jaws and paragnaths of proboscis pale in colour; paragnaths very small, widely scattered, and hard to see (e). Coloration variable: greenish, yellowish, pink, reddish.

At low water and in the shallow sublittoral, occupying a mucus tube in rock-crevices or kelp holdfasts. All around Britain; cosmopolitan.

16 OPHELIIDAE

Small worms having three distinct body-shapes: short and maggot-like, slender and torpedo-shaped, or with an anterior region appreciably broader than the posterior. There are relatively few segments and often a deep ventral gutter. Chaetae are all simple, hair-like bristles and parapods ill-developed, but fingerlike or paddle-shaped gills are obvious along each side of the body for at least half its length. Common in sandy beaches.

---

1. Body may have broad anterior region but is relatively slender posteriorly; posterior region has marked ventral gutter. Anus surrounded by a prominent hood or tube; ventrally, two long, stout anal papillae   **2**

   Body stout, maggot-like, broad throughout; ventral surface not markedly concave in section. Anal tube and papillae insignificant. May smell strongly of garlic when first collected   ***Travisia forbesi***

2. Gills (46–48 pairs) laterally on all but first and last two or three chaetigers (Fig. 6.11f). Prostomium conical, terminating in a single fingerlike median process. Anus surmounted by a dorsal hood with a toothed or fringed posterior edge   ***Ophelina acuminata***

   Fifteen pairs of gills in mid-region. Prostomium conical but without a prominent median process. Anus surrounded by a short tube with a toothed edge (Fig. 6.11h)   ***Ophelia bicornis***

Ophelia bicornis Savigny   FIG. 6.11

Thirty-two chaetigerous segments, 30–45 mm long. Body divided into a swollen anterior region (g) and a narrower posterior region with a marked ventral gutter. This posterior region bears 15 pairs of long, narrow, paddle-shaped gills inserted low on the body, lightly toothed along their upper edge and lacking in last seven segments. The last two or three segments appear telescoped. Anus surrounded by a short tube with a toothed edge (h); two large anal papillae. Normally pinkish, with iridescent glint; gills bright red. When disturbed, curls up to resemble a cooked and peeled shrimp. When breeding, males may appear milky white, females greenish grey.

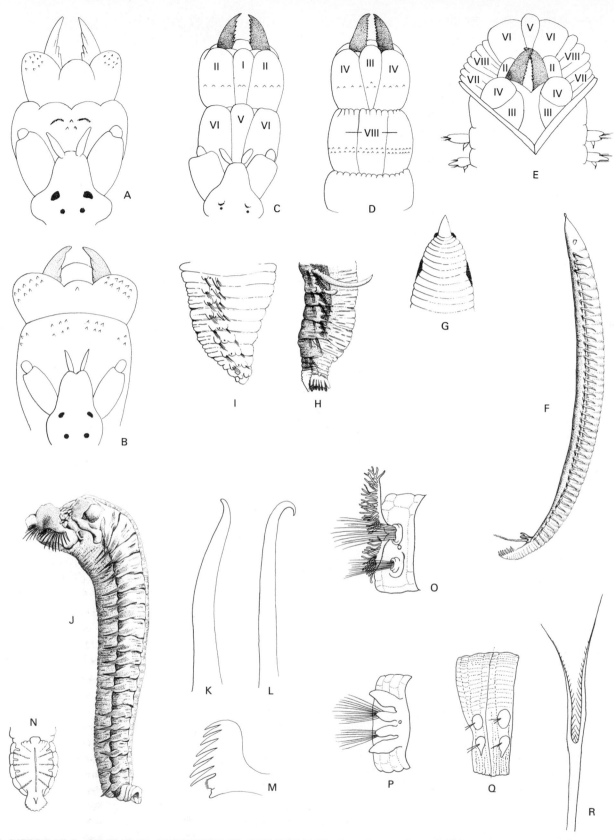

Fig. 6.11 (NEREIDAE 2, OPHELIIDAE, PECTINARIIDAE, SCALIBREGMIDAE) a. *Perinereis cultrifera*—ant. end with proboscis b. *Nereis zonata*—anterior end with proboscis c. Regions of nereid proboscis, dorsal d. Regions of nereid proboscis, ventral e. Regions of nereid proboscis, withdrawn and opened with a ventral longitudinal cut (c–e after O'Donnell) f. *Ophelina acuminata*—entire worm, lateral g. *Ophelia bicornis*—anterior end h. *O. bicornis*—posterior end i. *Travisia forbesi*—posterior end j. *Pectinaria belgica*—entire worm, lateral k. *P. belgica*—caudal crochet (after Fauvel) l. *P. auricoma*—caudal crochet (after Fauvel) m. *P. belgica*—uncinus (after Fauvel) n. *P. koreni*—caudal region, dorsal o. *Scalibregma inflatum*—parapod in branchial region (after Day) p. *S. inflatum*—posterior parapod (after Day) q. *Lipobranchus jeffreysi*—mid-region parapod r. *L. jeffreysi*—forked chaeta (after Fauvel)

On the lower shore, in coarse, mobile sand. English Channel and Atlantic coast of Europe.

Ophelina acuminata Oersted   FIG. 6.11
(includes *Ammotrypane aulogaster* Rathke)
About 50 segments, multiannulated; 25–60 mm long. Body slender, narrowing at each end, with a marked ventral gutter. Conical prostomium extended in a fingerlike median process slightly swollen at its tip. Long cirriform gills on all chaetigers but first and last two or three (f). Anus surmounted by a spoon-shaped hood, open ventrally, whose margin is divided into eight to ten little teeth; within this there are two large anal papillae with a single long cirrus between. Yellowish or pearly grey with bright red gills.

In the shallow sublittoral, on sand. European coasts from the Arctic to the Atlantic.

Travisia forbesi Johnston   FIG. 6.11
Body with 23–26 chaetigers, triannulated; 20–30 mm long. Body short, maggot-like, circular in section anteriorly, slightly narrower and quadrangular in section posteriorly; no marked ventral gutter. Integument reticulated. Prostomium small, oval, with an anterior conical process. Cirriform gills laterally in about 15 obvious pairs, from chaetiger 2, but becoming small posteriorly and missing from last two to five segments. Pygidium like an oval button amongst small anal papillae (i). Whitish or flesh-pink, may be encrusted with sand; a strong garlic-like smell when first collected.

At low water, in fine, clean sand. European coasts from the Arctic to the Atlantic.

17 ORBINIIDAE
Orbiniids (ariciids) are long worms with a slightly flattened and broader anterior region bearing lateral parapods and a rounded, more fragile posterior region bearing its parapods dorsally (Fig. 6.9j). Broad, lanceolate, simple gills are present dorsally on all but the first few segments; together with the cirri, chaetal bundles, and other appendages of the parapods, they can give the posterior region the appearance of an elongated toothbrush. The main genus *Orbinia* (= *Aricia*) has, as anterior neuropods, tori which contain crochets in several rows, fringed behind by a row of post-chaetal papillae (Fig. 6.9k); a number of segments at the junction of the anterior and posterior regions also have, on each side, a row of subpodial papillae which, in several segments, meet in the ventral mid-line. There are never fewer than five of such accessory papillae in each segment which bears them. In one or two of the less common species not listed here, one or more large, dark, spear-like bristles project from each neuropod of the last few anterior segments. Amongst these, *O. foetida* has a characteristic, strong smell of garlic when freshly collected. In *Scoloplos*, there are markedly fewer post-chaetal and subpodial papillae; crochets may be present on all, a few, or none of the anterior segments. A few members of the family (*O. norvegica* and *Naineris quadricuspida*) completely lack subpodial papillae. In all, tori and crochets are lacking from all but the first few posterior segments. The pygidium typically has two long, threadlike appendages.

---

1. Gills along dorsal surface from chaetiger 5. More than ten post-chaetal papillae form a fringe down neuropodial tori towards rear of anterior region, which contain large crochets in several rows. Numerous (17–33) segments in this mid-region also have a row of subpodial papillae, which encircle body ventrally in several (7–11) segments (Fig. 6.9g)   **2**
   Gills occur from chaetiger 9–17. Few (maximum three) or no post-chaetal papillae; all, some or no anterior neuropods contain crochets (but, in their absence, broken or worn large simple chaetae may superficially resemble them). No more than two subpodial papillae occur on only one to four segments of mid-region   ***Scoloplos armiger***

2. Subpodial papillae occur on chaetiger 22–42/55, encircling body ventrally on chaetiger 25–36; 12–25 post-chaetal papillae on best-developed tori   ***Orbinia latreilli***
   Subpodial papillae occur on chaetiger 17–34, encircling body ventrally on chaetiger 20–27; 10–15 post-chaetal papillae on best-developed tori   ***Orbinia sertulata***

Orbinia latreilli (Audouin and Milne Edwards)   FIG. 6.9
Anterior region of 30–40 chaetigers (g); altogether 300–400 segments, 300–400 mm long. Gills from chaetiger 5 (rarely, 6). Prostomium a blunt cone. Anterior neuropods swollen tori, typically with three or four rows of large yellow curved crochets (h), fringed behind by a row of 12–25 post-chaetal papillae (i), back to chaetiger 40/43. Subpodial papillae occur on chaetiger 22–42/55, forming a complete ventral belt (25–30 each side) on chaetiger 25–236. Anterior flesh-pink, posterior yellowish.

On lower shore in clean sand. West of Britain, North Sea, Channel and Atlantic coasts of Europe, Mediterranean.

Orbinia sertulata (Savigny)
(= *Aricia cuvieri* Audouin and Milne-Edwards)
Anterior region of 22–24 chaetigers; altogether up to 400 segments, up to 300 mm long. Gills from chaetiger 5. Prostomium a sharp cone. Anterior neuropods swollen tori, typically with three to five rows of large yellow curved chrochets, fringed behind by a row of 10–15 post-chaetal papillae, back to chaetiger 27/31. Subpodial papillae occur on chaetiger 17–34, forming a complete ventral belt (*c.* 12–15 each side) on chaetiger 20–27. Anterior dark red, posterior greyish brown.

At low water and in shallow sublittoral, on bottoms of sand or muddy sand. West of Britain, North Sea, Channel and Atlantic coasts of Europe, Mediterranean.

Scoloplos armiger (Müller)   FIG. 6.9
Anterior region of 12–20 chaetigers; altogether more than 200 segments, 50–20 mm long (j). Body elastic but thin and quite

fragile. Gills from chaetiger 9/17. Prostomium relatively large, conical or cylindrical. Anterior neuropods swollen tori with curved crochets in all, few, or none (but, where absent, stout curved capillary chaetae may resemble them if worn down or broken). Few or no post-chaetal papillae (k, *cf.* i); one to two subpodial papillae occur on two or three segments only (where present, such accessory papillae never exceed four per segment). Bright orange-pink, with main blood-vessels well visible.

At low water or in shallow sublittoral, in fine muddy sand, often amongst sea-grasses. West and north of Britain, Arctic, north-west Europe; Indian Ocean, Pacific, Antarctic.

18 OWENIIDAE

Head either without appendages or bearing a frilled membranous crown. Thoracic region made up of a chaetigerous buccal segment and three short segments bearing only dorsal hair-like chaetae. Abdominal region of long segments, becoming progressively shorter posteriorly, bearing ventrally rows of very numerous small crochets inserted in a long torus on each side (Fig. 6.8s). Pygidium small, rounded, slightly bilobed. Tube open but narrowing at each end.

---

1. Head with a frilled membranous crown surrounding mouth (Fig. 6.8t)   ***Owenia fusiformis***

     Head end rounded and obliquely truncated, lacking appendages of any kind (Fig. 6.8u)   ***Myriochele heeri***

Owenia fusiformis delle Chiaje   FIG. 6.8

Body with 20–30 segments, 30–100 mm long (s). Head bears a crown of six short, membranous processes cut into numerous frilly lobes, with a terminal three-lobed mouth at its centre (t). Tube encrusted with sand-grains or shell-fragments, each overlapping the more posterior one like a crudely tiled roof. The worm is able to move around while still in its tube. The tubes may be so numerous as to hold the sediment together, but many are usually empty. Body greenish or yellowish, with paler glandular bands; crown reddish.

At low water and in the shallow sublittoral. All around Britain, north-west Europe, Mediterranean; Indian Ocean, Pacific.

Myriochele heeri Malmgren   FIG. 6.8

About 27 segments, 20–30 mm long. Anterior end obliquely truncated; head rounded, without crown or other appendages. Mouth subterminal (u). Tube membranous, encrusted with small sand-grains not usually overlapping; may be very numerous in sediment. Yellowish.

Sublittoral, at moderate depths. North-west Britain, Arctic, north-west Europe, Mediterranean, Black Sea, Pacific, Antarctic.

19 PECTINARIIDAE

Also known as Amphictenidae. The body is relatively short and thick, divided into three regions. The blunt anterior end bears two comb-like bundles of stout golden spines (which are used for digging), crossing in the mid-line, and numerous prehensile tentacles surrounded by a cephalic veil; two pairs of tentacles and two pairs of feathery gills. It includes three segments bearing only bundles of hair-like bristles dorsally. The posterior (abdominal) region has 12–13 segments which, in addition, bear ventrally uncini with hooked teeth in numerous rows; it is of much the same thickness as the anterior region. A narrower, much shorter caudal region (scaphe) is divided from it by a marked constriction and is segmented, but lacks chaetae except a few crochets on each side around its base. The worm occupies a characteristic smooth, unattached tube open at each end, constructed of a single layer of sand-grains or shell fragments, cemented together so that their edges meet as closely as possible: it resembles a well-made old stone-built industrial chimney. It lives in sediments at low water and below, usually on fairly exposed sandy beaches, head down and with the smaller end of the tube protruding from the surface (see Holthe 1986).

---

1. Tube distinctly curved (17 segments bearing bundles of capillary chaetae)   ***Pectinaria auricoma***

     Tube straight or nearly straight   **2**

2. Fifteen segments bearing bundles of capillary chaetae; first three segments of caudal region carry a club-shaped papilla on each side (6.11n)   ***Pectinaria koreni***

     Seventeen segments bearing bundles of capillary chaetae; caudal region has no papillae   ***Pectinaria belgica***

Pectinaria (= *Amphictene*) *auricoma* (Müller)   FIG. 6.11

Seventeen segments with capillary chaetae dorsally, of which 13 (chaetigers 4–16) bear uncini; 20–40 mm long. No achaetous segments anterior to caudal region. Cephalic veil cut into long tongues, its dorsal edge crenellated. Comb of 10–15 spines on each side, with a flexible curved tip. Capillary chaetae of mixed types; uncini bear five or six rows of hooks above a series of very fine teeth. Crochets at the base of the caudal region are fine with a hooked point, eight to ten on each side (l). This region oval, with a membranous edge cut into lappets curving dorsally. A small conical anal cirrus. Pinkish white, gills bright red. Tube clearly curved, about 70–80 mm long.

At low water in sand and sublittorally on more muddy bottoms. European coasts from the Arctic to the Mediterranean; north-east Pacific.

Pectinaria belgica (Pallas)   FIG. 6.11

Seventeen segments with capillary chaetae dorsally, of which thirteen (chaetigers 4–16) also bear uncini; 30–70 mm long (j). No achaetous segments anterior to caudal region. Cephalic veil cut into a few long tongues, its dorsal edge entire. Comb of 8–15 spines on each side, with a very fine tip. Capillary chaetae of mixed types; uncini bear seven or eight rows of hooks above numerous very small ones (m). Crochets at base of caudal region stout, only slightly hooked, 6–12 on each side (k). This region an elongated oval, first few segments with a wavy margin, rest more or less smooth-edged. Anal cirrus very small. Pinkish white, gills carmine-red. Tube almost straight, about 90 mm long.

In muddy sand at low water and, more often, sublittorally. North-west Europe from Scandinavia to the Mediterranean; north-east Pacific (earlier reports more likely to be of *P. koreni*).

Pectinaria (= *Lagis*) *koreni* Malmgren   FIG. 6.11
Fifteen segments with capillary chaetae dorsally, of which twelve (chaetigers 4–15) bear uncini. Two achaetous segments anterior to caudal region. Comb of 10–15 spines on each side, with a flexible tip bent in a dorsal direction. Capillary chaetae of mixed types; uncini with a massive base and six to eight rows of thick hooks above four rows of little, indistinct teeth. Crochets at base of caudal region short, stout and with a blunt slightly hooked tip, three to seven on each side. This region an elongated oval with edges raised dorsally, on first three segments bearing a little club-shaped papilla on each side (n). A small conical anal cirrus; lobe surrounding anus cut into small teeth posteriorly. White with pink iridescence, gills carmine-red, ventral vessel red, visible by transparency. Tube slightly curved, about 80 mm long, always with a little mucous extension.

At very low water on long, open beaches, usually in very great numbers. Arctic and north-east Europe; Adriatic.

20 PHYLLODOCIDAE

A large family of long, thin, often quite large errant polychaetes in which the dorsal cirri of all but the first few segments are in a flattened leaf-like shape and held out vertically as a long fringe down each side of the animal (Fig. 6.12a) (hence the popular name 'paddleworms'). The prostomium is more or less pear-shaped, tapering anteriorly. It bears in front two pairs of short antennae. There are normally two small, dark eyes dorsally and the fifth, median antenna (if present) is usually placed just in front of them. At the back of the prostomium, on its dorsal surface or in an indentation of its rear edge, there may be a nuchal papilla like a domed button; rarely, there is a pair of nuchal organs resembling ear-flaps. The large, eversible proboscis lacks jaws but typically bears large papillae around its anterior margin and smaller ones on its outer surface; these are usually soft and rounded. In some species, much of the surface is smooth but may appear ridged or papillated if the proboscis is incompletely everted. The first two or three segments lack paddles (and, often, also lack chaetae) but the dorsal and some of the ventral cirri take the form of tentacles. These may be as short as the antennae but the more posterior ones are often moderately long, usually extending back fairly close to the body. The second of these segments is often fused with the first, at least dorsally, but they can be distinguished as separate in lateral or ventral view; less often, the first may be partly fused with the prostomium or appears partially to surround it like a collar. There are many body-segments (often several hundred), which are closely similar to each other. The ventral cirri are generally similar in shape to the dorsal paddles, but smaller. Between them lies a relatively simple parapodial mound bearing a single bundle containing a few jointed chaetae. These chaetae are much the same throughout the family, consisting of a long cylindrical shaft swollen at its outer end, into which is inserted a short flattened blade. The swollen joint and one edge of the blade are toothed. Simple chaetae may be present on the segments bearing tentacles. A pair of anal cirri, at the posterior end of the body, vary in form from short, thick paddles to cylindrical or threadlike tentacles. Phyllodocids are very active worms, primarily carnivorous, and they secrete large quantities of mucus. They are often brightly coloured and may bear patterns of dots and lines across their dorsal surface.

---

1. Head bears only four antennae (one pair on each side anteriorly, e.g. Fig. 6.12e)   **2**

   Head bears five antennae (one pair on each side anteriorly plus a median one dorsally, e.g. Fig. 6.13h)   **13**

2. Behind the head, there are two pairs of short conical tentacles on the first of two segments not bearing paddle-like dorsal cirri (e.g. Fig. 6.12b)   **3**

   There are three or four pairs of tentacles, which may be quite long (e.g. Figs. 6.13h, l); three segments do not bear paddles, although the division between the first two may be difficult to distinguish   **6**

3. Proboscis has numerous hard papillae, many bearing spines, around its proximal half (not visible if only partially everted). Shaft of compound chaetae bears two large spines at its joint with blade (Fig. 6.13b). Dorsal surface shows a pattern made up from brownish blotches   **Mysta picta**

   Proboscis more or less ridged and folded to produce soft papillae, but hard spiny ones are lacking. Shaft of compound chaetae bears only one large spine (Fig. 6.12k) or, if several, only one is prominent. Dorsal surface may have blotches but they do not form a well-marked pattern   **4**

4. Second body-segment bears a ventral cirrus on each side but lacks chaetae   **Eteone foliosa**

   Simple chaetae as well as ventral cirri present on second body-segment   **5**

5. Paddles in mid-region broader than long; prostomium also broader than long, narrowing only near front   **Eteone flava**

   Paddles in mid-region longer than broad (Fig. 6.12h); prostomium about as long as its width, narrowing well back towards eye   **Eteone longa**

6. Three pairs of tentacles borne on first two of three distinctly separate segments lacking paddle-like dorsal cirri; ventral pair of second segment flattened (Fig. 6.13g)   **Mystides limbata**

Four pairs of tentacles, all cylindrical but of variable length, borne on three segments lacking paddles; first segment more or less fused with second (there may appear to be only two such segments, especially from above) **7**

7. Tentacles long and slender: last pair reaches back beyond sixth body-segment. Nuchal papilla set unobtrusively in an indentation at rear of prostomium (Fig. 6.13d) **8**

Tentacles short and stout: last pair would reach no further than fourth body-segment if deflected rearwards. Nuchal papilla either set on prostomium (Fig. 6.13l) or absent **11**

8. Worm quite long (up to 300 mm), with paddles subrectangular in mid-body (Fig. 6.12j); prostomium heart-shaped, concave at sides; proximal part of everted proboscis bears small papillae in distinct rows down each side; in life, pale yellow, green, or brown dorsally **9**

Worm long or very long (up to 750 mm) with leaf-like paddles (Fig. 6.12a); prostomium pear-shaped, straight, or convex at sides; proximal part of everted proboscis bears small papillae diffusely arranged; in life, dark green with a metallic sheen dorsally **10**

9. Over 100 mm long, with more than 250 segments; in life, dorsal surface greenish yellow, with green paddles each having brown markings
Anaitides groenlandica

Under 100 mm long, 250 segments or fewer; in life, dorsal surface whitish or yellow, with brown paddles. Three brown blotches across each segment create a characteristic pattern *Anaitides maculata*

10. Worm long (up to 600 mm). Prostomium longer than broad, with more or less straight sides (Fig. 6.12a). In life, dorsal surface dark green with a bluish sheen; paddles brownish or yellowish *Phyllodoce lamelligera*

Worm very long (up to 750 mm). Prostomium broader than long, with convex sides (Fig. 6.13c). In life, dorsal surface very dark green-brown with a steel-blue iridescence; paddles green with a red-brown blotch
Phyllodoce laminosa

11. Nuchal papilla prominent, set on a narrow rearward projection of prostomium behind eyes
Parainitis kosteriensis

Nuchal papilla absent **12**

12. Worm moderately long (up to 100 mm), with fewer than 100 segments; in life, yellowish green with rust-coloured paddles *Genetyllis rubiginosa*

Worm long (up to 300 mm), with several hundred segments; in life, an iridescent blue or slate-grey, paddles green edged with yellow *Nereiphylla paretti*

13. Two nuchal organs present on posterior dorsal margin of prostomium, resembling ear-flaps
Notophyllum foliosum

Ear-like nuchal organs absent; nuchal papilla absent or indistinct **14**

14. First three segments lack paddle-like dorsal cirri (Fig. 6.12c); distinctly separate from each other, although first (bearing a pair of tentacles) may not otherwise be distinct from prostomium. The first obvious segment may thus appear to bear two pairs of short tentacles **15**

First three segments lack paddles but division between first two may be difficult to distinguish. The first obvious segment may thus appear to bear two pairs of short tentacles and one pair of moderate length (Fig. 6.13n) **17**

15. Worm small (12 mm long or less) *Eulalia pusilla*

Worm of moderate size (30–150 mm long) **16**

16. Last pair of tentacles long, reaching back to body-segment 10 or 12 (Fig. 6.12d), paddles elongated and pointed (Fig. 6.12i). In life, a uniform bright-green colour *Eulalia viridis*

Tentacles short and stout (last pair would reach no further than body-segment 4 if deflected to rear; Fig. 6.12c); paddles oval and blunt-ended (Fig. 6.12g); in life, yellowish or greenish yellow *Eulalia bilineata*

17. Ventral cirrus of second segment differs from other tentacles in having a flattened blade along one side, thus resembling a cleaver or chopping-knife (Fig. 6.13o) *Eumida macroceros*

Tentacles all of tapering cylindrical shape **18**

18. Worm of moderate length (60–150 mm), with several hundred segments; body marked with transverse lines of dark spots; proboscis has about 50 papillae around margin *Eumida punctifera*

Worm short (20–60 mm), with fewer than 150 segments; spots may be present but do not form a distinctive pattern; proboscis has about 20 papillae around margin **19**

19. Proboscis covered with numerous small papillae
Eumida fucescens

Proboscis smooth when fully extended (Fig. 6.13m)
Eumida sanguinea

Anaitides groenlandica Bergström FIGS. 6.12, 6.13
Body elongated but flattened, narrowing at each end, with 250–700 segments; 150–300 mm long. Prostomium heart-shaped, with a nuchal papilla in crevice between its lobes posteriorly. Four small antennae, two small eyes. Proboscis with rows of large flattened papillae distally, small rounded papillae proximally; 17 papillae surround its opening (Fig. 6.13d). First and second

tentacular segment indistinguishable dorsally but third clearly separate, bearing simple chaetae; four pairs of tentacles, longest reaching back to about 10th body-segment. Paddles of mid-region subrectangular, fairly elongated (Fig. 6.12j). Joint of compound chaetae fine-toothed. Anal cirri cylindrical. Greenish yellow with transverse bands of brown and blue; paddles greenish, heavily blotched with brown. In alcohol, yellow-grey with brown markings and bluish iridescence.

In sand and rock-crevices at low water; all around British Isles and north-west Europe, also Arctic; Sea of Japan.

Anaitides maculata FIG. 6.12
(Linnaeus, *non* de Saint-Joseph)

Body slender, with about 250 segments; 30–100 mm long. Prostomium heart-shaped, with a nuchal papilla in crevice between its lobes posteriorly. Four small antennae, two eyes of medium size. Proboscis transversely and longitudinally ridged distally to give appearance of large irregular papillae; flattened oval papillae proximally (e); 16–17 papillae surround its opening. First and second tentacular segments indistinguishable dorsally but third clearly separate, bearing simple chaetae; four pairs of tentacles, longest reaching back to 6th–10th body-segment. Paddles of mid-region subrectangular, broad but short. Joint of compound chaetae fine-toothed. Anal cirri cylindrical. Whitish or yellowish with transverse dark-brown bands; paddles brown. In alcohol, yellowish or brownish. Eggs dark orange or green.

In muddy sand, under stones and in mussel beds. All around British Isles and north-west Europe, also Arctic.

(N.B. *A. mucosa* (Oersted) is very similar but smaller; it may merely be a juvenile form of *A. maculata*.)

Eteone flava Fabricius

Body elongated but flattened, narrowing at each end, with about 300 segments; 40–120 mm long. Prostomium short, with concave sides; nuchal papilla indistinct. Four small antennae, two small eyes. Proboscis with more or less strongly marked transverse ridges; flaring out towards its opening, which is fringed with numerous medium-sized papillae. Two distinct tentacular segments; first has two pairs of short tentacles, second a pair of small ventral cirri and simple chaetae. Paddles broad, coming to a blunt point. Joint of compound chaetae finely toothed, terminating in a single large spine. Anal cirri broad, oval. Yellow or brick-red. In alcohol, lemon or brown.

In sand at low water and in the shallow sublittoral; around most of British Isles, north Atlantic to Arctic.

Eteone foliosa Quatrefages FIG. 6.12

Body slender, dorsally convex, with about 350 segments; 120–300 mm long. Prostomium a truncated cone, nuchal papilla indistinct. Four small antennae, two small eyes (not visible in alcohol-preserved specimens). Proboscis with ridges forming flattened papillae; short, widened towards its opening which has two fleshy lobes resembling lips, separated at each side by smaller papillae (b). Two distinct tentacular segments: first has two pairs of short, stout tentacles, second a pair of small ventral cirri but no chaetae. Paddles short but broad, not pointed; their

stalk extended across blade like a short finger. Joint of compound chaetae finely toothed, terminating in a single large spine (k). Yellowish white with little violet spots at base of parapods; brownish gut visible within. In alcohol, dirty white with iridescent sheen or brownish.

In clean sand or rock-crevices at low water; south-west Britain, Irish Sea, Atlantic coast of Europe.

Eteone longa (Fabricius) FIG. 6.12

Body flattened but very slender, with about 200 segments; 25–60 mm long. Prostomium conical, pinched in just in front of eyes. Four short antennae. Proboscis smooth or with small transverse ridges; flaring towards its opening which is surrounded by about 15 conical papillae. Two distinct tentacular segments: first has two pairs of short, stout tentacles, second a pair of ventral cirri and simple chaetae. Paddles rounded, oval (h). Joint of compound chaetae scarcely toothed, terminating in a single large spine. Whitish or pale grey, with brown blotches or broad transverse bands of brownish green. In alcohol, dark yellow with brownish paddles.

Offshore, around most of British Isles, north Atlantic to Arctic.

Eulalia bilineata Johnston FIG. 6.12

Body slender, narrowing at each end, with 100–150 segments; 30–90 mm long. Prostomium broad and rounded. Two medium-sized black eyes; five short antennae, two pairs anteriorly and a median one dorsally in front of eyes (c). Proboscis uniformly covered with scattered small papillae. Three tentacular segments: first separated from prostomium dorsally only by an ill-marked transverse groove and bears one pair of short tentacles. The next two segments bear simple chaetae and (respectively) two pairs and one pair of tentacles, also short (c). Paddles oval, bluntly pointed (g). Joint of compound chaetae covered with medium-sized teeth. Two anal cirri, cylindrical and fairly short. Mature female mid-green with a faint and broken median double line; male yellowish white.

At low water in crevices, under stones, and in kelp holdfasts; off-shore amongst old shells. Mostly on south and west coasts of Britain; North Sea, Channel, Atlantic, and Mediterranean coasts of Europe.

Eulalia pusilla Oersted

Body slender, with 65–80 segments; 8–12 mm long. Prostomium short and blunt-ended; two eyes, set well back. Five antennae, two short pairs anteriorly and a very short median one dorsally in front of eyes. Proboscis covered with small papillae, its opening surrounded by 24 larger, blunt ones. Three distinct tentacular segments bearing four pairs of short tentacles; last two also bear single chaetae. Paddles leaf-like, rounded. Jointed chaetae with a very finely toothed shaft. Two oval anal cirri. Brownish, with a longitudinal green line; paddles brown or green. Eggs green.

Offshore, from around south and west Britain; North Sea, Channel, north Atlantic coast of Europe.

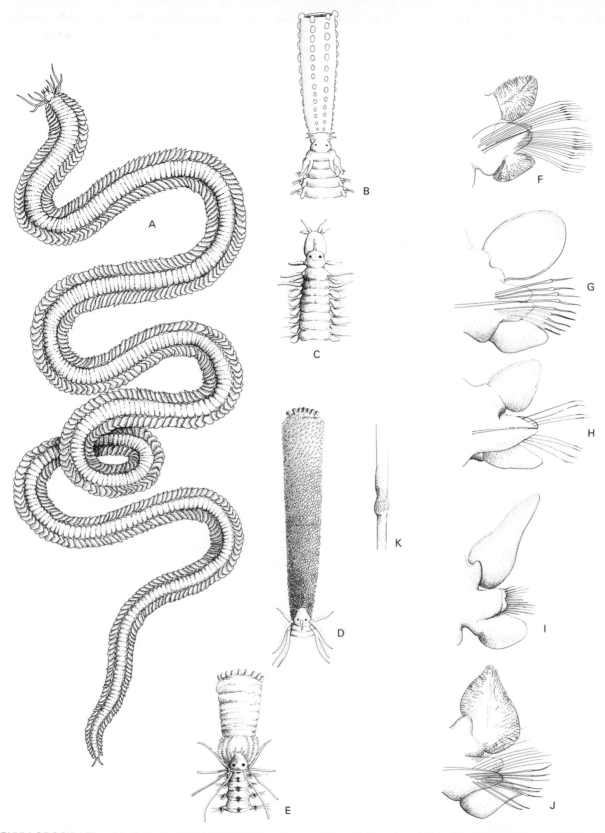

Fig. 6.12 (PHYLLODOCIDAE) a. *Phyllodoce lamelligera*—entire worm b. *Eteone foliosa*—anterior end with proboscis (after Day) c. *Eulalia bilineata*—anterior end (after McIntosh) d. *E. viridis*—anterior end with proboscis (after McIntosh) e. *Analtides maculata*—anterior end with proboscis (after McIntosh) f. *Mysta picta*—parapod (after McIntosh) g. *Eulalia bilineata*—parapod h. *Eteone longa*—parapod i. *Eulalia viridis*—parapod j. *Anaitides groenlandica*—parapod (after McIntosh) k. *Eteone foliosa*—detail of jointed chaeta

Eulalia viridis (O. F. Müller)   FIG. 6.12

Body straight-sided, with 60–200 segments; 50–150 mm long. Prostomium rounded in front, almost semicircular from above. Two eyes, five short antennae (four anteriorly, median one a little longer and set between eyes). Long cylindrical proboscis covered by very many small rounded papillae, its opening surrounded by 14–30 large ones, its base sometimes smooth or longitudinally striated (d). Three distinct tentacular segments bearing four pairs of stout tentacles, most posterior dorsal pair reaching back to 10th–12th body-segment. Last two tentacular segments also bear simple chaetae. Paddles elongated, narrowing to a point (i). Shaft of jointed chaetae with a coarsely toothed joint. Two anal cirri, stout or flattened. Bright mid- to deep-green, sometimes with black spots or transverse lines dorsally.

Very frequently recorded, perhaps because it is so obvious moving about in the open on intertidal rocks; also in kelp holdfasts, rarely in sediments or offshore. All around British Isles and north-west Europe; Mediterranean.

Eumida (= *Pirakia*) *fucescens* (de Saint-Joseph)

Body slender, narrowing at each end, with 95–100 segments; 20–30 mm long. Prostomium conical. Two black eyes; five short antennae, four anteriorly and one mid-dorsally well in front of eyes. Proboscis covered with numerous small rounded papillae, its opening surrounded by 20 reddish ones. Three tentacular segments, first indistinguishable from second dorsally. Four pairs of tentacles, anterior and ventral pairs short, posterior and dorsal pairs of medium length. The two posterior tentacular segments also bear simple chaetae. Paddles heart-shaped, pointed distally. Joint of compound chaetae coarsely toothed. Two long, cylindrical anal cirri. Light brown with regular darker spots; paddles brown or greenish. Eggs violet, mature males whitish.

Offshore; Irish Sea, Channel, Atlantic coast of Europe.

Eumida macroceros (Malmgren)   FIG. 6.13

Body broad, narrowing at each end, with about 170 segments; 30–80 mm long. Prostomium broad, oval from above. Two large black eyes, sometimes kidney-shaped. Five relatively long antennae, all inserted anteriorly (o). Proboscis cylindrical, covered with numerous small conical papillae, its opening surrounded by 48 larger rounded ones. Three tentacular segments, first distinct except when worm is tightly contracted. Four pairs of tentacles, ventral pair on second segment each have a flattened blade along one side, resembling a cleaver or chopping-knife (o). Last pair longer than the others, reaching back as far as 13th body-segment. The two posterior tentacular segments also bear simple chaetae. Paddles elongated, narrowing to an acutely pointed tip. Joint of compound chaetae with only a small patch of fine teeth; blade very long. Two long, stout anal cirri. Pale green, straw-yellow, or pale brown, with a darker blotch between eyes. Eggs green.

On the lower shore amongst bryozoans and hydroids; offshore, amongst old shells. Mainly on south and west coasts of Britain, North Sea and Atlantic coasts of Europe, also Mediterranean.

Eumida (= *Pirakia*) *punctifera* (de Saint-Joseph) FIG. 6.13

Body stout, narrowing posteriorly, with about 350 segments; 60–150 mm long. Prostomium heart-shaped. Two large eyes; five short antennae (n), median one (almost between eyes) with a dark blotch around its base. Proboscis cylindrical, very long, covered with very many small conical papillae, its opening surrounded by about 50 large rounded ones. Three tentacular segments, first indistinguishable from second dorsally. Four pairs of moderately long tentacles (n). The two posterior tentacular segments also bear simple chaetae. Paddles heart-shaped, with a thick stalk and an acutely pointed tip. Joint of compound chaetae with a few smallish teeth. Two stout anal cirri of moderate length. Greenish or yellowish, with one or two lines of brown or dark green spots dorsally across each segment; each paddle has a mass of brown spots at its centre. Mature females orange, eggs pink; mature males whitish.

At low water, under stones and in muddy gravel, also offshore. Mainly on south and west coasts of Britain, North Sea and Atlantic coasts of Europe, also Mediterranean.

Eumida sanguinea Malmgren   FIG. 6.13

Body stout, dorsally convex, with 60–140 segments; 30–60 mm long. Prostomium heart-shaped. Two fairly large black eyes; five antennae, paired anterior ones short, median one rather longer and inserted in front of eyes (m). Proboscis cylindrical, smooth when fully everted (m) but otherwise wrinkled, giving an irregularly papillated appearance; its opening surrounded by about 20 papillae. Three tentacular segments, first appearing fused with prostomium dorsally. Four pairs of tentacles, posterior ones quite long (reaching back to the 6th–8th body segment). The posterior two tentacular segments also bear simple chaetae. Paddles broad and bluntly pointed, on a thick stalk. Compound chaetae with a spiny joint and long blade. Two tapering anal cirri. Colour variable, from greyish white with brown spots through yellowish green to reddish brown with white transverse bands. In alcohol, olive or rust-coloured. Eggs green or reddish.

At low water, under stones or in kelp holdfasts; offshore amongst old shells. All around Britain and north-west Europe, Mediterranean; Arabian Gulf, Australasia.

Genetyllis rubiginosa (de Saint-Joseph)   FIG. 6.13

Body slender, narrowing posteriorly, with 50–60 segments; 10–100 mm long. Prostomium small, rounded, appearing to be mounted within first tentacular segment (j). Two large eyes, four stout antennae. Base of proboscis covered with numerous papillae, its opening surrounded by eight large ones. Three tentacular segments, first indistinguishable from second dorsally and scarcely more so ventrally. Four pairs of short, stout tentacles; two posterior tentacular segments also bear simple chaetae. Paddles heart-shaped, with an acutely pointed tip (j). Compound chaetae with a thickly toothed joint and short blade. Two tapering anal cirri. Yellowish green with two longitudinal lines, darker green or blue, down dorsal mid-line. Paddles dark yellow or rust-red with darker spots. In alcohol, body cinnamon with rust-red paddles.

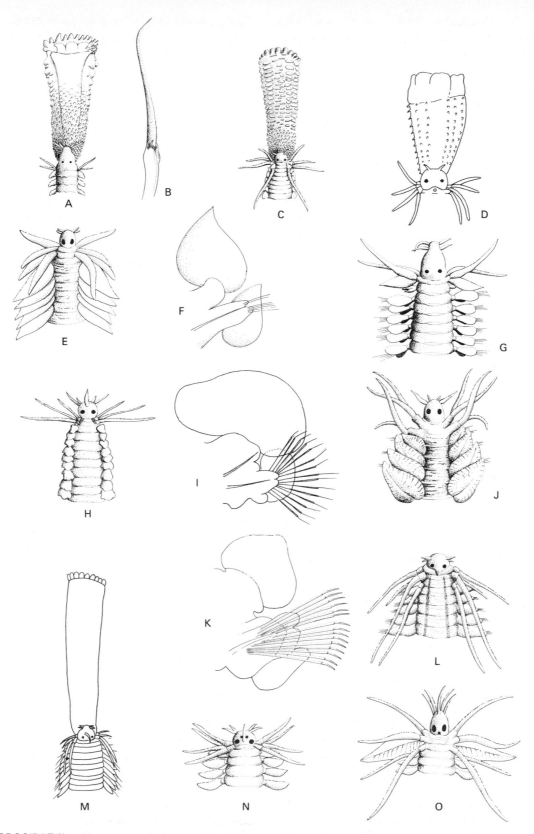

Fig. 6.13 (PHYLLODOCIDAE 2) a. *Mysta picta*—anterior region with proboscis b. *M. picta*—jointed chaeta c. *Phyllodoce laminosa*—anterior region with proboscis d. *Anaitides groenlandica*—anterior region with proboscis e. *Nereiphylla paretti*—anterior region (after Fauvel) f. *N. paretti*—mid-region parapod (after Fauvel) g. *Mystides limbata*—anterior region (after Fauvel) h. *Notophyllum foliosum*—anterior region i. *N. follosum*—mid-region parapod j. *Genetyllis rubiginosa*—anterior region k. *Parainitis kosteriensis*—mid-region parapod l. *P. kosteriensis*—anterior region m. *Eumida sanguinea*—anterior region with proboscis n. *E. punctifera*—anterior region o. *E. macroceros*—anterior region

Under stones or amongst algae along the sublittoral fringe, also offshore. Around the south and west coasts of Britain; Channel and Atlantic coasts of Europe.

Mysta picta (Quatrefages)   FIGS. 6.12, 6.13

Body flattened but slender, narrowing at each end, with 60–150 segments; 30–60 mm long. Prostomium triangular from above, truncated at its front and indented along each side. Two dark eyes, four short stout antennae. Proboscis with two rows of large, soft papillae down each side; flaring outwards towards its opening which is decorated, around ventral edge only, with a row of about 20 pointed papillae (Fig. 6.13a). Otherwise, the distal half is smooth. Its basal half (which may not be visible if the proboscis is only partly everted) is covered with numerous hard papillae, some flattened and others stalked, many of which are armed with chitinous spines or teeth. Two distinct tentacular segments: first has two pairs of short, stout tentacles, second a pair of small ventral cirri and simple chaetae. Paddles broad, oval or triangular in shape, with a blunt point and thick stalk (Fig. 6.12f). Joint of compound chaetae bears two large hooked spines as well as a few finer teeth (Fig. 6.13b). Two oval anal cirri. Colour very variable: pink or yellowish green with, on each segment, blotches in purple or rust which form a pattern of longitudinal and transverse lines. Each paddle has a brownish spot.

At low water amongst stones or algae; also offshore. Around most of the British Isles, Channel and Atlantic coasts of Europe, also Mediterranean.

Mystides limbata de Saint-Joseph   FIG. 6.13

Body slender, narrowing at each end, with 40–90 segments; 6–10 mm long. Prostomium an elongated cone, prolonged anteriorly to give the appearance of a snout (g). Two fairly large red eyes, four small stout antennae. Proboscis covered with large conical papillae, its opening surrounded by eight to ten papillae. Three distinct tentacular segments: first and second each bear dorsally a pair of cylindrical tentacles of moderate length. The second also has simple chaetae and a pair of flattened ventral cirri intermediate in form between tentacles and paddles (g). The third has some jointed chaetae and a pair of normal ventral cirri (like dorsal paddles, but much smaller), but no paddles dorsally. Paddles elongated, oval, with a blunt tip. Compound chaetae with a joint terminating in a large spine with a fan of smaller teeth to each side, the broad blade markedly toothed down one edge and obliquely striated. At maturity, the sexual segments also bear long, fine, oarlike simple chaetae. Two oval anal cirri. Light brown; eggs green. Offshore from shelly or coralline bottoms.

South and west coasts of Britain; Channel and Atlantic coasts of Europe.

Nereiphylla paretti (Blainville)   FIG. 6.13

Body slender, narrowing at each end, with several hundred segments; 150–300 mm long. Prostomium very small and rounded. Two large dark eyes, four small rather flattened antennae (e). Distal part of proboscis transversely ridged, its open-

ing surrounded by papillae; basal part covered with fine papillae. Three tentacular segments, first indistinguishable from second dorsally and scarcely more so ventrally. Four pairs of stout tentacles, last two flattened. The two posterior tentacular segments also bear simple chaetae. Paddles large: broad and heart-shaped in mid-body (f), narrower but longer anteriorly (e). Compound chaetae having a joint with a few small teeth and a short broad blade. Two leaf-like anal cirri. Colour variable— back bright blue with an iridescent sheen, slate colour, grey or yellow and blue; ventral surface yellow or pink, sometimes with a blue iridescence. Paddles green edged with yellow, tentacles yellow.

At low water under stones, also offshore. South-west Britain; North Sea, Channel, and Atlantic coasts of Europe, also Mediterranean.

Notophyllum foliosum Sars   FIG. 6.13

Body straight-sided and broad; dorsal surface convex, almost entirely hidden by the overarching paddles; 80–110 segments, 15–55 mm long. Prostomium rounded; two large eyes, each with a prominent lens. Five antennae, paired anterior ones a little flattened and inserted laterally, median one rather longer (h). Two ciliated nuchal organs extend back from posterior edge of prostomium, behind eyes, resembling ear-flaps. Proboscis has numerous papillae around its basal part; its opening surrounded by large rounded ones. Three tentacular segments, first difficult to distinguish from second dorsally. The two posterior dorsal tentacles are long, reaching back to 9th–10th body-segment. The two posterior tentacular segments bear simple setae, which are also present in the notopod of normal segments. Paddles kidney-shaped and very wide (i). Compound chaetae with a striated shaft, a strongly toothed joint and a long blade. Two anal cirri. Greenish grey, having green paddles edged with brown. In alcohol, brownish or greenish. Eggs greyish.

Offshore, amongst old shells, stones, and serpulid tubes. Around most of the British Isles, North Sea, Channel, and Atlantic coasts of Europe, also Mediterranean.

Paranaitis kosteriensis (Malmgren)   FIG. 6.13

Body rather wide, narrowing slightly at each end; dorsal surface convex. About 155 segments, 60–80 mm long. Prostomium with a blunt, rounded front, narrowing abruptly behind two large eyes to a rearward extension bearing the nuchal papilla. Four short antennae, inserted laterally (l). Proboscis with two longitudinal rows of papillae on each side at its base. Three tentacular segments, first enclosing posterior part of prostomium to each side in front and indistinguishable from second one, dorsally, behind. Four pairs of tentacles, two posterior dorsal ones rather longer (l). The third tentacular segment bears simple chaetae. Paddles kidney-shaped and very wide, with a thick stalk (k). Joint of compound chaetae coarsely toothed, with one spine markedly larger than rest. Two globular anal cirri. Back striped with transverse red or purple bands; paddles pale, with a spot of similar colour at their base.

Offshore, coastal and deep. Off the south and west coasts of Britain, North Sea, north Atlantic.

Phyllodoce lamelligera Johnston   FIG. 6.12

Body slender, with very many segments, 60–600 mm long (a). Prostomium an elongated, truncated cone. Two black eyes, four short antennae. Proboscis ridged longitudinally (so that it appears hexagonal in section) and also transversely; its opening surrounded by 16 papillae. Three tentacular segments, first indistinguishable from second dorsally. Four pairs of tentacles, two posterior dorsal ones moderately long (reaching back to 6th–8th body-segment). The posterior two tentacular segments bear simple chaetae. Paddles large, in an asymmetrical elongated leaf-shape. Compound chaetae with a joint covered by medium-sized teeth and a long straight blade. Two long cylindrical anal cirri. Dark green, with a blue metallic sheen. Paddles olive-green or brownish yellow. In alcohol, iridescent with brownish paddles.

Under large stones on the lower shore; in kelp holdfasts and offshore. Around the south and west coasts of Britain, Channel and Atlantic coasts of Europe, also Mediterranean; Pacific.

Phyllodoce laminosa Savigny   FIG. 6.13

Body slender, with several hundred segments; 150–750 mm long. Prostomium a rounded heart-shape, with a nuchal papilla visible in posterior indentation. Two large dark eyes, four short stout antennae (c). Distal part of proboscis ridged longitudinally (so that it appears hexagonal in section) and also transversely; its opening surrounded by 16–20 rounded papillae, the basal part covered with tightly packed small conical papillae not arranged in rows (c). Three tentacular segments, first indistinguishable from second dorsally. Four pairs of tentacles, most posterior dorsal pair long (reaching back to 14th–18th body-segment) (c). The posterior two tentacular segments bear simple chaetae. Paddles large and broad, in an asymmetrical leaf-shape with an acutely pointed tip. Compound chaetae with a coarsely toothed joint and a long straight blade. Two long cylindrical anal cirri. Very dark green, with a steel-blue iridescent sheen, transversely striped with green or brown bands. Ventral surface sometimes flushed with pink. Paddles pale or olive green with red-brown tinges. In alcohol, dark and iridescent with greenish- or purplish-brown paddles.

Under stones at low water or in damp rock-crevices. Around most of the British Isles, North Sea, Channel, Atlantic, also Mediterranean.

21 SCALIBREGMIDAE

Body usually either short and stocky or long and slender, often swollen anteriorly. Prostomium bilobed or two-horned. Segments annulated, integument usually wrinkled or reticulated. Parapods small but may have fairly prominent fingerlike cirri posteriorly; bearing hair-like and pitchfork (FIG. 6.11r) bristles but no crochets. Branched gills may be present anteriorly.

1. Body elongated, with 50–60 segments, all but first few 4-annulate. Fingerlike cirri, at least ventrally, on parapods of posterior half of body. Pygidium bears four or five medium-long cirri   **2**

Short, thickset, maggot-like, with about 30 triannulate segments. Parapods simple mounds, each with a bundle of chaetae but no appendages (Fig. 6.11q). Anus surrounded by short papillae   **Lipobranchus jeffreysi**

2. Body long (50–100 mm), swollen anteriorly then slender. Four pairs of branching gills dorsally on chaetigers 2–5 (Fig. 6.11o). Chaetae of first chaetiger similar to others. Parapods of posterior region bear fingerlike cirri dorsally and ventrally. Proboscis smooth, globular   **Scalibregma inflatum**

Body short (5–20 mm), slender, spindle-shaped. No gills. Notopod of first chaetiger bears a number of stout, blunt spines. In posterior half of body, fingerlike cirri are ventral only. Proboscis cylindrical and fringed with papillae   **Sclerocheilus minutus**

Scalibregma inflatum Rathke   FIG. 6.11

About 50–60 segments, first few triannulate, then 4-annulate; 50–100 mm long. Body lugworm-like, swollen anteriorly and then long and slender. Prostomium rectangular, with two short frontal horns; proboscis smooth and globular. Four pairs of branching gills dorsally on chaetigers 2–5 (o). From about chaetiger 16, fingerlike dorsal and ventral cirri (p). Pygidium bears four or five threadlike or fingerlike cirri. Purple-red with yellow blotches; eggs yellow.

At low water and in the shallow sublittoral, deep in sand or mud. From the Arctic all around Britain to Atlantic coast of Europe.

Also as a pelagic epitoke with longer chaetae.

Sclerocheilus minutus Grube

About 54 segments; chaetigers 2–4 biannulate, then divided into four annuli; 5–20 mm long. Body slender and spindle-shaped, convex dorsally and flattened ventrally. Prostomium T-shaped; proboscis cylindrical, fringed with papillae. Gills absent. First chaetiger bears a number of strong, blunt acicular spines in each notopodium. In posterior half of body, fingerlike ventral cirri are present and there is a button-like lateral organ between parapodial lobes. Pygidium bears four or five fingerlike or clubbed cirri. Reddish brown, mature females may be greyish white.

Shallow sublittoral, in the mud between stones and old shells. English Channel, Atlantic and Mediterranean coasts of Europe.

Lipobranchus jeffreysi McIntosh   FIG. 6.11

About 30 segments, triannulate; 20–25 mm long. Body short, thickset and maggot-like. Prostomium small and bilobed. Gills, acicular spines, and parapodial appendages are absent (q). Anus surrounded by short papillae. Coloration when alive flesh-pink.

Shallow sublittoral, in a thick tube of mud cemented with mucus, on muddy bottoms. Irish Sea, Firth of Clyde, North Sea, Atlantic coast of Europe.

22 SPHAERODORIDAE

Medium sized worms, long and thin, or very small, short and grub-like. The integument is covered by papillae, segmentation not being indicated externally by grooves or constrictions. Simple uniramous parapods with few chaetae are inconspicuous except for their dorsal cirri in the form of large spherical capsules. Amongst the small, stout forms, several more spherical tubercles lie between these cirri, aligned in longitudinal rows. The prostomium is indistinct, often more or less retracted, and bears only a few short tentacular papillae.

1. Elongated (10–60 mm), thin, with a single series of spherical capsules down each side of body (dorsal surface covered with smaller papillae) **2**

   Short (2–4 mm), stout, dorsal surface bears numerous series of spherical capsules **3**

2. About 120 chaetigers (as indicated by the spheres); chaetae simple **Sphaerodorum flavum**

   About 50 chaetigers; chaetae jointed **Sphaerodorum peripatus**

3. Eight to sixteen chaetigers, each bearing a row of six spheres dorsally **Sphaerodoridium claparedi**

   Seventeen to twenty-two chaetigers, each bearing ten to twelve spheres dorsally **Sphaerodoridium minutum**

Sphaerodorum flavum Oersted   FIG. 6.18
(includes *Ephesia gracilis* Rathke)

Body elongated and narrow, 10–60 mm long; *c.* 120 chaetigers. Four dark comma-shaped eyes dorsally, beneath skin at anterior end, whose apparent position varies according to extent to which prostomium is retracted (n). Mouth ventral, with a more or less cylindrical eversible proboscis closely covered with fine papillae. Integument bears scattered small papillae dorsally and ventrally. Parapods short and conical (p), each containing a few simple, stout, pointed chaetae (r). Dorsal cirri take the form of a large spherical capsule bearing a small pointed papilla (p); ventral cirri cylindro-conical. Pygidium with two spheres a little larger than the more anterior ones and a single anal cirrus. Pale yellow with a brown or pinkish tinge in the gut region; spheres whitish.

Amongst stones, shell-gravel, or coralline fragments at low water and sublittorally. All around Britain, north-east Atlantic, Mediterranean.

Sphaerodorum (= *Ephesia*) *peripatus*
(Clarapède *non* Johnston)

Similar to *S. flavum* but with about 50 chaetigers. Proboscis elongated, ventral cirri squatter and less pointed. Chaetae jointed, with a hooked terminal section; distal end of shaft may be finely toothed. Yellowish white.

In kelp holdfasts. Southern Britain, north-east Atlantic, Mediterranean.

Sphaerodoridium claparedi (Greeff)   FIG. 6.18

Body short and stout, *c.* 2 mm long; 8–16 chaetigers. Two eyes with lenses. Mouth ventral, proboscis globular. Striated gizzard visible externally (o). Dorsally, each segment bears a row of six large spherical capsules, of which the outermost at each end forms the dorsal cirrus of a parapod; these spheres are also aligned longitudinally. Ventrally, the globular papillae are smaller and arranged either irregularly or in four longitudinal rows. Each parapod is a ribbed elongated cone bearing two club-shaped papillae between which the chaetae emerge (q); these are jointed, with a long hooked end (s). Pygidium bears small papillae and a single anal cirrus. Yellowish white.

Amongst shells and algae at low water and sublittorally; may swim at the surface at night. South and west coasts of Britain, north-east Atlantic.

Sphaerodoridium minutum (Webster and Benedict)

Similar to *S. claparedi* but 2–4 mm long, with 17–22 chaetigers. There are 10–12 spherical capsules in each dorsal row, but only small scattered papillae ventrally. The pygidium bears two large globular papillae and a long cirrus.

Arctic waters, north-east and north-west Atlantic.

N.B. Further species of *Sphaerodoridium* are to be found in special European habitats, e.g. the Baltic (see Hartmann-Schröder 1971).

23 SPIONIDAE

Worms with a relatively elongated body not divided into distinct regions. Prostomium small, without antennae; its anterior end of variable shape even within a single species, may have a short frontal horn at each anterior corner; may have a small mid-dorsal occipital tentacle posteriorly. Eyes usually present. Two very long, usually sturdy palps which are very mobile in life and usually roll up spirally when the animal is disturbed. Proboscis poorly developed. Parapods biramous with leaf-like dorsal and ventral lobes. Dorsal gills, usually simple but rarely feathery, on a variable number of segments. These, and sometimes the extended dorsal lobes, arch over the dorsal surface, giving the animal the appearance of a pipe fitted with cooling-fins. In addition to the simple capillary chaetae, posterior segments also have shorter, stouter ones with a hooded tip which is usually hooked, having one to three teeth. The pygidium terminates in an anal funnel or numerous anal cirri. There may be one or more longitudinal, ciliated sensory grooves down the back and various glandular or genital pouches.

N.B. The palps and gills are readily autotomized. The palps are almost invariably lost when the worm is killed, thus removing the main character which identifies it as a spionid.

1. Chaetigerous segment 5 obviously different from all others, lacking gills and parapodial lobes but bearing a few extra-large chaetal spines

   Polydora (see key below)

No single anterior segment markedly different from its neighbours **2**

2. Gills present as elongated fingerlike processes more or less arching over dorsal surface and usually with bright red blood-vessels **3**

   Gills absent. Tufts of long silky threads laterally on chaetigerous segments 5–15

   Spiophanes bombyx

3. Gills commence from first or second chaetigerous segment and are present on at least front third of body (often more) **4**

   A large pair of gills may be present on chaetiger 2, but remainder commence between 11 and 20, and are present on no more than middle third of body (may be less); anus surrounded by four stout papillated processes. (Fig. 6.14h) ***Pygospio elegans***

4. Anus surrounded by a sucker-like or membranous funnel lacking cirri (Fig. 6.14i); in the posterior half of the body, a few short stout chaetae are present dorsally, together with long delicate capillary chaetae, as well as ventrally **5**

   Anus surrounded by threadlike or petal-like cirri; in posterior half of body, short stout chaetae are present only ventrally **6**

5. Gills present for almost whole length of body; prostomium extends rearwards in a blunt point but has no median tentacle (Fig. 6.14c); posteriorly, at least 20 segments have short stout chaetae ventrally before the dorsal ones appear ***Scolelepis squamata***

   Gills absent from about last third of body; prostomium has a short but distinct median tentacle (Fig. 6.14d); stout chaetae ventrally but not dorsally ***Scolelepis foliosa***

6. Gills present for almost whole length of body; prostomium has well-developed frontal horns (Fig. 6.14f) **7**

   Gills absent from about last half of body; prostomium rounded in front, lacking horns (Fig. 6.14e) ***Laonice cirrata***

7. Medium size (up to 60 mm long, 2 mm wide); six to eight short anal cirri; stout chaetae of posterior segments terminate in two hooded teeth (Fig. 6.14n), four or five in each neuropod ***Malacoceros fuliginosus***

   Large (100–160 mm long, 6 mm wide); 30 long anal cirri; stout chaetae of posterior segments terminate in three hooded teeth (Fig. 6.14o), 20–25 in each neuropod ***Malacoceros vulgaris***

Laonice cirrata (Sars) FIG. 6.14

Body long (90–120 mm), 3–5 mm wide, a little flattened; 160 chaetigers. Prostomium rounded anteriorly, with an occipital tentacle but no frontal horns (e). Two large eyespots. Sensory crest runs dorsally along first 28–30 chaetigers; 35–44 pairs of long cirriform gills from chaetiger 2. In gill-bearing segments,

dorsal lobe of each parapod is large, extending upwards like a pointed ear (l); it is independent of gill. From about chaetiger 25, mature adults bear genital pouches laterally. Stouter chaetae with two hooded teeth occur ventrally from 40th–50th chaetiger rearwards but are absent from notopods. Anus surrounded by *c*. 12 cirri. Yellowish in front, brownish towards the rear.

Sublittorally to considerable depths on bottom of muddy sand, shell gravel, or shingle. All around Britain; cosmopolitan.

Malacoceros (= *Scolelepis*) *fuliginosus* (Claparède)

Body long, rather slender (50–60 mm, up to 2 mm wide); 100–150 chaetigers. Prostomium with a pair of frontal horns and four eyes, extending rearwards in a crest but lacking an occipital tentacle (f). Palps banded. Fingerlike gills from the first chaetiger (although very small there), partly fused with the lobe of the notopod for the first third of the body (after which that lobe becomes small). No genital pouches. Stouter chaetae with two hooded teeth (n) occur ventrally from the 30th–45th chaetiger rearwards, four to five in each neuropod, but never dorsally. Pygidium with six to eight petal-like anal cirri. Salmon-pink, darker in front; when placed in an aquarium, rapidly covers itself with a flexible 'skin' of sandy mucus.

At low water, in galleries in muddy sand or under stones; may form dense groups in rich mud. Very active when disturbed, swimming in loose spirals. All round Britain, north-east Atlantic, Mediterranean.

Malacoceros vulgaris (Johnston) FIG. 6.14
(= *Scolelepis girardi* Fauvel)

Body stout (100–160 mm long, 6 mm wide) but fragile; 200–350 chaetigers. Prostomium broad and square, with pointed frontal horns and a small pointed rearward projection. No eyes in the adult. Gills extend from the first chaetiger along almost the entire body; in the first 30–40 segments, the lower part of each gill is fused with the top of the notopodial lobe. Stouter chaetae with three hooded teeth (o) occur ventrally from the 30th–40th chaetiger rearward, 20–25 in each neuropod, but not dorsally. Anus surrounded by 15–30 threadlike cirri. Pink or orange in front, greenish brown towards the rear; gills bright red.

At low water, in muddy sand under stones and amongst eelgrass; always well-spaced, does not occur in large numbers. Commonest in the south and west of Britain.

Polydora

Prostomium blunt in front, extending rearwards in a low crest. Palps long, slender, ciliated, very mobile. Longitudinal sensory grooves mid-dorsally. Dorsal lobes of parapods do not usually contribute to the gills; number of gills variable beginning from the seventh to ninth chaetiger, rarely from the second. Chaetiger 5 markedly different from all others, lacking gills and parapodial lobes but bearing extra-large chaetal spines dorsally. Short, stout chaetae ventrally from seventh or eighth chaetiger, tipped with two small hooded teeth; this type of chaeta absent dorsally (*cf.* certain other spionids) although large chaetae terminating in a hooked point may be present (*P. hoplura*). Well developed glandular pouches on some segments; seminal pouches also present when mature. Anus surrounded by a membranous funnel, complete or four-lobed. All species make a U-shaped tube from small particles (usually of mud, but may be whitish and calcareous if excavating in lithothamnia or other encrusting coralline algae): much of this tube may be embedded in a burrow excavated in limestone rock or shells. In life, the palps protrude, waving vigorously.

---

1. Dorsally on the 10–20 rearmost segments, large yellow chaetae with a pointed tip bent over like a meat-hook (Fig. 6.14p); of medium size (length 50 mm or more).   **P. hoplura**

   No such chaetae posteriorly; small (length 40 mm or less)   **2**

2. Dorsally from chaetiger 8 rearwards, tufts of numerous parallel fine chaetae which scarcely protrude from the surface   **P. flava**

   No such tufts of chaetae   **3**

3. Large chaetae on chaetiger 5 have a lateral tooth at their tip (Fig. 6.14r)   **4**

   Large chaetae on chaetiger 5 have no lateral tooth; tip hollowed on one side like a spoon (sim. Fig. 6.14s). Gills on most of the body segments   **P. caeca**

4. Gills from chaetiger 8 rearwards for more than half the remaining number of segments; over 20 mm long
                                                            P. ciliata

   Gills from chaetiger 10 (rarely 9) rearwards for fewer than half the remaining segments; 10 mm long or less
                                                             P. giardi

---

Polydora caeca (Oersted)

Body 20–40 mm long, 1 mm wide; 70–130 chaetigers. Chaetiger 5 has on each side dorsally four or five spoon-ended giant chaetae, lacking a lateral tooth, together with large lance-like chaetae. Gills from chaetiger 8 to one-half or two-thirds down the body. Yellowish or pale pink, in lithothamnia and kelp holdfasts.

In Most common in south-west Britain, Atlantic, Mediterranean; Indian Ocean.

Polydora ciliata (Johnston)   FIG. 6.14

Body 20–30 mm long, 0.7–1 mm wide; 60–180 chaetigers (a). Chaetiger 5 has on each side dorsally six or seven giant chaetae with a lateral tooth (r), together with large lance-like chaetae. Gills from chaetiger 7 to all but the ten rearmost ones. Yellowish brown.

In limestone rock and stones, old shells, or lithothamnia. All around Britain; Arctic, Baltic, Atlantic, Mediterranean, Indo-Pacific.

Polydora flava Claparède   FIG. 6.14

Body 20–45 mm long, slender; 100–150 chaetigers. Chaetiger 5 has on each side dorsally several spoon-ended chaetae, lacking

a lateral tooth (s), together with large lance-like chaetae. Gills from chaetiger 8 (rarely 7 or 9), often lacking from the last third of the body. Dorsally from chaetiger 8 rearwards, tufts of numerous parallel fine chaetae which scarcely protrude from the surface.

In coarse sand, rock-crevices, lithothamnia, and old shells. Most common in south-west Britain, north-east Atlantic, Mediterranean; Indo-Pacific.

Polydora giardi Mesnil

Body 8–10 mm long, 0.5 mm wide; 50–100 chaetigers. Chaetiger 5 has on each side dorsally four or five giant chaetae with a lateral tooth, together with large chaetae finned down one side. Gills from chaetiger 10 (rarely 9) to about 25, the first two or three pairs small. Yellowish or pink.

In lithothamnia and kelp holdfasts. South-west Britain, Channel, perhaps Mediterranean; north Pacific.

Polydora hoplura Claparède   FIG. 6.14

Body 50–60 mm long, 1–2 mm wide; 200 chaetigers or more. Chaetiger 5 has on each side dorsally several giant chaetae with a lateral tooth (q), together with large lance-like chaetae. Dorsally on the 10–20 rearmost segments, large yellow chaetae with a pointed tip bent over like a meat-hook (p). Reddish or yellowish.

Amongst serpulids and particularly oysters. Mostly in south-west Britain, north-east Atlantic, Mediterranean; southern Africa.

Pygospio elegans (Claparède)   FIG. 6.14

Body small and slender, 10–15 mm long, showing marked sexual dimorphism; 50–60 chaetigers. Prostomium narrow, extending posteriorly in a pointed process as far as chaetiger 2; two to eight small eyes, scattered in no clear pattern. Gills fringed for their entire length by an extension of the dorsal parapodial lobe (j); they begin from chaetiger 11–20 and number only 7–9 pairs in females but 20–28 pairs in males. In males, there is also a pair of large erect gills on chaetiger 2, which stand separate from the notopod. Behind the gilled region, parapodial lobes are much reduced. Short, stout chaetae with two hooded teeth occur ventrally from chaetiger 8, four to five in each neuropod. Glandular pouches ventrally from chaetiger 2 or 3, seminal receptacles (in females) from 12–13. Dorsal sense-organs rudimentary in females but well-developed on several segments in males. The pygidium ends in four stout papillated processes (i). Yellowish or greenish with a brown gut.

Occupies long flexible tube of fine sand-grains embedded in mucus; occurs in mud collected in rock-crevices or between old shells, from the mid-shore to the sublittoral. All around Britain, north-east Atlantic, Mediterranean; north Pacific.

Scolelepis (= Nerine) foliosa   FIG. 6.14
(Audouin and Milne Edwards)

Body stout (100–160 mm long, 6–9 mm wide) but fragile; 200–250 chaetigers. Prostomium small, with a little occipital tentacle

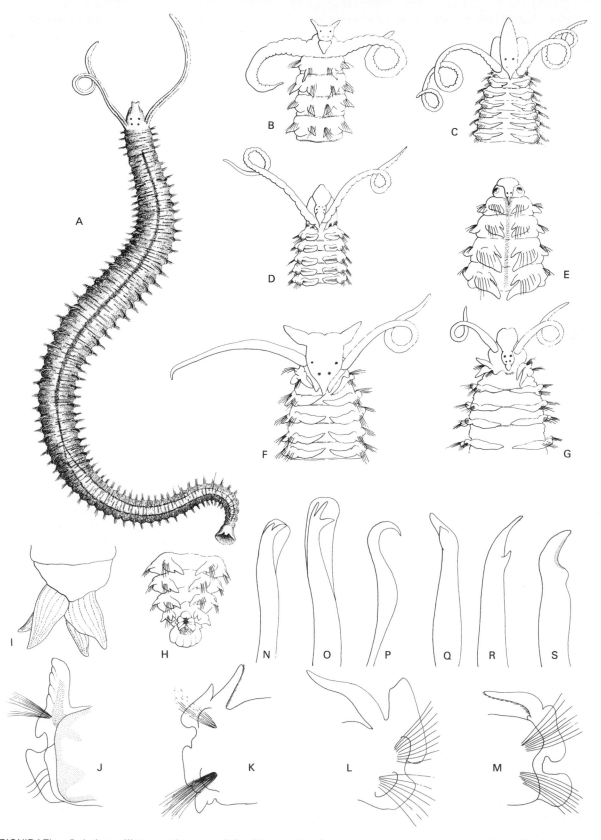

Fig. 6.14 (SPIONIDAE) a. *Polydora ciliata*—entire worm (after McIntosh) b. *Spiophanes bombyx*—anterior region c. *Scolelepis squamata*—anterior region (after Fauvel) d. *S. foliosa*—anterior region e. *Laonice cirrata*—anterior region, omitting palps (after Day) f. *Malacoceros fuliginosus*—anterior region g. *Spio filicornis*—anterior region h. *Scolelepis squamata*—pygidium (after Hartmann-Schröder) i. *Pygospio elegans*—posterior region j. *P. elegans*—parapod (after Day) k. *S. squamata*—parapod l. *L. cirrata*—parapod m. *S. filicornis*—parapod n. *M. fuliginosus*—posterior neurochaeta o. *M. vulgaris*—posterior neurochaeta p. *Polydora hoplura*—posterior notochaeta (l–p after Fauvel) q. *P. hoplura*—giant chaeta of 5th chaetiger r. *P. ciliata*—giant chaeta of 5th chaetiger s. *P. flava*—giant chaeta of 5th chaetiger (q–s after Day)

having a swollen base (d). Four small eyes in a transverse line, buried beneath the skin. Gills from chaetiger 2, very well-developed in the first 50–60 segments, where they are fringed almost to the top by an extension of the dorsal parapodial lobe; on more posterior segments this lobe is short and does not contribute to the long, slender gills. Gills absent from the last third of body. Short stout chaetae with a hooded tip occur from chaetiger 58–60 ventrally (about 20 per neuropod) and chaetiger 60–65 dorsally (about 10 per notopod). Pygidium ends in a short oblique anal funnel lacking cirri. Red in front, grey-green and almost transparent behind; gills bright red.

At low water, in clean or only slightly muddy sand, usually solitary; does not swim when disturbed. On most British coasts, north-east Atlantic; Mediterranean.

Scolelepis squamata (O. F. Müller)   FIG. 6.14
(= *Nerine cirratulus* Fauvel)

Body of medium length, slender; 50–80 mm long, 2–3 mm wide; 150–200 chaetigers. Prostomium an elongated cone which ends posteriorly in a stout, pointed process overhanging chaetigers 2 and 3. Four small eyes forming a large square. Palps particularly long. Gills from chaetiger 2 as far as the last seven or eight; dorsal lobe of parapod extended upwards like a pointed ear and forming a fringe to the gill for much of its length at front end of the worm, but becoming less and less developed posteriorly (k). Short stout chaetae with two hooded teeth from about chaetiger 40 ventrally (10–12 per neuropod) and 60–65 dorsally (2–5 per notopod). Pygidium ends in a delicate scalloped anal funnel (k). Bluish green with contrasting red blood-vessels in palps and gills; mature males whitish, females brighter green; when placed in an aquarium, rapidly covers itself with a flexible 'skin' of sandy mucus.

Mid- to lower shore in clean and mobile or only slightly muddy sand on exposed beaches; swims in spirals when disturbed. On most British coasts, north-eastern Atlantic, Mediterranean.

Spio filicornis (O. F. Müller)   FIG. 6.14

Body short and relatively thick (*c*. 30 mm long, 2 mm wide) but fragile; 80–90 chaetigers. Prostomium elongated, blunt in front and ending behind in a short stout pointed process (g). Four small eyes in a square. Palps relatively short and fat. Gills from the first to all but the last few chaetigers. Dorsal lobe of parapod extends only a short way up the anterior gills and is separate from the more posterior ones (m). Short stout chaetae with two hooded teeth (may be three in juveniles) ventrally only, from chaetiger 10–15 rearwards (6–9 per neuropod). Anus dorsal, between four petal-like cirri of which the dorsal pair are longer. Pink, with a brown gut and cream flecks laterally.

Low water and shallow sublittoral, in clean sand. On most British coasts, Arctic, Baltic, north-east Atlantic, Mediterranean; north Pacific.

Spiophanes bombyx (Claparède)   FIG. 6.14

Body slender (50–60 mm long, 1.5 mm wide), rather flattened dorsally; *c*. 180 chaetigers. Prostomium wide in front, with two long frontal horns, ending behind in a stout pointed process (b). Eyes may be absent or four forming a square. Palps thick and relatively short. Two longitudinal ciliated sensory grooves run down the dorsal mid-line; a ciliated ridge crosses these transversely on each segment. Gills are absent. The dorsal lobe of each parapod is extended upwards in a blade, folded back across the body, which becomes longer and more narrow on the most posterior segments. Chaetigers 5–15 bear laterally, between the two lobes of each parapod, a gland producing a tuft of long, twisted silky threads. From chaetiger 15 rearwards, each neuropod contains one large curved chaeta with a stippled blade. Short stout chaetae with two hooded teeth occur ventrally from chaetiger 15 but are absent dorsally. The pygidium bears two fingerlike anal cirri. Bright pink in front, then darker red or greenish brown.

At low water, in a slender but stiff sandy tube which protrudes slightly from the surface. On most British coasts, Atlantic, Mediterranean; north Pacific.

24 SYLLIDAE

Small active carnivorous worms found mostly amongst colonial sedentary animals and seaweeds, occasionally in a mucus tube; a few are interstitial in muddy sand. They typically have long, fingerlike, and often annulated dorsal cirri. All possess an eversible pharynx, usually armed with a single piercing tooth or a trepan (circlet of small teeth), connected to a barrel-shaped muscular proventriculus ('gizzard') which may be visible through the body-wall. The rounded head normally has four large eyes and bears three antennae followed by two pairs of tentacles; a pair of flattened ventral palps may be separate, joined at the base or wholly fused together in the mid-line. The parapods are uniramous, mostly with only a few jointed chaetae. Reproduction may be direct, the gametes often being released during epigamy (the swarming of adults modified for swimming), or by stolons budded from an asexual stock. These may form a chain behind the asexual individual and may be sexually dimorphic (Fig. 6.15l,m), the female (*saccocirrus*) brooding her developing eggs. Major divisions (sub-families) of this large group and their main characteristics are:

Syllinae—palps free for their entire length, antennae and cirri distinctly annulated (moniliform), ventral cirri present, reproduction usually by stolons (*Ehlersia*, *Haplosyllis*, *Syllis*, *Trypanosyllis*, *Tryposyllis*).

Eusyllinae—palps joined only at the base, antennae and cirri sometimes show superficial constrictions, ventral cirri present, reproduction by epigamy (*Amblyosyllis*, *Eusyllis*, *Odontosyllis*, *Pionosyllis*);

Exogoninae—palps fused for their entire length, antennae and cirri short, not annulated; ventral cirri present but may be indistinct, reproduction direct or rarely by stolons; often very small (*Brania*, *Eurysyllis*, *Exogone*, *Sphaerosyllis*);

Autolytinae—poorly developed palps fused and folded back ventrally (thus not readily visible), antennae and dorsal cirri (which may be absent except on the first chaetiger) not annulated, no ventral cirri, reproduction by sexually dimorphic stolons; number and arrangement of teeth may be an important feature, often requiring preserved specimens to be cleared (*Autolytus*, *Myrianida*, *Proceraea*).

---

1. Ventral cirri lacking   **2**

   Ventral cirri present   **7**

2. Antennae, tentacles, and dorsal cirri more or less elongated; anterior end of pharynx armed with a circle (trepan) of ten or more teeth (Fig. 6.15h,i; Fig. 6.16d–h)   **3**

   Antennae, tentacles, and dorsal cirri globular (Fig. 6.16i); further spherical tubercles across back; pharynx armed with a single tooth   ***Eurysyllis tuberculata***

3. Dorsal cirri (also, to some extent, antennae and tentacles) flattened, tongue-shaped; antennae short, median one up to twice as long as those on either side; trepan with 50–60 small teeth. May trail a long chain of stolons (Fig. 6.16q)   ***Myrianida pinnigera***

   Dorsal cirri, antennae, and tentacles cylindrical   **4**

4. Ciliary band across each segment dorsally; shaft of jointed chaetae thin   **5**

   Ciliary bands absent; shaft of jointed chaetae thick. Antennae and tentacles quite long; median antenna up to twice length of lateral ones. Trepan of ten large, alternating with ten small teeth (Fig. 6.16e)   ***Procerea picta***

5. Antennae short (about twice head-width), median one about same length as those on either side (Fig. 6.16a). All but most anterior dorsal cirri of uniform length, about equal to body-width. Trepan of ten blunt teeth, large but of varying size   ***Autolytus prolifer***

   Lateral antennae of short to medium length, median one 2–3 × as long (Fig. 6.16c)   **6**

6. All but most anterior dorsal cirri of uniform length, less than body-width. Trepan of 16–20 pointed teeth of equal size (Fig. 6.16g)   ***Autolytus aurantiacus***

   After the most anterior ones, length of dorsal cirri alternates between half body-width and about equal to body-width. Trepan of ten large blunt teeth, each separated by two or three small pointed ones (Fig. 6.16h)   ***Autolytus longeferiens***

7. Palps well-developed, fused together for most or all of length and clearly visible from above (Fig. 6.16j–l). Small (usually less than 6 mm and not more than 10 mm long)   **8**

   Palps fused together only at base, if at all (Fig. 6.15b); usually but not necessarily visible from above. Of medium size (usually more than 6 mm and often more than 10 mm long)   **14**

8. Antennae, tentacles, and dorsal cirri of medium length (about equal to body-width) and only moderately swollen near base; two pairs of tentacles. Very small (body length 1–3 mm)   **9**

   Antennae, tentacles, and dorsal cirri of varying length but often very short and swollen; only one tentacle on each side. Small (body length 2–10 mm)   **10**

9. Dorsal cirri with a square-cut tip (Fig. 6.16m); some jointed chaetae with a short, others with a long finely toothed blade bearing a larger single tooth at its tip   ***Brania pusilla***

   Dorsal cirri with a long, pointed tip (Fig. 6.16n); jointed chaetae all have a fairly long finely toothed blade bearing twin larger teeth at its tip   ***Brania clavata***

10. Antennae, tentacles, and dorsal cirri all of much the same length (up to half body-width), with a swollen base and pointed tip. Body may be encrusted with sand or mud   **11**

    Antennae, tentacles, and dorsal cirri more or less club-shaped, lacking a pointed tip; median antenna slightly or markedly longer, tentacles rudimentary, cirri short (much less than half body-width)   **12**

11. Body covered with papillae, often encrusted with sand or mud. Antennae, tentacles, and dorsal cirri about half body-width. Jointed chaetae with slender, finely toothed blades, some long, some of medium length (Fig. 6.16o)   ***Sphaerosyllis hystrix***

    Papillae only on parapods and anal segment. Antennae, tentacles, and dorsal cirri very short. Jointed chaetae with short, stout, more coarsely toothed blade (Fig. 6.16p)   ***Sphaerosyllis bulbosa***

12. Antennae all of medium length (at least half head-width). Jointed chaetae with a short double hook or a long delicate spine   ***Exogone gemmifera***

    Lateral antennae very short   **13**

13. Median antenna of medium length. Jointed chaetae with short, broad, finely toothed blades   ***Exogone hebes***

    Median antenna also very short. Jointed chaetae with a short, finely toothed blade, or a long, triangular spine   ***Exogone verugera***

14. Palps separate for their whole length; dorsal cirri (and usually antennae also) distinctly segmented (Fig. 6.15a, c)   **20**

    Palps fused at base; dorsal cirri and antennae not segmented, but may be superficially annulated (Fig. 6.15j, k)   **15**

15. Nuchal organs present, resembling elongated ear-flaps folded back across the tentacular segment (Fig. 6.15j); dorsal cirri annulated, length about four times body-width and coiled in a loose spiral. Body with fewer than 20 segments   ***Amblyosyllis formosa***

    Nuchal flaps absent; dorsal cirri may not be annulated and less than twice body-width in length. Body with 40 or more segments   **16**

16. Occipital flap present as a disc forming half or more of a circle, extending forwards dorsally across prostomium from tentacular segment (Fig. 6.15k). Front of pharynx bears small teeth in a row or ring, but no large tooth **17**

Occipital flap, if present, represented only by a narrow fold; a single large tooth present at front of pharynx (Fig. 6.15i) **19**

17. Antennae at least as long as head-width; longest tentacle about twice body-width. Dorsal cirri cylindrical, blunt-ended, alternately long and short. Body with up to 100 segments. Jointed chaetae with a short, smooth-edged hook (Fig. 6.15f, g) **18**

Antennae short (less than head-width); tentacles short (longest about equal to body-width). Dorsal cirri fusiform, with pointed tip, not alternating in length. Body with no more than 40 segments. Jointed chaetae with a long, finely toothed blade (*sim.* Fig. 6.15e) ***Odontosyllis gibba***

18. Antennae, tentacles, and anterior dorsal cirri slightly annulated. Each segment has a transverse granulated band dorsally. Hook of jointed chaetae single ***Odontosyllis ctenostoma***

Antennae, tentacles, and dorsal cirri smooth. No obvious body markings. Hook of jointed chaetae double ***Odontosyllis fulgurans***

19. Antennae and anterior cirri annulated; front of the pharynx bears a small, dark, toothed chitinous ring; jointed chaetae with a short blade (Fig. 6.15d) ***Eusyllis blomstrandi***

Antennae, tentacles, and cirri smooth; pharynx lacks a dark, toothed ring; some jointed chaetae with a long, narrow blade (Fig. 6.15e) ***Pionosyllis lamelligera***

20. Body flattened; pharynx with a single large tooth and a circlet of 10–12 small teeth (Fig. 6.15h) **21**

Body slender; pharynx with a single large tooth and sometimes also a circlet of soft papillae (Fig. 6.15b)

21. Body of medium length (8–12 mm); antennae of equal length; dorsal cirri uniformly short (less than body-width). ***Trypanosyllis coeliaca***

Body long (30–60 mm); median antenna longer than lateral ones; dorsal cirri at least as long as body-width, alternating with longer ones ***Trypanosyllis zebra***

22. Jointed chaetae present **23**
 Jointed chaetae lacking ***Haplosyllis spongicola***

23. All jointed chaetae have a short, stout blade **24**
 Many jointed chaetae have a very long, thin blade ***Ehlersia cornuta***

24. In the mid-region and posteriorly, stout chaetae present with a bifid end resembling a bird's open beak ***Syllis gracilis***

Stout chaetae with a simple blunt or pointed end (rarely, only delicately bifid) **25**

25. Alternate dorsal cirri thicker at the tip, curling back over dorsal surface and about as long as body-width; tooth at anterior end of pharynx ***Typosyllis krohni***
 Dorsal cirri narrowing towards tip **26**

26. Dorsal cirri not markedly alternating, all shorter than body-width; tooth near anterior end of pharynx ***Typosyllis armillaris***

Dorsal cirri alternating in length, all longer than body-width (Fig. 6.15a); tooth inserted about one-third of length of pharynx from its anterior end ***T. prolifera***

Amblyosyllis (= *Pterosyllis*) *formosa* (Claparède)

FIGS. 6.15, 6.16

Body 10–15 mm long, with 16 trapezoidal segments of which 13 bear chaetae (Fig. 6.16r). Two long nuchal organs project behind head like ciliated earflaps (Fig. 6.15j). Median antenna longer than lateral ones. Palps folded against ventral surface, well separated but scarcely visible from above. Tentacles long, in unequal pairs. Pharynx very long and slender, coiled several times when retracted, crowned with a circlet of six or seven two- or three-cusped teeth. Dorsal cirri very long, usually rolled in a loose spiral and annulated, as are the antennae. Ventral cirri flattened except on penultimate segment, where they are thread-like. Jointed chaetae with finely toothed bifid blade, long in dorsal but short in ventral ones. Simple chaetae also present in anterior region; penultimate segment achaetous. Chaetae modified for swimming present when sexually mature. Usually a creamy white, with two or more brown/violet stripes across back of each segment. In mature individuals, eggs green or brown; sperm white.

On the lower shore on green algae; also in shallow sublittoral amongst old shells. Around most of the British coast, Europe to the Mediterranean; southern Africa, Japan.

Autolytus aurantiacus (Claparède) FIG. 6.16

Body 8–10 mm long, narrowing at each end; 60–100 segments. Median antenna longer than lateral ones. Fused palps clearly visible, extending beyond head. Pharynx long and slender, coiled in one complete turn when retracted, crowned with 16–20 almost equal-sized teeth (g). Proventriculus spherical, marked with about 40 rows of violet spots. Dorsal tentacles about as long as lateral antennae, ventral ones shorter. Dorsal cirri of first chaetigerous segment at least as long as median antenna, of next segment about one-third or one-quarter this length, thereafter becoming much shorter (less than body-width). Jointed chaetae with a very short blade, bifid at the end. In each parapod of posterior half, one awl-shaped chaeta dorsally. Colourless or yellowish, often with a red spot below each parapod. Appendages of head and anterior segments orange-tipped. Eggs reddish purple.

On lower shore and in shallow sublittoral, under stones and

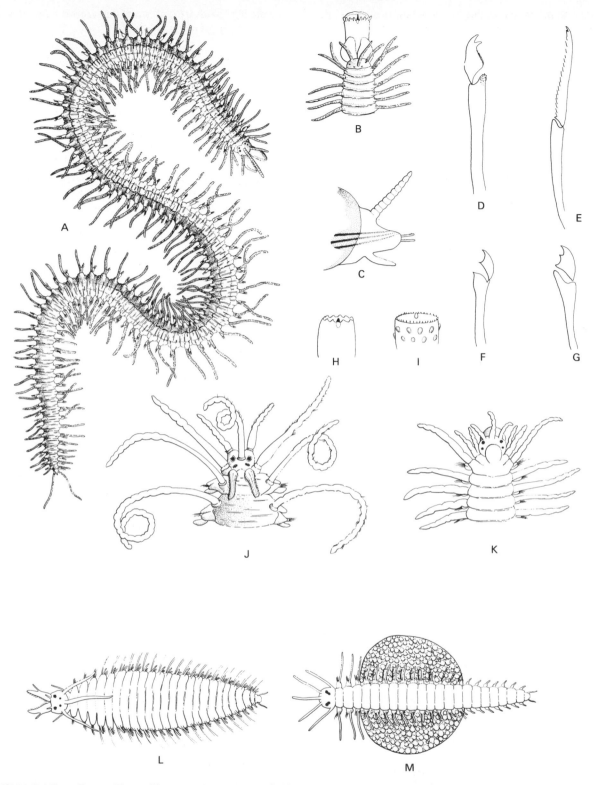

Fig. 6.15 (SYLLIDAE) a. *Typosyllis prolifera*—entire worm b. *Syllis gracilis*—anterior end c. *S. gracilis*—parapod (after Day) d. *Eusyllis blomstrandi*—jointed chaeta e. *Plonosyllis lamelligera*—jointed chaeta f. *Odontosyllis ctenostoma*—jointed chaeta (after Fauvel) g. *O. fulgurans*—jointed chaeta (after Fauvel) h. *Trypanosyllis zebra*—trepan i. *Eusyllis blomstrandi*—trepan j. *Amblyosyllis formosa*—anterior end (after Fauvel) k. *Odontosyllis gibba*—anterior end l. *Autolytus prolifer*—polybostrichus (male stolon) m. *A. prolifer*—saccocirrus (female stolon)

amongst algae. South and west coasts of Britain, Europe to the Mediterranean.

Autolytus longeferiens de Saint-Joseph FIG. 6.16

Body stout, 10–20 mm long, with 50–90 segments. Median antenna twice as long as lateral ones (c). Fused palps extending beyond head. Pharynx as long as body when extended, coiled in numerous turns when retracted, crowned with ten large blunt teeth each separated by two or three very pointed small ones (h). Proventriculus longer than broad, with 40–54 rows of spines. Dorsal tentacles as long as lateral antennae, ventral ones half as long. Dorsal cirri of first chaetigerous segment as long as dorsal tentacles, following ones alternating long and short (the longest not attaining length of the first). Jointed chaetae with a small two-hooked blade; also, on posterior half, one awl-shaped chaeta in each parapod dorsally. Orange; on anterior segments, three longitudinal red bands. Eggs greyish.

In kelp holdfasts. South-west Britain and Channel coasts.

Autolytus prolifer (O. F. Müller) FIG. 6.16

Body slender, 5–15 mm long; about 60 segments. Median antenna scarcely longer than lateral ones (a). Fused palps hardly extend beyond head. Retracted pharynx curled in an 'S' shape, crowned with about ten large unequal teeth (f). Proventriculus ovoid, with about 30 rows of spots. Dorsal tentacles about as long as antennae, ventral ones shorter. Dorsal cirri of first segment much longer than subsequent ones (a, b), which are all about equal to body-width. Jointed chaetae with a short bidentate blade; one awl-shaped chaeta in each parapod after the third. Whitish or yellowish with numerous rounded flecks, colourless or orange.

In kelp holdfasts and amongst stones or old shells in the shallow sublittoral. Around most of the British coast, especially in the south and west, North Sea, north-east Atlantic, Mediterranean.

Brania (= Grubea) pusilla Quatrefages FIG. 6.16

Body slender, 1–2.5 mm long; 28–35 chaetigers. Antennae small, swollen at base. Palps fused, rather hidden. Pharynx with a single tooth anteriorly, proventriculus with 12–15 rows of dots. Tentacles of an elongated flask-shape. Dorsal cirri spindle-shaped, with a square-cut end, containing two elongated yellowish bodies (m). Ventral cirri short and flattened. Jointed chaetae with blades terminating in a single tooth, some long and some short; acicula with a button-like swelling at end. In each parapod of last few segments, one simple chaeta dorsally and another ventrally, each finely toothed and bidentate. At maturity, the female develops long swimming chaetae and carries eggs or embryos ventrally, two per segment. Colourless, with a brown pharynx; eggs pink.

In kelp holdfasts, on smaller algae, and amongst shells or serpulid tubes on the lower shore and in the shallow sublittoral. Around most of the British coast, Europe to the Mediterranean.

Brania (= Grubea) clavata (Claparède) FIG. 6.16

Body cylindrical, 2–3 mm long; 25–35 segments. Antennae slightly swollen at base, extending well beyond palps, which are fused into a triangle projecting beyond head. Pharynx with a single tooth one-third of the distance back; proventriculus short. Tentacles fusiform, in unequal pairs. Dorsal cirri elongated, fusiform (n), longer in first chaetiger. Ventral cirri much smaller, flattened. Jointed chaetae with a long blade terminating in two teeth; acicula with a simple blunt end. In each parapod of last few segments, one curved simple chaeta. At maturity, the female develops long swimming chaetae and carries eggs in a transparent membrane dorsally, three to five per segment. Colourless, with a transverse brown band across several of the segments; mature males pale orange.

Amongst small algae and in kelp holdfasts on the lower shore and in the shallow sublittoral. South-west Britain, Europe to the Mediterranean.

Ehlersia (= Typosyllis) cornuta Langerhans

Body 10–15 mm long. Antennae annulated, subequal, extending well beyond the well-developed and widely separated palps. Pharynx very long when extended, with a single tooth inserted anteriorly; proventriculus long, with 30–35 rows of markings. Dorsal cirri annulated, alternately long and of medium length. Ventral cirri short. Jointed chaetae with a toothed blade, either very long and delicately bidentate at the tip or short and stoutly double-hooked; both sorts occur together in each parapod. In the last few segments, one simple sinuous chaeta occurs above and below them. Yellowish white or colourless.

At low water and in the shallow sublittoral, amongst serpulid tubes, bryozoans, and algae; very often in empty shells, commensal with hermit-crabs or sipunculids. Around most of the British coast, Arctic, north and south Atlantic, Mediterranean; Indian Ocean.

Eurysyllis tuberculata Ehlers FIG. 6.16

Body thick, 3–5 mm long; about 65 chaetigers. Antennae globular, around anterior edge of head. Palps fused, forming a lip above mouth but visible only from ventrally. Tentacles globular; tentacular segment also bears two dorsal tubercles (i). Pharynx surrounded by six large papillae anteriorly; at its opening, a circle of ten small teeth of equal size, together with a single large tooth. Proventriculus short, spherical. The gut has two large lateral diverticula in each segment. Four spherical tubercles distributed across dorsal surface of each segment; dorsal cirri are also spherical (i). Ventral cirri incorporated into the base of parapod, hard to distinguish. Jointed chaetae with blade terminating in a single point; on last few segments, each parapod also has a curved simple chaeta. Acicula have a swollen tip with a small, blunt spine.

At low water and in the shallow sublittoral, in kelp holdfasts, often encrusted with mud. South and west coasts of Britain, Europe to the Mediterranean.

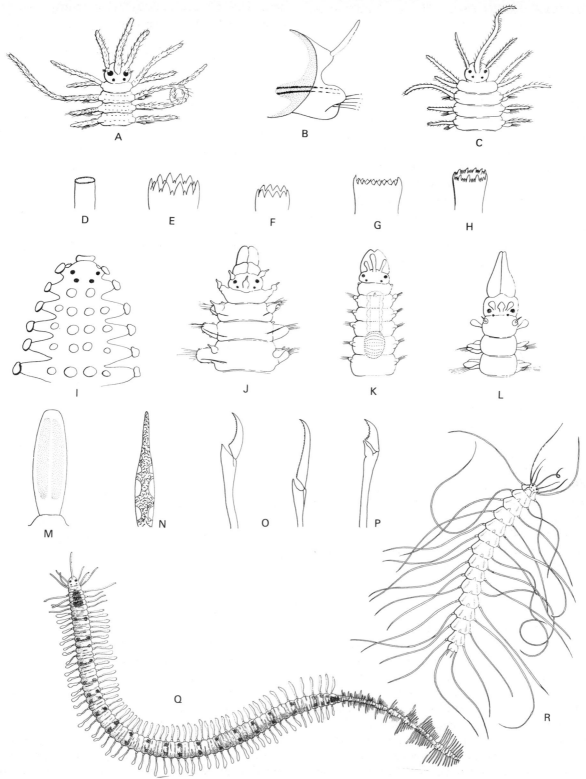

Fig. 6.16 (SYLLIDAE 2) a. *Autolytus prolifer*—anterior end b. *A. prolifer*—parapod (after Day) c. *A. longeferiens*—anterior end d. *Myrianida pinnigera*—trepan e. *Proceraea picta*—trepan (after Day) f. *Autolytus prolifer*—trepan (after Day) g. *A. aurantiacus*—trepan h. *A. longeferiens*—trepan i. *Eurysyllis tuberculata*—anterior end j. *Sphaerosyllis bulbosa*—anterior end k. *Exogone gemmifera*—anterior end (after Day) l. *E. verugera*—anterior end m. *Brania pusilla*—dorsal cirrus (after Day) n. *B. clavata*—dirsal cirrus (after Fauvel) o. *Sphaerosyllis hystrix*—jointed chaetae p. *S. bulbosa*—jointed chaeta q. *Myrianida pinnigera*—entire worm with train of stolons r. *Amblyosyllis formosa*—entire worm (after Day)

Eusyllis blomstrandi Malmgren   FIG. 6.15

Body thick but fragile, 6–10 mm long; about 50 segments. Median antenna longer than lateral ones. Palps long, oval, and well-separated. Pharynx surrounded by soft papillae anteriorly and crowned by a dark, finely toothed chitinous ring; also a single large conical tooth (i). Proventriculus elongated, with 50–55 rows of spots. Nuchal fold across posterior edge of prostomium. Upper pair of tentacles much longer than lower. First dorsal cirri longer than width of body, posterior ones shorter; antennae and anterior cirri with fairly distinct annulations, posterior cirri smooth. All ventral cirri short and stout. Jointed chaetae with a short, two-hooked blade (d); on last few segments, each parapod also has one simple chaeta dorsally and a bidentate one ventrally. Swimming chaetae also present when sexually mature. Orange or yellowish; tips of cirri brownish.

Amongst bryozoans, hydroids, and algae, often in a mucus tube. Northern and western coasts of Britain, Arctic, north-east Atlantic, Mediterranean.

Exogone gemmifera (Pagenstecher)   FIG. 6.16

Body cylindrical, 2–4 mm long; 24–33 chaetigers. Antennae short, stout, inserted in a straight line across front of head. Palps fused in a triangle, slightly indented in front (k). Pharynx narrow, with papillae anteriorly and a single conical tooth. Proventriculus globular (k). A single pair of tentacles, reduced to simple buttons. Dorsal cirri short, ovoid, missing from chaetiger 2. Ventral cirri very small and difficult to distinguish. In each parapod, a single simple blunt-ended chaeta dorsally; one jointed chaeta with a short, hooked end-element and, in posterior segments only, one simple curved chaeta ventrally. Long swimming chaetae also present when sexually mature. Eggs and embryos attached to ventral surface of female. Colourless or yellowish, eggs orange-red.

At low water and in the shallow sublittoral amongst algae, bryozoans, and ascidians. South and west coasts of Britain, Arctic, north and tropical Atlantic, Mediterranean; north Pacific.

Exogone hebes (Webster and Benedict)

Body narrow and wiry, 8–10 mm long; 30–44 chaetigers. Six little eyes arranged in two triangles, sometimes fused into an indeterminate mass. Antennae short and club-shaped, lateral ones often reduced to simple tubercles. Palps well-developed, fused into a rigid pointed snout. Pharynx long and narrow when extended, surrounded by ten papillae and with a single conical tooth anteriorly. Proventriculus elongated. Tentacles and dorsal cirri very small, club-shaped; ventral cirri cylindrical and bigger. Dorsal cirri missing from chaetiger 2. Parapods with two unequal lobes; one aciculum swollen terminally, the other slender with a curved point. Jointed chaetae with a short, broad, finely toothed blade having a single terminal hook; in addition, from chaetiger 8/10, a simple blunt-ended chaeta dorsally and, in the last few segments, a similar one ventrally. At sexual maturity, the male bears swimming chaetae. Eggs fixed to the parapods of the mature female. Creamy white.

At low water and in the shallow sublittoral, on sand or shell gravel and in sea-grass beds. On most British coasts, southern North Sea, north-east Atlantic.

Exogone verugera (Claparède)   FIG. 6.16

Body cylindrical, 3–8 mm long; 35–45 chaetigers. Antennae all reduced to simple pear-shaped papillae. Palps fused into a cone (l). Pharynx long and narrow when extended, bearing papillae and a single conical tooth anteriorly. Proventriculus elongated, with 25–28 rows of teeth. One pair of very short tentacles. Small ovoid dorsal cirri on all but chaetiger 2; ventral cirri even smaller. Acicula swollen at tip. In each parapod, one simple, curved, blunt-ended chaeta, one or two jointed chaetae with a strongly hooked blade and the others with a shorter end-element terminating in a single tooth; in last few segments, there is also another simple chaeta ventrally. Colourless.

At low water and in the shallow sublittoral. Along most of the British coast, southern North Sea, north-east Atlantic, Mediterranean; Pacific.

Haplosyllis spongicola Grube

Body 20–50 mm long, becoming slender posteriorly. Antennae annulated and fairly short. Palps large, close together at base but not fused. Pharynx long when extended, surrounded by ten soft papillae, with a single terminal tooth; rim often irregular. Proventriculus long. Dorsal cirri annulated, alternately long and of medium length; ventral cirri short and flattened. No jointed chaetae: in each parapod, three or four thick acicula terminating in a button-like swelling and two or three simple hooked chaetae with a single or double point, together with a very fine bristle. Reproduction by poorly developed stolons or direct. Orange or yellowish; on each side of last few segments, a large purplish blotch ventrally. Eggs violet, mature males purplish red.

At low water and in the shallow sublittoral, especially amongst sponges. Around most of the British coast; cosmopolitan.

Myrianida pinnigera (Montagu)   FIG. 6.16

Body thin, 15–30 mm long; 66 chaetigers (q). Median antenna long and leaf-like, lateral ones about half this length and narrower. Palps fused, folded back ventrally and extending little beyond head. Pharynx long and sinuous, making one or two complete turns when retracted, crowned by 50–60 little teeth of equal size (d). Proventriculus ovoid, with 32 rows of grey spines. Dorsal tentacles leaf-like, longer than the wedge-shaped ventral ones. Dorsal cirri also flattened, longer than width of body and inserted on a conical cirrophore. Jointed chaetae with a small blade having two teeth; from chaetiger 45 rearwards, there is also one fine hooked simple chaeta dorsally. Stolons may form a long chain of 15–30 individuals (q). White with large yellow, orange, or red blotches.

South-western coasts of Britain, Europe to the Mediterranean.

Odontosyllis ctenostoma Claparède   FIG. 6.15

Body thick but fragile, 10–20 mm long; 40–100 segments. Middle antenna often longer than lateral ones. Palps broad but short, folded under ventrally, separate to the base. Pharynx long when extended, crowned with six large teeth and with two lateral folds resembling ears. Proventriculus long. Tentacular segment has an occipital flap extending forwards over prostomium dorsally. Dorsal cirri thick, cylindrical, blunt-ended, alternately long and short, not annulated but often lightly grooved transversely. Ventral cirri leaf-like. Acicula stout, swollen at tip. Jointed chaetae small, with a short single-hooked blade (f). On last few segments, each parapod has a simple bristle dorsally and a hooked simple chaeta ventrally. At maturity, swimming chaetae are also present. Green or greenish yellow, with a speckled grey band across each segment; bioluminescent.

At low water and in the shallow sublittoral, amongst algae. Around most of the British coast, north-east and tropical Atlantic, Mediterranean.

Odontosyllis fulgurans Claparède FIG. 6.15
Body slim, 10–40 mm long; 35–100 segments. Antennae cylindrical, median one longer. Palps large, well-separated, and recurved. Pharynx very short, with six or seven large teeth curving rearwards and two lateral folds. Proventriculus three times as long as broad. Tentacular segment has an occipital flap extending forwards across prostomium, but this is not well-developed. Dorsal cirri cylindrical, smooth, alternating in length; those of chaetiger 1 much longer than following ones. Ventral cirri broad and short. Acicula stout, swollen at the tip. Blade of jointed chaetae with two small hooks (g). In the parapods of last few segments, one small simple chaeta dorsally. At maturity, swimming chaetae are also present. Pale yellow, orange, or reddish; eggs violet. Very bright green luminescence.

At low water and in the shallow sublittoral, amongst algae. South and west coasts of Britain, Europe to the Mediterranean.

Odontosyllis gibba (Claparède) FIG. 6.15
Body heavy but fragile, 5–25 mm long; 40 chaetigers. Antennae short, fusiform, and almost equal in length. Palps large, fairly prominent. Pharynx short and narrow, with six or seven large teeth and two lateral folds. Proventriculus short, spherical. Tentacular segment with an occipital flap extending dorsally over prostomium (k). Dorsal cirri fusiform, pointed, often weakly annulated. Ventral cirri short, conical. Acicula stout. Jointed chaetae with a long, finely toothed blade. On last few chaetigers, one simple bristle in each parapod. At maturity, swimming chaetae also present. Opaque white blotched with brown and violet.

At low water and in the shallow sublittoral, under stones and in kelp holdfasts. West coast of Britain, Europe to the Mediterranean.

Pionosyllis lamelligera de Saint-Joseph FIG. 6.15
Body slender, fragile, 6–7 mm long; 50–60 chaetigers. Median antenna longer than lateral ones. Palps long, divergent although fused at base. Pharynx with a smooth or slightly irregular edge, surrounded by ten soft papillae and bearing a single tooth anteriorly. Proventriculus short, with 22–25 rows of glands. Dorsal cirri of chaetiger 1 much longer than following ones, which are shorter than width of body. Antennae and cirri

smooth. Ventral cirri very small and flattened, except on chaetiger 1 where they are large and leaf-like. Acicula of first few chaetigers 'Y'-shaped. Some jointed chaetae have a long toothed blade with two small terminal teeth (e), others a very short bidentate hook. In the last few segments, parapods each have simple bristles and one large bidentate crochet. At maturity, swimming chaetae are also present. Colourless, sometimes with three purple-black bands across back of each segment (these persist in alcohol).

At low water, in tide-pools and also in the shallow sublittoral, in kelp holdfasts and amongst ascidians. Around most of the British coast, north-east Atlantic.

Procerea (= *Autolytus*) *picta* Ehlers FIG. 6.16
Body rounded, 10–25 mm long; 60–100 segments. Median antenna a little stouter and longer than lateral ones. Palps not visible from above. Pharynx sinuous, 'S'-shaped when retracted, crowned with ten large pointed teeth alternating with ten small ones (e). Proventriculus with 48–60 rows of brown spines. Dorsal tentacles a little larger than ventral ones, almost as long as lateral antennae. Dorsal cirri of chaetiger 1 larger than median antenna, rolling up spirally; those of chaetiger 2 much shorter, but still two or three times longer than following ones, which are of equal length (less than width of body). Jointed chaetae with a short, broad, bidentate blade. From chaetiger 34, each parapod also has one chaeta with a hooked blade, dorsally. Ventral surface pale pink, dorsal surface with violet/brown markings divided by white lines longitudinally and transversely. Antennae and tips of tentacles orange-brown.

At low water and in shallow sublittoral amongst algae and sponges or under stones. Around most of the British coast, north and tropical Atlantic, Mediterranean; Australasia.

Sphaerosyllis bulbosa Southern FIG. 6.16
Body 5–6 mm long, narrowing posteriorly; 48 chaetigers. Antennae very short, subequal, with a very swollen base. Palps fused together, long and broad (j). Pharynx with a single tooth anteriorly; proventriculus with 14 rows of spines. Dorsal cirri short, with a spherical base, then cylindrical, missing from chaetiger 2. Ventral cirri small and cylindrical. Small papillae on parapods and anal segment. Acicula stout, with a terminal button bearing a pointed tip. Jointed chaetae few, with a short toothed blade (p); one simple, sinuous chaeta dorsally in each parapod and, on a variable number of posterior segments, one ventrally too. Fawn or creamy white.

In the intertidal and shallow sublittoral. South and west coasts of Britain, north-east Atlantic.

Sphaerosyllis hystrix Claparède FIG. 6.16
Body straight-sided, 3–5 mm long, 30–40 segments; covered with little papillae and sometimes encrusted with sand or mud. Antennae shorter than palps, subequal, swollen at base. Palps fused together, triangular, longer than prostomium. Pharynx surrounded by brownish glands forming a tubular jacket, with a single tooth anteriorly; proventriculus short. Dorsal cirri with a spherical base extending into a tapering point, may be missing

from chaetiger 2. Ventral cirri very small, fingerlike. In each parapod from chaetiger 4 rearwards, a gland in the form of a rounded capsule filled with small rod-like particles. Acicula with tip bent at a right-angle. Jointed chaetae with a narrow finely toothed blade ending in a single large tooth, some long and others short (o). On a number of segments in middle and posterior regions, each parapod also has a strong, curved simple chaeta dorsally and ventrally. At maturity, males develop long swimming chaetae. Eggs or embryos are carried under a ventral membrane on females. Colourless or greyish.

On algae or amongst shells on muddy stores. Around most of the British coast, Europe to the Mediterranean.

Syllis gracilis Grube   FIG. 6.15

Body slim, 20–50 mm long. Antennae short, annulated; palps separate and stout. Pharynx long and slender when extended, with an irregular rim, bearing a single tooth anteriorly (b). Proventriculus fairly long. Dorsal cirri annulated, alternately short and of medium length. Ventral cirri conical (c). In anterior region, jointed chaetae have a broad blade with a finely toothed edge and long terminal tooth; they become shorter more posteriorly. In mid-region, thick simple chaetae with a bifid end resembling a bird's open beak also occur, together with curved simple chaetae. In parapods of last few segments, two awl-shaped simple chaetae are found, one dorsally and one ventrally. Pale yellow-brown, occasionally with lines of brown spots dorsally across anterior segments.

On the lower shore and in the shallow sublittoral, amongst sedentary organisms or old shells and in crevices. Around most of the British coast; cosmopolitan.

Trypanosyllis coeliaca Claparède

Body flattened, 8–12 mm long, with 60–90 short segments. Antennae annulated, short, subequal. Palps rounded, divergent. Pharynx surrounded by ten soft papillae and crowned by a trepan of ten inward-pointing teeth, also with a single large conical tooth. Proventriculus short. Gut with two large caeca in each segment. Dorsal cirri short, with a few annulations, all of much the same length. Ventral cirri flattened. Jointed chaetae with a bifid blade and, in each parapod of last few segments, also one simple chaeta with a bifid tip. Yellow; dorsal cirri full of yellow/green corpuscles.

On the lower shore, amongst old shells or in kelp holdfasts. South and west coasts of Britain, Europe to the Mediterranean.

Trypanosyllis zebra Grube   FIG. 6.15

Body flattened, 30–60 mm long, with numerous very short segments. Antennae annulated, median one longer than laterals. Palps elongated, well-separated. Pharynx surrounded by ten soft papillae and crowned by a trepan of 10–12 equal teeth, also with a single conical tooth which is hard to distinguish (h). Proventriculus long. Gut with two caeca in each segment. Dorsal cirri annulated, thick, alternately long and of medium length. Ventral cirri flattened. Jointed chaetae with a short, broad, finely toothed bifid blade and, in each parapod of last few segments, also one simple chaeta with a bifid tip. Whitish anteriorly, with

violet stripes across each segment; posteriorly, more yellowish. Cirri white or violet.

In the shallow sublittoral amongst old shells or in kelp holdfasts. South-western coasts of Britain, north-west Atlantic, Mediterranean; Indian Ocean, Japan.

Typosyllis (= Syllis) armillaris (Malmgren)

Body slender, 25–50 mm long, with numerous segments. Antennae annulated, median one longer than laterals, extending well beyond palps which are oval, separate but very close together. Pharynx with ten soft papillae and a large single tooth inserted well forwards. Proventriculus long. Dorsal cirri annulated, short (no more than body-width). Ventral cirri short and pointed. Jointed chaetae with a stout blade; those in mid-region have only a single terminal tooth but, towards front and rear ends of the worm, it is more or less clearly bifid. There are also one or two large conical acicula in each parapod and, in posterior segments, a simple pointed bristle. Reproduction by poorly developed stolons. Yellowish, occasionally with pink bands, or pinkish overall. Eggs violet, mature males bright pink.

On the lower shore and sublittorally, under stones or in kelp holdfasts. Around most of the British coast: cosmopolitan.

Typosyllis (= Syllis) krohni Ehlers

Body 15–30 mm long, thick but narrowing posteriorly. Antennae articulated and quite long. Palps large and separate. Pharynx with a single large tooth anteriorly. Proventriculus short. Dorsal cirri annulated, alternately short and long (long ones also thicker, with clubbed ends, tending to turn inwards across the back). Jointed chaetae thick, with a short, hooked blade (in first few chaetigers the blade may be longer and weakly bifid). In each parapod of the last few segments there is also a simple curved chaeta dorsally and one with a blunt tip ventrally. Anterior segments marked with brown/purple bands; cirri with scattered white spots. Eggs and sperm pink.

On the lower shore and sublittorally, amongst algae and under stones. South and west coasts of Britain, northern seas, Europe to the Mediterranean.

Typosyllis prolifera (Krohn)   FIG. 6.15
(includes Syllis armandi and Pionosyllis hyalina)

Body slender, 10–25 mm long, with numerous segments (a). Antennae annulated, median one longer than laterals. Palps long and well-separated. Pharynx broad and short, surrounded by 10–12 soft papillae and with a single large tooth about one-third of the way back. Proventriculus short and broad. Dorsal cirri annulated, alternating short and long. Jointed chaetae with a short, stout bidentate blade, posteriorly shorter and with more delicate terminal teeth. In each parapod of last few segments, also one simple, weakly bifid chaeta dorsally and another ventrally. Colour very variable: greyish, brownish, or reddish, sometimes with pink or orange markings anteriorly. Antennae and cirri with dark spots. Eggs and sperm violet/brown.

On the lower shore amongst algae, also in the shallow sublittoral and on the bottom offshore. South and west coasts of Britain, Europe to the Mediterranean; ? Indo-Pacific.

25 TEREBELLIDAE

Body with numerous segments divided into an inflated anterior region in which most segments have both notopods (with bundles of simple bristles) and neuropods (with uncini set in row/s down swollen ridges), usually bearing a series of glandular cushions along its ventral surface, and a more slender posterior region which more often has only uncini in neuropods. The head end is truncated, surrounded by various lobes, and bears numerous long, filiform, mobile tentacles which can be shortened but not withdrawn. Behind these there are normally one to three pairs of gills whose usual form resembles a much-branched bush. Occasionally, gills are lost during collection or in a previous accident. The uncini resemble a bird's head; the teeth are small and must be viewed at the right angle. These worms are common on the lower shore and in the shallow sublittoral, occupying a mucus-lined gallery or fragile tube loosely encrusted with detritus under a stone or in a large algal holdfast, or occasionally a more permanent tube of cemented sand-grains and shell-fragments; usually only their tentacles can be seen (see Holthe 1986).

1. Fifteen to twenty-five (in most, seventeen) anterior segments with bundles of bristles dorsally; the remaining segments (more than half body) with only uncini inserted on ridges or lappets ventrally. Gills variable   **2**

    At least thirty anterior segments have bristles dorsally as well as uncini ventrally, extending for half body-length and often more. Gills, if present, form two or three rows of numerous unbranched filaments   **11**

2. Gills bush-like, with a main stem repeatedly branching into finer filaments (Fig. 6.17b–d), inserted in pairs on two or three segments   **3**

    Gills either cirriform and unbranched or bear a series of lamellae (Fig. 6.17e, f)   **13**

3. Two pairs of gills   **4**

    Three pairs of gills   **7**

4. Stem of gills long, filaments forming a rounded tuft at end (Fig. 6.17d); segments bearing gills also have a small flap on each side, in the position of the neuropods in subsequent segments   ***Pista cristata***

    Gills branch from most of length of stem; no lateral flaps on the segments bearing gills   **5**

5. Neuropods are low swollen ridges throughout body. Anus surrounded by small papillae. Nephridial papillae (on some anterior segments between notopod and neuropod) not very prominent. Bristles have a slightly sickle-shaped end, finely toothed along inside of curve. Posterior half of body rolls into a tight spiral   ***Amphitritides gracilis***

Neuropods become progressively elongated into projecting lappets posteriorly. Rim of anus smooth. Nephridial papillae on each side of segments 6 and 7 may be prominent long tubes (Fig. 6.17c). Bristles have a simple tip like a narrow spear-head   **6**

6. Seventeen anterior segments with notopodial bristles. Gills large, with a long main stem   ***Nicolea venustula***

    Fifteen anterior segments with notopodial bristles. Gills small, main stem very short   ***Nicolea zostericola***

7. Seventeen anterior segments with notopodial bristles. Neuropods become progressively elongated into projecting lappets posteriorly   **8**

    Twenty-four to twenty-five anterior segments with notopodial bristles. Neuropods are short swollen ridges throughout body   ***Amphitrite figulus***

8. Two large triangular lobes (like a wing-collar) partly enclose head end. In last ten segments of anterior region, uncini are inserted in a double row back-to-back (with teeth pointing away from each other) (Fig. 6.18g). Tube strongly constructed from sand-grains and shell-fragments, with a fringe at its mouth (Fig. 6.18e)   ***Lanice conchilega***

    No large buccal lobes. Uncini of last ten anterior neuropods form either a double row face-to-face or a single row in which the teeth face in alternate directions (Fig. 6.18f). Tube, if present, is fragile and lacks a fringe   **9**

9. Large (up to 300 mm long, 20 mm wide) with 11–13 glandular cushions anteriorly along ventral surface and nine small nephridial papillae along each side (between notopods and neuropods). The bristles have a slightly sickle-shaped end, finely toothed along inside of curve (*sim.* Fig. 6.18b)   ***Amphitrite edwardsi***

    Medium-sized (not exceeding 150 mm), with 14–15 glandular cushions and six pairs of nephridial papillae. Bristles with a simple tip like a narrow spear-head   **10**

10. Up to 150 mm long, 8 mm wide, body soft and fragile. Pink, orange, or brown coloration, spotted all over with white. Beak of anterior uncini surmounted by two large teeth, then one to five smaller ones (Fig. 6.18j)   ***Eupolymnia nebulosa***

    Up to 60 mm long, 3 mm wide, body more rigid and quite strong. Coloration uniform, without white spots. Beak of anterior uncini surmounted by a single large tooth, then three smaller ones (Fig. 6.18i)   ***Eupolymnia nesidensis***

11. Gills absent. Some tentacles threadlike, others thicker and club-shaped; head partly surrounded by a prominent pleated collar. Integument smooth and translucent   ***Polycirrus caliendrum***

Numerous gill-filaments present. Tentacles of more or less uniform size and shape; cephalic lobe may be pleated but is ill-developed. Integument opaque and warty, especially after preservation　　　**12**

12. Two rows of gill-filaments across the dorsal surface, inserted on each side of segments 2 and 3 but not meeting in the middle　　　***Thelepus cincinnatus***

　　　Three rows of gill-filaments across the dorsal surface, inserted on each side of segments 2–4, the first meeting in the middle　　　***Thelepus setosus***

13. A single gill, made up of a short, stout main stem with four branches, each bearing a series of kidney-shaped lamellae (Fig. 6.17e)　　　***Terebellides stroemi***

　　　Six long cirriform gills arranged in pairs (Fig. 6.17f)
　　　　　　　　　　　　　　　　Trichobranchus glacialis

Amphitrite edwardsi (Quatrefages)　　　FIG. 6.18

Body with 100–150 segments, up to 250–300 mm long, not markedly narrowing posteriorly; 17 chaetigers in anterior region. Three pairs of many-branched gills. Segments 2–4 bear lateral flaps; 11–13 glandular cushions ventrally, nine pairs of nephridial papillae laterally on anterior segments. Posteriorly, neuropods become projecting lappets. Anus with a toothed rim. Bristles with a sickle-shaped, toothed end. Beak of uncini surmounted by six rows of smaller teeth (h). Salmon-pink or fawn overall, with dark red gills and orange-yellow tentacles.

Tube a cylindrical gallery, dug down into muddy sand (often amongst sea-grasses) at very low water. South and west coasts of Britain.

Amphitrite (= *Neoamphitrite*) *figulus* (Dalyell)　　FIG. 6.17 (includes *A. johnstoni* Malmgren)

Body 90–100 segments, up to 150–250 mm long (a). Twenty four (rarely 25) chaetigers in anterior region. Three pairs of many-branched gills. Segments 2 and 3 bear lateral flaps, which are only rudimentary on the 4th; 13–14 glandular cushions ventrally, 17–18 pairs of nephridial papillae laterally on anterior segments. Neuropods short but prominent ridges throughout body, not becoming lappets posteriorly. Anus with a finely toothed rim. Bristles with a sickle-shaped, toothed end. Beak of uncini surmounted by five large and then three rows of smaller teeth. Yellowish fawn or brown, with red gills.

Tube a simple gallery in muddy sand or the mud filling rock-crevices at low water; also amongst kelp holdfasts. Around much of Britain, north-west Europe, Mediterranean; north-west Atlantic, north-west Pacific.

Amphitritides (= *Amphitrite*) *gracilis* (Grube)　　FIG. 6.18

Body with 100–200 segments, 60–120 mm long, very soft, more or less of uniform diameter; posterior part tends to roll up tightly like a corkscrew. 17, 18, or 19 chaetigers in anterior region. Two pairs of many-branched gills. No lateral flaps in gill region; 11–13 glandular cushions ventrally, nine pairs of nephridial papillae

laterally on anterior segments. Neuropods not developed into lappets posteriorly. Small papillae surround the anus. Bristles with a sickle-shaped, toothed end (b). Uncini very small, with three to four rows of small teeth above the beak. Pale red or yellowish grey, with bright red gills and paler tentacles.

Makes a sinuous gallery in mud beneath stones or filling rock-crevices at low water. South and west coast of Britain, southern North Sea, north-east Atlantic, Mediterranean, Black Sea.

Eupolymnia (= *Polymnia*) *nebulosa* (Montagu)　　FIGS. 6.17, 6.18

About 100 segments, 50–150 mm long, body very rounded, soft, and fragile; 17 chaetigers in anterior region. Cephalic lobe forms a collar bearing very many little dark eyespots (Fig. 6.17b). Three pairs of many-branched gills. Lateral flaps well-developed on segments 2 and 3, smaller on 4. Four to fifteen glandular cushions ventrally, six pairs of nephridial papillae laterally on anterior segments (Fig. 6.17b). Posteriorly, neuropods becoming projecting lappets. Anus with a smooth rim or surrounded by very small papillae. Bristles with a simple lanceolate tip. Beak of uncini surmounted by two large teeth and then one to five small ones (Fig. 6.18f, j). Orange-grey, pink, or pale brown, spotted all over with white. Gills bright red, often also with white spots; tentacles pink or whitish with chalky rings.

Sandy tube without a fringe, attached to the underside of stones and old shells at low water and sublittorally. Around most of Britain, north-west Europe, Mediterranean; Red Sea, Arabian Gulf, Indian Ocean, Pacific.

Eupolymnia (= *Polymnia*) *nesidensis* (delle Chiaje)
　　　　　　　　　　　　　　　　　　　　　　FIG. 6.18

Body with 50–90 segments, 30–60 mm long, firm and fairly strong; seventeen chaetigers in anterior region, three pairs of many-branched gills. Lateral flaps on segments 2 and 3, smaller on 4. Fifteen glandular cushions ventrally, six pairs of nephridial papillae laterally on anterior segments. Posteriorly, neuropods become projecting lappets. Anus surrounded by a small fringe. Bristles with a simple lanceolate tip. Beak of uncini surmounted by a single large tooth, then three smaller ones (i). Uniformly dark brown, reddish, dark orange, yellowish green, or olive, with red gills and yellow tentacles; not spotted with white.

Tube encrusted with sand but fragile, entangled amongst algae or hydroids at low water or sublittorally. Around most of Britain, northern seas, north-west Europe, Mediterranean; north Pacific.

Lanice conchilega (Pallas) The Sand Mason　　FIG. 6.18

Body with 150–300 segments, up to 250–300 mm long, posterior region slender, fragile, and soft. Seventeen chaetigers in anterior region. Two erect triangular lobes, joined ventrally by a collar, surround the base of the tentacles. Three many-branched gills; a pair of otocysts and two foliaceous lobes occur in the gill region; 14–20 glandular cushions, prominent but not very distinct from each other, ventrally; five pairs of nephridial papillae laterally on anterior segments. Posteriorly, neuropods become projecting lappets. Anus with a smooth rim. Bristles with a simple lan-

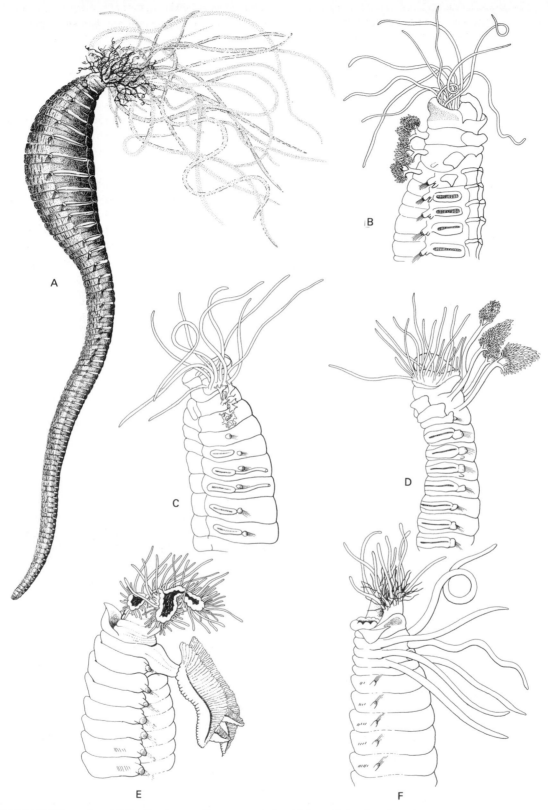

Fig. 6.17 (TEREBELLIDAE) a. *Amphitrite figulus*—entire worm (after McIntosh) b. *Eupolymnia nebulosa*—anterior end (after Fauvel) c. *Nicolea venustula*—anterior end d. *Pista cristata*—anterior end e. *Terebellides stroemi*—anterior end f. *Trichobranchus glacialis*—anterior end

ceolate tip. In the more rearward anterior segments, uncini are inserted in two rows with teeth facing away from each other (g); they have two large teeth above the beak and three smaller ones forming a high crest above these. Pink, yellowish, or brownish; when breeding, whitish or greenish. Glandular cushions dark red posteriorly. Gills blood-red, tentacles white. Preserved in alcohol, a prominent chalky band appears down each side.

Tube very characteristic, made from cemented sand-grains and shell-fragments with a ragged fringe at the mouth end (e). At low water and sublittorally to well offshore, may be very numerous on sandy beaches; also occurs in mud or mud-filled rock-crevices but appears favoured by moderate exposure to wave action. European shores from the Arctic to the Mediterranean; Arabian Gulf, Pacific.

Nicolea venustula (Montagu)   FIG. 6.17

Body with 50–70 segments, 30–60 mm long, soft and fragile. Seventeen chaetigers in anterior region. Tentacles of varied size (c). Two pairs of large gills with a long main stem. No lateral flaps in gill region. Thirteen to seventeen glandular cushions ventrally, nephridial papillae laterally very small on segment 3 but, in adult males, forming two long tubes extending from segments 6 and 7 (c). Posteriorly, neuropods become projecting fins. Anus with a smooth rim. Bristles with a simple lanceolate tip. Uncini with two to four teeth above the beak and two to five smaller teeth forming a crest above them. Brick-red, the dorsal surface marked with little white spots; gills bright red, tentacles violet.

Tube thin and transparent, encrusted with sand-grains and algae; amongst algae, hydroids, and old shells at low water and below tide-marks. European shores from the northern North Sea to the Mediterranean, circum-Arctic; Red Sea, southern Africa.

Nicolea zostericola (Oersted)

Body with 40–50 segments, 15–20 mm long (but reaching 65 mm in Arctic waters), body delicate; 15 chaetigers in anterior region. Tentacles of varied size. Two pairs of small gills with a very short main stem. No lateral flaps in gill region. About 15 glandular cushions ventrally (number and shape variable), lateral nephridial papillae very small on segment 3 but, in adult males, forming very long tubes extending from segments 6 and 7. Posteriorly, neuropods become projecting fins. Anus with a smooth rim. Bristles with a simple lanceolate tip. Uncini with one or two teeth above the beak and a few smaller teeth forming a crest above them. Uniform pink or fawn colour, with no white spots; gut bright red, visible by transparency.

At low water amongst red algae, hydroids, or sea-grasses to which the slender sandy tube is attached. When breeding, both male and female emerge from their tubes to spin a web of transparent threads; eggs enclosed in a cocoon attached to algae or hydroids. Cosmopolitan in northern seas, but records confused with *N. venustula*.

Pista cristata (Müller)   FIG. 6.17

Body with 70–100 segments, 30–90 mm long; 17 chaetigers in anterior region. Two pairs of gills with a long main stem and small branches forming a rounded tuft at the end (d). One of the gills is always noticeably larger than the other three. Lateral flaps present on segments 2–4; 17–20 glandular cushions ventrally, two pairs of nephridial papillae laterally on anterior segments (d). Posteriorly, neuropods become projecting fins. Anus with a smooth rim. Bristles with a short lancolate tip, some more curved and broader than others. Uncini with a row of five or six teeth above the beak, then several crests of smaller teeth. More or less uniform dark red, with brownish gills.

Tube membranous, covered with mud, shell-fragments, and algae, in fine sandy or muddy bottoms at low water and sublittorally. Cosmopolitan in northern seas, also south Atlantic and Antarctic.

Polycirrus caliendrum Claparède   FIG. 6.18

Body with 70–90 segments, of which 30–60 (sometimes up to 75) bear dorsal bristles; 30–100 mm long; readily autotomizes, particularly around segments 8–10, sealing the break so well that it does not appear to have been mutilated. Tentacles long and numerous, some threadlike, others thicker and club-shaped, surrounded at their base by a wide pleated collar. No gills. Eight to eleven paired glandular cushions ventrally. Six pairs of nephridia can be seen by transparency of the body-wall in the first six segments, first three much larger than last three. Anus surrounded by small lobes. Bristles simple, with a fine point; uncini have many small sharp teeth above the beak in the anterior region, only one tooth in addition to the beak posteriorly (k). Yellowish orange, eggs darker; luminescent blue or violet.

Temporary mucous tube, occurring amongst algae, hydroids, serpulid tubes, and old shells sublittorally, also in kelp holdfasts at low water. Western coasts of Britain and Europe, Mediterranean; Black Sea, north-east Pacific.

Terebellides stroemi Sars   FIGS. 6.17, 6.18

Body with 50–60 segments, 30–60 mm long, firm; 18 chaetigers in anterior region. Dorsally a single gill, consisting of four branches bearing kidney-shaped lamellae fused to a fat cylindrical main stem (Fig. 6.17e). No glandular cushions; segments 3–6 have a projecting anterior edge ventrally. Neuropods become projecting fins posteriorly. Bristles with a narrow fin, sometimes finely striated, and a simple point. The most anterior uncini are more like crochets but, in the following 12 segments, acquire a large beak surmounted by numerous smaller teeth; posteriorly they are of more usual design, with four to five teeth in a semicircle surmounting the beak (Fig. 6.18l). Flesh-coloured; adult males pale, females more pink. Gills blood-red.

Tube membranous, covered with mud or sand. At low water and sublittoral to well offshore, on bottoms of sand or mud, often amongst sea-grasses. Circum-Arctic, British and European shores to the Mediterranean; Australasia, Antarctic.

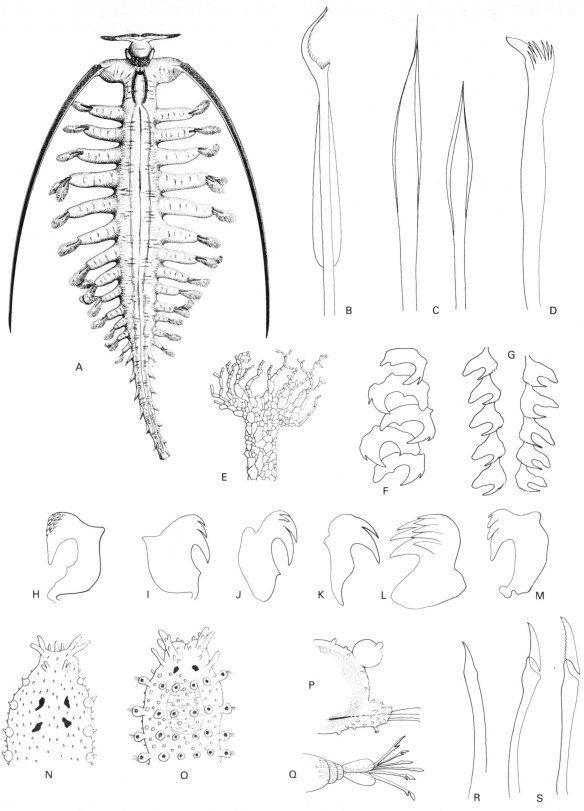

Fig. 6.18 (SPHAERODORIDAE, TEREBELLIDAE 2, TOMOPTERIDAE) a. *Tomopteris helgolandica* (after various authors) b. *Amphitritides gracilis*—'sickle' chaeta c. *Thelepus setosus*—lance-like chaeta (after Fauvel) d. *Trichobranchus glacialis*—crochet e. *Lanice conchilega*—top of tube f. *Eupolymnia nebulosa*—arrangement of uncini g. *Lanice conchilega*—arrangement of uncini (after Fauvel) h. *Amphitrite edwardsi*—uncinus (after Fauvel) i. *Eupolymnia nesidensis*—uncinus (after Fauvel) j. *E. nebulosa*—uncinus k. *Polycirrus caliendrum*—posterior uncinus l. *Terebellides stroemi*—uncinus (after Day) m. *Thelepus cincinnatus*—uncinus n. *Sphaerodorum flavum*—anterior end (after Fauvel) o. *Sphaerodoridium claparedi*—anterior end p. *S. flavum*—half TS to show parapod (after Day) q. *Sd. claparedi*—parapod (after Fauvel) r. *S. flavum*—chaeta s. *Sd. claparedi*—chaetae (after Fauvel)

Thelepus cincinnatus (Fabricius)   FIG. 6.18

About 100 segments, of which the most anterior 30–40 bear
dorsal bristles, which sometimes extend almost to the posterior
end; 100–200 mm long. Body of square section, often scattered
with warts on the dorsal surface anteriorly. Two rows of simple
filamentous gills on each side of the dorsal surface of segments
2 and 3, the first passing further laterally but neither meeting
in the middle. Four pairs of nephridial papillae laterally on
segments 4–7. Ventrally, glandular cushions very indistinct.
Neuropods become projecting fins posteriorly. Anus has a crenellated edge. Bristles either long, straight, and with a simple
point, or so short as barely to protrude, with a broad curved
lanceolate tip. Uncini with a beak surmounted by a pair of
teeth, then one in the middle flanked by two smaller ones (m).
Brownish, pink, or orange-yellow, paler on the underside. Gills
bright red, darker at the tips; tentacles orange or pale pink,
sometimes with red spots.

Tube membranous and sinuous, encrusted with loose
particles, amongst old shells and algal holdfasts at low water and
in the sublittoral to well offshore. Circum-Arctic, British and
European shores to the Mediterranean; west Atlantic, Caribbean, Antarctic.

Thelepus setosus (Quatrefages)   FIG. 6.18

Body with 80–120 segments, of which 30–60 anterior ones have
dorsal bristles and the 20–50 most posterior bear only uncini;
up to 100–150 (sometimes 200) mm long. Posterior region
slender and sinuous but not very fragile. Scattered white warts,
more or less prominent, occur particularly in this region and
become much more marked after preservation. Three rows of
simple filamentous gills on segments 2 to 4, the first passing
further down the sides and also meeting in the middle. Nephridial papillae laterally on segments 4–7; about 20 glandular
cushions ventrally, more or less distinct. Neuropods become
projecting fins posteriorly. Anus surrounded by six to eight small
lobes. Bristles either long, with a fine point, or shorter and more
spear-like (c). Uncini with a beak surmounted by a pair of large
teeth and two or three smaller ones. Colour variable—fawn,
yellowish brown, or yellow, often with fine white spots posteriorly. Gills bright red, tentacles orange-brown.

Tube thin and membranous, encrusted with loose particles.
At low water under stones or around sea-grasses; sublittorally
amongst serpulid tubes, old shells, and stones. South and west
coasts of Britain, Channel and Atlantic coasts of Europe; Red
Sea, Indian Ocean, Pacific.

Trichobranchus glacialis Malmgren   FIGS. 6.17, 6.18

Body with 60–70 segments, 20–30 mm long, rounded and of
much the same thickness throughout its length; 15 chaetigers in
anterior region. Six long, thick cirriform gills arranged in pairs
on segments 2–4 (Fig. 6.17f); small lateral flaps on 2 and 3.
Segments 2–5 bear no chaetae, although they have rudimentary
neuropodial ridges. No glandular cushions. Neuropods become
projecting triangular fins posteriorly. Anus with a smooth or

slightly lobed rim. Bristles with a simple, smooth point. Anteriorly, uncini are crochet-like with a large hooked beak and a
crest of little teeth (Fig. 6.18d), often covered by a transparent
striated hood; posteriorly they are very small, with concentric
semicircles of small teeth surmounting the beak. Orange-red;
gills bright red, tentacles violet, eggs yellow.

Tube membranous, covered with mud or fine sand, attached
to algae sublittorally. Circum-Arctic, scattered records along
European coasts to the Mediterranean; north-west Africa, sub-
Antarctic.

26 TOMOPTERIDAE

Small (2–60 mm long), transparent pelagic worms having a body
divided into three regions—head, trunk, and tail. In addition to
normal anterior antennae (divergent, as 'frontal horns') the head
carries a pair of tentacles, each enclosing a very long aciculum,
which curve backwards down each side of the body, reaching at
least half its length (a smaller, more anterior pair is present only
in juveniles). Eyes are usually well-developed and the head also
bears ciliated nuchal organs. An eversible pharynx may be quite
large but lacks teeth. The trunk is usually slender or flattened,
without obvious indications of segmentation other than the
elongated parapods, which have paddle-like distal extensions
but lack both chaetae and acicula. The tail may be short, bearing
rudimentary parapods, or long, without prominent appendages.
About a dozen species of the genus *Tomopteris* (and *Enapteris*,
probably juvenile stages of *Tomopteris*) may be found in plankton
hauls off the coasts of north-west Europe; their identity is
ultimately established by the presence and arrangement of
various groups of glands at the tip of the parapods.

They swim vigorously by rapid beating of the parapods (the
long tentacles seem to facilitate balance and buoyancy) and may
undergo diurnal vertical migrations, rising to the surface at
night. They are voracious predators of other planktonic organisms, with a wide geographical distribution.

Tomopteris helgolandica Greef   FIG. 6.18

Body 12–17 mm long, with 18–21 pairs of parapods; a quarter
of these are rudimentary, occurring in the tail region. Tentacles
extend back for about two-thirds of body-length. Parapods as
elongated cones with terminal fins in various shapes, usually
rounded.

North Sea, Irish Sea, Western Approaches, north and south
Atlantic, Mediterranean.

27 SABELLARIIDAE

Thick-walled tubes of cemented sand or shell-gravel, sometimes
aggregated and reef forming. Operculum of modified chaetae.
Numerous tentacular filaments near mouth on ventral side. A
pair of ciliated branchiae dorsally on most segments of thorax
and anterior abdomen. Abdomen distinguished by lateral fleshy
flaps bearing short saw-edged chaetae (uncini) and ventral to
these, tufts of fine chaetae. Post-abdomen lies folded forward in
a ventral abdominal groove with the anus facing anteriorly.

REFERENCES

Wilson, D. P. (1977). The distribution, development and settlement of the sabellarian polychaete *Lygdamis muratus* (Allen) near Plymouth. *Journal of the Marine Biological Association of the U. K.*, 57, 761–92.

1. Two anterior lobes each bearing half an oblique operculum, each half with two rows of chaetae; inner row simple spines and outer with flattened but slender blades   **Lygdamis murata**

   Lobes partially fused dorsally; operculum more or less at right angles to body axis with three rows of chaetae   **2**

2. Middle row of chaetae angular with the distal part lying transversely to axis of body   **Sabellaria alveolata**

   Middle row of chaetae sickle-shaped each with a leaf-like distal part projecting anteriorly   **Sabellaria spinulosa**

Lygdamis murata (Allen)   FIG. 6.19

About 13 cm long; thorax with four pairs of flattened chaetal sheaths; tube with an internal layer of regularly cemented fragments or thin flat stones and an outer layer of larger pieces of stone and shell.

Dredged from coarse gravel about 30–100 m off Plymouth; not common.

Sabellaria alveolata (Linnaeus)   FIG. 6.19

Length 30–40 mm; thorax with three pairs of flattened chaetal sheaths; inner and middle rows of opercular chaetae with asymmetrically angular spines pointing distally and transversely respectively, outer row each with a distal part flattened, flexible and with about five serrations across blunt distal margin. Tube made of cemented sand grains, often densely aggregated, their apertures forming a honeycomb pattern.

On lower shore and shallow sublittoral rocks adjacent to a sand table; southern species; both sides of Britain as far as Firth of Clyde and Berwick; western Ireland; locally abundant.

Sabellaria spinulosa Leuckhart   FIG. 6.19

Length 20–30 mm; as *S. alveolata* except middle row of opercular chaetae point distally, and outer ones tapered with several serrations each side. Others with less taper, with or without a median barb have been recorded; tubes similar to *alveolata*.

On rocks; sublittoral (occasionally LWS Menai Straits); boreal and warm temperate species; all coasts; locally abundant.

28 SABELLIDAE

Thin-walled tubes of mucoprotein with or without silt, sand, or fine shell, usually flexible; no operculum; distal crown of pinnate radioles, some species with a few apinnate tentacular filaments ventrally; most species with a membranous collar on first segment; thorax with dorsal bundles of long and short chaetae (shorter ones sometimes characteristic) and glistening ventral rows of hooked chaetae (uncini); minute companion chaetae (each in association with a thoracic uncinus) in many genera. Positions of chaetae and uncini reversed in abdomen; faecal groove passes from ventral to dorsal surface via the right side just behind thorax, otherwise bilaterally symmetrical; glandular surfaces often restricted to special areas, commonly the ventral surface forming subquadrangular shields or pads; some genera incubate their embryos. Found with all types of substratum, e.g. rock, mud, sand, algal holdfasts, and encrusting fauna (but never algal fronds) according to species.

REFERENCES

Banse, K. (1970). The small species of *Euchone* Malmgren (Sabellidae, Polychaeta). *Proceedings of the Biological Society of Washington*, 83, 387–408.

Banse, K. (1972). Redescription of some species of *Chone* Kroyer and *Euchone* Malmgren, and three new species (Sabellidae, Polychaete). *Fishery Bulletin*, 70, 459–95.

Ewer, D. W. (1946). *Sabella pavonina* Savigny var. *bicoronata* Hornell and the genus *Spirographis* Viviani (Polychaeta, Sabellidae). *Journal of the Marine Biological Association of the U. K.*, 26, 426–31.

Knight-Jones, P. (1983). Contributions to the taxonomy of Sabellidae (Polychaeta). *Zoological Journal of the Linnean Society*, 79, 245–95.

Knight-Jones, P. and Walker, A. J. M. (1985). Two new species of *Demonax* (Sabellidae: Polychaeta) from Liverpool Bay. *Journal of Natural History*, 19, 605–12.

Quatrefages, M. A. de (1966). *Histoire naturelle des Annelés marins et d'eau douce. Annélides et Géphyriens*, 2(1), 475.

1. Rows of uncini forming nearly complete girdles in a groove around each abdominal segment; radioles webbed for most of their length; tube gelatinous   **(Myxicolinae) 34**

   Rows of uncini prominent but no longer than one-third width of abdomen, commonly shorter; radioles with or without webbing; tube not gelatinous   **2**

2. Abdomen shorter than thorax, with only three to six segments   **(Some Fabriciinae) 28**

   Abdomen longer than thorax, more than 15 segments   **3**

3. Crown with two or more bare filaments adjacent to ventral radioles; companion chaetae absent; abdominal chaetae in transverse rows   **(Most Fabriciinae) 20**

   No such filaments present; companion chaetae usually present; abdominal chaetae in transverse rows or tufts   **(Most Sabellinae) 4**

4. Abdominal chaetae arranged in tight pencil-like tufts   **5**

   Abdominal chaetae of each tuft arranged in transverse rows   **9**

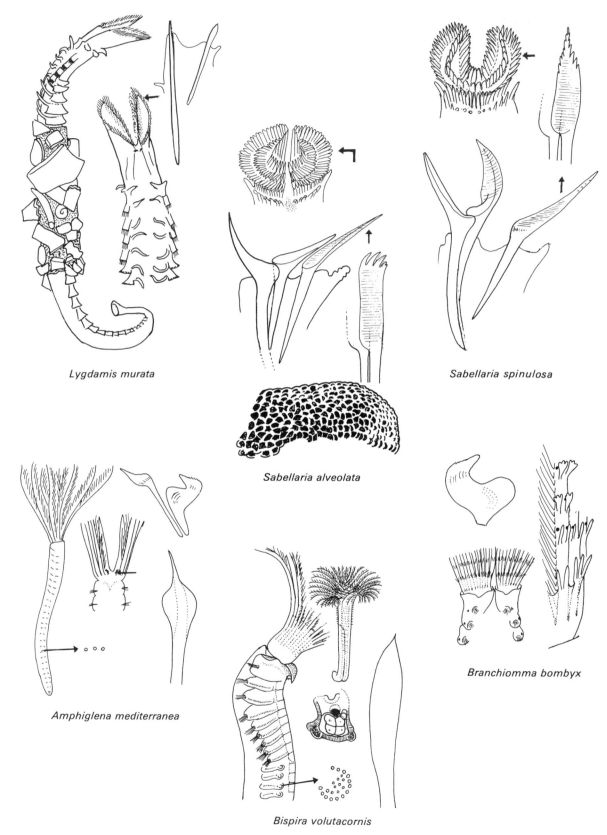

Lygdamis murata

Sabellaria alveolata

Sabellaria spinulosa

Amphiglena mediterranea

Bispira volutacornis

Branchiomma bombyx

Fig. 6.19

5. Abdominal chaetae arranged in a neat spiral **6**

   Abdominal chaetae of each tuft arranged in a C-shape with additional chaetae partially filling the arc **8**

6. Terminal part of each radiole slender but with a pale subdistal swelling *Sabella discifera*

   Terminal part of radiole tapered or blunt and without subdistal swelling **7**

7. Lateral collar margins not reaching transverse groove which marks base of crown: gap between dorsal margins smooth *Sabella pavonina*

   Lateral collar margins extend to groove which marks base of crown; gap between dorsal margins with distinct curved ridges each side of mid-line *Sabella spallanzanii*

8. Outer surface of each radiole bearing epithelial flaps (stylodes), each side of crown forming half circles; dorsal collar margins fused to sides of mid-line *Branchiomma bombyx*

   Without stylodes on radioles; crown forming spirals of up to three whorls each side in all but the smallest specimens; margins free and separated by distinct gap *Bispira volutacornis*

9. Collar absent *Amphiglena mediterranea*

   Collar distinct **10**

10. Dorsal collar margins widely separated **11**

    Collar fused to mid-dorsal groove **15**

11. Rows of thoracic uncini fairly short with a gap between their ventral ends and adjacent glandular shields **12**

    Rows of thoracic uncini long, their ventral ends indenting sides of shields **13**

12. Shorter thoracic chaetae spoon-shaped with a small distal point; tips of radioles tapered; lower shore *Perkinsiana rubra*

    Shorter thoracic chaetae with broad but tapered hoods; tips of radioles strap-like; offshore *Demonax torulis*

13. Shorter thoracic chaetae with narrowly tapered hoods *Demonax cambrensis*

    Shorter thoracic chaetae with broadly tapered hoods **14**

14. Terminal part of each radiole with parallel sides *Demonax langerhansi*

    Tips of radioles tapered *Demonax brachychona*

15. Collar with distinct dorso-lateral notches **16**

    Collar without dorso-lateral notches **18**

16. First thoracic segment about three times as long as those following; radioles without eyes *Potamethus murrayi*

First segment similar in length to others in thorax; radioles bearing distinct composite eyes **17**

17. Eyes compound, domed, and rust coloured, on outer sides of proximal halves of most dorsal radioles *Pseudopotamilla reniformis*

    Eyes bulbous and blackish brown, one near tip of all or most radioles, those on two radioles particularly conspicuous *Megalomma vesiculosum*

18. Collar with mid-ventral cleft; radioles with short blunt tips and basal webbing only 0.2 of radiole length; thoracic uncini S-shaped *Potamilla neglecta*

    Collar entire ventrally; radioles with filamentous or triangular tips; webbing 0.3–0.8 of radiole length; thoracic uncini like crochet hooks, with long shafts **19**

19. Radioles webbed for less than one-third of length and with long tapered tips *Chone cf. acustica*

    Radioles webbed for about three-quarters of length, with tips small, triangular, and flat *Chone fauveli*

20. Radioles webbed from one-half to three-quarters of their length **21**

    Radioles not webbed **26**

21. Posterior of abdomen funnel-shaped ventrally **24**

    Abdomen without funnel **22**

22. Collar with a finely scalloped margin *Chone cf. collaris*

    Collar margin smooth **23**

23. Posterior of abdomen with a fine filament; distal margin of collar covering base of crown; tip of each radiole triangular and flat *Chone filicaudata*

    Abdomen without filament; distal margin of collar not reaching base of crown; tip of each radiole long and finely tapered *Chone duneri*

24. Glandular areas obvious only on ventral surface **25**

    Glandular areas also on dorsal surface (abdomen) as narrow transverse bands *Euchone rubrocincta*

25. Glandular areas in each abdominal segment represented by four well-separated subcircular patches; worm more than 2 cm long *Euchone papillosa*

    These glandular areas represented by two pairs of closely aligned, transversely elongate patches; worm only a few mm long *Euchone southerni*

26. Ventral margins of crown with two or more tentacular filaments joined only at the base; anterior collar interrupted by dorsal groove **27**

    Margins with one filament each side joined across mid-line by a distinct membrane; anterior collar entire dorsally *Laonome kroyeri*

27. Abdomen blunt posteriorly   *Jasmineira elegans*

    Abdomen with small elongate process   *Jasmineira caudata*

28. Radioles each with the usual rachis and fine ciliated
    pinnules (few but long)   29

    Sturdy ciliated pinnules arise directly from anterior
    segment, not from a rachis   33

29. Abdomen with only three segments; abdominal
    uncini with small flattened shafts, elongate in side
    view   30

    Abdomen with five segments; abdominal uncini with
    truncated shafts, nearly square in side view   32

30. Distinct fleshy triangular lobe on antero-ventral
    surface of first segment, but true collar absent   31

    Collar present, its distal margin covering anterior
    margin of first segment   *Fabriciola* cf. *berkeleyi*

31. Tentacular filaments present at ventral margins of
    crown   *Fabriciola baltica*

    Tentacular filaments absent, represented only by
    small indistinct paired lappets   *Fabricia sabella*

32. Collar coinciding laterally and ventrally with anterior
    edge of first segment   *Oriopsis armandi*

    Collar not covering anterior margin of first segment
                                                 Oriopsis hynensis

33. Crown with four pairs of ciliated pinnules; chaetae
    with distal part twice as wide as shaft
                                             Manayunkia aestuarina

    Crown with eight to fifteen pairs of pinnules
                                              Manayunkia cursoria

34. Thorax indistinct (one to four segments); distinct eye-
    spots (one to four) each side of each segment; worm
    only a few mm long   *Myxicola aesthetica*

    Thorax distinct (seven to nine segments); eyespots
    absent; worm several cm long   35

35. Thoracic chaetae numerous, 100+ in small circular
    pads but scarcely visible under dissecting micro-
    scope; tips of radioles dull purple (pigment retained
    in preservative)   *Myxicola infundibulum*

    Thoracic chaetae fairly distinct but less numerous
    than in *M. infundibulum*; tips of radioles not differ-
    entially pigmented   *Myxicola sarsi*

Amphiglena mediterranea (Leydig)   FIG. 6.19

Up to 15 mm long; collar absent; eight to ten thoracic and up to
30 abdominal segments; about six radioles each side; a crescent-
shaped pigment patch (arrowed) at base of each dorsal lip but
fading in formalin; shorter thoracic chaetae spoon-shaped with

distal filament; short rows of compact S-shaped uncini with
companion chaetae; as few as three abdominal chaetae in each
group arranged transversely (arrowed); tube of mucus, readily
renewed.

In crevices of rock, holdfasts, sponges etc; intertidal and
shallow water; mainly southern, reaching Isle of Man; fairly
common.

Bispira volutacornis (Montagu)   FIG. 6.19

Up to 100 mm long, eight to nine thoracic and up to 100
abdominal segments; crown with up to 200 radioles which can
form up to three pairs of interlocking whorls; radioles with
paired longitudinal ridges (whitish), most with one or more
paired composite eyes (see cross-section) scattered on outer
surface; collar with two ventral lappets deeply pigmented except
for a white border and a wide gap between dorsal margins;
shorter chaetae from the more posterior thoracic segments, of
two types, one with a slender knee (see *Megalomma*) but the
outer ones flattened and obtuse distally (knife-shaped); thoracic
uncini and companion chaetae as in *Amphiglena* but forming long
rows especially in posterior half of thorax; abdominal chaetae
arranged in a C-shape partially infilled with chaetae (arrowed);
tube with a silt-mucoid outer layer.

Under rocky overhangs, sublittorally and in deep pools;
mainly southern, reaching Isle of Man; locally abundant.

N.B. Small specimens do not have bispiral crowns and have
been confused with the more northern forms *Sabella fabricii*
and *S. crassicornis*. These have abdominal chaetae in the same
arrangement as *Bispira* and should be placed in that genus. They
differ from *B. volutacornis* in having distinct gaps between all
thoracic tori and adjacent shields, and lack knife-shaped chaetae.

Branchiomma bombyx (Dalyell)   FIG. 6.19

Up to 50 mm long; eight thoracic and about 70 abdominal
segments; up to 25 radioles each side, the outer surfaces bearing
several paired composite 'eyes' and paired epithelial flaps (*stylodes*), those near the base tongue-like but majority with scalloped margins; collar short but covering base of crown, with a
shallow cleft ventrally, fused to the mid-line groove dorsally and
with or without a dorso-lateral notch; thoracic uncini truncated;
companion chaetae absent; thoracic chaetae like *Megalomma*;
arrangement of abdominal chaetae as in *Bispira*.

Under stones and shells; LWS and sublittoral; all coasts;
seldom abundant.

N.B. Small specimens have all stylodes tongue-like and may
be confused with *Branchiomma lucullana* (from Mediterranean
and perhaps Roscoff). *B. bombyx*, however, has dorsal lips
('palps', within base of crown) eight times as long as broad, and
a quarter of the length of radioles. In *B. lucullana* these are twice
as long as broad, and a tenth of the length of radioles.

Chone cf. *acustica* (Claparède)

About 30 mm long; eight thoracic and about 55 abdominal
segments; crown (from material in Paris and London museums,
type locality Naples, but type material not available) with
webbing extending less than one-third of its length, without

ventral apinnate tentacular filaments, but with enlarged pinnules on the most dorsal radioles, and with long free parts of radioles ending in long tapering filaments. Resembles *Chone fauveli* in the shapes of collar and chaetae.

Once amongst silted encrusting fauna on old wooden piles (now replaced) in Millbay Docks, Plymouth; shallow sublittoral; southern species; rare.

Chone cf. *collaris* Langerhans

About 15 mm long; crown webbed and similar to *Chone filicaudata* below; differs from other *Chone* species here in that the distal margin of the collar is scalloped; slightly different from the southern form described by Langerhans.

Dredged; soft bottom; North Sea.

Chone duneri Malmgren

Up to 17 mm long; eight thoracic and about 70 abdominal segments; each half of crown webbed for about two-thirds of length; eight radioles each side with long filamentous tips; dorsal radioles have enlarged pinnules basally; about three apinnate tentacular filaments adjacent to each of the two most ventral radioles; collar (without dorsal gap) set low on first segment, base of crown showing well above collar margins; chaetae as in *C. fauveli*.

Dredged, soft bottom; western Ireland, Shetlands; uncommon.

Chone fauveli McIntosh FIG. 6.20

Up to 120 mm long; eight thoracic and about 80 abdominal segments; crown webbed for about three-quarters of length with up to 36 radioles each side, each with a flanged tip like an elongated triangle; enlarged pinnules at base of dorsal radioles; no apinnate tentacular filaments; collar oblique in side-view with margin covering base of crown, fused to mid-dorsal groove and without a ventral cleft; 'glandular' girdle below 2nd thoracic chaeta, typical of *Chone*, *Euchone*, *Jasmineira*, and *Myxicola*; shorter thoracic chaetae with small rounded hoods; thoracic uncini with very long shafts; abdominal uncini truncated with an angular boss below peg; abdominal chaetae slender and arranged in transverse rows. Often misidentified as *C. infundibuliformis* (see Banse 1972).

Dredged, soft bottom; North Sea, Clyde Sea, Celtic Sea; locally common.

Chone filicaudata Southern

Up to 11 mm long; eight thoracic and 13 abdominal segments; crown webbed for two-thirds of length with eight radioles, somewhat resembles *Chone acustica* but differs in having five ventral apinnate tentacular filaments on each side and a short fine filament close to anus; other details like *C. fauveli*.

Dredged, soft substratum; western Ireland, Cumberland, Northumberland, Scotland; fairly common.

Demonax cambrensis Knight-Jones and Walker FIG. 6.20

Up to 86 mm long; eight thoracic and about 160 abdominal segments; about 20 radioles each side with tapered tips; shorter

thoracic chaetae very slender, hoods 7× as long as wide; companion chaetae (side-view figured), and uncini as *D. brachychona* and *D. langerhansi*.

Grab samples in mud, sand and gravel 26–27 m; Liverpool Bay; locally common.

Demonax langerhansi Knight-Jones FIG. 6.20

(= *Potamilla incerta* Langerhans *non Demonax incertus* Kinbert) Up to 10 mm long; five to seven (usually five) thoracic and about 58 abdominal segments; seven radioles on each side with tips slightly thickened, with whitish blotches in life; collar with obtusely pointed ventral lappets; shorter thoracic chaetae with broad hoods; thoracic uncini and companion chaetae like those described for *D. brachychona*. One of the species included in misidentifications of *Potamilla torelli* in warm and temperate waters.

In crevices in rock and encrusting fauna; lower shore and shallow sublittoral; southern species extending to south-west England, south-west Wales, and south-west Ireland.

Demonax brachychona (Grube) FIG. 6.20

Up to 25 mm long; four to eight thoracic and up to 130 abdominal segments and seven to nine unwebbed radioles on each side, with tapered tips; collar with two pointed ventral lappets and a fairly wide gap between dorsal margins; shorter thoracic chaetae with tapered hoods about 3× as long as broad; thoracic and abdominal uncini S-shaped (as *Amphiglena*) but thoracic companion chaetae with a bulbous toothed head and a fine filament at right angles to a fairly short shaft (see also *D. cambrensis* figure); slender abdominal chaetae arranged in transverse rows. One of the species misidentified as *Potamilla torelli* in warm and temperate waters.

In crevices of '*Lithothamnion*' and encrusted fauna; LW and shallow sublittoral; southern species extending to English Channel, South Wales, and southern Ireland.

Demonax torulis Knight-Jones and Walker FIG. 6.20

Up to 12 mm long; eight thoracic and about 40 abdominal segments, six radioles each side, each with a strap-like tip; shorter thoracic chaetae with broad hoods; companion chaetae with a toothed bulbous head and fine filament; thoracic uncini as for *D. langerhansi* except that they are in short rows and rather atypical of genus in not reaching the ventral shields.

Grab samples of mud, sand, and gravel, 26–27 m., Liverpool Bay; locally common.

Euchone papillosa (Sars) FIG. 6.20

Length 25 mm; eight thoracic and about 40 abdominal segments, crown webbed for two-thirds of its length, with 10–12 radioles each side (with tapered tips) and two pairs of apinnate tentacular filaments adjacent to ventral radioles; collar oblique in side view, with a dorsal groove and small ventral notch; shorter thoracic chaetae with broad hoods; thoracic uncini with long shafts; abdominal uncini similar to those figured for *Laonome kroyeri*; ventral abdomen with four characteristic glandular patches per segment; last ten posterior segments form a deep funnel-like groove ventrally.

Sublittoral muddy sand; northern species; closest record North Sea 56°43′N, 6°6′E.

Euchone rubrocincta (Sars)   FIG. 6.21

Up to 17 mm long; eight thoracic and about 30 abdominal segments; crown partially webbed, with tapered tips; shorter thoracic chaetae with narrow hoods 4 or 5× long as wide; thoracic uncini with long shafts; 11 or 12 posterior segments form funnel on ventral side, with a membranous anterior margin; glandular area mainly ventral but characteristically extends to the dorsal surface of abdomen as narrow pale bands transversely crossing the mainly red surface.

Sublittoral soft substratum; all coasts; locally common.

Euchone southerni Banse   FIG. 6.21
(= *Euchone rosea* Southern *non* Langerhans)

Only 4.4 mm long; eight thoracic and 12 abdominal segments, crown webbed for about two-thirds of length with five radioles each side (long tapered tips) and three pairs of apinnate tentacular filaments adjoining ventral radioles; collar fused to dorsal groove with ventral margin slightly indented; shorter thoracic chaetae with broad tapered hoods about 3× as long as wide; thoracic uncini with long shafts; last four segments (perhaps more) form a simple ventral funnel.

Soft substratum; depth 2–6 m; western Ireland.

Fabricia sabella (Ehrenberg)   FIG. 6.21

Up to 3 mm long; seven thoracic and three abdominal segments, three short radioles each side, each with about six pairs of pinnules and a tapered tip; without membranous collar but with a ventral 'mobile' triangular lobe projecting anteriorly partially obscuring paired, short apinnate processes; one pair of eyes flanking anal region and another pair on the first segment; shorter thoracic chaetae geniculate, the knee bulbous in both 'face'- and side-views; thoracic uncini with long shafts; abdominal uncini with shorter, thicker but flattened shafts (figured bottom right); mucus tube quickly secreted as worm crawls backwards.

In muddy holdfasts of turf algae; intertidal; all coasts; abundant.

Fabriciola baltica Friedrich   FIG. 6.21

As *Fabricia sabella* except that apinnate processes are long and tentacular (arrowed) and shorter thoracic chaetae are more slender at the 'knee' (side- and 'face'-views figured).

Surface mud, brackish water; sublittoral; head of Loch Etive, west Scotland; very abundant.

Fabriciola cf. *berkeleyi* Banse   FIG. 6.21

As *F. baltica* except that collar is distinct with distal margin covering base of crown and long dorsal 'margins' fused to mid-line groove. Usually intermixed with *Fabricia sabella*.

In muddy holdfasts of turf algae; intertidal; South Wales; locally common.

Jasmineira elegans Saint-Joseph   FIG. 6.21

Up to 20 mm; eight to nine thoracic and about 30 abdominal segments, six radioles and two to five ventral tentacular filaments each side, frequently sheds radioles but not the filaments or the sturdy base of crown; collar with mid-dorsal groove and without ventral cleft; shorter thoracic chaetae with tapered hoods 3× as long as wide; hooked thoracic uncini with long shafts; abdominal uncini almost S-shaped and generically characteristic (top right in figure); tube membranous, often coated with shell or sand.

In kelp holdfasts and crevices, (lower shore) and shell-gravel (sublittoral); all coasts; fairly common.

Jasmineira caudata Langerhans

As *J. elegans* but only about 5 mm long, with 17–20 abdominal segments and a characteristic filament posterior to anus.

Soft substratum; sublittoral; southern species; English Channel, Liverpool Bay, western Ireland.

Laonome kroyeri Malmgren   FIG. 6.21

Up to 56 mm long; eight to 12 thoracic and about 100 abdominal segments; six to eight pinnate radioles and one ventral tentacular (apinnate) filament each side, the latter characteristically joined together by a basal membrane; collar cleft ventrally and unusual in being entire (though very short) dorsally; shorter thoracic chaetae with spoon-shaped hoods and a distal point; thoracic and abdominal uncini similar in having a rounded breast (below peg) and a truncated 'shaft'; companion chaetae absent; glandular areas ventral but extending dorsally in first two segments.

Soft substratum; sublittoral; northern species; west and east coasts of Scotland, western Ireland; not common.

Manayunkia aestuarina (Bourne)   FIG. 6.21

Up to 6 mm long; eight thoracic and three abdominal segments, no pinnate radioles but instead eight sturdy ciliated pinnules arranged in pairs, and two ventral filaments with green blood sinuses; collar absent; shorter thoracic chaetae with tapered hoods 3× as long as broad; other chaetae and tube as *Fabricia sabella*.

In surface mud of estuaries; LW: Thames, Tyne, Tamar, Burry Inlet, Liffey; locally abundant.

Manayunkia cursoria (Quatrefages)

Up to 8 mm long; eight to 11 (?) thoracic and three abdominal segments; 16–30 ciliated pinnules; distal parts of shorter thoracic chaetae nearly as slender as shafts; other details as *Manayunkia aestuarina*.

In soft detritus on rock ledges and gutters; littoral; north-west France, perhaps Scilly Isles; not common.

Megalomma vesiculosum (Montagu)   FIG. 6.21

Up to 120 mm long; eight to nine thoracic and up to 200 abdominal segments; 30 radioles each side, each with a bulbous, subterminal eye on same side as the pinnules, two dorsal radioles each with a larger eye; collar with ventral cleft, dorso-lateral notches and dorsal groove, thoracic chaetae slender (side- and 'face'-view figured); thoracic (and abdominal) uncini S-shaped

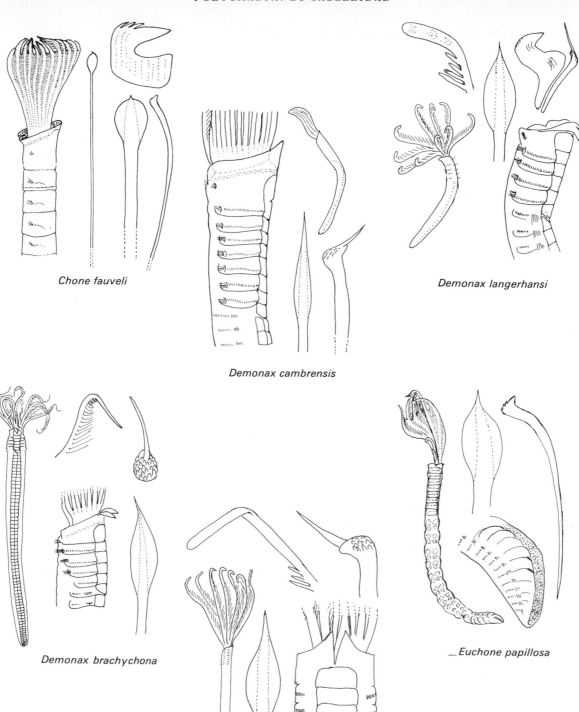

Chone fauveli

Demonax cambrensis

Demonax langerhansi

Demonax brachychona

Demonax torulis

Euchone papillosa

Fig. 6.20

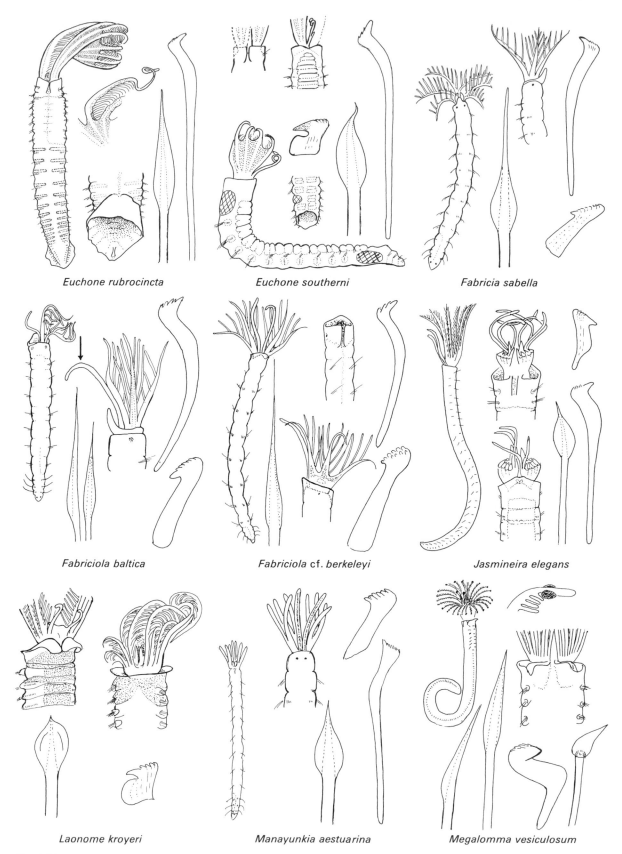

Euchone rubrocincta

Euchone southerni

Fabricia sabella

Fabriciola baltica

Fabriciola cf. berkeleyi

Jasmineira elegans

Laonome kroyeri

Manayunkia aestuarina

Megalomma vesiculosum

Fig. 6.21

and adjacent companion chaetae with a leaf-shaped blade; abdominal chaetae arranged in transverse rows; tube tough and covered with sand and shell particles.

In mud with stones and sand; lower shore and sublittoral in sheltered bays; southern species; south-west Wales, south-west England and Cornwall, western Ireland; locally abundant.

Myxicola aesthetica (Claparède) FIG. 6.22

About 26 mm long; thorax indistinct with one to four segments, abdomen with about 30, each with lateral eyespots; up to seven radioles each side, webbed for most of length, with flat triangular tips; chaetae in minute hair-like tufts which are difficult to distinguish; thoracic and abdominal uncini as figured for other *Myxicola* species but the abdominal ones with more teeth on crest and well spaced out within each girdle; worm moves rapidly backwards when disturbed with the crown then streamlined and new mucus tube readily secreted.

In rock-crevices and kelp holdfasts; lower shore and sublittoral; south Devon and Isle of Man; not common.

Myxicola infundibulum (Montagu) FIG. 6.22

Up to 200 mm but contracts by half when disturbed; up to 25 radioles each side of crown, webbed for most of length, leaving free purple/brown triangular tips (colour retained in preservative); eight thoracic and over 100 abdominal segments; chaetae fine and straight, and although numerous are difficult to see with a dissecting microscope, their presence indicated only by small circular pads each side of each segment (length of thorax best judged by change in direction of faecal groove); collar absent; distal part of biannulate first segment with a shallow lateral cleft and a triangular ventral lobe; 'glandular' girdle below the second fascicles of thoracic chaetae as in the larger Fabriciinae e.g. *Chone* and *Euchone*; hooked thoracic uncini (these may be absent in mature specimens) with long shafts and a smooth crest as in *M. sarsi*; abdominal uncini truncated; tube, (to left of figure) thick, gelatinous, transparent, carrot-shaped, and easily renewable.

In estuarine mud; lower shore and sublittoral; south-west Wales, south-west England; locally common.

Myxicola sarsi Krøyer FIG. 6.22

Up to 60 mm long; eight thoracic and about 70 abdominal segments; other characters as in *M. infundibulum* except for fewer radioles with tips not differentially coloured; biannulate first segment lacks lateral notches and the small size of the ventral lobe is emphasized by a transverse groove; thorax wider laterally and slim in side-view; thoracic tufts of chaetae easily distinguishable under dissecting microscope.

In fine muddy sand; sublittoral; northern species; north and east coasts of Scotland, north-east England, Isle of Man; fairly common.

Oriopsis cf. *armandi* (Claparède) FIG. 6.22

Up to 6 mm long; eight thoracic and five abdominal segments; crown with three slightly flanged radioles each side, each with about six pairs of pinnules and a long tapered tip; a ventral pair

of apinnate tentacular filaments; collar poorly differentiated; all thoracic chaetae slender; thoracic uncini long-shafted and similar to those of *Fabricia* but abdominal uncini different in having a wide but short and flattened shaft.

In muddy holdfasts of turf algae and muddy rock-crevices; intertidal; southern species; Anglesey, South Wales, south-west England, western Ireland.

Oriopsis hynensis Knight-Jones FIG. 6.22

As in *O. armandi*, except that radioles have more distinct flanges; collar distinct, set low on first segment, the distal margin well below the oblique anterior margin of that segment; abdominal uncini with a gouge-like boss beneath the anterior peg.

In algal holdfasts, e.g. *Laurencia* and *Codium*; just below LWM: Lough Hyne, southern Ireland; locally common.

Perkinsiana rubra (Langerhans) FIG. 6.22

Up to 80 mm long and slender; six to 11 thoracic and about 150 abdominal segments; five to ten radioles each side with reddish blood and fine tapered tips; collar with ventral cleft and a wide gap between dorsal margins; shorter thoracic chaetae with spoon-shaped hoods tapering distally; thoracic uncini somewhat S-shaped but with a shaft twice as long as distance between breast and crest; adjacent companion chaetae with leaf-shaped blades; abdominal uncini with shorter shafts; abdominal chaetae arranged in transverse rows each with a bulbous knee; tubes with a covering of sand and often shell-fragments near aperture. Often intermixed with *Pseudopotamilla reniformis* and *Demonax langerhansi* and one of three species often misidentified as *Potamilla torelli* in warm and temperate waters.

Bores into limestone rock or '*Lithothamnion*'; pools, lower shore and sublittoral; southern species; South Wales; locally abundant.

Potamethus murrayi (McIntosh) FIG. 6.22

Length over 40 mm; 15 radioles each side of crown; eight thoracic segments the first of which is 3 × the length of the others; collar with deep dorso-lateral notches and dorsal lamellae fused to sides of mid-dorsal groove (top left), oblique in side-view (bottom left), and with two large lappets ventrally, which are surmounted by large ventral sacs (top right); shorter thoracic chaetae with small rounded hoods tapering distally; thoracic uncini (and companion chaetae) with very long shafts.

Dredged; north of Hebrides; rare.

Potamilla neglecta (Sars) FIG. 6.22

Up to 45 mm long; eight thoracic and about 100 abdominal segments; 13 radioles each side with slight webbing at base, each with a short blunt tip; collar set low on first segment with a short dorsal groove, and long overlapping ventral lappets; dorsal lips blunt, without the usual midrib but each supported by a pinnule at the base of each dorsal radiole (generic character); shorter thoracic chaetae with broad tapered hoods; thoracic uncini and companion chaetae with moderately long shafts; tube brittle, a hard mucoid lining supported by a single layer of tightly packed sand-grains.

Dredged; Arctic species; reported west of Shetlands.

Pseudopotamilla reniformis (Bruguière) FIG. 6.22

Up to 120 mm long, slender; nine to 12 thoracic and up to 200 abdominal segments; up to 13 radioles each side of crown, with green blood, tapered tips and one to three rust-coloured compound eyes on the outer dorsal side of most radioles; ventral radioles shorter than others (top left) with few or no eyes; collar with ventral lappets and dorso-lateral notches forming pockets flanking mid-dorsal groove; shorter thoracic chaetae with spoon-shaped hoods; thoracic uncini and companion chaetae with moderately long shafts; tube of mucoid-silt, unusual in that distal part curls ventro-proximally when crown is withdrawn.

In narrow rock-crevices or boring in limestone, shells, or 'Lithothamnion'; pools, lower shore and sublittoral; widespread; all coasts; abundant locally.

Sabella discifera Grube FIG. 6.22
(= *S. variabilis* Langerhans and *Branchiomma linaresi* Rioja)

Up to 52 mm long, seven to eight thoracic and 50 abdominal segments; each side of crown with about ten radioles webbed basally, each with a very small, whitish, subterminal swelling of thickened epithelium; collar with long ventral lappets and a wide gap between dorsal margins; shorter thoracic chaetae very bulbous at the 'knee' in both side- and face-views; all uncini somewhat S-shaped but these and the companion chaetae have short shafts, the latter with leaf-like blades; abdominal chaetae arranged in a spiral (arrowed); tube of mucoid-silt; multiplies by fission.

On rocks, stones, and gorgonians; sublittoral in strong currents; South Wales, south Devon, Scilly Isles, and Roscoff; locally abundant.

Sabella pavonina Savigny FIG. 6.23

Often misnamed *Sabella penicillus*. Long slender body up to 300 mm long, 4 mm wide with up to 300 segments of which eight to 16 are thoracic. Crown webbed basally, one side usually larger and spiralling in from ventral edge in larger specimens (e.g. 40 stiff radioles on one side and 50 the other); first thoracic segment about twice as long as others with collar set low, the lateral margins extending only half-way to base of crown (top left and right), dorsal margins separated by a wide gap (centre bottom) and ventral margins forming two fleshy lappets below well-developed ventral sacs (centre top); thoracic ventral shields separated laterally from the tori by distinct gaps; uncini and arrangement of abdominal chaetae as figure for *S. discifera*; thoracic chaetae slender.

Found on all coasts with big populations in Menai Strait, Swansea Bay, and estuaries of Essex and Plymouth rivers. In sheltered locations the species tends to be more elongated (figure on left). On stones in sand and mud; sublittoral, locally abundant.

Sabella spallanzanii (Gmelin) FIG. 6.23

Up to 200 mm long and plump, (figured specimen 80 mm long, 6 mm wide); crown very asymmetrical in mature specimens, the left or right side forming one to three whorls; first thoracic segment short; lateral margins of collar extending to base of crown; gap between dorsal margins with paired crescent-shaped ridges flanking the mid-line groove; uncini as in *S. discifera* thoracic chaetae as in *S. pavonina*; abdominal chaetae arranged in spiral of two to three whorls (arrowed); thoracic ventral shields separated from the tori by an irregular gap, and chaetae in a diagonal series across the thorax (bottom right in figure).

On firm substrata; sublittoral; southern species; Channel Isles, Roscoff, and Cherbourg perhaps the northern limits.

29 SERPULIDAE

As Sabellidae, with distal crown and abdominal inversion of the thoracic arrangement of chaetae, but tubes are calcareous. Most species develop opercula, which are often characteristic in shape and usually single, on a dorsal radiole that usually loses or fails to develop its pinnules; the operculum arises on the left side but alternates between left and right in successive regenerations in some genera. The faecal groove passes around right side, as in Sabellidae; body otherwise bilaterally symmetrical; the distal collar on first segment extends symmetrically as 'thoracic membranes' down the dorsal side close to the left and right fascicles of chaetae, sometimes reaching only as far as segment 2, usually extending throughout thorax and often posteriorly to thorax as a ventral apron. The first segment usually bears collar chaetae but never uncini; the collar chaetae are often generically characteristic, some with or without a prominent boss with as few as two teeth, as in *Serpula*, or with numerous teeth (commonly called fin and blade chaetae) as in *Chitinopoma*. The fin is actually rounded, and the blade too is rounded in cross-section, as in simple bordered chaetae (figured for *Apomatus*). True blades are found in abdominal chaetae and the distal part of sickle chaetae which are present in some genera (e.g. *Apomatus*, but see figure of *Janua pagenstecheri*—Spirorbidae). Some species incubate but most have planktonic larvae; tubes usually attached to rocks, ships' hulls or kelp holdfasts, seldom to algal fronds.

REFERENCES

Bianchi, C. N. (1981). *Guide per il Riconoscimento delle specie Animali delle Acque Lagunari e Costiere Italiane*. **5**. *Policheti Serpuloidei*. Consiglio Nazionale delle Richerche, Geneva.

Hove, H. A. ten and Weerdenburg, J. C. A. (1978). A generic revision of the brackish-water serpulid *Ficopomatus* Southern, including *Mercierella* Fauvel, *Sphaeropomatus* Treadwell, *Mercierellopsis* Rioja and *Neopomatus* Pillai. *Biological Bulletin, Wood's Hole*, **154**, 96–120.

Nelson-Smith, A. (1967). *Catalogue of main marine fouling organisms*. *3, Serpulids*. OECD, Paris.

Thorp, C. H., Pyne, S. and West, S. A. (1987). *Hydroides ezoensis* Okuda, a fouling serpulid new to British coastal waters. *Journal of Natural History*, **21**, 863–77.

Zibrowius, H. W. (1969). Review of some little known genera of Serpulidae. *Smithsonian Contributions to Zoology*, **42**, 1–22.

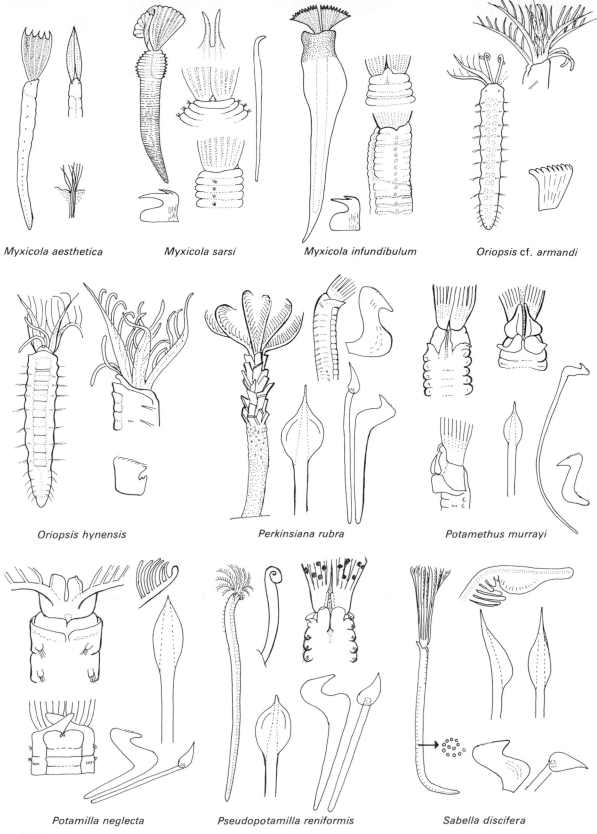

Myxicola aesthetica　　*Myxicola sarsi*　　*Myxicola infundibulum*　　*Oriopsis* cf. *armandi*

Oriopsis hynensis　　*Perkinsiana rubra*　　*Potamethus murrayi*

Potamilla neglecta　　*Pseudopotamilla reniformis*　　*Sabella discifera*

Fig. 6.22

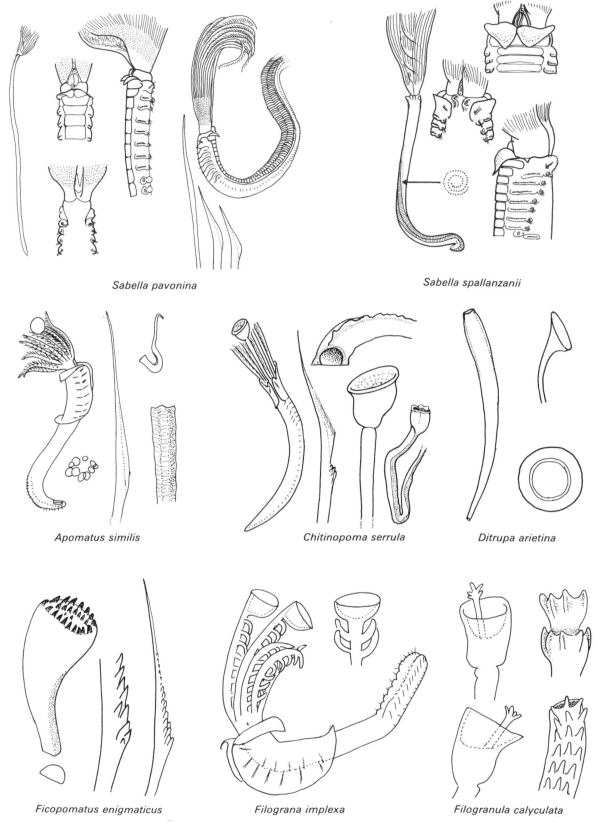

Sabella pavonina

Sabella spallanzanii

Apomatus similis

Chitinopoma serrula

Ditrupa arietina

Ficopomatus enigmaticus

Filograna implexa

Filogranula calyculata

Fig. 6.23

1. Tube not adhering to substratum, tusk-shaped and circular in cross-section **Ditrupa arietina**

   Tube adhering to substratum **2**

2. Lateral margins of thoracic membrane extending only as far as second chaetigerous segment **3**

   Thoracic membrane extending to last thoracic segment **4**

3. Operculum with a cup-shaped distal 'plate' and generally with a branched projection in the centre; tube with transverse rows of teeth pointing anteriorly. Where anterior portion of tube becomes erect these teeth form stacked ribbed cups **Filogranula calyculata**

   Operculum with a flat or concave horny distal plate without projections; tube with single ridge, sub-triangular in cross section; adults may have a single pair of calcareous brood chambers, one each side of aperture. More than one pair may be present **Chitinopoma serrula**

4. Tube translucent, vitreous, with one to three teeth at aperture and a single uneven longitudinal ridge, thus triangular in cross-section; first thoracic segment without chaetae **Placostegus tridentatus**

   Tube opaque, chalky, or porcellaneous **5**

5. Operculum present **6**

   Operculum absent **11**

6. Opercular peduncle with paired pointed lateral wings **7**

   Peduncle without lateral wings **8**

7. Opercular ampulla somewhat cup-shaped and deeper than the distal calcareous cap which may be flat or domed (seldom conical), with or without distal projections **Pomatoceros lamarcki**

   Ampulla a shallow dish-shape, rarely as deep as distal cap which is usually domed, often conical, and with or without distal projections **Pomatoceros triqueter**

8. Peduncle with pinnules **9**

   Peduncle without pinnules **12**

9. Tube >1 mm diameter, generally solitary; operculum spherical, often paired, one smaller than the other **Apomatus similis**

   Tubes generally aggregated forming a thin tracery over surface; operculum cup or bowl-shaped **10**

10. With two opercula, each an asymmetrical cup; tube diameter 0.5 mm **Filograna implexa**

    Single symmetrical operculum, with a small but bulbous ampulla and a distal cup; tube diameter 0.2 mm **Josephella marenzelleri**

11. Tube >2 mm diameter, generally solitary; radioles tapered distally, fairly smooth with bright red blotches (in life) and single lenticular units along their length **Protula tubularia**

    Tube about 0.5 mm diameter, often numerous, forming thick rope-like twisted assemblages in shallow water; radioles with swollen tips and each rachis with paired scalloped margins, representing rows of paired bulbous groups of lenticular units **Salmacina dysteri**

12. Opercular peduncle D-shaped or flattened in cross-section **13**

    Peduncle round in cross-section **14**

13. Peduncle smooth, stiff with the flat surface showing dorsally; operculum with many dark brown teeth; tube smooth **Ficopomatus enigmaticus**

    Peduncle ribbon-like and flexible, with oval annuli when preserved (contraction); operculum smooth, symmetrically domed or subconical; tube with rough or toothed ridges **Metavermilia multicristata**

14. Operculum asymmetrically domed or subconical; prominent glandular pad on dorsal side of last abdominal segments **Vermiliopsis striaticeps**

    Operculum funnel-like, with serrated circumference, with or without a central crown of spines **15**

15. Operculum a single straight-sided funnel about 4 mm across with 20–40 marginal serrations; crown red (young *Hydroides* opercula are similar, but crown is usually pale and banded with brown) **Serpula vermicularis**

    Operculum a double funnel, the basal one *Serpula*-like, the distal one a spiny crown **(Hydroides) 16**

16. Distal crown radially symmetrical **17**

    Distal crown not radially symmetrical **Hydroides dianthus**

17. Spines of crown without lateral teeth **Hydroides ezoensis**

    Spines with lateral teeth **18**

18. Centre of spiny crown with a small projection; collar chaetae with a finely toothed boss **Hydroides elegans**

    Centre of crown smooth; collar chaetae bearing one or usually two large teeth **Hydroides norvegica**

Apomatus similis Marion and Bobretsky   FIG. 6.23

Up to 30 mm long (13 mm figured); operculum a globular transparent vesicle on one or both second dorsal radioles (seven to 20 each side) which have short pinnules like the others in the crown; each rachis with about seven paired eyes consisting of irregular groups of eight to ten lenticular units (bottom of figure); collar chaetae bordered, scarcely geniculate with a slender knee, finely serrated and tapered distally; tube, just over 1 mm across, tapers, meanders, and bears fine transverse growth lines and indistinct longitudinal ridges.

On rock and shells; sublittoral; southern species: south-west Wales, Plymouth and Channel Isles.

Chitinopoma serrula Stimpson   FIG. 6.23
(= *Miroserpula inflata* Dons)

Up to 20 mm long (7 mm in figure); operculum with a flat or concave distal plate and a cup-shaped ampulla below; peduncle long, bare, and cylindrical, arises between first and second radioles of either right or left side; collar trilobed with dorso-lateral margins reaching only as far as segment 2; collar chaetae of two types, capillary and geniculate, the latter with a toothed fin and finely serrated blade; tube with an irregularly toothed medial keel; breeding specimens develop a calcareous brood-chamber on each side of aperture (figured bottom right).

On stones and shells; lower shore and sublittoral; northern species widespread in north Atlantic and parts of North Sea; may well occur in Scotland. Tubes of non-brooding specimens easily confused with young *Pomatoceros*.

Ditrupa arietina Müller   FIG. 6.23
Tube about 15 mm long and characteristic in being tusk-shaped, made of two layers (see transverse section), the outer thick and vitreous, the inner thin and opaque; operculum with a flattish lens-shaped plate; collar chaetae absent.

Lives unattached to substrata (sand or mud); sublittoral; Shetland, Celtic Sea, south-west Ireland.

Ficopomatus enigmaticus (Fauvel)   FIG. 6.23
(= *Mercierella enigmatica* Fauvel)

Operculum without a distal rim but with dark chitinous inwardly curved spines (figured specimen 1.2 mm diameter); peduncle arising near dorsal mid-line, D-shaped in cross-section with curved surface facing mouth; collar chaetae slightly geniculate with large teeth at knee and smaller but distinct ones along the distal taper; tube with fine transverse growth rings and occasional shelf-like annuli distally.

On hard substrata in the warmer and sometimes brackish water of estuaries, docks, lagoons, and power station outfalls. sublittoral; southern species, west and south coasts of England and Wales.

Filograna implexa Berkeley   FIG. 6.23
Two soft cup-shaped asymmetrically developed opercula (figured specimen 0.2 mm diameter) each on a pinnate peduncle/radiole; collar chaetae as *Chitinopoma*; tube fine with occasional growth rings, often forming shallow incrustations.

Crevices in rock, *Pentapora*, etc; sublittoral; south-west Wales and Plymouth (further records uncertain as *Salmacina dysteri* has often been synonymized with this species); locally abundant.

Filogranula calyculata (Costa)   FIG. 6.23
Operculum with asymmetrical cup-shaped 'plate' (figured specimen 0.2 mm diameter), with or without a central projection which bears irregular protuberances; collar chaetae as *Chit-*

inopoma; tube with a median and two lateral rows of pointed teeth positioned so as to form transverse rows of three teeth, anterior portion may become erect and growth then proceeds in spurts, resulting in formation of fluted nesting funnels.

Under edges of piled shale slabs; sublittoral; Abereiddy marine quarry, south-west Wales; southern species; locally common.

Hydroides dianthus (Verrill)   FIG. 6.24
Opercular basal funnel (figured specimen 1.5 m diameter) edged with 30–40 angular serrations and surmounted by a crown of large irregular spines curved towards radioles; collar chaetae scarcely geniculate, with two large teeth at knee and smooth taper distally; tube round in cross-section and fairly smooth.

On hard substrata; sublittoral; near Southampton; rare.

Hydroides elegans (Haswell)   FIG. 6.24
Operculum and tube as *H. dianthus* but distal crown with a small central projection and radiating spines with small lateral and other teeth; collar chaetae with a finely toothed boss (fin).

On hard substrata in many harbours worldwide e.g. Swansea, Shoreham; sublittoral.

Hydroides ezoensis Okuda   FIG. 6.24
Operculum as *H. elegans* but distal crown without central projection and spines without lateral teeth; collar chaetae as *H. dianthus*, tube with meandering growth rings irregularly coiled in one plane or in aggregations tightly parallel to each other with apertures towards open water.

On hard substrata, sublittoral; Japanese immigrant abundant in docks and marinas; Southampton, Hayling Island.

Hydroides norvegica (Gunnerus)   FIG. 6.24
Operculum and tube as *H. elegans*, but distal crown without central projection, and spines fused to each other for less than one-third of their length, collar chaetae with large teeth as in *H. dianthus*.

On hard substrata; usually sublittoral; all coasts; common.

Josephella marenzelleri Caullery and Mesnil   FIG. 6.24
The smallest British serpulid, just 2 mm long; operculum with distal cuticular cup about 0.1 mm diameter, with longitudinal ridges which give the effect of a scalloped or castellated margin under certain angles of illumination, cup distal to heart-shaped ampulla and pinnate peduncle; collar chaetae plain and bordered (as figured for *Apomatus*); tube about 0.2 mm in diameter and slightly flexible, usually part of a delicate tracery of tubes that are often branched (reproduction by scissiparity).

In rock clefts; sublittoral; southern species; Isle of Man, Dale and Abereiddy (south-west Wales), and Plymouth.

Metavermilia multicristata (Philippi)   FIG. 6.24
Distal part of opercular ampulla domed or conical (figured specimen 0.5 mm diameter), brownish (horny) in colour. It can be confused with *Vermiliopsis striaticeps*, but differs in that the long peduncle arising between radioles 1 and 2, is flattened,

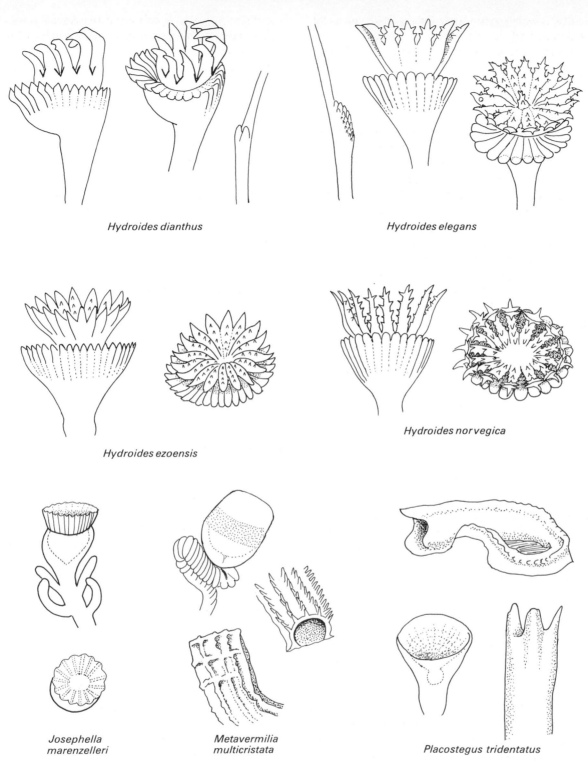

Hydroides dianthus

Hydroides elegans

Hydroides ezoensis

Hydroides norvegica

Josephella
marenzelleri

Metavermilia
multicristata

Placostegus tridentatus

Fig. 6.24

almost ribbonlike, but distinctly oval in cross-section even when contraction forms annulations. Dorsal side of last few segments is glandular but does not form a distinct pad as in *V. striaticeps*; collar chaetae plain (bordered) as in *Apomatus* but more slender; tube with five rough ridges or five longitudinal rows of sharp teeth.

On rock (shale); sublittoral; southern species; Abereiddy marine quarry, South Wales; locally common.

Placostegus tridentatus (Fabricius)   FIG. 6.24

Operculum with a brownish concave distal plate (figured specimen 2 mm diameter) bearing a knoblike projection within the funnel-shaped ampulla; collar chaetae absent; tube translucent; triangular in cross-section, with a median keel which extends over the aperture as a 'tooth', and flanges against the substratum which end as two additional teeth if the anterior becomes erect.

On stones and shell; dredged; coasts of Scotland; common.

Pomatoceros lamarcki (Quatrefages)   FIG. 6.25

Operculum with a cup-shaped ampulla, the distal plate concave or convex (figured specimens 1.2 mm diameter), with or without an eccentric projection which can be with or without distal protuberances, distal to thick smooth peduncle with a tapered wing on each side; collar chaetae, when present, like those figured for *Apomatus*; tube with a well-defined median keel and in adults two more vestigial ridges, one on each side.

On rocks; lower shore and shallow sublittoral; warm temperate species; widespread on rocky shores throughout Britain; very abundant.

Pomatoceros triqueter (Linnaeus)   FIG. 6.25

As *P. lamarcki* except the ampulla is shallow (dish-shaped) and the distal part often conical (with or without projections); tube with only a median ridge.

On rocks; mainly sublittoral; widespread species; all coasts; abundant, particularly adjoining deep water.

Protula tubularia (Montagu)   FIG. 6.25

Operculum absent; collar chaetae as figured for *Apomatus*; radioles have 15–25 paired red blotches concealing single lenticular units (side-view figured enlarged on right); thoracic membranes extensive; tube 2–8 mm diameter, smooth except for indistinct growth rings.

On hard substrata; sublittoral, Shetlands, Scotland, west and south coasts of England, Wales, Ireland, and Channel Isles; widespread but often solitary.

Salmacina dysteri (Huxley)   FIG. 6.25

Operculum absent; collar chaetae as in *Filograna*, radiole tips swollen (centre top), each rachis with paired scalloped 'ridges' with about 13 pairs of tightly packed lenticulate units (figured in plan view, centre bottom, and side view, to the right); tubes up to 0.5 mm diameter similar to those of *Filograna* except that they commonly make dense aggregations in the form of a rope-like mesh with tunnels.

On rock, lower shore, but mainly sublittoral in less sheltered areas; widespread on rocky coasts from Shetlands to Channel Islands; abundant.

Serpula vermicularis Linnaeus   FIG. 6.25

Operculum funnel-shaped (figured specimen 2.2 mm diameter) with radial grooves and 20–40 marginal serrations; collar chaetae with a boss bearing two large teeth and a smooth taper distally; tube with longitudinal ridges, but fairly smooth when erect and aggregated.

On rocks and shell; sublittoral in lagoons, inlets, fjords, and natural harbours; Shetlands, west and south coasts of Britain, western Ireland, and Channel Isles; often abundant.

Vermiliopsis striaticeps (Grube)   FIG. 6.25
(= in part *V. langerhansi* Fauvel)

Operculum asymmetrically domed or subconical (figured specimens less than 1 mm diameter), often with longitudinal striations; peduncle slender, stiff but annulated, arising near the dorsal mid-line; collar chaetae like those figured for *Apomatus*; tube about 2 mm diameter with about four longitudinal ridges and indistinct growth rings; dorsal side of the last 12 abdominal segments bears a prominent glandular pad. This character together with the shape and position of the peduncle, easily separates this species from *Metavermila multicristata*.

On hard substrata (shell and shale); sublittoral; Falmouth harbour and Roscoff.

30 SPIRORBIDAE

As Serpulidae with dorsal surface against substratum, and abdominal inversion of chaetal arrangement, but tubes coiled or helical, rarely evolute, sinistrally (clockwise) coiling species with operculum on left and change of direction of faecal groove on right, vice versa in dextrally coiling species. Mostly with three thoracic chaetigers, some with four, best assessed by counting the large glistening bands of uncini (tori) on the concave side. As there are no tori in the first chaetiger, two tori represent three chaetigers and three tori, four.

Sickle chaetae (figured for *Janua*) are common in Spirorbidae and, amongst British species, absent only in *Circeis* and *Neodexiospira*. The latter also has a character unique amongst British species in that the thoracic membranes are fused to form a tunnel dorsally whereas they are free in the other genera. The tunnel is best demonstrated with a fine pin, unless material is fresh when it is easily seen. Clove oil (after dehydration) helps to distinguish finer sculptural details of large talons, especially in preserved material, but it should not be used for opercular brood chambers as the extent of the finely calcified walls can be distorted.

Spirorbids have a much wider selection of substrata than serpulids, but are less tolerant of sand scour which hinders colonization. Larvae settle and metamorphose very quickly, there being virtually no planktonic stage.

Opercula are all drawn to the same scale except that of *Jugaria quadrangularis*, which has an operculum nearly as large in diameter as that of *Spirorbis tridentatus*, and is figured at half the scale of the other Spirorbidae.

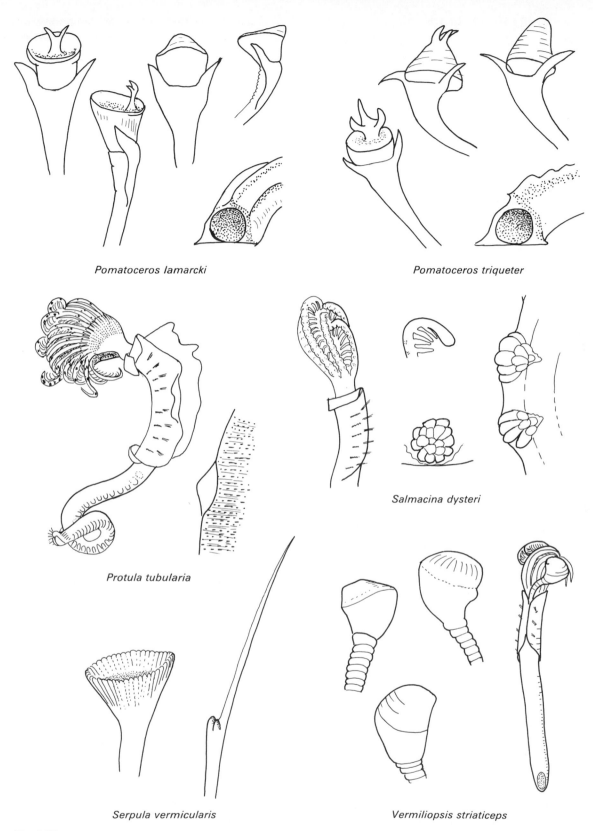

Pomatoceros lamarcki

Pomatoceros triqueter

Salmacina dysteri

Protula tubularia

Serpula vermicularis

Vermiliopsis striaticeps

Fig. 6.25

REFERENCES

Knight-Jones, P. (1984). A new species of *Protoleodora* (Spirorbidae: Polychaeta) from Eastern U.S.S.R., with a brief revision of related genera. *Zoological Journal of the Linnean Society*, **80**, 109–20.

Knight-Jones, P. and Knight-Jones, E. W. (1977). Taxonomy and ecology of British Spirorbidae (Polychaeta). *Journal of the Marine Biological Association of the U.K.*, **57**, 453–99.

Thorp, C. H., Knight-Jones, P., and Knight-Jones, E. W. (1986). New records of Tubeworms established in British harbours. *Journal of the Marine Biological Association of the U.K.*, **66**, 881–8.

1. Tube coiled dextrally (anticlockwise)   **2**

    Tube coiled sinistrally   **9**

2. Tube glassy or porcellaneous, eggs if present attached to inside of tube wall   **3**

    Tube opaque, somewhat chalky; incubation in a brood chamber, but non-brooding operculum may be present; two thoracic tori on concave side   **7**

3. Tube glassy or translucent, with longitudinal ridges; operculum bowl-shaped; three thoracic tori on concave side; on stones   ***Paradexiospira vitrea***

    Tube opaque or translucent, without ridges; operculum oblique in side-view with blunt talon towards (beneath) lower edge; two thoracic tori on concave side   (***Circeis***) *4*

4. Tube translucent, often helical; talon longer than radius of plate; on hydroids and bryozoans   ***Circeis spirillum***

    Tube opaque; talon shorter than radius of plate   **5**

5. On macroalgae   ***Circeis armoricana fragilis***

    On crustaceans and shell   **6**

6. On lobsters and crawfish   ***Circeis armoricana***

    With hermit crab *Pagurus bernhardus*; on abdomen or on surrounding shell   ***Circeis paguri***

7. Thoracic membrane not fused dorsally; non-brooding operculum with eccentric pin-shaped talon; brooding operculum with transparent wall

    Janua pagenstecheri

    Thoracic membrane fused dorsally to form a tunnel; non-brooding operculum with a flat peripheral talon; brooding operculum with light-reflecting or partially opaque wall   ***Neodexiospira* 8**

8. Non-brooding operculum with axe-shaped talon; brood chamber not much longer than diameter of plate; collar chaetae without cross striations

    Neodexiospira brasiliensis

    Non-brooding operculum with narrow talon; brood chamber longer than broad; collar chaetae with cross-striations   ***Neodexiospira pseudocorrugata***

9. Tube glassy or translucent and transversely ridged

    Protolaeospira striata

    Tube opaque, porcellaneous or chalky, without prominent transverse ridges   **10**

10. Operculum with talon   **11**

    Operculum forming brood chamber   **16 or 17**

11. Talon central, cone or pin-shaped   **12**

    Talon eccentric or peripheral, and vestigial, spatulate, or massive   **14**

12. Three thoracic tori on concave side; eggs incubated in tube; tube with one obtuse median ridge; talon pin or cone-shaped   ***Paralaeospira malardi***

    Two thoracic tori on concave side; tube with three indistinct longitudinal ridges; no eggs in tube   **13**

13. Talon sub-conical. Non-brooding operculum of

    Pileolaria berkeleyana

    Talon pin-shaped. Non-brooding operculum of

    Pileolaria heteropoma forma glabra

14. Talon peripheral and flat; may or may not be attached to brood chamber   **15**

    Talon not peripheral, but eccentric and either vestigial or massive; embryos when present in a string attached to the tube wall   (***Spirorbis***) **19**

15. Talon subquadrangular with a ventral spur; not attached to brood chamber; brownish patch on dorsal body surface (black in preservative). Non-brooding operculum of   ***Pileolaria militaris***

    Talon subtriangular or elongate and tapered proximally; usually attached to brood chamber; whitish, indistinct patch on dorsal body surface   (***Jugaria***) **16**

16. Opercular plate flat or concave, talon short (half diameter of plate) and subtriangular; after brood chamber formation, this operculum remains attached only by the proximal margin of talon   ***Jugaria granulata***

    Opercular plate convex, talon longer than diameter of plate, winged, and narrow, and bifid proximally; this operculum becomes completely fused to brood chamber formed below   ***Jugaria quadrangularis***

17. Brood chamber helmet-shaped and with distal spines

    Pileolaria militaris

    Brood chamber without distal spines   **18**

18. Brood chamber usually domed (seldom bilobed); body with two elongate bright orange patches dorsally (they fade in preservation); non-brooding operculum with central pin talon

    Pileolaria heteropoma forma glabra

Brood chamber asymmetrically bilobed; large diffuse patch across the dorsal body surface pinkish orange (fades in preservative); non-brooding operculum with blunt cone-shaped talon **Pileolaria berkeleyana**

19. Opercular plate with a slight thickening towards lower edge **20**

    Plate with bilobed or massive talon **21**

20. Tube smooth with small flange; body greenish brown; generally on *Fucus* **Spirorbis spirorbis**

    Tube without flange; body red; on stones or 'Lithothamnion' **Spirorbis rupestris**

21. Talon bilobed or like a horse's hoof; tube without longitudinal ridges **22**

    Talon rounded or pointed terminally; tube usually with longitudinal ridges **23**

22. Usually on *Corallina*; dorsal collar flaps only slightly asymmetrical **Spirorbis corallinae**

    Usually on other algae; dorsal collar flap much longer on convex side than on other side **Spirorbis inornatus**

23. Tube usually with three distinct smooth ridges forming three projections at mouth; talon with three distinct lobes; on stones, often on shore **Spirorbis tridentatus**

    Tube with three indistinct rough ridges, the inner one most prominent; talon with three pointed processes; on sublittoral stones, never on shore **Spirorbis cuneatus**

Circeis armoricana St Joseph FIG. 6.26

Opercular plate oblique, slightly concave (figured specimen 0.4 mm diameter); talon broad but short with an indentation proximally; collar chaetae geniculate with a sharp knee and teeth confined to the outer margin; larvae with two pairs of eyes, the lateral ones larger and bilobed; tube thick-walled and opaque, coil diameter up to 2 mm.

On *Homarus* and *Palinurus*, particularly in crevices on undersides; sublittoral; Swansea, Lundy, Anglesey, north-west Ireland.

Circeis armoricana fragilis Knight-Jones and Knight-Jones FIG. 6.26

Like *C. armoricana* but talon longer and occasionally serrated; tube slightly translucent, up to 1.5 mm coil diameter, showing faintly the orange pigment of worm within.

On *Laminaria* and *Saccorhiza* sublittorally in sheltered cold water; Isles of Scilly and Brittany (southern limit), Plymouth Sound, Fishguard, and Holyhead harbours, Loch Sween (Scotland), Lough Hyne (southern Ireland).

Circeis paguri Knight-Jones and Knight-Jones FIG. 6.26

Opercular plate markedly concave, the talon relatively long; collar chaetae as *C. armoricana* but larvae characteristic in having

three pairs of small rounded eyes; tube 0.6–1.3 mm coil diameter, translucent but colour of worm (pale yellow) does not readily show through.

In association with hermit crab *Pagurus bernhardus*, either attached to telson or to inside of shell that it inhabits; sublittoral; Swansea and Plymouth.

Circeis spirillum (Linnaeus) FIG. 6.26

Similar to *C. armoricana fragilis* but talon more slender in side-view; collar chaetae less geniculate with teeth not confined to margin and arranged in serried ranks across side (cross-striations); tube usually helically coiled as it grows away from narrow substrata, with translucent walls showing the orange body within.

On hydroids and bryozoans in strong currents; sublittoral; a widespread northern species; Guernsey, Plymouth, Swansea, Anglesey, and Scotland.

Janua pagenstecheri (Quatrefages) FIG. 6.26

Non-brooding operculum with eccentric pin-shaped talon; first brood chamber of a series includes this talon (most without), wall around embryos transparent and distal plate either flat or irregularly convex; collar chaetae geniculate with a rounded finely toothed knee; sickle chaetae (on right of figure) in third thoracic fascicle, with a similar knee but with a flat ribbed and marginally toothed blade distally; dorsal margins of collar not fused to form a tunnel; tube <2 mm coil diameter, dextral, with indistinct longitudinal ridges and a sloping flange.

On hard substrata and algae, intertidal and sublittoral. All coasts, common.

Jugaria granulata (Linnaeus) FIG. 6.26

Non-brooding operculum with a flat or concave distal plate and peripheral subtriangular talon, proximal margin of which remains attached to outer edge of the flat-topped brood chamber which has a helmet-shaped calcification; fin and blade collar chaetae finely toothed and without cross-striations; largest abdominal tori three-quarters of the way along abdomen; tube usually without longitudinal ridges, coil diameter 2 mm.

Under rocks and shells; sublittoral, in shallow water only in sheltered conditions; north temperate species; all coasts; common.

Jugaria quadrangularis (Stimpson) FIG. 6.26

Like *J. granulata* but talon wider and longer, with lateral wings and indentations, and is incorporated into the wall of the brood chamber; largest abdominal tori lie anteriorly.

On *Laminaria* sublittorally; near Inveraray, south-west Scotland; locally common.

Neodexiospira brasiliensis (Grube) FIG. 6.26

Non-brooding operculum with a peripheral axe-shaped talon, first brood chamber of a series includes this talon in the wall but most are without; cylindrical wall around embryos is calcified except for a proximal zone just above basal calcified disc; collar chaetae geniculate and with barely visible cross-striations associated with the toothed margin; sickle chaetae (see *Janua*) absent; thoracic membranes fused dorsally to form a tunnel (demonstrated by a fine pin in figure); tube 2 mm across with three indistinct longitudinal ridges.

On *Sargassum* and moored pontoons; sublittoral; widespread in warm temperate waters; Portsmouth Harbour; locally common.

Neodexiospira pseudocorrugata (Bush) FIG. 6.26

Like *N. brasiliensis* except that talon is narrow and flat; brood chamber wall longer and less opaque; collar chaetae with fairly distinct cross-striations and coarse teeth along the outer margin; tube smaller, 1.5 mm across.

Mainly on *Laminaria saccharina*, *Cystoseira*, and sublittoral Rhodophyceae; locally common in Channel Isles, Scilly Isles, Plymouth, Lundy, and south-east Ireland. Not found off Wales and Isle of Man.

Paradexiospira vitrea (Fabricius) FIG. 6.26

Orange pigment can be seen through the glassy usually ridged tube, 2.5 mm in coil diameter; operculum bowl-shaped and transparent except at slightly convex centre; three pairs of thoracic tori on concave side; collar chaetae with fins and coarsely toothed cross-striated blades.

In crevices under rocks in clear water; mostly sublittoral; arctic and north temperate species; Channel Isles, Scilly Isles, Plymouth (outside breakwater), Lizard, Isle of Man, west Scotland; not known from Wales; locally common.

Paralaeospira malardi Caullery and Mesnil FIG. 6.26

Opercular talon variable from a pin to cone-shape; collar chaetae with fin and finely serrated blades without cross-striations; three thoracic tori on concave side; tube 1.3 mm across with a single obtuse longitudinal ridge.

Under rocks; usually sublittoral, particularly *Laminaria* zone; possibly an immigrant from South Africa; Scilly Isles, Channel Isles, Cornwall, Plymouth, south-west Wales, Isle of Man, northern Scotland, southern Ireland; locally common.

Pileolaria berkeleyana (Rioja) FIG. 6.27
[(= *P. rosepigmentata* (Uchida)]

Non-brooding operculum with central talon forming a cone; brood chamber calcification helmet-shaped and bilobed distally, the side away from substratum being slightly more protuberant; live material readily distinguished from *P. heteropoma* by the large diffuse patch of milky orange-pink granules across the dorsal surface (fades in preservative); collar chaetae with fins and blades with coarse serrations and distinct cross-striations; tube with longitudinal ridges, coil diameter just over 1 mm.

On *Sargassum*, Portsmouth Harbour, and on walls of sea water aquarium system of Hayling Island Marine Laboratory, Portsmouth Polytechnic. Usually sublittoral, on hard substrata in and near harbours, widespread in warm and temperate waters.

Pileolaria heteropoma Zibrowius forma *glabra* FIG. 6.27

Non-brooding operculum with pin talon; brood chamber with helmet-shaped calcification distally domed (sometimes bilobed), lacking the eccentric distal point seen in Mediterranean and east Atlantic populations; live material easily distinguished from *P. berkeleyana* by twin elongate dorsal patches of vivid orange granules (they fade in preservative); collar chaetae with fins and blades, with serrations and cross-striations less distinct than those figured for *P. berkeleyana*, tube about 1 mm coil diameter with longitudinal ridges.

On underside of *Glycymeris* shells; 25 m depth; southern species; found off Stoke Point near Plymouth and the slopes of the Hurd Deep, English Channel; not common.

Pileolaria militaris Claparède FIG. 6.26

Non-brooding opercular talon (bottom left) with a ventral spur which may be with or without distal teeth (top left); brood chamber with helmet-shaped calcification and a ventro-distal semicircle of spines; dorsal surface of body bears a single rust-coloured patch which becomes and remains nearly black in preservative; collar chaetae with toothed fin and distal blade with coarse serrations and distinct cross-striations; tube up to 3 mm, fairly smooth with the last whorl rapidly widening.

Mainly on sublittoral Rhodophyceae; widespread in warm waters; Channel Isles, Plymouth, Gulland Rock, and Lundy Island (Bristol Channel); not common.

Protolaeospira striata (Quievreux) FIG. 6.27

Operculum with an oblique, slightly concave distal plate and a massive talon with lateral knobs and a small ventral spur; eggs incubated in a brood sac attached to an epithelial stalk arising from the thorax; collar chaetae similar to those of *Pileolaria*; tube over 2 mm diameter, transparent and easily overlooked.

Under stable rocks; sublittoral; widespread in warm European waters; Channel Isles and Scilly Isles, not common; northern record Gulland Rock, Padstow.

Spirorbis cuneatus Gee FIG. 6.27

Opercular plate slightly oblique, talon with three distinct points in face view, subconical in side view (bottom left) but slimmer in younger specimens (centre top); collar chaetae with fin, moderate serrations, and indistinct cross-striations on blade; tube opaque with a dull surface, coil diameter just over 1 mm, with three longitudinal ridges and a sloping flange from the outer ridge.

On rocks and shells; sublittoral; Mediterranean and east Atlantic species; south-west England, south-west Wales, and Scotland; locally common.

Spirorbis corallinae de Silva and Knight-Jones FIG. 6.27

Opercular plate flat (concave in young specimens) or domed, talon bilobed but conical in side view (left); collar chaetae with toothed fin and finely toothed blade (no cross-striations, similar to the largest chaeta figured for *S. tridentatus*); tips of radioles similar in length to adjacent pinnules; larvae with two pairs of eyes, the lateral ones composite and anterior ones small and round; tube about 1 mm coil diameter, smooth and with the

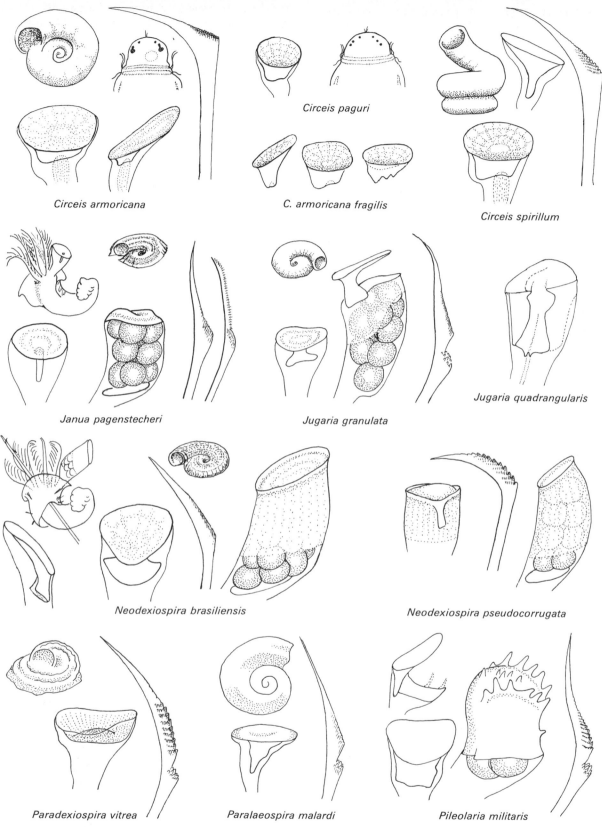

Circeis paguri

Circeis armoricana

C. armoricana fragilis

Circeis spirillum

Janua pagenstecheri

Jugaria granulata

Jugaria quadrangularis

Neodexiospira brasiliensis

Neodexiospira pseudocorrugata

Paradexiospira vitrea

Paralaeospira malardi

Pileolaria militaris

Fig. 6.26

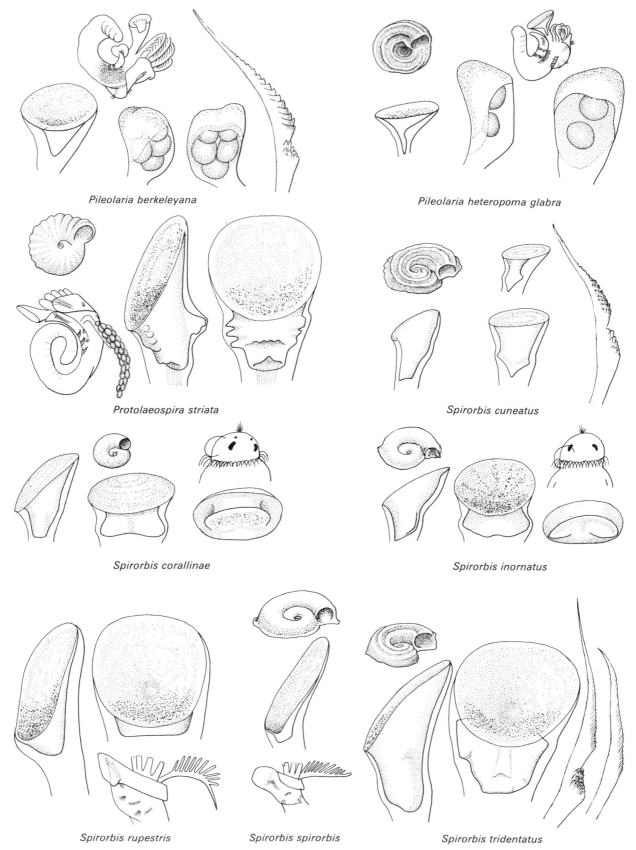

Pileolaria berkeleyana

Pileolaria heteropoma glabra

Protolaeospira striata

Spirorbis cuneatus

Spirorbis corallinae

Spirorbis inornatus

Spirorbis rupestris

Spirorbis spirorbis

Spirorbis tridentatus

Fig. 6.27

last whorl partially above the previous ones (owing to narrow substratum), walls porcellaneous.

Almost exclusively on *Corallina officinalis*; rock pools and shallow water; Scilly Isles, and Channel Isles to northern Scotland and Ireland.

Spirorbis inornatus L'Hardy and Quievreux   FIG. 6.27

As *S. corallinae* except that opercular plate remains concave in mature specimens; tips of radioles up to twice as long as adjacent pinnules; larvae lack the round pair of anterior eyes; porcellaneous tube nearly 2 mm across, usually coiled in one plane with a small flange close to substratum.

On *Laminaria* at St Michael's Isle (Cornwall), upper reaches of Milford Haven, Isle of Man, and Oban; on *Chondrus, Gigartina, Himanthalia* buttons, *Laminaria, Fucus serratus*, and other algae where there is plenty of gentle water movement; Channel Isles, south-west England, Roscoff, Wales, Ireland, Scotland, and Northumberland.

Spirorbis rupestris Gee and Knight-Jones   FIG. 6.27

Opercular plate very oblique, concave with shallow talon towards lower edge; body orange-red; tips of radioles two or three times as long as adjacent pinnules; collar chaetae with toothed fin and finely serrated blade (no cross-striations, similar to larger chaeta figured for *S. tridentatus*); tube up to 4.5 mm across when coiled in one plane, sometimes evolute and frequently with the last whorl ascending, especially when amongst '*Lithothamnion*'.

On rock particularly associated with *Phymatolithon polymorphum* L.; intertidal, common behind 'hanging' *Fucus*; a north temperate species. Scilly Isles, Channel Isles, Cornwall to Swanage (Dorset), south-west and north-west Wales, Isle of Man, Scotland, and Ireland.

Spirorbis spirorbis (Linnaeus)   FIG. 6.27

As *S. rupestris* except that body greenish with brown stomach; tips of radioles not much longer than adjacent pinnules; collar asymmetrical forming a large 'hinged' flap at dorso-convex margin; tube about 3 mm across, evenly coiled, shiny, and with a small peripheral flange.

On *Fucus*, especially *F. serratus*, occasionally on other algae, e.g. *Laminaria* and *Himanthalia* buttons, and stone; intertidal and shallow water; north temperate species; most rocky coasts; abundant.

Spirorbis tridentatus Levinsen   FIG. 6.27

Tuby shiny usually with rounded longitudinal ridges, coil diameter 3 mm, the last whorl widening abruptly towards mouth; talon conical in side-view (narrow in young specimens) and with indistinct lateral protuberances in 'face'-view; collar chaetae on convex side with a toothed fin separated by a gap from the finely toothed (non-cross-striated) blade, those in the concave fascicle smaller with a reduced gap or none at all as in simple bordered chaetae.

Under stones and in rock-crevices; lower shore and (more sparsely) to a depth of 20 m; north temperate species; abundant on most coasts (tolerates some sand abrasion).

B. Class **Oligochaeta**

Aquatic oligochaetes are generally similar to the more familiar earthworms, although much smaller and proportionally more slender. The anterior end usually lacks appendages or obvious sense-organs, although the prostomium may be elongated in a proboscis (separate from the mouth, unlike the eversible pharynx of many polychaetes) and some naidids may have simple eyespots. Typically, each segment behind the prostomium carries four bundles of chaetae, two in a dorso-lateral and two in a ventro-lateral position; sometimes they may be missing from a particular region (or even the whole body, in a few species not included here). Sexually mature worms develop a *clitellum* similar to the 'saddle' of an earthworm but less conspicuous, in the front third of the body: it covers up to six segments, normally in the region between the 5th (V) and 13th (XIII). In many species, the body-wall is translucent, so that internal organs can be seen. The location of these, and structures on the external surface, is indicated by giving the segments roman numbers starting with the peristomium as I (as for the clitellum, above).

Chaetae occurring in front of the clitellum are referred to as *anterior*, those behind it as *posterior*. They may be long, slender *hair chaetae* (found in the dorso-lateral bundles of Naididae and Tubificidae) or stouter *sigmoid chaetae* (as Fig. 6.29c), which are usually curved. These vary considerably in size, may have simple, bifid, or more elaborately toothed tips, and may be swollen into a *nodulus* about half-way along, at the level where they emerge from the body-wall (Fig. 6.29d). In the naidids, short chaetae accompanying the long hair-like ones are straighter and more delicate than most sigmoid forms and are called *needles* (Fig. 6.29b).

Oligochaetes are hermaphrodite; the nature and position of their complex reproductive structures are important in identification (see Fig. 6.28b,d,f). The female organs consist of paired *ovaries* attached to the anterior septum (dividing wall) of the ovarian segment (there is usually only one) and paired, ciliated *female funnels* on the posterior septum, which discharge released eggs through the inconspicuous *female pores*. The male organs comprise a normally single pair of *testes* in a segment anterior to the ovarian segment and *seminal vesicles* in which the sperm are matured. A pair of ciliated *male (sperm) funnels* form the opening of the *vasa deferentia* which pass the sperm into paired *atria* (sometimes a single atrium) in the next segment back, where they are stored. *Prostate glands* surround or are connected with the atria, which open to the exterior by a *male pore*, an eversible invagination of the body-wall known as a *pseudopenis*, or a true *penis* which retracts into a *cuticular sac* or *penis sheath* which may be thick and of a characteristic shape (Fig. 6.29r–t). These worms mostly cross-fertilize and, when they copulate, the exchanged sperm is stored in paired *spermathecae* (Fig. 6.29l–o) or (in species which lack these) ejected as *spermatophores* which are attached to the outside of the partner worm. Ventro-lateral bundles on spermathecal segments, or sometimes those bearing the male pores, may contain modified chaetae which facilitate this transfer. Aquatic oligochaetes often reproduce asexually: naidids produce chains of daughter individuals and tubificids can multiply by fission, at least in laboratory cultures. Self-fertilization is also possible, a single worm shedding both eggs and sperm into the same sort of cocoon which is secreted by the clitellum during copulation.

Marine or brackish-water oligochaetes, mostly associated with soft sediments, are small enough to become readily lost by normal sieving methods. Giere and Pfannkuche (1982) recommended the use of an 0.5 mm or smaller mesh-size, but commented that flotation with media denser than water, followed by centrifugation, is more convenient. They also gave details of elutriation methods, but reported that the seawater-ice extraction method used for meiofauna is unreliable for small oligochaetes. Initial investigation of a live specimen can be carried out by placing the animal beneath a cover-slip on a microscope slide, drawing off the surrounding water to flatten it gently and then introducing a little glycerin; active worms could be treated cautiously with one of the usual relaxing agents. Tynen and Nurminen (1969) commented that 'no satisfactory technique has been worked out for the examination of whole preserved littoral enchytraeids'. Initial preservation of separated specimens (or even an entire core sample) is best done using 5 per cent formalin; they should be stored in 70 per cent ethanol. Identification often calls for mounting in a clearing agent such as Amman's lactophenol, with slight flattening. Staining may be necessary to distinguish the male organs of small tubificids and, ultimately, dissection or sectioning may be required.

Many aquatic species are euryhaline, having been recorded most frequently in inland fresh waters but also occasionally in freshwater flows across seashores and at least in the reduced salinities found in estuaries or the upper parts of the Baltic Sea. Some predominantly terrestrial forms may, likewise, extend on to upper levels of the intertidal; conversely, species commonly recorded under algal wrack or other detritus stranded at high-water mark may survive well in soil on which this has subsequently been spread as fertilizer. Truly marine species feature relatively rarely in British records, but recent studies in various estuaries have swelled this number; yet more have been recorded from continental Europe, with a strong probability that they will eventually be found here, too. This section contains a selection of what appear to be the most frequently encountered British forms. Apart from the initial separation of the three major families, keys have not been provided because this would imply a degree of precision which is lacking in this simplified overview. Where a specimen obviously matches none of the descriptions given below, or the reader is unable to distinguish between two possible identifications, reference must be made either to the ingenious keys devised by Brinkhurst (1982) or the much fuller descriptions given by the authorities cited in that useful handbook.

REFERENCES

Brinkhurst, R. O. (1982). British and other marine and estuarine oligochaetes. *Synopses of the British Fauna* (N.S.) 21. London: Cambridge University Press, for the Linnean Society of London and the Estuarine and Brackish-Water Sciences Association.

Giere, O. and Pfannkuche, O. (1982). Biology and ecology of marine Oligochaeta, a review. *Oceanography and marine Biology annual Review*, 20, 173–308.

Nielson, C. O. and Christensen, B. (1959). The Enchytraeidae. Critical revision and taxonomy of European species. *Natura jutlandica*, 8–9, 1–160.

Tynen, M. J. and Nurminen, M. (1969). A key to the littoral Enchytraeidae (Oligochaeta). *Annales zoologici Societatis zoologico-botanicae fennicae*, 6, 150–155.

KEY TO FAMILIES

1. General resemblance to small, pale earthworm, with thick cuticle (Fig. 6.28a), often in top-shore detritus; few stout, simple-pointed chaetae (may be absent altogether). Spermathecae in segment V (remote from gonads and other reproductive structures which are in XI and XII, Fig. 6.28b)   *1. Enchytraeidae*

   More delicate than earthworms, with thin cuticle. Chaetae variable: all bifid or hair chaetae dorsally. Spermathecae in segment containing testes   2

2. Small (usually < 20 mm long), may have eyespots; often trailing a short chain of zooids. Pectinate chaetae rarely occur. Where present, gonads and related structures in two adjacent segments within the region IV–VIII (Fig. 6.28d)   *2. Naididae*

   Littoral and estuarine species usually longer than 20 mm, reddish (but offshore and meiobenthic ones much smaller, white); no eyespots, never with chain of zooids. Pectinate chaetae often present dorsally, with hair chaetae; otherwise hairs and simple-pointed chaetae dorsally in posterior segments or chaetae all bifid. Gonads and related structures in segments X and XI (Fig. 6.28f)   *3. Tubificidae*

I ENCHYTRAEIDAE

Predominantly terrestrial ('pot worms'). Many of the marine species are small and whitish, but transparent enough for internal structures to be seen under the microscope. Dorsal and ventral chaetae usually the same (Fig. 6.29c): sigmoid or straight, simple pointed or, rarely, bifid. They may occasionally be reduced in number or absent. The upper bundle is, in fact, normally located mid-laterally (Fig. 6.28b) but its chaetae are referred to as 'dorsal' for the sake of consistency. Paired salivary glands ('peptonephridia'), attached to the pharynx where it joins the oesophagus and extending rearwards free in the body cavity (Fig. 6.29m), of characteristic form but sometimes contracted or hard to see. Testes in segment XI, ovaries and male pores in XII, spermathecae in V; penial pulbs may be present but no penis or genital chaetae. Paired roundish glands, usually on the septa between IV–V, V–VI, and VI–VII (Fig. 6.29m), may be important in identification in some genera, although not used here.

Enchytraeus

Dorsal and ventral chaetae throughout the body, all straight. No dorsal pores. Peptonephridia unbranched. Spermathecae simple, the duct usually surrounded by small glands.

Enchytraeus albidus Henle

Medium to large (30–35 mm long), with 46–65 segments. Spermathecal duct long, thin, covered by a layer of glands (Fig. 6.29m). Recorded from Scotland and Ireland in decaying seaweed; cosmopolitan.

Enchytraeus buchholzi Vejdorsky

Small (5–10 mm long), with 24–40 segments. Spermathecal duct short, with a dense covering of glands which may appear as a rosette at its external aperture when contracted.

Recorded from Ireland; widely distributed, possibly cosmopolitan.

Enchytraeus capitatus Bülow

Medium (15–20 mm long), with 50–54 segments. Spermathecal duct short, with a small but distinct gland at its external aperture.

British records from storm beaches and sand-dunes, Ireland.

Enchytraeus minutus Nielsen and Christensen

Very small, with 26–27 segments. Spermathecal duct long, encased in fused glands (Fig. 6.29l).

Recorded from North Wales; widely distributed in Europe.

Fridericia

Dorsal and ventral chaetae throughout the body, all straight. Where numerous, they are arranged in pairs in each bundle, the central pair shorter than those flanking it (Fig. 6.28h); if there are only two, they are of equal length. The number per bundle in segments anterior to the clitellum varies little in a given species and is a good character. Dorsal pores present in all segments from about VII. Peptonephridia present, in various forms. Spermathecal bulb may have diverticula, its duct often having glands at the external aperture. *Distichopus* probably has priority as the name of this genus, but has been used by few authors.

Fridericia callosa (Eisen)

Worm 10–22 mm long, with 46–50 segments. Four chaetae per bundle (most anteriorly, six). Peptonephridia with three to six branches. Spermathecae without diverticula.

Recorded from North Wales and Ireland (also Siberia, Scandinavia, and the Baltic).

Fridericia paroniana Issel

Worm 8–12 mm long, usually with 38–45 segments. Two (rarely four) chaetae per bundle. Peptonephridia unbranched or with only one or two subterminal branches (as Fig. 6.29i). Two spermathecal diverticula (as Fig. 6.29n).

Recorded from Ireland (also north Europe and Italy).

Fridericia perrieri (Vejdovsky)

Worm 10–25 mm long, usually with 42–50 segments, four to eight (usually six) chaetae per bundle. Peptonephridia much branched (as Fig. 6.29k). Two spermathecal diverticula (Fig. 6.29n).

Recorded from North Wales (also Iceland, Scandinavia, Europe, East Africa).

Fridericia ratzeli (Eisen)

Worm 30–35 mm long, usually with 51–60 segments, five to eight chaetae per bundle. Peptonephridia much branched. About six to eight spermathecal diverticula (Fig. 6.29o).

Recorded from Ireland; widely distributed in Europe.

Fridericia striata (Levinsen)

Worm 10–20 mm long, usually 48–55 segments; six to eight chaetae per bundle. Peptonephridia much branched. Spermathecae without diverticula.

Recorded from North Wales (also North Europe, the Baltic, Italy).

Grania

Nematode-like worms. Chaetae single, stout, with a broad curved root-end resembling a hockey-stick (Fig. 6.29f); absent anteriorly and may be completely absent dorsally. Peptonephridia may be present or absent. Short spermathecal duct, lacking glands.

Grania maricola Southern

With 54–62 segments. Dorsal chaetae from XXIII/XXV, ventral chaetae from VI.

Recorded from Ireland, sublittoral.

Lumbricillus

Dorsal and ventral chaetae throughout the body, mostly sigmoid. Dorsal pores and peptonephridia absent. Spermathecae simple, with prominent glands usually at the external aperture of the

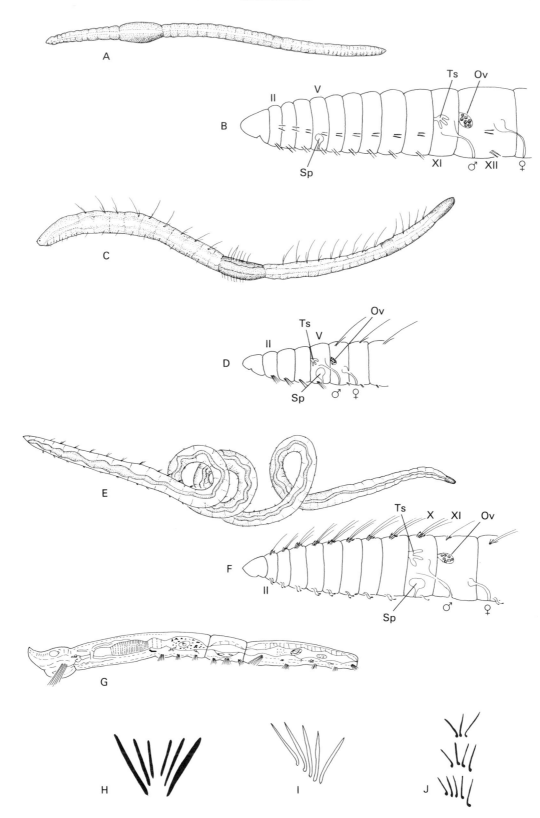

Fig. 6.28 (MARINE OLIGOCHAETA) a. Enchytraeid worm (entire) b. Enchytraeid worm (diagrammatic, to show reproductive structures and chaetae: Ov = ovary, Sp = spermatheca, Ts = testis, ♂ = male pore, ♀ = female pore; roman numbers indicate segments from peristomium as I) c. Naid worm (entire) d. Naid worm (diagrammatic, as b) e. Tubificid worm (entire) f. Tubificid worm (diagrammatic, as b) g. *Chaetogaster* sp., showing a chain of three individuals (after Grassé) h. *Fridericia* sp., chaetal bundle i. *Lumbricillus pagenstecheri*, chaetal bundle j. *Marionina spicula*, three anterior bundles (after Nielsen & Christensen)

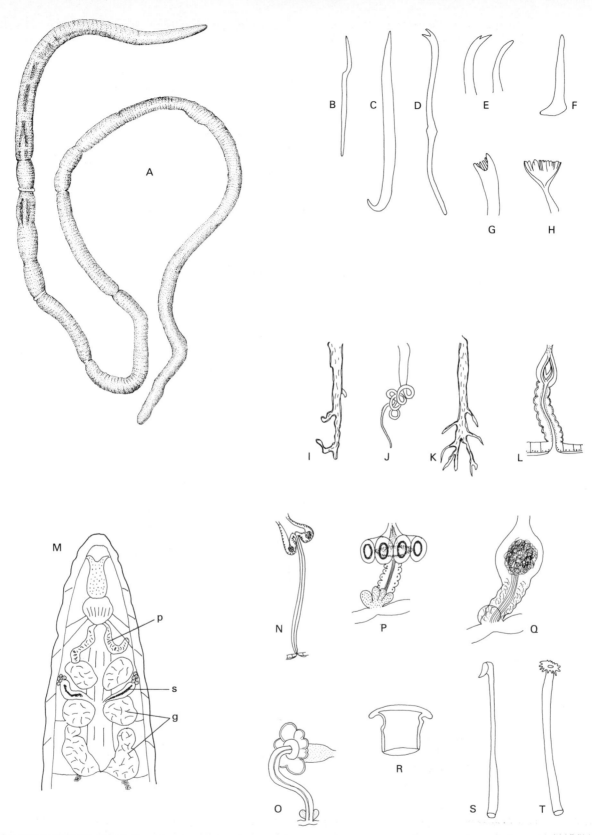

Fig. 6.29 (MARINE OLIGOCHAETA 2) a. *Tubificoides benedeni,* entire worm (after Brinkhurst) b. 'needle' chaeta of Naididae c. simple-pointed chaeta, slightly sigmoid (*Lumbricillus*—note hooked root-end) d. strongly bifid chaeta with nodulus (Naididae) e. weakly bifid and blunt-ended chaetae of *Chaetogaster* f. 'hockey-stick' chaeta of *Grania* g. pectinate chaeta (Tubificidae) h. palmate chaeta (*Tubifex costatus,* after Brinkhurst & Jamieson) i. stout, subterminally branched peptonephridium j. smooth, coiled peptonephridium k. multi-branched peptonephridium (i–k after Nielsen & Christensen) l. spermatheca of *Enchytraeus minutus* (after Brinkhurst) m. anterior end of *E. albidus,* showing septal glands (G), peptonephridium (P) and spermatheca (S) (after Nielsen & Christensen) n. spermatheca of *Fridericia perrieri* (after Brinkhurst) o. spermatheca of *F. ratzeli* p. spermatheca of *Marionina southerni* q. spermatheca of *M. spicula* (o–q after Nielsen and Christensen) r. penis-sheath of *Tubifex costatus* s. penis-sheath of *Linodrilus hoffmeisteri* (typical form, after Brinkhurst) t. penis-sheath of *L. hoffmeisteri* (flat-topped form, after Brinkhurst and Jamieson)

duct and sometimes also along it. Individual species are difficult to separate positively (this requires a mature specimen with sperm in the spermathecae) but details given below for the British species listed by Brinkhurst (1982) may enable a crude provisional identification to be made. Colour may be lost or modified in preserved specimens; numbers represent chaetae per anterior bundle, dorsal and ventral; British records are very patchy, given that lumbricillids have been widely recorded from elsewhere in Europe and from north-east America. Many are probably cosmopolitan.

1. Small (2–9 mm long), with about 25–30 segments.
    (a) White: *L. christenseni* Tynen and *L. knollneri* Nielsen and Christensen—chaetae straight, 2/2 in both; North Wales.
    (b) Reddish: *L. pumilio* Stephenson—chaetae sigmoid, 4–6/5–8; south-west England.
    (c) Orange: *L. scoticus* Elmhurst and Stephenson—chaetae sigmoid, 6–8/10–14; Scotland, North Wales, south-west England, Ireland.

2. Medium (10–18 mm long), with about 35–45 segments.
    (a) White: *L. dubius* (Stephenson)—chaetae straight, 2/2; Scotland.
        L. tuba Stephenson—chaetae slightly sigmoid, 2–4/3–5; Scotland, North Wales.
        L. helgolandicus (Michaelsen)—chaetae sigmoid, 3–6/5–7; North Wales.
        L. kaloensis Nielsen and Christensen (may be slightly reddish)—chaetae sigmoid, 3–6/4–7; North Wales, Ireland.
    (b) Reddish: *L. bulowi* Nielsen and Christensen—chaetae more or less straight, 2–3/2–3; North Wales, Ireland.
        L. arenarius (Michaelsen)—chaetae slightly sigmoid, 2–3/2–3; North Wales, Ireland.
        L. lineatus (O. F. Müller) (strong red)—chaetae sigmoid, 4–6/6–8; Scotland, North Wales, Ireland.
        L. semifuscus (Claparède) (bright red)—chaetae sigmoid, 2–7+/2–7+; Scotland, Ireland.
    (c) Yellow/brown: *L. pagenstecheri* (Ratzel)—chaetae slightly sigmoid, 4–6/5–7 (Fig. 6.28i): north-west England, North Wales, Ireland.
    (d) Black: *L. niger* Southern—chaetae sigmoid, 4–6/5–7; North Wales, Ireland.

3. Large (20–35 mm long), with about 40–65 segments.
    (a) Pink-grey: *L. reynoldsoni* Backlund—chaetae slightly sigmoid, 5–7/6–9; North Wales.
    (b) Red: *L. rivalis* Levinsen (colour intense in life)—chaetae sigmoid, 6–9/7–12; Scotland, Wales, Isle of Man, Ireland.
    (c) Green: *L. viridis* Stephenson—chaetae slightly sigmoid, 3/5–9; Scotland, North Wales, Ireland.

Marionina

Chaetae mostly straight; may be missing from certain segments, larger regions or occasionally the whole worm. Dorsal pores and peptonephridia absent. Spermathecal glands usually present along the duct, at its external aperture or both. Arrangement of septal glands may help identification of species: they are illustrated by Brinkhurst (1982) as 'pharyngeal glands'. Numerous species have been recorded from Scandinavia and elsewhere in northern Europe, some also from North America, but British records have been quite sparse.

Marionina appendiculata Nielsen
Worm 5–7 mm long, with about 28 segments. Chaetae throughout the body: sigmoid, arranged fanwise in bundles containing two to five (usually four except immediately anterior and posterior to the clitellum, where there are two). Spermathecal duct covered with an irregular glandular coating which may be difficult to see in a living worm.

Recorded from North Wales and south-east Ireland, likely to occur elsewhere in Britain on rocky shores.

Marionina preclitellochaeta Nielsen and Christensen
No dorsal chaetae, ventral chaetae in segments II–VI only. Spermathecal duct surrounded by glands at its external aperture.

Recorded from south-east Ireland but probably widespread in Britain.

Marionina sjaelandica Nielsen and Christensen
Chaetae throughout the body, two (rarely three) per bundle. Spermathecal duct covered with distinct small glands and surrounded by larger ones at its external aperture.

Recorded from North Wales.

Marionina southerni (Cernosvitov)
Worm 8–10 mm long, with 28–36 segments. Intensely white anteriorly, more translucent posteriorly. Chaetae throughout body (two per bundle) except dorsally on segment II (occasionally III) where they are missing. Diverticula surround the spermathecal bulb (Fig. 6.29p); the duct short, covered with small glands and surrounded by larger ones at its external aperture.

Recorded from south-west Scotland and North Wales.

Marionina spicula (Leuckart)
Worm 4–5 mm long, with 27–30 segments. Chaetae throughout body, usually three per anterior bundle, two or three per posterior one dorsally; four per anterior bundle, two or three per posterior one ventrally (Fig. 6.28j). Spermathecal duct covered by closely packed glands and with a larger one at its external aperture (Fig. 6.29q).

Recorded from North Wales.

Marionina subterranea (Knöllner)
About 6 mm long, with about 26 segments. Chaetae absent dorsally (bundles replaced by small swellings) but throughout the body ventrally, where each bundle contains two chaetae (rarely, a single one) with hooked root-ends. A rosette of glands surrounds the spermathecal duct at its external aperture.

Recorded from North Wales.

2 NAIDIDAE

Some freshwater species have a proboscis or gills; several bear eye-spots. Small, delicate, often transparent worms with chaetae of diverse form (Fig. 6.28c). Dorsally, these may be totally absent or, in many genera, missing from the first five or six segments; where present, they are usually long hair-chaetae and short needles (Fig. 6.29b). Ventral chaetae in these segments may be quite different from those further back but, in ventral bundles generally, chaetae are mostly bifid crochets with nodulus (Fig. 6.29d). Most reproduce asexually by pygidial budding, producing short chains of individuals; where gonads are (rarely) present, they occupy a more anterior position than in the tubificids (Fig. 6.28d). No penis, but penial chaetae may be present. Naidids found in estuaries are mostly freshwater forms capable of withstanding local or short-term saline intrusion; the few truly marine species are mainly epibenthic, often swim actively and do not extend far offshore.

Amphichaeta sannio Kallstenius

Small worm, found intertidally and sublittorally in brackish water. Mature specimens 1.5–1.7 mm long, with 13–14 segments; often in chains up to 4 mm long. Eyespots may be present on the well-developed prostomium. All chaetae are bifid, **beginning dorsally on segment III** (ventrally from II).

Europe (recorded in Britain from the Firth of Forth); west Pacific.

Chaetogaster

Worms of brackish water with a short, plump body **lacking dorsal chaetae** and eyes (Fig. 6.28g). A fan-like bundle of chaetae longer than the rest is inserted ventrally to each side of the mouth (on segment II); these, like the other ventral chaetae, are stout and bifid (Fig. 6.29e). Segment III is elongated. The anterior part of the worm is very contractile and is used in 'looping' locomotion, the rest of the body catching up by wriggling across the mud surface.

Carnivorous, taking small animals as well as ingesting algae and detritus.

Chaetogaster diaphanus Gruithhuisen

Worms 2.5–25 mm long, 14–15 segments.

Europe (including Britain and the Baltic), Asia, North America.

Chaetogaster langi Bretscher

Worm 0.9–2 mm long, 8–21 segments.

Europe (including Britain and the Baltic), Asia, Africa, North and South America.

Paranais litoralis (O. F. Müller)

Slender worm, living in intertidal and sublittoral mud both in brackish water and fully marine conditions; 9–14 mm long in life (much shorter when preserved) with 13–14 segments. No eyes, no nephridia. All chaetae are bifid, **beginning dorsally on segment V** (ventrally on II, where they are slightly larger and more numerous).

Europe (recorded in Britain from the Firth of Forth and the estuaries of the Tees and Clyde), north-east America, west Africa, Indian Ocean.

3 TUBIFICIDAE

Medium-sized reddish worms ('sludge worms' Fig. 6.28e) or very small white ones. Dorsal and ventral chaetae are of different forms unless all are bifid; crochets and hair-chaetae also occur. Testes and spermathecae are normally in segment X, ovaries and male organs in segment XI (Fig. 6.28f). Chitinous penis-sheaths usually present (Fig. 6.29r–t); there are often specialized genital chaetae. Asexual reproduction may occur by fragmentation (producing atypical worms regenerating missing sections) but not by budding. The larger species are usually littoral, living in muddy sediments surrounded by decaying organic material and able to withstand high levels of such pollution; when irritated, they tend to coil spirally. Small ones are mostly meiobenthic and have been recorded well offshore.

Clitellio arenarius (O. F. Müller)

Slender worm, 20–65 mm long, with 64–120 segments. Chaetae few (two to three per bundle anteriorly, one or two posteriorly), weakly bifid, absent ventrally from segment XI; sometimes only a single, larger one in ventral bundles on X and XII. Penis sheaths lacking, no prostate glands. Commonly found on the lower shore and in estuaries with *Tubificoides benedeni* (from which it is easily distinguished by its smooth cuticle).

Limnodrilus hoffmeisteri Claparède

The commonest and most widely distributed aquatic oligochaete, essentially a freshwater species but tolerant of saline conditions. Length 20–35 mm, with 55–95 segments. Chaetae all bifid, about seven in each anterior bundle but becoming fewer posteriorly. Penis sheaths long, narrow cylinders with a proximal flange sometimes having a scalloped edge, sometimes hood-like (Fig. 6.29s,t).

Cosmopolitan

Tubifex costatus (Claparède)

About 16 mm long, with 40 segments. Dorsal chaetae pectinate in anterior bundles (Fig. 6.29g), clearly bifid in posterior ones; between these (about segments V–XIV), they are palmate (i.e. very broadly pectinate, Fig. 6.29h) and numerous (7–11 per bundle). Ventral chaetae bifid. Penis sheaths short and tub-shaped (Fig. 6.29r).

In brackish waters all over Europe (scattered records from Britain).

Tubificoides (= Peloscolex) benedeni (Udekem)

Slender worm readily identified by its **papillated cuticle** covered with sediment particles; 15–55 mm long, with up to 100 segments (Fig. 6.29a). All chaetae either weakly bifid or simple-pointed (occasionally, short hair-chaetae in some bundles of small specimens). Penis sheaths cylindrical, with a rounded flange proximally and a recurved distal end (cannot be seen in a whole mount).

Commonly found with *Clitellio arenarius*; on the lower shore and sublittorally in sediments, from estuaries to some distance offshore.

Europe (recorded from major estuaries all around Britain), north-east America.

Tubificoides pseudogaster (Dahl)

Similar to *T. benedeni* but with a **smooth cuticle**; 8–22 mm long, with up to 75 segments. Dorsal bundles contain pectinate chaetae (Fig. 6.29g) and hair-chaetae; ventral clearly bifid. Penis sheaths resembling an elongated conical funnel, opening laterally at its distal end. Sublittoral, in brackish and marine waters.

Europe (recorded in Britain from the Firth of Forth and the estuaries of the Tees and Clyde), north-east America.

C. Class **Hirudinea**

Leeches are highly evolved annelids, with some cephalization, a constant number of segments, and a sucker at each end, used in 'geometrid' locomotion. They may be grouped with oligochaetes in the Clitellata, being hermaphrodite, with direct development within a cocoon secreted by a glandular girdle, the clitellum. All temperate marine leeches are Piscicolidae and they comprise more than half of that family. They lack jaws but have a protrusible pharynx and are thus Rhynchobdellida. They differ from other rhynchobdellids (the Glossiphoniidae, confined to freshwater) chiefly in having more conspicuous oral suckers, being blood-sucking rather than predatory. All known British species feed on fishes, occasionally leaving them to attach cocoons to rocks, shells, etc. Some occupy characteristic positions on their hosts (e.g. *Hemibdella* on *Solea* and *Sanguinothus* on *Taurulus*), but others are less specific. *Myoxocephalus scorpii* is attacked by at least four small species of leeches, which look rather similar but are placed in different genera.

The anterior part of a piscicolid (the *trachelosome*) consists of the *head* (= six fused segments), plus three *praeclitellar* and three *clitellar segments*. Its hind margin may be marked by a *clitellar constriction*. The rest of the body (the abdomen) has six *testicular*, six *caecal*, and three *anal segments*. The drawing of *Hemibdella* shows the gonads (lying intersegmentally) which characterize the testicular region. There are often only five pairs of testes, leaving more room for the ovary in the anterior part of that region. Between adjacent pairs of testes the gut may give off a succession of *segmental caeca*, which are easily seen during life in freshly collected specimens of transparent species (see drawings of *Oceanobdella*), because they are filled with red blood. Behind the testicular region there is a pair of particularly large caeca ('*postcaeca*'), which extend posteriorly almost to the anus. These may remain separate, or may fuse below the intestine to form a single *ventral caecum*. Fusion may be incomplete, leaving segmental fenestrae, through which muscles run dorso-ventrally.

Leeches should be examined whilst alive, for then the tissues may be transparent, revealing eyes (e.g. on fore sucker), spots (black spots—'ocelli' may occur on the hind sucker) and other markings which may not be visible after death. Some leeches have *pulsatile vesicles* segmentally arranged along each side of the abdomen. *Brumptiana* has these on all twelve segments of the testicular and caecal regions. *Branchellion*, *Calliobdella*, *Piscicola*, and *Trachelobdella* generally have them on the first eleven of those segments. From such external clues to segmentation there are obviously three annuli per mid-body somite in *Branchellion*, four in *Pontobdella*, six in most *Calliobdella*, and thirteen or fourteen in *Brumptiana*. Without segmental markings annulation is difficult to determine, but the testes can be seen after clearing (e.g. in cedar wood oil) and their centres mark the boundaries of somites, as shown in the drawing of *Heptacyclus*. Some leeches, however, would be difficult to identify or describe adequately without a complete series of transverse sections. Good sections are obtained after narcotizing with menthol and fixing in sea-water Bouin. For fixation the specimen should be laid out flat and straight, but not compressed unnaturally.

Taxonomically useful internal characters include the coelomic and genital systems. The former may include dorsal, ventral, lateral, and transverse lacunae linked with pulsatile vesicles. Genera that have a large male bursa may extrude it during coitus or fixation (figured here in *Platybdella*).

LITERATURE

Beneden, P. J. Van and Hesse, C. E. (1863). Recherches sur les Bdellodes et les Trematodes Marins. *Mémoires de l'Academie royale de Belgique*, **34**, 11–450.

Bennicke, S. A. B. and Bruun, A. F. (1939). *Pterobdellina jenseni*, a new ichthyobdellid. *Videnskabelige Meddelelser fra Dansk naturhistorisk Forening i Kjøbenhavn*, **103**, 517–21.

Brumpt, E. (1900). Reproduction des Hirudinées. Formation du cocoon chez *Pisciola* et *Herpobdella*. *Bulletin de la Société zoologique de France*, **25**, 47–51.

de Silva, P. H. D. H. and Burdon-Jones, C. (1961). A new genus and species of leech parasitic on the fish *Cottus bubalis*. *Proceedings of the Zoological Society of London*, **136**, 343–57.

Gibson, R. N. and Tong, L. J. (1969). Biology of the marine leech *Oceanobdella blennii*. *Journal of the Marine Biological Association of the U.K.*, **49**, 433–8.

Harding, W. A. (1910). A revision of the British leeches. *Parasitology*, **3**, 130–200.

Herter, K. (1935). Hirudinea. *Tierwelt der Nord – und Ostsee*, **29** (6c), 45–106.

Khan, R. A. and Meyer, M. C. (1976). Taxonomy and biology of some Newfoundland marine leeches. *Journal of the Fisheries Research Board of Canada*, **33**, 1699–714.

Knight-Jones, E. W. (1940). Occurrence of a marine leech *Abranchus blennii* n. sp. *Journal of the Marine Biological Association of the U.K.*, **24**, 533–41.

Leigh-Sharpe, W. H. (1914). *Calliobdella lophii*. *Parasitology*, **7**, 204–18.

Leigh-Sharpe, W. H. (1915). *Ganymedes cratere* n.g. et. sp. *Parasitology*, **8**, 1–10.

Leigh-Sharpe, W. H. (1916). *Platybdella anarrhichae*. *Parasitology*, **8**, 274–93.

Leigh-Sharpe, W. H. (1917). *Calliobdella nodulifera* Malm. *Proceedings of the Royal Physical Society, Edinburgh*, **20**, 118–22.

Leigh-Sharpe, W. H. (1933). Hirudinea of Plymouth. *Parisitology*, **25**, 255–62.

Llewellyn, L. C. (1965). Biology of the marine leech *Hemibdella soleae*. *Proceedings of the Zoological Society of London*, **145**, 509–28.

Llewellyn, L. C. (1966). Pontobdellinae in the British Museum. *Bulletin of the British Museum (Natural History) Zoology*, **14**(7), 391–439.

Llewellyn, L. C. and Knight-Jones, E. W. (1984). A new genus and species of marine leech. *Journal of the Marine Biological Association of the U.K.*, **64**, 919–34.

Sawyer, R. T. (1970). Juvenile anatomy and post-hatching development of *Oceanobdella blennii*. *Journal of Natural History*, **4**, 175–88.

Sawyer, R. T. (1985). *Leech biology and behaviour*. Clarendon Press, Oxford.

Srivastava, L. P. (1966). Three new leeches from Cottidae in British waters. *Journal of Zoology, London*, **150**, 297–318.

1 PISCICOLIDAE

Body usually more or less divided into trachelosome and abdomen. Both suckers usually cup-shaped.

---

1. Body with many conspicuous branchiae or tubercles **2**

   Body smooth or with a single fin or row of small vesicles on each side **5**

2. Body with leaf-like branchiae in a row along each side *Branchellion* **3**

   Body bears numerous tubercles *Pontobdella* **4**

3. Branchiae 31 pairs. Fore sucker two-thirds diameter of hind sucker *Branchellion borealis*

   Branchiae 33 pairs. Fore sucker half diameter of hind sucker *Branchellion torpedinis*

4. Fore sucker much wider than trachelosome. No tubercles in ventral mid-line *Pontobdella muricata*

   Fore sucker not much wider than trachelosome. Annulus with largest tubercles in each segment bears an unpaired tubercle mid-ventrally *Pontobdella vosmaeri*

5. Body with flattened fin along each side *Pterobdellina jenseni*

   Body without lateral fins **6**

6. Hind sucker about same width as hind end of body **7**

   Hind sucker much wider than hind end of body **8**

7. Fore sucker very large, nearly as wide as short flattened abdomen *Ganymedebdella cratere*

   Both suckers very small. Attached to spine on scale of *Solea vulgaris* *Hemibdella soleae*

8. With a row of 11–13 pulsatile vesicles along each side of body **9**

   Pulsatile vesicles absent or indistinguishable **14**

9. Abdomen broad, somewhat flattened and very distinct from narrow trachelosome. Suckers narrower than abdomen. Trachelosome bears four pairs of dorsolateral vesicles. In abdomen the four anterior pairs of vesicles are lateral or ventrolateral, the remainder are dorsolateral *Trachelobdella lubrica*

   Abdomen cylindrical or, if flattened, bearing a large hind sucker. Vesicles confined to abdomen and all lateral in position **10**

10. Fore sucker often with cross of pigment. Four eyes, often crescentic. Abdomen with transverse pigment bands. Hind sucker with 14 radiating pigment bands and a paramarginal ring of 14 black spots (ocelli). Fresh or brackish water *Piscicola geometra*

    Fore sucker without pigment cross. Eyes round, four or absent. Abdomen without transverse bands. Hind sucker without black spots. Marine **11**

11. Eyes four. Annuli thirteen or fourteen between successive vesicles. Hind sucker no wider than body. Abdomen with longitudinal streaks of pigment dorsally and a pair of small red spots associated with each pulsatile vesicle *Brumptiana lineata*

    Eyes four or absent. Annuli three or six between successive vesicles. Hind sucker wider than body **12**

12. Eyes four. Length about 20 mm. On shore fishes, e.g. *Taurulus* at Roscoff *Calliobdella punctata*

    Eyes absent. Length 25 mm. Sublittoral **13**

13. Length 25–50 mm. Hindsucker three or four times breadth of fore sucker. Abdomen swollen and trachelosome well-defined. On *Lophius piscatorius* *Calliobdella lophii*

    Length c. 30 mm. Hind sucker twice breadth of fore sucker. Abdomen rounded and trachelosome ill-defined *Calliobdella nodulifera*

14. Annuli seven (fourteen) per mid-body somite *Heptacyclus myoxocephali*

    Annuli two or three (six) per mid-body somite **15**

15. Annuli two per somite. Eyes four, each made up of several black spots *Janusion scorpii*

    Annuli three (six) per somite. If eyes are present, each is a simple, rounded or crescentic spot of pigment **16**

16. Hind sucker compressed laterally and capable of folding round a fin-ray. Body uniformly reddish, but with a narrow white band adjoining hind sucker. On *Taurulus bubalis* fins *Sanguinothus pinnarum*

    Hind sucker circular in outline **17**

17. Eyes absent. No ocelli on hind sucker. Male bursa large and thick-walled, resembling a penis when everted. Postcaeca fused for most of their length, with four fenestrae. On gills of *Anarrhichas lupus*
Platybdella anarrhichae

Eyes six or four. Paramarginal ocelli usually present on posterior sucker. Male bursa short and thin-walled, forming only a slight prominence even when everted. Postcaeca fused in not more than one or two places, often completely separate   **18**

18. Fore sucker inconspicuous, less than half width of hind sucker. Skin mostly transparent. Clitellar constriction separates trachelosome from abdomen
Oceanobdella **19**

Fore sucker discoid, at least half width of hind sucker. Skin opaque and pigmented. Clitellum not constricted, so trachelosome merges with abdomen
Malmiana **21**

19. Usually attached below head of Cottidae. Body unpigmented   ***Oceanobdella microstoma***

Usually attached behind pectoral fin of Blenniidae. Body with transverse stripes   **20**

20. On *Blennius pholis*   ***Oceanobdella blennii***

On *Zoarces* (and *Centronotus*?)   ***Oceanobdella sexoculata***

21. Six eyes. Hind sucker twice fore sucker diameter, without paramarginal ocelli   ***Malmiana bubali***

Four eyes. Hind sucker one and a half times fore sucker, with a paramarginal ring of 14 ocelli
Malmiana yorki

Branchellion borealis Leigh-Sharpe   FIG. 6.30
[Leigh-Sharpe 1933: 258]

Genus has each pair of branchiae arising from an annulus, and from the pulsatile vesicles wherever those occur, but this species has the first pair of vesicles lacking branchiae, which total only 31 pairs. Fore sucker bears light spots, in two semicircles of five and four, and is two-thirds width of hind sucker. Body length about 30 mm. Central annulus in each of the four anterior segments of trachelosome bears a row of four small warts dorsally.

On Rajidae. South-west Britain.

Branchellion torpedinis Savigny   FIG. 6.30
[HARDING 1910: 134]

Branchiae 33 pairs, the first arising from the anterior pulsatile vesicles. Fore sucker bears six eyes in a curved line, and is about half width of hind sucker. Body about 40 mm long. Central annulus in each segment of abdomen bears six light spots dorsally and four ventrally.

On Rajidae and occasionally teleosts. South-west Britain, Mediterranean, and West Africa.

Brumptiana lineata Llewellyn and Knight-Jones FIG. 6.30
[LLEWELLYN and KNIGHT-JONES 1984: 920]

Fore sucker bears two pairs rounded eyes, four white patches with posterior streaks and two white spots. Hind sucker large (fore/hind ratio 2:3), but no wider than abdomen, bearing 14 radiating markings but no ocelli. Body nearly 10 mm long, pale brown. Abdomen with dark pigment forming seven longitudinal lines dorsally. Pulsatile vesicles (12 pairs) each flanked by two red specks. Pairs 4, 6, 8, and 10 are white and there are similar white spots on the trachelosome (two pairs), flanked by red specks. Enlarged side-views show annulation and a spermatophore protruding from male aperture.

In mouth and nose of *Raja*. South-west Britain.

Calliobdella lophii Beneden and Hesse   FIG. 6.30
[LEIGH-SHARPE 1914: 206]

Length 50 mm. Both suckers large (fore/hind ratio 1:4). Without eyes or ocelli. Orange ring girdles body near genital apertures. Bursa eversible, to form penis. Abdomen somewhat flattened and wide, but less so than discoid hind sucker. Pulsatile vesicles 11 pairs. Annuli six per mid-body somite.

Ventro-laterally on *Lophius*. Norway to Mediterranean.

Calliobdella nodulifera (Malm)   FIG. 6.30
[LEIGH-SHARPE 1917: 118]

Like *C. lophii*, but smaller, fore/hind sucker ratio 1:2 and abdomen thinner, more cylindrical and merging into trachelosome imperceptibly.

Externally on a variety of fishes, especially gadoids. Iceland, Norway, Scotland.

Calliobdella punctata Beneden and Hesse
[BENEDEN and HESS 1863: 37]

Length 20 mm. Fore sucker, with white spots and two pairs of eyes, about two-thirds width of hind sucker, both suckers oval and relatively small. Body rust-coloured dorsally, lightly speckled with black, paler and pink ventrally; cylindrical and thin (breadth/length ratio 1:30), with a slight constriction near the genital apertures. Description incomplete. Pulsatile vesicles 14 or 15 pairs?

On *Taurulus*. Brittany. Probably absent from mainland Britain, but *Trypanosoma cotti*, of which it is the vector, infects *Taurulus* on Isles of Scilly.

Ganymedebdella cratere (Leigh-Sharpe)   FIG. 6.30
[LEIGH-SHARPE 1915: 4]

Length 8 mm. Fore sucker bowl-shaped, as wide as body (3 or 4 mm) and five times width of the small terminal hind sucker. Abdomen flattened and broadened, with three pairs of pulsatile vesicles. Postcaeca separate.

On a fish 'with a pronounced anal papilla'. Only one found? South Ronaldsway, Orkney.

Hemibdella soleae (Beneden and Hesse)   FIG. 6.30
[LLEWELLYN 1965: 515]

Length 10 mm. Both suckers small and terminal. No eyes. Body

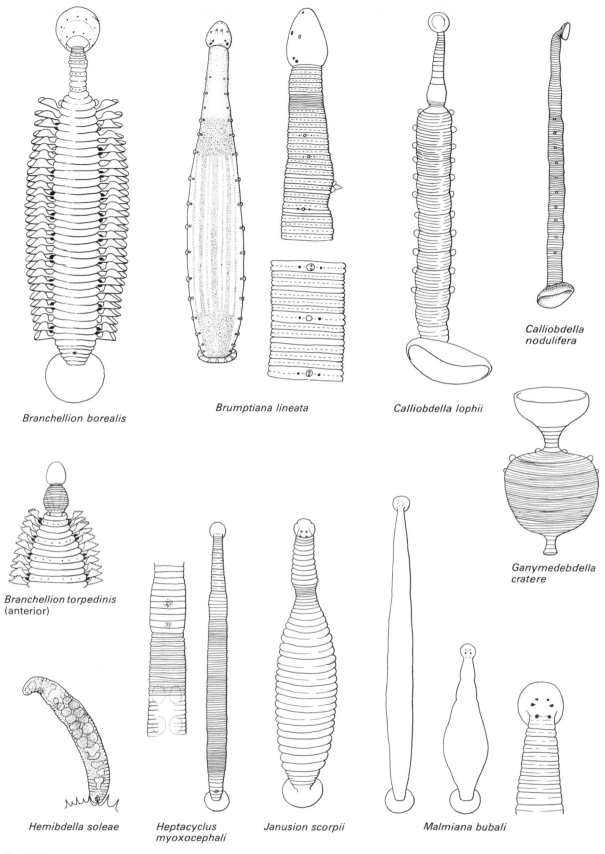

Branchellion borealis

Brumptiana lineata

Calliobdella lophii

Calliobdella
nodulifera

Ganymedebdella
cratere

Branchellion torpedinis
(anterior)

Hemibdella soleae

Heptacyclus
myoxocephali

Janusion scorpii

Malmiana bubali

Fig. 6.30

cylindrical. Annuli 12 per mid-body somite. Bursa large and protrusible. Coelom typical, but without vesicles. Postcaeca fused.

On *Solea vulgaris*, with hind sucker clamped around spine on ctenoid scale, as figured. West Europe and Mediterranean. Abundant off south-west Britain.

Heptacyclus myoxocephali Srivastava FIG. 6.30
[SRIVASTAVA 1966: 312]

Length 13 mm. Both suckers discoid, attached obliquely. Fore/hind sucker ratio 2:3. Body cylindrical. Annuli seven (fourteen) per mid-body somite. Bursa small. Testes five pairs, separated by minor enlargements of crop. Dorsal, ventral, and lateral lacunae, but no transverse communications or vesicles. Postcaecal cavities unfused.

On *Myoxocephalus scorpii*. Millport, Firth of Clyde.

Janusion scorpii (Malm) FIG. 6.30
[LEIGH-SHARPE 1933: 257]

Length 15 mm. Fore/hind sucker ratio 1:2. Eyes four, each composite. Distinct clitellar constriction. Annuli two per mid-body somite. Description incomplete.

On *Myoxocephalus*. Only three found? Plymouth.

Malmiana bubali Srivastava FIG. 6.30
[SRIVASTAVA 1966: 300]

Length 12 mm. Like *Heptacyclus* (see above), but with six eyes, abdomen more flattened (unusually so for *Malmiana* spp.), annuli three (six) per mid-body somite and four pairs of testes, which are separated by crop caeca and by transverse communications linking the dorsal and lateral lacunae.

On *Taurulus*. Only one found? Robin Hood's Bay, Yorkshire.

Malmiana yorki Srivastava FIG. 6.31
[SRIVASTAVA 1966: 308]

Like *M. bubali*, but with four eyes anteriorly, a ring of fourteen paramarginal ocelli on hind sucker, five pairs of testes, sphincter muscles around the crop, and dermal cells more rounded.

On *Taurulus*. Only one found? Scarborough Bay, Yorkshire.

Oceanobdella blennii (Knight-Jones) FIG. 6.31
[KNIGHT-JONES 1940: 535; GIBSON AND TONG 1969: 438; SAWYER 1970: 176]

Length 12 mm. Fore sucker 0.7 mm across when expanded. Eyes six. Hind sucker 1.7 mm, with some paramarginal spots, including one on each side of a mid-dorsal brown stripe. Body flattened when resting, often in sinuous but immobile curves (see small-scale figures), more cylindrical and threadlike when extended, marked in adults by transverse brown segmental stripes. White dermal cells show through transparent epidermis, especially dorso-laterally; so does the crop, with its caeca. Annuli three (six) per mid-body somite. Bursa small. Testes usually five pairs. Transverse communications as in *Malmiana*. Postcaeca usually separate.

On *Blennius pholis*, usually behind pectoral fins or (as unpigmented juveniles) in gill chamber. Locally common from Firth of Forth to Scarborough, and Mull to Crackington Haven (north Cornwall).

Oceanobdella microstoma (Johansson) FIG. 6.31
[KHAN and MEYER 1976: 1710]

Like *O. blennii*, but while resting it does not become so flattened, broadened, or sinuous, and it has a complete circle of about 12 paramarginal ocelli on hind sucker; otherwise lacks pigment, except for numerous creamy bodies seen through the skin (especially dorsally) and red blood in the crop caeca.

Ventrally under head of *Taurulus*, *Myoxocephalus*, and other Cottidae. Occasionally on shore in spring at Plymouth, Anglesey, and St. Andrews. Also west Sweden, Spitzbergen, Iceland, Greenland, Newfoundland, and Maine.

Oceanobdella sexoculata (Malm)
[KHAN and MEYER 1976:1711]

Leeches very like *O. blennii*, but smaller and not so flattened, occur behind pectoral fins of *Centronotus* at St. Andrews and occasionally in Northumberland. If dislodged they reattach to *Centronotus* and not to *Blennius*. Malm's species was from west Sweden, on *Gadus morhua* and *Zoarces*. It had a ring of ocelli on the hind-sucker, with one on each side of a green mid-dorsal stripe. In Scottish material the ring is usually incomplete. Newfoundland material has a complete ring, but each ocellus is in the middle of a radiating dark stripe.

Piscicola geometra (Linnaeus)
[HARDING 1910: 140]

Length 20–50 mm. Eyes four. Fore/hind sucker ratio 1:2. Hind sucker with ring of 14 ocelli, alternating with 14 radiating dark stripes. Annuli 14 per mid-body somite. Pulsatile vesicles 11 pairs. Bursa small, and spermatophores are deposited externally on a ventral copulation area developed posterior to clitellum when breeding (Brumpt 1900).

Holarctic in freshwater, and on *Pleuronectes flesus* and *Myoxocephalus* in Baltic (Herter 1935).

Platybdella anarrhichae (Diesing) FIG. 6.31
[LEIGH-SHARPE 1916:277]

Length 20–30 mm. Suckers discoid, without eyes or ocelli, fore/hind ratio 1:2 or 2:3. Abdomen cylindrical, merging with trachelosome. Annulation three (six) or indeterminate. No pulsatile vesicles, or lateral or segmental lacunae. Bursa large and may be extruded like a penis, as in the figures. Testes five pairs. Postcaeca fused, with five fenestrae. Epidermis lacks the small flask-shaped gland cells present in most Piscicolidae.

On gills and body of *Anarrhichas lupus*. North Sea, Iceland, and Greenland.

Pontobdella muricata (Linnaeus) FIG. 6.31
[LLEWELLYN 1966: 425]

Length 100–200 mm. Fore sucker equal to or much larger than hind, much wider than trachelosome, and with a distinct rim marked off by a groove. Annuli four per mid-body somite, with the main annulus larger than the others and bearing larger

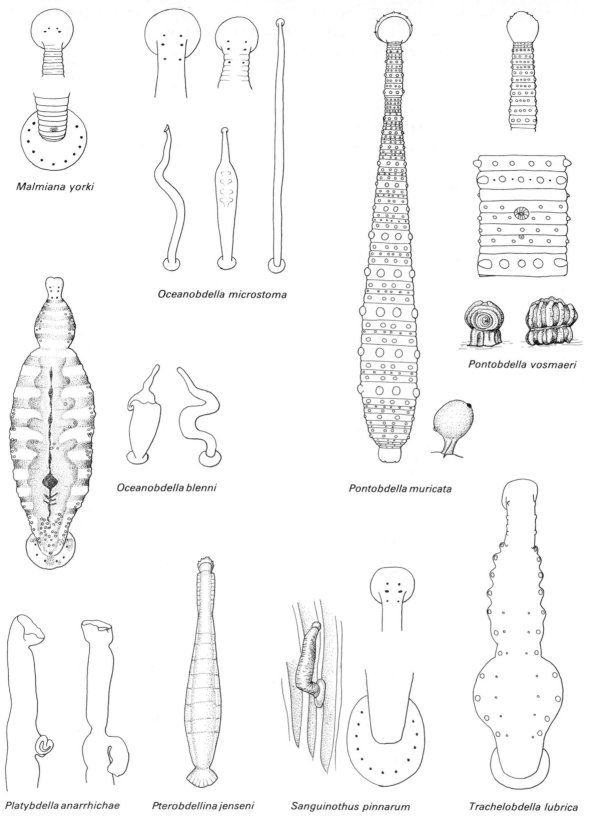

Malmiana yorki

Oceanobdella microstoma

Oceanobdella blenni

Pontobdella vosmaeri

Pontobdella muricata

Platybdella anarrhichae

Pterobdellina jenseni

Sanguinothus pinnarum

Trachelobdella lubrica

Fig. 6.31

tubercles (eight), none of them mid-ventral. Cocoons smooth and subspherical, on stalks (as figured).

On *Raja* and occasionally *Pleuronectes*. North Sea, Mediterranean, Iceland, Greenland.

Pontobdella vosmaeri Apathy   FIG. 6.31
[LLEWELLYN 1966: 427]

Length 80 mm. Like *P. muricata* but fore sucker not much wider than trachelosome, lacking paramarginal groove. Fore/hind ratio 1:2. Main annuli bear four tubercles dorsally and five ventrally, including a mid-ventral tubercle (enlarged drawing shows those near genital pores). Cocoons smaller than those of *P. muricata*, on broad pedestals and banded with corrugations (figured).

On *Raja*. Plymouth, Roscoff, Capri.

Pterobdellina jenseni Bennike and Bruun   FIG. 6.31
[BENNIKE and BRUUN 1939: 518]

Length 27–39 mm. Fore sucker with thickened rim, which bears four to six papillae on each side. Body subcylindrical, with a fin-like membrane along each side. Annulation seven (fourteen). Testes five pairs.

On *Raja*. Off Faeroes, depths > 400 m.

Sanguinothus pinnarum de Silva and   FIG. 6.31
Burdon-Jones
[DE SILVA and BURDON-JONES 1961: 344]

Length 7–12 mm. Hind sucker oval, usually clamped round a fin-ray (as figured). Fore/hind ratio about 1:2, with six eyes and fourteen ocelli respectively. Body uniformly reddish brown, with pale, almost white margins to the suckers and around the body next to the hind sucker. Annulation three (six) but indistinct. Bursa small. Testes five pairs. No pulsatile vesicles and no lateral or segmental lacunae. Postcaeca separate.

On fins of *Taurulus*, especially February to May. Firth of Clyde. Berwick-on-Tweed, West Anglesey.

Trachelobdella lubrica (Grube)   FIG. 6.31
[HERTER 1935: 51]

Genus has a small bursa, thick-walled vagina, flattened and broadened abdomen, eleven pairs of pulsatile vesicles, and a small terminal hind sucker. In this species the latter is radially marked, there are three to four pairs of 'non-pulsatile' vesicles dorso-laterally on the trachelosome, and the first four pairs of vesicles on the abdomen are located less dorsally than subsequent pairs. Length 4–30 mm. Specimen drawn here was from a goby near Naples.

On various teleosts. Mediterranean, west Africa, south Australia, and (doubtfully) North Sea.

7 PRIAPULIDA, SIPUNCULA, ECHIURA, POGONOPHORA, AND ENTOPROCTA

A. PRIAPULIDA

Unsegmented worms with a chitinous *cuticle*, small surface spines and *papillae*, a large body cavity and near-radial symmetry, except for paired gonads and nephridia, and a nerve cord regarded as ventral. The anterior body forms an *introvert*, in which the mouth is central. This is alternately pushed out and withdrawn to burrow, and prey is drawn in and swallowed during withdrawal, having been caught by curved teeth on the everted mouth and pharynx lining. The gut is simple and the anus terminal, except that a few genera have long tails arising ventrally to the anus. These bear many vesicular branches, which contain extensions of the coelom and are thought to be respiratory. Sexes are separate and cleavage radial, producing loricate larvae which stay in the adult environment.

Priapulids live in soft sediments. Only 15 living species are known and only one family occurs in cool seas. The others (Tubiluchidae and Maccabeidae) are meiofaunal, and tropical or Mediterranean so not treated here.

LITERATURE

Fischer, W. (1925). Echiuridae, Sipunculidae, Priapulidae. *Tierwelt der Nord-und Ostsee*, Lief I. Teil VId, 1–55.

Land, J. van der and Nørrevang, A. (1985). Affinities and intraphyletic relationships of the Priapulida. In *The origins and relationships of lower invertebrates* (ed. S. Conway Morris *et al.*). Systematics Association Special Volume **28**, Clarendon Press, Oxford, pp. 261–73.

Shipley, A. E. (1910). Gephyrea. In *Worms, rotifers and polyzoa*. Cambridge natural History Volume **2**, Macmillan, London, pp. 411–49.

I PRIAPULIDAE

Macrobenthic, with sperm of the type associated with external fertilization. Three of the four genera have tails. Two west European species.

1.	Without tail	***Halicryptus spinulosus***
	With tail	***Priapulus caudatus***

Halicryptus spinulosus von Siebold   FIG. 7.1
[SHIPLEY 1910, 433]
Body 20–30 mm long; mouth surrounded by a ring of five main teeth plus some smaller ones; introvert 0.1 of body length, and bears 25 longitudinal ribs; rest of body marked by about 100 rings, covered with small sharp spines.

In mud at depths 4–200 m in Sound and bays east of Denmark; holarctic?

Priapulus caudatus Lamarck   FIG. 7.1
[SHIPLEY 1910, 431]
Length usually 20–75 mm, sometimes more; mouth with seven rings each of five teeth; introvert 0.2–0.3 mm of total length, marked by 25 longitudinal ridges; rest of body with numerous rings, sometimes swelling posteriorly so that base of tail is partially enclosed.

In grey mud, sublittoral and up to mid-shore. Locally common, e.g. in Holyhead harbour, Menai Strait, Solent, Scandinavia; circumarctic; perhaps Antarctic.

B. SIPUNCULA

Unsegmented worms, with an anterior *introvert* which can be withdrawn into the *trunk*. When this is everted, by pressure of coelomic fluid, the *mouth* (m in Fig. 7.2) appears at the end. Dorsal to the mouth is a sensory prominence, the *nuchal organ* (no), which lies over the brain. A *ciliated fringe*, which is often emarginated to form *tentacles*, forms a ring round the mouth and/or a horseshoe round the nuchal organ. Extension of the tentacles involves an independent fluid pressure system powered by one or two *contractile vessels* (cv) which accompany the oesophagus, lying attached to its wall. The gut is long and U-shaped, with the two halves of the U twisted together, often round an axial strand, the *spindle muscle*. The *anus* (a) is dorsal, near the anterior end of the trunk. Two *nephridiopores* (np) open at about the same level, but ventro-laterally. The saclike *nephridia* (n), the dorsal and ventral pairs of *retractor muscles* of the introvert (drm, vrm) and the mid-ventral nerve cord can be seen internally, on opening up the coelom and moving aside the gut-loops; so can the *longitudinal muscle bands* formed in two British species on the inside of the body wall, but usually those body wall muscles form a continuous layer.

Cleavage is radial and some of the larvae resemble trochophores, but the group is isolated. It is remarkably homogeneous, but two classes are recognized.

Class I **Phascolosomatidea**

Tentacles all lie dorsal to mouth, forming a horseshoe round nuchal organ. Spindle muscle attached to body wall posteriorly. Two orders, each with one family.

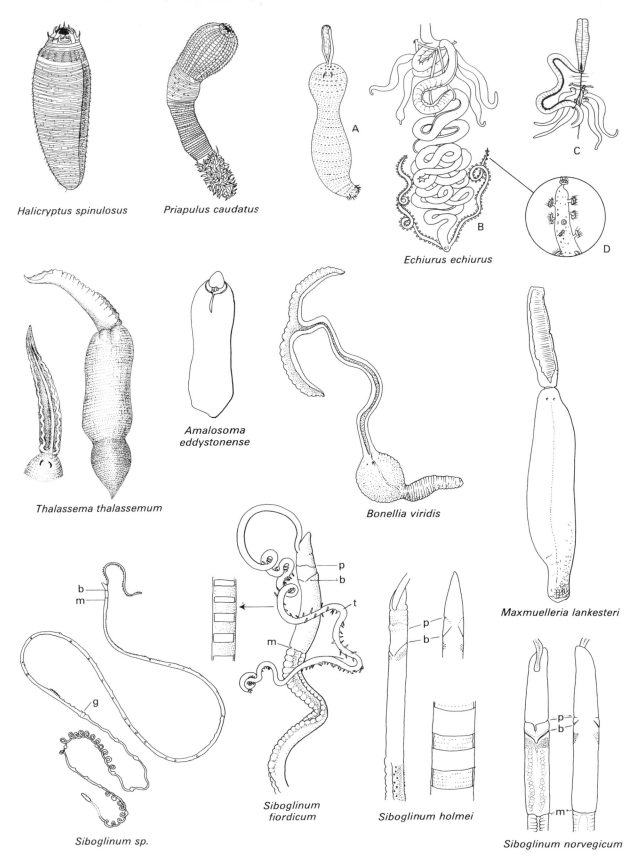

Halicryptus spinulosus

Priapulus caudatus

Echiurus echiurus

Thalassema thalassemum

Amalosoma eddystonense

Bonellia viridis

Maxmuelleria lankesteri

Siboglinum sp.

Siboglinum fiordicum

Siboglinum holmei

Siboglinum norvegicum

Fig. 7.1

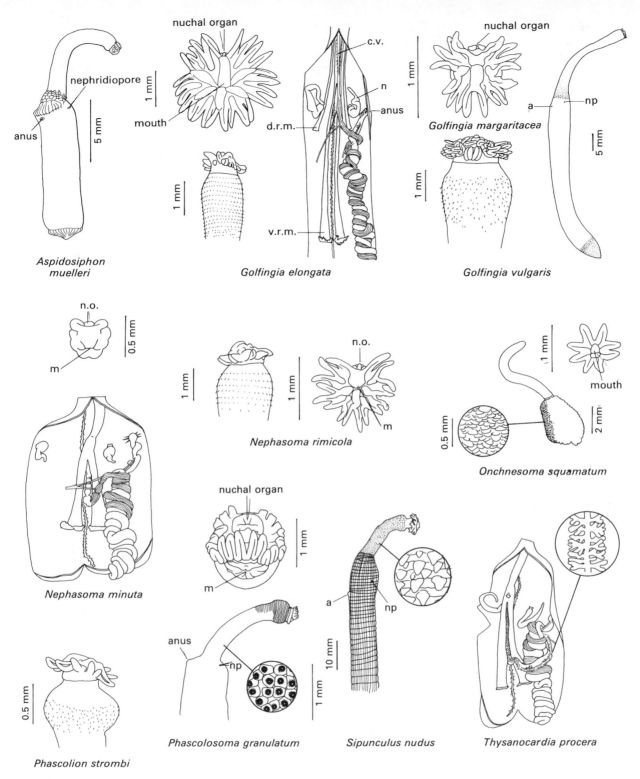

Fig. 7.2

Order 1 Aspidosiphonida
With horny epidermal shields at one or both ends of trunk.

Order 2 Phascolosomatida
Without epidermal shields.

Class II Sipunculidea
Tentacular fringe primarily surrounds mouth, although some dorsal tentacles may form a horseshoe round nuchal organ.

Order 1 Golfingiida

Longitudinal muscles form continuous layer inside body wall, not split up into bands. Three families.

Order 2 Sipunculida

With longitudinal muscle bands. One family.

Sipunculans burrow in mud, sand, or gravel on the lower shore or sublittorally. *Phascolion strombi* lives in old gastropod shells, and *Nephasoma minuta* in rock-crevices, with some other Golfingiidae. To narcotize, place worm in small quantity of cool sea-water and add powdered crystals of menthol. After 1 or 2 h add 80% alcohol a few drops at a time, until worm no longer responds to touch. Fix in 5% formaldehyde and store in 70% alcohol. To study anatomy open by dorsal cut along length of trunk, passing to one side of anus.

LITERATURE

British species were well-described by Gibbs (1977), more thoroughly than here. Later name changes are explained in recent papers. Figures have been redrawn from the sources cited for each species, or from Gibbs (1977).

Cutler, E. B. and Gibbs, P. E. (1985). A phylogenetic analysis of higher taxa in the phylum Sipuncula. *Systematic Zoology*, **34**, 162–73.

Gibbs, P. E. (1973). On the genus *Golfingia* (Sipuncula) in the Plymouth area, with a description of a new species. *Journal of the Marine Biological Association of the U.K.*, **53**, 73–86.

Gibbs, P. E. (1974). *Golfingia margaritacea* (Sipuncula) in British waters. *Journal of the Marine Biological Association of the U.K.*, **54**, 871–7.

Gibbs, P. E. (1977). British Sipunculans. *Linnean Society Synopses of the British Fauna*, (NS) **12**, 1–35. Academic Press, London.

Gibbs, P. E., Cutler, E. B., and Cutler, N. J. (1983). A review of the sipunculan genus *Thysanocardia* Fisher. *Zoologica Scripta*, **12**, 295–304.

Gibbs, P. E. and Cutler, E. B. (1987). A classification of the phylum Sipuncula. *Bulletin of the British Museum (Natural History) Zoology*, **52**, 43–58.

Stephen, A. C. and Edmonds, S. J. (1972). *The Phyla Sipuncula and Echiura*. British Museum (Natural History), London.

KEY TO BRITISH FAMILIES

1. Trunk with hard shield at each end — **1. Aspidosiphonidae**
   Trunk without shields — **2**

2. Tentacles all dorsal to mouth, almost enclosing nuchal organ — **2. Phascolosomatidae**
   Tentacles surround mouth or may be absent — **3**

3. Oral fringe wide, much folded, but not incised to form tentacles. Longitudinal muscles of body wall form bands — **5. Sipunculidae**
   Oral fringe forming tentacles or rudimentary. Longitudinal muscles of body wall form a continuous layer — **4**

4. Either inhabiting old gastropod shells; or with trunk rounded, its length less than twice its breadth and half length of slender extended introvert. Nephridium single — **4. Phascolionidae**
   Not in shells. Trunk length at least three times breadth, usually equalling length of introvert. Two nephridia — **3. Golfingiidae**

Class Phascolosomatidea

Order Aspidosiphonida

1 ASPIDOSIPHONIDAE

Ends of trunk chitinized to form anal shield anteriorly and caudal shield posteriorly, but otherwise like Phascolosomatidae. Two genera. One British species.

Aspidosiphon muelleri Diesing   FIG. 7.2

Length up to 80 mm; tentacles 10–12, short and united for much of their length, arranged round nuchal organ in a crescent; anal shield acts like operculum when introvert is withdrawn, so this species does not cement mouths of shells like *Phascolion* does.

In gastropod shells, serpulid tubes, and crevices, e.g. amongst coralline algae from LW to 1000 m depths. Rare in Britain, but recorded from Shetlands and Norway to Mediterranean.

Order Phascolosomatida

2 PHASCOLOSOMATIDAE

Differs from later families in having spindle muscle attached posteriorly and all tentacles enclosing nuchal organ. Three genera. One British species.

Phascolosoma granulatum Leuckart FIG. 7.2

Length up to 100 mm; tentacles 12–60, increasing with size, all forming dorsally-open horseshoe; introvert with many hooks anteriorly, arranged in 10–60 rings; the more posterior of these rings are often incomplete because of wear; body covered with domed papillae (shown enlarged) each capped by a dark ring round a clear spot; two nephridia; four retractor muscles; longitudinal muscles of body wall tend to form 20–30 anastomosing bands, but these are not readily seen in small specimens.

In muddy sand and gravel from shore crevices to 90 m depth. Common along Irish west coast, scarce in Hebrides, Orkneys, Shetland, and Norway. Ranges to Mediterranean, Cape Verde Islands, and Indo-West Pacific.

Class Sipunculidea

Order Golfingiida

3 GOLFINGIIDAE

Tentacles surround mouth or are mere rudimentary lobes. Spindle muscle attached anteriorly, near anus, but not posteriorly. Two nephridia. Three genera.

---

1. Everted introvert at least twice as long as trunk. Contractile vessel bears many branching villi
   Thysanocardia procera

   Introvert not much longer than trunk. Contractile vessel without villi **2**

2. Introvert bears many spine-like hooks near anterior end **3**
   Introvert without hooks **Golfingia margaritacea**

3. Usually with two pairs of retractor muscles, a ventral pair attached in posterior trunk on each side of nerve cord, and a shorter dorsal pair attached more anteriorly (*Golfingia*) **4**
   Lacking dorsal pair of retractors (*Nephasoma*) **5**

4. Trunk pigmented at each end. Introvert hooks arranged irregularly **Golfingia vulgaris**

   Trunk not pigmented at ends. Introvert hooks arranged in rings **Golfingia elongata**

5. Tentacles rudimentary. Nephridiopores posterior to anus **Nephasoma minuta**

   Tentacles well-formed. Nephridiopores anterior to anus **Nephasoma rimicola**

Golfingia elongata (Keferstein) FIG. 7.2

Length up to 150 mm; tentacles increase from eight to 36 during growth; introvert hooks arranged in up to 20 rings in juveniles less than 30 mm long (as figured), but adults may have only three or four as result of wear; retractor muscles usually four, but one or both of dorsal pair may be missing in aberrant individuals; specimens with both missing are distinguishable from *Nephasoma rimicola* by having more than 20 tentacles at lengths more than 30 mm.

In muddy sand or gravel from LW to 170 m depth. Juveniles up to 30 mm occasional in shore crevices with *Nephasoma* species. Common off Plymouth. Recorded from Skagerrak to Mediterranean.

Golfingia margaritacea (Sars) FIG. 7.2

Length in British populations up to 20 mm, with eight to 16 tentacles; introvert hooks absent; retractor muscles two pairs.

In muddy sand or gravel from LW crevices to 4600 m depth. Uncommon on shores of south-west Britain and west Scotland. Holarctic, perhaps bipolar. Off Norway reaches length of up to 300 mm, with over 100 tentacles, since additional tentacles develop in radial or longitudinal rows behind margin of oral disc.

Golfingia vulgaris (de Blainville) FIG. 7.2

Length up to 200 mm; tentacles increasing from 20 in a single circle at body length 10–15 mm, to 60–150 in three or more circles at lengths over 30 mm; introvert hooks arranged irregularly as figured; retractor muscles two pairs.

In muddy sand or gravel from LW to 2000 m depth, widespread round Britain and from northern Norway to West Africa and Mediterranean.

Nephasoma minuta (Keferstein) FIG. 7.2
[GIBBS 1977, 16 as *Golfingia*]

Length up to 15 mm; oral disc with two lobes flanking nuchal organ, and two to six round mouth; introvert hooks arranged irregularly, but may be lost through wear; retractor muscles one pair, ventral, and these are fused for much of their length.

Very common in rock crevices from mid-shore to 50 m depth; Shetland, Sweden, Britain, Brittany.

Nephasoma rimicola (Gibbs) FIG. 7.2
[GIBBS 1977, 18 as *Golfingia*]

Length up to 60 mm; tentacles increasing from eight in juveniles, and 16 in most adults over 20 mm long (as figured), to 20 in large specimens; introvert hooks arranged in six to ten rings (figured); only the ventral pair of retractor muscles is developed.

Fairly common in LW rock crevices in south-west Britain.

Thysanocardia procera (Möbius) FIG. 7.2
[GIBBS 1977, 20 as *Golfingia*]

Length up to 60 mm, but trunk only 15 mm; skin of trunk with irregular pattern of zigzag, mainly longitudinal folds; tentacles in radial rows and fairly numerous, up to 70; nuchal organ separated into two lobes by a longitudinal groove; introvert hooks absent; only the ventral pair of retractors is developed; distal half of contractile vessel bears many branching villi (see enlarged insert).

In muddy sand at depths 2–200 m; Skagerrak; Kattegat; northern North Sea; western Scotland; western Ireland; Milford Haven.

4 PHASCOLIONIDAE

Like Golfingiidae, but lacking left nephridium, spindle muscle, and some retractors. Two genera.

---

1. Living in old gastropod shells. Anus on trunk. Introvert bears hooks   *Phascolion strombi*

   Not in shells. Anus near mouth, on thin extended introvert, which lacks hooks   **2**

2. About eight tentacles surround mouth. Trunk covered with backward-directed scale-like protrusions   *Onchnesoma squamatum*

   Oral disc not forming tentacles or lobes. Trunk bears small papillae between flat or domed 'scales'   *Onchnesoma steenstrupi*

Onchnesoma squamatum (Koren and Danielssen) FIG. 7.2
Trunk rounded or pear-shaped, 2–7 mm long; introvert slender, 6–23 mm long; total length up to 30 mm; eight tentacles surround mouth; anus nearby, dorsal; rectum necessarily long; single retractor muscle has oesophagus attached to it for much of its length.

In mud or sand at 180–1000 m. Dredged, often in large numbers, from edge of shelf between Norway and Portugal. Also in west Atlantic and Mediterranean.

Onchnesoma steenstrupi Koren and Danielssen
Like *O. squamatum* except that scales do not point backwards, but are aligned to form longitudinal ridges posteriorly; tentacles are absent; oesophagus is not attached to retractor.

In mud or sand at 25–900 m. Distribution generally overlaps with *O. squamatum*, but in west Atlantic it seems to occupy a more northern belt.

Phascolion strombi (Montagu)   FIG. 7.2
Up to 50 mm long; tentacles eight to 16 when half-grown, 40–50 in large specimens which develop multiple circlets; introvert hooks irregularly arranged as figured; skin covered with papillae which are enlarged, conical, and pigmented in a band round middle of trunk; contractile vessel often as wide as oesophagus; main retractor muscle formed by complete fusion of dorsal pair: ventral pair narrower and similarly fused, except for a posterior division which allows attachment on each side of nerve cord.

In gastropod shells, cementing particles round shell mouth to leave narrow hole through which introvert may be protruded. Very common round all British coasts; panatlantic; Mediterranean; bipolar.

5 SIPUNCULIDAE

All with longitudinal muscle bands and most with coelomic extensions into body wall (for sipunculans lack a true blood-vascular system). Five genera, but only two species in shallow water off western Europe.

---

1. Introvert lacks spines; two contractile vessels, lacking villi; gut forms two spiralling U-loops; spindle muscle not attached posteriorly   *Sipunculus nudus*

   Introvert bears spines; contractile vessel single, bearing villi; gut forms one spiralling U-loop; spindle muscle attached posteriorly   *Siphonostoma arcassonense*

Siphonostoma arcassonense (Cuénot)
[STEPHEN AND EDMONDS 1972, 72]
Up to 540 mm long; introvert less than one-third of total length, with annular folds of skin at base enclosing papillae; introvert spines form 130–155 circles anteriorly; trunk smooth-skinned, with 23–24 anastomosing bands of inner longitudinal muscles; ventral retractor muscles inserted further back than dorsal pair.

In sand at LW near Cap Ferrat, Bay of Arcachon.

Sipunculus nudus Linnaeus   FIG. 7.2
Up to 350 mm long; oral disc much folded, but not incised to form tentacles, introvert without spines, but covered with triangular, backward-pointing papillae (shown enlarged); trunk marked with rectangular pattern of grooves in specimens more than 35 mm long; with up to 34 longitudinal muscle bands, fewer posteriorly; four retractor muscles all inserted at about level of anus; oesophagus bears one dorsal and one ventral contractile vessel.

In sand from LW to 700 m, from western Ireland and North Sea to Mediterranean, and in shallow, warm, and temperate waters worldwide. Very rare on British shores, but obtainable in Brittany (Morgat, Locquemeau).

C. ECHIURA

Coelomate worms which may be distantly related to annelids, because most possess at least a pair of *chaetae* and some have trochophore larvae. Adults however are unsegmented. The body is plump, with a posterior *anus*, and a *proboscis* extending forward from the anterior *mouth*. Like an annelid prostomium, the proboscis includes the brain, but it is long, soft, muscular, easily torn away, and often coloured differently from the rest of the worm. Its ventral surface forms a shallow ciliated channel along which mucus and detritus are brought to the mouth. The mouth is at the proboscis base and enclosed by the edges of the channel. On the ventral surface, close behind the mouth, there are usually two hooked chaetae and the pore(s) of one or more *nephridia*. The nephridia lie in the coelom, attached to the ventral wall, and act as genital ducts. The gut is much longer than the body, so follows a convoluted zigzag course. Two or more *anal vesicles*, bearing ciliated funnels or tubules, also lie in the coelom and connect with the cloaca.

The group is not divided into classes but four orders have been recognized.

Order 1 Echiurida

Longitudinal muscle fibres of body wall lie between layers of outer circular and inner oblique muscle fibres. Blood-vessels present. Both sexes of similar size. One family.

Order 2 Bonelliida

Like echiurids, but with dwarf males parasitic on the females. One family.

Order 3 Heteromyotida

Longitudinal muscles lie outside the circular and oblique layers. Blood-vessels present. Only one species, from Japan.

Order 4 Xenopneustida

Muscles as in echiuroids, but blood vessels absent. Comprises the Urechidae, known only from the Pacific Ocean. These have cloacal respiration and coelomocytes with haemoglobin.

Echiurans burrow into sand or mud, mostly at great depths, but some are found in shallow water, especially in rock crevices or under stones. They can be narcotized with menthol, fixed by 5% formaldehyde in sea-water, and preserved in 70% methanol. For study of internal anatomy the body is opened throughout its length by a mid-dorsal incision.

LITERATURE

Saxena, R. (1986). On *Amalosoma eddystonense* Stephen (Echiura). *Biological Memoirs*, **12**, 192–7.

Shipley, A. E. (1910). Gephyrea. *Cambridge natural History*, **2**, 411–49.

Southern, R. (1913*a*). Oligochaeta, Gephyrea, Hirudinea of Clare Island. *Proceedings of the Royal Irish Academy*, **31**, 1–14.

Southern, R. (1913*b*). Gephyrea of the coasts of Ireland. *Scientific Investigations, Fisheries Branch, Ireland*, **1912** (3), 1–46.

Stephen, A. C. (1956). *Amalosoma eddystonense* sp. n. a new species of Bonellidae. *Journal of the Marine Biological Association of the U.K.*, **35**, 605–608.

Stephen, A. C. and Edmonds, S. J. (1972). *The Phyla Sipuncula and Echiura*. British Museum (Natural History), London.

KEY TO BRITISH FAMILIES

1. Without sexual dimorphism. Anal vesicles elongated, with many small ciliated funnels attached directly to their surfaces. With at least a pair of antero-ventral chaetae. One genus has posterior chaetae as well **1. Echiuridae**

Most, perhaps all, with dwarf males living on or in females. Anal vesicles saclike, with ciliated funnels borne on tubules which usually branch. Some lack chaetae. None have posterior chaetae **2. Bonelliidae**

Order Echiurida

1 ECHIURIDAE

Includes nine genera and nearly 80 species, but few round Britain.

1. Two rings of chaetae surround anal region **2**

   Posterior chaetae absent **3**

2. Proboscis tip bilobed. Recorded only from depths exceeding 600 m ***Echiurus abyssalis***

   Proboscis tip not bilobed. Occurs in shallow water ***Echiurus echiurus***

3. With one pair of nephridia ***Thalassema arcassonense***

   With two pairs of nephridia ***Thalassema thalassemum***

Echiurus abyssalis Skorikow
[STEPHEN AND EDMONDS 1972, 411]

Resembling the next species but smaller, with pelagic larvae, and with each nephrostome attached not directly to its nephridium but to the body wall alongside.

Capri; west of Ireland (Southern 1913b).

Echiurus echiurus (Pallas) FIG. 7.1
[STEPHEN AND EDMONDS 1972, 412]

Proboscis 30–40 mm long, orange with brown streaks; body 70–110 mm long, greyish yellow, bearing 21–23 rings of papillae, each alternating with four or five rings of smaller papillae. With two anterior chaetae and two posterior circles, each of between five and nine chaetae. Figure B shows a dissection of the convoluted gut, with the pair of long anal vesicles. Anteriorly the gut partly obscures the two pairs of nephridia, but in Fig. C it is displaced to show the four nephrostomes, which are attached to the nephridia and have frilled edges. Anterior to these are the chaetal sacs of the anterior pair. These are joined transversely by an interbasal muscle, which has a blood-vessel looped round it, as shown in both B and C. Figure D is an enlarged view to show ciliated funnels attached near the end of an anal vesicle.

Holarctic, extending to Kattegat and North Sea. One recorded from shore debris at St. Andrews.

Thalassema arcassonense Cuènot
[STEPHEN AND EDMONDS 1972, 453]
Resembling the next species, but up to 110 mm body length, with one pair of nephridia and small chaetae not joined by an interbasal muscle.

Known only from Bay of Arcachon.

Thalassema thalassemum (Pallas)   FIG. 7.1
[SHIPLEY 1910, 433 as *T. neptuni*; Stephen and Edmonds 1972, 459]
Body length 20–70 mm; extensible proboscis 10–200 mm long, tapering to a point. Figures show whole animal from left side, with a ventral view of the anterior end to show the proboscis channel and the pair of ventral chaetae found in all species of the family. Chaetal sacs connected internally by a transverse interbasal muscle. Two pairs of nephridia. Anal vesicles also like those in *Echiurus*.

Mediterranean, extending to southern Britain. Very common in Devon and Cornwall, in rock crevices at LWST. Rarer in South Wales. One dredged off Isle of Man.

Order **Bonelliida**

2 BONELLIIDAE
With twenty-three genera, from eleven of which dwarf males have been described, living on or inside the females. Males not yet known from remaining genera.

---

1. Females lacking chaetae, but with a deep genital groove on mid-ventral surface, between mouth and nephridiopores   ***Amalosoma eddystonense***

   Females without distinct genital groove, but with a pair of antero-ventral chaetae connected internally by an interbasal muscle   **2**

2. Proboscis bifid. Single nephridium   ***Bonellia viridis***

   Proboscis truncate but not bifid. A pair of nephridia   ***Maxmuelleria lankesteri***

Amalosoma eddystonense Stephen   FIG. 7.1
[STEPHEN 1956, 606; Saxena 1986, 194]
Proboscis ovoid. Body of female up to 144 × 25 mm, mostly greenish, covered with darker papillae. One pair of nephridia which may be packed with ova. Male nearly 2 mm long with two curved chaetae, by which it is attached within genital groove.

Described from several incomplete specimens dredged near Eddystone Lighthouse and Rame Head, Plymouth, and from two dredged at over 4000 m depth in Gulf of Gascony.

Bonellia viridis Rolando   FIG. 7.1
[STEPHEN AND EDMONDS, 1972, 377]
Body up to 150 mm long, green and covered with papillae. Proboscis longer, extensible to over 1 m, bifid. One nephridium usually on right side. Anal vesicles saclike, with branches that end in ciliated funnels. Males nearly 2 mm long, lacking chaetae, ciliated all over, attached initially to female proboscis, later within pharynx, and eventually inside nephridium.

Very rare off Ireland and Norway, but common in shallow water of Mediterranean, e.g. off Chios.

Maxmuelleria lankesteri (Herdman)   FIG. 7.1
[STEPHEN AND EDMONDS 1972, 393]
Body up to 120 × 30 mm, green and papillate. Proboscis nearly as long, greenish. Two ventral chaetae with a strong interbasal muscle. Two nephridia. Anal vesicles saclike, covered with densely aggregated tubules. Male unknown.

Dredged sparsely in Irish Sea, west Scotland, Kattegat, Skagerrak. Not clearly distinguished from the Mediterranean form *Maxmuelleria gigas* (M. Müller), which was described earlier.

D. POGONOPHORA

Tubicolous, tentaculate, coelomate worms, which lack a gut. The tubes, mostly ringed and made of chitin and protein, are generally threadlike and so is the body. In mid-body there are usually two or three close-set girdles of *uncini*, whilst the hind end (the recently discovered *opisthosoma*) is short but many-segmented, with four blunt chaetae per segment. Because of these similarities to annelids the main nerve cord is now regarded as running mid-ventrally from a terminal brain, agreeing well with a view that the group also resembles hemichordates, having tentacle(s), heart, and excretory pores in antero-dorsal positions. Nevertheless the opposite orientation was used so consistently in descriptions of species before 1970 that it seems best to retain it here, with quote marks to imply disbelief. General body form and some details of anterior end are shown in sketches of *Siboglinum* species (Fig. 7.1) Behind the pinnate *tentacle* (t) there are often indistinct grooves (p and m), which mark off the second division of the body (*mesosoma*) from the *protosoma* and *metasoma*, respectively, corresponding with internal septa. The mesosoma usually bears more conspicuous cuticular grooves, forming the *bridle* (b). The bridle grooves run round each side obliquely, so tend to form V shapes in the mid-lines. The 'ventral' V, which points posteriorly, is particularly distinct. Opposite this an anteriorly pointing 'dorsal' V is formed in *Oligobrachia*, its point reaching the protosomal boundary groove. Usually, however, both the bridle and protosomal grooves are interrupted 'dorsally' by wide gaps. The metasoma, forming more than 90% of body length, first bears a series of so called metameric papillae flanking a 'ventral' furrow. The gonads overlap with this metameric region and extend back nearly as far as the *girdles* (g). The posterior half of the metasoma is full of chemoautotrophic bacteria held as symbionts. The sexes are separate, forming spermatophores or yolky eggs. Incubation within tube produces trimeric larvae with ciliation that is mostly 'dorsal'.

Class I Frenulatea

With a mesosomal bridle. Includes more than 70 species in 14 genera.

Order 1 Athecanephrida

Excretory portions of anterior coelomoducts widely separated, each adjoining lateral cephalic blood-vessel. Spermatophores spindle-shaped.

Order 2 Thecanephrida

Excretory portions of anterior coelomoducts close to each other, almost median, in a single sac formed by wall of 'ventral' blood-vessel. Spermatophores leaf-shaped.

Class II Afrenulatea

Lacking a bridle. Only one order.

Order 1 Vestimentiferida

Mesosoma with a cloak, like a collar cleft 'ventrally'. Only three species in two genera, found near volcanic vents emitting sulphide.

Most Pogonophora live at great depths, in or on soft sediments, forming crowded associations, but a few species are known from European shelf, slope, and fjords.

LITERATURE

Ivanov, A. V. (1963). *Pogonophora*. Academic Press, London.

Jones, M. L. (1981). *Riftia pachyptila* Jones: observations on the vestimentiferan worm from the Galapagos Rift. *Science, New York*, **213**, 333–6.

Nørrevang, A. (1970). On the embryology of *Siboglinum* and its implications for the systematic position of the Pogonophora. *Sarsia*, **42**, 7–16.

Southward, A. J., Southward, E. C., Dando, P. R., Barrett, R. L., and Ling, R. (1986). Chemoautotrophic function of bacterial symbionts in small Pogonophora. *Journal of the Marine Biological Association of the U.K.*, **66**, 415–37.

Southward, E. C. (1959). Two new species of Pogonophora from the northeast Atlantic. *Journal of the Marine Biological Association of the U.K.*, **39**, 439–44.

Southward, E. C. (1963). On a new species of *Siboglinum* (Pogonophora) found on both sides of the Atlantic. *Journal of the Marine Biological Association of the U.K.*, **43**, 513–7.

Southward, E. C. (1971). Recent researches on the Pogonophora. *Oceanography and Marine Biology Annual Review*, **9**, 193–220.

Southward, E. C. (1982). Bacterial symbionts in Pogonophora. *Journal of the Marine Biological Association of the U.K.*, **62**, 889–906.

Webb, M. (1963). *Siboglinum fiordicum sp. nov.* (Pogonophora) from the Raunefjord, western Norway. *Sarsia*, **13**, 33–44.

Webb, M. (1964). Additional notes on *Sclerolinum brattstromi* (Pogonophora) and the establishment of a new family, Sclerolinidae. *Sarsia*, **16**, 47–58.

KEY TO WEST EUROPEAN FAMILIES
(Unsuitable for wider area)

1. With only one tentacle. Tubes mostly ringed, alternately brown and clear		**2. Siboglinidae**
With more than one tentacle		**2**
2. With six to ten tentacles. Tubes black, with thicker rings		**1. Oligobrachiidae**
With two to four tentacles. Tubes brownish or pale		**3**
3. Without girdles. Tubes ringless, in rotting wood etc. in fjords		**4. Sclerolinidae**
With girdles. Tubes ringed light and dark brown		**3. Polybrachiidae**

Class Frenulatea

Order Athecanephrida

1 OLIGOBRACHIIDAE

Tentacles one to 12, usually six to 10. Three genera but only one European species.

Oligobrachia ivanovi Southward

[SOUTHWARD 1959, 439; IVANOV 1963, 160]

Tube black, with raised rings, 250×0.5–0.9 mm; body longer than 95 mm; seven tentacles, each with a double row of pinnules and all coiled together within tube; bridle forming complete Vs in both mid-lines.

One specimen at 1400 m depth off mouth of English Channel.

2 SIBOGLINIDAE

Tentacles one (*Siboglinum*, with many species) or two (*Siboglinoides*, with two species).

1. Tentacle with pinnules **2**

   Tentacle without pinnules **5**

2. With glandular patches just behind bridle **3**

   Without such patches just behind bridle **4**

3. Glandular patches oval and small **Siboglinum holmei**

   Glandular patches form long tracts which run alongside bridle and continue alongside 'ventral' mid-line throughout mesoma **Siboglinum atlanticum**

4. Bridle grooves fused 'ventrally' and nearly meeting 'dorsally' **Siboglinum ekmani**

   Bridle grooves separated by distinct mid-line gaps **Siboglinum fiordicum**

5. Glandular patches behind bridle are separated by wide mid-line gaps **Siboglinum inerme**

   Glandular patches behind bridle meet 'ventrally' **Siboglinum norvegicum**

Siboglinum atlanticum Southward and Southward
[IVANOV 1963, 263]

Tube 400 × 0.5 mm; body 112 mm, plus tentacle 20 mm long; head lobe not marked off distinctly from rest of protosoma; tentacle bears two rows of pinnules; bridle interrupted in mid-lines, with a pair of glandular patches in front of it 'ventrally', and long glandular tracts behind it extending throughout mesosoma.

In mud at 950–1800 m depth, south-west of Britain and north of Spain.

Siboglinum ekmani Jägersten
[IVANOV 1963, 185]

Tube 213 mm or longer × 0.12–0.16 mm; body 93 mm long, tentacle 8 mm, bearing two rows of pinnules; head lobe bounded by a pretentacular groove running right round protosoma; halves of bridle nearly meet 'dorsally' and fuse 'ventrally'; without glandular areas near bridle.

Mostly below 1000 m on Biscay slope, south-west of Britain; at 340 m in Skagerrak; at 120 m in Raunefjord near Bergen.

Siboglinum fiordicum Webb   FIG. 7.1
[WEBB 1963, 33]

Tube 243 × 0.21–0.39 mm with the usual light and dark brown rings, but colourless and unringed near each end; contractile body and tentacle were not measured overall, but protosoma and mesosoma (as far as m in figure) were 1.5–1.9 mm long; pinnules appear in one row when tentacle is extended, but two when it is contracted; head lobe marked off incompletely by

'dorsal' groove; bridle interrupted in both mid-lines and without nearby glandular areas.

In mud at 25–500 m near Bergen and Kristineberg.

Siboglinum holmei Southward   FIG. 7.1
[SOUTHWARD 1963, 514]

Tube 140 × 0.17–0.27 mm; body 70 mm, tentacle 15 mm long with pinnules in semi-double row; head lobe not clearly demarcated; bridle meeting 'ventrally' without fusing, and with wide gap 'dorsally'; behind it a pair of white glandular patches, shown stippled in figure.

In muddy sand at 150–400 m off Dingle Bay, Ireland; North Minch, Scotland; eastern U.S.A.

Siboglinum inerme Southward
[IVANOV 1963, 268]

Tube 65 × 0.13–0.18 mm; body 25 mm, tentacle 3 mm long, lacking pinnules; protosoma short, marked off by a post-tentacular groove (incomplete 'dorsally') from mesosoma which is four times as long; this groove and bridle are generally joined 'ventrally' by a mid-line furrow; bridle forms a shallow U 'ventrally' and is followed by a gland patch on each side.

At 500–1280 m south-west of Britain.

Siboglinum norvegicum Ivanov   FIG. 7.1
[IVANOV 1963, 251]

Tube 78 × 0.23–0.25 mm; body 39 mm, tentacle 11 mm long, lacking pinnules; head lobe not demarcated; protosoma nearly as long as mesosoma; bridle fused 'ventrally', forming a V, with glandular belt immediately following.

At 120 m depth west of Shetland Isles; at 1165 m west of Norway.

Order **Thecanephrida**

3 POLYBRACHIIDAE

Tentacles numbering from two to 268, but not fixed together in a tentacular cylinder or plate. At least 20 species in six genera.

Diplobrachia capillaris (Southward)
[IVANOV 1963, 378; SOUTHWARD 1959, 441]

Tube at least 120 × 0.10–0.17 mm, most of it marked by light and dark brown rings; body 55 mm long; tentacles two, three, or four, coiled spirally together within tube, each with double row of pinnules; bridle incomplete 'dorsally', forming a V 'ventrally' with two halves sometimes separate.

At about 500–1500 m south-west of Britain.

4 SCLEROLINIDAE

Lacking girdles of uncini. Excretory coelomoducts not studied, but the only genus has leaf-shaped spermatophores, as in Thecanephrida.

Sclerolinum brattstromi Webb
[WEBB 1964, 49]

Tube transparent, smooth-walled, ringless, and tough, up to

134 × 0.13 mm; body about 35 × 0.1 mm, plus two tentacles usually 0.4 mm long, lacking pinnules; bridle variable in extent, composed of several separate pieces; chaetae absent, but opisthosoma has up to 11 segments, mostly separated by septa and surface grooves; other body regions not delimited by grooves.

Tubes attached to rotting wood, old rope, etc. at 100–1230 m in fjords near Bergen.

E. ENTOPROCTA
(= Kamptozoa)

A clearly defined group of small, sessile, filter-feeding animals, many of which are colonial. The simplest entoprocts, however, are non-colonial though often gregarious, and found associated with sponges, bryozoans, polychaetes, and sipunculids, in all of which the host animal generates a feeding or respiratory water current of benefit to the commensal.

Each entoproct consists typically of a visceral region or *calyx* and a supporting *stalk*; in colonial forms the individuals or *zooids* are united, generally by a *stolon*. The stolon grows from its apices, branching and budding off successive zooids. In non-colonial forms daughter individuals are budded directly from the calyx, in time breaking free and settling nearby. The calyx is roughly globular and bears on its free face a ring of ciliated tentacles. These arise from the calyx margin, and their number is increased during life by additions made each side of a posterior gap until the maximum is reached. The tentacles are flexible and can be expanded for feeding or, in response to disturbance, folded down to lie inside the tentacular membrane which joins their bases. Contraction of a muscular sphincter within this membrane can then close the calyx tightly. Most of the volume of the calyx is occupied by the looped alimentary canal. It lies in the median plane, with both mouth and anus opening inside the tentacles. The anus is raised on a short papilla leaving a space, the *atrium*, between it and the mouth. Embryos develop in the atrium. The stalk is muscular and flexible, and the longitudinal muscles continue, with or without a break, into the calyx. The body cavity of stalk, calyx, and tentacles is a pseudocoel filled with gelatinous mesenchymatous tissue.

The classification adopted here was introduced by Emschermann (1972), whose paper also included a key to all genera in the phylum.

Order 1 Solitaria

Small, non-colonial forms often less than 0.5 mm high. The longitudinal muscles are continuous throughout both stalk and calyx. Daughter individuals are budded, and separate off, from the oral wall of the calyx. Commensals; though sometimes found freeliving in aquarium systems or on panels used for fouling studies.

Order 2 Coloniales

Colonial forms with zooids, often about 2 mm high, arising from a common basal plate (suborder Astolonata) or stolon (suborder Stolonata). The genera considered in this book belong to the latter. The calyx is separated from the stalk by a constriction, within whch lies the *pump-organ*, consisting of a stack of flat, stellate, contractile cells. Longitudinal muscles of the calyx (*atrial retractors*) and stalk are separate.

Commensal entoprocts are rarely discovered by accident, but can be found quite easily by collecting and examining suitable host animals (see below). There are many British species (list in Ryland, 1969), and some are common. Colonial entoprocts can be searched for on hydroids, bryozoans (such as *Scrupocellaria*), and delicate algae low on the shore, where they may be seen as a whitish fuzz over the surface. More often, however, they will be seen first when sorting material under a microscope. Particularly striking are the jerky, sweeping movements made by zooids from the base of their stalk. The structure of the stalk is important and separates two families. The number of tentacles is frequently employed in the discrimination of all entoproct species. For study purposes, therefore, some individuals (or zooids) must be preserved with the tentacles expanded. Isotcnic magnesium chloride (7.5% $MgCl_2.6H_2O$ in distilled water) added to an equal volume of sea-water is a suitable narcotic. Muscles are best seen in unfixed animals, but can be shown up clearly only by the use of phase contrast, interference, or polarizing microscopes.

REFERENCES

The treatment of colonial entoprocts in this book is complete, in view of the extensive confusion between the species, and based on the review of the Pedicellinidae by Ryland (1965) and an unpublished *Key for the identification of the Barentsiidae of the world* (1972) prepared by Dr. P. Emschermann. Commensal loxosomatids, as well as pedicellinids, can be identified using Nielsen's recent *Synopsis* (1989).

Atkins, D. (1932). The Loxosomatidae of the Plymouth area, including *L. obesum* sp. nov. *Quarterly Journal of Microscopical Science*, **75**, 321–91.

Eggleston, D. (1965). The Loxosomatidae of the Isle of Man. *Proceedings of the Zoological Society of London*, **145**, 529–47.

Eggleston, D. (1969). Marine fauna of the Isle of Man: revised lists of phylum Entoprocta (= Kamptozoa) and phylum Ectoprocta (= Bryozoa). *Report Marine Biological Station, Port Erin*, **81**, 57–80.

Eggleston, D. and Bull, H. O. (1966). The marine fauna of the Cullercoats district. 3a. Entoprocta. *Reports Dove Marine Laboratory*, (3rd series), **15**, 5–10.

Emschermann, P. (1972) *Loxokalypus socialis* gen. et sp. nov. (Kamptozoa, Loxokalypodidae fam. nov.), ein neuer Kamptozoentyp aus dem nördlichen Pazifischen Ozean. Ein Vorschlag zur Neufassung der Kamptozoensystematik. *Marine Biology*, **12**, 237–54.

Mariscal, R. N. (1965). The adult and larval morphology and life history of the entoproct *Barentsia gracilis* (M. Sars, 1835). *Journal of Morphology*, **116**, 311–38.

Nielsen, C. (1964). Studies on Danish Entoprocta. *Ophelia*, **1**, 1–76.

Nielsen, C. (1989). Entoprocts. *Synopses of the British Fauna* (N. S.), **41**. Leiden: E. J. Brill, for the Linnean Society of London and the Estuarine and Brackish Water Sciences Association.

Prenant, M. and Bobin, G. (1956). Bryozoaires, 1re partie: Entoproctes, Phylactolèmes, Cténostomes. *Faune de France*, **60**, 1–398.

Ryland, J. S. (1961). The occurrence of *Pseudopedicellina mutabilis* Toriumi (Entoprocta) in British waters, with a note on *Pedicellina nutans* Dalyell. *Annals and Magazine of Natural History*, (Series 13), **3**, 377–83.

Ryland, J. S. (1965). Some New Zealand Pedicellinidae (Entoprocta), and a species new to Europe. *Transactions of the Royal Society of New Zealand*, **6**, 189–205.

Ryland, J. S. (1969). A nomenclatural index to 'A history of the British marine Polyzoa' by T. Hincks (1880). *Bulletin of the British Museum (Natural History)*, Zoology, **17**, 207–260.

KEY TO FAMILIES

1. Non-colonial. Small entoprocts (often about 0.5 mm or less) generally found in aggregations commensally on worms, sponges, or bryozoans. Buds produced from the calyx.

    1. Loxosomatidae

    Colonial and stolonate. Freeliving. Buds not produced from the calyx   **2**

2. Zooid stalk of uniform structure, muscular and flexible   **2. Pedicellinidae**

    Zooid stalk at least partly rigid, supported by a muscular base and, in many cases, divided into two or more slender segments (internodes) by swollen muscular joints (nodes)   **3. Barentsiidae**

Order 1 Solitaria

1 LOXOSOMATIDAE

Non-colonial and normally commensal; with the characters of the order. Two principal genera, separated as follows:

1. Stalk terminating in a sucking disk; adult animal capable of movement from place to place. No foot gland in bud   ***Loxosoma***

    Adult cemented to host or substratum by base of the stalk; incapable of movement from place to place. A foot (cement) gland present in the bud (Fig. 7.3), persisting or disappearing in the adult   ***Loxosomella***

Loxosomella is the larger genus. No species are described here, but some of the commoner ones are listed below with their host organisms:

Loxosoma pectinaricola Franzén, on *Pectinaria belgica* (Polychaeta)

Loxosoma rhodinicola Franzén, on *Rhodine loveni* (Polychaeta)

Loxosomella atkinsae Bobin and Prenant, on *Phascolion strombi* (Sipuncula)

Loxosomella claviformis (Hincks), on *Aphrodita aculeata* and *Hermione hystrix* (Polychaeta)

Loxosomella compressa Nielsen and Ryland, on notopodial chaetae of *Gattyana cirrosa* and *Lagisca extenuata* (Polychaeta)

Loxosomella discopoda Nielsen and Ryland, on *Amphilepis norvegica* (Ophiuriodea)

Loxosomella fauveli Bobin and Prenant, on *Aphrodita aculeata* and *Hermione hystrix* (Polychaeta)

Loxosomella murmanica (Nilus), on *Phascolion strombi* (Sipuncula)

Loxosomella nitschei (Vigelius), on bryozoans.

Loxosomella nordgaardi Ryland, on bryozoans

Loxosomella obesa (Atkins), on *Aphrodita aculeata* (Polychaeta)

Loxosomella phascolosomata (Vogt), on *Golfingia* spp. (Sipuncula)

Loxosomella varians Nielsen, on *Nephtys* spp. (Polychaeta)

Descriptions of these and several others, and also bibliographies, will be found in Prenant and Bobin (1956) and Nielsen (1964, 1989).

Order 2 Coloniales

2 PEDICELLINIDAE

Colonial, with zooids arising from a creeping, branching stolon. Stolons usually septate, of alternating zooid-bearing and barren segments. Zooid stalks unjointed, flexible, entirely muscular. Muscles in stalk and calyx not continuous; atrial retractor muscles disposed all round the oral end of the calyx. British species are referable to the genus *Pedicellina*.

1. Zooids reaching or exceeding 2 mm in height; calyces strongly asymmetric; up to 24 tentacles   ***Pedicellina cernua***

    Zooids usually less than 1.5 mm in height, occasionally reaching 2 mm; calyces only slightly asymmetric; maximum number of tentacles between 15 and 21   **2**

2. Stalk glabrous; adult tentacle number 14–16 (–17)   ***Pedicellina nutans***

    Stalk hispid; adult tentacle number 16–21   ***Pedicellina hispida***

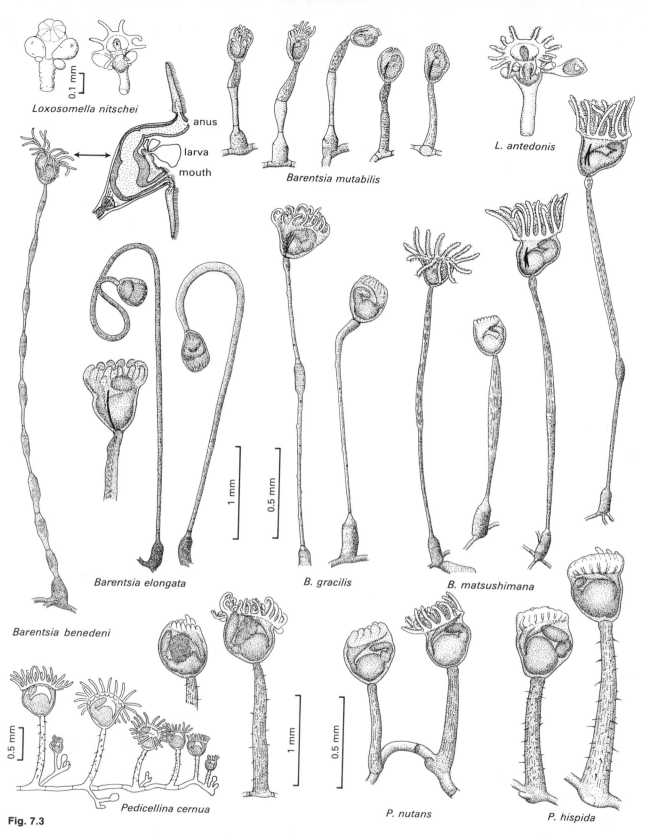

Loxosomella nitschei

anus
larva
mouth

Barentsia mutabilis

L. antedonis

0.1 mm

Barentsia elongata

B. gracilis

B. matsushimana

1 mm

0.5 mm

Barentsia benedeni

0.5 mm

Pedicellina cernua

Fig. 7.3

1 mm

0.5 mm

P. nutans

P. hispida

Pedicellina cernua (Pallas)   FIG. 7.3

Colonies often dense. Stolons creeping, about 60 μm in diameter, stalk parallel-sided or tapering very slightly towards the calyx; its height rarely more than twice that of the calyx; glabrous or hispid. Calyx about 0.5–0.6 mm high, large in relation to the stalk, somewhat compressed, strongly asymmetric in side view; up to 24 tentacles; anal papilla upright or reflected; glabrous or hispid.

The commonest and most conspicuous entoproct in British waters; on algae, hydroids, and bryozoans; low on the shore and from shallow water; all coasts.

Pedicellina hispida Ryland   FIG. 7.3

Stolons creeping, about 60 μm in diameter, often branching in cruciform manner at the zooid bases. Zooid stalks 1.0–1.5 mm in height, tapering from a basal width of about 200 μm to 80–100 μm at the calyx; two-and-a-half to three times the calyx height; hispid. calyx 250–500 μm high, somewhat asymmetric; about 20 tentacles; glabrous or slightly hispid.

On hydroids and bryozoans; from low on the shore on English Channel coasts. Perhaps present elsewhere but confused with the other species.

Pedicellina nutans Dalyell   FIG. 7.3

Colonies sometimes very dense. Stolons creeping, about 70 μm in diameter. Zooids generally about 1 (–2) mm in height. Stalks tapering, their diameter at the calyx about half that at the base, and the base diameter about 160 μm in a stalk 1.5 mm high and 100 μm in one 0.6 mm high; glabrous. Calyx usually 200–300 μm high (400–500 μm in some colonies), one-third to one-fifth of total height; bell-shaped, slightly asymmetric in side view; 12–15 (–17) tentacles; anal papilla reflected; glabrous.

Found in great abundance on small algae near ELWS on certain rocky shores; probably widespread but confused with *P. cernua*.

3 BARENTSIIDAE

Colonial, with zooids arising from a creeping or erect, branching stolon. Stolons septate, of alternating zooid-bearing and barren segments. Zooid stalks divided into alternating rigid sections (*internode*) and flexible muscular joins (*nodes*). Atrial retractor muscles in two orolateral series, converging V-like towards base of calyx. British species are referable to the genus *Barentsia*.

---

1. Stalk relatively short, two to three times as long as calyx; internode short, widening distally and becoming flexible, narrowing again towards calyx base; some zooids often with an undifferentiated (*Pedicellina*-like) stalk   ***Barentsia mutabilis***

   Stalk relatively long, usually many times longer than calyx (if short, then internode thin, not or scarcely widening distally, flexible just below calyx base); all zooids with a muscular base and variously differentiated stalk   **2**

2. Adult zooids usually with rigidly cuticularized internodes separated by joint-like nodes; if nodes absent, then stalk above base rigid and terminating below calyx in a sharply demarcated, flexible joint never constituting more than one-fifth of stalk length   **3**

   All zooids without intercalated nodes above base; lower portion (one-third to one-half) rigid; changing gradually to a flexible upper portion   **4**

3. Nodes and internodes numerous (5–20); internodes lacking pores; atrial retractor muscles in a broad band splaying-out basally; usually in brackish water
                                   Barentsia benedeni

   Usually one or two nodes (occasionally none or more than two); cuticle of internodes sparsely porous; two to five slender atrial retractor muscles on each side; marine only   ***Barentsia gracilis***

4. Zooids very tall (up to 15 mm); upper part of stalk flexible, with musculature confined to oral side; very motile, with stalk typically curling distally
                                   Barentsia elongata

   Zooids quite short, usually about 1–2 mm high (up to 4 mm); upper part of stalk flexible, but with symmetrical musculature; very motile, but the stalk not typically curling distally   ***Barentsia matsushimana***

Barentsia benedeni (Foettinger)   FIG. 7.3
(= *B. gracilis* Mariscal, 1965)

Colonies dense; stolons creeping, though sometimes arising from the zooid stalks. Adult zooids up to 10 mm in height. The stalk with 5–10 (–25) nodes; internodes 250–650 μm long, shorter, as long as or a little longer than nodes, without pores; nodes delimited distally by septa. Calyx trigonal, with the oral side strongly convex, tapering towards its base; 14–20 long tentacles. Atrial retractor muscles in a broad band on each side, fanning out basally.

On various substrata; euryhaline and tolerant of polluted water; most likely to be encountered on pier pilings etc. in estuaries and harbours.

Barentsia elongata Jullien and Calvet   FIG. 7.3
(*B. laxa* Eggleston and Bull, 1966)

Colonies dense, stolons creeping. Zooids very tall, 5–15 mm in height. Stalk with a muscular base but without nodes; long, thin, but slightly increasing in thickness distally; rigid proximally, flexible towards calyx, the flexible part with longitudinal muscles confined to the oral side, enabling upper region to curl, sometimes in several convolutions; pores lacking, the surface delicately and regularly annulate. Calyx bell-shaped, slightly asymmetric in lateral view; (10–) 12–16 (–20) tentacles. Atrial retractor muscles in a thin band on each side.

On firm substrata in shallow water; probably widely distributed. Has been found in aquaria.

Barentsia gracilis (M. Sars) FIG. 7.3

Stolon creeping. Zooids 2–3 (–5) mm in height. The stalk slender, without or with one or two nodes; internodes much longer than nodes, about 30 (–40) μm in diameter; pores usually present. Calyx up to about 350 μm high, more or less ovoid, quite strongly asymmetric in lateral view; 12–18 tentacles. Atrial retractor muscles in one to four slender bands on each side of calyx.

On shells (e.g. between ribs of *Pecten* and *Cardium* valves), crabs, hydroids, bryozoans, and algal stems; stenohaline, on the shore and in shallow water; all coasts; widespread, the commonest *Barentsia* on British coasts.

Barentsia matsushimana Toriumi FIG. 7.3

(= *B. laxa* Nielsen, 1964; Eggleston, 1969)

Colonies often extensive. Adult zooids small, seldom longer than 1–1.5 (–4) mm. The stalk slender, with a muscular base but no nodes; rigid proximally, flexible and transversely wrinkled distally; usually poreless; musculature never restricted to the oral side only. Calyx asymmetrical in lateral view; 12–14 tentacles. Atrial retractor muscles small, short, not reaching base of calyx, and widest proximally.

On firm substrata and algae from low on the shore into shallow water; apparently widely distributed though rarely reported. (North Sea coasts and Isle of Man).

Barentsia mutabilis (Toriumi) FIG. 7.3

[RYLAND 1961, as *Pseudopedicellina*]

Stolon creeping, 25–45 μm in diameter. Zooids to about 0.9 (–1.6) mm in height. The stalk 500–600 μm high, less than three times calyx height, usually with a muscular base, a biconcave rigid internode and a flexible subcalycal portion; internode usually with pores; stalk sometimes wholly non-rigid and muscular (as in *Pedicellina*). The two kinds of stalk may occur within the same colony. Calyx about 200 μm high, bell-shaped, very slightly asymmetrical in side view; 10–11 (–14) tentacles. Atrial retractor muscles one or two on each side of calyx, converging towards the base of the calyx.

On firm substrata; low in the intertidal zone or in shallow water; apparently uncommon.

8 CRUSTACEA I
ENTOMOSTRACA

PHYLUM CRUSTACEA

THE Crustacea exhibit a great diversity of structure, adaptation, and development. Freshwater and terrestrial species are common, but the greater majority of species are marine. Crustaceans occur in all marine habitats, from the supralittoral zone to the abyss; additionally, most holoplanktonic animals belong to the Crustacea, and the meroplankton largely consists of the larval stages of benthic Crustacea. The phylum comprises more than 30 000 species worldwide.

The crustacean body (Fig. 8.1) is segmented and organized into distinct regions. The segments, or *somites*, are typically compressed or depressed to a varying degree, but the dorsal *tergum*, ventral *sternum*, and lateral *pleuron* are usually recognizable. The body wall is basically chitinous and is most usually reinforced by calcium carbonate to form a rigid exoskeleton. Growth involves periodic moulting of the exoskeleton, necessitating hormone-controlled resorption of calcium salts, and their redeposition in the new-formed outer chitinous skeleton. The body regions comprise a *head, thorax,* and *abdomen*, with an additional tailpiece, the *telson*. In many crustaceans a number of anterior thoracic segments is fused with the head. The abdomen is variously developed throughout the phylum, and is often much reduced. In many groups a fold derived from the head extends posteriorly to form a characteristic *carapace* which covers most or all of the thorax.

Primitively, each body segment bears a pair of biramous appendages. In its simplest form the crustacean head has three pairs of appendages: the *antennule* (or *antenna 1*), the *antenna* (*antenna 2*), and the *mandibles*. The head is typically fused with two anterior thoracic segments, the appendages of which are modified as accessory feeding structures, the *maxillule* (*maxilla 1*) and the *maxilla* (*maxilla 2*). Thoracic and abdominal appendages show a wide range of modification throughout the phylum as a whole.

The crustacean limb (Fig. 8.1) consists of two segmented rami, the *exopodite* and the *endopodite*, rising from a peduncle of two articles, the *coxa* and the *basis*. Simple biramous limb structure persists in some primitive crustaceans, but in most groups the exopodite comprises the major functional unit of the limb, while the endopodite is reduced, or lost, or adapted to serve a separate function such as feeding, cleaning, or respiration. In some higher crustaceans, additional respiratory structures (*podobranchs* and *pleurobranchs*) are associated with the thoracic limbs.

Sexes are separate, with the exception of the sessile Cirripedia, in which hermaphroditism is generally the rule. The characteristic larval type is the *nauplius* (Fig. 8.1); it occurs as the first free-swimming larval stage in many crustaceans, while in others it occurs only in the earliest, brooded stages of development. A succession of often very specialized larval instars occurs in the later development of most crustaceans.

Crustaceans range in size from less than 0.5 mm to more than 1 m. Their morphological diversity, and wealth of adaptive features make them a difficult phylum to define satisfactorily, and crustacean classification has been the subject of much dispute. Morphological terms, consequently, are often confusing when used in comparative accounts of different classes or orders. A single, unified terminology for the Crustacea as a whole is desirable, but there is no consensus on this problem. In this and following chapters a simplified morphological terminology is utilized, with the sole intention of aiding the task of identification. It is not intended as support for any one opinion, but is adopted for purely practical purposes.

REFERENCES

Abele, L. G. (1982). *The biology of Crustacea.* **1,** *Systematics, the fossil record, and biogeography.* Academic Press, New York.

Abele, L. G. (1982). *The biology of Crustacea.* **2,** *Embryology, morphology and genetics.* Academic Press, New York.

Atwood, H. L. and Sandeman, D. C. (1982). *The biology of Crustacea.* **3,** *Neurobiology: structure and function.* Academic Press, New York.

Mantel, L. H. (1983). *The biology of Crustacea.* **5,** *Internal anatomy and physiological regulation.* Academic Press, New York.

Provenzano, A. J. (1983). *The biology of Crustacea.* **6,** *Pathobiology.* Academic Press, New York.

Provenzano, A. J. (1985). *The biology of Crustacea.* **10,** *Economic aspects: Fisheries and culture.* Academic Press, New York.

Sandeman, D. C. and Atwood, H. L. (1982). *The biology of Crustacea.* **4,** *Neural integration and behaviour.* Academic Press, New York.

Verberg, F. J. and Vernberg, W. B. (1983). *The biology of Crustacea.* **7,** *Behaviour and ecology.* Academic Press, New York.

Vernberg, F. J. and Vernberg, W. B. (1983). *The biology of Crustacea.* **8,** *Environmental adaptations.* Academic Press, New York.

A Class **Ostracoda**

In the Ostracoda the crustacean carapace is present as a bivalved shell into which the animal can withdraw completely. The two

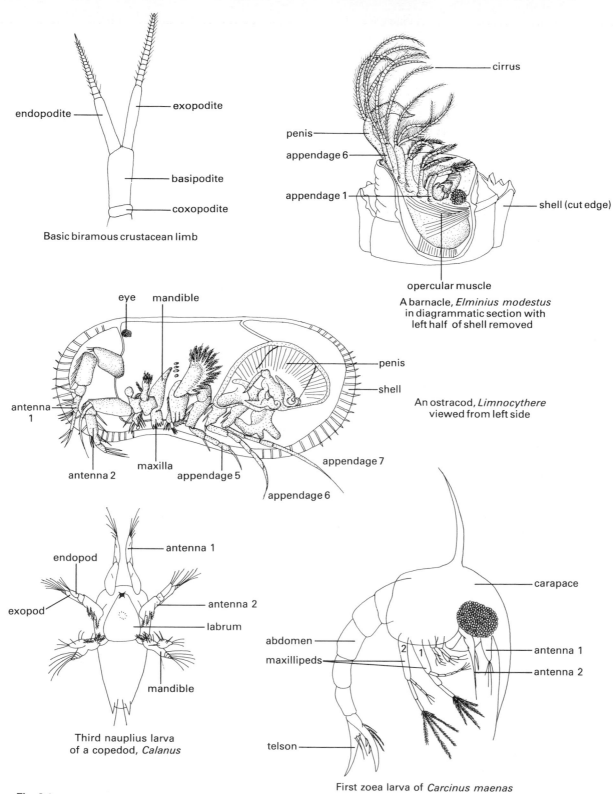

endopodite — exopodite

basipodite

coxopodite

Basic biramous crustacean limb

cirrus

penis

appendage 6

appendage 1

shell (cut edge)

opercular muscle

A barnacle, *Elminius modestus* in diagrammatic section with left half of shell removed

eye mandible

penis

shell

antenna 1

antenna 2 maxilla appendage 5

appendage 7

appendage 6

An ostracod, *Limnocythere* viewed from left side

endopod

antenna 1

exopod

antenna 2

labrum

mandible

Third nauplius larva of a copedod, *Calanus*

carapace

abdomen

maxillipeds

2 1

antenna 1

antenna 2

telson

First zoea larva of *Carcinus maenas*

Fig. 8.1

valves of the shell are closed by an adductor muscle which attaches to the centre of each valve. The shell is part of the exoskeleton and is thus shed and reformed at each moult. The body of the ostracod is highly modified, reduced in size, and largely coalesced with no externally visible segmentation. It

bears five to seven pairs of appendages, the terminology and homology of which varies between orders. Typically, there are two pairs of *antennae* and a pair of *mandibles*, with palps, arising from the indistinct head region. The first thoracic appendage is the *maxilla*, or *maxilla 1*, while the second (appendage 5) may be developed as *maxilla 2* or as the first walking leg. The remaining two pairs of appendages are developed as thoracic walking legs. The abdomen is devoid of appendages, but an unpaired, terminal *caudal furca* is situated anterior or posterior to the anus.

Ostracods are widespread in marine, brackish, and freshwater habitats. Most marine species are benthic, burrowing in, or crawling on, the substratum, but some are free-swimming and a few are planktonic. The following key will permit identification of common, intertidal benthic species.

REFERENCES

Athersuch, J. and Horne, D. J. (1984). A review of some European genera of the Family Loxoconchidae (Crustacea: Ostracoda). *Zoological Journal of the Linnean Society*, **81**, 1–22.

Brady, G. S. and Norman, A. M. (1889). A monograph of the marine and freshwater Ostracoda of the North Atlantic and of north western Europe. Section I, Podocopa, *Scientific Transactions of the Royal Dublin Society, Series II*, **4**, 63–270.

Brady, G. S. and Norman, A. M. (1896). A monograph of the marine and freshwater Ostracoda of the North Atlantic and of north western Europe. Part II. Sections II to IV, Myodocopa, Cladocopa and Platycopa. *Scientific Transactions of the Royal Dublin Society, Series II*, **5**, 621–746.

British Micropalaeontological Society. (1977–1989). *A Stereo Atlas of Ostracod Shells*. Vols. 4–15. London: British Micropalaeontological Society.

Hartmann, G. and Puri, H. S. (1974). Summary of neontological and paleontological classification of Ostracoda. *Mitteilungen aus dem Hamburgischen Zoologischen Museum und Institut*, **70**, 7–73.

Horne, D. J. (1982a). The vertical distribution of phytal ostracods in the intertidal zone at Gove Point, Bristol Channel, U.K. *Journal of Micropalaeontology*, **1**, 71–84.

Horne, D. J. (1982b). The ostracod fauna of an intertidal *Sabellaria* reef at Blue Anchor, Somerset, England. *Estuarine, Coastal and Shelf Science*, **15**, 671–8.

Horne, D. J. and Whittaker, J. E. (1985). A revision of the genus *Paradoxostoma* Fischer (Crustacea: Ostracoda) in British waters. *Zoological Journal of the Linnean Society*, **85**, 131–203.

Moore, R. C. (1961). *Treatise on Invertebrate Paleontology*. Part Q, *Arthropoda* 3, *Crustacea, Ostracoda*. Lawrence, Kansas: University of Kansas Press and the Geological Society of America.

Neale, J. W. *The taxonomy, morphology and ecology of recent Ostracoda*. Oliver and Boyd, Edinburgh.

Poulsen, E. M. (1969a) *Fiches d'identification du Zooplancton*, **115**, Ostracoda. I. Myodocopa. Suborder: Cypridiniformes. Families: Cypridinidae, Rutidermatidae, Sarsiellidae, Asteropidae. Counseil Permanent pour l'exploration de la mer, Copenhagen.

Poulsen, E. M. (1969b). *Fiches d'identification du Zooplancton*, **116**, Ostracoda. II Myodocopa. Suborder: Halocypridiformes. Families: Thaumatocypridae, Halocypridae. Conseil Permanent pour l'exploration de la Mer, Copenhagen.

Sars, G. O. (1928). Ostracoda. *An account of the Crustacea of Norway*, **9**, 1–277.

University of Leicester, Department of Geology. (1973–1975). *A Stereo Atlas of Ostracod Shells*. Vols. 1–2. University of Leicester.

University of Leicester, Department of Geology. (1976). *A Stereo Atlas of Ostracod Shells*. Vol. 3. Welwyn: Broadwater Press.

KEY TO REPRESENTATIVE SPECIES

1. Antennae 1 and 2 adapted for swimming. Two pairs of legs, more or less dissimilar, the second pair upturned into the shell. One simple eye (if present). Nearly always in *Laminaria* zone, very rare upshore ... **2**

   Antennae not adapted for swimming, but geniculate. Three pairs of legs, similar in structure and freely projecting from shell. Usually two eyes (occasionally confluent or absent). Intertidal and sublittoral ... **3**

2. Eye present; shell pellucid, with brown patches ... ***Propontocypris trigonella***

   Eye absent; shell bright purple/brown ... ***Pontocypris mytiloides***

3. Oral cone terminating with sucking disk ... **4**

   Oral cone without terminal disc ... **10**

4. Powerful, well-developed mandibles; sucking-disk incomplete ... ***Cytherois fischeri***

   Mandibles less well-developed; sucking disc complete ... **5**

5. Shell with upward-pointing, oblique posterior protuberance ... ***Paradoxostoma bradyi***

   Shell without such a proturbance ... **6**

6. Shell with broad, transverse violet band, extremities yellow, up to 0.5 mm
   Paradoxostoma pulchellum

   Shell differently coloured, larger **7**

7. Shell elongated, length about 2–2.5 times greatest height **_Paradoxostoma ensiforme_**
   Shell not so elongated **8**

8. Anterior part of shell base more or less straight; shell relatively elongated
   Paradoxostoma variabile

   Anterior part of shell base with a distinct concavity; shell relatively squat **9**

9. Shell extremely squat; concavity less deep **_Paradoxostoma abbreviatum_**
   Shell less squat; concavity very marked **_Paradoxostoma normani_**

10. Commensal, living in holes of _Chelura_ or _Limnoria_. Eyes absent, shell much expanded
    at base **_Cytheropteron humile_**
    Free-living **11**

11. Shell rhomboidal in shape, with small pits on surface; littoral **_Loxoconcha impressa_**
    Shell of different shape **12**

12. Shell with an obtuse posterior protuberance **13**
    Shell without this proturberance **16**

13. Shell very dark, almost black, with lighter areas **14**
    Shell brown or orange **15**

14. Shell with white tips and a white band across the back; posterior proturbance relatively
    short **_Cytherura gibba_**
    Shell with white tips only; posterior protuberance longer **_Semicytherura nigrescens_**

15. Extremely small (0.35 m); shell with teeth on anterior margin and areolar markings,
    brownish **_Hemicytherura cellulosa_**
    Shell with rib-like mesh reticulations, dark violet/brown **_Hemicytherura clathrata_**
    Shell with longitudinal striations, orange **_Semicytherura striata_**

16. Shell tumid and flattened at posterior end. Female with brood chamber within the shell.
    Antennae and legs with relatively moderate setae **_Xestoleberis aurantia_**
    Shell less tumid, with rounded posterior end. Female without brood chamber. Antennae
    and legs with stout setae **17**

17. Eyes fused; shell relatively elongate **18**
    Eyes separate; shell less elongate **19**

18. Shell with rather large pits on surface, becoming more elongated towards posterior
    end; yellowish brown, legs bright yellow   ***Leptocythere pellucida***

    Shell with smaller, more numerous pits; darker reddish brown, legs bright yellow
                                                                 Leptocythere castanea

19. Shell dark reddish brown, with relatively sparse hairs.   ***Cythere lutea***

    Shell lighter or patchy in colour, hairs more dense   **20**

20. Shell yellowish grey with irregular dark patches. Limbs dark yellow
                                                         Heterocythereis albomaculata

    Shell light brown. Limbs colourless   ***Hirschmannia viridis***

1 CYTHERIDAE

Shell ovate, subreniform, or subquadrangular; 0.4–0.9 mm long; right valve often overlapping left dorsally. Sculpture variable. A single V-shaped frontal scar, and a vertical row of four adductor scars. Three pairs of similar walking legs; antenna 1 with five or six joints, bearing bristles and claws; antenna 2 with well-developed spinneret bristle. Caudal furca small, sometimes indistinct, but always present, with two or three setae.

Cythere lutea Müller   FIG. 8.2

Shell subreniform, slightly tapered posteriorly, and somewhat angular, anterior margin smoothly rounded; up to 0.74 mm long, male smaller than female; smoothly calcified, with few large punctae.

Intertidal and shallow sublittoral, often in rock-pools, ranging into estuaries. All British coasts.

2 CYTHERURIDAE

Shell variable, usually dorsoventrally flattened, with caudal process; 0.3–0.7 mm long. Sculpture variably developed, often including longitudinal or vertical ribs. A single, V-shaped frontal scar, and a vertical row of four adductor scars. Three pairs of similar walking legs; antenna 1 with six joints (rarely five); antenna 2 with four or five joints, a spinneret bristle and two terminal claws. Caudal furca with three bristles or more.

Cytherura gibba (Müller)   FIG. 8.2

Shell elongate oval, greatest height close to anterior end, dorsal and ventral borders almost parallel; anterior border smoothly rounded, posterior border with short caudal process; 0.56 mm long; surface with bold reticulate ridges.

In brackish water habitats. All British coasts.

Cytheropteron humile Brady and Norman   FIG. 8.2

Shell small, up to 0.33 mm long, smooth, with prominent, wing-like, lateral projections. Shallow sublittoral, freeliving, or commensal in burrows of *Chelura* and *Limnoria*.

Hemicytherura cellulosa (Norman)   FIG. 8.2

Shell small, < 0.4 mm long, heavily calcified, with deep, reticulate pits or fossae; ventral border almost straight, dorsal border convex; well-developed caudal process. Eyespot distinct.

Intertidal and shallow sublittoral, among algae. Perhaps all British coasts. A similar species, *H. hoskini* Horne, distinguished by its fewer, larger, reticulate pits, is presently known from the Bristol Channel, among intertidal algae.

Hemicytherura clathrata (Sars)   FIG. 8.2

Larger than *H. cellulosa*, up to 0.62 mm long, with pronounced reticulations between fossae. Ventral margin markedly convex.

Semicytherura nigrescens (Baird)   FIG. 8.2

Shell elongate, greatest height close to midline, posterior border with well-marked caudal process, ventral border straight, dorsal border gently convex; 0.35–0.45 mm long; smooth-surfaced, with fine punctae or striations.

Intertidal and shallow sublittoral; among algae, often in rock-pools, and extending into estuaries and brackish habitats. All British coasts.

Semicytherura striata (Sars)   FIG. 8.2

Larger than *S. nigrescens*, > 0.5 mm long, broadened anteriorly; shell orange, with fine longitudinal striations.

Lower shore and subtidal, sometimes in rock pools.

3 HEMICYTHERIDAE

Shell elongate, subrectangular or oblong, obliquely rounded anteriorly; 0.5–1.2 mm long. Well-calcified, smooth, or with variable sculpture of pits, reticulations, or longitudinal ribs. With two or three anterior frontal scars, and a vertical row of four adductor scars. Three pairs of similar, geniculate, walking legs; antenna 1 with five joints; antenna 2 with well-developed exopod.

Heterocythereis albomaculata (Baird)   FIG. 8.2

Shell elongate oval, broadly fusiform in dorsal view; smoothly rounded anteriorly, slightly tapered posteriorly, 0.85–0.98 mm long; surface finely punctate, with larger, conspicuous pores.

Intertidal and shallow sublittoral, among algae. All British coasts.

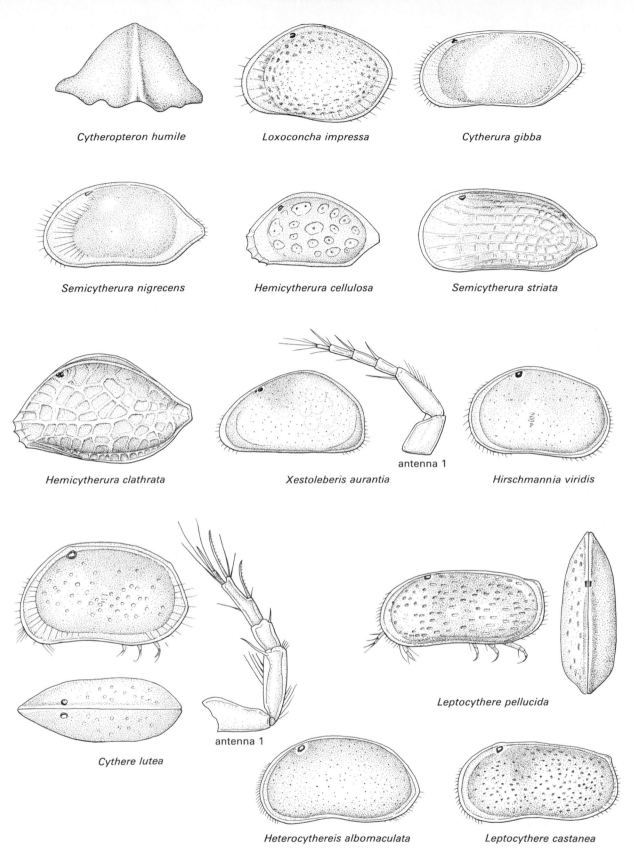

Cytheropteron humile

Loxoconcha impressa

Cytherura gibba

Semicytherura nigrecens

Hemicytherura cellulosa

Semicytherura striata

Hemicytherura clathrata

Xestoleberis aurantia

antenna 1

Hirschmannia viridis

Cythere lutea

antenna 1

Leptocythere pellucida

Heterocythereis albomaculata

Leptocythere castanea

Fig. 8.2

4 LEPTOCYTHERIDAE

Shell slender, small, oval to subquadrangular, with distinct posterior caudal angle; well-calcified, smooth or highly sculptured. A single V-shaped frontal scar, and a vertical row of four adductor scars. Three pairs of walking legs, increasing in length posteriorly. Antenna 1 with five articles; antenna 2 with two terminal claws and a well-developed spinneret bristle, caudal furca with two setae.

Leptocythere castanea Sars   FIG. 8.2

Shell elongate, highest close to anterior edge, posterior border rounded, with small caudal angle; dorsal border almost straight, ventral border concave; up to 0.7 mm long; sculpture of fine punctae.

In brackish and estuarine waters.

Leptocythere pellucida (Baird)   FIG. 8.2

Shell slender, elongate oval, somewhat angular posteriorly; greatest height close to midline; dorsal margin gently convex, ventral margin scarcely concave; caudal angle pronounced; 0.7 mm long; surface with coarse punctulation.

Intertidal and shallow sublittoral, sometimes occurring in estuaries.

5 LOXOCONCHIDAE

Shell short, rhomboidal, posterior margin obliquely rounded or with a dorsal caudal process; 0.4–0.8 mm long. Sculpture weakly developed. Three pairs of slender walking legs. Antenna 1 with five or six articles, slender, with weak claws; antenna 2 with two terminal claws. Caudal furca with one or two setae.

Loxoconcha impressa (Baird)   FIG. 8.2

Shell obliquely oval, greatest height close to midline; 0.6–0.7 mm long; light yellow.

Intertidal and shallow sublittoral, amongst seaweeds, common and often abundant; also in freshwater and brackish habitats. All British coasts.

Hirschmannia viridis Müller   FIG. 8.2

Shell reniform, parallel-sided in dorsal view, tapered anteriorly, rounded posteriorly; 0.45–0.55 mm long, surface finely pitted. Four adductor scars, the dorsalmost U-shaped; frontal scar U-shaped.

Intertidal and shallow sublittoral, among algae; often in brackish water. All British coasts; distributed from northern Norway to Biscay.

6 PARADOXOSTOMATIDAE

Shell elongate, laterally compressed and very slender, lightly calicifed, usually smooth; 0.3–0.9 mm long. No frontal scar, a vertical or oblique row of four or five adductor scars. Walking legs slender, of differing lengths. Antenna 1 with five or six joints; antenna 2 with well-developed spinneret bristle. Mouthparts modified, often forming a sucking disc.

Cytherois fischeri (Sars)   FIG. 8.3

Shell slender, elongate, markedly tapered anteriorly, 0.5–0.65 mm long.

Intertidal and shallow sublittoral, amongst algae; also in estuarine and brackish water habitats; common and often abundant. All British coasts.

Paradoxostoma abbreviatum Sars   FIG. 8.3

Shell short, high, broadly ovate in lateral view, 0.5–0.6 mm long, yellow or white. Posterior margin broadly rounded, with weak caudal process. Female slightly larger than male.

On littoral and sublittoral algae. All British coasts.

Paradoxostoma ensiforme Brady   FIG. 8.3

Shell elongate, subrhomboidal, narrowly rounded at each end, 0.7–0.85 mm long. Posterior margin with weak caudal process. White or light brown.

Intertidal and sublittoral, on algae and in sand. Recorded from scattered localities including Thames Estuary, Channel coasts, Herm, Bristol Channel, the Minch, Shetland, and western Ireland. Formerly confused with *P. anglorum* Horne and Whittaker, presently known from the Thames Estuary and the Essex coast.

Paradoxostoma normani Brady   FIG. 8.3

Small, subovate to subreniform, 0.45–0.5 mm long. With weak posterior caudal process. White, or light greyish brown.

Intertidal and sublittoral, among algae, including *Laminaria*. Reported from scattered localities on western coasts, from Skye to Herm, and from Robin Hood's Bay, Yorkshire.

Paradoxostoma bradyi Sars   FIG. 8.3

Shell strongly inflated, broadly ovate in lateral view, 0.65–0.75 mm long. Posterior margin with upwardly directed, oblique, caudal process. Deeply pigmented olive or chestnut brown.

Intertidal and sublittoral, among algae. Probably present on all British coasts; presently recorded from widely scattered habitats from Thames Estuary, Yorkshire, Northumberland, and all west coasts.

Paradoxostoma pulchellum Sars   FIG. 8.3

Shell small, compressed; dorsal margin evenly convex, ventral margin almost straight; 0.4–0.55 mm long. Posterior margin smoothly curved, no caudal process. Blue-black, with clear or golden-yellow extremities.

Intertidal and shallow sublittoral, amongst algae. Reported from southern and western coasts, from Dorset to the Hebrides.

Paradoxostoma variabile (Baird)   FIG. 8.3

Shell subovate, greatest height posterior to midline, 0.65–0.8 mm long. Colour variable, black to deep blue, brown, or red to grey.

Very common intertidally and sublittorally among algae. Also occurs in estuaries. All British coasts.

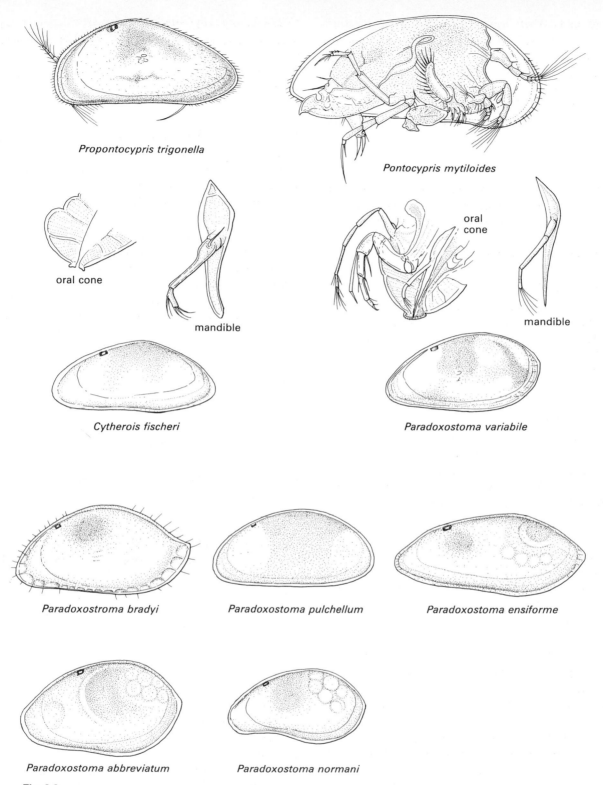

Propontocypris trigonella

Pontocypris mytiloides

oral cone

mandible

oral cone

mandible

Cytherois fischeri

Paradoxostoma variabile

Paradoxostroma bradyi

Paradoxostoma pulchellum

Paradoxostoma ensiforme

Paradoxostoma abbreviatum

Paradoxostoma normani

Fig. 8.3

7 XESTOLEBERIDAE

Shell subovate, dorsoventrally flattened, with curved dorsal margin; broadest posteriorly or with caudal process; left valve larger than right; 0.4–0.7 mm long. Lightly calcified, smooth or with weak sculpture. A single V-shaped frontal scar, and a vertical row of four adductor scars. Three pairs of walking legs, each with short, hooked claws. Antenna 1 with six articles, the terminal article stout; antenna 2 with strong spinneret bristle. Caudal fuca with two setae.

Xestoleberis aurantia (Baird)   FIG. 8.2

Shell thinly calcified, smooth, subreniform; strongly dimorphic, female larger and higher than male; 0.38–0.5 mm. Brownish orange when living.

Among seaweeds, often in rock-pools. Common on all British coasts.

X. nitida (Liljeborg) is larger (>0.5 mm), more distinctly triangular, and has a strongly biconvex outline in dorsal view. It replaces *X. aurantia* in brackish and lagoonal habitats.

8 PONTOCYPRIDIDAE

Shell variable, usually elongate, ovate to subtriangular, dorsally arched and ventrally concave; posterior more narrowly rounded than anterior; 0.5–1.3 mm long. Lightly calcified, smooth or with chitinous bristles. Five adductor scars in triangular pattern. Antennae 1 and 2 with long swimming bristles. Limb 5 leglike in female, forming a grasping hook in male; limb 6 forming a walking leg with one or two claws; limb 7 developed as a cleaning organ. Caudal furca with two terminal claws and four setae.

Pontocypris mytiloides (Norman)   FIG. 8.3

Shell subtriangular, greatest height close to midline, markedly tapered posteriorly; 1.00 mm long; purple coloured, the pigment often persisting in preserved material.

Lower shore and sublittoral.

Propontocypris trigonella Sars   FIG. 8.3

Shell rounded triangular, greatest length along ventral border, greatest height close to midpoint, 0.6–0.7 mm long; right valve larger than the left valve. Five adductor scars arranged in cluster or rosette. Eye prominent.

Sublittoral, recorded mostly from western Scotland. *P. pirifera* (Müller), less distinctly triangular in shape, may prove to be more widely distributed, among algae on British shores.

B Class **Copepoda**

The Copepoda is the second largest class of the Crustacea (after the Malacostraca). The class includes free-living, commensal, semi-parasitic, and parasitic forms. Most species are very small, often less than 0.5 mm. The body is more or less distinctly segmented, except in some parasitic genera, with a *head*, *thorax*, and *abdomen*. The Eucopepoda have only simple eyes (if present) whereas the Branchiura have two compound eyes. Two pairs of *antennae* are usually well-developed, and often used for loco-motion or prehension. The mouthparts consist of a pair of *mandibles, maxillae 1* and *2* and *maxillipeds*. The mandibles usually have a palp which is often biramous.

There are six thoracic segments, the first usually fused into the head. The last thoracic segment bears the genital apertures and is therefore often called the *genital segment*. The abdomen has five segments, some of which are nearly always fused. Very often the female apparently has one abdominal segment less than the male of the same species, due to a fusing of the first and second segments. The last abdominal segment bears two *furcal rami*, which are usually setose.

There is usually only one major articulation in the body, either between the fourth and fifth thoracic segments or fifth and sixth thoracic segments. It is therefore easier to regard the part of the body anterior to this division as the *metasome*, and the part posterior as the *urosome*. Each of the thoracic segments may bear a pair of appendages (legs), though those on the fifth and sixth segments are often modified or absent—indeed the pair on the sixth segment is nearly always lacking in freeliving forms.

The Eucopepoda are now divided into the eight orders: Calanoida, Harpacticoida, Misophrioida, Cyclopoida, Poecilostomatoida, Siphonostomatoida, Herpyllobioida, and Monstrilloida. The keys are for the identification of common genera only, which are likely to be found in the littoral or immediate sublittoral zone.

REFERENCES

Brumpt, E. (1987). Sur un Copepode nouveau (*Saccopsis alleni*, nova species, parasite de *Polycirrus aurantiacus* Grube). *Compte rendu hebdomadaire des séances de l'Academie des sciences, Paris*, **124**, 1464–5.

Delamare-Deboutteville, C. and Laubier, L. (1960). Les Phyllocolidae, une famille nouvelle de Copepodes parasites d'Annelides Polychaetes. *Compte rendu hebdomadaire des séances de l'Academie des sciences, Paris*, **251**, 2083–5.

Gotto, R. V. (1960). A key to the Ascidicolous Copepods of British Waters with Distributional Notes. *Annals and Magazine of Natural History* Ser. 13, **3**, 211–29.

Gotto, R. V. (1966). Copepods associated with Marine Invertebrates from the Northern Coasts of Ireland. *Irish Naturalists Journal*, **15**, 191–6.

Gotto, R. V. (1979). The association of copepods with marine invertebrates. *Advances in marine Biology*, **16**, 1–109.

Harzen, H. J. (1897). *Choniostomatidae*. Copenhagen.

Isaac, M. J. (1974). Copepoda monstrilloida from south-west Britain including six new species. *Journal of the Marine Biological Association of the U.K.*, **54**, 127–40.

Kabata, Z. (1979). *Parasitic Copepods of British Fishes*. Ray Society, London.

Malaquin, A. (1901). Le parasitisme évolutif des Monstrillides (Crustaces Copepodes). *Archives de Zoologie expérimental et génerale*, **9**, 81–232.

Sars, G. O. (1903). Copepoda Calanoida. *An Account of the Crustacea of Norway*, **4**, 1–171.

Sars, G. O. (1911). Copepoda Harpacticoida. *An Account of the Crustacea of Norway*, **5**, 1–449.

Sars, G. O. (1918). Copepoda Cyclopoida. *An Account of the Crustacea of Norway*, **6**, 1–225.

Sars, G. O. (1921). Copepoda Supplement. *An Account of the Crustacea of Norway*, **7**, 1–121.

Sars, G. O. (1921). Copepoda Monstrilloida and Notodelphyoida. *An Account of the Crustacea of Norway*, **8**, 1–91.

Wilson, C. B. (1932). The Copepods of the Woods Hole Region, Massachussetts. *Bulletin of the U.S. National Museum*, **158**, 1–635.

Yamaguti, S. (1963). *Parasitic Copepoda and Branchiura of Fishes*. Interscience, New York.

FREE-LIVING COPEPODA

---

1. Antenna 1 reaching at least as far as last segment of metasome   **2**

   Antenna 1 not reaching any further than segment 1 of metasome   **6**

---

2. Urosome, excluding furcal rami, shorter than metasome   Calanoida *3*

   Urosome, excluding furcal rami, more or less as long as metasome   ***Oithona***

---

3. Metasome consisting of five segments   **4**

   Metasome consisting of six segments   **5**

---

4. Furcal ramus at least five times long as wide   ***Temora***

   Furcal ramus much shorter   ***Acartia***

---

5. Metasome contracted anteriorly, giving the appearance of 'shoulders'   ***Centropages***

   Metasome rounded anteriorly; often in brackish pools   ***Eurytemora***

---

6. Antenna 1 consisting of less than ten segments (except *Halicyclops*, in brackish pools,
   see below); antenna 2 biramous; body usually cylindrical or ovoid, with less obvious
   division between metasome and urosome   Harpacticoida (see separate key)

   Antenna 1 consisting of at least ten segments; antenna 2 uniramous; metasome usually
   much wider than urosome   **7**

---

7. Mouthparts setose and used to scoop phytoplankton   **8**

   Mouthparts more robust and adapted for prehension and predation   **9**

---

8. Antenna 1 with six segments; in brackish pools   ***Halicyclops***

   Antenna 1 with at least ten segments   ***Cyclopina***

---

9. Urosome at least three-quarters length of metasome   ***Pseudanthessius****

   Urosome no more than half length of metasome   ***Ascomyzon****

*N.B. These two genera are parasitic, but sometimes found living freely from their hosts.

Order **Calanoida**

Acartia   FIG. 8.4

Length usually 1.0–1.3 mm, males slightly smaller than the females. The eye is well-developed and far forward. The metasome consists of five segments, the urosome three segments in the female and four in the male. Body very pale to colourless.

Centropages   FIG. 8.4

Length 1.3–1.8 mm, males slightly smaller than the females, with a prominent pincer on the fifth leg to transfer the spermatophore. Metasome contracted anteriorly, with a pair of spines on the posterior tips of the last (sixth) segment. The urosome consists of three segments in the female, four in the male.

Temora longicornis (Müller)   FIG. 8.4

Length 1.5 mm. Eye small. Metasome consists of five segments, and is wider anteriorly. The urosome consists of three segments in the female and five in the male. The furcal rami are extremely long.

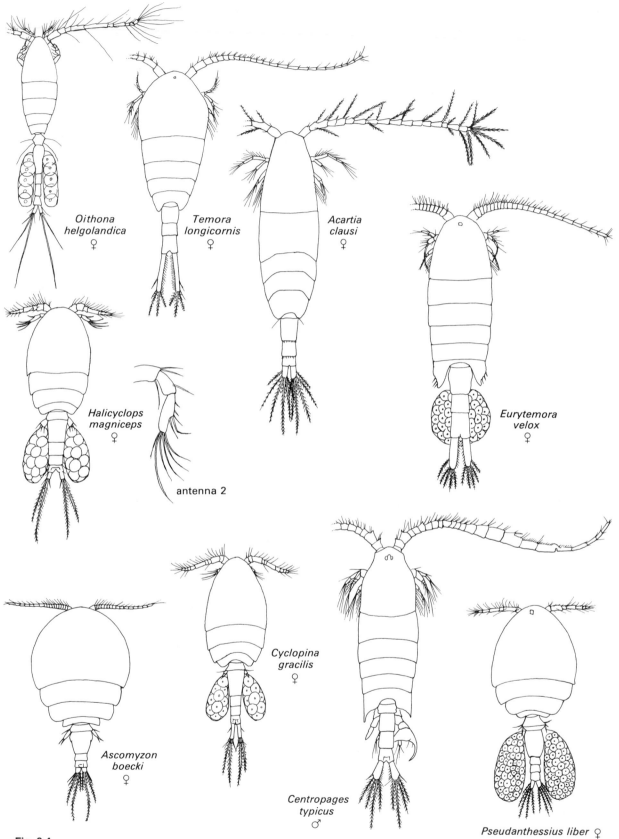

Oithona helgolandica ♀

Temora longicornis ♀

Acartia clausi ♀

Eurytemora velox ♀

Halicyclops magniceps ♀

antenna 2

Ascomyzon boecki ♀

Cyclopina gracilis ♀

Centropages typicus ♂

Pseudanthessius liber ♀

Fig. 8.4

Eurytemora FIG. 8.4

More elongate than the preceding genus; some species with a pair of spines or points on the posterior tips of the last (sixth) segment of the metasome. Urosome consists of three segments in the female, five in the male. Furcal rami elongate. A brackish water genus, often found in pools on salt-marshes.

Order Cyclopoida

Oithona FIG. 8.4

Rather delicate and slender, with an almost transparent body. First antennae very setose, and unusually long for a cyclopoid. Metasome of five segments; the urosome of five or six segments, and elongate.

Order Harpacticoida

Halicyclops FIG. 8.4

Length about 0.75 mm; body typical cyclopoid shape with short first antennae consisting of only six segments. Metasome of four segments, the urosome of five. In brackish water; often in rock-pools.

Cyclopina FIG. 8.4

More elongate than the preceding species. The metasome consists of four segments, the urosome of five. The furcal rami are elongate in some species. *C. gracilis* is sometimes found in rock-pools.

KEY TO GENERA

1. Maxilliped 2 non-prehensile (A in Fig. 8.5) — **2**
   Maxilliped 2 prehensile, with clawed, hand-like structure (D in Fig. 8.5) — **4**

2. Inner ramus of secondary natatory leg very elongated (B in Fig. 8.5) — *Longipedia*
   Second natatory leg more or less normal (C in Fig. 8.5) — **3**

3. Anterior of body somewhat dilated — *Bradya*
   Anterior of body not so — *Ectinosoma*

4. Body short and depressed, with urosome short, giving the body an isopod-like appearance — **5**
   Urosome obviously narrower than the metasome; and/or body elongated — **6**

5. Body shield-shaped. First natatory legs wide and flattened — *Porcellidium*
   Body more elongate. First natatory legs elongate — *Alteutha*

6. Thoracic segment 3 with a large dorsal plate-like extension, completely overlapping segment 4 and the articulation — *Aspidiscus*
   Thoracic segment 3 not so expanded — **7**

7. First pair of natatory legs similar in shape to second, third, and fourth pairs — *Tachidius*
   First pair of natatory legs dissimilar in shape from next three pairs (E in Fig. 8.5) — **8**

8. Segments of body sharply demarcated, giving a scalariform appearance — **9**
   Body not as described — **10**

9. Caudal rami short and lamellar — *Asellopsis*
   Caudal rami longer and cylindrical — *Laophonte*

10. Cephalic segment very large, almost half the body length; other segments very short.
    Bright red in colour   ***Metis ignea***
    Body not as described   **11**

11. Endopod of fourth natatory leg consists of one segment, or absent (A in Fig. 8.6)   **12**
    Endopod of fourth natatory leg consists of two segments (B in Fig. 8.6)   **13**
    Endopod of fourth natatory leg consists of three segments (D in Fig. 8.6)   **14**

12. First natatory leg prehensile with terminal claws   ***Evansula***
    First natatory leg non-prehensile, with setae only   ***Huntemannia***

13. Fifth leg consists of a single article, ending with a very large spine. Body very elongated
         Leptastacus
    Fifth leg consists of two articles, with setae and no spines   ***Mesochra***

14. Endopod of first leg consists of two segments (C in Fig. 8.6)   **15**
    Endopod of first leg consists of three segments (E in Fig. 8.7)   **19**

15. Exopod of first leg consists of one or two segments (C in Fig. 8.6)   **16**
    Exopod of first leg consists of three segments (B in Fig. 8.7)   **17**

16. Exopod of first leg shorter than endopod   ***Westwoodia***
    Exopod of first leg longer than endopod   ***Zaus***

17. Distal segment of leg 5 projects beyond proximal segment (C in Fig. 8.7)   **18**
    Distal segment of leg 5 does not project beyond proximal segment   ***Dactylopodella***

18. Furcal rami at least twice as long as broad   ***Stenhelia***
    Furcal rami about twice as broad as long   ***Microthalestris***

19. Exopod of first leg consists of one or two segments   ***Harpacticus***
    Exopod of first leg consists of three segments (A in Fig. 8.7)   **20**

20. Fifth leg consists of one obvious segment   ***Stenhelia***
    Fifth leg consists of two obvious segments (D in Fig. 8.7)   **21**

21. Exopod of first leg longer than endopod (F in Fig. 8.7)   **22**
    Exopod of first leg shorter than endopod (A in Fig. 8.8)   **23**
    Exopod and endopod of first leg more or less equal in length (D in Fig. 8.8)   **33**

22. Exopod of antenna 2 with four segments; fifth legs small, not reaching the ovisac; bright orange in colour, living in brackish pools **Tigriopus fulvus**

Exopod of antenna 2 with two segments; fifth legs large, reaching the ovisac; living in algae on the shore **Thalestris**

23. Division between metasome and urosome well-marked, with abrupt narrowing at thoracic segment 5 **24**

Division between metasome and urosome not well-defined; thoracic segments 4 and 5 of similar width **33**

24. Basal segment of endopod of first leg longer than entire exopod (A in Fig. 8.8) **25**

This segment equal to or shorter than exopod (C in Fig. 8.8) **26**

25. Exopod of antenna 2 with three segments **Dactylopusia**

Exopod of antenna 2 with one segment **Diosaccus**

26. Middle segment of endopods of second, third, and fourth legs each with two setae **Tisbe** (= Idya)

These segments with one seta each (B in Fig. 8.8) **27**

These segments without uniform setation **28**

27. Segments of urosome coarsely spinulose at hind edge; last segment with dorsal series of spinules **Nitocra**

Urosome segments less coarsely spinulose; last segment without dorsal series of spinules **Ameira**

28. Middle segment of endopod of second leg with one seta, that of third and fourth legs with two setae **Dactylopusia**

This segment of second and third legs with two setae, that of fourth leg with one seta **29**

This segment of second leg with two setae, those of third and fourth legs with one seta each **30**

29. Metasome wider than urosome **Diosaccus**

Metasome very slightly wider than urosome **Amphiascus**

30. Rostrum not visible from dorsal view **31**

Rostrum visible from dorsal view **32**

31. Metasome considerably wider than urosome **Machairopus**

Metasome very slightly wider than urosome **Thalestris**

32. Body more or less cylindrical in shape **Parathalestris**

Body more tapering **Stenhelia**

33. Exopod of antenna 2 with one segment; rostrum very small and immobile **Nitocra**

Exopod of antenna 2 with two segments; rostrum larger and may be mobile (G in Fig. 8.7) **34**

34. Body cylindrical in shape, metasome/urosome division not obvious; rostrum visible from dorsal view and mobile **Parathalestris**

Metasome/urosome division more obvious; rostrum immobile, not visible from dorsal view **Thalestris**

Longipedia FIG. 8.5

Slender body, consisting of four metasome segments (as in all genera) and six urosome segments. Last segment with dorsal terminal spines, the centre one being particularly robust. Inner ramus of second leg very elongated. Ovisac single.

Bradya FIG. 8.5

Urosome narrower than the metasome which is obviously wider and somewhat dorso-ventrally compressed. Outer ramus of second antenna well-developed. The urosome consists of five segments. Ovisac single.

Ectinosoma FIG. 8.5

Narrow body with little difference in width of metasome and urosome; rostrum robust. Urosome consists of five segments. Ovisac single. The animals of this genus remain floating on the surface film after being exposed to the air.

Porcellidium viride (Philippi) FIG. 8.5

Body extremely dorso-ventrally compressed and almost oval in shape. Metasome consisting of four segments, the urosome of two, the first of which is very wide. A single flattened ovisac. Lives amongst seaweeds on the shore. Length female 0.9 mm, male 0.6 mm.

Alteutha FIG. 8.5

Body more or less oval, four urosome segments. Ovisac single and extends anteriorly. Lives amongst *Laminaria*; it is a strong swimmer. Rolls up when disturbed.

Aspidiscus FIG. 8.5

The metasome is markedly wider than the urosome, with the last (fourth) segment attenuated dorsally, overlapping the first two urosome segments. Ovisac single. Found amongst *Laminaria*, to which it can attach itself very strongly.

Tachidius FIG. 8.5

The metasome is only slightly wider than the urosome; the genital segment of the female is partially divided into two. A single ovisac. The swimming legs are very well-developed, and the animal is very active. Sometimes found in brackish water.

Asellopsis FIG. 8.5

The body tapers very gradually, with the urosome almost as wide as the metasome. There is a pronounced rostrum in front of a well-developed eye. Sometimes found in rock pools. Length about 0.58 mm.

Laophonte FIG. 8.5

No obvious difference in width between metasome and urosome. Constrictions between the segments very marked. Inner ramus of first leg with a large claw-like, terminal segment. Single ovisac. Some species may be found in brackish water.

Metis ignea Philippi FIG. 8.6

Body more or less pear-shaped, with no obvious demarcation between the metasome and urosome. First (cephalic) segment very large – nearly half the body length. First pair of legs very robust with claw-like setae. Bright red in colour. Single ovisac. Sometimes found in rock pools. Length 0.55 mm.

Evansula incerta (Scott) FIG. 8.6

Body very slender and cylindrical in form. Prominent rostrum (in dorsal view) with sharp point at the tip. Furcal ramus long, with the apical seta swollen at the base, and kinked. Single ovisac. Length 0.84 mm

Huntemannia jadensis Poppe FIG. 8.6

Body tapers gradually; a well-defined rostrum, with a setose, rounded tip. Furcal ramus tipped with an extremely short spine which is about equal in length to the ramus. Found in tidal pools. Length 0.96 mm.

Leptastacus macronyx (Scott) FIG. 8.6

Cylindrical body shape. Fifth leg a single segment, with a stout spine which projects beyond the sides of the body when viewed dorsally. Furcal ramus long, with a stout apical seta, swollen at the base. Single ovisac. Body length 0.7 mm.

Mesochra FIG. 8.6

Body tapering, with five urosomal segments. Eye obvious, but not particularly well-developed. Rostrum small and rounded

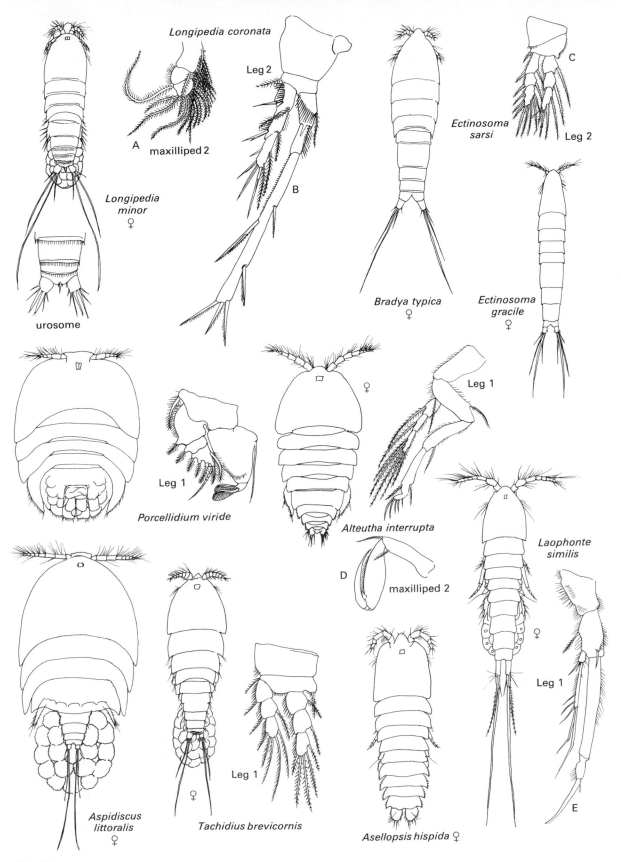

Longipedia coronata

A maxilliped 2

Leg 2

B

Longipedia minor ♀

urosome

Ectinosoma sarsi

Leg 2 C

Bradya typica ♀

Ectinosoma gracile ♀

Leg 1

Leg 1

Porcellidium viride

Alteutha interrupta ♀

D maxilliped 2

Laophonte similis ♀

Leg 1

E

Aspidiscus littoralis ♀

Tachidius brevicornis ♀

Leg 1

Asellopsis hispida ♀

Fig. 8.5

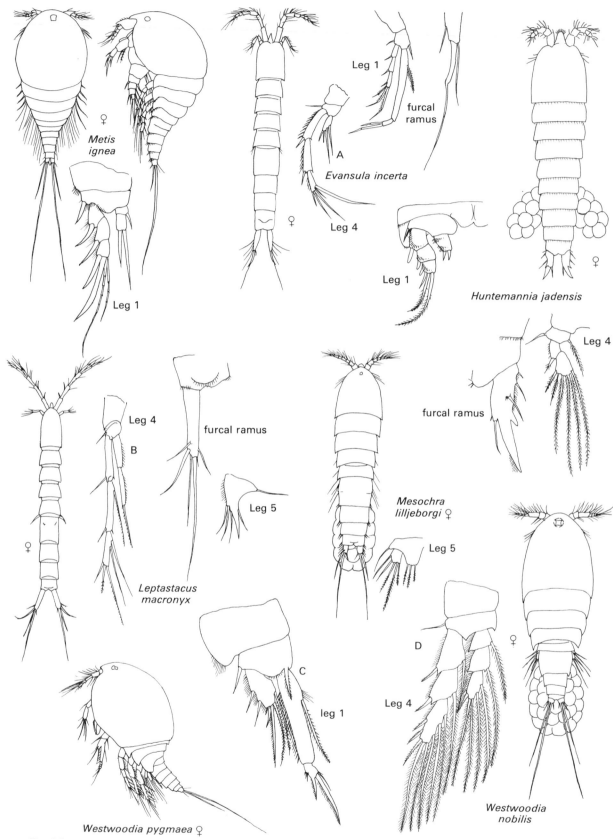

Metis ignea

Leg 1

Leg 1

Evansula incerta

A

Leg 4

furcal ramus

Leg 1

Huntemannia jadensis

Leg 4

Leg 4

B

furcal ramus

Leg 5

Leptastacus macronyx

furcal ramus

Mesochra lilljeborgi ♀

Leg 5

leg 1

C

D

Leg 4

Westwoodia nobilis

Westwoodia pygmaea ♀

Fig. 8.6

from dorsal view. Found in rock pools; some species also live in brackish water.

Westwoodia FIG. 8.6

Body somewhat pear-shaped, with large first (cephalic) segment. All metasomal segments project ventrally at the sides, giving rise to plate-like structures. Single ovisac. Often in pools and brackish ponds.

Zaus FIG. 8.7

A broad body with the metasome/urosome division very obvious. Metasomal segments produced laterally, and body dorso-ventrally flattened. Eye very obvious. Single ovisac. Sometimes stranded in pools.

Dactylopodella FIG. 8.7

First (cephalic) segment very large, more than half length of the metasome. The metasome/urosome division is well-marked. Eye obvious. Single ovisac.

Microthalestris FIG. 8.7

Body cylindrical, with the urosome similar in width to the metasome, though the division is evident. Rostrum very obvious from dorsal view. Last (sixth) urosomal segment with a dorsal prominence between the furcal rami which is most obvious in lateral view. Single ovisac. In rock-pools, often above high water.

Harpacticus FIG. 8.7

Body tapering, with an obvious metasome/urosome division. Rostrum broad in dorsal view. Outer ramus of third legs of male very robust. Single ovisac. Often in pools on the shore.

Stenhelia FIG. 8.7

Body tapers more or less uniformly; eye prominent; rostrum triangular with a broad base in dorsal view. Two sub-lateral ovisacs.

Tigriopus fulvus (Fischer) FIG. 8.7

Metasome/urosome division obvious. Eye quite prominent; rostrum wide and rounded. Single ovisac. A bright orange copepod found in rock-pools, often above high water. Length 1.2 mm.

Thalestris FIG. 8.7

Metasome/urosome division not very distinct. Eye very prominent and usually complex. Ovisac single, and more or less entirely covered by the large, flattened fifth legs of the female.

Dactylopusia FIG. 8.8

Body tapers more or less uniformly. Fourth metasomal segment with somewhat pointed postero-lateral edges. Rostrum broad and rounded in dorsal view. Ovisac single. Often in tidal pools, or amongst seaweeds.

Diosaccus tenuicornis (Claus) FIG. 8.8

First metasome segment longer than next three combined; all

metasomal segments with lateral margins produced ventrally and posteriorly. Rostrum extremely large. Metasome/urosome division pronounced. Two ovisacs. Often in tidal pools or amongst seaweeds. Length 0.8 mm.

Tisbe (= Idya) FIG. 8.8

Metasome much wider than urosome, somewhat pointed anteriorly, with a small rostrum, not obvious from dorsal view. Metasomal segments extended laterally. Eye obvious, but not prominent. Ovisac single. Often in tidal pools or amongst seaweeds.

Nitocra FIG. 8.8

Body more or less cylindrical, with metasome/urosome division not obvious. Eye small. Urosomal segments with postero-lateral spines; the last segment with spines across the postero-dorsal margin. Single ovisac. In brackish water or tidal pools.

Ameira FIG. 8.8

Similar to preceding genus, but the last abdominal segment without the spines across the postero-dorsal margin. Single ovisac. In pools or amongst seaweeds.

Amphiascus FIG. 8.8

Body tapers slightly; rostrum large and mobile. All metasomal segments with lateral margins produced posteriorly. Some species have a swelling and/or kink at the base of the largest furcal seta. Two ovisacs.

Machairopus minutus Sars FIG. 8.8

Metasome much broader than urosome, with all the metasomal margins produced laterally. Rostrum not obvious in dorsal view. Body white with two pink bands, one across the first segment and one across the anterior part of the urosome. Ovisac single. Amongst seaweeds and in sand. Length 0.65 mm.

Parathalestris FIG. 8.8

Body tapers more or less evenly, with the metasome/urosome division not obvious. Eye large. Ovisac single and very large, reaching as far as, or beyond the end of the furcal rami. Amongst seaweeds and sometimes in pools.

COMMENSAL AND PARASITIC COPEPODA

Commensalism and parasitism occur in all major taxonomic groups within the Copepoda, with the exception of the Calanoida and the Mesophrioida, and certain orders are entirely parasitic. The degree of consequent morphological adaptation varies greatly from family to family. In some this is expressed as a reduction of the abdomen, and an enlargement and modification of the thoracic appendages for grasping. In many other groups, however, the adult form is not readily recognizable as a copepod. In particular, among permanently attached species appendages are frequently reduced or lost, body segmentation is not apparent, and the organism appears as little more than a simple, saclike structure with grossly enlarged reproductive organs. The

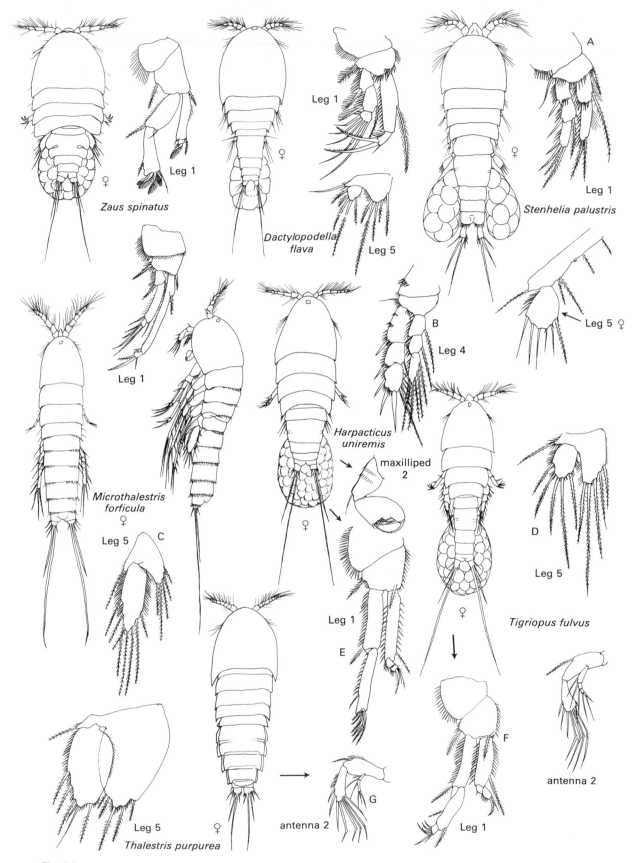

Zaus spinatus

Leg 1

Dactylopodella flava

Leg 1

Leg 5

Stenhelia palustris

A

Leg 1

Leg 5 ♀

B

Leg 4

Leg 1

Microthalestris forficula ♀

Leg 5

C

Harpacticus uniremis

maxilliped 2

Leg 1

E

D

Leg 5

Tigriopus fulvus

F

Leg 1

antenna 2

Leg 5

Thalestris purpurea

antenna 2

G

Fig. 8.7

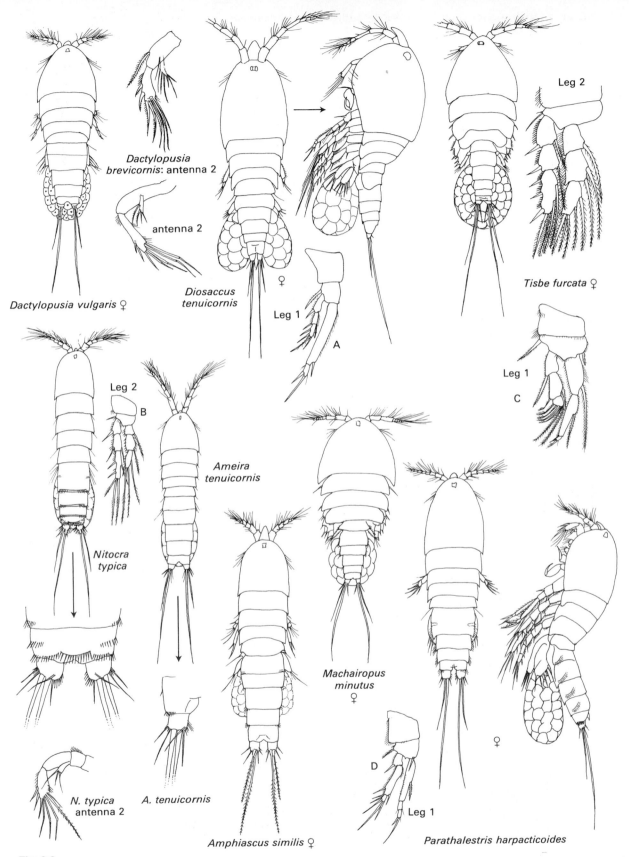

Dactylopusia brevicornis: antenna 2

antenna 2

Dactylopusia vulgaris ♀

Diosaccus tenuicornis ♀

Leg 1

A

Tisbe furcata ♀

Leg 2

Leg 1

C

Leg 2

B

Ameira tenuicornis

Nitocra typica

N. typica antenna 2

A. tenuicornis

Amphiascus similis ♀

Machairopus minutus ♀

D

Leg 1

♀

Parathalestris harpacticoides

Fig. 8.8

taxonomic affinity of such species is only revealed by study of their larval and juvenile stages.

There are very many species of parasitic copepod. Those associated with fishes are relatively well-studied, and have been the subject of several monographic treatments (Kabata 1979; Yamaguti 1963) but those parasitizing marine invertebrates are still poorly known. A comprehensive treatment of commensal and parasitic copepods is beyond the scope of this book. The following accounts are intended to illustrate the taxonomic and morphological diversity of this group of animals. Representative genera are figured, and the most frequently occurring species are noted, together with their usual hosts. For accurate identification of most species it will be necessary to consult specialist texts given in the reference list.

Order **Poecilostomatoida**

Acanthochondria   FIG. 8.9
Particularly associated with fish. The type species, *A. cornuta* (Müller) is primarily a parasite of flatfish in the North Atlantic. In British waters it is commonly reported on the Plaice *Pleuronectes platessa* (L.), Flounder *Platichthys flesus* (L.) and Dab *Limanda limanda* (L.) *A. limandae* (Krøyer) is restricted to the Dab; *A. soleae* (Krøyer) is similarly limited to the Sole *Solea solea* (L.), but may occur rarely on Brill *Scophthalmus rhombus* (L.). Both latter species have a restricted distribution in northeast Atlantic waters.

Bomolochus
Less modified than many other parasitic genera, species of *Bomolochus* are recognizably copepods. *B. soleae* Claus is a parasite of the Sole *Solea solea* (L.), in British and Mediterranean waters.

Ergasilus   FIG. 8.9
Species of this genus are characterized by a massively enlarged trunk region. They are parasites of both marine and freshwater fishes, and *E. gibbus* von Hardmann is a common parasite of the European Eel, *Anguilla anguilla* (L.).

Eunicicola   FIG. 8.9
The only British species, *E. clausi* Kurz, is an associate of the polychaete *Eunice harassii* Audouin and Milne Edwards.

Holobomolochus   FIG. 8.9
One species occurs in British waters, *H. confusus* (Stock), with a relatively unmodified body form, particularly broad anteriorly. *H. confusus* is a common parasite of the Cod *Gadus morhua* (L.) in the north-east Atlantic, and large specimens may contain several dozen of the parasite in their nasal cavities. It also occurs frequently in other gadoid fish, including Whiting *Merlangius merlangus* (L.), Coalfish *Pollachius virens* (L.), Ling *Molva molva* (L.), and Haddock *Melanogrammus aeglefinus* (L.), as well as the Lumpsucker *Cyclopterus lumpus* (L.), Ballan Wrasse *Labrus bergylta* Ascanius, Bib *Trisopterus luscus* (L.), and the Conger *Conger conger* (L.).

Lernentoma
The single species, *L. asellina* (Linnaeus), occurs in the northeast Atlantic region as a parasite of Gurnards (Triglidae), including the Grey Gurnard *Eutrigla gurnadus* (L.) and the Sapphirine Gurnard *T. lucerna* (L.). It has been reported rarely from the Plaice *Pleuronectes platessa* (L.) but does not occur on other species of fish.

Lichomolgus   FIG. 8.9
This large genus is particularly associated with ascidians. In the British sea area, *L. poucheti* Canu occurs in *Morchellium argus* (Milne Edwards), *L. forficula* Thorell in *Phallusia mamillata* (Cuvier) and *Ascidia mentula* Müller, *L. tenuifurcatus* Sars in *Diplosoma listerianum* (Milne Edwards) and the echinoderm *Labidoplax digitata* (Montagu), and *L. furcillatus* Thorell in *Ciona intestinalis* (L.). Both *C. intestinalis* and *Clavelina lepadiformis* (Müller) are host to *L. canui* Sars. *L. agilis* (Leydig) parasitizes a large number of opisthobranch molluscs, including *Doto coronata* (Gmelin), *Janolus cristatus* (delle Chiaje), *Archidoris pseudoargus* (Rapp), and *Aeolidia papillosa* (L.), while *L. leptodermata* Gooding is found in the Norway cockle, *Laevicardium crassum* (Gmelin).

Modiolicola   FIG. 8.9
Three species occur in British waters. *M. insignis* Aurivillus occurs in the mantle cavity of both the common Mussel *Mytilus edulis* (Linnaeus), and the Horse Mussel *Modiolus modiolus* (L.). *M. inermis* Canu and *M. maxima* Thompson are both associated with the Queen Scallop *Chlamys opercularis* (L.).

Mytilicola
The single British species, *M. intestinalis* Steuer is particularly associated with the Common Mussel *Mytilus edulis* (L.), some populations of which may have very high levels of infestation. It has also been reported from *Dosinia exoleta* (L.).

Pseudanthessius   FIG. 8.4
Two species are associated with echinoderms: *P. liber* (Brady and Robertson) occurs on *Echinus esculentus* L., and *P. sauvagei* Canu on *Echinocardium cordatum* (Pennant). *P. thorellii* (Brady and Robertson) is found in the Queen Scallop *Chlamys opercularis* (L.).

Sabelliphilus   FIG. 8.9
S. elongatus (Sars) is a parasite of the fanworm, *Sabella pavonina* Savigny.

Splanchnotrophus   FIG. 8.9
Species of *Sphanchnotrophus* have been reported from various opisthobranch seaslugs, including *Ancula gibbosa* (Risso), *Coryphella verrucosa* (Sars), *Aeolidia papillosa* (L.) and *Aeolidiella glauca* (Alder and Hancock). *S. gracilis* Hancock and Norman has been most frequently recorded, attached to *Acanthodoris pilosa* (Abildgaard, in Müller).

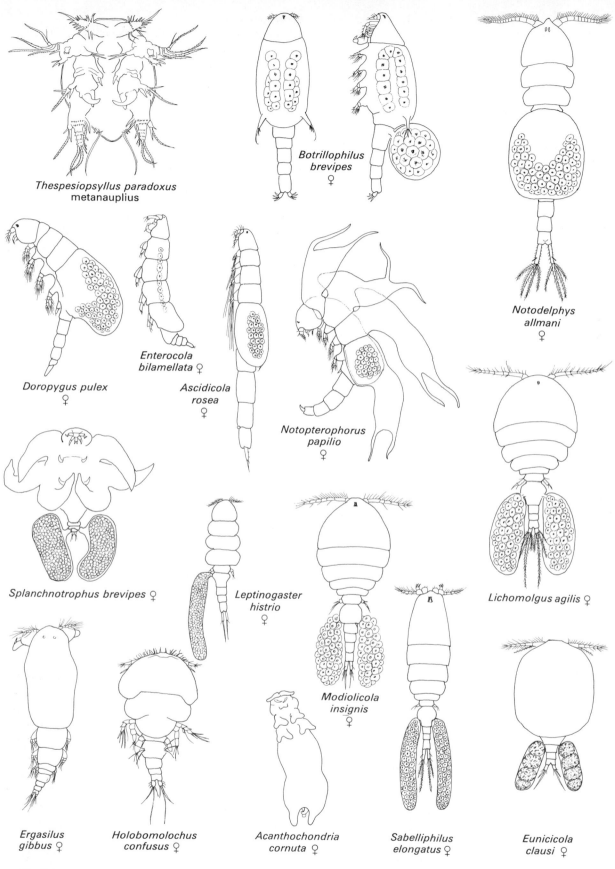

Thespesiopsyllus paradoxus
metanauplius

*Botrillophilus
brevipes*
♀

*Notodelphys
allmani*
♀

Doropygus pulex
♀

*Enterocola
bilamellata* ♀

*Ascidicola
rosea*
♀

*Notopterophorus
papilio*
♀

Splanchnotrophus brevipes ♀

*Leptinogaster
histrio*
♀

*Modiolicola
insignis*
♀

Lichomolgus agilis ♀

*Ergasilus
gibbus* ♀

*Holobomolochus
confusus* ♀

*Acanthochondria
cornuta* ♀

*Sabelliphilus
elongatus* ♀

*Eunicicola
clausi* ♀

Fig. 8.9

Order Cyclopoida

Ascidicola
FIG. 8.9

The only British species, *A. rosea* Thorell, is a parasite of the ascidians *Pyura squamulosa* (Alder), *Corella parallelogramma* (Müller), *Ascidia virginea* (Müller), and *Ascidiella aspersa* (Müller).

Botrillophilus
FIG. 8.9

Species of *Botrillophilus* are found in association with compound ascidians. *B. ruber* Hesse has been reported from many ascidian species, including *Aplidium proliferum* (Milne Edwards), *A. punctum* (Giard), *Botryllus schlosseri* (Pallas), *Botrylloides leachi* (Savigny), *Clavelina lepadiformis* (Müller), and *Morchellium argus* (Milne Edwards). *B. brevipes* (Sars) has been recorded only from *Botryllus schlosseri*.

Doropygus
FIG. 8.9

Two species are most frequently reported, *D. normani* (Brady) in *Pyura squamulosa* (Alder), and *D. pulex* Thorell in *Ascidiella scabra* (Müller).

Enterocola
FIG. 8.9

Several species recorded from Britain, usually as gut parasites of ascidians.

Lamippe
FIG. 8.10

L. rubicunda (Olsson) is found in association with the soft coral *Alcyonium digitatum* L.

Notodelphys
FIG. 8.9

Species of this genus are among the commonest parasites of the larger solitary ascidians. In British waters *N. allmani* Thorell has been reported from *Ascidia mentula* Müller and *Ascidiella aspersa* (Müller), *N. agilia* Thorell from *Corella paralellogramma* (Müller), *N. prasina* (Thorell) from *Phallusia mamillata* and *A. mentula*, and *N. elegans* from *Ciona intestinalis* (L.).

Notopterophorus
FIG. 8.9

The female of *Notopterophorus papilio* Hesse is immediately recognized by its striking morphology, but the smaller and rather nondescript male may be overlooked. *N. papilio* occurs, sometimes in large numbers, in the branchial cavity of *Ascidia mentula* (Müller).

Thespesiopsyllus
FIG. 8.9

The brittle stars *Ophiopholis aculeata* (L.), *Ophiothrix fragilis* (Abildgaard), and *Ophiura albida* Forbes are host to the larvae of *T. paradoxus* (Sars).

Order Siphonostomatoida

Artotrogus
FIG. 8.10

Body very broad. Female of *A. orbicularis* parasitizes dorid nudibranchs, but is also found free-living among algae.

Ascomyzon

Primarily parasites of echinoderms. *A. latum* (Brady) and *A. violaceum* (Claus) have been recorded on *Echinus esculentus* L., and *A. asterocheres* (Boeck) on *Asterias rubens* L.

Caligus
FIG. 8.10

A large genus of successful fish parasites, *Caligus* species are recognized by the broadly rounded cephalothorax. *C. curtus* Müller is common on gadoid fish, as well as percomorphs, flatfish, and even elasmobranchs. *C. elongatus* Nordmann has been recorded from more than 80 species of fish. *C. diaphanus* Nordmann is equally catholic in its choice of host, but *C. centrodonti* Baird is restricted to Perciformes, while *C. labracis* Scott is known only from the Ballan Wrasse *Labrus bergylta* Ascanius and the Cuckoo Wrasse *L. mixtus* L., and only from British waters.

Cancerilla
FIG. 8.10

Cancerilla tubulata (Dalyell) occurs on the brittlestar *Amphipholis squamata* (delle Chiaje) and *Ophiocomina nigra* (Abildgaard).

Clavella
FIG. 8.10

Three species of this genus of teleost parasites occur in British waters. *C. adunca* (Strom) is a common parasite of gadoid fish, including Cod *Gadus morhua* L., Whiting *Merlangius merlangus* (L.), Haddock *Melanogrammus aeglefinus* (L.), and Bib *Trisopterus luscus* (L.).

Haemobaphes
FIG. 8.10

Two species recorded from Britain. *H. cyclopterina* (Fabricius) parasitizes many fish species; *H. ambiguus* Scott occurs in the gill cavity of dragonets.

Hatschekia
FIG. 8.10

Six species are known to occur in British waters, but none seem to be common. *H. labracis* (van Beneden) may be common on the Ballan Wrasse *Labrus bergylta* (Ascanius) and the Cuckoo Wrasse *Labrus mixtus* L., but appears to have a limited distribution in the north-east Atlantic. *H. cluthae* (Scott) is known only from British waters, on the Goldsinny *Ctenolabrus rupestris* (L.) while *H. pygmaea* Scott and Scott has been recorded only on the Corkwing *Crenilabrus melops* (L.) and the Goldsinny, off western Scotland, and on the Corkwing at Plymouth.

Lepeophtheirus
FIG. 8.10

Very similar to *Caligus*. Species of *Lepeophtheirus* parasitize marine teleosts. Seven species occur in British waters. *L. pectoralis* (Müller) is a parasite of pleuronectid flatfish, in the north-east Atlantic; records from other species of fish probably result from transference of the parasite in trawled catches. *L. hippoglossi* (Krøyer) is principally associated with the Atlantic Halibut *Hippoglossus hippoglossus* (L.), but may occur rarely on Turbot *Psetta maxima* (L.), and Brill *Scophthalmus rhombus* (L.). The usual parasite of the latter two fish is *L. thompsoni* Baird.

Leptinogaster
FIG. 8.9

Two species may be encountered in bivalve molluscs: *L. pholadis* Pelseneer in *Pholas dactylus* L., and *L. histrio* (Pelseneer) in *Macoma balthica* (L.) and *Abra alba* (Wood).

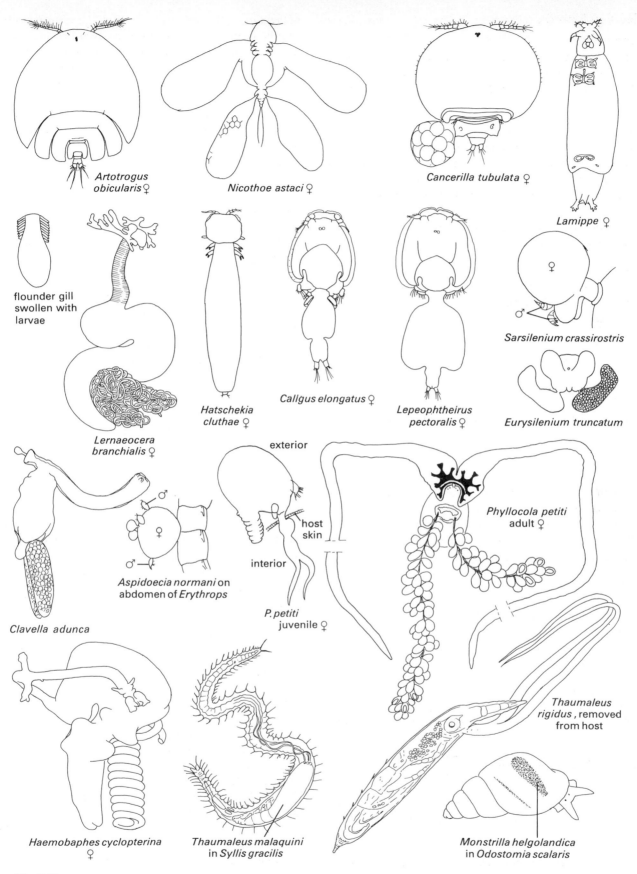

Artotrogus obicularis ♀

Nicothoe astaci ♀

Cancerilla tubulata ♀

Lamippe ♀

flounder gill swollen with larvae

Hatschekia cluthae ♀

Callgus elongatus ♀

Lepeophtheirus pectoralis ♀

Sarsilenium crassirostris

Eurysilenium truncatum

Lernaeocera branchialis ♀

Clavella adunca

Aspidoecia normani on abdomen of *Erythrops*

exterior

host skin

interior

P. petiti juvenile ♀

Phyllocola petiti adult ♀

Thaumaleus rigidus, removed from host

Haemobaphes cyclopterina ♀

Thaumaleus malaquini in *Syllis gracilis*

Monstrilla helgolandica in *Odostomia scalaris*

Fig. 8.10

Lernaeocera   FIG. 8.10

The life cycle of *Lernaeocera* involves two hosts. The copepodite stage of the parasite, little modified from the typical copepod plan, is usually associated with a flatfish, on which it undergoes a series of metamorphoses before moving as an impregnated female to its final host, a gadoid fish. This final, highly modified form of the parasite attaches to the ventral gill arches of the fish and penetrates as far as the ventral aorta; it is usually lethal to its host. *L. branchialis* (Linnaeus) chooses a pleuronectid flatfish as its intermediate host, and the mature females are most frequent on cod *Gadus morhua* L., Pollach *Pollachius pollachius* (L.), Coalfish *P. virens*, (L.), Haddock *Melanogrammus aeglefinus* (L.), and Whiting *Merlangius merlangus* (L.). Preferred intermediate and final hosts appear to vary throughout the northeast Atlantic, with the parasite occurring with highest frequency on one species in one part of the range, and on other species elsewhere. The Cod shows a high level of infestation throughout its geographical range. *L. lusci* (Bassett-Smith) is similar to *L. branchialis*, although smaller; its only known intermediate host is the Sole *Solea solea* (L.) but the final stages occur on numerous gadoid and other fishes. *L. minuta* (Scott) is less well-known; it occurs on the sand Goby *Pomatoschistus minutus* (Pallas).

Nicothoe   FIG. 8.10

The Common Lobster, *Homarus gammarus* (L.), is host to the only British species, *N. astaci* Audouin and Milne Edwards.

Order Herpyllobioida

Aspidoecia   FIG. 8.10

A. normani Giard and Bonnier parasitizes the mysid *Erythrops elegans* Sars.

Eurysilenium   FIG. 8.10

A single species, *E. truncatum* Sars, occurs in association with the scale worm *Harmothoe imbricata* (L.).

Sarsilenium crassirostris (Sars)   FIG. 8.10

S. crassirostris occurs on the scale worm *Harmothoe impar* (Johnston).

Order Monstrilloida

Monstrilla   FIG. 8.10

A large genus, most species of which are rarely reported, though probably quite widespread. *M. helgolandica* Claus occurs in the pyramidellid *Odostomia scalaris* MacGillivray, itself a commensal of *Mytilus edulis* L., and certain prosobranch gastropods.

Thaumaleus   FIG. 8.10

A large genus of annelidicolous parasites, *Thaumaleus* is widespread in British waters although infrequently recorded. *T. rigidus* (Thompson) occurs in association with the polychaetes *Polydora ciliata* (Johnston), *P. giardi* (Mesnil) and *Salmacina dysteri* (Huxley). *T. roscovita* (Malaquin) and *T. filogranarum*

(Malaquin), both formerly referred to *Cymbasoma*, are found with the tubeworm *Filograna implexa* Berkeley.

Incertae Sedis

Phyllocola   FIG. 8.10

A single species, *P. petiti* D.-Deboutteville and Laubier, has been reported from phyllodocid polychaetes, including *Eulalia expusilla* Pleijel.

C. Class Cirripedia

Cirripedia (barnacles and their allies) are highly modified crustaceans. Their free-swimming, bivalved cyprid larva has six pairs of thoracic swimming appendages and a pair of first antennae. The latter are used for selecting and attaching to a substrate. What happens next varies in the different Orders.

In the Thoracica or barnacles proper, the cyprid undergoes metamorphosis, the body performing a forward somersault bringing the thoracic limbs into the adult position as feathery *cirri*, used for plankton feeding. The bivalved *carapace* of the cyprid becomes the multi-plated *shell* of the barnacle enclosing a mantle cavity in which the *prosoma* (body) is suspended. The exoskeleton of barnacles is unique in not being completely shed at each moult; its calcareous plates, like the shells of molluscs exhibit concentric growth lines about an initial umbo from which striae radiate. The promosa and appendages have a flexible integument which is regularly moulted in typical fashion.

Appendages of the adult comprise the *cirri*, *mandibles*, and two pairs of *maxillae*. The first and second cirri are usually short and function as maxillipeds; the third to sixth are elongate and setate. Cirri can be completely retracted within the mantle cavity—coiling action is mediated by contraction of their offset longitudinal muscles. Extension is a hydraulic process, muscular contraction within the prosoma forcing coelomic fluid into the cirri. The abbreviated abdomen bears paired terminal *caudal appendages* flanking the median penis.

Most familiar barnacles are hermaphrodite and have paired testes located in the prosoma, and ovaries in the lining of the mantle cavity. The testes lead, via coiled vas deferens, to the single long penis which has annular thickening and is extremely extensile. The ovaries discharge eggs via paired oviducts equipped with oviducal glands which open at the bases of the first cirri. An oviducal gland encloses a batch of eggs in a membrane to form an egg lamella. Two lamellae are incubated in the mantle cavity, one on either side of the prosoma until they hatch as free-swimming nauplius larvae. These nauplii are usually planktotrophic and undergo six moults before achieving the cyprid stage. In gonochoristic species, the barnacle proper is female and dwarf males are parasitic within the mantle cavity. Some hermaphrodite species also employ such males, then referred to as complemental males.

The most generalized suborder of Thoracica is the Lepadomorpha in which the mantle cavity with its shell plates forms a 'head' or *capitulum* demarcated from a stalk or *peduncle* anchored to the substratum. The peduncle may or may not be armoured with plates. It has no cavity and contains the ovary. Two families comprise the Lepadomorpha.

The other two suborders of the Thoracica are the acorn, or stalkless barnacles (sometimes referred to as sessile barnacles). They are characterized by low conical shape on a roughly circular base. The rigid wall plates surround a central orifice protected by two pairs of moveable plates—the operculum. The first of these suborders is the Verrucomorpha, a small distinctive group with asymmetrical shape incorporating an operculum of only two plates, allowing the cirri to emerge at one side—suggested to be an adaptation for crevice dwelling. Balanomorpha, the third suborder of Thoracica, comprise the familiar barnacles including both the Chthamalidae and Balanidae. Normally there are six overlapping wall plates but these may be reduced in number or supplemented by accessory plates. The *carina* and *rostrum* are median; the other four are paired *carinolaterals* and *rostrolaterals*. The central sectors of plates are referred to as *parieties*, the overlapping parts as *alae* and the overlapped sectors as *radii*. The base or *basis* of a barnacle, where it is attached to the substratum, may be cuticular or, like the plates, calcified. The operculum of the Balanomorpha is symmetrical and consists of left and right 'doors' which open by moving apart, their outer edges tipping downwards within the wall plates. Each door consists of two plates—the *tergum* at the carinal end, and the anterior *scutum*—hinged together (Figs. 8.12, 8.13). The margins of the two doors, where they meet in the midline, are edged with a flexible *tergoscutal flap* which ensures a close fit. In life, these flaps are often distinctively coloured and aid in identification.

Finally, there are other orders of Cirripedia which are not immediately recognizable as barnacles. The Acrothoracica have plankton-catching cirri but lack shell plates. They are small reduced cirripedes found in burrows which they excavate in mollusc shells, corals etc. The order Rhizocephala have the distinctive cirripede nauplius and cyprid larvae but as adults are highly modified animals parasitic on crabs, hermit crabs, or even other barnacles. Another group of parasitic Crustacea, the Ascothoracida, once thought to be cirripedes, are now usually regarded as separate, since they have a different type of nauplius, sucking mouthparts, and thoracic limbs which are not modified as cirri. They are parasites of deepwater echinoderms and Cnidaria.

REFERENCES

Broch, H. (1960). *Fiches d'identification du Zooplancton*, **83**, Cirripedia (Thoracica). Fam. Lepadidae. Conseil Permanent pour l'exploration de la mer, Copenhagen.

Darwin, C. (1851). *A monograph on the subclass Cirripedia. 1. Lepadidae.* Ray Society, London.

Darwin, C. (1854). *A monograph on the subclass Cirripedia. 2. The Balanidae, Verrucidae etc.* Ray Society, London.

Hoeg, J. T. & Lutzen, J. (1985). Crustacea: Rhizocephala. *Marine Invertebrates of Scandinavia*, 6. Universitetsforlaget, Oslo.

Nillson-Cantell, C-A. (1978). Cirripedia Thoracica and Acrothoracica. *Marine invertebrates of Scandinavia*. Universitetsforlaget, Oslo.

Southward, A. J. (1963). Barnacles. *Catalogue of main fouling organisms*, *1*, OECD, Paris.

Southward, A. J. (1987). Barnacle biology. *Crustacean issues*, **5**. Balkema, Rotterdam.

Southward, A. J. (1976). On the taxonomic status and distribution of Chthamalus stellatus (Cirripedia), in the north-east Atlantic region: with a key to the common interdial barnacles of Britain. *Journal of the Marine Biological Association of the U. K.*, **56**, 1007–28.

Zevina, G. B. (1981). Barnacles of the suborder Lepadomorpha (Cirripedia Thoracica) of the world ocean. 1. Family Scalpellidae. *Opredeliteli Po Faune SSSR*, **127**, 1–398 (in Russian).

Zevina, G. B. (1982). Barnacles of the Suborder Lepadormpha (Cirripedia Thoracica) of the world ocean. 2. Family Lepadidae. *Opredeliteli Po Faune SSSR*, **133**, 1–221 (in Russian).

KEY TO FAMILIES

1. Cirripede which is a recognizable barnacle, with a carapace incorporating calcereous plates varying from massive to extremely reduced **2**

   Cirripede totally lacking calcareous plates. Either a minute form burrowing in gastropod shell or highly modified endoparasite on malacostracan host; lacking cirri but dispersing by cyprid larva **6**

2. Barnacle with a distinct flexible peduncle demarcated from the capitulum (stalked barnacle) **3**

   Barnacle without a flexible stalk (but may have rigid cup-shaped base); and having a distinct operculum (acorn barnacles) **4**

3. Stalked barnacle with usually five plates to the capitulum, these sometimes very reduced, perhaps only two visible **2. Lepadidae**

   Stalked barnacle with 13 or more capitular plates **1. Scalpellidae**

4. Operculum of only two plates opening to the side of the barnacle   **3. Verrucidae**

   Operculum of four plates placed more or less centrally on top of barnacle   **5**

5. Acorn barnacle in which the anterior wall plate or rostrum is little wider than the operculum and is overlapped by the flanking plates   **4. Chthamalidae**

   Acorn barnacle in which the rostrum if distinct is usually much wider the the operculum and always overlaps the flanking plates   **5. Balanidae**

6. Cirripede occupying a burrow it has excavated in the columella of the empty shell of a whelk (*Buccinum*) used by hermit crab   **6. Alcipidae**

   Cirripede parasitizing a crab, squat lobster, hermit crab, or a barnacle, recognizable as an external swelling usually attached to abdomen of host   **7. Sacculinidae**

Order **Thoracica**

Suborder **Lepadomorpha**

1 SCALPELLIDAE

Capitulum with more than five plates. Peduncle also armoured with many fine plates. Caudal appendages reduced or absent. Hermaphroditic or gonochoristic with dwarf males. Larvae planktotrophic or lecithotrophic.

1. Capitulum having thirteen distinct plates; carina with distinct angle near mid point   ***Scalpellum scalpellum***

   Capitulum having more than thirteen plates, including many small ones near junction with peduncle
                                              Pollicipes pollicipes

Scalpellum scalpellum (Linnaeus)   FIG. 8.11

Typical individuals have distinctively shaped capitulum larger than peduncle. Capitulum strongly compressed laterally and bearing 13 plates with variously aligned umbos. Peduncle with transverse rows of small imbricating plates.

Attached to hydroids, bryozoa, and rocks etc. sublittorally 10–500 m, east Atlantic, Iceland, Norway to West Africa, Azores, Mediterranean. British Isles, south and west coasts not uncommon.

Many other species of *Scalpellum* and *Arcoscalpellum* occur at greater depths (see Zevina 1981).

Pollicipes pollicipes Gmelin   FIG. 8.11

Peduncle generally much shorter than capitulum; overall length up to 30 mm. Capitulum laterally compressed with five prominent plates and a variable number of medium-sized and smaller, spine-like plates, all with terminal umbones. Peduncle tapers downwards to an expanded attachment point; surface of peduncle armoured with uniformly small plates.

On rocks or often anchored within empty *Balanus perforatus* shells, MSL to MLWN, on moderately exposed oceanic shores. France and Iberia, common at remote locations; formerly recorded from southwest Cornwall.

2 LEPADIDAE

Usually five plates to capitulum although in a few species they are greatly reduced and may even be absent in adults. Peduncle, which may be very long and contractile, never plated. Tergum with apical umbo; scutum and carina with basal umbos. Filamentary appendages usually present. Larvae planktotrophic.

1. Capitulum with five large calcareous plates   **2**

   Capitulum with two to five widely separated small plates or none at all   ***Conchoderma 6***

2. Carina (single median plate) angled at umbo, and expanded into disc-shaped base   ***Dosima***

   Carina not angled, and forked at base   ***Lepas 3***

3. Capitulum plates smooth or finely marked   **4**

   Capitulum plates, especially terga, strongly striated   **5**

4. Gap between carina and scutum narrow, small tooth on basal angle of right scutum; integument at base of capitulum even-coloured with peduncle; usually two filamentary appendages   ***Lepas anatifera***

   Gap between carina and scutum wide, no tooth on either scutum; integument between capitulum and peduncle yellow or pale coloured, three filamentary appendages each side   ***Lepas hilli***

5. Crest of scutum separates off a narrow ventral area; zero, one, or two filamentary appendages on each side   ***Lepas pectinata***

   Crest of scutum separates broad arched area, five or six filamentary appendages each side   ***Lepas anserifera***

6. Capitulum with two tubular 'ears' behind scuta, seven long filamentary appendages each side of body
                                           Conchoderma auritum

   Capitulum without 'ears'; capitulum grades into peduncle, five or six short filamentary appendages
                                           Conchoderma virgatum

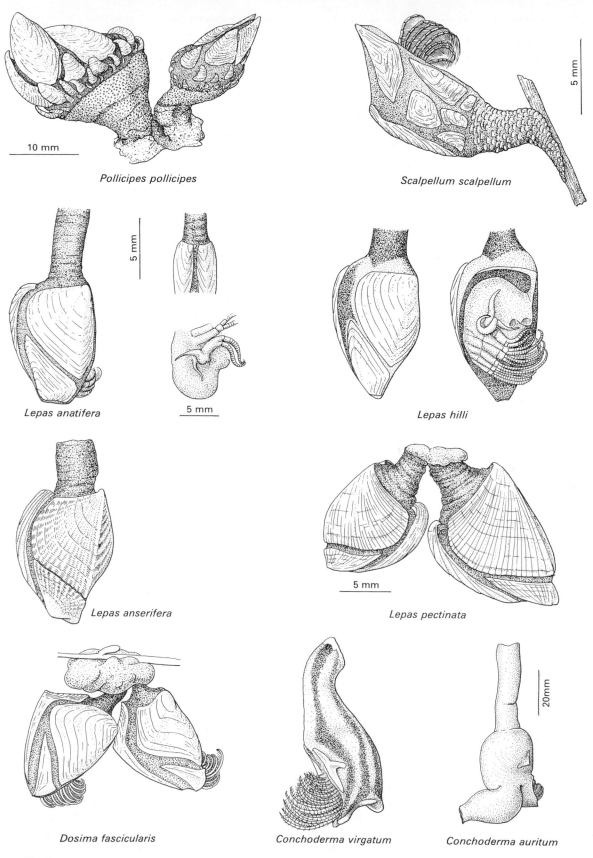

Pollicipes pollicipes

Scalpellum scalpellum

Lepas anatifera

Lepas hilli

Lepas anserifera

Lepas pectinata

Dosima fascicularis

Conchoderma virgatum

Conchoderma auritum

Fig. 8.11

Lepas anatifera Linnaeus   FIG. 8.11

Capitulum length up to 40(50) mm. Plates translucent white and usually smooth, integument between plates dark, even black. Carina sometimes transversely ridged, its forked base extending below scuta. Right scutum (but only rarely the left also) with umbonal tooth. Carina and scutum separated by distinct gap, but this gap narrower than that in *L. hilli*. Peduncle 40–850 mm, purplish brown, darkest adjacent to scutum.

Attached to large or small floating objects, cosmopolitan in warmer seas; the commonest species of *Lepas* to be stranded on south and west coasts of British Isles, rarely on east coast.

Lepas hilli (Leach)   FIG. 8.11

Capitulum up to 40 mm. Plates translucent, white, or bluish grey; forked base of carina barely overlaps scutum; no umbonal tooth on right (or left) scutum. Narrow gap between tergum and scutum; wide gap between carina and scutum. Peduncle variable in length, may be shorter than capitulum; dark coloured except for orange (or other pale colour) collar at base of capitulum.

Attached to floating objects. Cosmopolitan in warmer seas, but only rarely stranded in British Isles.

Lepas anserifera Linnaeus   FIG. 8.11

Large; capitulum up to 40 mm. Plates with radiating and transverse ribbing. Carina rather broad throughout length. Tergum trapezoid, more strongly striated than scutum. Scutum with smooth umbo, otherwise ribbed. Differs from *L. pectinata* in having a narrow secondary ventral area. Umbonal teeth on right scutum, sometimes on left too. Five or six filamentary appendages each side. Peduncle as long as capitulum; yellow or orange.

On large floating objects. Cosmopolitan in warmer seas, rarely stranded in British Isles (west coasts).

Lepas pectinata Spengler   FIG. 8.11

Small, capitulum only 15 mm. Plates ridged like those of *L. anserifera*. Carina wide near top, narrow near basal fork; sometimes elaborately spiny. Tergum triangular, also sometimes barbed. Scutum radially ridged, sometimes barbed. One or two filamentary appendages each side (sometimes none).

On large, or more often small, floating objects such as seaweed. Cosmopolitan in warmer seas. Often stranded on British Isles coasts (south and west).

Dosima fascicularis (Ellis and Solander)   FIG. 8.11

Capitulum usually 15–20 mm (up to 30 mm). Plates thin, smooth, and distinctively curved to give whole capitulum streamlined shape. Carina truly keeled, right-angled at umbo; basal part wide but not forked. Tergum triangular, nearly flat. Scutum well-separated from other plates with slight shelf at peduncular edge. Four or five filamentary appendages. Peduncle shorter than capitulum; pale yellowish to purplish brown; often has secreted float with texture of expanded polystyrene.

Attached to small or very small objects: weeds, straws, etc; supplemented in larger specimens by own float. Not often on

ships. Cosmopolitan in warmer seas. Often stranded on south and west coasts of British Isles, sometimes in large numbers.

Conchoderma auritum (Linnaeus)   FIG. 8.11

Capitulum about 30 mm long, with two distinctive tubular outgrowths ('ears'). Shell plates extremely reduced. Carina and terga rudimentary in young specimens, lost in adults. Scuta minute, V-shaped. Seven long filamentary appendages each side. Peduncle longer than capitulum.

Characteristically found attached to the whale barnacle *Coronula* (in turn on hump-back and other whales); also on ship hulls and buoys off British Isles coasts. Not uncommon on logs.

Conchoderma virgatum (Spengler)   FIG. 8.11

Capitulum about 35 mm, grades into peduncle. Colour grey with longitudinal bluish-black bands traversing capitulum and peduncle. The five shell plates all extremely small and peripheral. Carina straight and narrow. Tergum similar. Scutum Y-shaped. Five or six short filamentary appendages on each side.

On weeds, turtles, even fish; also on ships. Generally rare in British waters.

Suborder **Verrucomporpha**

3 VERRUCIDAE

Shell plates that compose the rigid wall include one tergum and one scutum; the other two wall plates are generally assumed to be the carina and rostrum. The operculum consists of a single rigid flat plate comprising the other tergum and scutum. Both right- and left-handed specimens are found. Basis usually membranous. Caudal appendages present. Larvae planktotrophic.

Verruca stroemia (O. F. Müller)   FIG. 8.12

Up to 3.5 (5) mm diameter. Shell has depressed shape, white to brownish. Hinge of operculum located on a diameter. All plates have radiating crests which interlock at interplate sutures. The crests in turn are ridged. Basis not calcified. Tergoscutal flaps pink or red.

On undersides of boulders, in crevices, on shells, algal holdfasts, etc.; LWST and sublittoral to over 500 m. Abundant on all coasts in British Isles; elsewhere Norway to Mediterranean, not Baltic.

Suborder **Balanomorpha**

4 CHTHAMALIDAE

Worldwide, the family includes genera with four, six, or eight wall plates. The British species have six. All these plates are solid. Caudal appendages present in some genera.

---

1. Orifice clearly kite-shaped with distinct obtuse angle at carinal end; length of tergum less than half length of scutum   ***Chthamalus montagui***

   Orifice more rounded at carinal end; tergum more than half length of scutum   ***Chthamalus stellatus***

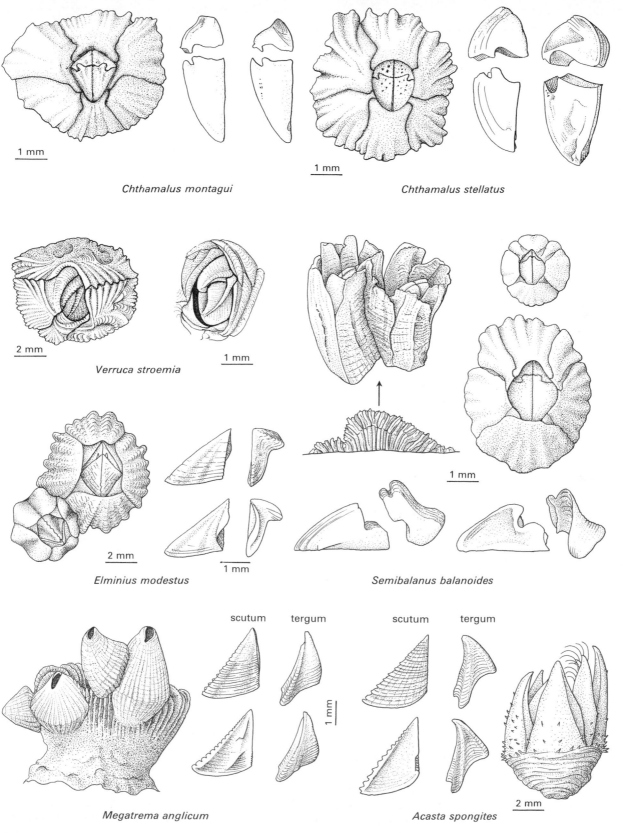

Chthamalus montagui

1 mm

Chthamalus stellatus

1 mm

Verruca stroemia

2 mm   1 mm

Elminius modestus

2 mm   1 mm

Semibalanus balanoides

1 mm

scutum   tergum   scutum   tergum

1 mm

Megatrema anglicum

Acasta spongites

2 mm

Fig. 8.12

Chthamalus montagui Southward   FIG. 8.12
[SOUTHWARD 1976, 1012]

Basal diameter up to 6 (10) mm. Brownish or greyish. Usually low conical. Surface nearly always corroded with sutures often obliterated. Opercular opening nearly always kite-shaped, junction between tergum and scutum close to carinal edge. Scutum much longer than broad.

Upper shore (above the next species) but with scattered individuals down to LWNT. South and west coasts of British Isles.

Chthamalus stellatus (Poli)   FIG. 8.12
[SOUTHWARD 1976, 1009]

Basal diameter up to 10 (15) mm. Light grey, often discoloured. Conical or flattened, usually corroded and sutures obliterated. Opercular opening broadly kite-shaped in juveniles, becoming oval or circular with age. Scutum apex usually a right angle; length usually less than $1\frac{1}{2} \times$ width.

Middle shore (below *C. montagui* but wide overlap); scattered individuals down to LWST. Abundant in Devon, Cornwall, and Channel Isles and exposed headlands including west coasts of Scotland and Ireland. Progressively less common elsewhere.

5 BALANIDAE

Wall of four or six plates, with rostrum overlapping the laterals. Carinolaterals narrow, sometimes absent. All wall plates fused in *Megatrema*. No caudal appendages.

1. Barnacle not attached to solid substrata but enclosed in live sponge.   ***Acasta spongites***

   Barnacle attached to a solid surface   **2**

2. Barnacle attached to live coral   ***Megatrema anglicum***

   Barnacle not on coral   **3**

3. Barnacle wall consisting of only four plates   ***Elminius modestus***

   Wall of six plates, although the dividing sutures are not always obvious   **4**

4. Base (basis) of barnacle forms a calcareous layer on the substratum   ***Balanus 5***

   Basis non-calcified, membranous   ***Semibalanus balanoides***

5. Wall shell plates striped or coloured with pink, purple, or brown (but may be corroded grey)   **6**

   Wall plates white (but may be corroded grey when old)   **8**

6. Part or all of shell strongly coloured but not strongly striped   **7**

   Large groups of pink or purplish stripes on white shell plates, large operculum, tergum blunt   ***Balanus amphitrite***

7. Whole shell of purple or pinkish colour when young, (sometimes slightly striped) obscured by grey corrosion in old specimens. Conical barnacle with very small orifice. Sutures often obscure   ***Balanus perforatus***

Half of barnacle (carinal half), uniformly dark pink; other half nearly white; clear sutures   ***Balanus spongicola***

8. Tergum blunt   **9**

   Tergum sharply pointed   **11**

9. Overlapping interapical areas on tergum and scutum. Tergoscutal flaps longitudinally striped cream on dark purple.   ***Balanus crenatus***

   No interapical areas; tergoscutal flaps mottled or with transverse bands   **10**

10. Orifice diamond-shaped; scuta simply striated. Tergoscutal flaps speckled; top edges of alae horizontal   ***Balanus improvisus***

    Orifice nearly triangular; scuta cross-striated; tergoscutal flaps banded brown on cream; top edges of alae oblique   ***Balanus eburneus***

11. Shell walls strongly ribbed, orifice relatively small; tergoscutal flaps with longitudinal stripes—yellow, brown, and yellow   ***Balanus balanus***

    Smooth walls; very large orifice; tergoscutal flaps white   ***Balanus hameri***

Balanus spongicola Brown   FIG. 8.13

Large, up to 15 mm diameter. Spectacular coloration: carinal half of shell strong reddish pink or purple, other half paler pink or white. Conical shape, circular outline with smooth margin. Wall plates heavy and smooth or striated, reflecting texture of substrate. Alae and radii obtuse, bordered. Orifice rather small and sharply edged. Operculum somewhat sunk; tergum sharply beaked with broad spur; tergoscutal flaps edged with orange, otherwise brown with three bands of cream. Basis of barnacle calcareous and porous.

Sublittoral, sometimes embedded in sponges but more often attached to shells of *Chlamys opercularis*. British Isles, southwest; quite common in English Channel but South Wales is its northern limit. Extends south to South Africa.

Balanus perforatus Bruguière   FIG. 8.13

Large, 15–30 (50) mm diameter; height similar. Various shades of purple to pink (partly as stripes) to white; dull grey colour when eroded. Usually conical (volcano-shaped); circular outline with simple margin. Wall plates slightly ribbed, very strongly built with narrow radii. Orifice usually very small but quite large in sublittoral specimens. Operculum often deeply sunk, tergum with well-marked beak and narrow spur. Tergoscutal flaps purple or brown with patches of blue and white. Basis of barnacle calcareous and porous.

MTL to sublittoral on rocks and on artificial structures including ships. Often abundant in south-west England. Northern limit is South Wales; not found east of Isle of Wight; not in Ireland. Southwards to Mediterranean and West Africa.

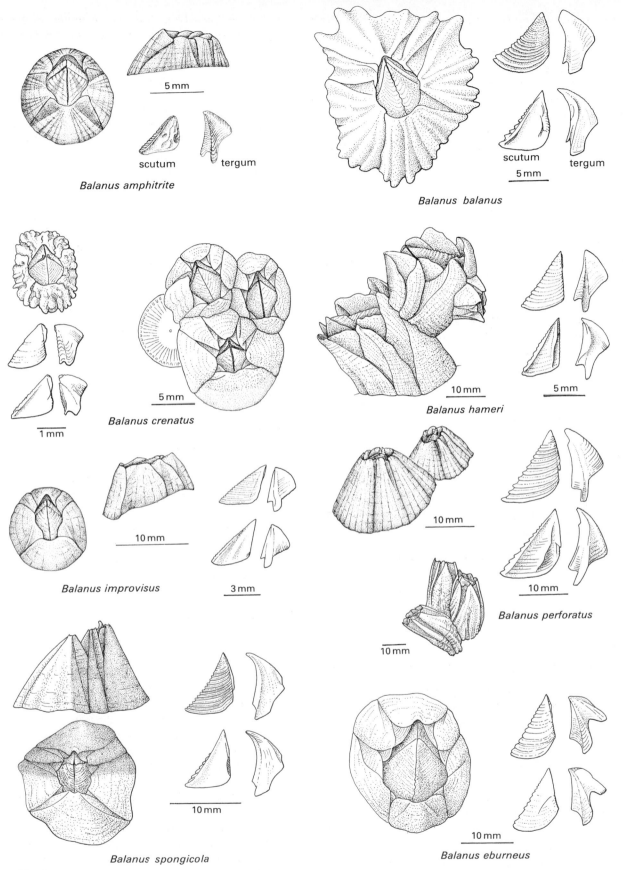

Balanus amphitrite

scutum tergum

5 mm

Balanus balanus

scutum tergum

5 mm

Balanus crenatus

5 mm

1 mm

Balanus hameri

10 mm 5 mm

Balanus improvisus

10 mm

3 mm

Balanus perforatus

10 mm

10 mm

10 mm

Balanus spongicola

10 mm

Balanus eburneus

10 mm

Fig. 8.13

Balanus amphitrite Darwin   FIG. 8.13

Medium sized; up to 10 (15+) mm. Plates pearly white or grey, each with several purplish to dark brown stripes. Generalized shape; slightly ovate, simple outline with large diamond-shaped orifice. Plates smooth and thin. Radii and alae nearly parallel with base. Scutum large with broad colour stripe radiating from umbo. Tergoscutal flaps white (sometimes tinged yellow or pink) with three black or purple spots. Basis calcareous, porous.

A tropical form, open sea and estuaries, intertidal and sublittoral. In British Isles only as introduced or fouling species. On ships and buoys, piers, etc., especially in docks warmed by generating station effluents. Elsewhere: Europe, West Africa, Mediterranean, Black Sea. Several closely related species worldwide.

Balanus balanus (Linnaeus)   FIG. 8.13

Large; up to 25 (30) mm. White or tinged brown. Conical shape, circular with irregular edge. Wall plates heavily ridged and strong; radii parallel. Orifice moderately sized, acutely angled at tergal end, rounded anteriorly. Operculum raised, tergum with prominent points, scutum with prominent ridges corresponding to growth lines. Tergoscutal flaps edged yellow, backed by brown stripe, followed by white stripe. Basis of barnacle solid and calcareous.

On rocks, stones, and shells; LWST to several hundred metres deep; occasionally on ships. British Isles: all coasts except Cornwall; abundant. Elsewhere, Arctic circle to North and Celtic Seas.

Balanus hameri (Ascanius)   FIG. 8.13

Large; up to 20 (30) mm and similar height. White or cream. Almost cylindrical. Clumps composed of young specimens settled on pre-existing ones. Wall plates with loose sutures. Free edges of radii oblique. Orifice very large, operculum only slightly sunk within. Tergum and scutum both ridged. Tergoscutal flaps large usually white. Basis of barnacle solid, calcareous.

On stones or shells, especially in currents; also on buoys and ships. 20–200 m; British Isles all coasts. Elsewhere: Arctic to North and Celtic Seas.

Balanus improvisus Darwin   FIG. 8.13

Moderate sized; up to 10 (15) mm; height less. White or cream, often superficially dirty. Low cone-shaped; slightly ovate; simple outline. Plates narrow, obliquely edged radii. Orifice narrow and diamond-shaped. Tergum with narrow spur. Tergoscutal flaps speckled white and pale purple. Basis calcareous and porous.

On stones, algae, and artificial substrates including ships; brackish water only, including estuaries and ports; MSL to sublittoral. British Isles, all suitable coasts, common, although retreating where in competition with *Elminius*. Elsewhere: Baltic (only barnacle there), Norway to Spain, Mediterranean and Black Sea.

Balanus eburneus Gould   FIG. 8.13

Large; up to 20 (30) mm, height similar. Plates cream or ivory. Steep-sided cone, round with smooth outline. Wall plates

smooth, alae and radii with free margins oblique (45°) and finely notched. Orifice large, with sharp edges. Operculum only slightly sunk. Tergum blunt-tipped; scutum with both radiate and transverse ridging. Tergoscutal flaps speckled brown on creamy white background. Basis of barnacle calcareous and porous.

Lower shore to sublittoral. In British Isles only as introduced or fouling species in brackish ports. Elsewhere: subtropical American. Introduced: Europe, Mediterranean, Black Sea.

Balanus crenatus Bruguière   FIG. 8.13

Moderately sized barnacle, up to 15 (20) mm. White, not eroded. Conical, or tubular when crowded. Wall plates usually smooth when young, irregularly ribbed when adult. Carina in profile slightly concave towards tip. Radii and alae with oblique rough edges. Orifice rather large, operculum flush; tergum blunt, with broad spur. Tergoscutal flaps yellow-edged, followed by brown, then another yellow stripe.

Lower shore to sublittoral on rocks, small stones, shells, artificial structures, and ships, British Isles all coasts: abundant. Arctic to west coast of France, as far as Bordeaux.

Semibalanus balanoides (Linnaeus)   FIG. 8.12

Up to 5–10 mm, rarely 15 mm, height varies with form. Shell white or cream to grey-brown. Low cone varying to tall tubular shape when crowded. Round to ovate outline with irregular margin. Wall plates smooth or ribbed; alae and radii oblique-edged. Orifice moderately sized, diamond-shaped; operculum nearly flush. Tergoscutal suture characteristically stepped (see Fig. 8.12) especially in adults. Tergum with very broad spur. Tergoscutal flaps white with brown spot at central groove. Basis of barnacle uncalcified and cuticular.

The commonest middle shore barnacle of rocky shores in the British Isles. On a wide variety of natural and artificial substrates including ships; sometimes found sublittorally.

Elminius modestus Darwin   FIG. 8.12

Mean basal diameter 5–10 mm. Opalescent greyish white when young, but may be drab greyish brown when old and eroded. Low conical shape, with an irregular margin and roughly circular when adult. Young specimens show clearly the four symmetrically placed wall plates, each with a median notch. Plates smooth when young. Orifice rather large, diamond-shaped; operculum flush; tergum with distinctively shaped spur; scutum with darker area radiating from umbo. Tergoscutal sutures straight when young; more sinuous; approaching shape in *Semibalanus* when old. Tergoscutal flaps white with orange-brown spot at centre, grey towards rostrum.

Intertidal and shallow sublittoral, especially estuarine but also open coast on a wide range of substrata including rocks, stones, shells, other crustacea, algae, and artificial structures including ships. Native in New Zealand. Introduced in Britain about 1940. Now in most north European ports.

Acasta spongites Darwin   FIG. 8.12

Mean basal diameter up to 5(8) mm. Shell white. Tall cone

rising from calcified cup-shaped basis. Outline subcircular. Wall plates fragile, spiny, with oblique alae and radii. Orifice large and ill-defined, operculum depressed. Tergoscutal flaps white.

Always associated with the sponge *Dysidea fragilis* in which it is embedded so that the cirri emerge from the surface of the sponge to feed. Sublittoral. South-west British Isles to West Africa; common.

Megatrema anglicum (Leach)   FIG. 8.12

Mean basal diameter up to 6 mm. Shell pink. Conical shell with circular outline arises from cup-shaped basis. Wall consists of a single structure derived from fused plates; longitudinally ribbed to give crenate outline at base. Orifice very small and offset to rostral aspect. Operculum depressed. Sublittoral, 5 to 30(50) m depth. Always associated with the non-hermatypic coral *Caryophyllia smithi*. West and south-west coasts of British Isles to West Africa, also Japan.

Order **Acrothoracica**

Tiny, burrowing, shell-less cirripedes with three to five pairs of cirri. Sexes separate.

6 ALCIPIDAE

Mantle (lacks shell plates) enclosed in chitinous sac, rounded, fixed to side of burrow, opens by a slit, Prosoma with four pairs of cirri. First cirri biramous maxillipeds, remaining three pairs are uniramous and with only four segments. Gonochoristic, dwarf males settle in or near female. Cyprid with six pairs of biramous thoracopods.

Trypetesa lampas (Hancock)

Occupies burrows in whelk shells (*Buccinum* and *Neptunea*) inhabited by the hermit crab *Pagurus bernhardus*. Burrows open on surface of columella of the body whorl of the shell; opening elongated and rounded at one end. Sublittoral. Probably all British coasts; also Southern Scandinavia to Mediterranean, and north America.

Order **Rhizocephala**

Controversy surrounds the relationship between this and other cirripede orders. Rhizocephala are always parasites of other crustaceans, mostly decapod, hosts. *Soma* (body) of parasite ramifies through host and produces large external reproductive sac or '*externa*' with characteristic shape. Soma and externa represent female adult having developed from a female cyprid larva via a kentrogon larva. Virgin externa is impregnated by a trichogon larva arising from the large male cyprid, whereupon ovary and testis both develop in the same externa. Eggs of two sizes hatch to produce male and female nauplius larvae of modified cirripede form, lacking gut and being gonochoristic and lecithotrophic rather than hermaphrodite and planktotrophic as in barnacles proper.

The figures accompanying this account (Figs. 8.14, 8.15) have been redrawn from the more comprehensive guide by Hoeg and Lutzen (1985).

A hyperparasite—the cryptoniscid isopod *Liriopsis*, is frequently present as an attendant sac attached to the rhizocephalan, especially in *Clistosaccus paguri*, *Peltogaster paguri*, *Tortugaster boschmai*, and *Lernaeodiscus ingolfi*.

KEY TO FAMILIES

1.	On prosoma (body) of barnacle	**1. Chthamalophilidae**
	On decapod crustacean	**2**
2.	On hermit crab	**3**
	Not on hermit crab	**7**
3.	Body 1–3 mm with circular outline, no mantle opening (immature)	**3. Clistosaccidae**
	Body cylindrical with subterminal stalk	**4**
4.	No cuticular shield around stalk	**5**
	Cuticular shield prominent on dorsal surface	**4. Peltogastridae**
5.	Stalk broad, almost one-fifth of externa length	**3. Clistosaccidae**
	Stalk narrower, less than one-tenth of externa length	**6**

| 6. | Width of body, less than one-third of length | **4. Peltogastridae** |
| | Body short and fat (immature) | **4. Peltogastridae** |

| 7. | On shrimps or prawns | **2. Sylonidae** |
| | Not on Caridea | **8** |

| 8. | On burrowing prawns (Thalassinidea) | **4. Peltogastridae** |
| | Not on burrowing prawns | **9** |

| 9. | On true crabs (Brachyura) | **6. Sacculinidae** |
| | On squat lobsters | **10** |

| 10. | Stalk on one side of externa | **4. Peltogastridae** |
| | Stalk at opposite end to mantle opening | **5. Lernaeodiscidae** |

1 CHTHAMALOPHILIDAE

Externa more or less rounded and featureless. Larvae hatch as modified cyprids lacking thoracic limbs. Parasites of balamorph barnacles. Two species.

On *Chthamalus*, internal body lobed	***Chthamalophilus***
On *Balanus improvisus*, branching roots within host	
	Boschmaella

Chthamalophilus delarge Bocquet-Vedrine   FIG. 8.14

Length 1–1.5 mm, white; nearly spherical, mantle opening almost opposite stalk. Normally solitary, but up to five at different stages on one host, suggesting gregariousness. One to 5% of hosts infected.

On *Chthamalus stellatus*, attached to side of body near cirri. Only recorded so far from north-west France (before the recognition in the area of two species of *Chthamalus* loc. cit.).

Boschmaella balani (Bocquet-Vedrine)

Very similar to *Chthamalophilus* but slightly larger and slightly elongate. Infection rate up to 90%, usually gregarious, up to 40 per host.

On *Balanus improvisus* attached to lining of mantle cavity. So far only recorded from western Europe.

2 SYLONIDAE

Externa slightly elongated parallel to axis of host. Two very small (left and right) mantle openings. Larva hatch as cyprids. One species.

Sylon hippolytes Kröyer   FIG. 8.14

Adults 4 mm on small host species, up to 15.2 mm long on large host. Whitish to pink. Initially spherical, broader and longer than adults. Stalk short and broad. Two small mantle openings appear when larvae are ready to hatch.

Occurs attached to sternite of abdomen of a wide range of shrimps and prawns found in the area. Detailed distributions unknown.

Recorded hosts include *Caridion gordoni*, *Crangon allmani*, *Dichelopandalus bonnieri*, *Eualus pusiolus*, *Spirontocaris lilljeborgi*, *S. spinus*.

3 CLISTOSACCIDAE

Body cylindrical. Small anterior mantle opening. Larvae hatch as cyprids. Parasitic on hermit crabs. One species.

Clistosaccus paguri Lilljeborg   FIG. 8.14

Size varies greatly with that of host: 2.5–26.0 mm in length. White. Originally circular, eventually elongate cylindrical with terminal mantle opening. Wide stalk two-thirds of length from mantle opening.

On abdomen of host, usually on left side. Up to 3% hosts infected. Half of these with only one, otherwise up to 10 on single host.

On *Pagurus bernhardus*, *P. pubescens*. Northern distribution.

4 PELTOGASTRIDAE

Diverse family. Body spherical to twisted elongate. Stalk always arises between posterior end and half way along dorsal side. Mantle opening at anterior extremity. Parasites of hermit crabs, squat lobsters and burrowing prawns.

| 1. | On hermit crabs | 2 |
| | Not on hermit crabs | 5 |

| 2. | Shield of thickened cuticle on parasite around stalk (*Peltogaster*) | 3 |
| | No shield | 4 |

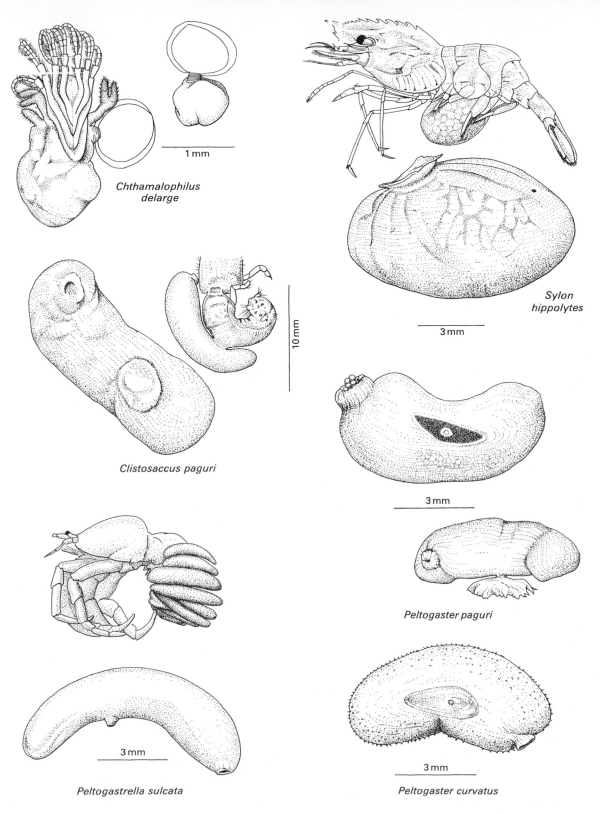

Chthamalophilus delarge

1 mm

Sylon hippolytes

3 mm

Clistosaccus paguri

10 mm

3 mm

Peltogaster paguri

Peltogastrella sulcata

3 mm

Peltogaster curvatus

3 mm

Fig. 8.14

3. Body covered in small spines **Peltogaster curvatus**

   Body smooth **Peltogaster paguri**

4. Body length about three times diameter, usually gregarious **Peltogastrella sulcata**

   Body not greatly elongated <4 mm juvenile **Peltogaster**

5. On burrowing prawns (Thalassinidea) **Parthenopea subterranea**

   Not on Thalassinidea **6**

6. Body symmetrical or nearly so. On *Galathea* **Galatheascus striatus**

   Strongly asymmetrical body; stalk on left side. On *Munida* **Tortugaster boschmai**

Peltogaster paguri Rathke FIG. 8.14

Length 2–15 (26) mm, brown-red colour, greenish when old. Elongate cylindrical, length 3 × width. Mantle aperture an elevated terminal and often lobulate structure. Narrow stalk, about half way from mantle opening. Prominent fusiform dark area (shield) around stalk on parasite. Up to 5% (usually less) of hosts infected. Usually single, multiples by chance up to four.

Attached to abdomen of hermit crabs usually left side. *Anapagurus chiroacanthus*, *P. cuanensis*.

Peltogaster curvatus Kossman FIG. 8.14

Length 4–16 mm, apricot-red. Like *P. paguri* but body armed with small spines. Up to 5.5% infection of *Pagurus cuanensis*. Gregarious, up to one-third of hosts carrying two to four parasites.

On *Pagurus cuanensis* and *P. prideauxi* (not *P. bernhardus*; scattered records, England and Iceland.

Peltogastrella sulcata (Lilljeborg) FIG. 8.14
(= *Peltogaster socialis* Müller; *Chlorogaster sulcatus* Lilljeborg)

Up to 11 mm; pinkish white, later apricot-red. Very long and thin, cylindrical, tapering posteriorly; curved; narrow stalk on concave side—smooth. Mantle opening terminal. Up to 14% of *Pagurus cuanensis* infected (Norway). Gregarious, occasionally single, but usually several, up to 30.

Not on *Pagarus bernhardus*. On *Anapagurus chiroacanthus*, *A. hyndmanni*, *A. laevis*, *Pagurus cuanensis*, and *P. prideauxi*.

Galatheascus striatus Boschma FIG. 8.15

Length usually less than 6 mm but occasionally up to 20. Egg-shaped with small stalk near middle, surrounded by oval shield two-thirds length of body. Mantle opening terminal.

Occurs singly on sternal aspect of 3rd or 4th abdominal segment of *Galathea strigosa*, *G. intermedia*, *G. dispersa*, *G. nexa*. Probably throughout British Isles.

Tortugaster boschmai Brinkman FIG. 8.15

Length up to 11 mm, cream-coloured. Asymmetrical shape, smooth or folded. Centrally placed, short broad stalk. Mantle opening at wide end. Singly or two together on 6th abdominal segment. Mantle opening to right side of host.

On *Munida sarsi* and (rarely) *M. rugosa*.

Parthenopea subterranea Kossmann FIG. 8.15

Maximum size 11 mm diameter. Pink or orange. Pea-shaped. Mantle opening usually to one side of host.

On *Callianassa subterranea*. In Scandinavia, probably in British Isles too.

5 LERNAEODISCIDAE

Body compact. Mantle opening opposite stalk or slightly displaced to one side. Parasites of squat lobsters.

---

1. Externally symmetrical **(Lernaeodiscus) 2**

   Mantle opening off centre **(Triangulus) 3**

2. On *Munida*, whitish **Lernaeodiscus ingolfi**

   On *Galathea squamifera*, reddish **Lernaeodiscus squamiferae**

3. On *Munida*, mantle opening to left **Triangulus munidae**

   On *Galathea*, opening to right **Triangulus galatheae**

Lernaeodiscus ingolfi Boschma FIG. 8.15

Maximum width 17 mm. Whitish colour, sometimes with red patch. Mantle opening very large and directed anteriorly on host. Short, posteriorly situated stalk, attached usually to 1st–4th abdominal segment. Recorded up to 0.5% of *Munida sarsi* infected. Occurs singly.

On *Munida sarsi* and less often, on *M. rugosa*.

Lernaeodiscus squamiferae Perez FIG. 8.15

Up to 5 mm wide, wine red colour. Oval and symmetrical with lateral lobes. Wide mantle opening

On *Galathea squamifera*. Rare.

Triangulus munidae Smith FIG. 8.15

Up to 15 mm wide, colour orange. Asymmetrical, mantle opening displaced towards left of parasite. Usually single, occasionally two or three; on 2nd–4th abdominal sterna.

On *Munida rugosa*.

Triangulus galatheae (Norman and Scott) FIG. 8.15

Up to 5.5 mm wide, lemon to orange. Asymmetrical, left side of body inflated. Mantle opening towards right sides of parasite and host. Usually only one per host.

On *Galathea intermedia*, *G. dispersa* and *G. nexa*. West coast of Britain and English Channel—common.

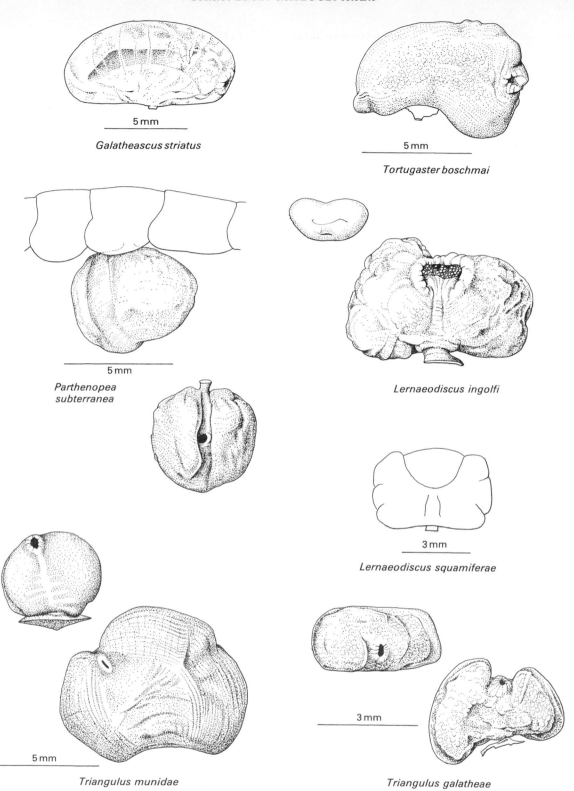

5 mm

Galatheascus striatus

5 mm

Tortugaster boschmai

5 mm

Parthenopea subterranea

Lernaeodiscus ingolfi

3 mm

Lernaeodiscus squamiferae

5 mm

Triangulus munidae

3 mm

Triangulus galatheae

Fig. 8.15

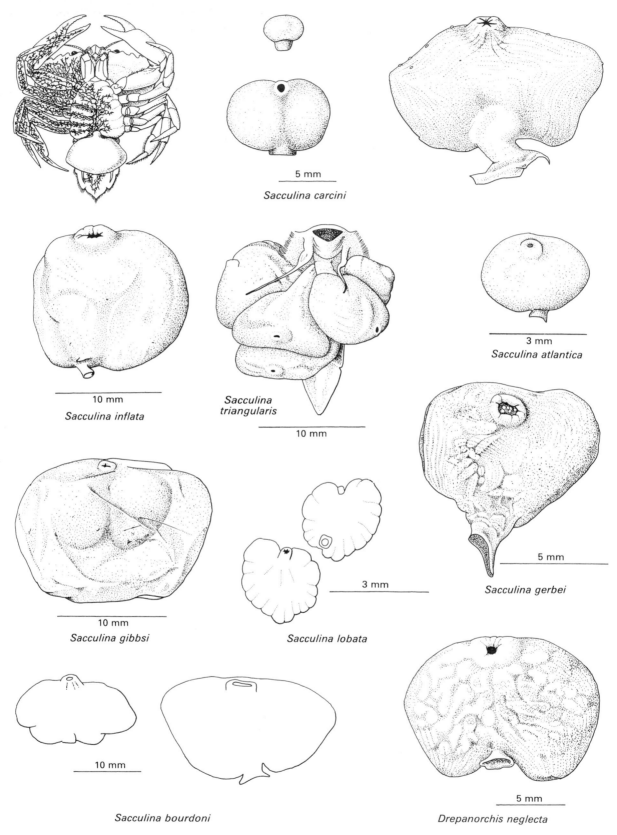

Sacculina carcini

Sacculina inflata

Sacculina triangularis

Sacculina atlantica

Sacculina gibbsi

Sacculina lobata

Sacculina gerbei

Sacculina bourdoni

Drepanorchis neglecta

Fig. 8.16

6 SACCULINIDAE

Body compact with mantle opening opposite or nearly opposite stalk. Parasites of true crabs.

---

1. On *Macropodia* or *Inachus*   **Drepanorchis neglecta**

   On other true crabs   **(Sacculina) 2**

2. On *Cancer pagurus*, stalk grades into body

        Sacculina triangularis

   Not on *C. pagurus*, stalk usually inconspicuous   **3**

3. On *Ebalia tuberosa*, body peripherally lobed

        Sacculina lobata

   Not on *Ebalia*   **4**

4. Body evenly rounded   **5**

   Body with shoulders   **6**

5. On the crab *Pisa*, mantle translucent   **Sacculina gibbsi**

   Not on *Pisa*   **7**

6. On *Xantho pilipes*   **Sacculina bourdoni**

   On *Carcinus, Macropipus, Pilumnus, Bathynectes, Liocarcinus*, and *Pirimella*   **Sacculina carcini**

7. On spider crab (Majidae)   **8**

   On *Xantho incisus, Pilumnus hirtellus*, or *Atelecyclus rotundatus*   **Sacculina gerbei**

8. Thick lips to mantle opening, on *Hyas*   **Sacculina inflata**

   No such lips, on *Dorynchus thomsoni*   **Sacculina atlantica**

Sacculina carcini Thompson   FIG. 8.16

Up to 26 mm. Cream when young, brown later. The best known British rhizocephalan. Symmetrical. Mantle aperture raised and slightly to left. Infection rate varies with host species, up to 50% or more; multiple infections (up to five) random. Infected *Carcinus* migrate to deeper water.

On *Carcinus maenas* and *Liocarcinus holsatus*, and a wide range of other Portunidae and Pirimelidae. Rarely found on *Liocarcinus puber* or *L. depurator*.

British Isles—abundant all coasts.

Sacculina inflata Leuckart   FIG. 8.16

15 mm across. Yellowish colour. Rounded shape; mantle aperture extensible with lobed rim. Surface with minute hairy papillae. Infection rate unknown.

On *Hyas araneus* and *H. coarctatus*. Rare.

Sacculina triangularis Anderson   FIG. 8.16

Up to 13 mm long. Pear-shaped with unusually long stalk grading into body of externa. Mantle opening small and simple.

On *Cancer pagurus*, often as multiple infection. Uncommon. British Isles, France, Sweden.

Sacculina gibbsi (Hesse)   FIG. 8.16

Up to 25 mm wide. Yellowish to brown. Rounded shape, mantle thin and opalescent.

On *Pisa armata*, English Channel. Rare

Sacculina atlantica Boschma   FIG. 8.16

Up to 3.5 mm. Yellowish grey. Simple shape, fairly smooth. Mantle opening on small papilla towards left. Infection rate not known.

On *Dorhynchus thomsoni*. Off south-west Britain.

Sacculina lobata Boschma   FIG. 8.16

Length 3.2 mm. Margin divided into rounded lobes. Infection rate not known.

On *Ebalia tuberosa* under the abdomen; rare.

Sacculina bourdoni Boschma   FIG. 8.16

Up to 18 mm wide. Irregular or grooved shape. Mantle opening on short tube. Less than 1% of hosts infected. Usually singly, sometimes two.

On *Xantho pilipes*. North-west France possibly also British Isles.

Sacculina gerbei Bonnier   FIG. 8.16

Up to 11 mm; light orange-brown. Fairly symmetrical. Mantle opening with thick protruding lips. Fine pattern of ridges on surface. Infection rates recorded are less than 1%. Singly or two or three.

On *Xantho incisus, Pilumnus hirtellus, Atelecyclus rotundatus*. Irish Sea, Ireland.

Drepanorchis neglecta (Fraise)   FIG. 8.16

Up to 14 mm, usually less yellowish, becoming browner. Infection rates up to 4.6% recorded in Irish Sea; 70% in Scandinavia—where multiple (up to four externae) observed.

On *Macropodia rostrata, M. tenuirostris, Inachus dorsettensis, I. phalangium, I. leptochirus*.

9 CRUSTACEA II
MALACOSTRACA PERACARIDA

C. Class **Malacostraca**

THE Malacostraca is the largest class of the Crustacea, with more than 19 000 species known from marine, freshwater, and terrestrial habitats. It is also the most familiar crustacean group, including the edible and economically important, crabs, lobsters, shrimps, and prawns, as well as a number of significant wood-destroying pests. The Malacostraca as a whole encompasses the broadest range of morphological and functional diversity, and displays a wealth of adaptive features. The largest crustaceans are the malacostracan spider crabs.

The malacostracan body plan comprises a, primitively, five-segmented *head*, often fused with the *thorax*, or *pereon*, of eight segments; the *abdomen*, or *pleon*, consists of a further six segments, or rarely seven. The head bears two pairs of antennae, usually well-developed, the first pair of which is typically biramous; there are two pairs of *maxillae* and up to three pairs of *maxillipeds*; compound eyes are usually present, often stalked, but may be absent. Each thoracic segment bears a pair of appendages, basically biramous but variously modifed, with a gill developed at the base of each appendage; the first three pairs are employed in feeding, while the rest are variously modified forming the locomotory *pereopods*. Each abdominal segment is similarly equipped with a pair of biramous appendages, the *pleopods* and *uropods*, modified for swimming or reproduction, or both functions, and occasionally for respiratory purposes. The last pair of abdominal appendages is often broadened, and with the last abdominal segment, the *telson*, constitutes a tail fan.

Malacostracans are mostly dioecious, although a few her-maphrodite species are known. Following copulation a considerable delay may lapse before fertilization and spawning. Eggs are usually retained by the female, within a thoracic brood chamber or attached to the pleopods. Life histories may be relatively simple, with direct development resulting in the hatching of juveniles, or very complex, involving often lengthy series of larval stages.

Malacostracan crustaceans occur abundantly in all marine habitats and display wide ecological diversity. Although a majority are particle-feeding scavengers, many feeding specializations occur, from planktonic filter feeders to macro-carnivores. Thus, the Malacostraca fulfill numerous significant roles in marine food webs.

Six superorders are recognized within the Malacostraca, only three of which are covered here. The Phyllocarida is a primitive group of small, predominantly filter-feeding malacostracans, of which only the order Leptostraca contains living representatives. In the Peracarida, exemplified by isopods and amphipods, the thoracic segments are typically distinct and a carapace is absent or only scarcely developed. Eggs are brooded in the *marsupium*, a brood chamber formed of a series of plates developed from the *coxae* of the thoracic limbs, and give rise to juveniles through direct development, with no intervening larval stages. The Euca-rida comprises the most familiar malacostracans, the crabs and their allies. In these the thorax is fused dorsally to a rigid carapace which displays no sign of segmentation. Eggs are typically brooded attached to the pleopods of the female and hatch as post-naupliar larvae which pass through a series of larval stages before metamorphosis to adult form.

Order **Leptostraca**

The leptostracans are the most primitive members of the Mala-costraca. Only ten living species are known although many fossil species have been described. The body is small, and the thorax and part of the abdomen is enclosed in a large bivalved *carapace* hinged along the mid-dorsal line. The carapace is attached to the head region of the animal by an adductor muscle. Anteriorly, a hinged and moveable *rostral plate* covers the head. The long antennae protrude anteriorly from the carapace, and in males the antennal flagellum is as long as the body. There are eight thoracic segments, each with a pair of biramous leaf-life append-ages; these are used for swimming and for feeding, and in the females may be modified for brooding eggs. The pleon comprises seven segments and terminates with a pair of long *furcal rami;* the first four pleon segments bear well-developed biramous appendages, segments five and six have reduced uniramous appendages, and segment seven is without appendages.

A single leptostracan occurs commonly in British coastal waters.

REFERENCES

Mauchline, J. (1984). Euphausiid, Stomatopod and Leptostracan Crus-taceans. *Synopses of the British fauna* (N.S.), **30**, Leiden: E. J.

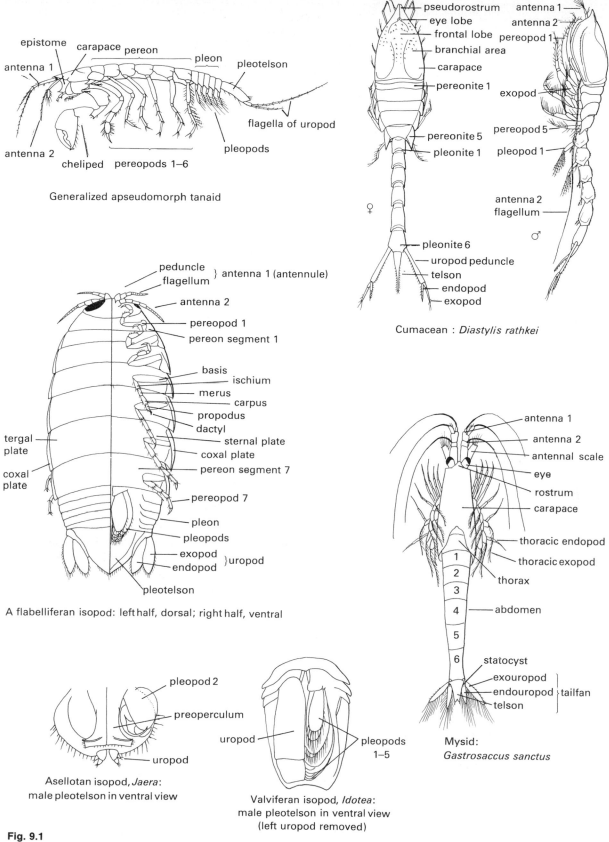

Generalized apseudomorph tanaid

Cumacean : *Diastylis rathkei*

A flabelliferan isopod: left half, dorsal; right half, ventral

Asellotan isopod, *Jaera*:
male pleotelson in ventral view

Valviferan isopod, *Idotea*:
male pleotelson in ventral view
(left uropod removed)

Mysid:
Gastrosaccus sanctus

Fig. 9.1

Brill, for the Linnean society of London, and the Estuarine and Brackish-Water Sciences Association.

Sars, G. O. (1896). Phyllocarida and Phyllopoda. *Fauna Norvegiae*, 1, 1–140.

I NEBALIIDAE

Nebalia bipes (Fabricius)   FIG. 9.2

Body up to 12 mm long, light brown, greenish, or dark brown, with red eyes; distinctly shrimp-like in appearance. Carapace smooth, proportionately shorter in female than male, rounded posteriorly, with conspicuous, projecting rostral plate anteriorly. Eyes large, stalked. Female antenna 1 with flagellum about as long as terminal three articles; antenna 2 flagellum less than twice length of antenna 1 flagellum, not reaching posterior edge of carapace. Male antenna 1 flagellum almost as long as carapace; antenna 2 flagellum very long, extending almost to tip of furcal rami.

Intertidal and shallow sublittoral; under stones, in decaying seaweed, in shaded rock-pools, frequently in crab pots or bait; often present in abundance. All British coasts; distributed from North Sea to Mediterranean.

Order Cumacea

Cumaceans are small peracaridan crustaceans, easily recognized by their structure. The broad anterior part of the body comprises the *carapace*, formed from the dorsal fusion of the head and the first three thoracic segments. Laterally, the carapace is produced into folds which enclose the anterior appendages of the animal. The anterior edge of the carapace is produced into two *pseudorostral lobes*, which together constitute the *pseudorostrum*. Below the pseudorostrum, on each side, the edge of the carapace has a distinct *antennal notch*, above an often prominent *anterio-lateral corner*. The single eye is situated posterior to the pseudorostrum, just anterior to the dorsal *frontal lobe* of the carapace. The remaining five thoracic segments comprise the *pereon*; the slender abdomen, or *pleon*, consists of six segments and a terminal *telson*. The anterior appendages consist of one or two pairs of *maxillae*, three pairs of *maxillipeds* and five pairs of *pereopods*. The pleon may have up to five pairs of *pleopods* in males, but female cumaceans lack pleopods entirely. The first antenna may have a brush of modified, jointed setae at the tip of the flagellum; referred to as *aesthetascs*, these appear to be sensory in function.

Sexual dimorphism is very marked in the Cumacea, and both carapace shape and sculpture may differ between the sexes. In the female, antenna 2 is rudimentary and there are no pleopods. The adult male has a well-developed antenna 2 with a long flagellum, and, with the exception of the Nannastacidae, has a number of pleopods. Immature males resemble the female, and the flagellum of antenna 2 increases in length with age.

Intertidal species of cumaceans are most easily found on the shore in areas of wet sand, particularly between ripple marks where water lies on the sand surface. Most species are retained by a 1 mm sieve. Alternatively, specimens may be obtained by puddling wet sand with an open hand, when the animals will emerge and swim in the surface water before reburying themselves. Some species are caught in inshore or surf plankton hauls, particularly at night when they may be attracted by a light. Plankton light traps, employing a towed net with a light source close to the mouth, will also catch cumaceans, particularly the males of certain species. Offshore, fine meshed bottom dredges may be used with good results.

REFERENCES

Fage, L. (1951). Cumacés, *Faune de France*, **54**, 1–136.

Jones, N. S. (1957). *Fiches d'Identification du Zooplancton*, No. 71–6. *Cumacea*. Conseil permanent International pour l'Exploration de la Mer, Copenhagen.

Jones, N. S. (1976). British Cumaceans. *Linnean Society Synopses of the British Fauna (New Series)*, No. **7**. London: Academic Press, for the Linnean Society of London.

Sars, G. O. (1878–79). Nye Bidrag til Kundskaben om Middelhavets Invertebratfauna. II. Middlhavets Cumaceer. *Archiv for mathematik og Naturvidenskab*, Kristiania, **3**, 461–512; **4**, 1–126.

Sars, G. O. (1900). Cumacea. *An Account of the Crustacea of Norway*, **3**, 1–115.

KEY TO FAMILIES

1. Telson absent, or so well fused with the last abdominal segment as to be separately indistinguishable   **2**

   Telson present and obvious, if only as a small plate   **3**

2. Male with five pairs of pleopods. Female with exopods on either pereopod 1, or on pereopods 1, 2, and 3   **1. Bodotriidae**

   Male without pleopods. Female with exopods on pereopods 1 and 2 only   **2. Nannastacidae**

3. Inner ramus of uropod with only one article   **3. Pseudocumatidae**

   Inner ramus of uropod with two or three articles   **4**

4. Telson with eight apical spines; the anus opening at its base **4. Lampropidae**

Telson with two apical spines; the anus opening part way along its length **5. Diastylidae**

I BODOTRIIDAE

No free telson on abdomen. Pleopods with a process on outer edge of inner ramus. Male with five pairs of pleopods, or occasionally only two or three pairs. Exopodites present on maxilliped 3 in both sexes. Male with exopodites on pereopod 1, or on pereopods 1–4, or only on pereopods 1, 2, and 3. Female with exopodites on pereopods 1–3, or pereopod 1 only, or on first two or first four pairs. Thoracic segments often reduced.

---

1. Exopodites on pereopod 1 only   **2**
   Exopodites on pereopods 1–3 or 1–4, sometimes rudimentary   **7**

2. First thoracic segment visible from above   **3**
   First thoracic segment fused with the carapace and not visible   **4**

3. Basis of pereopod 1 longer than the remaining articles together; last abdominal segment with two terminal setae   *Iphinoe trispinosa*
   Basis of pereopod 1 shorter than the remaining joints together; last abdominal segment with six terminal setae   *Iphinoe tenella*

4. Carapace with lateral horns   *Eocuma dollfusi*
   Carapace without lateral horns   **5**

5. Two folds along each side of carapace   *Bodotria pulchella*
   One fold along each side of carapace   **6**

6. Two joints on the inner ramus of uropod   *Bodotria scorpioides*
   One joint on the inner ramus of uropod   *Bodotria arenosa*

7. Exopods of pereopods 2 and 3 rudimentary   **8**
   These exopods well-developed   *Vaunthompsonia cristata*

8. Carapace with two lateral folds each side   *Cumopsis goodsiri*
   Carapace without lateral folds   **9**

9. Inner ramus of uropod with lateral spines and a thin apical spine   *Cumopsis longipes*
   Inner ramus of uropod without lateral spines, but with a stout apical spine   *Cumopsis fagei*

Iphinoe trispinosa (Goodsir)   FIG. 9.2

Body slender, up to 10 mm long, whitish or straw coloured. Adult female with two to six small teeth in middle of dorsal ridge of carapace; pseudorostrum acutely pointed. Male with dorsal ridge of carapace unarmed, and pseudorostrum blunt. Adult male with median spinous tubercle, and paired lateral tubercles, on ventral surface of pereon segment 2. Basis of pereopod 2 with bifid spur on inner edge. Two short setae on posterior body of last abdominal segment.

On fine sand; intertidal and coastal, but also offshore to 150 m. All British coasts; distributed from Norway to the Mediterranean, and the Canary Isles.

Iphinoe tenella Sars   FIG. 9.2

Body up to 8 mm long. Carapace in both sexes with prominent teeth along whole of dorsal crest, increasing in size anteriorly. Adult male without ventral tubercles on pereon segment 2. No spur on basis of pereopod 2. Last abdominal segment with six setae on posterior edge.

On muddy sand; intertidal and shallow sublittoral, to 30 m. Reported from Channel coasts, and southwards to the Mediterranean and west Africa.

Eocuma dollfusi Calman   FIG. 9.2

Body up to 7 mm long, smooth, lacking setae and spines. Carapace with paired, acute lateral horns, anteriorly directed, on dorso-anterior edge; most conspicuous in female. Distinct dorsal keel extends whole length of carapace. Pereon segment 1, and sometimes 2, fused with carapace. Pereopod 1 with process on inner distal edge; pereopod 2 basis and ischium fused. Uropod peduncle almost three times length of rami.

In sand, intertidal. Channel Isles only; distributed southwards to north-west Africa.

Bodotria arenosa Goodsir   FIG. 9.2

Body up to 7 mm, brownish yellow with a transverse white band on carapace. Well marked longitudinal dorsal ridge, and paired longitudinal lateral ridges, extending along length of carapace, and posteriorly to pereon segment 5; particularly well-marked in male. Uropod inner ramus with one article only.

In coarse sand; lower shore and shallow sublittoral, to 120 m. All British coasts; distributed from south-west Norway to Brittany.

Bodotria pulchella (Sars)   FIG. 9.2

Body up to 3.5 mm in male, 2.5 mm in female; whitish with brown speckles. Carapace rather squat, with dorsal longitudinal ridge, and two lateral ridges on each side, fusing towards posterior edge of carapace. Pereopod 2 basis with recurved spines on dorsal side. Uropod with inner ramus of two articles.

Shallow subtidal, to 70 m. Reported from scattered localities on western coasts, south of the Clyde Sea, and also from the Firth of Forth. Distributed from the southern North Sea to the Mediterranean and West Africa.

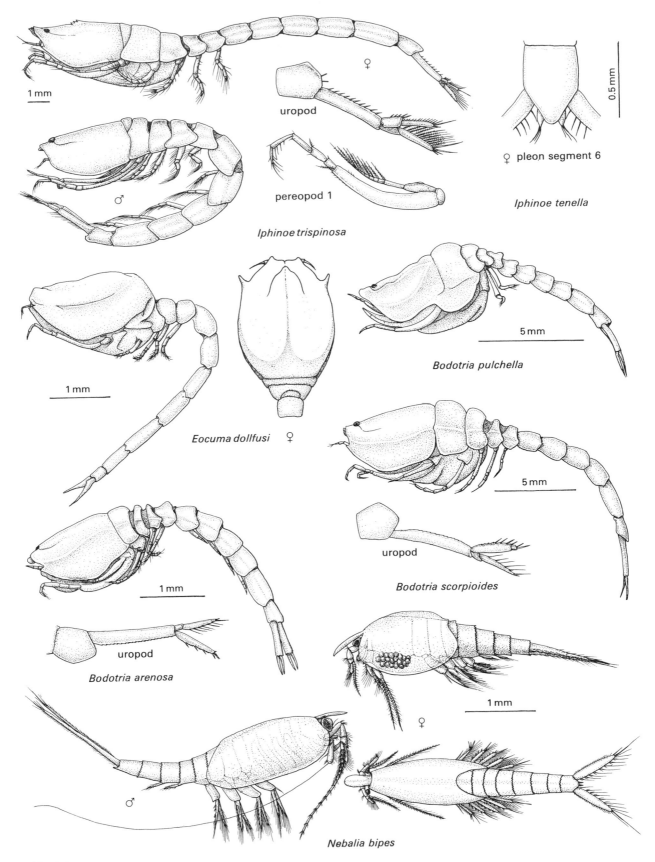

uropod

♀

0.5 mm

pereopod 1

♀ pleon segment 6

Iphinoe tenella

Iphinoe trispinosa

♂

5 mm

Bodotria pulchella

Eocuma dollfusi ♀

5 mm

1 mm

uropod

Bodotria scorpioides

uropod

Bodotria arenosa

1 mm

♀

♂

Nebalia bipes

Fig. 9.2

Bodotria scorpioides (Montagu)   FIG. 9.2
Body up to 7 mm long, light yellow with brown speckles. Carapace with dorsal longitudinal ridge and paired lateral ridges,
extending posteriorly on to first five pereon segments. Uropod
with inner ramus of two articles, the distal much shorter than
the proximal.

In fine sand, lower shore and shallow subtidal to 100 m. All
British coasts; distributed from Norway to western France.

Vaunthompsonia cristata Bate   FIG. 9.3
Body slender, up to 5 mm in male, 6 mm in female. Male with
smooth carapace and shallow antennal notch; female carapace
with dorsal median crest of two rows of small teeth, and conspicuous serrated antennal notch. Pereopods 1–4 of male, 1–
3 of female, each with well-developed exopodites. Antenna 2
flagellum of male extending posteriorly no further than pereon
segment 5.

Lower shore and shallow sublittoral, to 40 m, on coarse sand
and gravel. Southern and western shores only; distributed south
to the Mediterranean and west Africa.

Cumopsis fagei Bacescu   FIG. 9.3
Body up to 6 mm. Carapace without lateral folds, pereon segments smooth dorsally. Female uropod as long as combined
length of three posterior pleon segments, proximal segment of
exopod longer than distal segment, which terminates with a
strong spine but lacks spines on inner edge.

On exposed sandy beaches, predominantly intertidal but also
in shallow sublittoral. Distributed from Channel Isles to
Morocco, and perhaps occurring on extreme south-west shores
of Britain.

Cumopsis goodsiri (Van Beneden)   FIG. 9.3
Body up to 6 mm in female, 5 mm in male, with purplish brown
patches on carapace and pleon segment 5. Both sexes with a pair
of longitudinal ridges on each side of carapace, occasionally
faint; female with two semicircular folds on dorsal side of pereon
segment 2. Antenna 2 flagellum long, extending beyond end of
abdomen. Female uropod as long as posterior three segments of
abdomen, peduncle and inner ramus bearing variable number
of spines.

In fine sand, from mid-tidal level just into shallow subtidal
on sheltered beaches. All British coasts; distributed from North
Sea to Mediterranean and north-west Africa.

Cumopsis longipes (Dohrn)   FIG. 9.3
Body up to 6 mm long. Carapace smooth, lacking lateral ridges;
dorsal side of pereon segment 2 in female without folds. Female
uropod longer than posterior three segments of abdomen; peduncle with two or three spines on inner edge, three or four spines
on distal article of inner ramus.

Very similar to *C. goodsiri*, this species is only doubtfully
reported from the south coast of England.

2 NANNASTACIDAE
Pleon lacking both pleopods and telson. Male with exopodites

on maxilliped 3 and pereopods 1–4, rarely on pereopods 1, 2,
and 3 only. Female with exopodite on maxilliped 3 (rarely,
absent) and on pereopods 1, 2, rarely on pereopods 1–3, or
lacking completely. Uropod with inner ramus of one article only.

---

1. Dorsal surface of body with numerous tubercles and
   nodules   ***Nannastacus unguiculatus***
   Dorsal surface of body relatively smooth   **2**

2. Carapace with two depressions on each side
                               Campylaspis legendrei
   Carapace without lateral depressions   ***Cumella pygmaea***

Nannastacus unguiculatus (Bate)   FIG. 9.3
Body short and broad, up to 2 mm long; carapace with pronounced anterio-lateral processes, with numerous blunt or acute
tubercles, and short setae; female with prominent series of blunt
tubercles on posterio-lateral borders of carapace. Dorsal keel of
abdomen with distinct spines or coarse serrations. Female
uropod longer than combined length of posterior two pleon
segments; inner ramus more than twice length of peduncle, and
three times longer than outer ramus.

In coarse deposits, lower shore and shallow sublittoral. All
British coasts; distributed from Shetland to the Mediterranean.

Campylaspis legendrei Fage   FIG. 9.3
Body up to 4 mm; distinctive, with anteriorly tapered carapace
and very slender pleon; posterior margin of carapace extending
over first few pereon segments. Carapace finely rugose, with two
shallow depressions, separated by a slight ridge, on each side;
anterio-lateral corners rounded. Pereon segments 1 and 2 raised
dorsally. Maxilliped 2 dactyl with four spines; pereopod 2 dactyl
as long as carpus and propodus combined.

Reported from the Irish Sea, in coarse sand and shell-gravel,
at 25 m and 60 m, and intertidally at Concarneau.

Additional species of *Campylaspis* reported from scattered
offshore localities around Britain and Ireland are described by
Jones (1976).

Cumella pygmaea Sars   FIG. 9.3
Body up to 3 mm long. Female with laterally compressed carapace, arched dorsally, with a median keel of up to 12 anteriorly
directed teeth; anterio-lateral corners of carapace pronounced,
below a deep antennal notch. Male with dorsal edge of carapace
straight, without teeth. Female uropod with peduncle serrated
on inner edge; inner ramus shorter than peduncle but longer and
broader than outer ramus. Male antenna 2 flagellum extending
posteriorly to pleon segment 3.

In coarse sand and shell-gravels, shallow sublittoral. All
British coasts; distributed from Norway to Mediterranean and
Black Sea.

3 PSEUDOCUMATIDAE
Small telson present. Male with exopodites on maxilliped 3 and

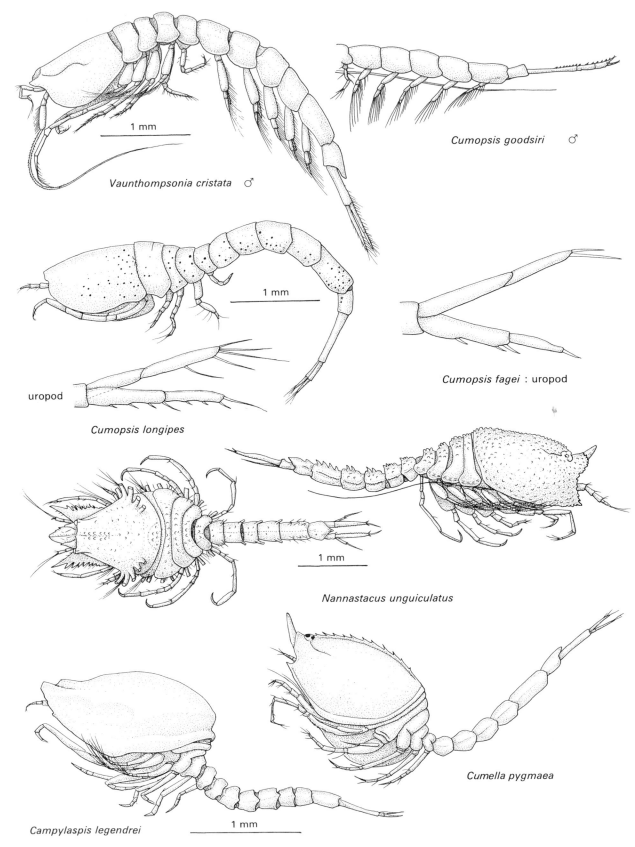

Vaunthompsonia cristata ♂

Cumopsis goodsiri ♂

uropod

Cumopsis longipes

Cumopsis fagei : uropod

Nannastacus unguiculatus

Cumella pygmaea

Campylaspis legendrei

Fig. 9.3

pereopods 1–4; female with exopodites on maxilliped 3 and pereopods 1, 2, poorly developed on pereopods 3, 4. Male with two rudimentary pairs of pleopods, or sometimes only a single pair. Pleopods without external process on inner ramus. Uropod with ramus of one article only.

---

1. Anterio-lateral angle of carapace with three teeth
   Pseudocuma similis

   Anterio-lateral angle of carapace without teeth **2**

2. Uropod peduncle with four feathery setae on inner edge; uropod inner ramus with about 12 spines
   Pseudocuma longicornis

   Uropod peduncle with one spine on inner edge; Uropod inner ramus with seven or fewer spines
   Pseudocuma gilsoni

Pseudocuma longicornis (Bate)   FIG. 9.4

Body up to 4 mm long, marked with dark brown patches. Carapace with three obliquely longitudinal folds on each side; dorsal edge convex in male, slightly concave in female; pseudorostrum acute, anterio-lateral corners without teeth. Pereon segments lacking dorsal keel or projections. Telson semicircular to semi-oval. Antenna 2 flagellum of male extending posteriorly at least as far as pleon segment 5. Uropod peduncle as long as outer ramus in female, shorter in male; inner ramus longer than outer, with about 12 spines on inner edge.

Intertidal and shallow sublittoral, occurring in brackish water and tolerant of very low salinities. All British coasts; distributed from northern Norway to the Mediterranean.

Pseudocuma gilsoni Bacescu   FIG. 9.4

Very similar to *P. longicornis*, of which it may be simply a neotonous male form. Distinguished by male antenna 1, which has a brush of aesthetascs on distal segment of peduncle, and by the shorter male antenna 2 flagellum. Additionally, only five to seven spines occur on the uropod inner ramus.

Reported from Liverpool Bay and the Belgian coast.

Pseudocuma similis Sars   FIG. 9.4

Body up to 5.5 mm, yellowish with light brown flecks. Similar to *P. longicornis*, distinguished by the carapace, which bears three small teeth on anterio-lateral corners. Telson broader than long, truncate in female. Uropod rami of almost equal length, both shorter than the peduncle.

Shallow sublittoral, but reported as deep as 360 m. All British coasts; a boreal species distributed from Norway to the Bay of Biscay.

4 LAMPROPIDAE

Large telson present, with terminal spines, and bearing anus at its base. Pleopods with external process on inner ramus. Male with three pairs of pleopods, or none, occasionally with one or two pairs; female typically lacking pleopods, rarely with one

pair. Exopodites present on maxilliped 3 and pereopods 1–4 in male; in female well-developed on maxilliped 3 and pereopods 1, 2; rudimentary on pereopods 3, 4. Uropod with inner ramus of three articles.

Lamprops fasciata Sars   FIG. 9.4

Body slender, male up to 7 mm, female up to 9 mm long; with more or less distinct transverse brownish bands. Carapace shorter than pereon, with three obliquely longitudinal folds on each side; pseudorostrum short and blunt. Pereon segments 2 and 3 together as long as carapace. Telson with five apical spines. Male lacking pleopods, with antenna 2 about half length of body. Female with rudimentary exopodites, each of two articles, on pereopods 3 and 4.

On sand, shallow sublittoral. All British coasts; distributed northwards to northern Norway.

5 DIASTYLIDAE

Telson present, often large, with two apical spines, or none. Pleopods sometimes small, without external process on inner ramus. Male with two pairs of pleopods, or none. Exopodites on maxilliped 3 and pereopods 1–4, or 1–2, in male; in female present or absent on maxilliped 3, present on pereopods 1–2, and occasionally as rudiments on pereopods 3–4. Uropod with inner ramus of three articles, or occasionally only two (or one) articles. Sexual dimorphism often marked.

---

1. Carapace with two to five more or less vertical folds
   Diastylis rugosa

   Carapace without vertical folds **2**

2. Pre-anal portion of telson about equal length to post-anal portion **Diastylis tumida**

   Pre-anal portion of telson shorter than post-anal portion **Diastylis bradyi**

Diastylis bradyi Norman   FIG. 9.4

Body up to 12 mm. Carapace with acute pseudorostrum, with up to two short apical spines in male; female with transverse lines of small denticles on sides of carapace. Posterio-lateral corners of pereon segment 5 produced as acute prolongations. Female with medial ventral spine on pereon segment 3. Pereopod 1 basis as long as remaining articles together, propodus less than twice length of dactyl.

On coarse deposits, often associated with mud, shallow sublittoral. All British coasts; distributed from southern North Sea to Biscay.

Diastylis rugosa Sars   FIG. 9.4

Body up to 9 mm, greyish white. Female carapace with three to five transverse folds on each side, and two pairs of conspicuous acute teeth fronto-dorsally. Male carapace with two transverse folds on each side, associated with a smooth, longitudinal ridge. Posterio-lateral corners of pereon segment 5 rounded in female,

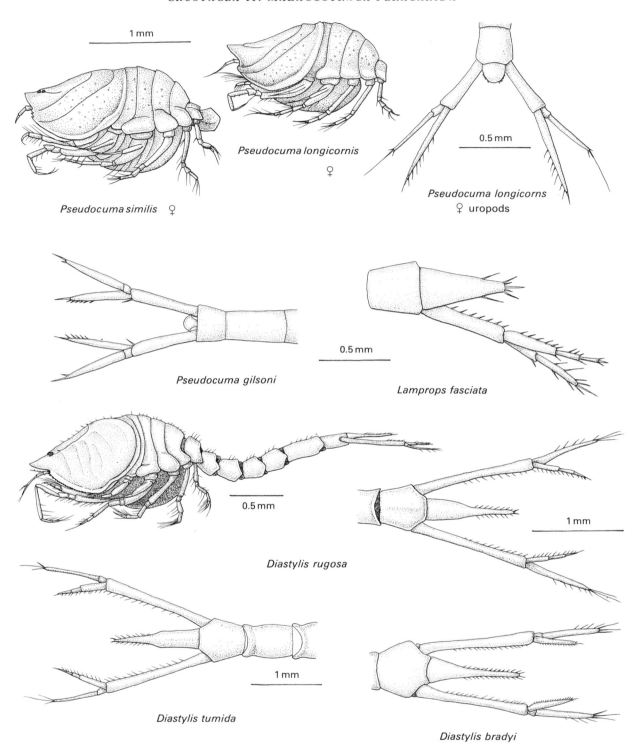

1 mm

Pseudocuma longicornis
♀

Pseudocuma similis ♀

0.5 mm

Pseudocuma longicorns
♀ uropods

Pseudocuma gilsoni

0.5 mm

Lamprops fasciata

0.5 mm

Diastylis rugosa

1 mm

1 mm

Diastylis tumida

Diastylis bradyi

Fig. 9.4

acutely pointed in male. Telson slightly shorter than uropod peduncle, with up to nine pairs of lateral spines.

Lower shore and shallow sublittoral, to 90 m; in muddy sand, and often in *Laminaria* beds. All British coasts; distributed from Norway to the Mediterranean,

Diastylis tumida (Lilljeborg)   FIG. 9.4
Body up to 10 mm, dull white. Carapace as broad as long,

with short pseudorostrum; usually smooth, but sometimes with minute denticles frontally in female; in male a transverse line below pseudorostrum, along lower edge of carapace to hind margin. Posterio-lateral corners of pereon segment 5 rounded in female, acutely pointed in male. Pereopod 1 basis shorter than remaining articles together, bearing a row of spines; propodus longer than carpus combined. Telson shorter than uropod peduncle, with eight or nine pairs of lateral spines.

Sublittoral, from 25 m to 1400 m, occasionally in shallower water. Reported sporadically from north-east and north-west coasts of Britain; distributed from northern Norway to the Azores.

Order **Tanaidacea**

Tanaids are small peracaridan crustaceans superficially resembling isopods, with which they were once classified. The tanaid body is dorso-ventrally flattened, or cylindrical and tends to be rather elongate. Anteriorly, the head and first two segments of the thorax are fused to form a *cephalothorax*, covered by a carapace which is produced into lateral folds enclosing a *branchial chamber*. Sessile eyes may be present, and the anterior edge of the carapace may be produced as a *rostrum*. The cephalothorax is followed by a six-segmented *pereon*, and a *pleon* of five segments which in some species are fused. The posterior *pleotelson* is formed from the fusion of a sixth pleon segment with the *telson*. The second fused thoracic segment bears a pair of chelate appendages, the *chelipeds*, and the following six pereon segments each bears a pair of ambulatory *pereopods*, usually all alike. Each pleon segment has a pair of *pleopods*, used in swimming, although these may be missing in the females of some species. Finally, a single pair of uniramous or biramous *uropods* is borne by the pleotelson. Sexes are separate and sexual dimorphism is often marked. Eggs are brooded in a *marsupium* on the ventral surface of the female and young are released as advanced juveniles, or *mancas*. Tanaids are small and often live in burrows or tubes in soft sandy or muddy substrate, or under stones, in crevices, and amongst red algae such as *Corallina* and *Laurencia*. They are generally inconspicuous and frequently overlooked. There are 30 shallow water species around the British Isles, eight of which may be found intertidally. Below 200 m species diversity is much higher.

REFERENCES

Bird, G. J. and Holdich, D. M. (1984). New deep-sea leptognathid tanaids (Crustacea, Tanaidacea) from the northeast Atlantic. *Zoologica Scripta*, **13** (4), 285–315.

Hassack, E. and Holdich, D. M. (1987). The tubiculous habit amongst the Tanaidacea (Crustacea: Peracarida) with particular reference to deep-sea species. *Zoologica Scripta*, **16** (3), 223–33.

Holdich, D. M. and Bird, G. J. (1986). Tanaidacea (Crustacea) from sublittoral waters off West Scotland including descriptions of two new genera. *Journal of Natural History*, **20**, 79–100.

Holdich, D. M. and Jones, J. A. (1983a). Tanaids. *Synopses of the British Fauna (N.S.)*, **27**. Cambridge University Press, for the Linnean Society of London.

Holdich, D. M. and Jones, J. A. (1983b). The distribution and ecology of British shallow-water tanaid crustaceans (Peracarida, Tanaidacea). *Journal of Natural History*, **27**, 157–83.

Sars, G. O. (1899). Isopoda. *An account of the Crustacea of Norway*, **2**, 1–270.

KEY TO FAMILIES

1. Antenna 1 with two flagella. Pereopod 1 stout, with flattened propodus. Male with single genital cone on pereon segment 6 **1. Apseudidae**

   Antenna 1 with only one flagellum. Pereopod 1 slender, similar to rest of pereopods. Male with two genital cones on pereon segment 6 **2**

2. Three pairs of pleopods present in both sexes. Pereopods without ischium. Uropods uniramous **2. Tanaidae**

   Five pairs of pleopods present, may be lacking in females. Pereopods with ischium. Uropods usually biramous **3**

3. Maxilliped bases distinct, not fused medially. Endopod of pleopod with conspicuous proximal seta on inner margin **3. Paratanaidae**

   Maxilliped bases fused medially to greater or lesser extent. Endopod of pleopod not as above **4**

4. Maxilliped bases fused proximally, separate distally. Female antenna 1 with three or four articles, male antenna 1 with up to seven articles **4. Leptognathiidae**

   Maxilliped bases fused to form a single plate. Female antenna 1 with four articles, male antenna 1 with six articles **5. Nototanaidae**

1 APSEUDIDAE

Body dorso-ventrally flattened, posteriorly tapered. Cephalothorax with prominent rostrum; ocular lobes distinct, eyes present or absent. Pereon segment 1 closely joined to carapace, all other pereon and pleon segments distinct. Antenna 1 with two flagellae, antenna 2 with one flagellum. Chelipeds often sexually dimorphic. Pereopod 1 flattened distally, with numerous propodial spines.

---

1. Rostrum parallel-sided with rounded apex, and
    apical spine   ***Apseudes latreillii***

    Rostrum triangular, with fine marginal denticulation
                                              Apseudes talpa

Apseudes talpa (Montagu)   FIG. 9.5

Body up to 8 mm long, opaque white. Cephalothorax as broad as long; with short, broadly triangular rostrum with denticulate margin and a distinct ventral keel. Eyes present. Anterio-lateral margins of pereon segments produced as short, rounded processes. Pleon segments with numerous setae; produced sharply laterally. Pleotelson as long as pleon. Chelipeds stouter in male than female, though not markedly dimorphic.

Middle and lower shore, into shallow sublittoral; in crevices, beneath stones, in *Laminaria* holdfasts and coralline algal turfs. South and west coasts of Britain, and western Ireland, southwards to north Africa.

Apseudes latreillii (Milne Edwards)   FIG. 9.5

Body up to 7 mm. Cephalothorax slightly longer than broad, with narrow, parallel-sided rostrum, produced apically into a single thin spine. Anterio-lateral margins of pereon segments rounded. Pleotelson shorter than pleon. Male cheliped stout, with prominent teeth on inner margins of propodus and dactylus; female cheliped slender, without teeth.

Middle and lower shore, and shallow subtidal; in crevices, in muddy gravel, beneath stones, in *Laminaria* holdfasts, coralline algal turfs, and the roots of *Zostera*. Reported from the Isles of Scilly and the Channel Isles, from Channel coasts, and from north-east England and eastern Scotland.

2 TANAIDAE

Body fusiform, anteriorly truncate, posteriorly rounded. Eyes well-developed. Three to five pleon segments. Antenna 1 with peduncle of three articles, with or without a small flagellum. Antenna 2 with six to eight articles. Pereopods without ischium; pleopods 4–6 with distinct claw. Three pairs of pleopods present. Uropods uniramous.

---

1. Uropod with three articles   ***Tanais dulongii***
    Uropod with four articles   ***Parasinelobus chevreuxi***

Tanais dulongii (Audouin)   FIG. 9.5

Body up to 5 mm long, often mottled with grey. Cephalothorax tapered and truncate anteriorly, slightly narrowed posteriorly. Pereon segment 1 much shorter than succeeding segments. Antenna 1 with four articles; antenna 2 with seven articles, the distal two very short. Cheliped typically with a tooth on inner margin of both propodus and dactylus, sometimes one or both missing; male often with more robust cheliped than female. Pereopods 4–6 with claw bearing a comb of stiff setae. Uropod with three articles.

Builds tube of sand, mud, and silt; intertidal and shallow subtidal, among barnacles, in crevices, under stones, in burrows formed by other organisms, among algal turfs, particularly *Corallina* and *Laurencia*; often on pier piles. A widespread and common species present on all British coasts; distributed from northern Norway to the Mediterranean, the east coasts of north and south America, and Australia, a distribution suggestive of association with fouling communities.

Parasinelobus chevreuxi (Dollfus)   FIG. 9.5

Body up to 6 mm long. Cephalothorax truncate anteriorly, broadest posteriorly. Pereon segments 1–3 of similar size. Antenna 1 with four articles; antenna 2 with six articles, articles 2 and 4 bearing distal fringe of stiff setae. Cheliped typically larger in male than female. Pereopods 4–6 without setal comb on claw. Uropod with four articles.

Builds long, parchment-like tubes in intertidal crevices; can be very abundant from middle to upper shore zones. Recorded from coasts of south Devon, Wales, and western Ireland; distributed southwards to north-west Africa.

3 PARATANAIDAE

British species display marked sexual dimorphism. Antenna 1 with three or four articles in female; with peduncle of two or three articles, and multiarticled flagellum, in male. Maxillipeds not fused medially. Cheliped with coxa situated behind proximal projection of basis. Pereopods with ischium; pereopods 4–6 with distal claw. Five pleon segments, each with biramous appendages. Uropods biramous.

---

1. Antenna 1 with ventral spine on article 2. Uropod
    outer ramus with one article only; inner ramus with
    four articles   ***Leptochelia savignyi***

    Antenna 1 without ventral spine on article 2. Uropod
    outer ramus with two articles; inner ramus of four to
    seven articles   ***Heterotanais oerstedti***

Heterotanais oerstedti (Krøyer)   FIG. 9.5

Body up to 2 mm long; rounded posteriorly, carapace anteriorly truncate in female, abruptly narrowed and elongate in male. Eyes prominent in both sexes. Pereon and pleon segments laterally rounded. Antenna 1 with three articles, lacking flagellum, in female; with three-articled peduncle and two-articled flagellum in male; antenna 2 with six articles. Male with massively enlarged

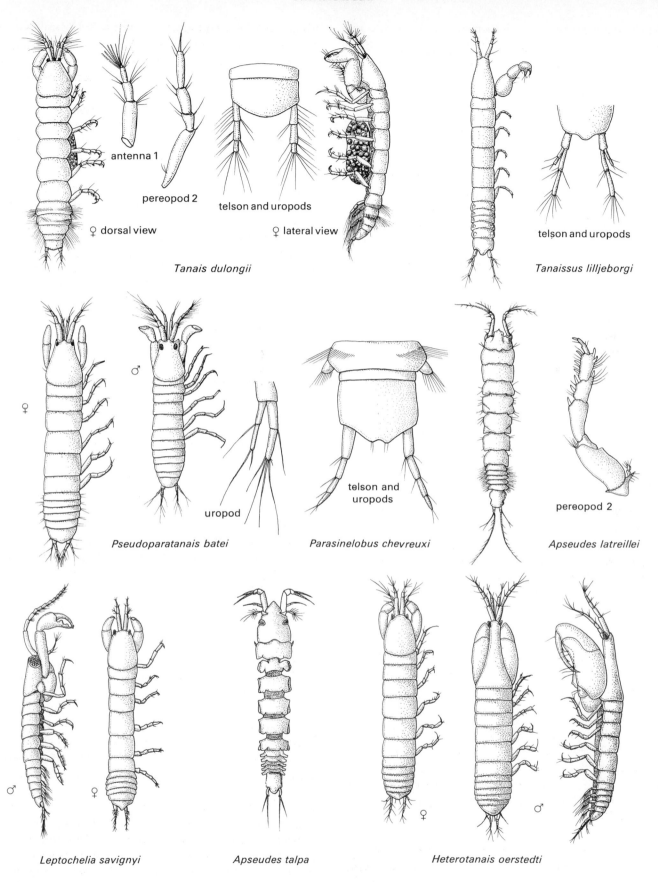

antenna 1

pereopod 2

telson and uropods

♀ dorsal view

♀ lateral view

Tanais dulongii

telson and uropods

Tanaissus lilljeborgi

♀

♂

uropod

Pseudoparatanais batei

telson and uropods

Parasinelobus chevreuxi

pereopod 2

Apseudes latreillei

♂ ♀

Leptochelia savignyi

Apseudes talpa

♀ ♂

Heterotanais oerstedti

Fig. 9.5

chelipeds, with prominent projection on carpus; female with smaller chelipeds. Pereopods 4–6 with bases much thicker than those of pereopods 1–3.

Builds tubes which are attached to algae, stones, and other hard substrata, or on mud surfaces, in sheltered conditions; lower shore and shallow sublittoral, to 10 m. Tolerant of low and varying salinity, from almost freshwater to fully marine. Reported from coastal, estuarine, and fluviatile habitats on south and east coasts of England, and South Wales; distributed from Norway to northern France.

Leptochelia savignyi (Krøyer) FIG. 9.5

Body up to 1.5 mm in male, 3 mm in female; rounded posteriorly, cephalothorax fusiform in female, more nearly quadrate in male. Pereon segments broadest posteriorly in male, more or less parallel-sided in female. Antenna 1 in female three- or four-articled, with single-articled flagellum, in male with two-articled peduncle and multiarticled flagellum. Antenna 2 with five or six articles. Male cheliped large, with two large teeth on inner margin of propodus and numerous spines on inner margin of dactylus; female cheliped relatively small. Pereopods 4–6 with bases thicker than in pereopods 1–3.

Builds tubes, attaching them to seaweed-covered surfaces, or among encrusting seaweeds and sea-grasses; intertidal and shallow subtidal. Recorded from shores of south-west England, the Channel Isles, and the south and west coasts of Ireland.

4 LEPTOGNATHIIDAE

Antenna 1 of female with three or four articles, in male with four to seven articles. Antenna 2 with five to seven articles in both sexes. Maxilliped bases fused to a variable extent. Chelipeds similar in males and females. Pleopods present or absent, highly variable.

Numerous species of this family have been described sporadically from British coasts. One common species is included here; Holdich and Jones (1983a,b) describe and illustrate all species recorded from British waters.

Pseudoparatanais batei (Sars) FIG. 9.5

Body up to 2 mm long in female, 1 mm in male; more or less parallel-sided in female, distinctly waisted between pereon segments 3 and 4 in male. Cephalothorax broadest posteriorly in female, broadened anteriorly in male; eyes well-developed, particularly large in male. Antenna 1 with three articles in female, six in male; antenna 2 with five articles in both sexes. Chelipeds similar in males and females. Pereopods 4–6 with bases broader than in pereopods 1–3. Uropod biramous, each ramus with two articles.

From lower shore to 100 m, among algae, in kelp holdfasts, hydroid clumps, crevices, muddy gravel, and shell deposits. Widely reported from most British coasts, except the south-east coast of England; distributed from Norway and Iceland south to the Mediterranean.

5 NOTOTANAIDAE

Antenna 1 in female with three or four articles, in male with five or six articles; antenna 2 with six articles. Maxilliped bases completely fused. Pleopods reduced or well-developed. Uropods biramous.

Tanaissus lilljeborgi (Stebbing) FIG. 9.5

Body up to 2.5 mm long, elongate and slender, rounded posteriorly; cephalothorax abruptly tapered anteriorly. No eyes. Antenna 1 with four articles in female, six articles in male; antenna 2 with six articles, shorter than basal article of antenna 1. Chelipeds large; propodus elongate in female, with dactyl forming chelate closure, shorter and broader in male with dactyl forming subchelate closure. Uropod biramous, each ramus of two articles, the inner ramus twice length of outer.

In sand, lower shore and shallow subtidal, often in abundance. Probably present on most British coasts; distributed from southern North Sea to northern France.

Order Mysidacea

Although abundant all round the British Isles, mysids are not common between tide marks and are often missed by shore collectors. Nevertheless, they have acquired a common name, 'Opossum Shrimps', which refers to the large ventral pouch, the *marsupium*, in which adult females carry eggs or developing young. The 29 species which have been recorded from depths of 20 m or less may be designated 'coastal'. More than 45 others occur in deeper water. One species (*Mysis relicta*) is restricted in Britain to deep freshwater lakes.

The order Mysidacea comprises two suborders, containing four families. The family Mysidae contains the vast majority of species and is the only family represented in coastal waters. All British coastal mysids are included in three of its subfamilies, the Siriellinae, Gastrosaccinae, and Mysinae.

Living mysids can be recognized by their more or less cylindrical form, shrimp-like appearance, free-swimming habit, and rather small size (Fig. 9.6A–D). Adults of the largest species attain a maximum length of 25 mm; the smallest species reaches no more than 6 mm. There is no separate larval form, early stages are carried by the female and released as juveniles which resemble the adults.

Most species are colourless and transparent or translucent, a few are normally red, or green. All have some chromatophores which are relatively larger and fewer than those of decapods. The chromatophores branch widely over the body and appendages, and pigments can be spread differentially so that part of an appendage might be coloured while the rest, and the body, remain transparent. The whole body can become dark, or change colour, so that some individuals look different from others in the same catch. A false appearance of coloration may be given by food in the gut showing through the transparent body tissue. Colour nearly always disappears or changes drastically in preserved material and is not used for identification.

The most distinctive characteristic of the Mysidae is a prominent *statocyst* in the swollen base of each endouropod (Fig. 9.6D, K). The mysid body has largely retained the primitive malacostracan arrangement; it consists of six fused head segments, eight thoracic segments, and six abdominal segments. The head is fused with the anterior thoracic segments, making a *cephalothorax*, with a *carapace* covering the head and most of the thorax dorsally and laterally. The large carapace is not attached to the posterior thoracic segments, and only partly overlaps the last one or two. The last few thoracic segments remain free but have very little mobility. The dorsal anterior margin of the carapace may be produced as a *rostrum*, usually small, sometimes virtually absent, and not serrated. The *abdomen* consists of six more or less similar, large, mobile segments, each with a posterior pair of appendages. The terminal *telson* is wider near its base than at the tip, unlike that of many Decapod larvae. Details of its form and armature are often important for identification (Fig. 9.6J, M, N).

The stalked eye consists of a set of many pigmented *ommatidia* delimited superficially by the *cornea* and mounted on a short or elongate mobile eyestalk (Fig. 9.6G). The corneal part is always conspicuous; in life it tends to be shiny, often golden-yellow with a black optical axis; in preserved specimens it goes dark. The other head appendages are: *antenna 1*, *antenna 2*; *mandible*; *maxilla 1* and *maxilla 2*. The antennae provide important key characters. Antenna 1 has a basal protopod of three distinct segments, collectively called the *peduncle*, bearing two long annulated *flagella*. Adult males have also a third, setose, projection, the *appendix masculina*. Antenna 2 has one long annulated flagellum, derived from the endopod and a flat, unsegmented lamellar arm, the *antennal scale*, which is the *exopod*. The antennal scale, like the telson, provides useful specific characters based on its shape and armature (Fig. 9.6D, H, I).

The thoracic limbs are biramous, with a basal protopod bearing a simple manipulatory or ambulatory *endopod* and a fringed natatory *exopod* (Fig. 9.6E, F). Euphausiids have similar limbs and at one time the two groups were known collectively as the 'Schizopoda'. The endopods of the first two or three pairs of thoracic limbs are modified as maxillipeds to assist feeding: the remainder are used for walking or holding on to weeds or pieces of food. They are never chelate, although in a few cases the terminal part may fold back to form a subchelate structure. The exopods of all eight thoracic limbs are elongated, thin and setose, and used for swimming. They maintain a constant rhythmic beat which propels the animal slowly forwards and also sets up respiratory and filter-feeding currents.

The first five pairs of abdominal appendages are the *pleopods*, the sixth pair, forming part of the tail fan, are the *uropods*. In females the pleopods are reduced to small, simple, setose processes; the males of some genera are similar when juvenile, but as they become sexually mature one or more pairs of pleopods become greatly modified and elongated. In other genera the males have large, biramous pleopods quite different from those of the female (Fig. 9.6A–C). The uropods are large flat fins, forming with the telson a strong tail fan. The uropod has lost most of its segmentation, so that its endopodite (the *endouropod*) and its exopodite (*exouropod*) each form a single flattened blade. Both blades provide key characters based on their form and armature. The exouropod is simple, flat, and paddle-shaped, its thin edge usually bearing a fringe of long setae; the outer edge may lack setae and bear a row of spines

instead. The distinction between setae and spines depends on their relative proportions; setae are very long, thin, and flexible, spines by comparison are shorter, stouter, and relatively rigid. In species with spines instead of setae on the outer edge of the exouropod, the basal part of the edge is smooth, without spines or setae. In the Siriellinae, an incipient suture divides a shorter distal part of the exouropod from a long proximal portion (Fig. 9.7N). The endouropod is smaller and less completely flattened than the exouropod. Its outer edge is thin and simple, but its inner margin is thick with a dorsal and ventral edge. It bears a continuous fringe of setae, and on the ventral inner edge a row of spines which are of great taxonomic importance. The swollen basal part of the endouropod bears a spherical *statocyst* containing a hard glassy *statolith*, a diagnostic feature of the Mysidae (Fig. 9.6D, K, L).

The sexes are separate. Maturing females develop, from the bases of the last two or three pairs of thoracic limbs, thin, curved, saucer-like plates (*oostegites* or *brood-lamellae*) which eventually overlap without fusing to form a large ventral brood pouch, the *marsupium* (Fig. 9.6A). Its development begins before sexual maturity is complete, so that a sub-adult condition is recognizable. Adult males develop a pair of papillae at the bases of the last pair of thoracic limbs on which the gonopores open. Males can be recognized by the form of the pleopods; in most genera, juvenile male pleopods are rudimentary and similar to those of the female, but with maturity one or two pairs become secondarily elongated. This secondary development begins before maturity, indicating a sub-adult stage. In these genera male and female juveniles look alike. In other genera, the large male pleopods and rudimentary female pleopods are evident even in juveniles; adult males are distinguished from juveniles only by the thoracic gonopore papillae and larger body size. A further character of adult males in the family Mysidae is the *appendix masculina* projecting from the end of the antenna 1 peduncle, just below the two flagella.

Mating and moulting are both normally nocturnal. A breeding female will release a brood of juveniles just before the moult and mate immediately after it. The male, apparently relying on chemical recognition at close quarters, seizes her from behind and adopts a mating position which varies between species. Sperm is shed either directly into the marsupium or is carried there by water currents set up by the mating pair. The next batch of eggs is released from the oviducts, opening near the bases of the sixth thoracic limbs, directly into the marsupium where fertilization occurs.

Early development takes place entirely within the marsupium and young are released as juveniles a few millimetres long. Juveniles adopt the same mode of life as adults, and individuals of all ages are likely to be found together in the same area. The offspring may mature and start breeding within a few months, while still growing, and thereafter will continue to grow towards a maximum size. The rate of growth, moulting, and breeding depend largely on temperature. Individuals live for one or two years.

All shallow-water mysids are to some extent eurythermic and euryhaline but the degree of tolerance varies considerably. Some are frequent in estuaries. One species, *Neomysis integer*, is characteristically associated with such conditions, being able to survive in almost fresh water. Most species swim slowly near the bottom, feeding on fine suspended matter, or chewing larger pieces of food including small animals. They may rest on weed or rocks, clinging on with the thoracic endopods, and a few species burrow into sand or mud. Open, moving water seems to be preferred, rather than pools, but several species occur in low shore pools. Mysids are frequently abundant just below LWS and may occur in large swarms. They also migrate tidally, diurnally, and seasonally, and greatest numbers are found at low tide, at night and in late summer. Most species rise towards the surface at night and may then be caught in a plankton net.

Mysids may be collected with a hand net in pools, or among seaweeds, but the best method of collecting them from the shore is by wading at low tide over a sandy bottom with a push-net of medium mesh (about 0.5–1 mm) or with a D-net hauled along the bottom on a long rope. From a boat, a net just running along the bottom will be suitable for daytime work; at night, oblique hauls, in which the net traverses the whole depth of water from bottom to top, are ideal for obtaining the maximum variety. Specimens should be killed by adding 40% formaldehyde to the seawater. A 4% solution in a clean tube will serve as a preservative. Alternatively, after being fixed in formalin they may be washed in freshwater then preserved and examined in 70% alcohol.

It is impossible to identify living, moving specimens without considerable experience. Microscopical examination of dead specimens is essential for certain identification. Precise adjustment of the light source is important when examining, for instance, spines on the endouropod. The spines on the ventral edge of the inner margin of the endouropod provide valuable specific characters but are difficult to see clearly because the margin is thick, having a dorsal edge fringed with setae. *The appendage should be examined upside down, as shown in Fig. 9.6K and the spines will be seen against a background of the dorsal setae.*

It is unwise to base a determination on a single character and all structures mentioned in a key couplet should be examined. The key may be used for young specimens and adults, but small juveniles are difficult to identify because of changes during growth in some features, such as the armature and relative proportions of appendages. As a general rule, specimens less than about 5 mm long should be treated with caution, bearing in mind that this represents an earlier stage for large species than for small ones. The smallest British species, *Erythrops elegans*, can be mature at that size.

LITERATURE

The older literature is dealt with in the monograph by Tattersall and Tattersall (1951), covering all the British Mysidacea. Nouvel (1951–63) has provided keys in French for the whole north-east Atlantic area. There have been a few changes in the British list since then, as noted by Makings (1977), who provides a condensed key to all British genera and a key to the coastal species which is used here with slight modification; and provides a general introduction to the group. Mauchline's

(1971*a*), account of the Clyde sea area summarizes much of his work on the biology of individual species. Another paper by Mauchline (1971*b*) provides information on seasonal movements and aggregation. Some idea of local distribution and abundance may be gained from fauna lists such as the Plymouth Marine Fauna (Marine Biological Association, 1957).

Makings, P. (1977). A guide to the British coastal Mysidacea. *Field Studies*, **4**, 575–95.

Makings, P. (1978). Two rare species of *Schistomysis* from South Wales. *Crustaceana*, **35**, 223–4.

Makings, P. (1981). *Mesopodopsis slabberi* (Crustacea, Mysidacea) at Millport, West Scotland, with the parasitic nematode *Anisakis simplex*. *Crustaceana*, **41**, 3: 310–2.

Marine Biological Association (1957). Plymouth Marine Fauna.

Mauchline, J. (1971*a*). *The fauna of the Clyde sea area. Crustacea: Mysidacea*. Scottish Marine Biological Association Dunstaffnage, Oban.

Mauchline, J. (1971*b*). Seasonal occurrence of Mysids (Crustacea) and evidence of social behaviour. *Journal of the Marine Biological Association of the U.K.*, **51**, 809–25.

Mauchline, J. (1980). The biology of mysids and euphausids. *Advances in marine Biology*, **18**, 1–677.

Nouvel, H. (1951–63). *Fiches d'Identification du Zooplancton*, No. **18–29**. *Mysidacea*. Conseil permanent International pour l'Exploration de la Mer, Copenhagen.

Tattersall, W. M. and Tattersall, O. S. (1951). *The British Mysidacea*. The Ray Society, London.

Mysidae

No gills. Carapace not attached to posterior thoracic segments. Male antenna 1 bears an 'appendix masculina' as well as the flagellum. Maxilla 1 without palp. First thoracic limb usually with well-developed exopod, second thoracic limb without a flat expansion of the merus. Endopods of thoracic limbs 3–8 with propodus, or carpus and propodus, usually divided into smaller segments. Two or three, rarely seven, pairs of oostegites in female, forming a characteristic marsupium. Male pleopods well-developed, biramous, or with one or more pairs rudimentary and one or more pairs secondarily enlarged as accessory sexual appendages; female pleopods rudimentary. Endouropod with statocyst.

---

1. Blade of telson (excluding spines) with apical cleft, i.e. distinctly notched or bifid at apex (Figs. 9.6J; 9.7S) **2**

   Telson without apical cleft, more or less rounded, pointed or truncate but not notched at the apex (Figs. 9.6M, N; 9.7T–X) (Spines at the tip may give a false impression if magnification is too low to distinguish them from blade of telson) **18**

2. Antennal scale with setae all round (Fig. 9.7G, H) **3**

   Antennal scale with a rather long smooth and naked outer margin. Remainder of edge, medial to this, bears setae (Figs. 9.6H; 9.7A–F) **4**

3. Apical cleft of telson with teeth inside. Endopod of thoracic limb 3 short, with a prehensile terminal claw ***Heteromysis formosa***

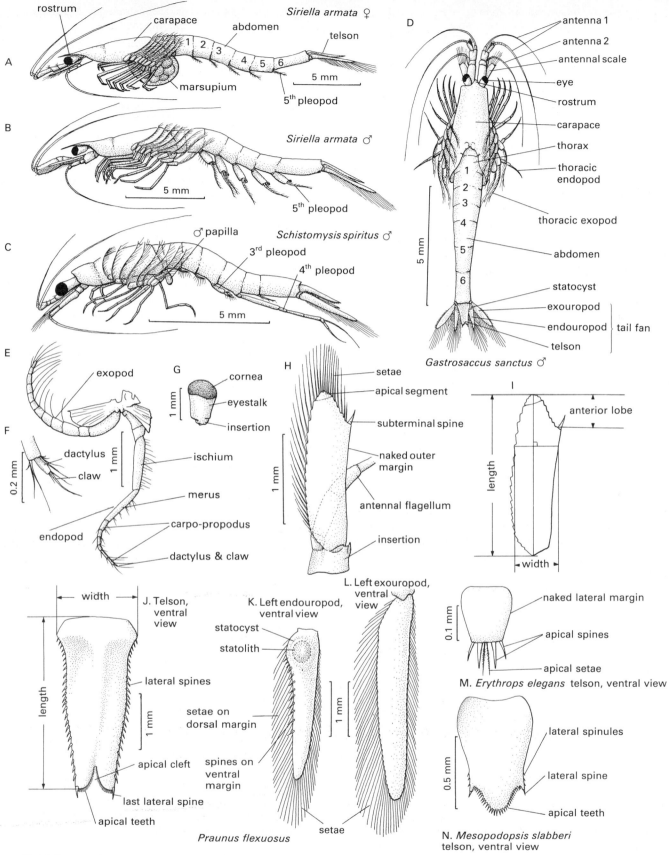

A Siriella armata ♀
rostrum, carapace, abdomen, telson, 5 mm, marsupium, 5th pleopod

B Siriella armata ♂
5 mm, 5th pleopod

C Schistomysis spiritus ♂
♂ papilla, 3rd pleopod, 4th pleopod, 5 mm

D Gastrosaccus sanctus ♂
antenna 1, antenna 2, antennal scale, eye, rostrum, carapace, thorax, thoracic endopod, thoracic exopod, abdomen, statocyst, exouropod, endouropod, telson, tail fan, 5 mm

E exopod

F dactylus, claw, 0.2 mm, ischium, merus, carpo-propodus, dactylus & claw, endopod, 1 mm

G cornea, eyestalk, insertion, 1 mm

H setae, apical segment, subterminal spine, naked outer margin, antennal flagellum, insertion, 1 mm

I anterior lobe, length, width

J. Telson, ventral view
width, length, lateral spines, apical cleft, last lateral spine, apical teeth, 1 mm

K. Left endouropod, ventral view
statocyst, statolith, setae on dorsal margin, spines on ventral margin

L. Left exouropod, ventral view
setae, 1 mm

Praunus flexuosus

M. Erythrops elegans telson, ventral view
naked lateral margin, apical spines, apical setae, 0.1 mm

N. Mesopodopsis slabberi telson, ventral view
lateral spinules, lateral spine, apical teeth, 0.5 mm

Fig. 9.6

Apical notch in telson without teeth or setae, smooth-edged inside. Endopod of thoracic limb 3 normal, like the others   ***Mysidopsis angusta***

4. Exouropod with spines, not setae, on outer margin; the spines absent from basal one-fifth or more of outer margin, leaving this part bare and smooth (Fig. 9.7L, M)   **5**

   Exouropod with setae, not spines, on outer margin. Setae occupy the whole margin from base to apex (Fig. 9.6L)   **9**

5. Abdominal segment 5 rather narrow when seen from above. In side-view it shows a dorsal ridge and spine-like median dorsal process at its posterior margin (Fig. 9.7I)   ***Gastrosaccus spinifer***

   Abdominal segment 5 may be narrowed, but lacks a dorsal ridge or median dorsal process   **6**

6. Telson with 20 or more lateral spines on each side. Outer margin of exouropod with 20 or more relatively small spines (Fig. 9.7M). Dorsal posterior margin of carapace straight, transverse (Fig. 9.7J)   ***Anchialina agilis***

   Telson with up to 14 lateral spines on each side. Outer margin of exouropod with 15 or less, relatively massive, spines. Dorsal posterior margin of carapace deeply concave when viewed from above (Fig. 9.6D)   **7**

7. Abdominal segment 5 narrow; nearly or quite as narrow as segment 6 (Fig. 9.6D). Telson about twice as long as broad, with five or six lateral spines on each side   ***Gastrosaccus sanctus***

   Abdominal segment 5 not as narrow as 6. Telson about three times as long as broad, with eight or more lateral spines on each side   **8**

8. Posterior margins of carapace with small lobes turning upwards and forwards   ***Gastrosaccus lobatus***

   Posterior margin of carapace with no such lobes   ***Gastrosaccus normani***

9. Smooth naked outer margin of antennal scale (about half length of scale) not ending in a spine, running smoothly into setose part (Fig. 9.7F). Telson has lateral spines restricted to apical half. Eyestalk shorter and smaller than large black corneal part of eye. Fresh specimens usually red   ***Hemimysis lamornae***

   Smooth naked outer edge of antennal scale ending in a small subterminal spine (Figs. 9.6H; 9.7A–E). Telson has lateral spines from base to apex (Figs. 9.6J; 9.7S). Eyestalk small but usually as large as corneal part of eye. Fresh specimens not normally red   **10**

10. Antennal scale rather parallel-sided, with short anterior lobe, which projects only slightly beyond base of subterminal spine, by twice length of spine or

less. Base of spine weakly constricted or articulated when seen under high magnification (Figs. 9.6H; 9.7A). Corneal part of eye extends beyond carapace   **11**

   Antennal scale broad, oval, with moderate anterior lobe (Fig. 9.7D, E) or narrow and elongated with long anterior lobe (Fig. 9.7B, C). Anterior lobe projecting well beyond base of subterminal spine, by more than twice length of spine. Base of spine with no trace of constriction or articulation. Corneal part of eye not reaching much beyond carapace (except in *Schistomysis spiritus*, which has anterior lobe of antennal scale several times longer than the subterminal spine)   **13**

11. Antennal scale about four times as long as broad, anterior lobe about twice as long as subterminal spine (Fig. 9.6H). Eyestalk slightly wider than long. Telson with 15–17 lateral spines. Chromatophores along ventral mid-line of abdomen, one on each segment; two chromatophores on telson, one on each blade of uropod. Living specimens red-brown to almost colourless   ***Praunus inermis***

   Antennal scale prominently long and strap-like; at least five times as long as broad, anterior lobe less than twice as long as subterminal spine (Fig. 9.7A). Eyestalk slightly or distinctly longer than wide. Telson with 18–28 lateral spines. Chromatophores along ventral mid-line of abdomen, two on each segment; four or more chromatophores on telson, several on each blade of uropod. Living specimens blackish, grey-brown, or green to almost colourless   **12**

12. Antennal scale only five or six times as long as broad, anterior lobe slightly longer than subterminal spine. Telson with 18–24 lateral spines. Three pairs of chromatophores on ventral surface of thorax, between legs; usually four chromatophores on telson and each exouropod, two on each endouropod. Living specimens almost colourless or pale to dark green   ***Praunus neglectus***

   Antennal scale seven or eight times as long as broad, anterior lobe at most as long as subterminal spine. Telson with 22–28 lateral spines. A separate pair of chromatophores on ventral surface of each thoracic segment, between legs. Usually more than four chromatophores on telson and four or more on each exouropod, three or four on each endouropod. Living specimens blackish, grey-brown, or yellowish to almost colourless   ***Praunus flexuosus***

13. Eyestalk longer than wide, like slightly tapering cylinder, eyes extend appreciably beyond margin of carapace. Distal third of endouropod very slightly incurved (Fig. 9.7O)   ***Schistomysis spiritus***

   Eyestalk not longer than wide, eyes not reaching appreciably beyond lateral margins of carapace. Endouropod either straight or with distal third markedly incurved   **14**

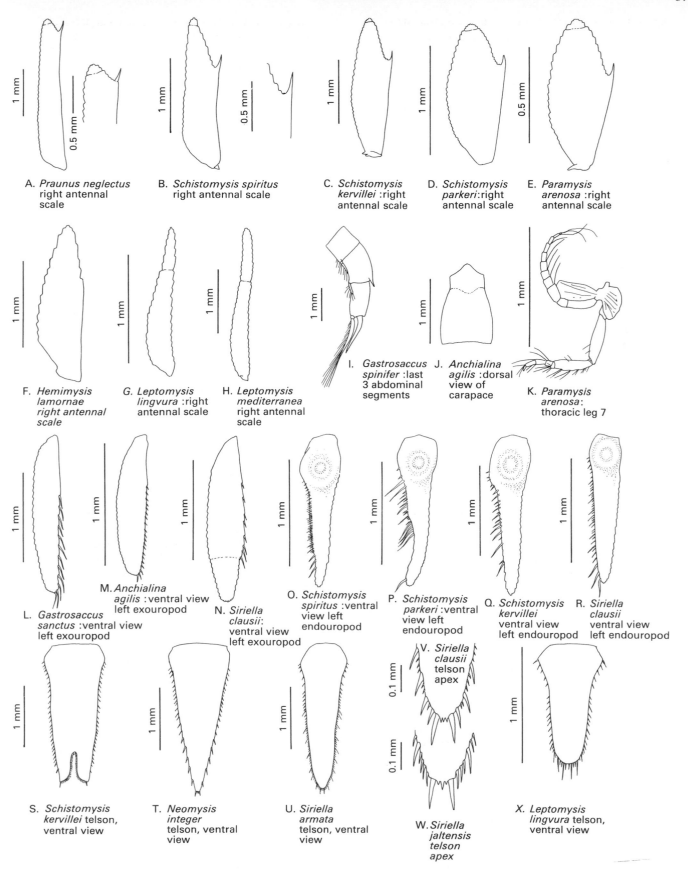

A. *Praunus neglectus* right antennal scale

B. *Schistomysis spiritus* right antennal scale

C. *Schistomysis kervillei* :right antennal scale

D. *Schistomysis parkeri*:right antennal scale

E. *Paramysis arenosa* :right antennal scale

F. *Hemimysis lamornae* right antennal scale

G. *Leptomysis lingvura* :right antennal scale

H. *Leptomysis mediterranea* right antennal scale

I. *Gastrosaccus spinifer* :last 3 abdominal segments

J. *Anchialina agilis* :dorsal view of carapace

K. *Paramysis arenosa*: thoracic leg 7

L. *Gastrosaccus sanctus* :ventral view left exouropod

M. *Anchialina agilis* :ventral view left exouropod

N. *Siriella clausii*: ventral view left exouropod

O. *Schistomysis spiritus* :ventral view left endouropod

P. *Schistomysis parkeri* :ventral view left endouropod

Q. *Schistomysis kervillei* ventral view left endouropod

R. *Siriella clausii* ventral view left endouropod

S. *Schistomysis kervillei* telson, ventral view

T. *Neomysis integer* telson, ventral view

U. *Siriella armata* telson, ventral view

V. *Siriella clausii* telson apex

W. *Siriella jaltensis* telson apex

X. *Leptomysis lingvura* telson, ventral view

Fig. 9.7

14. Distal third of endouropod markedly incurved. No spines on distal inner margin, which bears only setae, but strong spines proximally, and one on apex (Fig. 9.7P)   ***Schistomysis parkeri***

 Endouropod straight. Spines along most of inner margin from near base to near apex   **15**

15. Antennal scale more than three times as long as broad (Fig. 9.7C). Telson of adult with more than 24 lateral spines on each side. Eyestalk, from above, almost or quite as large as corneal part of eye (shrinkage of tissues away from cuticle may make it look smaller). Combined carpo-propodus of thoracic endopods divided into five or six sub-segments, basal one normal, longer than following sub-segment (as in Fig. 9.6E)   **16**

 Antennal scale oval, less than three times as long as broad (Fig. 9.7E). Telson of adult with less than 24 lateral spines on each side. Eyestalk from above only about half as big as corneal part of eye. Combined carpo-propodus of thoracic endopods divided into four or five sub-segments, basal one shorter than following sub-segment and very slightly bulbous (often difficult to see) (Fig. 9.7K)   **17**

16. Subterminal spine of antennal scale little more than half-way along length of scale. Spines on inner margin of endouropod extending, sparsely, almost to apex, increasingly larger from base to apex. Telson with about 26 lateral spines, evenly spaced, the last not particularly separated from the rest

 Schistomysis ornata

 Subterminal spine of antennal scale at about two-thirds length of scale from base (Fig. 9.7C). Spines on inner margin of endouropod irregular in size basally, long and short, stopping well short of apex (Fig. 9.7Q). Telson with about 30 lateral spines, a disproportionately larger gap between last lateral spine and preceding series (Fig. 9.7S)

 Schistomysis kervillei

17. Cleft of telson relatively wide and shallow: depth from one to one and a half times width between bases of last pair of lateral spines. Inner margin of endouropod with 13–18 spines in an irregular row, not nearly reaching apex. Telson with 13–18 lateral spines on each side   ***Paramysis nouveli***

 Cleft of telson rather deep; about one and a half times as deep as wide between bases of last lateral spines. Inner margin of endouropod with about 28 spines, some much larger than others, in a row extending almost or quite to apex. Telson with 17–23 lateral spines   ***Paramysis arenosa***

18. Telson characteristic: short, apex rounded, with numerous small teeth, flanked on each side by an angular shoulder bearing a strong spine (Fig. 9.6N). Eyestalks conspicuously long, cylindrical

 Mesopodopsis slabberi

 Telson not as described. Eyestalks not exceptionally long   **19**

19. Telson with truncate apex, narrow or broad; long, narrowing steadily towards almost pointed apex (Fig. 9.7T); or short and strongly truncate, almost trapezoidal (Fig. 9.6M)   **20**

 Apex of telson rounded (Fig. 9.7U–X)   **21**

20. Telson long, sides becoming straight towards apex, which is narrow, almost pointed. Antennal scale setose all round   ***Neomysis integer***

 Telson short, strongly truncated, almost trapezoidal. Antennal scale with naked outer margin   ***Erythrops elegans***

21. Exouropod divided, by a slight indentation and faint line, into a short distal segment and a longer proximal portion. Outer margin of proximal portion bearing spines, distal segment with setae instead of spines. (Line of division may be obscure, but distal and proximal portions are distinguished by shape and armature of exouropod) (Fig. 9.7N)   **22**

 Exouropod not divided, setose all round (Fig. 9.6L)   **25**

22. Rostrum long, tapering; normally projecting beyond anterior margin of eyes; reaching second basal segment of antenna 1 (shorter in juveniles). Eyestalk elongated, eyes extending beyond lateral margins of carapace. Telson with four or five (rarely three) small, equal apical spines between two large, last lateral ones. Exouropod rather long and parallel-sided, endouropod slightly incurving. Antennal scale long and almost parallel-sided   ***Siriella armata***

 Rostrum short; not, or barely, reaching anterior margin of eyes; reaching almost to middle, or less, of first basal segment of antenna 1. Eyestalks short and broad, not longer than wide. Telson with three tiny apical spines between two large, last lateral ones. Exouropod with slightly convex margins, endouropod straight (Fig. 9.7N, R). Antennal scale suboval   **23**

23. Three tiny apical spines of telson equal, or nearly so (Fig. 9.7V). Distal segment of exouropod about one and a half times as long as broad. Inner margin of endouropod with a series of large spines, all but distal three or four with smaller spines between

 Siriella clausii

 Three tiny apical spines of telson forming a trident: two very small ones flanking a larger median one (Fig. 9.7W). Distal segment of exouropod about twice as long as broad. Inner margin of endouropod with small spines between large ones, either restricted to basal region or continuing to apex   **24**

24. Outer margin of exouropod with 9–16 spines; inner margin of endouropod with a fairly regular series of spines graduated in size from base to apex, smaller ones interspersed only near base   ***Siriella jaltensis***

Outer margin of exouropod with 15–23 spines; inner margin of endouropod with two series: one of larger spines, the other of shorter, more numerous spines between longer ones, to apex **Siriella norvegica**

25. A dorsal fingerlike process on eyestalk, projecting outwards over edge of corneal part of eye. Two large, median dorsal humps on carapace. Telson not much longer than maximum width; with up to 18 very short spines on each side **Mysidopsis gibbosa**

No fingerlike process on eyestalk, no humps on carapace. Telson more than twice as long as wide, with 20 or more spines, often of varying size, on each side **26**

26. Telson without lateral spines on basal third, except for one or two near base. distal two-thirds strongly spinose. Endouropod with few spines near base on inner margin; apical half without spines
Acanthomysis longicornis

Telson with lateral spines from base to apex (Fig. 9.7X). Inner margin of endouropod spinose from near base to apex **27**

27. Integument microscopically scaly, looks bristly. Carapace notched on each side of rostrum base. Rostrum with slight convexity on each side behind tip **Leptomysis gracilis**

Integument normal, smooth. No notches in carapace near rostrum base. Edges of rostrum more or less concave all along **28**

28. Apical segment of antennal scale (best seen under low magnification) with ten setae or more on each side (best seen under high magnification). Rostrum relatively long, extending almost whole length of first basal segment of antenna 1 **Leptomysis mediterranea**

Apical segment of antennal scale with six setae or less on each side. Rostrum short, extending only half-way along first basal segment of antenna 1
Leptomysis lingvura

Acanthomysis longicornis (Milne Edwards) FIG. 9.8
Length 9 mm. Whole integument typically with minute scales, looking bristly, but this feature is variable (see also *Leptomysis gracilis*). Rostrum very short, pointed. Eyes prominent. Antennal scale narrow and tapering but not quite pointed. Female pleopods small, simple. Male pleopods small, fourth pair elongated but not quite reaching base of telson, with a terminal pair of unequal barbed setae. Telson long, tongue-shaped, with rounded apex, lateral spines absent from most of basal third, numerous on distal two-thirds. Base of endouropod with statocyst large, in relation to distal portion. Pigmentation sparse, dark brownish.

Near the bottom in moderate depths. Uncommon. Southern and western coasts of Britain, recorded from Scotland. Distributed south to the Mediterranean.

Anchialina agilis (G. O. Sars) FIGS. 9.7, 9.8
Length 9 mm. General appearance somewhat shrimp-like. Recognizable by relatively short, stout appearance and rather large carapace with straight hind margin. Rostrum well-developed, triangular, pointed. Eyes of moderate size, red to brownish. Antennal scale small, oval, with naked outer margin and subterminal spine. Females with very characteristic pleopods, much reduced to small angular plates. Those of male well-developed, natatory. Spines on outer margin of exouropod finer than in *Gastrosaccus*, needing close examination. Endouropod distinctly longer than exouropod; with many short and long spines on inner margin. Telson rather straight-sided, large; lateral spines fine, numerous. More or less transparent.

Normally near the bottom, swims actively. Shallow water to 100 m. Not usually taken from the shore except in night plankton. All British coasts. Distributed southwards to Mediterranean.

Erythrops elegans (G. O. Sars) FIGS. 9.6, 9.8
Length 6 mm; may be sexually mature at 5 mm. The only British species of *Erythrops* to occur in shallow water [*E. serrata* (11 mm), which might be taken rarely, has the naked outer margin of antennal scale strongly saw-toothed]. Living specimens of the genus have bright red eyes which fade in spirit. Corneal part of eyes prominent, wider than eyestalk, dorsoventrally compressed, thus appearing elongated laterally; with distinct individual ommatidia. Rostrum virtually absent, blunt. Subterminal spine of antennal scale strong, anterior lobe small. Thoracic endopods long and slender. Male pleopods well-developed, natatory. Female pleopods reduced, simple. Uropods extend far beyond short telson. Shape and armature of telson characteristic; no lateral spines, a pair of plumose apical setae medially between the apical spines. Body transparent, with bright pigmented spots.

At the bottom, on mud, sand, or shell-gravel. Siblittoral. Generally distributed around Britain, but not common. Ranges from Norway to the Mediterranean.

Gastrosaccus Norman
Moderate size. Appearance more shrimp-like than most mysids: thoracic region relatively stout compared with narrow middle region of abdomen. Eyes look relatively smaller than in most other genera. Rostrum slight. Antennal scale with naked outer margin and subterminal spine; anterior lobe short. Marsupium formed partly from anterior abdominal pleura. Female pleopods small. Male pleopods well-developed, biramous; third pair with very elongate exopod. Spines on outer margin of exouropod distinct but need careful scrutiny, and do not extend to base. Few long spines on inner margin of endouropod. Telson rather straight-sided, with up to 11 stout lateral spines on each side. Posterior margin of carapace often curiously ornamented, with little upturned lobes, as in *G. sanctus*, or a slight fringe as in *G. spinifer*. *G. normani* has neither of these and what was regarded as a variety with lobes has been distinguished as a distinct species, *G. lobatus*. Both *G. sanctus* and *G. lobatus* have forms with reduced lobes or none.

Gastrosaccus lobatus Nouvel   FIG. 9.8

Length 11 mm. Typical form distinguished from *G. normani* by presence of lobes on posterior margin of carapace. Telson with nine or ten lateral spines.

In the variety *armata* (not reported from Britain) the lobes on posterior margin of carapace are reduced (females) or absent (males); telson with 11–14 lateral spines instead of 9 or 10 in typical *G. lobatus* and *G. normani*.

Habits as *G. normani*. The two species occur together at Plymouth, *G. lobatus* being commoner inshore. Distribution southerly, limits not clear.

Gastrosaccus normani G. O. Sars

Length 11 mm. Smaller than *G. sanctus*, abdomen much less narrowed. Rostrum very short. Posterior margin of carapace without lobes. Telson more elongated with nine or ten lateral spines.

Bottom living, mostly offshore. A southern species, distributed from south-east England to the Mediterranean but recorded also from Scotland.

Gastrosaccus sanctus (van Beneden)   FIGS. 9.6, 9.7

Length 15 mm. Narrowing of abdomen fairly pronounced. Carapace deeply concave posteriorly; small upturned lobes on this margin rarely absent. Only six large lateral spines on each side of telson.

Burrows in mud or sand close inshore. Predominantly southern and western coasts, uncommon; rarer northwards to Scotland. Distributed southwards to Mediterranean.

Gastrosaccus spinifer (Goës)   FIGS. 9.7, 9.8

Length 21 mm. Immediately recognizable by narrowed abdomen with dorsally ridged fifth abdominal segment ending in a fingerlike spine. Posterior concavity of carapace with a slight fringe and minute lobation.

Bottom living, from close inshore to deep water. All British coasts, fairly common. Distributed from Norway to the Mediterranean.

Hemimysis lamornae (Couch)   FIGS. 9.7, 9.8

Length 13 mm. Rather small, very short rostrum. Antennal scale moderately broad, with basal half of outer margin smooth, no spine marking end of this part, which passes directly into setose part. Eyes very large, black and prominent; borne on smaller eyestalks. Female pleopods very small, simple. Male pleopods rather small, fourth pair with greatly elongated exopod, armed distally with two very long setae. Coloration distinctive, bright or dark red. Sometimes called the 'Midge Shrimp'.

Bottom living, avoiding light, usually among rocks and weed. From close inshore to >100 m. All British coasts but not common. Found in some marine aquaria, where it breeds freely. Distributed from Norway to the Mediterranean.

Heteromysis formosa Smith   FIG. 9.8

Length 8 mm. Unusual in structure and habits. General appearance robust, carapace short and broad without distinct rostrum, eyes moderately large but not projecting much beyond carapace.

Antennal scale rather small, slightly oval, with setae all round. Endopod of third thoracic limb different from all the others, shorter and stouter, with a prehensile terminal claw. Thoracic genital appendage of male large. Both male and female pleopods small and simple. Males with median thoracic sternal processes. Uropods relatively short and broad; inner margin of endouropod with a row of spines extending to apex. Telson with a fairly narrow cleft, toothed within. Lateral spines only along distal half of telson. Pale, somewhat translucent.

In cavities under stones, shells, in kelp holdfasts, usually on a muddy bottom. Lower shore to deep water. Uncommon. Reported sporadically, mostly from southern and western coasts. The similar *H. armoricana* Nouvel might be found in the west.

Leptomysis G. O. Sars

Moderately sized animals (15–20 mm). Rostrum fairly short, pointed. Telson smoothly rounded, with numerous, close, small and large spines from base to apex; lateral and apical spines not clearly separable, forming a continuous series. Antennal scale narrow, setose all round; division into apical and basal segments may be difficult to detect but is the best way of characterizing *L. mediterranea* and *L. lingvura*. Female pleopods reduced, small, slender; male pleopods strongly developed, natatory. Body pale or translucent with some pigmentation, or may be coloured reddish.

Leptomysis gracilis (G. O. Sars)   FIG. 9.8

Length 15 mm. Integument minutely scaled all over, appearing hispid (see also *Acanthomysis longicornis*). Rostrum triangular, sides bulging near middle, carapace with notch near base on each side. Apical segment of antennal scale with six setae or less on each side. Telson usually with a slight but characteristic constriction at base of a pair of large spines near apex. Perhaps these are thus equivalent to the last lateral spines.

Near the bottom or somewhat pelagic. Tends to keep away from the shore, in moderate depths, but also in estuaries. All British coasts. Distributed from southern Norway to the Mediterranean.

Leptomysis lingvura (G. O. Sars)   FIGS. 9.7, 9.8

Length 17 mm. Very similar to *L. gracilis* but with smooth integument and simple rostrum without notches in carapace. Apical segment of antennal scale with six or fewer setae on each side. Rostrum distinctly shorter than in the other two species. Often coloured reddish.

Littoral, or at the bottom in shallow water. All British coasts, common. Distributed from southern Norway to the Mediterranean.

Leptomysis mediterranea G. O. Sars   FIGS. 9.7, 9.8

Length 18 mm. Very similar to *L. lingvura*, but distinguished by the apical segment of antennal scale, which has ten setae or more on each side.

On or near the bottom, in shallow water, from tidal to deeper levels. Recorded mostly from southern and western coasts. Distributed from southern North Sea to the Mediterranean.

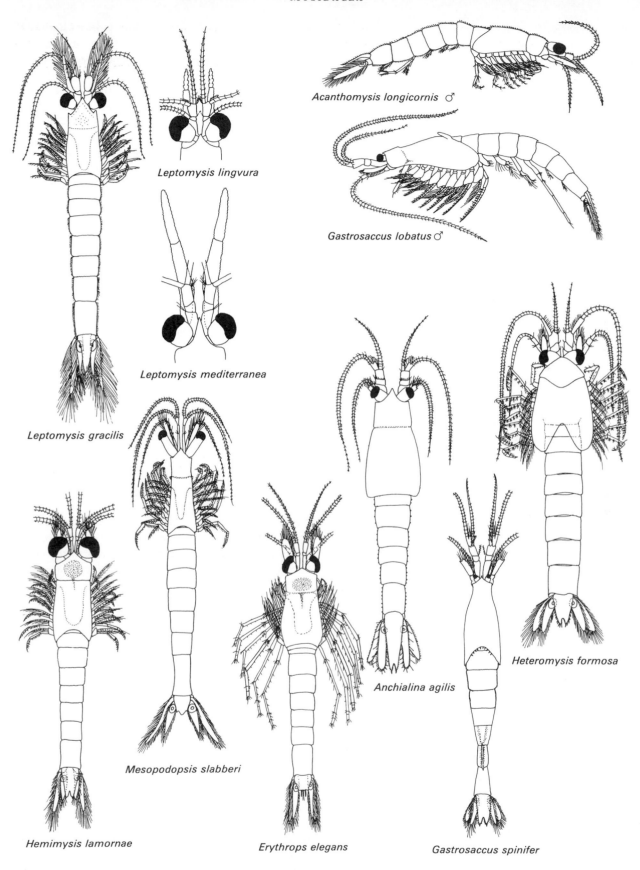

Leptomysis lingvura

Acanthomysis longicornis ♂

Gastrosaccus lobatus ♂

Leptomysis mediterranea

Leptomysis gracilis

Heteromysis formosa

Anchialina agilis

Hemimysis lamornae

Mesopodopsis slabberi

Erythrops elegans

Gastrosaccus spinifer

Fig. 9.8

Mesopodopsis slabberi (Van Beneden)   FIGS. 9.6, 9.8

Length 15 mm. General appearance very slender and delicate with exceptionally long eyestalks, carapace rather small. Antennal scale long and narrow with setae all round. Female pleopods very small; male pleopods small, fourth pair elongated, armed distally with two very long setae. Uropods very long compared with short, stout telson. Form of telson characteristic; the small lateral spinules may be absent. Transparent and colourless.

Swims freely in shallow brackish and estuarine waters, scarce offshore. All British coasts, common or abundant in most areas, recently confirmed in west Scotland (Makings 1981). Distributed from Scandinavia to West Africa, and in the Mediterranean.

Mysidopsis G. O. Sars

Only two species occur in shallow water, *M. angusta* and *M. gibbosa*. Antennal scale slender or of moderate width, setose all round. Rostrum short, almost lacking. Eyes large; a distinct, dorsal, fingerlike process extending from eyestalk partly over cornea. Female pleopods small, simple; male pleopods large, natatory. Exouropod very large compared with endouropod. Apex of telson rounded and truncate, or notched. A strong pair of black pigment spots at base of telson. General appearance somewhat short and thick compared with other genera. Rather small.

Mysidopsis angusta G. O. Sars   FIG. 9.9

Length 9 mm. Endouropod small compared with exouropod, but base very swollen, with large statocyst; a single strong spine on inner margin. Telson distinctive; small, dorsally concave, subtriangular, apex distinctly notched, the notch having smooth unarmed edges. About 15 lateral spines along each margin of telson. Colour slightly unusual, translucent above, purplish below.

Shallow water. Predominantly southern extending northwards to the Clyde, on the west, and the Moray Firth on the east. Not common. Distributed from southern Norway to the Mediterranean.

Mysidopsis gibbosa G. O. Sars   FIG. 9.9

Length 7 mm. Abdomen strongly curved, giving body a more marked sigmoid shape in lateral view than other mysids. Carapace rather short, of uneven form, with prominent anterior and posterior mid-dorsal humps. Telson short, deeply concave and scoop-shaped dorsally, smoothly rounded at tip with a prominent pair of apical spines and small lateral ones. Pigmentation variable, usually dark.

Near the bottom in shallow water. Mostly southern and western, extending to the Clyde, in the west, and the Firth of Forth in the east. Distributed from southern Norway to the Mediterranean.

Neomysis integer (Leach)   FIGS. 9.7, 9.9

Length 17 mm. Rostrum distinct, short, pointed. Antennal scale very long and narrow, tapering to a point, with setae all round. Female pleopods small, simple. Male pleopods small, fourth pair much elongated with a terminal pair of long, barbed setae. Endouropod with a short comb of spines near middle on inner ventral face. Telson long, tapering towards the almost pointed apex. Pale, translucent, some dark brownish pigment.

Occasionally in the open sea, but normally in brackish estuarine water, penetrating practically to the upper tidal limit. Recorded from hypersaline pools through all intermediate concentrations to the upper tidal limit. Reported as persisting for years in pools which have been cut off from the sea and become fresh, together with freshwater animals. All British coasts. Common, often abundant in appropriate conditions. Distributed from Arctic Norway to Spain.

Paramysis Czerniavsky

Rostrum very short or practically wanting. Antennal scale oval with rather large apical lobe and strong subterminal spine. Under high magnification this shows no trace of articulation at its base. Eyes rather large but with short stalks, and thus projecting only slightly. Combined carpo-propodus of thoracic endopod divided into four or five segments; basal one shorter than following sub-segment and very slightly swollen (may be difficult to see). Female pleopods very small, simple. Male pleopods not much larger, but fourth pair with elongated exopod bearing two very long claw-like distal setae.

P. helleri (G. O. Sars) was formerly recorded from Britain until *P. nouveli* and *P. bacescoi* were distinguished from it as new species. British records of *P. helleri* appear to be *P. nouveli*, true *helleri* occurring farther south and in the Mediterranean.

Paramysis arenosa (G. O. Sars)   FIGS. 9.7, 9.9

Length 10 mm. Eyestalks small and short. Inner margin of endouropod with up to 30 short and long spines, extending to apex. Telson with 17–23 spines on each side, apical cleft relatively deep and narrow. Body transparent with variable superimposed colours.

On sand, from the lower shore to 20 m or so. South and west coasts only, as far north as the Clyde. Fairly common. Distributed southwards to the Mediterranean.

Paramysis nouveli Labat

Length 11 mm. Very similar to *P. arenosa*. Eyestalks relatively slightly larger. Endouropod with only 13–18 spines on inner margin, stopping well short of apex. Telson with 13–18 lateral spines on each side, cleft more shallow and open. Coloration similar to *P. arenosa*.

Littoral and shallow water. Distribution similar to that of *P. arenosa*, but rare.

Praunus Leach

Rather large. Rostrum rounded, indistinct. Eyestalks long enough to carry eyes more or less entirely beyond carapace. Antennal scale tending to be elongated, naked outer margin extending almost whole length of scale. Subterminal spine has a basal constriction where it meets the scale, visible under high magnification. Proximal sub-segment of carpo-propodus of thoracic endopods normal. Female pleopods small, simple. Male

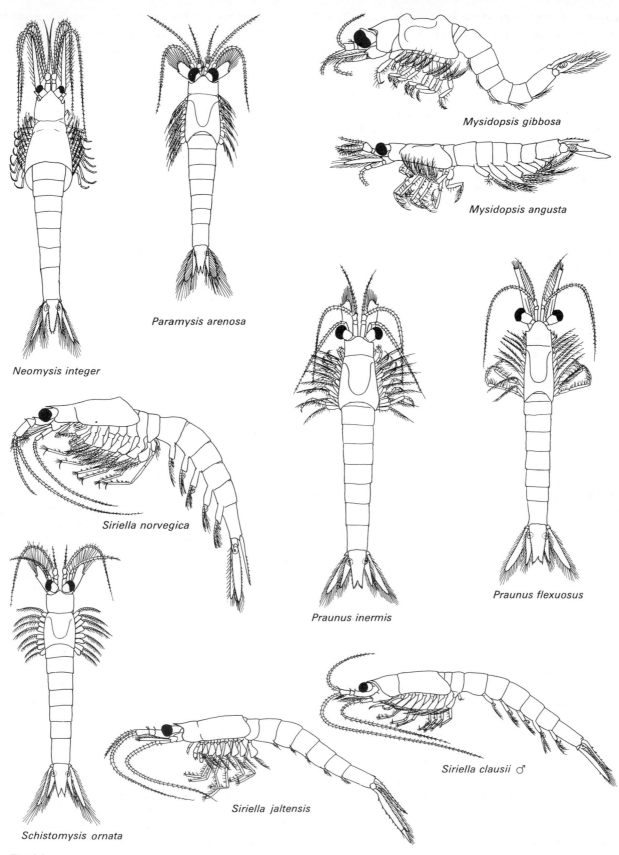

Neomysis integer

Paramysis arenosa

Mysidopsis gibbosa

Mysidopsis angusta

Siriella norvegica

Praunus inermis

Praunus flexuosus

Schistomysis ornata

Siriella jaltensis

Siriella clausii ♂

Fig. 9.9

pleopods small, fourth pair with very elongate exopod terminating in a thin prolongation which is knobbed at tip. Telson with 15–28 lateral spines on each side in adults, generally fewer in juveniles, increasing with growth. Form of the antennal scale is an unreliable character in young specimens, but chromatophores are useful as they do not increase with age. There is individual variation in the number of chromatophores on the tail fan of *P. flexuosus* and *P. neglectus* but the ventral thoracic ones seem to be constant in number and position.

Praunus flexuosus (Müller). The Chameleon Shrimp
FIGS. 9.6, 9.9

Length 24 mm. Antennal scale of adult distinct from all other British mysids except *P. neglectus*: very long and narrow, parallel-sided; anterior lobe so short as to be almost absent, shorter than subterminal spine. Eyes prominent. Inner margin of endouropod with 6–14 spines, not reaching apex. Telson with 22–28 lateral spines. Each thoracic segment with a distinct pair of ventral chromatophores, between the limbs; pigment usually more or less contracted to form eight pairs of prominent black spots in preserved material. The other two species have only two (*P. inermis*) or three (*P. neglectus*) ventral thoracic pairs of chromaphores although when expanded they spread along the other thoracic segments. One median dorsal and two median ventral chromatophores on each abdominal segment. Usually four chromatophores on telson, four or more on exouropods, three or four on endouropod. Transparent to almost black, variable; usually greyish sometimes yellowish.

Tends to swim slowly near the bottom, head upwards in a vertical position. Littoral pools and shallows, including brackish water. Widespread and common on all British coasts. Distributed northwards to Norway.

Praunus inermis (Rathke)
FIGS. 9.6H, 9.9

Length 15 mm. A smaller species than the other two but otherwise similar to them. Antennal scale much less elongated, anterior lobe extending beyond tip of subterminal spine. Eyestalks relatively shorter than in *P. flexuosus* and *P. neglectus*. Inner margin of endouropod with five or six spines, restricted to proximal region. Telson with 15–17 lateral spines. Best distinguished by its smaller complement of chromatophores: two ventral thoracic pairs, one dorsal and one ventral on each abdominal segment, two on telson, one on each blade of uropod. Pigmentation dark brownish.

Among weed in shallow water. Common all British coasts, but perhaps more abundant in the north. Distributed from Brittany to the White Sea.

Praunus neglectus (G. O. Sars)
FIG. 9.7

Length 21 mm. Very similar to *P. flexuosus*. Antennal scale less elongated, anterior lobe extending slightly beyond tip of subterminal spine. Telson with 18–24 lateral spines. Only three pairs of ventral thoracic chromatophores, though appearing more numerous when expanded. Chromatophores on the abdominal segments as in *P. flexousus*. Usually four chromatophores on telson, four on exouropod, two on endouropod.

Living specimens often bright green, making them instantly recognizable.

Mostly associated with weed in shallow water. Widespread on all British coasts.

Siriella Dana

Moderate to fairly large size (11–22 mm). Rostrum may be long or short, but strong and pointed. Eyes prominent, on well-developed eyestalks. Antennal scale with naked outer margin and strong subterminal spine. Pleopods of female reduced to small, simple, setose digits. Male pleopods fairly large, biramous. Divided exouropods characteristic of the genus. Telson with many short and long lateral spines, with a few small apical spines at the rounded tip providing useful specific characteristics. Usually pale and transparent.

Siriella armata (Milne Edwards)
FIGS. 9.6, 9.7

Length 22 mm, large but moderately slender. Easily identified by greatly produced rostrum, gently arching over bases of eyestalks, its slender pointed tip extending forwards beyond eyes (shorter in juveniles). Eyestalks noticeably long, eyes prominent. Exouropod long, proximal part parallel-sided; endouropod narrow and tapering, inner margin with a regular series of spines. Telson nearly always with four (rarely three or five) small, equal-sized, apical spines between the last, large lateral pair.

Swims near the bottom; littoral to 20 m. Common, present on all British coasts. Distributed southwards to the Mediterranean.

Siriella clausii G. O. Sars
FIGS. 9.7, 9.9

Length 11 mm. Smaller than *S. armata*, similar in general form but eyestalks and rostrum short. Telson with three small, equal-sized apical spines; rarely four as in *S. armata*. Exouropod rather broad. Inner margin of endouropod with alternating series of smaller and larger spines.

Swims near the bottom, distinctly littoral but extending to 30 m. Predominantly southern and western coasts, generally common. Distributed southwards to the Mediterranean.

Siriella jaltensis Czerniavsky
FIGS. 9.7, 9.9

Length 15 mm. Similar to *S. clausii* but with small unequal apical spines on telson forming a trident, and spines on inner margin of endouropod forming a uniform series.

The var. *brooki* Norman was at one time considered to be a distinct species but Tattersall and Tattersall (1951) consider both this and *S. gordonae* Zimmer to be forms of *S. jaltensis*.

Distribution similar to that of *S. clausii*, with which it is often found, but extends into much deeper water.

Siriella norvegica G. O. Sars
FIG. 9.9

Length 21 mm. Similar to, but often much larger than *S. clausii*. Three apical spines on the telson form a trident, as in *S. jaltensis*, but spines on inner margin of endouropod form two unequal series as in *S. clausii*.

Seldom littoral, offshore to 200 m. A northern species recorded mostly from the east coasts of Britain. Generally rare.

Schistomysis Norman

Fairly large species. Rostrum short or virtually wanting. Antennal scale oval to long and narrow, with naked outer margin, strong subterminal spine and well-developed anterior lobe. No trace of constriction at base of subterminal spine. Combined carpo-propodus of thoracic endopods divided into five to seven sub-segments, the proximal one normal, longer than the following sub-segment. Female pleopods very small, simple. Male pleopods small, fourth pair with elongated exopod bearing two very long distal setae. Telson with 24–30 lateral spines on each side.

Schistomysis spiritus (Norman). FIGS. 9.6, 9.7
The Ghost Shrimp

Length 18 mm, the most easily recognized member of the genus. Body long and slender. Eyes project noticeably beyond carapace, on cylindrical eyestalks. Antennal scale relatively long and narrow with long anterior lobe. Exouropod long and slender; endouropod incurving slightly at tip, inner margin with few spines apically, but densely spinose more proximally. Glassily transparent except for the eyes, though with chromatophores, and sometimes partly coloured red-brown.

Near the bottom in shallow water and estuaries. All British coasts, widespread and common, often occurring in very large shoals. Distributed northwards to Norway.

Schistomysis parkeri Norman FIG. 9.7

Length 10 mm. The only species of *Schistomysis* with a broad oval antennal scale with relatively short anterior lobe. General appearance less slender than *S. spiritus*. Eyestalks moderately short, eyes not extending much beyond carapace. Endouropod characteristic; distal portion distinctly incurved, with a single strong spine at apex; spines on inner margin irregular, absent from incurved portion.

Shallow water. South-west coasts including South Wales (Makings 1978), rare. Distributed south to West Africa.

Schistomysis ornata (G. O. Sars) FIG. 9.9

Length 19 mm. General appearance somewhat more robust than *S. spiritus*. Anterior lobe of antennal scale relatively longer. Eyestalks much shorter, eyes larger, but not extending much beyond carapace. Typically five sub-segments in carpo-propodus of thoracic endopods, followed by a very small dactylus and claw. In *S. kervillei* (below) there are normally six such sub-segments. Endouropod virtually straight, inner margin with rather sparse (about 16) spines extending to very near apex. Not so transparent as *S. spiritus*, with some variable pigmentation.

Near the bottom from deep water to close inshore, and in estuaries, but not extending into the intertidal. Common on all British coasts. Distributed from West Africa to Iceland.

Schistomysis kervillei (G. O. Sars) FIG. 9.7

Length 16 mm. Difficult to separate from *S. ornata*. The gap preceding the last lateral spine of the telson seems to be a good character, though not always as distinct as in Fig. 9.7. The position of the sub-terminal spine, indicating relative lengths of the naked outer margin and anterior lobe of the antennal scale, is usually distinctive, but not entirely reliable. The same is true of other characters, including the number of sub-segments in the carpo-propodus (typically six) though collectively they are likely to provide a determination.

In shallower water than *S, ornata*, and may occur at LWM. Few records, distributed from Kent to north-west Scotland.

Order **Isopoda**

The isopod body (Fig. 9.1) is usually dorso-ventrally flattened, and lacks a carapace. It comprises a head, or *cephalon*, a thorax, or *pereon*, of seven segments and an abdomen, or *pleon*, of six segments. The first, and rarely second, pereon segment is fused with the cephalon, and its appendages are modified as *maxillipeds*; the remaining pereon segments (except in the Arcturidae) bear more or less similar, uniramous *pereopods*, which function as walking legs. The coxae of the pereopods may be expanded as *coxal plates*, visible from above. Part or all of the pleon may be fused with the telson, forming a *pleotelson*. The pleon typically bears five pairs of biramous *pleopods*, which usually have a respiratory function, and a pair of uniramous or biramous *uropods*.

Sexes are separate, and marked sexual dimorphism occurs in a few species. In most families pleopod 2 in the male bears an *appendix masculina*; in others pleopods 1 and 2 are modified to form a combined copulatory structure in the male, while in the female pleopod 1 is missing and pleopod 2 is modified as a flattened *operculum* which covers the rest of the pleon appendages. Most isopods brood their embryos, either in a brood chamber formed of flattened plates (*oostegites*) developed on the bases of the first five pairs of pereopods, or in complex internal body pouches. The young are released as miniature adults, and in some species a succession of growth stages, or *instars*, is recognizable.

There are about 10 000 living species of Isopoda, classified in 9 suborders. They occur in terrestrial, freshwater, and marine habitats, and include some highly specialized parasitic forms. Intertidal species may be found at all shore levels, from among the barnacle belt, in crevices, beneath stones, on or under large macroalgae, within turfs of coralline algae and rhodophytes, among sessile animals such as sponges, hydroids, and bryozoans, and in sandy beaches. Very similar species may occupy distinctly separate microhabitats, and it is useful to know precisely where each sample was collected when commencing identification. Specimens may be fixed in 4% sea-water formalin and stored in 70% alcohol.

LITERATURE

Holdich, D. M. (1968). A systematic revision of the genus *Dynamene* (Crustacea: Isopoda) with descriptions of three new species. *Publicazioni della Stazione Zoologica de Napoli*, **36**, 401–26.

Holdich, D. M. (1970). The distribution and habitat preferences of the Afro-European species of *Dynamene* (Crustacea: Isopoda). *Journal of Natural History*, **4**, 419–38.

Holdich, D. M., Lincoln, R. J., and Ellis, J. P. (1984). The biology of terrestrial isopods. *Symposia of the Zoological Society of London*, **53**, 1–6.

Holthuis, L. H. (1956). Isopoda en Tanaidacea. *Fauna Van Nederland*, **16**, 1–280.

Jacobs, B. J. M. (1987). A taxonomic revision of the European, Mediterranean and N.W. African species generally placed in *Sphaeroma* Bosc, 1802 (Isopoda: Flabellifera: Sphaeromatidae). *Zoologische Verhandelingen*, **238**, 3–71.

Jones, D. A. (1970). Population densities and breeding of *Eurydice pulchra* Leach and *Eurydice affinis* Hansen in Britain. *Journal of the Marine Biological Association of the U. K.*, **50**, 635–55.

Jones, L. T. (1963). The geographical and vertical distribution of British *Limnoria* (Crustacea: Isopoda). *Journal of the Marine Biological Association of the U. K.*, **43**, 589–603.

Jones, M. B. and Naylor, E. (1971). Breeding and bionomics of the British members of the *Jaera albifrons* group of species. (Isopoda: Asellota). *Journal of Zoology*, **165**, 183–99.

Naylor, E. (1972). British Marine Isopods. *Linnean Society Synopses of the British Fauna*, (n.s.), **3**. Academic Press, London.

Sars, G. O. (1899). *An account of the Crustacea of Norway*, **2**. Isopoda.

KEY TO FAMILIES

1. Free-living, or parasitic on fish, not parasitic on Crustacea   **2**

     Entirely parasitic on Crustacea (Suborder Epicaridea)   **15**

2. Adults with five pairs of pereopods (Suborder Gnathiidea)   **1. Gnathiidae**

     Adults with seven pairs of pereopods   **3**

3. Uropods lateral or ventral   **4**

     Uropods terminal   **9**

4. Uropods ventral, hinged ventro-laterally to pleotelson to form opercular plates covering pleopods (Suborder Valvifera)   **5**

     Uropods lateral, flattened, and with pleotelson forming a tail fan (Suborder Flabellifera)   **6**

5. Pereopods all more or less alike   **6. Idoteidae**

     Pereopods 1–4 not ambulatory, resembling mouthparts and quite unlike 5–7   **7. Arcturidae**

6. Body markedly attenuated; uropod bases extending dorsally above telson with caudal fan somewhat cup-shaped   **2. Anthuridae**

     Body robust; uropod bases not extending above telson   **7**

7. Pleon with five distinct segments plus one fused with telson   **8**

     Pleon with less than five distinct segments, more than one fused with telson   **5. Sphaeromatidae**

8. Uropod rami tubular, outer ramus claw-like   **3. Limnoriidae**

     Uropod rami flattened, fan-like   **4. Cirolanidae**

9. Terrestrial, pleon usually with six distinct segments (Suborder Oniscoidea)   **10**

     Aquatic, pleon consisting of less than six segments (Suborder Asellota)   **12**

10. Antennal flagellum of ten or more articles **12. Ligiidae**

    Antennal flagellum of two or three articles **11**

11. Antennal flagellum of two articles **13. Armadillidiidae**

    Antennal flagellum of three articles **14. Halophilosciidae**

12. Uropods lacking peduncle; pereon with last three segments usually much smaller than first four; eyes when present on lateral extensions of head **13**

    Uropods with peduncle; pereon segments all subequal, no exaggerated posterior narrowing; eyes not on lateral extensions of head **14**

13. Molar process of mandible normal, strong, and truncated. Eyes present, on lateral extensions of head **9. Munnidae**

    Molar process of mandible weak and pointed (British genus, *Pleurogonium*, lacks eyes and head has no lateral extensions) **10. Pleurogonidae**

14. Antennal flagellum longer than peduncle **8. Janiridae**

    Antennal flagellum shorter than peduncle **11. Jaeropsidae**

15. Parasitic in decapod crustaceans (crabs, prawns, etc.) **16**

    Parasitic in other crustaceans (notably barnacles, isopods, ostracods, mysids, euphausiids) **17**

16. In gill chamber or attached to pleon of decapods. Female body with distinct segments, more or less asymmetrical and with seven pairs of pereopods. Oostegites present **15. Bopyridae**

    In visceral cavity of decapods. Female body without distinct segments, symmetrical and lobed; pereopods rudimentary or absent. Oostegites present **16. Entoniscidae**

17. On body or in brood chamber of mysids and euphausiids. Pereopods well-developed, numbering five pairs, crowded near mouth. Oostegites present **17. Dajidae**

    Notably from barnacles, isopods, and ostracods. Without pereopods and, uniquely in the suborder, without oostegites **18. Cryptoniscidae**

---

1 GNATHIIDAE

Male, female, and young (*praniza*) all of different form; each with only five pairs of ambulatory pereopods. Cephalon fused with two pereon segments, limbs of second fused segment modified as flattened *pylopods* (gnathopods). Last pereon segment reduced and without limbs. Male with large forcep-like mandibles which project in front of the cephalon. Females and late pranizas with pereon segments 3–5 fused and inflated, particularly in females which incubate the eggs internally. Adults benthic, pranizas often ectoparasitic on fish.

1. Male pylopod of five articles; adults usually in estuarine mudbanks ***Paragnathia formica***

    Male pylopod of two or three articles; adults usually in marine crevice-like situations **2**

2. Male with ridge over each eye ***Gnathia oxyuraea***

    Male without ridge over the eyes **3**

3. Lateral mandibular spine diverging from mandible ***Gnathia dentata***

    Lateral spine not diverging from mandible **4**

4. Front of cephalon with a shallow central concavity
    and a slight median forward projection   **Gnathia maxillaris**

    Front of cephalon with a deep central concavity and
    a small, acute median forward projection   **Gnathia vorax**

Gnathia dentata Sars   FIG. 9.10

Male with front of cephalon centrally tridentate and without a
concavity; lateral corners acutely pronounced. Cephalon broader
than long. Lateral tooth of mandible diverging markedly from
the mandible itself. Male body length 2.8–3.8 mm, females up
to 4.3 mm. In *Laminaria* holdfasts, LWST and below, south
and west coasts.

Gnathia maxillaris (Montagu)   FIG. 9.10

Not to be confused with *G. oxyuraea* which Sars (1899)
erroneously illustrated as *G. maxillaris*. Male with front of
cephalon having a shallow central concavity with only a slight
rounded median forward projection; lateral corners square,
cephalon wider than long. Lateral tooth of mandible closely
applied to mandible itself. Male body length usually 4.5–5.0 mm
or less.

  Adults in rock-crevices, dead barnacles, and *Laminaria* holdfasts; commonest intertidal gnathiid on south coasts.

Gnathia oxyuraea (Lilljeborg)   FIG. 9.10

Male with front of cephalon having a median tooth bordered by a
shallow concavity on each side; lateral corners square. Cephalon
broader than long and with a pronounced ridge over each eye.
Lateral tooth of mandible somewhat indistinct. Male body
length 2.4–5.4 mm; females 3.9 mm.

  Mainly sublittoral; common; all British coasts. Distributed
from the Barents Sea southwards to the Mediterranean.

Gnathia vorax (Lucas)   FIG. 9.10

Male with front of cephalon having a deep central concavity
with a fairly acute median forward projection; lateral tooth of
mandible closely applied to mandible itself. Larger than *G.
maxillaris*; 5–7 mm body length.

  Mainly sublittoral; sporadic, all British coasts. Distributed
from Greenland southwards to the Mediterranean.

Paragnathia formica (Hesse)   FIG. 9.10

Adult male pylopod of five articles; male, female, and praniza
body length ranging from 2.5–5 mm.

  Males, females, and late pranizas in sheltered estuaries or
inlets, usually around MHWN in mud cliffs at the edges of salt-
marsh. Early pranizas parasitic on inshore or estuarine flat-fish.
All British coasts. Widely distributed between Morocco and
Scotland.

2 ANTHURIDAE

Body long and narrow, subcylindrical. Pereonal somites longer
than wide. Pleon relatively short with uropodal exopods arching
dorsally and medially over the telson.

---

1. Telson subquadrate, widest posteriorly; marine
                                          Anthura gracilis

    Telson narrowing to a rounded apex; brackish
                                       Cyathura carinata

Anthura gracilis (Montagu)   FIG. 9.10

Eyes large. Female antennule 1 small, in male with elongate
flagellum densely clothed with filamentous setae. Telson
subquadrate, widest posteriorly. Females up to 11 mm body
length, males 4 mm.

  In crevices, among kelp holdfasts, and in empty tubes of
serpulid worms; LWST and shallow water; south and west
coasts only. Distributed from the Clyde Sea southwards to the
Mediterranean.

Cyathura carinata (Kröyer)   FIG. 9.10

Eyes small; antennule 1 small in both sexes; telson narrowing
to a rounded apex. Body length up to about 14 mm; whitish
with red-brown mottling.

  In brackish water habitats, usually in mud; southern coasts
only. Distributed southwards to the Mediterranean.

3 LIMNORIIDAE

British forms wood-boring. Uropod exopod much shorter than
endopod and with an apical claw; endopod elongate, apex blunt,
lacking claw.

---

1. Dorsal surface of posterior border of pleotelson
    tuberculate; central area of pleotelson with three
    tubercles   **Limnoria tripunctata**

    Dorsal surface of posterior border of pleotelson
    smooth, not tuberculate; central area of pleotelson
    with four tubercles or with an inverted Y-shaped
    carina   **2**

2. Central dorsal surface of pleotelson with an inverted
    Y-shaped carina   **Limnoria lignorum**

    Central dorsal surface of pleotelson with four
    tubercles   **Limnoria quadripunctata**

Limnoria lignorum (Rathke)   FIG. 9.10

Antennal flagellum of four articles; pleon somite 5 with a mid-
dorsal, longitudinal carina; pleotelson with an anteriorly situated
mid-dorsal longitudinal carina, which bifurcates posteriorly and
lacks tubercles; lateral crests of pleotelson slightly tuberculate,
dorsal surface of posterior margin not so. Body length up to
3.5 mm.

  When in company with the other species of *Limnoria*, *L.
lignorum* occurs at the base of exposed pilings or sublittorally
where the wood is kept wet and cool; all coasts. Ranges from
Norway to south of British Isles, and on the east and west coasts
of North America to 40° S.

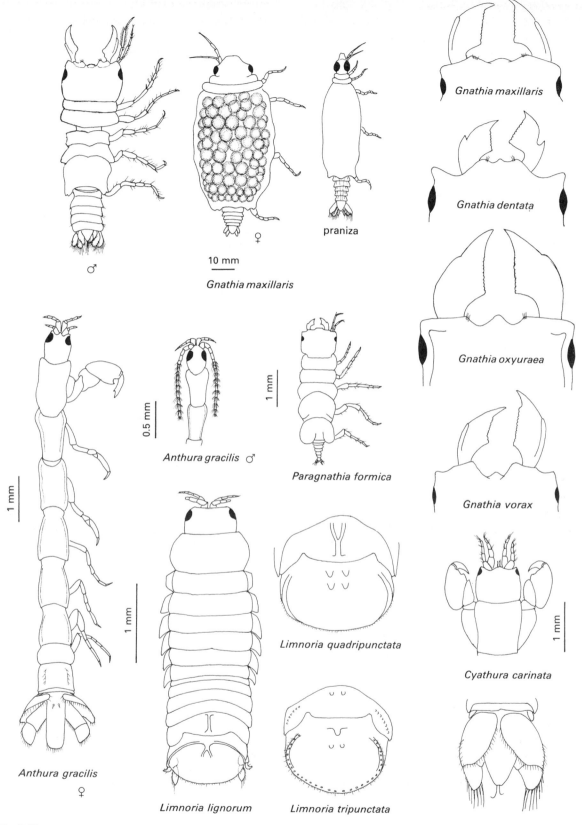

Gnathia maxillaris

Gnathia dentata

Gnathia oxyuraea

Gnathia vorax

10 mm

♂   ♀   praniza

Gnathia maxillaris

Anthura gracilis ♂

Paragnathia formica

Anthura gracilis ♀

Limnoria lignorum

Limnoria quadripunctata

Limnoria tripunctata

Cyathura carinata

Fig. 9.10

Limnoria quadripunctata Holthuis   FIG. 9.10

Antennal flagellum of five articles; pleon somite 5 with a Y-shaped carina on mid-dorsal surface; pleotelson with two pairs of tubercles; lateral crests of pleotelson and the posterio-dorsal margin lack tubercles. Body length up to 3.5 mm.

Tolerates more exposure to air and occurs higher on pilings than *L. lignorum*; south and west coasts only, from Kent to the Isle of Man, locally common on western coasts. Recorded also from New Zealand, South Africa, and California.

Limnoria tripunctata Menzies   FIG. 9.10

Antennal flagellum of five articles; pleon somite 5 with two anterior elevated nodes and sometimes a median posterior node; pleotelson with a triangle of three tubercles; lateral crests and posterio-dorsal margin of pleotelson tuberculate. Body length up to 4 mm.

Particularly in timbers near source of power station cooling water; locally common on south and west coasts. Widely distributed in temperate and tropical waters around the world.

4 CIROLANIDAE

Body with distinct coxal plates on pereon segments 2–7. Pleon with five distinct segments, plus one (the uropodal segment) fused with the telson. Uropods lateral, not arching dorsally, and with the pleotelson forming a terminal fan. Subfamily Cirolaninae well represented intertidally and inshore; for subfamilies ectoparasitic on offshore fish (Aeginae, Cymothoinae) see Naylor (1972).

---

1. Antennal peduncle of five distinct articles; uropodal peduncle produced backwards medial to endopod   **2**

    Antennal peduncle of four distinct articles; uropodal peduncle not produced backwards medial to endopod   **3**

2. Pleopod 1 with endopod normal, not heavily chitinized; peduncle broader than long; body not markedly elongate   ***Cirolana cranchii***

    Pleopod 1 with both rami heavily chitinized and forming an operculum; peduncle longer than broad; body markedly elongate   ***Conilera cylindracea***

3. Pleotelson posterior border narrow and concave, with two large spines at each corner   ***Eurydice spinigera***

    Pleotelson posterior border broad and slightly convex, with a pair of small spines towards each corner among plumose setae   **4**

4. Pereon segment 6 with posterior angle of coxal plate produced sharply backwards; black chromatophores on dorsal, lateral, and ventral surfaces   ***Eurydice pulchra***

    Pereon segment 6 with posterior angle of coxal plate acute but not produced sharply backwards; black chromatophores on dorsal surface only   ***Eurydice affinis***

Cirolana cranchii Leach   FIG. 9.11

Few plumose swimming setae on last three pereopods. Frontal lamina, between bases of antennae and antennules, small, pentagonal, less than twice as long as broad, and not visible from above.

Predominantly offshore but also on sand at LWST; south and west coasts only. Distributed from the Clyde Sea southwards to the Mediterranean.

Conilera cylindracea (Montagu)   FIG. 9.11

Characteristic, very long, cylindrical shape. Predominantly sublittoral in shell-gravel; locally common with *Cirolana cranchii* on fish bait in lobster pots.

Eurydice affinis Hansen   FIG. 9.11

Coxal plates of pereon segments 6 and 7 with posterior angles sharp but not produced into processes; pleotelson resembling *E. pulchra*, but body somewhat smaller and paler, with black chromatophores restricted to dorsal surface.

Occurs intertidally among *E. pulchra* in Bristol Channel and North Wales; locally common. Reported from Holland and the Atlantic coast of France, and widely from the Mediterranean.

Eurydice pulchra Leach   FIG. 9.11

Coxal plates of pereon segment 6 with posterior angle produced into fairly long processes, that of segment 7 smaller; pleotelson with posterior border fairly broadly rounded, with fairly long plumose setae and two small spines towards each corner. Males up to 8 mm; females up to 6.5 mm. Colour darker than *E. affinis* with numerous black chromatophores extending around the pleon.

Up to HWN in intertidal sand, swimming freely with the rising tide; all British coasts; common. Distributed from Norway to Morocco; absent from the Mediterranean.

Eurydice spinigera Hansen   FIG. 9.11

Pereon segments 2–6 with coxal plates produced into fairly long processes, those of segments 6 very long; pleotelson sharply narrowing posteriorly, posterior border emarginate with two conspicuous spines at each lateral corner. Body length up to 9 mm.

Predominantly sublittoral, but also at LWST in intertidal sand and among surf plankton; south and west coasts only. Distributed from the southern North Sea to the Mediterranean.

5 SPHAEROMATIDAE

Body oval in outline, readily rolling into a ball. Five anterior pleon segments all fused, usually with three sutures, the last two of which, or all three, are incomplete; pleon segment 6 fused with telson as a pleotelson which articulates freely with pleon. Coxal plates of pereon segments 2–7 fused with segment but suture lines may be evident. Uropods lateral; endopod rigidly fused with peduncle; exopod moveable. Sexual dimorphism apparent in some species, males of some of these bearing one or two backwardly directed projections on the posterior border of pereon segment 6.

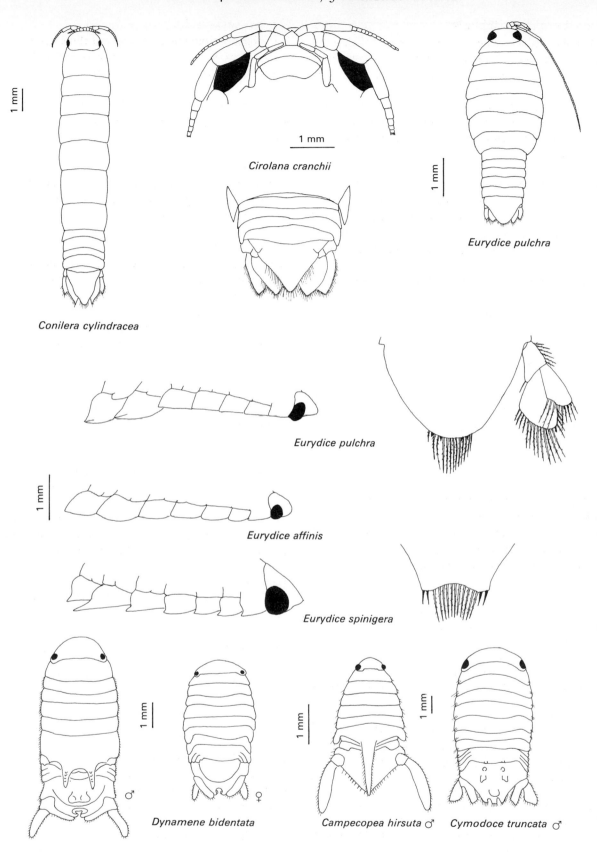

Cirolana cranchii

Eurydice pulchra

Conilera cylindracea

Eurydice pulchra

Eurydice affinis

Eurydice spinigera

Dynamene bidentata   Campecopea hirsuta ♂   Cymodoce truncata ♂

Fig. 9.11

1. Uropods with one ramus   2
    Uropods with two rami   3

2. Pereon segment 6 without projections
                            female *Campecopea hirsuta*
    Pereon segment 6 with posterior border bearing a
    single large backwardly directed median projection
                            male *Campecopea hirsuta*

3. Pereon segment 6 without projections   4
    Pereon segment 6 with posterior border bearing two
    backwardly directed projections [male *Dynamene*]   5

4. Pleotelson with posterior border notched, appearing
    tridentate or with a semicircular foramen in the mid-
    line   6
    Pleotelson with posterior border not notched,
    smoothly rounded or slightly acute   9

5. Pleotelson with two prominent hemispherical bosses
    which join at bases   male *Dynamene bidentata*
    Pleotelson with two bosses joined by a short stem;
    each boss with a prominent, apical, subsidiary pro-
    jection   male *Dynamene magnitorata*

6. Pleotelson posterior border with a semicircular
    foramen in mid-line at the posterior end of a channel
    in the mid-ventral line [female *Dynamene*]   7
    Pleotelson posterior border slightly or markedly tri-
    dentate   8

7. Pleotelson smoothly rounded in side-view
                            female *Dynamene bidentata*
    Pleotelson with a dorsal projection in side-view
                            female *Dynamene magnitorata*

8. Pleotelson posterior border with a marked tridentate
    process at the posterior end of a channel in the mid-
    ventral line   male *Cymodoce truncata*
    Pleotelson posterior border slightly tridentate
    (looked at from above median tooth partly obscures
    lateral teeth) at the posterior end of a channel in the
    mid-ventral line   female *Cymodoce truncata*

9. Exopod of adult uropod serrated   10
    Exopod of adult uropod at most slightly crenulate   11

10. Pereopods 1–3 and maxilliped palp with plumose
    setae. Maxilliped palp without lobes on articles 2–4
                                        Sphaeroma serratum
    Pereopods 1–3 and maxilliped palp with sparsely
    plumose setae. Maxilliped palp with prominent lobes
    on articles 2–4   *Lekanesphaera levii*

11. Pleotelson dorsal surface with two rows of elongate
    tubercles. Pereopod 1 propodus lacking distal setae
                                        Lekanesphaera hookeri

Pleotelson dorsal surface with small tubercles. Pereopod 1 propodus with two distal setae
                                        Lekanesphaera rugicauda

Campecopea hirsuta (Montagu)   FIG. 9.11

Sexually dimorphic. Rolls into a tight ball. Pleotelson rounded, without prominent tubercles, posterior border not notched, and without a posterior mid-ventral respiratory channel. Pereon segment 6 of male (but not female) with a long median, backwardly directed process. Pleopods 1–5 lamellar, not fleshy, and transversely corrugate; uropod of both sexes with a large exopod and lacking an endopod. Length up to 3.5 mm in female and 4.0 mm in male.

Exposed shores; MTL–HWN, among barnacles and *Lichina*, or in rock-crevices. South and west coasts only; locally common. Distributed southwards to West Africa.

Cymodoce truncata Leach   FIG. 9.11

Sexually dimorphic pleotelson: domed and smooth in females, with two 'bosses' and weakly tridentate posterior border; male with two prominent tubercles on pleon posterior border and five on dorsal surface of pleotelson, which has posterior border markedly tridentate. Pleopods 4 and 5 with exopod lamellar, endopod thick, fleshy and with transverse corrugations. Adult male body length 11 mm or more; female smaller.

Sometimes among algae, but adults characteristically in crevices and old mollusc borings; LWS. Sporadically distributed on south and west coasts from Isle of Wight, as far north as Shetland.

Dynamene bidentata (Adams)   FIG. 9.11

Markedly sexually dimorphic. Male with segment 6 overlapping 7 and produced into a prominent, backwardly directed, moderately rugose, bifid process. Pleotelson smooth in female, rugose in males, with a dorsal bilobed boss; respiratory channel sometimes closing ventrally. Pleopods 1–3 laminate, with apical setae, pleopod 2 of male without appendix masculina; pleopods 4 and 5 with exopod and endopod thick, fleshy, and with transverse folds. Length up to around 7 mm in male, 6 mm in female.

MTL–LWS. Juveniles among intertidal algae upon which they feed, and which they resemble in colour; adults in rock-crevices or the empty tests of *Balanus perforatus*, each male usually with several females which may be white or colourless when ovigerous. South and west coasts only; locally common.

Dynamene magnitorata Holdich

Similar to *D. bidentata* but male with characteristic pleotelsonic bosses joined by a short stalk and each with a subsidiary apical projection. Female with a mid-dorsal projection at posterior margin of pleotelson. Length up to 6 mm in male, 4.8 mm in female.

Juveniles amongst lower shore and upper sublittoral algae, particularly *Chondrus crispus* and corallines, the colour of which the isopod often matches. Adults in crevices, in tests of *Balanus crenatus*, amongst clumps of ascidians, and particularly within channels of encrusting sponges such as *Halichondria*; also in sponges associated with *Zostera* meadows. Mediterranean and Atlantic coasts of Africa, Spain, and France as far north as Guernsey where it is common on rocky coasts.

Lekanesphaera hookeri (Leach)   FIG. 9.12

Maxilliped palp with prominent lobes, fringed with smooth setae, on articles 2–4. Pereopod 1 with up to about 20 smooth setae on ischium and on merus; setae absent from distal region of propodus. Uropods with outer border of exopod almost smooth; pleotelson with two longitudinal rows of elongate tubercles, one on each side of mid-line, posterior border not extending beyond uropods. Male up to 10.5 mm and female 8.5 mm.

In brackish ditches in sheltered estuaries near limit of EHWS; most coasts except north-east; patchily distributed from the Mediterranean to northern Scotland.

Lekanesphaera levii (Argano and Ponticelli)

Maxilliped palp with prominent lobes, fringed with smooth setae, on articles 2–4. Pereopod 1 with up to 50 smooth setae on ischium, about 60 on merus, and three to eight in a distal row on the propodus. Uropods usually with six to seven slight serrations on outer margin of exopod; pleotelson with smooth dorsal surface, posterior border extending beyond uropod in large males. Formerly *Sphaeroma monodi* (see Jacobs 1987). Male up to 12.0 mm, female 8.0 mm.

Rock crevices and under stones, in brackish localities, between MTL and LWN. Southern coasts only, patchily distributed.

Lekanesphaera rugicauda (Leach)   FIG. 9.12

Maxilliped palp with prominent lobes, fringed with smooth setae, on articles 2–4. Pereopod 1 ischium with up to 30 smooth setae, merus with up to about 20, and propodus distal row with two (occasionally one). Uropod with outer edge of exopod almost smooth; pleotelson dorsal surface covered with very small tubercles, extending beyond uropods in adult males. Male up to 10.0 mm and female 7.5 mm.

In sheltered estuarine situations up to EHWS, usually in salt-marsh pools. All British coasts, very common.

Sphaeroma serratum (Fabricius)   FIG. 9.12

Maxilliped palp without lobes but with plumose setae on articles 2–4. Pereopod 1 ischium with up to about 60 plumose setae in two rows, propodus with a distal row of 15–20. Uropods with four to seven well-defined serrations on outer edge of exopod; pleotelson with smooth dorsal surface and not extending beyond uropods. Female ranging up to 10 mm and male to 11.5 mm.

In rock crevices or under stones around MTL, usually on open marine coasts, sometimes near freshwater seepages. Sometimes in crevices and under stones around HWS in sheltered locations. South and west coasts only, locally common. Distributed south to the Mediterranean and the Azores.

6 IDOTEIDAE

Body oval, oblong, or elongate; pereon segments and pereopods all more or less alike; pleon somites variously coalesced depending upon genus; uropods usually uniramous.

1. Pleon with no distinct segments; partial sutures (not visible from above) indicate almost complete fusion of pleon with telson — **2**

   Pleon of two or three distinct segments; remainder fused or partially fused with telson — **3**

2. Pereon lateral borders appearing serrated; pleotelson expanded laterally in the middle — **Synisoma lancifer**

   Pereon lateral borders straight and parallel; pleotelson narrowing evenly to an acute point — **Synisoma acuminatum**

3. Pleotelson with three complete segments and one partial suture. Isopod usually occupying a 'case' — **Zenobiana prismatica**

   Pleotelson with two complete segments and one partial suture. Free-living — **4**

4. Pleotelson apical border straight or concave — **5**

   Pleotelson apical border produced and more or less angulate in centre — **7**

5. Body markedly elongate; coxal plates very small, not reaching posterior border on any pereon segment — **Idotea linearis**

   Body not markedly elongate, coxal plates 3–7 reaching posterior border of pereon segment — **6**

6. Pleotelson with apical border concave, sides somewhat rounded. Cephalon lacking complete suture behind eyes — **Idotea emarginata**

   Pleotelson apical border and sides straight. Cephalon with distinct sinuous suture behind pronounced eyes — **Idotea metallica**

7. Pleotelson apical border tridentate or nearly so — **Idotea baltica**

   Pleotelson apical border not tridentate, almost invariably rounded laterally — **8**

8. Pleotelson sides slightly concave, apical margin with a pronounced, acute median process — **Idotea granulosa**

   Pleotelson sides straight or slightly convex, apical margin with at most an indistinct, blunt median process — **9**

9. Antenna with flagellum much shorter than peduncle; flagellum densely covered with fine setae in males — **Idotea pelagica**

   Antenna with flagellum longer than peduncle; flagellum not densely covered with fine setae in males — **10**

10. Body slender; length four or five times width in all but ovigerous females, which are wider. In brackish water — **Idotea chelipes**

    Body more robust; length little more than three times width. Sublittoral but often stranded among drift weed on the shore — **Idotea neglecta**

Idotea baltica (Pallas) FIG. 9.12

Adult pleotelson dorsally keeled, with more or less straight sides, tapering to a tridentate posterior border, with median process long and acute; less obvious in juveniles which have lateral corners obtusely angled. Male 10–30 mm body length; female 10–18 mm. Colour sometimes uniformly green or brown but often with white spots or longitudinal lines; female often darker than male.

Generally offshore, but occasionally among attached algae on the shore and often cast up in large numbers among drift weed. All British coasts. Widely distributed in north-east Atlantic region.

Idotea chelipes (Pallas) FIG. 9.12

Body slender. Unlike most species there is a single large aesthet-asc, not a pair, at the distal end of the aesthetasc series on antennule. Adult pleotelson with sides subparallel, slightly keeled posteriorly in mid-dorsal line, posterior border with a single, median tooth, hardly acute, and with obtusely rounded lateral corners. Male 5–15 mm body length; female 6–10 mm. Colour mostly uniformly green or brown, sometimes with white markings; females often darker.

A brackish water species; occurs among intertidal algae in sheltered estuaries or on green algae in sheltered brackish pools at or above high water mark. All British coasts; not common. Ranges from Norway southwards to the Mediterranean.

Idotea emarginata (Fabricius) FIG. 9.12

Pleotelson with sides slightly convex; adult posterior border emarginate, juveniles less so. Male 7–30 mm; female 9–18. Males often uniformly brown in colour, though sometimes with white markings; females generally darker in background colour, often with longitudinal lateral white bands, or alternating white and darker transverse bands.

Most common sublittorally on accumulations of detached algae; occasionally between tidemarks on attached algae or drift weed. All British coasts; locally abundant. Distributed along western European coasts from Norway to Spain.

Idotea granulosa Rathke FIG. 9.12

Adult pleotelson narrowing sharply at first, with concave lateral sides; posterior border with long, acute, median tooth and very obtusely rounded lateral shoulders; not keeled. Male 5–20 mm; female 6–13 mm. Mostly uniformly brown, red, or green, depending on the algae inhabited; occasionally with longitudinal white markings.

The common resident idoteid between tidemarks on all open but not excessively exposed coasts; large specimens on *Ascophyllum* and *Fucus*, and small specimens preferring smaller algae such as *Cladophora* and *Polysiphonia*. On all British coasts. Distributed from Arctic Norway to northern coast of France.

Idotea linearis (Linnaeus) FIG. 9.12

Body and appendages markedly slender; like *I. chelipes*, with a single aesthetasc, not a pair, at distal end of aesthetasc series

on the antennule. Adult pleotelson with sides slightly concave anteriorly, posterior border concave, and with a small median tooth in young specimens. Males 15–40 mm, females smaller. Colour green or brown, with darker or lighter longitudinal stripes; adult female often darker than male, frequently with paler markings around edges.

A sublittoral species occasionally cast up on the shore and often found swimming near the water's edge on sandy shores at low tide. South and west coasts of Britain. Distributed south to the Mediterranean, Morocco and the Canary Isles.

Idotea metallica Bosc FIG. 9.12

Cephalon with marked transverse sinuous furrow behind very prominent eyes. Coxal plates triangular. Pleotelson with sides and posterior border straight. Male 8–30 mm, female 9–18 mm. Colour uniformly greyish or brown.

Typically in Gulf Stream debris which may be stranded on open, west-facing coasts; rare.

Idotea neglecta Sars FIG. 9.12

Adult pleotelson with fairly straight sides converging posteriorly; posterior border with a median obtuse tooth, and obtusely rounded lateral shoulders; keeled. Male 8–30 mm, female 10–16 mm. Colour often uniformly brownish, sometimes with white longitudinal lateral markings, and occasionally with white marbling over the whole dorsal surface; adult females mostly darker than males.

Generally sublittoral on accumulations of detached algae or fish waste, but also between tidemarks on attached algae or among cast-up drift weed. All British coasts, locally common. Occurs on west European coasts from Norway to France.

Idotea pelagica Leach FIG. 9.12

Body short and stout. Pereopods all very robust, terminal claw relatively larger than in any other species. Adult males with antennae and pereopods 2–7 fringed with fine setae. Pleotelson broadly rounded, apical border with short, median, obtuse tooth; not keeled. Males 4–11 mm, females 7–10 mm. Colour merges well with typical background of barnacles, mostly dark purple-brown, with white diamond-shaped patches or elongated stripes down the mid-dorsal line, and with white markings along dorsal edges; females often darker.

Patchily distributed on exposed shores among mussels, barnacles, and stunted fucoid algae; HWNT–LWST. All British coasts. Distributed on west European coasts from Norway to France.

Synisoma acuminatum Leach FIG. 9.13

Body long, narrow, and subcylindrical. Coxal plates of pereon very small, barely visible from above. Pleotelson sides narrowing fairly evenly from the pereon articulation to an acute terminal projection. Up to 25 mm in length and rather less than 5 mm in breadth.

Typically among the alga *Halidrys siliquosa* in pools on rocky shores around MTL. South and west coasts only, locally frequent. Distributed south to the Mediterranean.

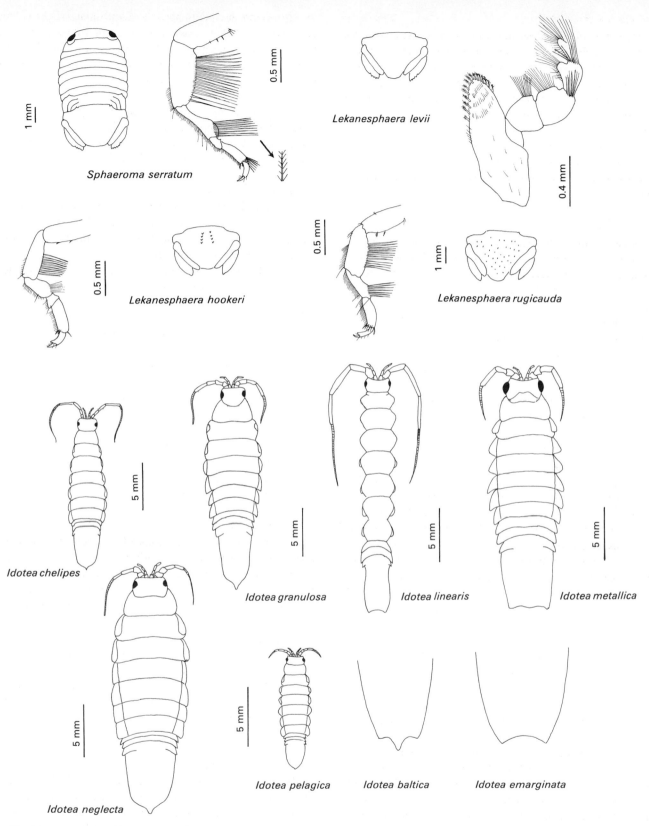

Fig. 9.12

Synisoma lancifer (Dollfus)   FIG.9.13

Pereon with coxal plates triangular, lateral borders appearing more or less symmetrically serrated; pleotelson sides markedly concave anteriorly and narrowing sharply to an elongate median projection. Male up to 22.5 mm body length, female smaller.

Among algae and under stones, particularly around LWST. South-western coasts only, rare. Ranging southwards to the Mediterranean.

Zenobiana prismatica (Risso)   FIG.9.13

Body slender, parallel-sided. Pleotelson of three distinct segments with evidence of a fourth in partial suture of the pleotelson; lateral borders of pleon fringed with setae. Up to 13.5 mm in length.

Typically in a case, in hollowed-out plant material such as *Zostera* stems, or in old worm tubes such as those of *Pomatoceros*; south and west coasts only, rare. Distributed from the Clyde Sea southwards to the Mediterranean.

7 ARCTURIDAE

Body subcylindrical and elongate, middle pereon segment enlarged. Pereopods 1–4 elongate, with long plumose setae, and directed towards the mouth; pereopods 5–7 short, stout, and adapted for clinging.

---

1. Middle pereon somite long and cylindrical
              Astacilla longicornis

   Middle pereon somite long, not cylindrical but with angled corners   ***Arcturella damnoniensis***

Arcturella damnoniensis (Stebbing)   FIG.9.13

Head with three conical tubercles; each pereon segment with at least one median tubercle; middle segment broad with angled corners, subequal in length to cephalon and anterior pereon segments. Pereopods 1–4 sparsely setose. Pleotelson with lateral borders deeply serrated. Female more strongly tuberculate than male and with larger triangular lobes on each side of segment 4. Up to about 10 mm body length.

Sublittoral, occasionally intertidal; south-west coasts only.

Astacilla longicornis (Sowerby)   FIG.9.13

Middle segment of pereon about twice length of anterior segments and cephalon. Female covered with small tubercles, two of which are conspicuous anteriorly on dorsal surface; male smooth and cylindrical. Pereopods 1–4 very densely setose. Female up to 30 mm body length; male up to 10 mm.

Occasional off most coasts, with sporadic intertidal records. Distributed from Norway southwards to Portugal.

8 JANIRIDAE

Body oval or elongate. Eyes, when present, dorsal. Pleon of one small, inconspicuous segment, others fused with telson to form a large, shield-shaped pleotelson. Uropod terminal or subterminal, with a peduncle, generally biramous; uropods styliform, articles cylindrical. Female pleopods covered by a plate-like operculum; males with a copulatory preoperculum.

---

1. Without eyes; interstitial, body narrow ***Microjaera anisopoda***
   With eyes; not interstitial. Body wider, oval   **2**

2. Uropods well-developed, slightly shorter or slightly longer than pleotelson, posterio-lateral borders of which are serrated   **3**
   Uropods small, barely if at all projecting beyond the pleotelson notch in which they are inserted. Pleotelson posterio-lateral borders not serrated   **4**

3. Antennae longer than body. Uropods longer than pleotelson. Pereon segments 2 and 3 with sinuous lateral borders   ***Janira maculosa***
   Antennae shorter than body. Uropods shorter than pleotelson. Pereon segments 2 and 3 with smooth lateral borders   ***Janiropsis breviremis***

4. Posterior border of pleotelson barely invaginated where uropods insert; ectocommensal on *Sphaeroma*   ***Jaera hopeana***
   Posterior border of pleotelson with deep invagination where uropods insert; free-living   **5**

5. Body widely oval, densely fringed with spines. Male preoperculum narrow and pointed   ***Jaera nordmanni***
   Body narrower, sparsely fringed with spines. Male preoperculum T-shaped   **6**

6. Male pereopods 6 and 7 with prominent lobes on carpus   ***Jaera albifrons***
   Male pereopods 6 and 7 without carpal lobes   **7**

7. Male pereopod 6 and 7 with a cluster of curved setae on distal portion of ischium   ***Jaera ischiosetosa***
   Male pereopod 6 and 7 without curved setae   **8**

8. Male pereopods 1–4 sparsely covered with curved setae on propodus, carpus, and merus. Pereopod 6 with carpal spine poorly developed, carpal spine of pereopod 7 well-developed   ***Jaera praehirsuta***
   Pereopods 1–4 sparsely covered with curved setae on propodus, carpus, and merus. Pereopods 6 and 7 both with carpal spine well-developed   ***Jaera forsmani***

Jaera albifrons Leach   FIG.9.13

Body narrowly oval in females, males smaller than females and broadest across posterior pereon segments; lateral margins of both sexes fairly sparsely fringed with spines. Eyes relatively large, situated laterally, particularly in males. Pleotelson posterior border fairly deeply excavate where uropods are inserted; preoperculum of male T-shaped with only slight lateral extensions to each arm. Pereopods of male diagnostic: 1–5 normal, 6 and 7 with distal region of carpus extended as a lobe fringed

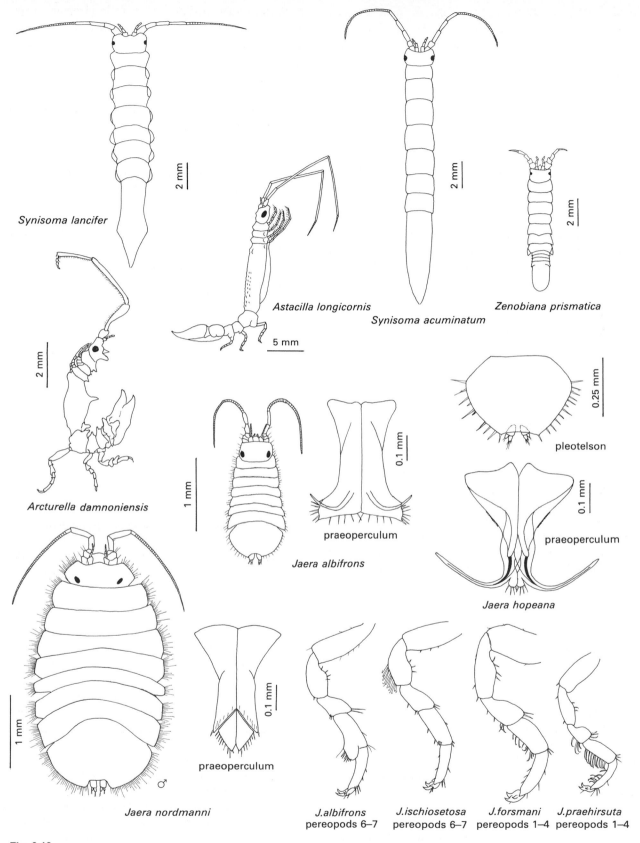

Synisoma lancifer

Astacilla longicornis

Synisoma acuminatum

Zenobiana prismatica

Arcturella damnoniensis

Jaera albifrons

praeoperculum

pleotelson

praeoperculum

Jaera hopeana

Jaera nordmanni

praeoperculum

J.albifrons
pereopods 6–7

J.ischiosetosa
pereopods 6–7

J.forsmani
pereopods 1–4

J.praehirsuta
pereopods 1–4

Fig. 9.13

with spines. Males up to 2.4 mm body length, females up to 5.0 mm.

Typically estuarine; most common at HWN beneath stones in areas which retain surface water at low tide. All British coasts, very common. Widespread in north-east Atlantic from French coasts northwards to Arctic waters.

Jaera forsmani Bocquet FIG. 9.13

Structurally resembles *J. albifrons* except in the nature of the pereopods of adult males: 1–4 have a few (usually six or less) curved setae on propodus, carpus and merus, 6 and 7 have no carpal lobe but have well-developed spines in its place. Male up to 3.4 mm, female up to 6.0 mm.

Least tolerant of reduced salinity; thinly distributed beneath stones in well-drained areas from HWN–LWS. South and west coasts only; not common.

Jaera ischiosetosa Forsman FIG. 9.13

Structurally similar to *J. albifrons* but with diagnostic adult male pereopods: 1–4 normal, 6 and 7 each with a dense cluster of curved setae on distal portion of the ischium. Male up to 2.7 mm, female up to 5.0 mm.

Very tolerant of reduced salinity; beneath stones in strong streams flowing over sheltered shores; LWN to above HWN. Most British coasts, locally common. Distributed from Russia southwards to Brittany.

Jaera praehirsuta Forsman FIG. 9.13

Structurally resembles *J. albifrons* but with diagnostic adult male pereopods: 1–4 with many curved setae on propodus, carpus, and merus; 7, but not 6, with a large spine on carpus; unlike *J. forsmani* the carpal spine of pereopod 6 is small. Male up to 3.0 mm body length, female up to 4.5 mm.

Among algae such as *Fucus serratus*; sheltered marine shores and estuaries; HWN–LWS. Most British coasts; occasional. Distributed from France to Norway.

Jaera hopeana Costa FIG. 9.13

Body fairly narrow, with very prominent spines fringing lateral margins. Pleotelson of males and females with only a very shallow invagination on posterior border where uropods are inserted. Preoperculum of male diagnostic, with narrow, elongated, terminal arms. Male about 1.5 mm body length; ovigerous females up to 2.0 mm.

Ectocommensal on *Sphaeroma serratum*; HWN–MTL; rare, south-west England.

Jaera nordmanni (Rathke) FIG. 9.13

Body broadly oval, flat, with sides densely setose. Eyes small and situated fairly medially on the head. Preoperculum of male diagnostic; narrow and pointed. Male length up to about 4.5 mm; female up to 3.5 mm.

Most tolerant of reduced salinity; MTL–EHWS, under stones in freshwater streams flowing down the shore. South and west coasts only, locally very common. Distributed from western Scotland south to the Mediterranean.

Janira maculosa Leach FIG. 9.14

Body oblong and flattened; anterior pereon segments laterally excavate, with bilobed coxal plates. Antennae longer than body. Pleotelson posterio-lateral borders serrated; uropods well-developed, longer than, or about equal in length to, pleotelson. Adult male with pereopod 1 normal, subequal to others; preoperculum expanded only slightly at tip. Male body length up to 10 mm; female up to 7 mm.

Among sponges, ascidians, hydroids, bryozoans and *Laminaria* holdfasts; LWST and below; most coasts, not uncommon. Distributed from Norway to Atlantic coast of France.

Janiropsis breviremis Sars FIG. 9.14

Body oblong and flattened; outline of anterior pereon segments smooth. Antennae shorter than body; uropods shorter than pleotelson. Adult male pereopod 1 and antennal peduncle larger than in female; male preoperculum flat and expanded into acute corners. Male body length 6 mm; female 4 mm.

Among sponges, hydroids, bryozoans, tunicates and *Laminaria* holdfasts, usually below tidemarks. Rare, reported sporadically from north-east, south and west coasts.

Microjaera anisopoda Bocquet and Levi FIG. 9.14

Body elongate, head subrectangular, without eyes. Pereon segment 1 large and partly embracing head. Pereopod 1 larger than remainder. Pleon oval and shield-shaped, with a sharp terminal projection; male preoperculum T-shaped. Females 1.4 mm long, males a little smaller; length 6 × width.

Interstitial in coarse sand and gravel; from MTL into sublittoral; extreme south-west coasts only; rare.

9 MUNNIDAE

Body short, narrowing sharply posteriorly; generally with pereon segments 5–7 much smaller than 1–4 and sharply marked off from them. Eyes on lateral extensions of head. Uropods small, lacking peduncle. Female pleopods covered by a plate-like operculum; males with a copulatory preoperculum.

1.	Appendages short; antennae less than half body length	***Paramunna bilobata***
	Appendages long; antennae at least as long as body	**2**
2.	Antennae as long as body	***Munna kroyeri***
	Antennae twice body length	***Munna minuta***

Munna kroyeri Goodsir FIG. 9.14

Antenna subequal in length to body, flagellum shorter than peduncle. Pleotelson with two to six large spines visible from above on each lateral border, posterior border not serrated. Uropod with distal, inward pointing, hooked process. Female up to 3 mm long, male 1.7 mm.

LWS and below; among sessile hydroids, bryozoans and *Laminaria* holdfasts. Reported sporadically from south-west, west, and north-west coasts; rare.

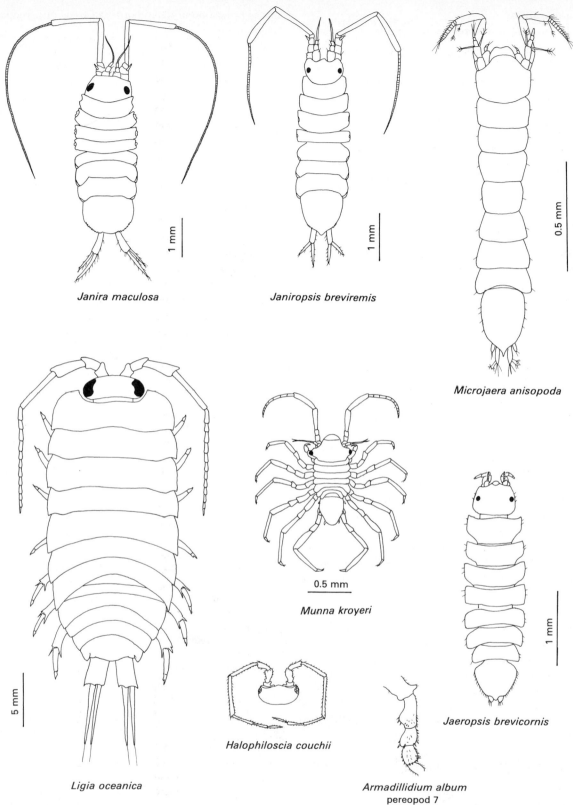

Janira maculosa

Janiropsis breviremis

Microjaera anisopoda

Munna kroyeri

Ligia oceanica

Halophiloscia couchii

Armadillidium album
pereopod 7

Jaeropsis brevicornis

Fig. 9.14

Munna minuta Hansen

Resembling *M. kroyeri* but with relatively more slender append-ages. Antennae almost twice length of body. Pleotelson with no more than one large spine on lateral borders; posterio-lateral borders serrated. Females scarcely reaching 3 mm body length; males smaller.

LWS and below; among sessile hydroids and bryozoans. Recorded on most British coasts, but rare.

Paramunna bilobata Sars

Appendages short; antennae less than half body length; head with pronounced bilobed frontal border. Up to 1 mm long.

Predominantly sublittoral, among gravel. Rare; west coasts.

10 PLEUROGONIDAE

Small isopods resembling Munnidae but with molar process of mandible reduced to narrow point, and not as a normal grinding process.

Pleurogonium rubicundum Sars

Resembles *Munna*, but with diagnostic lack of eyes.

Sublittoral, off north-east and north-west coasts; rare.

11 JAEROPSIDAE

Resembling Janiridae but with molar process of mandible reduced, elongate, and with no grinding surface. Antennae very short, with the antennal flagellum shorter than peduncle; coxal plates not visible from above.

Jaeropsis brevicornis Koehler   FIG. 9.14

Cephalon with bilobed mid-frontal region and median, jointed rostral projection. Antennule basal article large, inner distal border with a transparent serrated carina. Uropods very small, hardly visible from above; peduncle with a serrated carina on the outer border. Female 2–2.5 mm body length; male 1.5 mm.

LWS and below, among ascidians, encrusting algae, bryozoans and sponges. South and west coasts only; not common.

12 LIGIIDAE

Antennal flagellum with ten or more articles. Endopod of uropod joined to basis well beyond telson tip; exopod and endopod subequal and elongate.

Ligia oceanica (Linnaeus)   FIG. 9.14

Largest British oniscid isopod, up to 25 mm body length. Grey-green; juveniles mottled black.

In rock-crevices, caves, groynes, and quays at or above HWM; all British coasts, widespread and abundant.

13 ARMADILLIDIIDAE

Antennal flagellum of two articles. Uropod endopod fused to basis beneath telson, exopod rectangular, projecting only slightly beyond telson. Rolls into a ball.

Armadillidium album Dollfus   FIG. 9.14

Resembling common inland species *A. vulgare*, but with diag-

nostic projection of distal border of basis of pereopod 7. Body-length 6 mm.

Among debris and in burrows on sandy shores around strand line; Cumberland, southwards and eastwards to Norfolk and Yorkshire, and south-east Ireland.

14 HALOPHILOSCIIDAE

Antennal flagellum of three articles. Uropod endopod fused to basis beneath telson; exopod and endopod fairly elongate, unequal.

Halophiloscia couchii (Kinahan)   FIG. 9.14

Antennae very long. Body brown in colour.

Under stones around high water springs on rocky shores; south-west coasts; rare.

15 BOPYRIDAE

Parasitic in the branchial cavity or on the abdomen of decapods, mainly Macrura and Anomura. Body of female sometimes asymmetrical; pereon with distinct segments, seven pairs of pereopods and five pairs of oostegites, the first pair bilobed; pleon segments more or less distinct. Males small, with all seven pereon segments distinct and pleon segments distinct or fused; often found on female pleon.

Decapod Host	Parasite
Spirontocaris, Hippolyte	*Bopyroides hippolytes*
	Bopyrina giardi
Palaemon	*Bopyrus fougerouxi*
Callianassa	*Ione thoracica*
	Pseudione callianassae
Upogebia	*Gyge branchialis*
Galathea	*Pleurocrypta longibranchiata*
	Pleurocrypta marginata
Porcellana	*Pleurocrypta porcellanae*
Pagurus, Anapagurus	*Athelges paguri*
	Pseudione hyndmanni
	Pseudione proxima
Diogenes	*Pseudione diogeni*

Athelges paguri (Rathke)   FIG. 9.15

Female markedly asymmetrical; cephalon small, withdrawn into pereon; oostegites very large with anterior pairs elaborately folded and projecting beyond cephalon. Pleotelson narrowing abruptly, bearing four pairs of biramous, paddle-like pleopods; uropods as two very small tubercles on club-like posterior part of pleon. Male pleotelson unsegmented. Female up to 11 mm body length; male 4 mm.

Usually attached to abdomen, but occasionally in gill chambers, of the hermit crabs *Pagurus bernhardus* and *Anapagurus laevis*. All British coasts; local.

Bopyrina giardi Bonnier   FIG. 9.15

Female resembling *Bopyrus*, but pleon somites may show greater fusion and appear distinct on one side only; female with only

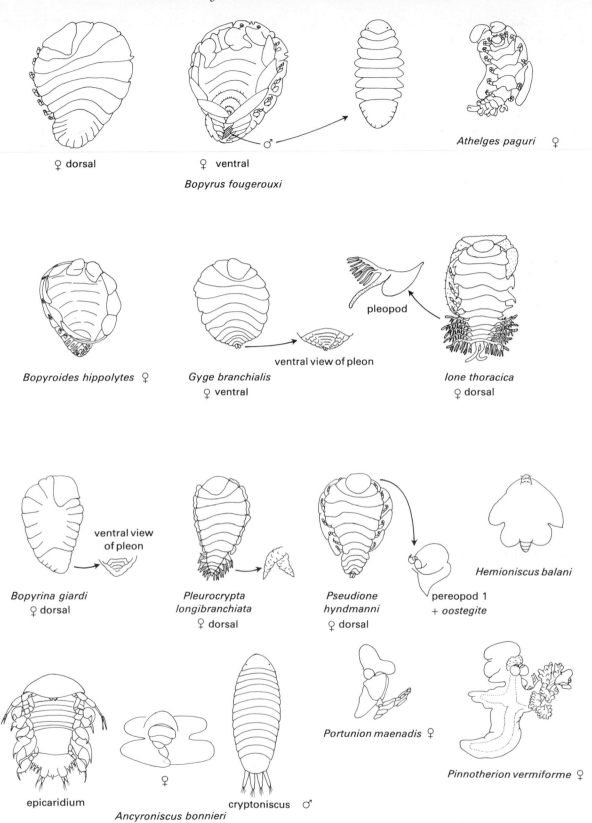

♀ dorsal

♀ ventral

Bopyrus fougerouxi

Athelges paguri ♀

Bopyroides hippolytes ♀

Gyge branchialis
♀ ventral

ventral view of pleon

pleopod

Ione thoracica
♀ dorsal

Bopyrina giardi
♀ dorsal

ventral view
of pleon

*Pleurocrypta
longibranchiata*
♀ dorsal

*Pseudione
hyndmanni*
♀ dorsal

pereopod 1
+ *oostegite*

Hemioniscus balani

epicaridium

♀

Ancyroniscus bonnieri

cryptoniscus ♂

Portunion maenadis ♀

Pinnotherion vermiforme ♀

Fig. 9.15

three or four (not five) pairs of uniramous pleopods, the most posterior very small. Male with uropods. Female 1.7 mm; male 0.7 mm.

Typically in the branchial chamber of *Hippolyte varians*. South and west coasts only; local.

Bopyroides hippolytes Kroyer   FIG. 9.15
Resembling *Bopyrus* but female pleon segments all distinct, and pleopods present only as five pairs of raised ridges. Female up to 11 mm, male 2.5 mm.

Typically offshore on *Spirontocaris*, but has been recorded intertidally from *Hippolyte varians*. South and west coasts only; local.

Bopyrus fougerouxi Giard and Bonnier   FIG. 9.15
Female asymmetrically oval; pereon somites distinct, pereopods small. Pleon somites fused in mid-line, sides without lateral projections; with five pairs of uniramous lamellar pleopods, lacking uropods. First oostegites large, remainder smaller and divergent, eggs partially enclosed by host carapace. Male pleotelson with segments fused. Female up to 11 mm body length; male 2 mm.

In the branchial chamber of *Palaemon serratus*, where it gives rise to the so-called 'face-ache' condition of the prawn. Most British coasts; locally not uncommon.

Gyge branchialis Cornalia and Panceri   FIG. 9.15
Female body oval; pleon segments distinct, with very small, vesicle-like uniramous pleopods; uropods as a very small pair of pointed terminal projections. Oostegites overlap ventrally in adult females. Male pleotelson with distinct segments; small uniramous uropods. Females up to 12 mm; males 5 mm.

Recorded from the gill chamber of the mud-burrowing decapods *Upogebia deltaura* and *U. stellata*; LW and below. South-west coasts only; rare.

Ione thoracica Montagu   FIG. 9.15
Female cephalon with prominent frontal lamella; pereon with distinct segments with prominent, pointed lateral projections. Oostegites overlapping, and covered with small pointed projections. Pleon segments distinct with six pairs of characteristic branched lateral processes, and five pairs of pleopods each with a lamellar endopod and cylindrical exopod. Uropods long and tubular. Male pleon segments fused, with six pairs of characteristic unbranched processes. Female body-length 6–7 mm, male smaller.

Recorded from the gill chamber of *Callianassa subterranea*, a predominantly sublittoral decapod burrowing in muddy sand. South and west coasts only; rare.

Pleurocrypta longibranchiata (Bate and Westwood)   FIG. 9.15
Female asymmetrically pyriform, cephalon lateral corners acute. Pereon with prominent lateral plates, more or less contiguous. Oostegites overlapping ventrally in adult. Pleon segments well-defined, with prominent lateral processes and well-developed,

biramous, tuberculate pleopods. Uropods present. Male with pleon segments fused. Female up to 8 mm, male 2 mm.

Probably the most regular parasite of intertidal *Galathea squamifera*. South-west, west, and north coasts; local.

Pleurocrypta marginata Sars
Resembles *P. longibranchiata* but female cephalon has a broad, flat frontal border, and the pereon has very wide, flattened, contiguous lateral plates. Pleopods short and smooth.

Recorded from *Galathea squamifera* and *G. intermedia*. South and west coasts; rare.

Pleurocrypta porcellanae Hesse
Resembles *P. longibranchiata* but recorded from the gill chamber of *Pisidia longicornis* taken subtidally. All British coasts; locally distributed and rare.

Pseudione callianassae Kossman
From the burrowing prawn *Callianassa subterranea*; predominantly sublittoral; south-west coasts; rare.

Pseudione diogeni Popov
Recorded from the hermit crab *Diogenes pugilator*; Channel Islands; rare.

Pseudione hyndmanni (Bate and Westwood)   FIG. 9.15
Mature female more or less asymmetrically pyriform; with distinct segments on pereon and pleon. Sides of pleon segments prominent and rounded; five pairs of short, smooth pleopods, biramous and lanceolate; uropods small, lanceolate. Oostegites large, completely enclosing brood chamber. Males with pleon of unfused segments.

In the branchial cavity of the hermit crabs *Pagurus bernhardus* and *P. pubescens*. South, west, and north coasts; local.

Pseudione proxima Bonnier
Differs from *P. hyndmanni* in having long, tuberculate pleopods projecting beyond sides of pleon; the posterio-lateral border of the maxilliped has two short processes; oostegite 1 with posterior process rounded and incurved.

One British record, from intertidal *Pagurus bernhardus*, at Plymouth.

16 ENTONISCIDAE
Almost always endoparasitic in the visceral cavity of Anomura and Brachyura, surrounded by a membrane of host origin and communicating with the brachial cavity of the host by a pore. Female body with only indistinct traces of segmentation, pereopods rudimentary or entirely absent, and with five pairs of oostegites arising somewhat dorsally owing to the considerable reduction of the dorsal body surface.

Decapod Host	Parasite
Eurynome	*Entionella monensis*
Pinnotheres	*Pinnotherion vermiforme*
Carcinus	*Portunion maenadis*

Entionella monensis Hartnoll
Recorded from the spider crab *Eurynome aspera*; predominantly sublittoral; Irish Sea; rare.

Pinnotherion vermiforme Giard and Bonnier   FIG. 9.15
Female pereon very short; ovary without external dorsal processes, but with two ventral processes, the posterior long and often extending into host pleon. Colour violet or blue. Male free in pereon and pleon of host, on the female abdomen, or in the female brood pouch. Length 1–3.5 mm.

Recorded from *Pinnotheres pisum* infecting the mussel *Mytilus*. Cornwall; local.

Portunion maenadis Giard   FIG. 9.15
Female pereon fairly long; ovary with two ventral and two dorsal processes. Size 3.2 mm. Male resembling that of *Pinnotherion* but with pereon segment 1 more distinct from cephalon.

Single British record from *Carcinus maenas*; Plymouth.

17 DAJIDAE
In incubatory chamber or on dorsal surface of mysids and euphausiids; rarely on Brachyura. Female body symmetrical; segments, when apparent, visible only in mid-dorsal region; pereopods well-developed but numbering only five pairs and crowded near mouth. Oostegites present but small with brood pouch often appearing bilateral. Pleopods small or absent.

A possible record of *Prodajus ostendensis* Gilson has been noted from the mysid *Gastrosaccus spinifer* on the east coast (Naylor 1972).

18 CRYPTONISCIDAE
Recorded particularly from barnacles, isopods, and ostracods. Female stage sac-like, with few distinct segments and lacking pereopods. Male (cryptoniscus) antennule 1 with basal article lamellar and often serrated; pereopods 3–7 usually slender with setiform dactyl; pleopods and uropods biramous. Unlike the Bopyridae, Entoniscidae, and Dajidae, which comprise the super-family Bopyrina, the Cryptoniscidae lack oostegites and incubate the brood internally. They are protandrous hermaphrodites, the cryptoniscus stage being male and the final highly modified stage being female.

Host	Parasite
Dynamene	*Ancyroniscus bonnieri*
Semibalanus,	*Hemioniscus balani*
Elminius	
Peltogaster	*Liriopsis pygmaea*

Ancyroniscus bonnieri Caullery and Mesnil   FIG. 9.15
Female a bilobed sac initially attaching to the gut, then protruding the head and anterior pleon into the brood pouch of the host isopod *Dynamene bidentata* where it feeds on the brood. On hatching, a microniscus stage and then an epicaridean stage attach to planktonic hosts before moulting to the cryptoniscus which locates the isopod host. South and west coasts; local.

Hemioniscus balani (Spence Bate)   FIG. 9.15
Female stage with middle part of body sac-like, with two or three lobes on each side; body-length reaching 8 mm.

In the mantle cavity of shore barnacles; south and west coasts; locally abundant in *Semibalanus balanoides*.

Liriopsis pygmaea Rathke
Female a constricted sac with an anterior lobe buried in the host and a projecting posterior lobe; the cryptoniscus lacks serrations on the basal article of the antennule.

Parasitizes *Peltogaster paguri*, a parasitic barnacle itself attached to the abdomen of the hermit crabs *Anapagurus laevis* and *Eupagurus cuanensis*. South and west coasts; rare.

Order **Amphipoda**
Amphipods are distinguished from other peracaridan crustaceans principally by the lack of a carapace. The body is typically laterally compressed, although cylindrical and dorso-ventrally depressed shapes also occur, and is divided into three regions: *head*, *pereon* (thorax, or mesosome) and *pleon* (abdomen, or metasome). Additionally, there is a terminal *telson*, attached dorsally to the last pleon segment. The head, which is actually fused with the first pereon segment, bears six pairs of appendages: *antennae 1*, *antennae 2*, *mandibles*, *maxillae 1*, *maxillae 2*, and *maxillipeds*. The pereon consists of seven visible segments, each of which bears a pair of uniramous appendages, *pereopods*; pereopods 1 and 2 are almost invariably modified as *gnathopods*. The pleon consists of six segments; the first three constitute the *pleosome*, and each bears a pair of biramous *pleopods*, the last three comprise the *urosome*, which typically bears three pairs of uniramous or biramous *uropods*. Females have a ventral brood pouch formed from a variable number of paired lamellae arising from the bases of pereopods 2–6.

This basic morphology varies widely throughout the Amphipoda, but the most marked divergence occurs among the suborder Caprellidea. These are recognized by their very attenuated, cylindrical bodies, and a reduction in number and type of appendages. The head is immoveably fused to the first two segments of the thorax; pereon segment 1 remains visible, however, and as usual bears the first pair of gnathopods. The pereon consists of seven segments but the pleon is rudimentary or absent; there are two pairs of gnathopods and three posteriorly situated pairs of pereopods (pereopods 5–7); pereopods 3 and 4 are variously developed or absent. The Hyperiidea are plump, rounded amphipods with enormously developed eyes. They are pelagic, and in British waters are frequently encountered in the gastric pouches of some jellyfishes (e.g. *Rhizostoma*).

KEY TO SUBORDERS

1. Body very attenuated, pleon usually vestigial. Head fused with pereon segment 1 (bearing gnathopod 1). Three pairs of terminal pereopods; pleopods and uropods lacking. Two or three pairs of gills; two pairs of brood lamellae   **Suborder Caprellidea** (p. 482)

   Body with pleon and pereon distinct. Head not fused with pereon segment 1. Pleopods and uropods present. More than three pairs of gills; four or five pairs of brood lamellae   **2**

2. Body rounded. Eyes often very large, occupying most of head. Maxillipeds without a palp. Coxae small or absent. Pelagic   **Suborder Hyperiidea** (p. 480)

   Eyes not occupying most of head, of variable size, sometimes apparently absent. Coxae present and typically relatively large. Maxillipeds with a palp. Benthic

   Suborder Gammaridea

Suborder **Gammaridea**

Gammaridean amphipods typically have laterally compressed body shapes although some are rather cylindrical, and a few distinctly dorso-ventrally depressed. The body is divided into a head, seven thoracic segments, and six abdominal segments. Older authorities referred to the head or *cephalon*, the *mesosome* (= thorax), and the *metasome* (= abdomen), with the last three abdominal segments constituting the *urosome*. Barnard (1969), in his world key to families and genera of marine gammarids, used the terms *pereon* (pereion or peraeon) and *pleon* for the thorax and abdomen, respectively. Since, universally, the thoracic limbs of amphipods are termed *pereopods* (pereopods or peraeopods) and the abdominal limbs *pleopods* and *uropods*, Barnard's terminology appears the more logical, and is followed here. The general features of gammaridean morphology are shown in Fig. 9.16.

A confusion exists concerning the terminology of the seven thoracic limbs. Some authorities numbered the pereopods from 1 to 7 while usually referring to the first and second pereopods as the first and second gnathopods. Others, including Barnard (1969), also termed the first and second thoracic limbs gnathopods, but the remaining limbs pereopods 1 to 5. In this case, the latter terminology seems the less logical since it suggests that the seventh thoracic (pereon) segment bears the fifth (rather than the seventh) pereopod. Lincoln (1979) numbers the thoracic limbs from 1 to 7, whilst denoting the first two pairs as gnathapods 1 and 2, and this terminology is followed here (Fig. 9.16).

The shape of the head has some significance at the family and genus levels. In shore and shallow water species the head usually bears a pair of round or reniform eyes situated laterally; rarely these may be indistinct (*Haustorius*), fused dorsally (Oedicerotidae), or supplemented by one or two further pairs. Deep water species may lack eyes. A number of families have a median, dorsal projection between the eyes, called the *rostrum*. Its presence, size, and shape has taxonomic significance at the family level. The head bears two pairs of antennae. *Antenna 1*, or antennule, has a *peduncle* composed of three articles, succeeded by a *flagellum* which may consist of a few or many articles. In many species the biramous derivation of the first antenna is indicated by the presence of an *accessory flagellum* at the distal tip of the third peduncle article; it may be uni- or multiarticulate, small or well-developed. *Antenna 2* has five peduncle articles and a variably articulate flagellum, but no accessory flagellum. Although the two pairs of antennae frequently show secondary sexual characters, their size and structure have considerable taxonomic significance at both family and genus levels. Occasionally their structure is diagnostic. (e.g. *Bathyporeia*).

The mouthparts of the Gammaridea are very variable and extremely important in classification. They have been used extensively in identification keys but because of their small size and complexity, they are much more useful to the skilled and well-equipped taxonomist than to the non-specialist. Accordingly, in this work, emphasis is placed either on the overall appearance of the mouthparts or on the structure of their most discernible components, especially the mandibles. Generally, mouthpart structures are here used in a confirmatory rather than diagnostic role.

The mouthparts comprise an upper lip, lower lip, and one pair each of *mandibles, first maxillae, second maxillae*, and *maxillipeds*. In peracaridean phylogeny the maxillipeds were originally the thoracic limbs of the first thoracic segment. In the fusion of this segment with the amphipod head they have assumed a role in the mouthpart apparatus. The maxillipeds are rarely absent in Gammaridea but are always missing in Hyperiidea. The overall structure of the mouthparts typically presents a quadrate appearance in sideview; rarely, they are arranged in a styliform or ventrally pointing conical manner (e.g. Acanthonotozomatidae, Lysianassidae). The mandibles are attached laterally to the mouth, adjacent to the lips, and in front of the remaining mouthparts. They may be recognized usually by the series of teeth, or *incisors*, at their anterio-distal ends. Generally, a *molar process* occurs on the medio-ventral surface of each mandible, usually with a ridged and toothed grinding surface. In the Liljeborgiidae the molar processes are reduced and smooth, while in forms with piercing and sucking mouthparts they are

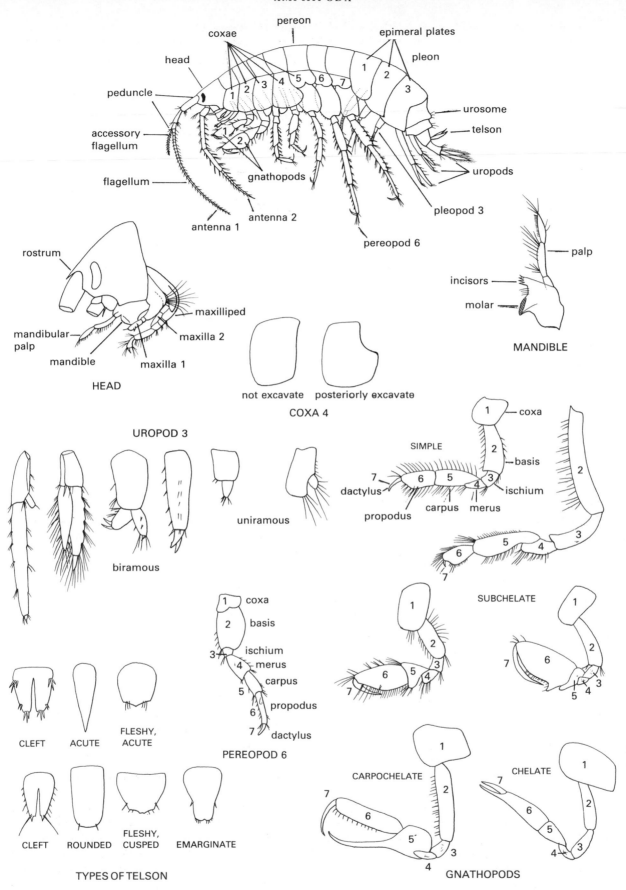

Fig. 9.16

absent. Most Gammaridea have single triarticulate *mandibular palps* attached dorso-laterally to each mandible. They are absent in some families, a fact useful in classification, and in the Corophiidae are reduced to one or two articles only.

The seven pereon segments carry the *pereopods*, the *gills* and, in females, the *brood lamellae*. Each pereopod is composed of seven articles, the first and most proximal is termed the *coxa*, and is followed by the *basis* (article 2), *ischium* (article 3), *merus* (article 4), *carpus* (article 5), *propodus* (article 6), and *dactylus* (article 7) (Fig. 9.16). The relative lengths, shapes, and structures of both whole pereopods and their individual articles have considerable taxonomic significance. In the Gammaridea the coxae have greater importance than in any other Malacostraca and in many species they are, structurally, more an integral part of the body than simply articles of the appendages. They resemble ventral, pleuron-like extensions of the pereon segments and usually contribute to the laterally compressed body shape. The shape of the posterior borders of the fourth coxae are especially useful in family diagnosis: in some the posterior border is smoothly convex, straight, or slightly concave; in others at least the dorsal part is strongly concave (*excavate*) (Fig. 9.16). The gills are generally attached to the medial surfaces of coxae 2–7, and in females the brood lamellae are similarly situated on coxae 2–5. In young females the lamellae are small buds but, with age, they grow longer and more heavily setose, with the setae interlocking to form a cradle enclosing the eggs.

The first two pairs of pereopods are usually termed the first and second *gnathopods* and usually one or both may be distally *chelate*, *subchelate*, or *carpochelate* (Fig. 9.16). In the basic subchelate condition the *dactylus* (article 7) is folded back on to the posterior distal border (*palm*) of the *propodus* (article 6); enlargement of the propodus and the presence of processes from the *carpus* (article 5) frequently complicate the arrangement, giving a carpochelate structure. A chelate gnathopod has the form of a true pincer similar to that of a crab or lobster claw. The gnathopods are usually larger than the other pereopods and the shapes of the articles are often useful taxonomic features. Frequently, however, the gnathopods show considerable sexual dimorphism, those of the male being the larger and/or more complex. Keys depending solely on the structure of the adult male gnathopods are not helpful when identification of juveniles and females is required.

In those families which burrow into sediments, pereopods 5–7 show adaptations to assist burrowing: they are armed with dense setae and strong spines, and often some articles are enlarged and compressed. Other gammaridean families construct dwelling tubes which are spun from strands of material secreted and probably manipulated by the third and fourth pereopods. The tubes may be limp, or stiff and erect, and may incorporate mud for reinforcement. The glands secreting the material are mainly concentrated on the *basis* and *merus* (articles 2 and 4, respectively) of the third and fourth pereopods and the yolky glandular tissue may be of a different colour to that of the adjacent musculature.

The three pleon segments, which may bear dorsal teeth, carry paired, biramous *pleopods* whose rami are multisegmented and strongly setose. The pleopods are used as paddles and gammarideans are generally good swimmers. The morphology of the pleopods has been largely ignored by taxonomists and their structure is rarely significant taxonomically. The *epimeral plates* project ventrally from each side of each pleon segment. Their shapes, particularly those of the ventral and posterior borders of the third pair, have considerable taxonomic value at the generic and specific levels.

The three *urosome* segments are usually separate and of more or less equal length. A degree of fusion between segments is not uncommon but the elongation of one segment is rare (Podoceridae). Dorsal teeth are more prevalent than on the pleon segments and the dorsal surface may also carry groups of spines and/or setae which have taxonomic importance. Each urosome segment bears a pair of biramous *uropods*. The proportions and structure of these, especially the third pair, are very variable between families. The third uropods may be *aramous*, *uniramous*, or *biramous*, with mono- or biarticulate, equal or unequal rami. The rami may be armed with hooks (Ampithoidae, Ischyroceridae, and rarely Corophiidae) but usually the armament, if present, consists of spines and/or setae. Rarely, one pair of uropods may be absent (Podoceridae).

The *telson* attaches above the anus to the posterio-dorsal surface of the third urosome segment and has great taxonomic value. It may be entire, notched, cleft, or emarginate, of variable size, and shows a wide range of ornamentation.

Although most species, especially the males, are good swimmers, the Gammaridea are essentially benthic. The typical body plan allows easy movement amongst masses of hydroids and algae, and gammaridean amphipods are among the most abundant macro-crustaceans in such habitats. On the shore amphipods frequently shelter beneath stones and one group, the Talitroidea, has developed a hopping mode of locomotion and inhabits the highest shore levels, sheltering amongst strandline debris. A number of families have adopted a tube-dwelling mode of life either on algae or hydroids or directly on the sea-bed. Sometimes tube dwelling is combined with a burrowing ability as in some of the Corophiidae. Some species burrow without forming even semi-permanent burrows; generally these inhabit marine sands but a few exploit coarser deposits in both the sublittoral and littoral zones. A number of families have penetrated estuaries and some species are typical of, and confined to, areas of low salinity.

Gammaridean amphipods take a wide range of food and exhibit a considerable number of feeding mechanisms. Many are omnivorous scavengers consuming both detritus and macrofoods. Some are herbivorous, although the majority of these concentrate on micro- rather than macro-algae, while a few are predatory macro-carnivores. Some have piercing and sucking mouthparts suggesting a specialized, perhaps ectoparasitic mode of life, but unlike some other crustacean groups, there are no radically degenerate endoparasitic amphipods. Some burrowing species scrape the flora from individual grains of sediment while others filter-feed either on plankton or meiofauna. Generally tube dwellers are also filter feeders, often using the antennae as feeding implements; however, large specimens of the tubicolous species *Jassa falcata* (Montagu) have also been seen to capture and feed upon other smaller amphipods.

The collection of rocky shore specimens requires little other than forceps and a small hand net. The most productive microhabitats are beneath stones, in crevices, and amongst algae, hydroids, barnacles, and other sessile marine organisms. A few species, notably in the genera *Leucothoe* and *Colomastix*, shelter with ascidians or sponges. Species burrowing in soft substrata should be gently sieved out of the sediment on a 1 mm or 0.5 mm mesh sieve. Amphipods rarely burrow deeper than 50 mm so that only the surface layers of the sediment need be sampled. Sublittoral samples may be collected using sediment grabs and fine mesh trawls. An Ockelmann sledge is useful on soft sublittoral sediments and a similar device towed by hand in the surf zone will also produce satisfactory catches, especially at night.

Amphipods can be successfully narcotized by placing them in a 7.5% solution of magnesium chloride in sea-water. Fixation is perhaps best achieved using 5% sea-water formalin but 70% ethanol is nearly as effective. For storage, specimens should be washed in tap water and transferred to a solution composed of 0.5% propylene phenoxetol, 4.5% propylene glycol, and 95% sea-water. More simply a solution of 70% ethanol which also includes a little glycerol may be used.

Examination of specimens requires both fine forceps and needles, and a binocular microscope equipped for transmitted and reflected illumination, capable of magnification to × 50.

Useful early works on the British Amphipoda include those of Bate and Westwood (1868), Norman and Scott (1906), and Stebbing (1906) but the premier English language work of that period is that of Sars (1894) which, although based on the Norwegian fauna, describes and illustrates a large number of British species. Subsequent to Sars, three other European works are useful in the identification of British species: Chevreux and Fage (1925) details French species, and Schellenberg (1942) describes the amphipod fauna of Germany; most recently Ruffo (1982, 1987) has begun to monograph the Mediterranean species. Barnard (1969) provided a world key to the families and genera of marine gammaridean amphipods, while, in an earlier work (1958), he indexed the world's families, genera, and species of gammarids. Lincoln (1979) described and figured most British species of gammaridean Amphipoda; Myers *et al.* (1979 *et seq.*) have since revised many genera, providing new keys for their identification.

The figures presented in Plates 9.17 to 9.46 have been redrawn from various sources, principally Lincoln (1979), Myers *et al.* (1979 *et seq.*), and Sars (1894).

REFERENCES

Barnard, J. L. (1958). Index to the families, genera, and species of the gammaridean Amphipoda. *Allan Hancock Foundation Publications, occasional paper, No.*, **19**. University of Southern California Press, Los Angeles.

Barnard, J. L. (1969). The families and genera of marine gammaridean Amphipoda. *Bulletin of the United States National Museum*, **271**. Smithsonian Press, Washington.

Bate, C. S. and Westwood, J. O. (1868). *A history of the British sessile-eyed Crustacea.* J. van Voorst, London.

Chevreux, E. and Fage, L. (1925). Amphipodes. *Faune de France*, **9**, Paris.

Fincham, A. A. (1970). Amphipods in the surf plankton. *Journal of the Marine Biological Association of the U.K.*, **50**, 177–98.

Fincham, A. A. (1971). Ecology and population studies of some intertidal and sublittoral sand-dwelling amphipods. *Journal of the Marine Biological Association of the U.K.*, **51**, 471–88.

Hughes, R. G. (1975). The distribution of epizooites on the hydroid *Nemertesia antennina* (L). *Journal of the Marine Biological Association of the U.K.*, **55**, 275–94.

Lincoln, R. J. (1979). *British Gammaridean Amphipods.* British Museum (Natural History), London.

Moore, P. G. (1973). The larger Crustacea associated with holdfasts of kelp (*Laminaria hyperborea*) in North-east Britain. *Cahiers de Biologie Marine*, **14**, 493–518.

Moore, P. G. (1978). Turbidity and kelp holdfast Amphipoda. 1. Wales and S.W. England. *Journal of Experimental Marine Biology and Ecology*, **32**, 53–96.

Myers, A. A. (1969). A revision of the amphipod genus *Microdeutopus* Costa (Gammaridea: Aoridae). *Bulletin of the British Museum Natural History* (Zoology), **17**, 91–148.

Myers, A. A. (1974). *Amphitholina cuniculus* (Stebbing), a little-known marine amphipod crustacean new to Ireland. *Proceedings of the Royal Irish Academy* (Series B), **74** (27), 463–69.

Myers, A. A. (1979). Studies on the genus *Lembos* Bate. 9. Atlantic species 6: *L. longipes* (Liljeborg), *L. websteri* (Bate), *L. longidigitans* (Bonnier), *L.* (*Arctolembos* sub. gen. nov.) *articus* (Hansen). *Bollettino del Museo civico di storia naturale di Verona*, **6**, 249–75.

Myers, A. A. and Costello, M. J. (1984). The amphipod genus *Aora* in British and Irish waters. *Journal of the Marine Biological Association of the U.K.*, **64** (2), 279–83.

Myers, A. A. and Costello, M. J. (1986). The amphipod sibling pair *Leucothoe lilljeborgi* and *L. incisa* in British and Irish waters. *Journal of the Marine Biological Association of the U.K.*, **66** (1), 75–82.

Myers, A. A. and McGrath, D. (1978). Littoral and benthic investigations on the west coast of Ireland, 8. (Section A: faunistic and ecological studies). A new species of amphipod, *Lembos denticarpus* sp.nov. (Aoridae), from Galway Bay. *Proceedings of the Royal Irish Academy* (Series B), **78** (8), 125–31.

Myers, A. A. and McGrath, D. (1979). The British and Irish species of *Siphonoecetes* Krøyer. (Amphipoda-Gammaridea). *Journal of Natural History*, **13** (2), 211–20.

Myers, A. A. and McGrath, D. (1980). A new species of *Stenothoe* Dana (Amphipoda, Gammaridea) from Maerl deposits in Kilkieran Bay. *Journal of Life Sciences, Royal Dublin Society*, **2** (1), 15–8.

Myers, A. A. and McGrath, D. (1981). Taxonomic studies on British and Irish Amphipoda. The genus *Photis* with the re-establishment of *P. pollex* (= *P. macrocoxa*). *Journal of the Marine Biological Association of the U.K.*, **61** (3), 759–68.

Myers, A. A. and McGrath, D. (1982a). Taxonomic studies on British and Irish Amphipoda. The genus *Gammaropsis*. *Journal of the Marine Biological Association of the U.K.*, **62** (1), 93–100.

Myers, A. A. and McGrath, D. (1982b). Taxonomic studies on British and Irish Amphipoda. Re-establishment of *Leucothoe procera*. *Journal of the Marine Biological Association of the U.K.*, **62** (3), 693–8.

Myers, A. A. and McGrath, D. (1983). The genus *Listriella* (Crustacea: Amphipoda) in British and Irish waters. *Journal of the Marine Biological Association of the U.K.*, **63** (2), 347–53.

Myers, A. A. and McGrath, D. (1984). A revision of the North-east Atlantic species of *Ericthonius* (Crustacea: Amphipoda). *Journal of the Marine Biological Association of the U.K.*, **64** (2), 379–400.

Myers, A. A., McGrath, D., and Costello, M. J. (1987). The Irish species of *Iphimedia* Rathke (Amphipoda: Acanthonotozomatidae). *Journal of the Marine Biological Association of the U.K.*, **67** (2), 307–21.

Norman, A. M. and Scott, T. (1906). *The Crustacea of Devon and Cornwall*. London.

Ruffo, S. (1982). The Amphipoda of the Mediterranean. Part 1. Acan-

thonotozomatidae to Gammaridae. *Memoires de l'Institut oceanographique, Monaco*, **13**, 1–364.

Ruffo, S. (ed.) (1987). The Amphipoda of the Mediterranean. Part 2.

Sars, G. O. (1894). *An account of the Crustacea of Norway*, 1, *Amphipoda* parts 1 and 2. Bergen.

Schellenberg, A. (1942). Krebstiere oder Crustacea IV: Flohkrebse oder Amphipoda. *Die Tierwelt Deutschlands*, **40**. Jena.

Stebbing, T. R. R. (1906). Amphipoda 1. Gammaridea. *Das Tierreich*, **21**. Berlin.

KEY TO FAMILIES

---

1. Body depressed. Pleon segment 3 with long dorsal spine. Uropods 1 and 2 with very different structure; uropod 3 with rudimentary inner ramus and massively enlarged outer ramus   **29. Cheluridae**

   Characters not combining as above   **2**

---

2. Body depressed. Head flat. Pereon and pleon segments with dorsal lumps. Coxae splayed. Antenna 1 and 2 short, accessory flagellum absent. Uropod 3 very small, without rami. Telson short and entire   **4. Phliantidae**

   Characters not combining as above   **3**

---

3. Coxal plates 1–3 successively shorter, coxal plate 4 larger than all others. Gnathopods simple, small, inconspicuous. Pereopod 7 with very broad basis, merus and carpus densely setose   **15. Argissidae**

   Characters not combining as above   **4**

---

4. Body often elongate, distinctly depressed or subcylindrical; urosome visibly depressed, segments often coalesced. Telson short, entire. Coxae short and serially separate or just touching. Mandible with a reduced palp. Uropod 3 very small, either uniramous or without rami; sometimes absent   **5**

   Characters not combining as above   **6**

---

5. Urosome segments 1 and 2 more or less of equal length   **28. Corophiidae**

   Urosome segment 1 more than twice length of 2   **31. Podoceridae**

---

6. Body almost cylindrical. Antenna 1 and 2 short with large peduncle articles but tiny flagella (three or fewer articles). Accessory flagellum absent. Mandibular palp absent. Coxae short but overlapping. Urosome segments 2 and 3 coalesced. Uropod 3 biramous. Telson entire, of medium length. Typically found in sponges   **5. Colomastigidae**

   Characters not combining as above   **7**

---

7. Body cylindrical and fat. Rostrum small or medium-sized, never hood-like. Accessory flagellum well-developed. Pereopod 7 as long or longer than 6. Pereopods fossorial (i.e. flattened, spinose, and setose). Telson cleft.   **14. Haustoriidae**

   Characters not combining as above   **8**

---

8. Body cylindrical but fusiform. Head elongate, dorso-ventrally flattened, with a large hood-like rostrum covering base of antenna 1. Pereopods fossorial. Pereopod 7 distinctly shorter than 6. Telson cleft **17. Phoxocephalidae**

   Characters not combining as above **9**

9. Head with conspicuous downturned rostrum, eyes more or less coalesced dorsally. Accessory flagellum absent or rudimentary. Pereopod 7 very much longer than 6. Ramus of uropod 3 scarcely longer than peduncle. Telson small and entire **16. Oedicerotidae**

   Characters not combining as above **10**

10. Head with conspicuous downturned rostrum; eyes large, not coalesced. Mouthparts arranged into a conical bundle pointing ventrally. Last pereon and all pleon segments produced dorsally into large paired teeth. Epimeral plate 3 with two large teeth on posterior border. Antennae subequal, accessory flagellum rudimentary. Gnathopods small. Telson entire and subquadrate **3. Acanthonotozomatidae**

    Characters not combining as above **11**

11. Pereopods 5–7 broad, flattened, spiny, and setose; pereopod 7 not markedly longer than 6. Antenna 1 geniculate, with enlarged first peduncle article bearing remainder of antenna on anterior ventral surface; *or* straight, with peduncle articles 1 and 2 together as long as rest of antenna. Accessory flagellum present. Telson cleft.

    14. Haustoriidae

    Characters not combining as above **12**

12. Body usually short and fat. Antenna 1 short, or very short, with stout peduncle; peduncle article 1 much larger and fatter than subsequent articles; flagellum scarcely longer than peduncle; accessory flagellum almost always present. Gnathopods usually small. Gnathopod 2 characteristic, with swollen propodus, rudimentary dactylus, and elongate ischium. Mandible with three-articled palp **1. Lysianassidae**

    Characters not combining as above **13**

13. Body usually short, fat, or compressed. Antenna 1 and 2 medium or short, almost equal length, or 1 much longer than 2. Accessory flagellum absent. Pereopod 1 coxa very small or rudimentary, partially hidden; pereopod 2–4 coxae grossly enlarged. Gnathopods variable but never chelate. Urosome segment 1 without a dorsal tooth. Uropod 3 uniramous or biramous. Telson entire **14**

    Characters not combining as above **16**

14. Uropod 3 biramous, longer than uropod 2. Rami uniarticulate **6. Amphilochidae**

    Uropod 3 uniramous. Ramus biarticulate **15**

15. Telson distinct, medium length. Antenna 1 and 2 subequal. Pereopod 5 with slender basis **8. Stenothoidae**

    Telson fused to urosome segment 3, which is fused to urosome segment 2. Pereopod 5 with expanded basis. Antenna 1 much longer than 2 **9. Cressidae**

16. Gnathopod 1 large, carpochelate; gnathopod 2 larger than 1, subchelate. Antenna 1 longer than 2. Accessory flagellum small, uniarticulate. Body slender. Coxae large. Uropod 3 biramous. Telson entire, triangular   **7. Leucothoidae**

    Characters not combining as above   **17**

17. With two, four, or six eyes. Urosome segments 2 and 3 coalesced; urosome usually with at least one sharp or blunt tooth. Uropod 3 biramous. Telson medium or long, deeply cleft. Accessory flagellum absent, rarely vestigial. Gnathopods small, sub-chelate, or simple   **18**

    Characters not combining as above   **20**

18. Head distinctly compressed, elongate, rostrum absent. Usually four, sometimes six or two eyes. Body strongly compressed, generally smooth dorsally. Pereopod 7 shorter and of different structure to 6   **2. Ampeliscidae**

    Head not especially flat or elongate. Rostrum present, large or small. Two eyes. Pereopods 6 and 7 broadly similar in structure   **19**

19. Antenna 1 shorter than 2. Rostrum large. Mandible with palp. Often with dorsal teeth on pleon and last pereon segment. Urosome segment 1 with two teeth dorsally; small anterior tooth separated from much larger posterior tooth by distinct cleft   **23. Atylidae**

    Antennae variable in length. Rostrum small. Mandible without palp. Teeth sometimes present on the pleon. Urosome segment 1 with single tooth, or nearly smooth
                                                                                    24. Dexaminidae

20. Accessory flagellum absent or rudimentary. Mandible with a palp. Coxa 4 excavate posteriorly. Uropod 3 biramous; rami usually at least twice length of peduncle, inner rami generally longer than outer. Telson entire but not fleshy, often triangular, usually about twice as long as wide, sometimes notched apically   **21**

    Characters not combining as above   **22**

21. Antenna 1 shorter than 2. Epimeral plate 3 with sharp or blunt point at posterio-ventral corner, often with denticulate or angular posterior border   **21. Calliopiidae** (Pt.)

    Antenna 1 longer than 2. Epimeral plate 3 with sharp or blunt point at posterio-ventral corner, posterior border smooth, usually convex   **22. Pleustidae**

22. Accessory flagellum absent. Uropod 3 uniramous, rami uniarticulate, shorter than, or subequal to, peduncle. Mandible without a palp   **23**

    Characters not combining as above   **24**

23. Telson short, entire. Antenna 1 shorter than peduncle of antenna 2. Large body size (10 mm); on strandline   **10. Talitridae**

    Telson short, cleft into two lobes. Antenna 1 longer than peduncle of Antenna 2 **11. Hyalidae**

24. Accessory flagellum present or absent. Uropod 3 biramous, rami small or very small, always shorter than peduncle; outer ramus frequently armed distally with one or two large hooked spines, or slightly curved and with only small teeth on disto-lateral border. Coxa 4 not excavate posteriorly. Telson entire, fleshy, and short, length never much more than width   **25**

    Characters not combining as above   **26**

25. Antenna 1 with peduncle article 3 very short, less than half length of article 2. Uropod 3 with quadrate, blunt rami armed with large hooks **25. Ampithoidae**

Antenna 1 with peduncle article 3 more than half length of article 2. Uropod 3 with triangular rami armed with either one hooked spine or with small disto-lateral teeth **30. Ischyroceridae**

26. Telson short and fleshy, quadrate or nearly circular, entire, or with a weak notch. Coxa 4 not excavate posteriorly. Accessory flagellum present or absent **27**

Telson elongate, flat, entire, or cleft. Coxa 4 emarginate posteriorly, except when small **28**

27. Gnathopod 1 usually larger than 2, complex and markedly subchelate, or carpochelate in male. Antenna 1 with peduncle article 3 shorter than article 1 **26. Aoridae**

Gnathopod 1 equal to or smaller than 2. Antenna 1 with peduncle article 3 equal to or longer than article 1, or if article 3 shorter than 1, then uropod 3 uniramous **27. Isaeidae**

28. Telson with shallow apical notch, but not obviously cleft. Coxa 4 deeply excavate posteriorly. Accessory flagellum well-developed, with three or more articles. Uropod 3 biramous, short, not exceeding length of uropod 1 **21. Calliopiidae** (pt.)

Telson cleft for at least one-third of its length **29**

29. Antenna 1 as long as, or longer than, antenna 2, with peduncle article 3 very short. Accessory flagellum with two articles. Gnathopods characteristic: powerfully subchelate, propodus as broad as long, freely articulating with produced apex of carpus. Telson longer than uropod 3 peduncle, subtriangular, partially cleft **20. Eusiridae**

Gnathopods not as described above **30**

30. Antenna 1 shorter than antenna 2. Accessory flagellum well-developed, with three or more articles. Mandible without molar process; mandibular palp with articles 1 and 3 of similar length. Gnathopods large, powerfully subchelate. Telson medium or long, deeply cleft, with bifid apex on each lobe **19. Liljeborgiidae**

Antenna 1 as long as, or longer than, antenna 2; if markedly shorter, then accessory flagellum with no more than two articles. Mandible with normal three-articled palp and molar process. Gnathopods variable. Telson short or medium, deeply cleft **31**

31. Uropod 3 extremely elongate, peduncle extending beyond tips of uropods 1 and 2; rami subequal, often foliaceous. Gnathopods small, simple, of similar size. Antenna 1 shorter than peduncle of antenna 2. Head with small rostrum, eyes large **18. Melphidippidae**

Uropod 3 not as described. Gnathopods large, subchelate **32**

32. Urosome with small groups of dorsal spines. Head with small rostrum, eyes usually large and reniform. Gnathopods 1 and 2 of similar size. Coxae large, overlapping **12. Gammaridae**

Urosome spines sparse or lacking. Head without rostrum, eyes small and rounded. Gnathopod 2 much larger than 1. Coxae short, not overlapping **13. Melitidae**

1 LYSIANASSIDAE

Body compact and usually smooth dorsally. Antenna 1 short or very short, peduncle article 1 very stout, much larger than subsequent articles. Accessory flagellum usually present, consisting of three or more articles, occasionally vestigial or with fewer articles. Mouthparts variable, sometimes styliform. Mandible with three-articled palp. Gnathopods normally small; gnathopod 2 mitten-shaped terminally with article 3 (ischium) elongate, article 5 (carpus) bulbous and scaled posteriorly, article 6 (propodus) swollen and scaly, article 7 (dactylus) small or rudimentary. Coxae usually long, sometimes one or more of the anterior pairs reduced and partially hidden. Uropod 3 with lanceolate rami; outer ramus often biarticulate, sometimes longer than inner. Telson entire or cleft.

A very large family with many British representatives. The majority occur in relatively deep water and only the commoner inshore species are keyed out below.

1. Mouthparts protruding, styliform. Gnathopod 1 powerful but simple. Gnathopod 2 without dactylus. Uropod 3 very small   *Acidostoma obesum*

   Characters not combining as above   **2**

2. Telson entire, or with a small posterior notch   **3**

   Telson deeply or shallowly cleft   **6**

3. Antenna 1 and 2 very short, more or less equal in length. Gnathopod 1 powerful, simple. Uropod 3 very short, outer ramus biarticulate   *Nannonyx goesi*

   Antenna 1 and 2 longer. Gnathopod 1 small, slender, simple or weakly subchelate. Uropod 3 relatively long, outer ramus with one or two articles   **4**

4. Coxal plate 1 less than half length of 2. Uropod 3 outer ramus with two articles   *Perrierella audouiniana*

   Coxal plate 1 almost as long as 2. Uropod 3 outer ramus with one article   **5**

5. Epimeral plate 3 with single tooth on posterior border. Antenna 1, peduncle article 1 without a tooth   *Lysianassa plumosa*

   Epimeral plate 3 not toothed posteriorly. Antenna 1 peduncle with tooth on inside edge of article 1   *Lysianassa ceratina*

6. Epimeral plate 3 produced posterio-ventrally as a long sharp point   **7**

   Epimeral plate 3 may be acutely angled posterio-ventrally, but not produced into a point   **8**

7. Head small, partly hidden by coxal plate 1. Gnathopods slender, propodus much shorter than carpus. Uropod 2 inner ramus without median constriction   *Hippomedon denticulatus*

   Head distinct. Gnathopods slender, propodus and carpus of equal length. Uropod 2 inner ramus with median constriction   *Tryphosites longipes*

8. Telson shallowly cleft, for less than one-third of its length. Gnathopod 2 propodus long and slender   *Orchomene humilis*

   Telson cleft for at least half of its length   **9**

9. Gnathopod 1 simple; ischium triangular, produced anteriorly into a point. Antenna 1 and 2 short, subequal in both sexes   *Socarnes erythrophthalmus*

   Gnathopod 1 simple, ischium not produced anteriorly. Antenna 2 longer than antenna 1 in male   **10**

10. Gnathopod 1 propodus very elongate; dactylus rudimentary, hidden in dense tuft of setae *Scopelocheirus hopei*

    Gnathopod 1 propodus not very elongate, dactylus distinct   **11**

11. Body with strong dorsal ridge; urosome segment 1 with projecting process. Antenna 1 peduncle article 1 with strongly produced distal process   *Lepidepecreum longicorne*

    Characters not combined as above   **12**

12. Gnathopod 1 with elongate ischium   *Tmetonyx cicada*

    Gnathopod 1 ischium not elongate   **13**

13. Gnathopod 1 slender, coxa distinctly tapered distally   *Tryphosella sarsi*

    Gnathopod 1 relatively stout, coxa not tapered distally   *Orchomene nana*

Acidostoma obesum (Bate and Westwood)   FIG. 9.17

Body stout, up to 7 mm. Head partly hidden by large first coxae. Mouthparts styliform, forming a conical, ventrally pointing bundle. Antenna 1 very stout in male. Accessory flagellum as long as antenna 1 flagellum. Gnathopod 1 simple, fairly large, propodus slightly longer than carpus. Gnathopod 2 lacking dactylus. Pereopods short and fat. Uropod 2 peduncle swollen. Uropod 3 very short, outer ramus with only one article. Telson short, cleft.

Mainly sublittoral, on muddy sand, apparently associated with sea anemones. Recorded from Moray Firth, Clyde and Argyll, Galway Bay, only; also from a few localities in the North Sea, from Brittany, and from the Bay of Naples.

A. sarsi Lincoln was formerly confused with this species, and is distinguished from it by its elongate telson, cleft for about half its length.

Hippomedon denticulatus (Bate)   FIG. 9.17

Body compressed, up to 14 mm. Head small, partly hidden by large first coxae. Antenna 1 short, peduncle robust, with articles 1 and 2 produced anterio-dorsally, accessory flagellum very small, indistinct; antenna 2 much longer than 1. Gnathopod 1 slender, simple; gnathopod 2 subchelate. Uropod 2 shorter than 1 and 3; uropod 3 with subequal rami, outer ramus biarticulate. Epimeral plate 3 with long curved tooth posterio-ventrally. Telson deeply cleft.

Sublittoral, in shallow water, burrowing in sand. All coasts.

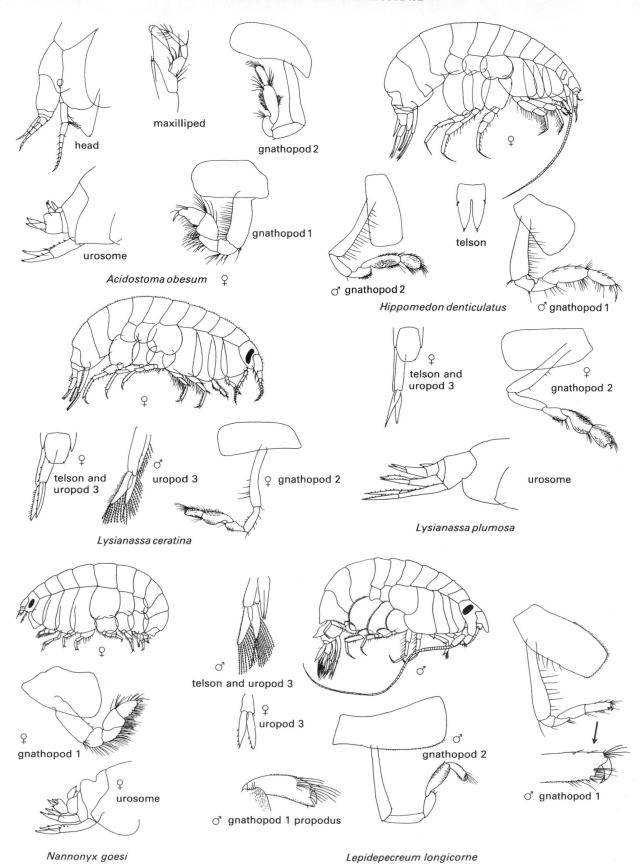

head

maxilliped

gnathopod 2

gnathopod 1

urosome

Acidostoma obesum ♀

♀

telson

♂ gnathopod 2

Hippomedon denticulatus

♂ gnathopod 1

♀

telson and uropod 3

♀ gnathopod 2

urosome

Lysianassa plumosa

♀

telson and uropod 3

♂ uropod 3

♀ gnathopod 2

Lysianassa ceratina

♀

gnathopod 1

♀ urosome

Nannonyx goesi

♂ telson and uropod 3

♀ uropod 3

♂ gnathopod 1 propodus

♂

gnathopod 2

♂ gnathopod 1

Lepidepecreum longicorne

Fig. 9.17

Lepidepecreum longicorne (Bate and Westwood)   FIG. 9.17
Body up to 8 mm long, white with orange patches; robust, strongly compressed, with a conspicuous dorsal keel. Head with small rostrum and strongly produced, downturned lateral lobes. Antenna 1 shorter than peduncle of antenna 2, peduncle article 1 produced and projecting anteriorly as an elongate rounded lobe. Antenna 2 in female with very short, four-articled flagellum; in male with slender flagellum as long as body. Gnathopod 1 slender, subchelate; propodus elongate with pair of large palmar spines. Gnathopod 2 as large as 1, slender, minutely chelate. Pereopods 5–7 robust, with basis and merus broadly expanded. Urosome segment 1 with pronounced keel; uropod 3 rami of similar length, with small spines in female, plumose setae in male. Telson very long and narrow, divided for three-quarters of length.

In shallow sublittoral. Reported sporadically from northern and western coasts, from Firth of Forth to Shetland, and southwards to the Channel Isles. Also on west coasts of Ireland.

Genus *Lysianassa*

Body compressed. Antenna 1 with peduncle article 2 relatively long. Coxae large. Gnathopod 1 simple, small; propodus and carpus nearly equal. Gnathopod 2 relatively long. Pereopods slender, each with large basis. Uropod 2 with outer ramus constricted or unconstricted. Outer ramus of uropod 3 uniarticulate. Telson entire.

Lysianassa ceratina (Walker)   FIG. 9.17
Body up to 10 mm; yellow with white flecks. Head with prominent lateral lobes; eyes large, oval to reniform. Antenna 1 with stout peduncle; article 1 with tooth on inner distal margin; flagellum of about nine articles, slightly shorter than peduncle. Antenna 2 in female as long as antenna 1, with flagellum of about ten articles; in male longer than body, with stout peduncle and very slender, filiform flagellum. Gnathopod 1 simple, propodus distally tapered with several short spines on inner posterior margin. Gnathopod 2 very slender, minutely subchelate. Coxal plates 1–4 elongate, forming a distinct shield. Epimeral plate 3 produced and broadly rounded distally. Uropod 1 elongate, with subequal rami; uropod 2 shorter than 1, with inner ramus distally constricted; uropod 3 with broad peduncle. Telson short and broad, distal margin straight.

Common among algae in shallow water. All coasts, locally abundant.

Lysianassa plumosa Boeck   FIG. 9.17
Body up to 12 mm; light yellow tinted with orange, or pink with yellow-brown patches. Head with prominent lateral lobes; eyes large, oval to reniform, purple or brown. Antenna 1 peduncle with broad article 1, lacking a tooth on inner distal margin; flagellum of about ten articles, as long as, or just shorter than, peduncle; accessory flagellum with three or four articles. Antenna 2 in female as long as antenna 1, with short flagellum of eight articles; in male longer than entire body, with slender, filiform flagellum. Gnathopod 1 simple, with distally tapered propodus bearing short spines on inner posterior margin. Gnathopod 2 very slender, minutely subchelate. Coxal plates 1–4 elongate, broad, forming a distinct shield; plate 1 produced anteriorly. Epimeral plate 3 with upturned tooth on posteriodistal margin. Uropod 1 elongate; uropod 2 with inner ramus distally constricted; uropod 3 with broad peduncle, and inner ramus slightly shorter than outer. Telson oval, with distal margin straight or slightly convex.

Sublittoral, to 800 m. Reported from Shetland southwards to Northumberland on the east coast, and to Scilly Isles on the west.

Nannonyx goesi (Boeck)   FIG. 9.17
Body short, metasome and urosome poorly developed. Up to 5 mm; yellowish, with orange bands. Mouthparts slightly conical. Antennae very short in female. Gnathopod 1 fairly large, simple; propodus and carpus short, stout, of equal length. Gnathopod 2 chelate; Coxae large. Epimeral plate 3 crenulate posteriorly. Uropod 3 very small, rami equal to or shorter than peduncle; external ramus biarticulate, longer than inner. Telson entire.

Sublittoral, amongst hydroids and in *Laminaria* holdfasts. South and west coasts.

N. spinimanus Walker, recorded from Anglesey and the Isle of Man, has a distinctly crenulate posterior margin to epimeral plate 3, and coarse spines on the posterior margin of gnathopod 1 propodus.

Genus *Orchomene*

First coxae not tapered distally. Antennae short and subequal in females, antenna 2 much longer than 1 in males. Gnathopod 1 subchelate, usually short and strong; ischium short but not triangular, carpus shorter than propodus, dactylus sometimes toothed on interior margin. Gnathopod 2 minutely chelate or subchelate. Uropod 3 with biarticulate outer ramus. Telson variable, entire or deeply cleft.

Orchomene humilis (Costa)   FIG. 9.18
Length 8 mm, whitish yellow speckled with red. Epimeral plate 3 quadrate, with crenulate posterior margin. Gnathopod 1 powerful, dactylus without a tooth on interior margin; gnathopod 2 with propodus long and slender. Uropod 3 more or less without spines in female, with plumose setae in male. Telson cleft for less than half its length, shallowly and widely in female, more narrowly and deeply in male.

Amongst sublittoral epibenthos and shells, sometimes in *Laminaria* holdfasts. All coasts.

Orchomene nana (Krøyer)   FIG. 9.18
Length 5 mm, greyish white. Epimeral plate 3 with smooth posterior margin and rounded posterio-ventral corner. Gnathopod 1 with dactylus toothed on interior margin; gnathopod 2 with propodus short, oval, and half length of carpus. Telson narrowly cleft nearly to its base.

Lower shore and sublittoral, on sandy and coarse grounds, in *Laminaria* holdfasts, or on dead crabs. All coasts.

Perrierella audouiniana (Bate) FIG. 9.18

Body up to 4 mm long; pale yellow, or white with red tints on pereon. Head with broad lateral lobes; eyes large and oval. Antenna 1 with enlarged peduncle article 1, four-articled flagellum, and small, two-articled accessory flagellum. Antenna 2 as long as 1, with robust peduncle, and tiny three-articled flagellum, shorter than peduncle article 5. Coxal plate 1 tiny, partly hidden by plate 2. Gnathopod 1 subchelate, but propodus oval with indistinct palm. Gnathopod 2 chelate, with elongate, slender propodus. Pereopods 3–7 short, stout, mostly devoid of spines and setae; propodus elongate, with distal tooth, dactylus large. Uropods 1 and 2 elongate, biramous; uropod 3 short, biramous. Telson short, truncate, with slightly concave distal margin.

Lower shores, amongst algae and sponges, to about 100 m. Western coasts, from Shetland to the Channel Isles, and west of Ireland.

Scopelocheirus hopei (Costa) FIG. 9.18

Body up to 10 mm long with orange markings. Head with lateral lobes produced anteriorly as blunt triangles. Antenna 1 short, scarcely longer than peduncle of antenna 2; peduncle article 1 stout, densely setose in male, articles 2 and 3 very short; flagellum of about ten articles, accessory flagellum of three articles. Antenna 2 longer in male than in female, with flagellum of about twenty-five articles. Coxal plates large. Gnathopod 1 slender, propodus as long as carpus, with minute dactylus hidden in dense tuft of setae. Gnathopod 2 slender, minutely chelate, with oval propodus. Pereopods 5–7 successively increasing in length; basis broadly expanded, all articles with stout spines. Uropod 3 elongate, with lanceolate rami, the outer ramus two-articled. Telson elongate, divided for three-quarters length, each lobe with one lateral and one apical spine.

Sublittoral, at least to edge of continental shelf, and sometimes deeper. Recorded off all British coasts.

Socarnes erythrophthalmus Robertson FIG. 9.18

Body up to 4 mm, translucent green, pink, or yellow-orange. Head with prominent, triangular, lateral lobes; eyes large, oval, bright red. Antenna 1 and 2 short in both sexes. Coxae large. Gnathopod 1 simple, carpus and propodus of equal length, ischium triangular with short anterior point; gnathopod 2 minutely subchelate, propodus half length of carpus. Pereopod 7 not longer than 6. Epimeral plate 3 rounded posteriorly. Uropod 3 outer ramus biarticulate. Telson deeply cleft.

Intertidal and shallow sublittoral, under stones or in sand. South and west coasts.

Tmetonyx cicada (Fabricius) FIG. 9.19

Body up to 25 mm; cream-coloured with reddish tints. Head with angular lateral lobes and elongate, irregular eyes. Antenna 1 shorter than 2, peduncle article 1 robust, articles 2 and 3 very short; flagellum with about sixteen articles, accessory flagellum with about seven articles. Antenna 2 longer in male than in female, with flagellum of about thirty articles. Coxal plates elongate, plate 1 narrower than rest, rectangular in outline.

Gnathopod 1 subchelate, ischium longer than merus, propodus and carpus of similar length, dactylus with tooth on inner margin. Gnathopod 2 weakly subchelate, propodus oval, shorter than carpus. Pereopods 3–4 with short and long spines on posterior edge of propodus. Pereopods 5–7 robust, basis broad with serrated posterior margin. Uropods 1–2 spiny; uropod 3 with inner ramus shorter than outer, both with numerous short setae. Telson deeply divided, each lobe with two lateral and one apical spine.

Offshore, from 50 to 3200 m, often in crab pots. A circumboreal species, reported on British coasts as far south as Yorkshire on the east, and the Channel Isles on the west. Also from Mayo, western Ireland.

Tryphosella sarsi Bonnier FIG. 9.18

Body up to 5 mm, white spotted with red. Coxa 1 distinctly tapered distally. Antennae short, subequal in female; antenna 2 longer than 1 in male. Gnathopod 1 slender, subchelate; ischium short but not triangular, carpus and propodus subequal, dactylus with tooth on inner margin. Gnathopod 2 minutely subchelate. Epimeral plate 3 quadrate, distal corner acutely rounded. Urosome segment 1 with weak dorsal hump in female, with deep depression and distinct rounded hump in male. Uropod 3 with outer ramus biarticulate. Telson triangular, deeply cleft, with one apical and two lateral spines on each lobe.

Sublittoral, all coasts.

Tryphosites longipes (Bate and Westwood) FIG. 9.19

Body up to 12 mm. Antenna 2 longer than 1 in male, 1 and 2 subequal in female. Coxae 1–4 large, elongate. Gnathopod 1 slender, subchelate, propodus shorter than carpus; gnathopod 2 slender, subchelate. Pereopods long, slender. Uropod 2 with inner ramus constricted medially, bearing a stout spine. Uropod 3 longer than 2, outer ramus biarticulate. Telson deeply cleft. Epimeral plate 3 with long curved point posterio-ventrally.

Sublittoral, on muddy sand. All coasts.

2 AMPELISCIDAE

Body laterally compressed. Accessory flagellum absent. Head elongate, without a rostrum. Two, four, or six eyes. Anterior coxae long. Pereon and pleon without dorsal teeth. Gnathopods simple, 2 longer and thinner than 1. Pereopod 7 shorter than, and structurally different from, 6. Urosome segments 2 and 3 coalesced. Uropod 3 biramous. Telson short or medium, deeply split. Builders of limp tubes on sandy and muddy sediments.

---

1. Pereopod 7 basis narrow posterio-distally; posterior border vertical, with setae on anterior border of posterio-ventral lobe up to its junction with ischium

   Haploops tubicola

   Peropod 7 basis considerably expanded posterio-distally; posterior border not vertical, no setae on anterior border on posterio-ventral lobe up to the junction with ischium

2

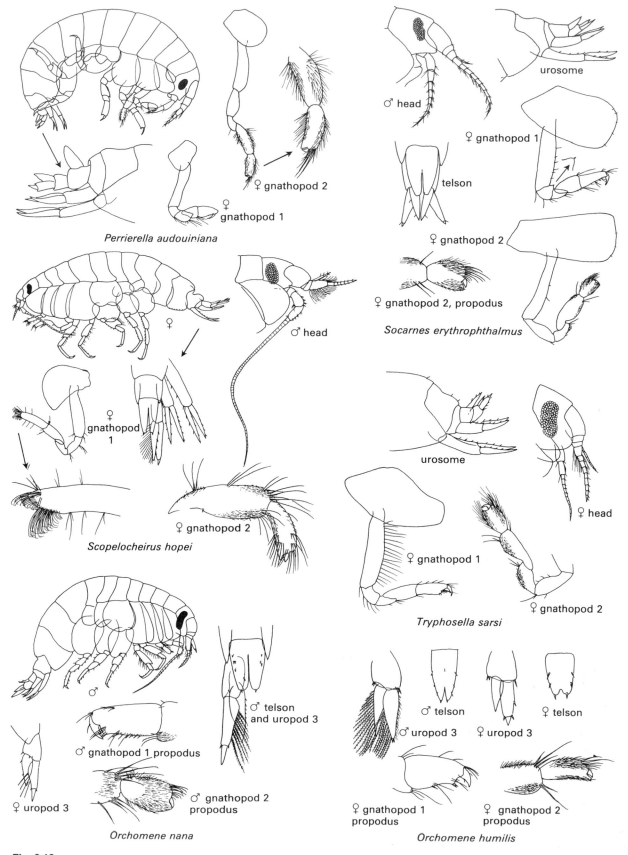

Perrierella audouiniana

♀ gnathopod 1

♀ gnathopod 2

♂ head

urosome

♀ gnathopod 1

telson

♀ gnathopod 2

♀ gnathopod 2, propodus

Socarnes erythrophthalmus

♂ head

♀ gnathopod 1

♀ gnathopod 2

Scopelocheirus hopei

urosome

♀ head

♀ gnathopod 1

♀ gnathopod 2

Tryphosella sarsi

♂ telson and uropod 3

♂ gnathopod 1 propodus

♀ uropod 3

♂ gnathopod 2 propodus

Orchomene nana

♂ telson

♀ telson

♂ uropod 3

♀ uropod 3

♀ gnathopod 1 propodus

♀ gnathopod 2 propodus

Orchomene humilis

Fig. 9.18

2. Epimeral plate 3 with long acute point at posterio-ventral corner. Pereopod 7 with ischium smaller or equal to merus. Merus produced posterio-ventrally **3**

 Epimeral plate 3 rounded or with very short point at posterio-ventral corner. Pereopod 7 with ischium larger than merus. Merus not produced posterio-ventrally **5**

3. Head with anterio-ventral margin nearly parallel with dorsal margin. Epimeral plate 3 with large median lobe posteriorly, as long as the sharply curved posterio-ventral tooth **Ampelisca brevicornis**

 Head with anterio-ventral margin oblique to dorsal margin. Epimeral plate 3 with small to moderate-sized median posterior lobe **4**

4. Urosome segment 1 with distinct dorsal projection (most prominent in males). Antenna 1 short: in female scarcely reaching beyond antenna 2 peduncle article 4, in male scarcely reaching distal half of antenna 2 peduncle article 5 **Ampelisca gibba**

 Urosome segment 1 with low dorsal keel, slightly angular terminally. Antenna 1 longer: in female reaching end of antenna 2 peduncle article 5, in male reaching considerably beyond antenna 2 peduncle **Ampelisca macrocephala**

5. Urosome segment 1 with very pronounced dorsal keel, acutely angled posteriorly. Telson with two rows of spines on dorsal surface. Antenna much shorter than (female), or slightly longer than (male), antenna 2 peduncle **Ampelisca typica**

 Urosome segment 1 with rounded dorsal keel. Telson with marginal spines but without dorsal spines. Antenna 1 never much shorter than antenna 2 peduncle **6**

6. Antenna 1 in both sexes considerably longer than antenna 2 peduncle. Antenna 1 peduncle article 2 more than three times length of article 3 **Ampelisca spinipes**

 Antenna 1 subequal to (female), or longer than (male), antenna 2 peduncle. Antenna 1 peduncle article 2 less than three times length of article 3 **7**

7. Anterior margin of head almost vertical; ventral margin oblique anteriorly, parallel to dorsal margin posteriorly. Coxa 4 as deep as broad, ventral margin oblique to anterior margin, posterior and anterior margins divergent. Female with antenna 1 equal to or shorter than antenna 2 peduncle **Ampelisca tenuicornis**

 Anterior margin of head oblique rather than vertical; ventral margin markedly oblique anteriorly, parallel to dorsal margin only in posterior third. Coxa 4 deeper than broad, ventral margin nearly transverse to anterior margin, posterior and anterior margins nearly parallel. Female with antenna 1 just longer than antenna 2 peduncle **Ampelisca diadema**

Genus *Ampelisca*

Two or three pairs of eyes. Mandibular palp article 3 variable in length. Pereopod 7 with posterior lobe of basis greatly expanded distally, posterior border oblique, anterior border of posterio-ventral lobe without setae near its junction with ischium; propodus not greatly expanded; dactylus lanceolate, not much less than half length of propodus.

Ampelisca brevicornis (Costa) FIG. 9.19

Length 12 mm, translucent white with scattered brown and/or yellow spots. Head with a concave ventral margin. Antenna 1 not reaching peduncle article 5 of antenna 2 in female; in male not extending beyond peduncle article 5 of antenna 2. Pereopod 7 with merus equal length to ischium; merus with long posterio-ventral lobe. Urosome segment 1 with small, rather rounded, dorsal keel. Epimeral plate 3 with long, curved acute point at posterio-ventral corner; posterior margin sinuous with median lobe as long as posterio-ventral point. Telson without spines on dorsal surface, but with marginal setae.

 Intertidal and sublittoral, on sandy mud. Common on all coasts.

Ampelisca diadema (Costa) FIG. 9.19

Length 10 mm, whitish with golden and yellow patches. Very similar to *A. tenuicornis*. Head with anterior margin oblique rather than vertical, ventral margin rather similar to *A. tenuicornis* but whole head not as deep as in that species. Antenna 1 similar to *A. tenuicornis* but longer than antenna 2 peduncle in both sexes. Coxa 4 much deeper than broad, ventral margin nearly transverse, shorter than posterior margin, anterior and posterior margins nearly parallel. Pereopod 7 similar to *A. tenuicornis*. Urosome segment 1 with deep dorsal depression followed by high rounded keel, in both sexes. Epimeral plate 3 with straight to convex posterior border and rounded posterio-ventral corner. Telson without dorsal spines but with four or five pairs of marginal setae towards tips of lobes.

 Sublittoral on fine silty and mixed sediments, often with *A. tenuicornis*. Northern and western coasts.

Ampelisca gibba Sars FIG. 9.19

Length 8 mm, translucent white with a few yellow speckles. Ventral margin of head parallel to dorsal margin posteriorly, becoming oblique anteriorly. Antenna 1 reaching end of peduncle article 4 of antenna 2 in female; in male reaching middle of peduncle article 5 of antenna 2. Pereopod 7 with ischium and merus of equal length; merus with long posterio-ventral lobe. Urosome segment 1 with high rounded keel, particularly prominent in male. Epimeral plate 3 with relatively short, curved, acute point at posterio-ventral corner; posterior margin sinuous but median posterior lobe shorter than posterio-ventral point. Telson without dorsal spines, but with marginal setae.

 Sublittoral, usually below 20 m, on mud and muddy sand. Recorded from Moray Firth, Channel Isles, and south and west Ireland.

Ampelisca macrocephala Liljeborg   FIG. 9.19

Length 14 mm, whitish with pink and yellow speckles. Head similar to *A. gibba*. Antenna 1 in female reaching end of antenna 2 peduncle; in male reaching considerably beyond antenna 2 peduncle. Pereopod 7 with ischium shorter than merus; merus with small posterio-ventral lobe. Urosome segment 1 with only a low dorsal keel, very slightly angular in male. Epimeral plate 3 with long, curved, acutely pointed tooth at posterio-ventral corner; posterior margin sinuous with a median lobe distinctly shorter than posterio-ventral tooth. Telson with four pairs of spines on dorsal surface and one pair of terminal setae.

On muddy sublittoral sands. A northern species which extends southwards into the Irish Sea and Celtic Sea (Fastnet), on the west, and to the Yorkshire coast on the east.

Ampelisca spinipes Boeck   FIG. 9.20

Length 15 mm, white to yellowish with faded orange patches and speckles. Ventral border of head oblique to dorsal margin for almost its whole length. Antenna 1 exceptionally long with peduncle article 2 three or more times length of article 3; in female antenna 1 considerably longer than antenna 2 peduncle, almost equal to half body length; antenna 1 in male longer than in female. Pereopod 7 similar to *A. typica*. Urosome segment 1 with deep dorsal depression followed by conspicuous rounded keel. Epimeral plate 3 with posterior border straight or convex, posterio-ventral corner quadrate, not produced. Telson without spines on dorsal surface, with only three pairs of terminal setae.

Sublittoral, on coarse sand and mixed bottoms. All coasts.

Ampelisca tenuicornis Liljeborg   FIG. 9.20

Length 8 mm, whitish, with carmine red patch on coxa 1, and yellow speckles. Anterior margin of head vertical distally, then oblique, ventral margin parallel to dorsal margin posteriorly, becoming oblique anteriorly. Antenna 1 with peduncle article 2 less than three times length of article 3; antenna 1 in female equal to or less than length of antenna 2 peduncle, in male distinctly longer than antenna 2 peduncle. Coxa 4 scarcely deeper than broad, lower margin oblique, longer than posterior margin, anterior and posterior margins divergent. Pereopod 7 with ischium about equal to combined length of merus and carpus. Urosome segment 1 in female with slight dorsal depression followed by low keel; in male depression distinct, keel high and rounded. Epimeral plate 3 with straight to convex posterior border; posterio-ventral corner quadrate, acute in female, rounded in male. Telson without spines on dorsal surface, with three pairs of marginal setae close to tips of lobes.

Sublittoral, on fine silty sediments. Often with *A. diadema*. All coasts.

Ampelisca typica (Bate)   FIG. 9.20

Length 10 mm, whitish with yellow and red patches. Head with posterio-ventral margin parallel to dorsal margin, anterio-ventral margin oblique to dorsal margin. Antenna 1 very short in female, reaching only middle of peduncle article 5 of antenna 2; in male reaching a little beyond peduncle article 5 of antenna 2. Pereopod 7 with ischium much larger than merus. Urosome segment 1

with conspicuous dorsal keel acutely angled posteriorly in both sexes. Epimeral plate 3 with posterior borders straight or slightly convex, posterio-ventral corners rounded and not produced. Telson with two rows of spines on dorsal surface, as well as marginal (not in male) and terminal state.

Sublittoral, on mixed and coarse bottoms. Recorded mostly on western coasts, from Shetland to the Bristol Channel.

Haploops tubicola Liljeborg   FIG. 9.20

Up to 10 mm, translucent pinkish white. Head with one pair of red eyes. Antenna 1 approximately half body-length. Mandibular palp article 3 as long as 2. Coxa 1 larger than 2 and 3. Pereopod 7 with posterior lobe of basis narrow, not expanded distally; posterior border of basis vertical, anterior border of posterio-ventral lobe bearing setae almost up to junction with ischium; propodus expanded and short, length less than twice width; dactylus spine-like, much less than half length of propodus.

Sublittoral, usually on clayey sediments. Northern coasts only; southwards to Northumberland on the east; and Isle of Man on the west.

3 ACANTHONOTOZOMATIDAE

Body short, stout, last pereon and all pleon segments produced posterio-dorsally into pointed paired teeth. Antennae short to medium length, subequal. Accessory flagellum rudimentary or missing. Head with well-developed rostrum. Mouthparts grouped into a ventrally pointing conical bundle; mandible with palps. Coxae 1–4 medium to large, convex anteriorly with single posterio-ventral point. Gnathopods small. Basis of pereopods 5–7 expanded, with one or two points on posterior border. Epimeral plate 3 with two large pointed teeth on posterior border. Uropod 3 rami longer than peduncle. Telson entire, slightly notched.

---

1. Pereopods 6 and 7 basis with proximal and medio-distal processes on posterior margin   ***Iphimedia spatula***

   Pereopods 6 and 7 without processes on posterior margin of basis, or with mediodistal process only   **2**

2. Epimeral plate 3 with two smooth, straight, equal-sized teeth on posterior border   ***Iphimedia obesa***

   Epimeral plate 3 with two crenulated, unequal teeth on posterior border, the mediodistal distinctly curved   **3**

3. Head with ventro-lateral margin deeply notched. Pleon segment 3 with dorso-posterior hump, and small, curved dorso-lateral teeth   ***Iphimedia perplexa***

   Head without ventro-lateral notch. Pleon segment 3 without hump, and with large, triangular dorso-lateral teeth   ***Iphimedia minuta***

Iphimedia minuta Sars   FIG. 9.20

Body up to 6 mm; colour variable, generally white with transverse yellow, orange or brown markings; eyes red. Pereon

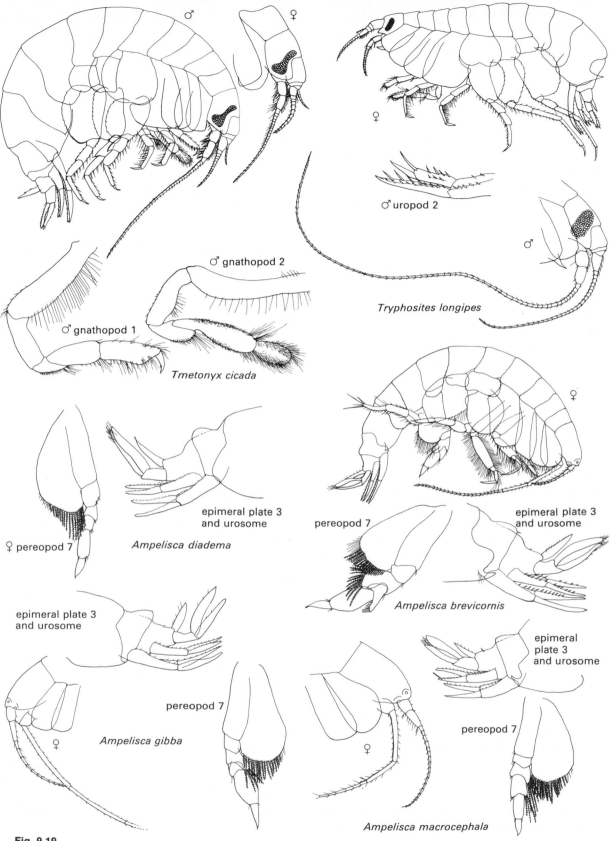

♂   ♀

♂ uropod 2

♂ gnathopod 2

♂ gnathopod 1

Tmetonyx cicada

♂

Tryphosites longipes

♀ pereopod 7

epimeral plate 3 and urosome

Ampelisca diadema

♀

pereopod 7

epimeral plate 3 and urosome

Ampelisca brevicornis

epimeral plate 3 and urosome

pereopod 7

Ampelisca gibba ♀

♀

epimeral plate 3 and urosome

pereopod 7

Ampelisca macrocephala

Fig. 9.19

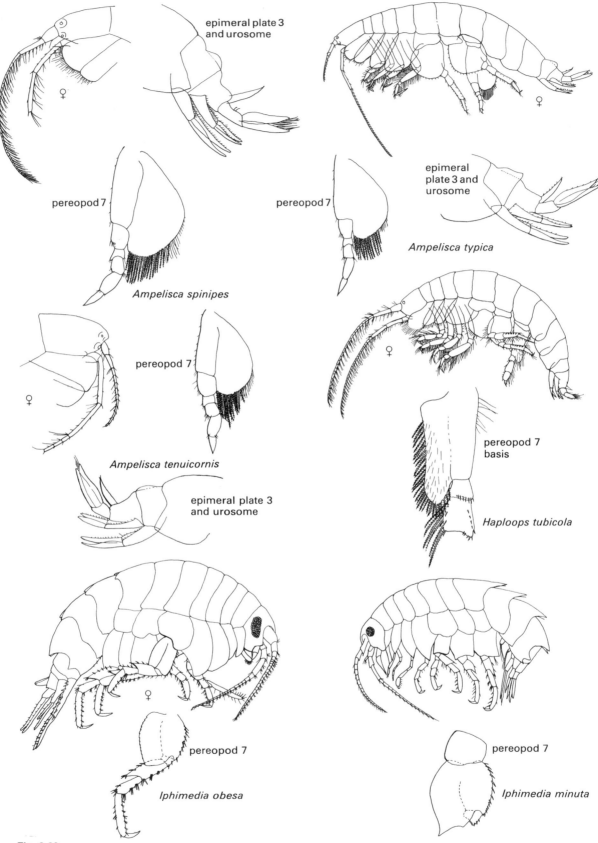

epimeral plate 3
and urosome

pereopod 7

Ampelisca spinipes

pereopod 7

epimeral
plate 3 and
urosome

Ampelisca typica

pereopod 7

Ampelisca tenuicornis

epimeral plate 3
and urosome

pereopod 7
basis

Haploops tubicola

pereopod 7

Iphimedia obesa

pereopod 7

Iphimedia minuta

Fig. 9.20

segment 7 and pleon segments 1–3 each with a pair of strong dorsal processes. Head with large curved rostrum. Antenna 1 about one-third body length, flagellum with about seventeen articles; antenna 2 slightly longer than 1. Gnathopods 1 and 2 both slender, feeble. Pereopods 5–7 with basis rounded proximally; pereopod 5 basis rounded distally; pereopod 6 basis with acute posterio-distal angle; pereopod 7 basis with produced, acute distal angle, and serrate posterior margin.

Lower shore and shallow sublittoral, amongst algae and hydroids. Common on all British coasts.

I. nexa Myers and McGrath, presently known from southern coasts of Ireland, and from Brittany, is similar to *I. minuta* and may prove to occur along the south-western coasts of Britain. It is distinguished from *I. minuta* principally by the strongly serrate margins to the basis of pereopods 6 and 7.

Iphimedia obesa Rathke FIG. 9.20

Body stout, up to 13 mm; colour variable, white or yellow with red or pink bands. Head with strong, curved rostrum. Maxilla 1 with well-developed biarticulate palp extending beyond external lobe. Pereon segment 7 and pleon segments 1–3 with paired dorsolateral teeth. Pereopods 5 and 6 basis with posterior margin evenly rounded, without teeth; pereopod 7 basis with triangular process or small tooth on posterio-distal margin. Epimeral plate 3 with two smooth, almost equal-sized teeth on posterior border, separated by wide gutter. Uropod 3 with inner ramus little longer than outer.

Shallow sublittoral, on hydroids and amongst algae. Common on all British coasts.

Iphimedia perplexa Myers and Costello FIG. 9.21

Body up to 6 mm. Head with strong, curved rostrum, and deep, ventrolateral notch between two acute processes. Pereon segment 3 and pleon segments 1–3 with small, paired dorsolateral teeth; pleon segment 3 with dorsal hump and dorsolateral teeth slightly curved. Epimeral plate 3 with wide gap between distal and mediodistal teeth, the latter distinctly curved. Pereopods 5–7 basis without proximal tooth; pereopod 7 basis with short posterio-distal tooth, and coarsely serrate posterior margin.

Described from southern and western coasts of Ireland, and from one locality in the Sound of Jura, west Scotland, in shallow sublittoral habitats.

Iphimedia spatula Myers and McGrath FIG. 9.21

Body up to 9 mm. Head with distinct but weakly curved rostrum, lateral lobes with two blunt processes. Pereon segment 7 and pleon segments 1–3 with well-developed, paired, dorsolateral teeth; pleon with distinct keel, developed as a distinct hump posteriorly on segment 3. Epimeral plate 3 with distal and mediodistal teeth, separated by narrow gap, the mediodistal tooth curved. Coxa 2 spatulate or truncate, coxa 3 quadrangular, coxa 7 with acute posterio-distal tooth. Pereopod 5 basis with proximal and mediodistal teeth, or with latter missing; pereopods 6–7 basis with proximal and mediodistal teeth; pereopod 7 basis with rounded distal lobe.

Sublittoral. Reported from Shetland, Galway Bay, Lundy, and the Brittany coast; perhaps more generally distributed along western coasts.

Iphimedia eblanae Bate, reported from Dublin Bay, Galway, the Atlantic coasts of France, and from Mediterranean localities, was previously confused with *I. spatula*. It is recognized by the pronounced medial teeth on pereon segment 7 and pleon segments 1–3, projecting between the dorsolateral teeth.

4 PHLIANTIDAE

Body dorsally depressed with at least the anterior coxae splayed. Antennae short, accessory flagellum absent. Mandible without a palp. Gnathopods simple, feeble. Uropod 1 normal, biramous; uropod 2 biramous in male, uniramous in female, uropod 3 very small, without rami, or absent. Telson short and entire.

Pereionotus testudo (Montagu) FIG. 9.21

Length 4 mm, yellowish green or orange with white patches, eyes red. Head flat. Pereon and pleon segments produced dorsally into humps.

Lower shore and shallow sublittoral, among coralline algae. Mediterranean; reaches northern limit in Channel Isles and western English Channel.

5 COLOMASTIGIDAE

Body almost cylindrical. Both pairs of antennae short with well-developed peduncles but tiny flagella (two or three articles only). Accessory flagellum absent. Mandible without a palp. Coxae short but overlapping, each with anterior border produced into blunt lobe. Gnathopod 1 simple, gnathopod 2 subchelate, considerably enlarged in male. Urosome segments 2 and 3 coalesced. Uropod 3 biramous. Telson entire, short to medium in length.

Colomastix pusilla Grube FIG. 9.21

Body depressed, up to 5 mm, yellowish, red, or brown, eyes red. Head large, broad, antenna 1 and 2 short, very robust, consisting largely of stout peduncle with minute flagellum. Gnathopod 1 short, slender; dactylus minute, hidden by setae on propodus. Gnathopod 2 in female with carpus and propodus almost equal in length; gnathopod 2 in male with massively enlarged propodus, dactylus short, robust.

Lower shore and sublittoral; associated with sponges, such as *Suberites*, *Halichondria*. Western and south-western coasts, and Shetland Isles.

6 AMPHILOCHIDAE

Body usually short and fat. Antennae medium to short, subequal. Accessory flagellum absent, rarely rudimentary. Rostrum conspicuous. Coxa 1 very small, partially hidden; coxa 2 sometimes small, usually large; coxae 3 and 4 large or immense, 4 excavate posteriorly. Mandible usually with palp of three articles. Gnathopods small or medium-sized, subchelate or nearly simple. Pereopods slender. Uropod 3 biramous, with elongate peduncle, longer than uropod 2. Telson entire, unarmed; usually long, triangular, sometimes immense.

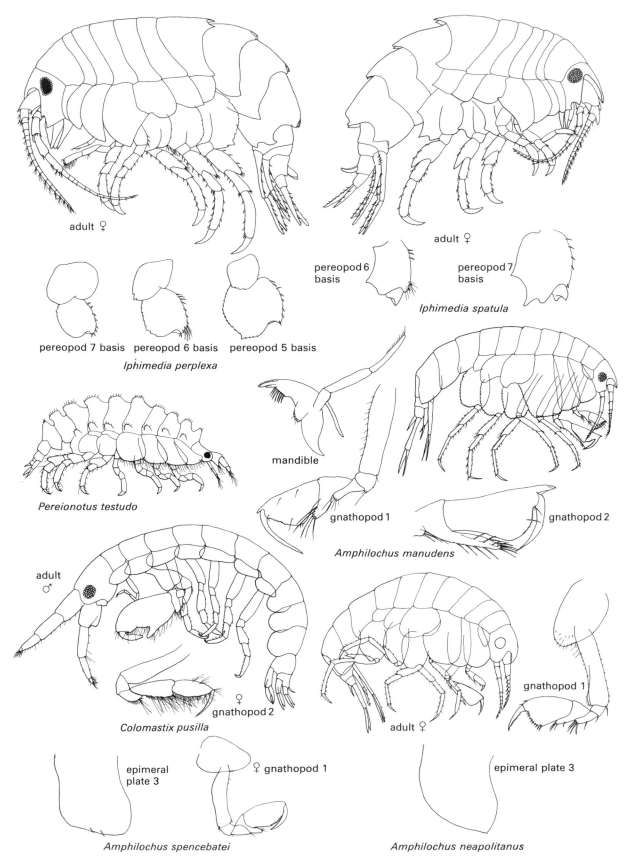

adult ♀

pereopod 6
basis

pereopod 7
basis

Iphimedia spatula

pereopod 7 basis   pereopod 6 basis   pereopod 5 basis

Iphimedia perplexa

Pereionotus testudo

mandible

gnathopod 1

gnathopod 2

Amphilochus manudens

adult
♂

gnathopod 2

Colomastix pusilla

adult ♀

gnathopod 1

♀ gnathopod 1

epimeral
plate 3

Amphilochus spencebatei

epimeral plate 3

Amphilochus neapolitanus

Fig. 9.21

1. Coxae 3 and 4 very large, with contiguous borders, completely hiding coxae 1 and 2. Telson greatly enlarged, fin-like **Peltocoxa damnoniensis**

   Coxae 3 and 4 moderately enlarged, overlapping, not hiding coxae 1 and 2 **2**

2. Gnathopods 1 and 2 small, simple or feebly subchelate. Mandible with prominent ridged molar **Gitana sarsi**

   Gnathopod 2 large, subchelate. Mandible with smaller rudimentary molar **3**

3. Telson minutely tridentate apically, longer than uropod 3 peduncle **Paramphilochoides odontonyx**

   Telson not tridentate apically, much shorter than elongate peduncle of uropod 3 **4**

4. Gnathopods 1 and 2 with propodus produced anterio-distally into a sharp tooth **Amphilochus manudens**

   Gnathopod 1 and 2 propodus not produced anterio-distally **5**

5. Antenna 1 much shorter than 2. Epimeral plate 3 rounded posterio-ventrally **Amphilochus spencebatei**

   Antenna 1 nearly as long as 2. Epimeral plate 3 slightly produced posterio-ventrally as a blunt tooth **Amphilochus neapolitanus**

Genus *Amphilochus*

Coxal plate 1 small, partly hidden by plate 2; plates 2–4 large, overlapping. Antenna 1 and 2 short. Gnathopods subchelate; gnathopod 2 larger than 1. Uropod 3 peduncle longer than rami. Telson usually fairly short, not tridentate apically, always shorter than uropod 3 peduncle.

Amphilochus manudens Bate FIG. 9.21

Length 5 mm, reddish brown with dark markings. Rostrum short. Coxae 2–4 with denticulate margins. Epimeral plate 3 produced posterio-ventrally as small sharp tooth. Telson three times as long as wide, terminating in sharp point.

Sublittoral on silty grounds and amongst hydroids. All coasts.

Amphilochus neapolitanus Della Valle FIG. 9.21

Length 4 mm, orange to yellow, greenish brown, or yellow-green marked with red and brown. Rostrum short and curved. Coxae slightly crenulate distally. Telson short, rather oval.

Lower shore and sublittoral. Southern coasts, Anglesey and Liverpool Bay. Rare.

Amphilochus spencebatei (Stebbing) FIG. 9.21

Length 3 mm, yellowish brown, sometimes with orange spots. Rostrum nearly straight, longer than peduncle article 1 of antenna 1. Coxae crenulate distally. Telson twice as long as wide.

Sublittoral on shelly hard ground. Reported from the Wash, English Channel, Irish Sea.

Gitana sarsi Boeck FIG. 9.22

Length 3 mm, white with broad brownish bands. Head with short, curved rostrum, broad at base. Mandible with conspicuous ridged and toothed molar process. Coxa 1 small, partly hidden; coxae 2–4 larger, elongate, overlapping; coxa 2 with distal crenulation. Gnathopods small, subequal, simple. Pereopods and uropods slender. Telson lanceolate, minutely tridentate apically, about two-thirds length of uropod 3 peduncle.

Intertidal and sublittoral, amongst algae, in *Laminaria* holdfasts, and amongst epibenthos. All coasts.

Paramphilochoides odontonyx (Boeck) FIG. 9.22

Length 4 mm. Head with large rostrum. Antenna 1 and 2 with long peduncle, short flagellum; accessory flagellum absent. Mandible with small, unridged molar. Gnathopods subchelate; carpus with pronounced anterior lobe, propodus approximately oval, dactylus long and curved, Gnathopod 2 larger than 1, dactylus with tooth on inner margin. Telson elongate, apically tridentate, slightly longer than uropod 3 peduncle.

Sublittoral, on muddy sand. All coasts.

P. intermedius (Scott) was formerly confused with this species. It differs in having a smooth, untoothed palm to gnathopod 2, and a small tooth on the distal angle of epimeral plate 3. It is probably quite widespread in British waters, although it was previously known only from the Firth of Forth.

Peltocoxa damnoniensis (Stebbing) FIG. 9.22

Body short, stout. Up to 3 mm, red to purple. Coxae 1 and 2 very small, hidden; coxae 3 and 4 grossly enlarged, with borders contiguous and abutting. Antennae very short, robust; antenna 1 peduncle stout; flagellum scarcely longer than peduncle article 1, with ventral fringe of long setae; accessory flagellum rudimentary, minute, uniarticulate. Gnathopods 1 and 2 dactylus with serrate margin. Telson very large, prominent, fin-like.

Lower shore and sublittoral, among algae on rocky shores. Southern and western coasts.

P. brevirostris (Scott), reported from the Irish Sea and the Bay of Biscay, differs from the above in lacking an accessory flagellum, and in the dactylus of gnathopods 1 and 2, which has three teeth instead of a serrated margin. The rostrum of *P. brevirostris* extends to the distal end of peduncle article 1.

7 LEUCOTHOIDAE

Body slender, slightly cylindrical. Antenna 1 as long as or longer than 2; both with long peduncle and relatively short flagellum. Accessory flagellum uniarticulate, very small. Mandible with palp, without molar process. Coxae large; coxa 1 not concealed. Gnathopods large. Gnathopod 1 distinctively carpochelate; gnathopod 2 powerfully subchelate, slightly smaller than 1. Gnathopod 2 propodus larger and more distinctly toothed in male than female. Uropod 2 shorter than 1 and 3. Uropod 3 biramous, with styliform rami shorter than peduncle. Telson entire, triangular.

1. Adult gnathopod 1 dactylus more than one-third length of propodus. Epimeral plate 3 with quadrate posterio-ventral corner, lacking a distinct tooth. Male gnathopod 2 propodus with crenulate margin to palm
Leucothoe spinicarpa

Adult gnathopod 1 dactylus less than one-third length of propodus. Epimeral plate 3 with well-marked tooth on posterio-ventral corner   **2**

2. Telson less than half as long as broad. Gnathopod 1 carpus with small, irregularly spaced teeth on anterior margin. Coxa 4 with angular anterior margin, often developing distinct anterio-ventral tooth
Leucothoe lilljeborgi

Telson twice as long as broad. Gnathopod 1 carpus with large, regularly spaced teeth. Coxa 4 rounded anteriorly, without tooth   *Leucothoe incisa*

Leucothoe spinicarpa (Abildgaard)   FIG. 9.22

Length 12 mm; pinkish, greenish, or white, translucent or opaque, eyes red. Coxa 4 without an anterio-ventral tooth. Dactylus of adult gnathopod 1 one-third to one-half length of propodus. Gnathopod 2 with small blunt teeth on palm of propodus and a projection above articulation with dactylus, no bifid distal tip on carpus. Epimeral plate 3 almost rectangular, without distinct tooth posterio-ventrally. Telson more than twice as long as broad.

Littoral and sublittoral, amongst algae and frequently in ascidians and sponges. All coasts.

Leucothoe lilljeborgi Boeck   FIG. 9.22

Length 5 mm; yellowish white, with pink or orange spots, translucent, eyes brownish. Coxa 4 with anterio-ventral corner lengthened into acute point. Dactylus of adult gnathopod 1 one-quarter length of propodus. Gnathopod 2 with propodus relatively slender, lacking teeth on palm, without a projection above articulation with dactylus; carpus with distal tip only indistinctly bifid, always armed with strong spine. Epimeral plate 3 with posterior margin deeply excavate ventrally and large curved tooth at posterio-ventral corner. Telson short, little longer than wide.

On sublittoral mud and sand. All coasts.

Leucothoe incisa Robertson   FIG. 9.22

Length 7 mm, greenish or yellowish white, eyes intense brick-red. Coxa 4 rounded anterio-ventrally. Dactylus of adult gnathopod 1 one-quarter to one-fifth length of propodus. Gnathopod 2 propodus with projection above articulation with dactylus; carpus with bifid distal tip, bearing a small spine. Epimeral plate 3 with deeply excavate posterior margin and large curved tooth at posterio-ventral corner. Telson more than twice as long as wide.

Lower shore and sublittoral, amongst rocks and sand. All coasts.

8 STENOTHOIDAE

Body short, fat, or compressed, usually smooth dorsally. Head with inconspicuous rostrum. Antennae subequal; accessory flagellum absent or vestigial. Coxa 1 very small, largely hidden; coxae 2–4 very large, plate-like; coxa 4 not posteriorly excavate. Gnathopods usually powerful, subchelate; gnathopod 1 rarely simple. Pereopod 5 basis slender. Urosome segment 1 not toothed dorsally. Uropod 3 uniramous, rami biarticulate. Telson entire, medium length, separate from last urosome segment.

---

1. Mandible without a palp   **2**

Mandible with a palp, either minute, uniarticulate, or moderately well-developed, with two or three articles   **5**

2. Antenna 1 peduncle with articles 1 and 2 produced anterio-dorsally. Coxa 2 triangular. Pereopod 7 merus markedly expanded posteriorly and posterio-distally   *Parametopa kervillei*

Antenna 1 peduncle articles 1 and 2 not produced anterio-dorsally. Coxa 2 quadrangular. Pereopod 7 merus expanded only posterio-distally   **3**

3. Uropod 3 peduncle much shorter than rami. Gnatho-pod 2 propodus quadrangular   *Stenothoe monoculoides*

Uropod 3 peduncle nearly equal to rami   **4**

4. Gnathopod 2 propodus elongate, with oblique, irregularly toothed palm   *Stenothoe marina*

Gnathopod 2 propodus elongate, slender, palm smooth along most of length, largely covered with short setae   *Stenothoe valida*

5. Mandible with tiny uniarticulate palp. Coxa 4 exceptionally large, extending posteriorly as far as coxa 7. Telson elongate oval, unarmed   *Stenula rubrovittata*

Mandible with small but distinct two- or three-articled palp   **6**

6. Gnathopod 2 propodus broad, with large palmar process and deeply indented palm   *Metopa alderi*

Gnathopod 2 propodus with small palmar process or spine, palm only lightly indented   **7**

7. Gnathopod 2 propodus with distinctly crenulate palm. Epimeral plate 3 with small tooth at posterio-ventral corner   *Metopa borealis*

Gnathopod 2 propodus with only minutely crenulate palm. Epimeral plate 3 with nearly square posterio-ventral corner   *Metopa pusilla*

Genus *Metopa*

Antennae short to medium. Accessory flagellum absent. Mandible with two- or three-articled palp but without a molar process. Coxae 2–4 large, forming a shield. Gnathopod 1 subchelate or simple, usually slender. Gnathopod 2 powerful, sub-

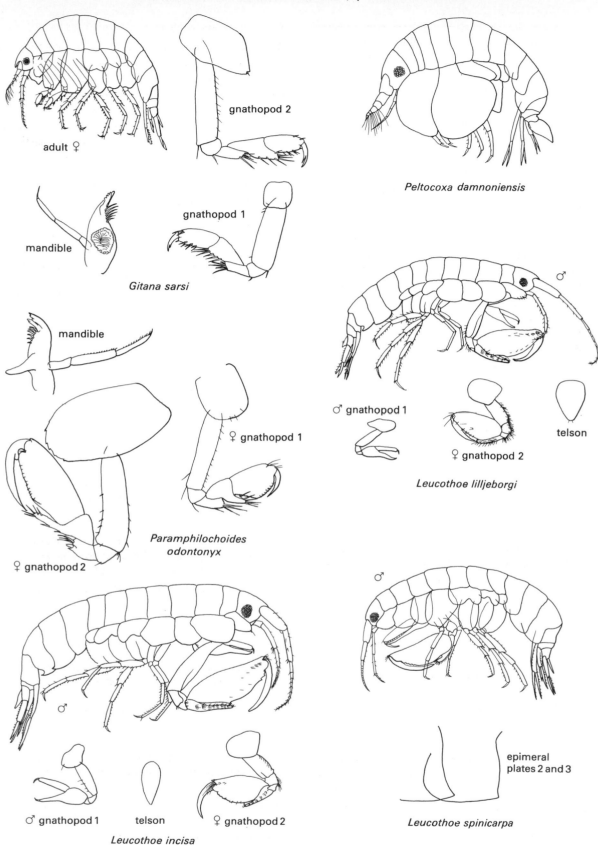

adult ♀

gnathopod 2

mandible

gnathopod 1

Gitana sarsi

Peltocoxa damnoniensis

mandible

♀ gnathopod 1

♂

♂ gnathopod 1

telson

♀ gnathopod 2

Leucothoe lilljeborgi

♀ gnathopod 2

Paramphilochoides odontonyx

♂

♂ gnathopod 1   telson   ♀ gnathopod 2

Leucothoe incisa

epimeral plates 2 and 3

Leucothoe spinicarpa

Fig. 9.22

chelate, much larger than 1. Pereopod 5 basis not expanded, pereopods 6 and 7 with basis expanded. Telson oval.

Metopa alderi (Bate)   FIG. 9.23

Length 7 mm, white with red patches or bands. Antenna 1 much shorter than 2. Gnathopod 2 large and powerful, especially in male; propodus broad, female palm delimited by a small to moderately large tooth and with a small sinus, in male palmar tooth and sinus much larger. Epimeral plate 3 nearly square at posterio-ventral corner. Telson oval and unarmed.

A northern sublittoral species occasionally reaching as far south as the English Channel and south-west Ireland.

Metopa norvegica (Liljeborg) is similar to this species. It is distinguished by its elongate, almost rectangular, gnathopod 2 propodus, and by the presence of dorsal spines on the telson; further, antenna 1 is longer than 2. *M. norvegica* has a similar distribution to *M. alderi* and may be locally abundant.

Metopa borealis Sars   FIG. 9.23

Length 5 mm. Antennae subequal, about one-third body length. Gnathopod 2 moderately powerful in male, smaller in female; propodus somewhat rectangular with oblique, distinctly crenulate palm delimited by a small tooth. Epimeral plate 3 with small tooth at posterio-ventral corner. Telson oval and unarmed.

A sublittoral species, commoner in the north but recorded as far south as the Channel Islands.

Metopa pusilla Sars   FIG. 9.23

Length 3 mm, greenish white with brown patches. Antennae more or less equal, about one-half of body-length. Gnathopod 2 moderately powerful in male, smaller in female; propodus broad distally with oblique, almost straight, slightly crenulate palm delimited by small tooth. Epimeral plate 3 slightly acutely angled posterio-ventrally. Telson oval with two or three pairs of spines dorso-laterally.

Among algae and hydroids in the shallow sublittoral. Probably all coasts.

Parametopa kervillei Chevreux   FIG. 9.23

Length 5 mm. Antennae short and subequal; antenna 1 with peduncle articles 1 and 2 slightly produced anterio-dorsally. Accessory flagellum absent. Mandible without palp or molar process. Maxilla 1 with uniarticulate palp. Coxa 2 large, triangular. Gnathopod 2 larger than 1; male with gnathopod 1 simple, 2 subchelate; both gnathopods subchelate in female. Pereopods 6 and 7 with basis and merus expanded posteriorly and posterio-distally. Epimeral plate 3 considerably extended posterio-ventrally, with rounded acute corner.

Shallow sublittoral, frequently in *Saccorhiza* holdfasts. South-western coasts.

Genus Stenothoe

Antennae usually subequal, short to medium length. Accessory flagellum absent. Mandible without molar process or palp. Maxilla 1 with distinct biarticulate palp. Gnathopods subchelate; gnathopod 1 smaller than 2. Pereopods 6 and 7 with

basis and merus somewhat expanded posteriorly and posterio-distally.

Stenothoe marina (Bate)   FIG. 9.23

Length 6 mm, whitish marked with yellow or pink. Antenna 1 about half body-length, equal to or little longer than 2. Coxa 2 not triangular. Gnathopod 1 and 2 merus with pronounced lobe; gnathopod 1 propodus oval with oblique, minutely denticulate palm delimited by two or three spines; male gnathopod 2 propodus elongately oval, palm crenulate, with numerous setae; female gnathopod 2 propodus less elongate with fewer setae. Pereopod 7 merus moderately expanded, extending posterio-distally as far as middle of carpus. Epimeral plate 3 produced posteriorly, posterio-ventral corner narrowly rounded. Uropod 3 peduncle about equal to length of rami. Telson oval with two or three pairs of spines dorso-laterally. Sublittoral among algae and hydroids. All coasts.

Stenothoe monoculoides (Montagu)   FIG. 9.23

Length 3 mm, whitish marked with red. Antennae short, subequal. Gnathopod 1 and 2 propodus rectangular, with palm slightly oblique, convex, smooth, delimited by small group of spines. Coxa 2 not triangular. Pereopod 7 merus only slightly expanded. Epimeral plate 3 produced posteriorly, acutely rounded posterio-ventrally. Uropod 3 peduncle only half length of rami. Telson oval and unarmed.

Intertidal and sublittoral, amongst algae and hydroids. Locally common. All coasts.

Stenothoe valida Dana   FIG. 9.23

Length 8 mm. Antenna 1 about half body-length, slightly shorter than 2. Coxa 2 somewhat triangular. Male gnathopod 2 propodus elongate, slender; palm straight, setose, smooth proximally, distally with a large curved tooth and small sinus. Female gnathopod 2 propodus with few setae on palm margin, delimited by small spine. Pereopod 7 merus considerably expanded, extending posterio-distally almost to end of carpus. Epimeral plate 3 produced posteriorly, narrowly rounded at posterio-ventral corner. Uropod 3 peduncle about equal to length of rami. Telson slightly angled at apex, armed with three or four pairs of spines dorso-laterally.

Shallow sublittoral, amongst hydroids. A warm water species recorded from southern coasts.

Stenula rubrovittata (Sars)   FIG. 9.23

Length 5 mm, whitish banded with red. Antennae short and stout. Accessory flagellum absent. Mandible with tiny uniarticulate palp, lacking a molar process. Coxa 4 exceptionally large. Gnathopod 1 weak, feebly subchelate. Gnathopod 2 much larger, subchelate. Pereopods 6 and 7 with basis expanded. Epimeral plate 3 produced posterio-ventrally, with rounded acute corner. Telson oval, unarmed.

Typically associated with hermit crabs (*Pagurus bernhardus*), also amongst sublittoral algae and hydroids. All coasts.

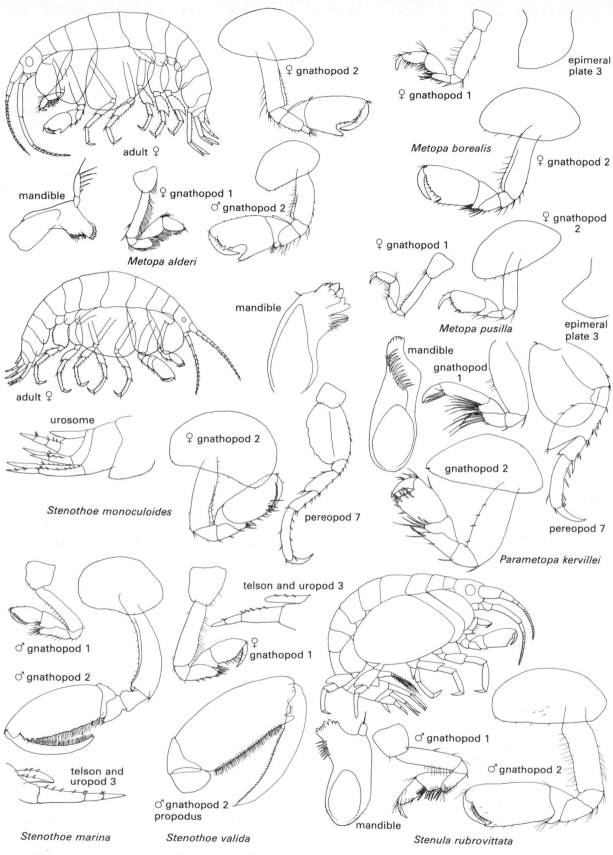

adult ♀

mandible

♀ gnathopod 1

♂ gnathopod 2

Metopa alderi

♀ gnathopod 2

♀ gnathopod 1

epimeral plate 3

Metopa borealis

♀ gnathopod 2

♀ gnathopod 1

mandible

Metopa pusilla

♀ gnathopod 2

epimeral plate 3

adult ♀

urosome

♀ gnathopod 2

mandible

Stenothoe monoculoides

pereopod 7

mandible

gnathopod 1

gnathopod 2

pereopod 7

Parametopa kervillei

♂ gnathopod 1

♂ gnathopod 2

telson and uropod 3

telson and uropod 3

♀ gnathopod 1

Stenothoe marina

♂ gnathopod 2 propodus

Stenothoe valida

mandible

♂ gnathopod 1

♂ gnathopod 2

Stenula rubrovittata

Fig. 9.23

9 CRESSIDAE

Body short and rather fat. Head with inconspicuous rostrum. Antenna 1 longer and stouter than 2. Accessory flagellum absent. Mandible with palp. Some pereon and pleon segments often with small dorsal teeth. Coxa 1 rudimentary, concealed. Coxa 4 large, posteriorly excavate. Gnathopod 1 small, simple; gnathopod 2 small, subchelate. Pereopod 5 basis expanded. Uropod 3 uniramous, rami biarticulate. Telson medium length, entire, fused to last pleon segment.

Cressa dubia (Bate)   FIG. 9.24

Length 3 mm, brown with paler markings. Head twice length of pereon segment 1; lateral lobes pointed, with single teeth on upper and lower margins. Coxae 2 and 3 with three to five teeth at posterio-ventral corners. Telson triangular, pointed, with one pair of marginal teeth.

Littoral and sublittoral, among hydroids and algae. All coasts.

10 TALITRIDAE

Body laterally compressed, smooth dorsally. Antenna 1 shorter than antenna 2 peduncle. Accessory flagellum absent. Mandible without a palp. Coxae medium-sized. Gnathopods variable; gnathopod 2 often large in male. Urosome segments not coalesced. Uropods short, relatively powerful; uropod 3 very short, uniramous, ramus shorter than, or subequal to, peduncle. Telson, short, entire.

Genus *Orchestia*

Antenna 1 shorter than antenna 2 peduncle. Antenna 2 without teeth on flagellum articles, peduncle article 5 a little longer than 4, with five to seven groups of spines dorsally. Coxa 1 broadly triangular. Gnathopod 1 small, subchelate; gnathopod 2 small, mitten-shaped in female, subchelate, large in male. Female gnathopod 2 basis lacking, or with few, spines on posterior border. Telson entire.

There are two common British marine species, but they show few morphological differences and females are especially difficult to distinguish.

Orchestia gammarella (Pallas)   FIG. 9.24

Length 18 mm; colour variable, red-brown to brown-green, marked with red stripes. Eyes round. Antenna 1 almost reaching distal end of peduncle article 4 of antenna 2. Male gnathopod 2 large, with palm of propodus convexly curved, delimited by a spine and not longer than ventral margin. Pereopod 7 merus and carpus expanded in older adult females. Pleopods with rami only half length of peduncles. Uropod 3 rami with two dorsal spines.

At and above strandline on open coasts and in estuaries, on shingle and rocky shores, in crevices, beneath algae and strand-line debris; also common in salt-marshes. All coasts.

Orchestia remyi roffensis Wildish and *O. cavimana* Heller are semi-terrestrial species, associated with fresh or brackish water. The former is known only from the type locality in the Medway estuary; the latter is a Mediterranean species reported from the upper Thames valley, and from isolated riverine localities in Norfolk, Yorkshire, and Cheshire. Both species are described by Lincoln (1979).

Orchestia mediterranea Da Costa   FIG. 9.24

Length 17 mm, colour variable but usually brownish-green, similar to *O. gammarella*. Rami of pleopods as long as or longer than peduncles, total length of each pleopod considerably greater than in *O. gammarella*. Male gnathopod 2 with propodus palm margin sinuous, oblique and longer than ventral margin. Telson without a posterior notch.

At and below the strandline, mainly on shingly and rocky shores, often in crevices. Often with *O. gammarella*, but less common in estuaries and salt-marshes. Probably on all coasts except perhaps the far north.

Talitrus saltator (Montagu)   FIG. 9.24

Length 20 mm, brown-grey. Antenna 1 just reaching distal end of peduncle article 4 of antenna 2. Flagellum of antenna 2 with teeth on some articles. Coxa 1 broadly rectangular. Gnathopod 1 spiny, simple; gnathopod 2 mitten-shaped. Uropod 3 with several stout spines on peduncle, rami with four dorsal spines, and one terminal spine equal to length of ramus.

On sandy shores, at strandline, beneath algae or other debris. All coasts.

1.	Antenna 2 with some flagellum articles produced into small teeth at the joints	**3**
	Antenna 2 with flagellum articles smoothly jointed	**2**
2.	Ramus of pleopods about half length of peduncle. Male gnathopod 2 with palm of propodus convexly curved, not longer than ventral margin, delimited by spine. Telson with very small posterior notch	***Orchestia gammarella***
	Ramus of pleopods as long as, or longer than, peduncle. Male gnathopod 2, with sinuous palm margin to propodus, oblique to and longer than ventral margin. Telson without posterior notch	***Orchestia mediterranea***
3.	Uropod 3 rami each with terminal spine, as long as ramus. Male with gnathopod 1 simple, gnathopod 2 small, mitten-shaped	***Talitrus saltator***
	Uropod 3 rami each terminated by a few short spines. Male gnathopod 2 large, subchelate	**4**
4.	Male gnathopod 2 propodus produced anterio-ventrally into a large hook. Female gnathopod 2 merus without a tooth. Uropod 3 rami shorter than peduncle. Telson longer than wide, with slight notch posteriorly	***Talorchestia deshayesii***
	Male gnathopod 2 propodus without hook. Gnathopod 2 merus with a short tooth in both sexes. Uropod 3 rami almost as long as peduncle. Telson as long as wide, without posterior notch	***Talorchestia brito***

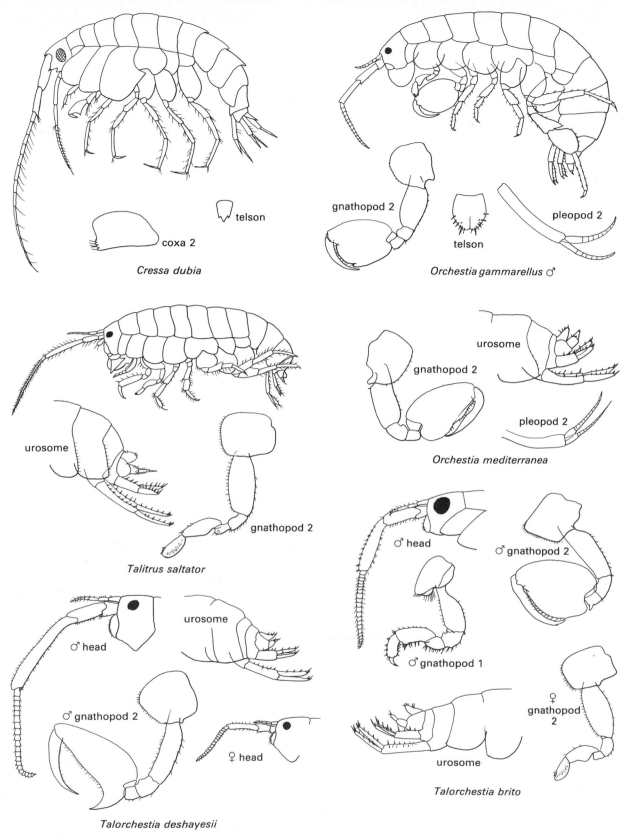

telson

coxa 2

Cressa dubia

gnathopod 2

telson

pleopod 2

Orchestia gammarellus ♂

urosome

gnathopod 2

Talitrus saltator

gnathopod 2

urosome

gnathopod 2

pleopod 2

Orchestia mediterranea

♂ head

♂ gnathopod 2

♂ gnathopod 1

♂ head

urosome

♂ gnathopod 2

♀ head

Talorchestia deshayesii

urosome

♀ gnathopod 2

Talorchestia brito

Fig. 9.24

Genus *Talorchestia*

Antenna 1 shorter than antenna 2 peduncle. Flagella articles of antenna 2 produced as teeth, peduncle article 5 longer than 4 and very spinous. Gnathopod 1 small, simple or poorly subchelate. Gnathopod 2 large and subchelate in male, small and mitten-shaped in female; basis of female gnathopod 2 with several spines on both anterior and posterior margins. Uropod 3 rami without dorsal spines, terminated by a few short spines. Telson entire.

Talorchestia brito Stebbing   FIG. 9.24

Length 15 mm, yellowish, sometimes marked with purple. Gnathopod 2 male large, subchelate; no hook on propodus, palm of propodus convexly curved, edged with short spines. In both sexes gnathopod 2 merus bears a short, stout tooth. Posterior border of epimeral plate 3 straight, posterio-ventral corner not pointed. Uropod 3 rami nearly as long as peduncle. Telson as long as wide, without a posterior notch.

Under stones on coarse sand, at and just below MHW. Uncommon; recorded from the Wash, Northumberland, Aberdeen, Swansea, and North Devon.

Talorchestia deshayesii (Audouin)   FIG. 9.24

Length 10 mm, pale brown with darker stripes, eyes black. Gnathopod 2 male large, subchelate with propodus produced anterio-ventrally into a large hook (rudiments of this visible in juvenile males). Gnathopod 2 female small, mitten-shaped, without a tooth on merus. Epimeral plate 3 with a slight point at posterio-ventral corner. Uropod 3 rami shorter than peduncle. Telson longer than wide, slightly notched posteriorly.

Beneath strandline algae and other debris on sandy and shingly shores, often extending above HWS. All coasts.

11 HYALIDAE

Body stout. Head without rostrum. Antenna 1 shorter than 2, but longer than antenna 2 peduncle. Gnathopods 1 and 2 subchelate; male with gnathopod 2 enlarged. Uropods short, stout; uropods 1 and 2 biramous, uropod 3 uniramous. Telson short, cleft into two lobes, unarmed or with few small spines. Jumping ability is a useful field character.

---

1. Pereopods 3–7 with large blunt spine on distal posterior border of propodus   ***Hyale pontica***

   Pereopods 3–7 not so armed   **2**

2. Gnathopod 2 male with broad propodus, palm only a little longer than ventral border. Gnathopod 2 female propodus with dorsal and ventral borders almost parallel, with broad lobe on carpus more or less as wide as long   ***Hyale nilssoni***

   Gnathopod 2 male propodus broad but more oval, with palm more than twice length of ventral border. Gnathopod 2 female with propodus nearly oval and lobe on carpus narrower, longer than wide   ***Hyale perieri***

Hyale nilssoni (Rathke)   FIG. 9.25

Length 7 mm, brown to vivid green. Gnathopod 2 male propodus broad, rather rectangular, palm only a little longer than ventral margin. Gnathopod 2 female propodus with approximately parallel dorsal and ventral margins, carpus with a fat lobe which is as wide as long. Pereopods 3–7 propodus without a large blunt spine. Pereopods 5–7 basis with only slight crenulations on posterior border.

Among intertidal algae on rocky and muddy shores from the *Pelvetia* level downwards. Excellent jumpers. All coasts including lower reaches of estuaries. Often common.

Hyale stebbingi Chevreux has only recently been accepted as distinct from *H. nilssoni*. It has been reported from Shetland, the Clyde Sea, and Fastnet, and may be widespread along western coasts. In *H. stebbingi*, epimeral plate 3 is quadrate, with straight posterior margin lacking a tooth; antenna 2 in the male has tufts of long setae on the inner surface.

Hyale perieri (Lucas)   FIG. 9.25

Length 13 mm; greenish, often with yellow, violet, or reddish brown bands. Pereopods 3–7 propodus without a large blunt spine. Pereopods 5–7 basis only slightly crenulated posteriorly. Gnathopod 2 male propodus broad but oval, palm twice length of ventral border. Gnathopod 2 female propodus rather oval, carpus with very narrow lobe, much longer than wide.

Amongst mud, algae, and mussel banks low on rocky shores, in rock-pools on exposed shores. South-western Britain and Ireland.

Hyale pontica (Rathke)   FIG. 9.25

Length 6 mm, brownish green. Gnathopod 2 male propodus broad, rather rectangular, palm only a little longer than ventral border. Gnathopod 2 female propodus with approximately parallel dorsal and ventral margins; carpus with narrow lobe which is longer than wide. Pereopods 3–7 with a large, blunt spine, marked with lateral striations, on distal posterior border of propodus. Pereopods 5–7 with posterior border of basis distinctly crenulate.

Intertidal and shallow sublittoral, amongst algae. Not a good jumper. All coasts but not especially common.

12 GAMMARIDAE

Body compressed, smooth dorsally except for the urosome which may bear small, often conspicuous, spines and/or setae. Head with small rostrum, large post-antennal sinus; eyes usually large, reniform. Antenna 1 and 2 well-developed; accessory flagellum elongate, multiarticulate. Mandible with elongate, three-articled palp. Coxae moderately large, overlapping; coxa 4 excavate posteriorly; coxae 5–7 with anterior lobe longer than posterior. Gnathopods 1 and 2 approximately equal-sized, subchelate, relatively well-developed. Pereopods with broad basis. Uropods 1–3 biramous; uropod 3 with biarticulate outer ramus, equal to, rarely much larger than, inner ramus. Telson cleft. Sexual dimorphism marked, reflected in antennae, gnathopods, pereopods, and uropods.

1. Uropod 3 inner ramus at least one-third length of outer ramus **2**

   Uropod 3 inner ramus small, less than one-third length of outer ramus **11**

2. Eyes small, more or less round. Antenna 2 male with a few short peduncular setae, each less than twice width of peduncle segment 4. Freshwater species, sometimes washed into brackish areas **[*Gammarus pulex* (L.) and *G. lacustris* Sars]**

   Eyes elongate, oval, or reniform, twice as long as wide. Antenna 2 male with many long peduncular setae, often more than twice width of peduncle segment 4. Brackish water and marine species **3**

3. Pereopod 7 basis with posterio-distal corner distinct from ischium, bearing only setae **4**

   Pereopod 7 basis with posterio-distal corner indistinct, bearing one or two spines as well as setae **5**

4. Uropod 3 inner ramus only one-third length of outer ramus. Epimeral plates 2 and 3 bearing few small setae, not set in notches. Mainly marine *Gammarus finmarchicus*

   Uropod 3 inner ramus more than half length of outer ramus. Epimeral plates 2 and 3 with few, relatively long setae posteriorly, set in small notches. Freshwater and brackish *Gammarus duebeni*

5. Mandibular palp article 3 with irregularly alternating short and long setae on ventral margin **6**

   Mandibular palp article 3 with regular, comb-like row of short to medium setae on ventral margin **8**

6. Antenna 1 peduncle with few (<10) groups of setae ventrally. Male antenna 2 peduncle with tufts of curled setae. Colour when live green/yellow, with deep blue, or black and gold, banding *Gammarus tigrinus*

   Antenna 1 peduncle with many (>15) groups of setae ventrally. Male antenna 2 peduncle lacking curled setae. Colour brown, yellow, or green with only indistinct banding **7**

7. Male pereopods 6 and 7 with posterior marginal setae and spines on merus and carpus about equal length. Adult male antenna 1 with five or six groups of setae on ventral surface of peduncle article 2, and two or three groups ventrally on article 3 (excluding terminal groups). Marine or brackish water *Gammarus salinus*

   Male pereopods 6 and 7 with posterior marginal setae on merus and carpus much longer than spines. Adult male antenna 1 with six to ten groups of setae on ventral surface of peduncle article 2, and three to six groups ventrally on article 3 (excluding terminal groups) *Gammarus zaddachi*

8. Uropod 3 inner ramus about one-half to two-thirds length of outer ramus. Adult male with long curled setae on antenna 2, gnathopods 1 and 2, and all pereopods. Brackish water *Gammarus chevreuxi*

   Uropod 3 with rami of about equal length. Curled setae absent, except perhaps on antenna 2 **9**

9. Mandibular palp article 3 with a row of ventral setae of constant length. Head with lateral lobes rather truncate, upper angle obtuse. Marine *Gammarus oceanicus*

   Mandibular palp article 3 with a row of ventral setae, increasing in length distally. Head lateral lobes not truncate, upper angle acute or nearly so **10**

10. Pereopod 7 basis only a little longer than wide, posterior margin angular. Urosome with small dorsal humps. Brackish water and marine *Gammarus crinicornis*

    Pereopod 7 basis about 1.5 times as long as wide. Urosome with prominent, angular dorsal humps. Epimeral plate 3 with several small setae on posterior margin *Gammarus locusta*

    Pereopod 7 basis much more than 1.5 times as long as wide. Urosome with prominent dorsal humps. Epimeral plate 3 with no more than one seta on posterior margin *Gammarus insensibilis*

11. Gnathopod 1 propodus larger than gnathopod 2 propodus. Gnathopod 2 carpus elongate *Eulimnogammarus obtusatus*

    Gnathopod 1 propodus not larger than gnathopod 2 propodus. Gnathopod 2 carpus short, more or less triangular **12**

12. Male with dense setae on coxae, pereopods, and epimeral plates. Body white *Pectenogammarus planicrurus*

    Male with sparser setation on coxae, pereopods, and epimeral plates. Body coloured **13**

13. Antenna 2 and uropod 3 outer ramus with dense setae **14**

    Antenna 2 with few setae, uropod 3 outer ramus lacking large setae *Chaetogammarus stoerensis*

14. Urosome with dorsal spines in transverse rows. Male uropod 3 with long but normal setae. Pereopod 7 merus about three times as long as wide *Chaetogammarus marinus*

    Urosome with few dorsal spines. Male uropod 3 with long plumose setae on outer ramus. Pereopod 7 merus about twice as long as wide *Chaetogammarus pirloti*

Genus *Chaetogammarus*

Antenna 1 longer than 2. Eyes elongate, usually reniform. Gnathopods subchelate; gnathopod 2 larger than 1. Coxae, pereopods 5–7, and dorsal surface of urosome more or less without setae. Pereopods spiny. Urosome with groups of spines dorsally.

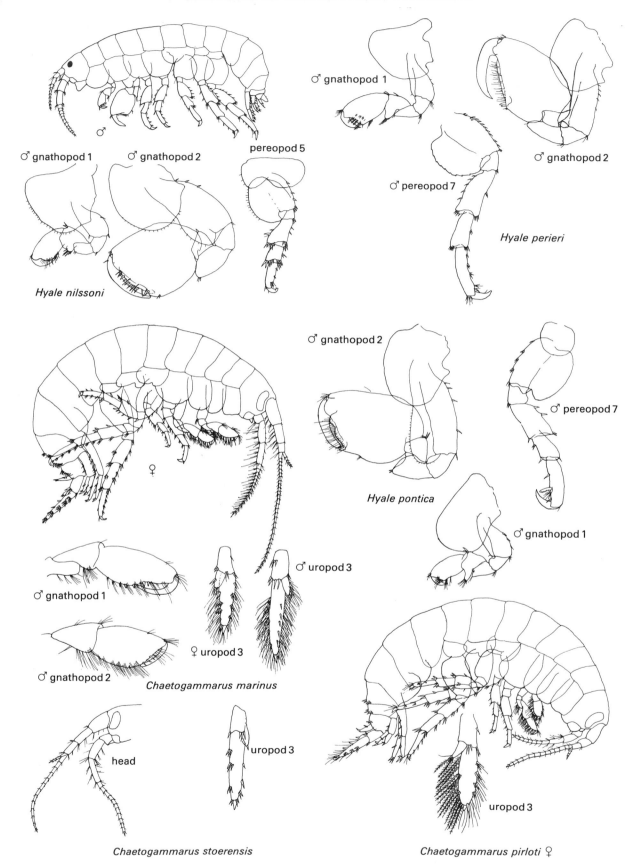

♂ gnathopod 1

♂ gnathopod 2

pereopod 5

Hyale nilssoni

♂ gnathopod 1

♂ gnathopod 2

♂ pereopod 7

Hyale perieri

♂ gnathopod 2

♂ pereopod 7

Hyale pontica

♂ gnathopod 1

♂ gnathopod 1

♂ gnathopod 2

♂ uropod 3

♀ uropod 3

Chaetogammarus marinus

head

uropod 3

Chaetogammarus stoerensis

uropod 3

Chaetogammarus pirloti ♀

Fig. 9.25

Uropod 3 outer ramus long, spiny, often with many setae; inner ramus small, scale-like.

Chaetogammarus marinus Leach   FIG. 9.25

Length up to 25 mm, dark green, sometimes marked with red or yellow. Head with lateral lobes broadly truncated, eyes slightly reniform. Antenna 2 densely setose, especially on flagellum. Pereopods 3 and 4 with few setae in male, rather more in female. Pereopods 5–7 spiny. Pereopod 7 basis with posterio-distal corner not produced, merus about three times as long as wide. Epimeral plate 3 with posterio-ventral corner produced as a point, posterior margin with several small setae. Urosome with numerous dorsal spines arranged in a transverse row across each segment. Uropod 3 inner ramus small, with spines and setae; male outer ramus with spines and many setae on both margins, but lacking plumose setae; female outer ramus with fewer setae, some of which may be plumose.

Intertidal, on sheltered shores beneath stones and amongst algae; sometimes in estuaries. All coasts.

Chaetogammarus pirloti (Sexton and Spooner)   FIG. 9.25

Length 14 mm; pale green, often tinged brown, pink, blue, or orange. Head with lateral lobes obliquely truncated, eyes slightly reniform. Antennae short; antenna 2 densely setose in male, moderately setose in female. Pereopods 3 and 4 with few setae in male, many setae in female. Pereopods 5–7 spiny. Pereopod 7 basis with posterio-distal corner not produced; merus broad, twice as long as wide. Epimeral plate 3 with posterio-ventral corner quadrate or slightly produced, with two or three small setae on posterior margin. Urosome with moderately prominent dorsal humps bearing small groups of spines. Uropod 3 inner ramus small, with plumose setae and spines; outer ramus large, spiny, with plumose setae on inner margins, and few (female) or many (male) normal setae on both margins.

Intertidal, on upper shore shingle and gravel subject to freshwater influence. Western and southern coasts, from Shetland to Dorset, also western Ireland.

Chaetogammarus stoerensis (Reid)   FIG. 9.25

Length 8 mm, pale green to greenish blue. Head with broad lateral lobes; eyes large, slightly reniform. Antenna 1 and 2 short, with few setae. Pereopods 3 and 4 sparsely setose, pereopods 5–7 sparsely spinose. Pereopod 7 basis with posterio-distal corner slightly produced; propodus distinctly longer than carpus. Epimeral plate 3 with quadrate posterio-ventral corner; posterior margin nearly straight, with few small setae. Urosome with a few dorsal spines. Uropod 3 inner ramus tiny, outer ramus broad, long, spiny, but lacking setae.

Intertidal, between HWN and LWN, on clean gravel in areas of freshwater run-off. All coasts.

Eulimnogammarus obtusatus (Dahl)   FIG. 9.26

Length 20 mm; brown to olive-green, sometimes tinged purple. Antenna 1 longer than antenna 2. Gnathopod 1 male with propodus larger than gnathopod 2 propodus. Gnathopod 2 carpus elongate. Urosome with small humps and groups of short

spines dorsally. Uropod 3 inner ramus less than one-fifth length of outer.

Intertidal. lower shore, on clean gravel and shingle, and amongst algae. All coasts.

Genus *Gammarus*

Head with lateral lobes truncated or rounded; eyes small and round, or large and reniform. Gnathopod 1 about equal size to, or smaller than, gnathopod 2. Epimeral plates 2 and 3 round, quadrate or slightly acute. Urosome with groups of spines and setae dorsally. Uropod 3 rami foliaceous, setose and/or spiny; inner ramus more than half length of biarticulate outer ramus. Telson cleft, with lateral and apical spines, with or without setae.

A large, mainly freshwater genus. Ten marine and two freshwater species occur in Britain but identification is difficult, many diagnostic features are seen only in adult males.

Gammarus chevreuxi Sexton   FIG. 9.26

Length 13 mm. Head with lateral lobes broadly truncated; eyes moderately large, reniform. Antenna 1 with few setae, peduncle with less than ten ventral groups of setae overall. Antenna 2 male with many setae, some long and curled. Male gnathopods, pereopod 3 and uropod 3 also with long, curled setae. Antenna 2 female with sparse, straight setae. Mandibular palp article 1 lacking setae, article 3 with ungraduated comb-like row of setae ventrally and one group of setae on outer surface. Pereopod 7 spiny, with few setae, basis with indistinct posterio-distal corner marked by two spines. Epimeral plates 2 and 3 with acute posterio-ventral corners, with only one or two short setae posteriorly. Urosome with very small dorsal humps. Uropod 3 inner ramus one-half to two-thirds length of article 1 of outer ramus.

Brackish water, particularly in coastal marshes. South-west only.

Gammarus crinicornis Stock   FIG. 9.26

Length 20 mm. Head with lateral lobes sloping forward, upper angles produced; eyes small, reniform. Antenna 1 peduncle with fewer than five ventral groups of setae (excluding apical tufts). Mandibular palp article 1 lacking setae, article 3 with one or two groups of setae on outer surface and ventrally a comb-like row of setae which gradually increase in length distally. Pereopod 7 basis only slightly longer than wide, with angular posterior margin. Epimeral plates 2 and 3 acutely produced posterioventrally, with concave posterior margins. Urosome with slight dorsal humps. Uropod 3 rami about equal length.

Mainly marine, occasionally estuarine, on exposed beaches, amongst algae in pools. South-west coasts.

Gammarus duebeni Liljeborg   FIG. 9.26

Up to 16 mm, yellowish green. Eyes reniform. Antenna 1 slightly longer than 2. Mandibular palp article 1 with at least one ventrodistal seta. Pereopods 5–7 basis armed with setae only, posterioventral corner distinct from joint with ischium. Epimeral plate 3 with setae (not spines) set in notches along nearly straight

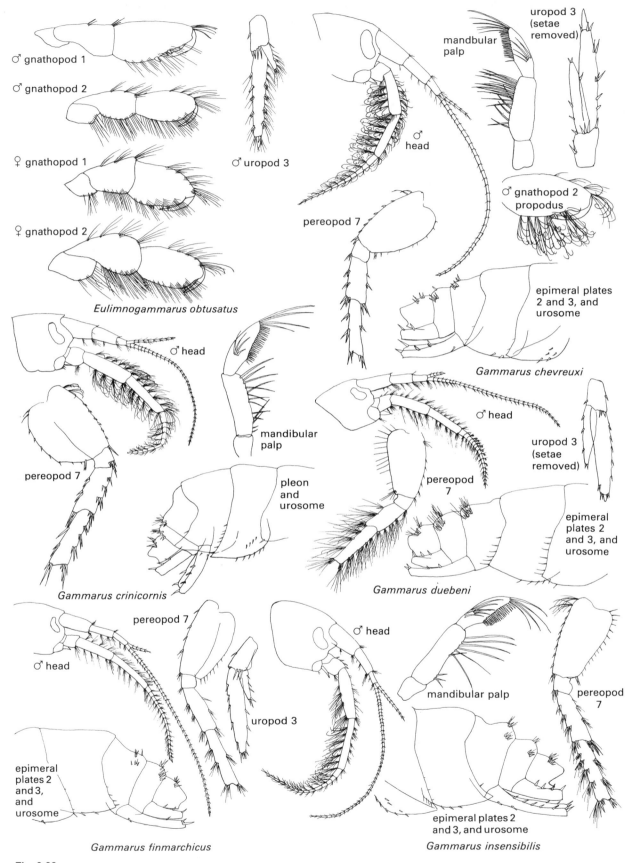

♂ gnathopod 1

♂ gnathopod 2

♀ gnathopod 1

♀ gnathopod 2

Eulimnogammarus obtusatus

♂ uropod 3

mandibular palp

uropod 3 (setae removed)

♂ head

pereopod 7

♂ gnathopod 2 propodus

epimeral plates 2 and 3, and urosome

Gammarus chevreuxi

♂ head

pereopod 7

mandibular palp

pleon and urosome

Gammarus crinicornis

♂ head

pereopod 7

uropod 3 (setae removed)

epimeral plates 2 and 3, and urosome

Gammarus duebeni

pereopod 7

♂ head

uropod 3

epimeral plates 2 and 3, and urosome

Gammarus finmarchicus

♂ head

mandibular palp

pereopod 7

epimeral plates 2 and 3, and urosome

Gammarus insensibilis

Fig. 9.26

posterior margin. Urosome with only small dorsal humps. Uropod 3 inner ramus more than half length of outer.

In brackish water, and in small streams crossing rocky shores; freshwater in Ireland, Isle of Man, Western Isles. All coasts.

Gammarus finmarchicus Dahl   FIG. 9.26

Adult male up to 20 mm, brown to yellow. Head with rather rounded lateral lobes, eyes narrowly reniform. Antenna 1 much longer than 2, with relatively few groups of peduncle setae; accessory flagellum about as long as peduncle article 2. Mandibular palp article 1 lacking setae, article 3 with a line of lateral setae and a comb-like row of uniformly long ventral setae. Pereopods 5–7 basis posterior margin armed with setae only, posterior ventral corner distinct from joint with ischium. Epimeral plate 3 with posterio-ventral margin nearly straight, bearing only a few small setae. Uropod 3 with inner ramus about one-third to half length of outer.

Intertidal, in pools. All coasts.

Gammarus insensibilis Stock   FIG. 9.26

Length 19 mm. Very similar to *G. locusta*. Distinguished by: curved or curled setae on inner surface of antenna 2; pereopod 7 basis more than 1.5 times as long as wide, with nearly straight posterior margin; epimeral plate 3 with no more than one seta on posterior margin.

Brackish water. Southern Europe and Mediterranean; reported from the Fleet, Dorset; New England Creek, Essex, and Lough Hyne, Ireland.

Gammarus locusta (Linnaeus)   FIG. 9.27

Length 33 mm. Head with lateral lobes sloping forward, upper angles produced; eyes moderately large, reniform. Antenna 1 peduncle article 1 with, or without, one ventral group of setae; article 2 with one or two groups, article 3 with or without one ventral group of setae (excluding apical tufts). Antenna 2 with numerous groups of peduncular setae. Mandibular palp article 1 lacking setae, article 3 with one to three groups of setae on outer surface and ventrally a comb-like row of setae which gradually increase in length distally. Pereopod 7 basis one to five times longer than wide, with indistinct posterio-distal corner armed with two slender spines; merus and carpus with setae twice length of adjacent spines. Epimeral plates 2 and 3 acutely produced posterio-ventrally, posterior margin concave with numerous short setae. Urosome with prominent, angular dorsal humps, Uropod 3 rami of nearly equal length, with numerous groups of spines and setae.

Marine. Middle shore to sublittoral, often abundant under stones and amongst algae. All coasts.

Gammarus oceanicus Sergerstrale   FIG. 9.27

Length 27 mm; uniform grey, yellow, or greenish brown with little patterning. Head with broadly truncated lateral lobes; eyes moderately large, reniform. Antenna 1 with few groups of setae. Antenna 2 with numerous groups of long, uncurled setae. Mandibular palp article 1 lacking setae, article 3 with two or three tufts of setae on outer surface and an ungraduated comb-like

row ventrally. Pereopod 7 basis with indistinct posterio-ventral corner armed with two spines, carpus with setae on anterio-distal margin longer than spines (setae sparse in female). Epimeral plates 2 and 3 slightly produced posterio-ventrally, with only one or two small posterio-marginal setae. Urosome with distinct, round dorsal humps. Uropod 3 inner ramus much narrower than outer ramus and only about three-quarters length; outer ramus with numerous groups of spines and setae on external margins.

Brackish water and marine, from MTL to sublittoral, often among algae. South-west, north, and north-east coasts.

Gammarus salinus Spooner   FIG. 9.27

Length 22 mm, brown or greenish brown with light banding. Head with lateral lobes broadly truncated; eyes large, reniform. Antenna 1 peduncle with numerous groups of setae ventrally. Mandibular palp article 1 with one to four apical setae, article 3 with three to five groups of setae laterally and a ventral row of irregular setae. Pereopod 7 merus and carpus with spines and setae of similar length on posterior margins; basis with indistinct posterio-distal corner armed with two spines. Urosome with only small dorsal humps. Uropod 3 inner ramus just shorter than article 1 of outer ramus.

Brackish waters, usually in more saline conditions than *G. zaddachi*. All coasts.

Gammarus tigrinus Sexton   FIG. 9.27

Length 12 mm, pale green to yellow (male) or blue (female), with distinct bands of green and deep blue, or black and gold. Head with lateral lobes broadly truncated; eyes large, reniform. Antenna 1 with few groups of setae on peduncle. Mandibular palp article 1 without setae, article 3 with one lateral and one ventral row of mixed long and short setae. Adult male with many long curled setae on antenna 2, and on some pereopods. Pereopods 6 and 7 basis armed with setae and spines. Urosome without dorsal humps. Uropod 3 inner ramus about three-quarters length of outer ramus.

Fresh and brackish waters. Western coasts, from the Clyde Sea to the Bristol Channel; reported from fresh water in north and west Midlands, and from Lough Neagh, Northern Ireland.

Gammarus zaddachi Sexton   FIG. 9.27

Length 22 mm, light grey, green, or yellow with darker bands. Head with truncated lateral lobes; eyes moderately large, reniform. Antenna 1 peduncle, in male, with at least 15 groups of setae ventrally (excluding apical tufts). Antenna 2 peduncle, in male, with numerous groups of long setae. Mandibular palp article 1 with one to five apical setae, article 3 with irregular ventral setae and three to five groups of setae on external surface. Pereopod 7 basis with indistinct posterio-distal corner armed with two spines and several setae. Epimeral plates 2 and 3 with acute posterio-ventral corners, posterior margins with several short setae. Urosome with small dorsal humps. Uropod 3 inner ramus about three-quarters length of article 1 of outer ramus.

Marine and brackish waters, lower shore and shallow sublittoral. All coasts.

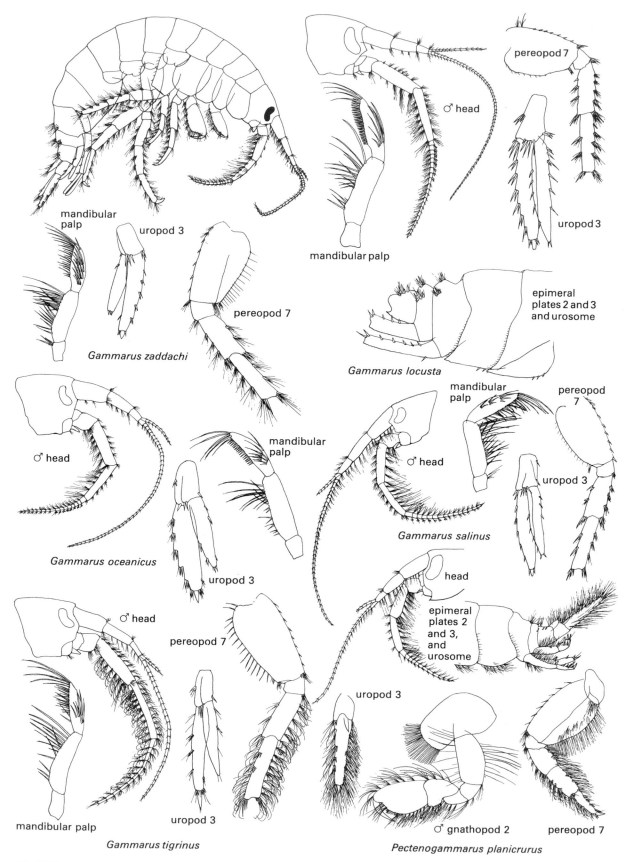

mandibular palp

uropod 3

pereopod 7

Gammarus zaddachi

♂ head

mandibular palp

uropod 3

Gammarus oceanicus

♂ head

mandibular palp

uropod 3

pereopod 7

Gammarus tigrinus

♂ head

mandibular palp

pereopod 7

uropod 3

mandibular palp

epimeral plates 2 and 3 and urosome

Gammarus locusta

mandibular palp

pereopod 7

♂ head

uropod 3

Gammarus salinus

head

epimeral plates 2 and 3, and urosome

uropod 3

♂ gnathopod 2

pereopod 7

Pectenogammarus planicrurus

Fig. 9.27

Pectenogammarus planicrurus Reid   FIG. 9.27

Length 9 mm; white, without patterning. Eyes elongate, reniform. Male with long, dense setal fringes on margins of pereopods and uropods, and along ventral margins of coxal plates. Female with sparser setation. Antenna 1 just longer than antenna 2. Gnathopod 2 larger than 1, carpus short, triangular. Pereopods short, strong, spiny. Uropod 3 with very small inner ramus.

Intertidal, on clean shingle. Southern Britain; Wash to Isle of Man, and southern Ireland.

13 MELITIDAE

Body usually elongate, compressed; pleon toothed or smooth dorsally, pereon and urosome usually smooth. Head without rostrum; eyes usually small and round. Antennae well-developed; antenna 1 usually much longer than 2; accessory flagellum present, often conspicuous. Mandible with large molar process, and long three-articled palp. Coxae contiguous, often short. Gnathopods subchelate; gnathopod 2 much larger than 1, especially in male. Pereopods variable. Epimeral plate 3 frequently toothed posteriorly. Uropods biramous; uropod 3 ramus variable. Telson cleft, often spiny. Sexual dimorphism apparent in antennae, gnathopod 2, and pereopods.

---

1. Uropod 3 inner ramus short, less than half length of outer — **2**

   Uropod 3 with rami more or less equal in length — **7**

2. Uropod 3 small, not projecting much beyond uropod 1; outer ramus about equal length to peduncle — ***Gammarella fucicola***

   Uropod 3 large, projecting well beyond uropod 1; outer ramus much longer than peduncle — **3**

3. Pleon without teeth dorsally — **4**

   Pleon with dorsal teeth on one or more segments — **6**

4. Urosome without teeth dorsally — ***Allomelita pellucida***

   Urosome with dorsal teeth on some segments — **5**

5. Head with both lateral lobes and post-antennal angles produced, with a cleft between. Telson with apical spines — ***Melita palmata***

   Post-antennal lobes of head not produced, cleft absent. Telson without apical spines — ***Melita hergensis***

6. Epimeral plate 3 with posterior and posterio-ventral borders distinctly serrated. Pleon with well-developed dorsal teeth — ***Melita gladiosa***

   Epimeral plate 3 with posterior and posterio-ventral borders smooth, or only slightly toothed. Pleon dorsal teeth small — ***Abludomelita obtusata***

7. Uropod 3 short, at most only just projecting beyond uropod 1; rami short and fat, scarcely longer than peduncle — ***Elasmopus rapax***

8. Uropod 3 projecting well beyond uropod 1, rami much longer than peduncle — **8**

8. Antenna 1 shorter than antenna 2 peduncle. Lateral lobes and post-antennal angles of head considerably produced — **9**

   Antenna 1 longer than antenna 2. Post-antennal angles of head not considerably produced — **11**

9. Male gnathopod 2 with dactylus crossing palm margin of propodus. Pereopods 5–7 slender. Epimeral plate 3 with a small tooth at posterio-ventral corner — ***Cheirocratus sundevallii***

   Male gnathopod 2 dactylus not crossing propodus palm margin — **10**

10. Male gnathopod 2 propodus with long palm margin bearing many setae. Pereopod 7 very slender. Epimeral plate 3 with usually a large tooth at posterio-ventral corner — ***Cheirocratus intermedius***

    Male gnathopod 2 propodus with short palm margin bearing few setae. Pereopod 7 merus, carpus, and propodus expanded and flattened — ***Cheirocratus assimilis***

11. Epimeral plate 3 with posterior margin very coarsely toothed — ***Ceradocus semiserratus***

    Epimeral plate 3 posterior margin not coarsely toothed — **12**

12. Pleon and urosome segments each with one or more dorsal teeth — ***Maerella tenuimana***

    Pleon and urosome smooth — **13**

13. Epimeral plate 3 with posterio-ventral margins serrated. Gnathopod 2 propodus narrowly oval — ***Maera othonis***

    Epimeral plate 3 with smooth margins, except for a distinct tooth at posterio-ventral corner. Gnathopod 2 propodus approximately quadrate. Uropod 3 rami less than twice length of peduncle — ***Maera grossimana***

Abludomelita obtusata (Montagu)   FIG. 9.28

Length 9 mm, brownish. Pleon and urosome segments variably toothed dorsally; pleon segment 2 usually with one large median and two smaller lateral teeth, segments 4 and 5 with small median teeth and two larger lateral teeth. Coxae 1–3 with small tooth at posterio-ventral corner; female coxa 6 distinctly bilobed anteriorly. Epimeral plate 3 with posterio-ventral corner acutely produced but weakly toothed. Uropod 3 outer ramus spiny, less than twice length of peduncle; inner ramus minute.

Sublittoral. All coasts.

Allomelita pellucida (Sars)   FIG. 9.28

Length 5–6 mm, white to grey. Smooth dorsally. Head with broadly rounded lateral lobes, eyes small. Antenna 2 about half length antenna 1; accessory flagellum very small. Female coxa

6 with rounded anterior lobe. Epimeral plate 3 more or less quadrate with acute posterio-ventral corner margins unserrated. Uropod 3 much larger in male than in female; outer ramus at least three times length of peduncle, spinose, and in male setose. Telson cleft, with apical spines on each lobe.

Amongst vegetation in shallow brackish water. Southern coasts, from Norfolk to Isle of Man.

Ceradocus semiserratus (Bate)   FIG. 9.28

Length 7 mm. Body slender, elongate, smooth dorsally. Antenna 1 much longer and more robust than antenna 2; accessory flagellum well-developed, with three articles. Mandibular palp article 2 twice length of 3. Maxilliped with four-articled palp. Coxae short; coxa 4 scarcely excavate posteriorly. Epimeral plate 3 with coarsely toothed posterior margin. Uropod 3 extending beyond uropod 1; rami subequal, lanceolate, uniarticulate. Telson cleft.

Sublittoral, on gravelly substrata. Mainly west coasts.

Genus *Cheirocratus*

Body slender; smooth dorsally, except for urosome, which may bear small teeth. Head with lateral lobes and post-antennal angles considerably produced, with a cleft between. Antenna 1 much shorter than 2; accessory flagellum small, with two or three articles. Maxilliped with large, four-articled palp. Coxae small; coxa 2 longer than others. Uropod 3 extending well beyond uropods 1 and 2; rami subequal, lanceolate, and uniarticulate. Telson widely cleft, with apical spines.

Cheirocratus assimilis (Liljeborg)   FIG. 9.28

Length 13 mm; pale yellow, marked with red. Very similar to *C. sundevallii*. Male gnathopod 2 propodus large, more or less rectangular; palm short, oblique, complexly sculptured, and sparsely setose, not crossed by dactylus. Pereopod 7 with merus, carpus, and propodus somewhat expanded and flattened.

Sublittoral. Reported from the Wash, Northumberland, the Clyde Sea, Isle of Man, western Channel, and the Channel Isles.

Cheirocratus intermedius Sars   FIG. 9.28

Length 10 mm; yellow with red markings. Very similar to *C. sundevallii*. Male gnathopod 2 propodus large, more or less oval, ventral margin sinuously concave with many long setae. Epimeral plate 3 usually with large tooth at posterio-ventral corner.

Sublittoral. Reported from the Wash, Shetland, Isle of Man, west Channel, the Channel Isles, and western Ireland.

Cheirocratus sundevallii (Rathke)   FIG. 9.28

Length 10 mm; yellow/orange with red markings. Gnathopod 2 male propodus large and oval, ventral margin convex, bearing many long setae, palm anterio-ventral, crossed by dactylus. Pereopods 5–7 slender; merus, carpus, and propodus not expanded. Urosome segment 1 with setae and three small teeth dorsally; segment 2 with setae and four teeth; segment 3 with

two setae, lacking teeth. Epimeral plate 3 with small tooth at posterio-ventral corner.

Sublittoral, on silty sand. All coasts.

Elasmopus rapax Costa   FIG. 9.29

Length 10 mm; yellow to deep blue, sometimes speckled. Body robust, smooth dorsally. Antenna 1 longer than antenna 2; accessory flagellum small, with about three articles. Epimeral plate 3 quadrate, posterior margin slightly toothed. Urosome without dorsal teeth. Uropod 3 short, projecting little beyond uropod 1; rami broad, short, spiny, outer just longer than inner. Telson cleft, lobes rounded terminally, with lateral spines.

In *Laminaria* holdfasts and among shallow sublittoral algae. Southern and western coasts.

Gammarella fucicola (Leach)   FIG. 9.29

Length 10 mm, yellow to brown. Body robust; pereon and pleon smooth dorsally, urosome carinate. Head with truncated lateral lobes and small round eyes. Antenna 1 much longer than 2; accessory flagellum well-developed, with four or five articles. Gnathopods subchelate; gnathopod 2 male very large. Epimeral plate 3 posterior margin more or less straight, with small tooth at posterio-ventral corner. Urosome segments 2 and 3 with paired dorsal spines. Uropod 3 not extending beyond uropod 1; outer ramus twice length of inner. Telson deeply cleft.

Intertidal and sublittoral, amongst algae. All coasts.

Genus *Maera*

Body slender, smooth dorsally. Antenna 1 much longer than antenna 2; accessory flagellum well-developed, with up to eight articles. Mandibular palp article 2 longer than 3. Maxilliped with four-articled palp. Uropod 3 long or short; rami subequal, lanceolate, uniarticulate. Telson cleft.

Maera grossimana (Montagu)   FIG. 9.29

Length 10 mm; yellowish, tinged with red. Eyes moderately large, oval. Antenna 1 peduncle article 1 longer than head. Coxae short, with smooth margins. Gnathopod 2 propodus expanded, more or less quadrate, with a distinct palm. Epimeral plate 3 with small tooth at posterio-ventral corner, margins smooth. Uropod 1 peduncle lacking median and proximal, submarginal spine. Uropod 3 rami broad, truncated, less than twice peduncle length, with numerous long spines.

Intertidal and sublittoral, under stones. South and south-west coasts.

Maera othonis (Milne Edwards)   FIG. 9.29

Length usually to 15 mm, rarely to 35 mm; whitish with pale red markings. Eyes small, oval to reniform. Antenna 1 peduncle article 1 as long as head. Coxa 1 acutely produced anteriorly, coxae 2 and 3 distinctly toothed posterio-distally. Gnathopod 2 propodus elongate, more or less oval. Epimeral plate 3 with acute tooth at posterio-ventral corner, posterio-ventral margin serrated. Uropod 1 peduncle with a small proximal, marginal spine. Uropod 3 rami long, lanceolate, sparsely spinose.

Shallow sublittoral, on sand and gravel. All coasts.

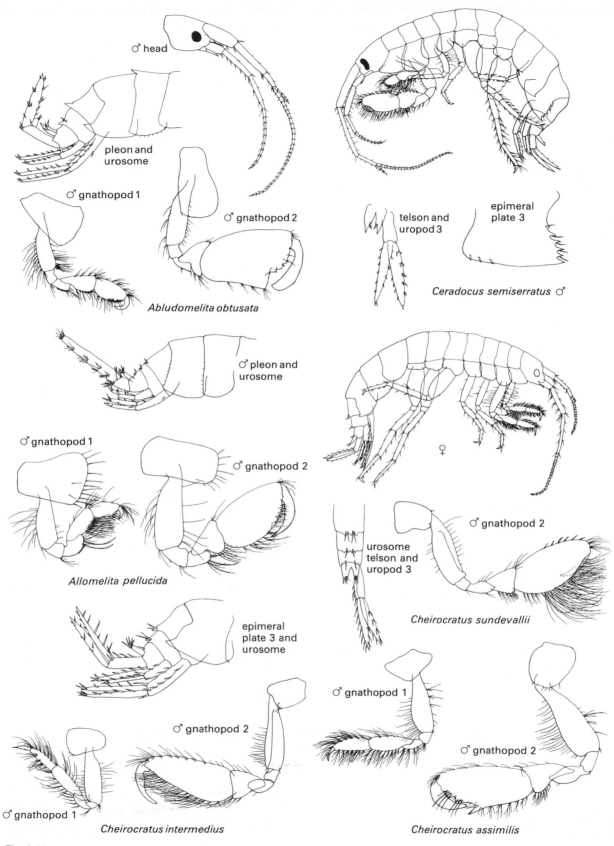

♂ head

pleon and urosome

♂ gnathopod 1

♂ gnathopod 2

Abludomelita obtusata

telson and uropod 3

epimeral plate 3

Ceradocus semiserratus ♂

♂ pleon and urosome

♂ gnathopod 1

♂ gnathopod 2

Allomelita pellucida

♀

urosome telson and uropod 3

♂ gnathopod 2

Cheirocratus sundevallii

epimeral plate 3 and urosome

♂ gnathopod 2

♂ gnathopod 1

♂ gnathopod 1

Cheirocratus intermedius

♂ gnathopod 1

♂ gnathopod 2

Cheirocratus assimilis

Fig. 9.28

Maerella tenuimana (Bate)   FIG. 9.29

Length 9 mm. Body slender; pleon segment 1 with at most one small dorsal tooth, segments 2 and 3 usually with three teeth each; urosome segments 1 and 2 usually with two dorsal teeth each, segment 3 usually with three teeth. Antenna 1 much longer than 2; accessory flagellum well-developed, with four or more articles. Mandibular palp articles 2 and 3 more or less equal length. Maxilliped with three-articled palp. Uropod 3 very large, extending well beyond uropod 1; rami subequal, lanceolate, uniarticulate. Telson deeply cleft.

Sublittoral, all coasts.

Genus *Melita*

Body compressed and slender. Pleon and urosome often with dorsal teeth and spines. Antenna 1 longer than 2; accessory flagellum variable, with two or more articles. Coxal plates small, or fairly large. Gnathopods subchelate; gnathopod 2 male larger than 1. Uropod 3 extending well beyond uropod 1; outer ramus uniarticulate, or with spine-like second article, inner ramus very small. Telson deeply cleft.

Melita gladiosa Bate   FIG. 9.29

Length 9 mm; brownish, with darker bands. Pleon and urosome segments each with three large dorsal teeth. Coxae 1–3 with small tooth at posterio-ventral corner. Female coxa 6 with at most a weakly bilobed anterior lobe. Epimeral plate 3 with posterio-ventral corner acutely produced, distinctly serrated. Uropod 3 outer ramus spiny, twice length of peduncle; inner ramus minute.

Sublittoral, on gravelly bottoms. South and south-west coasts.

Melita hergensis Reid   FIG. 9.30

Length 10 mm; blue-black, often with pale bands on limbs. Head with rounded lateral lobes, no cleft before post-antennal angles; eyes small, slightly oval. Antenna 2 peduncle much longer than antenna 1 peduncle; accessory flagellum with two to three articles. Gnathopod 2 male similar to *M. palmata*, but propodus less broad. Female coxa 6 with elongate anterior lobe. Epimeral plate 3 with posterio-ventral corner acutely produced, posterio-ventral margin weakly toothed. Urosome similar to *M. palmata*. Uropod 3 outer ramus very large, spiny; inner ramus minute. Telson cleft, with dorso-lateral spines, apical spines absent.

Intertidal, lower shore; on clean, fairly exposed, fully marine rocky shores. Southern coasts.

Melita palmata (Montagu)   FIG. 9.30

Length 16 mm; pale yellow to blue-grey, limbs banded. Head with lateral lobes rounded, separated by narrow cleft from produced post-antennal angle. Antenna 2 peduncle just longer than antenna 1 peduncle; accessory flagellum with two to four articles. Male gnathopod 2 with broad propodus, palm crossed by dactylus. Female coxa 6 with anterior lobe forming a hook. Epimeral plate 3 with posterio-ventral corner produced as a small tooth, posterio-ventral margin slightly toothed. Urosome segment 1 with single median dorsal tooth, segment 2 with two

dorso-lateral teeth. Uropod 3 outer ramus elongate, spiny; inner ramus minute. Telson cleft, with apical and internal marginal spines.

Marine and brackish water; intertidal and shallow sublittoral, among silty, stony habitats. All coasts.

14 HAUSTORIIDAE

Body either rounded or laterally compressed. Eyes distinct or indistinct. Antenna 1 shorter than antenna 2, peduncle modified or normal. Accessory flagellum present. If a rostrum is present then pereopod 7 longer than pereopod 6; some pereopods adapted for digging with some articles flattened, strongly spinose, and setose. Gnathopods feeble. Telson wholly or partly split. Burrowers in sand.

---

1. Body somewhat dorso-ventrally flattened to give rather rounded shape. Antenna 1 peduncle with articles normally arranged   **2**

   Body laterally compressed. Antenna 1 peduncle geniculate between articles 1 and 2: article 1 large, rest of peduncle depending at right angle from anterio-ventral corner   **6**

2. Pereopods 3–7 with only five articles, dactylus absent. Pereopod 6 propodus making forward-facing acute angle with distal border of carpus. Eyes indistinct   ***Haustorius arenarius***

   Pereopods 3–7 with six articles, dactylus more or less lanceolate. Eyes distinct   **3**

3. Uropod 1 rami strongly curved, smooth   ***Urothoe marina***

   Uropod 1 rami straight, or only slightly curved, often bearing spines or setae   **4**

4. Pereopod 5 carpus more than twice as wide as long, much broader than merus   ***Urothoe poseidonis***

   Pereopod 5 carpus only slightly wider than long, if at all   **5**

5. Antenna 1 accessory flagellum less than half length of primary flagellum   ***Urothoe elegans***

   Antenna 1 accessory flagellum more than half length of primary flagellum   ***Urothoe brevicornis***

6. Dorsal surface of urosome segment 1 with spines directed posteriorly and bristles directed anteriorly   **7**

   Dorsal surface of urosome segment 1 with anteriorly directed bristles only   **11**

7. Adults small (<3.5 mm). Epimeral plate 3 with only a single group of spines just above ventral margin   ***Bathyporeia nana***

   Adults larger. Epimeral plate 3 with more than one group of spines just above ventral margin   **8**

8. Epimeral plate 3, in adult female and juvenile male, with a well-developed tooth at posterio-ventral

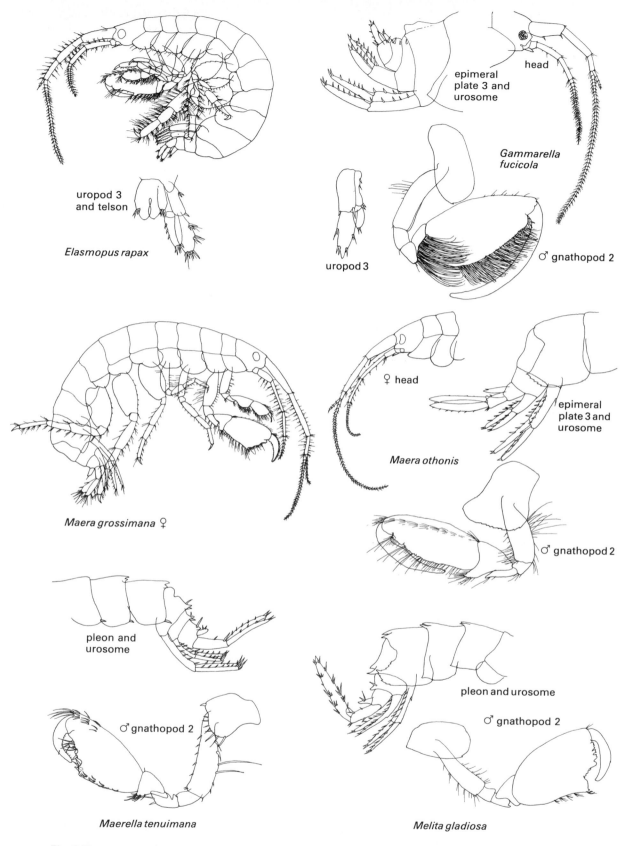

uropod 3
and telson

Elasmopus rapax

epimeral
plate 3 and
urosome

head

uropod 3

*Gammarella
fucicola*

♂ gnathopod 2

Maera grossimana ♀

♀ head

Maera othonis

epimeral
plate 3 and
urosome

♂ gnathopod 2

pleon and
urosome

♂ gnathopod 2

pleon and urosome

♂ gnathopod 2

Maerella tenuimana

Melita gladiosa

Fig. 9.29

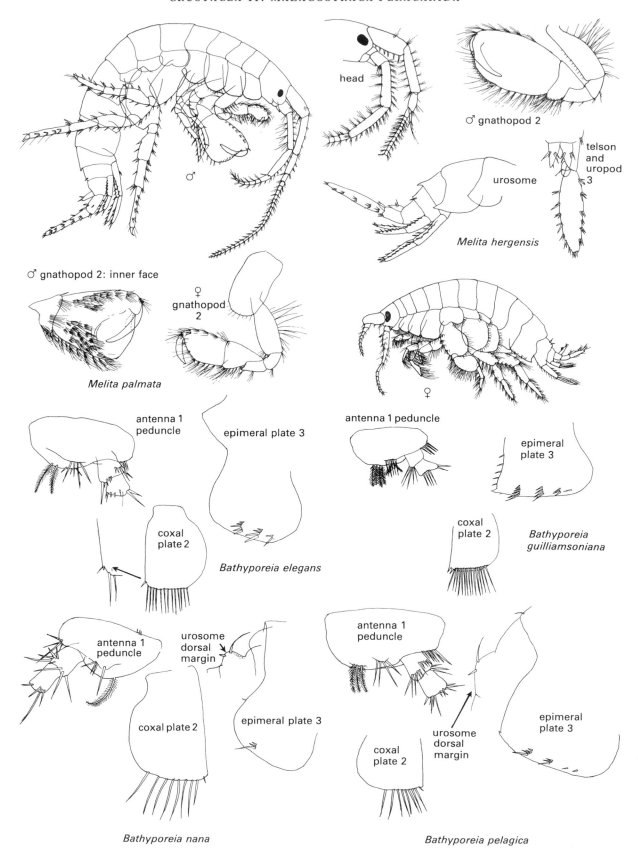

head

♂ gnathopod 2

urosome

telson and uropod 3

Melita hergensis

♂ gnathopod 2: inner face

♀ gnathopod 2

Melita palmata

♀

antenna 1 peduncle

epimeral plate 3

coxal plate 2

Bathyporeia elegans

antenna 1 peduncle

epimeral plate 3

coxal plate 2

Bathyporeia guilliamsoniana

antenna 1 peduncle

urosome dorsal margin

coxal plate 2

epimeral plate 3

Bathyporeia nana

antenna 1 peduncle

coxal plate 2

urosome dorsal margin

epimeral plate 3

Bathyporeia pelagica

Fig. 9.30

corner. Adult male with tooth reduced, may be indicated only by uneven border **9**

Epimeral plate 3 evenly rounded at posterio-ventral corner **10**

9. Epimeral plate 3 with well-developed tooth at posterio-ventral corner, extending beyond vertical margin of posterior border (reduced in males). Antenna 1 peduncle article 1 with more or less rounded tip; coxae 2 and 3 with tooth at posterio-ventral corner ***Bathyporeia guilliamsoniana***

Epimeral plate 3 with small tooth almost at posterio-ventral corner, not extending beyond vertical margin of posterior border (reduced in males). Antenna 1 peduncle article 1 with angular tip and more or less vertical anterior border; coxae 2 and 3 without tooth on posterio-ventral corner ***Bathyporeia pelagica***

10. Antenna 1 peduncle article 1 with sharply angular tip; coxae 2 and 3 with well-developed tooth at posterio-ventral corner ***Bathyporeia tenuipes***

Antenna 1 peduncle article 1 with rounded tip; coxae 2 and 3 with small tooth on posterio-ventral corner ***Bathyporeia elegans***

11. Antenna 1 peduncle article 1 with round, narrow tip. Epimeral plate 3 with not more than three groups of spines just above ventral border ***Bathyporeia pilosa***

Antenna 1 peduncle article 1 with semi-rounded, broad tip. Adult epimeral plate 3 with four to six groups of spines just above ventral margin ***Bathyporeia sarsi***

Genus *Bathyporeia*

Body laterally compressed. Eyes distinct. Antenna 1 geniculate between peduncle articles 1 and 2. Female with antenna 2 flagellum short; male with antenna 2 flagellum more than half body-length. Uropod 3 inner ramus very short, scale-like; outer ramus much longer. Telson completely split.

Bathyporeia elegans Watkin   FIG. 9.30

Length 5 mm. Dorsal surface of urosome segment 1 with one pair of posteriorly directed spines and anteriorly directed bristles. Epimeral plate 3 evenly rounded at posterio-ventral corner, with about four groups of spines just above ventral border. First segment of antenna 1 peduncle with evenly rounded tip. Coxa 1 with obtusely pointed tip and a small but distinct tooth on posterior border. Coxae 2 and 3 with small tooth at posterio-ventral corner, which usually does not reach to level of ventral border. Segment 2 of accessory flagellum about one-third length of segment 1.

In wet, fine, and often muddy sand from MLWN into the sublittoral. All coasts, common or abundant.

Bathyporeia guilliamsoniana (Bate)   FIG. 9.30

Length 8 mm. Dorsal surface of urosome segment 1 with a pair of posteriorly directed spines and anteriorly directed bristles. Epimeral plate 3 with a well-developed tooth at posterio-ventral corner extending beyond vertical margin of posterior border in female and juvenile male, somewhat reduced in adult male. First segment of antenna 1 peduncle with more or less rounded tip. Coxa 1 with pointed tip and a well-defined tooth, marked by a small bristle, on posterior border. Coxae 2 and 3 with well-defined tooth at posterio-ventral corner.

In wet, fine, and medium sand at and below MLWN but commonest in the shallow sublittoral. All coasts, often abundant.

Bathyporeia nana Toulmond   FIG. 9.30

Length 3 mm. Dorsal surface of urosome segment 1 with one pair of posteriorly directed spines and anteriorly directed bristles. Epimeral plate 3 rounded at posterio-ventral corner in adults (somewhat angular in juvenile male, with a distinct tooth in juvenile female), with a single group of two or three spines just above ventral border. First segment of antenna 1 peduncle with rounded tip. Coxa 1 with blunt point close by a single bristle. Coxae 2 and 3 without tooth at posterio-ventral corner.

In wet, fine, and often muddy sand from MLWS into the sublittoral. Sometimes abundant. First found on the Atlantic coast of France, now recorded from the Irish Sea, Bristol Channel, English Channel, and the North Sea.

Bathyporeia pelagica (Bate)   FIG. 9.30

Length 6 mm. Dorsal surface of urosome segment 1 with a pair of posteriorly directed spines and anteriorly directed bristles. Epimeral plate 3 with a small tooth almost at posterio-ventral corner not extending beyond vertical margin of posterior border in female and juvenile male; in adult male tooth is reduced to uneven border around posterio-ventral corner. First segment of antenna 1 peduncle with fairly angular tip, the anterior border vertical or receding. Coxa 1 with rounded tip and no tooth, only bristles, on posterior border. Coxae 2 and 3 without a tooth at posterio-ventral corner.

In wet, clean, fine to medium sand from above MTL into the shallow sublittoral. Stenohaline. All coasts, often abundant.

Bathyporeia pilosa Lindström   FIG. 9.31

Length 6 mm. Dorsal surface of urosome segment 1 without posteriorly directed spines but with anteriorly directed bristles. Epimeral plate 3 smoothly rounded at posterio-ventral corner, not more than three groups of spines just above ventral border. First segment of antenna 1 peduncle with narrow, rounded tip. Coxae without teeth; coxa 1 with relatively sharply pointed tip; coxa 2 rounded anteriorly, narrowing towards ventral border; coxa 3 rectangular.

In fine and medium sand from MHWN downwards but rarely sublittoral. Favours damp rather than wet sand and is normally commonest above the highest point of emergence of the beach water table. Euryhaline. All coasts, common to very abundant ($> 10\,000/m^2$).

Bathyporeia sarsi Watkin   FIG. 9.31

Length 8 mm. Dorsal surface of urosome segment 1 without posteriorly directed spines but with anteriorly directed bristles. Epimeral plate 3 smoothly rounded at posterio-ventral corner, with four or more groups of spines just above ventral border in adult; juvenile with three or fewer groups of spines. First segment of antenna 1 peduncle with broad and moderately rounded tip, anterior margin slightly receding. Coxae without teeth; a distinct ridge may occur at posterio-ventral corner of coxae 2 and 3; coxa 1 nearly rounded at tip, coxa 2 almost square, coxa 3 rectangular.

In fine and medium sand from MHWN downwards, sometimes into the sublittoral. Usually found at and below the highest point of emergence of the beach water table, usually commonest below *B. pilosa* but above *B. pelagica*. Somewhat euryhaline. Common to abundant from west Wales southwards and around into the North Sea. Not common in Irish Sea and apparently absent from north-west Scotland.

Bathyporeia tenuipes Meinert   FIG. 9.31

Length 6 mm. Dorsal surface of urosome segment 1 with paired posteriorly directed spines and anteriorly directed bristles. Epimeral plate 3 rounded at posterio-ventral corner, with numerous ($\simeq 9$) groups of spines just above ventral border. First segment of antenna 1 peduncle with sharply angular tip. Coxa 1 narrow with bluntly pointed tip, without a tooth on posterior border. Coxae 2 and 3 with pronounced tooth at the posterio-ventral corner.

In clean, fine sand, almost always sublittoral. From west Ireland southwards and around into the North Sea. Infrequent.

Haustorius arenarius (Slabber)   FIG. 9.31

Length 13 mm. Body rounded, fat, with very small urosome. Antenna 1 not geniculate. Eyes indistinct. Pereopods without dactylus but with other articles enlarged; pereopod 6 propodus making a forward-facing acute angle with distal border of carpus. Uropod 3 short, rami equal. Telson short, partially cleft.

In clean, medium to coarse sands. Intertidal, generally close to the highest point of emergence of water table. All coasts, including sandy estuaries. Common.

Genus *Urothoe*

Body rounded, urosome not especially reduced. Antenna 1 not geniculate. Antenna 2 flagellum short in female, in male more than three-quarters of body-length. Eyes distinct. Pereopods with more or less lanceolate dactylus. Uropod 3 rami of equal length. Telson split.

Urothoe brevicornis Bate   FIG. 9.31

Length 8 mm. Antenna 1 peduncle article 3 shorter than 1; articles 1 and 2 subequal; flagellum with eight articles. Accessory flagellum with seven articles. Pereopod 5 carpus only slightly wider than long. Telson a little longer than wide, with two pairs of median, marginal setae, two pairs of terminal setae and one pair of fine terminal spines.

On wet, clean, medium to fine sand from about MTL into the sublittoral. Probably stenohaline. Frequent but rarely numerous, commoner in the south.

Urothoe elegans Bate   FIG. 9.31

Length 4 mm. Antenna 1 peduncle article 3 shorter than 1; articles 1 and 2 subequal; flagellum with six articles. Accessory flagellum with three articles. Pereopod 5 carpus a little longer than wide. Telson with two pairs of median marginal setae, two pairs of terminal setae, and one pair of thick terminal spines.

On muddy sand and fine sediments, sublittoral. All coasts.

Urothoe marina (Bate)   FIG. 9.31

Length 8 mm. Antenna 1 flagellum with nine articles. Accessory flagellum with five to seven articles. Antenna 2 peduncle robust, spiny; flagellum of female two-articled, as long as peduncle article 5, in male as long as body. Pereopod 5 carpus only slightly broader than merus, slightly broader than long. Uropod 1 peduncle short, rami smooth, strongly curved. Telson as wide as long, each lobe with one apical spine and three or four setae.

Mostly sublittoral, sometimes at extreme low water, in coarse sand or gravel. All coasts.

Urothoe poseidonis Reibisch   FIG. 9.31

Length 6 mm. Antenna 1 flagellum small, shorter than peduncle article 3, with five articles. Antenna 2 flagellum of female small, two-articled, in male as long as body. Pereopod 5 basis short and very broad, carpus much broader than merus, at least twice as broad as long. Uropod 1 outer ramus slightly curved, with one or two groups of spines, inner ramus straight with up to three long setae. Telson broader than long, each lobe with two short apical setae.

Lower shore and shallow sublittoral, sometimes common on sheltered sandy beaches. Reported from the Wash, the English Channel, Channel Isles, and Bristol Channel.

15 ARGISSIDAE

Body compressed. Rostrum small or absent, eyes poorly defined or lacking. Coxal plate 1 large, plates 2 and 3 smaller than 1, plate 4 very much larger than 1. Antenna 1 shorter than 2, with tiny, two-articled accessory flagellum. Mandible with well-developed molar; palp small, article 3 longer than 1. Gnathopods 1 and 2 simple, propodus of both smaller and narrower than carpus. Pereopods 3 and 4 distinctly smaller than 5–7. Pereopods 5 and 6 with broad basis, pereopod 7 basis very expanded. Uropods biramous; uropod 3 rami broader than uropod 1 and 2 rami. Telson deeply divided.

Argissa hamatipes (Norman)   FIG. 9.32

Length up to 6 mm. Head with small rostrum, eye of four small units. Antenna 1 extending to end of antenna 2 peduncle article 4; flagellum with seven articles in female, longer in male, with elongate first article. Coxal plate 1 broad and rounded, plates 2 and 3 narrow and tapered, plated, plate 4 very large. Urosome smooth in female, in male with dorsal process on segment 2 and keel on segment 3.

Sublittoral, on soft sediments. Reported from numerous

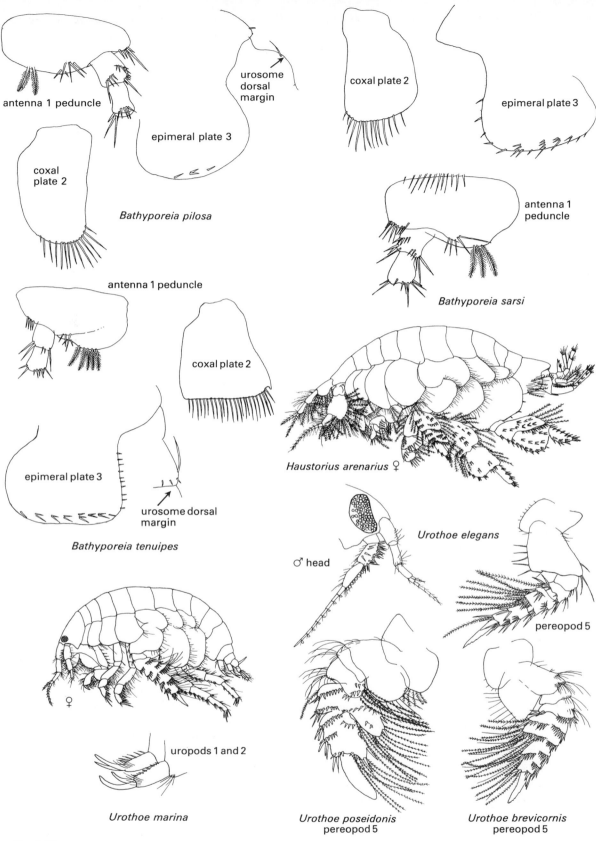

antenna 1 peduncle

urosome dorsal margin

epimeral plate 3

coxal plate 2

Bathyporeia pilosa

coxal plate 2

epimeral plate 3

antenna 1 peduncle

Bathyporeia sarsi

antenna 1 peduncle

coxal plate 2

epimeral plate 3

urosome dorsal margin

Bathyporeia tenuipes

Haustorius arenarius ♀

♂ head

Urothoe elegans

pereopod 5

Urothoe marina

uropods 1 and 2

Urothoe poseidonis pereopod 5

Urothoe brevicornis pereopod 5

Fig. 9.31

localities from the Wash to Shetland, and on southern and western coasts.

16 OEDICEROTIDAE

Body slightly or moderately cylindrical. Head with downcurved rostrum, usually conspicuous. Eyes distinct, partly or wholly coalesced. Accessory flagellum rudimentary or absent. Pereopods setose, 7 much longer than 6. Uropod 3 rami scarcely longer than peduncle. Telson short, entire or with shallow cleft or crenulations.

---

1. Gnathopod 2 chelate — **2**

   Gnathopod 2 subchelate or simple — **4**

2. Gnathopod 1 subchelate, stout; propodus with smooth distal border. Gnathopod 2 slender, carpus produced distally as long, slender process beneath propodus — **3**

   Gnathopod 1 subchelate, stout; distal border of propodus with about six small teeth. Gnathopod 2 slender, without distal process on carpus — ***Synchelidium haplocheles***

3. Gnathopod 1 propodus narrowly oval, only a slight angle between palm and hind margin. Pereopod 7 basis with distinctly convex posterior border — ***Pontocrates altamarinus***

   Gnathopod 1 propodus flatter, somewhat quadrangular, with distinct angle between palm and hind margin. Pereopod 7 basis with straight or sinuous posterior border — ***Pontocrates arenarius***

4. Gnathopods 1 and 2 subchelate, similar — **5**

   Gnathopods 1 and 2 subchelate, dissimilar; 1 stout with oval propodus and thick carpal process; 2 slender, elongate, with distal process on carpus closely underlying elongate propodus — ***Monoculodes carinatus***

5. Gnathopods 1 and 2 small, feeble; carpus with a very short distal process — ***Westwoodilla caecula***

   Gnathopods 1 and 2 elongate, slender; carpus produced distally as long, slender process underlying elongate propodus — ***Perioculodes longimanus***

Monoculodes carinatus (Bate)   FIG. 9.32

Length 10 mm, pale yellow with brown patches. Eyes coalesced but with median line of separation visible. Rostrum well-developed, downcurved. Gnathopod 1 subchelate, stout; carpal process robust, not contiguous with margin of propodus. Gnathopod 2 subchelate, slender; distal carpal process elongate, closely underlying propodus. Telson entire, slightly concave distally, with two distal spines.

Sublittoral, in fine sand; common. All British coasts.

Perioculodes longimanus (Bate and Westwood)   FIG. 9.32

Length 5 mm, translucent white. Eyes completely coalesced, reddish. Rostrum short, downcurved. Antenna 2 as long as body in male, less than half body-length in female. Gnathopods 1 and 2 subchelate, similar, with long carpal process lying beneath propodus. Telson entire.

In clean or muddy fine sand, from MLWS into sublittoral. Common. All coasts.

Genus *Pontocrates*

Eyes coalesced but with median line of separation sometimes visible, situated normally. Rostrum moderately sized, downcurved. Antenna 2 equal to body length in male, less than half body-length in female. Gnathopod 1 subchelate, stout; distal border of propodus smooth, underlain by distal carpal process. Gnathopod 2 chelate, long and slender; with long distal carpal process underlying propodus. Telson entire or with very slight posterior cleft.

Pontocrates altamarinus (Bate and Westwood)   FIG. 9.32

Length 7 mm; translucent white with orange/brown patches which usually persist even in preserved specimens. Antenna 1 female relatively long, equal to combined length of head and pereon segments 1–3; peduncle article 2 slender, as long as article 1; flagellum with eight articles, shorter than peduncle. Gnathopod 1 propodus large, narrowly oval; palm curved, fringed with small curved bristles and a few slender spinules, forming only a slight angle with much shorter hind margin; carpal process not projecting beyond propodus. Gnathopod 2 propodus distally tapered; thumb of chela only a little broader than dactylus; carpal process projecting beyond chela. Pereopod 7 basis with smoothly convex posterior border. Telson oval, distal border smooth or slightly cleft, with about five setae.

In fine and medium sand, lower shore and sublittoral. All coasts.

Pontocrates arenarius (Bate)   FIG. 9.32

Length 6.5 mm, translucent white. Antenna 1 female relatively short, about equal to twice length of head; peduncle article 2 shorter and much thinner than article 1; flagellum with nine articles, equal to length of peduncle. Gnathopod 1 propodus stout, somewhat quadrangular; palm with dense series of long stiff bristles, at distinct angle to longer hind margin; carpal process projecting beyond propodus. Gnathopod 2 very slender, thumb of chela only slightly broader than dactylus; carpal process projecting only slightly beyond chela. Pereopod 7 basis with straight or sinuous posterior border. Telson smoothly oval, with about two distal setae.

In sand from middle shore to sublittoral. All coasts.

Synchelidium haplocheles (Grube)   FIG. 9.32

Length 5 mm; white, banded or spotted with brown. Head with short downcurved rostrum, reaching to middle of antenna 1 peduncle article 1. Antenna 1 peduncle articles 2 and 3 subequal, much shorter than 1 in male, with flagellum as long as peduncle; antenna 1 female with articles 1 and 2 subequal, and short, five-

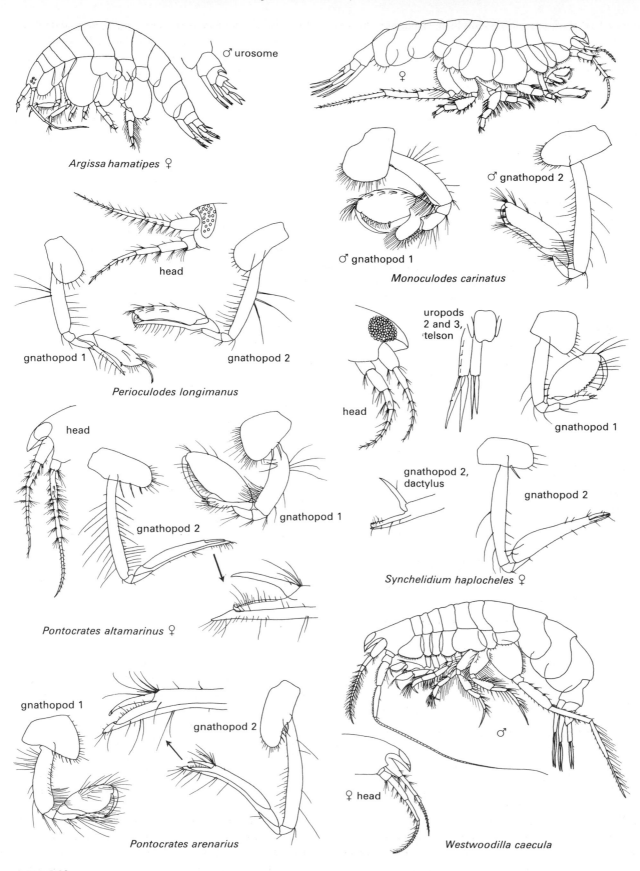

♂ urosome

Argissa hamatipes ♀

head

gnathopod 1

gnathopod 2

Perioculodes longimanus

♂ gnathopod 1

♂ gnathopod 2

Monoculodes carinatus

head

gnathopod 1

gnathopod 2

Pontocrates altamarinus ♀

uropods 2 and 3, telson

head

gnathopod 1

gnathopod 2, dactylus

gnathopod 2

Synchelidium haplocheles ♀

gnathopod 1

gnathopod 2

Pontocrates arenarius

♀ head

Westwoodilla caecula

Fig. 9.32

articled flagellum. Antenna 2 male with long, slender flagellum; antenna 2 female as long as antenna 1, peduncle articles 4 and 5 subequal, flagellum with seven articles. Gnathopod 1 carpal lobe elongate, with apical spine; propodus bearing about six teeth on palm. Gnathopod 2 without a carpal process, chela underlain by a distal process from the propodus. Telson entire, with distal concavity.

Sublittoral, in sand or mud. Reported from southern and western coasts, and from western Ireland.

Synchelidium maculatum Stebbing, reported from the Channel Isles, Dublin, and Anglesey, is distinguished from *S. haplocheles* by its smoothly rounded telson, and by gnathopod 2 propodus, which is distinctly swollen proximally.

Westwoodilla caecula (Bate) FIG. 9.32

Length 8 mm, white with red tint. Head elongate, anteriorly produced; rostrum small and straight, reaching end of antenna 1 peduncle article 1; eyes large, oval, Antenna 1 just longer than antenna 2 peduncle in female, with 15-articled flagellum; in male longer than antenna 2 peduncle, with densely setose 20-articled flagellum. Antenna 2 female with peduncle articles 4 and 5 of similar length, with short, 20-articled flagellum; antenna 2 male as long as body, with robust peduncle and elongate, filiform flagellum. Gnathopods 1 and 2 very similar, subchelate, with oval propodus and short, rounded, distal lobe on carpus. Pereopod 7 very elongate. Telson entire, rounded at tip.

Sublittoral. Widely reported, locally common; east coasts from Yorkshire to Shetland, on the west as far south as the Isle of Man, Dublin, and Fastnet.

17 PHOXOCEPHALIDAE

Body cylindrical, tapering at either end. Antennae short; accessory flagellum well-developed, with several articles. Head elongate with large hood-like rostrum enveloping bases of first antennae. Eyes separate or absent. Mandible with a palp. Gnathopods similar, small to medium-sized, subchelate. Pereopods spiny, adapted for burrowing. Pereopod 7 dissimilar to and shorter than 6; basis very expanded posteriorly. Uropod 3 biramous, external ramus biarticulate, longer than internal. Telson short or medium sized, always deeply split.

---

1. Pereopod 5 basis about as wide as ischium   **2**

   Pereopod 5 basis more than twice width of ischium   **4**

2. Epimeral plate 3 with a large sharp tooth at posterio-ventral corner   **3**

   Epimeral plate nearly rounded at posterio-ventral corner, marked only with two small teeth and a spine   ***Harpinia crenulata***

3. Posterior border of pereopod 7 basis with ten deeply cut teeth. Coxae 1 and 2 with a small tooth at posterio-ventral corner   ***Harpinia pectinata***

   Posterior border of pereopod 7 basis with eight or nine less distinct teeth. Coxae 1 and 2 without a tooth at posterio-ventral corner   ***Harpinia antennaria***

4. Rostrum pointed, very long, extending to end of antenna 1 peduncle. Eyes indistinct   ***Phoxocephalus holbolli***

   Rostrum projecting, flattened, but not extending as far as antenna 1 peduncle. Eyes large, distinct   **5**

5. Gnathopods 1 and 2 with more or less oval propodus   ***Metaphoxus pectinatus***

   Gnathopods 1 and 2 with distinctly quadrate propodus   ***Metaphoxus fultoni***

Genus *Harpinia*

Eyes absent. Antennae very short in both sexes. Antenna 2 peduncle article 4 with ventral lobe. Coxae bearing feathery distal setae; 4 produced posteriorly. Gnathopods similar. Pereopod 5 with basis scarcely wider than ischium. Pereopod 6 much the longest. Uropod 3 short, rami unequal in female, subequal in male. Telson short with rounded lobes.

Harpinia antennaria Meinert FIG. 9.33

Length 5 mm, translucent white. Pleon with many very short setae dorsally. Coxae 1 and 2 without teeth at posterio-ventral corners. Pereopod 7 basis with eight or nine moderately distinct teeth and short setae on posterior border. Epimeral plate 3 with a single large, sharp, curved tooth at posterio-ventral corner.

On muddy and silty sand, and mixed ground; sublittoral, rarely at ELWS. All coasts.

Harpinia crenulata (Boeck) FIG. 9.33

Length 4 mm, translucent white. Pleon with many very short setae dorsally. Coxae 1 and 2 without teeth at their posterio-ventral corners. Pereopod 7 basis irregularly denticulate posteriorly, with long setae. Epimeral plate 3 with two small teeth and a spine at posterio-ventral corner.

On muddy sand from depths of 10 m downwards. Recorded from Firth of Forth, the Minch, Clyde Sea, Isle of Man, Dublin, and western Ireland.

Harpinia pectinata Sars FIG. 9.33

Length 4 mm, translucent greyish white. Pleon without dorsal setae. Coxae 1 and 2 with a tooth at posterio-ventral corners. Pereopod 7 basis deeply denticulate posteriorly, with ten teeth and short setae. Epimeral plate 3 with a large, sharp, slightly curved tooth at posterio-ventral corner.

On muddy sand from 5 m downwards. All coasts.

Metaphoxus fultoni (Scott) FIG. 9.33

Length up to 3 mm; green with violet tint on pereon. Rostral hood flat, elongate, narrow, and rounded distally; eyes distinct. Antenna 1 short, peduncle article 1 robust, as long as combined length of 2 and 3; accessory flagellum well-developed, with three articles. Antenna 2 with very robust peduncle, female with short, three-articled flagellum, male with filiform flagellum as long as body. Gnathopod 1 with narrow rectangular propodus, palm convex. Coxal plate 1 only slightly broadened distally. Gnathopod 2 larger than 1, with broader rectangular propodus. Per-

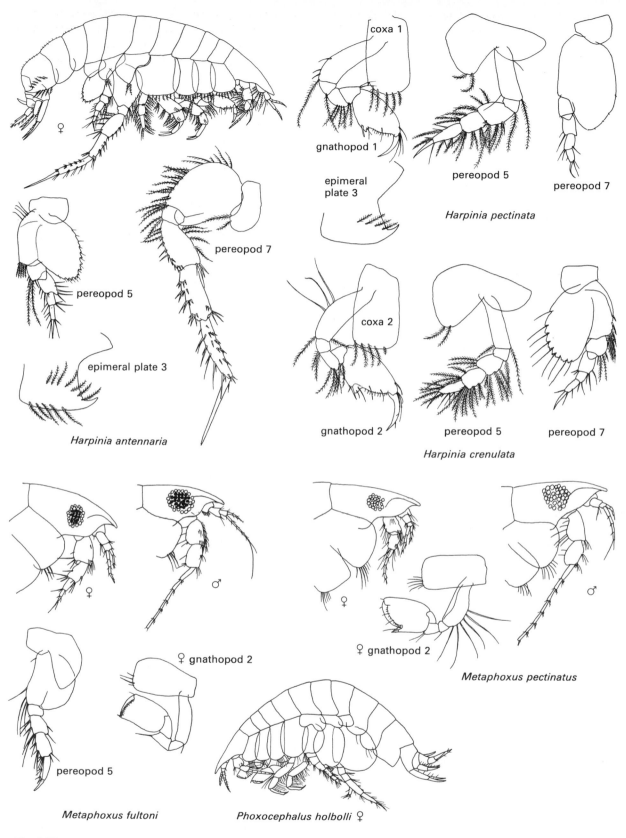

coxa 1

gnathopod 1

epimeral plate 3

pereopod 5

pereopod 7

Harpinia pectinata

pereopod 5

pereopod 7

epimeral plate 3

Harpinia antennaria

coxa 2

gnathopod 2

pereopod 5

pereopod 7

Harpinia crenulata

♀ gnathopod 2

♀ gnathopod 2

Metaphoxus pectinatus

pereopod 5

Metaphoxus fultoni

Phoxocephalus holbolli ♀

Fig. 9.33

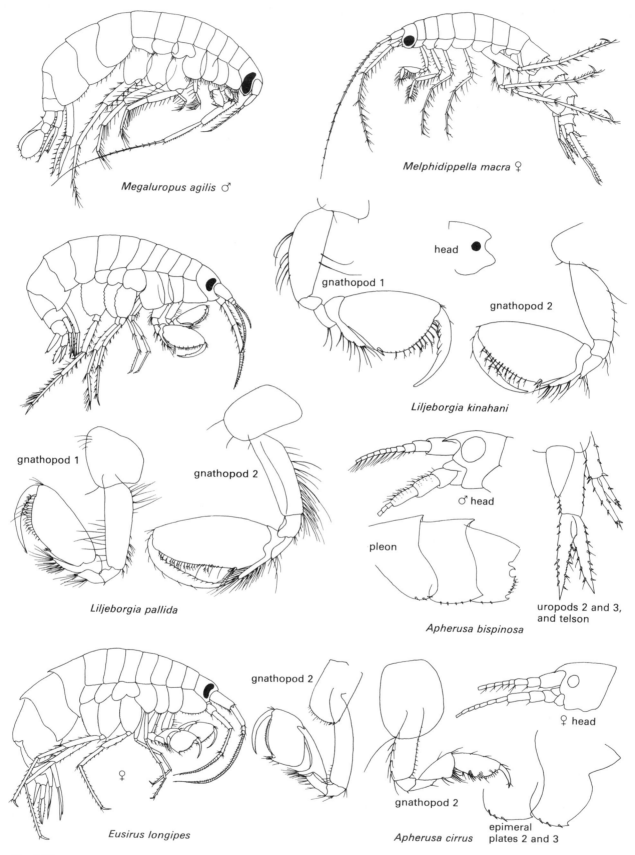

Megaluropus agilis ♂

Melphidippella macra ♀

head

gnathopod 1

gnathopod 2

Liljeborgia kinahani

gnathopod 1

gnathopod 2

Liljeborgia pallida

♂ head

pleon

uropods 2 and 3,
and telson

Apherusa bispinosa

gnathopod 2

♀ head

Eusirus longipes

gnathopod 2

Apherusa cirrus

epimeral
plates 2 and 3

Fig. 9.34

eopod 6 elongate, basis broad with densely setose anterior margin. Pereopod 7 basis very broad. Uropod 3 with few setae in female, inner ramus about half length of outer ramus article 1; in male with few long plumose setae on inner edges, inner ramus as long as outer ramus article 1. Telson elongate, deeply cleft, each lobe with two or three small apical setae.

Lower shore and shallow sublittoral. Recorded sporadically from both western and eastern coasts.

Metaphoxus pectinatus (Walker) FIG. 9.33

Length up to 3 mm; green-yellow to orange. Rostral hood flat, elongate, tapered, and rounded distally; eyes distinct. Antenna 1 short, peduncle article 1 robust, longer than combined length of 2 and 3; accessory flagellum well-developed, with three articles. Antenna 2 short in female, with robust peduncle and flagellum of four or five articles; in male with stout peduncle, as long as antenna 1 with elongate, filiform flagellum. Gnathopod 1 propodus broadly oval, with convex palm. Coxal plate 1 broad distally. Gnathopod 2 larger than 1, propodus broadly oval, with convex palm delimited by acute process and spine. Pereopod 6 much longer than 7, basis broad, with densely setose anterior margin. Pereopod 7 very broad. Uropod 3 sparsely setose in female, with inner ramus two-thirds length of outer ramus article 1; in male with plumose setae on inner edges, inner ramus as long as outer ramus article 1. Telson elongate, deeply cleft, each lobe with three or four small apical setae.

Lower shore and shallow sublittoral. Western coasts from Clyde Sea to Channel Isles, and off western Ireland.

Phoxocephalus holbolli (Kröyer) FIG. 9.33

Length 7 mm; pale brown to orange, with white flecks. Head with narrow, elongate rostral hood, extending to end of antenna 1 peduncle; eyes indistinct. Antenna 1 peduncle article 1 longer that articles 2 and 3 combined, flagellum of six articles, accessory flagellum elongate, with four articles. Antenna 2 slightly longer than 1 in female, with short, six-articled flagellum; in male with filiform flagellum as long as body. Gnathopods 1 and 2 with rounded, quadrate propodus, with oblique, convex palm. Gnathopod 2 slightly larger than 1. Pereopod 6 longer than 7, stout; pereopod 7 basis very broad, with serrate posterior margin. Uropod 3 female inner ramus three-quarters length of outer ramus article 1, sparsely setose; in male inner ramus about equal length to outer, with plumose setae.

Lower shore and sublittoral, in fine sand and mud. All coasts.

18 MELPHIDIPPIDAE

Pereon smooth, pleon often toothed dorsally. Head with small rostrum; lateral lobes broadly produced; eyes large. Antenna 1 equal to or shorter than 2. Accessory flagellum variable. Gnathopods feeble, more or less simple, similarly sized in both sexes. Pereopods long and slender. Uropods large; uropods 1 and 2 spiny; uropod 3 naked or spiny, with subequal, foliaceous, or lanceolate rami. Telson cleft or entire.

1. Antenna 1 much shorter than antenna 2. Uropod 3 rami oval, foliaceous ***Megaluropus agilis***

   Antenna 1 as long as, or longer than 2. Uropod 3 rami slender, lanceolate ***Melphidippella macra***

Megaluropus agilis Hoeck FIG. 9.34

Length 5 mm; mottled red, orange and white. Smooth dorsally, except for minute denticulation on posterio-dorsal margin of pleon segment 3. Head with sharp rostrum; lateral lobes considerably produced. Eyes especially large in male. Antenna 1 shorter than antenna 2 peduncle. Uropod 3 rami large, oval, foliaceous. Telson deeply cleft.

On sand, from LWS and sublittoral. All coasts.

Melphidippella macra (Norman) FIG. 9.34

Body very slender, up to 8 mm, red with white patches. Head with large bulging eyes. Antenna 1 longer than 2 in female, as long as 2 in male; peduncle article 1 stout, article 3 very small, flagellum long and slender. Coxal plates short, small; plates 5–7 scarcely touching. Pereon with dorsal tooth and lateral serrations on each segment. Gnathopods small, setose, simple or subchelate. Gnathopod 1 with slender, oval propodus; gnathopod 2 larger than 1 but with very slender, elongate propodus, and small dactylus. Pereopods 3 and 4 very slender, 5–7 stouter and longer. Uropod 3 very elongate, longer than 1 and 2, spinose; rami almost equal length, longer than peduncle. Telson divided for more than half its length, each lobe pointed distally with one long seta and several small, lateral setae.

Sublittoral. East coasts, from Yorkshire to Shetland, also Isle of Man, Dublin, and western Ireland.

19 LILJEBORGIIDAE

Antenna 1 distinctly shorter than 2. Accessory flagellum well-developed, with more than three articles. Rostrum small. Mandibular palp with three articles, 1 often as long as 3. Molar process of mandible without teeth or ridges. Gnathopods medium to large, subchelate. Pereopods 3 and 4 very thin. Pereopods 5 to 7 with basis expanded. Pleon and urosome segments usually with small teeth dorsally. Uropod 3 biramous, with subequal rami. Telson medium or long, deeply cleft, with bifid tips.

1. Eyes large. Pleon segments 1 and 2 each with a single tooth posterio-dorsally. Gnathopod 1 dactylus with ten teeth on inner surface ***Liljeborgia pallida***

   Eyes small. Pleon segments 1 and 2 each with three teeth posterio-dorsally. Gnathopod 1 dactylus with three teeth on inner surface ***Liljeborgia kinahani***

Genus *Liljeborgia*

Both gnathopods with carpus produced anteriorly into a long straight lobe; propodus large and oval; dactylus long, toothed on internal margin. Uropod 3 rami uniarticulate.

Liljeborgia kinahani (Bate)   FIG. 9.34

Length 3 mm, white or pink. Eyes small. Pleon segments 1 and 2 each with three teeth posterio-dorsally, segment 3 without teeth. Urosome segments 1 and 2 each with one posterio-dorsal tooth. Gnathopod 1 dactylus with three teeth on internal border. Gnathopod 2 dactylus with six teeth on internal border.

Sublittoral, on *Lithothamnion* and coarse gravel. Recorded from Firth of Forth, Clyde Sea, Isle of Man and English Channel.

Liljeborgia pallida (Bate)   FIG. 9.34

Length 6 mm, pale orange or white, with red or orange patch on pereon. Eyes large. Pleon segments 1 and 2 each with a single tooth posterio-dorsally, segment 3 without teeth. Urosome segment 1 with a single posterio-dorsal tooth, segments 2 and 3 without teeth. Gnathopod 1 dactylus with ten teeth on internal surface. Gnathopod 2 dactylus with 15 teeth on internal surface.

Sublittoral, rarely intertidal, among algae and stones. South and west Britain.

20 EUSIRIDAE

Body laterally compressed. Antenna 1 as long as or longer than 2, with peduncle article 3 very short. Accessory flagellum usually present, small, one or two articles only. Mandibular palp present. Gnathopods usually powerfully subchelate and characteristic: propodus as broad as long, attached to produced apex of carpus. Uropod 3 biramous, with elongate lanceolate rami. Telson usually longer than uropod 3 peduncle, subtriangular, partially cleft.

Eusirus longipes Boeck   FIG. 9.34

Length 13 mm, yellow marked with red. Eyes red, very large. Pleon segments produced posterio-dorsally into teeth. Epimeral plate 3 with posterior margin denticulate. Coxa 1 enlarged anteriorly.

Sublittoral, on mud and gravel. All coasts.

21 CALLIOPIIDAE

Body laterally compressed, often with a few teeth dorsally. Accessory flagellum present, well-developed or vestigial, or absent. Antenna 1 slender, medium to short, usually shorter than antenna 2, rarely equal to, or slightly longer. Rostrum small. Mandible with a palp. Coxae small to medium-sized, coxa 4 almost always excavate. Gnathopods feeble or occasionally moderately powerful, and more or less subchelate. Uropod 3 with elongate lanceolate rami, inner usually longer than outer. Telson entire, or slightly notched apically.

---

1. Accessory flagellum well-developed   **2**

    Accessory flagellum vestigial or absent   **3**

2. Dorsal carinae acutely produced posteriorly. Eyes
    occupying less than half side of head ***Gammarellus homari***

    Dorsal carinae not produced, scarcely acute. Eyes
    large, occupying more than half side of head
                                     Gammarellus angulosus

3. Gnathopods relatively feeble; carpus almost as long
    as propodus. With or without dorsal teeth   **4**

    Gnathopods more robust, carpus distinctly shorter
    than propodus. Body smooth dorsally
                                     Calliopius laeviusculus

4. Body smooth dorsally. Epimeral plate 3 with angular
    posterior border   ***Apherusa jurinei***

    Body with some dorsal teeth. Epimeral plate 3 with
    denticulate or convex posterior border   **5**

5. Last pereon and first two pleon segments with a
    posterio-dorsal tooth. Epimeral plate 3 complexly
    denticulate   ***Apherusa henneguyi***

    Last pereon segment without a dorsal tooth. Teeth
    present on pleon segments 1 and 2   **6**

6. Epimeral plate 3 smoothly convex posteriorly, with a
    tiny posterio-ventral tooth   ***Apherusa cirrus***

    Epimeral plate 3 with a minute or coarsely den-
    ticulate border   **7**

7. Epimeral plate 3 complexly denticulate. Pereopod 7
    basis with denticulate posterior border. Gnathopods
    slender; gnathopod 1 female with carpus longer than
    propodus   ***Apherusa bispinosa***

    Epimeral plate 3 simply denticulate or crenulate   **8**

8. Epimeral plate 3 simply denticulate. Pereopod 7
    basis without a denticulate posterior border
                                       Apherusa ovalipes

    Epimeral plate 3 with only slight crenulations on
    posterior border   ***Apherusa clevei***

Genus *Apherusa*

Antenna 1 usually shorter than 2, less than half body-length. Accessory flagellum absent. Gnathopods with carpus almost always longer than or equal to propodus. Gnathopod 1 with carpus lacking a posterior lobe. Body often with teeth dorsally on pereon and/or pleon. Epimeral plate 3 often with denticulate posterior border. Telson pointed, notched, or rounded.

Apherusa bispinosa (Bate)   FIG. 9.34

Length 6 mm. Colour variable, often deep red or violet with red eyes, or translucent white marked with black and/or green. Dorsal teeth present only on pleon segments 1 and 2. Eyes large and oval. Antenna 1 equal to half body-length, considerably shorter than 2. Coxa 1 angled anterio-distally. Gnathopods short, slender. Pereopod 7 basis with distinctly crenulated posterior border. Epimeral plate 3 with complexly denticulate posterior border: a sharp, sometimes bifid, proximal tooth followed by a gap and a number of distinct denticles ending in an acute posterio-ventral tooth. Telson triangular, twice as long as broad, with two distal setae.

In *Laminaria* holdfasts and among coralline algae, both littorally and sublittorally. All coasts.

Apherusa cirrus (Bate) FIG. 9.34

Length 6 mm. Reddish with black eyes. Dorsal teeth present only on pleon segments 1 and 2. Eyes small and round. Antenna 1 equal to half body-length, slightly shorter than 2. Coxae 1–3 rounded anteriorly. Pereopod 7 basis with smooth posterior border. Epimeral plate 3 with smoothly convex posterior border and a tiny tooth at posterio-ventral corner. Telson an elongated triangle, rounded at tip, with two distal setae.

Amongst algae, especially *Halidrys* and *Laminaria*. All coasts.

Apherusa clevei Sars FIG. 9.35

Length 3 mm. Very similar to *A. bispinosa* but with more robust gnathopods. Antennae and pereopods thinner, and posterior border of epimeral plate 3 only feebly crenulate.

Rare, mainly in bottom plankton hauls off southern shores, and from North Sea.

Apherusa henneguyi Chevreux and Fage FIG. 9.35

Length 7 mm. Last pereon and first two pleon segments produced dorsally into teeth. Eyes indistinct. Coxa 1 swollen distally, 2 and 3 rounded. Pereopod 7 basis with slightly concave and crenulate posterior border, and teeth at posterio-ventral corner. Epimeral plate 3 posterior border complex, with a distinct proximal tooth separated by a gap from a denticulate posterio-ventral border with a sharp posterio-ventral tooth. Telson triangular, with two distal setae.

On sand and mixed grounds at 49–60 m. South-west coasts.

Apherusa jurinei (Milne Edwards) FIG. 9.35

Length 6 mm. Colour very variable, whitish or yellow with bands of brown, crimson, or green giving, sometimes, a distinctly striped appearance. Body smooth dorsally. Eyes red, large and reniform. Antenna 1 equal to half body-length, almost as long as antenna 2. Coxae 1 to 3 quadrangular. Pereopod 7 basis with a crenulated posterior margin. Epimeral plate 3 posterior border angled in mid-region, with a small posterio-ventral tooth. Telson rounded-triangular, with two to four setae.

Common in *Laminaria* holdfasts and among other littoral and sublittoral algae. All coasts.

Apherusa ovalipes Norman and Scott FIG. 9.35

Length 6 mm. Dorsal teeth present only on pleon segments 1 and 2. Eyes large and rounded. Antenna 1 about half length of 2. Coxa 1 dilated distally. Pereopod 7 basis with smooth posterior border. Epimeral plate 3 with denticulate posterior border, no distinct proximal teeth, but with an acute tooth at posterio-ventral corner. Telson triangular, with minutely tridentate tip.

Among algae, generally in the sublittoral. Mainly southern coasts.

Calliopius laeviusculus (Krøyer) FIG. 9.35

Length 8 mm. Antennae more or less equal, short and thick; antenna 1 peduncle article 3 produced anterio-ventrally. Accessory flagellum absent. Gnathopods moderately robust; carpus much shorter than propodus, with a distinct lobe. Epimeral plate 3 with smooth, convex, posterior border and a small, sharp posterio-ventral tooth. Pereopod 7 basis with distinctly crenulate posterior border. Telson rounded triangular.

Among algae, lower shore and shallow sublittoral. Common. All coasts.

Genus *Gammarellus*

Body robust, carinate dorsally. Antennae of equal length. Accessory flagellum well-developed, Gnathopods 1 and 2 subchelate, similar. Pereopods powerful, spiny. Uropods 1 and 2 biramous, spiny; uropod 3 rami elongate, lanceolate, setose, uniarticulate. Telson entire, with terminal notch.

Gammarellus angulosus (Rathke) FIG. 9.35

Length 15 mm; yellowish, mottled with red or brown. Dorsal carinae not pronounced, scarcely produced posteriorly. Eyes very large, occupying more than half side of head.

Lower shore and sublittoral. Probably all coasts.

Gammarellus homari (Fabricius) FIG. 9.35

Length 35 mm; olive-green to yellow, marked with brown. Body stout, with large, acutely produced dorsal carinae on posterior pereon and pleon. Head with truncated lateral lobes; eyes round to reniform, occupying less than half side of head. Antenna 1 and 2 about one-third of body-length; accessory flagellum with five to seven articles. Coxae of moderate size. Epimeral plate 3 with convex posterior margins. Uropods 1 and 2 spiny, inner rami slightly longer than outer; uropod 3 rami lanceolate, setose, outer just longer than inner. Telson longer than broad, shallowly notched, with a few small spines.

Usually sublittoral. North Sea coasts.

22 PLEUSTIDAE

Body laterally compressed, smooth or with a few teeth dorsally. Antenna 1 longer than 2, equal to about three-quarters of body-length. Accessory flagellum absent. Rostrum medium-sized. Mandible with a palp. Gnathopods similar, small to moderately sized. Coxae medium or long; coxa 4 excavate posteriorly. Epimeral plate 3 not denticulate posteriorly but often with an acute posterio-ventral point. Uropod 3 biramous, with lanceolate rami much longer than peduncle; outer ramus usually shorter than inner. Telson entire, usually rounded triangular.

---

1. Maxilliped palp with well-developed distal process on article 3. Mandible with large, ridged molar process **Stenopleustes nodifer**

   Maxilliped palp article 3 without distal process. Mandible with poorly developed, unridged molar process **Parapleustes bicuspis**

Parapleustes bicuspis (Krøyer) FIG. 9.36

Length 12 mm; white or yellowish, with red or brown patches. Head with small rostrum; eyes large, oval, dark red. Body slender, with single, small, dorsal tooth on pleon segments 1 and 2. Coxal plates 1–3 with one or two small teeth on posterio-distal angle. Epimeral plate 3 with tooth on distal angle. Antenna

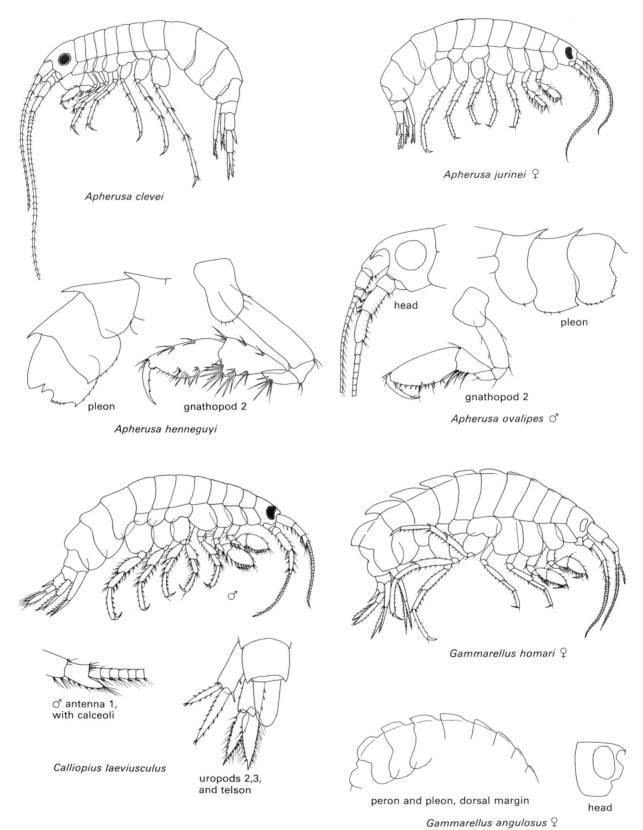

Apherusa clevei

Apherusa jurinei ♀

head

pleon

pleon   gnathopod 2

gnathopod 2

Apherusa henneguyi

Apherusa ovalipes ♂

♂ antenna 1,
with calceoli

Calliopius laeviusculus

uropods 2,3,
and telson

Gammarellus homari ♀

peron and pleon, dorsal margin

head

Gammarellus angulosus ♀

Fig. 9.35

1 flagellum about four times length of peduncle. Gnathopod 1 basis setose anteriorly, merus acute distally, propodus elongate oval with spinose palm. Gnathopod 2 slightly larger than 1. Uropod 3 outer ramus slightly more than half length of inner. Telson broadly rounded distally.

Sublittoral, to 120 m. A boreal species recorded from scattered localities on most British coasts.

Parapleustes assimilis (Sars) is smaller than *P. bicuspis*, up to 8 mm long, lacks dorsal pleon teeth and has no tooth on epimeral plate 3 distal angle.

Stenopleustes nodifer (Sars) FIG. 9.36

Length 5 mm; white with yellow-brown speckles, and dark brown on antenna 1 peduncle and uropods; or with dark red flecks on pereon and pleon. Head with small rostrum; eyes reniform, red. Body slender, with dorsal processes on pleon segments 1 and 2. Coxal plates 1–4 rounded, with tiny setae on surface. Gnathopod 1 basis with setose anterior margin; propodus suboval, with crenulate, convex palm bearing double row of four long spines. Gnathopod 2 slightly larger than 1; basis with anterior setae; propodus narrow-oval, with double row of six long spines on palm; carpus shorter than propodus. Pereopods 3 and 4 elongate, slender; pereopod 7 basis broad with finely serrate posterior margin. Uropod 1 rami subequal; uropod 2 with outer ramus shorter than inner; uropod 3 with smooth peduncle and spinose rami, outer ramus two-thirds length of inner. Telson elongate, rounded-triangular.

Sublittoral, to 300 m. West shores of Britain and Ireland, as far north as Antrim and the Firth of Clyde.

Stenopleustes latipes (Sars) is a larger species, up to 12 mm long. It is distinguished by its much larger, broader gnathopod 2 propodus, which has a sculptured edge to the palm, delimited by stout spines.

23 ATYLIDAE

Body compressed, pereon segments short, pleon segments long. Some body segments produced dorsally into keel-like, post-eriorly pointed teeth. Urosome segments 2 and 3 coalesced. Rostrum prominent. Eyes distinct and separate. Accessory flagellum vestigial or absent. Mandible with a distinct palp. Gnathopods subchelate, small. Uropod 3 biramous. Telson medium length, deeply split or cleft.

Atylus falcatus (Metzger) FIG. 9.36

Length 7 mm, translucent white with brown patches. Similar to *A. swammerdami* but pereopod 3 with dactylus very long, recurved, equal to combined length of propodus and carpus. Pereopod 4 small, with carpus, propodus and dactylus almost rudimentary; pereopods 5, 6, and 7 with propodus much shorter than carpus.

Sublittoral on shell or muddy sand; all British coasts but apparently not common.

Atylus guttatus (Costa) FIG. 9.36

Length 10 mm; reddish white with brown patches dorsally and on coxal plates. Eyes large. Rostrum nearly straight. Pereon and pleon with low dorsal keel. Coxae serrated distally; coxae 3 and 4 broad. Pereopod 5 basis with posterio-ventral corner produced as a triangular point. Telson with a deep median cleft, the two halves diverging distally.

Intertidal, and sublittoral to 75 m. A southern species, present on the Mediterranean and Atlantic coasts of western Europe, extending northwards to Irish Sea and southern North Sea.

Atylus swammerdami (Milne Edwards) FIG. 9.36

Length 8 mm; translucent white with brown patches. Pereon, and pleon segments 1 and 2, smooth dorsally; pleon segment 3 sometimes with a very small, dorsal, keel-like tooth. Urosome with two distinct teeth, the first small, the second large, separated by a deep notch. Pereopods 3 and 4 short, similar; 5, 6, and 7 with propodus as long as, or longer than, carpus.

Lower shore and sublittoral, generally on sand or amongst algae. Ubiquitous and often common.

Atylus vedlomensis (Bate and Westwood) FIG. 9.36

Length 8 mm; translucent, tinged yellow, with patches and irregular streaks of orange on the back, sides, and limbs. A keel-like tooth present dorsally on last pereon segment and on each pleon segment. Arrangement of urosome teeth similar to *A. swammerdami*. Rostrum somewhat downcurved. Coxae slightly serrated distally. Pereopod 5 basis with posterio-ventral corner produced into a hook. Telson with deep median split, the two halves not diverging distally.

On fine shelly sand and mud in shallow water. All British coasts, but commonest in the south.

24 DEXAMINIDAE

Body laterally compressed. Antennae usually medium or long, rarely very short. Accessory flagellum absent. One pair of eyes. Rostrum small. Mandible without a palp. Pleon usually with dorsal teeth. Urosome segments 2 and 3 coalesced. Gnathopods feeble, subchelate. Uropod 3 biramous. Telson deeply cleft, medium or long.

---

1. Distinct dorsal teeth present only on urosome segments **2**

   Distinct dorsal teeth present on whole of pleon and last pereon segments **3**

2. Pereopod 3 dactylus shorter than propodus ***Atylus swammerdami***

   Pereopod 3 dactylus very long, equal to combined length of propodus and carpus, recurved towards body ***Atylus falcatus***

3. Pereopod 5 basis with posterio-ventral corner produced into a hook; pereopod 6 basis produced at distal angle ***Atylus vedlomensis***

   Pereopod 5 basis with posterio-ventral corner produced into a triangular point; pereopod 6 basis not produced at distal angle ***Atylus guttatus***

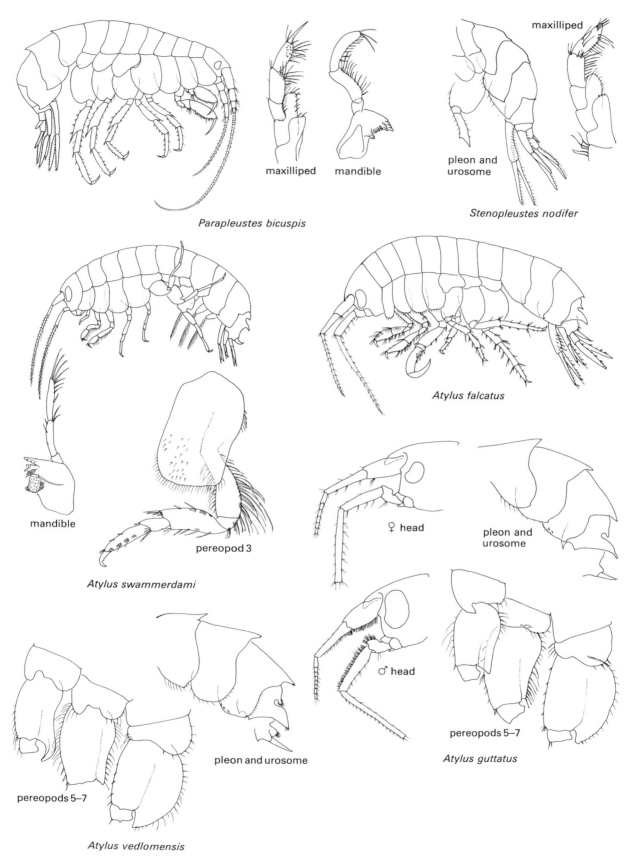

maxilliped

maxilliped   mandible

Parapleustes bicuspis

maxilliped

pleon and
urosome

Stenopleustes nodifer

mandible

pereopod 3

Atylus swammerdami

Atylus falcatus

♀ head

pleon and
urosome

♂ head

pereopods 5–7

Atylus guttatus

pereopods 5–7

pleon and urosome

pereopods 5–7

Atylus vedlomensis

Fig. 9.36

1. Adults very small, up to 2 mm. Pereopod 7 with merus and carpus expanded, bearing numerous long setae. Urosome segment 1 without a sharp dorsal tooth
Guernea coalita

   Adults 4–12 mm. Pereopod 7 merus and carpus not expanded, without numerous long setae. Urosome segment 1 terminating in a sharp posterio-dorsal tooth **2**

2. Pereopods 3–7 with merus longer than combined length of carpus and propodus **Tritaeta gibbosa**

   Pereopods 3–7 merus shorter than combined length of carpus and propodus **3**

3. Pereopod 7 basis with posterior margin expanded **Dexamine spinosa**

   Pereopod 7 basis with parallel margins, not expanded **Dexamine thea**

Genus *Dexamine*

Urosome segment 1 terminating in a sharp posterio-dorsal tooth. Antenna 1 longer than 2 in female, shorter or subequal in male. Rostrum small. Coxae medium-sized, rather rounded. Gnathopod 1 smaller than 2. Pereopods 3–7 with merus shorter than combined length of carpus and propodus. Epimeral plate 3 with a long posterio-ventral point. Telson much longer than wide.

Dexamine spinosa (Montagu) FIG. 9.37

Length 12 mm; whitish, marked with red, brown, violet, and orange. Eyes brown. Pleon segments 1–3 with single posterio-dorsal tooth. Pereopod 6 basis with a sinuous posterior border; pereopod 7 basis expanded, with a convex border. Uropod 3 rami twice length of peduncle.

Littoral and sublittoral; among *Laminaria* holdfasts, and other algae, in *Zostera*, and on sand or mud. All British coasts.

Dexamine thea Boeck FIG. 9.37

Length 5 mm; yellowish green marked with white. Eyes red. Much smaller than *D. spinosa* with pleon teeth less obvious. Pereopod 6 basis considerably expanded, with convex, slightly crenulate posterior border; pereopod 7 basis not expanded, posterior border approximately straight. Uropod 3 rami only a little longer than peduncle.

Intertidal and sublittoral, among algae, especially *Laminaria* holdfasts. South and west coasts, from Portland to the Clyde Sea; also coasts of Ireland.

Guernea coalita (Norman) FIG. 9.37

Adult up to 2 mm; usually opaque white, with red eyes. Urosome somewhat truncated, with segments rounded dorsally. Female antennae both very short; male antenna 2 much longer than 1. Coxa 5 larger than others. Pereopod 7 merus and carpus expanded, bearing numerous long setae. Telson a little longer than wide.

Sublittoral, in sand and gravel. Southern Britain, south North Sea to Irish Sea.

Tritaeta gibbosa (Bate) FIG. 9.37

Length 5 mm; brownish white, marked with brown patches. Pleon smooth dorsally in female, with small blunt teeth in male. Antennae subequal, about two-thirds of body-length. Coxae small, 3 and 4 acutely pointed at anterior and posterior ventral corners. Pereopods 3–7 merus longer than combined length of carpus and propodus. Epimeral plate 3 with only a small posterio-ventral point. Telson much longer than wide.

Usually sublittoral, among *Laminaria* holdfasts and other algae; often in sponges and ascidians. All British coasts.

25 AMPITHOIDAE

Body smooth dorsally. Antennae medium to long, 1 as long as or longer than 2. Accessory flagellum present or absent. Rostrum absent. Mandible with or without a palp. Coxae small to medium, coxa 4 not excavate posteriorly. Gnathopods well-developed, subchelate, 2 larger than 1, especially in male. Pereopod 5 frequently much shorter than 6 and 7. Uropod 3 biramous, with short quadrate rami always shorter than peduncle; outer ramus armed apically with one to three large hooked spines. Telson short, entire, fleshy; often with small cusps.

1. Head enlarged, globular, with distinct indentation at junction with antenna 1. Gnathopod 2 massive, with deeply concave palm **Amphitholina cuniculus**

   Head normal. Gnathopod 2 sometimes massive, but palm not, or only shallowly concave **2**

2. Mandible with palp **3**

   Mandible without palp. Pereopod 5 basis broadly expanded. Telson short, broad, truncated at apex **Sunamphithoe pelagica**

3. Pereopods 5–7 propodus scarcely expanded distally. Telson with two small apical cusps **4**

   Pereopods 5–7 propodus strongly expanded distally. Telson with two prominent curved spines and cusps **5**

4. Gnathopods 1 and 2 without distal lobe on ischium. Gnathopod 2 basis with a small lobe anterio-dorsally, propodus with only a slightly concave palm **Ampithoe (Ampithoe) rubricata**

   Gnathopod 2 in both sexes and gnathopod 1 in male with large lobe on inner distal margin of ischium. Gnathopod 2 basis with large anterio-dorsal lobe; propodus with a distinctly concave palm **Ampithoe (Ampithoe) ramondi**

5. Gnathopod 2 basis and ischium with distinct anterio-distal lobes **Ampithoe (Pleonexes) gammaroides**

   Gnathopod 2 basis with anterio-distal lobe in both sexes; ischium without a lobe **Ampithoe (Pleonexes) neglecta**

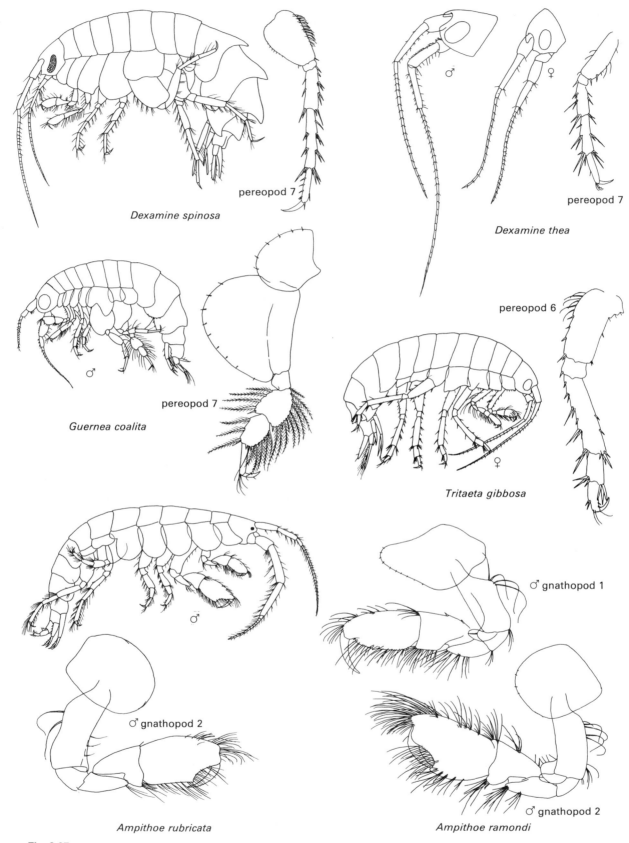

pereopod 7

Dexamine spinosa

pereopod 7

Dexamine thea

pereopod 7

Guernea coalita

pereopod 6

Tritaeta gibbosa

♂ gnathopod 1

♂ gnathopod 2

Ampithoe rubricata

♂ gnathopod 2

Ampithoe ramondi

Fig. 9.37

Genus *Ampithoe*

Accessory flagellum absent. Mandible with a slender three-articled palp. Gnathopods subchelate, 2 usually larger than 1. Uropod 3 outer ramus armed with a pair of large, curved spines. Telson short, fleshy, with two apical cusps.

Comprises the two subgenera *Ampithoe* and *Pleonexes*.

Ampithoe (Ampithoe) ramondi Audouin   FIG. 9.37

Length 13 mm, red-brown marked with white, to greenish marked with brown. Eyes fairly large. Uropod 3 without long dorsal setae on outer ramus. Telson weakly concave apically

Sublittoral, tube-building amongst shallow water algae. South and west coasts.

Ampithoe (Ampithoe) rubricata (Montagu)   FIG. 9.37

Length 20 mm, red to green, with light or dark markings. Eyes small. Uropod 3 outer ramus with group of long setae dorsally. Telson convex apically.

Littoral and sublittoral, very common, making tubes amongst algae and under stones. All British coasts.

Ampithoe (Pleonexes) gammaroides Bate   FIG. 9.38

Length 8 mm. Male gnathopod 2 propodus with straight palm. Antennae often exceeding half body-length, with few setae. Telson with two large curved hooks and a number of short setae.

Littoral and sublittoral, amongst algae. Probably on all coasts, although past confusion with *Ampithoe (Pleonexes) helleri* makes this uncertain.

Ampithoe (Pleonexes) helleri Karaman   FIG. 9.38

Length 5 mm. Gnathopod 2 basis with anterio-distal lobe in both sexes, ischium without lobe. Male gnathopod 2 propodus with sinuous palm. Antennae relatively short, reaching only one-third of body-length but with a moderate number of setae. Telson with two large curved hooks and just two setae.

Sublittoral, amongst shallow water algae. Southern and western coasts.

Amphitholina cuniculus (Stebbing)   FIG. 9.38

Length 4 mm, bright green. Body elongate, cylindrical. Head broad and swollen, rostrum absent. Antennae slender, 1 longer than 2. Accessory flagellum absent. Mandible without a palp. Gnathopod 2 very large, subchelate. Uropod 3 robust, outer ramus with two large spines, inner ramus with distal setae. Telson triangular with two curved distal cusps.

Burrows in stipes of *Alaria esculenta*. South and west coasts.

Sunamphitoe pelagica (Milne Edwards)   FIG. 9.38

Length 10 mm; greenish yellow or yellow with red markings. Accessory flagellum absent. Mandible without a palp. Gnathopod 2 male very large, much larger than 1; female with gnathopods subequal. Pereopods 5–7 propodus only slightly swollen distally; pereopod 5 basis considerably expanded; pereopods 6–7 basis only moderately expanded. Uropod 3 outer ramus with two apical hooks, inner ramus with one or two apical spines and several setae. Telson short, broad, apically truncated.

Intertidal and sublittoral, on algae. All coasts.

26 AORIDAE

Body smooth dorsally. Antenna 1 usually longer than 2, usually with an accessory flagellum. Rostrum vestigial. Mandible with a palp. Coxae of variable size and shape, coxa 4 not excavate posteriorly. Gnathopods large and subchelate, sometimes complexly so, 1 always larger than 2. Pereopod 7 conspicuously elongate. Uropod 3 biramous, short, rami as long as or longer than peduncle. Telson entire, fleshy and short, nearly circular or square.

Adult males may be readily identified by the structure of their gnathopods. In a number of species, however, identification of females is exceptionally difficult.

---

1. Gnathopod 2 basis with fringe of very long, plumose setae **2**

   Gnathopod 2 basis with very few, short setae **4**

2. Uropod 2 very short and spiny. Accessory flagellum long, with up to six articles   ***Leptocheirus hirsutimanus***

   Uropod 2 not very stout. Accessory flagellum small, with one or two articles **3**

3. Gnathopod 1 dactylus extending slightly beyond palmar margin of propodus. Pereopods 5–7 with basis at most only a little expanded posteriorly

        Leptocheirus pilosus

   Gnathopod 1 dactylus extending considerably beyond palmar margin of propodus. Pereopods 5–7 with basis distinctly expanded posteriorly

        Leptocheirus pectinatus

4. Male gnathopod 1 with merus produced anteriorly as a long, pointed process. Pereopod 7 with basis expanded, and excavate posterio-distally   ***Aora gracilis***

   Male gnathopod 1 with normal merus **5**

5. Male gnathopod 1 carpus with one or more stout processes on posterio-distal margin **6**

   Male gnathopod 1 carpus without posterio-distal processes **9**

6. Male gnathopod 2 chelate, the dactylus opposed by a stout spine on the propodus   ***Microdeutopus chelifer***

   Male gnathopod 2 not chelate **7**

7. Male gnathopod 1 carpus with two or more teeth on posterio-distal margin   ***Microdeutopus gryllotalpa***

   Male gnathopod 1 carpus with single large, posterio-distal tooth **8**

8. Male gnathopod 2 merus more than half length of carpus, with dense fringe of plumose setae

        Microdeutopus versiculatus

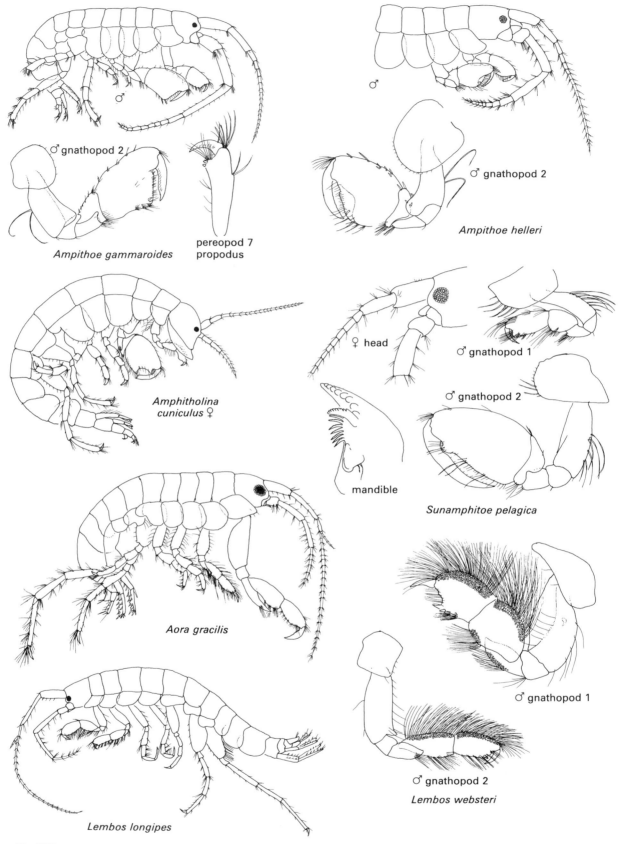

♂ gnathopod 2

Ampithoe gammaroides

pereopod 7
propodus

♂ gnathopod 2

Ampithoe helleri

*Amphitholina
cuniculus* ♀

♀ head

♂ gnathopod 1

♂ gnathopod 2

mandible

Sunamphitoe pelagica

Aora gracilis

♂ gnathopod 1

♂ gnathopod 2

Lembos websteri

Lembos longipes

Fig. 9.38

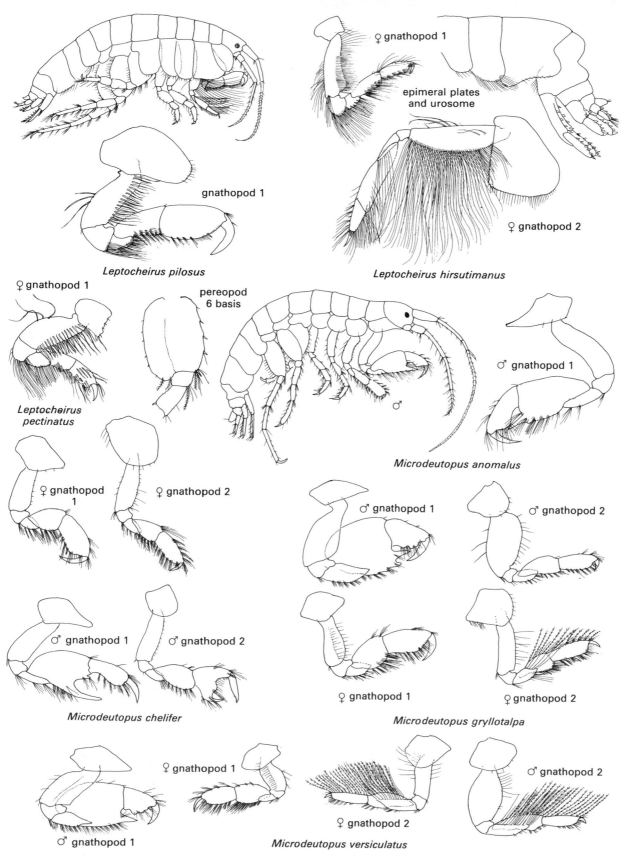

gnathopod 1

Leptocheirus pilosus

♀ gnathopod 1

epimeral plates and urosome

♀ gnathopod 2

Leptocheirus hirsutimanus

♀ gnathopod 1

pereopod 6 basis

Leptocheirus pectinatus

♀ gnathopod 1

♀ gnathopod 2

♂ gnathopod 1

Microdeutopus anomalus

♂ gnathopod 1

♂ gnathopod 2

♂ gnathopod 1

♂ gnathopod 2

♀ gnathopod 1

♀ gnathopod 2

Microdeutopus chelifer

Microdeutopus gryllotalpa

♀ gnathopod 1

♀ gnathopod 2

♂ gnathopod 2

♂ gnathopod 1

Microdeutopus versiculatus

Fig. 9.39

Male gnathopod 2 merus less than half length of carpus, with few, non-plumose setae

Microdeutopus anomalus

9. Male gnathopod 1 basis with tuft of very long setae posteriorly. Pereopods 3 and 4 with dactylus almost as long as propodus **Lembos longipes**

Male gnathopod 1 basis without long posterior setae. Pereopods 3 and 4 with dactylus only three-quarters as long as propodus **Lembos websteri**

Aora gracilis (Bate) FIG. 9.38

Length 6 mm; translucent yellow, or greenish white marked with brown. Eyes black. Body slender. Antenna 1 much longer than 2. Accessory flagellum well-developed. Gnathopod 1 very long, slender, merus prolonged into a long sharp point, carpus and propodus without teeth. Gnathopod 1 female almost simple, merus not produced, but with propodus longer than carpus. Gnathopod 2 in both sexes subchelate, not especially setose. Pereopod 6 basis expanded, posterior border straight proximally but excavate distally. Epimeral plate 3 with posterior border convex, and a small tooth at posterio-ventral corner. Uropod 3 rami subequal, longer than peduncle.

Intertidal and sublittoral, building tubes amongst algae and hydroids. All British coasts.

Genus *Lembos*

Similar to *Microdeutopus* but with accessory flagellum always well-developed. Gnathopod 1 male powerful, subchelate; merus and carpus without teeth; propodus not narrower but normally longer than carpus. Gnathopod 1 female much weaker, subchelate. Gnathopod 2 male subchelate, strongly setose anteriorly, with carpus equal to or longer than propodus. Uropod 3 rami equal, longer than peduncle.

Lembos longipes (Liljeborg) FIG. 9.38

Length 5 mm, white with pinkish bands. Accessory flagellum with two articles. Gnathopod 1 male with basis very large, convex posteriorly, with many long setae; carpus and propodus with long setae anteriorly, propodus larger than carpus, with two teeth on palm. Gnathopod 1 female feeble; propodus larger than carpus, nearly oval, without a well-defined palm. Gnathopod 2 male with basis not greatly expanded, without a hook anterio-distally; propodus smaller than carpus, both with many long setae anteriorly. Gnathopod 2 female with propodus larger than carpus, with a nearly transverse palm. Uropod 3 rami twice length of peduncle.

Sublittoral on hydroids and on coarse and muddy sands. Probably all British coasts but not usually common.

Lembos websteri Bate FIG. 9.38

Length 4 mm, yellowish brown with brown marks. Accessory flagellum with four articles. Gnathopod 1 male with basis, carpus, and propodus enlarged; palm of propodus with one sharp and one blunt tooth, and delimited by a spine. Gnathopod

1 female with propodus larger than carpus, with an oblique palm delimited by a spine. Gnathopod 2 male basis with a conspicuous, small, hooked tooth at anterio-distal corner; propodus shorter than carpus with numerous long setae anteriorly. Gnathopod 2 female similar to male but more slender and without a hook on anterio-distal corner of basis. Uropod 3 rami about 1.5 times length of peduncle.

Intertidal and sublittoral, frequently in *Laminaria* holdfasts, and amongst epibenthos. All British coasts.

Genus *Leptocheirus*

Antenna 1 usually shorter than 2. Accessory flagellum present. Coxa 2 large. Gnathopod 1 male subchelate, merus and carpus without teeth; gnathopod 1 female subchelate, extremely setose. Gnathopod 2 simple in both sexes, basis and carpus extremely setose, carpus not particularly expanded. Uropods 1 and 2 with peduncle produced into a long tooth dorsally, rami more or less spinose. Uropod 3 short, rami equal or unequal, one or both longer than peduncle.

Leptocheirus hirsutimanus (Bate) FIG. 9.39

Length 8 mm; opaque, with either orange or violet tinges. Eyes black. Antenna 1 slightly longer than 2. Accessory flagellum long, with six articles. Coxa 1 quadrangular, very small, hidden by large coxa 2. Gnathopod 1 propodus larger than carpus, palmar margin a little oblique and not shorter than dactylus. Gnathopod 2 propodus less than half length of carpus. Uropods 1 and 2 very stout; 2 with peduncle large and short, rami large with two rows of large spines.

Sublittoral on shelly gravel and sand. West and south coasts.

L. tricristatus (Chevreux), also reported from the south-west only, is distinguished from all other species of *Leptocheirus* by a distinct keel on urosome segment 1.

Leptocheirus pectinatus Norman FIG. 9.39

Length 3 mm, yellowish green. Eyes black. Antenna 1 longer than 2. Accessory flagellum very small, biarticulate. Gnathopod 1 female with basis short and stout; propodus shorter than carpus, quadrangular, with palm considerably shorter than dactylus. Gnathopod 1 male with carpus longer and larger than propodus, otherwise as in female. Gnathopod 2 with propodus half length of carpus. Uropod 2 not especially stout, rami longer than peduncle. Uropod 3 very small, rami shorter than peduncle.

Sublittoral on silty rough ground. Probably all British coasts.

Leptocheirus pilosus Zaddach FIG. 9.39

Length 4 mm, brownish red. Eyes black. Antenna 1 longer than 2. Accessory flagellum very small, uniarticulate. Coxa 1 not much smaller than 2. Gnathopod 1 female with propodus a little longer and broader than carpus, palmar margin convex and just shorter than dactylus. Gnathopod 1 male with basis, carpus and propodus large. Gnathopod 2 with propodus a little shorter than carpus. Uropod 2 not especially stout, rami equal to peduncle. Uropod 3 very small, with rami shorter than peduncle.

In brackish water, amongst *Ruppia maritima* or *Cordylophora lacustris*. Reported from the Wash and Norfolk, Plymouth,

Channel Isles, Anglesey, and the Isle of Man; also from Fastnet, Cork, and the northern Hebrides.

Genus *Microdeutopus*

Antenna 1 longer than 2. Accessory flagellum present, either small or well-developed. Gnathopod 1 male with carpus armed with one or more long teeth, wider and longer than propodus. Gnathopod 1 female subchelate. Gnathopod 2 variable, subchelate or nearly simple. Uropod 3 rami subequal, as long as or longer than peduncle.

Microdeutopus anomalus (Rathke)   FIG. 9.39

Length 8 mm. Antenna 1 longer than 2. Accessory flagellum with five articles. Gnathopod 1 (in mature males) large and powerful, carpus very enlarged, produced into a long curved tooth at the base of which are one or (rarely) two accessory teeth. Gnathopod 1 female with carpus shorter than propodus, which is broad distally, but narrows towards carpus. Gnathopod 2 male with carpus and propodus elongate; carpus broad. Gnathopod 2 female with propodus considerably longer and narrower than carpus. Uropod 3 with slender rami, as long as or longer than peduncle; outer ramus a little longer than inner, with only two spines on outer margin; inner ramus with four well-spaced spines on inner margin and two on outer.

Occasionally intertidal, usually sublittoral among weeds, shells, and bryozoans. Mainly south and west, but perhaps all British coasts.

Microdeutopus chelifer (Bate)   FIG. 9.39

Length 5 mm. Antenna 1 equal to or a little longer than 2. Accessory flagellum with two articles. Gnathopod 1 male powerful, carpus produced into one long tooth; gnathopod 1 female with carpus untoothed, shorter than propodus. Gnathopod 2 male with propodus much shorter and broader than carpus, palmar margin delimited by a tooth. Gnathopod 2 female similar to 1. Uropod 3 rami elongate, slender, about equal to peduncle; outer ramus slightly longer than inner, with two spines on outer margin, distal spine especially long; inner ramus with two well-separated spines on inner margin and one on outer. All rami terminate in a cluster of spines, one of which is much longer than the rest.

Amongst algae in shallow, tidal lagoons, sometimes in mid-shore rock pools. South-western coasts.

Microdeutopus gryllotalpa Costa   FIG. 9.39

Length 10 mm. Antenna 1 much longer than 2. Accessory flagellum with three articles. Gnathopod 1 male powerful, with carpus very expanded, nearly as broad as long, with two or four teeth posterio-distally, the distal longest; propodus short with sinuous posterior margin. Gnathopod 1 female with carpus and propodus subequal; carpus broadest. Gnathopod 2 female with basis expanded, crenulate and convex anteriorly; carpus and propodus subequal, carpus broadest; merus, carpus and propodus with long feathery setae anteriorly. Gnathopod 2 female with basis a little expanded and crenulate anteriorly; carpus elongate, subequal to propodus; merus, carpus and propodus

with feathery setae anteriorly. Uropod 3 peduncle as long as rami, outer ramus a little longer than inner; each ramus with a transverse row of closely spaced spines on outer dorsal margin, several variably spaced single and paired spines, and a group of fairly long terminal setae.

In rock pools amongst algae, amongst *Zostera*, in salt-marshes; also sublittorally with a variety of epibenthos, especially in docks. All British coasts but commonest in the south-west.

Microdeutopus versiculatus (Bate)   FIG. 9.39

Length 4 mm. Antenna 1 much longer than 2. Accessory flagellum small, uniarticulate. Gnathopod 1 male very powerful, carpus produced distally into a single tooth; gnathopod 1 female with carpus and propodus nearly equal-sized, densely covered by setae posteriorly. Gnathopod 2 fairly similar in both sexes: merus well-developed, extending along much of length of carpus, which is a little longer than propodus; anterior margins of merus, carpus, and propodus clothed in dense, slightly feathery setae. Uropod 3 rami subequal, as long as peduncle; outer ramus with transverse row of three closely grouped spines dorsally on outer margin and a single spine basally; inner ramus with a similar group of three spines and, on inner margin, a series of well-spaced spines; terminal setae of each ramus fairly long.

Littoral and sublittoral amongst algae, hydroids and other epibenthos. Northwest, west, and south coasts.

27 ISAEIDAE

Body smooth dorsally. Antenna 1 usually with peduncle article 3 equal to or longer than 1. Rostrum absent. Mandible with a palp. Coxa 4 not excavate posteriorly. Gnathopods usually powerful, subchelate, 1 equal to or smaller than 2. Uropod 3 short, biramous, rarely uniramous; rami as long as or longer than peduncle, without hooks or teeth. Telson entire, short, fleshy; nearly circular or square.

---

1. Uropod 3 uniramous. Gnathopod 2 male with propodus palm bearing one small proximal and two distal teeth. Gnathopod 2 female subchelate, propodus with distinct palm   ***Microprotopus maculatus***

   Uropod 3 biramous   **2**

2. Uropod 3 with inner ramus much shorter than outer   **3**

   Uropod 3 with subequal rami   **5**

3. Eyes at the extremity of very produced, rounded lateral lobes of head. Pereopods 3 and 4 with elongate propodus, about twice length of carpus
   Photis longicaudata

   Head lateral lobes less produced, angular rather than rounded, eyes not quite at the extremity. Pereopods 3 and 4 with stout propodus, only slightly longer than carpus   **4**

4. Male gnathopod 2 basis with anterio-proximal lobe. Coxa 2 excavate posterio-ventrally; coxa 3 strongly convex anteriorly   ***Photis pollex***

Male gnathopod 2 basis with anterio-distal lobe.
Coxa 2 evenly rounded; coxa 3 weakly convex anteriorly   **Photis reinhardi**

5. Accessory flagellum well-developed, conspicuous,
with three or more articles   **6**

   Accessory flagellum very small or absent   **10**

6. Pereopods 3–7 slightly subchelate, distal portion of
propodus swollen   **7**

   Pereopods simple   **8**

7. Eye large, occupying most of lateral lobe of head.
Epimeral plate 3 with distinct distal tooth and straight
proximal margin   **Isaea montagui**

   Eye small, occupying only part of lateral lobe of head.
Epimeral plate 3 with minute distal tooth and convex
proximal margin   **Isaea elmhirsti**

8. Antenna 1 peduncle with article 3 shorter than article
1   **Protomedeia fasciata**

   Antenna 1 peduncle with article 3 as long as, or
longer than article 1   **9**

9. Up to 10 mm long. Male gnathopod 2 dactylus closing
along palm of propodus. Uropod 1 rami about equal
length   **Gammaropsis maculata**

   Up to 3 mm long. Male gnathopod 2 dactylus closing
across inner face of propodus. Uropod 1 outer ramus
shorter than inner   **Gammaropsis palmata**

10. Accessory flagellum absent. Gnathopod 2 carpus
short, considerably less than half length of propodus   **11**

   Accessory flagellum uni- or biarticulate, article 1
elongate. Gnathopod 2 carpus longer, not much less
than half length of propodus   **Megamphopus cornutus**

11. Pereopods 3 and 4 with merus equal to combined
length of carpus and propodus. Uropod 3 rami equal
to peduncle, without terminal spines   **Gammaropsis sophiae**

   Pereopods 3 and 4 merus a little shorter than combined length of carpus and propodus. Uropod 3 rami
shorter than peduncle, each armed terminally with
one spine   **Gammaropsis nitida**

Genus *Gammaropsis*

Body slender. Head lateral lobes somewhat produced. Antenna
1 with peduncle article 3 equal to or longer than 1. Accessory
flagellum present, with three or more articles, or absent. Mandible with very large palp. Gnathopods subchelate. Uropod 3
biramous, rami equal but of variable length, usually equal to or
longer than peduncle.

Gammaropsis maculata (Johnston)   FIG. 9.40

Length 10 mm, pale yellow with darker bands. Antenna 1 longer
than 2; accessory flagellum with six articles. Gnathopod 1 propodus equal to carpus, oval, without a well-defined palm.

Gnathopod 2 large, propodus twice length of carpus. Pereopod
5 basis expanded to a greater degree than on pereopods 6 and
7. Uropod 3 rami a little shorter than peduncle.

Intertidal and sublittoral among hydroids, algae, and *Laminaria* holdfasts. Mostly southern shores, often common in south-
west.

Gammaropsis nitida (Stimpson)   FIG. 9.40

Length 7 mm. Antennae subequal. Coxa 1 larger than in *G.
sophiae*. Gnathopod 1 slender, propodus a little smaller than
carpus, dactylus long. Gnathopod 2 male propodus large, with
a less sinuous, oblique palm which has only one small notch;
dactylus long. Gnathopod 2 female similar to male but with
propodus less enlarged. Pereopods 3 and 4 with merus a little
shorter than combined length of carpus and propodus. Uropod
3 rami shorter than peduncle, terminally spined. Epimeral plate
3 with posterio-ventral corner slightly produced as an obtuse
tooth.

Sublittoral, often in the shells of *Buccinum* inhabited by
hermit crabs (*Pagurus*), otherwise amongst hydroids. Probably
all British coasts.

Gammaropsis palmata (Stebbing and Robertson) FIG. 9.40

Length 3 mm, white with light brown bands. Antenna 1 less
than half body-length; Accessory flagellum with up to six
articles; antenna 2 as long as 1. Gnathopod 1 propodus slightly
longer than carpus, palm delimited by thin spine. Female
gnathopod 2 slightly larger than 1, dactylus larger than palm of
propodus. Male gnathopod 2 much larger than 1, dactylus
curved, closing across inner surface of robust propodus. Pereopods 5–7 basis broad, distally tapered.

Sublittoral. Recorded from east and south coasts of England,
west Scotland and western Ireland.

Gammaropsis sophiae (Boeck)   FIG. 9.40

Length 6 mm, banded with yellow and red. Antennae subequal.
Coxa 1 small. Gnathopod 1 slender, propodus oval, as long as
carpus. Gnathopod 2 male propodus very large, with very
sinuous, deeply notched, oblique palm; dactylus large. Gnathopod 2 female with carpus short; propodus large, oval, palm
finely crenulate. Pereopods 3 and 4 with merus large, equal to
combined length of carpus and propodus. Epimeral plate 3
rounded posteriorly, with a tiny tooth at posterio-ventral corner.
Uropod 3 rami equal to peduncle, unarmed terminally.

Sublittoral on silty ground and on decapods (*Maja*). Southern
coasts.

Isaea elmhirsti Patience   FIG. 9.40

Length 6 mm; yellowish brown with dark patches. Head with
angular lateral lobes; eyes oval, small, occupying about half
surface area of lateral lobes. Antenna 1 half body-length, flagellum of twelve articles, accessory flagellum of six articles;
antenna 2 shorter than 1, flagellum of about ten articles.
Epimeral plate 3 with minute tooth on distal angle, and convex
posterior margin. Gnathopod 2 much larger than 1. Pereopods 3
and 4 with elongate oval propodus; pereopods 5–7 with elongate

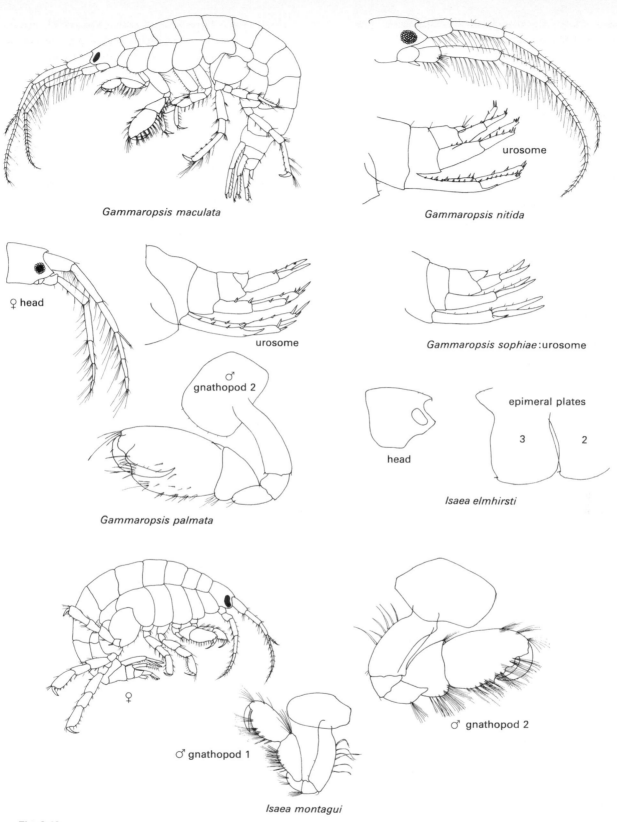

Gammaropsis maculata

Gammaropsis nitida

urosome

♀ head

urosome

Gammaropsis sophiae:urosome

♂ gnathopod 2

Gammaropsis palmata

head

epimeral plates

3   2

Isaea elmhirsti

♀

♂ gnathopod 1

♂ gnathopod 2

Isaea montagui

Fig. 9.40

propodus dilated distally. Uropod 3 biramous; rami uniarticulate, longer than peduncle.

Sublittoral, on mouthparts, appendages, and sternum of the lobster, *Homarus gammarus* (Linnaeus). Recorded from Firth of Forth, the Minch, Clyde Sea, and western English Channel; also from Galway Bay.

Isaea montagui Milne Edwards FIG. 9.40

Length 6 mm; reddish brown, or with red and yellow banding. Head with large angular lateral lobes, occupied by very large, oval, bright red eyes. Antenna 1 one-third of body-length, larger than 2; flagellum with twelve articles, accessory flagellum with six articles. Epimeral plate 3 with small but distinct tooth on posterio-distal corner, posterior margin straight. Gnathopod 2 larger than 1. Pereopods 3 and 4 with elongate, oval propodus; pereopods 5–7 slightly subchelate, with propodus dilated distally. Uropod 3 biramous; rami uniarticulate, longer than peduncle.

Sublittoral, frequently associated with the spider crab, *Maja*. South-west Britain, from Portland to the Isle of Man; also Western Ireland.

Megamphopus cornutus Norman FIG. 9.41

Length 5 mm. Body slender. Eyes large. Antenna 1 shorter than 2; accessory flagellum small, with one or two articles. Antenna 1 peduncle article 3 equal to or longer than article 1. Gnathopods subchelate in male, nearly simple in female. Gnathopod 2 male propodus large, elongate. Epimeral plate 3 rounded posteriorly. Uropod 3 biramous; rami subequal, longer than peduncle. Telson concave distally.

Sublittoral on coarse, silty bottoms. Probably all coasts.

Microprotopus maculatus Norman FIG. 9.41

Length 2 mm, dark brown with pale bands. Antennae short, accessory flagellum biarticulate. Gnathopod 1 male subchelate, slender. Gnathopod 2 male propodus very large, palmar margin slightly concave, delimited proximally by a small tooth and distally by two larger teeth; dactylus large and curved. Gnathopod 1 female slender, slightly subchelate. Gnathopod 2 female propodus enlarged and somewhat quadrangular, palm sinuous but distinct. Pereopods 3 and 4 with basis slightly enlarged. Pereopods 5–7 with basis very enlarged, oval. Epimeral plate 3 prolonged, rounded, slightly crenulate posteriorly. Uropod 3 uniramous, ramus a little longer than peduncle. Telson small, quadrangular.

Among algae and on sand, littoral and shallow sublittoral. All British coasts.

Genus *Photis*

Antennae subequal. Accessory flagellum absent or comprising a vestigial scale. Eyes near the ends of the produced lateral head lobes. Gnathopods subchelate, larger in male than in female. Pereopod 5 short, dactylus inverted and denticulate on internal margin. Uropod 3 outer ramus biarticulate, much longer than inner ramus. Telson small and triangular.

Photis longicaudata (Bate and Westwood) FIG. 9.41

Length 6 mm, whitish with brown bands. Head lateral lobes very produced with eyes at their rounded extremities. Gnathopod 1 propodus oval, palm margin not well-defined. Gnathopod 2 propodus large, palmar margin sinuous but untoothed; larger in male than female. Epimeral plate 3 rounded posterio-ventrally. Uropod 3 outer ramus longer than peduncle.

Sublittoral, rarely littoral, on coarse grounds and muddy sand. All British coasts.

Photis pollex Walker FIG. 9.41

Length 3.5 mm. Head lateral lobes only moderately produced, angular; eyes small, dark brown. Antenna 1 less than half body-length, flagellum about half length of peduncle, with five articles; antenna 2 flagellum about as long as peduncle article five. Gnathopod 2 coxa concave posteriorly, basis with large anterio-proximal lobe.

Sublittoral, on both coarse and fine sediments. Western coasts; recorded Dublin Bay, Liverpool Bay, and Mull of Kintyre, but probably quite widely distributed.

Photis reinhardi Krøyer FIG. 9.41

Length 5 mm. Head lateral lobes produced, angular terminally; eyes not quite at extremity. Gnathopod 1 propodus somewhat quadrangular, with a well-defined palm. Gnathopod 2 male propodus enlarged, palm sinuous and delimited by a large tooth. Gnathopod 2 female similar to male but with propodus palm lacking tooth. Epimeral plate 3 rounded posterio-ventrally. Uropod 3 peduncle as long as, or longer than, outer ramus.

Lower shore and sublittoral, in *Laminaria* holdfasts and among algae. North Sea.

Protomedeia fasciata Krøyer FIG. 9.41

Length 8 mm; white with dark brown banding. Head with short, angular lateral lobes; eyes small and round. Antenna 1 half body-length; flagellum of up to twenty articles, slender, longer than peduncle; accessory flagellum with five to seven articles. Antenna 2 much shorter than 1, with short flagellum of about seven articles. Male gnathopod 1 basis with large posterio-distal lobe; propodus about as long as carpus, oval, with minutely toothed palm delimited by one long spine; dactylus shorter than palm of propodus. Male gnathopod 2 very robust; basis broad, with prominent anterior ridge; carpus broad, with tufts of long setae on posterior margin; propodus broad, but smaller than carpus, with long setae on posterior margin, palm short, bearing stout spine; dactylus longer than palm. Pereopods 3 and 4 with propodus and dactylus very slender; pereopods 5–7 successively longer, with elongate basis. Uropods 1 and 2 spinose, with stout ventral tooth on peduncle; uropod 3 rami as long as peduncle. Telson rounded, with small hook on each distolateral angle, and two short setae.

Sublittoral. North-east coasts, from Yorkshire to Shetland; also recorded from Isle of Man.

28 COROPHIIDAE

Body usually dorso-ventrally depressed, occasionally somewhat elongate or cylindrical. Urosome segments always distinctly

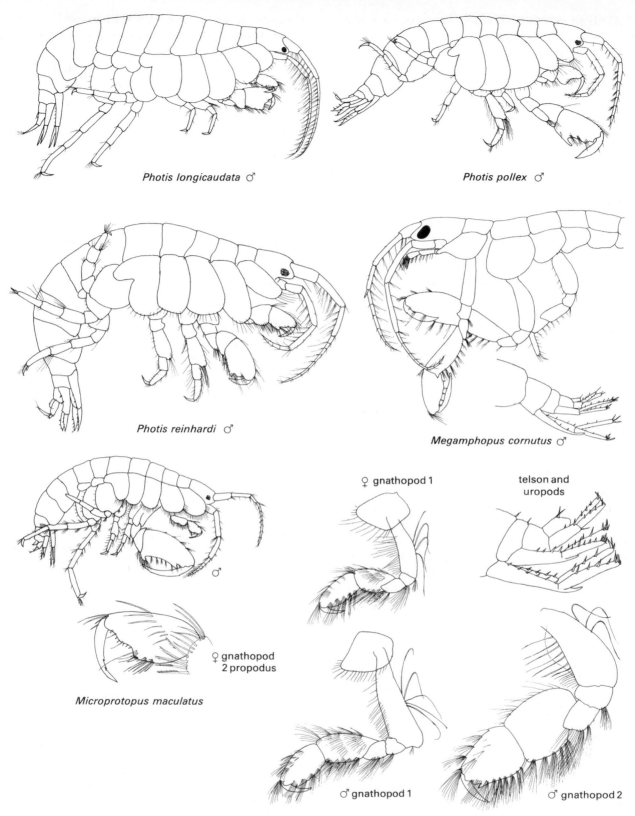

Photis longicaudata ♂

Photis pollex ♂

Photis reinhardi ♂

Megamphopus cornutus ♂

Microprotopus maculatus

♀ gnathopod 2 propodus

♂

♀ gnathopod 1

telson and uropods

♂ gnathopod 1

♂ gnathopod 2

Protomedia fasciata

Fig. 9.41

depressed, some or all may be coalesced. Antennae variable, accessory flagellum usually absent, occasionally present but small. Mandibular palp present, sometimes reduced to two or one article(s). Coxae short, usually separate from each other or just touching. Gnathopods variable, one pair often complexly subchelate. Uropod 3 small, variably uniramous, sometimes with hooked rami, or with peduncles produced distally to give a pseudobiramous appearance. Telson entire, fleshy; circular, very broad and short, or symmetrically trapezoidal. Many species construct tubes while a few make semi-permanent burrows in the sediment.

Numerous British species. Some are marine, a number are exclusively estuarine. In many species it is convenient to key out males and females separately, primarily using the structure of the antennae.

1. Gnathopod 2 merus and carpus elongate, about equal size, longitudinally fused. Antenna 1 peduncle article 3 shorter than 1; accessory flagellum absent. Mandibular palp with two articles   **5**

    Gnathopod 2 merus and carpus not elongate, or subequal. Accessory flagellum present. Mandibular palp with one or three articles   **2**

2. Pereopods 3 and 4 basis elongate, slender. Epimeral plates 1–3 acutely pointed. Antenna 1 peduncle article 1 longer than 3. Mandibular palp with three articles   **3**

    Pereopods 3 and 4 basis broad and flattened. Epimeral plates 1–3 rounded. Antenna 1 peduncle articles 1 and 3 subequal. Mandibular palp with 1 article   **4**

3. Gnathopod 2 carpus smaller than propodus. Eyes well-developed   ***Unciola crenatipalma***

    Gnathopod 2 carpus much larger than propodus. Eyes rather indistinct   ***Unciola planipes***

4. Uropod 1 inner ramus much shorter than outer ramus; uropod 3 peduncle with moderately long setae, and a small spine less than half length of ramus. Antenna 2 peduncle article 3 with dorso-lateral strip of pigment   ***Siphonoecetes striatus***

    Uropod 1 inner ramus scarcely shorter than outer ramus; uropod 3 peduncle with very long setae, and a stout spine half or more length of ramus. Antenna 2 peduncle with proximal pigment on all articles   ***Siphonoecetes kroyeranus***

5. Urosome segments separate and freely articulating   **6**

    Urosome segments fused   **8**

6. Rostrum small; lateral lobes of head produced, acutely pointed. Eyes imperfectly developed and replaced by patches of opaque white pigment   ***Corophium affine***

    Lateral lobes of head rounded. Eyes black but small   **7**

7. Uropod 1 with single row of spines along outer edge of peduncle, not replaced proximally by setae. Uropod 3 rami not eccentrically placed on peduncle   ***Corophium volutator***

    Uropod 1 with two rows of spines along outer edge of peduncle, outer row replaced proximally by setae. Uropod 3 rami not eccentrically placed on peduncle   ***Corophium arenarium***

    Uropod 1 with one or two rows of spines on outer edge of peduncle, never replaced proximally by setae. Uropod 3 rami eccentrically attached to peduncle   ***Corophium multisetosum***

8. Lateral borders of urosome with notches into which uropods 1 and 2 are inserted   **9**

    Lateral borders of urosome smooth. Uropods 1 and 2 inserted ventrally   **16**

9. Lateral lobes of head acutely pointed, eyes small. Burrowers in sand   ***Corophium crassicorne***

    Lateral lobes of head truncate or rounded, eyes well-developed. Tube builders on hard substrata   **10**

10. Antenna 2 with two terminal teeth on peduncle article 4, the smaller above the larger   **11**

    Antenna 2 peduncle article 4 armed only with spines   **13**

11. Rostrum long, acutely pointed, about one-third length of antenna 1 peduncle article 1, which has a blunt process on inner border opposite midpoint between middle and tip of rostrum   ***Corophium insidiosum*** male

    Rostrum shorter and more triangular   **12**

12. Antenna 1 peduncle article 2 longer than the five-articled flagellum. Antenna 2 with two or three spines on peduncle article 4 and no processes on article 5   ***Corophium sextonae*** male

    Antenna 1 peduncle article 2 shorter than the seven- to ten-articled flagellum. Antenna 2 without spines on peduncle article 4 and with two processes on peduncle article 5   ***Corophium acherusicum*** male

13. Antenna 2 peduncle article 4 with four to six spines set in a single row on a flange   ***Corophium sextonae*** female

    Antenna 2 peduncle article 4 with spines set in pairs, except for the terminal spine   **14**

14. Antenna 2 peduncle article 4 with three pairs of spines and one terminal spine   ***Corophium acherusicum*** female

    Antenna 2 peduncle article 4 with two pairs of spines and one terminal spine   **15**

15. Antenna 1 peduncle article 1 with sharply curved spines proximally on lower and inner edges   ***Corophium bonellii*** female

    Antenna 1 peduncle article 1 with straight spines only   ***Corophium insidiosum*** female

16. Antenna 2 peduncle article 4 with a large curved terminal tooth, and a small tooth or lobe above it **17**

    Antenna 2 without terminal teeth on peduncle article 4 **18**

17. Antenna 2 with a long pointed process near middle of peduncle article 5   ***Corophium acutum*** male

    Antenna 2 without median process on peduncle article 5   ***Corophium lacustre*** male

18. Antenna 1 with three spines on peduncle article 1. Antenna 2 with three spines on peduncle article 4 and one spine on article 5   ***Corophium acutum*** female

    Antenna 1 with one spine on peduncle article 1. Antenna 2 with two spines on peduncle article 4, no spines on article 5   ***Corophium lacustre*** female

---

Genus *Corophium*

Antenna 1 with peduncle article 3 shorter than 1 and shorter than the flagellum. Accessory flagellum absent. Antenna 2 equal to or longer than 1, thickened, and, especially in male, with flagellum much shorter than peduncle article 5; peduncle article 4 usually with a distal tooth. Mandibular palp with two articles. Coxae short and separate. Gnathopods small; 1 subchelate; 2 simple, very setose, with merus and carpus elongate and fused longitudinally. Uropod 3 flattened, ramus equal in length to peduncle. Telson trapezoidal.

Corophium acherusicum Costa   FIG. 9.42

Length 5 mm, yellowish brown. Rostrum short and pointed; lateral lobes of head rounded, eyes well-developed. Antenna 2 female with peduncle article 4 bearing ventrally usually three pairs of spines and a single terminal spine; occasionally up to four additional spines alongside or between paired spines. Antenna 2 female with peduncle article 5 bearing two, rarely three, ventral spines. Antenna 1 male with seven- to ten-articled flagellum, longer than peduncle article 2. Antenna 2 male with peduncle article 4 lacking spines, armed terminally with a large curved tooth beneath one or two smaller teeth; peduncle article 5 with small process near base and a large blunt process terminally. Urosome segments fused, with lateral borders notched.

A tube builder on algae and hydroids attached to floating objects. South and south-west coasts.

Corophium acutum Chevreux   FIG. 9.42

Length 4 mm; yellowish, with brown markings on head and coxae. Eyes large, black; rostrum short, triangular. Lateral lobes of head elongate, rounded. Antenna 1 female with peduncle article 1 armed with three spines ventrally. Antenna 2 female with peduncle article 4 bearing three ventral spines; article 5 with one ventral spine. Antenna 2 male with a large curved terminal tooth on peduncle article 4, surmounted by a smaller

tooth or lobe; peduncle article 5 with a long, centrally placed, pointed process on lower margin. Urosome segments fused, lateral borders forming a smooth convex curve.

A tube builder among sponges and *Laminaria* holdfasts. Littoral and sublittoral, often in harbours and lower reaches of estuaries. South and south-west Britain, and south-west Ireland.

Corophium affine Bruzelius   FIG. 9.42

Length 4 mm; pale yellow, without any other pigment. Rostrum small, lateral lobes of head acutely pointed and rather produced. Eyes imperfectly developed, marked by patches of white pigment. Antenna 2 female relatively feeble, peduncle article 1 produced anterio-ventrally, peduncle article 4 without a terminal tooth. Antenna 2 female large and strong, with a large terminal tooth on peduncle article 4, surmounted by complex of small blunt teeth. Pereopod 7 basis scarcely expanded, slightly concave posteriorly. Urosome segments distinct and freely articulating with each other. Uropod 3 peduncle and rami narrow.

A burrower in sublittoral muddy sands. A northern species penetrating as far south as the Irish Sea.

Corophium arenarium Crawford   FIG. 9.42

Length 6 mm, whitish with brown markings. Eyes small and black. Rostrum triangular, lateral lobes of head rounded and short. Antenna 1 female peduncle article 1 with two spines proximally on lower edge, followed by three setae and a terminal spine. Antenna 2 female with peduncle article 4 bearing a small spine on inner surface and a spiniferous process terminally which extends just beyond end of article. Antenna 1 male with lower edge of peduncle article 1 armed with two small spines and three setae; inner edge slightly crenulate. Antenna 2 male with powerful articles: article 4 armed terminally with a long tooth. Pereopod 7 basis oval. Urosome segments distinct and freely articulating with each other. Uropod 1 with two row of spines on outer edge of peduncle, outer row being replaced proximally by setae. Uropod 3 with ramus not eccentrically placed on peduncle.

A builder of semi-permanent burrows in sand or muddy sand rather than mud. Generally littoral, often estuarine. Southern Britain (Norfolk to Irish Sea).

Corophium bonellii (Sars)   FIG. 9.42

The male is unknown and the species may well be parthenogenetic. The following description therefore applies to the female.

Length 5.5 mm. Rostrum short, triangular. Lateral lobes of head rounded; eyes black, well-developed. Antenna 1 peduncle article 1 shorter than combined length of articles 2 and 3, armed ventrally with three large straight spines distally, and one or two sharply curved spines proximally; inner margin of article 1 also armed with one to three spines, the proximal one sharply curved and short; flagellum with a maximum of eight articles. Antenna 2 peduncle article 4 armed ventrally with two pairs of spines and one terminal spine; article 5 usually with two spines, proximal spine may be as large as distal, or smaller, or absent.

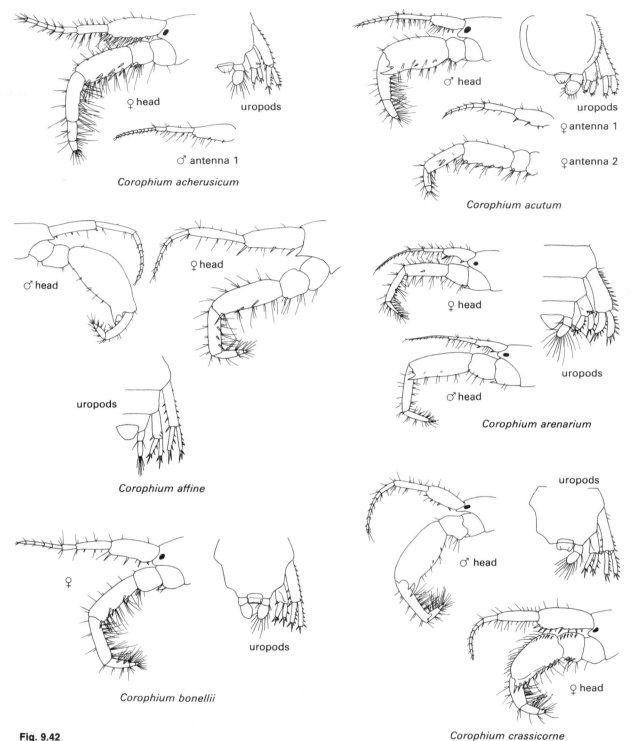

Corophium acherusicum

Corophium acutum

Corophium affine

Corophium arenarium

Corophium bonellii

Corophium crassicorne

Fig. 9.42

Urosome segments fused, lateral borders partially notched for insertion of uropods 1 and 2.

A tube builder, common in *Laminaria* holdfasts and on other algae and hydroids, littorally and sublittorally on all coasts. Displaced by *C. sextoni* in the Plymouth area.

Corophium crassicorne Bruzelius   FIG. 9.42
Length 5 mm, brown. Rostrum short and pointed. Lateral lobes of head acutely pointed; eyes small and poorly developed.

Antenna 2 female with peduncle article 4 nearly crescent-shaped in section, the concavity facing inwards and upwards; with a row of six to eight spines on ventral margin. Antenna 2 male peduncle article 4 with two terminal teeth, the smaller above the larger; peduncle article 5 with a single small tooth on ventral margin. Urosome segments fused, with lateral borders notched.

A burrower in muddy sand, LWS and subtidal. All British coasts.

Corophium insidiosum Crawford FIG. 9.43

Length 4.5 mm. Lateral lobes of head rounded, elongate. Eyes black, well-developed. Rostrum short and pointed in female, long and acutely pointed in male. Antenna 1 female peduncle article 1 shorter than combined length of 2 and 3, armed with straight rather than curved spines; flagellum with seven articles. Antenna 2 female peduncle article 4 with two pairs of spines and a single terminal spine on ventral border; peduncle article 5 with one median spine; flagellum composed of three articles. Antenna 1 male peduncle article 1 keeled ventrally, with a small terminal spine, and symmetrical blunt process on inner margin opposite a point between middle and tip of rostrum; flagellum with ten articles. Antenna 2 male with two terminal teeth on peduncle article 4, the lower being the larger; peduncle article 5 without teeth or spines; flagellum with three articles. Urosome segments fused, with lateral borders notched.

A tube builder on algae and other substrata, generally in areas of lowered salinity. South coast of Britain, Denmark, and Germany.

Corophium lacustre Vanhöffen FIG. 9.43

Recorded in Britain only from a few localities in Norfolk. A tube builder on plants, especially *Cordylophora lacustris*, in low salinity waters (almost 0‰–15‰).

Corophium multisetosum Stock FIG. 9.43

Length 8 mm, whitish with brown markings. Eyes black. Rostrum short and triangular. Female with lateral lobes of head rounded, shorter than rostrum; male lateral lobes more triangular, with rounded tips, longer than rostrum. Antenna 1 female with lower edges of peduncle article 1 armed with three spines, and about 14 setae between second and third spines. Antenna 2 female with peduncle article 4 armed with one spine and a very long terminal tooth, extending one-third length of article 5. Antenna 1 male with peduncle article 1 armed on lower edge with three to five small spines and numerous setae. Antenna 2 male large, peduncle article 4 armed terminally with a long tooth. Pereopod 7 basis oval. Urosome segments distinct and freely articulating with each other. Uropod 1 with one or two rows of spines on peduncle, outer row not replaced proximally by setae. Uropod 3 with rami eccentrically placed on peduncle.

A builder of semi-permanent burrows in mud or sand, and a tube builder on sessile objects. Inhabits the upper regions of estuaries in salinities often <1‰ and rather lower than those preferred by *C. volutator* and *C. arenarium*. Sometimes common with *C. lacustre*. Southern Britain (Norfolk to Wales).

Corophium sextonae Crawford FIG. 9.43

Length 4.5 mm; greyish white, with two darker bars across each segment, and on the antennae and head. Eyes large and black. Rostrum short, acutely pointed. Lateral lobes of head long and rounded. Antenna 2 female peduncle article 4 with a ventral flange armed with four to six spines set in a single row; peduncle article 5 with one to two ventral spines; flagellum with three articles. Antenna 1 male with five-articled flagellum, shorter than or equal to peduncle article 2. Antenna 2 male with few setae; peduncle article 4 with large terminal tooth set beneath smaller one, with two to three short spines ventrally; peduncle article 5 without process; flagellum with three articles. Urosome segments fused, with lateral borders notched.

A tube builder common in shallow dredgings and *Laminaria* holdfasts from south and south-west coasts. Also recorded from the Netherlands.

Corophium volutator (Pallas) FIG. 9.43

Length 8 mm, whitish with brown markings. Eyes small and black. Rostrum and lateral lobes of head short and rounded. Antenna 1 female with two, rarely three, well-developed spines, separated by three to four setae on the lower edges of peduncle article 1. Antenna 2 female without a spine on inner surface of peduncle article 4; terminal tooth on article 4 strong, extending just beyond end of article. Antenna 1 male with peduncle article 1 bearing two, rarely three, small spines on lower edge and distinct crenulations on inner edge. Antenna 2 male with powerful peduncle articles; article 4 armed with a terminal tooth. Pereopod 7 basis rather oval in shape. Urosome segments distinct and freely articulating with each other. Uropod 1 with single row of spines on outer edge of peduncle, not replaced proximally by setae. Uropod 3 with ramus not attached eccentrically to peduncle.

Intertidal. A builder of semi-permanent burrows in mud, usually in estuaries. All British coasts.

Genus *Siphonoecetes*

Antenna 1 peduncle article 3 more or less equal to 1, and subequal to or shorter than flagellum. Accessory flagellum absent. Antenna 2 longer and stronger than 1, with flagellum shorter than last peduncle article. Mandibular palp uniarticulate. Coxae somewhat pointed distally, serially separate and bearing many setae. Gnathopods subchelate, never massive. Uropod 3 with distally produced peduncle, longer than the eccentrically positioned ramus. Telson round, as wide as long.

Siphonoecetes kroyeranus Bate FIG. 9.43

Length up to 5.5 mm; body slender, with diffuse brown pigmentation, head with irregular distal brown patch on dorsum, articles of both antennae pigmented proximally, unpigmented distally. Antenna 1 flagellum with three to five well-developed articles and a rudimentary terminal article. Gnathopod 2 propodus oval, with sloping palm equal to half length of posterior margin. Uropod 1 rami subequal, of similar shape, although inner ramus sometimes a little shorter and broader than outer. Uropod 3 peduncle with distal spine, at least equivalent to half length of ramus, occasionally almost as long as ramus; very long setae between spine and ramus.

Shallow sublittoral, on sand, building tubes of sand-grains. At present recorded from eastern Scotland, the west Channel coast, and west and south-west Ireland.

Siphonoecetes striatus Myers and McGrath FIG. 9.43

Length up to 8 mm. Body stout, white, with light brown pigmentation distributed in definite pattern; antenna 2 peduncle

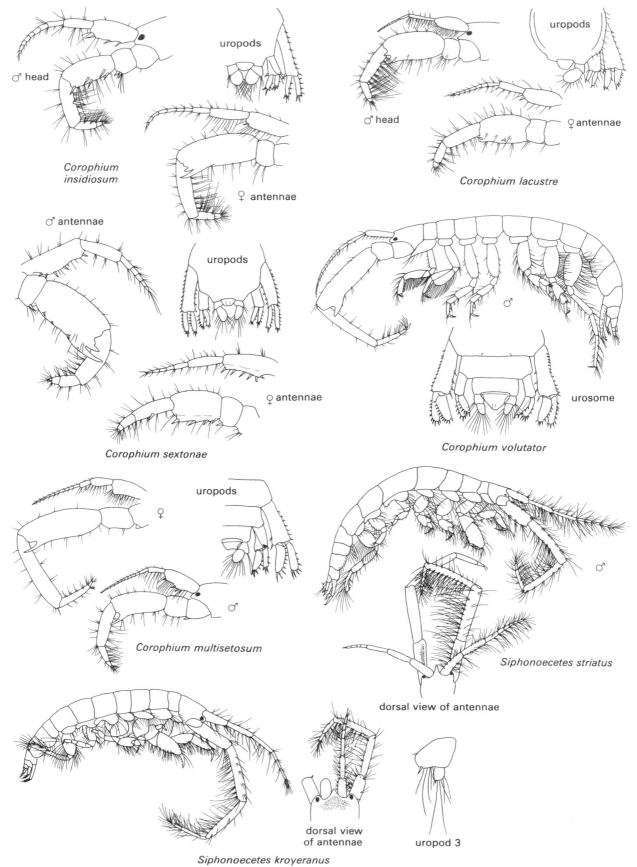

♂ head

uropods

Corophium insidiosum

♀ antennae

♂ head

uropods

♀ antennae

Corophium lacustre

♂ antennae

uropods

♀ antennae

Corophium sextonae

♂

urosome

Corophium volutator

♀

uropods

♂

Corophium multisetosum

♂

dorsal view of antennae

Siphonoecetes striatus

dorsal view of antennae

uropod 3

Siphonoecetes kroyeranus

Fig. 9.43

article 3 with longitudinal strip of brown on inner dorsolateral surface, article 4 with small patch of brown proximally on inner dorsolateral surface. Antennal flagellum with six to seven, rarely five, well-developed articles and a rudimentary terminal article. Gnathopod 2 propodus subrectangular, palm short, much less than half length of posterior margin. Uropod 1 rami very unequal; inner ramus short, pear-shaped. Uropod 3 peduncle with small distal spine, less than half length of ramus, a series of moderately long setae between ramus and spine.

Sublittoral, 50–200 m, in empty shells of *Dentalium* or empty tubes of *Ditrupa*, on sandy bottoms. Presumably known from western coasts only; reported from Shetland, south-west Ireland, and the Celtic Sea, Fastnet, Galway Bay.

Genus *Unciola*

Body slender, somewhat elongate. Antenna 1 with peduncle article 1 longer than 3; flagellum more or less equal to peduncle. Accessory flagellum present but small. Antenna 2 stronger, although slightly shorter, than 1; flagellum more or less equal to length of peduncle article 5. Mandibular palp with three articles. Coxae short and serially separate. Gnathopod subchelate, 1 larger than 2. Uropod 3 with peduncle somewhat produced distally, a little longer than the eccentrically positioned, unhooked rami. Telson rounded and short.

Unciola crenatipalma (Bate)   FIG. 9.44
Length 7 mm; yellow and orange, fading to translucent white. Gnathopod 2 with carpus smaller than propodus. Eyes well-developed.

Sublittoral, usually among muddy stones and shells. Quite common in southern Britain, apparently absent in the north.

Unciola planipes Norman   FIG. 9.44
Length 6 mm; yellow and orange, fading to white. Gnathopod 2 with carpus much larger than propodus. Eyes somewhat indistinct.

Sublittoral. A northern species which has been recorded on sand in the Irish Sea.

29 CHELURIDAE
Body depressed. Antennae short: 1 with uniarticulate accessory flagellum; 2 with flagellum largely composed of one clavate article. Mandible with a palp. Coxae small. Urosome segments immoveably fused together, segment 3 very large. Uropods 1–3 radically different from each other: 1 normal with long peduncle terminated by two short rami; 2 with foliaceous peduncle, with or without rami; 3 with short peduncle, greatly enlarged outer ramus, inner ramus scale-like or absent. Telson entire.

Chelura terebrans Philippi   FIG. 9.44
Length 6 mm, brown to cream. Pleon segment 3 with long backwardly pointing dorsal spine. Gnathopods small. Uropod 2 with two rami, uropod 3 with a scale-like inner ramus.

In driftwood, on pier piles and other structures, intertidal and sublittoral. Settles in wood after preliminary attack by gribbles (*Limnoria* spp.).

30 ISCHYROCERIDAE
Body laterally compressed, smooth dorsally. Antenna 1 peduncle article 3 more than half length of 2. Accessory flagellum present or absent. Rostrum absent. Mandible with a palp. Coxa 4 not excavate posteriorly. Gnathopods powerfully subchelate. Uropod 3 usually not projecting beyond 1 and 2, uniramous or biramous with small or very small, rather triangular rami, always shorter than peduncle; outer ramus with one hooked spine distally and/or small distolateral teeth. Telson fleshy, subcircular or nearly square.

Adult males may be identified using the following key. Juvenile males and females are very difficult to identify and may not key out readily.

1.	Uropod 3 uniramous	**2**
	Uropod 3 biramous	**5**
2.	Male gnathopod 2 coxa with stridulating ridges, carpus with two teeth on posterio-distal margin in adults (rarely only one). Coxa 2 widely separated from coxae 1 and 3	**3**
	Male gnathopod 2 coxa without stridulating ridges, carpus with only one tooth on posterio-distal margin. Coxa 2 more or less contiguous with coxae 1 and 3	**4**
3.	Gnathopod 1 basis slender; gnathopod 2 carpus with two teeth (in old males the inner tooth may be just a rounded process)	***Ericthonius punctatus***
	Gnathopod 1 basis broad, with anterior flange; gnathopod 2 with one slender tooth, or with one main tooth and a small accessory tooth	***Ericthonius difformis***
4.	Pereopod 5 basis elongate, posterior margin slightly concave with evenly rounded lobe distally. Antenna 2 peduncle elongate and slender, articles 4 and 5 longer than combined length of head and pereon segments 1 and 2. Uropods 1 and 2 very elongate and slender	***Ericthonius fasciatus***
	Pereopod 5 basis almost as broad as long, posterior margin straight with posterio-distal margin almost a right angle. Antenna 2 peduncle stout, articles 4 and 5 shorter than combined length of head and pereon segments 1 and 2. Pereopod 3 stout, with rounded basis	***Ericthonius rubricornis***
5.	Accessory flagellum an indistinct tubercle. Coxae 1 and 2 equal in length	***Parajassa pelagica***
	Accessory flagellum distinct, uni- or biarticulate. Coxae 1 and 2 not equal in length	**6**
6.	Accessory flagellum uniarticulate. Coxa 1 less than half length of 2; coxa 5 not longer than 6	***Microjassa cumbrensis***
	Accessory flagellum biarticulate. Coxa 1 at least three-quarters length of 2; coxa 5 much longer than 6	**7**

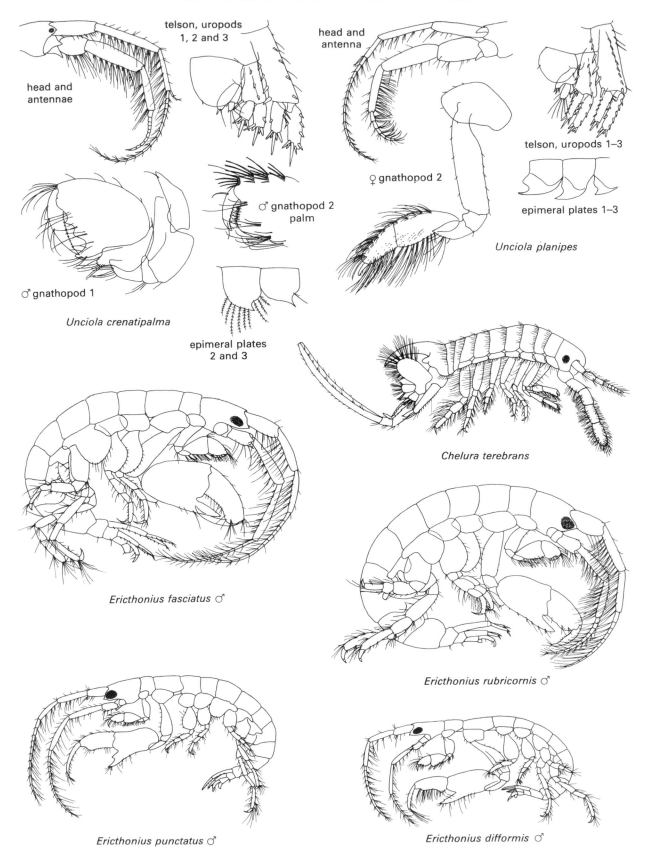

head and
antennae

head and
antenna

telson, uropods
1, 2 and 3

♀ gnathopod 2

telson, uropods 1–3

epimeral plates 1–3

Unciola planipes

♂ gnathopod 2
palm

♂ gnathopod 1

Unciola crenatipalma

epimeral plates
2 and 3

Chelura terebrans

Ericthonius fasciatus ♂

Ericthonius rubricornis ♂

Ericthonius punctatus ♂

Ericthonius difformis ♂

Fig. 9.44

7. Male gnathopod 2 often with distal process on palm of propodus, but lacking proximal tooth. Uropod 3 outer ramus with straight terminal spine and a number of small distolateral teeth

Ischyrocerus anguipes

Male gnathopod 2 propodus with small distal tooth and large proximal process. Uropod 3 outer ramus with hooked spine distally, and one to three distolateral teeth   **8**

8. Gnathopod 2 basis with long setae on anterior margin (male and female)   **9**

Gnathopod 2 basis without long setae on anterior margin (male and female)   **10**

9. Gnathopod 2 male with single thumb-like process; setae simple   **Jassa marmorata**

Gnathopod 2 male with two large proximal processes; setae plumose   **Jassa ocia**

10. Gnathopod 2 male (in large specimens) with bilobed propodal process. Body up to 5 mm long   **Jassa pusilla**

Gnathopod 2 male (in large specimens) with simple propodal process. Body up to 12 mm long   **Jassa falcata**

Genus *Ericthonius*

Antenna 1 with peduncle article 1 shorter than 3, flagellum more or less equal to peduncle; accessory flagellum absent. Antenna 2 slender, as long as antenna 1, with flagellum as long as peduncle. Mandibular palp with three articles. Coxae short, at most just touching serially. Female gnathopods subchelate; male gnathopod 2 much enlarged, carpochelate. Uropod 3 with hooked rami. Telson very short and wide with a spiny patch on each side.

Ericthonius difformis Milne Edwards   FIG. 9.44

Length 10 mm; body very slender, greyish with brown spots. Eyes large. Antenna 1 of variable length, accessory flagellum minute. Antenna 2 shorter than 1, peduncle article 5 longer than 4, flagellum longer than article 5. Male gnathopod 1 coxa small, rounded-triangular, widely separate from coxa 2; basis broad, with anterior flange, no posterior process. Male gnathopod 2 coxa much broader than long, with anterior stridulating ridges; basis slender, broadened distally, carpus slightly convex anterioproximally, posterio-distal process moderately deflected, with one large tooth, and sometimes accessory tooth distally; propodus with irregular posterior margin, sometimes with distinct proximal lobe, lacking cutting edge; dactylus at least three-quarters length of propodus. Pereopod 3 basis widest mediodistally, anterior margin convex.

Shallow sublittoral, amongst algae and hydroids, and often associated with *Zostera*. Distribution incompletely known; reported from south-western coasts, but probably more widely distributed.

Ericthonius fasciatus (Stimpson)   FIG. 9.44

Length 10 mm; yellowish, with a single dark, reddish brown band on each body segment. Eyes large. Antenna 1 two-thirds of body-length, flagellum shorter than peduncle, accessory flagellum minute, with two or three setae at apex. Antenna 2 larger than 1, peduncle article 5 longer than 4, flagellum shorter than articles 4 and 5 combined. Male gnathopod 1 coxa small, slightly excavate, overlapping coxa 2; basis slender, without anteriodistal lobe, no process on posterior margin. Male gnathopod 2 coxa broader than deep, lower edge strongly excavate, without stridulating ridges; basis very elongate; anterior margin of carpus strongly convex proximally in juveniles, later slightly convex proximally and slightly concave distally, posterio-distal process at most slightly deflected, anterior margin with discontinuity; propodus with posterior margin finely ridged; dactylus elongate, slender. Pereopod 3 basis widest medio-distally, anterior margin evenly convex. Pereopod 5 basis stout, but length at least one and one-half times breadth.

Sublittoral, building tubes of fine sediment. Only recently redescribed by Myers and McGrath (1984); presently known from a few localities in the North Sea and the Irish Sea, but probably widespread around the British Isles.

Ericthonius punctatus (Bate)   FIG. 9.44

Length 10 mm. Eyes large. Antenna 1 two-thirds of body-length, flagellum about as long as peduncle, accessory flagellum a simple tubercle with two setae. Antenna 2 slightly longer than 1, peduncle article 5 slightly longer than 4, flagellum about as long as articles 4 and 5 together. Male gnathopod 1 coxa small and rounded, widely separate from coxa 2; basis very slender, without posterior process. Gnathopod 2 coxa rounded, with stridulating ridges on distal margin; basis broadened distally; carpus strongly convex anterio-proximally, posterio-distal process strongly deflected, with two teeth separated by rounded depression; propodus lacking posterior marginal lobes or serrations; dactylus elongate. Pereopod 3 basis widest medially, with evenly convex anterior margin.

Sublittoral, building tubes amongst algae and hydroids. Common on all British coasts.

Ericthonius rubricornis (Stimpson)   FIG. 9.44

Length 10 mm; body stout, mottled dark grey. Eyes large. Antenna 1 half or less body-length, flagellum shorter than peduncle, accessory flagellum minute. Antenna 2 slightly longer than 1, peduncle articles 4 and 5 about equal length, flagellum shorter than articles 4 and 5 together. Male gnathopod 1 coxa small, rounded, overlapping coxa 2; basis slender, with strong anterio-distal lobe, no posterior process. Male gnathopod 2 coxa much broader than deep, lower edge moderately to markedly excavate, without stridulating ridges; basis elongate; carpus strongly convex anterio-proximally, posterio-distal process scarcely deflected, anterior margin straight or evenly concave; propodus with smooth or weakly ridged posterior margin; dactylus stout. Pereopod 3 basis widest medially, anterior edge evenly convex. Pereopod 5 basis square, with straight distal edge.

Sublittoral. Distribution imperfectly known, due to previous confusion with *E. difformis* and *E. fasciatus*. Reported from east coast of Scotland, and north-east England, and perhaps limited to northern coasts.

Ischyrocerus anguipes (Krøyer)   FIG. 9.45

Length 8–10 mm; colour variable, usually banded. Similar to, and difficult to distinguish from, species of *Jassa*. Accessory flagellum biarticulate and relatively elongate, almost as long as article 1 of antenna 1 flagellum. Coxa 1 more than three-quarters length of 2; coxa 5 longer than 6. Male gnathopod 2 propodus lacking a large proximal palm or projection. Uropod 3 outer ramus with or without an unhooked terminal spine, usually with small, blunt, recurved, lateral denticles near tip.

Abundant in *Laminaria* holdfasts (north-east coast), also among intertidal and sublittoral epibenthos. All British coasts.

Genus *Jassa*

Accessory flagellum biarticulate, distinct, although clearly shorter than article 1 of antenna 1 flagellum. Eyes small to medium-sized. Coxa 1 more than three-quarters length of 2; coxa 5 longer than 6. Male gnathopod 2 propodus usually with a large proximal tooth on palm. Uropod 3 outer ramus with a hooked spine distally and one to three large, sharp, curved, disto-lateral teeth. Telson triangular.

Jassa falcata (Montagu)   FIG. 9.45

Length 7 mm; yellow-grey, strongly marked with brown, red, or black depending on habitat colour. Eyes small, round, and dark. Coxa 1 angular, elongated anteriorly; coxa 2 longer than deep but with anterior margin much shorter than posterior margin of coxa 1. Epimeral plate 3 with a minute tooth at posterio-ventral corner. Uropods 1 and 2 with outer ramus shorter than inner. Uropod 3 with peduncle much longer than rami: outer ramus with a strong, hooked terminal spine usually bearing two distolateral denticles. Telson small, triangular, with two setae on each side of apex.

The antennae and gnathopods show considerable variation. In the adult male, gnathopod 2 propodus is greatly enlarged, with a proximal projection from the palm which is never bifid. In adult females also the propodus is enlarged, but the palm margin is concave rather than straight and there is no proximal projection.

Intertidal and sublittoral. Builds tubes among algae and hydroids, and on solid structures. An important fouling species. Often abundant on buoys, ships, and in harbours. In *Laminaria* holdfasts and similar habitats. Widespread and common. All British coasts.

Jassa marmorata Holmes   FIG. 9.45

Length 10 mm, grey with brown markings. Very similar to *J. falcata* but with proportionately shorter, more robust antennae. Gnathopod 2 basis with fringe of long setae on anterior margin. Coxal plate 2 angular, with posterio-ventral corner produced. Gnathopod 2 male with single, elongate propodal process.

Among algae and epibenthic assemblages, on rafts, buoys, and similar structures. Reported from isolated localities on south-east and south coasts of Britain, probably more widespread but only recently regarded as specifically distinct from *J. falcata*.

Jassa ocia (Bate)   FIG. 9.45

Length 4 mm. Similar to *J. pusilla*. Male gnathopod 2 characteristic: propodus very enlarged, with sinuous palm and two proximal projections. Female gnathopod 2 broadly similar to male but much smaller.

Intertidal, amongst sponges and *Laminaria* holdfasts. South and west coasts.

Jassa pusilla (Sars)   FIG. 9.45

Length 4 mm. Similar to *J. falcata* but more robust. Male gnathopod 2 with bifid palmar process on propodus; female gnathopod 2 with palm less convex than in *J. falcata*.

Sublittoral, on sponges and hydroids. All British coasts.

Microjassa cumbrensis (Stebbing and Robertson) FIG. 9.45

Length 2 mm, brown. Eyes large. Antenna 2 longer and stouter than 1. Accessory flagellum uniarticulate, very small. Coxa 1 small, less than half length of 2, and partly concealed; coxa 5 not longer than 6. Epimeral plate 3 acutely angled posteriorly. Telson triangular.

Sublittoral, on coarse grounds, among hydroids. Western coasts only.

Parajassa pelagica (Leach)   FIG. 9.45

Length 5 mm, greyish with bands of brown. Eyes small. Antennae short and robust, with dense whorls of long setae. Antenna 1 about one-third of body-length, accessory flagellum represented by an indistinct tubercle; antenna 2 much longer than 1, very robust. Coxae 1 and 2 equal in length; coxa 5 longer than 6. Epimeral plate 3 rounded posteriorly. Telson approximately triangular.

Common in *Laminaria* holdfasts and similar habitats. All British coasts.

31 PODOCERIDAE

Body dorso-ventrally depressed, usually slender. Accessory flagellum present or absent. Mandible with palp. Coxae small, not touching. Urosome segments markedly depressed, segment 1 more than twice length of 2. Pleon segment 6 sometimes apparently fused with 5. Uropods variable. Telson entire and rounded.

---

1. Body oval, depressed. Pereopods 3–7 all more or
   less of similar length. Two pairs of biramous uropods
                                              Podocerus variegatus

   Body elongate, slender, depressed. Pereopods 3 and
   4 much smaller than 5–7   **2**

2. Pereopods 3 and 4 with slender, parallel-sided basis.
   Pereopods 5–7 elongate   ***Dulichia falcata***

   Pereopods 3 and 4 with broad, oval basis. Pereopods
   5–7 not greatly elongate   **3**

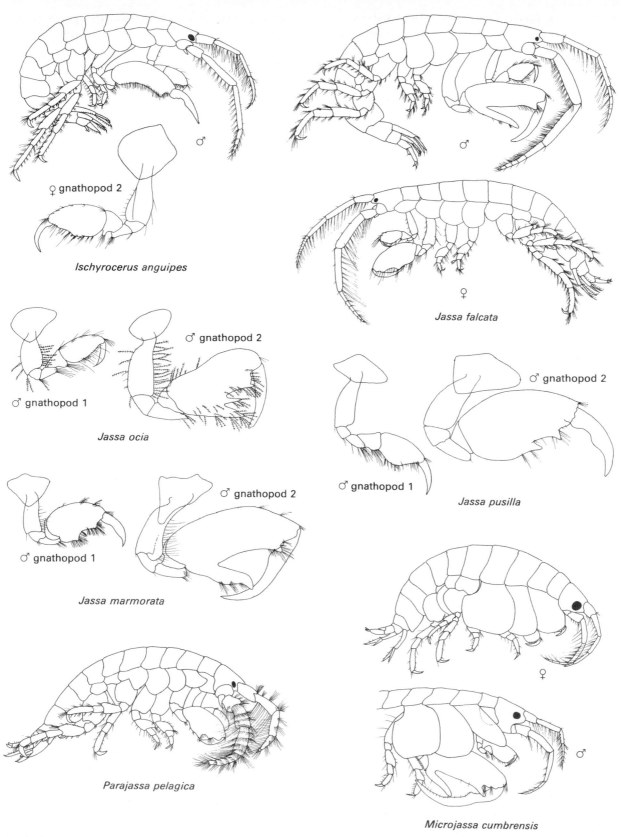

♀ gnathopod 2

♂

Ischyrocerus anguipes

♂ gnathopod 1

♂ gnathopod 2

Jassa ocia

♂ gnathopod 1

♂ gnathopod 2

Jassa marmorata

Jassa falcata

♀

♂ gnathopod 1

♂ gnathopod 2

Jassa pusilla

Parajassa pelagica

♀

♂

Microjassa cumbrensis

Fig. 9.45

3. Male coxa 1 spiniform, coxa 2 normal. Female
   gnathopod 2 dactylus more than half length of propodus   **Dyopedos monacanthus**

   Male coxa 1 normal, coxa 2 spiniform. Female
   gnathopod 2 dactylus less than half length of propodus   **Dyopedos porrectus**

Dulichia falcata (Bate)   FIG. 9.46

Length 8.5 mm; body very slender, white with red mottling.
Head elongate, with large round eyes. Antenna 1 longer than
body, slender, flagellum equal to length of peduncle article 3,
with five articles; accessory flagellum minute, with three articles.
Antenna 2 about two-thirds length of 1, flagellum shorter than
peduncle article 5. Coxae very small. Gnathopod 1 small, simple,
with propodus shorter than carpus. Female gnathopod 2 similar
to 1, but propodus longer than carpus. Male gnathopod 2 very
large; basis with large anterio-distal lobe; propodus elongate,
with large proximal process on palm and acute distal tooth.
Pereopods 5–7 elongate, carpus and propodus spinose; pereopod
7 may be very elongate. Uropods 1 and 2 outer ramus three-
quarters length of inner; uropod 1 rami each with long apical
spine. Telson rounded, shorter than uropod 2 peduncle.

Sublittoral, 20–700 m; on algae, hydroids, bryozoans, and
other epibenthos. recorded from north-east England, Scotland,
Clyde Sea, and Bristol Channel; North Devon appears to be its
southerly limit.

Dyopedos monacanthus (Metzger)   FIG. 9.46

Length 7.5 mm; body slender, light yellow with brown patches.
Head elongate, with large, round, protruding eyes. Antenna 1
about as long as body; flagellum equal to three-quarters length
of peduncle article 3, with five articles; accessory flagellum very
small, with three articles. Antenna 2 about three-quarters length
of 1. Coxae small; coxa 1 in male with spiniform anterio-distal
process. Gnathopod 1 small, simple, carpus longer than
propodus. Female gnathopod 2 small; carpus triangular; propodus oval, much longer than carpus; dactylus more than half
length of propodus. Male gnathopod 2 very large; basis with
stout anterio-distal lobe; propodus massive, densely setose, palm
with spiniform proximal process, and triangular distal tooth;
dactylus stout. Pereopods 3 and 4 small, basis oval; pereopods
5 and 6 elongate, carpus spinose, dactylus minute; pereopod 7
may be very elongate. Uropods 1 and 2 peduncle outer edge and
rami minutely toothed; outer ramus just shorter than inner.
Telson rounded.

Sublittoral. Recorded from Thames Estuary, north to Shetland, also from Bristol Channel and Channel Isles.

Dyopedos porrectus Bate   FIG. 9.46

Length 6.5 mm; body slender, white with narrow brown bands.
Head elongate, with large, rounded oval, protruding eyes.
Antenna 1 slightly longer than body, flagellum as long as peduncle article 3, with five articles, accessory flagellum very small,
with three articles. Antenna 2 two-thirds length of 1. Coxae very
small; coxa 2 in male with spiniform anterio-distal process.
Gnathopod 1 small, simple, carpus longer than propodus.

Female gnathopod 2 small; carpus triangular; propodus oval,
twice length of carpus; dactylus less than half length of propodus.
Male gnathopod 2 very large; basis with large anterio-distal lobe;
propodus narrow, elongate, palm with straight, long proximal
process and rounded or triangular distal tooth; dactylus stout.
Pereopods 3 and 4 small, basis oval; pereopods 5–7 not greatly
elongate, carpus spinose, dactylus very small. Uropods 1 and 2
with outer ramus two-thirds length of inner. Telson rounded.

Sublittoral, often associated with hydroids and bryozoans.
Recorded from Northumberland, north to Shetland, from the
Clyde Sea, Anglesey, and the Bristol Channel.

Podocerus variegatus Leach   FIG. 9.46

Length 4 mm, brownish red. Antenna 1 shorter than 2, accessory
flagellum present. Eyes prominent. Pereon normal. Pereopods
3 and 4 with basis not expanded. Gnathopod 2 large, subchelate;
male propodus oval, two and a half times as long as wide; female
propodus more circular, only one and a half times as long as
wide. Urosome with three segments; uropods 1 and 2 biramous;
uropod 3 without rami. Telson rounded, with four to five long
setae.

Lower shore and shallow sublittoral, on algae and sponges,
particularly in pools with *Corallina*. Western and southern
coasts.

Suborder **Hyperiidea**

Hyperiid amphipods are characterized by short, sometimes
slender, but typically fat or swollen bodies. The head is very
deep, rounded, and almost globular, with large, often strikingly
coloured eyes occupying the whole of the two sides of the head.
The pereon is often deep, rounded laterally and dorsally, and
somewhat compressed laterally; the pleon is usually slender
and the urosome well-developed, often elongate. Marked sexual
dimorphism occurs: the male has elongate, slender antennae,
while in the female both pairs of antennae are very short. The
maxilliped lacks a palp. Gnathopods are poorly developed and
differ between sexes; perepods 3–7 are typically slender, and in
all pereopods the coxa is very small, and sometimes absent.
Pleopods are well-developed, often powerful. Uropods are
laminar, biramous and lack spines.

Hyperiids have planktonic life cycles, the adult is frequently
associated with species of Scyphozoa.

Hyperia galba (Montagu)   FIG. 9.46

Length 12 mm; light translucent brown, with enormous green
eyes. Body plump, rounded. Head rounded, short and deep,
with eyes occupying whole of each side. Female with antennae
very short, subequal; peduncle of three articles attached to
immoveable basal segment, flagellum scarcely longer than peduncle. Male with long slender antennae; antenna 2 longer than
1, about two-thirds of body-length. Gnathopods 1 and 2 small,
simple; carpus with acute, projecting, disto-ventral lobe.
Uropods 1–3 broad, laminar; rami lanceolate, with finely denticulate margins.

In *Rhizostoma, Aurelia,* and other scyphozoa. All British
coasts. Widespread and common.

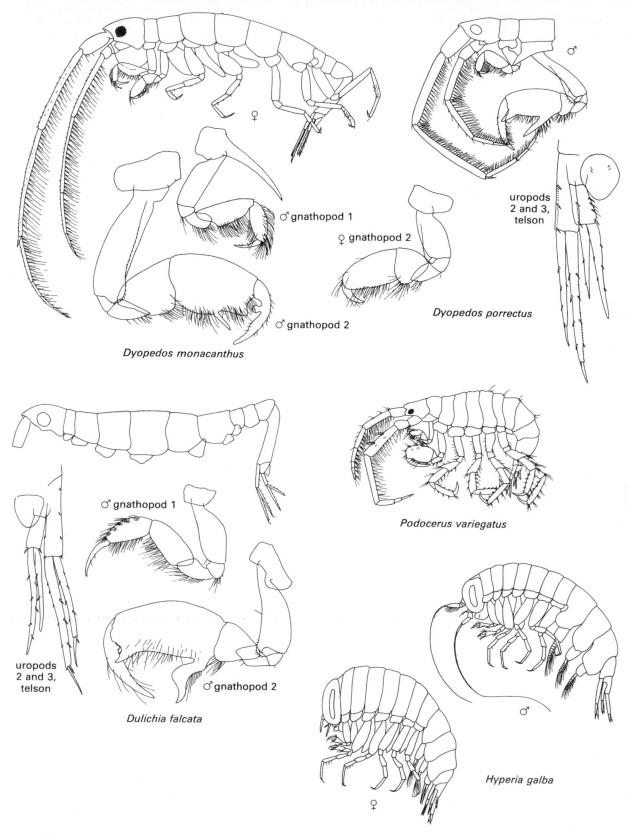

♂ gnathopod 1

♀ gnathopod 2

♂ gnathopod 2

Dyopedos monacanthus

uropods
2 and 3,
telson

Dyopedos porrectus

♂ gnathopod 1

uropods
2 and 3,
telson

♂ gnathopod 2

Dulichia falcata

Podocerus variegatus

Hyperia galba

Fig. 9.46

Suborder **Caprellidea**

The caprellids are amphipods in which the body is elongate and slender, the appendages reduced in number and, with few exceptions, the ability to swim or move rapidly has been lost. Caprellids tend to be slow-moving, often blending well with their surroundings. They are frequently found clinging to algae, hydroids, and Bryozoa, on buoys and pontoons, and may be found on the shore, in the shallow sublittoral, and even at depths approaching 5000 m. Certain species are opportunistic feeders and consume detritus, carrion, and protozoa, whereas others may actively prey on small crustacea. Some species may practise both feeding methods and others are known to be commensal with other marine invertebrates such as starfish.

The structure of a caprellid is less complex than that of a gammaridean amphipod. The animal may be divided into a *head*, a thorax or *pereon*, and an *abdomen*. The head and pereon segment 1 may be completely or partially fused and the length of segment 1 may vary appreciably. *Antenna 1* is longer than *antenna 2*. Antenna 1 has a three-jointed peduncle and a multi-articulate flagellum. Antenna 2 has a peduncle of three or four joints and a shorter flagellum, normally of two articles. Antenna 2 may bear parallel rows of long, so-called '*swimming*' *setae* on the central border of the peduncle and flagellum; these setae are of taxonomic importance. The presence or absence of a *mandibular palp* is also important, and when present this slim palp normally projects upwards between the peduncles of antennae 2. The pereon may be smooth or may possess dorsal and/or lateral *tubercles* or sharp *spines*. A pair of round or club-shaped *gills* is normally found on the ventro-lateral borders of segments 3 and 4, and may be present on segment 2 in some species. The *gnathopods* are normally larger than other pereopods and modified into grasping claws, with a moveable finger and an opposing cutting edge. The pereopods may be completely absent from segments 3 and 4, or may be reduced to minute appendages. Pereopods 5, 6, and 7 are normally of approximately equal length and are used for holding on to the substratum while the animal feeds with the gnathopods. The *propodus* of the posterior pereopods may bear one or two spines on its inner surface, these

being termed '*grasping*' *spines*. The small abdomen may be furnished with lobes and/or articulated appendages, or may be without either, differences between the sexes being usual. Although the abdomen is of taxonomic importance, its minute size makes it a difficult feature to observe. Female caprellids develop paired *lamellae* on the ventral borders of pereon segments 3 and 4, and these lamellae enlarge to form a *brood-pouch* for the developing eggs. The presence or absence of setae on the borders of the lamellae varies between species and is of some taxonomic value. Development of the embryos is completed within the brood-pouch and miniature caprellids eventually emerge. Female caprellids can be recognized by the presence of these brood lamellae, which may appear as small oval plates on immature forms. Male caprellids of a species are normally larger than females.

The following key and descriptions apply only to fully-grown adult animals, since juveniles often do not show features which are taxonomically important in the adults. Female adults often differ from males in several respects, and these differences are noted in the descriptions. The colour of an animal is an unreliable character, and many of the following species exhibit various colours when alive.

Caprellids should be narcotized in 7.5% magnesium chloride, then fixed in 5% neutral sea-water formalin. They should be stored in 70% ethanol, propylene phenoxetol, or neutralized formalin. Examination should be carried out with a binocular microscope, at up to × 50 magnification, although higher power will be necessary to examine the abdomen.

REFERENCES

Bocquet, C. and Peltier, A-M. (1964). Redescription de l'amphipode *Caprella erithizon* Mayer. *Bulletin de la Société linnéene de Normandie*, (10) **4**, 152–65.

Chevreux, E. and Fage, L. (1925). Amphipodes. *Faune de France*, **9**, 1–438, Lechevalier, Paris.

McCain, J. C. (1968). The Caprellidae (Crustacea: Amphipoda) of the Western North Atlantic. *Bulletin of the U.S. National Museum*, **278**, i–vi, 1–147.

KEY TO SPECIES

1. Gills on segments 2, 3, and 4. Pereopods 3 and 4 six-segmented, pereopod 5 five-segmented   **Phtisica marina**

   Gills on segments 3 and 4 only. Pereopods 3 and 4 greatly reduced or absent   **2**

2. Pereopods 3 and 4 minute, reduced to two segments. Mandibular palp of three segments. Head and pereon segments 1 and 2 with strong, forwardly directed spines   **Pseudoprotella phasma**

   Pereopods 3 and 4 absent, or represented only by a single minute seta. Mandibular palp present or absent   **3**

3. Mandibular palp present   **4**

    Mandibular palp absent   **5**

4. Antenna 2 flagellum with two segments. Body robust, usually spinose. Abdomen of male and female with two pairs of biarticulate appendages plus a pair of lobes. Pereopods 3 and 4 absent. Northern species, probably not occurring south of Shetland

    Aeginina longicornis

    Antenna 2 flagellum with three segments. Body slender, smooth. No abdominal appendages or lobes: replaced by median plaque in male, absent in female. Pereopods 3 and 4 absent. Southern and western coasts   *Parvipalpus capillaceous*

5. Pereopod 5 with six segments, about equal in size to 6 and 7. Pereopods 3 and 4 absent   **6**

    Pereopod 5 reduced, minute, with only two segments. Pereopods 3 and 4 represented only by a single seta. Often in association with starfish   *Pariambus typicus*

6. Antenna 2 with short setae ventrally, not arranged in parallel rows. Head bulbous and skull-shaped   *Caprella acanthifera*

    Antenna 2 with long setae ventrally, arranged in parallel rows   **7**

7. Prominent ventral spine arising between insertions of gnathopod 2 on each side

    Caprella equilibra

    No ventral spine between insertions of gnathopod 2   **8**

8. Head with prominent anteriorly directed triangular projection anterior to eye   **9**

    Head without triangular projection; smooth or with spine(s) or tubercle(s)   **10**

9. Carpus of pereopods 5–7 with medial ventral row of small tubercles, and parallel row of setae. Gnathopod 2 inserted in middle of segment, propodus one and a half times longer than wide in male   *Caprella periantis*

    Carpus of pereopods 5–7 without row of tubercles, but with row of setae. Gnathopod 2 inserted in posterior half of segment, propodus four times longer than wide in male

    Caprella fretensis

10. Head and pereon segments smooth, or with varying numbers of small pointed tubercles   **11**

    Head and pereon segments with sharp, anteriorly directed dorsal spines; or large, prominent, rounded, dorsal tubercles on pereon segments only. Tubercles more prominent in posterior segments

    12

11. Ratio of total body-length to length of pereopod 2 basis normally > 13. Dorsal surface of pereon segments 1–4 usually with pointed tubercles; head usually with at least a single tubercle. Head and pereon tubercles unpaired, although bifid single tubercles may appear as a pair. Peduncle of antenna 1 rarely with numerous setules

    Caprella septentrionalis

    Ratio of total body-length to length of gnathopod 2 basis normally < 13. Dorsal surface of pereon segments 1–4 usually smooth, head infrequently with small tubercle or pair of tubercles. When present, tubercles on pereon segments 1–4 normally paired and wide apart. Peduncle of antenna 1 often with numerous setules   *Caprella linearis*

12. Antenna 1 flagellum with six to eight articles. Head and pereon segments 1 and 2 with long, pointed, anteriorly directed spines; segments 3–5 with shorter spines. Ventrolateral spines prominent on segments 2–5. Small species, maximum length 4.5 mm .... ***Caprella erithizon***

Antenna 1 flagellum with eleven to thirteen articles (rarely ten). All pereon segments, except 1 in male, bearing large rounded tubercles, becoming more numerous on posterior segments. Maximum length approximately 15 mm .... ***Caprella tuberculata***

---

1 CAPRELLIDAE

Phtisica marina Slabber .... FIG. 9.47

Head rounded, smooth. Body smooth, slender. Antenna 1 from half to equal body-length, flagellum with up to 20 articles. Antenna 2 approximately equal to antenna 1 peduncle; flagellum of three to six articles, sparse, short, ventral setae on peduncle and flagellum. Gnathopod 1 propodus with four or five grasping spines, margin without serrations but with numerous short spines; dactyl not serrate. Gnathopod 2 propodus often with two unequal grasping spines, sometimes only larger spine present; palm with numerous short spines and few setae; propodus often with inflated appearance in older males. Gills elliptical, on segments 2, 3, and 4. Pereopods 6 and 7 six-segmented, propodus with two proximal grasping spines, one medial spine, one distal spine. Abdomen of male with two pairs of articulate appendages and one pair of pyriform appendages. Female abdomen with two pairs of articulate appendages, one pair of lobes, and an anterior raised projection, Brood pouch of female without setal fringe on lamellae. Maximum length 20 mm (male) and 16 mm (female).

Usually sublittoral, on hydroids and algae, or attached to floating objects and buoys. Known to swim occasionally, especially at night. All British coasts.

Pseudoprotella phasma (Montagu) .... FIG. 9.47

Head with large, anteriorly directed spine dorsally. Pereon segment 1 with similar spine; segment 2 with two spines in middle, one spine on posterior margin. Usual spine formula 1–1–2–1 for head and first two pereon segments, but other variations are known. Pereon segment 3 with small triangular tubercle dorsal to insertion of pereopod, and two small rounded dorsal tubercles mid-way along segment. Small triangular tubercle dorsal to insertion of pereopod, and two small rounded dorsal tubercles mid-way along segment. Small rounded dorsal tubercle, or occasionally a spine, at junction of pereon segments 3 and 4; tubercles on segment 4 as on 3; segment 5 with small lateral triangular tubercle one-third length along each side. Antenna 1 about two-thirds length of body, flagellum of 18–26 articles. Antenna 2 flagellum with 2 articles; peduncle and flagellum with short setae widely spaced. Pereopods 3 and 4 minute, two-segmented, with long terminal seta. Pereopods 5, 6, and 7 six-segmented, about equal length. Gnathopod 2 inserted one-third to one-half length along segment; basis with downwardly directed spine on distal anterior edge. Gills ovoid,

on segments 3 and 4 only. Abdomen with two pairs of non-jointed appendages in male, without appendages in female. Brood pouch of female with anterior pair of lamellae entirely setose, posterior pair setose only on posterior half. Maximum length 25 mm (male) and 20 mm (female).

Usually sublittoral, often on algae and large hydroids. All British coasts, probably more common in south.

Aeginina longicornis (Krøyer) .... FIG. 9.47

Head separated from pereon segment 1 by suture. Spination of head and pereon segments variable, from almost smooth to spinose. Antenna 1 as long as or slightly longer than body, flagellum with up to 26 articles. Antenna 2 reaches almost to distal end of antenna 1 peduncle segment 2; short setae on all segments. Gnathopod 1 with triangular propodus; grasping margin of propodus and dactyl slightly serrate; propodus with one pair of grasping spines. Gnathopod 2 inserted about half-way along segment in male or in anterior third of segment in female; basis and ischium with strong distal anterior projection; palm of propodus with proximal poison tooth and distal notch, tooth, and rectangular projection; carpus with posterio-distal projection. Gills elliptical, on segments 3 and 4 only. Lateral spines over insertions of gnathopod 2. Pereopods 5–7 six-segmented, increasing in length posteriorly, each propodus with pair of proximal grasping spines. Abdomen of male and female with two pairs of biarticulate appendages and one pair of lobes. Maximum length 54 mm (male) and 34 mm (female).

Sublittoral. An Arctic species, which reaches its southernmost limits around Shetland.

Parvipalpus capillaceous (Chevreux) .... FIG. 9.47

Head and body smooth, without spines or tubercles; eyes large. Small lateral spine at base of gnathopod 2. Antenna 1 about one-third of body-length, flagellum of nine articles in male, five in female. Antenna 2 peduncle slightly longer than that of antenna 1, flagellum of three articles, scattered short setae on ventral borders. Gnathopod 2 inserted in anterior quarter of segment; palm of propodus with distal poison tooth and proximal tooth. Gills short, oval, second pair inserted in proximal third of segment 4. Pereon segment 5 longest, with pereopod 5 inserted in posterior quarter. Pereopod 5 propodus with strong distal spine; pereopods 6 and 7 propodus unarmed. Abdomen without appendages, replaced by large median plaque. Female gnathopod 2 propodus without poison tooth. Abdomen without median

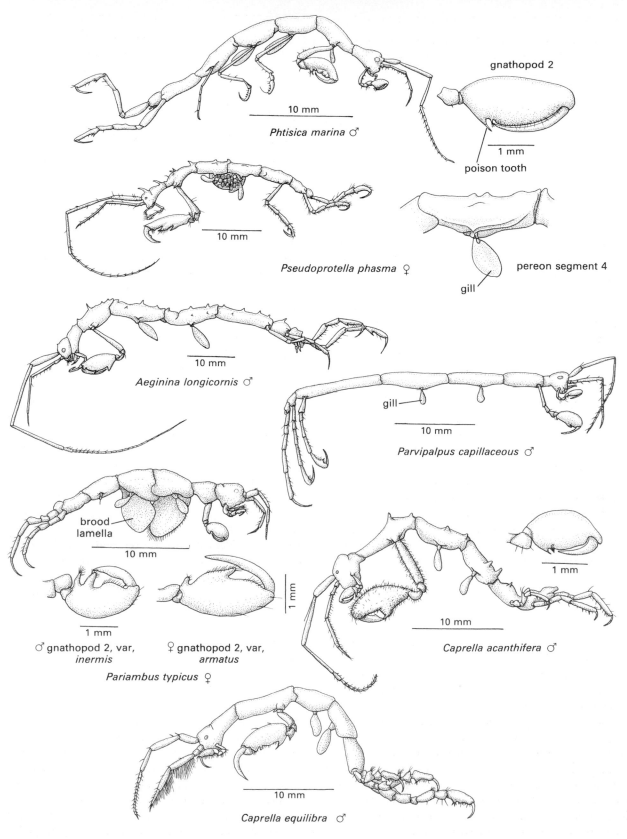

gnathopod 2

10 mm

Phtisica marina ♂

1 mm

poison tooth

Pseudoprotella phasma ♀

10 mm

pereon segment 4

gill

Aeginina longicornis ♂

10 mm

gill

10 mm

Parvipalpus capillaceous ♂

brood lamella

10 mm

1 mm

♂ gnathopod 2, var, *inermis*

♀ gnathopod 2, var, *armatus*

1 mm

Pariambus typicus ♀

1 mm

10 mm

Caprella acanthifera ♂

10 mm

Caprella equilibra ♂

Fig. 9.47

plaque. Both pairs of brood lamellae setose on interior edges, largest setae on anterior pair, few on posterior pair. Maximum length 7 mm (male) and 5 mm (female).

Sublittoral. Rare, known only occasionally from Isle of Man, Bristol Channel, south-west Ireland, and west coast of Scotland. Found also on French Atlantic coast.

Pariambus typicus (Krøyer)   FIG. 9.47

Head and body smooth, without tubercles or spines; body stout in female more slender in male. Antenna 1 about one-third to one-half length of body, flagellum of eight articles. Antenna 2 with short ventral setae; about as long as antenna 1 peduncle. Mandible without palp. Gnathopod 1 with short obtuse spine on distal merus, plus one or two distal setae; carpus triangular. Gnathopod 2 inserted near middle of segment; palm of propodus armed with strong proximal poison spine and large sub-median tooth; dactyl slightly sinuous on inner border. Gnathopod 2 female without sub-median tooth. Gills small, oval, on segments 3 and 4 only. Pereopods 3 and 4 represented by single seta only. Pereopods 5 minute, comprising two segments with long terminal seta. Pereopods 6 and 7 with six articles. Abdomen in male with plaque and pair of vestigial lobes, female without lobes. Anterior pair of incubatory lamellae setose. Maximum length 7 mm (male) and 6 mm (female).

Two varieties are known to occur around British coasts, distinguishable by certain characteristics evident in the males:

var. *armatus:* with a tubercle on peduncle article 3 of antenna 1; without a deep indentation on palm of gnathopod 2. Strong proximal spine on pereopods 6 and 7 propodus. Recorded infrequently from the southern and eastern coasts of Britain and from the Scilly Isles.

var. *inermis:* no tubercle on antenna 1; with deep indentation on palm of gnathopod 2. No spines on perepods 6 and 7 propodus. All British coasts, the more frequently encountered variety. Sublittoral, but may occur on the lower shore. On coarse sandy substrata, but often found on the aboral surface of the starfish *Asterias rubens* and *Crossaster papposus*.

Caprella acanthifera Leach   FIG. 9.47

Head smooth, domed, and skull-shaped. Body stout, with varying numbers of small, paired dorsal tubercles on all segments except 1; tubercles may be elongate in large specimens. Posterior regions of segments 2, 3, and 4 often with single tubercle behind a pair. Antenna 1 about two-thirds of body-length, covered sparsely with short setae not arranged in parallel rows; flagellum of two articles. Mandible without palp. Gnathopod 1 propodus with proximal spine. Gnathopod 2 inserted in posterior third of segment, often massive in large males; palm of propodus concave, with proximal spine and median tooth. In old and large males and females, segment 2 and gnathopod 2 may be covered in dense, fine setae. Gills club-shaped, on segments 3 and 4 only. Pereopods 3 and 4 absent. Pereopods 5–7 with pair of grasping spines on propodus, and two to four accessory spines proximal to grasping spines. Female gnathopod 2 inserted in

anterior half of segment; anterior incubatory lamellae setose. Abdomen with pair of lobes and pair of biarticulate appendages in male, in female without either. Maximum length 13 mm (male) and 8 mm (female).

Midshore level to sublittoral. Frequent in rock pools and gullies, on algae, hydroids, and Bryozoa. All British coasts, possibly more frequent in north.

Caprella equilibra Say   FIG. 9.47

Head and body smooth dorsally, except for paired tubercles occasionally present on pereon segment 5. Head flattened anteriorly. Strong lateral anteriorly directed spines at base of gnathopod 2. Antero-lateral spines on pereon segments 3 and 4; segments 1 and 2 elongate in male. Antenna 1 about half body-length, flagellum of 13–15 articles. Antenna 2 one-fifth to one-third of body-length, flagellum of 2 articles; ventral border of peduncle with two parallel rows of long setae, shorter setae on flagellum. Strong ventral spine between insertions of gnathopod 2. Mandible without palp. Gnathopod 1 propodus with two proximal grasping spines; grasping margin of dactyl and propodus serrate. Gnathopod 2 with short, stout basis, distal anterior margin produced into triangular projection; palm of propodus with single proximal grasping spine, large, rectangular distal tooth and more proximal tooth. Gills oval or elliptical, on segments 3 and 4 only. Pereopods 5–7 propodus with two proximal grasping spines. Abdomen of male with one pair of appendages and one pair of lobes; female with lobes only. Brood lamellae with posterior border of anterior lamella only setose. Maximum length 23 mm (male) and 12 mm (female).

Sublittoral, usually associated with floating buoys, pontoons. All British coasts.

Caprella periantis Leach   FIG. 9.48

Head with anteriorly directed triangular projection anterior to eye. Body stout, smooth. Antenna 1 about one-third of body-length, flagellum up to 15 articles. Antenna 2 usually longer than peduncle of antenna 1, central border of peduncle and flagellum with two parallel rows of long setae. Mandible without palp. Gnathopod 1 propodus with two proximal grasping spines; grasping margins of dactyl and propodus serrate. Gnathopod 2 inserted in mid-segment; propodus with proximal poison tooth, palm setose and concave in male, slightly convex in female; grasping margin of dactyl serrate. Gills circular, oval, or elliptical; on segments 3 and 4 only. Pereopods 5–7 propodus with pair of proximal grasping spines; palm concave. Abdomen of male with one pair of appendages and one pair of lobes; female with lobes only. Pereopods 5–7 carpus with median ventral row of small tubercles and parallel row of setae. Maximum length 15 mm (male) and 12 mm (female).

Intertidal and sublittoral, usually on buoys or associated with sponges and hydroids. Southern and south-western coasts, English Channel.

Caprella fretensis Stebbing   FIG. 9.48

Head with triangular projection anterior to eye. Body smooth, except for a few small tubercles on posterior segments. Pereon

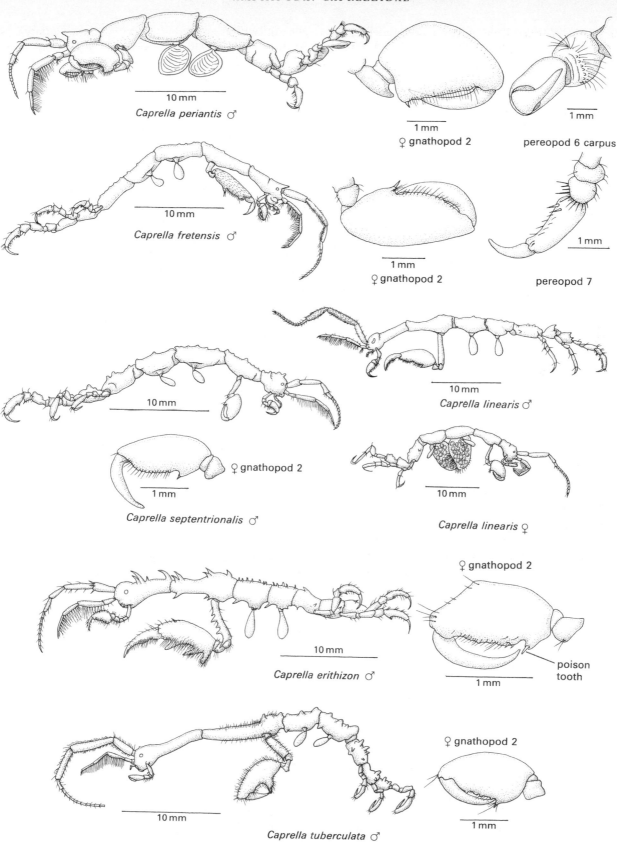

Caprella periantis ♂

10 mm

♀ gnathopod 2

1 mm

pereopod 6 carpus

1 mm

Caprella fretensis ♂

10 mm

♀ gnathopod 2

1 mm

pereopod 7

1 mm

Caprella linearis ♂

10 mm

Caprella septentrionalis ♂

♀ gnathopod 2

1 mm

10 mm

Caprella linearis ♀

10 mm

♀ gnathopod 2

poison tooth

Caprella erithizon ♂

10 mm

1 mm

♀ gnathopod 2

Caprella tuberculata ♂

10 mm

1 mm

Fig. 9.48

segments 1 and 2 elongate in male. Antenna 1 about half body-length, ventral surface of peduncle articles 2 and 3 with rows of fine, short setae in male; flagellum with 12–14 articles. Antenna 2 about equal length of peduncle segments 1 and 2 of antenna 1; ventral borders of peduncle and flagellum with two parallel rows of long setae. Mandible without palp. Gnathopod 2 inserted in posterior half of segment in male, centre in female. Gnathopod 2 propodus in male 3.5–4 times longer than broad, frequently covered with dense mat of fine setae; palm straight, with median tooth and small distal tooth; dactyl tip extends to median tooth. Pereopods 5–7 propodus with two proximal grasping spines; carpus with transverse row of setae ventrally. Abdomen with one pair of appendages and one pair of lobes in male, lobes only in female.

Southern and south-western coasts, Irish Sea, and English Channel. ELWS–sublittoral.

Caprella septentrionalis Krøyer   FIG. 9.48

Head usually with single spine or tubercle. Body spination variable, but usually with spines or tubercles on all segments, larger on anterior segments and always unpaired, although bifid single tubercles may occur. Antenna 1 peduncle articles 1 and 2 rarely setose in male; flagellum of up to sixteen articles. Antenna 2 at least as long as peduncle of antenna 1, ventral margin with two parallel rows of long setae; flagellum of two articles. Mandible without palp. Gnathopod 1 propodus with two proximal grasping spines, grasping margins of propodus and dactyl serrated. Gnathopod 2 propodus with proximal poison tooth on palm and small tooth on inner surface; distally with small tooth, notch, and rectangular projection. Ratio of total length to length of basis of gnathopod 2 usually greater than 13. Gills usually elliptical, occasionally oval or grossly inflated. Pereopods 5–7 propodus with pair of proximal grasping spines. Abdomen with paired appendages and lobes in male, lobes only in female. Maximum length 31 mm (male) and 24 mm (female), normally less.

Intertidal and shallow sublittoral, sometimes amongst *Corallina* in rock-pools. A northern species, occurring in Scottish waters, but not known further south.

This species is easily confused with *C. linearis*, and no simple distinction can be made between the two species. The ratio of gnathopod 2 basis to total body-length is one suggested by McCain (1968) for western Atlantic specimens, and tests on British specimens show it to work fairly reliably. The difference in geographical range also helps identification except in the north of Britain. Although the observations on tubercles are fairly reliable, exceptions can occur.

Caprella linearis (Linnaeus)   FIG. 9.48

Head and body segments normally smooth; tuberculations always paired when present. Pereon segment 5 with pair of antero-lateral tubercles, two small anterior dorsal tubercles, and four posterio-dorsal tubercles, Pereon segments 1 and 2 elongate in male. Antenna 1 often with setose peduncle in male, flagellum of up to 15 articles (male) or 20 articles (female). Antenna 2 shorter than articles 1 and 2 of antenna 1, ventral surface

with two parallel rows of long setae; flagellum of two articles. Mandible without palp. Ratio of total length to length of gnathopod 2 basis usually less than 13. Gnathopod 2 propodus with small tooth adjacent to poison tooth, and two distal projections separated by a deep cleft. Distal projections smaller and closer together in female. Gills elliptical. Pereopods 5–7 propodus with pair of proximal grasping spines. Maximum length 22 mm (male) and 14 mm (female). Occasionally larger specimens are found.

ELWS to sublittoral. Often on buoys among hydroids and Bryozoa. All British coasts.

Caprella erithizon Mayer   FIG. 9.48

Head and pereon segments 1 and 2 with long, anteriorly directed spines. Pereon segments 3–5 with shorter anteriorly directed spines; prominent ventro-lateral spines on segments 2–5. Antenna 1 about half body-length, flagellum of six to eight articles; ventral margin of flagellum with setae on articulations. Antenna 2 about two-thirds length of antenna 1; flagellum with two articles, ventral border with two parallel rows of long setae. Mandible without palp. Gnathopod 2 inserted in posterior half of segment in male, in anterior half of segment in female; propodus with large proximal tooth, prominent distal tooth, and anteriorly directed median tooth. Female gnathopod 2 propodus with proximal poison tooth only. Gills oval. Pereopod 5–7 propodus with pair of proximal grasping spines and series of distal spines on palm. Abdomen with one pair of appendages and one pair of lobes in male, lobes only in female. Maximum length 4.5 mm (male) and 4 mm (female).

Intertidal and shallow sublittoral, often on Bryozoa. Rare. Known only from south-west coasts and English Channel.

Caprella tuberculata Bate and Westwood   FIG. 9.48

Head normally with very short dorsal spine in centre. All body segments, except segment 1 in male, with strong and numerous dorsal tubercles. These occur first on the posterior of segment 2, and become more numerous and pronounced on more posterior segments. Segments 1 and 2 elongate in male, each about twice length of segment 3. Antenna 1 about half body-length, flagellum of 11–13 articles. Antenna 2 little more than one-third length of antenna 1; flagellum with two articles, ventral surface with two parallel rows of long setae. Mandible without palp. Gnathopod 2 inserted in posterior half of segment in male, in anterior half in female; palm of propodus in male with large median protuberance bearing small proximal tooth and larger distal tooth; palm and outer edge often covered with fine setae. Female gnathopod 2 with palm of propodus straight, with proximal tooth and two rudimentary teeth. Gills club-shaped. Pereopods 5–7 basis with four tubercles; palm of propodus with proximal pair of grasping spines plus two or three pairs of short spines. Abdomen with one pair of appendages and one pair of lobes in male, lobes only in female. Anterior brood lamellae setose all round, posterior pair with posterior edges only setose. Maximum length 15 mm (male) and 10 mm (female).

Sublittoral, often on buoys, flotsam, and large hydroids. All British coasts, but scarce.

Class **Crustacea Malacostraca**

Order **Decapoda**

THE Decapoda is the largest natural grouping within the Mala-costraca. In all decapods the thoracic segments are fused dorsally to a *carapace*, a fold of which extends ventrally on each side of the animal, enclosing the gills and constituting a *branchial chamber*. The maxilla has a large, modified endopodite, the *scaphognathite*, which drives water through the branchial chamber by rhythmic beating.

Classification within the Decapoda presents some problems. Most frequently, the order is divided simply into two suborders, the swimming decapods, or Natantia, and the walking decapods, or Reptantia, and this arrangement is maintained by many authorities. However, a more natural classification recognizes the suborders Dendrobranchiata and Pleocyemata. In Dend-robranchiate decapods the gills are subdivided to form arbor-escent tufts, the first three pairs of pereopods are chelate, and eggs, which are not carried by the female, hatch as nauplii larvae. The Pleocyemata have unbranched gills, show variable chelation of the second and third pereopods, and their eggs, which develop attached to the female pleopods, hatch as zoeae larvae. The Dendrobranchiata comprises the single infraorder Periaeidea, which together with three infraorders of the Pleocyemata con-stitute the Natantia. In British waters natant decapods are rep-resented by the infraorder Caridea only. The remaining four infraorders of the Pleocyemata constitute the Reptantia, and representatives of all four groups occur in the British sea area.

Suborder **Dendrobranchiata**

Infraorder **Caridea**
[Natantia]

The natant Decapods have retained an elongate body shape (Fig. 10.1). The body is divisible into three regions: head, thorax (or *pereon*) and abdomen (or *pleon*). Fusion of some of the head segments with the pereon gives a *cephalothorax*. This and the remaining pereon segments are usually covered by the *carapace*, which also extends ventro-laterally to cover the gills, viscera, and the bases of the thoracic limbs. Sculpturing and spination of the carapace differ between and within families. The anterior extension of the carapace into a 'beak' or *rostrum* is a common feature amongst natantians. The rostrum is often armed with teeth on its dorsal and ventral borders, and it may be straight, or curving upwards or downwards. It is taxonomically important, although in some families, e.g. Pandalidae, its great length often results in it snapping off when the animal is caught in a net. Anteriorly the head possesses a pair of stalked *eyes*, plus a pair of sensory *antennules* (or first antennae) and a pair of *antennae* (or second antennae). The antennules are usually biramous, although in the Paleamonidae they are triramous. The basal three segments of the antennule form the *peduncle* and the first of these is usually produced antero-laterally into a process called the *stylocerite*. The antennae are usually much longer than the antennules, the exopod being produced into a scale-like process, the *scaphocerite*. The mouthparts comprise one pair of *mandibles*, two pairs of *maxillae* and three pairs of *maxillipeds*. The man-dibles grind and crush food, and usually consist of a *molar process*, plus an *incisor process* and a *palp*. Either or both of the latter two structures may be absent, and in *Pasiphaea* the molar process and palp are absent. The three maxillipeds are derived from the first three pairs of thoracic limbs of the primitive form, and the third maxilliped is usually the least modified. The five pairs of *pereopods* are used for locomotion; the anterior two or three pairs usually terminate in a claw or *chela*, which assists in feeding, and in offence and defence. The structure of a pereopod is outlined in Fig. 10.1. In some families, (e.g. Pasiphaeidae) all the pereopods bear *exopods*, whereas in others (e.g. Hip-polytidae) exopods are absent, or present only on some limbs (e.g. Crangonidae). *Epipods* may also be present (e.g. *Alpheus*) or absent (e.g. *Crangon*). The carpus of pereopod 2 is subdivided in some families (e.g. Hippolytidae) but not in others (e.g. Palaemonidae) and this feature is of taxonomic importance. Each pleon segment bears a pair of biramous *pleopods*, enabling the animal to swim by means of their rhythmic beating. The *endo-pods* of pleopods 2–5 usually have a short *appendix interna*, bearing hooks and presumably assisting in locomotion by coup-ling together adjacent pleopods during swimming. The sixth pleopods are considerably flattened and expanded to form the *uropods*, which, with the tail or *telson*, make up the tail-fan of the animal.

The sexes are separate and secondary sexual features are noticeable in adult natantians. The first pleopods differ, and usually the endopod of pleopod 2 of the male bears an *appendix masculina* which aids in copulation. In some families (e.g. Cran-gonidae) there are sexual differences between the antennular rami, and in most cases the female of a species is larger than the

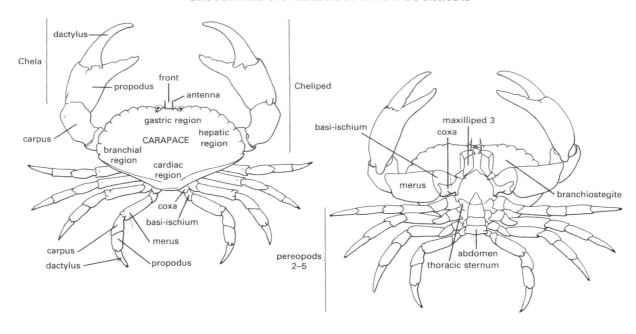

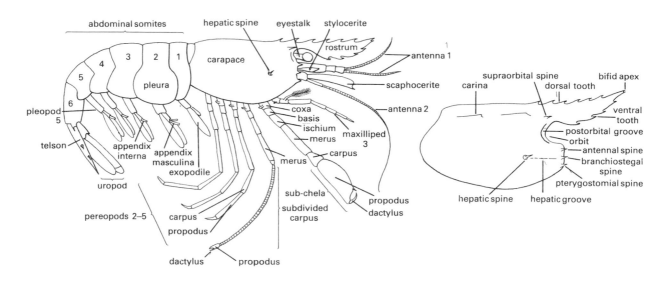

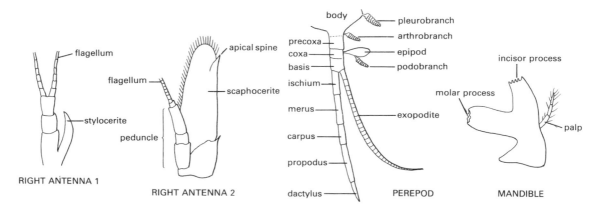

Fig. 10.1

male. Eggs are carried externally by the females, attached to long setae which develop on the pleopods for this purpose. Planktonic *zoeae* larvae metamorphose through *post-larval* stages to the adult form, the number of zoeae and post-larvae varying between species.

Natant Decapods occur in freshwater, brackish water and estuarine environments, although most are exclusively marine. *Palaemonetes* inhabits brackish pools in northern Europe, whereas in Mediterranean regions it is found in freshwater habitats. Some species are adapted to life in a fluctuating estuarine environment, e.g. *Crangon crangon* and *Palaemon longirostris*. Many species are encountered on the shore and in the shallow sublittoral zone, although natant Decapods are also well-represented in catches from the bathypelagic regions. Members of many families are benthic in habit (e.g. Crangonidae, Alphaeidae), whereas others (e.g. Oplophoridae, a deep water family) are pelagic and make extensive diurnal vertical migrations. A few natantians are found in specific associations with other animals (e.g. *Typton*). Most natant Decapods are predacious, many being omnivorous and often scavenging for food. They are preyed upon to a great extent by fish, and to a lesser extent by other invertebrates such as coelenterates and octopods. Active fisheries also account for large numbers of certain species, e.g. *Pandalus, Crangon*.

Specimens can be narcotized successfully prior to fixation by replacing the sea-water in which they are kept by a 7.5% solution of magnesium chloride in sea-water. If this is not available, CO_2 can be added to the sea-water via a soda siphon, or the animals can be placed in a freezer overnight and fixed after thawing. Fixation is probably best carried out in 5% sea-water formalin solution, specimens being kept in this solution for about 24 h. They may then be washed in tap water and transferred to a solution made up of: propylene phenoxetol 0.5 ml, propylene glycol 4.5 ml, sea-water 95 ml. This mixture is not unpleasant to handle, and specimens do not dry out. It must not be used as a fixative, but only after fixation has taken place. If these chemicals are not available, specimens may be transferred from formalin, through a wash to 70 per cent ethanol to which a little glycerol has been added.

Specimens should be examined with the aid of a binocular microscope, and magnifications of up to × 50 may be required in the examination of mouthparts.

REFERENCES

Al-Adhub, A. H. Y, and Williamson, D. I. (1975). Some European Processidae (Crustacea, Decapoda, Caridea). *Journal of Natural History*, 9, 693–703.

Allen, J. A. (1967). *The Fauna of the Clyde Sea area. Crustacea: Euphausiacea and Decapoda, with an illustrated key to the British species.* Scottish Marine Biological Association, Millport.

Bacescu, M. S. (1967). Decapoda. *Fauna Republic populare Romane*, 4, 1–356.

Balss, H. (1956). Decapoda. In: *Klassen und Ordnungen das Tierreichs*, (ed. H. Bronns), 5 Bd., 1 Abt., 7 Buch, (11–13): 1369–70.

Christiansen, M. E. (1972). *Crustacea Decapoda*. Tifotkreps, pp. 1–71, Figs. 1–91. Universitetsforlaget, Oslo.

Fincham, A. A. and Wickins, J. F. (1976). *Identification of commercial prawns and shrimps.* London, British Museum (Natural History), Publ. No. 779: 1–7.

Greve, L. (1963). The genera *Spirontocaris, Lebbeus, Eualus* and *Thoralus* in Norwegian waters (Crustacea Decapoda). *Sarsia*, 11, 29–42..

Holthuis,L. B. (1946). Notes on the genus *Pandalina* (Crustacea, Decapoda) with the description of a new species from European waters. *Zoölogische mededeelingen, Leiden*, 26, 281–6.

Holthuis, L. B. (1950). Decapoda (K. ix) A. Natantia, Macrura Reptantia, Anomuras en Stomatopoda (K. x). *Fauna van Nederland*, 15, 1–166.

Holthius, L. B. (1955). The recent genera of Caridean and Stenopodidean shrimps (Class Crustacea, Order Decapoda. Supersection Natantia) with keys for their determination. *Zoölogische verhandelingen, Leiden*, 26, 1–157.

Kemp, S. (1910). The Decapoda Natantia of the coasts of Ireland. *Scientific Investigations of the Fisheries Branch. Department of Agriculture for Ireland*, 1908, 1: 1–190.

Lagardere, J-P. (1969). Les crevettes du Golfe de Gascogne (Region Sud). *Tethys*, 1 (4): 1023–48.

Lagardere, J-P. (1971). Les crevettes des cotes du Maroc. *Travaux de l'Institut scientifique cherifien*, No. 36: 1–140.

Nouvel, H. and Holthius, L. B. (1957). Les Processidae (Crustacea Decapoda Natantia) des eaux Européennes. *Zoölogische verhandelingen Leiden*, 32: 1–53.

Simpson, A. C., Howell, B. R., and Warren, P. J. (1970). Synopsis of biological data on the shrimp *Pandalus montagui* Leach 1814. *F.A.O. Fisheries Reports*, 57, 1225–49.

Silvertsen, E. and Holthuis, L. B. (1956). Crustacea Decapoda (the Penaidea and Stenopodidea excepted). *Report on the Scientific Results of the 'Michael Sars' North Atlantic Deep-Sea Expedition*, 1910, 5, (12), 1–54.

Smaldon, G. (1979). British coastal shrimps and prawns. *Synopses of the British Fauna* (N.S.), 15. London: Academic Press for the Linnean Society of London, and the Estuarine and Brackish Water Sciences Association.

Tiews, K. (1970). Synopsis of biological data on the common shrimp, *Crangon crangon. F.A.O. Fisheries Reports*, 57, 1167–224.

Zariquiey Alvarez, R. (1968). Crustaceos Decapodos Ibericos. *Investiacion Pesquera*, 32, 1–510.

KEY TO FAMILIES

1. Pereopod 1 chelate or simple   **2**
   Pereopod 1 subchelate   **7. Crangonidae**

---

2. Fingers of chelae of pereopods 1 and 2 slender, with pectinate cutting edges
                                                                                          1. Pasiphaeidae
   Cutting edges of chelae not pectinate   **3**

---

3. Pereopod 2 carpus subdivided into two or more segments   **4**
   Pereopod 2 carpus not subdivided. Pereopod 1 with well-developed chela   **2. Palaemonidae**

---

4. Pereopod 1 chela distinct, at least on one side   **5**
   Pereopod 1 chela microscopically small or absent   **6. Pandalidae**

---

5. Both of first pair of pereopods chelate   **6**
   Only one of first pair of pereopods chelate, the other ending in a simple curved dactyl
                                                                                          5. Processidae

---

6. First pair of chelae short, not swollen; tips of fingers usually dark coloured. Eyes free,
   not covered by carapace. Pereopod 2 carpus with more or less than five segments,
   but never with five segments   **4. Hippolytidae**
   Tips of fingers of first pair of chelae not dark coloured. Pereopod 1 stronger than 2,
   chelipeds swollen and often unequal. Eyes partly or wholly covered by carapace.
   Pereopod 2 carpus with five segments   **3. Alpheidae**

---

1 PASIPHAEIDAE

Rostrum short, sometimes represented by a spine arising behind frontal margin of carapace. Mandibular palp present or absent. Maxilliped 2 with article 7 attached terminally to article 6, exopod rudimentary or absent. First two pairs of pereopods longer and much stouter than the others; chelae elongate, with slender dactyl and propodus; carpus short, unsegmented. Exopods on all pereopods, often very long; present (often very small) on maxilliped 3; often forming chief part of maxilliped 1. Eggs often large, development abbreviated.

---

1. Pleon with distinct dorsal carina. Rostrum slender, in form of spine, with inferior margin concave. Basis of pereopod 2 with 7–12 spines, Telson cleft at apex
                                         Pasiphaea multidentata

   Pleon without dorsal carina. Rostrum short, triangular, and upturned, apex pointed. Pleon segment 6 with dorsal posteriorly directed spine. Telson slightly convex at apex   ***Pasiphaea sivado***

Pasiphaea multidentata Esmark   FIG. 10.2

Length up to 110 mm, colour milky white, smaller specimens transparent. Rostrum slender, spinous, with inferior margin concave. Stylocerite twisted, acutely pointed. Scaphocerite (including apical spine) more than half length of carapace; outer margin evenly convex throughout length with long, stout apical spine exceeding lamellar portion. Maxilliped 3 extends to distal end of scaphocerite; exopod present. Mandible without palp or molar process. Pereopods 1 and 2 chelate; chelae slender with pectinate cutting edges. Pereopods 1–5 with exopods; pereopod 2 basis with 7–12 spines. Pleon segments with distinct dorsal carina. Telson narrow, cleft at apex.

Off west and south-west coasts, 10–2000 m.

Pasiphaea sivado (Risso)   FIG. 10.2

Length up to 100 mm; colour translucent, with pink or red spots. Rostrum short, triangular, and upturned with pointed apex; arises behind anterior margin of carapace. Stylocerite twisted, acutely pointed, with spine at apex. Outer margin of scaphocerite slightly convex, apical spine stout, exceeding lamellar portion. Maxilliped 3 about 1.25 × length of scaphocerite; exopod present. Mandible without palp or molar process. Pereopods 1 and 2 chelate; chelae slender with pectinate cutting edges; exopods present on pereopods 1–5; pereopod 2 merus with variable number of spines. Pleon segments without dorsal carina. Pleon segment 6 with dorsal, posteriorly directed spine. Telson slightly convex at apex.

West coasts, not in Channel or North sea, 20–500 m.

2 PALAEMONIDAE

Rostrum compressed, usually dentate. Carapace with antennal spine, with or without hepatic and branchiostegal spines. Eyes developed. Mandible with or without palp, incisor process and molar process separated by cleft. Maxilliped 2 with article 7 attached lateral to article 6. Maxilliped 3 with exopod, with or without arthrobranch or pleurobranch. Pereopod 1 with well-developed chela, but smaller than that of pereopod 2; pereopod 2 carpus unsegmented. Pereopods without epipods; maxillipeds 1 and 2 with epipods. Telson tapering. Six or seven gills plus two epipods.

1. Rostrum very short, unarmed. Antennules biramous, pereopod 2 asymmetrical, with swollen chelae, living in sponges **Typton spongicola**

   Rostrum well-developed, with teeth on dorsal and ventral borders. Antennules triramous, perepod 2 symmetrical, chelae slender **2**

2. Mandible with palp **3**

   Mandible without palp. Rostrum straight, four to six dorsal teeth, two ventral teeth. One dorsal tooth behind posterior edge of orbit **Palaemonetes varians**

3. Mandibular palp with three segments **4**

   Mandibular palp with two segments. Rostrum straight, or very slightly upcurved; seven to nine dorsal teeth, three (rarely two to four) ventral teeth. Three (occasionally two) of the dorsal teeth behind posterior edge of orbit. Dactyl of pereopod 2 one-third of propodus **Palaemon elegans**

4. Rostrum straight, with dorsal teeth extending into distal third. Pereopod 2 carpus equal to or slightly longer than merus **5**

   Rostrum with distinct upward curve, dorsal teeth not extending into distal third. Six or seven dorsal teeth, four or five ventral teeth; two of the dorsal teeth behind posterior edge of orbit. Pereopod 2 merus 1.25 × length of carpus **Palaemon serratus**

5. Rostrum straight or very slightly upcurved. Seven to eight dorsal teeth, three or four (rarely five) ventral teeth; two of the dorsal teeth behind posterior edge of orbit, second tooth about 1.5 × more distant from first than from next. Pereopod 2 carpus equal to or slightly longer than merus **Palaemon longirostris**

   Rostrum straight, five or six dorsal teeth, three (rarely two or four) ventral teeth; one dorsal tooth behind posterior edge of orbit, second tooth often directly above edge. Pereopod 2 carpus about 1.2 × length of merus **Palaemon adspersus**

Palaemon adspersus Rathke   FIG. 10.2

Length up to 70 mm; body uniform yellowish-grey, pigment spots on lower half of rostrum, distinctive. Rostrum extending well beyond scaphocerite; straight, with five or six dorsal teeth, three (rarely two or four) ventral teeth; one dorsal tooth behind posterior edge of orbit, second often directly above edge. Carapace with antennal and branchiostegal spine. Antennules tri-ramous; shorter ramus of outer antennule exceeds length of peduncle, fused for one-third its length to longer flagellum. Outer edge of stylocerite very slightly convex, anterior edge convex. Maxilliped 3 about half length of scaphocerite, exopod present. Mandible with three-articled palp and incisor process. Pereopod 2 dactyl little over half length of propodus; carpus about 1.2 × length of merus. Telson with two pairs of lateral spines.

Shallow sublittoral; south and south-east coasts only.

Palaemon elegans Rathke   FIG. 10.3

Length up to 63 mm; thorax and pleon usually bearing dark yellow-brown bands. Rostrum straight or very slightly upcurved; seven to nine dorsal teeth, three (rarely two or four) ventral teeth; three (occasionally two) of dorsal teeth behind posterior edge of orbit. Carapace with antennal and branchiostegal spine. Antennules triramous; shorter ramus of outer antennule about equal in length to peduncle, fused for about two-fifths its length to longer flagellum. Outer edge of stylocerite straight or very slightly concave; anterior border convex, becoming markedly concave adjacent to apical spine. Scaphocerite extends to proximal half of pereopod 2 propodus; apical spine not exceeding lamellar portion. Maxilliped 3 about half length of scaphocerite, exopod present. Mandible with two-articled palp and incisor process. Pereopod 2 dactyl one-third length of propodus; carpus equal to or very slightly longer than merus. Telson with two pairs of lateral spines.

Intertidal; all coasts, possibly scarcer in North.

Palaemon longirostris Milne Edwards   FIG. 10.3

Length up to 77 mm; usually almost colourless, but speckled with small red chromatophores when viewed closely. Rostrum straight or very slightly upcurved, projecting beyond tip of scaphocerite. Seven or eight dorsal teeth, three or four (rarely five) ventral teeth; two of dorsal teeth behind posterior edge of orbit, second tooth about 1.5 × more distant from first than from next distally. Antennules triramous; shorter ramus of outer antennule about two-thirds length of peduncle, fused for about one-third its length to longer flagellum. Stylocerite border slightly concave, anterior border convex. Scaphocerite extends to distal half of pereopod 2 carpus; apical spine not exceeding lamellar portion. Maxilliped 3 with exopod. Mandible with three-articled palp and incisor process. Pereopod 2 dactyl about

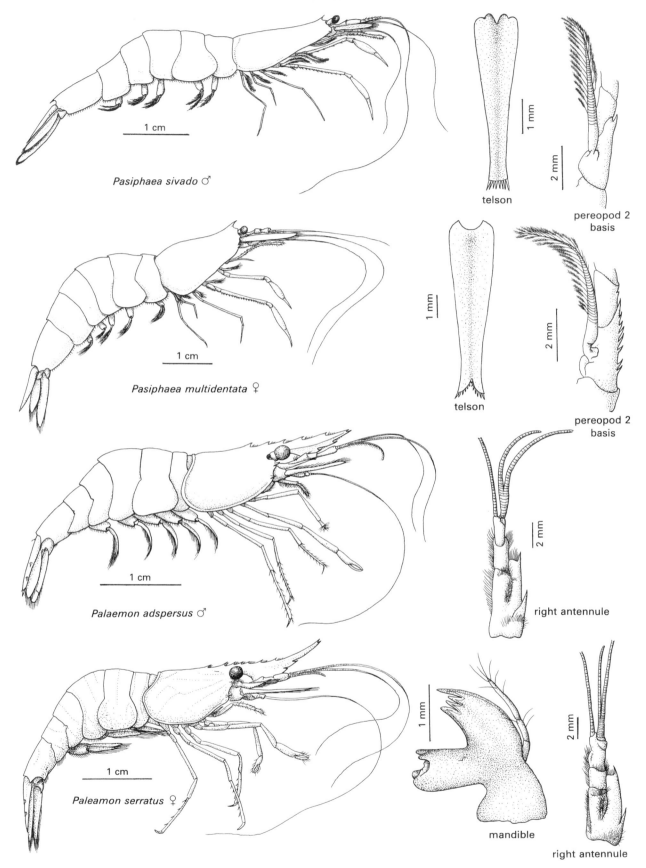

Pasiphaea sivado ♂

telson

pereopod 2
basis

Pasiphaea multidentata ♀

telson

pereopod 2
basis

Palaemon adspersus ♂

right antennule

Paleamon serratus ♀

mandible

right antennule

Fig. 10.2

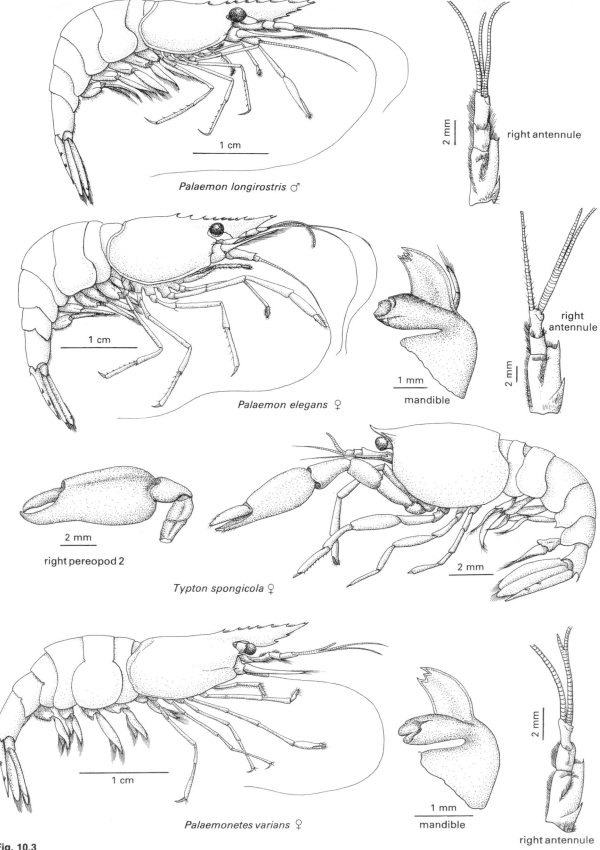

1 cm

2 mm right antennule

Palaemon longirostris ♂

1 cm

1 mm
mandible

2 mm

right
antennule

Palaemon elegans ♀

2 mm

right pereopod 2

2 mm

Typton spongicola ♀

1 cm

1 mm
mandible

2 mm

Palaemonetes varians ♀

right antennule

Fig. 10.3

two-fifths length of propodus, but variable; carpus equal to or very slightly longer than merus. Telson with two pairs of lateral spines.

Estuarine and brackish water species; south and south-east coasts only.

Palaemon serratus (Pennant)   FIG. 10.2

Length up to 110 mm; colour variable, pereon and pleon often banded with brownish red, plus horizontal lines on pereon. Rostrum with distinct upward curve, dorsal teeth not extending into distal third. Six or seven dorsal teeth, four or five ventral teeth; two of dorsal teeth behind posterior edge of orbit. Carapace with antennal and branchiostegal spine. Antennules triramous; shorter ramus of outer antennule about six-sevenths length of peduncle, fused for one-fifth to one-quarter its length to longer flagellum. Outer edge of stylocerite very slightly concave, anterior border virtually flat, spine long and stout. Scaphocerite extends to half length of pereopod 2 dactyl, or to tip of dactyl in juveniles; spine does not exceed lamellar portion. Maxilliped 3 extends to half length of scaphocerite or slightly less; exopod present. Mandible with three-articled palp and incisor process. Pereopod 2 dactyl about half length of propodus; merus 1.25 × length of carpus. Telson with two pairs of lateral spines.

Intertidal to 40 m; frequently on west and south coasts, scarce on north-east coast north of Thames.

Palaemonetes varians (Leach)   FIG. 10.3

Length up to 50 mm; almost colourless. Rostrum straight, four to six dorsal teeth, two ventral teeth; one of the dorsal teeth behind posterior edge of orbit. Carapace with antennal and branchiostegal spine. Antennules triramous; shorter ramus of outer antennule about four-fifths length of peduncle, fused for about three-quarters of its length to longer flagellum. Outer edge of stylocerite slightly concave, anterior border straight, spine short and stout. Scaphocerite extends into proximal half of pereopod 2 propodus (or to half length of dactyl in juveniles); spine not exceeding lamellar portion. Maxilliped 3 extends to little over half length of scaphocerite, exopod present. Mandible without palp, with incisor process. Pereopod 2 dactyl little over one-third length of propodus; carpus about 1.2 × length of merus, but occasionally up to 1.7 × length of merus. Telson with two pairs of lateral spines.

Brackish or almost freshwater pools and ditches, salt-marshes; all coasts, but scarce in northern Scotland.

Typton spongicola Costa   FIG. 10.3

Length up to 25 mm; yellow-red or orange. Rostrum short, unarmed. Carapace with prominent supra-orbital spine, about two-thirds length of rostrum in adults. Antennules biramous; antennular peduncle 1.6–2.3 × length of rostrum; stylocerite very small. Scaphocerite rudimentary, about one-half to two-thirds length of eye. Maxilliped 3 stout, about two-thirds length of antennular peduncle. Mandible without palp, incisor process reduced or absent. Pereopod 2 asymmetrical, chelae swollen. Pleon segment 6 with pointed lateral process and posteriorly

directed process on each side, plus small median posteriorly directed tooth. No appendix masculina on endopod of pleopod two of male. Telson with two, rarely three pairs of lateral spines; tip slightly convex.

Sublittoral, 8–90 m, living in sponges; south-west coast only, very scarce.

3 ALPHEIDAE

Rostrum small, reduced or absent, never spinose. Carapace sometimes with supra-orbital and pterygostomial spines, but no antennal spine. Anterior projections of carapace usually forming hood over the short-stalked eyes and partially or wholly concealing them in dorsal view. Mandible with two-articled palp and incisor process. Maxilliped 2 with article 7 attached laterally to article 6. Maxilliped 3 with exopod, epipod present or absent. Pereopod 1 usually strong, robustly chelate, often asymmetrical, especially in the male. Pereopod 2 usually with five-segmented carpus, minutely chelate. Pereopod 5 with series of spines on outer, posterior surface of article 6. Pereopods 3–5 with simple dactyl, or with not more than two accessory denticles. Telson linguiform, usually rather short and broad; anal tubercles may be present. An articulated process at base of uropod in some genera. Gills: five pleurobranchs, one arthobranch, rudimentary or absent on maxilliped 3, plus two to eight epipods.

---

1. Eyes completely covered in dorsal view by projecting anterior margins of carapace, forming orbital hoods. Rostrum short, not reaching distal end of basal article of antennular peduncle. No articulated process on segment 6 at base of uropods **2**

   Eyes only partially covered by projecting anterior margins of carapace. Rostrum well-developed, reaching beyond distal end of basal article of antennular peduncle. An articulated process on segment 6 at base of urorods. ***Athanas nitescens***

2. Orbital hoods produced into a short spine over each eye. Chela of pereopod 1 without longitudinal carina, dactyl articulating with propodus by lateral and oblique movement ***Alpheus macrocheles***

   Orbital hoods with rounded margins, without spines. Chelae of first pereopods markedly dissimilar in size and shape, articulation of dactyl normal ***Alpheus glaber***

Athanas nitescens (Leach)   FIG. 10.4

Length up to 20 mm; colour variable, may be green, blue, or red-brown, often with white dorsal stripe. Rostrum straight, unarmed, extending little beyond distal end of basal article of antennular peduncle; apex acutely pointed. Carapace with anterior projections which partly cover eyes in dorsal view; projections with two lateral spines plus small dorsal lobe. Stylocerite acutely pointed, two-thirds to three-quarters length of scaphocerite. Scaphocerite as long as antennular peduncle; apical spine stout, exceeding lamella portion. Maxilliped 3 about equal in length to scaphocerite; epipod and exopod present. Mandible with two-articled palp and incisor process. Pereopods 1–3 with

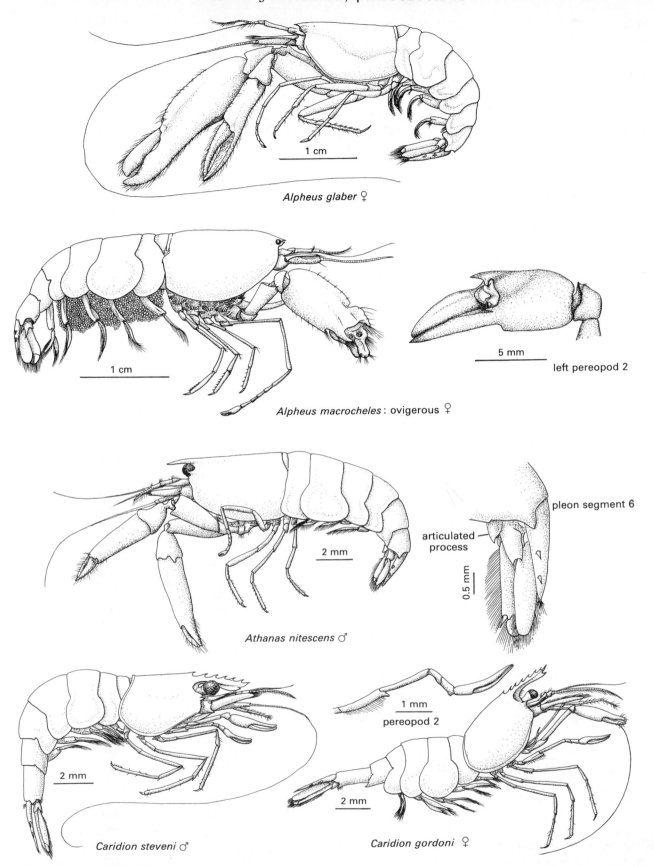

Alpheus glaber ♀

Alpheus macrocheles: ovigerous ♀

left pereopod 2

5 mm

1 cm

pleon segment 6

articulated process

0.5 mm

Athanas nitescens ♂

2 mm

pereopod 2

1 mm

Caridion steveni ♂

Caridion gordoni ♀

2 mm

Fig. 10.4

epipods; perepod 1 with reduced exopod. Pereopod 2 carpus with five segments. Pleon segment 6 with articulated process at base of uropods. Telson with two pairs of lateral spines.

Lower shore to about 60 m; south and west coasts, scarce in north-east.

Alpheus glaber (Olivi) FIG. 10.4

Length up to 43 mm; usually red dorsally, with lateral borders of carapace and pleon white. Rostrum narrow, straight, unarmed, does not extend to basal article of atennular peduncle; apex acutely pointed. Carapace with anterior projections completely covering eyes in dorsal view, projections lacking spines. Stylocerite acutely pointed, about one-third length of scaphocerite. Scaphocerite as long as antennular peduncle, outer margin concave, apical spine exceeding lamellar portion. Maxilliped 3 slightly longer than scaphocerite; exopod and epipod present. Mandible with two-articled palp and incisor process. Pereopods 1–4 with epipods; chelae of first pereopods dissimilar in size and shape, articulation of dactyl normal. Pereopod 2 with five-segmented carpus. Pleon somite 6 without articulated process at base of uropods. Telson with two pairs of lateral spines.

Sublittoral, 33–550 m; south and west coasts only, scarce.

Alpheus macrocheles (Hailstone) FIG. 10.4

Length up to 35 mm; orange-red. Rostrum short, not reaching to distal end of basal article of antennular peduncle. Carapace with projecting anterior margins completely covering eyes in dorsal view; projections formed into short spine over each eye. Stylocerite acutely pointed, extending to distal end of basal article of antennular peduncle. Scaphocerite as long as antennular peduncle, or slightly longer; apical spine stout, slightly incurved, exceeding lamellar portion; outer margin concave. Maxilliped 3 about as long as antennal peduncle; epipod and exopod present. Mandible with broad, two-articled palp and incisor process. Pereopods 1–4 with epipods; first pereopods with asymmetrical chelae, without longitudinal carinae, dactyl articulating with propodus by lateral and oblique movement. Pereopod 2 with carpus of five segments, most proximal segment 1.75–2 × length of next segment. Pleon segment 6 without articulated process. Telson with two pairs of lateral spines, apex convex.

Lower shore to 185 m; south coast only, very scarce.

4 HIPPOLYTIDAE

Rostrum long or short. Supra-orbital spine present or absent. Mandible with or without palp, with or without incisor process. Maxilliped 2 with article 7 attached laterally to article 6. Exopod of maxilliped 1 with flagellum. Maxilliped 3 with or without exopod. Exopods absent from all pereopods. One to seven pairs of epipods. Pereopod 1 usually not much longer than others, but sometimes sexually dimorphic, chelate. Pereopod 2 carpus with two or more segments. Telson tapering more or less acutely. Gills five to six, with varying number of epipods.

1. Pereopod 2 carpus comprising two segments *(Caridion)* 5

   Pereopod 2 carpus comprising more than two segments **2**

2. Pereopod 2 carpus comprising three segments *(Hippolyte)* 6

   Pereopod 2 carpus with more than three segments **3**

3. Pereopod 2 carpus comprising six segments. Mandibular palp absent. Epipods on perepods 1 and 2. *Thoralus cranchii*

   Pereopod 2 carpus comprising seven segments **4**

4. Pereopod 2 carpus seven-segmented, carapace without supra-orbital spines *(Eulalus)* 7

   Pereopod 2 carpus seven-segmented, carapace with one or two supra-orbital spines **8**

5. Rostrum nearly straight, about half length of carapace and always slightly longer than antennular peduncle; five to ten dorsal teeth (usually seven or eight), one ventral tooth (rarely two or three). Maxilliped 3 always longer than scaphocerite by as much as the last two articles. Sublittoral *Caridion gordoni*

   Rostrum curving downwards slightly, deeper than *C. gordoni*; slightly shorter than antennular peduncle; five to seven dorsal teeth, one ventral tooth. Maxilliped 3 only slightly longer than scaphocerite. Shore and shallow sublittoral *Caridion steveni*

6. Rostrum longer than carapace, usually without dorsal tooth at base in adults; often present in small specimens, and in adults as a small tubercle. Rostrum 2.25 × length of antennular peduncle. Maxilliped 3.25 × length of scaphocerite, little more in large specimens. Scaphocerite 4.5 × longer than broad. *Hippolyte inermis*

   Rostrum almost as long as carapace, always with dorsal tooth at base; 1.5 × length of antennular peduncle, little more in large specimens. Maxilliped 3 half length of scaphocerite, 3 × longer than broad *Hippolyte varians*

   Rostrum almost as long as carapace in adults, less in juveniles. Posterior dorsal border of rostrum with two to four teeth; rostrum half to two-thirds length of antennular peduncle. Maxilliped 3 about half length of scaphocerite. Scaphocerite about 2.8 × longer than broad. Carapace and pleon segments with tufts of setae dorsally. Very scarce. *Hippolyte longirostris*

7. Rostrum twice length of antennular peduncle, little more in large specimens; five to seven dorsal teeth, three to five ventral teeth. Epipods on pereopods 1 and 2. Mandibular palp two-articled *Eualus gaimardii*

   Rostrum equal to or little over half length of antennular peduncle; four dorsal teeth; tip bi- or tridentate (rarely a single point). Epipods on pereopods 1 and 2. Mandibular palp two-articled *Eualus occultus*

Rostrum half length of antennular peduncle; two to five dorsal teeth; tip a single point (rarely bidentate). Epipods on pereopods 1–3. Mandibular palp two-articled **Eualus pusiolus**

8. Carapace with one supra-orbital spine. Maxilliped 3 without exopod. Inner basal part of eyestalk without tubercle. Rostrum with five to seven dorsal teeth, two to four ventral teeth **Lebbeus polaris**

Carapace with two supra-orbital spines. Maxilliped 3 with exopod. Tubercle on inner basal part of eyestalk **9**

9. Dorsal rostral teeth extend almost to posterior edge of carapace; teeth may have serrated margins in large specimens. Apex of rostrum with two points, with arcuate space or smaller teeth between. Pleon segment 3 produced posteriorly into a very distinct hooked 'tooth' over segment 4 **Spirontocaris spinus**

Dorsal rostral teeth extend only to two-thirds length of carapace. Apex of rostrum with one point, with successive teeth on ventral border posterior to the apical point. Pleon segment 3 only slightly produced into a 'tooth' over segment 4 **Spirontocaris lilljeborgi**

Caridion gordoni (Bate) FIG. 10.4

Length up to 27 mm; transparent, with red chromatophores on carapace. Rostrum nearly straight, about half length of carapace, slightly longer than antennular peduncle; five to ten dorsal teeth (usually seven or eight), one ventral tooth (rarely two or three). Carapace without supra-orbital spines, but with antennal spine. Stylocerite narrow, acutely pointed, two-thirds length of antennular peduncle or slightly less. Scaphocerite outer margin straight or slightly concave, apex acutely rounded, spine not exceeding lamellar portion. Antennal flagellum about three-quarters length of body. Maxilliped 3 longer than scaphocerite by as much as last two articles, exopod present. Mandible with three-articled palp and incisor process. Pereopod 2 carpus two-segmented; pereopods 1–4 with epipods. Pleon segment 4 usually without ventro-posterior tooth in female. Telson with two pairs of lateral spines.

Sublittoral 10–500 m; all coasts.

Caridion steveni Lebour FIG. 10.4

Length up to 27 mm; red, with diffuse yellow. Rostrum curving slightly downwards, little shorter than antennular peduncle; five to seven dorsal teeth, one ventral tooth. Carapace without supra-orbital spines, but with antennal spine. Stylocerite narrow, acutely pointed, half to two-thirds length of antennular peduncle. Scaphocerite outer margin straight, apex less acute than *C. gordoni*, spine not exceeding lamellar portion. Antennal flagellum usually as long as body, sometimes little shorter. Maxilliped 3 only slightly longer than scaphocerite, exopod present. Mandible with three-articled palp and incisor process. Pereopod 2 carpus two-segmented. Pereopods 1–4 with epipods. Pleon segment 4 with ventro-posterior tooth in both sexes. Telson with two pairs of lateral spines.

Lower shore to 30 m; all coasts.

Eualus gaimardii (Milne Edwards) FIG. 10.5

Length up to 100 mm; translucent, with reddish brown spots and markings. Rostrum twice length of antennular peduncle; five to seven dorsal teeth, three to five ventral teeth. Carapace without supra-orbital spine, but with antennal and pterygostomial spine. Stylocerite acutely pointed, two-thirds length of antennular peduncle or little more. Scaphocerite outer margin straight, becoming slightly concave towards apex; twice length of antennular peduncle, apical spine not exceeding lamellar portion. Maxilliped 3 equal to or slightly shorter than scaphocerite, exopod present. Mandible with two-articled palp and incisor process. Pereopods 1 and 2 with epipods; pereopod 2 carpus with seven segments. Pleon segment 4 with acute ventroposterior spine. Telson with three to five pairs of lateral spines.

From ELWS to 300 m; north, north-west, and north-east coasts only.

Eualus occultus (Lebour) FIG. 10.5

Length up to 22 mm. Colour variable, may be dark brownish-green, with stripes of red-brown on body and extremities. Rostrum equal to or little over half length of antennular peduncle, occasionally slightly less; two to four dorsal teeth, tip bi- or tridentate, rarely a single point. Carapace without supra-orbital spine, with antennal spine. Stylocerite acutely pointed, about two-thirds length of antennular peduncle. Scaphocerite outer margin slightly concave, apical spine equal to or slightly shorter than lamellar portion; scaphocerite extends to about half length of last article of maxilliped 3, sometimes slightly less. Maxilliped 3, 1.5–1.6 × length of scaphocerite, exopod present. Mandible with two-articled palp and incisor process. Pereopods 1 and 2 with epipods; pereopod 2 carpus with seven segments. Telson usually with four or five pairs of lateral spines, occasionally two or three pairs.

From LWS to about 80 m. South and west coasts only.

Eualus pusiolus (Krøyer) FIG. 10.5

Length up to 28 mm; colour variable, green, red-brown, pink, speckled. Carapace about half length of antennular peduncle, less in juveniles; two to five dorsal teeth, tip a single point (rarely bidentate). Carapace without supra-orbital spines, but with antennal spine. Stylocerite acutely pointed, two-thirds length of antennular peduncle. Scaphocerite outer margin slightly concave; 1.3 × length of antennular peduncle, spine exceeding lamellar portion or equal in length. Maxilliped 3 up to 1.25 × length of scaphocerite, exopod present. Mandible with two-articled palp and incisor process. Pereopods 1–3 with epipods; perepod 2 carpus seven-segmented. Telson usually with four or five pairs of lateral spines.

From ELWS to about 500 m; all coasts, possibly scarcer in south.

Lebbeus polaris (Sabine) FIG. 10.5

Length up to 90 mm, usually 60–70 mm; pale, with red and yellowish markings on carapace and pleon, tips of chelae brownish black. Rostrum almost straight, or very slightly downcurved, 1–1.5 × length of antennular peduncle; five to seven dorsal teeth

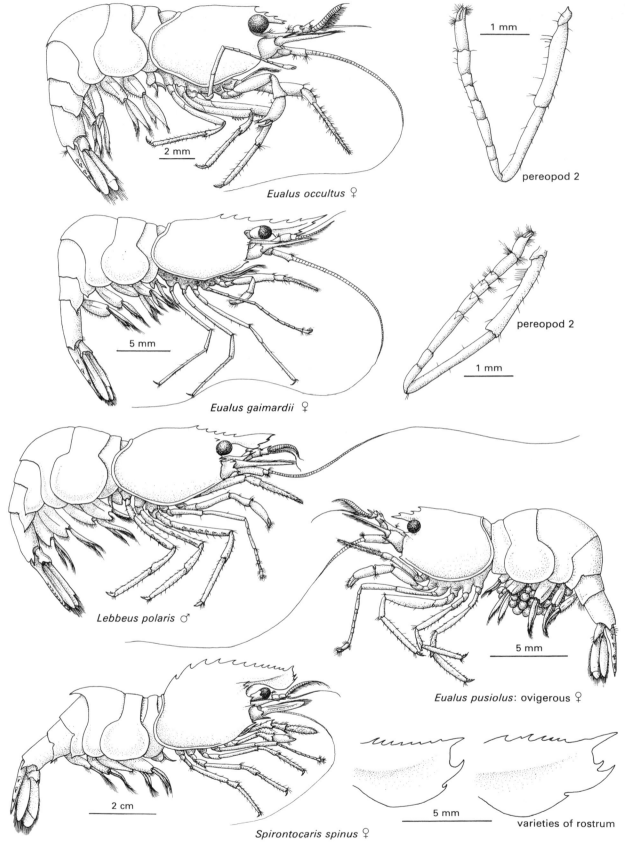

Eualus occultus ♀

pereopod 2

1 mm

2 mm

Eualus gaimardii ♀

pereopod 2

1 mm

5 mm

Lebbeus polaris ♂

5 mm

Eualus pusiolus: ovigerous ♀

2 cm

Spirontocaris spinus ♀

5 mm

varieties of rostrum

Fig. 10.5

(rarely four, eight, or nine), two or three of these behind posterior edge of orbit; two or four ventral teeth (rarely one or five). Carapace with antennal and pterygostomian spines, plus one supra-orbital spine. Stylocerite acutely pointed, two-thirds to three-quarters length of antennular peduncle, or slightly more in large specimens. Antennular peduncle with strong, anteriorly directed spine on lateral border. Scaphocerite broad, outer border straight or very slightly concave, apical spine not exceeding lamellar portion. Maxilliped 3 with epipod. Mandible with molar, incisor process, and two-articled palp. Pereopods 1 and 2 with epipods; pereopod 3 with reduced setobranch. Pereopod 2 carpus seven-segmented. Pleon segment 4 with small ventro-posterior spine, segment 6 with strong, acute, posterio-ventral projection, and additional projection on each side of telson insertion. Telson with eight to eleven pairs of lateral spines; not evenly spaced, and variable, often with different numbers on each side, from four or five to eleven or twelve, sometimes in double rows on each lateral border of telson.

Sublittoral, from 0–930 m, most usually 30–300 m. Reaches southern limit of its distribution off Shetland; formerly reported off the Hebrides.

Spirontocaris lilljeborgi (Danielssen)   FIG. 10.6

Length up to 74 mm; usually bright red, sometimes mottled brownish-red. Rostrum about 1.5 × length of antennular peduncle; dorsal rostral teeth extend along about two-thirds length of carapace, making an angle of about 30° with posterior border of carapace; apex of rostrum normally a single acute point, with series of smaller teeth posterior and ventral to point; ventral border less convex than in *S. spinus*. Carapace with two supra-orbital spines; antennal spine, branchiostegal and pterygostomian spine present. Stylocerite acutely pointed, three-quarters to five-sixths length of antennular peduncle. Scaphocerite outer margin very slightly convex; apical spine exceeds lamellar portion. Maxilliped 3, 1–1.25 × length of scaphocerite, exopod present. Mandible with two-articled palp and incisor process. Pereopods 1–3 with epipods; pereopod 2 carpus seven segmented. Pleon segment 3 only slightly produced into 'hook' over segment 4. Small tooth on ventro-posterior border of pleon segment 4. Telson with three or four pairs of lateral spines.

Sublittoral, 20–1000 m; north-east and north-west coasts, scarce in south.

Spirontocaris spinus (Sowerby)   FIG. 10.5

Length up to 60 mm; usually bright red. Rostrum about 1.5 × length of antennular peduncle; dorsal rostral teeth extend almost to posterior border of carapace, making an angle of about 45° with posterior border; dorsal teeth occasionally serrated in large specimens. Apex of rostrum with two points, with arcuate space or series of small teeth between; ventral border deeply convex. Carapace with two supra-orbital spines, plus antennal, branchiostegal and pterygostomian spines. Stylocerite acutely pointed, equal to or slightly longer than antennular peduncle. Scaphocerite outer margin straight or very slightly convex; apical spine exceeds lamellar portion. Maxilliped 3 about equal in length to scaphocerite, little more in large specimens; exopod

present. Mandible with two-articled palp and incisor process. Pereopods 1–3 with epipods; pereopod 2 carpus seven-segmented. Pleon segment 3 produced into very distinct hooked 'tooth' over segment 4; ventro-posterior border of segment 4 with robust tooth. Telson with three to five pairs of lateral spines.

Sublittoral, 20–400 m; north-east and north-west coasts, apparently absent from south and south-west coasts.

Hippolyte inermis Leach   FIG. 10.6

Length up to 42 mm; usually green, ocasionally crimson or brown specimens. Rostrum 2–2.25 × length of antennular peduncle, longer than carapace; usually without tooth at base, but a single small tooth may be present in juveniles or a small tubercle in adults. Carapace with one supra-orbital spine, plus pterygostomial and hepatic spine. Stylocerite acutely pointed, three-fifths length of antennular peduncle. Scaphocerite little over twice length of antennular peduncle, 4.5 × longer than broad, spine not exceeding lamellar portion. Maxilliped 3 little over one-quarter length of scaphocerite; exopod present. Mandible without palp, with incisor process. Pereopod 2 carpus three-segmented. Telson with two pairs of lateral spines.

LWS, about 50 m; south and west coasts only.

Hippolyte longirostris (Czerniavsky)   FIG. 10.6

Length up to 20 mm; colour variable, greenish brown, almost transparent with flecks of red-brown. Rostrum almost as long as carapace, half to two-thirds length of antennular peduncle; posterior dorsal border of rostrum with two to four teeth. Carapace with one supra-orbital spine, plus antennal and hepatic spines; fascigerous tufts present on carapace and pleon segments dorsally. Stylocerite acutely pointed, about half length of antennular peduncle, less in juveniles. Scaphocerite about 2.8 × longer than broad; spine not exceeding lamellar portion. Maxilliped 3 about half length of scaphocerite; exopod present. Mandible without palp, with incisor process. Pereopod 2 carpus three-segmented. Telson with two pairs of lateral spines.

Lower shore. Channel coast only, probably more frequent in south-west.

Hippolyte varians Leach   FIG. 10.6

Length up to 32 mm; colour variable; red, brown, green, flecked reddish-brown, almost transparent. Rostrum almost as long as carapace, about 1.5 × length of antennular peduncle, less in males; single dorsal tooth at base. Carapace with one supra-orbital spine, plus antennal and hepatic spine; fascigerous tufts occasionally present on dorsal carapace and pleon segments. Stylocerite acutely pointed, little over half length of antennular peduncle. Scaphocerite 3 × longer than broad; spine not exceeding lamellar portion. Maxilliped 3 half length of scaphocerite or slightly more, exopod present. Mandible without palp but with incisor process. Pereopod 2 carpus with three segments. Telson with two pairs of lateral spines.

Lower shore to 150 m, but most frequent intertidally; all coasts.

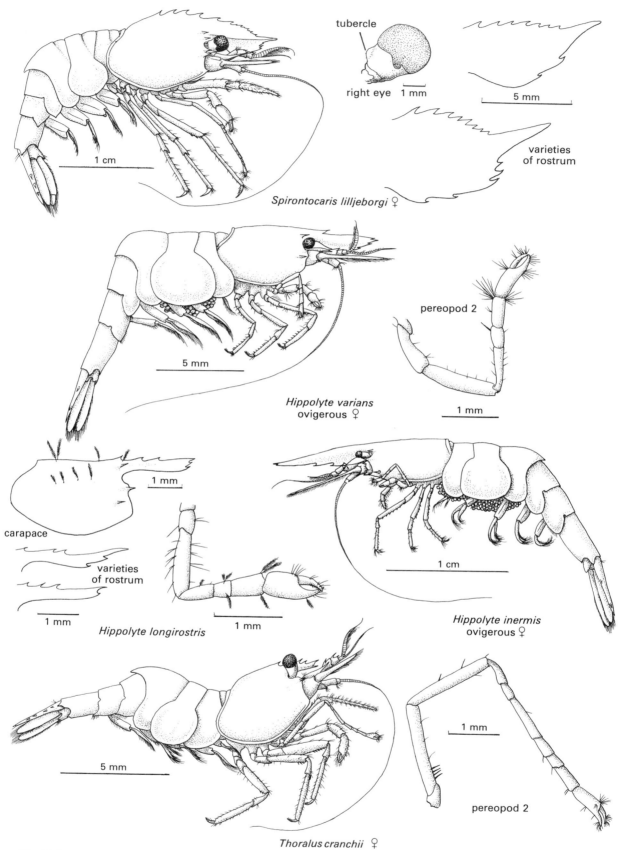

tubercle

right eye   1 mm

5 mm

varieties of rostrum

Spirontocaris lilljeborgi ♀

pereopod 2

Hippolyte varians ovigerous ♀

1 mm

carapace

1 mm

varieties of rostrum

1 mm

1 mm

Hippolyte longirostris

1 cm

Hippolyte inermis ovigerous ♀

5 mm

1 mm

pereopod 2

Thoralus cranchii ♀

Fig. 10.6

Thoralus cranchii (Leach)   FIG. 10.6

Length up to 22 mm; usually semi-transparent with purplish brown blotches; occasionally dark brownish-green. Rostrum little over half length of antennular peduncle; three or four (rarely five or six) dorsal teeth, tip bi- or tridentate (rarely a single point). Carapace without supra-orbital spines, but with antennal spine. Stylocerite acutely pointed, two-thirds length of antennular peduncle. Scaphocerite outer margin straight or very slightly concave; apical spine only very slightly shorter than lamellar portion. Maxilliped 3 extends to just beyond tip of scaphocerite, exopod present. Mandible without palp, with incisor process. Pereopods 1 and 2 with epipods; pereopod 2 carpus six-segmented. Telson with two to seven pairs of lateral spines, usually with four pairs.

From lower shore to about 70 m; all coasts.

5 PROCESSIDAE

Rostrum short, unarmed. Mandible without incisor process or palp. Maxilliped 2 with article 7 attached laterally to article 6. Maxilliped 3 large, pediform, with exopod. Exopods absent from all pereopods, or present only on pereopod 1. Pereopods without epipods. First pair of pereopods asymmetrical, one simple and one chelate. Second pair of pereopods usually unequal, one much longer than the other, both chelate; carpus and merus multiarticulate. Telson channelled. Gills: five plus two epipods.

---

1. Stylocerite with tooth on anterior external corner. Ventro-posterior corner of pleon segment 5 rounded or angular, but without distinct tooth   **2**

   Stylocerite without tooth on anterior external corner. Ventro-posterior corner of pleon segment 5 with at least one tooth directed posteriorly. Pereopod 2 *left*: merus 5–7 articles, carpus 17–20 (to 22) articles. Pereopod 2 *right*: merus 12–18 (to 21) articles, carpus 30–34 (to 39) articles.   ***Processa edulis* subsp. *crassipes***

2. Second pereopods equal in length, merocarpal articulation reaching half-way along eye. Pereopod 2 merus of four or five articles, carpus of 11 (to 15) articles. Tooth of stylocerite below lamellar portion   ***Processa parva***

   Second pereopods clearly unequal in length   **3**

3. Rostrum, in profile, deepest in middle. Pleon segment 5 ventrally convex; segment 6 with prominent ventro-posterior spine. Margins of scaphocerite nearly parallel, scaphocerite reaching to distal end of antennular peduncle or little further   ***Processa nouveli* subsp. *holthuisi***

   Rostrum deepest, in profile, in posterior half. Pleon segment 5 ventrally straight; segment 6 with short ventro-posterior tooth. Scaphocerite reaching beyond antennular peduncle by half maximum scaphocerite width. Inner margin of scaphocerite sinuous, outer margin slightly convex   ***Processa canaliculata***

Processa canaliculata Leach   FIG. 10.7

Length up to 74 mm; dull whitish, with greenish tinge at anterior end of carapace. Rostrum deepest in posterior half, in profile, often slightly downcurved at tip, dorsal terminal tooth more than half length of ventral. Carapace with antennal spine. Stylocerite with tooth on anterior external corner, tooth less than $0.15 \times$ width of stylocerite. Scaphocerite longer than antennular peduncle by more than half maximum scaphocerite width; inner margin sinuous, outer margin slightly convex. Maxilliped 3 about $1.3 \times$ length of scaphocerite, exopod present. Mandible without palp or incisor process. Pereopod 1 with small arthrobranch at base in adults, occasionally absent in juveniles. Pereopod 2 *right*: carpus 41–43 segments, merus 16–19 (rarely up to 24) segments; pereopod 2 *left*: carpus 18–22 (rarely up to 28) segments, merus 4–8 (rarely up to 11 segments). Ventro-posterior corner of pleon segment 5 ventrally straight, without tooth; pleon segment 6 with short posterio-ventral tooth. Anterior palp of lateral spines on telson arise well behind anterior transverse row of setae.

Shallow sublittoral to about 200 m; west, south-west and north-east coasts.

Processa nouveli subsp. *holthuisi* Al-Adhub and Williamson   FIG. 10.7

Length up to 51 mm; whitish, spotted variably with purple and red. Rostrum deepest in middle, in profile; dorsal terminal tooth less than half length of ventral. Carapace with antennal spine. Stylocerite with tooth on anterior external corner, width of tooth $0.3 \times$ greatest width of stylocerite. Scaphocerite extends to distal tip of antennular peduncle or little further, margins nearly parallel. Maxilliped 3 about $1.5 \times$ length of scaphocerite, exopod present. Mandible without palp or incisor process. Length of eye $1–1.25 \times$ length of rostrum; width of eye in dorsal view $1.5–1.8 \times$ width of scaphocerite. Pereopod 1 without arthrobranch, occasionally with small tubercle in place of arthrobranch. Pereopod 2 *right*: carpus 29–42 segments, merus 10–20 segments; pereopod 2 *left*: carpus 15–19 segments, merus 5 segments. Pleon segment 5 ventrally convex; pleon segment 6 with prominent acute ventro-posterior spine. Anterior pair of lateral spines of telson arise close to anterior transverse row of setae.

For details of other subspecies see Al-Adhub and Williamson (1975). Sublittoral, 30–230 m; west coast, central and northern North Sea.

Processa edulis subsp. *crassipes*   FIG. 10.7
Nouvel and Holthuis

Length up to 44 mm; whitish, with pale green hue. Rostrum slightly downturned, little shorter than eye; ventral tooth at tip longer than dorsal. Carapace with antennal spine. Stylocerite without tooth on anterio-exterior corner; antennular peduncle with middle segment $1.5 \times$ longer than broad. Scaphocerite with outer margin virtually straight, lamellar portion exceeding apical spine. Maxilliped 3 about $1.75 \times$ length of scaphocerite, exopod present. Mandible without palp or incisor process. Pereopod 1 without arthrobranch at base. Eye globular, as wide as long. Pereopod 2 *right*: carpus 30–34 (rarely up to 39) segments, merus

12–18 (rarely up to 21) segments. Pereopod 2 *left*: carpus 17–20 (rarely up to 22) segments, merus 5–7 segments. Merocarpal articulation of right pereopod 2 not reaching beyond distal extremity of penultimate segment of maxilliped 3. Ventro-posterior corner of pleon segment 5 with at least one tooth directed posteriorly, occasionally two or three small teeth dorsal to large one. Telson with two pairs of lateral spines.

For details of other subspecies see Nouvel and Holthius (1957).

Lower shore to 20 m; south and west coasts only.

Processa parva Holthius   FIG. 10.7
Length up to 33 mm. Rostrum slightly downcurved at tip, dorsal tooth slightly shorter than ventral. Carapace with antennal spine. Stylocerite with short tooth on anterio-exterior corner; tooth not exceeding lamellar portion. Mandible without palp or incisor process. Second pereopods of equal length; carpus 11 (rarely 12–15) segments, merus 4 (rarely 5) segments; merocarpal articulation reached half-way along eye. Ventro-posterior corner of pleon segment 5 rounded, without tooth; ventral border convex. Pleon segment 6 with prominent posterio-ventral spine. Anterior of two pairs of lateral spines on telson level with anterior setal fringe.

Shallow sublittoral to 100 m; North Sea, not known in Channel or Irish Sea.

6 PANDALIDAE

Rostrum well-developed. Mandible deeply cleft into molar and incisor portions, palp usually three-articled. Maxilliped 2 with article 7 attached laterally to article 6. Exopod of maxilliped 1 with flagellum. Maxilliped 3 with or without exopod; exopods absent from all pereopods. Epipods on maxillipeds 1–3, present or absent on pereopods 1–4. Pereopod 1 simple, or microscopically and imperfectly chelate; pereopod 2 minutely chelate, with bi-, tri- or multiarticulate carpus; pereopods 3–5 long and slender. Telson acute.

1. Rostrum as long as, or longer than carapace, curving upwards   **2**

   Rostrum not more than half carapace length, virtually straight, with seven or eight dorsal teeth and two (occasionally three) ventral teeth. Carpus of right pereopod 2 comprises four segments
                                          Pandalina brevirostris

2. Maxilliped 3 without an exopod   **(*Pandalus*) 3**

   Maxilliped 3 with exopod. Rostrum with nine or ten dorsal teeth (rarely eight), and seven (rarely six or eight) ventral teeth. Carpus of right pereopod 2 with five segments (very rarely six or seven)
                                          Dichelopandalus bonnieri

3. Carpus of right pereopod 2 comprises 20 or more segments   **4**

   Carpus of right pereopod 2 comprises five segments. Rostrum with nine (rarely eight) dorsal teeth and six

(rarely seven) ventral teeth. Scaphocerite narrowing towards tip, about one-third to one-half length of rostrum, with outer edge slightly concave
                                          Pandalus propinquus

4. Rostrum with 12–16 dorsal teeth and six to eight ventral teeth. Dorsal teeth extend into anterior third of rostrum. Lamellar portion of scaphocerite extends beyond apical spine. Carpus of right pereopod 2 comprises 23–36 segments   ***Pandalus borealis***

   Rostrum with 10–12 dorsal teeth and five to six (rarely seven) ventral teeth. Dorsal teeth do not extend beyond middle of rostrum. Apical spine of scaphocerite exceeds lamellar portion. Carpus of right pereopod 2 comprises 20–22 segments
                                          Pandalus montagui

Pandalina brevirostris (Rathke)   FIG. 10.7
Length up to 33 mm; whitish, with many red and yellow chromatophores. Rostrum virtually straight, not more than half length of carapace; seven or eight dorsal teeth, four or five of these behind posterior edge of orbit; posterior five to six dorsal teeth moveable; two, occasionally three ventral teeth. Carapace with antennal and pterygostomian spine. Stylocerite broadly rounded, shorter than eye. Scaphocerite outer margin slightly convex, apical spine exceeding lamellar portion. Maxilliped 3, 1–1.2 × length of scaphocerite; epipod present. Mandible with three-articled palp and incisor process; lateral lobe on proximal segment of palp. Pereopods 1–4 with epipods; carpus of right pereopod 2 with four segments; carpus of left pereopod 2 with 14–20 segments. Telson with six to nine pairs of lateral spines.

Holthuis (1946) describes a similar, deep water, species *P. profunda*. Sublittoral, 10–100 m; all coasts.

Pandalus borealis Krøyer   FIG. 10.8
Length up to 120 mm or larger; pale red, pleon often deeper red. Rostrum upcurved, 12–16 dorsal teeth, normally four of these behind posterior edge of orbit; six to eight ventral teeth. Dorsal teeth extend into anterior third of rostrum. Carapace with strong antennal spine, small pterygostomian spine. Stylocerite broadly rounded, shorter than eye. Outer margin of scaphocerite very slightly convex, lamellar portion exceeding apical spine. Maxilliped 3 five-sixths length of scaphocerite, epipod present. Mandible with three-articled palp and incisor process; lateral lobe on proximal segment of palp. Pereopods 1–4 with epipods and arthrobranchs; carpus of right pereopod 2 with 25–26 segments; carpus of left pereopod 2 with 50–60 segments. Telson with 8–11 pairs of lateral spines.

Sublittoral, 20–600 m; north-east coast only.

Pandalus montagui Leach   FIG. 10.8
Length up to 160 mm, but usually less than 100 mm; semitranslucent with patches of red on carapace and pleon. Rostrum upcurved, 10–12 dorsal teeth, normally four of these behind posterior edge of orbit; five or six (rarely seven) ventral teeth. Dorsal teeth do not extend into anterior half of rostrum. Cara-

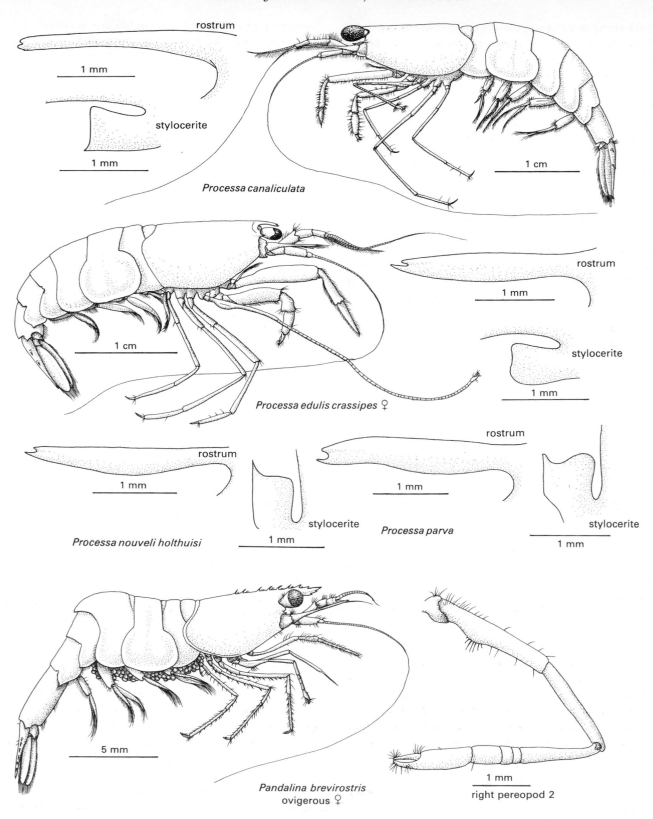

rostrum

1 mm

stylocerite

1 mm

1 cm

Processa canaliculata

rostrum

1 mm

stylocerite

1 mm

1 cm

Processa edulis crassipes ♀

rostrum

1 mm

stylocerite

1 mm

Processa nouveli holthuisi

rostrum

1 mm

stylocerite

1 mm

Processa parva

5 mm

Pandalina brevirostris
ovigerous ♀

1 mm

right pereopod 2

Fig. 10.7

pace with strong antennal spine and small pterygostomian spine. Stylocerite broadly rounded, shorter than eye. Apical spine of scaphocerite exceeds lamellar portion. Maxilliped 3 five-sixths length of scaphocerite, epipod present. Pereopods 1–4 with epipods and arthrobranchs; carpus of right pereopod 2 with 20–22 segments; carpus of left pereopod 2 with 50–65 segments. Mandible with three-articled palp and incisor process; lateral lobe on proximal segment of palp. Telson with five to seven pairs of lateral spines.

Sublittoral, 5–230 m, usually 20–150 m; all coasts.

Pandalus propinquus G. O. Sars   FIG. 10.8

Length up to 150 mm, but usually less than 100 mm; pale red. Rostrum strongly upcurved, nine (rarely eight) dorsal teeth, normally three of these behind posterior edge of orbit; six (rarely seven) ventral teeth. Carapace with strong antennal spine, small pterygostomian spine. Stylocerite broadly rounded, shorter than eye. Scaphocerite narrows towards tip, outer margin slightly concave; one-third to one-half length of rostrum, apical spine exceeding lamellar portion. Maxilliped 3 is four-fifths to five-sixths length of scaphocerite, epipod present. Mandible with three-articled palp and incisor process; proximal article of palp with lateral lobe. Pereopods 1–4 with epipods and arthrobranchs; carpus of right pereopod 2 with five segments, carpus of left pereopod 2 with 25–30 segments. Telson with five or six pairs of lateral spines.

Offshore, 40–2000 m; all coasts, possibly scarcer in northeast.

Dichelopandalus bonnieri Caullery   FIG. 10.8

Length up to 160 mm, usually less than 100 mm; pale reddish, tip of rostrum bright red. Rostrum upcurved, nine or ten (rarely eight) dorsal teeth, normally three of these behind posterior edge of orbit, although third may be directed over edge in juveniles; seven (rarely six or eight) ventral teeth. Carapace with strong antennal spine, small pterygostomian spine. Stylocerite broadly rounded, shorter than eye. Scaphocerite outer margin straight, but often slightly concave in juveniles; apical spine slightly exceeds lamellar portion. Maxilliped 3 three-quarters to four-fifths length of scaphocerite, epipod and exopod present. Mandible with three-articled palp and incisor process; lateral lobe on proximal article of palp. Pereopods 1–4 with arthrobranchs and epipods; carpus of right pereopod 2 with five (rarely six or seven) segments; carpus of left pereopod 2 with 38–45 segments, although normally about 30 in juveniles. Rarely these pereopods are reversed, i.e. right with 38–45 segments. Telson with six to eight pairs of lateral spines.

Sublittoral to 33 to 400 m; south and west coasts, less common in North Sea, not in Channel.

7 CRANGONIDAE

Rostrum short or spiniform. Carapace sometimes more or less sculptured. Eyes well-developed. Mandible simple, without palp. Maxilliped 2 with article 7 small, attached obliquely at apex of article 6. Maxilliped 3 with exopod, epipod present or absent. Pereopod 1 strong, subchelate; pereopod 2 slender, sometimes reduced, in one genus absent; pereopod 3 slender, pereopods 4 and 5 more robust, sometimes with dilated dactyls. Telson tapering. No epipods on pereopods. Exopods on pereopods, if present, on pereopod 1 only. Gills: five to eight plus two or three epipods.

---

1. Pereopod 2 extends to about three-quarters length of propodus of pereopod 1. Pereopod 2 dactyl less than half length of propodus   **8**

   Pereopod 2 extends at most to proximal quarter of propodus of pereopod 1, often less. Pereopod 2 dactyl half length of propodus or more   **2**

2. Pereopod 1 with small exopod. Stylocerite acutely pointed   **3**

   No exopod on pereopod 1. Stylocerite rounded or truncate   **4**

3. Two spines on first lateral carina of carapace, one spine on second carina. Endopods of pleopods 2–5 with appendix interna in both sexes

       Pontophilus norvegicus

   Three spines on first lateral carina of carapace, two spines on second carina. Endopods of pleopods 2–5 with appendix interna in both sexes   ***Pontophilus spinosus***

4. Rostrum with rounded or triangular apex   **5**

   Rostrum with truncate or emarginate apex   **7**

5. Carapace with one or three spines on median line   **6**

   Carapace with two spines on median line, posterior spine may be reduced to a tubercle. Appendix interna absent from endopods of pleopods 2–5 in both sexes

       Pontophilus bispinosus

6. Carapace with one spine on median line, slightly in advance of lateral spine on each side. Rostrum broadly triangular at apex. Appendix interna absent from endopods of pleopods 2–5 in both sexes

       Pontophilus trispinosus

   Carapace with three spines on median line, small tubercle usually before anterior spine. Six (rarely five) spines on first lateral carina, two (rarely three) spines on second lateral carina. Appendix interna on endopods of pleopods 2–5 in males only

       Pontophilus echinulatus

7. Rostrum broadly truncate at apex. One spine on median line of carapace. Stylocerite broadly rounded. Endopods of pleopods 2–5 without appendix interna in both sexes   ***Pontophilus fasciatus***

   Rostrum truncate and emarginate at apex. One spine, plus posterior depressed spine, on median line of carapace. Usually five ridges on first lateral carina; spine and posterior ridge on second lateral carina. Scaphocerite with spine half-way along outer edge.

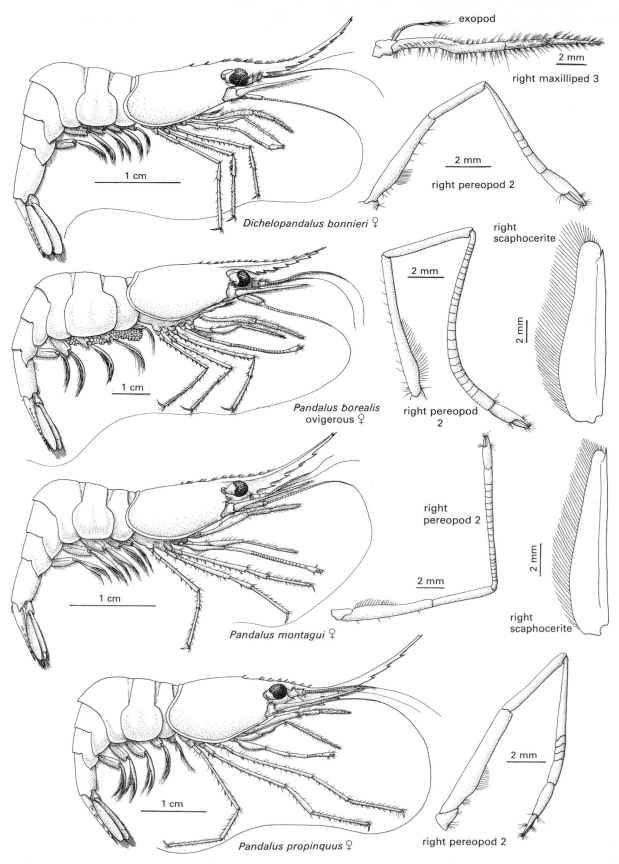

exopod

right maxilliped 3

right pereopod 2

Dichelopandalus bonnieri ♀

right scaphocerite

right pereopod 2

Pandalus borealis ovigerous ♀

right pereopod 2

right scaphocerite

Pandalus montagui ♀

right pereopod 2

Pandalus propinquus ♀

Fig. 10.8

Endopods of pleopods 2–5 with appendix interna in male, pleopods 2–4 with appendix interna in female **Pontophilus sculptus**

8. Pleon segment 6 smooth on dorsal side **Crangon crangon**

Pleon segment 6 with deep dorsal longitudinal groove and parallel carinae **Crangon allmani**

Crangon allmani Kinahan

FIG. 10.9

Length up to 75 mm, usually less; brownish grey. Rostrum about half length of eye, narrow with rounded apex. Median line of carapace with forward-directed spine in anterior quarter; antennal, pterygostomian and hepatic spines present. Stylocerite acutely pointed, two-fifths length of antennular peduncle. Apical spine of scaphocerite exceeds lamellar portion. Maxilliped 3, 1–1.2 × length of scaphocerite; exopod and arthrobranch present. Mandible without palp or incisor process, mandibular teeth sharply pointed. Pereopod 2 extends to three-quarters length of propodus of pereopod 1; pereopod 2 dactyl one-quarter length of propodus. Pleon segment 6 with deep dorsal longitudinal groove and two parallel carinae. Endopods of pleopods 2–5 two-articled, without appendix interna; endopod of pleopod 2 one-fifth to one-quarter length of exopod in male, and one-quarter to one-third length of exopod in female. Telson with two pairs of small lateral spines.

Sublittoral, 10–250 m; all coasts.

Crangon crangon (Linnaeus)

FIG. 10.9

Length up to 90 mm; mottled grey or brownish. Rostrum about half length of eye, or slightly more, narrow with rounded apex. Median line of carapace with forward-directed spine in anterior quarter; antennal, pterygostomian and hepatic spines present. Stylocerite acutely pointed, two-fifths to one-half length of antennal peduncle. Apical spine of scaphocerite exceeds lamellar portion. Maxilliped 3 about equal in length to scaphocerite; exopod and arthrobranch present. Mandible without palp or incisor process, mandibular teeth sharply pointed. Pereopod 2 extends to three-quarters length of pereopod 1 propodus; pereopod 2 dactyl one-quarter length of propodus. Pleon segment 6 smooth dorsally. Endopods of pleopods 2–5 two-articled, without appendix interna; endopod of pleopod 2 one-fifth length of exopod in male or one-quarter length of exopod in female. Telson with two pairs of small lateral spines.

From MTL to about 50 m; all coasts.

Pontophilus norvegicus (M. Sars)

FIG. 10.9

Length up to 75 mm; mottled reddish-brown. Rostrum narrow, triangular, with small, anteriorly directed tooth on each lateral border; extends to anterior margin of eye. Carapace with three anteriorly directed spines on median line. Two spines on first lateral carina, one spine on second lateral carina. Stylocerite acutely pointed, about half length of antennular peduncle. Apical spine of scaphocerite slightly shorter than lamellar portion. Maxilliped 3 about 1.5 × length of scaphocerite, exopod present. Mandible without palp or incisor process; mandibular teeth

acutely pointed. Pereopod 1 with small exopod; pereopod 2 extends to half length of pereopod 1 merus; pereopod 2 dactyl about half length of propodus. Endopods of pleopods 2–5 with appendix interna in both sexes; endopods of pleopod 2 five-sixths length of exopod in both sexes. Telson with two pairs of small lateral spines.

Sublittoral, 50–500 m; northern and western coasts.

Pontophilus spinosus (Leach)

FIG. 10.9

Length up to 52 mm; mottled reddish-brown with greenish markings on carapace. Rostrum triangular, with small anteriorly directed tooth on each lateral border; extends to anterior margin of eye. Carapace with three anteriorly directed spines on median line, three spines on first lateral carina, two spines on second lateral carina. Stylocerite acutely pointed, about half length of antennular peduncle. Apical spine of scaphocerite slightly longer than lamellar portion. Maxilliped 3 about 1.5 × length of scaphocerite, exopod present. Mandible without palp or incisor process, mandibular teeth acutely pointed. Pereopod 1 with small exopod; pereopod 2 extends to half length of pereopod 1 merus; pereopod 2 dactyl about half length of propodus. Endopods of pleopods 2–5 with appendix interna in both sexes; endopods of pleopod 2 four-fifths to five-sixths length of exopod in both sexes. Telson with two pairs of small lateral spines.

Sublittoral, 12–150 m; all coasts.

Pontophilus bispinosus Hailstone

FIG. 10.9

Length up to 26 mm; pale mottled grey or reddish. Rostrum narrow, triangular, with rounded apex, extending to about two-thirds length of eye. Carapace with two spines on median line; antennal and pterygostomian spine present. Stylocerite broad diamond shape, rounded. Apical spine of scaphocerite equal to or slightly longer than lamellar portion. Maxilliped 3, 1–1.3 × length of scaphocerite; exopod and arthrobranch present. Mandible without palp or incisor process, mandibular teeth with rounded tips. Pereopod 2 extends to proximal quarter of propodus of pereopod 1; pereopod 2 dactyl two-thirds length of propodus, often little more. Endopods of pleopods 2–5 two-articled, without appendix interna; endopods of pleopod 2 three-fifths length of exopod in both sexes. Telson with two pairs of small lateral spines.

Sublittoral, 5–400 m; all coasts.

The variety *neglectus* (G. O. Sars) differs in having the second spine in the median line of the carapace reduced to a tubercle, the carapace is also smoother than in *P. bispinosus*.

Pontophilus echinulatus (M. Sars)

FIG. 10.9

Length up to 45 mm; greenish, with red-brown gastric region. Rostrum triangular, narrow, with rounded apex; extends almost to anterior margin of eye. Carapace with three spines on median line, small tubercle usually in front of anterior spine; five or six ridge-like spines on first lateral carina, two or three on second lateral carina. Stylocerite broad, rounded, diamond-shaped, slightly longer than eye. Scaphocerite with outer margin slightly concave, apical spine stout, exceeding lamellar portion. Maxilliped 3, 1.3–1.5 × length of scaphocerite; exopod and arthro-

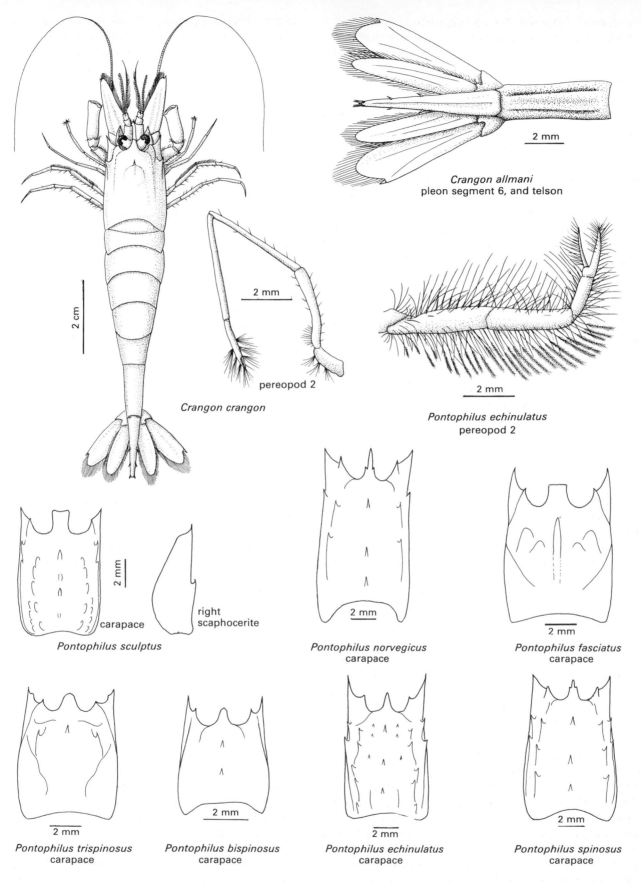

Crangon allmani
pleon segment 6, and telson

2 mm

pereopod 2

Crangon crangon

Pontophilus echinulatus
pereopod 2

2 mm

carapace

right
scaphocerite

Pontophilus sculptus

Pontophilus norvegicus
carapace

Pontophilus fasciatus
carapace

Pontophilus trispinosus
carapace

Pontophilus bispinosus
carapace

Pontophilus echinulatus
carapace

Pontophilus spinosus
carapace

Fig. 10.9

branch present. Mandible without palp or incisor process, tips of mandibular teeth rounded. Pereopod 2 extends to proximal quarter of propodus of pereopod 1; pereopod 2 dactyl about five-sixths length of propodus. Endopods of pleopods 2–5 comprise single article plus appendix interna in male, single article without appendix interna in female; endopod of pleopod 2 two-thirds length of exopod in male or half to three-fifths length of exopod in female. Telson with two pairs of small lateral spines.

Offshore, 60–900 m; west and north-east coasts.

Pontophilus fasciatus (Risso)   FIG. 10.9

Length up to 19 mm; whitish, with usually dark brown band on pleon segments 4 and 6. Rostrum broad, squarely truncate at apex, extending almost two-thirds length of eye. Carapace with one spine on median line, in anterior quarter, plus large and small lobe lateral to spine. Stylocerite broadly rounded with flattened anterior margin. Scaphocerite apical spine not exceeding lamellar portion. Maxilliped 3 with exopod and arthrobranch; extending to just beyond tip of scaphocerite. Mandible without palp or incisor process. Pereopod 2 extends to proximal quarter of propodus of perepod 1; pereopod 2 dactyl three-quarters length of propodus. Endopods of pleopods 2–5 two-articled, without appendix interna in both sexes; endoped of pleopod 2 four-fifths length of exopod in male, or half length of exopod in female. Telson with two pairs of small lateral spines.

Lower shore and shallow sublittoral to about 50 m; all coasts.

Pontophilus sculptus (Bell)   FIG. 10.9

Length up to 24 mm; colour variable, brick-red, brown, pleon sometimes whitish. Rostrum broad, truncate and emarginate at apex; extends three-quarters length of eye. Carapace with one spine plus one depressed spine on median line; first lateral carina with five low ridges, second lateral carina with anterior spine, and ridge posterior to it. Stylocerite rounded, broadly diamond-shaped, slightly longer than eye. Scaphocerite with apical spine exceeding lamellar portion, plus spine at about mid-point of outer margin. Maxilliped 3, 1.3–1.5 × length of scaphocerite; exopod and arthrobranch present. Mandible without palp or incisor process, tips of mandibular teeth rounded. Subchelar spine of pereopod 1 mobile. Pereopod 2 extends to proximal quarter of propodus of pereopod 1; perepod 2 dactyl three-quarters length of propodus. Endopods with appendix interna on pleopods 2–5 in male, pleopods 2–4 in female. Endopod of pleopod 2 three-fifths length of exopod in male, or two-fifths to one-half length of exopod in female. Telson with two pairs of small lateral spines.

Sublittoral, 10 to about 230 m; all coasts, possibly more frequent in south.

Pontophilus trispinosus Hailstone   FIG. 10.9

Length up to 27 mm; yellowish brown, mottled. Rostrum broad, with triangular, rounded apex; extends half to three-quarters length of eye. Carapace with one spine on median line, in anterior third, plus one lateral spine each side of, and slightly posterior to, median spine. Stylocerite broadly rounded, slightly longer than eye. Scaphocerite apical spine not exceeding lamellar

portion. Maxilliped 3, 1.25 × length of scaphocerite; exopod and arthrobranch present. Mandible without palp or incisor process, tips of mandibular teeth rounded. Pereopod 2 extends to distal end of carpus of pereopod 1; pereopod 2 dactyl about three-quarters length of propodus. Endopods of pleopods 2–5 two-articled, without appendix interna in both sexes; endopod of pleopod 2 two-fifths to one-half length of exopod in male, or one-third to two-thirds length of exopod in female. Telson with two pairs of small lateral spines.

From lower shore to about 40 m; all coasts.

Suborder **Pleocyemata** [Reptantia]

The reptant decapods comprise four infraorders of widely different form. They are predominantly marine, although estuarine, freshwater, and coastal-terrestrial species occur. Marine Reptantia are distributed from the supralittoral to abyssal depths, but are most abundant in the shallow waters of the continental shelf seas, where they have adapted to a very broad range of habitats. They are primarily scavengers, feeding on both plant and animal remains, but many are predators of molluscs, fish, and other crustaceans, while some are microphagous detritus feeders, or have even adopted a filter feeding existence.

The infraorders Astacidea and Palinura (Fig. 10.10), comprising the lobsters and crawfish (or crayfish), are characterized by a cylindrical or slightly flattened carapace, and an elongate, cylindrical, or compressed abdomen enclosed within a heavily calcified exoskeleton. Typically, they have a well-developed tailfan. In the crawfish (Palinura), the carapace is fused ventrally with a solid plate extending beneath the bases of the antennae, distal to the mouth; the first four pairs of pereopods usually bear simple, terminal claws. In the lobsters (Astacidea) the carapace is not fused ventrally, and the first three pairs of pereopods are chelate; typically, the chelae of the first pereopods are much larger than those of the following two pairs. The infraorder Anomura is a very diverse group, including the porcelain crabs, squat lobsters, and hermit crabs (egs. Figs. 10.15, 10.16). As in the Astacidea, the anomuran carapace is not ventrally fused, the first pair of pereopods often bear large chelae, and many anomurans are superficially similar either to lobsters, or to the true crabs (Brachyura). However, in all anomurans the fifth pair of pereopods, and sometimes the fourth, is reduced in size and generally concealed by the carapace. The Brachyura, or true crabs, are characterized by a flattened, heavily calcified carapace (Fig. 10.1), ventrally fused in front of the mouth. The abdomen is small, folded beneath the carapace, and concealed. The first pereopods are developed as massive chelae, and the remainder end in simple claws.

A surprising variety of reptant decapods may be found on Small spider crabs may be quite common among tufts of red algae, or on clumps of hydroids or erect bryozoans, and emerge when samples are teased out and left quietly in bowls of seawater. Fewer species occur on sandy shores, or on estuarine muds, but night-time collecting at low tide on a sandy shore can be rewarding. Shallow water dredging will yield many more species, and hydroid tufts, large bryozoans, and dead shells should be carefully searched for the more cryptic species. Careful handling is required, as most decapods will freely shed limbs when distressed. Also, in mixed samples large species will frequently crush, or even eat, smaller animals. If specimens are requested for preservation they should be first narcotized, and this is best achieved through asphyxiation, either by the gradual dilution of sea-water with fresh-water, or by simply leaving the specimen in a bowl of sea-water, in a warm place. Several hours may be required before the specimen is completely narcotized. The most useful fixatives are 70 per cent ethanol and 5 per cent sea-water formalin; large specimens may require several days for adequate fixation, with regular changes of fixative. For long term storage, 70 per cent ethanol or 1 per cent propylene phenoxetol are the best preservatives.

REFERENCES

Allen, J. A. (1967). *The fauna of the Clyde Sea area. Crustacea: Euphausicea and Decapoda with an illustrated key to the British species.* Scottish Marine Biological Association, Millport.

Balss, H. (1926). Decapoda. *Tierwelt der Nord- und Ostsee*, Lief **6**. Teil 10, Heft 2, 1–112.

Bouvier, E. L. (1940). Décapodes Marcheurs. *Faune de France*, **37**, 1–404.

Christiansen, M. E. (1969). *Marine Invertebrates of Scandinavia*, No. 2 Crustacea, Decapoda, Brachyura. Universitetsforlaget, Oslo, pp. 1–143.

Edwards, E. (1978). *The Edible Crab and its Fishery in British Waters.* Fishing News Books Ltd., Surrey.

Forest, J. (1978). Le genre *Macropodia* Leach dans les eaux atlantique européenes (Crustacea, Brachyura, Majidae). *Cahiers de Biologie marine*, **19**, 323–42.

Glaessner, M. F. (1969). Decapoda. In: Moore, R. E. (editors), *Treatise on Invertebrate Palaeontology*, Part R, Arthropoda 4, (ed. R. C. Moore). Geological Society of America and University of Kansas Press.

Holthius, L. B. and Heerebout, G. R. (1976). Crustacea-Kreeftachtigen de Nederlandser Decapoda (Garnalen, Kreeften en Krabben). *Wetenschappelijke Mededeelingen. K. Nederlandse Naturhistoriche Vereniging*, **11**, 1–56.

Ingle, R. W. (1980). *British Crabs.* Oxford and London: Oxford University Press and British Museum (Natural History).

Ingle, R. W. (1983). Shallow-water Crabs. *Linnean Society Synopses of the British Fauna* (N.S.), **25**, Cambridge and London: Cambridge University Press for the Linnean Society of London and the Estuarine and Brackish Water Sciences Association.

O'Ceidigh, P. (1962). The marine Decapoda of the counties Galway and Clare. *Proceedings of the Royal Irish Academy*, **62**, 151–74.

Selbie, C. M. (1915). The Decapoda Reptantia of the coasts of Ireland. Part I. Palinura, Astacura, and Anomura (except Paguridea). *Scientific Investigations of the Fisheries Branch. Department of Agriculture for Ireland*, **1914**, No. 1, 1–116.

Selbie, C. M. (1921). The Decapoda Reptantia of the coasts of Ireland. Part II. Paguridea. *Scientific Investigations of the Fisheries Branch. Department of Agriculture for Ireland*, **1921**, 1–68.

Warner, G. F. (1977). *The biology of crabs.* Elek Science, London.

Zariquiey Alvarez, R. (1968). Crustaceos Decapodes Ibericos. *Investigacion Pesquera*, **32**, 1–510.

KEY TO FAMILIES

1. Abdomen long and symmetrical with well-developed tail-fan — **3**

   Abdomen short, or if long, curved asymmetrically — **2**

2. Fifth pereopods (and sometimes fourth) much smaller than anterior ones — **10**

   Fifth pereopods similar to anterior ones; abdomen comparatively small, flattened, lacking pronounced tail-fan — **14**

3. Chelae present on first three pairs of pereopods — **4**

   No chelae on third pereopods — **5**

4. Chela present on fourth pereopods; eyes very small and immoveable — **2. Polychelidae**

   No chelae on fourth pereopods; eyes large and movable — **1. Nephropidae**

5. Carapace shiny; shelf over eyes — **6**

   Carapace smooth apart from spiny rostrum, no shelf over eyes — **7**

6. Antenna ending in long flagellum; carapace dorsally convex — **3. Palinuridae**

   Antenna wide, with blade-like flagellum; large carapace, dorsally depressed — **4. Scyllaridae**

7. Pleura of abdominal segments large, no thalassinian line   **5. Axiidae**

   Pleura generally small; thalassinian line on carapace   **8**

8. Exopodite of uropod with articulated outer article   **6. Laomediidae**

   Uropod exopodites (and endopodites) simple   **9**

9. First pereopods (chelae) equal in size; large triangular rostrum   **8. Upogebiidae**

   First pereopods unequal; very small rostrum   **7. Callianassidae**

10. Abdomen asymmetrical and usually soft; uropods if present, asymmetrical   **11**

    Adbomen reduced and curved ventrally, but provided with distinct pleura and terga
    and symmetrical uropods   **12**

11. Abdomen modified for occupying gastropod shell   **9. Paguridae**

    Abdomen asymmetrical and tightly reflexed under cephalothorax as in Brachyura; no
    tail-fan   **10. Lithodidae**

12. Telson with one or two transverse sutures; tail-fan normally folded under last segment;
    abdomen curved under rear of carapace; scale on third article of antennal peduncle
                                                                     12. Chirostylidae

    Telson has three pairs of lobes; no scale on third article of antennal peduncle   **13**

13. Carapace longer than broad; abdomen only loosely reflexed; rostrum large, triangular,
    and spiny   **11. Galatheidae**

    Crablike, carapace almost circular; abdomen tightly reflexed under sternum; rostrum
    small   **13. Porcellanidae**

14. Third maxillipeds tapering, to fit within the triangular mouth area   **16. Leucosiidae**

    Third maxillipeds distally wide, fitting within a quadrangular mouth area   **15**

15. Last pereopods small and held dorsally; first article of antenna mobile, with con-
    spicuous excretory pore; female opening coxal; pleopods on first female abdominal
    segment   **16**

    Last pereopods held normally; first article of antenna fused to carapace, its excretory
    pore hidden; female openings sternal; no pleopods on first female abdominal segment   **17**

16. Antennules and eyes retract into sockets; gill associated with last pereopod   **14. Dromiidae**

    Antennules and eyes not retractile; no gill associated with last pereopod   **15. Homolidae**

17. Carapace drawn forward into a pronounced, often bifid rostrum   **18**

    Front of carapace usually wide, without prominent rostrum   **19**

18. Antenna has enlarged second and third articles, fused to underside of carapace edge
                                                                         17. Majidae

Antenna has small second and third articles, not fused to, or extending to, carapace
edge **18. Parthenopidae**

---

19. Carapace slightly longer than wide; antenna longer than carapace width **19. Corystidae**

Carapace usually wider than long; antenna shorter than carapace width **20**

---

20. The carpus of the third maxilliped arises at inner margin of merus **21**

The carpus of the third maxilliped arises near the centre of the merus margin **27**

---

21. Last pereopod, especially the dactylus, flattened for swimming **22. Portunidae**

Dactylus of last pereopod not flattened for swimming **22**

---

22. Carapace almost circular, the margin with a dense fringe of hair **20. Atelecyclidae**

Carapace hexagonal, square or broadly oval, not particularly hairy **23**

---

23. Single median lobe to front edge of carapace **24**

Pair of median lobes **25**

---

24. Carapace wider than long; five sharp teeth on each side **(part of) 22. Portunidae**

Carapace much wider than long: about nine or ten broad lobes or teeth each side
21. Cancridae

---

25. Eyestalk length about one-third width of carapace **25. Goneplacidae**

Eyestalk length much less than one-third width of carapace **26**

---

26. Front of carapace with a small central pair of acute lobes; fifth pereopod longer than
first (chela) **24. Geryonidae**

Front of carapace with central pair of broad lobes; last pereopod not longer than chela
23. Xanthidae

---

27. Carapace nearly circular; eyes very small, commensal crab **26. Pinnotheridae**

Carapace nearly square; eyes conspicuous; free-living crabs **27. Grapsidae**

Infraorder **Astacidea**

1 NEPHROPIDAE

Carapace having post-cervical (transverse) and branchiocardiac (oblique) grooves, which are sometimes contiguous. Last thoracic segment fused to carapace. Chelae on first three pereopods. Eyes moveable. Includes subfamilies Nephropinae and Homarinae in British waters.

---

1. Small unpigmented eyes; no antennal scale
Nephropsis atlantica

Large pigmented eyes; antennal scale present **2**

2. Very large, kidney-shaped eyes, broader than the eyestalks; antennal scale leaf-like *Nephrops norvegicus*

Large eyes, the same width as eyestalks; spine-like antennal scale *Homarus gammarus*

Nephropsis atlantica Norman FIG. 10.12

Length up to about 103 mm, female 75 mm, abyssal-red in colour. Carapace hairy with strong cervical groove; rostrum robust with lateral spines. Small eyes close together beneath rostrum. Low median keel to abdominal terga. Antennal flagellum up to 2.5 × body length. No antennal scale. Massive chelae on first legs, slightly unequal in both sexes; larger in male.

Off western coasts of British Isles, unconsolidated bottoms at 1600–1700 m, not uncommon; elsewhere northern Scotland to Cape Verde and Cape of Good Hope; Arabian Sea.

Nephrops norvegicus (Linnaeus). Norway Lobster, Dublin Bay Prawn, Scampi, Langoustine   FIG. 10.10
Length up to 240 mm; pale orange. Carapace with distinct postcervical groove and longitudinal spinose keels. Rostrum long and spinose. Abdomen with transverse grooves. Eyes very large, well-pigmented and kidney-shaped, broader than stalks. First legs with very long slender keeled chelae.

In shallow burrows, in soft sediments, at 200–800 m; British Isles, all coasts, common; elsewhere Norway and Iceland to Morocco and Mediterreanan.

Homarus gammarus (Linnaeus). Common Lobster   FIG. 10.10
Length variable, up to 500 mm; blue coloured above with coalescing spots; yellowish below. Carapace and abdomen generally lacking strong spines or ridges and only slightly granular. Rostrum rather short and spiny. Strong gastro-orbital groove with below it, the cervical groove. Chelae large, hetero-chelous.

Rocky substrate, LWST to 60 m; British Isles, all coasts, common; elsewhere Lofoten Isles to Morocco, Mediterranean, Black Sea.

Infraorder Palinura

2 POLYCHELIDAE
Carapace depressed, longer than broad, with deep orbital indentations. Lateral margins of carapace well-defined, toothed or spiny; medial keel strong; well-marked cervical groove. Eyes reduced. First four or all five pereopods chelate; telson narrow; uropods lack transverse suture. All deep water species.

1. Double ridge on tergum of abdominal segment 6; spines on posterior edge of carapace   2

   No ridge on abdominal segement 6; no spines on posterior edge of carapace   **Polycheles granulatus**

2. Paired median rostral spines; no row of spines on terga   3

   Rostral spine single; row of spines on posterior edge of abdominal terga   **Polycheles typhlops**

3. Chelipeds (pereopod 1) shorter than body, jagged keel on abdominal tergum 6   **Stereomastis grimaldi**

   Chelipeds much longer than body; keel on abdominal tergum 6 low and smooth   **Stereomastis sculpta**

Polycheles typhlops Heller   FIG. 10.11
Overall length 70(90) mm. Carapace fringed with spines of decreasing size from fronto-lateral margin for three-quarters of

length. Orbital socket encroached by a lobed projection from its exterior border. The single rostral spine followed in mid-line by three other single spines and then five pairs of spines. Abdominal terga 2–5 with flat forward-pointing keels in mid-line; abdominal tergum 6 with double median ridge. Chelipeds (pereopod 1) longer than whole body including telson. All five pairs of pereopods chelate, except last pair in males.

Deep water species, 100–1500 (sometimes 2000) m. British Isles: off west coast of Ireland; elsewhere south to Cape Verde, Mediterranean.

Polycheles granulatus Faxon   FIG. 10.11
Overall length 76(112) mm. Full length of carapace edged with spines of similar size. Orbital socket not encroached laterally. A pair of median rostral spines; double row of granules runs length of carapace median keel; otherwise no spines on carapace surface. Abdominal terga with smaller flat keels than in *P. typhlops*, only that of segment 2 with sharp forward-directed point. Chelipeds longer than body including telson.

Deep water, 1400–2100 m. British Isles: off south-western Ireland; elsewhere south to Madeira and Canaries, also Panama and Hawaii.

Stereomastis sculpta (S. I. Smith)   FIG. 10.11
Overall length of male 68(124) mm. Similar to *Polycheles*. Carapace with median keel running from rostrum to posterior edge, furnished with single or twinned spines in order from the rostum:- 2:1:2:1:2:2:2. Low, forward-hooked keels on abdominal segments 1–5; smooth, low keel on segment 6. Chelipeds much longer than whole body.

Deep water, 500–3000 m. Off western coast of Ireland; elsewhere Iceland to South Africa, West Indies, Arabian Sea, Mediterranean.

Stereomastis grimaldi (Bouvier)   FIG. 10.11
Length of typical female 74 mm. Carapace with median keel similar to that of *S. sculpta* but with the following spine series:- 2:1:1:2:1:2:2:2. Keels on abdominal terga 1–5 with sharp projecting points, especially those of segments 3–5. Tergum 6 with a double jagged ridge. Chelipeds shorter than whole body.

Deep water, about 1500–2500 m. Off western coast of Ireland; elsewhere Iceland, Biscay, South Africa, North America, Pacific.

3 PALINURIDAE
Carapace slightly compressed, without lateral ridges. Antenna base without scaphocerite; fused to epistome; antennal flagellum very long and strong. Pereopods without chelae. Two British species.

1. Pereopod 1 similar in size to the others; without spines on upper edge of propodus and carpus but with a row of spines on lower edge of merus   **Palinurus mauretanicus**

   Pereopod 1 stouter than others. Upper edges of pro-

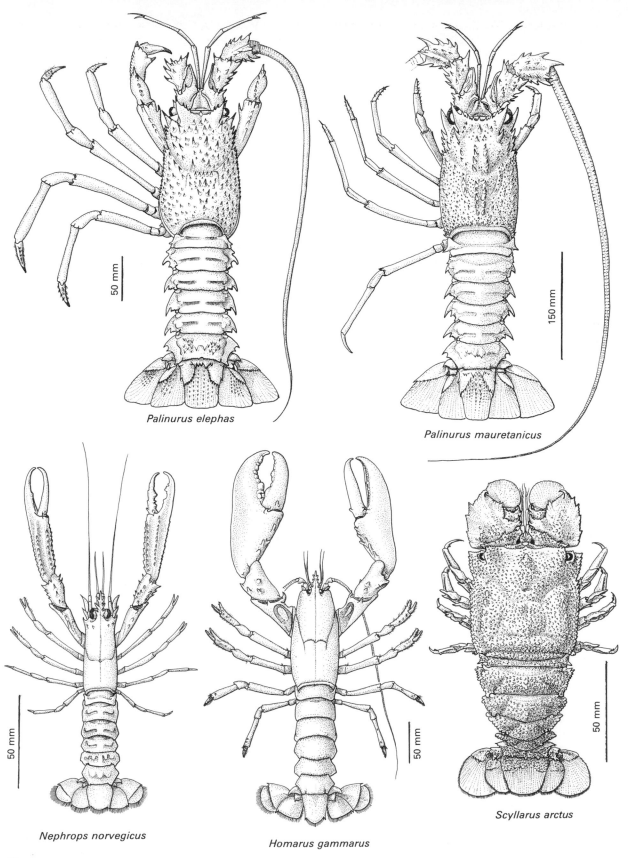

Palinurus elephas

Palinurus mauretanicus

Nephrops norvegicus

Homarus gammarus

Scyllarus arctus

Fig. 10.10

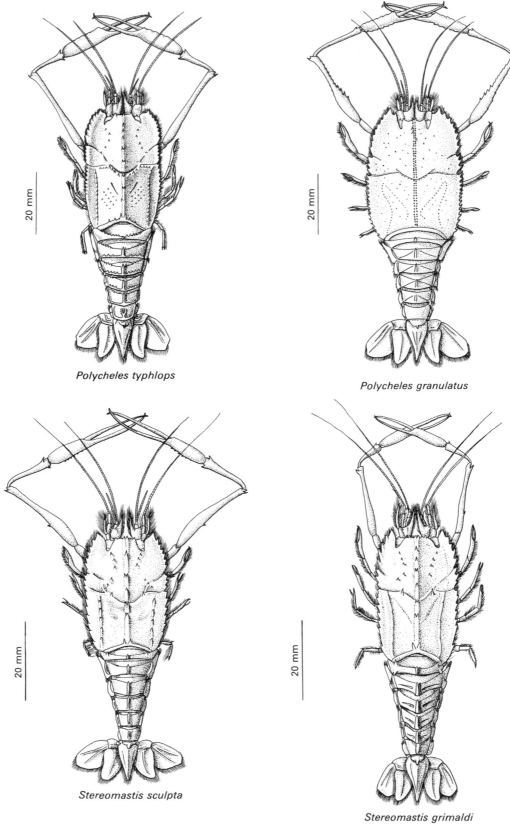

Polycheles typhlops

Polycheles granulatus

Stereomastis sculpta

Stereomastis grimaldi

Fig. 10.11

podus, carpus and merus all bear spines; lower edge
of merus with a single apical spine **Palinurus elephas**

Palinurus elephas (Fabricius). Common crawfish, spiny
lobster, langouste FIG. 10.10
Length up to 500 mm, usually 250–350 mm; adults reddish
brown with yellow spots. Carapace covered with forward-
directed spines; supra-orbital spines particularly prominent.
Antennal stalks very heavy and spiny; flagellum stout, tapering,
and longer than body. Pereopod 1 subchelate; row of spines on
upper crest of merus characteristic. Reddish eggs, September to
October; hatching in six months as phyllosoma larvae.

Mainly rocky bottoms from 20 to 70 m. South and west coasts
of the British Isles, common; elsewhere south to Azores and
Mediterranean.

Palinurus mauretanicus Gruvel FIG. 10.10
Length up to 750 mm, usually about 450 mm; light wine-red
with whitish spots. Very similar to the last species. Carapace
more swollen and bearing a prominent double row of large
spines extending its entire length. Pereopod 1 distinctive, not
subchelate, slightly shorter than in *P. elephas*, bearing a row of
spines on median crest of lower side of merus.

On various substrata, generally rocky; deeper than last species,
200–300 m; deeper in Mediterranean, but recorded at 20–50 m
off West Africa.

South-west Ireland; elsewhere south to Senegal and Mediterranean.

4 SCYLLARIDAE

Carapace rather flattened, front corners prominent. Antennae
short, flagella reduced to broad, lobed plates. Pereopod 1 similar
to other pereopods.

Scyllarus arctus (Linnaeus) FIG. 10.10
Length up to 114 mm; dark chestnut with yellow spines and
scales, brown underside, light blue and orange bands in articulation of abdomen. Carapace almost as broad as long. Antennules
similar to other Palinura but antennae represented by massive
flat plates without flagella. A sluggish species; can retreat fast
by flexing large tail-fan.

Shallow sublittoral, down to 50 m. British Isles, only in far
south off Plymouth; elsewhere south to Madeira, Azores, and
Mediterranean.

Infraorder **Anomura**

5 AXIIDAE

The first of four families of the superfamily Thalassinoidea.
Members of this superfamily are all small, mostly burrowing
Anomura with smooth carapaces; there may be a few spines
associated with the rostrum but never the thorn-like extensions
of the carapace over the eyes seen in the Palinuridae. The Axiidae
are thalassinians that lack the '*thalassinian line*' (characteristic of
the other three families). The abdominal pleura are large. The

first pereopods bear large, often asymmetrical, chelae. The third
pereopods are not chelate.

Two genera of the family are represented in British waters.
In *Axius* the body is compressed laterally; the carapace lacks a
median ridge and the exopodites of the uropods lack sutures.
Calocaris has an almost cylindrical body with a pronounced
median dorsal ridge to the carapace and a suture to the exopodites of the urorods.

---

1. Body laterally compressed; no dorsal ridge on carapace; no suture on uropod exopod; eyes pigmented
   Axius stirhynchus

   Body cylindrical; suture on uropod exopod; eyes
   unpigmented; median dorsal ridge extends full length
   of carapace **Calocaris macandreae**

Axius stirhynchus Leach FIG. 10.12
Overall body length about 72 mm. Rostrum triangular, terminal
spine not extended; margins slightly ridged and furnished with
short blunt teeth; hairy. Chelae large and unequal; manus
1.5 × length of fingers; tips of fingers cross when closed; dactyl
bears a well-marked ridge and is more hairy than finger of
propodus; cutting edges minutely serrate; a few crushing
tubercles on larger chela. Pereopod 4 longest. No ridges on
uropods.

Burrows in mud or sand, at LWST to shallow sublittoral.
Confined to south-west British Isles; uncommon; elsewhere to
Spain and Mediterranean.

Calocaris macandreae Bell FIG. 10.12
Up to 40 mm long. Carapace with median ridge; rostrum slightly
upturned, its strong, toothed margins continuing on to the
carapace; eyes large. Chelipeds long and unequal; fingers up to
twice length of manus, compressed and covered with tufts of
setae; minutely serrate cutting edges, except proximal part of
dactyl; tips crossed. Only exopodite of uropod has transverse
suture. Said to be simultaneous hermaphrodite (non self-fer-
tilizing).

Burrows in mud at 35–1400 m; western coasts of British Isles;
elsewhere ranges from Iceland and Norway to Mediterranean;
also North America, Arabian Gulf, Indian Ocean, and Pacific.

6 LAOMEDIIDAE

The second family of the Thalassinoidea. Together with the
third and fourth families, the Callianassidae and Upogebiidae,
the Laomediidae are characterizied by possessing a '*thalassinian
line*' dorso-laterally on the carapace, parallel to the mid-line;
the abdominal pleura are small. Unlike the Callianassidae and
Upogebiidae, the Laomediidae bear *transverse sutures* to the
exopods and *endopods* of the *uropods*, and pereopods 1–3 bear
gills.

Represented in Britain by a single species, *Jaxea nocturna*.

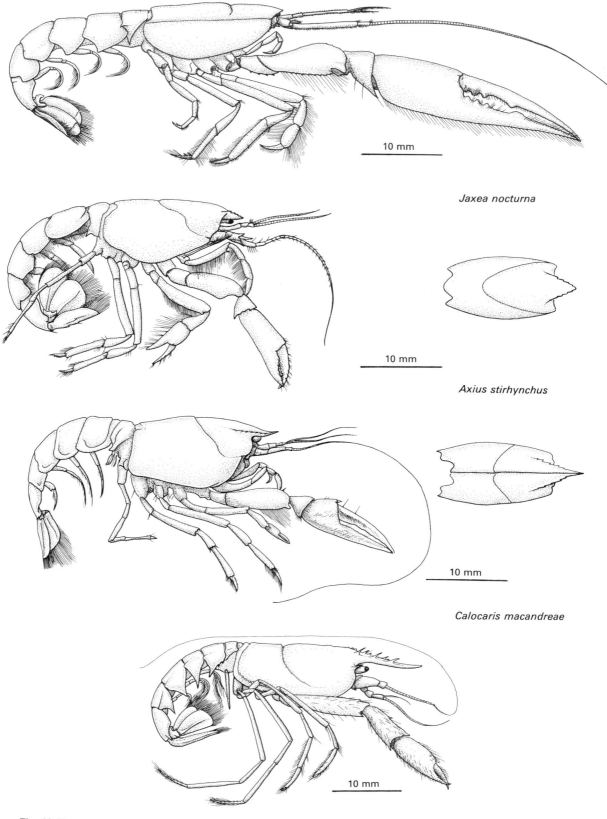

10 mm

Jaxea nocturna

10 mm

Axius stirhynchus

10 mm

Calocaris macandreae

Fig. 10.12

10 mm

Nephropsis atlantica

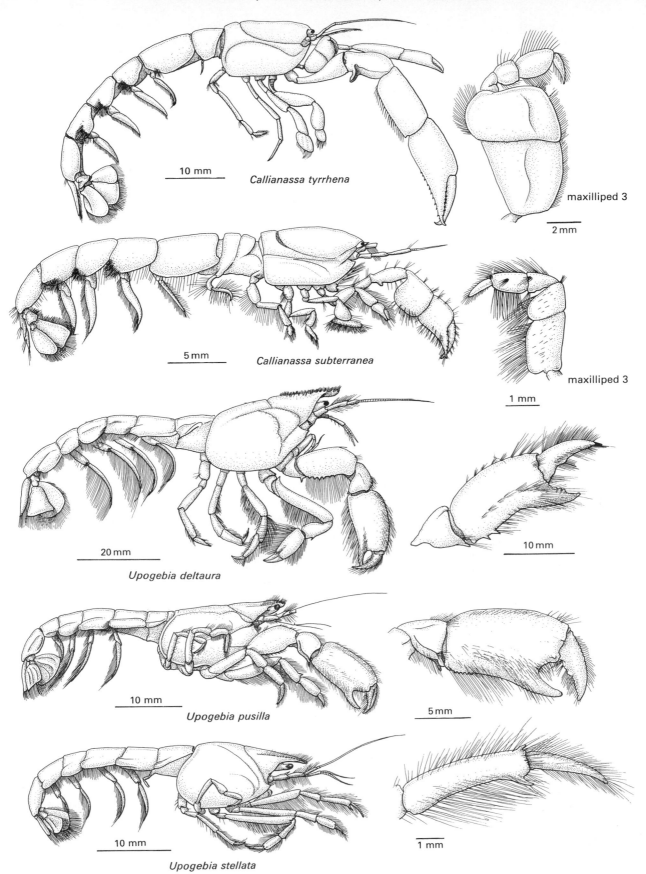

Callianassa tyrrhena

10 mm

maxilliped 3

2 mm

Callianassa subterranea

5 mm

maxilliped 3

1 mm

Upogebia deltaura

20 mm

10 mm

Upogebia pusilla

10 mm

5 mm

Upogebia stellata

10 mm

1 mm

Fig. 10.13

Jaxea nocturna (Chiereghin) FIG. 10.12

Overall length of body 40–60 mm; pinkish white with yellow or chestnut hairs. Typical thalassinoid anomuran, characterized by enormous equal-sized chelae, longer than whole carapace. Transverse sutures are present on both exopods and endopods of uropods. Eyes minute and hidden by the rostrum.

Burrows in mud, sublittoral, 10–50 m. Off west coasts of British Isles, scarce; most often seen as fragments in fish stomachs or as planktonic larvae. Elsewhere south to Mediterranean, particulary in the Adriatic.

7 CALLIANASSIDAE

The third family of the superfamily Thalassinoidea is characterized by possession of the '*thalassinian line*' which extends to the front of the carapace. The rostrum does not extend as far as the antennal peduncle; the chelipeds are unequal, and pleopods 3, 4, and 5 have the subterminal article (propodus) expanded, plate-like, and fringed with hairs.

---

1. Telson much shorter than uropod; maxilliped 3 almost as wide as long (except for three slender terminal segments) *Callianassa tyrrhena*

   Telson as long as uropod; maxilliped 3 slender *Callianassa subterranea*

Callianassa tyrrhena (Petagna) FIG. 10.13

The larger of the British species; body length up to 67 mm; whitish with pink or blue spots, sometimes greenish grey. Rostrum practically absent, eyes small and close together. The third maxillipeds form an operculum, their lower articles (merus and ischium) being broad and flat. Chelipeds unequal, left sometimes the larger; fingers cross at tips; joint between carpus and merus narrow but not wasp-waisted; outgrowth on merus curved, serrate, and sharp. Lower margin of chela hairy; bristles on dactyl. Pereopod 3 dactyl rectangular, plate-like. Telson considerably shorter than uropods.

Burrows in muddy sand, 5–20 m or deeper. Perhaps all coasts of British Isles, not uncommon; elsewhere south Norway to Mediterranean.

Callianassa subterranea (Montagu) FIG. 10.13

The smaller species, up to 40 mm overall length; pale puce, sometimes quite dark. Rostrum minute. Third maxillipeds leg-like, not forming an operculum. Chelipeds massive, the finger-tips not crossing markedly; the joint between carpus and merus wasp-waisted; merus bears curved and serrated outgrowth; propodus and merus very hairy on lower edge. Pereopod 3 dactyl elongated, plate-like. Telson as long as uropods.

Burrows in sandy mud; LWST down to 20 m; southern coasts of British Isles, common; elsewhere southwards, probably to Mediterranean.

8 UPOGEBIIDAE

These have resemblances to the callianassids but with the following differences: the cervical groove (rather than the thalassinian line) extends to the front edge of the carapace, the rostrum extends beyond the peduncles of the antennules, the chelipeds are similar in size, and all the pleopods are slender.

---

1. No ocular spine; thumb of chela as long as dactyl *Upogebia deltaura*

   Ocular spine present, thumb much shorter than dactylus of chela **2**

2. Propodus of chela wide; thumb subterminal *Upogebia pusilla*

   Propodus of chela narrow; thumb almost terminal *Upogebia stellata*

Upogebia deltaura (Leach) FIG. 10.13

Largest of the three species; overall body length 80 mm or exceptionally 150 mm. Colour dirty yellow, tinged white, green, or red. Very similar to *U. stellata*, but lacks ocular spines; front of carapace including rostrum hairy above. Chelipeds equal and quite robust; the moveable dactyl only slightly longer than 'thumb', no pronounced fringe of hairs along edge of manus, and only a short spine on outer extremity of carpus; abdomen broader and more softly membranous than *U. stellata*.

Uses burrows of other animals; LWST–40 m; perhaps all coasts of British Isles, common, often with *U. stellata*. Elsewhere, Norway to Spain and Mediterranean, and Black Sea.

Upogebia pusilla (Petagna) FIG. 10.13

Adult body length up to about 45 mm. The carapace is generally more slender than the other species; there is a well-marked ocular spine and the lateral margin is strongly notched where the cervical groove meets it. Chelipeds distinctively long, with relatively heavy chelae; dactyl more than twice length of thumb, which is set back subterminally on the manus; there is a short dense fringe of hairs behind thumb.

Burrows in sand and muddy sand, shallow sublittoral; British Isles: uncommon, probably only in south; elsewhere Norway to Spain, Mediterranean and Black Sea.

Upogebia stellata (Montagu) FIG. 10.13

Adult body length up to 50 mm; yellowish white, often orange spotted. Carapace with strong cervical groove; anterior lateral border with a distinctive ocular spine; well-developed hairy rostrum. Chelipeds equal in size, long and slender; the moveable finger (dactyl) up to 1.5 × length of thumb; central margin of manus with dense rows of hairs; outer extremity of carpus with a long spine. Abdomen narrower and more rigidly chitinized than in *U. deltaura*.

In burrows, LWST to shallow sublittoral; British Isles, all coasts, commonest of three species. Elsewhere south-west Norway to Spain and Mediterranean.

9 PAGURIDAE

The Paguridae, or hermit crabs are anomurans adapted to living in gastropod shells; growing crabs move to progressively larger shells. The abdomen is asymmetrical and twisted to fit the shell's dextral coil. Typically the last pleopod on the left side is converted into a hook for anchoring the body to the spiral columella. In most genera all the right pleopods are absent in both sexes, those of the left (apart from the last) are lost in males but present for egg carrying in females. In keeping with its protection by the mollusc shell the abdomen of pagurids is soft, its exoskeleton lacking the usual calcification. The first pereopods are chelate, the right being larger than the left in most species. The fourth and fifth pereopods are generally poorly developed.

The hermit crab and its shell are frequently the habitat for specific associated animals; coelenterates or sponges on the outside, polychaetes sharing the shell cavity, and spirorbids or acrothoracican cirripedes occupying the columella.

In the less advanced genera, several features show variation from the typical form. The chelae may be equal or subequal in size (exceptionally the left is larger as in *Diogenes*). The action of the chelae fingers is parallel to the longitudinal plane of the body rather than across it (*Parapagurus*, *Nematopagurus*).

Only the anterior (calcified) part of the carapace is shown in the accompanying figures.

---

1. Third maxillipeds contiguous at base   **2**

   Third maxillipeds widely separate   **3**

2. Chelipeds subequal   ***Clibanarius erythropus***

   Left cheliped much larger than the right

        Diogenes pugilator

3. Abdominal segments 1 and 2 of male bear broad uniramous pleopods. Female genital opening on left pereopod 3   ***Parapagurus pilosimanus***

   No paired pleopods in male; female genital openings on both third pereopods   **4**

4. Abdominal segment 1 of female has pair of two-jointed pleopods. Male right pleopod 5 has long protruding filamentous vas deferens

        Nematopagurus longicornis

   No paired pleopods in female; vas deferens not ending in long filament   **3**

5. Chelae almost equal in length; both vas deferens protrude   ***Catapaguroides timidus***

   Left chela smaller than right; neither, or only left, vas deferens projecting   **6**

6. Vas deferens not protruding; more than four spines (except in *P. pubscens*, with four) on each side of rear margin of telson   **9**

   Four spines on each side of telson; rostrum wide and rounded   **7**

7. Eyestalk short, about half length of hard carapace

        Anapagurus laevis

Eyestalk long, more than half length of hard carapace   **8**

8. Stalk of antennule three times length of eyestalk; right chela almost hairless   ***Anapagurus hyndmanni***

   Antennule stalk one and a half times length of eyestalk; right chela hairy   ***Anapagurus chiroacanthus***

9. Right chela setose   **10**

   Right chela bald   **12**

10. Manus of right chela with two depressions

         Pagurus sculptimanus

    Manus of right chela without depressions   **11**

11. Rostrum rounded; right chela enclosed in dense plumose setae, with carpus as long as manus

         Pagurus cuanensis

    Rostrum pointed; short setae of right chela arranged in minute groups arising from tubercles; carpus as long as whole chela   ***Pagurus pubescens***

12. Sharp pointed rostral region   **13**

    Rostral region rounded   **14**

13. Manus of right chela smooth and shining   ***Pagurus carneus***

    Manus of right chela tuberculate   ***Pagurus bernhardus***

14. Manus of left chela armed with toothed keel

         Pagurus variabilis

    Manus of left chela not so armed   ***Pagurus prideauxi***

Diogenes pugilator (Roux)   FIG. 10.14

Carapace length up to 11 mm; greenish tinted. Left chela considerably larger than right, narrower in the male than in the female and more outwardly orientated. Propodus and carpus of chela short, covered with sharp teeth; in the male these articles are more elongated, and covered with small granulations which turn into teeth near the upper edge.

Inhabits fairly sheltered sandy bottoms; LWST to 35 m; south and west coasts of British Isles, common. Elsewhere from Holland to Angola, Mediterranean, Black Sea, and Red Sea.

Parapagurus pilosimanus Smith   FIG. 10.14

Carapace length about 19 mm; reddish with some yellow. Antennular peduncle much longer than ocular peduncle; ophthalmic scale long and narrow. Pereopod 4 subchelate; pereopod 5 ends in a small chela. Males have a pair of two articled sexual pleopods on abdominal segments 1 and 2, the second being spatulate; remaining three pleopods biramous, left side only. Female lacking right genital pore; pleopods on left side only, biramous except last.

Deep water species, 500–4000 m; off west coast of Ireland, rare; otherwise cosmopolitan, including Biscay and Mediterranean.

Catapaguroides timidus (Roux)   FIG. 10.14

A small hermit crab, carapace length about 5 mm. Rostrum triangular, similar sized to anterio-lateral teeth; occular peduncles subcylindrical, about as long as antennular peduncles. In females the first pleopods are lacking. The males have sexual tubes arising from the usual openings; the left one is short, conical, and curved; the right is strong, wide, and curved from right to left over the base of the abdomen.

Amongst *Zostera* spp., *Posidonia* sp., and algae; intertidal to 80 m. Extreme south-west British Isles, Channel Isles (?), uncommon; elsewhere Roscoff to Canaries; abundant in Mediterranean.

Clibanarius erythropus (Latreille)   FIG. 10.14

Carapace length about 15 mm. Rostrum small, acute, and slightly protruding. Chelae with thick fingers bearing horny, black tips and covered by wide, blunt tubercles and hairiness, which also occurs on antennal peduncles and pereopods 2 and 3. Eyes extend slightly beyond antennal peduncles. Triangular ophthalmic scales with toothed horizontal prolongation.

In intertidal pools and on sand, gravel, and algae in shallow sublittoral, to 40 m; Channel Isles only, uncommon; formerly sporadic South Devon and Cornwall; elsewhere Brittany to Azores, Mediterranean and Black Sea.

Nematopagurus longicornis Milne Edwards and Bouvier   FIG. 10.14

Carapace length about 7 mm; body variably coloured, pinkish yellow to black; pereopods 2 and 3 marked with red longitudinal lines. Rostrum wide, rounded slightly in advance of anterio-lateral teeth. Ocular peduncles thick and short. Chelae with horny nail, and long bunches or setae arranged across manus and front edge of carpus. Chelipeds unequal in size, with fingers mobile across the body axis. Female with a pair of pleopods on abdominal segment 1, left pleopod only on segment 2. Male bears three non-sexual pleopods, left side only.

Occurs at medium depths, 70–800 m. Off west coasts of British Isles; elsewhere south to Cape Verde, Azores, Mediterranean.

Anapagurus chiroacanthus (Lilljeborg)   FIG. 10.14

Carapace length about 6 mm. Rostrum rounded, flanked by rounded anterio-lateral teeth to carapace. Antennule peduncle 1.5 × length of eyestalk. Abundant hair covering carapace, chelae, and legs. Sexual tube of male on left side only; slightly curved.

Shallow, sublittoral species; British Isles: localized in northern North Sea, and apparently Guernsey; elsewhere from Norway to Spain and Mediterranean.

Anapagurus hyndmanni Thompson   FIG. 10.14

Carapace length about 10 mm. Gently rounded rostrum flanked by sharp anterio-lateral teeth. Right cheliped has carpus almost as long as propodus; no basal tubercle on upper side. Carpus of pereopods toothed on upper edge. Last article of antennular peduncle longer than in other species. Ocular peduncle does not

reach base of article 3 of antennular peduncle; this article longer than the first two articles together.

Associated with sand, mud, or gravel in shallow sublittoral, LWST to 35 m. British Isles, all coasts, uncommon. Elsewhere north Biscay to Portugal.

Anapagurus laevis (Bell)   FIG. 10.14

Carapace length about 7 mm. Anterio-lateral edge of carapace has very conspicuous tooth. Eye reaches base of article 3 of antennular peduncle, which is three times longer than article 2. Right cheliped of male reaches four times the length of thorax. Ophthalmic scale wide and rounded in the distal region, with a small apical spine.

On substrata of muddy sand or gravel, 20–200(400) m. All British coasts, very common. Elsewhere Norway to Senegal, Azores, Mediterranean.

Pagurus bernhardus (Linnaeus)   FIG. 10.15

Carapace length about 35 mm, intertidal specimens smaller; reddish. Chelipeds covered with uniformly distributed granules or small teeth. Propodus of right chela with two rows of larger granulations, starting at the base and converging towards the middle.

On rocky and sandy substrata; MTL to 140 m (occasionally 500 m). Very common off all British coasts. Elsewhere from Iceland and Norway to Portugal; also on American Atlantic coasts.

Any small gastropod shell may be occupied; large specimens are usually found in shells of *Buccinum undatum*. Commensals include *Calliactis parasitica*, *Hydractinia echinata*, *Nereis fucata*, *Trypetesa lampas*; parasites: *Clistosaccus paguri* and *Peltogaster curvatus*.

Pagurus carneus Pocock   FIG. 10.15

Carapace length about 15.5 mm. Chelipeds hairless and shiny on dorsal surface; lateral edge of right chlela with a sharp keel.

Deep water only, 100–1000 m; off west coast of Ireland, localized. Elsewhere south to west Africa.

Pagurus cuanensis Thompson   FIG. 10.15

Carapace length about 15.6 mm, pale reddish brown with darker spots and some white, legs predominantly red. Upper surface of right chela strongly hairy, covered with conical teeth, more developed in the mid-line.

Shallow sublittoral, LWST to 175 m. All British coasts, common; elsewhere Norway to South Africa, Mediterranean.

Pagurus prideauxi Leach   FIG. FIG. 10.15

Carapace length about 14 mm; muddy red colour with paler spots; chelae salmon-pink. Upper surface of right chela regularly convex with a slight protruding part, and a slightly raised longitudinal region; blunt tubercles and small granules distributed evenly over both dorsal surface and sides.

On sand, mud, or gravel, LWST to 40 m (exceptionally 400 m); all British coasts, locally very common, elsewhere Norway to Cape Verde; Mediterranean. Adults often accompanied by commensal cloak anemone, *Adamsia palliata*.

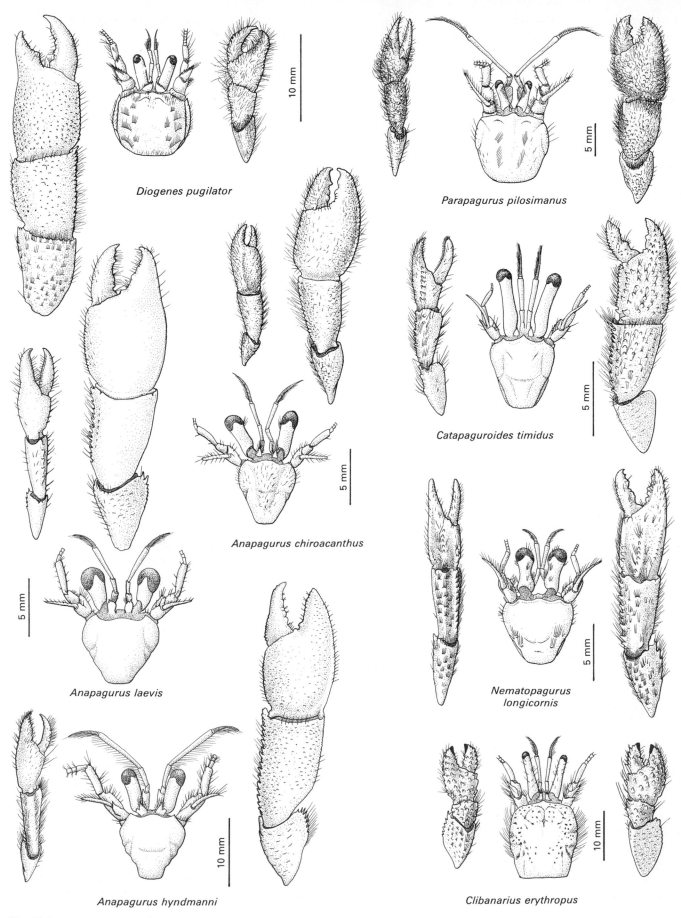

Diogenes pugilator

Parapagurus pilosimanus

Catapaguroides timidus

Anapagurus chiroacanthus

Anapagurus laevis

Nematopagurus longicornis

Anapagurus hyndmanni

Clibanarius erythropus

Fig. 10.14

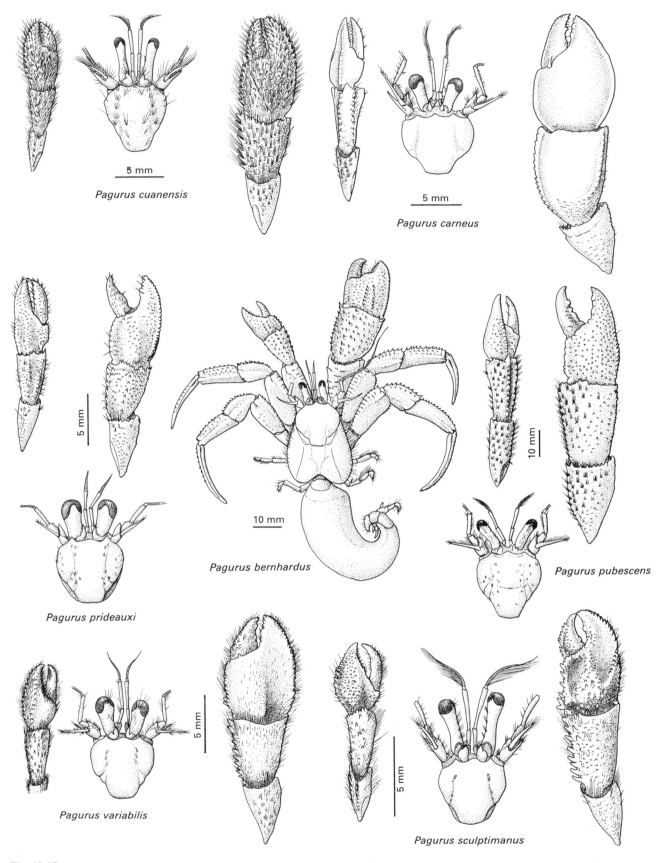

Pagurus cuanensis

Pagurus carneus

Pagurus prideauxi

Pagurus bernhardus

Pagurus pubescens

Pagurus variabilis

Pagurus sculptimanus

Fig. 10.15

Pagurus pubescens Krøyer FIG. 10.15

Carapace length about 20.5 mm; chela (propodus) 20(31) mm. Front of carapace with a central, acutely pointed rostrum flanked laterally by two slightly shorter and less acute anterio-lateral teeth. Right cheliped larger than left, three times length of carapace; propodus and carpus about equal length, both with bunches of setae arising from tubercles; setae longer on carpus.

Shallow sublittoral, 8–500(100) m; sand, mud, or rock, not uncommon. A northern species, north and west coasts of Britain, including Irish Sea; elsewhere Norway, Iceland.

Pagurus sculptimanus Lucas FIG. 10.15

Carapace length about 8.5 mm; reddish yellow with darker spots in the gastric region. Upper surface of right chela granulated and slightly hairy; propodus with two characteristic depressions separated by a large elongated ridge extending on to finger; a larger tubercle near base, and another below dactyl.

A shallow sublittoral species: 20–70 m; off south and south-west coasts of British Isles, not uncommon. Elsewhere south to Senegal, Mediterranean.

Pagurus variabilis (Milne Edwards and Bouvier)

FIG. 10.15

Carapace length 15–19 mm. Anterio-lateral teeth of carapace in advance of rounded rostrum. Article 2 of the antennal peduncle drawn out as a spine which reaches beyond base of its last article. Right chela bears a median keel.

Offshore, 40–50 m; all British coasts, common; elsewhere Norway to White Cape, Mediterranean.

10 LITHODIDAE (Stone Crabs)

Large and crablike with a well-calcified carapace. Right chela larger than left; fifth pereopods very small and hidden. Abdomen, particularly of female, strongly asymmetrical, reflecting the pagurid ancestry. Mostly in deep water.

---

1. Rostrum simple, or if bifid, only minutely so at tip; length of spines on pereopods mostly less than diameter of limb **Lithodes maja**

   Rostrum bifid, many limb spines much longer than diameter of limb **Neolithodes grimaldi**

Lithodes maja Linnaeus FIG. 10.19

Carapace width up to 120 mm. Carapace almost circular with a well-defined rim of irregular spines; scattered spines on dorsal surface and also on limbs.

Offshore; from 10 to 600 metres; locally common; northern species extending not much further south than Isle of Man.

Neolithodes grimaldi (Milne Edwards and Bouvier)

FIG. 10.19

Carapace width up to 110 mm. Whole crab orange to red in colour. Carapace pear-shaped with rostrum of two strong spines, with similar long spines numerous on carapace.

Deep water species; from 500–2000 m deep off the western coasts of the British Isles and considerably further north and south.

11 GALATHEIDAE

Carapace longer than wide; rostrum triangular or elongated. Sternum of last thoracic segment free from carapace. Abdomen curved under cephalothorax.

Two subfamilies are represented in the British Sea area:-

Galatheinae: Carapace lightly calcified with a well-marked transverse suture. Eyes well-developed. Antennal peduncle with articles 2 and 3 fused. Exopodite of maxilliped 1 with flagellum. Telson with numerous sutures, making three pairs of lobes around a central one; one pair of lobes much larger than others.

Munidopsinae: Carapace well-calcified, usually without strong transverse suture. Eyes reduced. Antennal peduncle with articles 2 and 3 fused. Exopodite of maxilliped 1 without flagellum. Telson with numerous sutures and three pairs of lobes.

---

1. Carapace lightly calcified; posterior male pleopods blade-like, with small endopods. Intertidal or shallow sublittoral **2**

   Carapace heavily calcified; posterior male pleopods styliform. Deep water species (more than 300 m); telson with numerous sutures and three pairs of lobes **8**

2. Rostrum broad, flattened, triangular, and toothed on each side **4**

   Rostrum a simple spine accompanied by long supra-orbital spines **3**

3. Eyes small. Dactyls of pereopods 2–4 less than half length of propodus; chelipeds very hairy; intense reddish colour. Large species **Munida rugosa**

   Eyes large. Dactyls of pereopods 2–4 more than half length of propodus; chelipeds sparsely covered with short hairs. Pale colour. Small. Carapace grooves granular, posterior edge of carapace with numerous spines (up to 12). **Munida intermedia sarsi**

4. Basal joint of antennule with three massive spines **5**

   Basal joint of antennule with two such spines **Galathea intermedia**

5. Manus of chela with few spines; pereopods 2–3 with epipodite **6**

   Manus covered with spines; pereopods 2–5 without epipodite **Galathea strigosa**

6. Merus of maxilliped 3 longer than ischium, chela with scaly tubercles **Galathea squamifera**

   Merus of maxilliped 3 about same length as ischium; chelae covered with hairs or scales fringed with short setae **7**

7. Abdominal segments with single transverse furrow; rostrum concave above, few setae **Galathea nexa**

   Abdominal segments with three transverse furrows; rostrum thickly clothed in setae or scales **Galathea dispersa**

8. Rostrum tridentate; cheliped twice length of carapace **Munidopsis tridentata**

   Rostrum spiniform; cheliped much less than twice length of carapace **9**

9. Cheliped longer than carapace and rostrum; transverse cardiac ridge with central spine; forward-pointing median spines on three abdominal segments **Munidopsis curvirostra**

   Cheliped about same length as carapace and rostrum; no cardiac ridge or spine; no abdominal spines **Munidopsis crassa**

Subfamily **Galatheinae**

Munida rugosa (Fabricius) FIG. 10.16

Overall length of adult body, with abdomen extended, about 60 mm; carapace length, including rostrum, about 30 mm; pinkish yellow, with edges and transverse grooves reddish, some red spines. Carapace with few spines on posterior margin; rostrum proper a single untoothed spine, flanked by two shorter supra-orbital spines. Chelipeds very long.

Stony bottoms, LWST to 150 m; all British coasts, fairly common; elsewhere Norway to Madeira, Mediterranean.

Munida intermedia var. *sarsi* Brinkman NOT FIGURED

Carapace length about 16.5 mm including rostrum. Carapace sparsely covered with short hairs; posterior edge with numerous spines (up to 12); edges of carapace grooves granular. Eyes large. Pereopods 2–4 with dactyl more than half length of propodus.

This is in need of taxonomic revision, but is almost certainly a separate species from the larger *M. intermedia* Milne Edwards and Bouvier, found in the Mediterranean and off neighbouring Atlantic coasts.

Offshore, at depths of 100–300 m; west coast of Ireland; elsewhere Norway and Iceland south to Portugal.

Galathea dispersa Bate FIG. 10.16

Length of whole body, of adult male, 35(45) mm; colour varies from red to dull yellow, sometimes with white spotting, never any blue. Carapace narrower than *G. nexa* and more hairy; lateral spines more unevenly spaced and less protruding; rostrum also narrower and pilose; tubercles at base of apical tooth hidden by hairs. Abdominal segments marked by a central transverse groove, with lesser furrows in parallel, in front and behind; all grooves furnished with fringes of setae. Antennal peduncle without a spine on article 2. Merus of maxilliped 3 with central spine smaller than in *G. nexa*; chelipeds closely covered with fringed scales. Eggs carried in spring.

Sublittoral, depths of 10–500 m; all British coasts, common; elsewhere, Norway and south Iceland to Madeira and Canaries, Mediterranean.

Galathea intermedia Lilljeborg FIG. 10.16

Small; length of whole body about 18 mm; carapace 8.5 mm; mainly salmon-red. Rostrum narrow, especially in males; paired lateral teeth protruding very little from edge. Transverse postrostral groove arched forward centrally, with a pair of distinctive setae in a separate smaller groove just behind it.

Sublittoral, 15–20 m (exceptionally 25 m); all British coasts, very common; elsewhere Norway to Dakar and Mediterranean.

Galathea nexa Embleton FIG. 10.16

Overall body length of male about 40 mm, female about 30 mm; reddish green with darker spots, bluish spots on labrum. Carapace longer than wide, narrower anteriorly; lateral edge spines sharp and prominent; with transverse grooves; setate but not closely so. Rostrum relatively shorter than in *G. dispersa*, each lateral tooth bears a single seta; a few tubercles are just visible on concave upper surface posterior to apical tooth. Abdominal segmental groves fringed with fine setae. Article 2 of antenna bears a spine (lacking in *G. dispersa*). Spines of chelae and pereopods stronger than in *G. dispersa*.

Sublittoral, 25–270 m; south and west coasts of British Isles, uncommon; elsewhere southwards to Tenerife and Mediterranean.

Galathea squamifera Leach FIG. 10.16

Overall length of adult about 65 mm; carapace 32 mm; dark chestnut-brown with greenish tinge; spine tips red; juveniles reddish. Apical spine of rostrum stands out from, but is larger than the lateral spines, one epigastric spine on each side; carapace shiny between grooves and scattered short hairs, chelae closely covered in scale-like tubercles; merus of maxilliped 3 bears a distal row of spines, the end ones longest.

LWST to shallow sublittoral, juveniles deeper (30–70 m); all coasts of British Isles, common; elsewhere Norway to Azores and Mediterranean.

Galathea strigosa (Linnaeus) FIG. 10.16

Large, overall body length about 90 mm, carpace up to 53 mm; vivid red with patches and bands of bright blue. Rostrum has a long apical spine and is covered with fringed scales; three epigastric spines on each side, middle one longest; carapace grooves densely pilose. Merus of maxilliped 3 with two strong spines.

From shallow sublittoral to 600 m; gravelly and rocky bottoms; all British coasts, very common; elsewhere from North Cape, Scandinavia to Spain, Canaries, Mediterranean, and Red Sea.

Subfamily **Munidopsinae**

Munidopsis crassa Smith FIG. 10.17

Overall length of body up to 100 mm. Front edges of carapace oblique; lateral edges parallel. Edges of rostrum bearing small teeth. Basal article of antennal peduncle bears two fine spines, inner one being the stronger.

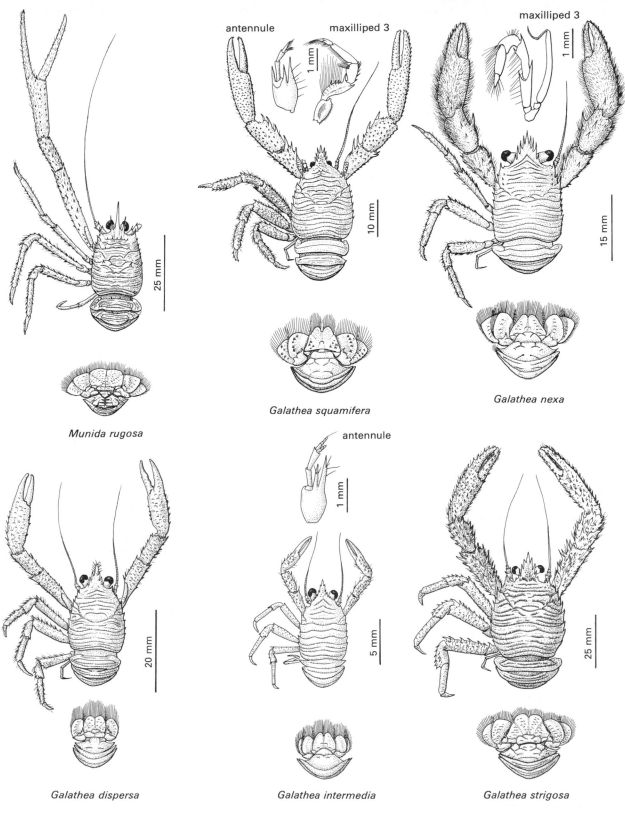

antennule   maxilliped 3

1 mm

25 mm

Munida rugosa

10 mm

Galathea squamifera

maxilliped 3

1 mm

15 mm

Galathea nexa

antennule

1 mm

20 mm

Galathea dispersa

5 mm

Galathea intermedia

25 mm

Galathea strigosa

Fig. 10.16

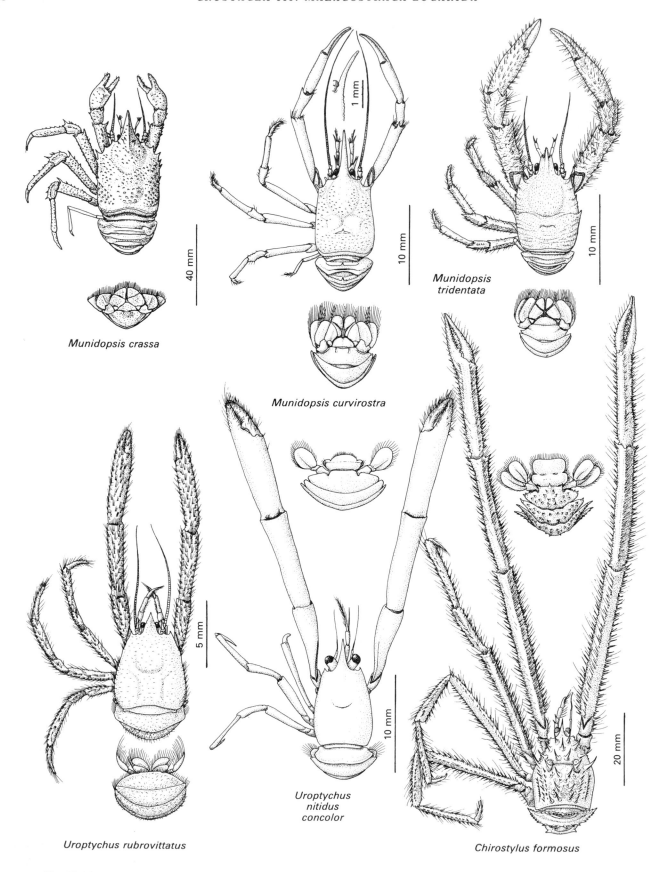

Munidopsis crassa

Munidopsis curvirostra

Munidopsis tridentata

Uroptychus rubrovittatus

Uroptychus nitidus concolor

Chirostylus formosus

Fig. 10.17

Deep water, 3000 to 4700 m; English Channel only, rare; elsewhere Biscay, and off North American coasts.

Munidopsis curvirostra Whiteaves   FIG. 10.17

Overall length of body 31(35) mm. Carapace rectangular, slightly tapering forwards; patchily covered with minute tubercles; anterior margins with two narrow, blunt teeth; lateral edges smooth, lacking spines as viewed from above; one small central spine in cardiac region. Rostrum very long, upcurved, tapering. Eyes quite large but unpigmented. Chelipeds long, slender, and slightly unequal; carpus much shorter than manus, bearing a small distal spine on its outer aspect; a few distal spines and hairs on merus. Dactyls of pereopods hairy, carpi also slightly hairy.

Deep water, 350–1800 (2300) m; off south-west Ireland, rare; elsewhere, North Atlantic.

Munidopsis tridentata (Esmark)   FIG. 10.17

Overall body length of male 20 mm; carapace 11 mm; cheliped about 22 mm. Carapace with poorly marked grooves and short hairy striae. Rostrum with parallel sides, terminating in lateral rostral spines. Abdominal segments with transverse groove but no spines. Antennal flagellum longer than carapace. Chelipeds longer than other pereopods and carapace; pereopods 2–4 with upper edges of carpus and merus toothed.

In deep water, around 2000 m; off west coasts of British Isles, not uncommon; elsewhere deep water off coasts from Norway to Azores and Cape Verde; also Indo-Pacific.

12 CHIROSTYLIDAE

Carapace well-calcified, without transverse suture. Antennal peduncle with articles 2 and 3 not fused; often a spine on article 3. Exopodite of maxilliped 1 with flagellum. Telson with one or two sutures, more reduced than in the Galatheidae and tucked over the last abdominal segment.

---

1. Rostrum in the form of a spine; carapace very spiny; chelipds often more than five times length of carapace and rostrum   ***Chirostylus formosus***

    Rostrum flat and triangular; cheliped less than four times length of carapace   **2**

2. Carapace hairy; chelae covered with scales bearing hairs   ***Uroptychus rubrovittatus***

    Carapace bald; chelae smooth except at tips   ***Uroptychus nitidus concolor***

Uroptychus nitidus concolor (Milne Edwards and Bouvier)   FIG. 10.17

Overall body length about 38 mm; carapace length 15 mm; cheliped 56 mm; reddish purple, sometimes red anteriorly, legs brick-red. Carapace edges not toothed; cheliped surfaces smooth and generally hairless. Pereopods 2–4, with a row of mobile spines on lower edges of propodus.

Deep water species, 500–1800 m; off west coast of Ireland, not uncommon; elsewhere, southwards to Cape Verde, Canaries and Azores.

Uroptychus rubrovittatus (Milne Edwards)   FIG. 10.17

Overall body length about 22 mm; carapace length 7 mm; chelipeds 38 mm. Carapace and rostrum with finely toothed edges. Pereopods 2–4 without mobile spines on propodus.

Deep water species, 300–1400 m; west coast of Ireland; elsewhere, from south Iceland to Azores and Canaries, probably not uncommon.

Chirostylus formosus Filhol   FIG. 10.17

Overall body length 44–52 mm; chelipeds about 120 mm; scarlet body and limbs, brown eyes. Carapace tapers posteriorly, widest immediately behind cervical groove; front triangular, with strong supra-orbital spines flanking central rostrum; carapace bears many long spines, but is otherwise smooth. Chelipeds five to six times length of carapace; thin, cylindrical and spiny.

Deep water species, 800–1700 m; off west coast of Ireland, rare; elsewhere south to Canaries.

13 PORCELLANIDAE

Carapace nearly circular, crablike, flat, smooth; front quite wide. Antennae very long. Maxilliped 3 with flattened ischium and merus. Abdomen very reduced and thin; flexed under cephalothorax. Pereopod 5 extremely thin and tucked under carapace.

---

1. Chelipeds with dense fringe of long setae on outer edge; chelae very large   ***Porcellana platycheles***

    Chelipeds devoid of setae; chelae narrow   ***Pisidia longicornis***

Porcellana platycheles (Pennant). Porcelain Crab   FIG. 10.18

Carapace length up to 15 mm; greyish brown above, underside dirty yellowish/white. Carapace nearly circular, slightly longer than broad, with setose posterior margins; front with slightly advanced, acute median tooth, flanked by smaller acute submarginals. Chelipeds unequal, massive, compressed; propodus densely fringed with long setae. Pereopods heavily setose. Distal edges of abdominal segments setose.

Undersides of boulders; intertidal; all British coasts, north as far as Shetland, abundant; elsewhere North Sea, Holland to White Cape, Canaries, Mediterranean.

Pisidia longicornis (Linnaeus)   FIG. 10.18

Carapace length 8 (10) mm. Dark maroon or olive. Carapace almost circular, slightly convex, smooth and bald; front three-lobed; median lobe with longitudinal furrow, serrated terminally. Antennae very long and slender. Eyes deeply sunk. Chelipeds unequal, large, compressed, not setose; fingers slightly twisted, meet only at tips.

Rock or gravel substrata, also in the bryozoan *Pentapora foliacea*, and amongst other colonial forms; intertidal to 100 m;

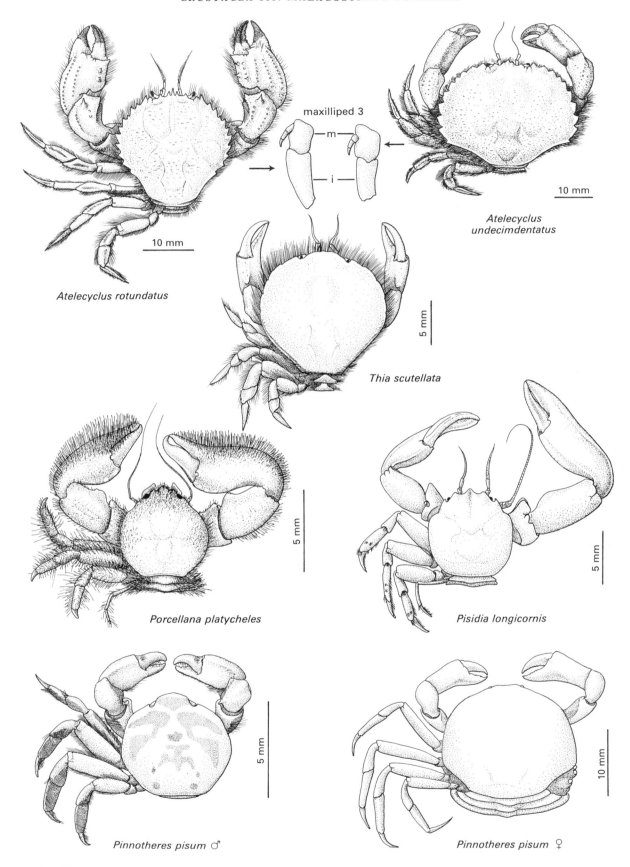

maxilliped 3

m

i

Atelecyclus undecimdentatus

10 mm

Atelecyclus rotundatus

10 mm

Thia scutellata

5 mm

Porcellana platycheles

5 mm

Pisidia longicornis

5 mm

Pinnotheres pisum ♂

5 mm

Pinnotheres pisum ♀

10 mm

Fig. 10.18

abundant on all British coasts; elsewhere, Norway to Angola, Canaries, and Mediterranean.

Infraorder **Brachyura**

14 DROMIIDAE

Carapace with shallow orbits, convex, more or less circular, front with three teeth, the middle one small and deflexed. Antennal stalk with four articles. Pereopod 1 with strong chelae, pereopods 4 and 5 reduced. Uropods vestigial. Abdomen wide, usually with seven segments.

Only one genus and species in British Isles.

Dromia personata (Linnaeus)   FIG. 10.19

Carapace of male up to 53 mm long, breadth 67 mm; dark brown with pink chelae. Body often covered with a sponge. Carapace sub-globose, length/breadth ratio 4/5; whole body and legs covered with velvet-textured pile; front with three teeth, central one small and lower than other two. Chelae stout and equal, smaller in female. Pereopods 4 and 5 subdorsal, shorter than the others, subchelate; male pereopod 5 with long penis. Abdomen of both sexes with all segments free; first pair of pleopods and vestiges of uropods present.

Rocky or stony substrata, 10–30 m (to 100 m); uncommon around British Isles: south coasts, northern North Sea, Anglesey; elsewhere south to West Africa, Azores, Mediterranean.

15 HOMOLIDAE

Carapace longer than broad, with longitudinal lines. No orbits, eyestalks jointed. Long antennal flagellum. Maxilliped 3 leg-like. Pereopod 5 reduced, dorsal. One species in British Isles.

Paromola cuvieri (Risso)   FIG. 10.19

Carapace length 160 (215) mm; light reddish, with dark chelae. Carapace longer than broad; front with three similar spines; whole surface covered with small spines. Chelae slender, in male three times length of carapace, in female not much longer than carapace. Pereopod 5 much shorter than others, subdorsal and subchelate. Abdomen seven-segmented, both sexes possess pleopod 1.

Deep water, 150–345 m. Off west coasts of British Isles only, rare; elsewhere, from West Norway to Mediterranean, Azores, and West Africa.

16 LEUCOSIIDAE

Eyes and orbits very small. Third maxillipeds completely filling buccal frame.

---

1. Abdominal segments 3–6 fused in both sexes. Surface of carapace raised in the form of a 'plus'-sign. Pleopod 1 of male with terminal tufts of hair   ***Ebalia tuberosa***

    Abdominal segments 3–5 fused in male, 4–6 in females. No 'plus'-shaped elevation. Male pleopod 1 without hairs   **2**

2. Pereopods furnished with teeth or long tubercles   ***Ebalia granulosa***

    Pereopods finely granular, not toothed   **3**

3. Dactylus of chela very much shorter than manus. Lateral margins of carapace edged with large tubercles   ***Ebalia nux***

    Dactylus of chela not much shorter than manus of propodus. Carapace not edged with large tubercles   **4**

4. Carapace slightly broader than long; branchial region strongly inflated   ***Ebalia tumefacta***

    Carapace about as long as broad; branchial region elevated but not inflated; granular   ***Ebalia cranchii***

Ebalia tuberosa (Pennant)   FIG. 10.20

Carapace length 13 (17) mm. Colour variable, light orange to reddish brown, sometimes spotted white. Carapace rhomboid, slightly broader than long; surface with many prominent tubercles, smaller at front; widest part anterior of half-way; contours of surface in form of a 'plus'-sign; posterior margin convex in female, shallowly concave in male. Male pleopod 1 with terminal hairs. Pereopods slender, often tuberculate; chelipeds more robust and longer in male. Abdominal segments 3–6 fused.

On gravel and stony bottoms; intertidal (rare) to 190 m; all British coasts, common; elsewhere, west Norway to north-west Africa, Azores, and Mediterranean.

Ebalia nux Milne Edwards   FIG. 10.20

Carapace length 6 (12) mm. Brick-red with darker red spots. Carapace as broad as long, widest half-way back, with numerous bead-like tubercles; front straight, with small central notch; orbits inset from margin in female. Posterior margin of carapace concave in both sexes. Chelipeds equal, very long and slender, more robust in male. Pereopods 2–5 slender, strongly tuberculate. Abdominal segments 3–5 fused in male; 4–6 in female.

Deep water, on mud and sand, 80–3000 m; British Isles, Celtic Sea, and off Hebrides; elsewhere south to Cape Verde, Azores, and Mediterranean.

Ebalia tumefacta (Montagu)   FIG. 10.20

Carapace length 10 (12) mm. Colour variable, reddish to yellowish grey, often spotted red; otherwise variegated brown (black), or banded pink or orange. Carapace broader than long, minutely tuberculate; anterio-lateral margin forming an almost straight line. Pair of branchial prominences and median cardiac prominence, all very much larger in female; group of tubercles in gastric region of male. Posterior carapace margin notched in male, only faintly notched in female. Chelipeds equal, propodus swollen, longer in male. Abdominal segments 3–5 fused in male; 4–6 in female.

On muddy sand, gravel, or stones, 2–15 m; probably all British coasts, very common; elsewhere south Norway to north-west Africa; not Mediterranean.

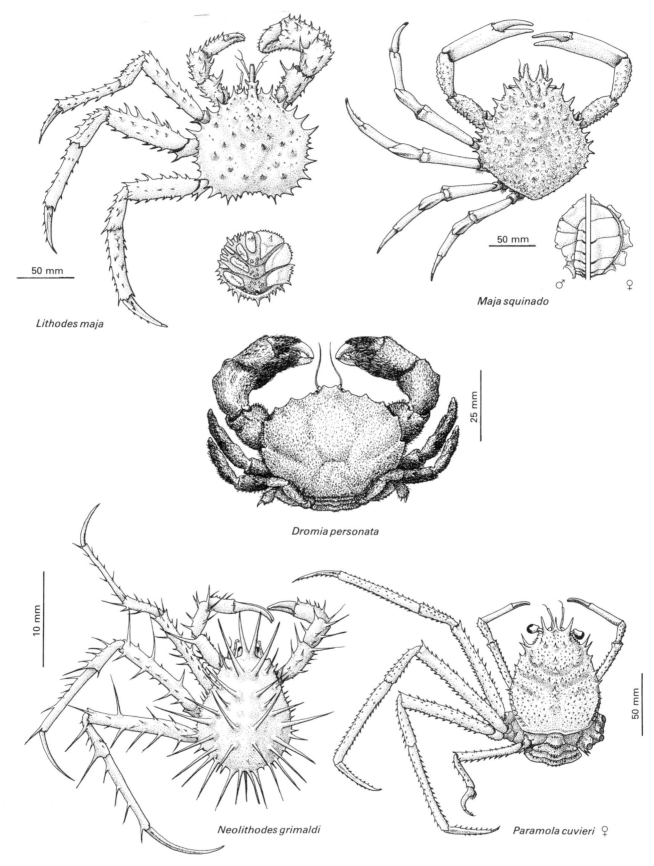

Lithodes maja

Maja squinado

♂ ♀

Dromia personata

Neolithodes grimaldi

Paramola cuvieri ♀

Fig. 10.19

Ebalia granulosa Milne Edwards FIG. 10.20

Carapace length 9.5 (11) mm. Yellowish with two spots on carapace. Carapace as broad as long, with low tubercles; front notched, biconvex; anterio-lateral margins sinuous and cristate. Prominences similar to *E. tumefacta* but lower, posterior margin slightly bifid in female, deeply so in male. Chelipeds equal, stout; margins of merus and propodus sharply cristate, merus with poorly defined tubercles. Chelipeds longer, and propodus more inflated in males. Pereopods 2–5 thin; merus often with spine-like tubercles. Abdominal segments 3–5 fused in male; 4–6 in female.

Shallow sublittoral, 20–3000 m; off west Scottish coast, west Ireland, rare; elsewhere south to Spain and Mediterranean.

Ebalia cranchii Leach FIG. 10.20

Carapace length 8 (11) mm. Colour variable, reddish yellow to reddish white with dark red spots; legs yellowish. Carapace may be slightly longer than broad; front variable, often only faintly notched. Surface tubercles flat to bead-like. Distinctive prominences often capped by tubercles. Posterior margin of carapace more prominently notched in male. Chelipeds equal, stout, moderately tuberculate; merus margin sharp but not cristate; longer, with propodus more inflated in male. Pereopods 2–5 thin, granular or finely tuberculate.

On muddy sand and gravel, 5–100 m; all British coasts, not uncommon; elsewhere west Norway to West Africa, Mediterranean.

17 MAJIDAE

Antennal peduncle well-developed, article 2 elongated and fused to underside of carapace. Chelipeds not longer than other pereopods but very mobile and used for (amongst other things), attaching pieces of weed, sponge and other sedentary organisms to the hooked setae. Four subfamilies are represented:-

Oregoninae (two species): with broad, flattened post-orbital spines and a broad telson in the male.

Inachinae (nine species): having long eyestalks but no orbits. Basal article of antennal peduncle is elongated. Very long, slender, spidery legs.

Pisinae (five species): a cupped post-orbital spine and supra-orbital eave usually forms the orbit into which the eye can be partially retracted. Base (article 2) of antennal peduncle broad. Pereopods relatively stout.

Majinae (one species): cornea completely concealed in orbit when eye is retracted. Orbit composed of supra-orbital eave and associated spines. Base of antennal peduncle (article 2) broad and furnished with anterior and posterior spines. Pereopods strongly built.

---

1. Basal article of antennal peduncle (segments 2 and 3) more than twice as long as broad **5**

   Length of basal article of antenna less than twice width **2**

2. Eye retractile into orbit concealing cornea when viewed from above. Very broad basal article to antenna ***Maja squinado***

   Cornea of retracted eye still at least partly visible from above **3**

3. Post-orbital spine flattened and expanded laterally; telson of male very wide, fitting into a slot in abdominal segment 6 **4**

   Post-orbital spine not flattened or expanded laterally, telson of male rounded-triangular **13**

4. Hepatic region not dilated laterally, only a slight swelling ***Hyas araneus***

   Hepatic region dilated laterally, forming with post-orbital region a lyriform shelf, carapace margin contracted between it and branchial region ***Hyas coarctatus***

5. Orbital spines present; eyestalks retractile **6**

   No orbital spines; eyestalks not retractile **7**

6. No supra-orbital spine **8**

   Supra-orbital spine present ***Dorhynchus thomsoni***

7. Rostrum short, extending to end of first free segment of antenna ***Achaeus cranchii***

   Rostrum extending well beyond end of first free segment of antenna **10**

8. Gastric region of carapace with four small tubercles in a transverse row, behind which is a strong median spine ***Inachus dorsettensis***

   Gastric region with only two small tubercles in transverse row, behind which is a median spine **9**

9. Distinct U-shaped cleft separating rostral horns, male thoracic sternum with callosity ***Inachus leptochirus***

   Very narrow slit between rostral horns. Male thoracic sternum lacks callosity ***Inachus phalangium***

10. Anterior edge of antennule socket visible from above, between rostrum and antennal peduncle. Dactyl of pereopods 4 and 5 very strongly arched, nearly forming a semicircle. Rostrum very short, upswept ***Macropodia linaresi***

    Anterior edge of antennule socket not visible from above between rostrum and antennal peduncles. Dactyl of pereopods 4 and 5 moderately arched **11**

11. Rostrum upswept, extending beyond extremity of antennal peduncle. Always some strong spine-like teeth on basal article of antenna ***Macropodia tenuirostris***

    Rostrum at most extending to extremity of antennal peduncle. Basal articles of antenna smooth or with some tubercles or variously developed teeth **12**

12. Rostrum straight or slightly upswept; basal article of antenna always smooth ***Macropodia rostrata***

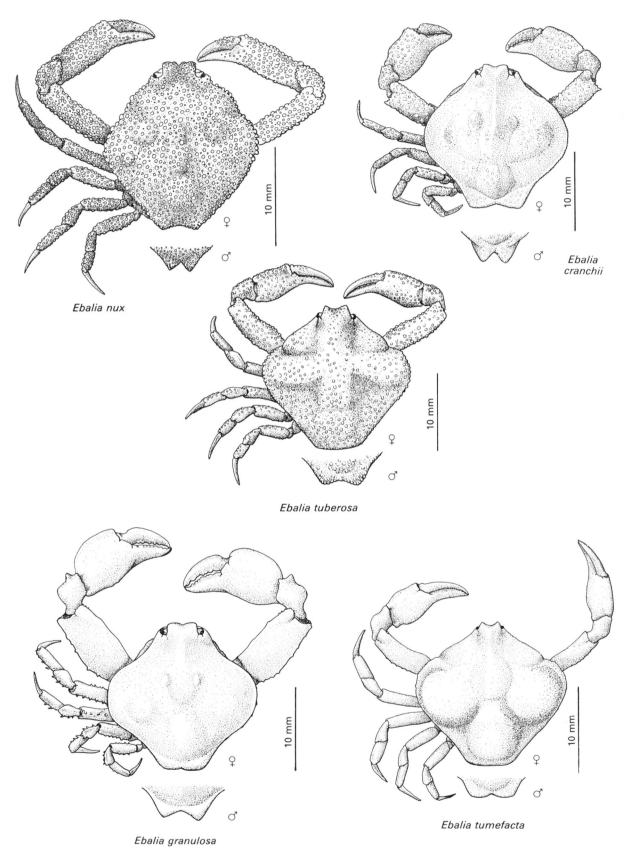

Ebalia nux

Ebalia cranchii

Ebalia tuberosa

Ebalia granulosa

Ebalia tumefacta

Fig. 10.20

Rostrum more or less arched downwards; basal article of antenna nearly always bearing teeth

Macropodia deflexa

13. Supra-orbital eave extends forward as a preorbital spine **14**

Supra-orbital eave not extended so **15**

14. The two rostral processes strongly divergent from base **Rochinia carpenteri**

Rostral processes not so divergent **16**

15. Tubercles at posterior margin of carapace usually fused into a crescent-shaped group **Eurynome aspera**

Tubercles at posterior margin not fused

Eurynome spinosa

16. One branchial tooth **Pisa armata**

Two or more branchial teeth **Pisa tetraodon**

Subfamily **Oregoninae**

Hyas araneus (Linnaeus) FIG. 10.24

Carapace, of large male, length 105 mm, breadth 83 mm; reddish brown; dirty white underside. Carapace rounded posteriorly, uneven and tuberculated; only slightly contracted behind post-orbital tooth. Rostrum triangular, formed of two close-set horns each bearing two rows of hooked setae. Eyes not entirely covered when retracted. Basal article of antenna fused to carapace, longer than broad, tapering anteriorly. Chelipeds shorter than pereopods 2–5. Telson of male distinctively wide. Scattered hairs, some hooked, on carapace and limbs.

On hard and sandy bottoms, LWST to 50 m (occasionally to 350 m); all British coasts, common. A northern species; Spitzbergen, Iceland, Norway to English Channel; also Greenland and North America.

Hyas coarctatus Leach FIG. 10.24

Carapace, of a large male, length 61 mm, breadth 44 mm; similar colour to *H. araneus*. Carapace contracted behind post-orbital shelf. Rostral horns slightly longer and less close than in *H. araneus*, converging at tips. Sides of basal article of antenna parallel rather than tapering. Chelipeds longer than in *H. araneus*, exceeding other pereopods in older specimens. Outer regions of pereopods often furry except for claw.

On hard and sandy bottoms, LWST to 50 m (occasionally to 500 m), often deeper than *H. araneus*. All British coasts, common. Another northern species, Spitzbergen and Norway to Brittany; also Greenland and North America.

Subfamily **Inachinae**

Dorhynchus thomsoni Thomson FIG. 10.21

Carapace (typical female) length 10 mm, breadth 8 mm; reddish white. Carapace furnished with many more marginal spines than *Inachus* spp., including one spanning the eyestalk; others occur on both hepatic and branchial margins; principal tubercles of dorsal surface similar to *Inachus*. Rostrum upturned. Eyestalks with a few tubercles. Chelipeds equal; more slender in female; all articles spiny, except dactyl. Pereopods long, pereopod 2 three times carapace length, bearing hooked and straight spines; merus of each pereopod with a terminal thorn.

Offshore, 100–2100 m; Shetland north to Faroes; elsewhere, from Iceland to West Africa, Mediterranean.

Inachus dorsettensis (Pennant) FIG. 10.21

Carapace, of a large male, length 30 mm, breadth 27 mm; greyish or light brown with reddish spots. Carapace surface with very consistent pattern of spines, including a distinctive transverse row of four. Rostrum short, the two horns separated by a U-shaped cleft. Short-stalked eyes; sharp post-orbital spine. Antenna with long, slender, tuberculated basal article. Chelipeds equal, more swollen in males. Successive pereopods shorter. Some hairs and hooked spines on carapace and limbs.

Stony, sand, or mud substrata; shallow sublittoral, 6–100 m; all British coasts, common; elsewhere, north Norway to South Africa, Mediterranean.

Inachus phalangium (Fabricius) FIG. 10.21

Carapace, of large male, length 20.5 mm, breadth 17.5; brownish yellow. Similar to *I. dorsettensis* but carapace spines less prominent, and the middle two of the transverse row missing. Rostrum blunt and flat with narrow gap.

On stony, sandy, and shell substrata, shallow sublittoral, 11–55 m; all British coasts, frequent; elsewhere, Norway to West Africa, Cape Verde, Mediterranean.

Inachus leptochirus Leach FIG. 10.21

Carapace, of large male, length 28 mm, breadth 24 mm; colour variable, yellowish or greyish brown. Very similar to *I. phalangium*. Distinct but narrow U-shaped gap between rostral horns. Hepatic region lacks the prominent marginal spines seen in the other two species, but small ones sometimes present. Thoracic sternum of male bears a callosity sited in front of reflexed telson.

On mud and muddy sand, 32–230 m; all British coasts, scarce; elsewhere, Faeroes, to West Africa, Azores, Mediterranean.

Achaeus cranchii Leach FIG. 10.21

Carapace, of typical male, length 11 mm, breadth 9 mm; pale reddish brown. Carapace with distinctive outline, swollen in hepatic and branchial regions; no orbital or hepatic spines. Rostrum short, notched, reaching no further than first moveable article (4) of antenna. Eyes on long, non-retractile stalks. Chelipeds spiny, equal, fatter in males. Pereopods shorter than those of *Inachus*, last three pairs ending in a sickle-like dactyl with spinulous inner edge. Many hooked setae on body and limbs.

Offshore 20–70 m; west coasts only, rare; elsewhere, south to West Africa, Azores, and Mediterranean.

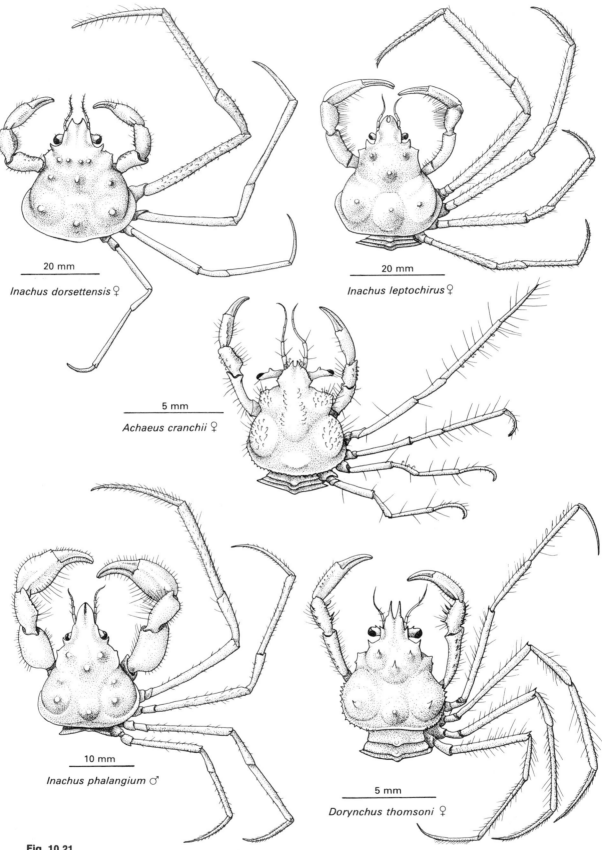

20 mm

Inachus dorsettensis ♀

20 mm

Inachus leptochirus ♀

5 mm

Achaeus cranchii ♀

10 mm

Inachus phalangium ♂

5 mm

Dorynchus thomsoni ♀

Fig. 10.21

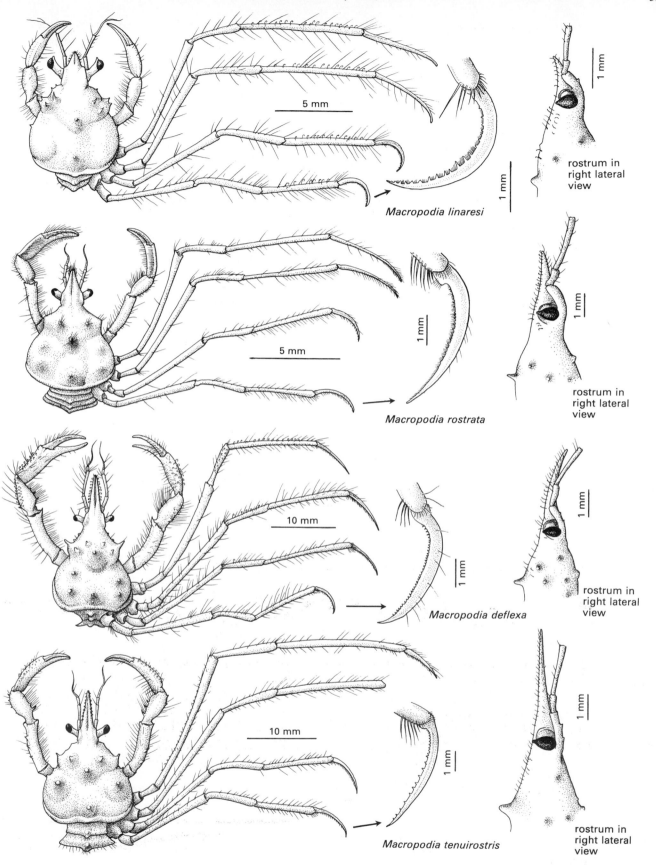

5 mm

1 mm

Macropodia linaresi

1 mm

rostrum in
right lateral
view

5 mm

1 mm

Macropodia rostrata

1 mm

rostrum in
right lateral
view

10 mm

1 mm

Macropodia deflexa

1 mm

rostrum in
right lateral
view

10 mm

1 mm

Macropodia tenuirostris

1 mm

rostrum in
right lateral
view

Fig. 10.22

Macropodia rostrata (Linnaeus)   FIG. 10.22

Carapace, of large male, length 22 mm, breadth 15 mm; brown tinged with grey, yellow, or red. Carapace lacks spines between eyes and hepatic tubercles. Rostrum somewhat shorter than antennal peduncle and slightly upcurved. Basal segment of antennal peduncle (articles 2 and 3) devoid of spines. Merus of pereopod 2 longer than whole carapace; dactyl of last pereopod has very small spines on only the proximal two-thirds.

On hard or mixed substrata, shallow sublittoral, 4–90 m; all British coasts, common; elsewhere, Norway to West Africa, Azores, Mediterranean.

Sometimes infected with the rhizocephalan cirripede *Drepanorchis neglecta*, as are other species of the genus.

Macropodia linaresi Forest and Zariquiey   FIG. 10.22

Carapace length, average 7.7 mm. Carapace with two small spines between eyestalks and hepatic tubercles. Rostrum slightly upturned and only just reaching terminal article (5) of antennal peduncle. Basal segment of antennal peduncle (articles 2 and 3) bearing at least two spines. Merus of pereopod 2 about as long as carapace; dactyl of last pereopod sickle-shaped and furnished with strong spines throughout its length.

Shallow sublittoral, south coasts of British Isles, not uncommon; elsewhere south to Spain, Mediterranean.

Macropodia deflexa Forest   FIG. 10.22

Carapace, average male length 29 mm; average female length 25 mm. Colour greyish brown; young striped pink. Carapace with at least two small spines between eye and hepatic tubercle. Rostrum extending slightly less far than last article of antennal peduncle; often slightly decurved. Basal article of antennal peduncle spiny. Merus of pereopod shorter than whole carapace; dactyl of last pereopod less curved than in *M. linaresi* and furnished with much smaller but more numerous spines throughout greater part of its curving inner face.

Shallow sublittoral 15–90 m; on sandy and weedy grounds. South and all west coasts of British Isles, elsewhere probably southwards.

Macropodia tenuirostris (Leach)   FIG. 10.22

Carapace, large female, length 19 mm, breadth 11 mm; reddish brown. Carapace with one small spine between eye and hepatic tubercle. Rostrum longer than whole antennal peduncle. Basal segment of antennal peduncle (articles 1 and 2) with two or three conspicuous sharp spines. Merus of pereopod 2 longer than whole carapace and rostrum; dactyl of last pereopod only slightly curved and bearing small, mostly widely spaced spines throughout its length.

Shallow water, LWST to 168 m; all British coasts, common; elsewhere, Faeroes Banks southwards at least to Portugal.

Subfamily Pisinae

Eurynome aspera (Pennant)   FIG. 10.23

Carapace, of large male, length 17 mm, breadth 13 mm; light rose intermixed with a tint of bluish grey. Carapace longer than broad, covered with large, irregular warty tubercles; distinctive amongst these is a fused group in gastric region and a partly fused series bordering posterior margin; an oval group in cardiac region has two large tubercles at its anterior end. Rostral horns taper from a widened basal region to form a V-shaped cleft. Long chelipeds, and merus of rather short pereopods 2–5 also tuberculate.

On stony sand and shell substrata, sublittoral, mostly 12–40 m (occasionally 2–120 m); all British coasts, common; elsewhere, west Norway to West Africa; Mediterranean.

Eurynome spinosa Hailstone   FIG. 10.23

Carapace, of large male, length 17 mm, breadth 11 mm. Very similar to *E. aspera* but tubercles generally smaller. Tubercles bordering posterior margin of carapace generally not fused; oval group in cardiac region completed anteriorly by a large median tubercle. Tapering rostral horns very wide at base, diverging apically with a wide gap between.

On stony, gravel, and shell substrata, 20–85 m; south and west coasts of British Isles, scarce; elsewhere, south to Spain and Azores, Mediterranean.

Pisa armata (Latreille)   FIG. 10.23

Carapace, of typical male, length 30 mm, breadth 18 mm; dull reddish brown. Dorsal surface with velvet-like pile. Carapace with distinctive posterior-lateral (branchial) spines, also pre- and post-orbital spines; lateral border with one other major spine; a large median posterior spine. Rostral horns parallel at base, slightly diverging at tips; cleft narrow. A small intercalary spine present between other orbitals. Eyes very small.

Shallow sublittoral; south and west coasts of British Isles, scarce; elsewhere, southern North Sea to West Africa, Mediterranean.

Pisa tetraodon (Pennant). Four-horned spider crab

FIG. 10.23

Carapace length (excluding rostrum), of typical male 34 mm; brownish red. Very similar to *P. armata* but lacking velvet covering. Carapace with three large spines each side between post-orbitals and posterior-laterals; very reduced posterior-median spine; pre-orbital spine larger than in the other species.

Shallow sublittoral, down to 50 m; south and south-west coasts of British Isles, not uncommon; elsewhere to Gibraltar and Mediterranean.

Rochinia carpenteri (Thomson)   FIG. 10.23

Carapace, of typical female, length 72 mm, breadth 42 mm; pale pink, darker in front, paler on the depressed tubercles. Convex, pear-shaped carapace bearing several low tubercles with pre- and post-orbital spines, but no intercalary spines; also a sharp branchial spine. Rostral horns long, slender, and diverging. Chelipeds almost as slender as pereopods 2–5. Carapace bears hooked setae, and also dense layer of vesiculate setae.

Offshore, 180–400 m; British Isles, off Scotland; elsewhere, Norway and Iceland to West Africa.

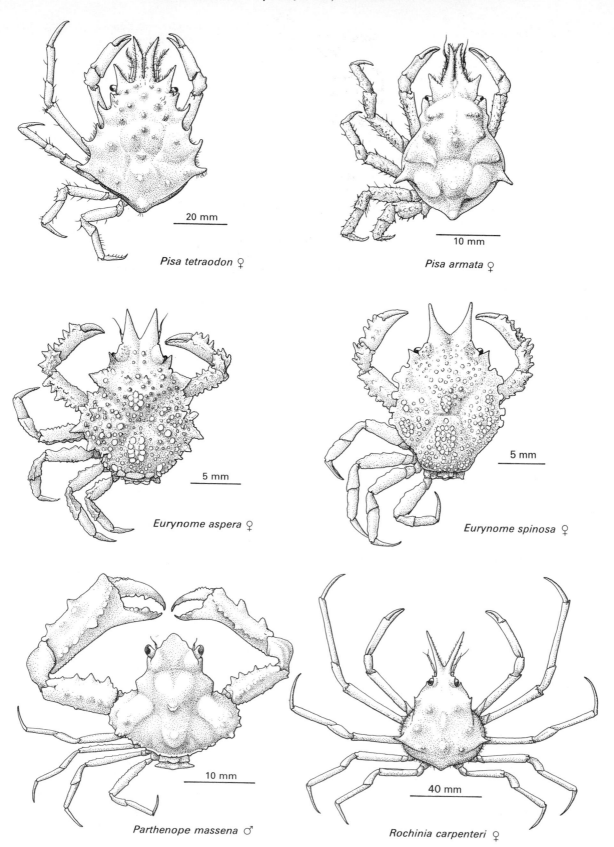

20 mm

Pisa tetraodon ♀

10 mm

Pisa armata ♀

5 mm

Eurynome aspera ♀

5 mm

Eurynome spinosa ♀

10 mm

Parthenope massena ♂

40 mm

Rochinia carpenteri ♀

Fig. 10.23

Subfamily **Majinae**

Maja squinado (Herbst). Spider-Crab of   FIG. 10.19
commerce

Carapace, of large specimen, length 200 mm, breadth 150 mm;
cheliped 450 mm; red, brownish red, or yellowish. Very large
crab often covered with attached algae. Circular, convex carapace bordered by strong tapering spines; dorsal surface with
many shorter, sharp spines. Rostrum of two stout divergent
horns. Distinctive orbital spines. Chelipeds not much thicker
than pereopods 2–5 except in larger males. Many strong setae
and hooked hairs, especially on spines.

On various substrata, down to 50 m; abundant on west and
south-west British coasts, less common in North Sea; elsewhere
south to Cape Verde, Mediterranean.

18 PARTHENOPIDAE

Very similar to the Majidae but chelipeds much larger than
other pereopods. Eyes small. Basal segment of antennal peduncle
not extended forward.

Only one British species.

Parthenope massena (Roux)   FIG. 10.23

Carapace, average length 14 mm, breadth 15 mm, brown or
brownish red. Small, knobbly crab with large chelae. Triangular
carapace with large inflated areas laterally; smoothly tuberculate.
Rostrum rounded-triangular, not bifid. Eyes bounded by post-
orbital spine. Chelipeds long, unequal, irregular; large tubercles
on outer surfaces; pereopods 2–5 slender.

A southern, sublittoral species (30–100 m) with northern limit
in Brittany and therefore to be expected in Channel Isles; elsewhere south to Congo, Mediterranean.

19 CORYSTIDAE

Burrowing crabs with the carapace longer than broad. Antennae
long, stiff, and hairy; interlocking to form a sand-proof inhalant
respiratory water tube.

One species in British waters.

Corystes cassivelaunus (Pennant).   FIG. 10.24
Masked Crab

Carapace, of large female, length 39 mm, breadth 29 mm; pale
red, grading into yellowish white. Dorsal surface minutely
granulated; markings sometimes give impression of a face; lateral
margin with four teeth, of which the second is largest. Chelipeds
of male more than twice length of carapace; those of female
about as long as carapace.

Sandy, soft bottoms, LWST to 90 m; all British coasts, very
common; elsewhere, Sweden to Portugal, Mediterranean.

20 ATELECYCLIDAE

Crabs with generally almost circular carapace. Anterio-lateral
margins with well-developed teeth.

| 1. Frontal region of carapace toothed | **2** |
| Frontal region of carapace without teeth | ***Thia scutellata*** |

---

2. Carapace covered with coarse granules bearing
hairs; merus of maxilliped 3 as long as ischium;
carapace wider than long   **Atelecyclus undecimdentatus**

Carapace with only very small granulations, confined
to gastric region and with very few hairs; merus of
maxilliped 3 much shorter than ischium, carapace at
most slightly wider than long   **Atelecyclus rotundatus**

Atelecyclus rotundatus (Olivi)   FIG. 10.18

Carapace length 28 (39) mm. Reddish brown, legs light brown;
chelae fingers black. Carapace almost circular, about as broad
as long, with numerous, short, transverse, granular striae; front
with three acute teeth, central the longest; anterio-lateral margin
with nine to eleven acute teeth with tuberculate edges. Chelipeds
equal, male with two spines on upper edge of manus. Pereopods
2–5 moderately developed, slightly flattened.

Sandy and gravel bottoms, sublittoral, 12–300 m; probably
all British coasts, not uncommon; elsewhere Norway to South
Africa.

Atelecyclus undecimdentatus (Herbst)   FIG. 10.18

Carapace length up to 50 mm; broadly oval, much broader than
long, dorsal surface tuberculate and thinly clothed in short hairs;
front with three small acute lobes; anterio-lateral margins with
nine to eleven acute teeth with tuberculate edges. Lateral
margins of carapace densely hairy. Chelipeds equal, compressed.
Pereopods 2–5 moderately well-developed.

Sublittoral (rarely LWST) to 30 m. English Channel, rare;
elsewhere, south to West Africa, Mediterranean.

Thia scutellata (Fabricius)   FIG. 10.18

Carapace length 20(22) mm; pale pink, with brown markings.
Carapace heart-shaped, slightly broader than long, convex,
smooth, with densely setose margins; front faintly three-lobed;
eyes and orbits very small; anterio-lateral margins with three
or four indistinct teeth. Chelipeds equal, slightly compressed.
Pereopods 2–5 compressed, hairy.

LWST and shallow sublittoral to 45 m; burrowing in sand
and mud; all British coasts (and North Sea?), not uncommon;
elsewhere, Sweden, Holland to West Africa, Mediterranean.

21 CANCRIDAE

Carapace wide and oval; front to lateral border lobed (or
toothed).

| 1. Carapace edged with rounded lobes | ***Cancer pagurus*** |
| Carapace lobes with small sharp teeth | ***Cancer bellianus*** |

Cancer pagurus Linnaeus. 'Edible Crab'   FIG. 10.24
of commerce

Carapace, of typical male, up to length 92 mm, breadth 150 mm,
large specimens up to breadth of 250 mm; reddish brown; chela
fingers black. The wide, oblong-shaped carapace is distinctively

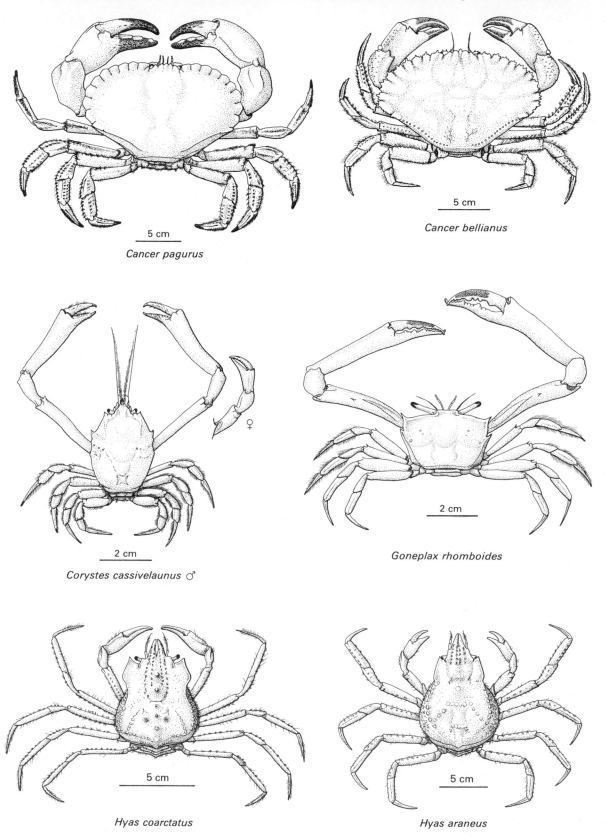

Cancer pagurus

Cancer bellianus

Corystes cassivelaunus ♂

Goneplax rhomboides

Hyas coarctatus

Hyas araneus

Fig. 10.24

marked along its fronto-lateral margins with ten rounded lobes; the surface is smooth and bald with a row of granules parallel to lateral margins. Chelae slightly unequal in shape and toothing; somewhat smaller in females. Tufts of stiff hairs in rows on pereopods, dactyls ending in spine-like tips.

Mid-tide to shallow sublittoral (100 m); rocky bottoms; all British coasts, abundant; elsewhere, north Norway to West Africa, Mediterranean.

Cancer bellianus Johnson   FIG. 10.24

Carapace of typical adult male, length 95 mm, breadth 147 mm; pale brown, spotted red. The ten marginal lobes each furnished with about three or four sharp teeth; surface rougher than *C. pagurus*. Cheliped carpus with two spines on upper margin; outer surface of carpus and manus tuberculate; dactyl furrowed. Pereopods more uniformly hairy than in *C. pagurus*.

Subtropical; sublittoral, shelf and upper continental slope 37–620 m; off west coasts of British Isles; elsewhere, Shetland to Portugal.

22 PORTUNIDAE

Carapace usually broader than long, broadest at last pair of anterio-lateral teeth; front margin usually with an uneven number of teeth, often three; usually five anterio-lateral teeth, but up to nine. Eyes and orbits prominent. Carpus of chelipeds usually with strong acute carpal processs. Dactyl of last pereopod usually flattened, often oval-shaped forming a paddle used for swimming.

Four subfamilies are recognized here:-

Pirimelinae (one species): carapace slightly broader than long, fronto-lateral margin with five teeth; frontal margin three-lobed. Dactyl of all pereopods including, last, conical rather than flattened.

Portuninae (one species): carapace very broad, with four to nine teeth. Chelipeds long and robust, usually longer than second pereopod.

Polybiinae (eleven species): carapace not particularly broad; three to five anterio-lateral teeth. Ridges on endostome continue on to epistome. Dactyl of last pereopod sub-oval to lanceolate.

Carcininae (three species): carapace not particularly broad; four or five anterio-lateral teeth. Ridges on endostome do not continue on to epistome. At least one pair of pereopods longer than chelipeds.

---

1. Carapace with nine teeth each side   ***Callinectes sapidus***

   Carapace with five teeth each side   **2**

2. Dactyl of pereopods 2–4 slightly flattened   **5**

   Dactyl of pereopods 2–4 long and conical   **3**

3. Dactyl of pereopod 5 narrowly conical, as other dactyls   ***Pirimela denticulata***

   Dactyl of pereopod 5 flattened   **4**

4. Dactyl of pereopod 5 slightly broader than that of pereopods 2–4   ***Carcinus maenas***

   Dactyl of pereopod 5 broad and flat   **6**

5. Carapace slightly longer than wide, weakly toothed, but front trilobed   ***Portumnus latipes***

   Carapace wider than long, strongly toothed, but front with single strong tooth, not trilobed   ***Xaiva biguttata***

6. Front with even number of teeth, last lateral tooth long and pointed   **8**

   Front with odd number of teeth, or many small irregular teeth, or none   **7**

7. Pereopods 2–4 with broad and flattened dactyl   ***Polybius henslowi***

   Dactyl of pereopods 2–4 long and conical   **9**

8. Front of carapace simple; manus of chela with two carinae, one of which bears a single tooth   ***Bathynectes longipes***

   Front of carapace with four teeth; manus of chela with five longitudinal carinae armed with teeth   ***Bathynectes superba***

9. Front of carapace with seven to ten unequal teeth   ***Liocarcinus puber***

   Front with three teeth or lobes, or toothless   **10**

10. Front entire (toothless)   ***Liocarcinus arcuatus***

    Front with three lobes or teeth   **11**

11. Front with three blunt lobes, the middle one longest   **12**

    Front with three teeth which may be blunt or sharp, all similar   **13**

12. Front projecting; dactyl of pereopod 5 without distinct median rib; carapace usually smooth and almost hairless   ***Liocarcinus pusillus***

    Front lobed, not projecting; dactyl of pereopod 5 with strong median rib; carapace and parts of limbs covered by transverse rows of hairs arising from crenulated streaks   ***Liocarcinus corrugatus***

13. The fifth anterio-lateral tooth of carapace at least twice as long as others; carapace wide and tuberculate   ***Macropipus tuberculatus***

    Posterior anterio-lateral tooth not markedly different from others   **14**

14. Carapace with minute rows of hairs arising from transverse granular lines   ***Liocarcinus depurator***

    Carapace smooth   **15**

15. Front with three similar teeth, the middle often the shortest; cheliped carpus has no tooth on outer edge   ***Liocarcinus marmoreus***

Middle of three front teeth just longest; cheliped carpus with tooth at outer angle **Liocarcinus holsatus**

Subfamily **Pirimelinae**

Pirimela denticulata (Montagu) FIG. 10.25

Carapace length 15 mm, breadth 18 mm; blackish violet, margins red, whitish tubercles; chelipeds and legs banded brown and yellow. Carapace slightly broader than long, minutely granular; frontal margin with pronounced, rounded acute, median lobe, and smaller acute sub-median lobes. Orbits with well-marked fissures; five prominent, cristate, acute teeth on anterio-lateral margins. Chelipeds equal; rather small, especially in females; carpal processes small. Pereopods slightly compressed.

LWST to 180 m, gravel and sand; all British coasts, common; elsewhere, Norway to West Africa, Mediterranean.

Subfamily **Portuninae**

Callinectes sapidus Rathbun. Blue Crab FIG. 10.25
of U.S.

Carapace length 77 (90) mm, breadth (including spines 177 (225) mm. Greyish or bluish-green; red points to spines and fingers. Carapace breadth more than twice length; surface granular; front with two low, triangular lobes and a downward deflected, acute median lobe, also inner orbital teeth; fronto-lateral edge with nine teeth, the last much longer than others. Chelipeds strong, merus armed with three stout spines; outer surface of propodus with five strong keels. Pereopods 2–5 flattened; pereopod 5 with paddle-shaped propodus and dactyl, length/breadth ratio of dactyl 2.3, rounded terminally.

Various shallow substrata. A north-east American species, introduced in Europe; scattered records from Denmark to Mediterranean. Firmly established in east Mediterranean.

Subfamily **Polybiinae**

Polybius henslowi Leach FIG. 10.25

Carapace length 39 (44) mm. Reddish brown. Carapace flat and circular, slightly broader than long; five low broad teeth on anterio-lateral margin; five nearly similar teeth on front between orbits. Antennae short. Chelipeds strong, equal; carpus with sharp spike. Pereopods 2–5 flattened, dactyl always quite broad; propodus and dactyl of last pereopod paddle-shaped, length/breadth ratio 1.7, obtusely rounded terminally.

Truly a swimming crab; shallow inshore waters. British Isles: especially south coasts, common; elsewhere to Morocco, Mediterranean.

Bathynectes maravigna (Prestandrea) FIG. 10.25

Carapace length about 44 mm, breadth about 70 mm. Lively orange-red. Carapace broader than long, finely granular; front with bifid median lobe flanked by rounded sub-median lobes; five anterio-lateral teeth, the last much longer than the others. Chelipeds slightly unequal; two keels on upper side of propodus, outer with up to nine spines; carpus elaborately spined. Pereopods 2–4 slender; 5 with flattened, broadly lanceolate dactyl, length/breadth ratio 2:7; sharply pointed.

Shelf and slope species, 200–1500 m; Shetland, Irish Sea, Hebrides, not uncommon; elsewhere, Norway, Faeroes, to South-West Africa, Mediterranean; in western Atlantic from Florida to Massachusetts.

Bathynectes longipes (Risso) FIG. 10.25

Carapace length 16(24) mm, breadth about 24 mm. Brilliant reddish brown, sometimes blotched. Similar shape and texture to *B. maravigna*. Front with four barely discernible lobes; teeth on anterio-lateral border curved forwards; last one less than twice length of others. Chelipeds unequal; outer keel of upper surface of propodus lacking spines; carpus lacking the numerous spines of *B. maravigna*. Pereopods 2–4 slender; 5 with narrowly paddle-shaped dactyl, length/breadth ratio 3.7 sharply pointed.

Offshore 20–150 m, sand; south coasts of Britain, Bristol Channel, rare; elsewhere south to North Africa, Mediterranean.

Liocarcinus puber (Linnaeus). Velvet Fiddler FIG. 10.26
or Devil Crab

Carapace length 50 (65) mm, breadth about 66 mm. Blue, obscured by brown pubescence, red prominences. Carapace dorsal surface flattened and pubescent; frontal margin with up to ten narrow unequal teeth, middle two often larger; anterio-lateral margin with five sharp, forward-pointing teeth. Chelipeds equal, strong, pubescent; spine on outer margin of carpus as well as usual spike-like carpal process; smaller spines on anterior edge of carpus; propodus with keels formed of transverse row of tubercles. Pereopods 2–5 strong with keels on outer segments; dactyl of last pereopod flattened, lanceolate, length/breadth ratio 2.7, sharply pointed with median keel.

On stony and rock substrata; intertidal and shallow water, occasionally to 70 m. All British coasts, widespread and very common; elsewhere west Norway to West Africa, Mediterranean, Black Sea.

Liocarcinus arcuatus (Leach) FIG. 10.26

Carapace length 22 (29) mm, breadth about 30 mm; brown, limbs lighter. Carapace gently convex, with minute transverse ridges; frontal margin between eyes entirely without teeth, hairy; five teeth of anterio-lateral margin alternating in size, third the largest. Chelipeds equal, rather smooth. Pereopods 2–5 moderately developed; dactyl of last pereopod flattened, narrowly lanceolate, length/breadth ratio 2.8, bluntly pointed.

On sandy and stony substrata, 2–108 m; south and west coasts of British Isles, common.

Liocarcinus corrugatus (Pennant) FIG. 10.26

Carapace length 33(43) mm, breadth about 41 mm. Brownish red with patches of red or yellow. Carapace with numerous, strong, transverse, hairy ridges; frontal margin with prominent, rounded, median lobe, flanked by broad sub-median lobes reaching the orbits; anterio-lateral teeth prominent and equal. Chelipeds equal, propodus with two keels on dorsal surface and three on outer face. Margins of pereopods 2–5 hairy, outer segments keeled; last pereopod robust, propodus rounded, dactyl lanceo-

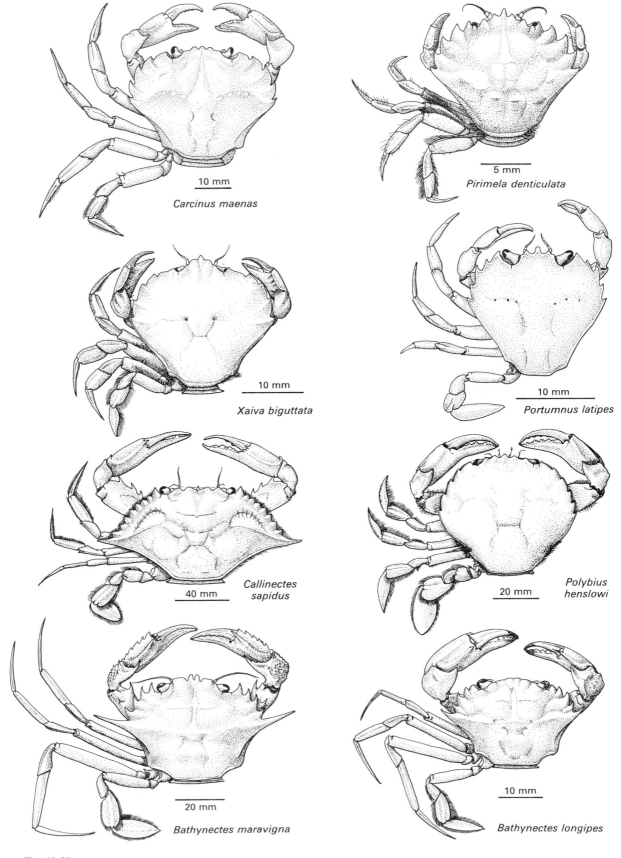

10 mm

Carcinus maenas

5 mm

Pirimela denticulata

10 mm

Xaiva biguttata

10 mm

Portumnus latipes

40 mm

Callinectes sapidus

20 mm

Polybius henslowi

20 mm

Bathynectes maravigna

10 mm

Bathynectes longipes

Fig. 10.25

late, keeled, and hairy, length/breadth 2.3, acutely pointed terminally.

On stones and gravel 1–100 m; south and west coasts of British Isles, uncommon; elsewhere south to North Africa, Mediterranean.

Liocarcinus pusillus (Leach) FIG. 10.26

Carapace length 20 (23) mm. Variable colour; yellow, variegated with red-brown to uniform brown. Carapace gently convex, smooth to granular; frontal margin protruding, with a low median lobe and broader sub-median lobes; teeth of anteriolateral margin slightly unequal, the fifth sharply acute, the others slightly rounded, arranged as two pairs. Chelipeds equal, carpal process acute but not greatly extended. Pereopods 2–5 of moderate build; propodus and dactyl of last pereopod paddle-shaped, dactyl without median carina, length/breadth ratio 2.9, with acute tip.

On stones, gravel, and rough ground, also sand; intertidal to 100 m; all British coasts, common; elsewhere, north Norway to West Africa, Canaries, Mediterranean.

Liocarcinus depurator (Linnaeus). Swimming Crab
FIG. 10.26

Carapace length about 40 mm, breadth about 51 mm. Pale reddish-brown, tip of last pereopod violet. Carapace relatively flat, with numerous transverse, hairy, crenulations; front of carapace with a median lobe slightly more prominent than two similar flanking lobes; orbits wide; teeth of anterio-lateral margin acute, slightly curved; posterior margin of carapace broad. Chelipeds equal; outer margin of carpus with two obtuse lobes; carpal process long and acute. Pereopods 2–4 of rather slight build, pereopod 5 strongly paddle-shaped, dactyl lacking a keel, length/breadth ratio 2.0, obtuse or rounded terminally.

Soft, sandy and mixed bottoms, LWST to 450 m; all British coasts, very common; elsewhere, Norway to West Africa, Mediterranean.

Liocarcinus holsatus (Fabricius) FIG. 10.26

Carapace length 30 (37) mm, breadth about 38 mm. Brownish grey, tinged with green. Very similar to *L. depurator* but lacking transverse crenulations on carapace; three similar-sized lobes on frontal margin, central one sometimes shortest; orbits smaller than in *L. depurator*; last tooth of fronto-lateral margin projects laterally; posterior edge of carapace narrower than in *L. depurator*. Chelipeds equal, stout; outer margin of carpus with two obtuse lobes and an acute lobe at posterior angle; long sharp carpal process. Pereopods 2–5 of rather slight build; merus of last pereopod not extending beyond mid-point of merus of pereopod 4; dactyl of pereopod 4 sub-oval, length/breadth ratio 1.9, faint median keel, acute termination.

On hard and mixed bottoms; 6–350 m; all British coasts, widespread and often very common; elsewhere north Norway to Spain and Canaries; not Mediterranean. Host to the parasitic cirripede *Sacculina carcini* in some areas.

Liocarcinus marmoreus (Leach) FIG. 10.26

Carapace length 30 (35) mm, breadth about 35 mm. Marbling patterns of reddish yellow, light brown. Carapace surface smooth; frontal margin with three similar-sized lobes; teeth of fronto-lateral margins similar. Chelipeds equal, moderately built; outer margin of carpus without strong processes; carpal process robust and acute. Pereopods rather slight; merus of last pereopod extending beyond middle of merus of pereopod 4; dactyl of last pereopod with a faint keel; length/breadth ratio 2.3, obtuse or rounded extremity.

On fine sand and gravel, LWST to 200 m; east and west coasts of British Isles, common; elsewhere Denmark to Spain and Azores. Apparently replaced by closely related species in Mediterranean.

Macropipus tuberculatus (Roux) FIG. 10.26

Carapace length about 34 mm, breadth about 56 mm. Yellowish grey with scattered pink bands or spots. Carapace relatively broad and flat, surface coarsely tuberculate; front with three similar acute teeth, central one longest; orbits with marked V-shaped incision; anterio-lateral margin with four similar acute teeth, followed by a much longer, laterally directed fifth tooth. Chelipeds equal; moderately developed; carpus with a very long acute carpal process, and a spine on outer margin. Pereopods 2–5 long and thin; paddle-shaped last pereopod with two keels on propodus and one on dactyl, length/breadth ratio of dactyl 2.1; termination barely acute.

Offshore, 80–400 m; off west coasts of British Isles; elsewhere west Norway to north Spain, Azores, Mediterranean.

Subfamily **Carcininae**

Carcinus maenas (Linnaeus). Shore Crab, FIG. 10.25
Green Crab

Carapace length 55 (60) mm, breadth about 73 mm; males slightly larger than females, maximum size (after terminal anecdysis) varies with locality. Colour variable, adults dark green, mottled to grey, with green or puce (brick-red) legs and underside; juveniles variable, often speckled or with central white or black triangle or other strong pattern. Carapace much broader than long, minutely granular; frontal margin with three gently rounded lobes, central one slightly advanced, flanked on each side by a lower smaller prominence which forms the mesial angle of the orbit; orbital margin incised; five teeth on anterio-lateral margin conspicuous and sharp. Chelipeds unequal, carpal process acutely pointed, outer margin of carpus not spiny. Pereopods 2–5 smooth; moderately strong dactyl of last pereopod scarcely wider than first three but compressed with setose margin.

Ubiquitous intertidally, including splash zone pools, saltmarshes, and estuaries, also in shallow sublittoral down to 200 m; all British coasts, abundant; elsewhere north Norway and Iceland to West Africa, north-east Americas and Indo-west Pacific.

Sacculina carcini, a parasitic cirripede is common, especially on sublittoral specimens.

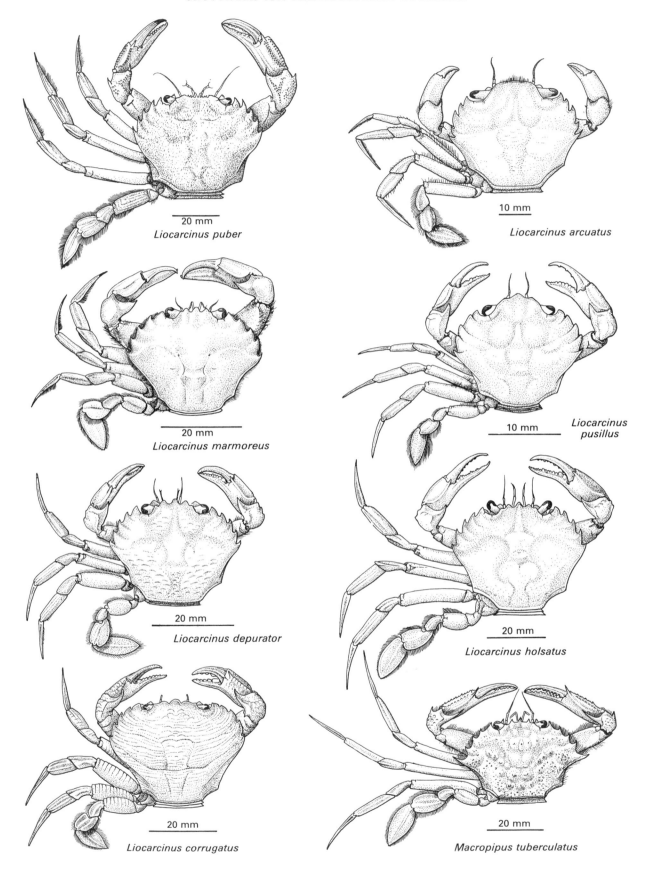

20 mm
Liocarcinus puber

10 mm
Liocarcinus arcuatus

20 mm
Liocarcinus marmoreus

10 mm
Liocarcinus pusillus

20 mm
Liocarcinus depurator

20 mm
Liocarcinus holsatus

20 mm
Liocarcinus corrugatus

20 mm
Macropipus tuberculatus

Fig. 10.26

Xaiva biguttata (Risso)   FIG. 10.25

Carapace length about 23 mm, breadth about 23 mm. Colour variable, dull greenish yellow to white with large brown patches; dactyl sometimes violet. Carapace only slightly wider than long; frontal margin protrudes as three obtusely rounded lobes, the median slightly in advance; orbits and eyes small; the first of five anterio-lateral teeth has a concave outer face. Chelipeds equal; inner edge of carpus hairy. Pereopods 2–5 of moderate build; propodus of pereopod 4 wide, with cristate outer margin. Last pereopod lanceolate, dactyl bearing a median keel.

On gravel and sand, intertidal or shallow sublittoral; south and west coasts of British Isles, sparse; elsewhere south to Cape Verde, Mediterranean.

Portumnus latipes (Pennant)   FIG. 10.25

Carapace length about 20 mm; reddish with white shading. Carapace as broad as long, heart-shaped, smooth; frontal margin with three small sub-acute teeth, the median slightly in advance; orbits large; fourth of the five anterio-lateral teeth small. Chelipeds slightly unequal; dorsal edge of carpus and chela sharp and hairy. Pereopods 2–5 flattened, edges hairy; dactyl of last pereopod broadly lanceolate, length/breadth ratio 2.9, with rounded acute tip.

Sandy bottoms, LWST to shallow sublittoral, 150 m; all British coasts, except for north, common; elsewhere, North Sea to North Africa, Mediterranean, Black Sea.

23 XANTHIDAE

Carapace broader than long; oval or sub-rectangular. Frontal region broad.

1. Outer surface of cheliped carpus spiny or tuberculated   **2**

   Chelipeds without spines or tubercles on carpus   **5**

2. Carapace largely covered by hairs   **3**

   Carapace not hairy   **4**

3. Manus of major cheliped almost entirely smooth, no distal spine on carpus of pereopods 2–5
   Pilumnus hirtellus

   Manus of major cheliped spiny on its outer face; pereopods 2–5 all with spine at distal end of carpus
   Pilumnus spinifer

4. Front two-thirds of carapace covered by large irregular tubercles   **Pilumnoides perlatus**

   Surface of carapace sculptured but not tuberculate
   Monodaeus couchi

5. Anterio-lateral margin of carapace with five teeth, the first forming the outer angle of the orbit   **6**

   Anterio-lateral margin of carapace with four teeth similarly counted   **7**

6. Pereopods 2–5 have thick fringe of hairs on carpus (and merus)   **Xantho pilipes**

   Pereopods 2–5 have very few hairs on carpus
   Xantho incisus

7. Basal segment of antenna (articles 2 and 3) not in contact with margin of front   **Rhithropanopeus harrisii**

   Basal segment of antenna in contact with front
   Neopanope sayi

Pilumnoides perlatus (Poeppig)   FIG. 10.27

Carapace length 9 (18) mm. Dark brown, whitish, posteriorly brownish; chelipeds of small specimens grey, fingers brown or olive. Carapace almost circular, convex; anterior two-thirds tuberculate; front broad, bilobed; anterio-lateral margin with about eight, sometimes bilobed, teeth. Basal segment of antenna (article 2) not in contact with front margin of carapace. Chelipeds large, unequal, with tuberculate chela and carpus. Pereopods 2–5 strong and distally hairy.

Exotic species from South America, occasionally introduced by shipping to European ports.

Pilumnus hirtellus (Linnaeus)   FIG. 10.27

Carapace length 9 (15) mm. Brownish red (or purplish); fingers light brown; legs banded purple and yellowish white. Carapace broader than long, convex, smooth with conspicuous club-shaped setae; front straight, with median notch and serrated edges. Anterio-lateral margin with five unequal, sharp, teeth. Chelipeds large and very unequal, carpus spiny; manus of larger chela smooth or slightly tuberculate; manus of smaller chela always tuberculate or spiny. Pereopods 2–5 quite strong; carpus rarely with small distal spine. Chelipeds and legs with long club-shaped setae.

Rock and stony bottoms, LWNT to 70 m; all British coasts, very common intertidally; elsewhere, west Norway to north Africa, Cape Verde, Mediterranean, Black Sea.

Pilumnus spinifer Milne Edwards   FIG. 10.27

Carapace, of typical female, length 9 mm, breadth, 12 mm. Similar to *P. hirtellus*. Front margin curved and more deeply serrated. Both chelipeds, including dactyl, spiny. Pereopods 2–5 all with sharp distal spine on carpus.

North African and Mediterranean species; occasionally shipborne to north European ports.

Rhithropanopeus harrisii (Gould)   FIG. 10.27

Carapace, of typical male, length 12 mm, breadth 15 mm. Yellowish green, with black spots. Fingers of chelipeds whitish. Carapace hexagonal, front edge straight and bearing two rows of minute tubercles; four low teeth to anterio-lateral margin. Basal segment of antennal peduncle (article 2) touching front margin. Chelipeds unequal, rather smooth. Margins of pereopods 2–5 hairy.

North-east American, brackish water, species introduced into south Baltic, Dutch and other European estuaries, and particularly docks warmed by power station effluents, e.g. Swansea and Southampton.

Neopanope sayi (Smith)   FIG. 10.27

Carapace length 13 (23) m. Generally reddish brown; fingers of chelae dark brown to black. Carapace oval, convex, minutely granular; front convexly curved, with small median notch; four cristate teeth to anterio-lateral margin. Basal segment (article 2) of antenna in contact with carapace front. Chelipeds very unequal in male only; smooth but minutely tuberculate.

North American species introduced into various European coastal situations frequented by shipping. Flourished in dock at Swansea at a time when this received warm power-station effluent.

Monodaeus couchi (Couch)   FIG. 10.27

Carapace length 13 (18) mm. Reddish brown, yellowish grey below, cheliped fingers black or brown. Carapace oval, relatively flat, with tiny transverse tubercle rows; front relatively straight, with very small median notch; anterio-lateral margin with four strong, tuberculate, acute teeth. Chelipeds quite stout, unequal (in male); carpus and propodus with tuberculate keels. Pereopods 2–5 with spinulate merus; distal segments densely hairy.

On sand, sandy mud, and gravel, 10–100 m, south and south-west coasts, British coasts, Irish Sea, rare; elsewhere, south to Cape Verde and Azores, Mediterranean.

Xantho pilipes Milne Edwards   FIG. 10.27

Carapace length 15 (21) mm. Yellowish with red markings, fingers of chelipeds brown. Carapace oval, flat, widest at last anterio-lateral tooth; front almost straight, with faint median notch; anterio-lateral margin with four, more or less obtuse teeth, all hairy on underside, last two with fringed hairs, last three separated by inward running grooves. Chelipeds stout, slightly unequal. Pereopods 2–5 stout, slightly flattened; margins of merus, carpus, and propodus of pereopods 4 and 5 fringed with long hairs.

Stone, shell, and sand bottoms, LWST to 110 m; Shetland and all west coasts, south coast as far as Suffolk, very common; elsewhere, west Norway, Sweden to West Africa, Mediterranean.

Xantho incisus Leach   FIG. 10.27

Carapace length 16 (22) mm. Yellowish brown with darker patches, fingers of chelipeds black. Very similar to *X. pilipes*. Anterio-lateral teeth more obtuse, none fringed with hairs. Carapace often widest at fourth tooth. Pereopods 2–5 with margins of merus, carpus, and propodus bald or at most sparsely setose.

On rocky shores, LWST to 40 m; more southern than last species, south and west British coasts, widespread and often abundant; elsewhere south to Cape Verde, Azores and Canaries, Mediterranean.

24 GERYONIDAE

Carapace broader than long. Anterio-lateral margins with three to five teeth. Last leg longer than cheliped.

| 1. | Anterio-lateral margin with three teeth | ***Geryon tridens*** |
| | Anterio-lateral margin with five teeth | ***Geryon affinis*** |

Geryon tridens Krøyer   FIG. 10.28

Carapace length 40 (80) mm. Reddish brown, legs lighter. Carapace surface faintly rough; front with four low teeth, outer ones representing mesial angle of orbit. Chelipeds slightly unequal, moderately stout. Pereopods 2–5 long and thin, dactyl strongly depressed.

On soft bottoms, offshore, 82–1500 m; south of Ireland; elsewhere north Norway to North Sea, Biscay, Mediterranean. Usually deeper further south.

Geryon affinis Milne Edwards and Bouvier   FIG. 10.28

Carapace length about 155 mm. Dull yellowish with patches of red and brown, dactyl edged dark brown. Carapace surface punctuate and tuberculate; front with four acute teeth, outer ones representing mesial angle of orbit. Chelipeds slightly unequal, moderately stout. Pereopods 2–5 long and thin, dactyl not strongly depressed.

Deep water, continental slope species, 400–2000 m; reported off Rockall; elsewhere Iceland, Norway (rare), to West and South Africa; Florida; south Atlantic; Indian Ocean.

25 GONEPLACIDAE

Crabs with a wide rectangular carapace and very long chelipeds. One species in British waters.

Goneplax rhomboides (Linnaeus)   FIG. 10.24

Carapace, of typical male, length 20 mm, breadth 34 mm, cheliped 100 m; female, length 11 mm, breadth 18 mm. Reddish yellow. Carapace rectangular, with prominent spines at front corners; central margin flat and smooth. Eyes on long retractable peduncles. Chelipeds of males four or five times length of carapace; shorter in female.

Burrows in muddy sand; 8–80 m; all British coasts, common; elsewhere, south to South Africa, Mediterranean.

26 PINNOTHERIDAE

Carapace often thin and translucent. Eyes small. Ischium of maxilliped 3 sometimes fused with merus. Commensal with other invertebrates.

1.	Carapace more or less round. Ischium and merus of maxilliped 3 fused; dactyl sub-terminal	**2**
	Carapace angular. Maxilliped 3 with no fusion of merus and ischium, dactyl terminal	
		Asthenognathus atlanticus

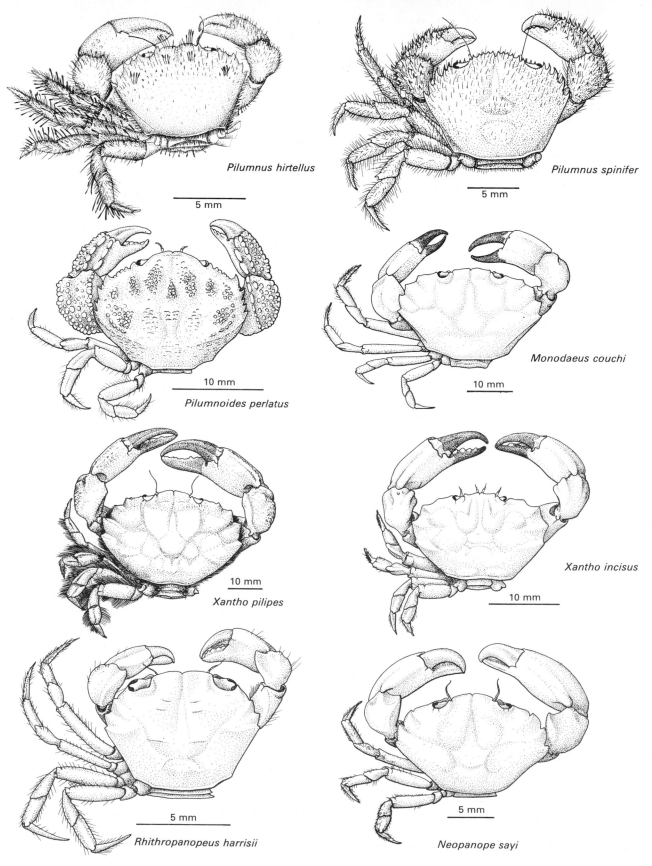

Pilumnus hirtellus

5 mm

Pilumnus spinifer

5 mm

Pilumnoides perlatus

10 mm

Monodaeus couchi

10 mm

Xantho pilipes

10 mm

Xantho incisus

10 mm

Rhithropanopeus harrisii

5 mm

Neopanope sayi

5 mm

Fig. 10.27

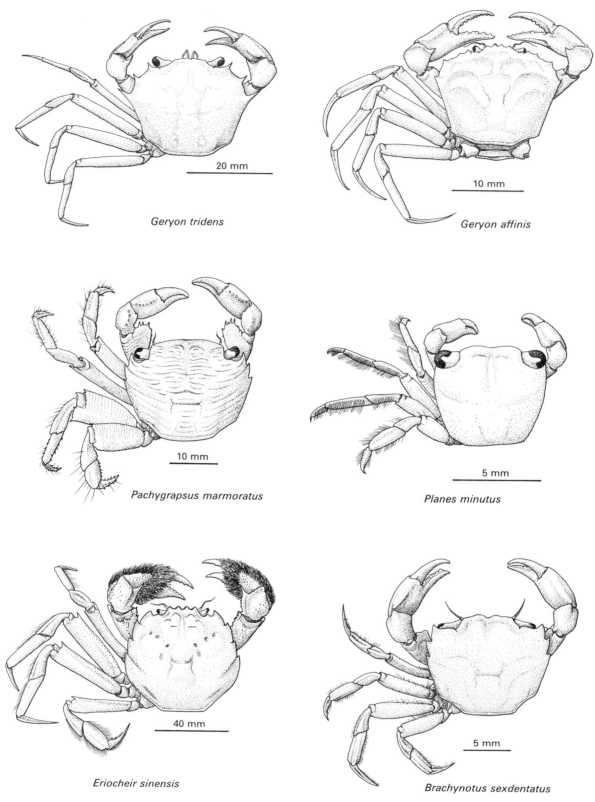

Geryon tridens

20 mm

Geryon affinis

10 mm

Pachygrapsus marmoratus

10 mm

Planes minutus

5 mm

Eriocheir sinensis

40 mm

Brachynotus sexdentatus

5 mm

Fig. 10.28

2. Dactyl of pereopods 2–5 strongly curved, half length of propodus. Front of male carapace extended forward **Pinnotheres pisum**

Dactyl of pereopods 2–5 only slightly curved, more than half length of propodus. Front of male carapace not extended **Pinnotheres pinnotheres**

Pinnotheres pisum (Linnaeus) FIG. 10.18

Carapace, of typical male, length 6 mm, female length 13 mm. Male pale yellowish grey with symmetrical darker markings. Female translucent, revealing yellow internal organs and red gonads. Carapace smooth. Antennae minute. Chelipeds equal. Pereopods 2–5 with short curved dactyl, not much more than half length of propodus. Male carapace hard, opaque with projecting front margin; chela with swollen manus; pereopods 2–5 with long setae when young. Female carapace translucent, front deflected downwards; chela manus not swollen; pereopods 2–5 slender with setose margins.

Parasitic; in mantle cavity of live lamellibranchs: *Modiolus modiolus* abundant; *Mytilus edulis* rare. Also occasional in *Spisula, Glycymeris, Venus* and *Venerupis*. All British coasts; elsewhere, Norway to West Africa and Mediterranean.

Pinnotheres pinnotheres (Linnaeus)

Carapace average length, male 7 mm, female 12 mm. Brown. Carapace smooth. Antennae minute. Chelipeds equal. Pereopods 2–5 with dactyl as long as propodus. Male carapace hard and opaque; front hardly projecting or deflected; pereopods 2–5 moderately stout and covered with long setae. Female carapace poorly calcified, soft, translucent; front deflected downwards; pereopods 2–5 slender.

Parasitic in mantle cavity of lamellibranchs: commonest in *Pinna*, also in *Modiolus* and oysters. Also in tunicates: *Ascidia mentula, Ascidiella aspersa*. South-west British Isles, scarce; elsewhere, south to Gabon, Mediterranean.

Asthenognathus atlanticus Monod

Carapace average length, male 8 mm; female 8.2 mm. Yellowish to brownish red, lateral regions sometimes bluish. Propodus of legs banded red. Carapace broad, minutely punctate; front slightly bifid when small. Antennae well-developed. Chelipeds equal. Pereopods 3 and 4 longer than 2 and 5; merus, carpus, and propodus broad. Chela with manus inflated in male; slender in female.

Commensal with *Amphitrite edwardsi*; probably in Channel Islands; elsewhere in France and south to Gulf of Guinea; rare. This species is described and figured by Ingle (1980).

27 GRAPSIDAE

Carapace usually more or less rectangular; lateral margins not clearly separable into anterior and posterior regions. Two subfamilies:-

Grapsinae: carapace front strongly deflected. Pronounced ventral notch on outer margin of orbit. Lower edge of orbit curves down to buccal frame. Inner margins of third maxillipeds separated by a wide rhomboid-shaped gap.

Varuninae: carapace front only moderately deflected. No notch at outer margin of orbit; ventral margin usually with suborbital crest. Third maxillipeds separated by a rather narrow rhomboid-shaped gap.

---

1. Lateral notch at lower side of orbit margin **2**

No lateral notch to lower side of orbit margin **3**

2. Carapace distinctly striated; margin with three teeth **Pachygrapsus marmoratus**

Carapace almost smooth; margin with two teeth **Planes minutus**

3. Mat of hairs on manus of chela; carapace narrowing anteriorly **Eriocheir sinensis**

Manus of chela without mat of hairs; carapace narrowing posteriorly **Brachynotus sexdentatus**

Subfamily **Grapsinae**

Pachygrapsus marmoratus (Fabricius) FIG. 10.28

Carapace length 22 (36) mm. Violet brown to almost black; variable patterning of yellow brown. Carapace almost square, slightly broader than long; with distinct gently oblique striae; frontal edge almost straight, wide, unnotched; three acute teeth on lateral margin. Chelipeds equal, large. Pereopods 2–5 with prominent merus, with keeled upper edge and distal spine; dactyl with small spines.

Essentially a Mediterranean species; has occurred in the area intertidally.

Planes minutus (Linnaeus). Gulf Weed Crab FIG. 10.28

Carapace length 10(17.5) mm. Variable colour; mottled with light greenish-yellow on darker olive ground-colour, imitating *Sargassum* encrusted with patches of Bryozoa. Carapace almost square; front wide, faintly blotched; one lateral spine. Chelipeds equal, smooth; merus serrated terminally. Pereopods 2–5 with lower edges of propodus and dactyl spiny, upper edges with fringe of setae.

Associated with floating 'Gulf Weed' (*Sargassum* spp.), pieces of which are occasionally cast ashore on European coasts, from the Channel coasts to Portugal and Mediterranean. Native in Sargasso Sea, Florida Straits.

Subfamily **Varuninae**

Eriocheir sinensis Milne Edwards FIG. 10.28

Carapace length 56 (62) mm. Greyish green to dark brown, legs lighter. Carapace almost square, convex; front with four conspicuous teeth separated by three curved notches, the central deepest; four lateral teeth; both frontal and lateral teeth themselves finely serrate. Chelipeds robust, equal, carpus process long and sharp; palm with dense tuft of long setae. Legs with distal spine on merus; outer segments fringed with setae.

Freshwater, river crab; returns to saline water in estuaries for breeding; British Isles: River Thames, River Ouse, rare; elsewhere Baltic Sea to France; introduced to Europe in 1912 by shipping trade with China. A pest species, causing damage to river banks and fishing nets.

Brachynotus sexdentatus (Risso)   FIG. 10.28
Carapace length 10 (18) mm. Olive-green, speckled with black, chelipeds and legs light olive or grey, mottled black. Carapace broader than long, convex; frontal region wide and faintly bilobed; orbits wide; three lateral teeth. Chelipeds equal; much larger in male. Pereopods 2–5 thin, slightly hairy.

Mediterranean species, littoral to 90 m. British Isles: survives in docks warmed by power station effluents; presumably introduced by shipping; previously at Swansea.

11 CHELICERATA, UNIRAMIA, AND TARDIGRADA

A. CHELICERATA

Class Arachnida

Order Pseudoscorpiones

PSEUDOSCORPIONS have a superficial resemblance to true scorpions, with their characteristic, large, chelate pedipalps. However, they differ from true scorpions in their size (all British species are under 4 mm long), and the fact that they lack a telson and sting. All are predatory.

The body is divided into two regions (Fig. 11.1), namely an anterior *prosoma* bearing two pairs of *ocelli* (= eyes), and the body appendages; and a posterior *opisthosoma*. The prosoma is armoured dorsally by a *carapace* bearing the ocelli, the anterior margin is often serrated forming a species characteristic *epistome*. Ventrally, the prosoma is armoured by the leg *coxae*. The first pair of body appendages are the *chelicerae*—complex two segmented pre-oral structures; basically they comprise a large basal segment which is produced to form a *fixed digit*, and a subapical *moveable digit* which extends parallel with the fixed digit and acts against it to form a chelate pincer. The two digits are ornamented with a number of structures, including *serrula interior* and *flagellum* on the fixed digit; and *serrula exterior* and *galea* on the moveable digit (Fig. 11.1). The complexity of the chelicerae is a result of their carrying out a number of varied roles, they not only function during feeding, but also in silk production and grooming.

The mouth lies posterior to the chelicerae, and is protected ventrally by the *palp coxae*—the basal segments of the conspicuous pedipalps (Fig. 11.1). The palps are six-segmented and terminate in a large chela, comprising a basal *hand* which extends to form a fixed digit; and a moveable digit or *finger*. The palps have a number of functions, including sensory (they are equipped with sensory *trichobothria*), prey capture, and immobilization (in some species the palps may have venom glands), and they have a variety of social functions (including mating, defence, fighting, and nest building). Behind the palps are four pairs of walking legs, with five to seven segments, including immoveable basal *coxa, trochanter, femur* (1 and 2), *tibia*, (*metatarsus*) and *tarsus* (Fig. 11.1); the tip of the tarsus or *pretarsus* is equipped with two *claws* and an *arolium* (Fig. 11.1).

The opisthosoma is distinctly segmented, bears no appendages, and is broadly fused to the cephalothorax, it is armoured with twelve pairs of dorsal *tergites* and ten pairs of ventral *sternites*, separated by lateral *pleural membranes*. The *genital orifice* is between sternites 2 and 3, with the second forming the *genital operculum* (Fig. 11.1). Sexual dimorphism is obscure, often only indicated by a more elaborate cheliceral galea in the female.

A detailed account of the biology of the group is given by Weygoldt (1969).

Several families have been recorded from the littoral zone throughout the world, usually associated with air pockets in crevices, etc. (Roth and Brown 1976); however, only three species, representing two families, have been recorded from British shores (Evans and Browning 1954).

TECHNIQUES

Collection, preparation, and preservation is basically similar to that described for the smaller Araneae, except that a hammer and chisel may be required to find *Neobisium maritimum* in littoral crevices.

KEY TO BRITISH LITTORAL PSEUDOSCORPIONS

1. All legs with two tarsal segments; palp finger as long as hand; over 3 mm long
   Neobisium maritimum

   Legs 1 and 2 with one tarsal segment, 3 and 4 with two; palp finger longer than hand; always under 2 mm long **2**

2. Teeth on fixed digit of palp small, truncate, and set close together; epistome present; posterior eyes smaller than anterior pair   ***Chthonius halberti***

Teeth on fixed digit of palp large, triangular, and widely separated; epistome absent; all eyes large   ***Chthonius tetrachelatus***

REFERENCES

Evans, G. O. and Browning, E. (1954). Pseudoscorpiones. *Synopses of the British Fauna*, No. 10. Linnean Society, London.

Roth, V. D. and Brown, W. D. (1976). Other intertidal air-breathing arthropods. In: *Marine insects*, (ed. L. Cheng). North-Holland Publishing Co., Amsterdam and Oxford.

Weygoldt, P. (1969). *The biology of Pseudoscorpions.* Harvard University Press, Cambridge, Mass.

1 NEOBISIIDAE

Neobisium maritimum (Leach)   FIG. 11.1

This species is by far the most common on British shores, easily identified by its size, and the features outlined in the key.

Occurs in crevices in the littoral zone, to below MTL. Frequently found in silk cocoons where it hibernates in winter, moults, or broods eggs.

South and west coasts only.

2 CHTHONIIDAE

Chthonius halberti Kew   FIG. 11.1

Length 1.2 mm. Characters as outlined in the key; in addition the fixed digit of the palp is nearly twice as long as the hand.

Only recorded from Eire, the type locality, where it was found in the upper littoral and supralittoral zones.

Chthonius tetrachelatus (Preyssler)   FIG. 11.1

Length 1.3–1.9 mm. Characters as outlined in the key; in addition, the fixed digit of the palp is longer than the hand, and the dorsal surface of the hand has a distinct depression.

Occasionally occurs in the supralittoral among tidal debris, but is common in non-littoral habitats. Widely distributed throughout Britain.

Order Araneae

The Araneae, or spiders, are arachnids having the body divided into two distinct regions, namely an anterior *prosoma* bearing the *ocelli* (=eyes), mouthparts, and *palps*, and a posterior *opisthosoma* equipped with the openings of the respiratory and reproductive systems, the anus, and the characteristic *spinnerets*. These two regions are separated by a narrow waist or *pedicel* (Fig. 11.2).

The prosoma is armoured dorsally by a *carapace* and ventrally by an anterior *labium* and posterior *sternum*. The carapace may be divided into an anterior head occupied by the ocelli, and a post-ocular thoracic region; these two regions may be separated by a *fovea*. Three or four pairs of ocelli are present (all British littoral forms have four pairs, designated as *anterior medians*, *posterior medians*, *anterior laterals*, and *posterior laterals*). These are arranged in two or three rows, forming the *ocular quadrangle*; if the lateral eyes of a row are further forward than the medians, then the row is described as *procurved*, if the median eyes are further forward, then the row is described as *recurved* (Fig. 11.2).

The area anterior to the eyes is termed the *clypeus*, below and anterior of which extend the paired *chelicerae*, each comprising a basal piece, or *paturon*, often armed with distal teeth, and a moveable digit or *fang* equipped with a poison duct for prey immobilization (Fig. 11.2). Spider chelicerae are of two basic types. The *paraxial* type project forward horizontally, with the fang articulating in a plane parallel with the median plane of the body. Only one British species has this arrangement, namely *Atypus affinis* (suborder Orthognatha, Mygalomorph spiders) which is rare and non-littoral; all of the littoral and supralittoral representatives have *diaxial* chelicerae, which project downwards with the fangs articulating in a transverse plane (suborder Labidognatha, Araneomorph spiders).

Posterior of the chelicerae are the *pedipalps*, each consisting of a five-segmented, free *palp* and a basal *endite*, or *maxilla*, which is used during feeding. The distal segment of the palp (=*tarsus*) of the female is simple and may have a distal *claw*, but that of the mature male is modified for sperm transfer, being equipped with a tarsal *copulatory organ* and tibial *apophyses* (structures of great taxonomic importance) (Fig. 11.2).

There are four pairs of *legs* attached to the prosoma, each with seven free segments: proximal *coxa*, *trochanter*, *femur*, *patella*, *tibia*, *metatarsus*, and distal *tarsus*. The segments may be ornamented with *spines* and/or *hairs*, together with specialized *trichobothria* (Fig. 11.2). Some tarsi and/or metatarsi may be equipped with a ventral brush of stiff, short hairs termed a *scopula*, or a dorsal/dorsolateral series of curved setae arranged like a comb, termed a *calamistrum*, may be present on metatarsus 4 (Fig. 11.3).

The abdomen may vary in shape from spherical to elongate oval, and is equipped with ventral slits leading to the *booklungs*, the *anus*, and two or three pairs of *spinnerets* below the anus. The latter produce silk, used to form a 'dragline', or the characteristic web to capture prey, a 'parachute' for dispersal, or 'swathing threads' to bind and immobilize prey. In front of the spinnerets may be a plate, or *cribellum* (Fig. 11.3), but this only occurs in species possessing a calamistrum.

Spiders are dioecious and development is direct to miniature adults or spiderlings, which undergo a number of moults to become adults.

In the tropics and subtropics, some spiders occur in the lower littoral, where they retreat to air pockets among coral heads or similar structures during periods of tidal inundation. All known

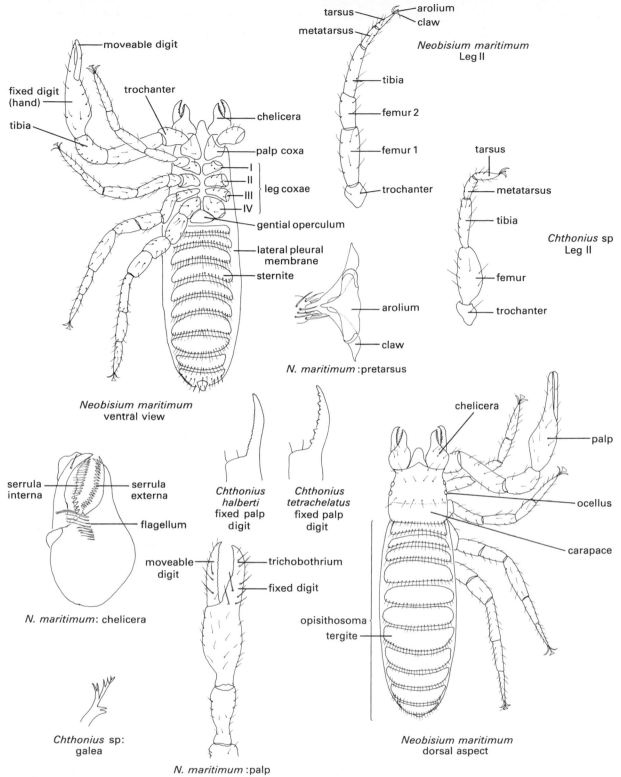

Fig. 11.1

British species occur in the supralittoral and extreme upper littoral zones, among beach litter on rocky and sandy shores. A few species occur in salt-marshes, where they are often associated with flowering plants, and climb up the stems during the flood tide, or retreat to air pockets in crevices or under stones to avoid inundation. However, some species can trap a thin air film around parts of the abdomen and survive short periods of inundation.

A majority of the species which occur in the upper littoral and supralittoral zones on British shores are also found in nonlittoral habitats, and are often referred to as having a 'coastal' distribution. Only the commoner species are keyed out here.

Others may be found in the upper supralittoral, especially species associated with sandy habitats, such as sand dunes and gravel heathlands.

TECHNIQUES

Shore dwelling spiders usually occur in the supralittoral among debris, stones, and shingle. They are best collected by hand, using a small jar for the larger species. Small specimens are best captured using an entomologist's aspirator, while the smallest may be picked up with a small paintbrush dipped in fixative. Alternatively, fall traps may be used. If live material is required, specimens are best stored individually, to prevent cannibalism, in suitable vials, with a piece of damp tissue paper to prevent desiccation.

Specimens should be fixed as soon as possible to prevent shrinkage, either with 70% ethyl alcohol or by means of an entomologist's killing bottle (using cyanide or ethyl acetate fumes). This latter method has the advantage in that the legs are fixed in the extended position. Material may then be stored in 70% ethyl alcohol, with 5% glycerol added to prevent dehydration, though this may result in loss of colour patterns. Colour may be preserved using a mixture of ethyl alcohol (50 parts), formalin (10 parts), glycerol (5 parts), distilled water (35 parts).

For identification, specimens are best viewed in 70% ethyl alcohol, although some structures—particularly the female epigyne, the male palp tarsus, and the location of the tarsal trichobothria—may be difficult to see. This can be overcome by clearing specimens in 90–95% lactic acid at 50°C for a few hours to several days (depending upon the size of the specimen), and then viewing in lactic acid; this renders the body semi-transparent, but destroys colour patterns, and often distorts the shape of the opisthosoma. Specimens cleared in lactic acid may be stored in alcohol or made into permanent microscope preparations using Hoyer's medium as described in the section on Acari.

In the following key, the structure of the epigyne is viewed ventrally, and that of the male palp on the inner lateral surface. The characters used in the key are only reliable for mature adult specimens; juveniles, and adults which have just completed the final moult, and in which the typical colour patterns have not yet developed, may be difficult to determine.

REFERENCES

Bristowe, W. S. (1939). *The comity of Spiders*. Ray Society, London.
Bristow, W. S. (1958). *The world of Spiders*. Collins, London.
Lockett, G. H. and Millidge, A. F. (1951). *British spiders*, Vol. 1. Ray Society, London.
Lockett, G. H. and Millidge, A. F. (1953). *British spiders*, Vol. 2. Ray Society, London.
Savory, T. H. (1977). *Arachnida*, Edn. 2. Academic Press, London.

KEY TO FAMILIES

1. Calamistrum on metatarsus 4, cribellum present (Fig. 11.3); male has a characteristic apophysis at base of palp tibia   **1. Dictynidae**

   Calamistrum and cribellum absent   **2**

2. Tarsi each with two claws (median claw absent)   **3**

   Tarsi each with three claws (median claw may be very small) (Fig. 11.3)   **4**

3. Eight eyes arranged in three rows, all rounded; carapace massive and square-fronted; chelicerae with one conical tooth on each margin; body generally black and shiny   **2. Salticidae**

   Eight eyes arranged in two rows, posterior medians oval; carapace flat and broad; chelicerae with two teeth on each margin; whole body covered by fine grey pubescence giving it a characteristic 'mousy' appearance   **3. Gnaphosidae**

4. Eight eyes arranged in three rows; carapace rounded anteriorly, tarsi with trichobothria   **4. Lycosidae**

   Eight eyes arranged in three rows; carapace of male may be elevated as a hump; tarsi lacking trichobothria   **5. Linyphiidae**

Aranean morphology: *Oedothorax fuscus*

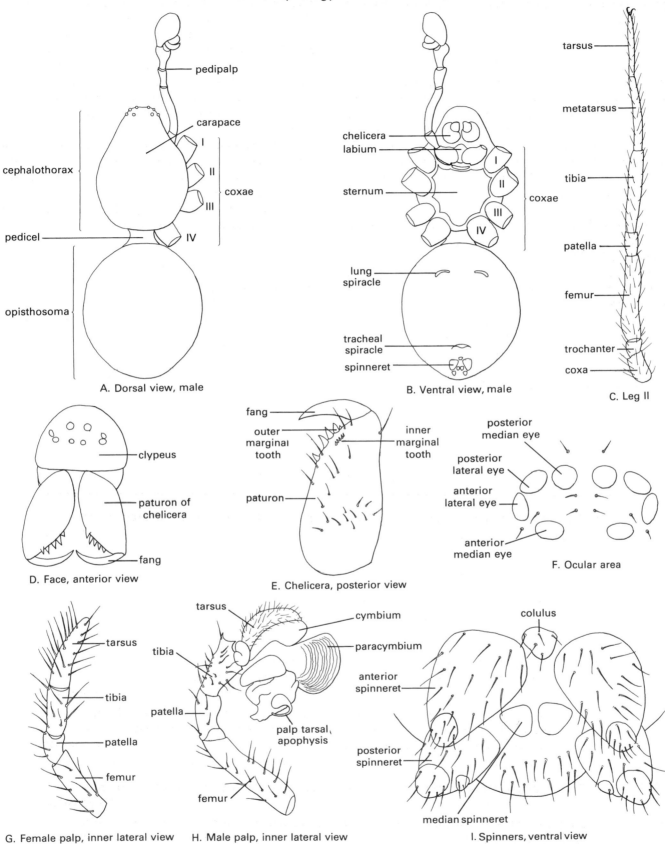

A. Dorsal view, male

B. Ventral view, male

C. Leg II

D. Face, anterior view

E. Chelicera, posterior view

F. Ocular area

G. Female palp, inner lateral view   H. Male palp, inner lateral view   I. Spinners, ventral view

Fig. 11.2

1 DICTYNIDAE

Head broad and elevated, equipped with two almost straight rows of eyes. Chelicerae strong, sometimes modified in the male, and with the distal edge concave, also with a lateral condyle; female palp tarsus has a pectinate claw. Opisthosoma has a parallel-sided cribellum, the anterior spinnerets are well-separated. Legs equipped with three tarsal claws, usually toothed, and a calamistrum; tarsal trichobothria present, legs robust and of near equal length.

Only one British littoral species.

Dictyna major Menge   FIG. 11.3

Female 3.0–3.5 mm long, male 2.5–3.0 mm. The male is easily recognized by the basal apophysis on the palp tibia, the female has a characteristic trifid marking on the dorsum of the opisthosoma.

Occurs on the shore in the supralittoral, among tidal debris, and on sand during the summer. North of England and Scotland only.

2 SALTICIDAE (Jumping Spiders)

Carapace large, truncate anteriorly, bearing four pairs of eyes arranged in three rows, forming a large ocular quadrangle. Male palp has apophyses on the tibia and sometimes on the femur. Cribellum absent. Legs short and equipped with two tarsal claws and a claw tuft, calamistrum absent; leg 1 is always the thickest (cf. other spiders where leg 4 is usually the thickest, or all are of equal thickness).

Only one British littoral species.

Euophrys browningi Millidge and Lockett   FIG. 11.3

Female 2.5–2.8 mm long, male 2.5–2.8 mm. Thorax longer than head, ocular trapezium twice as broad as long and parallel-sided. Chelicerae with one tooth on both inner and outer margins. Carapace of the male black and shiny, becoming dark brown posteriorly; in the female there is an additional light median stripe in the foveal region, though this may be indistinct. Male palp tibial apophysis long and slightly recurved distally. Opisthosoma is dark with lighter mottling. Legs with numerous spines, all segments with pale bands on a brown background, although tarsus 1 is generally pale yellow in colour.

Occurs in the supralittoral among gravel and tidal debris on sheltered coasts. South-east England only.

3 GNAPHOSIDAE

Head with two rows of eyes, posterior medians usually irregular in shape. Chelicerae toothed, and equipped with characteristic chitinous ridge. Usually a dark grey or black colour. Cribellum absent. Legs long with femoral and tibial spines; tarsal trichobothria present; calamistrum absent; tarsi with two claws.

Only one British littoral species.

Haplodrassus minor (O. P. Cambridge)   FIG. 11.3

Female 4.0 mm long, male 3.7 mm. This species is highly distinctive with a broad flattened carapace and elongate opisthosoma covered by a fine dense pelage, giving it a 'mousy' appearance.

Occurs only on the south coast of England, among shingle and in tidal debris.

4 LYCOSIDAE (Wolf Spiders)

Chelicerae robust, with toothed margins; body generally elongate and covered with thick fine hairs. Four pairs of eyes arranged in three rows, posterior medians characteristically large. Male palp tibia lacking an apophysis. Cribellum absent. Legs long with trichobothria and three claws on each tarsus, calamistrum absent. Often very active at night.

Two genera and four species occur on British shores.

---

1. Head with sloping sides; clypeus narrow, equal in width to diameter of each anterior median eye, and less than twice diameter of each anterior lateral eye (Fig. 11.3); metatarsus 4 as long as corresponding patella and tibia combined; legs long and slender, attenuated apically; male chelicera usually with a characteristic external excrescence on fang (Fig. 11.3)   ***Trochosa rucicola***

   Head with near vertical sides, and overall elevated appearance; clypeus wide, at least twice diameter of each lateral eye, and usually twice diameter of each anterior median eye (Fig. 11.3); metatarsus 4 longer than length of corresponding patella and tibia combined; legs stout and relatively short compared to length of body; male chelicera lacking external excrescence on fang   **2**

2. Epigyne of female with a conspicuous plate, having prominent posterior lobes (Fig. 11.3); male palp tarsal apophysis elongate, blunt (Fig. 11.3); lateral pale colour bands on carapace discontinuous
                                          Lycosa arenicola

   Epigyne of female with conspicuous plate, having prominent posterior lobes (Fig. 11.3); male palp tarsal apophysis elongate, blunt (Fig. 11.3); lateral pale colour bands on carapace continuous around head   ***Lycosa purbeckensis***

   Epigyne of female equipped with chitinous tongue, shaped like a mushroom (Fig. 11.3); male palp tarsal apophysis elongate, pointed (Fig. 11.3); lateral pale colour bands on carapace continuous or broken by faint transverse bars   ***Lycosa pullata***

Lycosa arenicola O. P. Cambridge   FIG. 11.3

Female 6–8 mm long, male 5.5–6.5 mm. Carapace very dark brown, almost black, with three paler bands including a lighter (often indistinct) median stripe and two broken lateral bands. Male palp tarsus with a characterstic tapering apophysis and a minute distal claw. Opisthosoma dark brown, with a median pale stripe surrounded by smaller light patches. Legs brown with pale annulations.

Southern counties of England only, occurs among shingle and debris on the shore but also extensively in non-littoral habitats.

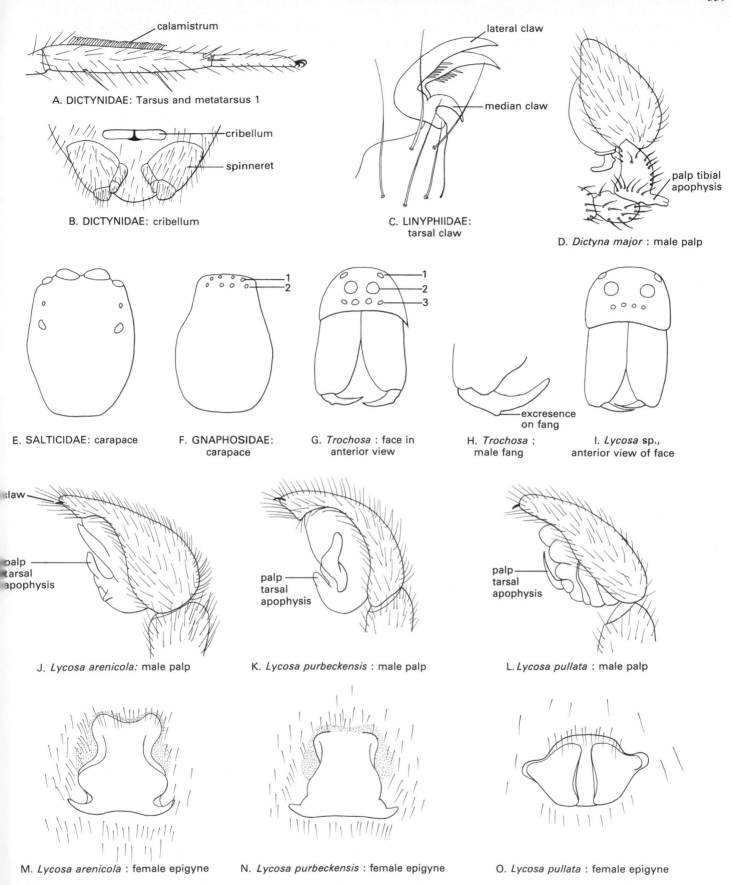

A. DICTYNIDAE: Tarsus and metatarsus 1

B. DICTYNIDAE: cribellum

C. LINYPHIIDAE: tarsal claw

D. *Dictyna major* : male palp

E. SALTICIDAE: carapace

F. GNAPHOSIDAE: carapace

G. *Trochosa* : face in anterior view

H. *Trochosa* : male fang

I. *Lycosa* sp., anterior view of face

J. *Lycosa arenicola:* male palp

K. *Lycosa purbeckensis* : male palp

L. *Lycosa pullata* : male palp

M. *Lycosa arenicola* : female epigyne

N. *Lycosa purbeckensis* : female epigyne

O. *Lycosa pullata* : female epigyne

Fig. 11.3

Lycosa pullata (Clerck) FIG. 11.3

Female 4–6 mm, male 4–5 mm. Head black, carapace dark brown, broken by a light median band which is short but dilated anteriorly, lateral bands broken or continuous. Male palp with a small distal claw and an elongate, pointed tarsal apophysis. Opisthosoma rust-brown with black markings.

Common and widespread in tidal debris, and in non-littoral habitats, especially during the summer.

Lycosa purbeckensis (F. O. P. Cambridge) FIG. 11.3

Female 7–9 mm, male 6–7 mm, Carapace and abdomen dark brown, almost black, with a lighter median and paired lateral bands on the carapace which continue around the head. Male palp with a minute distal claw and an elongate, sharp, pointed tarsal aophysis. Legs dark brown with pale streaks and blotches, but not distinct bands; tarsi and metatarsi with long hairs.

Widely distributed on mud flats, especially on estuarine shores. Local but abundant.

Trochosa ruricola (De Geer) FIG. 11.3

Female 10–14 mm long, male 7.5–9 mm. Male chelicera usually with a highly characterstic small excrescence on the outer margin. Carapace dark brown with three lighter bands, including a broad median and two even, narrow lateral bands. Male palp tarsus with a small distal claw, tibia elongate. Opisthosoma mottled light olive-brown. Legs stout, pale brown or beige in colour.

Often found in salt-marshes, but also extensively in non-littoral habitats, throughout the year.

5 LINYPHIIDAE

An odd assemblage of species loosely bound together by a common structure of the male palp. The head, especially that of the male, may be elongated to form a lobe, and bear protuberances or *sulci* (grooves). Two rows of eyes. Abdomen without a cribellum. Tarsi each with three claws, tarsal trichobothria and calamistrum absent; metatarsi with one dorsal trichobothrium. The morphology of this family is complex and heterogenous, though they are usually minute spiders.

---

1. Metatarsus 4 with a trichobothrium (Fig. 11.4) **2**

   Metatarsus 4 without a trichobothrium **4**

2. Tibia 4 with two dorsal spines (Fig. 11.4); male chelicera armed with a large cylindrical tubercle, just above the outer row of teeth **Halorates reprobus**

   Tibia 4 with one dorsal spine (Fig. 11.4) **3**

3. Carapace of male elevated anteriorly to form conspicuous setate hump behind eyes (Fig. 11.4); male palp tibial apophysis long; palp tarsal apophysis long (approximately half length of segment) (Fig. 11.4) **Acanthophyma gowerensis**

   Carapace of male only slightly elevated anteriorly; male palp tibial apophysis short, palp tarsal apophysis very short **Oedothorax fuscus**

4. Carapace of male produced anterior to ocular area as a hairy cornicule, with a hat-like extension (Fig. 11.4); in female produced to form a small point above anterior median eyes (Fig. 11.4) **Praestigia duffeyi**

   Carapace not produced in this manner, point absent **5**

5. Tibiae 1–3 each with two, and tibia 4 with only one dorsal spine; lateral margins of carapace serrated, especially in male; palp femur of male with large ventral teeth-like serrations, palp patella with apophysis (Fig. 11.4) **6**

   Tibiae 1–4 each with one spine dorsally; lateral margins of carapace smooth; palp femur of male lacking ventral serrations, palp patella lacking apophysis **7**

6. Male palp tibial apophysis bifid and pointed (Fig. 11.4); male chelicera with small teeth; female chelicera with row of teeth extending almost whole length of digit anterio-laterally (Fig. 11.4). **Erigone longipalpis**

   Male palp tibial apophysis blunt; male cheliceral teeth pronounced; female with three or four small outer cheliceral teeth (Fig. 11.4) **Erigone arctica v. maritima**

7. Tibiae and metatarsi 1 and 2 with seven or eight pairs of long ventral spines; male carapace with post-ocular sulci (Fig. 11.4) **Perimones britteni**

   Tibiae and metatarsi 1 and 2 lacking ventral spines (Fig. 11.4); male carapace lacking post-ocular sulci **8**

8. Trichobothrium on metatarsus 1 inserted in proximal half of segment, tibiae 1 and 2 each with one dorsal spine; palp tibia of male with very long apophysis (Fig. 11.4); clypeus of male projects forward of ocular area in lateral view **Trichoncus hackmani**

   Trichobothrium on metatarsus 1 inserted in distal half of segment, tibiae 1 and 2 without ventral spines; palp tibial apophysis of male short; clypeus of male not projecting forward of ocular area in lateral view **Silometopus curtus**

Acanthophyma gowerensis (Lockett) FIG. 11.4

Female 2.7–3.3 mm long, male 2.6–3.1 mm. The head of the male is raised into a lobe, with prominent sulci behind the posterior lateral eyes, and with numerous curved bristles. Carapace brown/black. Opisthosoma elongate and black, with four prominent, lighter dorsal dots and a dense covering of setae. Legs rust or orange-brown with pale tarsi, claws weakly pectinate.

Occurs in salt-marshes among debris and on vegetation. Gower peninsula and Ireland.

Erigone arctica (White) var. *maritima* Kulczynski

FIG. 11.4

Female 2.3–1.75 mm long, male 2.5 mm. Margins of carapace toothed; chelicerae with three or four small warts on the outer

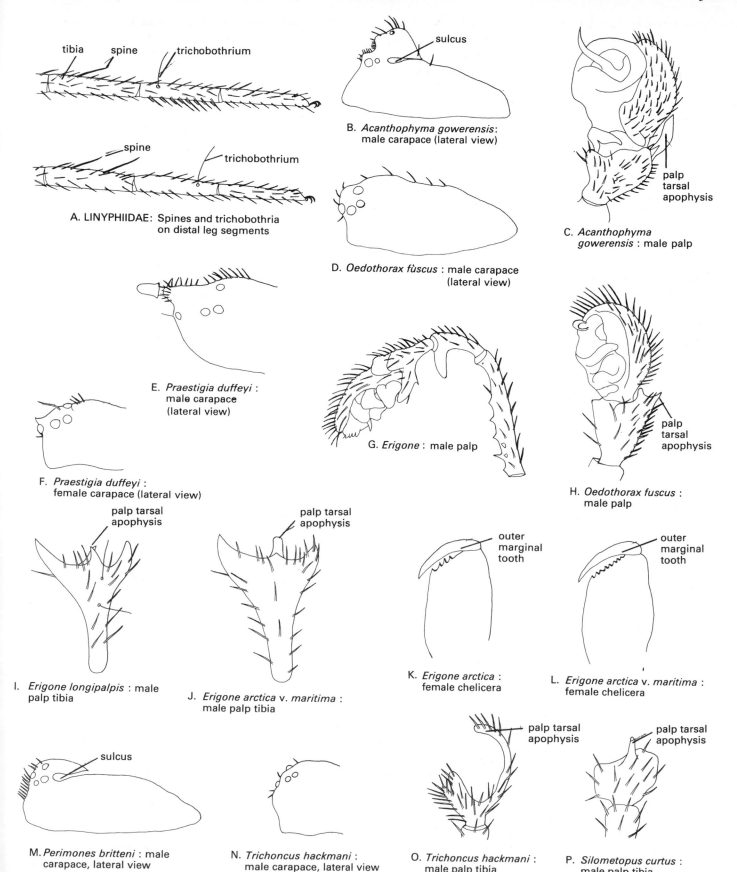

A. LINYPHIIDAE: Spines and trichobothria on distal leg segments

B. *Acanthophyma gowerensis*: male carapace (lateral view)

C. *Acanthophyma gowerensis* : male palp

D. *Oedothorax fuscus* : male carapace (lateral view)

E. *Praestigia duffeyi* : male carapace (lateral view)

F. *Praestigia duffeyi* : female carapace (lateral view)

G. *Erigone* : male palp

H. *Oedothorax fuscus* : male palp

I. *Erigone longipalpis* : male palp tibia

J. *Erigone arctica* v. *maritima* : male palp tibia

K. *Erigone arctica* : female chelicera

L. *Erigone arctica* v. *maritima* : female chelicera

M. *Perimones britteni* : male carapace, lateral view

N. *Trichoncus hackmani* : male carapace, lateral view

O. *Trichoncus hackmani* : male palp tibia

P. *Silometopus curtus* : male palp tibia

Fig. 11.4

margin, more pronounced in the male. The male palp is characteristic, with femoral spines, tibial and patellar apophyses.

Occurs on the shore in tidal debris, among stones and algae in the upper littoral zone, and in estuaries. Widespread and locally common.

Erigone longipalpis (Sundevall)   FIG. 11.4

Female 2.5–3.0 mm long, male 2.5–3.0 mm. Female has a row of warts extending the whole length of the chelicera, male has numerous small warts anteriorly. Male palp with femoral spurs and pronounced patellar and tibial apophyses. Trochanter and femur 1 equipped with a few small teeth.

In tidal debris, among algae and stones in the upper littoral zone. Widespread throughout Britain, but not common.

Halorates reprobus (O. P. Cambridge)   FIG. 11.4

Female 3.4 mm long, male 2.5–3.0 mm. The male chelicera has a large tubercle just above the outer row of teeth. Carapace is brown with lighter striae, opisthosoma dark brown, legs brown.

Occurs in salt-marshes, and on mud flats, under stones in the upper littoral zone. Widespread but uncommon.

Oedothorax fuscus (Blackwall)   FIGS. 11.2, 11.4

Female 2.5 mm long, male 2.0 mm. Carapace orange-yellow with darker striae and fovea, elevated in the male. Abdomen grey or almost black with a pale median band, legs yellow-brown.

Widespread among plants in salt-marshes.

Perimones britteni (Jackson)   FIG. 11.4

Carapace of the male with the head slightly elevated, with lateral sulci and numerous short bristles, coloured deep orange-brown with dark foveae. Opisthosoma brown-black. Legs brown and becoming paler distally.

Occurs in salt-marshes and non-littoral habitats. Widespread but uncommon.

Praestigia duffeyi Millidge   FIG. 11.4

Female 1.8–2.0 mm long, male 1.6–1.8 mm. Carapace of the male is characteristic, being equipped with an anterior corniculate and a hat-like extension, the female has a small spine in the same position, coloured brown-black. Male palp tibia with a long curved apophysis. Opisthosoma dark brown to black, legs brown with grey distal segments, claws toothless.

Occurs in salt-marshes and other brackish water habitats. South-east England only.

Silometopus curtus (Simon)   FIG. 11.4

Female 1.5 mm long, male 1.3–1.4 mm. Carapace yellow-brown with black foveae and striae, head not elevated. Opisthosoma grey to black with four prominent red dots. Legs brown to pale yellow.

Occurs in salt-marshes amongst angiosperms, and on the coast, especially in estuarine areas. Widespread.

Trichoncus hackmani Millidge   FIG. 11.4

Female 1.0–2.2 mm long, male 1.8–2.0 mm. Carapace with dark brown radiating striae. Male with a long palp tibial apophysis. Opisthosoma black, legs brown to yellow-brown.

Occurs in beach litter and shingle. On the south coast only.

Order **Acarina**

The acari are a group of primarily terrestrial arachnids occupying a wide range of niches, from soil to stored products, and even includes parasitic species. A large number of species are found near freshwater, but comparatively few are associated with the marine environment below EHWS. The majority of marine forms are intertidal, occurring between the tide marks EHWS to ELWS, although one family, the Halacaridae also occurs sublittorally. Few studies exist on the marine acari, hence knowledge of the British fauna is incomplete. Many 'littoral' records are inaccurate, sometimes referring to tidal debris in the supralittoral zone where conditions are very similar to those in soil and leaf litter. Some families which have been only sporadically recorded from tidal debris are omitted from this key, but approximately 100 species are found regularly below EHWS.

The acari are arachnids in which the *prosoma* is fused to the *opisthosoma*; segmentation is usually absent or considerably reduced, although some Prostigmata and Cryptostigmata show divisions of the *idiosoma*. The body consists of an anterior *gnathosoma* bearing the mouthparts and *palps*, which articulates with the main body or *idiosoma* (Fig. 11.5). The palps have a maximum of six segments, or *palpomeres*, but the number may be reduced to as few as two as a result of fusion; they may be simple, or modified, for example to become raptorial (Figs. 11.9, 11.12). The main feeding organs are the *chelicerae*, which are primitively chelate but may be modified, for example to become stylettiform. The integument of the idiosoma may be sculptured or regionally sclerotized (armoured) to form a series of *shields*, on both the dorsal and ventral surfaces (Fig. 11.5). The idiosoma may bear sense-organs, e.g. *eyes*, sensory setae or *sensilla*, and *lyrifissures*. Many species have *stigmata*, or spiracles, and *tracheae*; most Mesostigmata have in addition a pair of *peritremes* exterior of the leg coxae and running anteriorly.

The *genital* and *anal shields* are associated with the genital and anal orifices respectively, on the venter of the idiosoma. Adults have four pairs of legs, usually with six segments including a proximal *coxa*, *trochanter*, *femur*, *genu*, *tibia* and a distal *tarsus* (Fig. 11.5). Some segments may be fused; for example in the Astigmata, the coxae may be fused to the ventral surface of the body, reducing the leg to only five free segments or *podomeres* (Fig. 11.16). In some Mesostigmata and Prostigmata other segments, especially the femora and tarsi, may show subdivision due to the fusion of lyrifissures, forming *basifemur*, *telofemur*, *basitarsus*, and *telotarsus*, respectively (Figs. 11.6, 11.9). Juveniles may have fewer legs—larvae have only three pairs—or legs with fewer segments, for example leg 4 of the halacarid protonymph has only five podomeres. The legs terminate in an *ambulacrum* consisting of *claws* and/or *pulvillus* or *empodium* (Figs. 11.5, 11.9). The legs may also bear sensory sensilla and lyrifissures, especially on the tarsi. The gnathosoma, idiosoma, and appendages may have simple or modified setae.

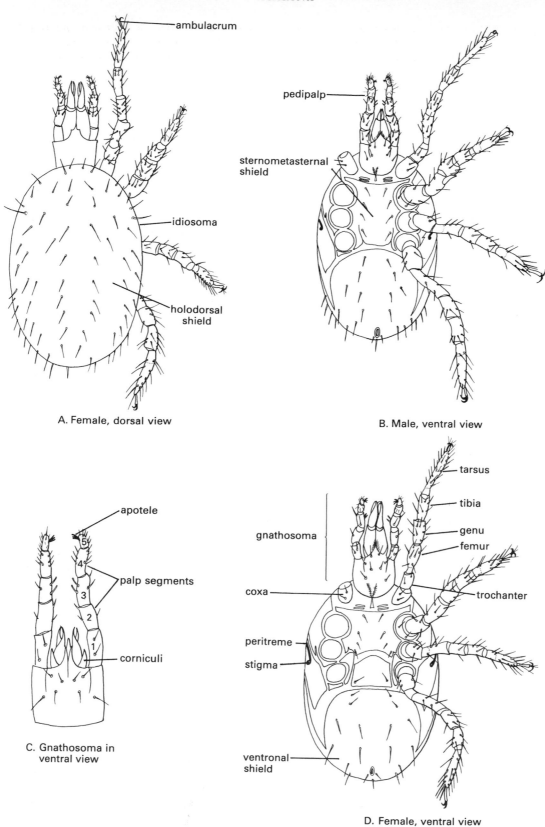

A. Female, dorsal view

B. Male, ventral view

C. Gnathosoma in ventral view

D. Female, ventral view

CYRTOLAELAPIDAE: *Hydrogamasus*

Fig. 11.5

SAMPLING TECHNIQUES

Casual searching on the shore for individual acari is unsatisfactory because they are minute animals and random searching usually fails to locate the smaller species. For qualitative and quantitative studies, more efficient collecting techniques are required, their suitability depending upon the habitat. Mites running over open rock surfaces, especially on the upper shore, may sometimes be picked up using a brush dipped into a fixative. A more efficient method is to suck them up using an aspirator or 'pooter', and then if necessary to transfer them to fixative.

Littoral algae and lichens may support large populations, particularly of Halacaridae. Samples of alga and lichen should be collected in suitable containers and acari extracted in the laboratory using either narcotized sea-water (3–5% chloroform in sea-water) or hypersaline (commercial grade salt dissolved in tap water to a specific gravity of 1.2 at 20°C). The sample is tipped into a large container and at least 10 times the sample volume of chloroform sea-water or hypersaline added, and stirred vigorously for 2 mins. The mites release their grip on the substrata, becoming suspended in the chloroform sea-water, or floating to the top of the hypersaline solution. The plant material is removed and the narcotic solution, containing mites and other small arthropods, is strained through bolting silk (125 μm mesh). The damp bolting silk should be examined on a glass plate under a low power light microscope; any mites may be removed with fine forceps and transferred to fixative.

Crevices may be opened using a hammer and chisel, crowbar, or other suitable implement. Sediment should be scraped out using a solid blade scalpel and stored in a suitable container, residues may be removed by washing out the crevice with a wash bottle and a small nylon scrubbing brush. In the laboratory, the sediment is placed in hypersaline, stirred and allowed to settle out, when the acari will float to the surface. They may be picked off the surface meniscus under incident illumination, or strained through bolting silk. Restraint must be practised since a crevice, once opened, is destroyed and only an absolute minimum should be examined.

Many species of intertidal acari occur on the underside of boulders and large stones, and in the sediment surrounding them. The best method of collection is by scrubbing the stones or boulders in a bucket of sea-water, using a small nylon scrubbing brush. The sediment suspension is then filtered in the laboratory, or, in the field, may be washed through a 125 μm mesh bronze sieve and transferred to a suitable container for extraction in the laboratory. Some Halacaridae, Amernothroidea, and Ascidae are found between barnacles or within their empty shells, especially where the barnacles are columnar as a result of crowding. Removed from the substratum, the barnacles are placed in hypersaline or chloroform sea-water and mites extracted as described above. Mussels removed as clumps from the substratum, should be individually separated and dropped into hypersaline. This ensures that all mites living between the byssal threads are liberated and extracted from the sample.

Acari can be extracted from sand, mud, or gravel sediments by one of two methods, depending upon the volume of the sediment sample. Small samples, up to 250 ml, may be taken using a corer, placed in a 500 ml screw-top container and topped up with chloroform sea-water. The container is shaken vigorously and the sediment allowed to settle out; the supernatant is poured through bolting silk. Large samples, up to 1000 ml, should be extracted in a Ladell extractor funnel with compressed air used to agitate a hypersaline-sediment suspension (Evans et al. 1961). The hypersaline is then filtered through bolting silk as before. Tidal debris can be extracted using either a hypersaline medium or by means of Tullgren funnels. Although a very useful device, the Tullgren funnel is unsuitable for extracting inactive species. Salt-marsh plants may be treated in a similar manner to littoral algae, and soil samples can be extracted using a Tullgren funnel.

Acari can be extracted from sublittoral material including algae, encrusting and fouling organisms, rocks, and sediments using the appropriate methods described previously. All sublittoral material must however be treated with the utmost care to prevent any acari from being washed off the material during collection. Sublittoral mites are generally rarer than those of the intertidal zone, and all of them belong to the family Halacaridae.

Alcohol-based fixatives cause tissue shrinkage and hardening, as well as buckling of the integument, thus making clearing and examination difficult. A much better fixative is Koenike's fluid, consisting of glacial acetic acid (10 per cent), glycerol (50 per cent) and distilled water (40 per cent). This does not cause tissue shrinkage, or buckling of the integument, nor does it make the animals brittle and prone to damage during preparation.

Most acari cannot be identified from living material, the body must be cleared in lactic acid (50–90 per cent depending on the degree of sclerotization) on a hotplate (single specimens in temporary mounts) or in an oven (larger batches of vials of lactic acid). Temperature for clearing should not exceed 50°C, to prevent damage to the cleared integument. Examination is best carried out in lactic acid temporary mounts so that orientation of the specimens can be varied to examine various diagnostic features. Heavily sclerotized specimens, such as some Cryptostigmata, may require bleaching in sodium perborate or hydrogen peroxide. Newell (1947) suggested enzymic clearing of Halacaridae, but this is not now recommended. Specimens should be stored in vials of 70% ethyl alcohol, to which 5% glycerol may be added to prevent drying out; alternatively permanent preparations may be made using Hoyer's medium compounded from crystalline gum arabic (= Acacia) (30 g), chloral hydrate (50 g), glycerol (20 ml), and distilled water (50 ml). Hoyer's medium is an aqueous solution, and any preparations require sealing by ringing with an insoluble sealant such as Glyceel or clear nail polish.

Further information on preparation of acari may be obtained from Evans and Browning (1955), Evans et al. (1961), Krantz (1978), and from Newell (1947) specifically for the Halacaridae.

REFERENCES

Andre, M. (1946). Halacariens marins. *Fauna de France*, **46**, 1–152.

Balogh, J. (1972). *Oribatid genera of the world*. Akademiae Kiado, Budapest.

Evans, G. O. and Browning, E. (1955). Techniques for the preparation of mites for study. *Annals and Magazine of Natural History*, (Ser. 12), **8**, 631–5.

Evans, G. O., Sheals, J. G., and Macfarlane, D. (1961). *The terrestrial Acari of the British Isles*. I. *Introduction and biology*. British Museum (Natural History), London.

Evans, G. O. and Till, W. M. (1979). Mesostigmatic mites of Britain and Ireland (Chelicerata: Acari—Parasitiformes). An introduction to their external morphology and classification. *Transactions of the Zoological Society of London*, **35**, 139–270.

Green, J. (1960). A checklist of British marine Halacaridae (Acari) with notes on two species of the sub-family Rhombognathinae. *Journal of the Marine Biological Association of the U.K.*, **39**, 63–9.

Green, J. and Nacquitty, N. (1987). Halacarid mites. *Linnean Society Synopsis of the British Fauna* (new series), **36**. Leiden: E. J. Brill, for the Linnean Society of London and the Estuarine and Brackish water Sciences Association.

Halbert, J. N. (1915). Clare Island Survey. Part 39, II. Acarinidia: II Terrestrial and marine Acarina. *Proceedings of the Royal Irish Academy*, **31**, 45–136.

Halbert, J. N. (1920). The Acarina of the seashore. *Proceedings of the Royal Academy*, **35**, 106–52.

Hyatt, K. H. (1980). Mites of the subfamily Parasitinae (Mesostigmata: Parasitinae) in the British Isles. *Bulletin of the British Museum (Natural History), Zoology*, **38**, 273–378.

Karg, W. (1971). Acari (Acarina), Milben. Unterordnung Anactinochaeta (Parasitiformes). Die freilebenden Gamasina (Gamasides), Raumilben. *Tierwelt Deutschlands*, **59**, 1–475.

King, L. A. L. (1914). Notes on the habits and characteristics of some littoral mites of Millport. *Proceedings of the Royal Physical Society of Edinburgh*, **19**, 129–41.

Krantz, G. W. (1978). *A manual of Acarology*. 2nd edn. Oregon State University, Corvallis, Oregon.

Michael, A. D. (1884). *British Oribatidae*, Vol. I. Ray Society.

Michael, A. D. (1888). *British Oribatidae*, Vol. II. Ray Society.

Michael, A. D. (1901). *British Tyroglyphidae*, Vol. I. Ray Society.

Newell, I. M. (1947). A systematic and ecological study of the Halacaridae of eastern North America. *Bulletin of the Brigham Oceanographic Collection, Yale University*, **10**, 1–232.

Pugh, P. J. A. (1985). *Studies on the biology of the British littoral Acari*. Ph.D. Thesis, University of Wales.

Schubart, H. (1975). Morphologische Grundlagen für die Klarung der Verwandtschaftshbeziehungen innerhalb der Milbefamilie Ameronothridae (Acari: Oribatei). *Zoologica, Stuttgart*, **123**, 23–91.

Thor, S. (1931). Acarina—Bdellidae, Nicoletiellidae, Cryptognathidae. *Das Tierreich*, **56**, 1–87.

Thor, S. (1933). Acarina. Tydeidae, Ereynetidae. *Das Tierreich*, **60**, 1–84.

Thor, S. and Willmann, C. (1941). Acarina. Prostigmata 6–11. Eupodidae, Penthalodidae, Rhegidiidae, Pachygnathidae. *Das Tierreich*, **71**, 1–186.

Turk, F. A. (1953). A synonymic list of the British Acari (parts I and II). *Annals and Magazine of Natural History*, (12) **6**, 1–26; 81–99.

Willmann, C. (1931). Moosmilben oder Oribatiden, Cryptostigmata. *Tierwelt Deutschland*, **22**, 79–200.

KEY TO SUBORDERS

(BASED UPON ADULTS)

1. Palp with two- or three-tined claw or apotele at base of tarsus; stigmata positioned exterior to leg coxae, associated with elongate peritremes. A tritosternum with pilose lacinae usually present (Fig. 11.8)

   (I) Mesostigmata

   Palp apotele absent, stigmata if present, not positioned as above   **2**

2. Palps small, two-segmented, closely applied to lateral margins of gnathosoma; leg ambulacra with empodial claw and associated pulvillus. (Fig. 11.16)

   (IV) Astigmata

   Palps variable, with three to five segments; leg ambulacra variously modified, but usually with two true claws and/or an empodium   **3**

3. Gnathosoma with conspicuous rutella (Fig. 11.13); chelicerae usually chelate and dentate; palps simple, one pair of idiosomal sensilla present, inserted into conical bothridia (absent in some Ameronothroidea). Usually heavily armoured or sclerotized

   (III) Cryptostigmata

   Gnathosoma only rarely with rutella, chelicerae variously modified, e.g. stylettiform, hook-like, etc.; palps simple, modified to form a thumb claw complex, or raptorial. Idiosomal sensilla usually present (except in Halacaridae), but not inserted into conical bothridia. Only rarely heavily sclerotized, usually unarmoured

   (II) Prostigmata

I. Suborder **Mesostigmata**

A large group with many littoral and supralittoral representatives. Members of this group are mostly predatory or scavenging, feeding on other arthropods and their eggs, nematodes, or carrion. The idiosoma is ornamented with sclerotized shields of taxonomic importance, separated by areas of unsclerotized integument. The gnathosoma and coxa 1 articulate with the idiosoma via a large cavity in the idiosoma, the *gnathopodal cavity*. The palps have five free segments and a two- and four-tined *apotele* or claw, the gnathosoma bears horn-like *corniculi* and a dorsal *gnathotectum*, the chelicerae are chelate and the moveable digit in the male may bear a *spermatodactyl* or a *spermatotreme* (Fig. 11.6D,E).

The dorsum of the idiosoma may have one or more shields. The venter has an intercoxal genital orifice and a subterminal genital orifice, together with a *tritosternum* and a variety of shields depending upon species, sex, and stage of development. The legs have six segments including moveable coxae, though some segments, namely femora and tarsi, may show fusion of lyrifissures which divide the podomeres into basi – and telofemur and basi- and telotarsus. Leg 1 is usually sensory and may occasionally lack an ambulacrum, legs 2 and 4 may bear spurs and excrescences—especially in the male. The latero-ventral or lateral surfaces of the adults and nymphs bear the stigmata and their associated peritremes.

The life cycle has four stages: larva, protonymph, deuteronymph, and dioecious adults, which may be identified as follows:

1.	Three pairs of legs	*Larva*
	Four pairs of legs	2
2.	Intercoxal region armoured with an unbroken intercoxal shield, genital orifice absent	3
	Intercoxal region armoured by one or more shields, some associated with a pre-sternal or intercoxal genital orifice	4
3.	Palp trochanter with one ventral seta	*Protonymph*
	Palp trochanter with two ventral setae	*Deuteronymph*
4.	Genital orifice usually pre-sternal, circular, and armoured with one or two shields; chelicerae may have a spermatodactyl or spermatotreme on the moveable digit. Leg 2 usually with spurs	*Male*
	Genital orifice usually intercoxal, in the form of a transverse slit, and armoured by discrete genital and sternal shields; chelicerae not bearing any processes as described above. Leg 2 usually lacking spurs	*Female*

KEY TO FAMILIES

(BASED ON ADULTS)

1.	Tarsi 2 to 4 with dorsal lyrifissures in distal two-thirds of each podomere, not closely associated with peripodomeric fissure (Fig. 11.6A)	2
	Tarsi 2 to 4 with dorsal lyrifissures in proximal one-third of each podomere, closely associated with peripodomeric fissure (Fig. 11.6B)	16
2.	Female with paired sternal shields, peritremes dorsal (Fig. 11.8E,H)	**14. Thinozerconidae**
	Female with a single sternal shield, peritremes lateral or ventral	3
3.	Body conspicuously elongate, palp tibia and tarsus fused; tritosternum reduced, lacking pilose lacinae. Parasitic in the nostrils of seals (Fig. 11.7G,H)	**8. Halarachnidae**
	Body ovoid or pyriform, palp tibia and tarsus not fused; tritosternum variable, but usually with pilose lacinae—rarely absent. Freeliving, at least as adults	4
4.	Female typically with triangular genital shield flanked by a pair of metasternal shields. Male chelicera with spermatotreme on moveable digit (Fig. 11.6E)	**13. Parasitidae**
	Female without large metasternal shields flanking genital shield. Male chelicera with spermatodactyl on moveable digit, or lacking any additional sperm transfer processes, as in the female (Fig. 11.6C,D)	5

5. Apotele on palp tarsus closely associated with a scale-like appendage (Fig. 11.8C,D)
12. Veigaiidae

Apotele on palp tarsus lacking a scale-like hyaline appendage **6**

6. Peritreme joins stigma posteriorly via a loop; tarsus 1 lacking claws (Fig. 11.6H)
1. Machrochelidae

Peritreme joins stigma anteriorly or anterio-laterally, not via a loop; tarsus 1 usually with claws **7**

7. Tarsus 2 with one or two distal spurs (Fig. 11.6K,L) **3. Pachylaepidae**
Tarsus 2 lacking any such spurs **8**

8. Dorsum of idiosoma armoured with two shields **9**
Dorsum of idiosoma armoured with only one shield **12**

9. Sternal shield of female separated from podal shields (Fig. 11.7A,D) **5. Halolaelapidae**
Sternal shield of female fused with podal shields **10**

10. Palp apotele with three tines **9. Rhodacaridae**
Palp apotele with two tines **11**

11. Podal shields with refractive nodules; female with sternometasternal shield (Fig. 11.7I)
11. Digamagellidae

Podal shields lacking refractive nodules; female with sternal shield (Fig. 11.7B,E) **6. Ascidae**

12. Dorsal surface with maximum of two pairs of *J*-series setae, i.e. *J2* and *J5*; *J4* are absent (Fig. 11.6M,N) **4. Phytoseidae**
Dorsal surface with two to five pairs of *J*-series setae, i.e. *J4* is always present (Fig. 11.5A) **13**

13. Palp apotele with three tines (Fig. 11.5) **10. Cyrtolaelapidae**
Palp apotele with two tines **14**

14. Female genital shield flask- or tongue-shaped, with one or more pairs of setae. Male typically with holoventral shield (Fig. 11.7C,F) **7. Laelapidae**
Female genital shield wedge-shaped, or with posterior margin slightly convex, never with more than one pair of setae. Male typically with ventrianal shield **15**

15. Genu and tibia 1 with one anterio-lateral seta (*al.1*) (Fig. 11.6) **12. Eviphididae**
Genu and tibia 1 with two anterio-lateral setae (*al.1* and *al.2*) (Figs. 11.6, 11.7) **6. Ascidae**

16. Tibia 1 with three dorsal setae; genua 2 and 3 with one anterio-lateral seta; base of the tritosternum usually longer than broad (Fig. 11.8F,I) **15. Uropodidae**
Tibia 1 with four dorsal setae; genua 2 and 3 with two anterio-lateral setae; base of tritosternum usually broader than long (Fig. 11.8G,J) **16. Polyaspididae**

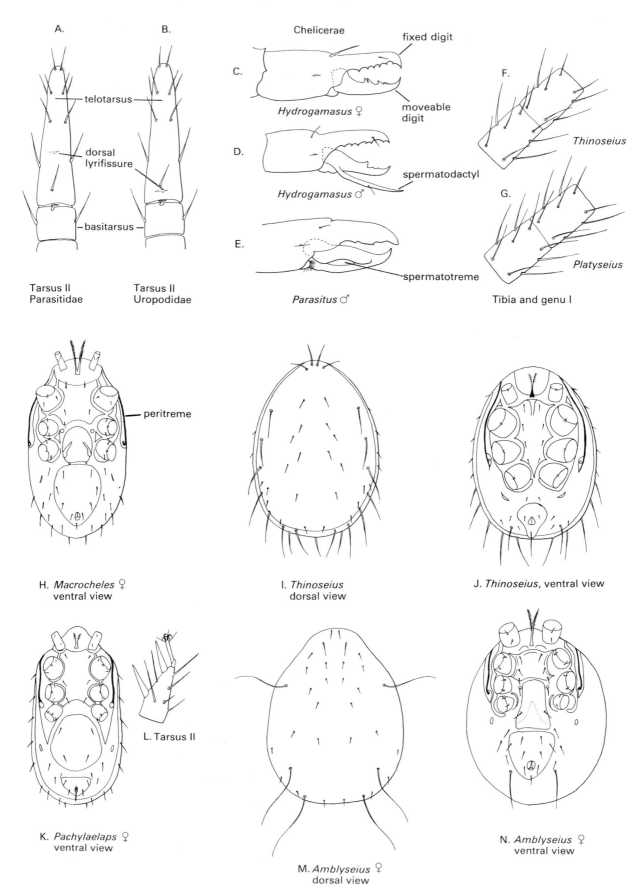

A.

B.

telotarsus

dorsal
lyrifissure

basitarsus

Tarsus II
Parasitidae

Tarsus II
Uropodidae

Chelicerae

fixed digit

C.

Hydrogamasus ♀

moveable
digit

D.

Hydrogamasus ♂

spermatodactyl

E.

Parasitus ♂

spermatotreme

F.

Thinoseius

G.

Platyseius

Tibia and genu I

peritreme

H. *Macrocheles* ♀
ventral view

I. *Thinoseius*
dorsal view

J. *Thinoseius*, ventral view

K. *Pachylaelaps* ♀
ventral view

L. Tarsus II

M. *Amblyseius* ♀
dorsal view

N. *Amblyseius* ♀
ventral view

Fig. 11.6

1 MACHROCHELIDAE   FIG. 11.6H

Length 0.5–1.5 mm. Leg 1 characteristically lacking an ambulacrum, peritreme loops posteriorly to join on to the stigma; female genital shield truncated anteriorly and posteriorly. Legs 2 and 4 of the male are spurred. Predatory.

Under stones resting on mud, sand, etc. and also in tidal debris, and in the supralittoral zone to around HWN. Also recorded from salt-marshes and non-littoral habitats. May be dispersed by insects.

e.g. *Machrocheles* Latreille

2 EVIPHIDIDAE   FIG. 11.6IJ

Length 0.4–0.85 mm. Dorsal shield reduced and weakly sclerotized in the female, normal in the male; both sexes with an anal shield.

From tidal debris in the supralittoral, and non-littoral habitats.

e.g. *Thinoseius* Halbert

3 PACHYLAELAPIDAE   FIG. 11.6K,L

Length 0.8–0.9 mm. Ventral surface of the female almost totally covered by armouring, genital-ventral shield almost abutting on to the anal shield.

From tidal debris in the supralittoral down to the *Pelvetia* and *F. spiralis* zones; also found in decaying vegetable matter in non-littoral habitats. May be associated with insects.

e.g. *Pachylaelaps* Berlese, *Onchodellus* Berlese

4 PHYTOSEIDAE   FIG. 11.6M,N

Length 0.2–0.4 mm. A rather heterogenous assembly of species. With a holodorsal shield and a characteristic posteriorly truncate genital shield, armouring usually thin, apotele on the palp tarsus with two tines.

Recorded from the supralittoral, usually in tidal debris. However, most species are non-littoral and are found on vegetation where they feed upon phytophagous mites.

e.g. *Amblyseius* Berlese, *Typhlodromus* Scheuten

5 HALOLAELAPIDAE   FIG. 11.7A

Length 0.8–0.85 mm. Two dorsal shields, female sternal shield narrow and not fused to the endopodal shields; genital shield with one pair of setae; genital and anal shields well-separated in the female, male with a ventrianal shield.

Found under stones, on algae (e.g. *Fucus*), in crevices, from HWS down to the *Laminaria* zone, where they occur among algal holdfasts; apparently more common on the lower shore. Also recorded from salt-marshes, e.g. among *Salicornia* roots and decaying organic matter. Many terrestrial species amongst humus and other concentrations of organic material. Littoral species may be dispersed by amphipods.

e.g. *Halolaelaps* Berlese and Trouessart, *Saprogamasellus* Berlese and Trouessart.

6 ASCIDAE   FIG. 11.7B,E

Length 0.35–0.7 mm long. A wide range of morphology is exhibited by this family, as suggested by the key.

Found under stones, among tidal debris and lichens in the supralittoral; in the littoral zone especially among barnacles and in crevices, down to the *F. serratus* zone; also from salt-marshes and terrestrial habitats. Some species may be associated with insects.

e.g. *Antennoseius* Berlese, *Arctoseoides* Willmann, *Arctoseius* Thor, *Iphidozercon* Berlese, *Lasioseius* Berlese, *Leioseius* Berlese, *Neojordensia* Evans, *Platyseius* Berlese.

7 LAELAPIDAE   FIG. 11.7C,F

Length 0.4–0.7 mm. Complex and varied morphology.

In crevices and under stones in the upper littoral, *Pelvetia*, and *F. vesiculosus* zones, also from salt-marshes and among decaying organic matter in supralittoral tidal debris, and in non-littoral habitats.

e.g. *Hypoaspis* Canestrini, *Ololaelaps* Berlese, *Pseudoparasitus* Oudemans.

8 HALARACHNIDAE   FIG. 11.7G,H

The body is elongate, with a reduced and undivided dorsal shield; tritosternum and sternal shield reduced.

Parasitic in the external nares of seals.

e.g. *Halarachne* Allmann.

9 RHODACARIDAE   FIG. 11.8B

Length 0.38–0.5 mm. Two dorsal shields, body narrow.

Found in crevices, under stones, and among tidal debris in the supralittoral, down to the *F. spiralis* zone. Some species have been recorded from sandy shores and many from non-littoral habitats.

e.g. *Rhodacarellus* Willmann, *Rhodacarus* Oudemans.

10 CYRTOLAELAPIDAE   FIG. 11.5

Length 0.5–0.8 mm. Holodorsal shield is fused with the ventrianal shield posteriorly.

Found in crevices, among barnacles, under stones, among the byssal threads of mussels, and on fucoid algae; all shore levels from the *Pelvetia* to the *Laminaria* zones.

e.g. *Hydrogamasus* Berlese.

12 VEIGAIIDAE   FIG. 11.8C,D

Length 1.0–1.4 mm. With a unique, hyaline, scale-like structure on the palp tarsus, in close proximity to the apotele.

In many terrestrial habitats, although the two genera listed are usually associated with wet or damp environments. All shore levels from the *Pelvetia* to the *Laminaria* zones, but especially common in the lower littoral; usually in crevices, among barnacles, and occasionally on open rock.

e.g. *Cyrthydrolaelaps* Berlese, *Gamasolaelaps* Berlese.

13 PARASITIDAE   FIG. 11.8A

Length 0.7–1.5 mm. Easily recognized by the structure of the female genital shield which is large, triangular, and flanked by a pair of metasternal shields; male chelicera equipped with a spermatotreme, leg 2 armed with often large spurs.

From tidal debris in the supralittoral zone; also in the littoral,

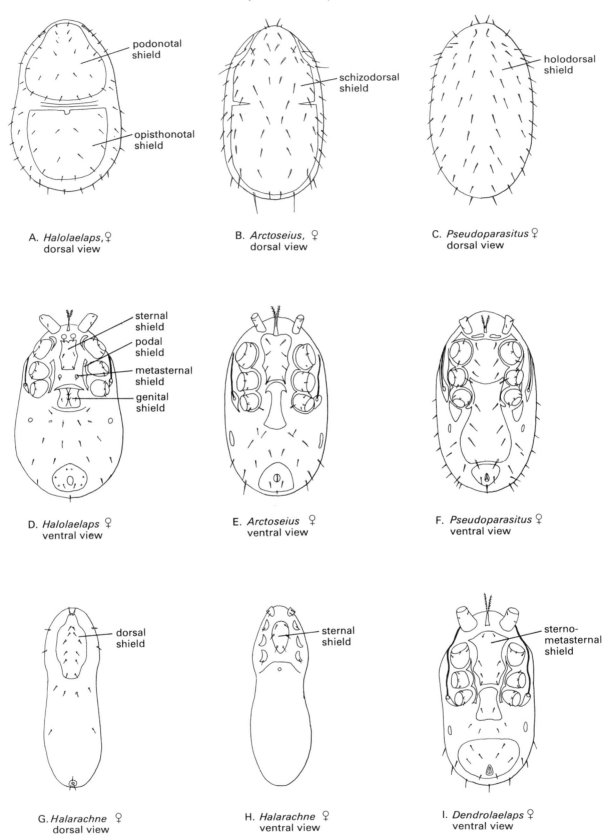

A. *Halolaelaps,* ♀
dorsal view

B. *Arctoseius,* ♀
dorsal view

C. *Pseudoparasitus* ♀
dorsal view

D. *Halolaelaps* ♀
ventral view

E. *Arctoseius* ♀
ventral view

F. *Pseudoparasitus* ♀
ventral view

G. *Halarachne* ♀
dorsal view

H. *Halarachne* ♀
ventral view

I. *Dendrolaelaps* ♀
ventral view

Fig. 11.7

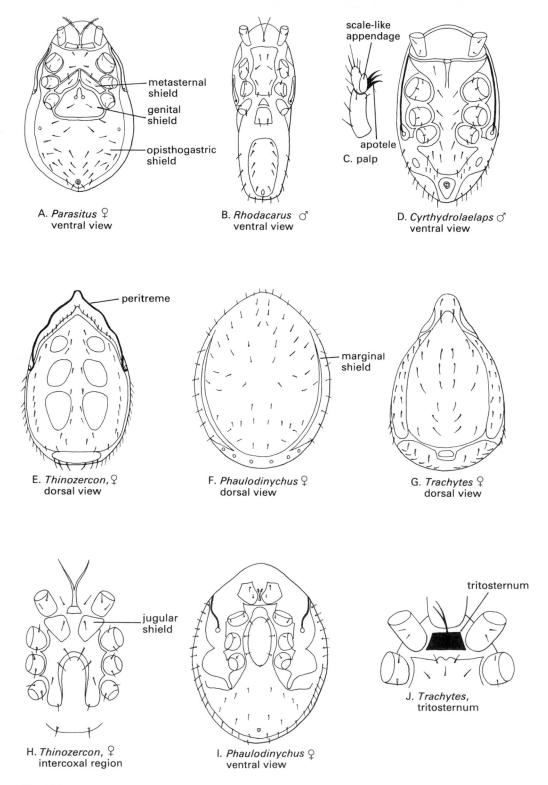

Fig. 11.8

in crevices, under stones, and among algae down to the *F. serratus* zone; also recorded from salt-marshes. A large number of species, some occurring in both littoral and non-littoral habitats. Most of the littoral species are predatory.

e.g. *Cornigamasus* Evans and Till, *Gamasodes* Oudemans, *Holoparasitus* Oudemans, *Paragamasus* Hull, *Parasitus* Latreille,

Pergamasus Berlese, *Trachygamasus* Berlese, *Vulgarogamasus* Tichomirov.

14 THINOZERCONIDAE FIG. 11.8E,H

Length 1.0–1.4 mm. The female has highly characteristic paired sternal shields and dorsal peritremes.

Occurs under stones, in crevices, and among debris in the supralittoral and *Pelvetia* zones.

e.g. *Thinozercon* Halbert.

15 UROPODIDAE   FIG. 11.8F,I

Length 0.6–1.0 mm. With one dorsal shield or with a separate pygidial shield; marginal shields free or fused dorsally. Tritosternum base longer than broad.

Found in tidal debris and in the littoral down to the *F. spiralis* zone; usually under stones, but occasionally in crevices. Deuteronymphs may have a phoretic association with *Talitrus* spp. and some insects. There are many terrestrial species in this family.

e.g. *Dinychus* Kramer, *Phaulodinychus* Berlese, *Uropoda* Latreille.

16 POLYASPIDIDAE   FIG. 11.8G.J

Length 0.2–0.5 mm. Large dorsal shield, with small pygidial shields, marginal shields present and may be fused at the anterior ends, otherwise separate; tritosternum base broader than long.

From tidal debris, salt-marshes, and non-littoral habitats.

e.g. *Trachytes* Michael.

II. Suborder **Prostigmata**

A very large group of diverse forms; the taxonomy of the littoral species is provisional but practical.

Stigmata at the bases of the chelicerae, or on the anterior of the idiosoma (absent in the Halacaridae); gnathosoma may be sunk into the idiosoma, or may protrude anteriorly. The palps may range from very reduced to very large, simple, elbowed or modified to become prehensile (Figs. 11.9A; 11.12C,E), the palp tibia and tarsus may combine to form a *thumb claw complex* (Fig. 11.11H). The chelicerae may be chelate or stylet-like. Sensory organs are very diverse, including eyes, and a variety of tactile/sensory sensilla which may be grouped together in specialized sensory areas, for example the *crista metopica* (Fig. 11.11H,J) on the dorsum of the idiosoma; or the *rhagidial organs* (Fig. 11.10J,K) on the leg tarsi. Members of this group are usually weakly sclerotized, the leg tarsi are usually equipped with two claws and a pulvillus or empodium. Sexual dimorphism is extremely variable.

Most littoral Prostigmata are predatory, feeding upon small arthropods, their eggs, nematodes, etc. Some are scavengers, while the Rhombognathinae (Halacaridae) are herbivorous.

KEY TO FAMILIES

(BASED ON ADULTS)

1. Palp with a distinct thumb claw complex (Fig. 11.11H)   **10**

   Thumb claw complex absent or indistinct   **2**

2. Prodorsal sensilla absent; leg femora undivided; usually with four dorsal and four ventral shields, may be modified as a result of fusion or division   **30. Halacaridae**

   Prodorsal sensilla present, inserted in distinct bothridia (Fig. 11.10B); leg femora subdivided   **3**

3. Tarsus 1 with recumbent sensilla in depressions (Fig. 11.10J,K)   **4**

   Tarsus 1 with erect or bent sensilla (Fig. 11.11E), never recumbent or in depressions, sometimes absent   **7**

4. Dorsum sclerotized, with a prominent V-shaped suture (Fig. 11.10N)   **21. Penthalodidae**

   Dorsum not sclerotized in this manner   **5**

5. Chelicerae with large, equally developed digits; leg tarsi with T-shaped rhagidial organs (Fig. 11.10J–L)   **20. Rhagidiidae**

   Moveable cheliceral digit modified, may be stylet-like; the fixed digit with several processes; rhagidial organs simple or elbowed basally (Fig. 11.10I)   **6**

6. Anus ventral; femur 4 may be swollen   **19. Eupodidae**

   Anus terminal or dorsal; femur 4 never swollen   **22. Penthaleidae**

7. Hypostome produced to form a snout; palps prominent and geniculate (elbowed) (Fig. 11.9A,B) **24. Bdellidae**

Hypostome not produced to form a snout **8**

8. Idiosoma with less than 15 pairs of setae **23. Tydeidae**

Idiosoma with more than 20 pairs of setae (usually many) **9**

9. Leg tarsi with two true claws and an empodium; hysterosomal setae pilose (Fig. 11.10A,D) **17. Pachygnathidae**

Leg tarsi lacking true claws, empodium claw-like; hysterosomal setae branched and shrub-like (Fig. 11.10E,G) **18. Nanorchestidae**

10. Body hypertrichous, setae often resembling a dense pelage; one or two pairs of prodorsal sensilla in a crista metopica (Fig. 11.11F,H) **12**

Relatively few body setae, arranged in transverse rows; prodorsal sensilla absent (if present then never on a crista metopica) **11**

11. Palp tibia with one claw, idiosoma ornamented with at least two shields **25. Stigmaeidae**

Palp tibia with two claws; idiosoma ornamented with only one shield **26. Anystidae**

12. Crista metopica with two pairs of sensilla; coxae 1 and 2 discrete (Fig. 11.11F–H) **27. Erythraeidae**

Crista metopica with one pair of sensilla; coxae 1 and 2 contiguous (Fig. 11.11J) **13**

13. Area sensilligera in front of eyes **29. Podothrombiidae**

Area sensilligera behind eyes **28. Tromidiidae**

17 PACHYGNATHIDAE FIG. 11.10A–D

Length 0.2–0.4 mm. Soft bodied, whitish, and usually with a striated integument; prodorsum with an anterior epistome bearing a pair of sensilla, separated from the hysterosoma by a suture—the *sejugal furrow*. Palps five-segmented, without a thumb claw; legs 1 and 2 separated from 3 and 4, the tarsi equipped with two claws and an empodium. Predatory.

In crevices and tidal debris in the supralittoral zone, may also occur in salt-marshes. Many species occur in non-littoral habitats, especially soil.

e.g. *Pachygnathus* Duges.

18 NANORCHESTIDAE FIG. 11.10E–G

Length 0.1–0.4 mm. Soft bodied, reddish in colour, with a finely striated integument, may show signs of segmentation. Palps without a thumb claw, epistome absent. Leg coxae grouped anteriorly; leg 4 modified for jumping; tarsi equipped with claw-like empodia only, no true claws. Predatory.

In crevices, from the supralittoral down to the *F. spiralis* zone. Many related species in non-littoral habitats. Herbivorous.

e.g. *Nanorchestes* Topsent and Trouessart.

19 EUPODIDAE FIG. 11.10H

Length 0.2–0.4 mm. Soft bodied, usually greenish in colour with red or black legs. Fast movers, and accomplished jumpers. The body is pear-shaped, tapering posteriorly; the integument is finely striated; one pair of prodorsal sensilla. The prodorsum is separated from the hysterosoma by a furrow. Tarsi each with two claws and a 'haired' or pincushion empodium.

Littoral species often occur in the mid and lower littoral, in crevices and under stones, they come out on to the open shore to forage. Many terrestrial species.

e.g. *Eupodes* Koch.

20 RHAGIDIIDAE FIG. 11.10I–K

Length up to 1.5 mm. Brightly coloured, usually pink or orange with red or black flecks on the legs, very fast moving. Body soft and elongate, the prodorsum and hysterosoma separated by a furrow. Legs long, with 1 and 2 separated from 3 and 4. Tarsi each with two claws and a 'haired' or pincushion empodium; palps four-segmented and without a thumb claw. Predatory.

In the littoral, down to the *F. spiralis* zone, also in the

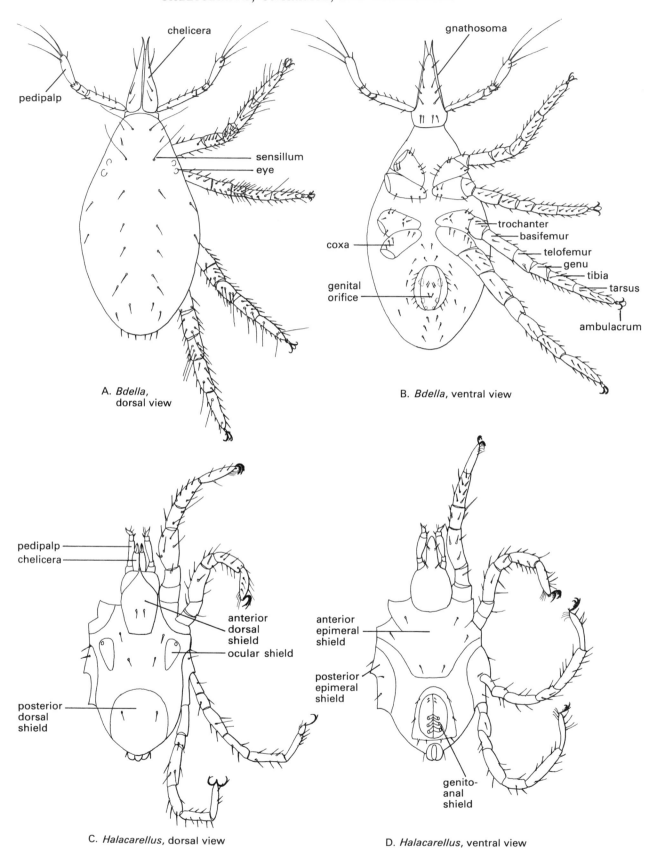

A. *Bdella*, dorsal view

B. *Bdella*, ventral view

C. *Halacarellus*, dorsal view

D. *Halacarellus*, ventral view

Fig. 11.9

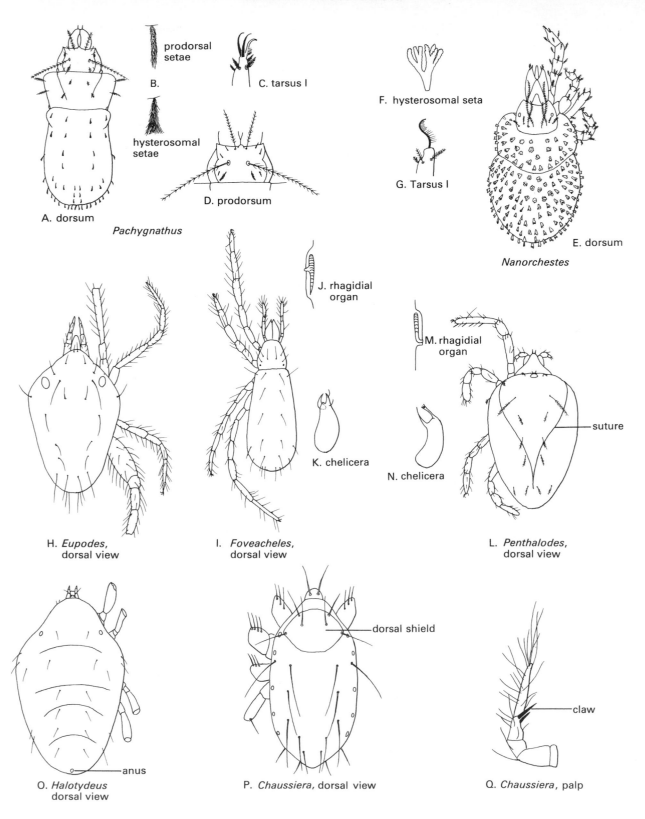

B. prodorsal setae

C. tarsus I

hysterosomal setae

D. prodorsum

A. dorsum

Pachygnathus

F. hysterosomal seta

G. Tarsus I

E. dorsum

Nanorchestes

J. rhagidial organ

K. chelicera

H. *Eupodes*, dorsal view

I. *Foveacheles*, dorsal view

M. rhagidial organ

N. chelicera

suture

L. *Penthalodes*, dorsal view

anus

O. *Halotydeus* dorsal view

dorsal shield

P. *Chaussiera*, dorsal view

claw

Q. *Chaussiera*, palp

Fig. 11.10

supralittoral in crevices, under stones, and among tidal debris. Many species occur in non-littoral habitats.

e.g. *Foveacheles* Zacharda, (= *Rhagidia* Thorell), *Robustocheles* Zacharda.

21 PENTHALODIDAE   FIG. 11.10L

Length 0.35–0.8 mm. Darkly coloured (sometimes black) with red markings and red legs; strongly sclerotized with reticulate or punctate sculpturing. Prodorsum and hysterosoma separated by a furrow; setae relatively few and short; legs long and thin, tarsi with two true claws and a 'haired' or pincushion empodium. Predatory.

Under stones in the supralittoral and *Pelvetia* zones; also from terrestrial habitats.

e.g. *Penthalodes* Murray.

22 PENTHALEIDAE   FIG. 11.10M–O

Length up to 1.6 mm. Soft bodied, usually brightly coloured, fast moving. The body is ovoid or pear-shaped, with relatively few setae. Anus dorsal or terminal; tarsi with two claws and a 'haired' or pincushion empodium. Predatory.

In the littoral from *Pelvetia* down to the *F. spiralis* zone, in crevices and under stones embedded in sand or mud, often seen foraging on open rock surfaces; many non-littoral species.

e.g. *Halotydeus* Berlese.

23 TYDEIDAE   FIG. 11.11A

Length up to 0.3 mm. Red, brown, or green in colour. Soft bodied, ovoid, ornamented with rows of punctate spots, relatively few setae. Prosoma with one pair of sensilla, separated from the hysterosoma by a furrow. Tarsi with two claws and a 'haired' or pincushion empodium. Predatory.

In the supralittoral and upper littoral (*Pelvetia*) zones, usually in crevices, under stones, tidal debris, and also found in salt-marshes.

e.g. *Lasiotydeus* Berlese, *Retetydeus* Thor.

24 BDELLIDAE   FIG. 11.9A,B

Length up to 3.5 mm. Usually bright red in colour, soft bodied with a finely striated integument; hypostome elongate and projecting anteriorly, hence the common name 'snout mites'. Littoral species do not have a furrow separating the prosoma and the hysterosoma; prosoma bears two pairs of elongate sensilla and two pairs of 'eyes'. Chelicerae very elongate; palps geniculate (= elbowed); tarsi with two claws and a 'haired' or pincushion empodium. Predatory.

On the open shore running among barnacles, algae, and rocks; in crevices and under stones in the supralittoral zone, and in the littoral down to the *F. serratus* zone. Many terrestrial species (including some littoral species which also occur in non-littoral habitats).

e.g. *Bdella* Latrielle, *Cyta* von Heyden, *Hoplomolgus* Berlese, *Neomolgus* Oudemans.

25 STIGMAEIDAE   FIG. 11.11B–E

Length 0.25–0.5 mm. Orange in colour; furrow between prosoma and hysterosoma; dorsal shields present, the unsclerotized integument between the shields finely striated. One or two pairs of 'eyes'. Tarsi with two claws and a rayed pulvillus. Mostly predatory, and highly active.

In the supralittoral and littoral (*Pelvetia*) zones, usually in crevices and under stones; also found in salt-marshes.

e.g. *Cheylostigmaeus* Willmann, *Stigmaeus* Koch.

26 ANYSTIDAE   FIG. 11.10P,Q

Length 0.8–1.0 mm. Reddish brown in colour, prosomal/hysterosomal furrow absent; soft bodied, with a broad anterior shield. Epistome bears a pair of elongate sensilla; palp tibia with two large internal spines. Predatory.

In the upper littoral, under stones, but also found extensively in non-littoral habitats.

e.g. *Chaussiera* Oudemans.

27 ERYTHRAEIDAE   FIG. 11.11F–H

Length 1.0–2.0 mm. Usually coloured red; soft bodied, ovoid, with a shallow depression between the prosoma and hysterosoma. Prosoma bears an anterior crista metopica equipped with two pairs of elongate sensilla, the anterior pair being on a frontal prominence or epistome. One or two pairs of 'eyes' present. Body and legs densely clothed in setae; palps with a thumb claw process: tibia with a strong claw, the tarsus (= thumb) pear-shaped. Leg coxae 1 and 2 discrete from 3 and 4; tarsi with two claws but no empodium. Predatory.

On open rock surfaces and among barnacles in the upper littoral and supralittoral zones, especially during the summer; also in crevices and under stones on the shore. Many species, including some of the shore-frequenting species occur in non-littoral habitats. Larvae may be associated with insects or amphipods.

e.g. *Balaustium* von Heyden, *Erythraeus* Latreille.

28 TROMBIDIIDAE   FIG. 11.11I–K

Length 1.2–2.0 mm. Usually red in colour, no furrow between prosoma and hysterosoma; easily recognized by the dense pelage of plumose setae on the body and appendages. Palps five-segmented, with a thumb claw complex. Anterior prosoma with a crista metopica bearing one pair of sensilla behind the 'eyes'. Predatory, though the larvae may be associated with insects.

Under stones in the upper littoral and supralittoral zones, many species in non-littoral habitats.

e.g. *Microtrombidium* Haller.

29 PODOTHROMBIIDAE

Length 1.0–1.7 mm. Reddish in colour; body subcylindrical or elongate in outline. Prosomal crista metopica with one pair of sensilla, inserted in front of two pairs of 'eyes'. Body setae sparse, spiniform, or barbed. Predatory, though larvae may be associated with insects.

Under stones in the upper littoral and supralittoral zones, many species in non-littoral habitats.

e.g. *Podothrombium* Berlese.

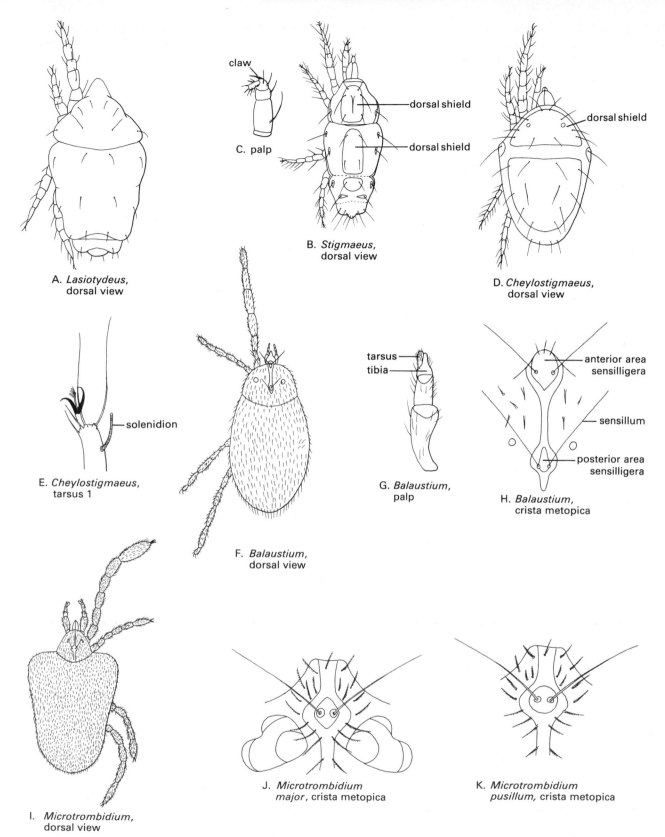

C. palp

claw

dorsal shield

dorsal shield

B. *Stigmaeus*,
dorsal view

dorsal shield

D. *Cheylostigmaeus*,
dorsal view

A. *Lasiotydeus*,
dorsal view

solenidion

E. *Cheylostigmaeus*,
tarsus 1

tarsus
tibia

G. *Balaustium*,
palp

anterior area
sensilligera

sensillum

posterior area
sensilligera

H. *Balaustium*,
crista metopica

F. *Balaustium*,
dorsal view

I. *Microtrombidium*,
dorsal view

J. *Microtrombidium
major*, crista metopica

K. *Microtrombidium
pusillum,* crista metopica

Fig. 11.11

30 HALACARIDAE

Length 0.15–1.5 mm. Idiosoma somewhat depressed, armoured with discrete shields (usually eight in number), i.e. anterior and posterior dorsals, paired oculars (absent in the Actacarinae), anterior epimeral, paired posterior epimerals, and a single genito-anal shield. Palps may be simple or raptorial, all adults have three pairs of genital papillae. This is the only family of acari that can be said to be truly marine, all species living either totally submerged or at least covered by a film of water throughout their lives; a few species occur in fresh or brackish water, but none are terrestrial. Halacarids move around by crawling, they cannot swim yet occur from the upper reaches of the littoral zone down to the deep ocean. Most are freeliving, but a few are parasitic in the larval and nymphal stages, on echinoderms for example.

Approximately 50 species have been recorded from British waters, though this may not be the total number present, since relatively little work has been done on the British fauna. Considerably more species are found in adjacent areas of continental Europe.

KEY TO SUBFAMILIES OF HALACARIDAE

(BASED ON ADULTS)

1.	Palps small, closely applied to lateral margins of capitulum (Fig. 11.12D)	**2**
	Palps large and prominent, not closely applied to lateral margins of capitulum (Fig. 11.12B,E)	**3**
2.	Ocular shields present, may be fused with other dorsal shields	*Rhombognathinae*
	Ocular shields present	*Actacarinae*
3.	Leg 1 modified as a prehensile structure	*Simognathinae*
	Leg 1 not modified as a prehensile structure	**4**
4.	Palps and capitulum together form a prehensile structure (Fig. 11.12B,C,E)	*Lohmannellinae*
	Palps and capitulum do not form a prehensile structure	**5**
5.	Only internal genital papillae present (Fig. 11.12G)	*Halacarinae*
	Both internal and external genital papillae present	*Porohalacarinae*

Subfamily *Actacarinae*

Length 0.1–0.15 mm. Very similar to the Rhombognathinae, but with massive palps and no ocular shields.

Recorded from adjacent continental European waters, but as yet unrecorded from Britain.

e.g. *Actacarus* Schulz.

Subfamily *Halacarinae*   FIGS. 11.9C,D, 11.12G

Length 0.3–1.5 mm. Palps four-segmented and widely separated on the lateral margins of the capitulum.

Common in the littoral and sublittoral zones on both algae and hard substrates. Predatory.

e.g. *Agauopsis* Viets, *Arhodeoporus* Newell, *Copidognathus* Trouessart, *Halacarellus* Viets, *Halacarus* Gosse.

Subfamily *Lohmannellinae*   FIG. 11.12B,C,E

Length 0.75–1.0 mm. Palps four segmented, articulating against lateral margins of capitulum to form a pincer-like structure used to capture prey. Predatory. Littoral to abyssal.

e.g. *Lohmannella* Trouessart, *Scaptognathus* Trouessart.

Subfamily *Porohalacarinae*   FIG. 11.12H

Similar to the Halacarinae, but with a subterminal anus, and external genital papillae.

From estuarine, brackish, and fresh water.

e.g. *Caspihalacarus* Viets.

Subfamily *Rhombognathinae*   FIG. 11.12A,D

Length 0.28–0.5 mm. Short hypostome, with a pair of short broad-based palps, closely applied to lateral margins of capitulum. Herbivorous, usually on littoral algae, but also among barnacles and in crevices; not common in the sublittoral environment.

e.g. *Isobactrus* Newell, *Metarhombognathus* Newell, *Rhombognathides* Viets, *Rhombognathus* Trouessart.

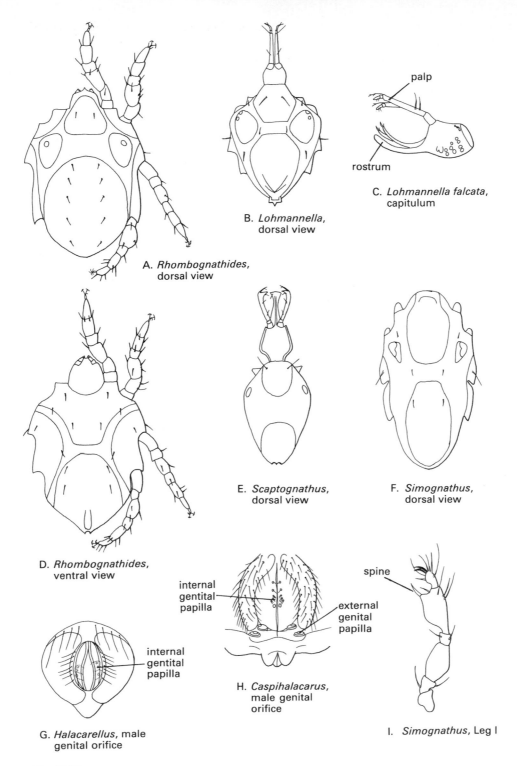

palp

rostrum

C. *Lohmannella falcata*,
capitulum

B. *Lohmannella*,
dorsal view

A. *Rhombognathides*,
dorsal view

E. *Scaptognathus*,
dorsal view

F. *Simognathus*,
dorsal view

D. *Rhombognathides*,
ventral view

internal
gentital
papilla

internal
gentital
papilla

external
genital
papilla

spine

H. *Caspihalacarus*,
male genital
orifice

G. *Halacarellus*, male
genital orifice

I. *Simognathus*, Leg I

Fig. 11.12

Subfamily *Simognathinae* FIG. 11.12F, I

Length 0.5–0.6 mm. Palps three-segmented (palpomeres 2 and 3 fused) and generally crescent-shaped; leg prehensile, armed with large spines on tibia, and large claws on tarsus, which together form a pincer used to capture prey. Rostrum short and triangular; armouring heavy. Predatory.

In the littoral zone on algae, also sublittoral.
e.g. *Simognathus* Trouessart

III. Suborder **Cryptostigmata**

A large group of usually dark coloured mites with a well-sclerotized or leathery integument. The body consists of an anterior gnathosoma set in an anterior cavity of the idiosoma termed the *camerostome*. The idiosoma may be divided into an anterior *proterosoma* covered by the *prodorsum*, and a posterior *hysterosoma* covered by the *notogastral shield* or *notogaster*; these two regions are separated by the *sejugal furrow* (Fig. 11.13C). Some primitive forms may have several small shields in place of the notogaster.

The prodorsum is ornamented with up to six pairs of setae including the characteristic *sensilla* inserted into conical *bothridia* (Fig. 11.13J), very useful diagnostic features, though absent in some Ameronothroidea. In addition the prodorsum may bear a pair of rib-like *costulae*, or more prominent lath-like *lamellae*, that may be fused (*synlamellate*) or connected by a *translamella* (Fig. 11.13E–H).

The notogaster is ornamented with up to 16 pairs of setae, and may also have *areae porosae* (= porose areas), *pori*, or *sacculi*— collectively termed *octolactic organs* (Fig. 11.13C). In addition there may be lateral or anterio-lateral *pteromorphae*, all of which are important diagnostic features.

The ventral surface is armoured with a *ventral shield* together with paired *genital* and *anal shields*, bearing *genital* and *anal setae*, respectively; in addition these may be flanked by *aggenital* and *adanal setae* that may be inserted on *aggenital* and *adanal shields*, or on the ventral shield (Fig. 11.13B). The disposition of these shields and the arrangement of their setae are key diagnostic features. The legs have five free segments and one to three claws. Sensory organs include sensilla on the body and the legs. The life cycle has six stages including prelarva, larva, protonymph, deuteronymph, tritonymph, and dioecous adults. Parthenogenesis and larviparity are common phenomena even among the littoral species. Sexual dimorphism is usually confined to differences in the external genitalia.

The Cryptostigmata are mostly herbivorous, hence most littoral species are found among decaying vegetation in tidal debris, and also in salt-marshes. Some Ameronothroidea occur in the littoral zone among barnacles, lichens, and in crevices, where they feed upon microphytes. Many species have been recorded in the supralittoral zone, but very few in the littoral zone.

KEY TO SUPERFAMILIES

(BASED UPON ADULTS)

1. Leg genua similar in shape, subequal in size to corresponding tibiae **2**

   Leg genua differently shaped from, and considerably shorter than, corresponding tibiae (Fig. 11.13A) **3**

2. Ptychoid: proterosoma can 'jack-knife' into the hysterosoma; idiosoma laterally compressed (Fig. 11.14A–B) **Phthiracaroidea**

   Aptychoid: proterosoma and hysterosoma immoveably fused together; idiosoma dorso-ventrally depressed (Fig. 11.14C) **Nothroidea**

3. Pteromorphae present (Fig. 11.13C) **11**

   Pteromorphae absent **4**

4. Genital shields with minimum seven pairs of genital setae; genital and anal shields contiguous or nearly so (Fig. 11.14D–G) **Hermannioidea**

   Genital shields with maximum six pairs of genital setae; genital and anal shields discrete (Fig. 11.13G–I) **5**

5. Lamellae present (Fig. 11.13F–H) **6**

   Lamellae absent, or at most with linear costulae (Fig. 11.13E) **8**

6. Translamella present (Fig. 11.15B) **Passalozetoidea**

   Translamella absent **7**

7. Four pairs of genital setae; four pairs of areae porosae (Fig. 11.15I,J) **Oribatuloidea**

   Five or six pairs of genital setae; two pairs of areae porosae, or none (Fig. 11.14E,H) **Liacaroidea**

8. Tarsi with two claws (Fig. 11.15B)   ***Passalozetoidea***

   Tarsi with one or three claws   **9**

---

9. Anterior margin of the hysterosoma interrupted medially by a lenticulus (Fig. 11.13A,B)
     Ameronothroidea

   Anterior margin of hysterosoma entire, lenticulus absent   **10**

---

10. Tarsi with one claw   ***Oppioidea***

   Tarsi with three claws   ***Oribatuloidea***

---

11. Ptermorphae auriculate, i.e. extend both forward and backward from hingeline, moveable (Fig. 11.15H)   ***Galumnoidea***

   Ptermorphae not auriculate   **12**

---

12. Chelicerae peloptoid, i.e. elongate with relatively small digits; notogaster covered by thick cerotegument, bearing a number of fusiform notogastral setae (Fig. 11.15C,D)
     Pelopoidea

   Chelicerae not peloptoid; cerotegument usually absent; notogaster smooth and thin, but tanned   **13**

---

13. Lamellae extremely broad, often meeting or fusing medially, covering a major portion of the prodorsum; translamella absent (Fig. 11.15E)   ***Oribatelloidea***

   Lamellae variable, if broad, then a translamella is present   **14**

---

14. Genital shield with a maximum of five pairs of genital setae; lamellae attenuated anteriorly; translamella usually absent, only faint if present; pteromorphae inconspicuous and protrude laterally (Fig. 11.15I,J)   ***Oribatuloidea***

   Genital shield with six pairs of genital setae; lamellae not conspicuously attenuated anteriorly; translamella usually present; pteromorphae curved ventrally around lateral margin of idiosoma (Fig. 11.15F,G)   ***Ceratozoidea***

Superfamily *Ameronothroidea*   FIG. 11.13A,B

Length 0.5–0.7 mm. Aptychoid; notogaster hemispherical or flattened, with a leathery integument; no suture between proterosoma and hysterosoma. Pteromorphae absent, sensilla either very small and club-shaped or absent; one pair of prominent dorsal pores present; lamellae usually absent, or at most only represented by a pair of linear costulae. Leg tarsi with one or three claws. Key setal distribution: five pairs of genitals, one pair of aggenitals, two pairs of anals, three pairs of adanals, ten or fifteen pairs of notogastrals.

Under stones, in crevices, among barnacles, *Mytilus* byssal threads, and *Lichina* in the littoral zone down to the *F. serratus* zone, from tidal debris and lichens in the supralittoral zone, and in salt-marshes.

e.g. *Ameronothrus* Berlese.

Superfamily *Carabodoidea*   FIG. 11.15A

Length 0.4–0.5 mm. Aptychoid; hysterosoma heavily sclerotized and roughly sculptured, or at least punctate. Pteromorphae absent, sensilla club-shaped with pyriform heads; genital and anal shields discrete; lamellae narrow; leg tarsi with one claw.

Under lichens growing on rocks in the supralittoral zone, also in non-littoral habitats.

e.g. *Carabodes* C. L. Koch

Superfamily *Ceratozetoidea*   FIG. 11.15F,G

Length 0.3–0.7 mm. Aptychoid; hysterosoma rounded and usually heavily sclerotized, ornamentation varying from highly polished to finely punctate. Pteromorphae may or may not be hinged and moveable; sensilla long and setiform, lanceolate or with a club-like apex. Lamellae usually large and blade-like, with or without a translamella; four pairs of area porosae on

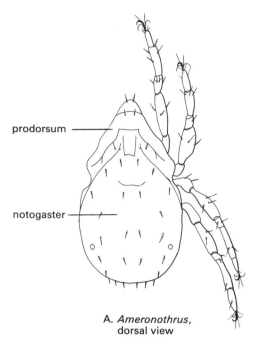

prodorsum

notogaster

A. *Ameronothrus*,
dorsal view

camerostome

genital shield

ventral shield

anal shield

ambulacrum

B. *Ameronothrus*,
ventral view

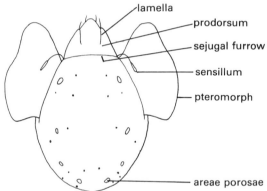

lamella
prodorsum
sejugal furrow
sensillum
pteromorph

areae porosae

C. generalized higher Cryptostigmatid mite,
dorsal view

D. Cryptostigmatid gnathosoma,
ventral view

E.
prodorsum with
costulae

F.
prodorsum with
lamellae

G.
prodorsum with
lamellae and
translamella

H.
prodorsum with
fused lamellae
(synlamellae)

I. Cryptostigmatid chelicera

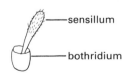

sensillum

bothridium

J. Cryptostigmatid sensillum

Fig. 11.13

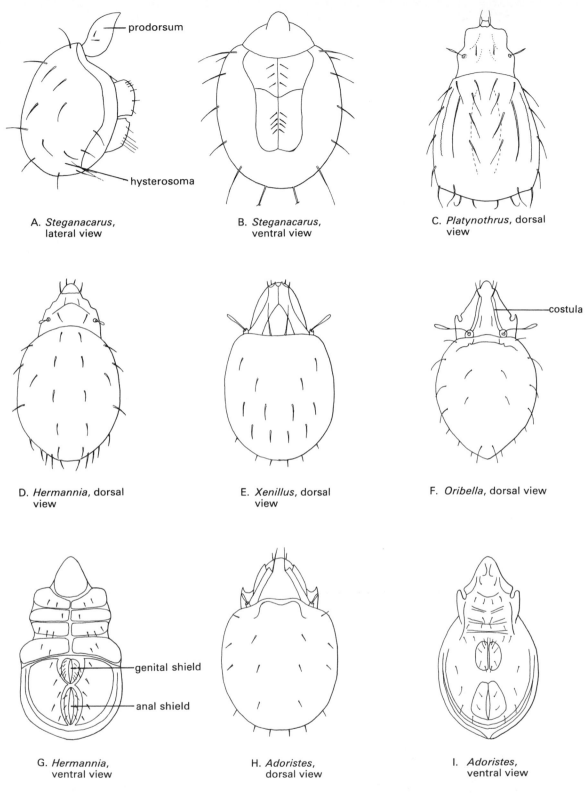

A. *Steganacarus*, lateral view

B. *Steganacarus*, ventral view

C. *Platynothrus*, dorsal view

D. *Hermannia*, dorsal view

E. *Xenillus*, dorsal view

F. *Oribella*, dorsal view

G. *Hermannia*, ventral view

H. *Adoristes*, dorsal view

I. *Adoristes*, ventral view

prodorsum

hysterosoma

costula

genital shield

anal shield

Fig. 11.14

notogaster; leg tarsi with one or three claws. Key setal distribution: six pairs of genitals, one pair of aggenitals, two pairs of anals, three pairs of adanals, 10, 11, or 14 pairs of notogastrals.

In the supralittoral and extreme upper littoral (*Pelvetia*)

zones, under stones and in crevices, also found extensively in non-littoral habitats.

e.g. *Ceratozetes* Berlese, *Chamobates* Hull, *Euzetes* Hull, *Fuscozetes* Sellnick, *Minunthozetes* Hull, *Mycobates* Hull,

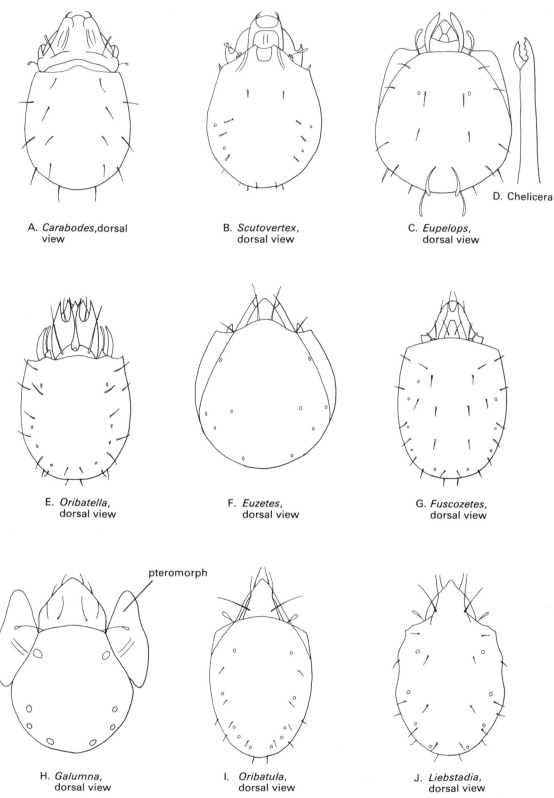

A. *Carabodes*, dorsal view

B. *Scutovertex*, dorsal view

C. *Eupelops*, dorsal view

D. Chelicera

E. *Oribatella*, dorsal view

F. *Euzetes*, dorsal view

G. *Fuscozetes*, dorsal view

pteromorph

H. *Galumna*, dorsal view

I. *Oribatula*, dorsal view

J. *Liebstadia*, dorsal view

Fig. 11.15

Punctoribates Berlese, *Sphaerozetes* Berlese, *Trichoribates* Berlese.

Superfamily *Galumnoidea*

FIG. 11.15H

Length 0.7–0.8 mm. Aptychoid: hysterosoma rounded, almost spherical, heavily sclerotized and polished. Pteromorphae moveable, very large, with prominent anterior and posterior projections; sensilla long and lanceolate; ten pairs of area porosae or alveoli; lamellae reduced to a line or absent; leg tarsi with three claws. Key setal distribution: six pairs of genitals, one pair of aggenitals, two pairs of anals, three pairs of adanals, ten pairs of notogastrals.

Under stones in the supralittoral zone, and in non-littoral habitats.

e.g. *Galumna* von Heyden

Superfamily *Hermannioidea* FIG. 11.14G
Length 0.8–0.9 mm. Aptychoid; hysterosoma strongly convex and well-sclerotized with an ornamentation of coarse ridges and fine reticulation. Pteromorphae absent, sensilla of variable size, spatulate, fusiform, or club-shaped; genital and anal shields contiguous. Lamella absent, leg tarsi with one claw. Key setal distribution: six pairs of genitals, two pairs of anals, three pairs of adanals, sixteen pairs of notogastrals.

Among lichens, under stones or mud and gravel, and in tidal debris in the supralittoral zone, also from salt-marshes and non-littoral habitats.

e.g. *Hermannia* Nicolet

Superfamily *Liacaroidea* FIG. 11.14H,I
Length 0.45–0.9 mm. Aptychoid; hysterosoma subcylindrical or slightly depressed, well-sclerotized, with a reticulate ornamentation. Pteromorphae absent, sensilla clavate, genital and anal shields contiguous. Lamellae wide, convergent or continguous; leg tarsi with three claws. Key setal distribution: five or six pairs of genitals, one pair of aggenitals, two pairs of anals, three pairs of adanals, eleven or twelve pairs of notogastrals.

From tidal debris and non-littoral habitats.

e.g. *Adoristes* Hull, *Xenillus* Robineau-Desvoidy

Superfamily *Nothroidea* FIG. 11.14C
Length 0.6–0.9 mm. Aptychoid: hysterosoma cylindrical or dorsoventrally depressed and well-sclerotized. Pteromorphae absent, sensilla of variable size; genital and anal shields contiguous. Lamellae absent or represented by fine ridges; leg tarsi with one or three claws. Key setal distribution: nine to twenty-five pairs of genitals, two pairs of aggenitals, two or three pairs adanals.

From tidal debris, salt-marshes, and terrestrial habitats.

e.g. *Camisia* von Heyden, *Platynothrus* Berlese

Superfamily *Oppioidea* FIG. 11.14F
Length 0.3–0.35 mm. Aptychoid; hysterosoma heavily sclerotized and glabrous (= shiny), granulate or finely lined. Pteromorphae absent; sensilla lanceolate or club-shaped, may be ciliate (setate); true lamellae absent, although narrow ridges or costulae may be present; leg tarsi with one claw. Key setal distribution: four to six pairs of genitals, six pairs of aggenitals, two pairs of anals, three pairs of adanals, nine or ten pairs of notogastrals.

In tidal debris in the supralittoral, may also occur in the extreme upper littoral (*Pelvetia*) zone; also from salt-marshes and non-littoral habitats.

e.g. *Oppia* C. L. Koch, *Oribella* Berlese

Superfamily *Oribatelloidea* FIG. 11.15E
Length 0.2–0.6 mm. Aptychoid: hysterosoma strongly rounded, sclerotized but smooth. Pteromorphae immoveable, i.e. not hinged; sensilla long and setulate. Lamellae very large, covering a major part of prodorsum and fused medially; four pairs of area porosae; leg tarsi with one or three claws. Key setal distribution: six pairs of genitals, one pair of aggenitals, two pairs of anals, three pairs of adanals, ten pairs of notogastrals.

In the supralittoral under stones, also in salt-marshes and non-littoral habitats.

e.g. *Oribatella* Banks, *Parachipteria* van der Hammen

Superfamily *Oribatuloidea* FIG. 11.15I,J
Length 0.45–0.6 mm. Aptychoid; hysterosoma spherical to elongate ovoid, heavily sclerotized, smooth or finely sculptured; pteromorphae immoveable or absent; sensilla long, club-shaped or lanceolate. Lamellae long and ribbon-shaped, a faint translamella may be present; two to four pairs of area porosae or sacculi on the hysterosoma; leg tarsi with one or three claws. Key setal distribution: four pairs of genitals, one pair of aggenitals, two pairs of anals, three pairs of adanals, 10, 12, or 14 pairs of notogastrals.

From crevices, under boulders, and in tidal debris in the supralittoral and extreme upper littoral (*Pelvetia*) zones, also extensively from non-littoral habitats.

e.g. *Liebstadia* Oudemans, *Oribatula* Berlese, *Scheloribates* Berlese

Superfamily *Passalozetoidea* FIG. 11.15B
Length 0.5–0.6 mm. Aptychoid: notogaster ovoid, heavily sclerotized and roughly sculptured. Pteromorphae absent; sensilla variable, usually setiform or spatulate. Two pairs of area porosae; lamellae bridged by a translamella; leg tarsi with three claws. Key setal distributions: five pairs of genitals, one pair of aggenitals, two pairs of anals, three pairs of adanals, nine to ten pairs of notogastrals.

Under stones in the littoral zone, also in tidal debris in the supralittoral, from salt-marshes and in non-littoral habitats.

e.g. *Scutovertex* Michael

Superfamily *Pelopoidea* FIG. 11.15C,D
Length 0.5–0.6 mm. Aptychoid; hysterosoma rounded and quite heavily sclerotized. Pteromorphae moveable, extending anteriorly from hinge with the hysterosoma. Interlamellar setae usually prominent and spatulate; some hysterosomal setae may be fan-shaped. Sensilla usually small, mostly conical and distally setulate; four pairs of area porosae on notogaster; anterior margin of hysterosoma overhanging prodorsum; chelicerae very long and narrow; lamellae rarely bridged by a translamella; leg tarsi with three claws. Key setal distribution: six pairs of genitals, one pair of aggenitals, two pairs of anals, three pairs of adanals, seven to ten pairs of notogastrals.

In tidal debris, salt-marshes, and non-littoral habitats.

e.g. *Eupelops* Ewing, *Pelops* C. L. Koch

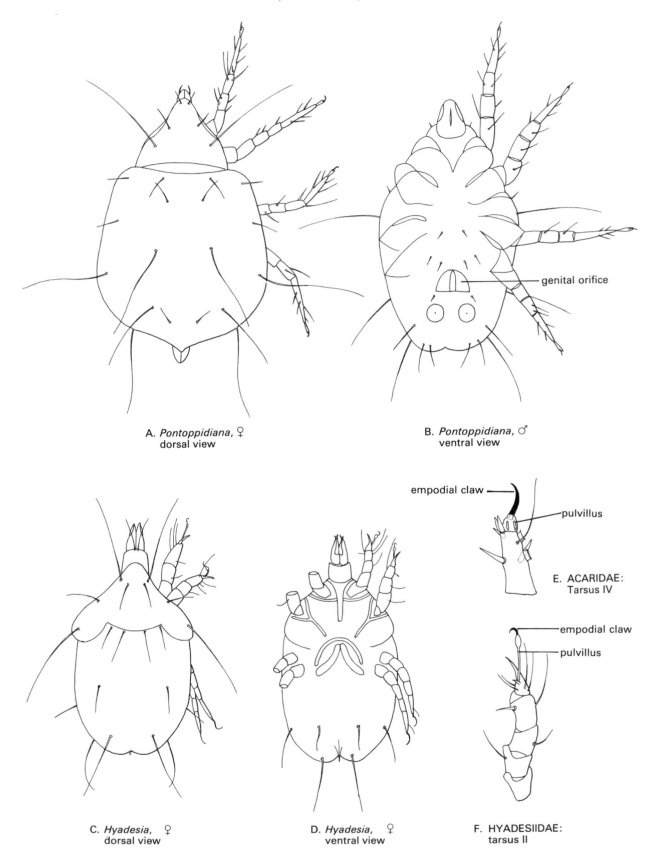

A. *Pontoppidiana*, ♀
dorsal view

B. *Pontoppidiana*, ♂
ventral view

genital orifice

empodial claw

pulvillus

E. ACARIDAE:
Tarsus IV

empodial claw

pulvillus

C. *Hyadesia*, ♀
dorsal view

D. *Hyadesia*, ♀
ventral view

F. HYADESIIDAE:
tarsus II

Fig. 11.16

Superfamily *Phthiracaroidea* FIG. 11.14A,B

Length 0.9–1.5 mm. Ptychoid; hysterosoma laterally compressed and heavily sclerotized with a reticulate ornamentation. Pteromorphae absent, sensilla present but may be minute; anal shields strongly convex, protruding considerably in lateral view, contiguous with genital shields. Lamellae absent, leg tarsi with one, two, or three claws. Key setal distribution: four pairs of genitals, four pairs of anals, less than sixteen pairs of notogastrals.

In tidal debris, and extensively in non-littoral habitats.

e.g. *Steganacarus* Ewing

IV. Suborder **Astigmata**

Usually small and weakly sclerotized; gnathosoma small, protruding prominently from the anterior of the idiosoma; palps are small and consist of only two palpomeres; chelicerae chelate. Legs with five free segments, coxae are fused to the venter; stigmata and peritremes are absent, as are idiosomal sensilla. Life cycle has five or six free stages: (prelarva), larva, protonymph, sessile hypopus, tritonymph, and dioecious adults. Two major groups within the suborder, one of which is parasitic, and the other freeliving; only the second is considered here.

KEY TO FAMILIES

(BASED ON ADULTS)

1. Tarsi 1 and 2 normal, with a sessile pulvillus and an empodial claw (Fig. 11.16A,B,E)
31. Acaridae

   Tarsi 1 and 2 claw-like, with a stalked pulvillus and a minute distal empodial claw (Fig. 11.16C,D,F)
32. Hyadesidae

31 ACARIDAE FIG. 11.16A,B,E

Length 0.3–0.8 mm. Body divided into an anterior propodosoma and posterior hysterosoma by a suture; integument smooth; epimerae 1 and 2 fused to the sternal shield. Tarsi equipped with empodial claw on a sessile pulvillus; tarsi 4 of male with suckers. Genital orifice intercoxal. Usually detritivores or herbivores.

Among tidal debris and lichens in the supralittoral zone, also found in salt-marshes and extensively in non-littoral habitats.

e.g. *Pontoppidania* Oudemans, *Rhizoglyphus* Claparède, *Tyrophagus* Oudemans

32 HYADESIIDAE FIG. 11.16C,D,F

Length 0.3–0.5 mm. Body divided into propodosoma and hysterosoma by a suture, integument soft and finely striated. Tarsi 1 and 2 claw-like, with a small empodial claw on a long stalked pulvillus. Genital orifice posterior to coxae 4.

In pools among algae, in crevices, and among barnacles in the littoral zone, also from salt-marshes and brackish water habitats.

e.g. *Hyadesia* Megnin

B. PHYLUM PYCNOGONIDA

The Pycnogonida are often referred to as sea spiders. They occur commonly on rocky shores which provide a stable substratum for attachment and are a source for the pycnogonid's principal foods—hydroids and bryozoans.

Most sea spiders have a narrow elongate body divided into a number of segments (Fig. 11.17). At the anterior end there is a *cephalon* with a *proboscis*, bearing a terminal mouth. On the dorsal side of the cephalon there is a *tubercle* bearing the eyes, one pair directed forwards and the other pair posteriorly. The first *trunk* segment is fused with the cephalon and the last segment has an *abdomen* or *anal process*, with a terminal anus. In most adults the trunk segmentation is visible externally.

The appendages consist of a pair of *palps* carrying sense-organs, *chelifores* which may have terminal, functional *chelae*, used for food gathering or perhaps gripping the substratum, *ovigerous legs*, and four pairs of *ambulatory* (walking) or *natatory* (swimming) *legs*. Some juvenile stages have fewer than four pairs of legs and cannot be identified with this key. Some species are without palps or chelifores, or both. In some species the ovigerous legs are present only in the males, whilst in others, although present in females, they are reduced. The terminal segments of the ovigerous legs may bear a number of serrated spines which help them to fulfil their secondary function of cleaning the surface of the body, their primary function being to carry the eggs. Each body segment has a prominent *lateral process* with which the legs articulate. These consist of three *coxae*, a *femur*, two *tibiae*, a *tarsus*, a *propodus*, and a *terminal claw*, with some *auxiliary claws* associated with it or the propodus.

During the breeding season, females can be identified readily by the presence of eggs in their femurs but, at other times of the year, some species are difficult to sex and may require the presence of both sexes so that the relative length of ovigers can be compared.

Littoral pycnogonids can be most readily collected by scraping small seaweeds, hydroids, bryozoans, and algal holdfasts from the rocks. These should be allowed to stand in bowls of seawater before sorting. Many of the pycnogonids will walk out as the oxygen content of the water falls, and others can be extracted by shaking the material into the water. After sorting, specimens should be narcotized with a few drops of ethyl acetate added to the water and then, after 10–15 mins, placed in hot Bouins fixative. They can thus be preserved in an extended state and stored in 70% alcohol, or mounted on slides with Canada balsam after dehydration with alcohol.

The present key has been confined to the adults because early larval stages are difficult to distinguish from one another. Some are carried by the adults. Later larval stages may differ from the adults in the number of legs, and the structure of other appendages, such as chelifores.

Bouvier, E. L. (1923). Pycnoginides. *Faune de France*, **7**. Paris.

Crothers, J. H. (1966). *Dale Fort Marine Fauna*. Field Studies Council.

Fry, W. G. (1978). A classification within the pycnogonids. *Zoological Journal of the Linnean Society*, **63**, 35–58.

King, P. E. (1974). *British sea spiders*. Linnean Society Synopses of the British Fauna (New Series), No. 5. Academic Press, London.

King, P. E. (1986). A revised key to the adults of littoral pycnogonids in the British Isles. *Field Studies*, **6**, 493–516.

Stock, J. H. (1952). Revision of the European representatives of the genus *Callipallene* Flynn. *Beaufortia*, **13**, 1–15.

REFERENCES

Bamber, R. N. (1982). Variation in *Nymphon brevirostre* (Hodge), and the status of *N. rubrum* (Hodge) (Arthropoda: Pycnogonida). *Biological Journal of the Linnean Society*, **17**, 275–88.

KEY TO FAMILIES

Chelifores (see Fig. 11.17) can be observed from the dorsal surface and palps from the ventral surface.

1.	Chelifores and palpi present	**2**
	Palpi, or both chelifores and palpi, absent	**3**
2.	Palpi five-segmented. Chelae of chelifores conspicuous, over-reaching proboscis	**1. Nymphonidae**
	Palpi eight- or nine-segmented. Chelae small, chelifores shorter than proboscis	**2. Acheliidae**
3.	Chelifores present, palpi lacking	**4**
	Both chelifores and palpi lacking	**5**
4.	Ovigerous legs ten-segmented in both sexes	**6. Callipallenidae**
	Ovigerous legs five- or six-jointed in males; absent in females	**6**
5.	Body slender, legs about twice as long as body. Auxiliary claws present (Fig. 11.19). Ovigerous legs seven-segmented (present in male only)	**4. Endeidae**
	Body stout, legs stout, little longer than the body. Auxiliary claws absent. Ovigerous legs nine-jointed (present in males only)	**5. Pycnogonidae**
6.	Auxiliary claws laterally placed, small compared with size of main claw, or absent	**7. Anoplodactylidae**
	Auxiliary claws dorsally placed, large compared with size of main claw	**3. Ammotheidae**

1 NYMPHONIDAE

Members of this family have a slender body with a relatively short and wide proboscis. Chelifores are two-jointed, having functional chelae with fingers bearing prominent teeth. Palps and ovigerous legs are present in both sexes. Several species have been observed swimming and are amongst the most active pycnogonids. There is considerable controversy regarding the validity of some species.

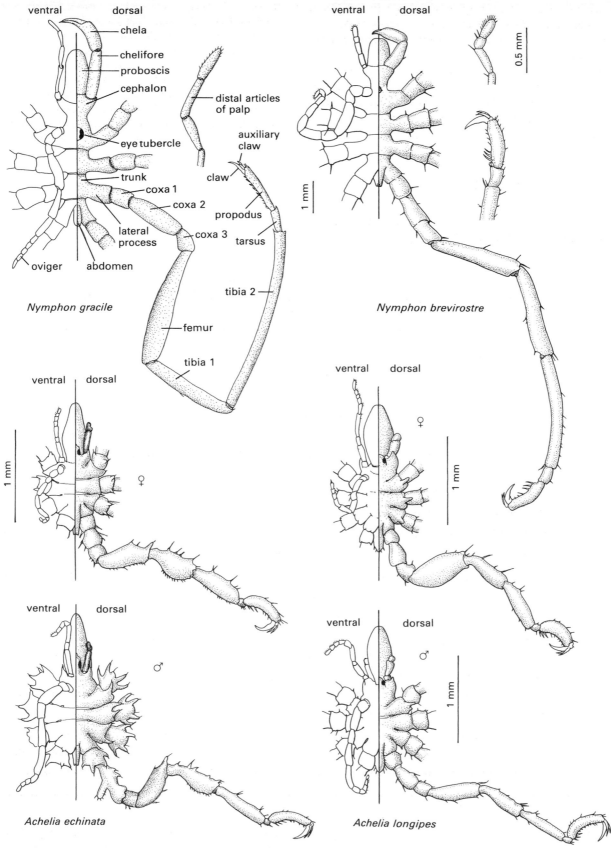

ventral   dorsal

chela
chelifore
proboscis
cephalon

distal articles of palp

eye tubercle

auxiliary claw

trunk

claw

coxa 1

coxa 2

propodus

lateral process

coxa 3

tarsus

oviger   abdomen

tibia 2

Nymphon gracile

femur

tibia 1

Nymphon brevirostre

0.5 mm

1 mm

ventral   dorsal

♀

Achelia echinata

ventral   dorsal

♀

ventral   dorsal

♂

ventral   dorsal

♂

Achelia longipes

1 mm

Fig. 11.17

1. Abdomen longer than fourth pair of lateral processes. Body and legs covered thickly in hairs　***Nymphon hirtum***

   Abdomen not longer than fourth pair of lateral processes. Body bare, although legs may have some spines　　　　**2**

2. Terminal and penultimate segments of palps equal in length　***Nymphon gracile***

   Terminal segments of palps approximately twice as long as subterminal segments　***Nymphon brevirostre***

Nymphon hirtum Fabricius

Length of body from tip of proboscis to abdomen 1 mm.

Most frequently sublittoral. Although usually found in the cold seas of the north Atlantic, Iceland, Greenland, and Spitzbergen, it sometimes reaches the northern parts of the British Isles and has been recorded from Shetland, Northumberland, and Scotland.

Nymphon gracile Leach　　　　FIG. 11.17

Slender, smooth body, 4 mm long with elongate limbs three or four times as long as body. Proboscis elongate, twice as long as wide. Terminal and penultimate segments of palps equal in length. Propodus and tarsus subequal in length; propodus has a number of spines with three slightly longer ones half-way along length. Ovigerous legs are prominent in both sexes and are used to clean the surface of the body.

N. gracile is a shallow water species around most European Atlantic coasts from Norway to Morocco. Occurs in the littoral zone during the summer months.

Nymphon brevirostre Hodge　　　　FIG. 11.17

Legs three and a half times as long as body. Proboscis short and stout. Thoracic segments broader than long. Terminal segment of palp longer than penultimate. Propodus longer than tarsus, slightly bent, with a series of spines consisting of a few short spines and three longer ones near its proximal end.

All British coasts; distributed from the Arctic to Brittany.

2 ACHELIIDAE

Achelia echinata and *A. longipes* are clearly defined species, though views differ regarding the generic name of the latter. *A. simplex* has only been recorded from the shore of the Isle of Man, western Ireland, and Millport. *A. hispida* seems closely related to *A. longipes* and was described as a variety of that species. A form resembling *A. hispida* was called *A. longipes* by Bouvier (1923). There are sufficient morphological differences to suggest that three distinct species may be recognized. Immature forms of all species have fewer palp segments than the adults, have functional chelae on their chelifores, and lack outwardly visible body segmentation. *A. laevis* characteristically lacks body segmentation in a manner similar to juveniles.

1. Palps with nine segments. Male coxal projections, bearing genital openings, small　　　　**2**

   Palps with eight segments. Male coxal projections prominent on second coxae of third and fourth pairs of legs　　　　**3**

2. Only one complete suture on trunk segments. Chelifores at most half as long as proboscis　***Achelia longipes***

   Two sutures on trunk segments. Chelifores more than half as long as proboscis　***Achelia hispida***

3. No articulation or sutures visible on trunk　***Achelia laevis***

   Articulation or sutures separate at least two trunk segments　　　　**4**

4. No suture between third and fourth segments. Lateral processes and legs with spine-bearing projections
   Achelia echinata

   A feebly distinct suture between third and fourth segments. No spine-bearing projections on lateral processes and legs　***Achelia simplex***

Achelia longipes Hodge　　　　FIGS. 11.17, 11.18

Body approximately 2 mm long, legs 8 mm. Body smooth, not spiny, joint between segments 2 and 3 frequently indistinct. A prominent pointed dorsal tubercle on each lateral projection. Proboscis with widest point near middle of length, the three lips around mouth, although beak-like, somewhat blunter than in *A. echinata*. Palps with nine segments.

This species is thought to be more southern in its distribution than *A. echinata*. Reported from west coasts of Ireland, South Wales, North Wales, east coast of Britain, Plymouth.

Achelia hispida Hodge　　　　FIG. 11.18

Body approximately 2.5 mm long. Similar to *A. longipes* but with more spines. This is more obvious in males than females. Two sutures visible on trunk, instead of one in *A. longipes*: spines at front of cephalon, abdomen, and chelifores all relatively longer. Male projections and dorsal protuberances on lateral processes longer than in *A. longipes*, eye tubercle differently shaped and trunk longer.

Probably a southern species since it has only been recorded from the west coast of Ireland, and from Pembrokeshire and Lundy Island.

Achelia laevis Hodge　　　　FIG. 11.18

Body 1.5 mm long. Slightly smaller than other members of the genus in British waters. No visible trunk segmentation.

This species has not been recorded frequently but may have a distribution similar to that of *A. echinata*. However, much more data is needed.

Achelia echinata Hodge　　　　FIGS. 11.17, 11.18

Body 2 mm long. Two distinct sutures visible externally. Proboscis as long as body, broadest one-third of distance from

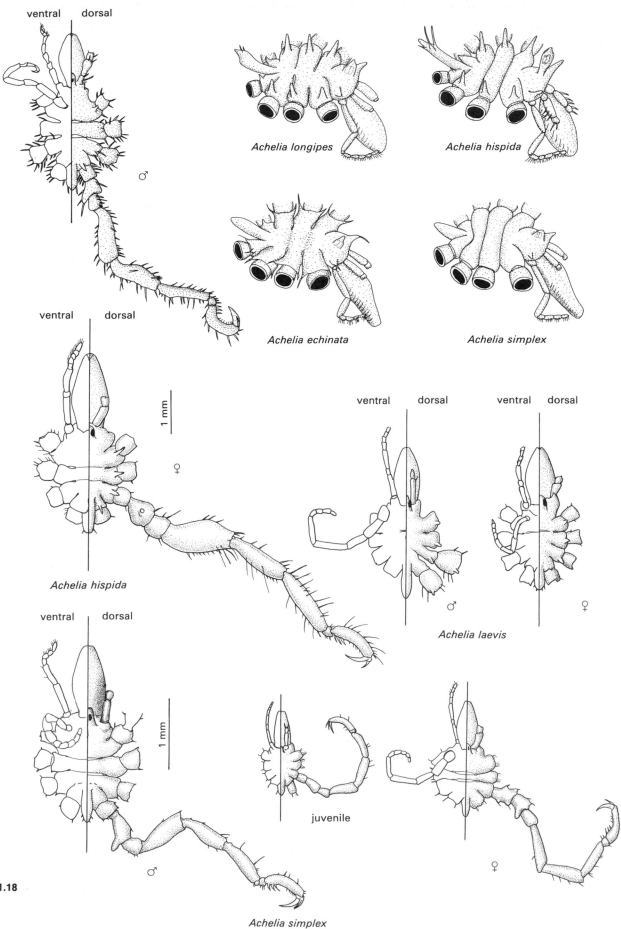

ventral dorsal

Achelia longipes

Achelia hispida

Achelia echinata

Achelia simplex

ventral dorsal

1 mm

Achelia hispida

ventral dorsal   ventral dorsal

Achelia laevis

ventral dorsal

1 mm

juvenile

Achelia simplex

Fig. 11.18

proximal end, tapering towards mouth. Palps with eight segments. Legs with a number of spines, characteristically one pair on each of lateral processes and two pairs on each first coxa; larger in male which, in addition, has a prominent projection on second coxae of third and fourth pairs of legs. Ovigerous legs with nine segments, present in both sexes, though slightly smaller in female. Ocular tubercle sub-conical with a sharp terminal spine.

Of wide occurrence throughout the British Isles.

Achelia simplex (Giltay) FIG. 11.18

Body 1.0–1.25 mm long. Two sutures visible externally on trunk: between cephalon and second segment, and, less distinct, between third and fourth segments. No conspicuous protuberances on lateral processes of body segments. Ocular tubercle with rounded summit. Palps with eight segments, ovigers ten. Recorded at ELWS at Galway, Isle of Man, and Millport.

3 AMMOTHEIDAE

Originally this family included the genus *Achelia*, which has now been placed in a family of its own. *Phoxichilidium femoratum*, previously in the Phoxichilidiidae, is now considered to belong in the Ammotheidae.

Phoxichilidium femoratum (Rathke) FIG. 11.19

Body length 2–3 mm, with legs almost three times as long. Proboscis cylindrical, almost constant width throughout its length. Chelifores with chelae reaching beyond tip of proboscis. Ovigerous legs with five segments. Cement glands open from a series of depressions along femur. Abdomen short, hardly as long as either of the hind pair of lateral processes. Heel of propodus armed with four large, single teeth, and a pair which is usually smaller. There are well-developed, dorsally situated auxiliary claws.

Widespread from the north Atlantic, Greenland, and Norway to France.

4 ENDEIDAE

The body is elongate with long legs, each with a well-developed, arched propodus bearing pronounced heel and sole spines. There are well-developed auxiliary claws. In the adult there are neither chelifores nor palps, though the juvenile six-legged and early eight-legged forms have long, slender chelifores with a small chela at the tip.

---

1. Auxiliary claws at least half as long as main claws. Mouth surrounded by numerous spines
   Endeis charybdaea

   Auxiliary claws less than half as long as main claws. Mouth with few spines around it **Endeis spinosa**

Endeis spinosa (Montagu) FIG. 11.19

Body 3 mm long. Smaller than *E. charybdaea*. Tip of proboscis slightly tapered, circular in cross-section, with fewer spines around mouth. Auxiliary claws relatively shorter compared with length of main claw. Male femurs with 19–20 cement gland ducts.

Occurs in the littoral zone, and to depths of 12 m in the sublittoral zone. Widespread on British coasts.

Endeis charybdaea (Dohrn) FIG. 11.19

Body 5–6 mm long. Proboscis cylindrical proximally, widening distally, with a swollen region almost half-way along it. Apex oval in cross-section, then tapered slightly before being further enlarged to form a bulbous tip. Mouth surrounded by concentric rows of irregularly arranged spines. Male with 25–26 cement glands on femur, visible during period of egg release by females.

Usually occurs in sublittoral zone, below 13 m, mainly around south-west coasts.

5 PYCNOGONIDAE

Pycnogonum littorale (Strøm) FIG. 11.20

Body 5 mm long, sturdy. No chelifores or palps in either adults or juveniles; nine-segmented ovigerous legs present only in males, appearing at an early stage of development as buds, number of segments increasing as growth proceeds. Proboscis conical, never longer than trunk. Abdomen truncate at posterior end. Legs slightly shorter than body, terminating with a claw; no auxiliary claws. Genital apertures situated on ventral surface of second coxae of hind legs of male, but on dorsal surface of same coxae in females.

Widespread in the British Isles.

6 CALLIPALLENIDAE

The identification of the European members of this family is very difficult. Stock (1952) reviewed the European representatives in the genus *Callipallene*, the only British genus of this family. [There is an unconfirmed record of *Pallenopsis* sp. from Milford Haven (Crothers 1966)]. The characters Stock used were: shape of the neck, curvature and armature of the propodus, length of the claw and auxiliary claw, and the length of, and distance between, the lateral processes. He divided the genus into three species – *Callipallene brevirostris*, *C. phantoma* and *C. emaciata*. However, British records are confused and there is some doubt as to which species occur in the British Isles.

---

1. Sole of propodus straight, auxiliary claws at most half as long as principal claw, usually less. Neck long and slender with distal end distinctly set off from rest
   Callipallene phantoma

   Sole of propodus curved. Auxiliary claws at least half as long as principal claw, usually more. Neck much shorter 2

2. Sole of propodus slightly curved. Auxiliary claws more than two-thirds as long as principal claw
   Callipallene brevirostris

   Sole of propodus strongly curved. Auxiliary claws about half as long as principal claw
   Callipallene emaciata

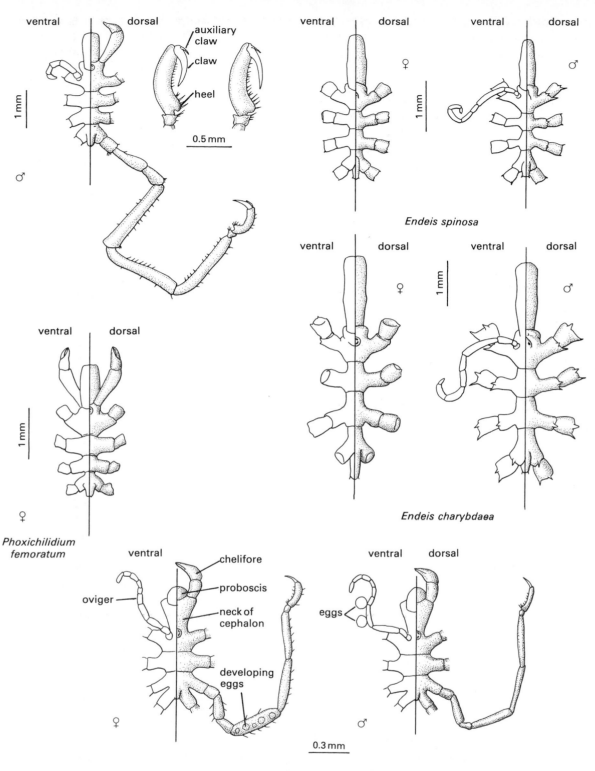

ventral   dorsal   auxiliary claw   claw   heel
0.5 mm
♂
1 mm

ventral   dorsal
♀
1 mm

Endeis spinosa

ventral   dorsal
♂
1 mm

ventral   dorsal
♀
1 mm

ventral   dorsal
♂

Endeis charybdaea

ventral   dorsal
♀
1 mm

Phoxichilidium femoratum

oviger   ventral   chelifore   proboscis   neck of cephalon   developing eggs
♀

eggs   ventral   dorsal
♂
0.3 mm

Callipallene brevirostris

Fig. 11.19

Callipallene brevirostris (Johnston)   FIG. 11.19

Body 1–5 mm long; legs four times as long as body. Proboscis short, rounded at distal end. Cephalon long, wider anteriorly. Trunk segment 2 short and wide, segments 3 and 4 fused, abdomen relatively small. Ovigerous legs with ten segments, all short except segments 3 and 4; this appendage longer in male than in female. Femur of female proportionately wider than in male.

Essentially sublittoral, but occurs occasionally in the littoral zone. Widespread around Britain.

Callipallene emaciata (Dohrn)

This species is characterized by its auxiliary claws, which are half as long as the principal claws, combined with a strongly curved propodal joint.

Distribution incompletely known but recorded mainly from southern regions.

Callipallene phantoma (Dohrn)

Body 2 mm long, a considerable proportion being taken up by the neck, which is long and narrow but widens considerably at anterior end. Legs four times length of body. Proboscis cylindrical, with a bluntly rounded distal end. Trunk segment 2 considerably longer than wide, segments 3 and 4 fused; with a short abdomen. Femur shorter than tibia on leg 2 but longer than tibia on leg 1. Ovigerous legs with ten segments, all short except segments 3, 4 and 5; segment 3 shorter than either segments 4 and 5.

Essentially sublittoral but occurs occasionally in the littoral zone. Widespread around Britain.

7 ANOPLODACTYLIDAE

1. Eye tubercle not projecting forwards beyond cephalon. No dorsal protuberances on lateral processes. Propodus without lamellae. Ovigerous legs with five or six segments   **2**

    Eye tubercle projects beyond cephalon. Protuberances present on lateral processes. Propodus with a cutting lamella. Ovigerous legs with six segments   **3**

2. Ovigerous legs with five segments. Proboscis straight at end with slight angles at corners. Abdomen slightly longer than fourth pair of lateral processes   ***Anoplodactylus virescens***

    Ovigerous legs with six segments. Proboscis with conspicuous angles at corners. Abdomen more than twice length of lateral processes of last trunk segment   ***Anoplodactylus angulatus***

3. Anterior part of cephalon long and narrow, overhanging posterior part of proboscis. Auxiliary claws small and laterally positioned. Protuberances on lateral processes without a spine at apex. Cutting lamellae of propodus short, preceded by four to six small teeth   ***Anoplodactylus petiolatus***

Cephalon short and wide; does not overhang proboscis. Auxiliary claws absent. Protuberances on lateral processes with spine at apex. Cutting lamellae of propodus long, preceded by one or two small teeth   ***Anoplodactylus pygmaeus***

Anoplodactylus angulatus (Dohrn)   FIG. 11.20

Body 1–2 mm long, with legs three times this length. Proboscis broad, with conspicuous angles at distal end, when viewed from dorsal surface, caused by ventrolateral protuberances. Ovigerous legs with five segments. Cephalon broad, ocular tubercle with a small point. Body segments broad, with thick lateral processes. Abdomen more than twice length of very short last lateral processes. Proboscis with two large teeth and three setae, preceding a row of teeth on sole. Small, laterally placed auxiliary claws on legs.

Mainly south-west in distribution.

Anoplodactylus pygmaeus (Hodge)   FIG. 11.20

Small species, body length 0.7–1 mm; legs two and a half times as long as body. Proboscis rounded at end, with a subterminal constriction. Cephalon broad, with a long ocular process extending anteriorly. Ovigerous legs with six segments. General shape more compact than *A. petiolatus*. Abdomen approximately twice as long as last pair of lateral processes. Small dorsal protuberance on each lateral process, each with a terminal spine. Propodus with two spines on heel, and one or two spines, and a long cutting lamella, on sole. No auxiliary claws.

A common shallow-water species, distributed from Denmark to the Azores.

Anoplodactylus petiolatus (Krøyer)   FIG. 11.20

Slender body, 1–1.5 mm long; legs three times as long as body. Proboscis with a rounded end. Ovigerous legs with six segments. Long neck, with a long ocular tubercle. Body segments broad, with wide lateral processes; abdomen long and narrow, reaching well beyond last lateral processes, which have a dorsal protuberance which lacks a terminal spine. Propodus with two large spines and a smaller pair, with four to six spines and a short cutting lamella on sole. There are small, laterally placed, auxiliary claws.

Widely distributed around Britain.

Anoplodactylus virescens Hodge   FIG. 11.20

Body 1 mm long, with legs three times this length. Proboscis bluntly truncate. Ovigers with five segments. Cephalon broad with an extremely blunt ocular tubercle. Body segments broad, with thick lateral processes. Abdomen a short rounded knob, reaching oliquely slightly beyond the very short, last lateral processes. Heel of propodus with two or three large spines, and a row of teeth on sole. Auxiliary claws are small and laterally placed.

Mainly southern in distribution.

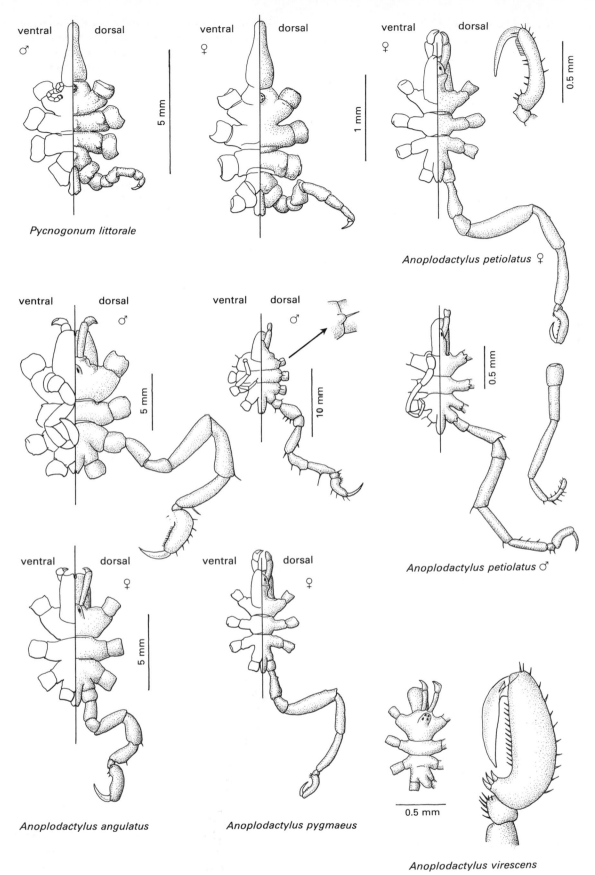

ventral   dorsal
♂

Pycnogonum littorale

5 mm

ventral   dorsal
♀

1 mm

ventral   dorsal
♀

0.5 mm

Anoplodactylus petiolatus ♀

ventral   dorsal   ♂

5 mm

ventral   dorsal   ♂

10 mm

0.5 mm

Anoplodactylus petiolatus ♂

ventral   dorsal
♀

5 mm

ventral   dorsal
♀

Anoplodactylus angulatus

Anoplodactylus pygmaeus

0.5 mm

Anoplodactylus virescens

Fig. 11.20

C. PHYLUM TARDIGRADA

The phylum Tardigrada contains more than 500 species of small multicellular animals, between 50 and 1200 µm long, which occur most commonly in the surface water of mosses, lichens, liverworts, and some angiosperms. They move with a characteristic bear-like, lumbering gait and have been popularly described as 'water bears'. Marine forms occur mainly in the interstitial water between sand-grains, though *Echiniscoides sigismundi* (Schultze) has been recorded at various times on *Enteromorpha*, in the mantle cavity of mussels, and on the opercular plates of *Semibalanus balanoides* (L.).

The tardigrades can be divided into two distinct types: those with plates on their dorsal cuticle, and those without plates. In all species the body is elongate, often cylindrical in shape, or in cross-section convex dorsally and flattened ventrally. There is a distinct anterior region which may bear *eyespots* and *cephalic appendages*. There are four pairs of stumpy *legs*, all of which may not be visible when the animal is observed from above. Each of the legs is equipped with *claws* of variable type and number, although most marine forms have 'toes' with distal *adhesive discs*.

The cuticle, which consists of up to seven layers, contains tanned proteins other than chitin and extends into the foregut and rectum. Amongst essentially terrestrial species, members of the Macrobiotidae, and similar types, generally have a smooth cuticle, except for a superficial segmentation; in some species there may be small refractive pores scattered regularly over the dorsal surface, a fine or coarse granulation, or various arrangements of spines and/or swellings. In the Echiniscidae the dorsal surface of the body is covered with a series of cuticular plates and there may be a variety of appendages on head and body.

The Macrobiotidae are without either cuticular plates or appendages of the *Echiniscus* type, and also lack cephalic/buccal appendages. The Milnesiidae, comprising the monotypical genus *Milnesium*, possess six rostral and two latero-ventral papillae.

The internal body plan of tardigrades is very simple. The *mouth* is terminal or subterminal, and may be surrounded by cuticular thickenings, the *peribuccal lamellae*. It leads to a straight, slightly curved, or undulating *buccal tube*, followed by a bulbous muscular *pharynx* (*pharyngeal bulb*). The buccal tube is pierced by a pair of pointed *stylets* which are everted through the mouth and used to pierce plant or animal cells. The pharynx opens into the *oesophagus*, the length of which varies markedly between species. The *midgut* is large and may extend over half the total body-length. The *hindgut* or rectum is short and opens into a small cavity, which in Eutardigrada is a true *cloaca*, visible as a transverse or longitudinal slit on the ventral surface of the body between the third and fourth pairs of legs. The body cavity is fluid-filled and contains a large number of 'cavity globules' or *coelomocytes* which are believed to have a storage function. The *nervous system* consists of a large, lobed *cerebral ganglion* from which two connectives pass, one to each side of the pharynx, to the *sub-pharyngeal ganglion*, which is one of a chain of five *ventral ganglia* each united by two longitudinal *nerves*.

The single *gonad* is an elongate sac above the gut. In the male there are two vasa deferentia, each with a small *seminal receptacle*. The female has a single *oviduct* which curves from the right to the left side of the intestine. The oviduct in the female and the vasa deferentia in the male may share a common opening with the anus, i.e. a *cloaca* (in Eutardigrada) or may have a separate opening between the third and fourth pair of legs. Some species consist solely of females but in most males comprise 10% of the total population. Apart from a tendency on the part of the males to be smaller there is little or no sexual dimorphism.

Estimates of the life-span of tardigrades vary between 3 and 30 months. The animal may moult up to twelve times during its life, reaching sexual maturity after the second or third moult. The peak of reproductive activity occurs between May and November although females with eggs, casts with eggs, or free eggs can be found in small numbers throughout the year.

One of the most remarkable properties displayed by tardigrades is their ability to enter a resistant state referred to as the *tun*, in which they are able to withstand a wide range of environmental stresses of both a chemical and physical nature. This dormant state has been variously described as anabiosis, cryptobiosis, and recently anhydrobiosis. When the surrounding water dries up the tardigrade will readily enter this dormant state, and when water is again available recovery occurs. This phenomenon has not been recorded in marine species.

Interstitial marine tardigrades usually occur at mid-tide level and below, particularly in the damp ripples lying across the beach, at a depth of up to 10 cm. Crisp and Hobart (1954) recorded *Echiniscus sigismundi* from the opercular plates of *Semibalanus balanoides* covered with green algae. Most pieces of moss in the terrestrial environment contain tardigrades. The yellow or grey *Xanthoria* species of lichen often yield a rich tardigrade fauna, particularly *Hypsibius* (*Hypsibius*) *oberhaeuseri* (Doyère) even when collected from rocks in the splash zone on the sea shore. In *Ramalina* spp., a grey-green, stiff, upright, branching lichen also found on the sea shore, tardigrades are confined to the basal 'holdfast' portion.

After collection moss or lichen samples should be placed in polythene bags with adequate data labels and the bags left open so that the contents can slowly air dry. They can then be stored in a cool, dry place for long periods without deterioration of the specimens or growth of mould. Aquatic mosses can be similarly treated but angiosperms, algae, and bottom samples can only be kept for short periods and should be sorted as soon as possible. Marine sand samples can be preserved with 5% sea-water formalin if they have to be stored.

Dried samples should be allowed to soak in tap water for 24 h before the tardigrades are extracted. This allows encysted and cryptobiosed individuals to recover before extraction. To the sample is added an equal volume of 4% acetic acid or 20% ethyl alcohol for 10 min. This narcotizes the specimens, which relax and fall away from the plant material.

The simplest method of recovering tardigrades from moss or lichen is to squeeze the material dry over a Petri dish, resoak it and allow it to stand for several minutes, then wring again. This process should be repeated several times. An elaboration of this method involves soaking the plant material, enclosed in a bag of bolting silk, in narcotizing agent and squeezing it out over a fine mesh membrane on which the microfauna collects. For extracting marine species, the sand sample is mixed with 10% $MgCl_2$ narcotizing agent and allowed to stand for 10 min. By agitating and swirling rapidly the material can be forced into suspension and after allowing a short time for the larger particles to settle the supernatant is poured off through a fine nylon membrane, which collects the meiofauna. The mixing and decanting process is repeated several times.

One problem with formalin-fixed marine material is that the animals are usually in an irreversibly contracted state. Since an aid to identification when sorting is their manner of locomotion, the use of fresh material is preferable and the animals quickly recover from the effect of $MgCl_2$.

Asphyxiated animals are better for permanent or semi-permanent preparations. This state can be induced by keeping them in suitable containers with distilled water or deoxygenated sea-water, depending upon from which habitat they have been obtained. A wide range of proprietary makes of mountant is available but Faure's Medium (Gum chloral) is particularly suitable.

Specimens may be transferred to Faure's Medium from water and will readily fix and clear. There may be some initial distortion but this disappears within a few days. To facilitate subsequent observation a dye, such as lignin pink, may be added to the mountant. Gum chloral will harden but other mountants may not attain the same degree of permanence, consequently the coverslip should be ringed with stiff Canada balsam or Laktoseal.

Examination and species determination often requires a microscope equipped with oil immersion. All measurements refer to fully extended, asphyxiated individuals, the body length being the distance between the most anterior tip and the junction of the fourth pair of legs.

Quantitative estimates of moss-living tardigrades can be made using the Boisseau apparatus (Morgan and King 1976).

REFERENCES

Boaden, P. J. S. (1963). The interstitial fauna of some North Wales beaches. *Journal of the Marine Biological Association of the United Kingdom*, **43**, 79–96.

Boaden, P. J. S. (1966). Interstitial fauna from Northern Ireland. *Veröffentlichungen des Instituts für Meeresforschung in Bremerhaven*, **11**, 125–30.

Crisp, D. J. and Hobart, J. (1954). A note on the habitat of the marine tardigrade *Echiniscoides sigismundi* (Schultze). *Annals and Magazine of Natural History*, **7**, 554–60.

Green, J. (1950). Habits of the marine tardigrade *Echiniscoides sigismundi*. *Nature*, **166**, 153–4.

Gray, J. S. and Rieger, R. M. (1971). A quantitative study of the meiofauna of an exposed sandy beach, at Robin Hood's Bay, Yorkshire. *Journal of the Marine Biological Association of the United Kingdom*, **51**, 1–19.

Harris, R. P. (1972). The distribution and ecology of the interstitial meiofauna of a sandy beach at Whitsand Bay, East Cornwall. *Journal of the Marine Biological Association of the United Kingdom*, **52**, 1–18.

King, P. E., Fordy, M. R., and Morgan, C. I. (1981). The marine flora and fauna of the Isles of Scilly—Tardigrada. *Journal of Natural History*, **15**, 145–50.

McIntyre, A. D. and Murison, D. J. (1973). The meiofauna of a flatfish nursery ground. *Journal of the Marine Biological Association of the United Kingdom*, **53**, 93–118.

Moore, C. G. (1979). The distribution and ecology of psammolittoral meiofauna around the Isle of Man. *Cahiers de Biologie Marine*, **20**, 383–415.

Moore, P. G. (1977). Additions to the littoral fauna of Rockall, with a description of *Araeolaimus penelope* sp. nov (Nematoda: Axonolaimidae). *Journal of the Marine Biological Association of the United Kingdom*, **57**, 191–200.

Morgan, C. I. (1976). Studies on the British tardigrade fauna: some zoogeographical and ecological notes. *Journal of Natural History*, **10**, 607–32.

Morgan, C. I. (1980). Notes on the distribution and abundance of the Irish marine Tardigrada, including two additions to the Irish fauna. *Irish Naturalists Journal*, **20**, 129–72.

Morgan, C. I. and King, P. E. (1976). *British Tardigrades. Synopses of the British Fauna (New Series)*, No. 9. Linnean Society of London, Academic Press.

Morgan, C. I. and Lampard, D. J. (1986). A wealth of water bears. *The Arran Naturalist*, **9**, 24–30.

Morgan, C. I. and Lampard, D. J. (1986). *The Fauna of the Clyde Sea Area. Phylum Tardigrada*. Occasional Publication No. 3. University Marine Biological Station, Millport, Isle of Cumbrae.

Morgan, C. I. and O'Reilly, M. (1988). Tardigrada from Tanera Mor, Summer Isles, North-west Scotland, including a description of *Megastygarctides setoloso* new species and a revised key for the identification of Scottish marine species. *Glasgow Naturalist*, **21**, 445–54.

Murray, J. (1911). Arctiscoida. *Proceedings of the Royal Irish Academy*, **31**, 1–16.

Pollock, L. W. (1971). On some British marine Tardigrada, including two new species of *Batillipes*. *Journal of the Marine Biological Association of the United Kingdom*, **51**, 93–103.

Ramazzotti, G. and Maucci, W. (1983). Il Phylum Tardigrada, 3rd edn. *Memorie dell'Istituto Italiano di Idrobiologia dott. Marco de Marchi*, **41**, 1–1012.

KEY TO SPECIES

The species treated here are those which are most likely to be encountered in littoral marine habitats. Excluded are: species normally associated with freshwater or terrestrial habitats which may occur accidentally in the littoral zone, particularly where fresh water crosses the shore; uncommon species; sublittoral forms. Morgan and Lampard (1986) and Morgan and O'Reilly (1988) provide keys which are more comprehensive.

1. With lateral cirrus at position A (Fig. 11.21)   **2**

   Without lateral cirrus at position A. Species usually associated with terrestrial or freshwater habitats; refer to Morgan and King (1976).

2. Legs without claws and terminated with digits, bearing elongate, rounded, or oval flattened expansions   **3**

   Legs without digits but terminated with 5 to 11 claws inserted directly on to leg
                                                                              Echiniscoides sigisimundi

3. Digitate leg terminated with elongate, paddle-shaped expansions   ***Orzeliscus belopus***

   Digitate leg terminated with round or oval expansions   **[Genus *Batillipes*] 4**

4. Animals without a caudal appendage   **5**

   Animals with a caudal appendage   **6**

5. Caudal end swollen, with slight facetting   ***Batillipes tubernatis***

   Caudal end gently rounded   ***Batillipes acaudatus***

6. Caudal appendage a single spine   **7**

   Caudal appendage consists of more than one spine   **9**

7. Caudal appendage a long spine, placed dorsally, terminating in a membranous sack; the sack may be inflated   ***Batillipes bullacaudatus***

   Caudal appendage a simple spine, slender and short, inserted directly into the extreme caudal end of the body   ***Batillipes mirus***

8. Caudal appendage consisting of three spines of equal length inserted directly on to the caudal end   ***Batillipes littoralis***

   Caudal appendage consisting of a central long spine, surrounded by several small spines at the base   ***Batillipes phreaticus***

I BATILLIPEDIDAE

Batillipes tubernatis Pollock   FIG. 11.21

Length 165–190 μm. Cuticle transparent with distinct, uniformly dispersed pores. Slight projection often present between head and first pair of legs, otherwise body outline does not taper towards anterior end. Cephalic appendages consist of a single

median cirrus (18 μm); paired internal (20 μm) and external (13 μm) cirri, one of each pair on either side of head. The internals more dorsally placed than externals with respect to anterior margin of body; clavae (12 μm) and lateral cirri A (24 μm), one of each on either side of head, with a common large, conical, base. Laterally only cirri E (18 μm) present, located latero-dorsally and slightly anterior to fourth pair of

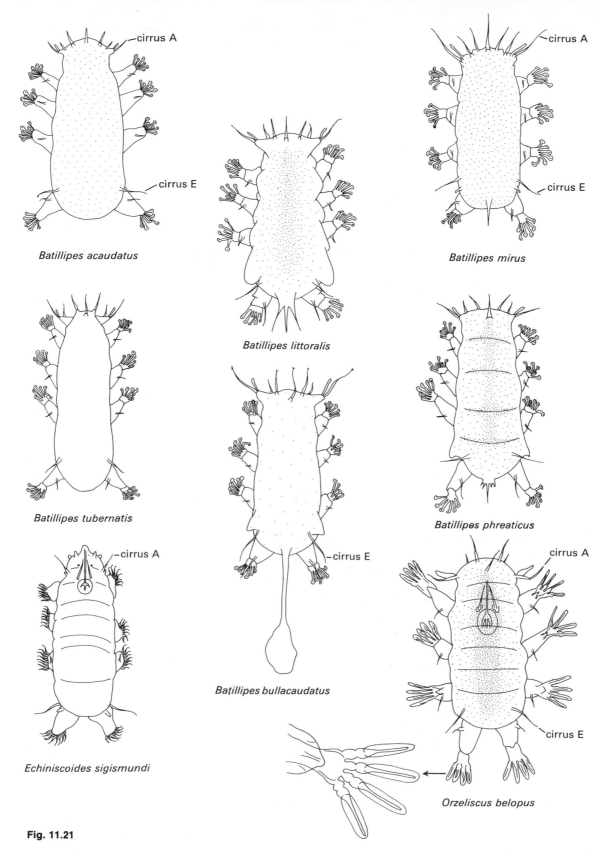

Batillipes acaudatus

Batillipes littoralis

Batillipes mirus

Batillipes tubernatis

Batillipes phreaticus

Batillipes bullacaudatus

Echiniscoides sigismundi

Orzeliscus belopus

Fig. 11.21

legs. Each leg with a stout spine, longer on second pair (12 μm) than on others (6.5 μm). Legs slightly telescopic distally, each bearing six 'toes', arranged as in *Batillipes mirus*, with four central toes in two rows of two, the internal pair shorter and placed more ventrally than external pair; remaining two toes laterally placed, one on either side of central rows.

Recorded from the Gower Peninsula; Filey Beach and Stoupe Beck Beach, Yorkshire; the Clyde Sea area and Loch Ewe, Scotland; the Isle of Man.

Batillipes acaudatus Pollock   FIG. 11.21

Length 185–195 μm. Cuticle smooth and transparent, with distinct uniformly arranged pores. Cephalic appendages consisting of: median cirrus (14–15 μm); internal cirri (16 μm); clavae (8 μm) and lateral cirri A (15–17 μm). Body with smooth outline lacking caudal appendages, but slight lateral projections often occurring between first, second, and third pairs of legs. Dorsolateral cirrus (E) present above fourth pair of legs, and all legs bear a short spine, usually more fully developed on fourth pair (often 10 μm long). Legs slightly telescopic distally, bearing six toes.

Recorded from the Gower Peninsula, Filey Beach and Stoupe Beck Beach, Yorkshire, and the Clyde Sea area.

Batillipes mirus Richters   FIG. 11.21

Length 100–720 μm, most frequently around 400–600 μm. Juveniles 100 μm or less. Usually without eye-pigment. Body colourless, cuticle smooth, poorly developed cuticular folds and inconspicuous external segmentation. Buccal aperture ventral and subterminal with cephalic appendages dorsal to it, consisting of: single median cirrus; two median internal and two median external cirri, one of each positioned either side of slightly shorter median cirrus, internal medians a little above, and external medians a little below, rostral margins of body with a cephalic papillus between them on each side. Cirrus A long, bristle-like, accompanied by long, curved, club-like clavus, both sharing a small cuticular basal projection. Laterally, a bristle-like projection present between third and fourth pairs of legs and also a median caudal cirrus. Small lateral marginal spines sometimes present near base of lateral bristles.

Legs of three distinct parts, retractile into broad basal portion, terminal portion bearing six 'toes' better developed on first and fourth pairs of legs. The four central 'toes' arranged in two rows, internal row composed of shorter toes orientated ventrally, longer external toes orientated dorsally. Distal end of each 'toe' expanded in a palette shape often reinforced with a median longitudinal bar.

Recorded from many locations on the western European coastline, including Firemore Bay, Loch Ewe, and the Clyde Sea area Scotland, and Whitford sands, Gower Peninsula, South Wales.

Batillipes phreaticus Renaud-Debyser   FIG. 11.21

Dimensions 170 × 75 μm. Cuticle usually finely striated. Body tapering slightly towards head; projections on lateral margins of caudal end of body give it a rather bulky appearance. Cephalic

appendages consist of: median cirrus (15 μm) immediately dorsal to anterior margin of body; internal (22 μm) and external (15 μm) buccal cirri with slightly protruding papillus between them on each side; highly characteristic clavus, curved, refractive, and speckled with dark spots. Cephalic appendages, mounted on cuticular projections, often 2–3 μm in height. Lateral cirri A 30–32 μm long. Slender spine (25–28 μm) present in a dorsolateral position above each of fourth pair of legs. Each pair of legs with a bristle, especially well-developed on fourth pair (up to 25 μm). Legs with six unequal toes each with an oval, concave palette. Caudally, a long straight spine (up to 25 μm) present with a variable number of secondary spines around its base.

Recorded from Filey Beach and Stoupe Beck Beach, Yorkshire; Isles of Scilly; Isle of Man; Clyde Sea area.

Batillipes bullacaudatus McGinty and Higgins   FIG. 11.21

Length up to 130 μm. The body outline undulates slightly between each of the first three pairs of legs while there is an acute lateral projection on each side between the third and fourth pair of legs; the animal tapers slightly from these projections towards the neck. Cuticle transparent, with regularly arranged pores. Cirrus E a filament (22 μm), inserted posterio-dorsally on lateral projection. Caudal region slightly flattened, with a long spine, inserted slightly dorsally to the margin of the body, terminating in a saclike bulbous membrane. Cephalic appendages long consisting of; lateral cirri (28 μm); clavae (13 μm); cirri (14 μm) inserted on cephalic papillae; internal cirri (20 μm); dorsal median cirrus (20 μm) lacking a pedestal. The lateral, internal, and median cirri usually terminate in three small hairs. Buccal tube straight, pharyngeal bulb subspherical. Each of the first three pairs of legs bears a short spine. The spine on each of the fourth legs is long (28 μm), extending past the toes, and terminates with short hairs.

Recorded from the Clyde Sea area.

Batillipes littoralis Renaud-Debyser   FIG. 11.21

Length up to 200 μm, width (excluding appendages) up to 80 μm; animal with a stumpy appearance. Body outline undulating with prominent posteriorly directed projections between third and fourth legs. Body tapers slightly from the caudal end towards the neck. Cuticle transparent and finely granulate. Cirrus E a long filament inserted posterio-dorsally to the lateral projection. Caudal region gently curved with a characteristic appendage inserted slightly dorsally to margin of body. Caudal appendage consists of three spines of equal length, or with the central slightly longer, almost reaching the end of the fourth pair of legs. Cephalic appendages consisting of: lateral cirri (35 μm); clavae (18 μm); short external cirri (12 μm); internal cirri (21 μm); median cirrus (17 μm). The pedestals of external cirri, lateral cirri, and clavae are well-developed. Buccal apparatus similar to *B. mirus*. Short fine spines are present on the first three pairs of legs, while those on the fourth pair of legs are longer (up to 24 μm) extending to the toes. The fourth pair of legs also carry a small backward pointing projection, on the anterior lateral margin.

Recorded from the Clyde Sea area and Solway coast.

2 HALECHINISCIDAE

Orzeliscus belopus du Bois-Reymond Marcus FIG. 11.21

Dimensions 200 × 90 μm giving a very stumpy appearance. Cuticle distinctly granulate, with granulations larger and coarser along mid-line than on flanks. Cephalic appendages complex, consisting of: one dorsal median cirrus (16 μm); two median internal (buccal) cirri (16 μm); two median external cirri (16 μm) positioned between anterior margin and buccal aperture; two lateral cirri at corners of rostral margin (25 μm) with a tapering clavus (15 μm) positioned near base of each; two disc-like cephalic papillae, one each side between internal and external cirri; a blunt projection behind each lateral cirrus with accompanying clavus. Buccal aperture surrounded by a rounded plate; buccal tube about 25 μm, 2 μm in diameter. Bulb short, oval, with rods crinkled. Caudal cirrus (30 μm) above each of fourth pair of legs and each of first three pairs of legs bearing a papillus (9 μm) and terminating with a small seta. Legs long, divided into three portions, a sculpted proximal part, narrowing to median part and terminating with characteristic expansion bearing four 'toes' each 15 μm long and 2 μm in diameter. Each 'toe' consisting of globular base with finger-like keeled extremity, often hollow at tip and with adhesive ventral surface.

Recorded from Yorkshire, Solway coast, Clyde Sea area, and Loch Ewe, Scotland.

3 ECHINISCOIDIDAE

Echiniscoides sigismundi (Schultze) FIG. 11.21

Length 100–340 μm, but majority around 200 μm; juveniles, 100 μm or less. Transparent, reddish, or colourless with large black eyespots. Cuticle thin and smooth with transverse dorsal folds. Buccal aperture subterminal. Bulb short, oval, slightly broader posteriorly. Median cirri and cephalic papillae absent; cephalic appendages consist of short, spinose lateral cirri A, associated with a small clavus, and minute internal and external buccal cirri, situated above and below anterior cephalic margin. Cuticular spine present in equivalent position to lateral appendage E between third and fourth pair of legs. Papillus present at point of insertion of fourth legs, third legs bear a short spine. Head with blunt projections on either side, giving the animal a rather square-ended appearance. Five to nine claws (rarely 11), equal-sized, smooth, without spurs. Eggs oval (maximum diameter 45 μm) occasionally spherical, colourless, or reddish, deposited singly or in masses.

Recorded feeding on the chlorophyllic contents of *Enteromorpha* from the North Sea, Atlantic, and Mediterranean coasts. British records include: the west coast of Ireland; North Wales; in the mantle cavity of *Mytilus edulis* at Whitstable; in the crevices of the plates of the barnacle *Semibalanus balanoides*, from mainly west coast locations of the British Isles.

D. MYRIAPODA

Class Chilopoda

Order Geophilomorpha

Littoral and supralittoral represenatives of the Chilopoda are confined to the order Geophilomorpha which are long, worm-like burrowing centipedes. They are predaceous, with the first pair of walking legs converted to poison claws. *Hydroschendyla submarina* feeds on polychaete annelids and *Strigamia maritima* on isopods, amphipods, enchytraeid annelids, periwinkles, and barnacles. Geophilids usually occur in moist soil but some have been recorded in the upper littoral zone on sandy shores under rejectamenta, or in crevices or empty barnacle shells on rocky shores. The body is somewhat dorso-ventrally flattened, the genital opening is at the posterior end of the body and there is a pair of legs on each trunk segment. The basal segment of each leg is the *coxa*. On each segment there is a dorsal *tergite* and a ventral *sternite* with a number of lateral *pleurites*. The tergite is often divided transversely into a smaller anterior *pretergite* and a larger posterior *metatergite*. The sternite is similarly divided into a *presternite* and a *metasternite*. In most British species each trunk sternite from about the fourth backwards has a transverse pit or fossa on its anterior margin, which increases in size up to segments eight or nine and then becomes smaller on the last few sternites. Corresponding with this fossa there is a small peg on the posterior border of the preceding sternite. The combination of peg and fossa is known as the *carpophagus structure*.

REFERENCES

Blower, J. G. (1985). Millipedes. *Synopses of the British Fauna*, no. 35. Leiden: E. J. Brill, for the Linnean Society of London, and the Estuarine and Brackish Water Sciences Association.

Eason, E. H. (1964). *Centipedes of the British Isles*. Frederick Warne, London.

KEY TO SPECIES

1. Coxal pores distributed over ventral surface of coxa ***Strigamia maritima***

   Coxal pores largely concentrated along edge of adjacent metasternite or opening into pits **2**

2. Two coxal pores on each side	*Hydroschendyla submarina*
More than two coxal pores on each side	**3**

3. Without carpophagus structure	*Necrophloeophagus longicornis*
With carpophagus structure	*Geophilus fucorum serauti*

Hydroschendyla submarina (Grube)   FIG. 11.22

About 30 mm long and 1.2 mm broad, but may reach 40 mm. Number of trunk segments: 45–51 (male), 47–53 (female), most usually 47 (male) and 49 (female). Reddish brown in colour. Basal node of poison claw absent or rudimentary. Longitudinal sternal gutters not strongly marked. Last legs with apical claws absent or rudimentary.

Usually in rock crevices in intertidal zone. Recorded from Cornwall, Devon, Yorkshire, Clare Island, Channel Islands.

Strigamia maritima (Leach)   FIG. 11.22

Up to 40 mm long and 1.5 mm broad, but usually smaller than this. Number of trunk segments: 47–49 (male) and 49–51 (female). Red colour. Pleurites of last trunk-segment distinct from adjacent pretergite.

Occurs in shingle banks, rock crevices around high water mark, and between rock and overlying seaweed. Also above high water.

Widely distributed; reported from all coasts of Britain and Ireland.

Geophilus fucorum serauti Brolemann   FIG. 11.22

Slender pale species, 30 mm long, 0.8 mm broad. Trunk segments 51–53 (male), 51–57 (female). Poison claw with crenulate concavity, about 14 scallops. Antennae about five times as long as breadth of head. Carpophagus fossa, where fully developed, occupying no more than three-quarters breadth of sternite, usually less. Claw of second maxillary teleopodite well-developed. Fewer than 65 pairs of legs. Coxal pores opening ventrally only.

Occurs around high-tide mark, often associated with *Strigamia maritima* but never in such large numbers. Reported from Caernarvonshire, Isle of Man, Galway.

Necrophloeophagus longicornis (Leach)   FIG. 11.22

About 30 mm long and 0.9–1.0 mm broad, but may reach 45 mm. Number of trunk segments: 49–55 (male), 51–57 (female). Bright yellow colour with head and forcipular segment distinctly darker. More than three coxal pores on each side. Poison claw with crenulate concavity. Fewer than 65 pairs of legs.

In addition to occasional records on the sea shore it occurs commonly in gardens, woodland, grassland, and mountains; geographically widespread in the British Isles.

Class **Diplopoda**

The body consists of a head followed by a trunk consisting of a number of leg-bearing segments, some of which are double, one or more legless or *apodous rings* and a tail piece or *telson*. The head has paired *antennae*, groups of *ocelli*, a pair of *mandibles*, and a lower lip or *gnathochilarium* formed from the first maxillae. The first trunk segment is the *collum* and all the rest have a narrow anterior section, the *prozonite*, and a wider posterior *metazonite*. In some species the metazonite of the *pleurotergite* is produced laterally or dorso-laterally into lobes or keels, the *paranota*. Stink glands open on some segments by *ozopores*. Legs near the posterior end of males are usually modified for transferring the sperm to the female. These are referred to as *gonopods*.

KEY TO SPECIES

1. Head, collum, and tergites with two transverse rows of serrated hollow spines, a lateral tuft of similar spines on each pleurite except first; two long brushes of spines terminally. Adults with collum followed by nine tergites, thirteen pairs of legs   *Polyxenus lagurus*

Without serrated spines on tergites and pleurites, setae on trunk, if present, simple. Tergites strongly arched, hiding ventrally placed pleurites and sternites, or with pleurites incorporated into a pleurotergal arch or three-quarter cylinder, or sternites may be joined to the pleurotergal arch to give a cylindrical sclerite. Pleurotergites with or without lateral or dorsolateral expansions or paranota   **2**

2. Ocelli may occupy a triangular field, or form a single line, or a single line augmented anteriorly by two or three extra ocelli. Longitudinal striae confined to ventral half of

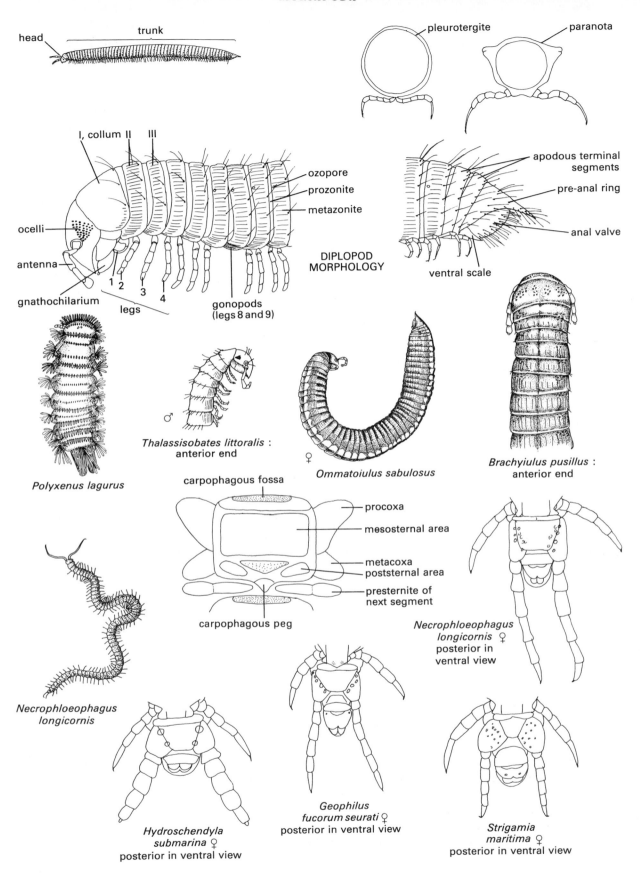

head

trunk

pleurotergite

paranota

I, collum II III

ozopore

prozonite

metazonite

ocelli

antenna

gnathochilarium

1 2 3 4

legs

gonopods
(legs 8 and 9)

DIPLOPOD
MORPHOLOGY

apodous terminal
segments

pre-anal ring

anal valve

ventral scale

Polyxenus lagurus

♂ *Thalassisobates littoralis* :
anterior end

♀ *Ommatoiulus sabulosus*

Brachyiulus pusillus :
anterior end

carpophagous fossa

procoxa

mesosternal area

metacoxa
poststernal area

presternite of
next segment

carpophagous peg

*Necrophloeophagus
longicornis* ♀
posterior in
ventral view

*Necrophloeophagus
longicornis*

*Hydroschendyla
submarina* ♀
posterior in ventral view

*Geophilus
fucorum seurati* ♀
posterior in ventral view

*Strigamia
maritima* ♀
posterior in ventral view

Fig. 11.22

ring up to the level of ozopores. Long and thin; length/breadth ratio males 20–30:1, females 15–30:1; adults usually thinner than 0.7 mm. Never with caudal projection. Gonopods never retracted into lumen of seventh ring **Thalassisobates littoralis**

Ocelli usually present in a triangular field. Longitudinal striae or flutings extend around whole of ring; a distinct suture divides prozonite from metazonite. Short and fat; length/breadth ratio of males 10–14:1, females thicker. Adult males usually thicker than 0.7 mm. With or without caudal projections. Gonopods usually completely retracted within lumen of seventh ring (except *Brachyiulus pusillus*) **3**

3. Telson produced as a pointed tail extending beyond posterior level of anal valves **Ommatoiulus sabulosus**

Telson either clubbed, or rounded and not obviously produced or, if pointed (*Brachyiulus*), not extending beyond level of anal valves **4**

4. Apex of telson distinctly club-shaped or smoothly rounded, not projecting. Metazonites without fringing setae **Cylindroiulus latestriatus**

Apex of telson pointed, obtuse, roof-like, very slightly projecting over anal valves. Small species, adults less than 14 mm long and 1.0 mm wide. Two dorsolateral yellow-cream bands extending along length of animal. Metazonites fringed with setae **Brachyiulus pusillus**

Polyxenus lagurus (Linnaeus)   FIG. 11.22
Dorso-ventrally flattened, lacks calcification, light amber coloured, clothed in dark brown setae, prominent lateral tufts on every pleurite, except the first, and two long terminal brushes on telson.

Occasionally in coastal regions at roots of halophile plants, beneath lichens and moss on boulders.

Thalassisobates littoralis (Silvestri)   FIG. 11.22
Pale greyish white with dark brown ozodenes. Setae fringing metazonites prominent.

Under stones between HWN and HWS in fine gravel associated with *Geophilus fucorium* and *Strigamia maritima* (Blower 1985). Grange-over-Sands, Menai Straits, Isle of Man, Devon, Norfolk.

Ommatoiulus sabulosus (Linnaeus)   FIG. 11.22
Orange, reddish, rust-brown, or dark red-brown. Median-dorsal third of the upper hemicircle of each segment has two lighter bands of straw-coloured lighter pigment on either side of median-dorsal band. Bands may be broken into a series of segmental spots.

A wandering species which occurs in a wide range of habitats. Duneland or sometimes foreshore; Ainsdale, Newborough Warren, Anglesey, Gower.

Cylindroiulus latestriatus (Curtis)
Light brown with darker ozadenes. Metazonite striae widely spaced. Anal valves usually with three setae.

Occurs in coastal areas. Fixed or semi-fixed dunes at roots of marram grass, on the shore in roots of sea pink and other halophytes. Surrey, Suffolk, Devon, Cornwall, northern England generally; Ireland, Scotland, Wales.

Brachyiulus pusillus (Leach)   FIG. 11.22
Colour pattern similar to that of *Ommatoiulus sabulosus* but colour darker brown and stripes lighter yellow rather than orange.

Widespread, including coastal habitats, England, Wales, Scotland, and northern Ireland.

E. Hexapoda

Class **Collembola**

Collembola are mainly soil dwellers and are extremely numerous as individuals and species. They require a moist environment and are mainly saprophagous, although some eat soil nematodes. There are two suborders of Collembola, the Symphypleona, characterized by their short globular, indistinctly segmented bodies, and the Arthropleona with elongate cylindrical and clearly segmented bodies. Most littoral species belong to the second suborder. It is further subdivided into the Podomorpha and Entomobryomorpha.

The collembolan body is divided into three tagmata: the *head*, the *thorax*, consisting of three segments, and the *abdomen* with six segments. The body is generally covered with setae of various forms and some species may have scales. The head bears the *antennae* which usually consist of four segments varying in length between species. Groups of one to eight *ocelli* may be present on each side of the head, and in many species a *post-antennal organ* is present between the ocelli and the antenna. The mouthparts are situated within a pouch formed by ventrolateral extensions of the head capsule. The thorax has three pairs of *legs*, one to each segment. Each leg ends in a *terminal claw*, usually bearing *teeth*. An *empodium* is usually present. The abdomen has a bilobed structure known as the *ventral tube* on the ventral surface of segment 1, the name Collembola, meaning 'gluey-peg' refers to this projection which enables the animal to attach itself to the substratum. It also functions in osmoregulation. There is a '*springing organ*' or *furcula* on the fourth abdominal segment, although in many species this is reduced or absent. The furcula is held in a cocked position under the body by a hook-like structure, the *retinaculum*, situated on the third abdominal segment.

The sexes are similar. The reproductive system is simple, the gonads consisting of a pair of large sacs with short ducts which unite to form the vagina in the female or the ejaculatory canal in the male. Eggs are laid singly or in batches. Moulting continues in adult life and maturity is attained when a certain size is reached. There are often five to seven immature stages and there may be fifty moults during life though frequency depends, to a large extent, upon temperature.

A number of keys to the Collembola have been published, but these refer either to a particular family, or to a localized geographical area. The present key includes those species which have been recorded from littoral habitats around the British Isles, recognizing that information regarding distribution is extremely limited.

REFERENCES

Bagnall, R. S. (1949). Notes on the British Collembola. *Entomologist's Monthly Magazine*, **85**, 51–61.

Delamare-Deboutteville, C. (1953). Collemboles marins de la zone souterraine humide des sables litteraux. *Vie et Milieu*, **4**, 290–319.

Gisin, H. (1960). *Collembolenfauna Europas*. Museum d'histoire Naturelle, Geneve.

Gough, J. J. (1979). A key for the identification of the families of Collembola recorded from the British Isles. *Entomologist's Monthly Magazine*, **113**, 193–7.

Lubbock, J. (1873). *Monograph of the Collembola and Thysaneura*. Ray Society, London.

KEY TO FAMILIES

1. Pronotum with some setae, body generally stout, antennae short — **2**

   Pronotum small, without setae, usually hidden under mesonotum, habitus slender, antennae rather long — **4**

2. Pseudocelli present, antennal segment 3 with complex sense-organ, eyes absent, usually white — **1. Onychiuridae**

   Pseudocelli absent — **3**

3. Chewing mouthparts with well-developed molar plate (visible after clearing or squashing) not projected in a cone — **2. Hypogastruridae**

   Mouthparts usually without molar plate, often projected in a cone — **3. Neanuridae**

4. Body with smooth or ciliated setae. Abdominal segments 3 and 4 usually subequal, 4–6 sometimes fused. Furca often reduced — **4. Isotomidae**

   Body often with scales or densely ciliated. Abdominal segment 4 most appreciably longer than 3. Furca well-developed — **5. Entomobryidae**

1 ONYCHIURIDAE

1. Furca reduced to a single fold — *Onychiurus tullbergi*

   No trace of furca — **2**

2. Rudimentary empodium at most one-sixth as long as claw — *Onychiurus thalassophila*

   Longer empodium one-third length of claw, often thin at tip and wider at base — **3**

3. Posterior border of head with four pseudocelli — *Onychiurus halophilus*

   Posterior border of head with two pseudocelli — *Onychiurus debilis*

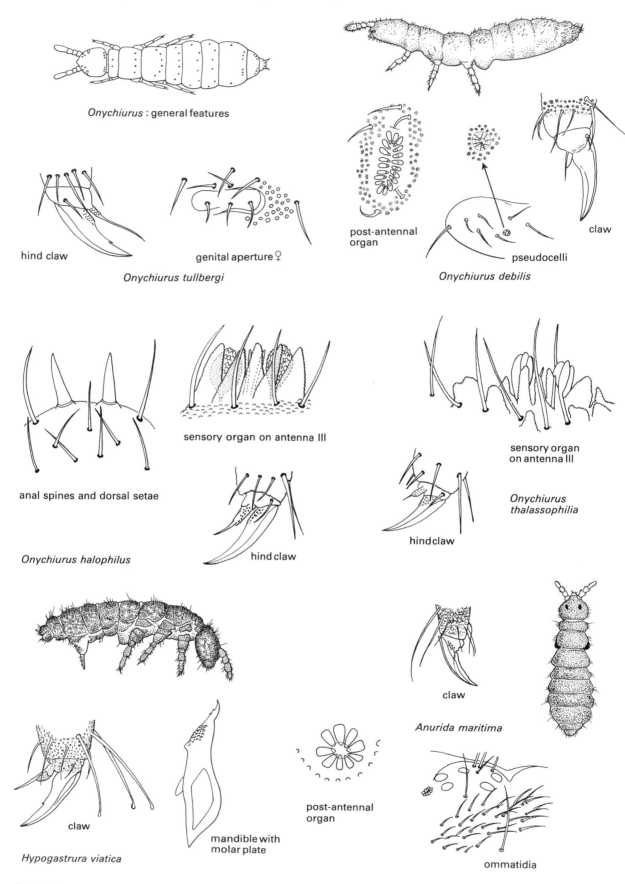

Onychiurus : general features

hind claw

genital aperture ♀

Onychiurus tullbergi

post-antennal organ

pseudocelli

claw

Onychiurus debilis

anal spines and dorsal setae

sensory organ on antenna III

hind claw

Onychiurus halophilus

sensory organ on antenna III

hindclaw

Onychiurus thalassophilia

claw

Anurida maritima

claw

Hypogastrura viatica

mandible with molar plate

post-antennal organ

ommatidia

Fig. 11.23

Onychiurus tullbergi (Bagnall)   FIG. 11.23

Length 2 mm. Usually white. Antennal segment 3 with complex sense-organ consisting of five papillae, four guard setae, two large globular granulated sense clubs, and a pair of long, thin, sense rods. Eyes absent, pseudocelli present. Post-antennal organ with 26–30 vesicles with distinctly thickened basal attachment zones. Antennal base area distinct, with finer granules. Furcal rudiments present, a distinct integumentary ridge bearing four short setae. Claw with strong inner tooth below centre, no outer teeth; a long basal seta to each side; unguis tapering and reaching to level of claw apex on hind feet but slightly shorter on other feet; both claw and unguis granulate dorsally. Genital aperture of male with 10–12 short setae arranged irregularly in transverse rows anterior to pore, three minute setae inside tip of pore and the two flanking setae further removed. Genital aperture of female as in Fig. 11.23.

Recorded from Scottish coasts (Gisin 1960).

Onychiurus thalassophila (Bagnall)   FIG. 11.23

Length 1.5 mm. Usually white. Antennal segment 3 with complex sense-organ consisting of two sense clubs, longitudinally lamellated, giving them a characteristic petal-like appearance; also with two long, thin, widely separated sense rods, 12–13 low papillae of varying shapes and six guard setae. Pseudocelli present. Post-antennal organ with 20–24 broad vesicles often touching or overlapping, each with two distinct basal chitinous thickenings. Anal spines almost straight, on well-separated papillae. Genital aperture flanked by two, small, widely spaced papillae, each covered by numerous short setae. Furcal rudiments entirely absent. Sparse covering of short, curved setae. Claw basally granulate, without teeth but with a long basal seta to each side; unguis reduced with a stout basal granulated section bearing a sharp needle-like process, the whole reaching to about one-third down inner margin of claw.

Recorded from coasts of Scotland and England (Gisin 1960).

Onychiurus halophilus (Bagnall)   FIG. 11.23

Length 1.5 mm. Usually white. Antennal segment 3 with complex sense-organ similar to O. tullbergi. Post-antennal organ with 24–30 vesicles with basal attachment 'circles' quite distinct. Pseudocelli present. Anal spines on short papillae, the spines pointed, more or less straight, and with associated setae. Furcal ridge present, marked by four irregular rows of very short setae. Claw and unguis granulated basally; claw without teeth but with very long basal setae to each side; unguis with stout basal granulated half and apical needle-like extension, the whole about two-thirds length of claw.

Recorded from Northumberland coast.

Onychiurus debilis (Moniez)   FIG. 11.23

Length 1.5 mm. White in colour. Antennal segment 3 with complex sense-organ bearing five papillae. Pseudocelli present. Skin finely granulated over whole body. Post-antennal organ with eighteen vesicles. Claw toothless. Anal spines almost straight, about the same length as the empodium.

Recorded from Northumberland and Yorkshire coasts.

2 HYPOGASTRURIDAE

Hypogastrura viatica (Tulberg)   FIG. 11.23

Length 1.9 mm. Blue-violet in colour. Antennal segment 4 with fine sensory papillae. Eight eyes on each side of head. Claw with small inner teeth. Empodium with broad basal lamellae. Tenaculum with three + three teeth. Dens with six setae. Anal spines almost straight, about one-third length of claw.

All British coasts, among seaweed and in salt-marshes.

3 NEANURIDAE

1.	Post-antennal organ absent	**Friesea acuminata**
	Post-antennal organ present	**2**
2.	Eyes absent. White or yellowish species	**3**
	Eyes present. Grey-blue species	**5**
3.	Plump species. Abdomen segment 4 about half as long as broad. Mandibles with smooth face. Setae on antenna 1 stout, serrate, longer than olfactory setae of antenna segment 4. Abdomen without ventral papillae but with six to eight minute setulae less than half as long as adjacent setae	**Anuridella thalassophila**
	Slender species. Abdomen segment 4 more than half as long as broad. Mandibles with serrate faces	**4**
4.	Olfactory setae on antenna segment 4 club-shaped, variable in proportion, extending anteriorly and to a lesser extent posteriorly, more than twice as plump as adjacent setae. Mandible head with fine denticulation between stout apical and basal teeth but reduced or absent proximal to latter. Subcoxal process present on leg 3. White	**Anuridella calcarata**
	Olfactory setae on antenna segment 4 similar in size and shape, without posterior projection, about twice as plump as adjacent setae. Mandible head with coarse teeth especially on concave margin of base. Subcoxal process of leg 3 absent. Yellowish white	**Anuridella marina**
5.	Three eyes on each side of head. Base of mandible head with more than 20 'ciliated fingers'. Maxillary lamellae with marginal teeth and rows of fine ciliations.	**Anuridella denisi**
	Five eyes on each side of head. Base of mandible head with small number of smooth, sharply pointed teeth. Maxillary lamellae with marginal teeth but without ciliations. Post-antennal organ with five to ten vesicles arranged in a circle. Antenna 4 segment with six olfactory setae. Male with more than 150 genital setae. Tibiotarsus with two acuminate subapical setae. Dark blue-black	**Anurida maritima**

Anurida maritima (Guerin)   FIG. 11.23

Length 3 mm, blue-black in colour. Dense covering of long stout setae on dorsal surface. Abdominal segment 6 with six spine-

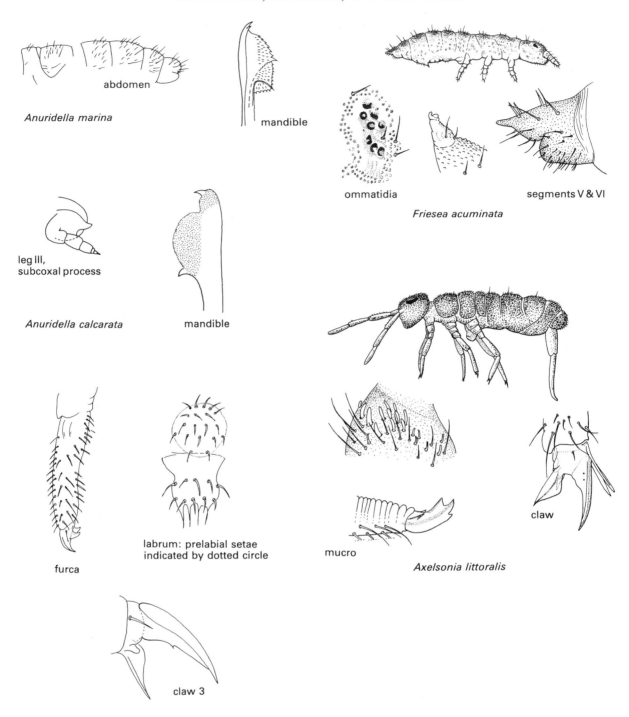

Anuridella marina

abdomen

mandible

ommatidia

segments V & VI

Friesea acuminata

leg III,
subcoxal process

Anuridella calcarata

mandible

furca

labrum: prelabial setae
indicated by dotted circle

mucro

claw

Axelsonia littoralis

claw 3

Archisotoma megalops

Fig. 11.24

like setae directed backwards in a series of four + two. Mandible with four large and two small teeth. Post-antennal organ with five to ten vesicles. Furca and tenaculum absent. Anal spines absent. Up to five ommatidia on each side of head (5 + 5 or 3 + 3). Antennae with trilobed sense organ situated towards inner side of each apical segment.

Recorded from Hayling Island, Hants; Tynemouth, Northumberland; Anglesey; Church Reef, Wembury, Plymouth;

Gower coast. Common and generally distributed, widespread on Atlantic coasts.

Anurida denisi (Bagnall)

Length 2 mm, blue in colour. Bristles finer, less dense, and not spine-like as in *A. maritima*. Mandible with three small teeth at tip. Post-antennal organ with fifteen vesicles. Furca and tenaculum absent. Ommatidia three + three. Antenna with trilobed apical sense organ. Empodial appendage of foot absent. Recorded from the Atlantic coasts of England and Ireland.

Anuridella calcarata (Denis) FIG. 11.24

Length 1.2 mm, white in colour. Mandible with single curved apical tooth and sub-apical lobe-like expansion. Ommatidia absent. Post-antennal organ with 20 irregular vesicles. Antennal segment 4 with a three-lobed sense organ and three thick sensory setae. Last abdominal segment abnormally long. Median lamella of maxillae head projecting beyond the apex.

On rocky shores. Reported from Dalmeny Estate, Scotland; Whitburn, Durham; east Yorkshire; Cloughey, Co. Down, Ireland.

Anuridella marina (Willem) FIG. 11.24

Length 1.0–1.9 mm, yellowish white in colour. Three maxillary lamellae distinguishable in lateral view. Post-antennal organ with 17–20 vesicles. Mandible with a single curved apical tooth and sub-apical lobe-like expansion. Ommatidia absent. Three-lobed apical antennal organ.

Rocky shores on the Atlantic coast of England; reported from Angelsey; Dub Reef, Port Erin; Dalmeny Estate, Scotland; Gower coast.

Anuridella thalassophila (Bagnall)

Length 1–1.35 mm. Colour white. Post-antennal organ with 12–18 vesicles. Abdomen segment 5 with row of eight setae in front of a row of six setae. Abdomen segment 4 with one median + two lateral swellings.

Recorded from Dalmeny Estate, Scotland; south Queensferry; Torryburn, Fife; Barra; Northumberland and Durham coasts; Flamborough Head and Danes Dyke, Yorkshire; Dittisham and Torquay, south Devon.

4 ISOTOMIDAE

1. Abdominal segments 5 and 6 fused, with one or two long thin 'hairs' on each side (bothriotrichae). Manubrium with few hairs **2**

   Abdominal segments 5 and 6 separated, without bothriotrichae **3**

2. Claws with teeth on inner surface of claw **Archisotoma megalops**

   Claws without teeth on inner surface of claw **Archisotoma nigricans**

3. Dens clumsy, with two or more hairs in front **4**

   Front of manubrium with hairs **5**

4. Skin clearly granulated **Proisotoma crassicauda**

   Skin practically smooth **Proisotoma admaritima**

5. Abdomen without bothriotrichae **Isotoma maritima**

   At least abdominal segment 4 with one or two pairs of very thin smooth bothriotrichae. Claws with long teeth **Axelsonia littoralis**

Friesea acuminata (Denis) FIG. 11.24

Length 1.5 mm. Colour white. Ommatidia eight + eight. Claw toothless. Furca reduced or absent. Abdominal segment 6 with three anal spines.

Occurs mainly in sandy intertidal habitats. Reported from Dorset and Essex.

Archisotoma megalops (Bagnall) FIG. 11.24

Length 2.0–2.3 mm; brown in colour with greyish-black markings. Antenna 1.25 × median length of head. Segment 3 of antenna with a pair of strong, curved sensory rods, subtending from chitinous fold; segment 4 with several curved sensory rods, a terminal lobe, and sub-apical papilla. Six ommatidia. Post-antennal organ very narrow, 0.65–0.7 × width of antennal segment 1. Head of maxilla with a galea but lamella with a larger and longer median lamella extending beyond apex of galea, very strongly ciliate. Two smaller lateral but elongate lamellae, also strongly fringed. Manubrium with a few setae.

Occurs on the coast of England and Scotland, in littoral sub-soil and salt-marshes.

Archisotoma nigricans (Bagnall)

Length 0.9–1.0 mm; dark greyish black with paler mottlings. Intermediate body segments with irregular transverse paler belts of colour at interstices. Antennae 1.4 × length of head. Post-antennal organ exceptionally elongate, parallel-sided, transverse length about 6 × diameter of nearest ommatidia. Furcula less stout than in other species, reaching to beyond middle of sternum II. Weak body setae, thorn-like spine on hind tibio-tarsus. Apical swelling on antennal segment 2, exceptionally long sensory rods on antennal segment 3. Manubrium with few setae.

Occurs in littoral subsoil and salt-marshes on the east coast of England.

Axelosonia littoralis (Moniez) FIG. 11.24

Length 2.0 mm, dark greyish-black. Short, stout body broadest in region of abdominal segments 3 and 4. Antennae longer than length of head. Distinctive organ on antennal segment 3 consisting of two sensory clubs subtending from a cuticular fold and supported by approximately 15 short, blunt, sensory rods. Furca long, relative length of manubrium, dentes, and mucro being 20:35:4; mucro with five teeth. Abdominal segments 3 and 4 subequal. Ommatidia 1–6 large, arranged in contiguous or subcontiguous pairs, 7 and 8 small.

Reported from Canvey Island, Essex, under stones below HWM, usually in black tenacious mud; Allhallows, Kent; Hayling Island, Hants; Gower coast.

Isotoma maritima (Tullberg) FIG. 11.25

Length 1.5–2.5 mm, grey to blue-grey in colour. Antennae long and slender. Eight ocelli on each side of head. Post-antennal organ only twice the size of one ommatidium.

All British coasts.

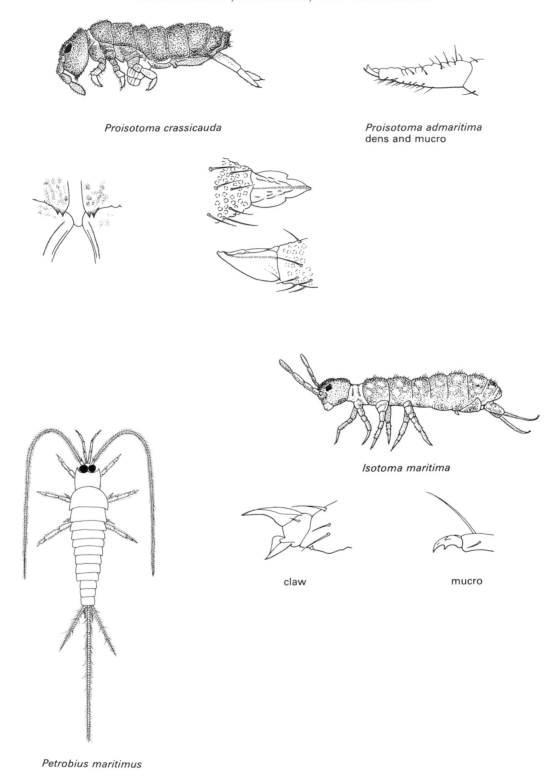

Proisotoma crassicauda

Proisotoma admaritima
dens and mucro

Isotoma maritima

claw

mucro

Petrobius maritimus

Fig. 11.25

Proisotoma admaritima Murphy   FIG. 11.25
Length 1.32 mm; deep blue-black in colour with paler appendages. Smooth cuticle with a scattered covering of moderately
short, smooth, pointed setae. Ocelli eight + eight of similar size,
arranged on a common black-coloured eye patch. Post-antennal
organ 1.2–1.4× diameter of an ocellus, broadly elliptical in
shape. Claws with no inner or lateral teeth. Empodium slightly
longer than half length of inner edge of claw. Furcula short,
reaching only to middle of abdominal segment 2. Relatively
short thick dens with a few setae. Dentes clumsy with two or
more setae in front.

On the coast of Scotland. Isle of Cumbrae, Millport: Keppel

pier on surface of rock-pools in splash zone, and about HWM springs.

Proisotoma crassicauda (Tullberg)   FIG. 11.25

Length 1.5 mm; blackish violet in colour with bright spots. Post-antennal organ narrow and elliptical. Relatively short thick dens with a few setae. Manubrium with two + two apical setae.

In wrack and under stones on the coast of England.

5 ENTOMOBRYIDAE

Pseudosinella halophila (Bagnall)

Length 1.5 mm, white or yellowish in colour. Antennae twice as long as head. Body often with microscopic scales or densely packed setae. Abdominal segment 4 usually appreciably longer than 3. Well-developed furca. Rami of tenaculum quadridentate, claw short and stout. Empodium large, 0.7 × length of inner claw, margin more than twice as broad as basal third. Setae short, thin, pointed, and less than 0.4 × length of claw.

Kent, Cooden Beach, under stones uncovered at low tide; south Devon, Kingsteignton.

Class **Insecta**

An insect body is divided into three regions or tagmata, a *head*, *thorax* and *abdomen*. Each of these consists of a number of segments which have undergone different degrees of fusion, six completely fused in the head, three distinct ones in the thorax, the *prothorax, mesothorax*, and *metathorax* and a slightly variable number in the abdomen. The body is covered by a thickened cuticle and each segment has an upper *tergum*, a lower *sternum* and lateral *pleuron*. These may be subdivided into a number of *sclerites*. The head bears one pair of *antennae*, paired *mandibles* and *maxillae*, and a single *labium*. In some species the mouthparts are adapted to chewing as in the beetles, whilst in others they are modified in a number of ways, such as for piercing and sucking in the Hemiptera and some Diptera. The thorax usually has three pairs of segmented legs. These are modified to a varying degree, but each consists basically of a *coxa, trochanter, femur, tibia*, and a number of *tarsal* segments. The tips of the walking legs may have one or more claws, or be otherwise modified. Wings are usually present on the *meso-* and *meta-thoracic* segments. Some insects are apterous and have never possessed wings. These are referred to as the Apterygota, and include the Thysanura which may occur in the splash zone. The Pterygota consist of insects which have wings or have secondarily lost them. Most other orders of insects belong to this group. The venation and structure of the wing, i.e. whether membranous or leathery, are important characters in identification.

Most insects lay eggs. These hatch into larvae which in most orders differ from the adults; in the Apterygota larvae hatch into forms resembling miniature adults but which are not sexually mature. Because they are enclosed by cuticle the larvae need to moult in order to grow. In some orders, the Exopterygota, they have a number of moults, with stages or *instars* between them, until they reach the adult form or *imago*. The Hemiptera belong in this group. In the Endopterygota the larvae have a series of stages with a pupal stage preceding the imago. The Coleoptera and Diptera belong to this group. Representatives of almost all insect orders have been recorded at some time or another from the intertidal zone but the only species which occur regularly, and spend some of their time in the intertidal zone belong to the Thysanura, Hemiptera, Coleoptera, or Diptera. Almost any insect which occurs in fresh water may sometimes be found in brackish water.

REFERENCES

Chinery, M. (1973). *A field guide to the insects of Britain and northern Europe*. Collins, London.

Cheng, L. (1976). *Marine insects*, Elsevier-North Holland, Amsterdam.

Subclass **Apterygota**
Order **Thysanura**

Thysanurans, or bristle-tails, are among the most primitive of the apterygote insects. They may be recognized by their elongate, spindle-shaped bodies, broadest anteriorly, threadlike antennae, and by the last abdominal segment, which bears a slender tailpiece, or *epiproct*, flanked by two, equally long, *cerci*.

Two large, metallic coloured thysanurans are common on British coasts, on rocky shores above mean HWM.

---

1.   Sub-coxae of male abdominal segment 8 prolonged into rounded lobes   **Petrobius brevistylis**

      Sub-coxae of male abdominal segment 8 not prolonged   **Petrobius maritimus** [Fig. 11.25]

Subclass **Pterygota**

Keys to pterygote insects are confined to a determination of families with littoral representatives. Specialist keys will be needed to determine species.

Order **Hemiptera**
Suborder **Heteroptera**

Representatives of the true bugs, Heteroptera, occur on rocky shores and salt-marshes. Many of the intertidal forms belong to the Saldidae. Most have been derived from freshwater and occasionally terrestrial habitats. A few are apterous but most have two pairs of wings, the hind pair are membranous but the front pair are partially hardened and called *hemelytra*. The hardened area is divided into several regions, *clavus, corium, cuneus*, and *embolium*. The anterior segment of the thorax, the *prothorax* is large and prominent with the *pronotum* occupying most of the visible parts of the thorax when viewed from above. A prominent triangular region, the *scutellum*, which is part of the *mesothorax*, lies between the wings when they are folded. The head is variable in shape, the *antennae* never have more than five segments, *compound eyes* are present and sometimes *ocelli* on the dorsal surface of the head. The mouthparts are characterstic with the *mandibles* and *maxillae* in the form of needle-like stylets held in a groove of the *labrum*. The composite structure is referred to as a *rostrum*.

REFERENCES

Southward, T. R. E. and Leston, D. (1959). *Land and water bugs of the British Isles*. Frederick Warne, London.

KEY TO FAMILIES
WITH LITTORAL REPRESENTATIVES

1. Antennae, shorter than head, usually concealed	**1. Corixidae**
Antennae longer than head, not concealed	**2**
2. Corium and pronotum covered with net-like pattern	**3**
Corium and pronotum without net-like pattern	**4**
3. Pronotum projecting back and covering scutellum, head and pronotum black; forewing membrane not distinct	**2. Tingidae**
Pronotum not projecting back, scutellum exposed, head and pronotum usually green or brown, forewing membranous area distinct, with cross-veins	**3. Piesmidae**
4. Ocelli absent	**4. Miridae**
Ocelli present	**5**
5. Rostrum three-segmented, labrum large, extending over base of rostral segment 1; generally black, oval bugs with white markings, or reddish brown with reduced forewings	**5. Saldidae**
Rostrum four-segmented; labrum smaller, brownish or otherwise coloured	**6. Lygaeidae**

1 CORIXIDAE FIG. 11.26

Most species occupy fresh water and estuarine habitats. Mainly herbivorous. Body dorsally flattened; swims with dorsal surface uppermost. Rostrum concealed, and/or two-segmented; antennae with three or four segments. Anterior legs shortened, used as scoops to gather food; fore and hind tarsi clawless, the latter two-segmented.

2 TINGIDAE FIG. 11.26

Lacebugs. Lace-like reticulation on the pronotum and forewings a distinguishing feature. Not usually associated with the maritime zone but *Agramma laeta* (Faller) often occurs on salt-marshes.

3 PIESMIDAE FIG. 11.26

Not considered as typically intertidal but *Piesma quadratum* Fieber occurs on salt-marshes.

4 MIRIDAE FIG. 11.26

Most representatives are not maritime but *Lopus decolor* (Fallen), *Conostethus frisicus* Wagner and *C. brevis* Reuter occur on salt-marshes.

5 SALDIDAE FIG. 11.26

Oval-shaped, legs of moderate length with large coxae. Tarsi three-segmented, claws apical and symmetrical, without arolia. Short wide head, bearing ocelli and large compound eyes, long four-segmented antenna and backwardly directed, four-segmented rostrum. Usually dull, black or brown, *Saldula palustris* (Douglas) occurs on estuarine mudflats. *Aepophilus bonnairei* (Signoret) is unique in the Saldidae in that the hemelytra do not cover the abdomen, it lacks ocelli and has relatively small eyes. It occurs in crevices near low water.

6 LYGAEIDAE FIG. 11.26

Small, dark or brightly coloured. Antennae inserted well down on sides of head, narrow or oval in outline when viewed from above.

Order **Coleoptera**

Body usually covered with a tough cuticle. Head with biting mouthparts, *mandibles*, *maxillae*, and *labium*, sometimes on a projection of the head, *rostrum*. The paired antennae vary in structure between families and genera. Usually two pairs of wings, the hind pair sometimes reduced or absent; the front

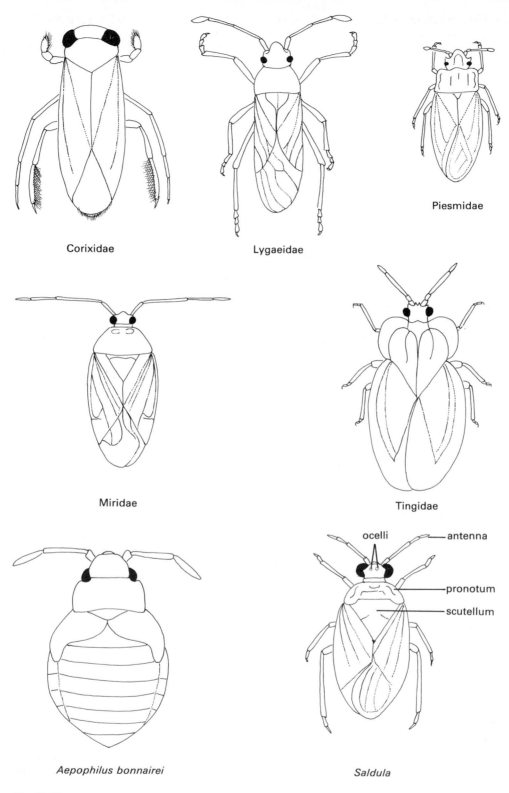

Corixidae

Lygaeidae

Piesmidae

Miridae

Tingidae

Aepophilus bonnairei

Saldula

ocelli — antenna
pronotum
scutellum

Fig. 11.26

pair form thickened *elytra* to protect the hind pair, and are particularly useful in burrowers or crevice dwellers. Most have elytra which cover the abdominal segments, but in some genera they are short leaving several abdominal segments and the terminal *pygidium* exposed. In contrast to the Heteroptera the elytra meet in the mid-line and do not overlap. The legs are similar to those of other insects, usually with five *tarsal* segments although these are sometimes reduced in number. The *coxae* are particularly important taxonomically and in the burrowing forms show a number of variations.

REFERENCES

Fowler, W. W. (1887–1913). *The Coleoptera of the British Islands.* (6 vols). London.

Joy, N. H. *A practical handbook of British beetles* (2 vols). Frederick Warne, London.

Linssen, E. F. (1959). *Beetles of the British Isles* (2 vols). Frederick Warne, London.

Unwin, D. M. (1984). A key to the families of British Coleoptera. *Field Studies*, **6**, 149–97.

KEY TO FAMILIES OF COASTAL COLEOPTERA

1. Reduced mouthparts, head with a rostrum (Fig. 11.27J). Tarsi 5:5:5, segment 4 sometimes small — **1. Curculionidae**

   Mouthparts not reduced, head without a rostrum (Fig. 11.27A–D) — **2**

2. Hind tarsi with the same number of segments as the foretarsi (Fig. 11.27A) — **7**

   Hind and fore tarsi with different numbers of segments — **3**

3. Tarsi 5:5:4 — **4**

   Tarsi 4:5:5, elytra truncate — **12**

4. Front coxal cavities open behind (Fig. 11.27H) — **5**

   Front coxal cavities closed behind (Fig. 11.27I) — **6**

5. Head strongly and suddenly contracted at base (Fig. 11.29A) — **2. Anthicidae**

   Head not strongly or suddenly contracted at base. Middle coxae large, body long and narrow (Fig. 11.29B) — **3. Oedemeridae**

6. Eyes notched at the front. Abdomen with five visible sternites (Fig. 11.29C) — **4. Tenebrionidae**

   Eyes not notched — **26**

7. Tarsi 5:5:5, all segments full size — **16**

   Tarsi 4:4:4 or apparently so — **8**

   Tarsi 3:3:3 or apparently so — **11**

8. Tarsi 4:4:4 — **9**

   Tarsi really 5:5:5, segment 4 very small and hidden by the lobes of segment 3 (Fig. 11.27E) — **10**

9. Elytra not truncate (Fig. 11.27L) — **5. Heteroceridae**

   Elytra truncate (Fig. 11.27G) — **12**

10. Less than 3 mm, shining, convex. Three-segmented antennal club — **6. Phalacridae**

    Not like this (Fig. 11.27K, 29D) — **7. Chrysomelidae**

11. Elytra truncate, revealing at least three tergites (Fig. 11.27G)   **12**

    Elytra not truncate (Fig. 11.27A)   **13**

12. Abdomen flexible and with seven or eight sternites visible (Figs. 11.27G, 11.28K)

                                                                   8. Staphylinidae

    Abdomen rigid, elytra short. Antennae clubbed. 'Ant-like' appearance (Fig. 11.29E)

                                                                   9. Pselaphidae

13. Wings with fringes (Fig. 11.28F)   **14**

    Wings not fringed   **15**

14. Wings broad. Tarsi 4:4:4, segment 3 small and hidden in a notch in segment 2
    (Fig. 11.29F)   **10. Corylophidae**

    Wings narrow. Tarsi 3:3:3 (Fig. 11.28F, 11.29G)   **11. Ptiliidae**

15. Tarsi 4:4:4, segment 3 very small (Fig. 11.27F)   **12. Coccinellidae**

    Tarsi 3:3:3   **13. Lathrididae**

16. First abdominal sternite completely divided by hind coxal cavities (Fig. 11.28A, 11.27D).
    Outer lobe of maxilla palpiform. Antennae usually filiform   **17**

    First abdominal sternite not completely divided by hind coxal cavities (Fig. 11.28B).
    Outer lobe of galae not palpiform. Antennae various   **19**

17. Not aquatic. Projecting setae at fixed points. Antennae mostly pubescent. Hind coxae
    not extending laterally to meet sides of elytra (Fig. 11.27A,B, 11.28A)   **14. Carabidae**

    Aquatic. Without such projecting setae. Antennae practically glabrous, hind coxae
    extending laterally to meet sides of elytra   **18**

18. Posterio-ventral edge of hind coxae produced into large plates covering basal abdomi-
    nal sternites (Fig. 11.28D), elytra with large punctures in regular rows, scutellum hidden

                                                                   15. Haliplidae

    Posterio-ventral edge of hind coxae not so developed (Fig. 11.28C), elytra without such
    regular rows of punctures   **16. Dytiscidae**

19. Nine-segmented antennae. Apical three to five segments expanded on one side to
    form a lamellate club (Fig. 11.28L). Tarsi always 5:5:5   **17. Scarabaeidae**

    Antennae not lamellate   **20**

20. Hind legs modified for swimming. Antennae short and palpi long   **21**

    Hind legs not modified for swimming   **22**

21. Antennal club five-segmented. Abdomen with six or seven sternites visible. Less than
    3 mm. Not very convex or rounded   **18. Hydraenidae**

    Antennal club three-segmented. Abdomen with five visible sternites   **19. Hydrophilidae**

22. Elytra truncate and exposing at least three tergites (Fig. 11.27G)   **12**

    Elytra not truncate, or exposing only the pygidium (Fig. 11.27A)   **23**

23. Abdomen with seven or eight visible sternites   **20. Cantharidae**

    Abdomen with fewer than seven visible sernites   **24**

24. Abdomen with five visible sternites   **26**

    Abdomen with six visible sternites   **25**

25. Longer than 4 mm. Green in colour   **21. Melyridae**

    Shorter than 4 mm. Variable in colour but not green. Dorsally quite convex (Fig. 11.29I)

                                                                            22. Leiodidae

26. Truncate elytra exposing only the pygidium. Antennae clubbed and elbowed   **23. Histeridae**

    Elytra not truncate   **27**

27. Femur attached to the end of the trochanter (Fig. 11.28G)   **24. Ptinidae**

    Femur attached to the side of the trochanter (Fig. 11.28H)   **28**

28. Prosternum has a spine which fits into a groove in the metatarsum   **29**

    Possesses no such spine   **25. Cryptophagidae**

29. Prothorax loosely jointed to the mesothorax and moving freely on it. Hind angles
    prolonged into teeth   **26. Elateridae**

    Prothorax not moveable, firmly fixed to the mesothorax.   **27. Throscidae**

---

1 CURCULIONIDAE (Weevils)   FIG. 11.27J

Head extended anteriorly to form a rostrum to which the elbowed antennae are attached. Size of rostrum varies between species. The elytra cover the entire dorsal surface of the abdomen. Herbivorous.

e.g. *Philopedon plagiatus* (Schaller). Sandy places on the coast and rarely inland.

2 ANTHICIDAE   FIG. 11.29A

Small species, superficially resembling ants. The head is strongly contracted behind the eyes, prothorax oval in shape.

e.g. *Anthicus* spp., beneath stranded algae in salt-marshes.

3 OEDEMERIDAE   FIG. 11.29B

Soft-bodied, elongate and subparallel-sided. The prothorax is narrower than the elytra and the antennae long and slender.

Nacerdes melanura (Linnaeus) is the only coastal species; it is yellowish red, has prominent eyes and occurs on seashore timber and at the mouths of large rivers.

4 TENEBRIONIDAE   FIG. 11.29C

The 5:5:4 tarsal arrangement distinguishes this family. When viewed from above the first joint of the antenna is partly hidden because the antennae are attached under the side of the head. Most species are glabrous.

e.g. *Phylan gibbus* (Fabricius), *Phaleria cadaverina* (Fabricius) (Fig. 11.27) and *Cylindrinotus pallidus* (Curtis). All found on sandy coasts. *P. cadaverina* is common beneath strandline debris.

5 HETEROCERIDAE   FIG. 11.27L

Shape is more or less ovate, with flattened body, covered with a dense coat of short setae. Brown and black in colour with dull yellow bands or spots.

Seven coastal species of genus *Heterocerus* Fabricius inhabit salt-marshes.

6 PHALACRIDAE

Convex and glabrous, usually 1–3 mm in length.

One species is recorded from the shore, *Phalacrus brunnipes*

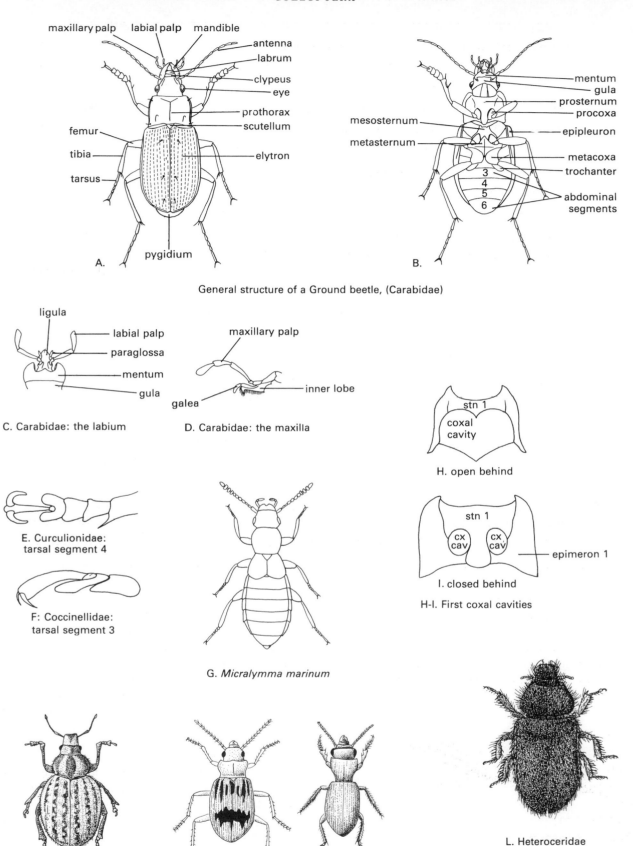

A.

maxillary palp   labial palp   mandible
antenna
labrum
clypeus
eye
prothorax
scutellum
femur
tibia
elytron
tarsus
pygidium

B.

mentum
gula
prosternum
procoxa
mesosternum
epipleuron
metasternum
metacoxa
trochanter
3
4
5
6
abdominal segments

General structure of a Ground beetle, (Carabidae)

C. Carabidae: the labium

ligula
labial palp
paraglossa
mentum
gula

D. Carabidae: the maxilla

maxillary palp
inner lobe
galea

E. Curculionidae: tarsal segment 4

F: Coccinellidae: tarsal segment 3

G. *Micralymma marinum*

H. open behind

stn 1
coxal cavity

I. closed behind

stn 1
cx cav
cx cav
epimeron 1

H-I. First coxal cavities

J. Curculionidae

Eurynebria complanata   *Broscus cephalotes*
K. Carabidae

L. Heteroceridae

Fig. 11.27

(Brisout), which is black and 1.5–2 mm. It lives on the banks of rivers and on the coast.

7 CHRYSOMELIDAE   FIG. 11.29D

Less than 8.5 mm in length, oval in shape. Some species brightly coloured.

Five British species have been recorded from coastal habitats: *Macroplea mutica* (Fabricius), in brackish water; *Chrysolina haemoptera* (Linnaeus), on sandy coasts; *Phaedon conannus* (Stephens), *Crepidodea impressa* (Fabricius), and *Cassida vittata* (de Villers) in salt-marshes.

8 STAPHYLINIDAE   FIGS. 11.27G, 11.28K

Family with the largest number of coastal species, around 65. Easily recognized by the abbreviated elytra and black colour.

Some species occur well down the intertidal zone, for example, *Micralymma marinum* (Strom), in rock-crevies; *Diglotta marina* (Haliday), on rocky and sandy shores; *Bledius spectabilis* (Kraatz) in salt-marshes. Many other species are characteristically found on strandlines, such as *Aleochara algarum* (Fauvel), *Myrmecopora sulcata* (Kiesenwetter), and *Cafius xantholoma* (Gravenhorst).

9 PSELAPHIDAE   FIG. 11.29E

Very small ant-like species with abbreviated elytra and elbowed, clubbed antennae.

Two British species are recorded from salt-marshes: *Brachygluta helferi* (Schmidt-Goebl) and *Brachygluta simplex* (Waterhouse).

10 CORYLOPHIDAE   FIG. 11.29F

Oval and less than 1 mm in length.

The one British species occurring on the coast, *Corylophus cassidordes* (Marsham), has a red and yellow thorax with black elytra; it is found in vegetable refuse, including strandline algae.

11 PTILIIDAE   FIG. 11.29G

Very small, oval, less than 1 mm in length. Wings narrow, with long fringe of setae sometimes projecting from beneath elytra.

Two British species occur on the seashore beneath seaweed, *Actidium coarctatum* (Haliday) and *Ptenidium punctatum* (Gyllenhal).

12 COCCINELLIDAE (Ladybirds)

Convex, with head partly retracted into the thorax. Most species are brightly coloured and often have prominent spots on the elytra.

Coccinella septempunctata (Linnaeus) is ubiquitous and often common on the coast, *Tytthaspis sexdecimpunctata* (Linnaeus) occurs in marshes.

13 LATHRIDIDAE

Small, elongate, oval beetles, 1–3 mm in length. Distinguished by the 3:3:3 tarsal arrangement. Four British species belonging to the genus *Corticana* Marsham are found beneath vegetable refuse, including seaweed.

14 CARABIDAE, (Ground Beetles)   FIG. 11.28I,J,M

Around 50 coastal species are known, almost exclusively predacious.

Aepopsis robinii (Laboulbene) and *Aepus marinus* (Ström) live permanently between the tidemarks in crevices and beneath stones: 2 mm long, yellow-brown, with small eyes and slightly abbreviated elytra. *Cillenus laterale* (Samouelle) is a fully intertidal species which lives in a variety of habitats, but is abundant in salt-marshes; *Lymnaem nigropiceum* (Marsham) and three species of *Tachys* Dejean occur beneath stones. *Nebria complanata* (Linnaeus) and *Broscus cephalotes* (Linnaeus) are found beneath strandline debris on sandy shores (Fig. 11.27K).

15 HALIPLIDAE   FIG. 11.28D

Small, convex, yellow-brown in colour, often with black spots. One species, *Haliplus apicalis* (Thomson) occurs in ditches sometimes flooded by the tide.

16 DYTISCIDAE   FIG. 11.28C

Large family with smooth, oval bodies and flattened hind legs used as paddles.

Two British species recorded from brackish ponds and ditches; *Agabus conspersus* (Marsham) and *Coelambus parallelogrammus* (Ahrens).

17 SCARABAEIDAE   FIG. 11.28E,L

Thick sculptured cuticles, often convex and rounded in shape; characterized by lamellate antennae.

Seven coastal species occur in Britain. e.g. *Aegialia arenaria* (Fabricius), found beneath strandline debris.

18 HYDRAENIDAE

Small, elongate beetles with long palpi and short antennae.

Species of *Octhebius* Leach live in brackish water ditches and occasionally among strandline algae.

19 HYDROPHILIDAE

Convex, oval beetles with clubbed antennae and long maxillary palps.

Several species in brackish water, and some species of *Cerycon* Leach occur beneath strandline algae.

20 CANTHARIDAE, (Soldier Beetles)

Elongate, soft bodied.

Cantharis rufa (Linnaeus) occurs beneath strandline algae.

21 MELYRIDAE   FIG. 11.29H

Elongate, oval species, soft bodies.

Two species, *Dolichosoma lineare* (Rossi) and *Malachius vulneratus* (Abeille) occur in salt-marshes. Both are green and 4–5 mm long.

22 LEOIDIDAE   FIG. 11.29I

Small, convex, oval and shiny.

Hydnobius perrisi (Fairmaire) and *Liodes dubia* (Kugelann) occur in sandy coastal habitats, including strandline algae.

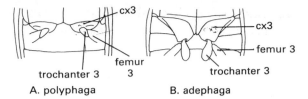

A. polyphaga

B. adephaga

A Hind coxa in adephaga and polyphaga

C. Dytiscidae   D. Haliplidae
metasternum and abdomen in ventral view

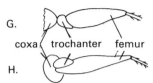

G.   Ptinidae

coxa   trochanter   femur

H.   Cryptophagidae

Femur attached to end (above)
or side (lower) of trochanter

E. Scarabaeid
antenna

F. Ptiliid wing

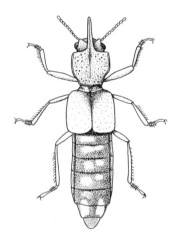

I. *Aepus marinus*

J. *Aepopsis robinii*

K. *Bledius spectabilis*

L. *Aegialia arenaria*

M. *Cillenus*

Fig. 11.28

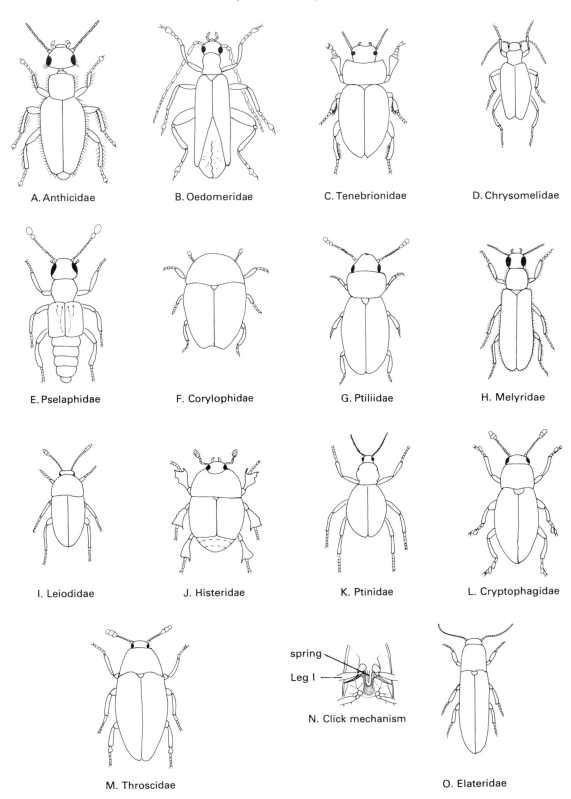

A. Anthicidae

B. Oedomeridae

C. Tenebrionidae

D. Chrysomelidae

E. Pselaphidae

F. Corylophidae

G. Ptiliidae

H. Melyridae

I. Leiodidae

J. Histeridae

K. Ptinidae

L. Cryptophagidae

M. Throscidae

spring

Leg I

N. Click mechanism

O. Elateridae

Fig. 11.29

23 HISTERIDAE FIG. 11.29J

Oval, often black, 0.5–1.0 mm, associated with decaying material.

Two species occur on the coast, *Halacritus punctum* (Aube), in vegetable refuse, and *Baekmanniolus maritimus* (Stephens) in dung.

24 PTINIDAE (Spider Beetles) FIG. 11.29K

Long legs; resemble spiders with large abdomen and the head hidden from above.

Ptinus palliatus (Perris) may be found in old wooden posts on the sea-shore.

25 CRYPTOPHAGIDAE FIG. 11.29L

Yellowish brown, oval and covered with fine pubescence.

Atomaria fuscipes (Gyllenhal) occurs in vegetable refuse, including stranded seaweed.

26 ELATERIDAE (Click Beetles) FIG. 11.29N,O

Elongate; can produce a clicking sound and jumping action by rapid movement of a prosternal spine into a groove on the mesosternum.

Agriotes sordidus (Illiger) lives on sandy coasts.

27 THROSCIDAE FIG. 11.29M

Similar to *Elateridae*, but mostly smaller and none able to 'click'.

Troxagus elateroides (Heer) occurs in salt-marshes.

Order **Diptera**

An extremely large order. Most flies feed on liquids although their mouthparts, modified for this purpose, vary considerably throughout the order. On the head the compound eyes are large, and ocelli are present in some species. The structure of the antennae is important in classification, in particular some may have a conspicuous bristle or *arista*. The head and thorax also have *setae*, *vibrissae* or *bristles*, in specific positions. In some there is a facial depression bounded by a *ptilinal suture*. There may also be a crescent-shaped mark above the bases of the antennae, the *lunule*. The bulk of the thorax consists of the wing-bearing *mesothorax*. The lateral aspect of the thorax has a number of clearly defined areas, the *pleural plates* or *pleurites*; the wings arise from the *pteropleuron*. The dorsal surface is divided into three divisions, the *prescutum*, *scutum*, and *scutellum*. The two former may be separated by a transverse *suture*.

There is one pair of wings, the venation of which is important in classification. Close to the front margin is the *sub-costa* (*Sc*), and often a small cross vein, the *humeral* vein. Behind this may be a series of other long veins, the *radius* (*R*), *costa* (C), *media* (*M*), *cubitus* (*Cu*), and *anal vein* (*A*), with a number of cross-veins (*Y-M*) and enclosed areas of wing, or cells, the *discal cell* and *cubital cell*. The base of the wing sometimes has a number of small flaps, the *squamae*. The legs possess the normal insect compliment of segments but some terminate with a median lobe or *arolium* and others with two lobes or *pulvilli* between the claws.

REFERENCES

Chinery, M. (1973). *A field guide to the insects of Britain and western Europe*. Collins, London.

Colyer, C. N. and Hammond, C. O. (1951). *Flies of the British Isles*. Frederick Warne, London.

Oldroyd, H. (1954). Diptera, 1. Introduction and Key to families. *Handbooks for the identification of British Insects*, **9**, 1. Royal Entomological Society, London.

Suborder **Nematocera**

Antennae of imago many segemented (Fig. 11.30A), usually longer than head and thorax; segments usually similar, no arista. Pleural suture of mesothorax straight. Discal cell generally absent, cubital cell, when present widely open (Fig. 11.30B). No frontal lunule or ptilinum.

KEY TO FAMILIES

1.	Costa extending right round wing (Fig. 11.30B), though weaker along posterior margin	**2**
	Costa confined to anterior margin of wing	**4**
2.	Thorax with V-shaped suture on mesonotum (Fig. 11.31J). Intermedian cell usually present	**1. Tipulidae**
	Thorax without V-shaped suture. Intermedian cell absent (Fig. 11.31L,M). Ocelli absent or vestigial	**3**
3.	Wings not specially setaceous or scaly. Antennal segment 2 short and thick, distal segments filamentous	**2. Dixidae**
	Wings setaceous or scaly	**3. Culicidae**

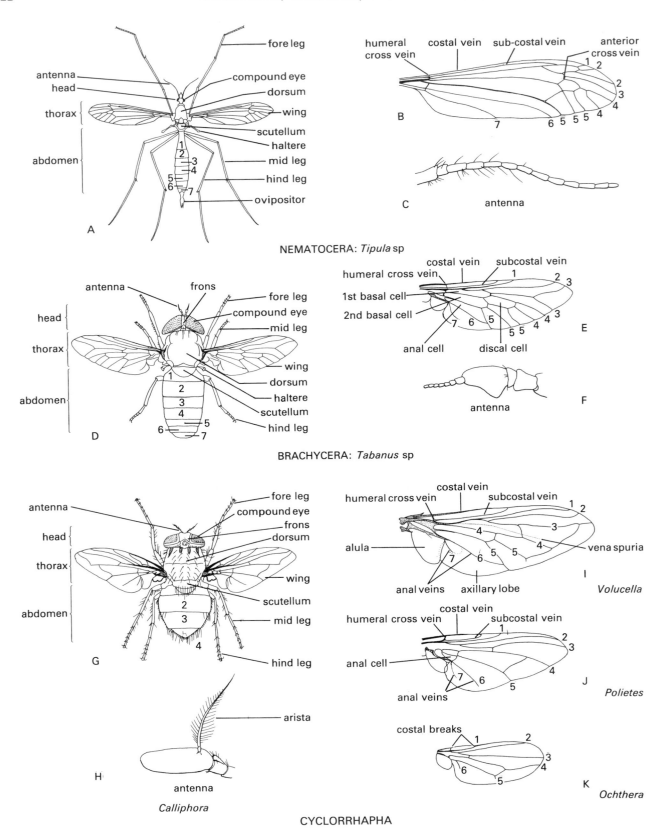

NEMATOCERA: *Tipula* sp

BRACHYCERA: *Tabanus* sp

Volucella

Polietes

Ochthera

Calliphora

CYCLORRHAPHA

Fig. 11.30

4. Vein M_{1+2} forked (Fig. 11.31K), Mandibles present. Fore legs normal   **4. Ceratopogonidae**

    Vein M_{1+2} simple (Fig. 11.31N). Mandibles absent. Fore legs elongate   **5. Chironomidae**

---

1 TIPULIDAE   FIG. 11.30A–C, 11.31J

Suture on top of thorax V-shaped; 10–12 longitudinal veins or branches reach the wing margin. Veins 6 and 7 long, reaching wing margin.

   e.g. *Limonia* (*Geranomyia*) *unicolor* (Haliday) on rocky, intertidal shores.

2 DIXIDAE   FIG. 11.31L

Antennae with 14 segments; male antennae not plumed; no scales on wings and legs.

   e.g. *Dixella attica* Pandazis.

3 CULICIDAE (Mosquitoes)   FIG. 11.31M

Antennae with 13 segments; male antenna plumed. Posterior cross-vein present.

   e.g. *Ochlerotatus caspius* (Pallas), *O. detritus* (Haliday), *O. dorsalis* (*Meigen*). *Anopheles labrauchiae atroparvus* (van Thiel), breeds in coastal saline waters and carried 'ague' until late 19th century.

4 CERATOPOGONIDAE   FIG. 11.31K

Minute flies, sometimes with broad-wings; mouthparts short and adapted for piercing. Wings usually held over body at rest. Sometimes with small spines beneath hind femora. Vein 4 forked.

   e.g. *Dasyhelea flavoscutellata* (Zetterstedt), *Monoculicoides nubeculosus* (Meigen).

5 CHIRONOMIDAE

Non-biting midges; delicate gnat-like flies, often with head overhung by thorax; mouthparts poorly developed; wings usually narrow, and generally held apart at rest.

   e.g. *Clunio marinus* Haliday 1.5 mm in length, wingless females; larvae in burrow tubes of particles of sand and seaweed beneath water. *Psammathiomyia pectinata* Deby; *Thalassomyia fravenfeldi* Schiner; *Halocladius fucicola* (Edwards). Intertidal on rocky shores.

Suborder **Brachycera**

Antennae of imago shorter than thorax (Fig. 11.30D), generally three-segmented with terminal arista (Fig. 11.30F). Pleural suture twice bent. Discal cell usually present. Cubital cell contracted before the wing-margin or closed (Fig. 11.30E). No frontal lunule or ptilinum.

KEY TO FAMILIES

---

1. Arolium pad-like, nearly or quite as large as the two pulvilli (Fig. 11.31O)   **1. Stratiomyidae**

   Arolium replaced by a hair-like empodium or absent (Fig. 11.31P)   **2**

---

2. Cu_1 and 1A separate or meeting near the wing-margin. C extending to hind margin   **3**

   Cu_1 and 1A meeting near base of wing. C not extending to hind margin   **2. Asilidae**

---

3. Vein R_1 meeting C at or beyond middle of fore margin, cross-vein r-m close to base (Fig. 11.31V). Colours not metallic   **3. Empididae**

   Vein R_1 meeting C at or before middle of fore margin, cross-vein r-m close to base (Fig. 11.32C). Colours often metallic   **4. Dolichopodidae**

---

1 STRATIOMYIDAE (Soldier Flies) FIG. 11.31O,Q; 11.32S

Small to fairly large flies (3–20 mm), often with metallic coloration, flattened, without bristles. Discal cells usually small, antennal segment 3 annulated, scutellum sometimes with spines. At rest wings folded over abdomen, one over the other.

   e.g. *Nemotelus* spp. larvae develop in brackish pools.

2 ASILIDAE (Robber flies)   FIG. 11.31R, 11.32R

Medium to large flies, usually narrow body with strong bristly legs. e.g. *Philonicus albiceps* (Meigen). Coastal sand dunes, prey peculiar to seashore.

3 EMPIDIDAE (Dance Flies)   FIG. 11.31S–V

Small to medium-sized, mostly bristly flies; head nearly spherical. Proboscis usually rigid, sometimes very long. Usually a notch present on anterior margin of the eyes.

4 DOLICHOPODIDAE   FIG. 11.32A–C

Small, bristly, often metallic, bluish or greenish flies; head long in profile, higher than wide; proboscis usually short and stout. Vein 4 sometimes kinked and sometimes forked.

   e.g. *Thinophilus flavipalpis* (Zetterstedt), *Aphyrosylus celticer* Haliday, *A. ferox* Haliday, *Hydrophorus oceanus* (Macquart).

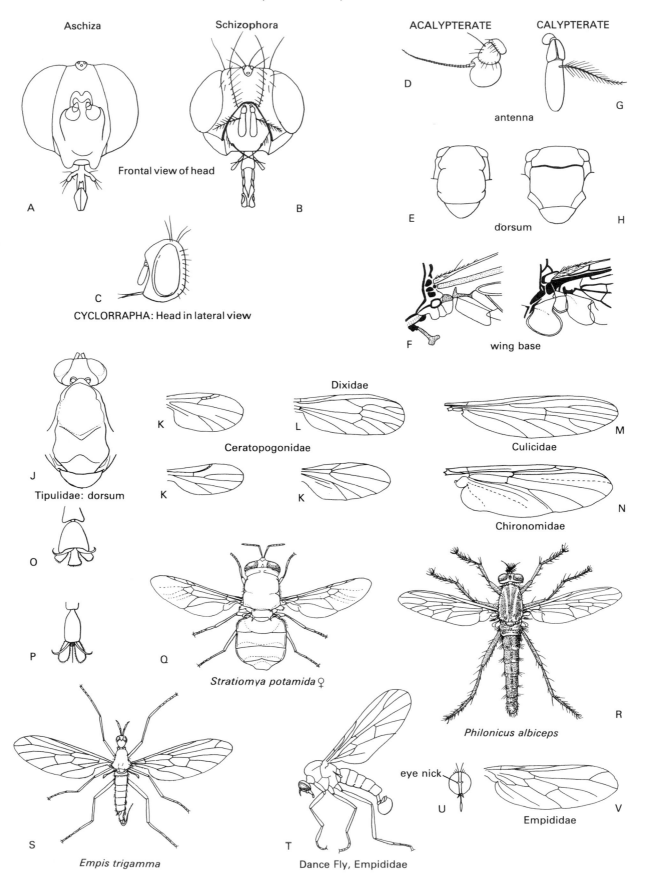

Aschiza

Schizophora

Frontal view of head

ACALYPTERATE

CALYPTERATE

D

G

antenna

E

H

dorsum

F

wing base

C

CYCLORRAPHA: Head in lateral view

J

Tipulidae: dorsum

K

Dixidae

L

Ceratopogonidae

M

Culicidae

K

K

N

Chironomidae

O

P

Q

Stratiomya potamida ♀

R

Philonicus albiceps

S

Empis trigamma

T

Dance Fly, Empididae

U

eye nick

V

Empididae

Fig. 11.31

Suborder **Cyclorrhapha**

Antenna of imago three-segmented with a dorsally positioned arista (Fig. 11.30H). Pleural suture twice bent. Discal cell almost always present. Cubital cell contracted or closed. Head usually with a frontal lunule and usually a ptilinum.

Section A *Aschiza*

Frontal suture absent: lunule often indistinct or absent—ptilinum absent. Cell Cu elongated extending more than half-way to wing-margin (Fig. 11.30J).

KEY TO FAMILIES

1. Venation characteristically reduced, only C, R, and M present as darkened veins near wing base, other venation decolorized, no discal or cubital cell. Wingless forms common

    1. Phoridae

    Venation more complete **2. Syrphidae**

1 PHORIDAE

Minute to small greyish-black, brownish, or yellowish flies with humped-back appearance. Frons wide, usually with strong, upcurved bristles, eyes separate in both sexes. Venation abnormal. Veins 1–3 strong and crowded basally; other veins running from vein 3 to the margin, weak, vein 2 may be absent.

2 SYRPHIDAE (Hoverflies) FIG. 11.30I

Small to large, often brightly coloured flies; cross-veins closing the sub-apical and discal cells mostly in line forming a false margin to the wing. Sub-apical cell always fully closed.
    e.g. *Eristalinus aenus* (Scopoli).

Section B *Schizophora*

Frontal structure and lunule distinct; ptilinum always present (Fig. 11.31B). Cell Cu short or vestigial.

1. Antennal segment 2 above without a distinct external groove (Fig. 11.31D). Theca not developed at base of proboscis. Subcostal vein usually reduced. Squamae usually small or vestigial (Fig. 11.31F) *Acalyptratae*

    Antennal segment 2 above with a distinct external groove (Fig. 11.31G). Theca developed at base of proboscis. Subcostal vein complete. Squamae well-developed (Fig. 11.31I) *Calyptratae*

KEY TO FAMILIES: ACALYPTRATAE

1. Costa complete   2
    Costa more or less interrupted either at the end of Sc or R_1 4

2. Vibrissae present   **1. Sepsidae**
    Vibrissae absent   3

3. Tibiae with pre-apical bristles   **2. Coleopidae**
    Tibiae without pre-apical bristles   **3. Chamaemyiidae**

4. Costa more or less interrupted well before end of R_1 at point where Sc ends or would end if complete   5
    Costa more or less interrupted at end of R_1; Sc, if complete, ending at the same point   6

5. Sc complete   **4. Heleomyzidae**
    Sc vestigial or absent   **5. Sphaeroceridae**

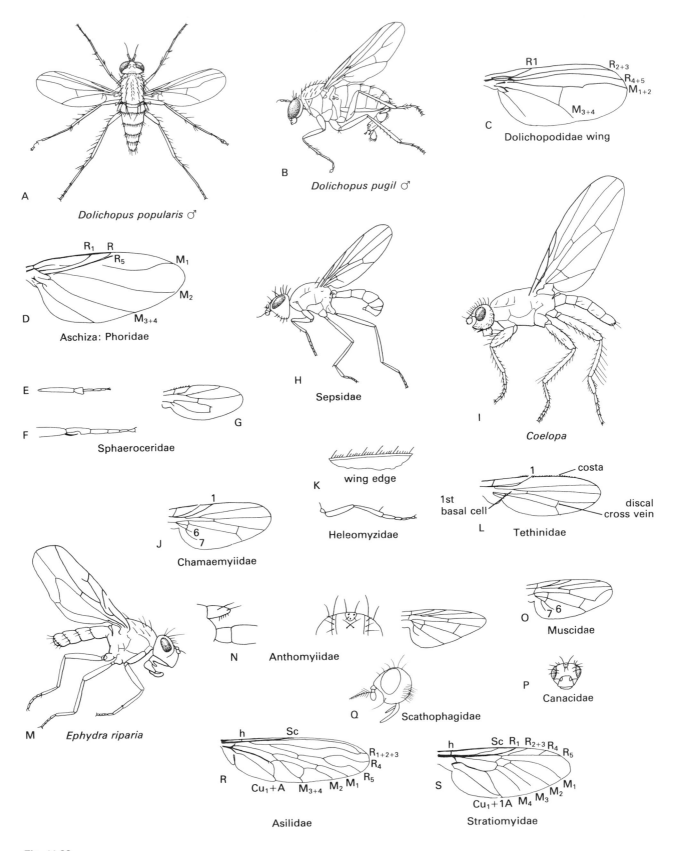

A   *Dolichopus popularis* ♂

B   *Dolichopus pugil* ♂

C   Dolichopodidae wing

D   Aschiza: Phoridae

F   Sphaeroceridae

H   Sepsidae

I   *Coelopa*

K   wing edge

J   Chamaemyiidae

Heleomyzidae

L   Tethinidae

M   *Ephydra riparia*

N   Anthomyiidae

O   Muscidae

Q   Scathophagidae

P   Canacidae

R   Asilidae

S   Stratiomyidae

Fig. 11.32

6.	Costa interrupted at end of humeral vein as well as at end of R$_1$	**6. Ephydridae**
	Costa interrupted only at end of R$_1$	**7**

7.	Vibrissae absent	**7. Canacidae**
	Vibrissae present even if small	**8. Tethinidae**

1 SEPSIDAE   FIG. 11.32H

Small, black or brownish-black flies, sometimes metallic and shining. Some have wings with dark apical spots. Eyes small, oval, with space below eye equal to about twice height of eye. Posterior spiracle (the respiratory opening just below and to the front of the haltere) always with at least one bristle.

e.g. *Orygma luctuosum* Meigen occurs on drift line.

2 COLEOPIDAE   FIG. 11.32I

Small to medium-sized rather flattened flies, very bristly or setaceous, feet large; sub-costa complete, reaching the costa.

e.g. *Coleopa frigida* (Fabricius), *C. pilipes* Haliday, *Oedoparia buccata* Fallen, *Malacomyia sciomyzina* (Haliday) on drift line.

3 CHAMAEMYIIDAE   FIG. 11.32J

Generally very small, greyish or yellowish-grey, heavily dusted flies; vein 6 very weak, vein 7 more developed, running about half-way to the wing margin. Post-vertical bristles convergent or absent.

e.g. *Chamaemyia flavipalpis* Haliday. Common on seashores.

4 HELEOMYZIDAE   FIG. 11.32K

Small to medium-sized yellowish, brownish or grey flies. Costa of wing with a series of spines, distinct from Costal cilia.

e.g. *Heterocheita buccata* (Fallen) and *Helcomyza ustulata* Curtis typical of the drift line.

5 SPHAEROCERIDAE   FIG. 11.32F,G

Minute to small, usually black or brown flies. Mouth opening wide. Frontal femora often enlarged, hind tibia sometimes with large apical claw. Tarsal sgment 1 of hind legs less than one and a half times as long as segment and usually dilated. Second basal and discal cells not separated by cross-vein. Veins 4 and 5 often fade apically.

e.g. *Leptocera* (*Thoracochaeta*) *zostera* (Haliday), a permanent inhabitant of beds of seaweed; *Scatomyza littorea* Fallen.

6 EPHYDRIDAE   FIG. 11.32M

Costa of wing broken distinctly near the humeral cross-vein and again near the end of vein 1; wings sometimes patterned. Basal cell 2 not separated from discal cell. Arista bare, or plumose with setae on upper side only.

e.g. *Ephydra ripari* Fallen, a common coastal species. Salt flats and brackish pools near shore.

7 CANACIDAE   FIG. 11.32P

Very small, greyish or greyish-brown, bases of antennae widely separated, arista short, eyes small and lengthened horizontally.

e.g. *Canace nasica* Haliday, *Xanthocanace ranula* (Loew).

8 TETHINIDAE   FIG. 11.32L

Small to very small greyish or brownish flies. Costa broken near end of vein.

KEY TO FAMILIES: CALYPTRATAE

1.	Lower squama large, as long as or longer than the upper	**2**
	Lower squama short, at most half the length of the upper	**1. Scathophagidae**

2.	Vein 6 reaches the wing margin	**2. Anthomyiidae**
	Vein 6 and 7 short, do not reach wing margin	**3. Muscidae**

1 SCATHOPHAGIDAE   FIG. 11.32S

Back of head rounded, with fine, pale hair below. Medium to large, predatory flies. Lower squama reduced to a narrow strip. Eyes well-separated in both sexes.

e.g. *Scathophaga littorea* Fallen, *Ceratinostoma ostiorum* Haliday.

2 MUSCIDAE   FIG. 11.32O

Veins 6 and 7 short, their paths not convergent. Never with crossed bristles and fine pale hair under the scutellum.

e.g. *Lispe tentaculata* (Degeer).

3 ANTHOMYIIDAE   FIG. 11.32N

Frons (forehead) often with a pair of crossed bristles and fine pale hairs pointing downwards from the underside of scutellum.

e.g. *Fucellia fucorum* (Fallen), *F. maritima* (Haliday).

INDEX OF TECHNICAL TERMS

TAXONOMIC INDEX

Correct names of species and genera are given in *italic*.
Synonyms and the names of families and higher taxa are given in roman.